OBSTETRICAL PRACTICE

By

ALFRED C. BECK, M.D.

PROFESSOR OF OBSTETRICS AND GYNECOLOGY, LONG ISLAND COLLEGE
OF MEDICINE; OBSTETRICIAN AND GYNECOLOGIST-IN-CHIEF,
LONG ISLAND COLLEGE HOSPITAL, BROOKLYN

MORE THAN ONE THOUSAND ILLUSTRATIONS

FOURTH EDITION

BALTIMORE

THE WILLIAMS & WILKINS COMPANY

1947

Composed and Printed at the
WAVERLY PRESS, INC.
for
The Williams & Wilkins Company
Baltimore, Md., U. S. A.

This Book is Dedicated to the Memory of

JOHN OSBORN POLAK

LATE PROFESSOR OF OBSTETRICS AND GYNECOLOGY

THE LONG ISLAND COLLEGE OF MEDICINE

PREFACE TO FOURTH EDITION

Those advances in the field of medicine which have a bearing on obstetrics have been reviewed for the purpose of keeping the text up to date. Such alterations and additions as were required and could be made within the limits of the text will be found in their appropriate chapters.

The observations made on the new early human ova and the conclusions which have been drawn from these observations have led to the deletion of considerable old material and its replacement by new text and new illustrations. In fact, the sections on implantation and placentation have been almost completely rewritten and simplified. Much of this work has been borrowed from the Contributions to Embryology of the Carnegie Institute. It is fitting therefore that the author acknowledge his deep sense of gratitude to Drs. G. L. Streeter, G. B. Wislocki, G. W. Corner, C. H. Heuser, A. T. Hertig, J. Rock and J. I. Brewer, who have done so much to further our knowledge in this field. Most of the illustrations for this new material were redrawn from their Carnegie Contributions. Because the original photomicrographs could not be reproduced in a text of this character, the student is referred to the original articles for the details which are so well illustrated in the Carnegie publications.

The great promise which the use of penicillin offers in the prevention of congenital syphilis is discussed in the section on syphilis and pregnancy. The use of this remarkable preparation also has been included in the discussion of the treatment of puerperal infection.

A chapter on Analgesia, Amnesia and Anesthesia has been added. In the discussion of the various routines which have been advocated, the author has been careful to consider the safety factor of both the mother and child as well as the laudable effort to relieve the suffering of childbirth.

PREFACE TO FIRST EDITION

The purpose of this book is to present the essentials of obstetric practice to undergraduate students and young practitioners as concisely as is consistent with the requirements of a textbook. Disproven theories and the conflicting factors which have led to controversy accordingly are not discussed. For the sake of clearness also, historical data and the names of those who have made important contributions to obstetric progress have been omitted from the text. References to these contributions, however, are noted by number and are grouped at the end of their respective chapters. At the Long Island College of Medicine, these omissions are covered by elaborations of the text that are made in the classroom and, in addition, each student is required to present the biography of some noted obstetrician or must review the literature on an assigned subject in obstetrics at one of the senior conferences.

Especial attention has been given to the details of prenatal care. These represent the accepted views on the subject and their merit has been observed for twenty-three years in our prenatal clinic and in private practice.

The mechanism of labor has received much consideration. Experience with postgraduate students has shown that most of their difficulties in obstetric deliveries have been due to their lack of knowledge of the mechanism of labor. In order that this subject might be more readily understood, many original drawings have been made to illustrate the various steps involved in each stage of labor under normal and abnormal circumstances.

The chapter on the toxemias has been kept as simple as possible in order that specific and unmistakable directions might be given for the care of the toxic patient. In the absence of sound information concerning the causes of the various toxemias, confusing theoretical considerations have been avoided and deductions have been made from clinical experience.

Long association with a large general hospital has shown the importance of the medical and surgical complications in obstetrics. As a result, a relatively large portion of the text is devoted to a consideration of the effect of pregnancy on the more common medical and surgical diseases as well as their effects on the products of conception. In this work the author has had the advantage of consultation and association with specialists in the different branches of medicine and the accumulated experience of such an association is advantageously used throughout this chapter.

In the section on operative obstetrics, the details of the usual obstetric operations are profusely illustrated and series of drawings show the successive steps of each procedure.

Simple drawings have been used whenever possible to illustrate the text and, in many places, series of illustrations have made possible the elimination of lengthy descriptions. Most of these drawings were made by the author in the course of the past ten years. Many of them are original; others have been redrawn and, in some instances, modified from various sources in the obstetric literature. In the caption under each of the later drawings the name of the author from whom it was redrawn is given in grateful acknowledgement of this aid. In order that the drawings might not have an amateur appearance, a professional illustrator, Mr. Alfred Feinberg, was engaged to go over the sketches. All of his work was done in the presence of the author and, as a result, the original conceptions are faithfully preserved. Much credit is due Mr. Feinberg, not only for his artistic ability, but for his great patience and understanding. Without the latter, the author's time and finances would not have permitted the luxury of over one thousand illustrations.

The author wishes to acknowledge his appreciation of the instruction he received from the three great American teachers under whom it has been his privilege to have studied, Doctors Reuben Peterson, J. Whitridge Williams and John Osborn Polak. In fact, much that is contained in this book consists of their teachings modified in places as a result of the author's experience in the direct or indirect supervision of over twenty thousand obstetric cases.

He is also grateful to his secretary, Miss Louise M. Deuschle, for the careful preparation of the manuscript and wishes to acknowledge his indebtedness to Doctors George W. Phelan and Arthur C. Jacobson for their kindness in reading the manuscript and correcting the proofs, and to the College photographer, Mr. James Dunn, whose assistance was invaluable in the preparation of those illustrations which were redrawn from photographs.

The author also is grateful to the publishers for their many courtesies and their constant effort to produce a satisfactory book at a price within the means of the average student.

CONTENTS

ix

AMBROISE PARÉ
1510–1590
Paris

Paré was the greatest surgeon of his time. He reintroduced podalic version and stimulated the entrance of trained men into obstetric practice. His treatise on obstetrics appeared in connection with "A Short Compendium on Anatomy" (1550) and his teaching had a great influence on the development of modern obstetrics.

CHAPTER I

THE OVARIAN CYCLE

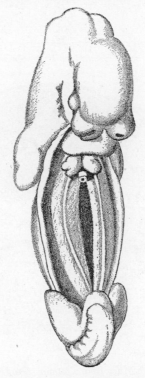

FIG. 1.—Embryo at five weeks, showing the genital
ridge on each mesonephros (Bumm).

DEVELOPMENT OF THE OVARIES

In order that the ovarian changes which precede pregnancy and recur
periodically after puberty may be better understood, the development of the
ovary will be briefly reviewed. Very early in embryonic life, the coelomic
epithelium on the ventromesial surface of each mesonephros becomes distinctly
altered. The cells proliferate rapidly and invade the underlying mesenchyme
to form a solid mass several cells thick. As this mass penetrates more deeply
into the mesonephros, it also becomes elevated and projects into the body cavity.
These altered portions of the mesonephroi are the anlagen of the sex glands and,
accordingly, are termed the genital ridges (Fig. 1). In the female, the middle
third of each genital ridge gives rise to an ovary.

1

The cells of the ovarian portion of the genital ridge become larger and more cuboidal in shape. Those at the periphery are arranged in a fairly distinct layer which is to become the future ovarian epithelium. Beneath this surface layer, the cells soon are differentiated into two types—large spherical and small cuboidal. The large spherical cells have a clear cytoplasm and a large nucleus. They are the primitive ova. The more numerous small cuboidal cells have a denser cytoplasm and are destined to form the epithelium of the future graafian follicles (1) (Fig. 2).

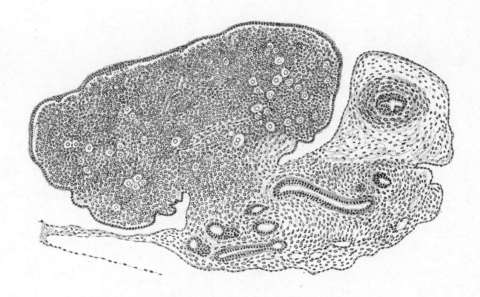

Fig. 2. Section of an ovary from a 50 mm. fetus (Keibel and Mall)

The origin of the primordial germ cells is not settled. Some observers believe that they are derived directly from the blastomeres of early cleavage and as germ cells migrate into the developing ovary (2, 3). Such cells have been observed in the vicinity of the yolk sac and entoderm of the intestines (4, 5). Others deny the early segmentation of the germ cells but believe that they are formed from the coelomic epithelium of the genital ridges (6, 7). Still others admit that some germ cells do originate from the early blastomeres but that they subsequently degenerate, while the germ cells which mature into ova are derived from the coelomic epithelium (8, 9). Both regional and extraregional origin, with persistence of ova derived from both sources, is claimed by a fourth group (10, 11). More recently, it has been suggested that new ova are formed periodically even after puberty (11, 12).

Septa from the underlying connective tissue with their blood vessels soon invade the genital ridge and divide it into epithelial islands. At the same time, the proliferating epithelium grows into the stroma between the denser connective tissue trabeculae (Fig. 3). The latter epithelial cells, however, soon degenerate and leave only cord-like groups in the medulla. Unlike their analogues in the

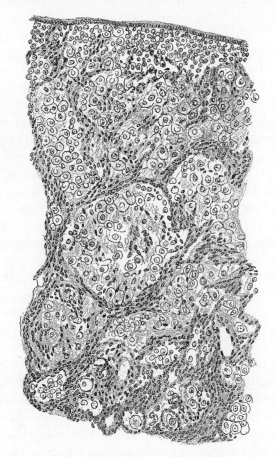

FIG. 3. Section of an ovary from an 80 mm. fetus, showing epithelial islands formed by the invasion of connective tissue trabeculae (Keibel and Mall).

testes, these medullary cords do not serve as excretory tubules later in life. In places, particularly cephalad, the epithelial tubes penetrate still further to form the rete ovarii which almost entirely disappears in the fully developed ovary. During fetal life, these rete cords may communicate with the tubules from the wolffian body just as do those of the rete testis. This communication, however, disappears early, and its absence is one of the points of differentiation between the primitive sex glands.

CHANGES IN THE FOLLICLE AND CORPUS LUTEUM

The dormant follicle consists of a primitive ovum surrounded by a single layer of flat epithelial cells (Fig. 4). Such follicles are present in great numbers at birth and throughout the reproductive period (13, 14, 15).

When a follicle develops, the flattened peripheral cells become cuboidal and proliferate to several times their original number to form a single layer of cuboidal cells that line the follicle. This is the first stage in the development of the membrana granulosa. The ovum likewise increases in size, and its nucleus is considerably enlarged (Fig. 5). Proliferation of the granulosa cells continues, and within a short time several layers may be seen in the place of the original one. A thin, clear zone, the zona pellucida, appears on the inner margin of these cells and surrounds the ovum. Coincidently, the connective tissue, adjacent to the follicle, is arranged in a circular manner to form the tunica interna (Fig. 6).

Further proliferation of the membrana granulosa results in rapid growth of the follicle. Spaces soon appear between groups of cells and in these, liquor folliculi accumulates. This follicular fluid is thought to be secreted by the granulosa elements (16, 17). Small vessels appear in the connective tissue surrounding the granulosa layer and vascularize this tunic (Fig. 7).

Coalescence of the fluid-filled spaces leads to a lateral displacement of the ovum, which is surrounded by a mass of nurse cells—the discus proligerous. As the vascularization of the connective tissue tunic increases, its cells proliferate and arrange themselves in two layers. Those in the tunica interna are somewhat altered and grow considerably larger. The outer layer, tunica externa, resembles the connective tissue of the ovarian stroma, but is circularly arranged. Enlargement of the ovum continues, as it is preparing for the splitting-off of the first polar body (Fig. 8).

Up to the time of puberty, the follicles develop largely in the deeper portions of the ovarian cortex. They never reach the surface and consequently fail to rupture. Sooner or later, however, retrogressive changes take place. These are characterized by a degeneration of the granulosa cells. The ovum likewise degenerates and is absorbed or broken up by the phagocytic granulosa cells. With the complete disappearance of the granulosa elements, the follicle contracts and is infiltrated by connective tissue, so that only a small scar remains where the former follicle existed—an atretic follicle.

Many follicles, even after puberty, terminate in the manner described. After puberty, however, some of them develop near the surface of the cortex. As maturity is approached, they are forced toward the periphery and undergo rotation so that the cumulus which originally was nearer the medulla comes to lie adjacent to the future site of rupture. The thin outer layer of the follicle wall and its covering of ovarian tissue then ruptures and the ovum is extruded (18).

FIG. 4. Dormant follicles.

FIG. 5. Beginning follicular development.

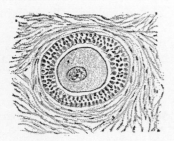

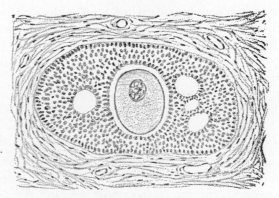

FIG. 6. Enlarging ovum, zona pellucida, proliferating stratum granulosum, early tunica interna.

FIG. 7. Vacuolization of granulosa layer. Vascularization of tunica interna. Figures 4, 5, 6 and 7 are of the same magnification. Note the progressive enlargement of the follicle, the ovum and its nucleus.

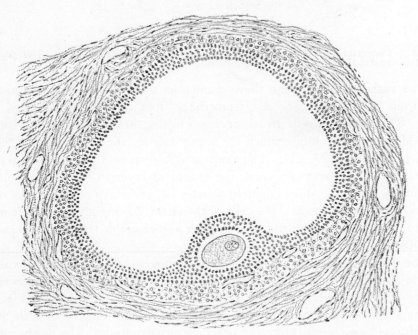

FIG. 8. Well developed follicle with discus proligerous and changed theca interna. The magnification is two-thirds that of the preceding figures.

DEVELOPMENT OF THE CORPUS LUTEUM

Following rupture of the follicle and expulsion of the ovum, a corpus luteum is formed. The life history of the latter is divided into four stages: proliferation, vascularization, maturity, and retrogression (19, 20, 21, 22).

The stage of hyperemia or proliferation follows immediately after the expulsion of the ovum and the liquor folliculi. As the cavity shrinks, the walls of the follicle are thrown into folds, and the site of rupture is closed by fibrin which soon becomes organized (21). The previously described vascularization of the theca continues, and the cells of this layer become much larger. Proliferation likewise is observed in the granulosa layer, which is separated from the theca by a vascular zone (Fig. 9). At this stage, however, the granulosa cells remain relatively small.

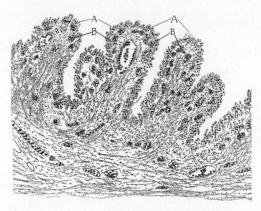

FIG. 9. Corpus luteum—Proliferation. Folds in the wall of the collapsed follicle. Thin granulosa layer (A) internal to the vascular zone of the theca interna (B).

The vascularization stage shows numerous vessels entering the granulosa layer from the adjacent theca. Hemorrhage from these fills the lumen with blood. The granulosa cells greatly increase in size, are polyhedral and contain the yellow pigment granules which are responsible for the characteristic color of the corpus luteum (23, 24). They now are known as lutein cells. Marked hyperplasia and hypertrophy cause the granulosa layer to become convoluted. In addition, it is divided into numerous zones by fine fibrils of connective tissue and vessels from the theca. The cells of the latter, having given up their nutriment to the granulosa elements, grow smaller and resemble the earlier theca cells (Fig. 10).

The stage of maturity reveals a well developed and markedly convoluted lutein layer through which vessels and trabeculae of connective tissue pass to the limiting membrane which separates the lutein cells from the lumen (Fig. 11). This stage corresponds to the premenstrual phase in the endometrial cycle and is reached about one week before the onset of menstruation. The newly formed vessels in the Lutein layer are tortuous and distended with blood for about eight

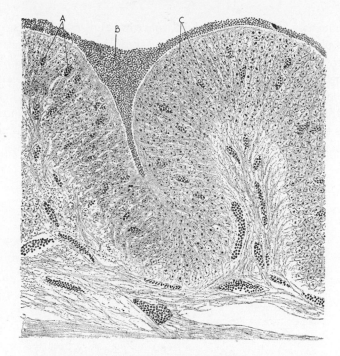

FIG. 10. Corpus luteum—Vascularization. Vessels entering the granulosa layer (*A*). Hemorrhage into the lumen (*B*). Granulosa cells increased in number and size, and containing lutein (*C*). Theca cells smaller and less prominent.

FIG. 11. Corpus luteum—Maturity. Lutein layer convoluted. Connective tissue trabeculae passing through lutein layer to the limiting membrane between the lutein elements and the blood in the lumen.

days. Subsequently they are straight, narrow and contain relatively little blood. This observation has led to the assumption that the activity of the corpus luteum is limited largely to the first eight or ten days of its life and that the changes which occur in the endometrium for several days thereafter are due to the effect of the progesterone which has already been secreted. Additional support for this theory is afforded by the fact that the artificial menstruation which follows the withdrawal of progesterone in ovariectomized animals does not occur until several days after the last injection of progesterone is given. A

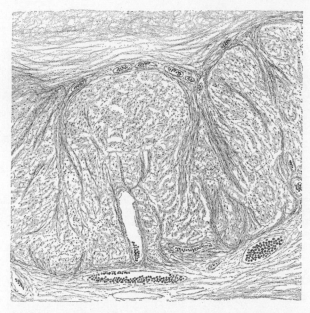

Fig. 12. Corpus luteum—Retrogression. Lutein layer becomes hyalinized as the cells lose their pigment and shrink. Limiting membrane grows thicker and gradual organization takes place.

gradual increase in the phospholipid content of the corpus luteum also has been observed up to the 10th day. On the grounds that the phospholipid content varies with the functional activity it likewise has been concluded that the functional activity of the corpus luteum reaches its maximum by the 10th day (24a).

If pregnancy occurs the growth of the corpus luteum continues until it reaches its maximum size about the fourth month of gestation. It may then occupy a very considerable portion of the ovary. Hyperemia and other evidences of secretory activity likewise persist as decidua forms within the uterus. Subsequently retrogressive changes analogous to those seen in the absence of pregnancy are observed.

The stage of retrogression begins several days prior to the onset of the menstrual flow. Fatty changes appear in the lutein layer as the cells shrink and lose their pigment (Fig. 12). The limiting membrane becomes thicker and

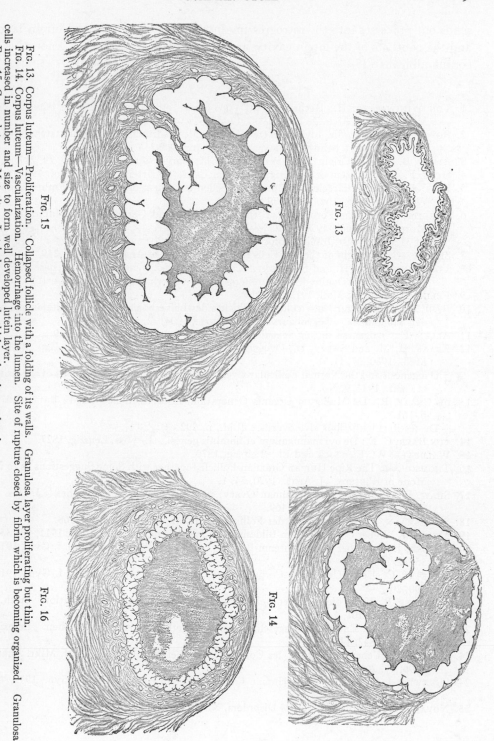

Fig. 13

Fig. 15

Fig. 16

Fig. 14

Fig. 13. Corpus luteum—Proliferation. Collapsed follicle with a folding of its walls. Granulosa layer proliferating but thin.
Fig. 14. Corpus luteum—Vascularization. Hemorrhage into the lumen. Site of rupture closed by fibrin which is becoming organized. Granulosa cells increased in number and size to form well developed lutein layer.
Fig. 15. Corpus luteum—Maturity. Lutein layer greatly thickened and convoluted.
Fig. 16. Corpus luteum—Retrogression. Lutein layer shrinking and losing its pigment. Limiting membrane between it and the blood clot in the lumen increasing in size and participating in the gradual organization of the corpus luteum.

sends out processes into the retrogressing lutein layer until both the lutein layer and the contents of the lutein cavity are organized to form what is known as a corpus albicans (25).

REFERENCES

1. Von Winiwarter, H.: Recherches sur l'Ovogenèse et l'Organogenèse de l'Ovaire des Mammifères. Arch. de Biol., 1900, 17, 33.
2. Boveri, T.: Ueber die Bildungstätte der Geschlechtsdrüsen und die Entstehung der Genitalkammern beim Amphioxus. Anat. Anz., 1892, 7, 170.
3. Allen, B. M.: The Origin of the Sex Cells of Chrysemys. Anat. Anz., 1906, 29, 217.
4. Heys, F.: The Problem of the Origin of Germ Cells. Quarterly Rev. of Biol. 1931, 6, 1.
5. Fuss, A.: Ueber extraregionäre Geschlechtszellen bei einem menschlichen Embryo von 4 Wochen. Anat. Anz., 1911, 39, 407.
6. Hargitt, G. T.: The Formation of the Sex Glands and Germ Cells of Mammals. J. Morph. & Physiol., 1926, 42, 253·
   Abst 31 Wistar Inst. Bibliographic Service, 1929, Nov.
7. Simkins, C. S.: Origin of the Sex Cells in Man. Am. J. of Anat., 1928, 41, 249.
8. Von Winiwarter, H. and Sainmont, G.: Nouvelles recherches sur l'Ovogenèse et l'Organogenèse de l'Ovaire des Mammifères (chat). Arch. de Biol., 1909, 24, 165.
9. Felix, A.: Keibel & Mall, 1912, 2, 882.
10. Böhi, U.: Beiträge zur Entwicklungsgeschichte des Leibeshöhle und der Genitalanlage bei den Salmoniden. Gegenbaurs Morph. Jahrb., 1904, 32, 505.
11. Allen, E.: Ovogenesis during Sexual Maturity. Am. J. Anat., 1923, 31, 439.
12. Evans, H. M. and Swezy, O.: Ovogenesis in the Mammalia. Proc. Soc. Exp. Biol. & Med., 1930, 27, 11.
    Ovogenesis and the Normal Follicular Cycle in Adult Mammalia. Memoirs of the Univ. of Calif., 1931, 9, No. 3.
13. de Graaf, R.: De Mulierum Organis Generationi inservientibus. Lugd., Batav. 1677, p. 161.
    De testibus mulieribus sive ovariis. Ibid., p. 292.
14. von Baer, C. E.: De ovi mammalium et hominis genesi. L. Voss, Leipzig, 1827.
15. Waldeyer, W.: Eierstock und Ei. Leipzig, 1870.
16. Thomson, A.: The Ripe Human Graafian Follicle together with Some Suggestions as to its Mode of Rupture. J. Anat., 1920, 54, 1.
17. Shaw, W.: Ovulation in the Human Ovary: its Mechanism and Anomalies. J. Obs. & Gyn. Brit. Emp., 1927, 34, 469.
18. Strassmann, E.: Warum platzt der Follikel? Arch. f. Gyn., 1923, 119, 168.
19. Meyer, R.: Ueber Corpus luteum-Bildung beim Menschen. Arch. f. Gyn., 1911, 93, 354.
20. Miller, J. W.: Ueber Corpus-luteum-Bildung beim Menschen. Zentralbl. f. Gyn., 1911, 35, II, 1089.
21. Ruge, II, C.: Ueber Ovulation, Corpus luteum und Menstruation. Arch. f. Gyn., 1913, 100, 20.
22. Schröder, R.: Ueber die zeitlichen Beziehungen der Ovulation und Menstruation. Arch. f. Gyn., 1913, 101, 1.
23. Bischoff, T. L.: Entwickelungsgeschichte der Säugethiere und des Menschen. Leipzig, L. Voss, 1842, 14, 575.
24. Sobotta, J.: Ueber die Bildung des Corpus luteum bei der Maus. Arch. f. Mikr. Anat., 1896, 47, 261.
24a. Brewer, J. I.: Studies of the Human Corpus Luteum. Am. J. Obs. & Gyn., 1942, 44, 1048.
25. Novak, E.: Menstruation and Its Disorders, N. Y., 1931.

CHAPTER II

THE MENSTRUAL CYCLE

CYCLIC CHANGES IN THE ENDOMETRIUM

THE ENDOMETRIUM undergoes alteration throughout the menstrual cycle. As a result of these changes, the cycle is divided into the following phases (1, 2):

Menstrual—1st to the 4th day.

Postmenstrual—4th to the 10th day.

Interval—10th to the 24th day.

Premenstrual—24th through the 28th day.

THE MENSTRUAL PHASE is the stage during which the menstrual flow takes place. It lasts about three days and is characterized by necrosis, hemorrhage, desquamation, and beginning regeneration. From the histological standpoint therefore this is the terminal phase of the previous endometrial cycle.

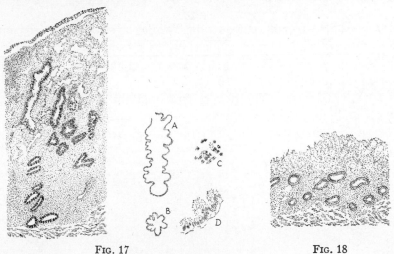

FIG. 17   FIG. 18

FIG. 17. Endometrium on the first day of the menstrual phase. *A*. Longitudinal section of gland. *B*. Cross-section of gland. *C*. Stroma cells. *D*. Gland epithelium.

FIG. 18. Endometrium on the second day of the menstrual phase. Often, only the basal layer of inactive gland terminals remains.

On the first day, the cells stain poorly and are necrotic. The capillaries are engorged and the glands are distended with their secretion. Edema is observed in the stroma, which likewise is infiltrated with leukocytes (Fig. 17). Soon hemorrhage occurs, and the continuity of the surface epithelium is broken. This is followed by desquamation which, at times, extends down to the basal layer (Fig. 18). In the latter part of the menstrual phase, regeneration begins. The glandular epithelium in the basal layer proliferates and grows out over the stroma, which becomes completely epithelialized by the first day of the postmenstrual phase.

11

THE POSTMENSTRUAL PHASE lasts about one week after the cessation of the flow. During this time, proliferation of the cellular elements completes the regeneration of the endometrium. The latter is smooth, pale, and measures .5 to 1 mm. in thickness. The surface epithelium is of the low columnar type.

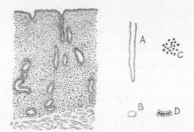

FIG. 19. Endometrium in the postmenstrual phase. *A.* Longitudinal section of gland. *B.* Cross-section of gland. *C.* Stroma cells. *D.* Gland epithelium.

The glands are short, straight, narrow tubes, while the stroma cells are small and are almost completely filled by their nuclei. The glands are inactive throughout this phase and glycogen, which was stored in the endometrium during the premenstrual stage is no longer present (3) (Fig. 19).

THE INTERVAL PHASE extends over approximately two weeks and is characterized by a gradually increasing activity of the endometrium. Early in this phase, the epithelium grows taller and the glands become wider and slightly

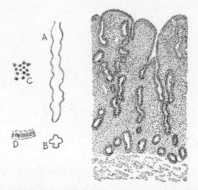

FIG. 20. Endometrium in the interval phase. *A.* Longitudinal section of gland. *B.* Cross-section of gland. *C.* Stroma cells. *D.* Gland epithelium.

tortuous, but the stroma remains compact. Later, the epithelial cells are of the tall columnar type and the glands become larger and very tortuous. On cross-section, they are cruciform. Congestion of the capillaries and increasing glandular activity likewise are observed (Fig. 20).

THE PREMENSTRUAL OR PROGESTATIONAL PHASE is one of marked hyperemia and secretory activity. It lasts slightly less than one week. During this stage, the endometrium undergoes its greatest development and reaches a thickness of 5 to 8 mm. This marked thickening causes it to be thrown into folds and gives it a velvety appearance.

The glands are distended and considerably convoluted. On section, they have a typical sawtooth or corkscrew appearance. Various stages of secretory activity are observed in the glandular epithelium. In places, the cells are filled with fine granules, while in others they are frayed out and show globules of secretion. Owing to the proliferation of its cellular elements, the epithelium has a tufted arrangement which, on cross-section, is quite characteristic. A marked increase in the cytoplasm of the stroma cells causes them to be greatly enlarged. This is particularly noticeable near the surface and around the glands, where, occasionally, they are suggestive of those found in typical decidua. The vessels are engorged and the endometrium is edematous and infiltrated with leukocytes (Fig. 21).

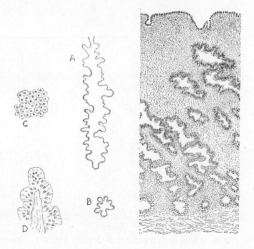

FIG. 21. Endometrium in the premenstrual phase. *A* .Longitudinal section of gland. *B*. Cross-section of gland. *C*. Stroma cells. *D*. Gland epithelium.

At this time, mucin, lipoids, a tryptic ferment and a large quantity of glycogen are demonstrable (3, 4). Should pregnancy occur, these progressive changes continue and the endometrium is transformed into a typical decidua.

If pregnancy does not occur, necrosis, hemorrhage and desquamation of the next menstrual phase follow.

Throughout the menstrual cycle, the basal layer of the endometrium, which contains the extremities of the glands, remains inactive excepting during the stage of regeneration, when proliferation of the gland epithelium leads to the epithelialization of the regenerated endometrium.

CIRCULATORY CHANGES IN THE ENDOMETRIUM. Two types of arteries supply the endometrium. One of these is made up of straight narrow vessels which penetrate and supply the basalis but do not extend beyond this area. The other is made up of spiral arteries which pass outward and supply most of the endometrium. These spiral arteries enter the mucous membrane as continuations of the straight arteries which extend radially from the vascular zone of the myometrium and proceed through the endometrium in a tightly coiled tortuous course. They give off very few branches and end abruptly in numerous small terminal arterioles (Fig. 22A). While little or no change occurs in the straight vessels, the coiled arteries undergo marked alterations during the menstrual cycle (5 & 6).

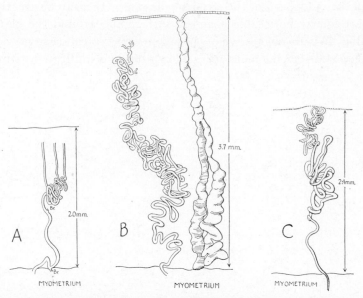

FIG. 22. Projection reconstructions of coiled arteries during the ovulatory menstrual cycle of the monkey (Daron)
A. Early proliferative phase. The endometrium is 2 mm. thick. The artery is markedly coiled in the middle third of the mucosa.
B. Late pre-gravid phase. Note the marked elongation of the artery, its small number of branches and its length in relation to the height of the endometrium.
C. Menstrual phase. Constriction of the vessel before it enters the endometrium is marked in comparison with the calibre of the coiled portion of the artery.

In the proliferative stage, the arteries extend little more than half way through the mucosa but, in the late pre-gravid phase, they reach almost to the epithelium (Fig. 22A & B). In other words, the hyperplasia and hypertrophy of the stroma and glands proceed more rapidly than do the growth and differentiation of the arteries in the first half of the cycle. Later, the reverse seems to occur and a rather marked disproportion between the thickness of the endometrium and the length of the vessels is observed. Because of this disproportionate lengthening of the arteries, they are compressed from end to end and are more markedly coiled, as many as eight new coils appearing in the 24 hours preceding menstruation. The increased coiling of the arteries and the marked vasodilatation appears to slow the circulation in the functional zone and may cause an increase in capillary permeability with consequent edema and diapedesis of both leucocytes and erythrocytes. This therefore may be the normal method by which the pabulum bed for the implantation of the ovum is prepared. Beginning 6 to 12 hours before menstruation and persisting throughout the period of flow, the radial arteries, which are the precursors of the spiral arteries, become constricted and, as a result, a very abrupt change in the diameter of the lumen is observed as the artery passes from the myometrium into the endometrium (Fig. 22C). Coiled vessels which measure 25 to 40 μ in the endometrium are thus constricted to 7 μ or less in the region of the myometrium. This marked constriction of the myometrial segments may lead to anemia and necrosis of the terminal vessels and the adjacent endometrial elements which they supply. It accordingly has been suggested that the blood which is lost during menstruation comes from the damaged terminals of the coiled arteries. This theory, however, has been opposed on the ground that the damaged vessels in the desquamated zone are always occluded. It also has been observed that material injected into the arteries during menstruation does not pass into the uterine cavity while it does when the veins are injected. As a consequence, it seems reasonable to conclude that menstrual blood is venous in origin (5 & 6).

The straight arteries in the basal zone are not affected during the various phases of the menstrual cycle. They therefore are not damaged in the stage of menstruation and the basal zone from which regeneration occurs continues to be well nourished throughout the period of menstrual flow (5 & 6).

Because estrin and progestin are associated with the functioning of the endometrium and because their withdrawal is followed by menstruation, a relationship between these hormones and the vascular changes described is assumed but the details of this relationship are as yet unknown.

The phenomenon of menstruation has been studied by means of endometrial transplants into the anterior chamber of the eyes of animals. In them, all of the above observations have been noted. In addition to the vasoconstriction which begins 6 to 12 hours before the onset of the flow and persists throughout the first day, subepithelial hematomata are formed and project slightly above the surface as small papillae. These papillae then rupture and from them hemorrhage continues for 25 to 70 minutes. More hematomata are subsequently formed and these again rupture. Only part of the transplant, accordingly, bleeds at one time. No tissue is desquamated during the first few hours and only small bits of epithelium and superficial stroma are shed during the first day. In cases of profuse hemorrhage, some of the deeper stroma becomes detached after this time. Observations on transplants also indicate that re-epithelization occurs as an outgrowth of the epithelium from the free extremities of the glands (6).

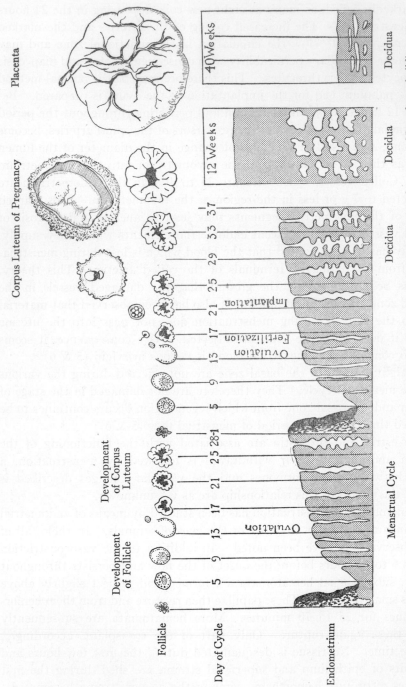

Fig. 23. Correlation between the cyclic changes that occur in the endometrium and those observed in the ovary. Note that rebuilding or proliferative phase of the endometrial cycle corresponds with the development of the graafian follicle and the secretory phase with that of the corpus luteum. Menstruation follows soon after the corpus luteum regresses. In the event that pregnancy occurs, the corpus luteum continues to grow and reaches its maximum development by the fourth month. Under the influence of its secretion the endometrial changes progress to form a typical decidua of pregnancy. After the fourth month, the function of the corpus luteum is taken over by the placenta, the secretion of which prolongs the life of the decidua. Because of the pressure of the expanding uterine content, however, the decidua ultimately becomes flattened to but a fraction of its maximum thickness observed at the third month.

CORRELATION OF THE MENSTRUAL AND OVARIAN CYCLES

As the follicle develops, regeneration of the endometrium takes place.

Rupture of the follicle with the expulsion of the mature ovum—ovulation—occurs in the middle of the intermenstrual period—about the 13th or 14th day. Regardless of the length of the cycle it is thought that ovulation occurs about 14 days before the end of the cycle, i.e., 14 days before the menstrual flow appears.

The corpus luteum develops for 8–10 days after ovulation. It then shows evidence of regression and probably ceases to secrete its hormone progesterone.

Maturity of the corpus luteum is synchronous with the beginning premenstrual changes that are observed in the endometrium (2, 7). The correlation between the menstrual and ovarian cycles is well shown in Figure 23.

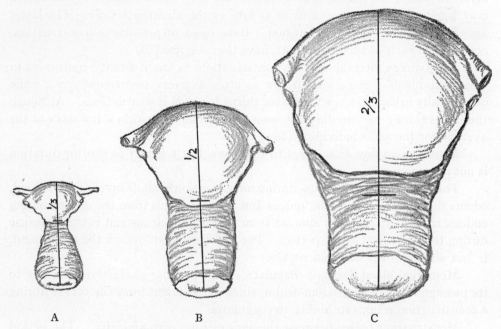

FIG. 24. Relative size of the cervix and uterus at different ages.
A. The uterus of a newborn infant. The ratio of body to cervix is 1 to 2.
B. The uterus at puberty. The ratio of body to cervix is 1 to 1.
C. The uterus of an adult woman. The ratio of body to cervix is 2 to 1.

MENSTRUATION may be defined as the hemorrhagic phase of the cyclic changes which occur in women. It is characterized by a periodic, bloody, genital discharge which recurs at regular intervals from puberty to the menopause, excepting during pregnancy and lactation.

PUBERTY is the transition period between girlhood and womanhood. It is accompanied by the onset of menstruation and definite changes in those structures which are concerned with the physiology of reproduction. At this time, the girl is conscious of the distinction between the sexes, and the secondary sex manifestations become apparent. The breasts develop, the hips become rounded and the body loses its angular outline as it takes on the graceful curves that are characteristic of the adult female figure. Hair grows in the axillae and over the mons, and a deposition of fat so increases the size of the labia majora that they partially conceal the labia minora.

In the ovaries follicles periodically reach their fullest development, rupture, and expel their almost completely matured ova.

The body of the uterus develops more rapidly than the cervix. As a result, the length of the former soon equals and finally exceeds that of the latter (Figs. 24A, B, C). Its endometrium also begins the previously described cycle of changes that commonly are observed throughout the period of sexual activity.

The age of onset of the first menstruation varies between the twelfth and fifteenth years, the average being 13.9 years (8). Occasionally, menstruation may begin as early as the ninth or as late as the nineteenth year. The latter ages of onset, however, are unusual. Rare cases of precocious menstruation, occurring as early as the second year, have been reported (9).

The average interval between menstruations is about twenty-eight days in most individuals. Some women flow as often as every twenty-one days, while occasionally others go a few days over thirty between menstruations. Although the interval may vary in different women, it usually is within a few days of the average for the same individual (10, 11).

Most women flow from three to five days, but a longer or shorter duration is not uncommon.

The discharge which occurs during menstruation is made up of altered blood, edema fluid, uterine secretion, mucus and tissue detritus from the desquamating endometrium. It varies in amount from two to six ounces and is most profuse during the early part of the period. The average blood loss, on the other hand, is but slightly over one ounce (12).

Menstrual blood does not coagulate. This peculiar characteristic is due to its passage through the endometrium, since blood taken from the cervix during a menstruation retains its ability to coagulate.

Menstruation ceases between the ages of forty-five and fifty. The period in a woman's life at which this takes place is known as the **Menopause**. It may occur as early as the thirty-fifth or as late as the fifty-fifth year (13). A late puberty usually is followed by an early menopause. In addition to the cessation of menstruation, the menopause is accompanied by a loss of the reproductive function and retrogressive changes in the genitalia.

CAUSE OF MENSTRUATION. Removal of the ovaries is followed by an artificial menopause. The ovaries, therefore, are essential to menstruation.

If they are removed in the last half of the menstrual cycle, a final menstruation follows within a few days, but their removal earlier in the cycle has no such effect. From this it is concluded that the ovaries contain a substance or substances which causes the premenstrual changes in the endometrium and the removal of which is responsible for the menstrual flow. When the ovary which contains the corpus luteum is removed, or when the corpus luteum itself is destroyed, in the latter part of the menstrual cycle, premature menstruation also occurs (14).

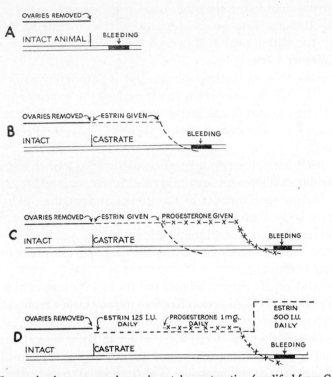

FIG. 25. The ovarian hormones and experimental menstruation (modified from Corner).
A. Bleeding follows removal of ovaries.
B. Estrin administration prevents the bleeding which follows removal of the ovaries but its discontinuance is followed by bleeding (Allen, 1927–1928).
C. Progesterone prevents estrin-deprivation bleeding but its discontinuance is followed by bleeding (Smith and Engle, 1932) (Hisaw, 1935) (Corner, 1938).
D. Bleeding occurs after discontinuance of progesterone in spite of continued and more intensive estrin treatment (Corner, 1937–1938) (Zuckerman 1937) (Hisaw and Green, 1938).

Menstruation in the monkey occurs without ovulation and without the development of the corpus luteum. It therefore is thought to be under the control of the follicular hormone (17). In this animal, injections of estrin cause changes in the endometrium similar to those observed in the interval stage and menstruation follows shortly after these injections are discontinued (18). The addition of progesterone, however, is necessary to produce premenstrual endometrial changes in monkeys previously treated with estrin (15, 20). Following oöphorectomy in women, the administration of estrin and progesterone have an effect similar to that observed in monkeys (21). Proliferation of the endometrium followed by premenstrual or progestational changes, accordingly, are produced by the injection of large amounts of estrin and progesterone and their withdrawal leads to a temporary menstrual flow (22) Fig. 25A, B, C, D.

From these observations, it seems reasonable to conclude that the changes in the endometrium which take place up to and perhaps slightly after rupture of the follicle are the result of the influence of the follicular hormone, estrin, while the premenstrual changes, on the other hand, are due to the supplementary action of the corpus luteum hormone, progesterone. The menstrual flow accordingly is caused by the withdrawal of progesterone in the ovulatory cycle and estrin in the anovulatory cycle.

The anterior lobe of the hypophysis also is intimately associated with the genital function. Its removal leads to atrophy of the ovaries and the accessory sex organs. The changes in the latter, however, are secondary to failure of the ovaries to function. Hypophysectomy, therefore, has an effect similar to that of castration (24).

On the other hand, the administration of anterior lobe to immature animals leads to follicular development, ovulation and luteinization (24, 25, 26), together with the premature development of the uterus and vagina. The anterior lobe of the pituitary body, therefore, is essential and acts through its ability to stimulate follicular development and luteinization.

The action of these hormones during the early part of pregnancy is interesting in this connection.

The removal of the corpus luteum results in a failure of the endometrium to produce decidua (27). Abortion likewise follows either removal of the corpus luteum or hypophysectomy in the early months of pregnancy, but may be prevented if progestin is administered after either of these operations (27, 28, 29).

This evidence shows that the corpus luteum which is responsible for the premenstrual changes in the endometrium is also essential to its further development into the decidua of pregnancy. It is possible to delay parturition and prolong pregnancy in animals by the injection of progesterone or the gonadotropic hormone of pregnancy urine (30, 31).

REFERENCES

1. HITSCHMANN, F. AND ADLER, L.: Der Bau der Uterusschleimhaut des geschlechtsreifen Weibes mit besonderer Berücksichtigung der Menstruation. Monatschr. f. Geburtsh. u. Gyn., 1908, 27, 1.
2. SCHROEDER, R.: Ueber die zeitlichen Beziehungen der Ovulation und Menstruation. Arch. f. Gyn., 1913, 101, 1.
3. ASCHHEIM, S.: Ueber den Glykogengehalt der Uterusschleimhaut. Zentralbl. f. Gyn., 1915, 39, 65.
4. FRANKL, O. AND ASCHNER, B.: Zur quantitativen Bestimmung des tryptischen Fermentes in der Uterusmukosa. Gyn. Rundschau. Berl. u. Wien, 1911, 5, 647.
5. DARON, G. H.: The Arterial Pattern of the Tunica Mucosa of the Macacus Rhesus Uterus. Anat. Rec., 1932, 52, Suppl. 9 & 1936, 58, 348.
6. MARKEE, J. E.: Menstruation in Intraocular Endometrial Transplants. Contrib. to Embryol., Carnegie Inst., 1940, 28, 233.
7. MEYER, R.: Ueber Corpus luteum Bildung beim Menschen. Arch. f. Gyn., 1911, 93, 354.
8. NOVAK, E.: Menstruation and Its Disorders, N. Y., 1931.

9. LENZ, J.: Vorzeitige Menstruation, Geschlechtsreife und Entwicklung mit besonderer Berücksichtigung der Skelettentwicklung. Arch. f. Gyn., 1913, 99, 67.

10. FLUHMAN, C. F.: The Length of the Human Menstrual Cycle. Am. J. Obst. & Gyn., 1934, 27, 73.

11. AREY, L. B.: The Degree of Normal Menstrual Irregularity. An Analysis of 20,000 Calendar Records from 1500 Individuals. Am. J. Obst. & Gyn., 1939, 37, 112.

12. BARER, A. P., FOWLER, W. W. AND BALDRIDGE, C. W.: Blood Loss during Normal Menstruation. Proc. Soc. Exper. Med., 1935, 32, 1458.

13. SANES, K. I.: The Age of Menopause. A Statistical Study. Trans. Sec. Ob. Gyn. & Abd. Surg., A.M.A., 1918, 258.

14. FRAENKL, L.: Die Function des Corpus Luteum. Arch. f. Gyn., 1903, 68, 438.

15. CORNER, G. W. AND ALLEN, W. M.: Physiology of the Corpus Luteum. Production of a Special Uterine Reaction (Progestational Proliferation) by Extracts of the Corpus Luteum. Am. Jnl. Physiol., 1929, 88, 326.

16. SMITH, P. E. AND ENGEL, E. T.: Experimental Evidence Regarding the Role of Anterior Pituitary in the Development and Regulation of the Genital System. Am. J. Anat., 1927, 40, 159.

17. ALLEN, E.: The Menstrual Cycle of the Monkey, Macacus Rhesus. Observations on Normal Animals, the Effects of the Removal of the Ovaries and the Effect of Injections of Ovarian and Placental Extracts into the Spayed Animals. Contrib. to Embryol. No. 98 Carnegie Inst., 1927, 19, 1.

18. ROBERTSON, D. C., MADDUX, W. P. AND ALLEN, E.: Ovarian Hormone Effects in Ovariectomized Monkeys. Endocrinol., 1930, 14, 77.

19. HISAW, F. L., MEYER, R. K. AND FEVOLD, H. L.: Production of a Premenstrual Endometrium in Castrated Monkeys by Ovarian Hormones. Proc. Soc. Exp. Biol. & Med., 1930, 27, 400.

20. CORNER, G. W.: The Ovarian Hormones and Experimental Menstruation, Am. J. Obst. and Gyn., 1939, 38.

21. WERNER, A. A. AND COLLIER, W. D.: The Effect of Theelin Injections on the Castrated Woman. J. A. M. A., 1933, 100, 633.

22. KAUFMAN, C.: Therapeutics with Ovarian Hormones, J. Obs. & Gyn. Br. Emp., 1935, 42, 409.

23. ZUCKERMAN, S.: Proc. Roy. Soc. Lond., 1937, 13, 124, 150.

24. SMITH, P. E. AND WHITE, W. E.: The Effect of Hypophysectomy on Ovulation and Corpus Luteum Formation in the Rabbit. J. A. M. A., 1931, 97, 1861.

25. ENGEL, E. T.: Pituitary-gonadal Relationship and the Problem of Precocious Sexual Maturity. Endocrinol., 1931, 15, 405.

26. ASCHHEIM, S. AND ZONDEK, B.: Hypophysenvorderlappenhormon und Ovarialhormon im Harn von Schwangeren. Klin. Wchnschr., 1927, 6, 1322.

27. LOEB, L.: Ueber die Bedeutung des Corpus Luteum für die Periodizität des sexuellen Zyklus beim weiblichen Säugetierorganismus. Deutsch. Med. Wchnschr., 1911, 37, 17.

28. CORNER, G. W.: Physiology of the Corpus Luteum. 1. The Effect of Very Early Ablation of the Corpus Luteum upon Embryos and Uterus. Am. Jnl. Physiol., 1928, 86, 74.

29. ALLEN, W. M. AND CORNER, G. W.: Physiology of Corpus Luteum VII. Maintenance of Pregnancy in Rabbit after very early Castration by Corpus Luteum Extracts. Proc. Soc. Exp. Biol. & Med., 1930, 27, 403.

30. HECKEL, G. P. AND ALLEN, W. M.: Prolongation of Pregnancy in the Rabbit by the Injection of Progesterone. Am. J. Obst. & Gyn., 1938, 35, 131.

31. SNYDER, F. F.: The Prolongation of Pregnancy and Complications of Parturition in the Rabbit Following Induction of Ovulation near Term. Bull. J. Hopk. Hosp., 1934, 54, 1.

CHAPTER III

RELATION OF MENSTRUATION TO OVULATION; FERTILIZA-
TION; AND IMPLANTATION

OVULATION is the term applied to the expulsion of an ovum from a mature graafian follicle. Tissues removed simultaneously from the uterus and ovary show that ovulation occurs in the interval phase of the mentrual cycle (1, 2). Most observers believe that it takes place around the 13th or 14th day after the beginning of the last menstruation. Likewise, all human ova that have been recovered from the fallopian tubes have been obtained in the middle of the inter-menstrual cycle (3).

This opinion has been further substantiated by observing the effect of pituitary extract on uterine contractions. Injections of pituitary extract cause the uterus to contract when it has been previously sensitized by estrin. On the other hand, this action is inhibited by progestin. It has been shown that up to the fifteenth day uterine contractions may be thus produced but after this date they are inhibited. It therefore is thought that the follicle secretes estrin up to a short time before the fifteenth day and that after the fifteenth day the corpus luteum is sufficiently developed to produce the inhibiting progestin. Ovulation, accordingly, must occur a short time before the fifteenth day (4).

MATURATION OF THE HUMAN OVUM has not been fully observed. In most mammals studied, the first polar body is given off before the follicle ruptures. Similar changes probably take place in the human ovum before it leaves the ovary (3). In the monkey, the extrusion of the second polar body occurs in the tubes (5).

MIGRATION OF THE OVUM. It is generally believed that the ovum, after its extrusion from the ovary, is caught in a capillary current which flows between the peritoneal surfaces of the pelvic organs and that it is carried by this current to one of the abdominal ostia of the Fallopian tubes. Experimental proof of the existence of such a current is afforded by the observation that India ink injected into the peritoneal cavity of animals can be found in the tubes within a short time thereafter. Similarly, dye injected into the pouch of Douglas, ultimately finds its way into the vagina. Perhaps the best evidence of this method of transmission is the fact that uterine pregnancies have occurred after the removal of the tube on one side and the ovary on the other. It formerly was thought that the direction of the capillary current was due to the action of the cilia which are present on the tubal epithelium. Since many of the ciliated cells are replaced by secretory cells soon after the follicle ruptures, the cilia are least numerous when they are most needed. For this reason, the peristaltic

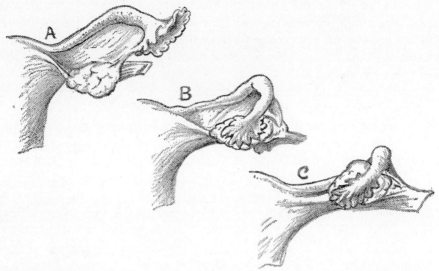

Fig. 26. Movement of tube and ovary during ovulation (Westman). The straight tube A becomes bow-shaped B, C and the ovary rotates upward B, C and downward as a result of contraction and relaxation of its ligaments.

action of the tubal musculature which causes rhythmic contractile waves toward the uterus are now thought to be responsible for the sucking-in of the ovum-laden capillary stream (6, 7).

The transit of the ovum from the ovary to the tube may and, at times, probably is effected by a much simpler mechanism. Observations made on monkeys through a laparoscope and special Roentgen studies of women indicate that the tube which ordinarily is more or less straight (Fig. 26A) curves in a bow-shaped manner around the upper pole of the ovary during ovulation with the result that the abdominal ostium and its blood-distended and stretched-out fimbriae are brought into relation with the surface of the ovary (Fig. 26B). Due to the alternate contraction and relaxation of the musculature in the ovarian ligaments, the ovary then moves upward and downward and rotates from side to side on its long axis so that its various surfaces are successively turned toward the fimbriated extremity of the tube (Fig. 26C). In such circumstances, an ovum extruded from the ovary will be transferred almost directly from the ruptured follicle to the Fallopian tube (8, 9).

MIGRATION OF THE SPERMATOZOA. The seminal fluid ejaculated into the vagina during coitus contains millions of actively motile spermatozoa. From the upper vagina some of these migrate through the uterus to the tubes. The upward journey through the cervix and uterus is accomplished in slightly over one hour and is largely the result of their own motility. Pregnancy, therefore, occasionally follows the discharge of semen on an unruptured hymen even though its orifice is only a few milimeters in diameter.

THE VIABILITY OF THE OVUM AND SPERMATOZOON has been variously estimated. The ovum probably dies within a short time after it leaves the ovary.
Up to the present, all ova recovered from the fallopian tubes show evidences of
degeneration, even though they were obtained within a few days after the estimated date of ovulation (3).

In some animals, the life of the spermatozoon is very short, while in others it
lives for several months. Human spermatozoa have been kept alive in test
tubes for as long as one week. Observations made on seminal fluid removed
from the vagina show that they die within a few hours after coitus if they remain
in contact with the vaginal fluids. Unquestionably, their life is much longer in
the uterus and the tubes from which they have been recovered as late as two
weeks after coitus (10). It is generally believed, however, that coitus, to be
fruitful, must take place within two or three days of the time of ovulation.

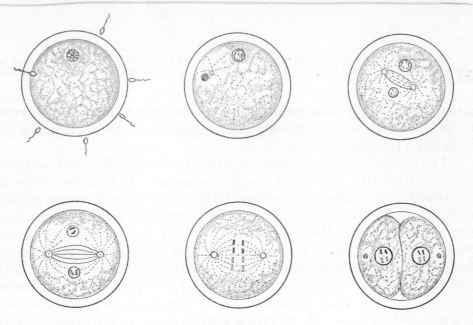

FIG. 27. Fertilization of an ovum.

FERTILIZATION. The union of a spermatozoon and a mature ovum is known
as fertilization. This union usually takes place in the outer third of the fallopian
tube.

One of the numerous sperms that commonly surround the ovum, passes
through the zona pellucida, and thereafter the latter becomes impenetrable to
other spermatozoa. Following penetration, the tail ceases to vibrate and disappears while the head and neck advance toward the center of the egg (Fig. 27).

The head increases in size and becomes spherical to form the male pronucleus.
As it approaches the female pronucleus, the neck piece, which contains the cen-

trosome, divides and the resulting pair of centrosomes arrange themselves between the two pronuclei preparatory to their union to form the first cleavage nucleus. Thus the ovum, which contains only half the original number of chromosomes, receives an equal amount of nuclear material from a similarly reduced male cell.

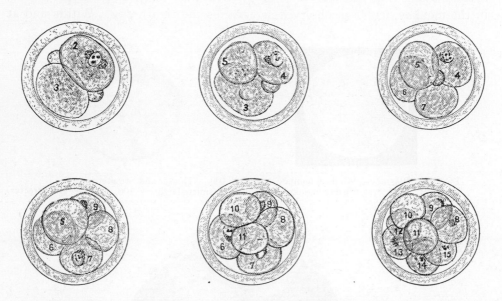

FIG. 28. Early cleavage of the ovum in the monkey (Lewis and Hartman). 1 cell stage from ovulation to 24 hours. 2 cell stage from 24 hours to 26 hours. 3 and 4 cell stages from 36 hours to 48 hours. 5 to 8 cell stages from 48 hours to 72 hours. 9 to 16 cell stages from 72 hours to 96 hours.

SEGMENTATION. Early cell division has not been observed in the human subject. It, however, is believed to be similar to that which occurs in other mammals. In the monkey, the fertilized egg has been washed out of the tube and artificially cultivated (11) (Fig. 28). Under such conditions, the first cleavage takes place in 24 to 26 hours. Mitotic spindles then form in the first two blastomeres but one daughter cell divides before the other with the result that a three-cell stage is observed for a brief interval. Within a few hours, however, cleavage of the second daughter cell occurs. Continued division results in the formation of 9 to 16 blastomeres within three to four days after fertilization, at which time, in the living animal, the ovum reaches the uterine cavity.

Throughout the early cell division, no growth takes place. Accordingly, succeeding blastomeres become smaller as development proceeds and the entire mass of cells is included within the zona pellucida. It, therefore, is no larger than the original mature ovum 0.13 to 0.20 mm. (3).

BLASTULA FORMATION. As the daughter cells divide, the material from which the embryo is to develop seems to be segregated in certain cells—formative cells—and that which is concerned with the development of the auxiliary structures is collected into others—the auxiliary cells. For a time, division of the auxiliary cells is accelerated and they form a single-celled covering for the lagging formative cells. From this uni-cellular envelope, fluid is then secreted and its accumulation soon leads to the formation of the blastodermic vesicle which, in the monkey, has been observed as early as the eighth day. Within and at

FIG. 29A. Blastocyst, 9th day, monkey ovum, × 100.   (Heuser and Streeter).
FIG. 29B. Blastocyst, 9th day, monkey ovum, by transmitted light, × 100.   (Heuser and Streeter)

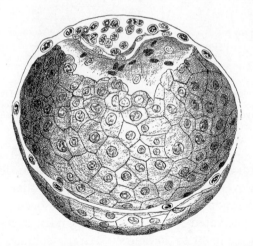

FIG. 29C. Blastocyst, 9th day, monkey ovum, reconstruction based on serial photographs.   Formative cells are shown as the lighter mass at upper or embryonic pole, × 250.   (Heuser and Streeter).

one extremity of this fluid-filled sac, the formative material is collected as an inner cell mass which is in apposition with the covering auxiliary cells (Fig. 29A, B, C).

IMPLANTATION of the human ovum usually takes place in the upper part of the uterus and occurs with equal frequency on the anterior and posterior walls. Occasionally, however, the ovum is implanted laterally, and, in rare instances,

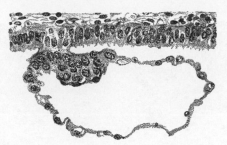

FIG. 29D. Blastocyst, 9th day, monkey ovum, attaching itself to the endometrium.   At the zone of attachment the uterine epithelium is less well stained and the nuclei appear to be loosened up, indicating a beginning cytolysis, ✕ 250.   (Heuser and Streeter).

the implantation site is in the lower segment, in which circumstance the placenta may encroach upon the internal os and give rise to serious or even fatal hemorrhage during pregnancy and labor.

Implantation is thought to occur six days after the ovum is fertilized. Three to four of these are considered necessary for its passage through the Fallopian tube.   During the remainder, the ovum lies free in the uterine cavity and is developing into a blastodermic vesicle.

Just as segmentation and blastula formation have not been observed in man, knowledge of the earliest stage in implantation also is lacking.   For this reason, it will be necessary to supply a description of this phase as it occurs in the monkey. On the 8th day (in the monkey) the zona pellucida disintegrates and the auxilliary cells in the vicinity of the dormant inner cell mass multiply rapidly to form a ring of trophoblast about this portion of the ovum.   Soon thereafter, the newly formed trophoblastic ring attaches itself to the endometrium.   At the site of attachment the cytoplasm of the epithelial cells becomes pale and the cell nuclei seem to move toward the attached trophoblastic elements (12) (Fig. 29D).   As cytolysis progresses the epithelial nuclei are released and they become engulfed by the rapidly expanding trophoblast.   Within a short time the area of attachment is greatly enlarged and as a consequence the ovum becomes flattened.   As human material is available for the study of most of the subsequent stages, the remainder of this discussion is based largely upon observations made on early human ova.

SOLID TROPHOBLASTIC PLATE STAGE.   Soon after the ovum attaches itself to the surface of the endometrium (6th to 7th day in man) the superficial cells of the latter are destroyed and absorbed by the adjacent blastocyst.   Thus nourished, the trophoblast cells in contact with the endometrium proliferate rapidly and increase in size to form an extensive **solid trophoblastic plate** beneath the embryonic area.   As the surface endometrial epithelium about the site of implantation has only begun to proliferate at this time, the opposite or abembryonic pole of the flattened ovum is free in the uterine cavity and its cells

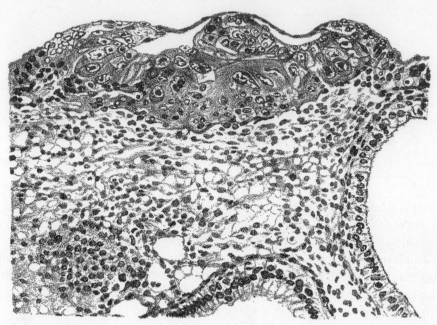

FIG. 30. Implantation—solid trophoblastic plate stage of development (Hertig and Rock, 7½ day human ovum), × 333. The flattened blastocyst is partially implanted in the endometrium. Adjacent to the implantation site, the endometrial epithelium still shows evidence of degeneration in that its nuclei have lost their chromatin and appear hydropic. Some attempt, however is being made by the maternal epithelium to repair the defect as occasional mitotic figures indicate. Beneath the embryonic area the cells in contact with the endometrium have destroyed and absorbed the superficial elements of the latter. Their resulting proliferation and growth has led to the formation of an extensive **solid trophoblastic plate.** That portion of this plate which is adjacent to the blastocyst cavity contains large irregular pale staining cells which have distinct cell outlines—**cytotrophoblast.** The more remote and greater part of the plate is made up of multi-nucleated cytoplasm without definite cell-outlines **syncytiotrophoblast, or plasmoditrophoblast,** with occasional large dividing intermediary cells which are thought to be in the process of transition from cytotrophoblast to syncytiotrophoblast. The opposite pole of the ovum is free in the uterine cavity. Its cells accordingly are not in contact with the endometrium. Lacking pabulum from this source they retain the flat mesotheloid character of the original blastocyst wall. The embryonic area consists of a bilaminar disk dorsal to which is a small cleft, the primordial amniotic cavity between it and the cytotrophoblast. The endometrial pattern is that of the 22nd day of the menstrual cycle with some edema of the stroma immediately beneath the implanted ovum.

lacking pabulum from the endometrium retain the flat mesothelioid character of the original blastocyst wall (Fig. 30). Even at this early stage (7½ days) the solid trophoblastic plate shows considerable differentiation. Adjacent to the blastocyst cavity the cells are large, pale staining and have distinct cell outlines— **cytotrophoblast,** while the more remote and greater part of the plate is made up of masses of multinucleated cytoplasm without cell outlines—**syncytiotrophoblast or plasmoditrophoblast,** with occasional large dividing intermediary cells which are thought to be in the process of transition from the parent cytotrophoblast to syncytiotrophoblast (13).

LACUNAR STAGE. As the ovum insinuates itself further into the endometrium the degenerating cells of the latter furnish nutriment to more and more of the

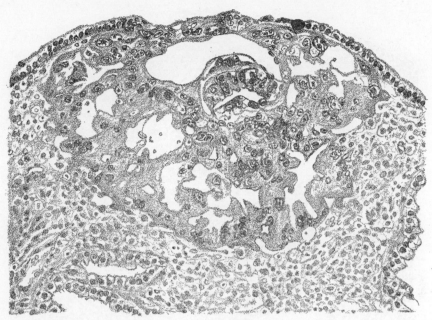

FIG. 31. Implantation—lacunar stage of development (Hertig and Rock), 9½ day human ovum) × 200. The ovum is two-thirds implanted in the superficial portion of the endometrium and the site of penetration is partially closed by proliferating endometrial epithelium. As more and more of the periphery of the ovum comes into contact with destroyed endometrial tissue, the nutriment furnished by the latter leads to alterations in the entire blastocyst wall which are characteristic of all phases of early trophoblastic differentiation. The most noteworthy of these is the formation of large intercommunicating spaces or lacunae in the rapidly growing peripheral trophoblast. Hence the designation of this phase of development as the **lacunar stage**. These lacunae are most prominent at the embryonic pole where the syncytium is more mature and contains phagocytosed and partially digested remnants of maternal tissue. In other sections of the same ovum nearby blood sinusoids are being opened by the trophoblast with the result that small amounts of blood have entered some of the lacunae. At the abembryonic pole the trophoblast consists mostly of cytotrophoblastic elements with some transitional cells and scant syncytium. Syrrounding the chorionic cavity is an irregular layer of cytotrophoblast cells. The amniotic cavity is now quite distinct and its dorsal wall shows amniogenic cells being delaminated from the cytotrophoblast. The embryonic disk contains primitive ectodermal cells adjacent to the amniotic cavity and a layer of endodermal cells which cover the opposite or ventral surface. The endometrium is characteristic of the 26th day of the menstrual cycle. The glands are serrated and moderately active. Beneath the surface epithelium and about the spiral arteries a predecidual reaction is evident. Edema of the stroma is somewhat more marked than ordinary for this stage of the premenstrual cycle.

trophoblastic envelope with the result that by the 9th day the entire blastocyst wall has become altered and shows the various phases of early trophoblastic differentiation (Fig. 31). The most noteworthy of these is the presence of large intercommunicating spaces or lacunae in the rapidly growing peripheral trophoblast—hence the designation of this phase as the **lacunar stage of development**. These lacunae are most prominent at the embryonic pole of the ovum where the syncytium is more mature and contains remnants of phagocytosed and partially digested maternal tissue which have been taken up by pseudopodia projecting into the maternal stroma (13).

The rapidly expanding trophoblast continues to invade the underlying stroma and erodes contiguous maternal vessels from which blood enters the lacunae.

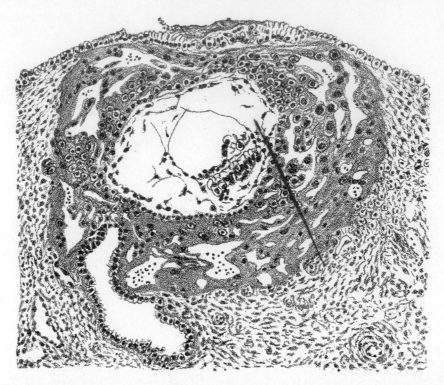

FIG. 31A. Implantation—lacunar stage of development (continued) (Hertig and Rock, 11½ day human ovum), × 133.   The ovum is almost completely buried within the endometrium.   All but a small portion of the defect at the site of penetration has been repaired by regenerating epithelium which in places is several cells thick.   A small overlying coagulum completes the closure of the unrepaired defect.   The peripheral syncytiotrophoblast forms approximately three-fourths of the entire tropho- blastic shell.   It contains many intercommunicating lacunae (precursers of the intervillous space) which have been partially filled with blood from eroded contiguous maternal vessels.   A large gland is being surrounded by the invading syncytium and the epithelium in its upper portion is showing the effect of this trophoblastic invasion.   Bounding the chorionic cavity is a fairly well defined cytotrophoblast which merges outwardly with the syncytiotrophoblast and inwardly with the primitive extraembryonic mesoblast to both of which it is giving origin.   In places irregular masses of proliferating cytotrophoblast project out into the syncytiotrophoblast to form what probably would eventually have become primary chorionic villi.   The embryo consists of two opposed disks of cells ectoderm and endoderm: the former bounded dorsally by the partially formed amnion and the latter bounded ventrally by the extraembry- onic coelom.   The endometrial pattern is that of the 25th day of the menstrual cycle.   Predecidual changes are seen in the stroma beneath the ovum and about the spiral arteries.

Thus the nutrient elements of the mother's blood are brought into direct contact with the ovum, whose absorption surface has been extensively increased by the formation of the enlarging anastomosing lacunae. This more suitable source of nutriment also is favored by an underlying network of large thin-walled en- dothelial-lined sinusoids which are derived from the surrounding arteriovenous capillary system.

The cytotrophoblast prior to the formation of the lacunae is relatively remote from the endometrium and the source of nutriment which the degenerating cells of the latter furnish.   After the lacunae are formed and their connection with

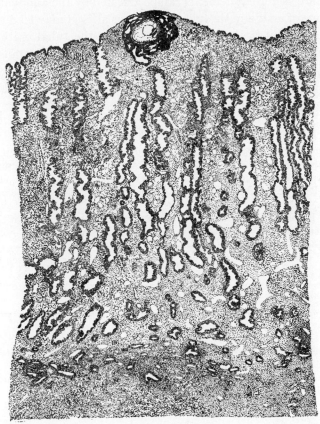

FIG. 31B. Implantation (Hertig and Rock, 11½ day human ovum), × 20, showing the general architecture of the endometrium at this stage of implantation. The ovum is almost completely imbedded in the superficial compact portion of the endometrium. The glands and stroma are characteristic of the 25th day of the menstrual cycle with some edema immediately beneath the implanted ovum.

each other and the maternal sinusoids is established not only is the absorption surface of the ovum greatly increased but the nutrient elements in the mother's blood are brought into closer proximity to the underlying or basally placed cytotrophoblast. The cytotrophoblast which encircles the chorionic cavity, accordingly, proliferates rapidly and sends out into the syncytiotrophoblast buds of cells which project into the lacunar spaces (Fig. 31A). These cytotrophoblastic buds now in direct contact with the maternal blood continue their proliferation to form solid masses which are to become the primary chorionic villi and are observed in most early ova at about the 14th day (14).

During the period in which the ovum passes through the tube, the ciliated tubal epithelium, acting under the influence of the corpus luteum, is transformed largely into secretory cells, the secretion of which is thought to furnish protection and some essential factor to the segmenting egg. This transformation of ciliated cells into secretory elements can be arrested by the removal of the ovaries, and the passage of an ovum through a tube thus altered may lead to its degeneration. The corpus luteum, through its action on the tubal epithelium, accordingly, is essential to the life of the fertilized ovum during its transit through the tube (15). Removal of the corpus luteum shortly after fertilization also inhibits the growth of the blastocyst but this inhibiting effect can be prevented by the injection of progesterone (16, 17).

REFERENCES

1. MEYER, R.: Ueber die Beziehung der Eizelle und des befruchteten Eies zum Follikelapparat, sowie des Corpus luteum zur Menstruation. Ein Beitrag zur normalen und pathologischen Anatomie und Physiologie des Ovariums. Arch. f. Gyn., 1913, 100, 1.
2. SCHRÖDER, R.: Ueber die zeitlichen Beziehungen der Ovulation und Menstruation. Arch. f. Gyn., 1913, 101, 1.
3. ALLEN, E., PRATT, J. P., NEWELL, Q. U., AND BLAND, L.: Recovery of Human Ova from the Uterine Tubes. Time of Ovulation in the Menstrual Cycle. J. A. M. A., 1928, 91, 1018.
4. KNAUS, H.: Ueber die Bedeutung von Untersuchungen an der isolierten Gebärmutter für das Geschehen in vivo. Zentralbl. f. Gyn., 1928, 52, 2566.
5. CORNER, G. W.: Ovulation and Menstruation in Macacus Rhesus. Contrib. to Embryol. Carnegie Inst. No. 75, 1923, 15, 73.
6. KOK, F.: Experimentelle Untersuchungen über die pharmakologische Beeinflussung der Eileiter-Muskulatur. Arch. f. Gyn., 1927, 132, 7.
7. v. MICULICZ-RADECKI, F.: Der Eiauffangsmechanismus bei der Frau und die sich daraus ergebenden Schlussfolgerungen für die operative Behandlung der Sterilität. Arch. f. Gyn., 1936, 141, 128.
8. CAFFIER, P.: Studien zum Eitransport beim Menschen. I. Der Eiabnahme-mechanismus. Zentralbl. f. Gyn., 1936, 60. 1873.
9. WESTMAN, A.: Investigations into the Transit of Ova in Man. J. Obs. & Gyn. Brit. Emp., 1937, 44, 821.
10. NÜRNBERGER: Klinische und experimentelle Untersuchungen über die Lebensdauer der menschlichen Spermatozoen. Monatschr. f. Geburtsh. u. Gyn., 1920, 53, 87.
11. LEWIS, W. H. AND HARTMAN, C. C.: Early Cleavage Stages of the Egg of the Monkey (Macacus Rhesus), Contrib. to Embryol. Carnegie Inst. No. 143, 1933, 24, 187.
12. WISLOCKI, G. B. AND STREETER, G. L.: On the Placentation of the Macaque (Macaca Mulatta) from the Time of Implantation until the Formation of the Definitive Placenta. Contrib. to Embryol. Carnegie Inst., No. 160, 1938, 27, 1.
13. HERTIG, A. T. AND ROCK, J.: Two Human Ova of the Previllous Stage Having a Developmental Age of About 7 to 9 Days Respectively. Contributions to Embryol., Carnegie Inst., 1945, 41, 67.
14. HERTIG, A. T. AND ROCK, J.: Two Human Ova of the Previllous Stage Having an Ovulation Age of About Eleven and Twelve Days Respectively. Contributions to Embryol., Carnegie Inst., 1941, 39, 127.
15. WESTMAN, A.: Studies of the Function of the Mucous Membranes of the Uterine Tube. Acta Obst. et Gyn. Scandin., 1930, 10, 288.
16. CORNER, G. W.: Physiology of the Corpus Luteum. Am. J. Physiol., 1928, 86, 74.
17. ALLEN, W. M. AND CORNER, G. W.: Physiology of the Corpus Luteum. Am. J. Physiol., 1929, 88, 340.
18. HEUSER, C. H. AND STREETER, G. L.: Development of the Macaque Embryo. Contrib. to Embryol., Carnegie Inst., 1941, 29, 17.

CHAPTER IV

CHRONOLOGICAL DEVELOPMENT OF PREGNANCY

THE END OF THE FIRST LUNAR MONTH

The end of the first lunar month, after the beginning of the last menstruation, has now been reached.

During the month just past the following events have taken place in the order given:

1st to 4th day—Menstrual phase of the endometrial cycle.

4th to 10th day—Postmenstrual phase accompanied by the development of the follicle.

14th day—Ovulation probably took place around this date and was followed almost immediately by fertilization.

14th to 18th day—Migration of the segmenting ovum through the tube to the uterine cavity.

18th to 21st day—Transformation of the ovum into the blastodermic vesicle with the loss of the zona pellucida and implantation into the endometrium.

21st to 28th day—Endometrium beginning to change into decidua. Rapid growth of the ovum with the development of a marked plasmoditrophoblast. Nutriment is supplied by histiotroph through osmosis—the histiotroph stage.

At the end of the first lunar month the following changes are noted.

Ovum

THE OVUM is about sixteen days old and measures 2 to 3 mm., i.e., it is smaller than a BB shot.

THE EMBRYONIC AREA is 0.15 to 0.20 mm. thick.

THE AMNION, YOLK SAC, ECTODERM, MESODERM AND ENTODERM as well as an extraembryonic body cavity are present. Most of these have been noted in the Miller ovum, twelve days of age, and the Bryce-Teacher ovum, fourteen days of age. They are all present in the Peters' ovum, which is about seventeen days old, and was found in the uterus of a woman who committed suicide thirty days after the beginning of her last period (Fig. 32).

The egg has been implanted about one week, and is receiving abundant nutriment by osmosis from the embryotroph.

33

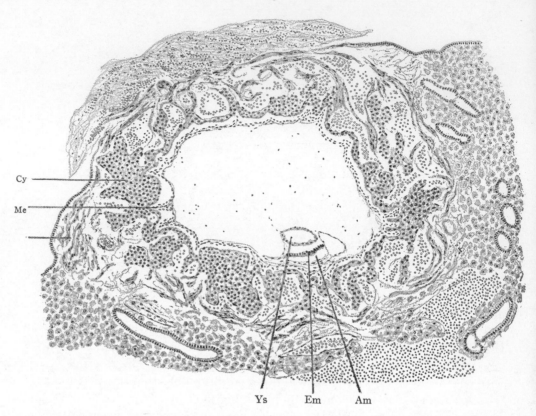

FIG. 32. Peters Ovum. Cytotrophoblast (*Cy*) many cells thick projecting into plasmoditropho-blast (*Pl*). Mesoderm (*Me*). Yolk sac (Ys). Embryonic area (*Em*). Amnion (*Am*).

Uterus

THE UTERUS is somewhat enlarged and slightly softened. On bimanual examination, however, these changes cannot be distinguished from those that are observed in the uterus just before a normal menstruation.

THE ENDOMETRIUM continues to hypertrophy to form the decidua vera.

THE SITE OF IMPLANTATION is closed but is not sufficiently elevated above the adjacent thickened endometrium to be distinguishable (Fig. 33).

Ovary

Development of the corpus luteum continues with a resultant increase in its size.

Symptoms

AMENORRHEA, or the cessation of menstruation, is the chief symptom observed by the patient at this time.

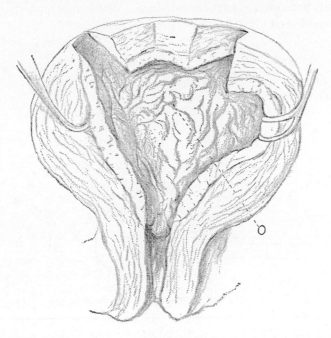

FIG. 33. The uterus thirty days after the beginning of the last period—natural size (Peters). *O*, site of implantation.

THE END OF THE SIXTH WEEK

THE OVUM measures 2 to 2½ cm. in diameter (the size of a large marble).

THE EMBRYO is 1 cm. long and has curved laterally to form a cylindrical mass. It likewise has curved forward on its long axis so that the head and tail almost meet on the ventral surface. The anlagen of the heart, brain, limbs, oral fossae, ears and nasal fossae have appeared.

THE AMNION is considerably larger and there is present a definite body stalk which contains the allantois and the trunks of the chorionic vessels.

THE YOLK SAC is beginning to be pinched off by the ventral bending of the embryo.

THE CHORION. The cytotrophoblast has become more active, and definite outgrowths extend into the blood lacunae. In these outgrowths mesodermal elements likewise have developed. Vascularization also has been effected, so that each villus now consists of a vascularized core of mesoderm surrounded by an inner layer of cytotrophoblast—the Langhans' layer—and an outer covering of plasmoditrophoblast—the syncytium. At the end of the sixth week (after the beginning of the last period, when the ovum is about four weeks old), the circulatory system between the embryo and the chorion has been completed and pulsations of the heart have begun.   The hemotroph stage, therefore, is definitely established (Fig. 34).

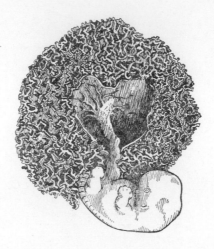

IG. 34. The ovum and embryo at the sixth week (Kollman).

HE ENDOMETRIUM continues to hypertrophy and is now 6 to 8 mm. in thickness.   Two distinct layers are to be distinguished—the compact and the alveolar.   The development of the endometrium has not kept pace with that of the ovum.   As a result, the latter, covered by a thin layer of decidua, bulges into the cavity of the uterus.   That portion of the decidua which covers the projecting wall of the ovum is termed the decidua capsularis.   The part which lies between the ovum and the uterine musculature is the decidua basalis, while the remainder which lines the uterine cavity is known as the decidua vera.

Uterus

SIZE.   Enlargement of the uterus continues as a result of hypertrophy and hyperplasia of its muscle fibers, together with an increase in elastic tissue.   The blood vessels also are enlarged and engorged.   This appreciable increase in the size of the whole uterus may be detected by bimanual examination (Fig. 35).

SHAPE.   The shape of the uterus is still pyriform although it is beginning to become more or less ovoid.

CONSISTENCY.   The whole uterus, together with the cervix, is somewhat softened.   In the body, the degree of softening varies in different parts.   This irregular softening can be felt by the examining fingers and makes possible a tentative diagnosis of pregnancy.

POSITION.   At this time, the normal anteflexion of the uterus is increased.

CERVIX.   The cervix is slightly softened and its glands are more active and give rise to a rather profuse, whitish vaginal discharge.

URINE. The urine when injected into animals produces the characteristic changes seen when the Aschheim-Zondek test is positive.

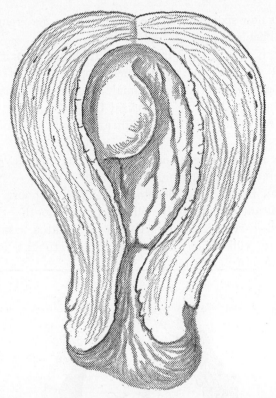

FIG. 35. The uterus at the end of the sixth week, showing the ovum with its covering of decidua capsularis projecting into the uterine cavity (Bumm). The decidua vera is well developed (natural size).

Symptoms

MORNING SICKNESS. About 50 per cent of all pregnant women are nauseated or complain of vomiting, especially in the morning, hence the term "morning sickness". This symptom grows worse for about one month, after which it progressively improves and finally disappears at the end of the third month.

FREQUENCY OF URINATION. The enlarged and more anteflexed uterus causes an increased desire to urinate which grows worse for a short time. When the uterus rises out of the pelvis at the end of the third month, this symptom usually disappears.

BREAST SYMPTOMS. Many women state that their breasts are enlarged and feel different at this time. They describe this symptom as a feeling of fullness or numbness in the region of the breasts. More marked breast changes, however, are observed at a slightly later period.

THE END OF THE SECOND LUNAR MONTH

Ovum

THE OVUM is now six weeks of age and measures 5 x 3 cm., i.e., it is about the size of a small hen's egg.

THE EMBRYO is about $2\frac{1}{2}$ cm. in length. Its limbs are fairly well developed and the external genitals have made their appearance. The indifferent sex glands have become differentiated into male and female gonads. Histological examination of them at this time will reveal the sex of the fetus. The form of the embryo now resembles that of an adult and from this time on it is referred to as a fetus.

THE AMNION is much larger and extends to the inner layer of the chorion, completely obliterating the extraembryonic body cavity.

THE CHORION beneath the decidua capsularis is poorly nourished, and, owing to the resultant atrophy of its villi, becomes smooth—the chorion laeve. On the other hand, that which is adjacent to the decidua basalis shows marked development of its villi which ultimately enter into the formation of the placenta—the chorion frondosum (Fig. 36).

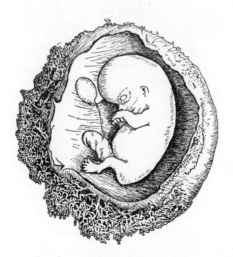

FIG. 36. Ovum and embryo at the end of the second month (Kollman).

Uterus

SIZE. Hypertrophy and hyperplasia continue and result in considerable enlargement of the uterus. It now measures 10 x 6 cm. (Fig. 37).

SHAPE. The uterus is almost ovoid in shape. When relaxed, it loses its characteristic symmetry.

CONSISTENCY. The whole organ is softer, but in the isthmic portion it is much more compressible. Hegar's sign of pregnancy, accordingly, is obtainable at this time.

INTERMITTENT CONTRACTIONS. The uterus may be felt to contract and relax intermittently—Braxton Hicks' sign of pregnancy.

THE CERVIX is considerably softened. Its consistency resembles that of the lips, while in the nonpregnant state it is as firm as the tip of the nose—

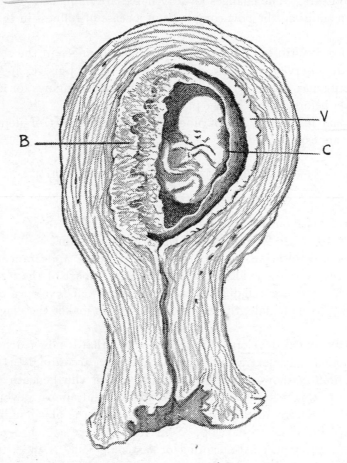

FIG. 37. The uterus at the end of the second month—natural size (Bumm). *V*, decidua vera; *C*, decidua capsularis; *B*, decidua basalis.

Goodell's sign of pregnancy. The glands of the cervix are very active and cause an increase in the vaginal discharge.

VAGINA. The increasing congestion of the vagina gives it a purplish hue—Chadwick's sign of pregnancy.

THE BREASTS are enlarged, their superficial veins are engorged, the nipples show an increased erectility, and the primary areola of pigmentation is darker and contains enlarged sebaceous glands—Montgomery's follicles.

Symptoms

MORNING SICKNESS is at its worst at this time.

PTYALISM. Occasionally, the salivary glands are hyperactive and in rare instances they may cause almost constant expectoration.

BLADDER IRRITABILITY. The increased desire to urinate continues and, like morning sickness, usually is worse at the end of the second lunar month.

THE BREASTS. The changes already noted are frequently observed by the patient. In addition, she now complains of a sense of fullness in the mammary glands.

NERVOUS SYMPTOMS. Occasionally, peculiar changes in the sense of taste and smell are observed. Certain odors become very repulsive, and alterations in the appetite may occur. There may be cravings or longings for unusual substances never before desired by the patient.

Emotional instability is not uncommon, and periods of depression and excitability are experienced.

THE END OF THE THIRD LUNAR MONTH

Ovum

THE OVUM is about the size of a tennis ball (Fig. 38).

THE FETUS is 7 to 9 cm. long and weighs about 30 gm.

Centers of ossification, which began to make their appearance as early as the sixth week, are now evident throughout a large part of the fetal skeleton. The fingers and toes are well differentiated and show well developed nails at their extremities. In the female, the presence of a uterus makes the diagnosis of sex possible.

THE AMNION has developed to such an extent that it now reaches and fuses with the chorion. The extraembryonic body cavity, accordingly, is obliterated.

THE CHORION shows continued atrophy of the villi beneath the decidua capsularis. In this region, therefore, it is smooth and almost devoid of villous projections. Adjacent to the decidua basalis, where the blood supply is abundant, the villi continue to develop. Some of them are attached to the endometrium and are known as anchoring or fastening villi. Others terminate in the intervillous spaces where they receive nutriment from the maternal blood— nourishing villi.

THE DECIDUA capsularis is in contact with the decidua vera, and the uterine cavity is almost completely obliterated. Further penetration of the chorionic elements has greatly diminished the thickness of the decidua basalis. The decidua vera, on the other hand, has reached its greatest development and is about 1 cm. thick. On section, it shows two well defined layers. The upper of these is made up of the hypertrophied stroma cells and is known as the decidua compacta. The glands have been crowded to a deeper level and the interglandular substance is diminished, so that this layer now has a spongy appearance. Accordingly, it is known as the alveolar or spongy layer of the decidua.

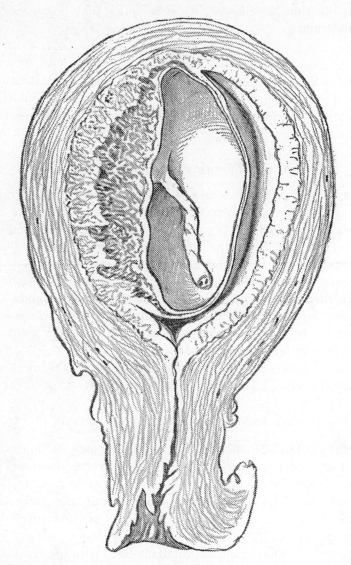

FIG. 38. Section of the uterus through the implanted ovum at the end of the third month—natural size (Bumm).

Uterus

SIZE. The uterus at the end of the third month is 13 x 10 x 7½ cm. (Fig. 38).

SHAPE. It has lost its former pyriform shape and is now ovoid.

CONSISTENCY. The entire uterus is symmetrically softened and resembles, in consistency, the relaxed biceps muscle.

THE BREASTS continue to enlarge and the pigment changes become more intense. At this time, a yellowish, sticky secretion may be expressed from the nipples—colostrum.

Symptoms

Morning sickness has disappeared as has the bladder irritability which was complained of in the second month. With the loss of these troublesome symptoms, the patient develops a sense of well being which makes her view with optimism the remainder of her pregnancy.

THE END OF THE FOURTH LUNAR MONTH

THE FETUS is 10 to 17 cm. long and weighs 108 gm. The external genitalia are sufficiently differentiated to make possible the diagnosis of sex.

THE DECIDUA capsularis is in contact with the decidua vera, and the decidua basalis has become united with the chorion frondosum to form the placenta.

THE UTERUS is 15 x 12½ x 10 cm. and is globular in shape. The presence of a relatively large amount of amniotic fluid gives it a cystic consistency.

Between the fourth and fifth months, the **fetal heart sounds** are audible. They are more rapid than the **uterine souffle** which is synchronous with the maternal pulse. At this time, the movements of the child, likewise, may be heard—**choc fetal or fetal shock sounds.**

SYMPTOMS. Between the fourth and fifth month, the mother may feel movements of the fetus. This is known as **quickening.**

THE END OF THE FIFTH LUNAR MONTH

THE FETUS is 18 to 27 cm. long and weighs 280 gm. A thin, white, cheesy material is now found on parts of its body—the vernix caseosa. Its face is wrinkled and the eyelids are open.

THE CHORION. The chorionic villi show a diminution in the cells which make up Langhans' layer. Accordingly, most villi are now covered by only a thin layer of syncytium.

THE DECIDUA. The decidua capsularis is fused with the decidua vera.

THE UTERUS is 17½ x 15 x 12 cm. and is changing from a globular to an ovoid shape (Fig. 39).

On vaginal examination, passive movements of the fetus may be obtained—**internal ballottement.**

THE BREASTS show a second zone of pigmentation, peripheral to the original primary areola. In this region, the pigment is unevenly distributed and has a mottled appearance—**the secondary areola of pigmentation.**

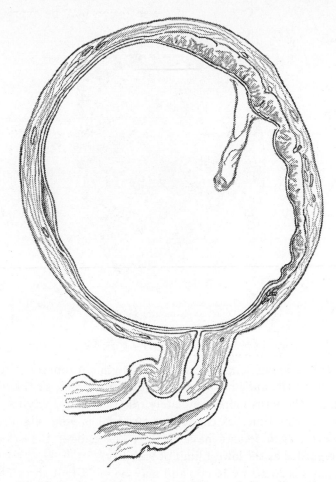

FIG. 39. Section of the uterus at the fifth month (Bumm). $\times\frac{1}{2}$

THE END OF THE SIXTH LUNAR MONTH

THE FETUS is 31 cm. long and weighs about 650 gm. If born at this time, it may survive for a few hours. Its skin is thin, shiny, and reddish in color (Fig. 40).

THE UTERUS is 21 x 16 x 15 cm. and extends to the level of the umbilicus. Its shape is more or less ovoid.

The abdomen is slightly distended and the depression which usually is seen at the umbilicus is obliterated. A thin area of pigmentation may be observed in the midline between the symphysis and the umbilicus—the linea nigra.

Often the parts of the child may be distinctly felt, and palpation of the fetus at this time may be sufficiently definite to enable one to make a positive diagnosis of pregnancy.

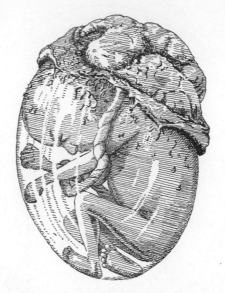

FIG. 40. Ovum at six months (Kollman). ✕½

THE END OF THE SEVENTH LUNAR MONTH

THE FETUS is 36 cm. long and weighs 1200 gm. From now on, the ratio of the child's bulk to the amount of amniotic fluid increases, so that, as the pregnancy advances, the fetus more completely fills the uterine cavity. Should the child be born at this time, its chance for survival is very slight. In rare instances, however, such fetuses have lived. The end of the seventh month, therefore, is regarded as the lowest limit of viability.

THE UTERUS is 26 x 18 x 16 cm. and may be felt about three fingerbreadths above the umbilicus.

As the abdomen continues to enlarge, the deeper layers of the skin are torn and give rise to purplish red zigzag marks which are known as the striae gravidarum.

Auscultation occasionally reveals a bruit which is synchronous with the fetal heart rate—the funic souffle.

THE END OF THE EIGHTH LUNAR MONTH

THE FETUS is 40 cm. long and weighs 1600 gm. Its chances for survival are much greater than are those of a seventh month fetus, although there is a popular fallacy to the contrary.

THE UTERUS is 29 x 21 x 17½ cm.

Pressure symptoms resulting from the rapidly growing uterus are not uncommon. These consist of constipation, gastric distress, and interference with the return circulation from the lower extremities, which, if marked, may cause varicosities in the latter and edema of the ankles.

THE END OF THE NINTH LUNAR MONTH

THE FETUS is 44 cm. long and weighs 2500 gm. If born at this time, it should survive.

THE UTERUS is $32\frac{1}{2}$ x 23 x $21\frac{1}{2}$ cm. and extends almost to the ensiform cartilage.

The enlargement of the abdomen is very marked and leads to a protrusion of the umbilicus and an increase in the striae of pregnancy.

Likewise, descent of the diaphragm is interfered with and, as a result, difficult breathing or shortness of breath is a common complaint in the latter months of pregnancy.

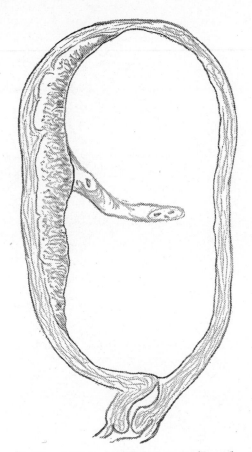

FIG. 41. Cross-section of a full term uterus (Bumm). $\times\frac{1}{3}$

THE END OF THE TENTH LUNAR MONTH

THE FETUS is 50 cm. long and weighs 3200 gm.

THE UTERUS, which measured $7\frac{1}{2}$ x 5 x $2\frac{1}{2}$ cm. and weighed 50 to 60 gm. before pregnancy, now measures 35 x 24 x $21\frac{1}{2}$ cm. and weighs 1000 gm. At the same time, its capacity has increased from 2 to 4 cc. to over 4000 cc. (Fig. 41).

In women who are pregnant for the first time, the presenting part sinks into the pelvis about two weeks before the end of gestation. This is known as **lightening.** When it occurs, the patient experiences greater ease in breathing and notes that her waist line is smaller. At the same time, the pressure symptoms above noted are aggravated. Varicosities of the veins and edema of the ankles, accordingly, are not uncommon as term approaches. Lightening also is responsible for an increase in the irritability of the bladder, and the patient again has a more frequent desire to urinate.

CHAPTER V

THE FETAL MEMBRANES

THE CHORION

The ovum is in the blastodermic vesicle stage and is about 6 days old when as a result of the erosive action of its trophoblast it penetrates the superficial layer of the endometrium and is partially implanted. That portion of the blastocyst wall which is in direct contact with the maternal tissues is thus nourished by the destroyed endometrial cells and proliferates rapidly to form a **solid trophoblastic plate.** In the $7\frac{1}{2}$ day ovum this plate is already differentiated into an irregular proximal layer of large pale cells with definite cell outline—**cytotrophoblast** and peripheral masses of multinucleated cytoplasm without cell outline—**syncytiotrophoblast** or **plasmoditrophoblast** (1) (Figs. 30 and 42).

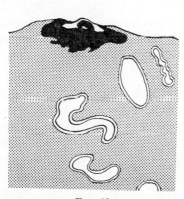
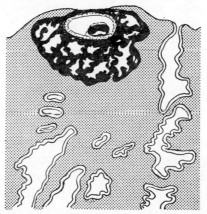

FIG. 42   FIG. 43

FIG. 42. Early trophoblast. Solid trophoblastic plate stage. Hertig and Rock, $7\frac{1}{2}$ day human ovum, $\times$ 133.

FIG. 43. Early trophoblast. Lacunar stage. Hertig and Rock, $9\frac{1}{2}$ day human ovum, $\times$ 133.

Deeper penetration of the ovum is associated with increased destruction of the endometrium, the degenerating cells of which furnish nutriment—**histiotroph** to more and more of the blastocyst wall. As a consequence, the entire wall becomes altered and on the 9th day shows large intercommunicating spaces or **lacunae** in the rapidly growing peripheral syncytium (Figs. 31 and 43). Enlargement of these spaces soon converts the trophoblast into a sponge like mass which as development proceeds shows a progressive thinning of its syncytial trabeculae. As expansion of the trophoblast continues its invasion of the underlying stroma is accompanied with erosion of maternal vessels which brings the maternal blood stream into communication with the lacunae. The nutrient elements of the mother's blood are thereby brought directly to the greatly

47

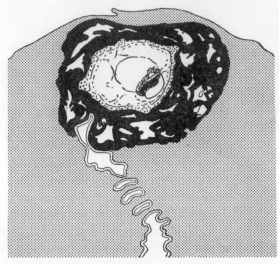

FIG. 44. Early trophoblast.   Rapidly proliferating cytotrophoblast with buds projecting **into the** syncytium.   Hertig and Rock, 11½ day human ovum, × 133.

increased absorption surface of the ovum.   At the same time, there is developed from the adjacent maternal arteriovenous capillary system an underlying network of large thin-walled endothelial lined sinusoids which greatly favor this additional and more suitable source of nutriment.

Prior to the lacunar stage, the proximal cytotrophoblast is relatively remote from the endometrial stroma and its source of nutriment.   After the lacunae are formed however and their connection with each other and the maternal sinusoids is established not only histiotroph but the nutrient elements of the mother's blood are brought into close proximity to the cytotrophoblast which encircles the chorionic cavity.   The basally placed cytotrophoblast accordingly proliferates rapidly and by the 11th day sends out buds of cells which project into the blood contained spaces in the sponge like syncytium (2) (Figs. 31a and 44).

The cytotrophoblast buds, now in direct contact with the maternal blood continue their proliferation to form solid masses of cells which are to become the primary chorionic villi and are observed in early ova on about the 11th day (Fig. 45a).   Within a short time the central portion of the primary villus loosens up and gives rise to a reticular core of mesoblast which seems to originate from the cytotrophoblast about the periphery and at the tip of the villus (Fig. 45b). As the syncytiotrophoblast covering of the villi also has been observed to arise from the cytotrophoblast it is thought that the cytotrophoblast is the parent of both the mesodermal core and the syncytial covering of the villus.

Soon multinucleated angioblastic strands appear within the mesoblastic core.   The cells about the periphery of these strands become elongated to form endothelium while the cytoplasm of some of their central elements undergoes vacuolization and thus gives rise to the future vessels of the villi.   At the same

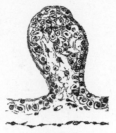

FIG. 45A   FIG. 45B

FIG. 45A. Development of a villus—schematic.   Trophoblastic bud projecting out from chorionic plate.

FIG. 45B. Development of a villus—schematic.   Core of mesoblast originating in situ in tropho-blastic bud.

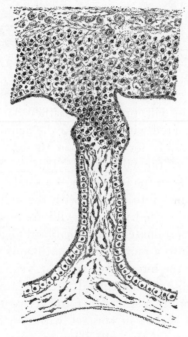

FIG. 45C

FIG. 45C. Development of a villus—schematic.   Angioblastic strands originating in situ in the proximal portion of a villus which contains a mesodermal core surrounded by an inner layer of cytotro-phoblast and an outer layer of syncytium.   Distal to the mesodermal core, the cytotrophoblast is active giving rise to proximal elements below, and a distal cell column above, which is in contact with the endometrium.   Lateral projections of this cell column join similar projections from adjacent villi to form the trophoblastic shell.

time, other central cells are transformed into blood cells.   Thus the blood vessels, plasma and blood cells are developed in-situ in the mesodermal core of the chorionic villi (4).   These vessels later join with similar vessels which have been formed in the mesoderm surrounding the chorionic cavity and in this manner the chorionic plate and its villi are vascularized Fig 45 C.

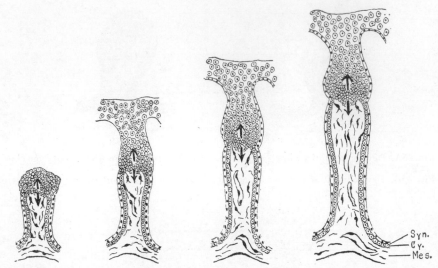

FIG. 46. Diagram showing the growth of a villus.   The cells of the villous tip proliferate and give rise to a distal cytotrophoblast column above and the proximal elements of the villus below.

The extremities of the villi projecting as they do into the blood contained lacunae are favorably situated with regard to the acquisition of nutriment from the maternal blood.   Possibly for this reason the greatest activity is observed in the cellular elements of the villus tips.   This proliferation from the distal portion of the villus results in the formation of a solid column of cytotrophoblast cells which ultimately comes into contact with the maternal tissue.

About the end of the second week the villi are observed to give off definite branches many of which terminate within the blood filled lacunae.   As the latter have become converted into a more or less continuous space the area about the villi is now referred to as the **intervillous space.**   Near the zone of juncture with the endometrium the cell columns spread out laterally and unite with lateral expansions from neighboring columns to form a trophoblastic shell which surrounds the entire ovum and is in contact with the endometrium (Fig. 45c). In the junction zone many of the cells show evidence of degeneration and the extremities of the cell columns are more or less edematous.   These degenerating elements apparently are constantly replaced by new cells which grow outward from the distal ends of the villi.   The growth of the villi accordingly proceeds in two directions, outward and inward from the cytotrophoblast cells at their distal ends.   Some of the cells grow outward to replenish the cell columns while others growing inward give rise to the mesoblastic elements which add to the length of the villous cores (Fig. 46) (3, 4, 5).

In summary, it may be stated that the trophoblast has been differentiated into a chorionic plate which surrounds the chorionic cavity and from which many branching villi project into the blood filled intervillous space while others extend

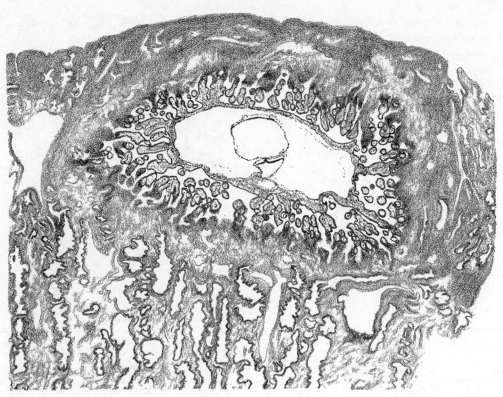

Fig. 47. 18½ day, Jones-Brewer ovum I, × 60.   The ovum is implanted in the decidua compacta which is sharply defined from the spongy zone.   The glands in the compacta are scattered and narrowed whereas in the spongiosa they are dilated, tortuous and contain secretion.   The venous sinuses about the ovum are dilated.   The chorionic villi have cones of mesoderm and many of them are branched. They are most actively proliferating at their tips as is shown by the fact that the villi are more deeply stained in this region.   Many cytotrophoblast cell columns which have grown out from the villous tips have reached the maternal stroma and their lateral projections have joined to form the peripheral trophoblastic shell.   The junction zone is less dense and somewhat edematous.   It contains endometrial and cytotrophoblast cells in various stages of regression as well as island of syncytium and small amounts of fibrinoid material.   The yolk sac is larger than the amniotic cavity.   The embryo contains a primitive streak and groove.

across this space to the underlying endometrium.   The extremities of the latter spread outward and unite with similar extensions from neighboring villi to form a trophoblastic shell which surrounds the entire ovum and is in contact with the maternal stroma.   Each villus consists of a column of cytotrophoblast in the center of which is a vessel bearing mesodermal core and covering which is a thin layer of syncytiotrophoblast (Fig. 47).

The union of the chorionic and embryonic vascular systems is completed when the heart begins to function, so that by the sixth week of pregnancy the circulation between the chorion and the embryo is established.   At this time, therefore, the histiotroph phase is supplanted by the hemotroph stage.

The circulation in the villus is carried on through the vessels in its mesodermal core.   Each villus has its own artery which terminates in capillaries that ultimately are collected into the veins of the villus (Fig. 48).   The fetal blood, which circulates in the villus, therefore, never comes into contact with the maternal blood that fills the intervillous spaces.   The latter are lined by syn-

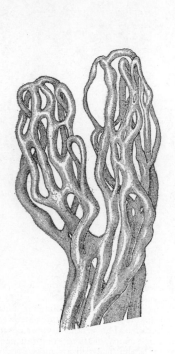

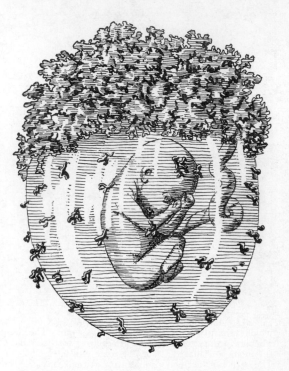

FIG. 48. The vascular system of
a villus (Kollman).

FIG. 49. Ovum at the fourth month showing luxuriant chorion frondosum and atrophic villi of the chorion laeve (Kollman).

cytium, except where they communicate with the maternal vessels (Fig. 47). The blood in these spaces, accordingly, is always in contact with endothelium or fetal syncytium.   Since the latter has the same faculty of inhibiting clotting as the former, the maternal blood in these lacunae remains in a liquid state.

The ovum, growing more rapidly than the decidua, bulges into the uterine cavity and pushes before it a thin layer of decidua capsularis.   Owing to the poor circulation in the latter, the underlying chorion is inadequately nourished and its villi atrophy, so that by the third month, it is quite smooth—**chorion laeve.** Those villi, which are adjacent to the decidua basalis, have a much more abundant food supply.   They accordingly continue to develop and enter into the formation of the fetal portion of the placenta—**chorion frondosum** (Fig. 49).

The chorion frondosum gradually increases in thickness and in area until about the middle of pregnancy, after which its growth is largely due to a length-

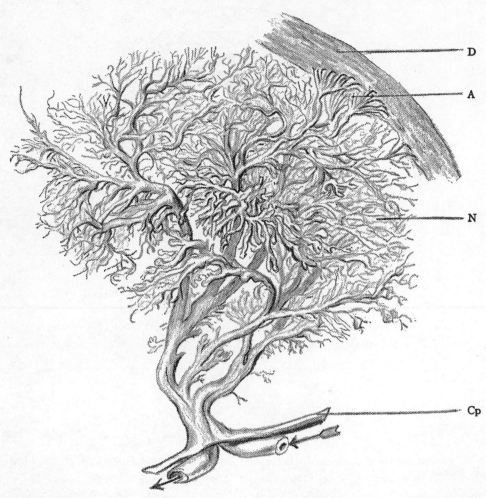

FIG. 50. The villous tree (Kollman). *D*, decidua; *A*, anchoring villi; *N*, nourishing villi; *Cp*, chorionic plate.

ening of the villi. At this time, the villi show multiple branches, most of which end freely in the intervillous space, like the branches of a tree, while others are attached to the adjacent decidua (Fig. 50). In places, buds, comprised of trophoblastic elements, lie free in the intervillous space. Some of these, as a consequence, enter the maternal circulation and are carried to the capillaries of the lungs.

That portion of the chorion from which the villi arise is known as the chorionic plate. In the early stages of pregnancy, it consists of a layer of syncytium and cytotrophoblast covering the primitive mesoderm, which contains the chorionic vessel trunks. Later, the trophoblastic elements are replaced by a fibrinoid material from which the fully developed villi project into the intervillous space.

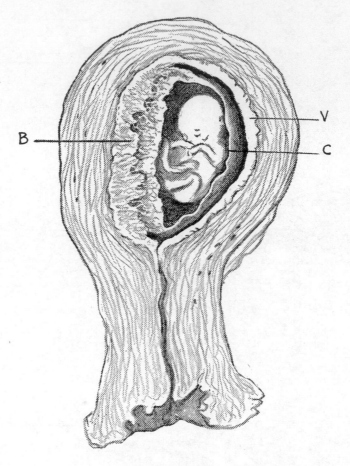

Fig. 51. Section of a pregnant uterus at eight weeks. *C*, decidua capsularis; *B*, decidua basalis; *V*, decidua vera.

THE DECIDUA

The endometrium at the time of implantation is in the secretory phase of the menstrual cycle—22nd day in the case of the 7½ day ovum. Aside from evidences of degeneration in the adjacent epithelium and stroma cells, it shows little response to the presence of the ovum except for a possible increase in the edema of the neighboring stroma. Soon an underlying network of thin-walled sinusoids develops beneath the ovum. As these are invaded by the trophoblast, maternal blood not only enters the lacunae but is extravasated into the surrounding tissues thereby adding materially to the ovum's source of nutriment. Toward the end of the first week after implantation changes similar to those which occur just before the onset of menstruation are observed. It is thought that the intermittent contractions of the spiral arteries, which favor an increase in the permeability of the capillaries with a resultant diapedesis of red cells and edema at that time, constitute one of the methods by which pabulum is provided for the early stages of implantation.

Although regeneration of the surface epithelium at the site of penetration is not complete until about the third week, the defect is essentially closed within a few days. This is accomplished partly by the regeneration of the endometrial epithelium and partly by the formation of the fibrinoid closing coagulum. The implantation accordingly is completely interstitial by the end of the second week. Within a few days after the first period is skipped, the stroma cells become greatly enlarged and are in intimate contact with each other; the glands are markedly increased in size, serrated and distended with secretion. In other words, a typical decidual reaction is observed (Fig. 47).

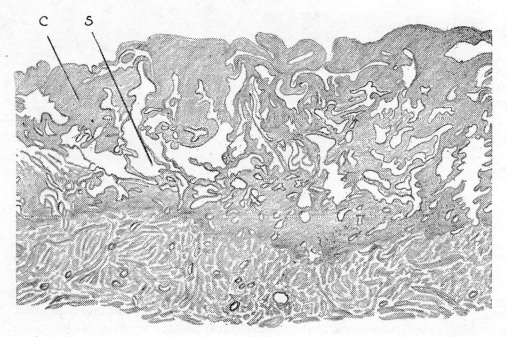

FIG. 52. The decidua vera at the seventh week. *C*, stratum compactum; *S*, stratum spongiosum.

Abundantly nourished the ovum grows rapidly and exerts pressure in all directions on the surrounding decidua. Laterally the glands are displaced and narrowed. The endometrium at its base is compressed and the thin covering layer bulges outward into the uterine cavity. The superficial layer which separates the ovum from the uterine cavity is now referred to as the **decidua capsularis.** The deeper portion, lying between the ovum and the uterine musculature is termed the **decidua basalis** and the remainder of the endometrial lining of the uterus is known as the **decidua vera** (Fig. 51).

THE DECIDUA VERA soon shows two distinct layers—a dense stratum compactum and an alveolar stratum spongiosum (Fig. 52).

The compact layer consists largely of altered stroma cells which have an epithelioid appearance and are greatly enlarged, some of them measuring as much as 50μ (Fig. 53). These cells are closely packed and crowd all but the necks of the glands into the deeper zone of the endometrium.

The spongy or alveolar layer is made up of distended, tortuous glands, the development of which has progressed considerably beyond the stage shown in the premenstrual endometrium. Their high columnar epithelial cells show evidence of secretory activity and project as papillae into the lumen. Between the glands are thin septa of connective tissue which contain occasional decidual cells (Fig. 54).

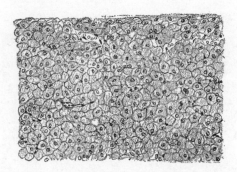
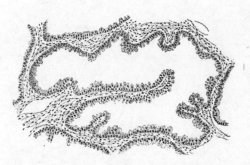

FIG. 53   FIG. 54

FIG. 53. Higher magnification of the decidual cells which make up the stratum compactum.
FIG. 54. Higher magnification of a gland from the stratum spongiosum.

After the second month, the gland cavities become smooth and broad owing to the stretching of the entire decidua which accompanies the growth of the uterus. Later, they are flattened and elongated, and are lined by low epithelial cells which somewhat resemble endothelium.

As pregnancy progresses, the spongy layer is transformed into a thin network of gland spaces, separated by fragile trabeculae of interglandular substance. It is in this zone that cleavage takes place when the decidua is separated and expelled after labor (Figs. 55 and 56).

The terminal portions of the glands remain more or less unchanged. The portion of the decidua in which they are contained is referred to as the basal or inactive layer from which regeneration of the endometrium takes place after pregnancy, just as it does in the ordinary menstrual cycle.

THE DECIDUA CAPSULARIS, within a short time after closure of the site of implantation, is converted into a thin, smooth layer of fibrin and connective tissue, which, as the ovum grows, becomes stretched and is poorly nourished. By the fourth month, this thin decidual covering of the greatly enlarged ovum comes into contact with the decidua vera of the opposite side and completely obliterates the uterine cavity. Later, fusion of these two decidual structures occurs, and at term no evidence of the capsularis is demonstrable even on microscopic examination (9).

THE DECIDUA BASALIS (Serotina), which is to form the maternal portion of the placenta, is similar in structure to the decidua vera but, owing to the destructive action of the trophoblast and the pressure of the growing ovum, its compact layer is considerably diminished in thickness. The outer part is made up largely

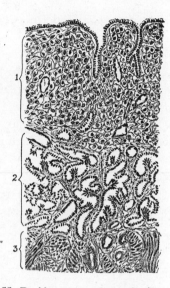
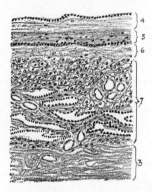

FIG. 55. Decidua vera at 3 months (Bumm).   FIG. 56. Decidua vera at 5 months (Bumm).

1. Stratum compactum.   2. Stratum spongiosum.   3. Muscle.   4. Amnion.   5. Chorion.   6. Decidua capsularis fused to compacta of Decidua vera 7.

of canalized fibrin which contains trophoblastic and decidual elements in various stages of degeneration—Nitabuch's fibrin layer—beneath which decidual cells form a typical stratum compactum. Relatively large vessels pass outward through this layer to communicate with the intervillous space. The spongy layer is thinner and possesses fewer glands. In places, clusters of trophoblast cells or syncytial giant cells may be observed in the interglandular substance.

THE PLACENTA

At the end of the third month, when the chorion laeve is well differentiated from the chorion frondosum, the latter structure, combined with the underlying decidua basalis, is termed the **placenta.** The tissues of the placenta, therefore, are both fetal and maternal.

THE FETAL PORTION of the placenta consists of the chorionic membrane from which numerous multibranched villi are suspended. Most of these terminate in the intervillous space where they receive nourishment from the maternal circulation. Others penetrate the decidua and act as anchoring villi.

Each villus has a mesodermal core which contains the terminal vessels of the chorionic trunks and is surrounded by an inner layer of Langhans' cells and an outer covering of syncytium (10).

Between the villi, the chorionic plate consists of mesoderm covered by cytotrophoblast and syncytium.

As pregnancy advances, the cytotrophoblast gradually disappears so that the villi in the latter months are covered by only a single layer of syncytium (Fig. 57). Similarly, the trophoblast cells which cover the chorionic plate are replaced by fibrinoid material, except at the periphery of the placenta, where a narrow band remains as the subchorial closing ring. The zone in which fetal and maternal cells meet also is converted into an area of canalized fibrin which contains degenerated trophoblast and decidual cells—a typical no-man's land between the invading trophoblast and the defending decidua.

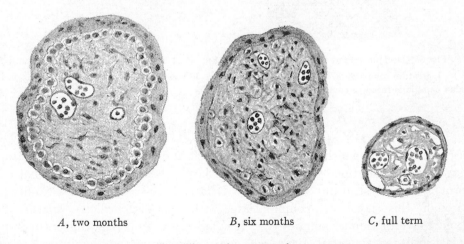

A, two months   B, six months   C, full term

FIG. 57. Villi at various stages of pregnancy.

THE MATERNAL PORTION of the placenta is that part of the decidua to which the chorion frondosum is attached. It is so intimately associated with the terminal villi that separation from the fetal elements is mechanically impossible. This portion of the decidua, **decidua basalis,** grows thinner as the compact layer is eroded and the glands of the spongy layer become flattened as this layer is compressed by the expanding ovum. Ultimately, the once luxuriant stratum compactum almost completely disappears and is replaced by canalized fibrin in which may be seen altered decidual cells and trophoblastic elements. In the alveolar layer, the interglandular substance is reduced and, as the flattening of the glands increases, the stratum spongiosum is converted into a frail network of decidual tissue.

CIRCULATION IN THE PLACENTAL SITE. Beneath the placental site the spiral arteries of the endometrium become greatly dilated and after loosing the muscle elements in their walls, terminate in funnel shaped openings which communicate with the intervillous space. Blood leaves the placental lake or intervillous space by way of the enlarged marginal sinus which communicates with a rich plexus of large maternal veins in the neighboring decidua (10a, 15). At the placental site, therefore, there is produced a **physiological arteriovenous fistula** which grows larger as pregnancy advances. Arterial blood, accordingly, is shunted into the venous system without passing through intervening capillaries and, as a result, may cause changes in the maternal circulation similar to those observed in other large arteriovenous fistulae.

TABLE I

AVERAGE PERCENTAGE SATURATION WITH OXYGEN OF BLOOD COMING FROM UTERUS

(Barcroft et al.)

Days of fetal life	6	10	14	18	22	26	30
Pregnant side	80	80	75	70	50	40	28
Non-pregnant side	60	60	60	65	67	68	69

At first the blood which flows through the placental lake is but slightly altered by its contact with the villi but later, when the growth of the fetus is accelerated, marked changes take place. Some idea of the magnitude of these changes may be derived from observations made on rabbits (11). The ovary on one side was removed so that, after mating, the uterus on the side operated upon contained no fetuses while the one on the opposite side harbored the products of conception. Samples of blood withdrawn from the vein coming away from the pregnant and non-pregnant uteri were then compared and it was noted that, early in pregnancy, the blood which is shunted from the arterial to the venous side through the placental lake of the pregnant uterus, leaves the vein of that uterus with a higher oxygen saturation (80%) than is present in the blood which passes through the capillaries of the non-pregnant uterus (60%). This higher saturation on the pregnant side shows that relatively little oxygen is taken up by the placenta in the first trimester of gestation. Later, however, as the fetal requirements are increased, the blood which leaves the pregnant side is less than half as saturated as that which comes from the non-pregnant uterus (see Table I)

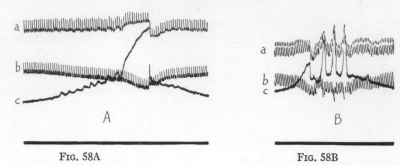

FIG. 58A

FIG. 58B

Pressure Curves Early in Labor   Pressure Curves Late in Labor

(a) Pressure in Brachial Artery, (b) Maternal Placental Blood Pressure, (c) Intrauterine Pressure
(Woodbury, Hamilton and Torpin)

THE MATERNAL PLACENTAL BLOOD PRESSURE has been determined by deducting the intrauterine pressure from the pressure in the brachial artery and it has been studied under varying conditions by means of a differential manometer (12). Figures 58A and 58B show in graphic form the results of these studies early and late in labor. The curve a is a tracing from a manometer connected with a needle in the brachial artery and curve c represents a simultaneous recording of the intrauterine pressure obtained by attaching a simple manometer to one end of a balloon-tipped catheter which had been passed into the fundal portion of the uterine cavity. By connecting one of these systems with the front chamber of a differential manometer and the other with the rear chamber, the difference between the two pressures or the effective head of the maternal arterial pressure to the placenta was accurately ascertained and recorded as curve b. From these curves the values shown in Table II were then calculated.

TABLE II

THE EFFECT OF LABOR PAINS ON THE EFFECTIVE PLACENTAL BLOOD PRESSURE (mm. Hg.)
(Woodbury, Hamilton and Torpin)

	A EARLY IN LABOR			B LATE IN LABOR		
	Brachial Blood Pressure	Intra-uterine Pressure	Placental Blood Pressure	Brachial Blood Pressure	Intra-uterine Pressure	Placental Blood Pressure
Before pains..................	90/50 minus 20 =		70/30	150/100 minus 25 =		125/75
Height of pain before "bearing-down"......................	95/60 minus 65 =		30/−5	150/100 minus 55 =		95/45
While "bearing-down".........	120/83 minus 120 =		0/−37	205/165 minus 160 =		45/5
Immediately after "bearing-down"......................	65/43 minus 65 =		0/−23	140/100 minus 55 =		85/45
Three seconds later...........	95/65 minus 50 =		45/15	150/110 minus 55 =		95/55

Early in labor, pressure in the brachial artery increases from 90/50 mm. Hg. between pains to 120/83 mm. at the height of a bearing-down effort and, as the contraction of the uterus becomes more intense, the pulse rate is somewhat slowed (Fig. 58Aa). Simultaneous determination of the intrauterine pressure shows a gradual increase from 20 mm. before the onset of a labor pain to 65 mm. at its acme and 120 mm. during a bearing-down effort (Fig. 58Ac). By deducting the intrauterine pressure from the maternal arterial pressure, the effective placental blood pressure is found to be 70/30 mm. before a pain, 30/−5 mm. during a uterine contraction and 0/−37 in the course of a bearing-down effort (Fig. 58Ab). At the height of a contraction, therefore, the diastolic pressure in the placental site is almost or completely obliterated and, in the course of a bearing-down effort, the pressure relationships may be reversed. The blood in the placental lake, accordingly, is then stagnant or is being forced onward into the uterine veins or backward into the arterial system (Table IIA). Since bearing-down efforts do not ordinarily occur early in labor, these extreme reversals of pressure are unusual. Later in labor, when they result from a natural reflex, they are of short duration. At that time, the arterial pressure likewise is somewhat more elevated so that in spite of the increased intrauterine pressure which they induce, a sufficient pressure head is maintained to insure adequate irrigation of the placenta (Fig. 58B and Table IIB).

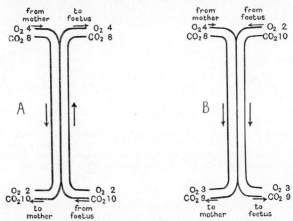

FIG. 59. Effect of maternal and fetal blood streams flowing in opposite and the same directions (Mossman).

A	B
Foetal and Maternal Blood Flowing in Opposite Directions	Foetal and Maternal Blood Flowing in Same Direction

BLOOD CURRENTS IN THE PLACENTA. It has been shown in some animals that the maternal and fetal blood streams flow in opposite directions, the maternal blood flowing from the fetal surface toward the uterus and the fetal blood from the uterine toward the fetal side (13, 14). Maternal blood of low oxygen tension which is about to leave the placenta, accordingly, is contiguous with fetal blood of still lower tension which is entering the placenta. As the fetal blood passes through its capillaries, therefore, it takes up oxygen in increasing amounts and leaves the placenta with an oxygen tension almost equal to that of maternal arterial blood. The great advantage of this arrangement is illustrated in Fig. 59. Although the human placenta is unlike that of the animals in which such an arrangement is demonstrable, the tendency of the two bloods is to flow in opposite directions at the time when the greatest interchange between the two circulations takes place. The maternal arterial stream which enters the placental lake is directed toward the chorionic plate and the force of its current bends the villi backward upon themselves. As a consequence, the fetal blood coursing through the terminal villous capillaries tends to flow in a direction opposite to that of the maternal current. As the maternal blood passes beyond the limits of the intercotyledonary septa and reaches the region of the chorionic plate, it is deflected laterally and finally leaves the placental lake by way of the marginal sinuses which empty into the uterine veins (15) (Fig. 60).

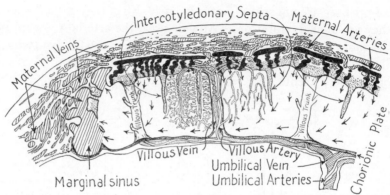

Fig. 60. Schematic representation of placental circulation (modified from Spanner). Blood enters the placental lake from the maternal arteries (solid black) and flows toward the chorionic plate until it passes the limits of the intercotyledonary septa (stippled projections). It then flows along the chorionic plate and leaves the placental lake by way of the marginal sinus (shaded area on left). The villous branches and their vessels are bent upon themselves so that their extremities point toward the chorionic plate. In places some of the villous veins show areas of constriction.

The placenta progressively grows in thickness and in breadth. Its size, however, is not increased proportionately with the uterine enlargement in the various periods of gestation. Up to the middle of pregnancy, the placental site enlarges more rapidly than does the internal surface of the uterus. In the last half of pregnancy, it fails to keep pace with uterine expansion. Accordingly, at the third month it covers one-third of the internal surface of the uterus. By the fifth month this is increased to one-half, but at term its area again is about one-third that of the uterus.

The placenta, at the end of pregnancy, is an irregularly oval, friable mass which measures about 18 x 16 x 2½ cm. and weighs approximately 600 gms. Its internal or fetal surface is smooth and glistening (Fig. 61A). Beneath the transparent amnion, branches of the umbilical vessels radiate over the tough, grayish, somewhat granular chorionic plate to which the umbilical cord is attached.

The external or maternal surface is rough and purplish red in color. It is divided by furrows into distinct areas or cotyledons and is covered by remnants of the decidua basalis (Fig. 61B).

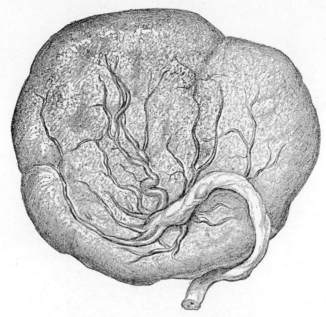

FIG. 61A. Fetal surface of the placenta.

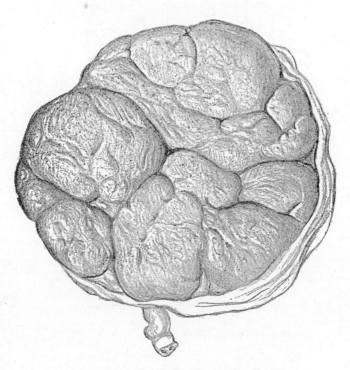

FIG. 61B. Maternal surface of the placenta.

Amnion

Chorionic plate

Fibrinoid material

Villi and Intervillous spaces

Decidua

Muscle

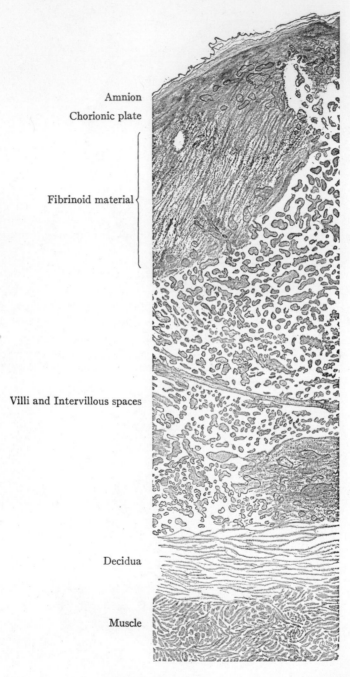

FIG. 62. Cross-section of placenta at the sixth month.

Cross-section shows an inner tough layer, the chorionic plate, and an outer friable membrane, the decidua, between which a thick, spongy mass of villi makes up the bulk of the placenta.

The microscopic picture of a well developed placenta is as follows (Fig. 62): On the fetal surface, a single layer of columnar cells, with a few fibrils of connective tissue, makes up the amnion, which is loosely attached to the underlying chorionic membrane. The latter structure consists of fibrinoid material from which the trunks of the villi are suspended in the intervillous spaces. The branches of these trunks rebranch repeatedly and extend in all directions, so that the bulk of the placenta resembles an inverted forest. Accordingly, on cross-section, the villi are cut longitudinally, transversely and obliquely. Unlike those in the earlier stages, the villi are smaller and contain relatively large vessels. The Langhans' cells have almost completely disappeared and the denser stroma is covered by only a thin layer of syncytium. In places, fibrinoid material has replaced the whole or parts of villi. Between the villi are the intervillous spaces which, more correctly, should be called the intervillous space, since it is a single chamber into which the villi are suspended. These spaces contain maternal blood and occasional syncytial buds or the fibrin which has replaced such buds. Most of the villous branches terminate in these blood lacunae. Some of them, however, penetrate Nitabuch's fibrin layer and act as anchoring villi. The latter layer of canalized fibrin, which contains remnants of trophoblast and decidual cells, extends across the proximal surface of the decidua. External to it are patches of the stratum compactum, and adjacent to these may be seen the flattened gland spaces of the stratum spongiosum. Many maternal vessels, which communicate with the intervillous spaces pass through the altered decidua.

PHYSIOLOGY OF THE PLACENTA

As might be expected from the placenta's many and important associations with the development and growth of the fetus, its weight has a definite relationship to that of the child at the various periods of gestation but, since the growth of the child is more rapid than that of the placenta, the ratio of fetal weight to placental weight changes from month to month (16). At term it is as 5.3 is to 1. Because the placentae of twins are relatively small, the fetal-weight placental-weight ratio in multiple pregnancies is considerably above this figure.

Computations from serial section reconstructions have shown the combined surface of all the villi to be approximately 6.5 square meters and the aggregate length of the villi has been estimated at 18 kilometers (17). These figures should give some idea of the large area that is available for absorption in the average placenta. No doubt such an extensive absorption surface is beyond the average fetal requirement as is indicated by the fact that twin fetuses survive in spite of their relatively small placentae. The excess surface, on the other hand, serves as a reserve in case of damage to isolated groups of villi and may be the means of saving the life of the child when the placenta becomes partially detached or when infarction occurs.

TABLE III

PERCENTAGE OF THE TOTAL ASH

(Needham)

	P_2O_5	SO_3	Cl	CaO	MgO	K_2O	Na_2O	FE	SI_2O_3
Placenta................	15.0	1.7	21.0	14.0	0.8	11.0	39.0	0.008	7.0
Fetus.................	37.65	1.2	5.7	41.9	1.3	5.1	9.0	0.72	

Comparison of the total ash of the mature human placenta with that of the fetus at term is shown in Table III. From this it may be seen that the placenta contains much less calcium, phosphorus and iron than does the fetus but it has a higher sodium and chlorine content (18).

The placenta may be considered as a wall which separates the maternal and fetal circulations but through which certain constituents pass, unaltered or altered, from one side to the other. One side of this wall is made up of the fetal endothelial lining of the villous capillaries. The other side consists of a single or double layer of trophoblastic epithelium, which covers the villus. Between these, more or less connective tissue intervenes. While the fetal endothelial side probably functions like the endothelium in other fetal capillaries, the cells derived from the trophoblast on the opposite side of the wall may well retain some of the properties possessed by the trophoblast during the early life of the ovum. It may be remembered that the trophoblast at that time was an active structure able to destroy maternal tissue and prepare the debris for absorption. There are present, therefore, certain facilities, fetal or maternal or both, which are capable of preparing for absorption some of the blood constituents which otherwise could not pass through the barrier. In addition, the maternal side possesses facilities for the storage of such elements as must be held in reserve for future metabolic needs.

It may be well at this point to recall that all mammalian placentae are not alike (Fig. 63) (20). At one extreme is the hemoendothelial type exemplified by the rat, in which only a thin layer of fetal capillary endothelium separates the fetal and maternal blood streams (Fig. 63A). At the other extreme is the epitheliochorial placenta of the horse and pig in which the placental barrier is made up of a maternal partition consisting of endothelium, connective tissue and epithelium as well as a fetal partition composed also of epithelium, connective tissue and capillary endothelium (Fig. 63E). It is obvious that the latter may not permit the passage of many substances which are easily transmitted by the former. Because the human placenta (Fig. 63B) differs from that of most

animals, placental function in man cannot be accurately determined by animal
experimentation. Great caution, therefore, should be used in transferring to
human physiology conclusions which are derived from observations on animals.

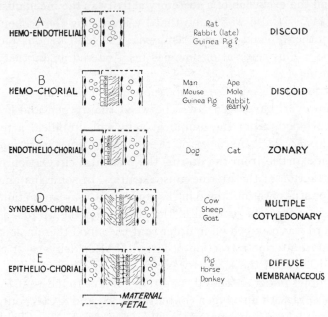

FIG. 63. Variations in the Placental Barrier in Different Animals (Mossman—Grosser)

RESPIRATION. Long before adequate facilities for blood analyses were
available, it was observed that the blood in the umbilical vein was bright red
while that in the umbilical arteries was dark, and, from this observation, the
bright red blood which leaves the placenta was thought to contain more oxygen
than that which is brought to the placenta. The placenta, accordingly, was
regarded as the organ which purified the fetal blood. Subsequent research has
proved that **oxygen from the maternal circulation diffuses through the placental
barrier to the fetal blood and carbon dioxide passes in the opposite direction.**
The interchange of these gases in the placenta has been carefully investigated in animals. In the goat, the average oxygen content of the blood from
the umbilical vein has been found to be 7.96 vol. % and that from the umbilical
arteries, 2.94 vol. %, while the carbon dioxide averaged 29.9% and 41.5% respectively. The fetal blood, accordingly, takes up oxygen and gives off carbon
dioxide as it passes through the placenta (21). The oxygen tension of the
maternal goat's arterial blood (from aorta) is 60 mm. and that of the fetal venous
blood (from umbilical arteries) is 15 mm. With a gradient of 45 mm., diffusion
from the mother's blood through the placental barrier to the fetal blood no doubt
takes place. The tensions for carbon dioxide in the same bloods are 43 mm. and
61 mm. While a difference of 18 is smaller than that for oxygen, it is sufficiently

large to favor diffusion of carbon dioxide from the fetal to the maternal circulation, since the diffusion constant for carbon dioxide is greater than that of oxygen (22). **The differences in tension are sufficient to favor the acceptance of diffusion and the exclusion of a secretory activity as the mechanism of gaseous interchange (21).** It also was found that by increasing the carbon dioxide tension of the mother's blood through asphyxia, the fetal venous blood absorbed carbon dioxide. This reversal of flow has been offered as another argument in favor of diffusion (21).

Similar complete studies are impossible in the human subject. Marked differences, however, have been noted between the oxygen and carbon dioxide content of the bloods from the umbilical vein and umbilical arteries at birth (23, 24, 25, 26, 27, 28). As most of these observations were made after the child had been expelled from the uterus, the placental circulation no doubt was altered by retraction of the uterine musculature. In some instances, however, the material for study was obtained in the course of Cesarean sections done under local anesthesia. Prior to removal of the child from the uterus, a 12-inch segment of the cord was clamped off in order that the blood therein contained might be isolated before uterine retraction occurred. After delivery of the child, the blood retained between the clamps was removed and examined. By thus collecting the samples under antenatal conditions, it was found that the fetal blood enters the placenta with an oxygen content of 6.3% and a CO_2 content of 56.2% and leaves it with 13.3% oxygen and 48.4% CO_2 (26, 27, 28) (Table IV). The differences in the fetal arterial and fetal venous bloods in the human subjects are so like those observed in the more satisfactory goat experiments that similar conclusions as to the mechanism of gaseous interchange are warranted.

The character of the fetal blood at term indicates that respiration through the placenta probably is much less satisfactory than it is through the lungs in after-life, for it resembles the blood picture of an individual who visits the higher altitudes and necessarily lives in an atmosphere of low oxygen tension. The red blood count and hemoglobin are above the customary figures for the average adult. As a result, the oxygen capacity of the fetus is greater than that of the mother. On the other hand, the degree of saturation is considerably less. Although the average oxygen capacity of fetal arterial blood is 20.8 vol. %, it is only 50 to 80% saturated, while the maternal blood has an oxygen capacity of 15.4 vol. % and is 95% saturated (26, 29).

Since the blood removed from the umbilical vein at the time of Cesarean section was only 63% saturated and since such a degree of saturation is obtained when blood is exposed to an oxygen tension of 33 mm. of mercury, it has been suggested that the oxygen tension of the blood to which the circulation in the villi is exposed does not exceed 40 mm. or less than half that to which adult blood is subjected in its passage through the pulmonary circulation (26) (See also Table I, p. 59).

TABLE IV
OXYGEN AND CARBON DIOXIDE
Content of Fetal Blood as it Enters and Leaves the Placenta
(Eastman)

	UMBILICAL ARTERIES	UMBILICAL VEIN
	vol. %	vol. %
Oxygen.	6.3	13.3
Carbon Dioxide.	56.2	48.4

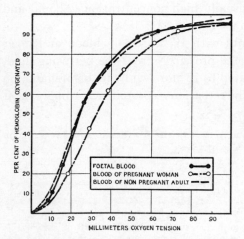

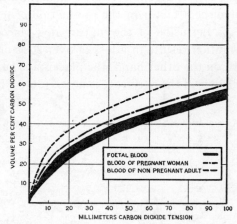

FIG. 64A. Oxygen Dissociation Curves, Mother and Fetus (Eastman)

FIG. 64B. CO₂ Dissociation Curves, Mother and Fetus (Eastman)

At very low and very high tensions, fetal blood takes up less oxygen and gives up more of this gas to the tissues than adult blood. Adult blood becomes 95% saturated at an oxygen tension of 75 mm. whereas fetal blood requires a tension of 90 mm. for similar saturation. The situation is reversed in the middle range. There is a marked difference between fetal blood and the blood of the pregnant woman, the curve of the latter being definitely shifted to the right. Fetal blood, accordingly, takes up more oxygen than does that of the mother. The carbon dioxide curve of fetal blood follows a lower level than that of the mother's blood and is considerably lower than the curve of the non-pregnant adult's blood. Fetal blood, therefore, releases CO₂ more readily than does that of the mother.

As has been mentioned, the dissociation curves of maternal and fetal bloods differ from each other and from the blood of non-pregnant adults, the most pronounced change being in the blood of the mother. Without entering into the details of these differences, it is sufficient for purposes of the present discussion to state that at any given tension between 25 mm. and 60 mm., oxygen is released more readily by the maternal blood and is taken up more effectively by the fetal blood (Fig. 64A). On the other hand, the reverse is true of carbon dioxide, which is given off more readily by the blood of the fetus (Fig. 64B). **These changes in the dissociation relationships which enable fetal blood to absorb oxygen and release carbon dioxide more readily than maternal blood are most advantageous from the standpoint of placental interchange (29, 30).**

NITROGEN METABOLISM. There is little or no change in the percentage of nitrogen in the human placenta at different periods of gestation (31, 32). Analysis of the maternal and fetal portions of the placentae of those animals in which the two parts are separable, however, shows a progressive increase in the nitrogen percentage of the fetal portion while that of the maternal side remains quite constant (19). Possibly the same is true in the human subject, the fetal gain being offset by the loss of maternal tissue, which, in the beginning, contains more nitrogen than the growing fetal elements (33). The protein split-product, albumose, has been found in the placenta (34) and amino acids are abundant. Of the latter, argenine is present in an unusually high concentration (22.5%) and may be a factor in the production of fetal nucleins (31, 35).

Perfusion of the mature dog placenta with 1% casein in blood or Ringer solution results in a loss of over 20% of the protein N from the perfusing fluid. If, on the other hand, the placenta is heated to 75° for two hours beforehand, no change in the perfusate is noted (36). The retention of protein accordingly must

TABLE V

AMINO ACID N, NON PROTEIN N, UREA N AND URIC ACID N IN THE MATERNAL AND FETAL BLOOD
(Plass and Matthew)

	WHOLE BLOOD		PLASMA		CORPUSCLES	
	Fetus	Mother	Fetus	Mother	Fetus	Mother
	mg. %	mg. %	mg. %	mg. %	mg. %	mg. %
Amino Acid N....................	8.2	6.1	6.4	4.5	10.3	9.1
Non Protein N....................	35.5	28.9	23.1	20.1	47.4	46.1
Urea N.........................	9.7	9.7	10.1	10.2	9.4	8.8
Uric Acid N.....................	2.6	2.5	2.8	2.6	2.5	2.3

be associated with some vital activity on the part of the placenta. When the placenta is perfused with Ringer solution alone, amino acids are accumulated in the perfusate but if a fairly large amount of amino acid is added to the perfusing fluid, 10 to 30% of it is lost in passage through the placenta (37). **Amino acid, therefore, can pass through the placenta by diffusion.** This conclusion is further substantiated by the observation that maternal hyperaminoacidemia resulting from some abnormal condition is accompanied by an increase in the amino acids of the fetus (38). Likewise, alanin injected into the vein of the pregnant animal causes a rise in the amino acid content of both the maternal and fetal blood (39, 40).

Amino acid N, non protein N, urea N and uric acid N determinations made on samples of human blood taken immediately after delivery from the mother's vein and from the umbilical cord are shown in Table V (41). The fetal blood is richer in amino acid than is that of the mother. As may be observed, 1.9 mg. per 100 cc. or 42% more amino acid is found in the fetal plasma. While the amino acids probably pass through the placental barrier by diffusion, they are retained in excess on the fetal side by some special fixation mechanism. Non protein N likewise is somewhat higher in the fetal than in the maternal blood (41, 42, 43). Plasma proteins, on the other hand, are more concentrated on the maternal side (43). Due to the large size of their molecules, albumin and globulin do not pass through the placenta but are probably built up from the amino acids by the fetal tissues. The waste products, creatine, creatinine, urea and uric acid, have about the same values in both circulations (41, 42, 44). If the blood urea of the mother rises as a result of disease, the urea content of the fetal blood also is increased (45). The same effect may be produced by the injection of urea into the maternal blood stream (44, 46). The transmission of urea and uric acid, accordingly, is effected by diffusion. Because the placenta has an unusually high urea content and is able to manufacture urea readily, it has been suggested that the placenta may have the ability to prepare some of the fetal nitrogenous waste products for excretion (47).

From the foregoing observations, it is reasonable to assume that **amino acids and probably non protein nitrogen pass through the placenta by diffusion as do the usual waste products—creatine, creatinine, urea and uric acid.** There is, therefore, no great need for the assumption of a vital capacity on the part of the placenta in the transmission of essential nitrogenous elements. Some of the citations, on the other hand, indicate that the placenta may, at times, play a more than passive rôle, particularly as regards the larger protein molecules, and additional support is given to this conclusion by the fact that proteolytic ferments resembling pepsin, trypsin and erepsin have been found in the placental tissues (48, 49).

CARBOHYDRATE METABOLISM. The part played by the placenta in the metabolism of the carbohydrates varies in different periods of gestation. Its glycogen content is greatest in the early months when it anticipates the liver as a carbohydrate storehouse. After the pancreatic isles of Langerhans and the liver have developed, however, the placenta becomes less and less important in this respect and its glycogen decreases from 2.75% at three months to 1.05% at term, while that of the liver increases from 1.8% to 29.5% in the same period (50, 51, 52). Although glycogen is stored mostly in the maternal portion of the placenta, the placenta does not give up its glycogen as readily as does the maternal liver. Ordinarily, factors which raise or lower the maternal blood sugar affect it but slightly. Carbohydrate feeding, injections of glucose, insulin and adrenalin fail to influence the glycogen stored in the placenta even though they may cause marked alteration in the glycogen of the maternal liver. Repeated doses of thyroid extract and insulin, however, ultimately affect the placental glycogen as do also extreme cases of disordered metabolism in the mother (53).

Perfusion of the placenta with blood and glucose leads to the loss of 18% to 33% of the sugar from the perfusing liquid and this ability to take up glucose is destroyed when the placenta is heated to 75° for two hours (36, 54). A loss of glycogen, on the other hand, is observed when the placenta is perfused with glucose-free Ringer solution (55). These observations, together with the finding of amylolytic and glycolytic enzymes (56) in placental tissue, indicate that the placenta may be able to take up glucose from the mother's blood, store it as glycogen and subsequently break down the latter when the fetus draws upon the stored-up reserve.

Estimations of the glucose content of fetal and maternal blood show a higher concentration on the maternal side and, when the sugar level is artificially raised in the blood of the mother, a corresponding fetal rise is noted (57, 58, 59). As may be observed in Table VI, the fetal blood which leaves the placenta is considerably richer than that which is brought to the placenta by the umbilical arteries. The fetal blood, accordingly, takes up glucose and the sugar thus absorbed probably passes through the placenta by diffusion.

TABLE VI

GLUCOSE AND LACTIC ACID

(Bell et al.)

	MATERNAL VEIN	UMBILICAL VEIN	UMBILICAL ARTERY
	mg. %	mg. %	mg. %
Glucose....................................	106	84.4	75.2
Lactic Acid................................	38	54	68

Lactic acid is more concentrated in the fetal circulation than it is in that of the mother (58). Since it is present in greater amounts in the umbilical arteries than in the umbilical vein, this catabolic end product of carbohydrate metabolism must pass through the placenta to the mother's blood.

FAT METABOLISM. The percentage of fat in the placenta decreases with the progress of gestation and is reduced over 50% at term (60). When considered in relation to the weight of the fetus, however, the placental fats and lipoids are at their highest level by the end of the fourth month. Thereafter, as the fetus gains more rapidly in weight, they fall abruptly (61). Although the fat percentage of the placenta diminishes as pregnancy advances, the total amount of fats and lipoids increases from 0.1 gm. at two months to 2.8 gm. at term as a result of the marked growth of the placenta (61).

TABLE VII

FAT AND LIPOIDS

Maternal and Fetal Blood

(Slemons and Stander)

	FATTY ACIDS	PHOSPHATIDS	CHOLESTEROL
	mg. 100 cc.	mg. 100 cc.	mg. 100 cc.
Maternal blood.............................	690–1120	265–350	190–330
Fetal blood.................................	500–815	210–290	120–200

Blood taken simultaneously from the mother and from the umbilical cord immediately after delivery shows a much higher concentration of fat, phospholipid and cholesterol on the maternal than on the fetal side of the placenta (Table VII) (62, 63). This high content of fatty substances in the mother's blood and in the placenta has been compared with the fat storage in the developing hen's egg. "If we may imagine the lipoids of the egg stored not in the yolk but in the blastoderm or some analogous structure and not stored there from the beginning but put there during the growth of the embryo, as the mammalian mother is in a position to do, then the correlation is not so far-fetched as it appears at first sight" (64).

Because the maternal blood contains much more fat than that of the fetus, it has been suggested that fatty substances are not transmitted through the placenta but are synthesized from carbohydrates by the fetal tissues. While such a synthesis may take place, some fat must pass through the placenta, since the fetal blood is richer in lipids when it leaves than when it enters this organ.

One group of investigators noted in a series of 16 cases that, without exception, the concentration of phospholipid was greater in the human umbilical vein blood than in that from the umbilical arteries. Blood coming from the placenta averaged 204 mg. per 100 cc. while that entering the placenta showed 160 mg. An average of 44 mg. or 22%, accordingly, was taken from the placenta and retained by the fetus (65).

Except in two instances, the same observation was made concerning free cholesterol, the average of which was 64 mg. per 100 cc. in the umbilical vein blood and 55 mg. in that of the umbilical arteries. Thus 9 mg. or 14% went to the fetus from the placenta (65).

The findings with regard to ester cholesterol differed somewhat from those of free cholesterol and phospholipid. In all cases in which the blood coming from the placenta contained more than 10 mg. per 100 cc., the fetus took up ester cholesterol from the umbilical vein blood but, when the concentration fell below this level, fetal ester cholesterol was passed on to the blood in the umbilical artery. In other words, when the concentration in the blood coming from the placenta was above a certain level (10 mg. per 100 cc.) absorption by the fetus took place and when the concentration fell below this minimum, the reverse occurred (65).

In nine instances, the neutral fat concentration was higher in the umbilical vein than in the artery and the reverse was true in the remaining six cases (65).

The same investigators clamped the cord immediately after birth and took blood from the umbilical vein at that time and again when the placenta separated. The second specimen invariably showed a higher concentration of phospholipids. It also contained more free cholesterol in 75% of the cases, more ester cholesterol in 66% and more neutral fat in 50% (65).

The presence of a higher concentration of lipid substances in blood coming from the placenta than in that going to the placenta indicates that the placenta furnishes added fatty substances and this conclusion is further supported by the observation that samples taken from the cord at birth and again at the time of placental separation show higher concentration of fat and lipoids in the second specimen (65).

Although an increase in the fats of the mother's diet may not cause an increase in the blood fats of the fetus, the feeding of certain fats to pregnant animals does influence the iodine values of the fetal fat. If a fat with a low iodine number is given, the fat stores in the mother will have lower iodine numbers than when she is otherwise fed. The same effect also is observed in the fetus, but to a lesser degree. Fats with high iodine values, on the other hand, cause high values in the maternal fat and a somewhat lesser increase in that of the fetus (66, 67, 68). If the fetal fats were entirely synthesized from the carbohydrates, this relationship between the iodine values of the food and the stored fat would not obtain.

MINERAL METABOLISM. Examination of blood from the mother's vein and from the umbilical cord immediately after birth shows essentially the same values for sodium (69), potassium (70) and magnesium (71) but the fetal blood is found to be richer in calcium (69, 71, 72) and in inorganic and organic phosphorus (73). Lipoid phosphorus (73), on the other hand, is more abundant on the maternal side of the placenta. All of these substances, with the possible exception of lipoid phosphorus, are thought to pass freely through the placental barrier but calcium and phosphorus, like amino acid, are held in excess in the fetal blood.

IRON. On the basis of histologic findings in early pregnancy, it has been suggested that red blood cells are broken up and absorbed by the chorionic epithelium. This evidence becomes less and less marked and finally disappears as gestation progresses. Since most of the fetal iron is taken up from the mother after all evidence of such a mechanism has disappeared, the greater part of the iron which goes to the fetus must pass through the placenta in some other way (74, 75). Perhaps, when more is known concerning the so-called loosely held iron of the blood, it may be found that this is the source of the iron which passes through the placenta.

VITAMINS. In spite of their importance, very little investigative work has been done on the permeability of the placenta to the various vitamins. As a result, most of the evidence concerning the passage of these important dietary constituents from the mother to the fetus is of a more or less indirect nature.

Vitamin A is never found, except in traces, in the fetal blood and carotene is present in only small quantities. The maternal blood, on the other hand, always contains large amounts (76, 77). After the third month, both carotene and vitamin A increase in the fetus and carotene is present in the placenta (77, 78). The liver, however, is the only fetal organ in which are stored sufficient amounts of this vitamin to permit quantitative estimation. It contains 14–17 units per gram in contrast with an average of 220 units per gram in healthy adults (79, 80, 81). While the liver reserve is slight at birth, it rises rapidly in the first few months of life in well-fed infants. Before birth, on the other hand, little or no increase in the vitamin A content of the fetus can be accomplished by increasing the mother's intake. In the rabbit, it has been shown that a reserve of 10 units in the fetal liver may be acquired during the storage of 1000 units in the mother's liver but that the fetal reserve can be raised to only 40 units by increasing the mother's storage to 50,000 units (82, 83). From these observations, it is clear that the passage of vitamin A and carotene from the maternal to the fetal circulation is accomplished with great difficulty and cannot be explained by simple physiochemical changes. It also is not probable that either pro vitamin or vitamin A are synthesized by the fetal tissue, since the fetus occasionally is born without either of these substances.

Information concerning **vitamin B** also is more or less indefinite. During pregnancy, less vitamin B_1 is found in the various organs of the rabbit than is present in the non-pregnant state. With this depletion of the maternal stores, there is, however, an accumulation in the placenta and fetus. It, therefore, is thought that vitamin B_1 is transmitted from the mother to the fetus through the placenta (84, 85). Although direct evidence of placental transmission is lacking, this deduction is strengthened by the observation that rabbits fed on diets deficient in vitamin B_1 use up their reserves much more rapidly when they are pregnant than when they are not and, at the same time, the vitamin content of the placenta and fetus also is greatly diminished. When vitamin B is withheld completely during the first half of pregnancy, all fetuses are aborted and its withdrawal after the middle of gestation leads to the birth of off-spring lacking in vigor. Permeability of the human placenta is indicated by the observation that the new born infant's blood shows a concentration similar to that of the mother even when the latter has been increased by intramuscular injections of Vitamin B_1 just before labor (85a). Although the placenta's permeability to **vitamin B_2** has not been demonstrated, the relatively low molecular weight of riboflavin favors the assumption that it may pass from the mother to the fetus through the placenta.

Vitamin C. While the values of ascorbic acid in the fetal and maternal bloods vary with different observers, all are agreed that the concentration on the fetal side of the placenta is greater than that on the maternal side (86, 87, 88). One observer found an average of 1.07 mg. of ascorbic acid per 100 cc. in the umbilical cord blood and only 0.26 mg. per 100 cc. in the maternal blood (88). The higher values on the fetal side suggest that vitamin C may be entirely synthesized by the fetus but this conclusion is hardly tenable in view of the fact that the fetal value of 1.07 mg. diminished to 0.27 mg. ten days after birth. Passage of vitamin C from the mother to the fetus through the placenta is also indicated by the presence of considerable ascorbic acid in the placenta (89) and by the observation that blood which comes from the placenta in the umbilical vein contains more ascorbic acid (1.9–3.6 mg.) than that which is brought to the placenta by the umbilical arteries (0.7–2.1 mg.). Considerable vitamin C accordingly must be taken up from the placenta and need not be accounted for on the basis of fetal synthesis. While the evidence concerning placental transmission of the other vitamins is indefinite, without a doubt **vitamin C is capable of passing from the mother to the fetus through the placenta** even though it may also be synthesized by the fetus.

Vitamins D and E. To date, the passage of vitamins D and E through the placenta apparently has not been investigated. Since the structural formulae suggested for these two vitamins indicate that their molecules are very large ones, their passage through the placenta might be doubted. On the other hand, the fact that they are fat-soluble indicates that they, like the maternal fatty substances, may pass through the placenta irrespective of the size of their molecules.

INTERNAL SECRETIONS—ESTRIN. The estrogenic hormones, estriol and emmenin (estriol glucuronide), are present in large quantities (1000–2000 mouse units) in the placenta (90, 91, 92, 93, 94). Because the estrogenic content of the urine in early pregnancy diminishes after double oophorectomy and then rises to normal several months later (95, 96), an extra-ovarian source of these hormones is assumed and the placenta has been suggested as this source (97). That the placenta may secrete estrogenic substances is also indicated by the fact that large amounts of the hormone were found in the urine of a woman who had a recurrence of a chorioepithelioma three months after the original tumor and both ovaries had been removed (98).

Estrin is found in diminishing amounts in the blood and urine of newly born infants for about five days after birth (99, 100, 101). Its subsequent absence in demonstrable amounts has led to the suggestion that the estrogenic substance present at birth is not derived from the fetus but is transmitted from the mother's blood through the placental partition or comes directly from the placenta itself. In support of this view may be offered the changes observed in the uterus during fetal and neonatal life. After the 20th week, the cervix grows much more rapidly than does the corpus uteri and, at term, it comprises about two-thirds of the entire uterus. Following delivery, on the other hand, when the stimulating influence of estrin presumably is lacking, the cervical portion becomes relatively and absolutely smaller and the uterus returns to a size comparable with that observed at the seventh month (102).

Soon after birth, many female infants have a temporary bloody vaginal discharge associated with changes in the uterine and cervical epithelium, both of which may be explained on the basis of estrin withdrawal. Similarly, the breasts of male and female mature fetuses are developed under the influence of estrogenic hormones but they retrogress after the first few days of neonatal life, thereby indicating a loss of estrin. In this connection, it is of interest to note that the breast development which results from this stimulus is adequate for secretory activity and, in some cases, "witch's milk" is produced even in male infants when a sufficient amount of lactogenic pituitary secretion also has been carried over from the mother to the child. **From these observations, it may be assumed that estrin is secreted by and readily passes through the placenta.**

PROGESTERONE. In some animals, removal of the ovaries (progesterone) at any time during gestation, results in the interruption of pregnancy. In man, on the other hand, oöphorectomy may not be followed by abortion if the operation is done after the first trimester. For this reason, it is thought that the function of the ovaries is taken over by the placenta, which then produces the essential corpus luteum hormone—progesterone.

Although the urine fails to show any progesterone during pregnancy, it does, at that time, contain pregnandiol-glucuronidate, a metabolic end-product of progesterone which is recoverable from the urine after the experimental injection of progesterone (89, 90). Up to the 60th day of pregnancy, pregnandiol is present in amounts normal for the menstrual cycle (4–10 mg. per liter). Thereafter, it increases progressively to 40 mg. per liter by the 150th day and 73–80 mg. per liter by the eighth month. Within 24 hours postpartum, it disappears entirely from the urine (106). Since the progressive increase in pregnandiol apparently occurs at the time of diminishing ovarian activity and since it disappears entirely within 24 hours after delivery, progestin also may have an extra-ovarian source and this source may be the placenta. Such an hypothesis is supported by the observation that in the rat, an animal which invariably aborts after removal of the ovaries, the ovaries may be removed without effect provided all but one of the fetuses in the litter have been previously removed (107, 108). In other words, the combined placentae of all are able to replace the ovaries even in the rat if the fetal load is reduced. **These observations indicate that progestin also may be secreted by the placenta.**

GONADOTROPIC HORMONES. Shortly after the onset of pregnancy, gonadotropic substances are found in the mother's blood and urine and these persist until after the expulsion of the fetus and placenta at the end of gestation (109). There is therefore a definite association between the presence of the gonad-stimulating hormones and the placenta and this association is further indicated by the observation that the urine is positive for these hormones in hydatidiform mole even after the embryo is absorbed, as well as in cases of malignant chorionic new growths known as chorioepitheliomata (110). It also remains positive for some time after the delivery of a full term abdominal pregnancy when the placenta is left within the abdomen (111).

The injection of placental extracts into young animals causes ripening and luteinization of the Graafian follicles (90, 112), the same effect as is produced by injections of blood and urine from pregnant women or by extract injections and implants of the anterior lobe of the pituitary (113, 114). In hypophysectomized animals, on the other hand, the action of both placental extract and pregnancy urine is less effective in stimulating the follicle than it is in inducing luteinization (115, 116). From this data, it has been suggested that the gonad-stimulating substances in the urine and in the placenta are identical but that they differ from those in the anterior lobe which are capable of causing pronounced follicle stimulation as well as luteinization. Their action, however, may not be entirely dependent upon the pituitary since the hypophysis may not have a gonadotropic action during pregnancy, as is shown by the fact that implants of the pituitary gland removed from women after the fourth month of gestation have no effect on the gonads of immature animals (118, 119).

As pregnancy progresses, the placenta contains an increasing amount of gonad stimulating substances—1144 mouse units at 7 weeks, 1132 mouse units at 11 weeks and 5800 mouse units at term but the increase is less than the increase in the placental weight over the same period (120). The percentage concentration of these hormones, accordingly, is less at term than in the first trimester. In addition to storing gonadotroph, the placenta also is able to manufacture this substance since cultures of placental tissue in vitro have been shown to secrete the gonad stimulating hormone (121) and the cells responsible for its secretion are the cytotrophoblast or Langhans cells.

Notwithstanding the fact that the placenta contains large amounts of prolan, only 20 units per liter are found in the fetal serum at birth and none is present after the fifth day (122, 123). It therefore can hardly be said that this hormone passes through the placenta readily. Evidence in corroboration of this has been obtained by injecting the chorionic gonad stimulating substance of pregnancy urine and the gonadotropic hormone of the hypophysis into the fetuses of pregnant animals. Although direct injection of these substances into control pregnant animals stimulated ovulation, injections into the fetus failed to affect the mother's ovaries. **It may be stated, therefore, that the placenta does not readily permit the passage of chorionic gonadotroph (124, 125).** Similarly, the placenta seems impermeable to the thyrotropic hormone of the hypophysis. While large doses of this substance given to pregnant guinea pigs cause changes in the thyroid gland of the mother, they have no effect on those of the fetuses. Because the newly born is particularly sensitive to the colloid-stimulating action of this hormone, its passage through the placenta, therefore, does not take place (126, 127, 128).

Apparently, the lactogenic hormone of the anterior-pituitary passes through the placenta since it has been recovered from the urine of newborn babies within the first week of life. When present in sufficient amounts, it stimulates the mammary glands of both male and female infants to secrete "witch's milk" for a short time after birth (129).

PARATHORMONE. If parathyroid secretion passes through the placenta, its injection into the fetus should raise the calcium values of the maternal blood as well as those of the fetus. When fetuses of pregnant dogs are so injected, the fetal serum calcium, which ordinarily is 1–2 mg. per 100 cc. higher than maternal calcium, becomes 4–7 mg. higher than the calcium of the maternal blood. On the other hand, injections of parathormone into the mothers cause a rise in their serum calcium above the level of the fetal blood (130). **The placenta, accordingly, must be regarded as impermeable to parathyroid secretion.**

THYROXIN. Removal of the thyroid gland from pregnant animals is followed by thyroid hyperplasia in the young (131, 132) and the feeding of thyroid substance to pregnant rabbits induces histologic changes in the glands of the fetuses (127, 133, 134). These experiments, together with the observation that thyroxin given to pregnant guinea pigs causes an increase in metabolism of the newborn offspring (135), indicate that the **thyroid hormone passes through the placenta**.

ADRENALIN. Injections of adrenalin into the fetus have no effect on the maternal blood sugar level (136, 137). From this it would seem that adrenalin does not pass through the placenta. On the other hand, direct injections of the hormone into the fetal heart (138) or into the umbilical artery (139) cause a temporary rise in the mother's blood pressure and the degree and duration of this rise varies with the amount of adrenalin given. **Adrenalin, accordingly, passes from the fetus to the mother through the placenta.** Although no change in fetal blood pressure is observed after the injection of adrenalin into the mother's vein, it still may be possible that adrenalin can pass through the placenta from mother to the fetus since the hormone is so unstable that the small amount used may be changed before it reaches the fetus.

INSULIN. Some diabetic women seem to improve when they become pregnant. This improvement, however, is suddenly interrupted on the death or delivery of the child (140). The presence of a living fetus, therefore, is thought to have a beneficial influence in certain cases of diabetes. Because the improvement usually is not observed until after the fetal pancreas has developed, it has been suggested that insulin from the fetus passes through the placenta and aids the diabetic mother (141). On the other hand, the maternal benefit has been attributed solely to the added utilization of sugar by the fetus (142).

The effect on the fetus of insulin injected into the mother likewise has been interpreted differently by different observers. Such injections are followed by a lowering of the maternal blood sugar with a somewhat less marked fall in that of the fetus and the depression of the sugar level in the fetus as well as in the mother has been offered as further proof of the passage of insulin through the placenta (143, 144). Those who disagree with this hypothesis claim that the fetal effect is due to the loss of fetal sugar through the placenta as a result of insulin hypoglycemia in the mother. This conclusion is further supported by the observation that the injection of insulin several weeks after delivery may greatly lower the mother's blood sugar and cause hypoglycemic shock while the same dose, injected several weeks before the end of pregnancy, is followed by a less marked hypoglycemia and no shock (145). Glucose, accordingly, must pass from the fetus through the placenta when the mother's blood sugar is greatly reduced by insulin.

Injections of insulin into the fetus cause a fall in the mother's blood sugar as well as in that of the fetus and this observation has been added to the previous arguments in favor of the passage of insulin through the placenta (144, 146). On the other hand, the lowering of the maternal sugar level again may be due to the added fetal demands for sugar caused by the effect of insulin on the fetus (147).

As has been noted, the added utilization of glucose by the fetus may explain all of the observations enumerated, without assuming that insulin passes through the placenta. **The placenta, accordingly, may be impermeable to the passage of insulin.** In this connection, evidence of a positive nature is offered by the fact that the response of the maternal blood sugar to fetal injections of insulin is independent of the amount of insulin given. Regardless of the number of units injected into the fetuses of pregnant dogs, the maternal blood sugar level cannot be lowered below 80 mg. % and the depression in the sugar level of the mother ceases when the placental circulation is interrupted (148).

DRUGS, ETC. The placenta also has been found to be permeable to alcohol, chloroform, ether, morphine, hyoscin, atropine, physostigmine, pilocarpine, ephedrine, the barbiturates, arsphenamine, sulphanilimide, penicillin and various salts of sodium, potassium, copper and bismuth (149, 150, 151, 151a).

MICRO-ORGANISMS. The human placenta is generally regarded as an efficient barrier against the transmission of bacteria but cases are occasionally reported in which the organisms of anthrax (152), tuberculosis (153, 154), leprosy (155), typhoid fever (156), pneumonia (157, 158) and pyogenic infections (159, 160) have passed from the mother to the fetus. **Such instances, however, are very infrequent and are thought to result from injury to the placenta.** In them the placental elements may be involved in the pathological process as is sometimes observed in miliary tuberculosis and infections with streptococci, or the injurious effect of the mother's illness on the chorionic epithelium may increase its permeability sufficiently to allow organisms, particularly motile ones like B. typhosis, to penetrate the placenta and infect the child. Transmission of malaria is very rarely observed (161) but the spirocheta pallida often invades the placenta after the middle of pregnancy and gives rise to placental syphilis and congenital lues.

The viruses of small pox, measles, chicken-pox and rabies (162) readily pass through the placenta and, as a result, often cause intrauterine infection of the child when these diseases occur during pregnancy. In former years, when small pox was quite prevalent, living children not infrequently were born with pockmarks as evidence of their having survived intrauterine infection.

TOXINS, ANTITOXINS, AGGLUTININS, ETC. The placenta is impermeable to the toxins of tetanus and diphtheria (163) but permits the passage of antitoxins (163, 164, 165, 166, 167), agglutinins (168, 169, 170), bacteriolysins (171) and complement fixing antibodies. Accordingly, the infants of mothers having an immunity to diphtheria, scarlet fever, measles, etc., are born with a temporary passive immunity toward these diseases. In this connection, it is interesting to note that the H and O agglutinins of typhoid fever pass unequally through the placenta, the O form passing much less readily than does the H form (168).

Immunity to pertussis usually is lacking at birth.   As a result, precautions are always taken to protect newborn infants from contact with those who are suffering from this disease, which is very serious in the first year of life.

THE AMNION

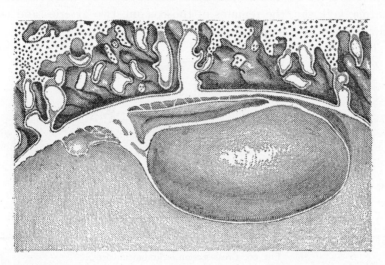

FIG. 65. The Mateer ovum.   A reconstruction (Streeter).   Note the anchoring villi attached to the decidua and the nourishing villi free in the blood space.   Also observe the amnion above, yolk sac below the embryonic area, body stalk and coelomic cavity.

In the earliest human ovum ($7\frac{1}{2}$ days) the amniotic cavity appears as a small closed space between the cytotrophoblast and the dorsal aspect of the embryonic disk.   This cavity is soon lined by cells which apparently are delaminated from the cytotrophoblast and give rise to the future epithelial lining of the amniotic membrane.   As development proceeds the amnion and yolk sac with the intervening embryonic disk are attached to the chorion by a narrow bridge of mesoderm—the body stalk (Fig. 65).   Shortly after the circulation between the chorionic villi and the embryo is established, the growth of the yolk sac is arrested but the amnion continues to enlarge and completely surrounds the embryo, yolk sac and body stalk.   By the end of the second month it fills the chorionic sac and later becomes loosely attached to the mesoderm of the latter, thus completely obliterating the coelomic cavity.

In early embryonic life, the ectodermal cells which line the amnion are low, but by the fourth month they become cuboidal and in the latter part of pregnancy are columnar.   The amniotic cavity is filled with a fluid the functions of which will be considered in chapter VI.

At birth, the amnion is a thin, transparent, avascular membrane which may easily be separated from the chorion.

THE UMBILICAL CORD

The primitive mesodermal body stalk, containing the allantois, receives a remnant of the extraembryonic body cavity and the yolk stalk as the enlarging amnion obliterates the coelomic cavity. At the same time, the amnion envelops the elongated body stalk which is to become the umbilical cord. Early in pregnancy, therefore, the cord consists of embryonic connective tissue which contains the allantois, yolk sac, the remains of the coelom, two arteries and two veins, and is surrounded by a single layer of ectodermal cells.

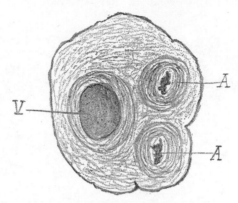

FIG. 66. Cross-section of umbilical cord

Later, the umbilical veins fuse to form a single afferent trunk which passes upward in the falciform ligament of the liver. The two arteries are given off from the hypogastric arteries in the fetal pelvis and, after passing upward on the abdominal wall, enter the cord at the umbilicus. These vessels traverse the cord in a somewhat spiral direction and, in places, bulge beyond its surface.

At term, the umbilical cord is about 50 cm. long and 1 to 2 cm. in diameter. It usually is eccentrically attached to the fetal surface of the placenta.

On cross-section, a covering layer of ectoderm, several cells thick, is observed. The bulk of the cord is made up of a mucoid embryonic connective tissue, Wharton's jelly, which contains the umbilical vein and two umbilical arteries (Fig. 66).

REFERENCES

1. HERTIG, A. T. AND ROCK, J.: Two Human Ova of the Previllous Stage. Contrib. to Embryol., Carnegie Inst., 1945, 41, 67.
2. HERTIG, A. T. AND ROCK, J.: Two Human Ova of the Previllous Stage. Contrib. to Embryol., Carnegie Inst., 1941, 29, 127.
3. JONES, H. O. AND BREWER, J. I.: A Human Ovum in the Primitive-Streak Stage. Contrib. to Embryol., Carnegie Inst., 1941, 29, 159; also S. G. O. 1935, 60, 657.
4. HERTIG, A. T.: Angiogenesis in the Early Human Chorion and in the Primary Placenta of the Macaque Monkey. Contrib. to Embryol. Carnegie Inst., No. 146, 1935, 25, 37.
5. WISLOCKI, G. B. AND STREETER, G. L.: On the Placentation of the Macaque (Macaca Mulata) from the Time of Implantation until the Formation of the Definitive Placenta. Contrib. to Embryol. Carnegie Inst., No. 160, 1938, 1.

6. STREETER, G. L.: A Human Embryo (Mateer) of the presomite Period. Contrib. to Embryol. Carnegie Inst., No. 43, 1920, 9, 389.

7. FRIEDLÄNDER, C.: Physiologisch-Anatomische Untersuchungen über den Uterus, Leipzig, 1870.

8. ENGLEMANN, G. J.: The mucous membrane of the uterus with especial reference to the development and structure of the decidua. Am. J. Obs., 1875–76, 8, 30.

9. MINOT, C.: Uterus and Embryo. I. Rabbit; II. Man. J. Morphol., 1889, 2, No. 3, 341.

10. LANGHANS, T.: Untersuchungen über die menschliche Placenta. Arch. f. Anat. u. Physiol. Anatomische Abtheilung, 1877, 55, 188.

10a. KEARNS, P. J.: Changes in the Uterine and Placental Circulations during Different Stages of Pregnancy. Am. J. Obst. and Gyn., 1939, 38, 400.

11. BARCROFT, J., FLEXNER, L. B., AND McCLURKIN, T.: Output of the Foetal Heart in the Goat. J. Physiol., 1934, 82, 498.

12. WOODBURY, R. A., HAMILTON, W. F. AND TORPIN, R.: The Relationship between Abdominal, Uterine and Arterial Pressures during Labor. Am. J. Physiol., 1938, 121, 640.

13. TAFANI, A.: La Circulation dans le Placenta de Quelques Mammiferes. Arch. Ital. di Biol., 1887, 8, 49.

14. MOSSMAN, H. W.: The Rabbit Placenta and the Problem of Placental Transmission. Am. J. Anat., 1926, 37, 433.
    Comparative Morphogenesis of the Fetal Membranes and Accessory Uterine Structures. Contrib. to Embryol. Carnegie Inst., No. 158, 1937, 26, 129.

15. SPANNER, R.: Mütterlicher und kindlicher Kreislauf der menschlichen Placenta und seine Strombahnen. Ztschr. f. Anat. und Entwickl., 1935–36, 105, 163.

16. CALKINS, L. A.: Placental Variation. Am. J. O. & G., 1937, 33, 280.

17. DODDS, G. S.: The Area of the Chorionic Villi in Full Term Placentae. Anat. Rec., 1922, 24, 287.

18. NEEDHAM, J.: Chemical Embryol. Cambridge, 1931, 3, 1460.

19. FENGER, F.: The Chemical Composition of the Placenta. J. Biol. Chem., 1917, 29, 9.

20. MOSSMAN, H. W.: The Rabbit Placenta and the Problem of Placental Transmission. Am. J. Anat., 1926, 37, 433.

21. HUGGETT, A. S.: Foetal Blood-Gas Tensions and Gas Transfusion Through the Placenta of the Goat. J. Physiol., 1927, 62, 373.

22. KROGH, A.: On the Mechanism of the Gas-Exchange in the Lungs. Skand. Arch. f. Physiol., 1909–10, 23, 248.

23. COHNSTEIN, J. AND ZUNTZ, N.: Untersuchungen über das Blut, den Kreislauf und die Athmung beim Säugethier-Fötus. Archiv. f. Physiol., 1884, 34, 173.

24. BELL, W. B., CUNNINGHAM, L., JOWETT, M., MILLET, H. AND BROOKS, J.: The Metabolism and Acidity of the Foetal Tissues and Fluids. Br. Med. J., 1928, 1, 126.

25. HASELHORST, G.: Zum plazentaren Kreislauf unter der Geburt. Ztschr. f. Geb. u. Gyn., 1929, 95, 32, 224, 400.

26. EASTMAN, N. J.: Foetal Blood Studies. I. The Oxygen Relationships of Umbilical Cord Blood at Birth. Bull. J. Hopk. Hosp., 1930, 47, 221.

27. EASTMAN, N. J.: Foetal Blood Studies. III. The Chemical Nature of Asphyxia Neonatorum and Its Bearing on Certain Practical Problems. Bull. J. Hopk. Hosp., 1932, 50, 39.

28. HASELHORST, G. AND STROMBERGER: Über den Gasgehalt des Nabelschnurblutes vor und nach der Geburt des Kindes und über den Gasaustausch in der Placenta. Ztschr. f. Geb. u. Gyn., 1932, 102, 16.

29. GOLDBLOOM, A. AND GOTTLIEB, R.: Icterus Neonatorum. III. The Oxygen Capacity and Saturation of the Mother and Fetus. J. Clin. Invest., 1930, 9, 139.

30. EASTMAN, N. J., GEILING, E. M. K. AND DeLAWDER, A. M.: Foetal Blood Studies IV. The Oxygen and Carbon Dioxide Dissociation Curves of Foetal Blood. Bull. J. Hopk. Hosp., 1933, 53, 246.

31. EHRENBERG, R. AND LIEBENOW, W.: Über chemische Altersveränderungen der menschlichen Placenta. Arch. f. Physiol. (Pflüger's) 1923, 201, 387 .

32. WEHEFRITZ, E.: Über chemische Altersveränderungen der menschlichen Placenta und ihre Beziehungen zum Problem des Geburtseintrittes. Arch. f. Gyn., 1926, 124, 511.
33. NEEDHAM: Chemic. Embryol. Cambridge, 1931, 3, 1462.
34. BASSO, G. L.: Ueber Autolyse der Placenta. Arch. f. Gyn., 1905, 76, 162.
35. HARDING, V. J. AND FORT, C. A.: The Amino Acids of Mature Human Placenta. J. Biol. Chem., 1918, 35, 29.
36. LIEPMANN, W. AND SCHULZ, E.: Neue Ergebnisse zur Plazentar-und Eklampsieforschung. Deutsche. med. Wchnschr., 1921, 47, 1417.
37. DELLAPIANE, G.: Sul Metabolismo degli idrati di carbonio nella Placenta. Boll. de Soc. Ital. di Biol. Sper., 1925–26, 1, 117. (See also Reference 40.)
38. MORSE, A.: The Amino Acid Nitrogen of the Blood in Cases of Normal and Complicated Pregnancy and also in the New Born Infant. Bull. J. Hopk. Hosp., 1917, 28, 199.
39. SCHLOSSMANN, H.: Beiträge zur Biologie der Plazenta. IV. Über die Durchlässigkeit der Plazenta für Amniosäuren. Arch. f. Exper. Path., 1932, 166, 81.
40. LUCK, J. M. AND ENGLE, E. T.: The Permeability of the Placenta of the Rat to Glycine, Alanin and Urea. Am. J. Physiol., 1929, 88, 230.
41. PLASS, E. D. AND MATTHEWS, C. W.: Placental Transmission. III. Amino Acids, Non Protein Nitrogen, Urea and Uric Acid in Fetal and Maternal Whole Blood Plasma and Corpuscles. Bull. J. Hopk. Hosp., 1925, 36, 393.
42. HELMUTH, K.: Beiträge zur Biologie des Neugeborenen. Arch. f. Gyn., 1924, 123, 57.
43. POMMERENKE, W. T.: Placental Interchange. I. On the Concentration of Certain Nitrogenous Substances in the Blood Before and After Passing Through the Placenta. J. Clin. Invest., 1936, 15, 485.
44. HUNTER, A. AND CAMPBELL, W. R.: The Placental Transmission of Creatine and Creatinine. J. Biol. Chem., 1918, 34, 5.
45. SLEMMONS, J. M. AND MORRISS, W. H.: The Non Protein Nitrogen and Urea in the Maternal and Fetal Blood at the Time of Birth. Bull. J. Hopk. Hosp., 1916, 27, 343.
46. BRANDSTRUP, E.: Recherches sur le passage de substances chimiques de la mère au foetus à la fin de la gestation. Bull. Soc. Chim. Biol., 1931, 13, 172.
47. HAMMITT, F. S.: The Urea Content of Placentas from Normal and Toxemic Pregnancies. J. Biol. Chem., 1918, 34, 515; 1918, 36, 569; 1919, 37, 105.
48. MAEDA, K.: Zur Kenntnis der Fermente in der Placenta. Biochem. Ztschr., 1923, 143, 347.
49. NEEDHAM, J.: Chem. Embryol. Cambridge, 1931, 3, 1514. (Contains summary tables of various nitrogen bodies.)
50. BERNARD, C.: Leçons sur les Phenomènes de la Vie. Paris, 1879.
51. LOCHHEAD, J. AND CRAMER, W.: The Glycogenic Changes in the Placenta and the Foetus of the Pregnant Rabbit: A Contribution to the Chemistry of Growth. Proc. Roy. Soc. B., 1908, 80, 263.
52. CLOGNE, R., WELTI, M. AND PICHON, M.: Dosage du glycogène dans le placenta. Bull. Soc. Chim. Biol., 1924, 6, 788.
53. HUGGETT, A. ST. G.: Maternal Control of the Placental Glycogen. J. Physiol., 1929, 67, 360.
54. VON OETTINGEN, K.: Beitrag zum Kohlehydratstoffwechsel der normalen menschlichen Placenta. Monatschr. f. Geb. u. Gyn., 1924, 67, 41.
55. DELLAPIANE, G.: Sulla funcione della plazenta. Riv. Ital. di Ginecol., 1926, 5, 328.
56. LIEPMANN, W. AND BERGELL, P.: Verhandlung der Gesellschaft für Geburtsh. u. Gyn. zu Berlin. Zeitschr. f. Geb. u. Gyn., 1905, 54, 366.
57. MORRISS, W. H.: The Obstetrical Significance of the Blood Sugar with Special Reference to the Placental Interchange. J. Hopk. Hosp. Bull., 1917, 28, 140.
58. BELL, W. B., CUNNINGHAM, L., JOWETT, M., MILLET, H. AND BROOKS, J.: The Metabolism and Acidity of the Foetal Tissues and Fluids. Br. M. J., 1928, 1, 126.
59. SCHLOSSMANN, H.: Beiträge zur Biologie der Placenta. I. Die Durchlässigkeit der Placenta für Traubenzucker. Zeitschr. Exper. Med., 1930, 72, 401
60. BIENENFELD, B.: Beitrag zur Kenntnis des Lipoidgehaltes der Placenta. Biochem. Ztschr., 1912, 43, 245.

61. WATANABE, H.: Über die Lipoidsubstanzen der Placenta in Verschiedenen Schwanger-schaftsmonaten mit Besonderer Berücksichtigung ihrer Mengenverhältnisse. Jap. J. Biochem., 1923, 2, 369.
62. SLEMMONS, J. M. AND STANDER, H. J.: The Lipoids of the Maternal and Fetal Blood at the Conclusion of Labor. Bull. J. Hopk. Hosp., 1923, 34, 7.
63. HELMUTH, K.: Beiträge zur Biologie des Neugeborenen. Arch. f. Gyn., 1926, 127, 293.
64. NEEDHAM, J.: Chemical Embryol. Cambridge, 1931, 3, 1476.
65. BOYD, E. M. AND WILSON, K. M.: The Exchange of Lipids in the Umbilical Circulation at Birth. J. Clin. Invest., 1935, 14, 7.
66. BECKENBACH, W. AND RUPP, H.: Das Verhalten der Fette bei ihrem Durchtritt durch die Placenta. Klin. Wchnschr., 1931, 10, 63.
67. SINCLAIR, R. G.: The Permeability of the Rat Placenta to Fat. Am. J. Physiol., 1933, 103, 73.
68. CHAIKOFF, I. L. AND ROBINSON, A.: Studies in Fetal Fat. I. The Influence of High and Low Fat Diets on the Quantity of Fat Formed in the Fetus of the Rat. J. Biol. Chem., 1933, 100, 13.
69. VON OETTINGEN, K.: Vergleichende Untersuchungen des mütterlichen und kindlichen Blutes. Arch. f. Gyn., 1927, 129, 115.
70. SPIEGEL, R.: Kalium und Calcium im Cyclus und während der Gestation. 1930, Arch. f. Gyn., 1930, 143, 248.
71. BOGERT AND PLASS: Placental Transmission. I. The Calcium and Magnesium Content of Fetal and Maternal Blood Serums. 1923, J. Biol. Chem., 1923, 56, 297.
72. KRANE, W.: Kalium und Kalzium im mütterlichen und kindlichen Serum sowie im Gesamtblut von Mutter und Kind. Ztschr. f. Geb. u. Gyn., 1930, 97, 22.
73. PLASS AND TOMPKINS: Placental Transmission. II. The Various Phosphoric Acid Com-pounds in Maternal and Fetal Serum. 1923, J. Biol. Chem., 1923, 56, 309.
74. CUNNINGHAM, R. S.: Studies in Placental Permeability. II. Proc. Soc. Exper. Biol. and Med., 1923, 20, 343.
75. BRUNSCHWIG, A. E.: Notes on Experiments in Placental Permeability. Anat. Rec., 1927, 34, 237.
76. GAEHTGENS, G.: Der Übergang von Carotin und Vitamin A aus dem mütterlichen in den kindlichen Blutkreislauf. Arch. f. Gyn., 1937, 164, 398.
77. ASCHOFF: Über den Karotingehalt menschlicher Gewebe (Leber- und Fettgewebe). Verhandl. deutsch. Path. Gesellsch., 1934, 27, 145.
78. GAEHTGENS, G.: Der Gehalt der Placenta an Carotin und Vitamin A. Arch. f. Gyn., 1937, 164, 588.
79. ELLISON, J. B. AND MOORE, T.: The Vitamin A Reserves of the Human Infant and Child. In Health and Disease. Biochem. J., 1937, 31, 165.
80. DANN, W. J.: The Transmission of Vitamin A from Parents to Young in Mammals. Biochem. J., 1932, 26, 1072.
81. GAEHTGENS, G.: Carotin und Vitamin A in der fetalen Leber und im Fruchtwasser. Klin. Wchnschr., 1937, 16, 1073.
82. DANN, W. J.: The Transmission of Vitamin A from Parents to Young in Mammals. III. Effect of Fat Content of Diet During Pregnancy on the Transmission of Vitamin A to the Fetal Rat. Biochem. J., 1934, 28, 634.
83. DANN, W. J.: The Transmission of Vitamin A from Parents to Young in Mammals. IV. Effect of Liver Reserve of Mother on Transmission of Vitamin A to the Fetal and Suckling Rat. Biochem. J., 1934, 28, 2141.
84. SHIN, H.: Studies on Pregnant and Puerperal Infant Beri-Beri. I. Vitamin B Content of Urine and Various Tissues of Normal Rabbits Fed with Complete Diet. J. Chosen Med. Assn., 1932, 22, 1011.
85. SHIN, H.: Studies on Infant Beri Beri: Vitamin Content of Urine and Various Tissues of Pregnant Rabbit, Fetus and Show. J. Ch. Med. Assn., 1932, 22, 1143.

85a STRÄHLER, F.: Untersuchungen über den Vitamin B_1-Stoffwechsel gesunder und polyneuritiskranker Schwangerer und Wöchnerinnen. Deutsch. med. Wchnschr., 1938, 64, 1137.

86. ABT, A. F., FARMER, C. J. AND EPSTEIN, I. M.: Normal Cevitamic (Ascorbic) Acid Determinations in Blood Plasma and Their Relationship to Capillary Resistance. J. Pediat., 1936, 8, 1.

87. WAHREN, H. AND RUNDQVIST, O.: Ueber den Ascorbinsäuregehalt des Blutes von Mutter und Frucht. Klin. Wchnschr., 1937, 16, 1498.

88. BRAESTRUP, P. W.: Studies of Latent Scurvy in Infants. III. J. Nutrition, 1938, 16, 363.

89. NEUWEILER, W.: Ueber den Gehalt der Plazenta an Vitamin C. Schweiz. med. Wchnschr., 1935, 16, 539.

90. ASCHNER, B.: Ueber brunstartige Erscheinungen (Hyperämie und Hämorrhagie am weiblichen Genitale) nach subkutaner Injektion von Ovarial oder Plazentarextrakt. Arch. f. Gyn., 1913, 99, 534.

91. DOISY, E. A., RALLS, J. O., ALLEN, E. AND JOHNSTON, C. G.: The Extraction and Some Properties of an Ovarian Hormone. J. Biol. Chem., 1924, 61, 711.

92. COLLIP, J. B.: Further Observations on an Ovary-stimulating Hormone of the Placentae. Canad. M. A. J., 1930, 22, 761.

93. COLLIP, J. B., BROWNE, S. L. AND THOMSON, D. L.: The Relation of Emmenin to Other Estrogenic Hormones. J. Biol. Chem., 1932, 97, XVII.

94. ALLEN, E., PRATT, J. P. AND DOISY, E. A.: The Ovarian Follicular Hormone: Its Distribution in Human General Tissue. J. A. M. A., 1925, 85, 399.

95. WALDSTEIN, E.: Frühkastration in der Schwangerschaft. Zur Genese des Ovarialhormons. Zentralbl. f. Gyn., 1929, 53, 1305.

96. PROBSTNER, A.: Zur Frage der innersekretorischen Tätigkeit der Plazenta. Endokrinol., 1931, 8, 161.

97. CORNER, G. W.: The Sites of Formation of Estrogenic Substances in the Animal Body. Physiol. Rev., 1938, 18, 154.

98. DE SNOO, K.: Chorionepitheliom der Tube Hormon Bildung vom isolierten Trophoblasten (Menformon). Zentralbl. f. Gyn., 1928, 52, 2703.

99. JOSEPH, S.: Zur Biologie der Brustdrüse beim Neugebornen. Monatschr. f. Geb. u. Gyn., 1929, 83, 219.

100. NEUMANN, H. O.: Schwangerschaftsreaktion im Neugeborenen Organismus. Sitzungsb. d. Gesellsch z. Beförd. d. ges. Naturw. zu Marburg., 1930, 65, 61.

101. BRUHL, R.: Das Vorkommen von weiblichen Sexualhormon und Hypophysenvorderlappenhormon im Blute und Urine von Neugeborenen. Klin. Wchnschr., 1929, 8, 1766.

102. SCAMMON, R. E.: Prenatal Growth and Natal Involution of the Human Uterus. Proc. Soc. Exp. Biol. and Med., 1926, 23, 687.

103. HAIN, A. M.: The Physiology of Pregnancy in the rat: Further Data On the Passage of Hormones Via the Placenta and the Mother's Milk. Quart. J. Exp. Physiol., 1936, 26, 29.

104. VENNING, E. M. AND BROWNE, J. S. L.: Isolation of a Water-Soluble Pregnandiol Complex from Human Pregnancy Urine. Proc. Soc. Exper. Biol., 1936, 34, 792.

105. VENNING, E. M. AND BROWNE, J. S. L.: Urinary Excretion of Sodium Pregnandiol Glucuronidate in the Menstrual Cycle (an Excretion Product of Progesterone). Am. J. Physiol., 1937, 119, 417.

106. BROWNE, J. S. L., HENRY, J. S. AND VENNING, E. M.: The Corpus Luteum Hormone in Pregnancy. J. Clin. Invest., 1937, 16, 678.

107. HATERIUS, H. O.: Reduction of Litter Size and Maintenance of Pregnancy in the Oophorectomized Rat: Evidence Concerning the Endocrine Rôle of the Placenta. Am. J. Physiol., 1936, 114, 399.

108. KIRSCH, R. E.: A Study on the Control of the Length of Gestation in the Rat with Notes on the Maintenance and Termination of Gestation. Am. J. Physiology, 1938, 122, 86.

109. Aschheim, S. and Zondek, B.: Hypophysenvorderloppenhormon und Ovarialhormon im Harn von Schwangeren. Klin. Wchnschr., 1927, 6, 1322.

110. Heidrich, L., Fels, E. and Matthias, E.: Testikuläres Chorionepitheliom mit Gynäkomastie und mit einigen Schwangerschaftserscheinungen. Brun's Beitr., 1930, 150, 349.

111. Ware, H. H. and Main, R. J.: An Abdominal Pregnancy Near Term With Successful Termination: Retained Placenta and Observations on the Postpartum Excretion of Prolan. Am. J. O. & G., 1934, 27, 756.

112. Murata, M. and Adachi, K.: Über die künstliche Erzeugung des Corpus luteum durch Injektion der Plazentarsubstanz aus frühen Schwangerschaftsmonaten. Zeitschr. f. Geb. u. Gyn., 1927, 92, 45.

113. Evans, H. M. and Long, J. A.: The Effect of the Anterior Lobe Administered Intraperitoneally upon Growth, Maturity and Oestrus Cycles of Rat. Anat. Rec., 1921, 21, 62.

114. Smith, P. E. and Engle, E. T.: Experimental Evidence Regarding The Rôle of the Anterior Pituitary in the Development and Regulation of the Genital System. Am. J. Anat., 1927, 40, 159.

115. Hill, M. and Parkes, A. S.: Studies on Ovulation. V. The Action of the Ovulation-Producing Substance of Urine of Pregnancy on the Hypophysectomized Rabbit. J. Physiol., 1931, 71, 36, 40.

116. Leonard, S. L. and Smith, P. E.: Effects of Injecting Pregnancy-Urine Extracts in Hypophysectomized Rats. Proc. Soc. Exper. Biol., 1933, 30, 1248.

117. Fevold, H. L. and Hisaw, F. L.: Interactions of Gonad-Stimulating Hormones in Ovarian Development. Am. J. Physiol., 1934, 109, 655.

118. Philipp, E.: Die Wirkung von Hypophysenvorderlappen und von Placenta auf die Uterusschleimhaut beim Kaninchen. Zentralbl. f. Gyn., 1931, 55, 929.

119. Saxton, J. and Loeb, L.: Thyroid-Stimulating and Gonadotropic Hormones of the Human Anterior-Pituitary Gland at Different Ages and in Pregnant and Lactating Women. Anat. Rec., 1937, 69, 261.

120. Zondek, B.: Die Hormone des Ovariums und des Hypophysenvorderlappens. Berlin, 1931.

121. Gey, G. O., Seegar, G. E. and Hellman, L. M.: The Production of a Gonadotropic Substance (Prolan) by Placental Cells in Tissue Culture. Science, 1938, 88, 306.

122. Bourg, R. and Legrand, G.: Etude comparative de la teneur en gravidine du placenta et des humeurs maternelles et ovulaires au cours de l'accouchement normal et pathologique.

123. Joseph, S.: Zur Biologie der Brustdrüse beim Neugebornen. Monatschr. f. Geb. u. Gyn., 1929, 83, 219.

124. Wislocki, G. B. and Snyder, F. F.: Note on the Failure of Anterior Lobe Extract to Pass from Fetus to Mother. Proc. Soc. Exp. Biol. and Med., 1932, 33, 30, 196.

125. Lévy-Solal, E., Walther, P. and D'Alsace, J.: Les Hormones de Grossesse, Traversent-elles le Placenta? Compt. Rend. Soc. Biol., 1934, 115, 272.

126. Aron, M.: Sur l'imperméabilité du Placenta à La Substance Prehypophysaire active sur la glande thyroïde. Compt. Rend. Soc. Biol., 1930, 103, 151.

127. Ujiie, S.: Über die Beziehungen des Nebenschilddrüsen und Schilddrüsenhormons zwischen Mutter und Fötus. J. Expt'l. Med., 1932, 20, 34.

128. Schittenhelm, A. and Eisler, B.: Zur Frage der Übertragung des thyreotropen Hormons durch die Placenta und die Milch. Ztschr. f. d. ges. Expt'l. Med., 1934, 35, 95, 124.

129. Lyons, W. R.: The Hormonal Basis for Witch's Milk. Proc. Soc. Exp. Biol. & Med., 1937, 37, 207.

130. Hoskins, F. M. and Snyder, F. F.: The Placental Transmission of Parathyroid Extract. Am. J. Physiol., 1930, 104, 530.

131. Halstead: An Experimental Study of the Thyroid Gland of Dogs, with Especial Consideration of Hypertrophy of This Gland. J. H. Hosp. Reports, 1896, 1, 373.

88 OBSTETRICAL PRACTICE

132. EDMONDS, W.: Thyroid of Puppy of Thyroidless Bitch. Tr. Path. Soc. London, 1901, 51, 221.
133. TAKAHASHI, T.: Über den Einfluss der Schildrüsenfunktionsstörung der Mutter auf die innersekretorischen Organe des Fetus oder des Säuglings. Berichte über ges. Biol., 1930, 53, 389.
134. CENTANNI, G.: Sulle modificazioni regressive della tiroide materna e fetale in seguito somministrazione esogena del suo secreto. Berichte u. ges. Biol., 1930, 56, 128.
135. DÖDERLEIN, G.: Experimenteller Hyperthyreoidismus und seine Wirkung auf Fortpflanzung und Nachkommenschaft. Arch. Gyn., 1928, 133, 680.
136. SNYDER, F. F. AND HOSKINS, F. M.: Calcium Content of Maternal and Foetal Blood Serum following Injections of Parathyroid Extract in Foetuses in Utero. Proc. Soc. Exper. Biol. & Med., 1928, 25, 264.
137. RUPP, H.: Die Durchlässigkeit der Placenta und Eihäute für Antigine, Antikörper und Inkrete. Arch. f. Gyn., 1930, 143, 80.
138. CATTANEO, L.: Contribution expérimentale à L'étude du Passage des Hormones Foetales à Travers le Placenta. (Les Hormones des Glandes surrénalales et l'hormone Hypophysaire Postérieure.) Arch. Ital. de Biol., 1931, 86, 1, 33.
139. SCHLOSSMAN, H.: Beiträge zur Biologie der Placenta. III. Die Durchlässigkeit der Plazenta für Adrenalin. Arch. f. Exper. Path., 1932, 166, 74.
140. NEVINNY, H. AND SCHRETTER, G.: Zuckerkrankheit und Schwangerschaft. Arch. f. Gyn., 1930, 140, 397.
141. LAMBIE, C. G.: Diabetes in Pregnancy. J. O. & G., Brit. Emp., 1926, 33, 563.
142. STANDER, H. J. AND PECKHAM, C. H.: Diebetes Mellitus and Pregnancy. Am. J. O. & G., 1927, 14, 313.
143. ARON, M.: Sur le Passage de l'insuline à travers le placenta. Compt. rend. Soc. Biol., 1929, 100, 844.
144. COREY, : Placental Permeability to Insulin in the Albino Rat. Physiologic. Zool., 1932, 5, 36.
145. BRITTON, S. W.: Maternal and Fetal Blood Sugar Changes under Various Experimental Conditions. Am. J. Physiol., 1930, 95, 178.
146. PACK, G. T. AND BARBER, D.: The Placental Transmission of Insulin from Fetus to Mother. Am. J. Physiol., 1930, 92, 271.
147. OLOW, J.: Über den Übergang von Insulin aus dem Fötus in die Mutter. Biochem. Z., 1930, 217, 475.
148. SCHLOSSMANN, H.: Beitrage zur Biologie der Plazenta. II. Ist die Plazenta für Insulin durchlässig? Arch. f. Exper. Path., 1931, 159, 213.
149. NEEDHAM, J.: Chemical Embryol. Cambridge, 1931, 4.
150. SCHLOSSMANN, H.: Der Stoffaustausch zwischen Mutter und Frucht durch die Placenta. München, 1933, p. 54.
151. SPEERT, H. AND BABBITT, D.: The Passage of Sulphanilimide Through the Human Placenta. Bull. J. Hopk. Hosp., 1938, 63, 337.
151a. GREEN, H. J. AND HOBBY, G. L.: Transmission of Penicillin through Human Placenta. Proc. Soc. Exper. Biol. & Med., 1944, 57, 282.
152. ROSTOWZEW, M. J.: Ueber die Uebertragung von Milzbrandbacillen beim Menchen von der Mutter auf die Frucht bei Pustula maligna. Ztschr. f. Geb. u. Gyn., 1897, 37, 542.
153. WHITMAN, R. C. AND GREENE, L. W.: A Case of Desseminated Miliary Tuberculosis in a Stillborn Infant. Arch. Int. Med., 1922, 29, 261.
154. McCORD, J. R.: A Probable Case of Direct Intrauterine Transmission of Tuberculosis from Mother to Baby. Am. J. O. & G., 1930, 19 826.
155. PINEDA, E. V.: The Presence of Mycobacterium Leprae in the Placenta and Umbilical Cord. J. Phillipine I. M. A., 1928, 8, 67.
156. HICKS, H. T. AND FRENCH, H.: Typhoid Fever and Pregnancy with Special Reference to Fetal Infection. Lancet., 1905, 1, 1491.
157. BOCHENSKI, K. AND GROEBEL, M.: Ein Fall von intrauterin acquirierter Pneumonie. Monatschr. f. Geb. u. Gyn., 1905, 22, 490.

158. MÜLLER, C.: Kongenitale Pneumonie als Ursache von Totgeburt. Arch. f. Gyn., 1932, 150, 482.
159. PHILIPP, E.: Experimentelle Studien zur Frage der kongenitalen Trupanosomen und Spirochateninfektion. Arch. f. Gyn., 1928, 133, 573, 679.
160. SLOBOZIANU, H. AND HERSOVICI, P.: La transmission de placentaire de l'infection gonococcique chez le foetus. Gynec. et Obstet., 1933, 28, 601.
161. FORBES, R. P.: Congenital Malaria. Am. J. Dis. Child., 1923, 25, 130.
162. HERRMANN, O.: Plazentare Uebertragung der Wut. Zeitschr. Immuniättsforsch u. Exper. Therap., 1928, 58, 371.
163. NATAN-LARRIER, L., RAMON, G. AND GRASSET, E.: Recherches sur le passage des toxins et des antitoxines à travers le Placenta. Compt. Rend. Acad. Soc. Biol., 1927, 96, 241.
164. POLANO, O.: Der Antitoxinübergang von der Mutter auf das Kind. Ztschr. f. Geb. und Gyn., 1904, 53, 456.
165. RUH, H. C. AND McCLELLAND, J. E.: Comparison of Diphtheria Immunity in the Mother and in the Newborn. Am. J. Dis. Child., 1923, 25, 59.
166. KUTTNER, A. AND RATNER, B.: The Importance of Colostrum to the Newborn Infant. Am. J. Dis. Child., 1923, 25, 413.
167. TEN BROECK, C. AND BAUER, J. H.: The Transmission of Tetanus Antitoxin Through the Placenta. Proc. Soc. Exper. Biol. & Med., 1923, 20, 399.
168. TIMMERMANN, W. A.: The Transference of H and O Typhoid Agglutinin From Mother to Child. Ztschr. f. Immunitätsforsch. u. exp. Therap., 1931, 70, 388 or 399.
169. NEILL, J. M., GASPARI, E. L., RICHARDSON, L. V. AND SUGG, J. Y.: Diphtheria Antibodies Transmitted from Mother to Child. J. Immunol., 1932, 22, 117.
170. TOOMEY, J. A.: Agglutinins in Mother's Blood, Baby's Blood, Mother's Milk and Placental Blood. Am. J. Dis. Child., 1934, 47, 521.
171. WILSON, M. G., WHEELER, G. W. AND TRASK, M. M.: Antistreptolysin Content of Blood Serum of Children: Its Significance in Rheumatic Fever. Proc. Soc. Exper. Biol. & Med., 1934, 31, 1001.
172. VON SPEE: Epidiaskopische Demonstration eines jungen Stadiums der menschlichen Eieinbettung. Verhandl. d. deutsch. Gesellsch. f. Gyn., 1906, p. 421.
173. HEUSER, C. H. AND STREETER, G. L.: Development of the Macaque Embryo. Contrib. to Embryol., Carnegie Inst., 1941, 29, 17.

CHAPTER VI

PHYSIOLOGY OF THE FETUS

NUTRITION AND ELIMINATION. Shortly after implantation, the ovum is surrounded by maternal blood, altered decidual elements (which have been destroyed by the erosive action of the trophoblast), glycogen (which is present in the endometrium at this time), and secretion from the adjacent endometrial glands, all of which furnish abundant nutriment. Until the circulation in the villi and chorionic plate is developed and communicates with that of the embryo, the latter receives its nourishment from these materials by osmosis.

With the establishment of the cardiovascular system, the essential food elements are carried by the newly formed circulation to the embryo and waste products are returned to the villi. The chorionic villi, therefore, are responsible for the interchange of food and waste material between the maternal and the fetal circulations.

Nutrition and elimination are thus carried on in the placenta and, in this respect, the function of the latter may be likened to that of the alimentary tract, lungs, liver and kidneys in later life. See Chapter V.

RESPIRATORY SYSTEM. Rhythmic respiratory movements have been observed before the end of the first trimester in sheep. They are derived from a general mass movement of an extensor type by the dropping out of the movements of the head and limbs and are somewhat similar to the gasps which occur at the late stages of poisoning by minimal lethal doses of hydrocyanic acid vapor (1). When studied under satisfactory experimental conditions later in pregnancy, **these respiratory movements are not unlike those observed soon after birth.**

After cutting the spinal cord so that the abdomen may be opened without the use of anesthesia, laparotomy in a saline bath permits visualization of fetal respiratory movements before and after the uterus is incised. In this manner, the placental circulation is not disturbed and the effect of anesthesia is eliminated. Observations of this character made on rabbits show the respiratory movements of the full-term fetus (32 days) to occur about 30 times per minute. In prematures (30 days) the rate is less than half as rapid and, in post-matures (34 days), it is often twice as fast as at term. Soon after birth, breathing is greatly accelerated, the rate in some instances reaching 180 per minute (2).

When the maternal experimental animal breathes a gas mixture of low oxygen content, the fetal respiratory movements are depressed even though those of the mother are stimulated. **Anoxemia, therefore, leads to fetal apnea.** Possibly some of the instances of apnea occurring during and immediately after parturition may be explained on this basis (2). In other words, the decrease in the placental circulation which results from the increasing uterine contractions, may cause a lowering of the oxygen in the fetal blood and thereby depress respiratory movements to such an extent that resuscitation at the time of birth may be difficult or impossible.

Hyperventilation of the mother also depresses the respiratory movements of the fetus unless a sufficient amount of carbon dioxide is introduced in the gas mixture. **Acapnia, like anoxemia, accordingly, causes apnea and a certain level of carbon dioxide is essential for the maintenance of fetal respiratory movements.** On the other hand, an excess of carbon dioxide sufficient to accelerate the mother's respiration has little or no effect upon the movements of the child (2).

The fetal respiratory system also is peculiarly sensitive to the various drugs which produce analgesia and anesthesia. Pentobarbital sodium, when given in amounts sufficient to produce anesthesia or perceptibly to alter respiration or the reflexes of the maternal animal, results in immediate depression or abolition of fetal respiratory movements. A similar depressing effect follows the use of phenobarbital, paraldehyde, chloral hydrate, nitrous oxide and divinyl ether. Cyclopropane, given with oxygen, however, seems to have little or no depressing action when administered over as long a period as 30 minutes (2).

Similar rhythmic movements have been observed through the abdominal walls of women in the latter months of pregnancy and were formerly thought to be respiratory in nature (3) but this interpretation was abandoned because fetuses observed at operation usually were in a state of apnea. The development of a more satisfactory operative technique, however, has demonstrated the unquestionable presence of respiratory movements and has shown that the condition of apnea ordinarily seen at operation probably is due to the depressing effect of the anesthetic administered to the mother (2).

Further proof of the true nature of these movements is afforded by the finding of amniotic fluid contents in the alveoli of the lungs (4) and by the observation that India ink may be found in the fetal lungs within a few minutes after it has been injected into the amniotic sac (5).

If in the course of the animal experiments previously described, the fetal head is raised above the fluid in the saline bath, the respiratory movements continue. With the escape of fluid from the mouth and nares, the onset of the breathing of air instead of fluid is marked by a change in the color of the blood in the umbilical artery from blue to bright red. Thus, **post-natal respiration is thought to be a continuation of intrauterine respiratory activity** and not an abrupt transition from a state of apnea (2). It, therefore, is a common experience to observe typical respiratory movements in living fetuses that are aborted before the 28th week of pregnancy.

CIRCULATION. Blood from the placenta is carried to the fetus by the umbilical vein.   It then enters the inferior vena cava either directly by way of the ductus venosus or indirectly through the hepatic veins after circulating through the liver.   This oxygenated blood, therefore, mingles with the venous blood from the liver and lower part of the body before it reaches the heart.   On reaching the

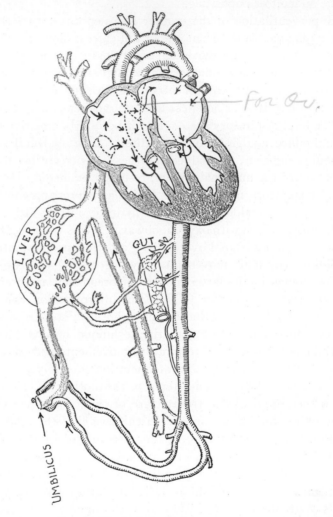

FIG. 67. The fetal circulation.

right auricle, it is further mixed with venous blood from the superior vena cava, and a part is forced through the foramen ovale into the left auricle while the remainder passes through the tricuspid valve into the right ventricle.   The latter portion enters the pulmonary arteries and is either shunted into the aorta by way of the ductus arteriosus or passes through the lungs and is returned by the pulmonary veins to the left auricle where it mingles with the blood which has passed through the foramen ovale. The contents of the left auricle are expelled into the left ventricle from which the blood is forced into the aorta and systemic vessels (6, 7, 8) (Fig. 67). The blood is then returned to the placenta by the hypogastric branches of the internal iliac arteries.

Soon after birth the umbilical extremities of the hypogastric vessels cease to pulsate and their obliteration follows within a few days. Likewise, a rapid closure of the umbilical vein and ductus venosus is observed but the ductus arteriosus and foramen ovale remain patent for some time. As respiration is established, the pulmonary circulation becomes more active, and less blood is shunted through the ductus arteriosus, with the result that the latter becomes progressively smaller and after about eight weeks is finally obliterated. Similarly, the foramen ovale closes within a short time after birth as a result of the greater pressure in the left auricle which follows the increase in the pulmonary circulation.

BLOOD VOLUME determinations made by the dye method on fetal sheep at various periods of intrauterine life show the volume of blood in the fetal circulation (fetus and placenta) expressed as a percentage of the weight of the fetus, to be 20-40% near the end of the first half of pregnancy. This large proportion of blood appears to diminish as the ratio of fetal growth to placental growth increases and, at term, the figure is reduced to 14-15%. Since the fetal circulation includes the placental circulation, the blood volume should be compared with the combined weights of the fetus and the placenta. When considered as a percentage of the weight of the fetus plus that of the placenta, accordingly, the blood volume is found to be rather uniform through most of fetal life, increasing but slightly from 8% in the first half of gestation to 9.6% late in pregnancy (9).

As the placental circulation in early gestation forms a much greater proportion of the whole vascular bed than it does later on, the relative amount of blood in the placenta diminishes with the progress of pregnancy. The blood in the fetal circulation, accordingly, is almost equally divided between the fetus and the placenta in the middle of gestation, whereas three-fourths of it is in the fetus and only one-fourth in the placenta as term is approached (10). A large part of the blood in the placental circulation is taken up by the fetus during and immediately after birth (11).

BLOOD PRESSURE. The arterial pressure rises as development proceeds. In the fetus of the sheep, it increases from 20 mm. Hg. near the end of the first trimester to 76 mm. in the last and during parturition it is further elevated to reach 95-100 mm. in the newly-born offspring (11).

CARDIAC OUTPUT is progressively augmented as the age of the fetus increases. Expressed as a percentage of the weight of the tissues through which the blood circulates, the number of cubic centimeters of blood which circulate per minute in the fetus of the sheep early in the second half of pregnancy is 6% of the combined fetal and placental weights, and 17% at term. **At the end of gestation, accordingly, almost three times as much blood flows through each gram of tissue as in the middle of pregnancy.** If, as previously stated, the blood volume is around 9% of the weight of the fetus and placenta, about two-thirds of the total blood should make the circuit of the vascular bed in each minute during the early period and twice the total volume at the end of gestation. The approximate correctness of these calculated values, is shown by the experimental observation that the actual cardiac output at 89 days (period of gestation 150 days) was **26 cc.** per minute or **55%** of the total blood volume of 47 cc., while at 150 days, it was **257 cc.** or **163%** of a total volume of 157 cc. In other words, **the actual cardiac output was almost ten times as great at the end of gestation as it was earlier in pregnancy and the proportion of the total volume which circulated in one minute was increased from one-half to over one and one-half times** (10).

WORK DONE BY THE HEART. The work done by the heart as determined by multiplying the minute output by the pressure against which it is expelled is tremendously increased in the last half of fetal life. Since the arterial pressures in the animals used in the experiment in which the cardiac output was shown to have increased almost ten times, were 30 mm. in the early period and 70 mm. at term, the proportionate increase in work done by the heart was as 30:700, or more than twenty fold (10).

PULSE RATE. The fetal heart tones indicate a pulse rate in the human subject varying from 120 to 150 and averaging 135 per minute. During contractions of the uterus in pregnancy, and especially in the course of parturition, the rate may change considerably but in the intervals of relaxation, the customary rate for the individual is restored. While resuscitation is being effected immediately after birth, the pulse may become markedly slowed but, when respiration is satisfactorily re-established, the rate rises to about 110 per minute.

ERYTHROCYTES. The erythrocyte count is very low in early fetal life and increases with growth and development. From a value below one million in the first trimester, it rises to over three million in the second and reaches 4,500,000 to 5,500,000 at term. The relative scarcity of red blood corpuscles in early pregnancy is somewhat counterbalanced by their greater size, the mean corpuscular volume being as great as five times the normal in very young fetuses. The large red cells diminish in size as gestation advances and as the number of erythrocytes increases. At birth, however, they are still larger than those of the adult cells.

There is present a great degree of anisocytosis but this also diminishes with fetal development. Macroblasts and numerous normoblasts likewise are observed and polychromatophilic cells and reticulocytes are common. The proportion of nucleated forms is high in very young fetuses but decreases rather

rapidly as pregnancy advances.   Reticulocytes also diminish with fetal development but their reduction is more gradual than is that of the nucleated cells.
Along with the rise in the red cell count, the hemoglobin is definitely and progressively increased as pregnancy advances.   Although values as low as 8 gm. per
100 cc. are found early in pregnancy, as much as 19 gm. have been recorded
at the time of birth (12, 13, 14, 15, 16, 17).   In the preceding chapter, the difference between the oxygen dissociation curves of the mother and of the fetus
was described and it was stated that fetal blood absorbs oxygen more effectively
than does that of the mother.   Due possibly to a lower serum base and a higher
hemoglobin content, the carbon dioxide curve of the fetal blood tends to be
lower than that of the mother, indicating thereby the greater ease with which
fetal blood releases carbon dioxide. This ability of the fetal blood to absorb
oxygen more effectively and release carbon dioxide more readily than does maternal blood, greatly facilitates the interchange of these gases in the placenta.   At
the same time, it is not so favorable to the interchange of gases between the
blood and the fetal tissues.

LEUCOCYTES.   The full-term fetus has a slight leucocytosis, the white blood
cells averaging from 16,000 to 19,000.   Among these, the polymorphonuclears
often are diminished to around 50% and the lymphocytes are increased to over
40% (13).

METABOLIC RATE.   It has been estimated that the fetus of the sheep
utilizes about 0.0026 cc. of oxygen per gram of body weight per minute.   This
figure is extremely low when compared with the rate of 0.0057 to 0.028 cc. per
gram per minute for adult sheep.   **A fetal rate of from one-tenth to one-half that
of the adult is accounted for by the fact that the fetus is surrounded by amniotic
fluid and has no cooling surface.**   It therefore is under no necessity to keep up
its own body temperature (10).   The presence of a low metabolic rate also is
indicated by the flaccid condition of the fetus in utero, in contradistinction to
the increase in tone that occurs when it is lifted out of its warm surroundings.
These changes in tone are demonstrable by observing, with an amplification
technique, the electric waves generated in the muscles (10).

ALIMENTARY TRACT.   Deglutition is possible as early as the 28th week and
the presence of vernix caseosum, lanugo and skin epithelium in the intestinal
tract shows that these materials are swallowed while the fetus is within the
uterine cavity.   Ptyalin, pepsin, rennin and trypsin are present at birth and
meconium is found in the intestines early in fetal life.   That intestinal peristalsis
apparently does not occur to any great extent is shown by the absence of meconium in the amniotic fluid except in cases of intrauterine asphyxia.

LIVER.   The liver is relatively much larger in newborn infants than it is
in adult life, and its great size is an indication of its importance to the fetus.
Little, however, is known concerning hepatic function at this time.   As was
mentioned in the discussion of carbohydrate metabolism in the placenta, the

liver takes over the function of glycogen storage about the end of the first trimester. At this time, the isles of Langerhans in the pancreas are capable of functioning and a marked change in the metabolism of the carbohydrates occurs. Before the pancreatic and hepatic functions are established, free glucose in the embryo exceeds the fetal glycogen by 150 per cent. Soon thereafter, however, the ratio is reversed and glycogen is over one and one-half times as abundant as free glucose. While little or no glycogen is present in the liver before the fourth month, it makes up 29.5 per cent of the dry liver at term (18). Since bile and its derivatives are found in the intestinal tract as early as the fourth month, biliary function must be present before this time and probably antedates the glycogen function of the liver. It should be recalled that a part of the umbilical vein blood with its high oxygen content passes directly through the liver tissue and this gives the liver cells first call upon the oxygen supply of the fetus. Thus the liver is in a most advantageous position to play its part in fetal metabolism.

KIDNEYS. The presence of urine in the amniotic fluid and spontaneous urination within a few minutes after birth demonstrate that the kidneys are capable of functioning in fetal life. Urine likewise is often observed in the bladders of premature infants and its chemical analysis reveals the presence of urea, uric acid, creatinine and chlorides. On the other hand, fetuses born with imperforate urethrae do not have distended bladders. It may therefore be concluded that while the kidneys are capable of functioning before birth, they probably are inactive.

MUSCULAR ACTIVITY is manifested about the middle of pregnancy by the active fetal movements. These often are quite vigorous and, at times, cause the fetus to turn through an arc of 180° or more. As a result, the head may be found in relation to the pelvic brim on one day and in the opposite pole of the uterus on another. Nothing is known concerning the exciting cause of these movements aside from the fact that in cases of asphyxia they often become very vigorous just before intrauterine death.

GROWTH OF THE FETUS. The following table shows the average length and weight of the fetus at the various periods of gestation (19, 20):

Week	Length cm.	Weight gm.
8	3.	1.1
12	9.8	18.
16	18.	89.
20	25.	273.
24	31.5	625.
28	37.1	1150.
32	42.5	1640.
36	47.	2339.
40	50.	3175.

Since the length is less variable than the weight, it is a more accurate guide to the age of the fetus. For ordinary purposes, it may be stated that up to the fifth month, the length of the fetus is equal to the square of the month in centimeters and after the fifth month it is five times the month (Haas's rule).

THE FULL TERM CHILD is pinkish white in color and lacks the glistening appearance which is characteristic of prematurity. It usually is partially or wholly covered with a whitish material which somewhat resembles cream cheese— **vernix caseosa.** This is derived from the epithelial cells of the skin and the secretion of the sebaceous glands, and is most abundant in the folds of the groins and axillae. There is a well marked development of the cartilages of the nose and ears as a consequence of which these structures are less flabby and stand out more prominently than in premature infants. The breasts are capable of engorgement which, in the male as well as in the female, is quite noticeable on the second or third day after birth. The external genitalia are clearly differentiated and, in the male, the testes may be felt within the scrotum. Well developed nails also are observed to extend beyond the tips of the fingers and toes. Certain centers of ossification have been taken as evidence of maturity but data in this connection are conflicting. Probably the best criteria of maturity are the length and weight of the fetus. All infants measuring over 45 cm. and weighing over 2500 gm., accordingly, are considered mature. In addition, the relation of the shoulder circumference to that of the head in the occipitofrontal plane is helpful since the girth of the shoulders equals or exceeds that of the head after maturity is reached (21).

AMNIOTIC FLUID. Throughout most of its intrauterine life, the fetus is more or less surrounded by amniotic fluid, the exact origin of which is not fully understood.

SOURCE. It has been suggested that the fetal kidneys are the source of amniotic fluid because the latter contains a small amount of urea and because of the presence of urine in the bladder at birth. While the kidneys may, at times, be a source of part of the amniotic fluid, it must have some other origin, since the amniotic cavity is filled with fluid before the urinary tract is capable of functioning and it also is present in those cases in which the urethra is imperforate. In addition, injections of phloridzin are not followed by the appearance of sugar in the amniotic fluid, although the drug can be recovered from the tissues of the fetus (22).

The occurrence of larger amounts of amniotic fluid in edematous women has led some to believe that it may be a transudate from the maternal vessels. This, however, is disproved by the fact that the freezing point of amniotic fluid differs from that of the maternal serum (23).

The secretory theory as to the origin of the amniotic fluid is based upon the finding of amniotic cells which appear to have a secretory function (24, 25, 26), and is strengthened by the foregoing proofs that it is not a transudate from the maternal vessels and does not normally come from the fetal kidneys.

Under abnormal circumstances, it may have other origins, and the occurrence of excessive amounts of amniotic fluid is common in uniovular twins and in those fetal malformations in which parts of the brain and spinal cord are exposed.

CHARACTERISTICS. The liquor amnii is a pale and clear fluid with a slightly alkaline reaction and a specific gravity of 1008. More than 98 per cent of its bulk is water and the remainder consists of small quantities of inorganic salts, urea, uric acid, creatinine, lanugo, sebaceous material and epithelial cells. It progressively increases in amount up to the seventh month when the total quantity may be 1000 to 1500 cc. After the seventh month, the liquor amnii gradually diminishes until at term it averages less than 700 cc. Since the fetus gains rapidly in size during this period in which the amount of amniotic fluid decreases, the relation between the bulk of the fetus to that of the surrounding fluid is greatly altered. As a consequence, the incidence of head presentations increases as the fetal and uterine ovoids become more nearly of the same size.

FUNCTIONS. The amniotic fluid is a source of **fluid** and to a slight extent furnishes **food** to the fetus. It serves as a means of distributing the pressure equally in all directions whenever the uterus is subjected to **external violence** and protects the fetus from the **pressure effects of the muscular walls** which surround it. Serving as an insulator, it also protects the child against temperature changes. During parturition, the fetus is again protected against the **pressure effects of the uterine contractions** and at the same time, **molding of the uterus** is prevented. The hydrostatic action of the bag of waters likewise aids in the **dilation of the maternal soft parts** and greatly **lessens the trauma of labor.** After the passages are dilated and the membranes rupture, the liquor amnii serves, to some extent, as a **lubricant** and following the delivery of the child, the gush of hind waters **flushes the passages** and washes away infectious material that may have entered the vagina during labor.

REFERENCES

1. BARCROFT, J. AND BARRON, D. H.: The Genesis of Respiratory Movements in the Fetus of the Sheep. J. Physiol., 1936–37, 88, 56.
2. SNYDER, F. F. AND ROSENFELD, M.: Direct Observation of Intrauterine Respiratory Movements of the Fetus and the Rôle of Carbon Dioxide in their Regulation. Am. J. Physiol., 1937, 119, 153.
3. AHLFELD, F.: Die intrauterine Tätigkeit der Thorax-und Zwerchfellmuskulatur, Intrauterine Atmung. Monatschr. f. Geb. u. Gyn., 1905, 21, 143.
4. FARBER, S. AND SWEET, L. K.: Amniotic Sac Contents in the Lungs of Infants. Am. J. Dis. Child., 1931, 42, 1372.
5. SNYDER, F. AND ROSENFELD, M.: Intra-Uterine Respiratory Movements of the Human Fetus. J. A. M. A., 1937, 23, 1946.
6. POHLMAN, A. G.: The Course of the Blood Through the Heart of the Fetal Mammal, with a Note on the Reptilian and Amphibian Circulations. Anat. Rec. 1909, 3, 75.
7. KELLOGG, H. B.: The Course of the Blood Flow through the Fetal Mammalian Heart. Am. J. Anat., 1928, 42, 443.
   Studies on the Fetal Circulation of Mammals. Am. J. Physiol., 1929–30, 91, 637.

8. PATTEN, B. M., SOMMERFIELD, W. A. AND PAFF, G. H.: Functional Limitations of the foramen ovale in the Human Fetal Heart. Anat. Rec., 1929–30, 44, 165.
9. ELLIOTT, R. H., HALL, F. G. AND HUGGETT, A. S. G.: The Blood Volume and Oxygen Capacity of Fetal Blood in the Goat. J. Physiol., 1934, 82, 160.
10. BARCROFT, J.: Fetal Circulation and Respiration. Physiological Rev., 1936, 16, 103.
11. BARCROFT, J.: Respiratory and Vascular Changes in the Mammal Before and After Birth. Lancet, 1935, 2, 647.
12. LUCAS, W. P., BRADFORD, F. D., COX, H. R., JONES, M. R. AND SMYTH, F. S.: Blood Studies in the New-Born. Am. J. Dis. Child., 1921, 22, 525.
13. LIPPMAN, H. S.: A Morphologic and Quantitative Study of the Blood Corpuscles in the New-Born Period. Am. J. Dis. Child., 1924, 27, 473.
14. KROLL, W.: Untersuchungen über embryonale Blutbildung beim Menschen. Ztschr. f. mikr-anat. Forsch., 1929, 18, 199.
15. ZEIDBERG, L. D. A.: A Quantitative Determination of the Changes in Hemoglobin Concentration, Volume of Red Cells and Basophilia in the Blood of Rabbit Fetuses at Various Stages During the Last Third of Pregnancy. Am. J. Physiol., 1929, 90, 172.
16. VON DESEÖ, D.: Beiträge zur Kenntnis der fetalen Blutentwicklung beim Rinde. Arch. f. d. ges. Physiol., 1929, 221, 326.
17. WINTROBE, M. M. AND SCHUMACKER, H. B., JR.: Comparison of Hematopoiesis in the Fetus and During Recovery from Pernicious Anemia Together with a Consideration of the Relationship of Fetal Hematopoiesis to Macrocytic Anemia of Pregnancy and Anemia in Infants. J. Clin. Invest., 1935, 14, 837.
18. NEEDHAM, J.: Chemical Embryology, 1931–2, 1022 & 1031.
19. SCAMMON, R. E. AND CALKINS, L. A.: The Development and Growth of the External Dimensions of the Human Body in the Fetal Period. Minneapolis, 1929.
20. STREETER, G. L.: Weight, Sitting Height, Head Size, Foot Length, and Menstrual Age of the Human Embryo. Contrib. to Embryol. Carnegie Inst., No. 55, 1920, 11, 143.
21. HOLZBACH, E.: Ueber den Wert der Merkmale zur Bestimmung der Reife der Neugeborenen. Ein Versuch zur Aufstellung neuer Gesichtspunkte in der Frage der Altersbestimmung. Monatschr. f. Geburtsh. u. Gyn., 1906, 24, 429.
22. SCHALLER, L.: Ueber Phloridzindiabetes Schwangerer Kreissender und Neugeborener und dessen Beziehungen zur Frage der Harnsekretion des Fötus. Arch. f. Gyn., 1898, 57, 566.
23. ZANGMEISTER, W. U. MEISSL, T.: Vergleichende Untersuchungen über Mütterliches und kindliches Blut und Fruchtwasser nebst Bemerkungen über die fötale Harnsekretion. Münch. Med. Wchnschr. 1903, 50, 673.
24. BONDI, J.: Zur Histologie des Amnionepithels. Zentralbl. f. Gyn., 1905, 29, 1073.
25. MANDL, L.: Weitere Beiträge zur Kenntniss der sekretorischen Tätigkeit des Amnionepithels. Ztschr. f. Geburtsh. u. Gyn., 1906, 58, 249.
26. KEIFFER, H.: Recherches sur la physiologie de l'amnios humain. Gyn. et Obs., 1926, 14, 1.

FRANCOIS MAURICEAU
1637–1709
Paris

Mauriceau was the leading French obstetrician of his time.

He originated the Mauriceau maneuver used in breech extraction.

His work, "Traite des maladies des femmes grosses," published in Paris in 1668 and translated into English by Hugh Chamberlen was well illustrated and set the standard for obstetric practice.   In it he corrected many of the erroneous teachings of former times and gave directions as to the conduct of normal labor, version and the management of placenta praevia.

CHAPTER VII

CHANGES IN THE MATERNAL ORGANISM

UTERUS

SIZE. The enlargement of the uterus during pregnancy is one of the most remarkable instances of growth encountered in physiology (Fig. 68). From an organ measuring 7.5 x 5 x 2.5 cm., it develops into an enormous muscular sac, the dimensions of which are 35 x 25 x 22 cm. Its capacity, accordingly, is increased several hundred times—to over 4,000 cc.

This change is a progressive one, and the degree of enlargement is sufficiently constant for each month to enable the experienced obstetrician to estimate the duration of pregnancy from the size of the uterus.

SHAPE. Up to the sixth week, the uterus retains its usual pyriform outline, which gradually changes to ovoid in the latter part of the second month and becomes spherical in the third. By the middle of pregnancy, its contour again becomes ovoid, and remains so until the greater lengthening of the transverse fundal diameter in the last month again gives it a pyriform appearance.

CONSISTENCY. Pregnancy also causes a progressive softening of the uterus. At first this is more or less uniform and is largely due to congestion. As early as the sixth week, however, the ovum is large enough to have an influence on the consistency and probably is responsible for the varying degrees of softening that are then demonstrable. More marked softening of the lower uterine segment leads to greater compressibility of the isthmus, which, by the end of the second month is detected as Hegar's sign. As the changes in the uterine wall progress, it becomes more and more yielding, so that by the fourth month the consistency of the uterus is that of its content. At this time, fluctuation is evident and the uterus feels like a sac filled with fluid. After the sixth month, the fetus occupies a relatively larger part of the ovum, and, as pregnancy advances, may be felt with increasing ease through the soft and yielding uterine wall.

POSITION. Early in pregnancy the normal anteflexion and anteversion of the uterus are accentuated and the whole organ descends slightly in the pelvis. Later, a tendency to dextroversion and considerable torsion toward the right is observed. These changes frequently may be shown in a cesarean section. On opening the abdomen in the course of this operation, the left round ligament often is found nearer the midline, indicating a torsion of the uterus toward the right.

WEIGHT. Along with the alterations in size, shape and consistency, a

101

great increase in the mass of the uterus is observed.   Its weight of from 30 to 60 gm. before pregnancy increases some twenty-fold, to 1,000 gm. at term.

Hypertrophy and hyperplasia of the muscle and connective tissue, together with general vascular engorgement, lead to an early increase in the thickness of the uterine wall (1).   This, however, is soon counteracted by the rapidly growing ovum, so that by the fifth month the wall of the uterus is not over 0.5 cm. thick.

During the latter part of pregnancy, it is possible to learn something about the arrangement of the muscle fibers which cannot be traced in the nonpregnant uterus.   Three layers are described: a thin external, another thin internal, and a thick middle layer (2).

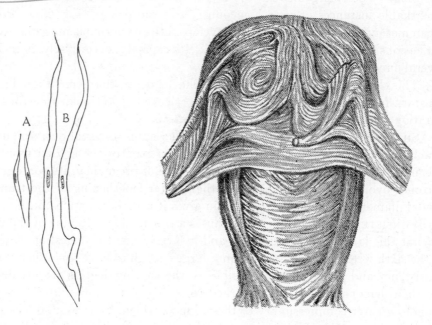

FIG. 68. Muscle cells (A) before and (B) during pregnancy.

FIG. 69. External layer of uterine muscle (Hélie).

The external layer is made up largely of muscle fibers which interlace across the midline and extend from the lower uterine segment upward over the fundus (Fig. 69).

The inner layer is external to the endometrium.   Its fibers pass obliquely upward on the anterior and posterior walls and are joined to similar fibers that arch over the fundus, and to others that encircle the tubal orifices and the internal os (Fig. 70).

Between these thin muscle plates is a thick middle layer which contains the greater part of the uterine musculature.   It is made up of an interlacing network of fibers which, as a whole, has a somewhat circular or transverse arrangement (Fig. 71).

The vessels pass through the spaces between the muscle trabeculae and, as a result, are **compressed** and **twisted** and **kinked** when the uterus contracts and retracts at the end of labor. This layer, accordingly, not only furnishes the greater part of the force that is derived from the uterine contractions during labor, but efficiently ligates the vessels that supply the open sinuses in the placental site after the contents of the uterus have been expelled.

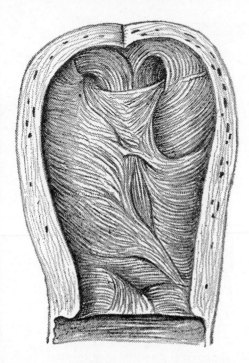
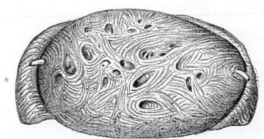

FIG. 70. Internal layer of uterine muscle (Hélie).   FIG. 71. Middle layer of uterine muscle (Hélie).

On the anterior and posterior surface of the uterus, fibers, resembling those found in the conducting system of the heart muscle, have been described, and it has been suggested that they may function in a similar manner. These fibers are very sensitive and contract more vigorously when they are stimulated. Following intramuscular injections of pituitary extract, contractions of the uterus seem to start in this region and spread out over the remainder of the organ. This structure, accordingly, has been referred to as "the pacemaker of the parturient uterus" (3, 4).

CERVIX

The cervix undergoes changes little short of those described in connection with the body of the uterus. Its muscle fibers diminish in number, but those that remain undergo hypertrophy while the connective tissue becomes less dense and is considerably altered. In addition, the circulation in the cervix is greatly augmented by a marked increase in its vessels as a result of which the cervix at term is almost cavernous in structure.

The mucosa is thickened and its glands become greatly enlarged with a corresponding diminution in the interglandular substance. On section, it accordingly has a honeycombed appearance (Figs 72 to 75). The thick mucous secre-

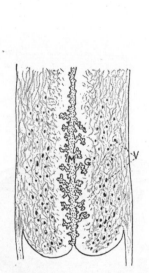

FIG. 72. The normal cervix (Stieve).

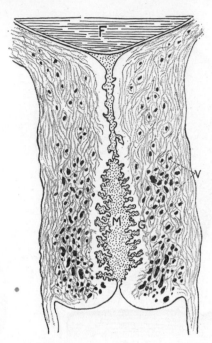

FIG. 73. The cervix at the second month of pregnancy (Stieve). *F*, forewaters; *G*, glands; *V*, vessels; *M*, mucus.

tion from these enlarged glands completely fills the cervical canal and aids in preventing the ascent of pathogenic bacteria into the uterine cavity. Early in labor, this plug of mucus with most of the honeycombed mucosa is expelled as a cast of the cervical canal and is known as the mucous plug (5). These changes in the mucosa contribute to the characteristic softening of the cervix.

As pregnancy progresses, the cervix gives the impression of being considerably shortened, although frozen section measurements show very little change in its length. Near term the external os enlarges and in women who have borne children it often admits two fingers with ease.

PARAMETRIUM

The unstriped muscle of the parametrium undergoes hypertrophy and is augmented by outgrowths from the vessel walls. As a result of both of these factors, its usefulness as a support is increased. The most striking change in this tissue, however, is the peculiar activity of the mesenchymal cells. These, at first, are more numerous in the vicinity of the blood vessels. Later, they change into clasmatocytes and monocytes which acquire phagocytic properties and lie between the connective tissue fibers. As term approaches, they become more numerous and probably are a part of the protecting mechanism which guards the maternal organism against infection during labor (6).

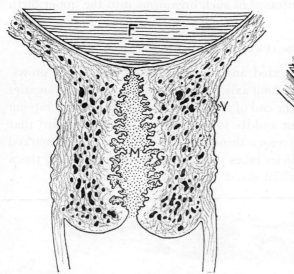 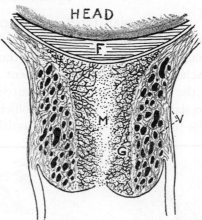

FIG. 74. The cervix at the third month of pregnancy (Stieve). *F*, forewaters; *G*, glands; *V*, vessels; *M*, mucus.

FIG. 75. The cervix at term (Stieve). *F*, forewaters; *G*, glands; *V*, vessels; *M*, mucus.

ROUND LIGAMENTS

The round ligaments are elongated and considerably enlarged, often reaching the size of a finger in the last trimester. Their insertion into the uterus in the early part of pregnancy is near its superior surface. Later, however, owing to the greater development of the uterine musculature in the region of the fundus, the attachment is much nearer to the middle of the uterus. This observation, accordingly, is significant in that it not only indictates the asymmetrical growth of the uterus, but, at times, proves valuable in the differentiation between a pregnancy and a soft tumor.

VAGINA

The vagina is congested and, as a result, changes its color to a purplish blue. There is, likewise, a marked thickening of the mucosa, the surface of which, due to hypertrophy of its papillae, becomes rough or granular. In the surrounding connective tissue, alterations also occur which render the vaginal canal more dilatable in labor (7). Owing to this change, women who complain during a gentle vaginal examination in the early months of pregnancy, often experience no discomfort when a much more thorough examination is made six weeks before the expected date of confinement.

The vaginal secretion is abundant and has an acid reaction. It is thought that this secretion inhibits the growth of pathogenic bacteria. Accordingly, it is a factor in preventing the entrance of such organisms into the upper birth passages (8, 9).

FALLOPIAN TUBES AND OVARIES

The fallopian tubes are elongated and congested. As the uterus grows, they lie more or less parallel to its long axis. For the same reason, the ovaries occupy an altered position. By the end of the first trimester, the corpus luteum reaches its maximum development and its total bulk may equal one-third that of the entire ovary. Ovulation ceases throughout pregnancy, and a marked atresia of partially developed follicles takes place, with an increase in the theca cells to form the so-called interstitial gland (10, 11, 12).

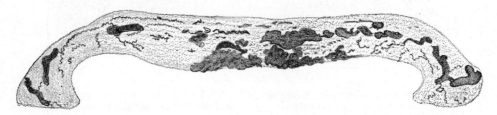

FIG. 76. Cross-section of placental site. Injected specimen (Beker and Van Steenis).

PELVIC VESSELS

The uterine and ovarian vessels are larger in diameter, elongated and more tortuous. Similarly, their lumina become enlarged to form large sinuses which are numerous and well developed in the region of the placental site. In a cesarean section, this area is incised whenever the placenta is anterior and some of these immense blood spaces are seen to be almost as large as a finger. Following delivery, the vascular trunks are tortuous, greatly dilated, and bulge out from the thin walls of the broad ligament (Figs. 76 and 77).

ABDOMINAL WALLS

As the uterus grows, the abdominal walls become distended. The umbilicus is flush with the skin surface at the sixth month and protrudes in the latter part of pregnancy. If proper support is not given to the enlarging uterine tumor,

the deeper layer of the skin is torn and purplish pink streaks appear on its surface—striae gravidarum.   A narrow band of pigment usually is seen in the
midline between the symphysis and the umbilicus, and a similar area of pigmentation often encircles the latter.

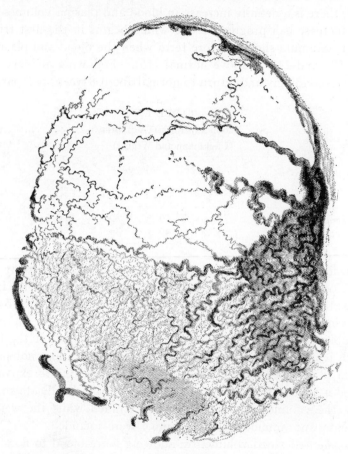

FIG. 77. Vessels of pregnant uterus. Injected specimen. Note density of placental site (Beker
and Van Steenis).

BREASTS

The mammary glands become enlarged soon after the first period is skipped.
This change is due to glandular hypertrophy and hyperplasia in preparation for
lactation, together with the deposition of fat between the lobules and in the
panniculus.   In the second month, the primary areola of pigmentation is deepened and contains hypertrophied, sebaceous glands.   The first evidence
of secretory activity appears at the end of the first trimester, when a yellowish
fluid—colostrum—may be expressed from the nipples.   Several months later,

increasing pigment changes lead to the formation of a secondary areola about the nipples.

BLOOD AND CIRCULATION

BLOOD AND PLASMA VOLUMES. During pregnancy and especially in the second half, there is a definite increase in blood and plasma volumes (13, 14, 15, 16). This increase is a progressive one which begins in the first trimester and reaches its maxiumum shortly before term when the blood and plasma volumes average 22.5% and 24.8% above normal (16). Following delivery, the values decrease correspondingly and return to normal about 8 weeks postpartum.

TABLE I

BLOOD AND PLASMA VOLUMES

(Dieckmann and Wegner)

	ANTEPARTUM				POSTPARTUM	
	8–15 weeks	16–25 weeks	26–35 weeks	36–40 weeks	2–6 days	10–25 days
Blood, cc. per kgm.	77.3	79.5	80.4	80.9	77	82.1
Plasma, cc. per kgm.	47.3	49.5	49.7	49.8	49.9	50.1

Even when expressed in cubic centimeters per kilogram of body weight, the figures for blood and plasma volumes show a slight but progressive increase and indicate that the vascular bed is expanded beyond the needs of the growing uterus, mammary glands and other tissues which add to the weight of the pregnant woman (Table I). If consideration is given to the fact that the dye (Congo Red), which is used in these volumetric determinations, does not pass through the placenta, it will be seen that the volume increase due to expansion of the vascular bed is much greater than the values in Table I indicate since, in their calculation, the volume of fetal blood was excluded while the weights of the fetus, placenta and amniotic fluid (6 kgm.) were included.

The augmented blood volume, by allowing more blood to flow through the placental lake in the latter half of pregnancy, when the retroplacental oxygen tension is relatively low, facilitates the interchange of gases between the maternal and fetal circulations. During and immediately following labor, it also is held in reserve in the dilated vascular system and this reserve, together with the fluid retained in the tissues, enables the parturient woman to withstand blood losses which might otherwise prove fatal.

Although the need for a better placental interchange and the need for a greater ability to withstand hemorrhage is met by an increase in blood volume, these needs are not the cause of the volume changes observed in pregnancy since the latter occur long before either need arises. If, as was mentioned in Chapter III, the placental lake is regarded as an indirect arteriovenous fistula, the increase in blood volume may perhaps be explained on this basis, since similar volume changes are known to follow such fistulae in other parts of the body.

TABLE II

SERUM PROTEIN

(Dieckmann and Wegner)

	ANTEPARTUM			POSTPARTUM	
	10–15 weeks	26–35 weeks	36–40 weeks	2–6 days	10–25 days
Gm. per 100 cc..........................	6.77	6.42	6.51	6.13	6.8
Gm. per kgm..........................	3.13	3.15	3.20	2.99	3.25

PLASMA PROTEINS are diminished in concentration and the greatest change in this respect occurs early in the last trimester (17, 18, 19). The average percentage of serum proteins is 6.77 in the first trimester and 6.42 at 26–35 weeks. As term approaches, it gradually increases and reaches normal eight weeks postpartum (Table II) (19). Although this reduction in concentration is too slight to be of significance, blood studies of the same women throughout pregnancy indicate a trend which, under abnormal conditions, may be sufficiently accentuated to cause marked changes in water balance. Late in pregnancy, therefore, a rapid gain in weight due to water retention, with or without visible evidence of edema, often is accompanied by too great a reduction of the plasma proteins. The normal decrease is to a large extent only relative and is due to the fact that the serum protein has not kept pace with the increase in plasma volume. When allowance is made for the latter change, it is found that there is an actual gain in the total amount of serum protein which amounts to 13.7% at 26–35 weeks and 18.3% at term (19).

SERUM ALBUMIN is decreased from 4.34 gm. per 100 cc. early in pregnancy to an average minimum of 3.83 at 33 weeks and rises to 4.07 at term. This reduction in the serum albumin is sufficient to account for the fall in the total plasma proteins (18) and it is the albumin fraction which is largely affected by those late complications of pregnancy in which water retention is a prominent factor.

SERUM GLOBULIN. The concentration of serum globulin undergoes a slight gain which is most marked on the third day postpartum (18). While the cause of this peculiar increase is not known, it is of interest to note that the greatest gain takes place at the time when the secretion of colostrum is most plentiful and that globulin is the most abundant protein constituent of this early breast secretion.

FIBRINOGEN is both relatively and actually increased (18). From 0.4% at 10 weeks, it increases to 0.43% at 26–35 weeks and 0.48% at term. The total amount of fibrinogen naturally is even more markedly augmented and its value at term is 40% above that observed early in pregnancy (19). The increase in fibrin has been attributed to the entrance of chorionic elements into the blood stream.   Whatever the cause, it is most fortunate that this constituent of the blood, which is associated with clotting, is augmented at the time of delivery when the danger of profuse hemorrhage is greatest.   Loss of blood and trauma during labor cause a still further increase in the fibrin content of the plasma which, no doubt, is a factor in the prevention of profuse bleeding in the early days of the puerperium (20, 21, 22).

SEDIMENTATION TIME.   The suspension stability of the red cells decreases as pregnancy advances with the result that the sedimentation time drops to 40 minutes during labor and 20 minutes during the first week postpartum (22). The similarity of the curves for fibrin and the sedimentation time leads to the inference that the increased sinking velocity of the red blood cells may be due either to the increase in fibrin or to the same factors which underlie its cause.

TABLE III

ERYTHROCYTE, HEMATOCRIT AND HEMOGLOBIN VALUES

(Dieckmann and Wegner)

	ANTEPARTUM			POSTPARTUM	
	10–15 weeks	26–35 weeks	36–40 weeks	2–6 days	10–25 days
Erythrocytes..........................	4,380,000	3,910,000	4,200,000	3,850,000	4,240,000
Hematocrit, %........................	39.8	36.9	38.1	38.0	40.1
Hemoglobin, gm. per 100 cc.............	13.8	12.2	12.4		11.78
Hemoglobin, gm. per kgm...............	10.52	9.28	9.15	9.23	10.90

RED CELL COUNT.   Due to the dilution which accompanies the increase in blood volume, the erythrocyte count is decreased during pregnancy but returns to normal within a few weeks after delivery.   The number of cells per cubic milli-meter is little changed during the first trimester.   Soon, thereafter, it begins to decrease and reaches an average minimum of 3,910,000 at 26–35 weeks.   During the last month, the red cell count gradually increases to an average of 4,200,000 at term and returns almost to normal by the end of the third week postpartum (23, 24).

HEMATOCRIT READING.   The cell volume as determined by the hematocrit likewise decreases during pregnancy (17, 23, 25).   The average reading in the first trimester is 39.8 or 7% below normal and falls to an average minimum of 36.9 or 14% below normal at 26–35 weeks.   During the last month, it again rises to 38.1 or 11 per cent below normal.   Although the concentration of erythro-cytes is diminished, their total volume is increased 20% (23).

HEMOGLOBIN.   The amount of hemoglobin per 100 cc. of blood is also reduced and is lowest at 26–35 weeks at which time an average of 12.2 gm. per 100 cc. (15% below normal) is observed.   It then increases slightly or remains stationary until term is reached.   Like the decrease in cell volume, the reduction ın hemoglobin is only a relative one, since the total amount is increased 13%. From the fact that a 20% gain in total cell volume occurs while the total hemoglobin is increasing only 13%, it would seem that, during pregnancy, the red cells are manufactured more readily than the hemoglobin and, because the red cells return to normal sooner after delivery than does the hemoglobin, the same conclusion may be applied to the puerperium (23).

The red cell, hematocrit and hemoglobin determinations, as ordinarily made, are misleading in that they indicate a "physiological anemia of pregnancy" (26). Instead of being reduced the total number of red cells, the total cell volume, and the total amount of hemoglobin in the body of the pregnant woman are increased. Their increases, however, are less than the increase in blood volume. For this reason, the values of each per 100 cc. of blood are reduced. Because increasing concentration during and soon after labor causes marked alterations in volume, blood counts at that time are quite unreliable.

All of the previously discussed blood changes reveal the presence of a distinct tendency toward anemia during pregnancy and this tendency is not surprising when one considers (1) the possible hemolytic effect of the trophoblast, (2) the demands of the fetus for iron, and (3) the probable deficiency of blood-forming materials in the mother's diet. For these reasons, the blood changes require careful consideration during the periods of antenatal and postpartum supervision.

OXYGEN AND CARBON DIOXIDE DISSOCIATION CURVES. During pregnancy, the blood oxygen and carbon dioxide dissociation curves are somewhat altered (29, 30). In the middle portion of the oxygen curve, a definite shift to the right is observed and the carbon dioxide curve tends to be lower than that of normal adult blood. The mother's blood, accordingly, gives up oxygen more readily than it does in the non-pregnant state and the same holds true for carbon dioxide but to a lesser degree (30). The fact that oxygen is given up more readily by the maternal blood and is absorbed more easily by the blood of the fetus is most advantageous for the interchange of this essential gas in the placenta.

THE WHITE BLOOD CELLS average 10,000–11,000 in pregnancy and the count remains more or less constant throughout gestation. Some women have a leucocytosis of 15,000 or over while others show little or no change from the low normal values. Both of these extremes, however, are much less common than the intermediate group which maintains a slight elevation above normal levels. This tendency to maintain a normal or slightly elevated count indicates an increased production of leucocytes which is equal to or greater than the increase in blood volume; otherwise the concentration of white cells would be reduced as much as are the plasma proteins, red cells and hemoglobin. A further and, at times, rather marked leucocytosis occurs during and immediately after parturition, the greatest change being observed when the labor is long. Part of this increase in white cells may be due to the concentration of the blood which accompanies and follows labor but most of it no doubt is caused by a definite increase in the production of leucocytes since counts of 20,000–30,000 are not unusual at the end of prolonged labors and on the first day after delivery. The white cell count remains considerably elevated until the third day of the puerperium after which it falls rapidly and reaches normal by the end of the first week postpartum (31, 32, 33).

THE SPECIFIC GRAVITY of the blood is essentially normal in the early months after which it progressively declines as pregnancy advances. With the approach of term, however, the trend changes and it again rises to normal at the time of delivery (34, 35, 36). These changes parallel the alterations in cell volume, which, as noted above, is at first reduced and then increases toward the end of gestation.

WATER CONCENTRATION. The fact that the cell volume, the plasma proteins and the specific gravity tend to diminish during pregnancy and rise at the time of labor, while the blood volume follows an opposite trend indicates a blood dilution during gestation with prompt elimination of the excess water at the time of delivery. This conclusion is further supported by observations made on the water concentration of the plasma and whole blood. Such observations show changes which are the reverse of those followed by the specific gravity, cell volume and plasma proteins (36). In other words, the water concentration of the whole blood is increased during pregnancy but falls to almost normal levels as term is reached.

TABLE IV

CONDUCTIVITY, TOTAL BASE, CO_2, pH AND TOTAL NaCl

(Dieckmann and Wegner)

	ANTEPARTUM				POSTPARTUM	
	10–15 weeks	16–25 weeks	26–35 weeks	36–40 weeks	2–6 days	10–15 days
Conductivity of serum in per cent NaCl....	0.780	0.786	0.782	0.771	0.776	0.775
Conductivity as gm. NaCl per kgm.....	0.34	0.38	0.36	0.36	0.36	0.40
Total base millimolls....................	156		150	152	154	151
CO_2, vol. %...........................	54		55	53	58	54
pH......................................	7.40		7.39	7.38	7.39	7.39
NaCl, mg. per 100 cc...................	604	605	609	612	595	602

CONDUCTIVITY, TOTAL BASE, CO_2, pH, TOTAL NaCl. After the 16th week, there is a definite reduction in the electrolyte concentration of the serum and this reduction increases as pregnancy advances. Following delivery, a gradual return to normal is observed. When the conductivity of the serum is expressed in percentage of sodium chloride, the value for the 16th to 25th week is 0.786%. This drops to 0.771% at term and returns to 0.775% by the 15th day postpartum

(37). Total base naturally follows a similar course decreasing from 156 milli-molls at 10–15 weeks to 150 millimolls at 26–35 weeks after which it rises to 152 millimolls at term and 154 millimolls 2–6 days after delivery. If the variations in the total amount are considered instead of the changes in concentration there is an increase in conductivity and total base of 16.8% and 18% respectively at 26–35 weeks and these figures rise to 22.7% and 20.6% by the end of gestation. The increase in electrolytes and total base therefore is essentially equal to the increase in plasma volume (37). The carbon dioxide content of the serum like-wise is decreased 6–10% by volume below normal values. The acid base rela-tionship in pregnancy, accordingly, is one of a compensated alkali or carbon dioxide deficit, the pH remaining quite unchanged (37, 38, 39, 40, 41). The mechanism by which this compensated alkali or carbon dioxide deficit is brought about is not understood. It has been suggested, however, that the increased pulmonary ventilation which is present during pregnancy reduces the carbon dioxide and that total base undergoes a compensatory reduction (42, 43). The observation that the urine before delivery is less acid (pH 5.80) than after (pH 4.60) seems to support this hypothesis (44). The concentration of sodium chloride tends to increase slightly up to the end of pregnancy and falls off some-what after delivery. The average concentration of sodium chloride in the serum early in pregnancy is around 600 mg. per 100 cc. and this figure increases slightly up to term after which it is somewhat reduced (37).

UREA, URIC ACID, CREATININE, NON-PROTEIN NITROGEN. The blood urea is considerably decreased during pregnancy, its value at term being 12.5 mgm. per 100 cc. or about 1/3 less than normal. Non-protein nitrogen also is somewhat reduced. An average of 28 mgm. per 100 cc. (10% below the normal value) is found in the last trimester. The amount of uric acid and creatinine, on the other hand, are unchanged, 3 mgm. of the former and 1–2 mgm. of the latter being present throughout gestation.

BLOOD CHANGES DUE TO THE RH FACTOR. When the mother's blood is Rh negative and that of the father Rh positive, the fetal blood may be Rh positive and may cause the formation of immune isoantibodies in the maternal blood. Should the mother have a transfusion subsequently, a transfusion reaction sufficiently serious to cause her death may occur. Should she become pregnant again these immune isoantibodies passing through the placenta often cause the death of the fetus with abortion or late stillbirth. Should the child be born alive, it may subsequently die from erythroblastosis fetalis.

CHANGES IN THE VASCULAR SYSTEM. During pregnancy, the arterial loops of the capillaries contract more frequently and the contractions last much longer than in the non-pregnant state. As a result, the venous ends of the capillary loops become dilated and the circulation in them is temporarily arrested (45, 46). Evidence of increased vasoconstriction may also be revealed in the retinal arteri-oles. Pronounced alterations of this character are common in toxemia and general contraction of the capillaries with spasm of the arterioles of the retina may be present some little time before edema and elevation of the blood pressure are observed (47, 48).

The veins of the pelvis and lower extremities are distended and there is an increasing tendency toward varicosities in the legs, about the vulva and around the anus. Attention has already been called to the marked dilatation of the veins in the broad ligaments, the aggregate diameters of which exceed those of the veins into which they empty. These enlarged vessels serve as safety devices which allow the blood, forced from the placental site, to collect in their expanded channels before entering the narrower iliac veins. By permitting an expansion of the vascular bed, they guard against too great a pressure increase in the placental site and thus prevent separation of the placenta when the uterus contracts (49).

BLOOD PRESSURE. When compared with suitable controls, the systolic pressure in uncomplicated pregnancies tends to be relatively low. Observations made upon a large number of cases show mean values of 112 mm. to 116 mm., the lowest levels occurring in the middle of gestation and the highest during the last month (50). Up to the last trimester, the diastolic pressure also is lower than in the non-pregnant state. Thereafter a gradual rise is observed and this reaches its maximum in the final weeks of pregnancy. Pulse pressure also tends toward the low normal range, gradually falling from a mean of 43 mm. in the middle period to 36 mm. as term is approached (50, 51).

THE PULSE RATE is slightly elevated. Observations in uncomplicated cases show the rate to be slightly higher than in non-pregnant control groups, the mean pulse being 84 per minute (50).

CARDIAC OUTPUT as determined by the acetylene method progressively rises as pregnancy advances. Although the rate of increase is greatest in the early months, the minute volume reaches its highest level (over 50% above normal) several weeks before term and then tends to decline somewhat below its maximum values (52, 53, 54).

CARDIAC ENLARGEMENT. Upward displacement of the diaphragm leads to an alteration in the position of the heart so that, on percussion, cardiac enlargement is suspected. The question of hypertrophy, therefore, has led to considerable controversy. Autopsy material shows the heart in pregnancy to be slightly heavier than in the non-pregnant state (55, 56, 57). X-ray examination, in some cases, likewise is thought to reveal a lengthening of the longitudinal and transverse diameters as early as the fifth month (58, 59). On the other hand, part of the enlarged shadow may be due to cardiac dilatation resulting from the increase in blood volume. Because of the disturbance in water balance which commonly occurs in pregnancy, some of the enlargement also may be caused by an increase in the interstitial and pericardial fluids as is occasionally noted in myxedema. In addition, some observers have noticed a progressive tendency toward left axis deviation in the electrocardiogram from the second to the sixth months. The axis remains about the same in the seventh and eighth months and definitely shifts back to the right in the ninth month. A further shift to the right is commonly noted after parturition (60, 61, 62, 63). Some interpret these electrocardiographic changes as the result of left ventricle hypertrophy in the first six months with similar changes in the right ventricle during the last trimester (61, 63). Others incline to the belief that they are the result of changes in the position of the heart (60, 62). In the last trimester, a complete inversion of Lead III may occur and it is thought to be due to the transverse position of the heart at that time (62, 64).

While the work of the heart should be increased by (1) the rapid gain in body weight, (2) the changes in the peripheral vessels, (3) the increased metabolism and (4) the augmented blood volume, a somewhat compensatory lessening of the work of the heart is effected by the diminution in the viscosity of the blood which results from blood dilution. **The circulatory adjustments to pregnancy, accordingly, are adequate in normal cases.** Because of the greater load placed upon the heart, however, circulatory diseases in general and mitral stenosis in particular are serious complications during gestation.

Marked as are the blood and circulatory changes of pregnancy, no satisfactory explanation of their cause has been discovered. It has been suggested that many of these alterations may be explained on the basis of a modified arteriovenous fistula at the placental site (65). When such fistulae in other parts of the body are sufficiently large, they cause circulatory adjustments similar to those observed during gestation. Some of the pregnancy changes which might be explained in this manner are (1) the acceleration in the pulse rate, (2) the decrease in the blood pressure, (3) the elevated venous pressure in the pelvis and lower extremities, (4) the increased cardiac output, (5) the augmented blood volume, (6) the loud placental murmur (uterine souffle) heard over the pregnant uterus. In addition, it has been shown that blood taken from the uterine vein in animals has more oxygen than the blood in the right ventricle (49, 65). Some of these changes also are corrected during a uterine contraction just as pressure over a large arteriovenous fistula results in partial restoration of the normal circulation. Likewise the obliteration of the placental site after parturition may explain the rapid return to normal of some of the above noted alterations, an effect not unlike that produced by the surgical correction of a large arteriovenous leak.

SPLEEN. Somewhat before the middle of pregnancy, the spleen, in the dog, commences to shrink and the reduction in its size continues until four days before term is reached. After delivery, it again becomes turgid and, by the 20th day postpartum, returns to its normal proportions. This change in the size of the spleen parallels the increase in blood volume necessitated by the expansion of the vascular bed. Since similar contraction of the spleen occurs at high altitudes and during exercise when the oxygen capacity of the blood is raised, it may be possible that the splenic changes in pregnancy assist the circulatory system in satisfying the greater oxygen requirements of the pregnant organism (66).

RESPIRATORY SYSTEM

Throughout the respiratory tract, capillary engorgement occurs and the mucous membranes of the nasopharynx and accessory sinuses frequently are hyperemic and edematous. Similar changes in the larynx affect the vocal cords, and, as a result, singers often observe a change in their voices during pregnancy.

Upward pressure of the growing uterus on the diaphragm should interfere with respiration. This, however, is counteracted by a compensatory broadening of the chest wall and a change from abdominal to thoracic breathing. Although a decrease of as much as 4 cm. has been observed in the vertical diameter of the chest, increases in the antero-posterior and transverse diameters more than compensate for the vertical shortening. Coincident with these changes, the substernal angle is broadened from 68.5° in the first trimester to 103.5° at term and the circumference of the thoracic cage is enlarged 5–10 cm. (67, 68, 69). Instead of being diminished, therefore, the vital capacity is increased from 3260 cc. in the early months to 3450 cc. by the end of gestation (69, 70, 71). A slight acceleration in the rate of respiration, together with a distinct rise in tidal air, causes a 43–45% increase in the minute volume of respired air. While

FIG. 78. Dilatation of the right ureter and the pelvis of the right kidney (Schumacher).

the percentage of oxygen absorbed and CO_2 given off is somewhat less than normal, the total volume of these gases exchanged is augmented because of the increased volume of air respired per minute (72, 73, 74, 75).

URINARY TRACT

During pregnancy, changes in the urinary tract are observed.   In the early months, bladder irritability is common, until the uterus rises out of the pelvis. Ureteral dilatation, particularly on the right side and above the pelvic brim, frequently occurs after the middle of pregnancy.   This may result from the changes in the muscular layers that have been noted in the pelvic portion of the ureter or from the increased angulation of that part of the ureter which is adjacent to the cervix.   The latter occurrence is more common on the right side because of the dextroversion and right-sided torsion of the uterus.   Along with ureteral dilatation, x-ray studies have demonstrated rather marked dilatation of the pelvis of the kidney, the capacity of which often is more than doubled (76, 77) (Fig. 78).   Such an alteration in the ureter and kidney pelvis favors infection, and pyelitis, therefore, is not unusual as a complication of pregnancy. At times, there are changes in the kidney peculiar to pregnancy.   Cloudy swelling in the convoluted tubules and capillary engorgement in the glomeruli constitute the picture that often is referred to as the kidney of pregnancy.

ALIMENTARY TRACT

The secretions of the mouth show a relatively high degree of acidity due possibly to the regurgitation of gastric fluids which commonly occurs in pregnant women.   As a result of this change in reaction, the salivary glands are stimulated to secrete an abundance of saliva which sometimes becomes excessive in nervous women.   The increased acidity of the oral secretions, together with a possible depletion of the maternal calcium by the growing fetus, are said to favor dental caries.   In former times, decay of the teeth was so common that every woman expected to lose a tooth every time she became pregnant.   If the teeth really are more susceptible to caries, modern oral hygiene and careful attention to the diet should eliminate this so-called hazard of pregnancy.

Peculiarities in the sense of smell and taste at times occur.   To some women, certain odors become obnoxious and the smell of cooking food is repugnant. Others at times crave articles of diet to which they are not accustomed and occasionally their perverted appetite leads to a longing for clay, sand, chalk and other such anomalous substances.   The desire for ordinary foods, on the other hand, is greatly increased and most pregnant women have difficulty in limiting their food intake.

Nausea and vomiting are common in the early months of pregnancy.   This disturbance of the alimentary tract occurs so frequently that it is considered one of the symptoms of gestation and, because of its predilection for the morning hours, it is termed "morning sickness." Nausea and vomiting are associated with the chorionic activity of the growing ovum and the change in the carbohydrate metabolism which is observed in early pregnancy. The acid products of trophoblastic action accumulate during the night in consequence of the carbohydrate shortage which results from the night's fast and the glycogen depletion of the liver. A mild ketosis is thus produced and the normal pH of the blood is maintained by the reduction of the hydrochloric acid of the gastric juice through vomiting and through regurgitation of the neutralizing duodenal contents.

For the reasons given, a relative hypochlorhydria is frequently observed in the first trimester of pregnancy. Analysis of the gastric secretion after a night's fasting shows a decrease in or a total absence of free hydrochloric acid and a normal or increased amount of total chlorides (78). The hypochlorhydria, however, is promptly overcome by the taking of food. This lack of acidity, accordingly, is not due to a diminished activity of the gastric mucosa but to the neutralizing effect of regurgitated material from the small intestine. In this connection, it may be stated that the gradient in irritability of the intestines is flattened in some pregnant animals and reversed in others (79), an observation which has led to the suggestion that nausea and vomiting may at times be due to a reversal of the intestinal gradient in pregnant women.

In the latter months, pressure effects are observed in the lower intestines and constipation is frequent. The appendix also is displaced upward and reaches the level of the iliac crest by the sixth month (80).

Alterations in liver function are observed and certain liver lesions are characteristic of pregnancy toxemias. The glycogen metabolism frequently is disturbed and an inability to store glycogen results in glycosuria and the rapid onset of acetonuria if carbohydrates are withdrawn.

X-ray studies of the gall-bladder show a definite delay in its emptying time. This delay may be as long as six hours but is shortened by the injection of atropine (81). Alteration in the vegetative nervous system is thought to be responsible for this change, which, together with the increase in the cholesterol content of the blood, may be a factor in the causation of cholelithiasis, a condition found more commonly in women who have borne children.

OSSEOUS SYSTEM

Postmortem findings and x-ray studies show bony growths on the inner surface of the skulls of pregnant women. These growths have been termed puerperal osteophytes (82) and are present in 50 per cent of the skulls examined at autopsy and 33 per cent of those studied by the x-ray.

The growing fetus requires 0.1 to 0.4 gms. of calcium daily in the last half of pregnancy (83, 84). If the mother's diet does not supply this amount, her osseous structures may make up the deficiency. Dental caries is very common and possibly is due to dietary deficiencies as well as a lack of proper mouth hygiene.

The pelvic joints are more mobile and considerable separation of the symphysis as well as of the sacroiliac synchrondroses may be demonstrated by means of the x-ray.

The posture changes as pregnancy progresses, and the head and shoulders are thrown backward to compensate for the forward displacement of the growing uterus.

DUCTLESS GLANDS

With increasing developments in endocrinology, the relationship between the ductless glands and the physiology of reproduction is being more fully appreciated. During pregnancy, histologic changes have been described in the hypophysis, thyroid, parathyroid, suprarenals and the ovaries, and the fruits of much research have added considerably to our understanding of the subject. As a result, relationships which, clinically, have been known to exist, have been explained in a more scientific manner.

THE THYROID GLAND during pregnancy is frequently enlarged. This is due to parenchymatous changes and increased vascularity. Histologically, hyperplasia of the glandular epithelium is observed. The cells become columnar and give to the lining of the acini a tufted appearance. An increased tendency toward the storage of colloid likewise is common. There is a steady increase in blood iodine from 15.5 $\gamma\%$ at 2 months to 24.9 $\gamma\%$ at nine months. Within two weeks after delivery, it again falls to 17.7 $\gamma\%$ (85).

Hyperfunction of the thyroid has been assumed from the observation that tadpoles develop much more rapidly in the presence of blood from pregnant women (86).

The basal metabolic rate increases in the latter part of pregnancy and returns to normal within a few weeks after delivery. This change in metabolism is thought to be due in part to hyperactivity of the thyroid gland.

When the thyroid is removed from a pregnant animal, the pregnancy is prolonged, the offspring are underdeveloped, and their thyroids frequently are hypertrophied (87).

Clinical evidence of the relation of the thyroid to pregnancy is furnished by the observations made on cases of hypothyroidism and hyperthyroidism that become pregnant. Patients in whom symptoms of hypothyroidism are present suffer from an aggravation of these symptoms during pregnancy, although occasionally the fetus supplies the deficiency and the symptoms are ameliorated. This clinical evidence indicates that even under the stimulus of pregnancy the hypofunctioning gland cannot be aroused to increased activity, and the requirements of the pregnancy rob the mother of her already insufficient amount of thyroid secretion.

The well-known tendency of hypothyroid cases to abort and their ability to carry their pregnancies to term when fed thyroid extract, likewise shows the need for increased thyroid secretion in pregnant women.

Symptoms of hyperthyroidism grow worse during pregnancy and occasionally are so aggravated that partial thyroidectomy or abortion is necessary.

THE PARATHYROID GLAND undergoes hypertrophy and hyperplasia (88). The concentration of the hormone, parathormone, roughly parallels the fetal calcium requirements. High values are found between the 15th and 35th weeks and normal or subnormal values are present before parturition (89). If the glands are partially removed during pregnancy, tetany follows, while the same experiment has no effect on nonpregnant animals (90).

Clinically, the appearance of tetany has been observed during gestation and in some women it seemingly can occur only through the influence of pregnancy.

Hypofunction of the parathyroids produces tetany through an alteration of the calcium metabolism and the administration of calcium and parathormone gives immediate relief.

HYPOPHYSIS. The pituitary body is considerably enlarged during pregnancy. Its greatest change is observed in the last month and it returns to normal within a short time after delivery. The weight of the gland increases with succeeding pregnancies. In multiparae, accordingly, weights of over 1500 mgm. have been noted (91, 92, 93). Rarely pressure on the optic chiasm causes temporary hemiamopsia which disappears soon after birth (94).

The principal alteration is found in the anterior lobe which may become twice its normal size. As pregnancy advances, there develops from the chromophobes an actively granulating and degranulating cell, whose granules are not distinguishable, except in size and number, from those of the typical acidophile cells. This is the so-called "pregnancy cell" which is actually an acidophile in a high degree of activity (95). It remains in an active secretory phase throughout pregnancy and reverts again to the chromophobe state soon after delivery. The basophile cells appear to be quite normal in the early part of pregnancy During the middle period, they are present as large granulating forms and, in the last trimester, they show a progressive increase in mitachondria and a marked depletion of their granules (95). With fixation methods which preserve mitachondria, both types of granule-depleted cells resemble acidophiles; otherwise, they appear as large chromophobes. Failure to appreciate these differences, due to preparation, formerly led to considerable confusion as to the actual cellular changes which accompany pregnancy (95). Even though the cells are depleted, changes in the Golgi apparatus and increased mitachondria indicate **an increased cellular activity during pregnancy** (95).

In addition to its effect on carbohydrate metabolism and the elaboration of thyrotrophic and adrenotrophic hormones which help to alter the metabolic processes during pregnancy, the anterior lobe of the hypophysis produces two hormones which are of great importance in relation to reproduction. These are the gonad-stimulating substances and prolactin.

Prolactin. It has been definitely established that the factor which is responsible for the actual secretion of milk is a product of anterior lobe activity (96). This hormone, "prolactin" or "galactin" is present in the last half of pregnancy and its continued production after parturition is dependent upon the stimulus furnished by suckling. Further discussion of this interesting substance and its relation to lactation is continued in Chapter XVI.

Gonadotrophic Hormones. The gonad-stimulating substances produced by the hypophysis are responsible for the development and luteinization of the Graafian follicles. It is generally believed that two separate hormones are secreted, the one, stimulating follicular development and the other causing the luteinization of the corpus luteum. In spite of the increased activity of the cells of the hypophysis during pregnancy, little or no gonad-stimulating substance is present in the excised gland. Just as the hyperactive thyroid contains less thyroxin than the normal gland, so the pituitary in pregnancy, by giving off its secretion as soon as it is formed, fails to store the hormone in the cytoplasm of its cells. A gonad-stimulating substance resembling that produced by the anterior lobe, is elaborated by the placenta (98).

Gonadotrophic hormone is found in the blood serum shortly after the onset of pregnancy and it increases rapidly in amount to reach a peak of 300 rat units per 100 cc. by the end of the second month. Soon thereafter, it again falls and, by the fourth month, has dropped to a comparatively low level at which it tends to remain until shortly before the end of gestation when, in some cas es, a moderate rise is observed. The excretion of gonadotrophic hormone in the urine follows a similar course, a total of about 30,000 rat units being excreted in the course of 24 hours at the end of the second month (100, 101, 117) Fig. 78C, page 124. The presence of these gonad-stimulating substances in the urine during pregnancy forms the basis of the well-known Aschheim-Zondek test for pregnancy.

Changes in the anterior lobe of the pituitary similar to those observed in pregnancy have been reproduced in non-pregnant animals by the injection of placental extract. It, therefore, is thought that the trophoblast is the activating factor (102).

Removal of the hypophysis results in the termination of pregnancy, but the latter may be made to continue to term by the administration of corpus luteum extract.

The posterior lobe contains a powerful oxytocic hormone (103). The changes in this portion of the gland during pregnancy are insignificant and its removal is without effect on either pregnancy or labor.

OVARIES. As was noted in the discussion of menstruation, the ovary is responsible for the elaboration of two important internal secretions. One of these, "estrin," was first obtained from the fluid of the developing follicle and is best known because of its ability to induce estrus in spayed animals. The other, "progestin" is elaborated by the corpus luteum.

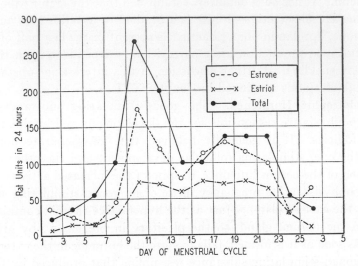

FIG. 78A. Excretion of estrogenic substances in the urine during the menstrual cycle (Smith and Smith).

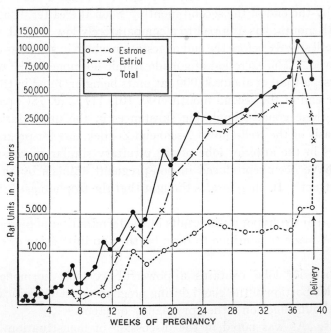

FIG. 78B. Excretion of estrogenic substances in the urine during pregnancy (Smith and Smith).

Estrogens are also produced by other ovarian tissues and by the placenta. They are found in varying amounts in the blood and urine during pregnancy and the menstrual cycle. Several substances having estrogenic properties have been described. Of these, **estradiol,** a dihydroxyestrin, is thought to be the primary ovarian estrogen (104). From it, **estrone,** a ketohydroxyestrin, is supposed to be produced and the reaction is regarded as reversible. The latter, in turn, is thought to be converted into **estriol,** a trihydroxyestrin, but, for this conversion, the presence of the uterus is necessary and its endometrium must be under the controlling influence of progestin (105, 106). Estradiol is ten times as potent as estrone and estrone is more estrogenic than estriol.

Assays of total estrogen in the urine during the menstrual cycle show the excretion to be greatest 12 to 13 days preceding the onset of menstruation, i.e., early in the period of luteal activity with low levels just before the menstrual flow and during follicle ripening (Fig. 78A) (107).

During pregnancy, the amount of estrogenic substances in the urine is greatly increased. Soon after the first period is skipped, the estrin level is elevated considerably above its peak in the menstrual cycle and this increase continues progressively until the last month when a rather marked fall is observed shortly before parturition. Excretion is greatly accelerated about the 28th week and is most marked during the last trimester, the rate rising from 40,000 to 50,000 rat units per day to over 100,000 in the last month (107, 108, 109). It is of interest to note that this is the time when many of the alterations in the blood and circulation occur. It also is the period in which toxemia and disturbances in water balance are most frequent. Throughout pregnancy, almost all of the total estrin excreted is in the combined form. Just before labor and coincident with the abrupt fall in the total estrogen level, however, there seems to be an increase in the free estrogenic substances in the urine (108). Most of the total estrogen also is made up of estriol, the increased excretion of which indicates a progressive increase in progestin secretion (107) (Fig. 78B).

The estrogen content of the blood rises from an insignificant figure in the first trimester to as much as 100 rat units per 100 cc. in the last month. While the increase is progressive after the third month, most of the rise in the blood estrin curve is observed after the 28th week, the general trend resembling that of the excretion in the urine (101).

The importance of these estrogenic substances in the physiology of reproduction is shown by the many functions that have been attributed to them by competent investigators. The most essential of these functions are as follows:

1. Estrin is responsible for the proliferative changes in the endometrium which take place during the menstrual cycle. In this connection it also is an essential preliminary to the action of progestin but, when given in excessive amounts, it may prevent the customary progestin effect (111, 112).

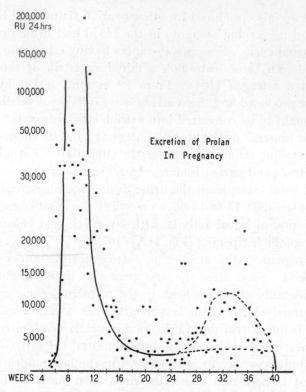

FIG. 78C. Excretion of prolan in the urine during pregnancy (J. S. L. Browne).

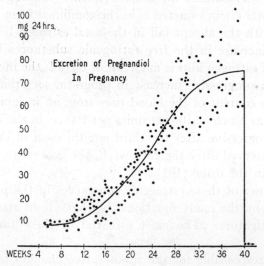

FIG. 78D. Excretion of pregnandiol in the urine during pregnancy (J. S. L. Browne).

2. The withdrawal of estrin, on the other hand, has been suggested as a cause of menstruation. After proper preparation of the endometrium in oophorectized animals, the withholding of the estrogen results in bleeding analagous to anovulatory menstruation (113).

3. The estrogenic substances are growth-promoting in that they bring the uterus to a state of sexual maturity. They, therefore, stimulate the growth of the uterus in immature animals and prevent uterine atrophy after castration. This function is also manifest in pregnancy when the estrin-induced hyperemia aids in the hypertrophy of the muscle and connective tissue cells of the uterus (114).

4. The estrogens are said to play a part in the development of rhythmic contractions in the myometrium and they sensitize the uterus to the action of posterior pituitary extract (115).

5. The development of the breasts, likewise, is largely influenced by estrin which is responsible for the growth of the duct system and, with progestin, has considerable to do with the building up of the glands (116).

6. The sudden drop in the high level of combined estrogens in the urine with a synchronous increase in the free estrin has been suggested as a factor in the initiation of labor (108).

PROGESTERONE is produced by the corpus luteum during the luteal phase of the menstrual cycle and by the corpus luteum of pregnancy during the period of its continued activity in the first three or four months of gestation. It also is elaborated in increasingly large amounts by the placenta which seems to take over some of the functions of the ovary.

Progesterone is not excreted as such in the urine but its metabolic end product, pregnandiol glucuronidate, is found in varying amounts during pregnancy. Up to the 60th day, pregnandiol is present in amounts normal for the menstrual cycle (4 mg.–10 mg. per liter). Thereafter, it increases to 40 mg. by the 150th day and 80 mg. by the eighth month. Within 24 hours after delivery, it disappears entirely from the urine (117) Fig. 78D. Since only 25 mg. of pregnandiol are recovered from the urine when 50 mg. of progesterone are injected into the mother, it has been suggested that the amount of progesterone secreted is equal to twice the pregnandiol excretion. If this is so, the above values should be doubled to represent the progesterone secreted at the various periods of gestation (118). The ineffectualness of ordinary progestin therapy is also evident from these figures. As one rabbit unit is equivalent to approximately 1 mg., at least 8–20 rabbit units should be given early in pregnancy if complete substitution is desired. The chief functions of progestin in the physiology of reproduction are:—

1. During the menstrual cycle, progestin causes the secretory or pre-gravid changes in the endometrium after the latter has undergone preliminary preparation by estrin (119).

2. Withdrawal of progesterone also has been suggested as a cause of menstruation. If the endometrium of an oöphorectomized monkey is subjected to the influence of progesterone and this influence is withdrawn by discontinuing the injections, bleeding not unlike that of ovulatory menstruation follows within two days. It is well known that the removal of the corpus luteum precipitates a premature menstruation. Such bleeding, however, may be prevented by the injection of 5 rabbit units or approximately 5 mg. of progesterone. From this observation may be derived some idea of the amount of progesterone that is produced by the human corpus luteum during the menstrual cycle (120).

3. The presence of progesterone and its action on the endometrium is thought to facilitate the metabolic conversion of estrone to estriol (106, 121).

4. Continued development of the pre-gravid endometrium into the decidua of pregnancy is under the controlling influence of progesterone (122).

5. It has been suggested that progesterone maintains the tubal secretions which sustain the life of the ovum during its passage through the tube (123).

6. Progesterone, possibly through its action on the endometrium, is thought to influence the formation of the blastocyst in the early ovum prior to its implantation (106).

7. Progesterone is essential to the maintainance of pregnancy (124). Removal of the ovaries of some animals is followed by the interruption of pregnancy. This can be prevented by the injection of sufficient amounts of the essential hormone of the corpus luteum. When present in excessive amounts, on the other hand, progesterone is able to prolong gestation beyond the expected date of confinement (125).

8. Mammary development, particularly that of the alveolar system, is influenced by progesterone but preliminary estrin preparation is necessary.

9. Progesterone also renders the uterus refractory to pituitrin (126, 127). The use of estrin and progesterone, on the other hand, bring about relaxation (128).

ADRENAL GLANDS. The adrenal cortex is hypertrophied and contains an increased amount of lipoid substance during pregnancy. Its cytology has been carefully studied in sheep (129). By means of special staining and fixation methods, variations have been shown to occur in the percentage of light and dark cells in the zona fasiculata and zona reticularis and in the amount of lipoid in the cells of the zona glomerulosa and zona fasiculata. The number of dark cells is great early and late in pregnancy and the amount of lipoid diminishes less rapidly after oestrus in animals which have become pregnant than in those which have not. There also is a great increase in lipoid late in pregnancy but it diminishes as the number of dark cells increases and is considerably reduced after parturition. If, as has been suggested, the dark staining is an indication of depletion or degeneration (130, 131), and the lipoid material represents either the substance from which cortical hormone is produced or the vehicle in which it is stored, **there is an increased activity throughout pregnancy and this is particularly true early and late in gestation.** Frequent fluctuations in the number of chondriosomes also point to more marked changes in secretory activity than are observed in the non-pregnant state. The great increase in lipoid late in pregnancy and its reduction just before and after parturition, indicate the utilization of this lipoid material for the production of secretion about the time of labor.

METABOLISM

Pregnancy seems to have a favorable effect upon metabolism; otherwise the maternal organism would not be able to provide for the increasing needs of the gravid state. These needs include the assimilation and storage of sufficient tissue-building materials to provide for:

1. The replacement of tissue loss due to wear and tear.
2. The development and growth of the fetus, fetal membranes and placenta.
3. The preparatory changes essential to parturition—uterine hypertrophy and hyperplasia.
4. The preparatory changes requisite for successful lactation—mammary development and the storage of milk-forming materials.

Not only are these requirements of pregnancy fully satisfied but the mother's body often is enriched by an appreciable surplus of stored metabolic products. This is particularly true if she is in good health and is given the benefit of an ample balanced diet. The favorable effect of pregnancy on the utilization of essential food elements also is shown by the tendency toward greater retention in those women who have a deficiency when they become pregnant than is observed in normal individuals. When the diet is inadequate, on the other hand, such deficient women are made worse and the fetus likewise may suffer from the deficiency.

WEIGHT. If the diet is well balanced and not restricted in amount, the average woman gains 20–25 pounds during pregnancy. In the early months, the weight may remain stationary or even fall slightly as a result of morning sickness and the metabolic adjustments which take place during the first trimester. Following this, the appetite improves and a general feeling of well-being is experienced with the result that the mother progressively gains in weight until shortly before the end of gestation. The greatest gain occurs during the 6th and 7th months when an average monthly increment of 4–5 pounds may be observed. In the last two months, a weekly increase of one pound is common but a loss of from 1 to 3 pounds not infrequently occurs during the final week of pregnancy.   About fifteen of the twenty to twenty-five pounds may be accounted for as follows: child 7 lb., placenta $1\frac{1}{2}$ lb., amniotic fluid $1\frac{1}{2}$ lb., uterus 2 lb., breasts, blood and retained fluid 3 lb.   The remainder is stored largely as fat.

Metabolic balance studies of different women during pregnancy frequently show rather marked individual variation even though the investigations are carried out under similar circumstances as to diet, surroundings and other experimental conditions.   Certain complicating diseases also may so alter the findings as to make them unreliable.   The same is true when the subject is deficient in the substance under investigation.   In such an event, the abnormally large storage of the deficient substance must be interpreted in the light of the underlying conditions; otherwise the findings again will be misleading.   In spite of these objections, balance studies are contributing much to our knowledge of the metabolism of pregnancy and are aiding in the scientific explanation of well-known clinical observations.

PROTEIN METABOLISM.   It formerly was thought that the mother's proteins were utilized in the development of the fetus even when the diet was abundant (132) and this erroneous concept led to the belief that "gestation constitutes a sacrifice of the individual for the species" (133, 134).   Carefully conducted experiments in animals, however, have shown that, "given sufficient rations, the healthy mother's body can supply the needs of the developing fetus without drawing upon its own capital even when the needs are extreme" (135, 136). Although some of the experimental animals retained small amounts of nitrogen immediately after fertilization, all of them had a slight negative balance in the early months and later stored nitrogen in progressively increasing amounts as pregnancy advanced.   The negative phase corresponded to the time of more or less indiscriminate chorionic activity but recovery from this nitrogen loss appeared soon after the development of the placenta was completed and growth of the fetus had begun.   Although the period of greatest accumulation corresponded to the months of greatest fetal growth, the total amount of nitrogen retained greatly exceeded the nitrogen content of the newborn offspring.

Extensive studies of nitrogen metabolism in pregnant women also have been made and it has been shown that their nitrogen output likewise is less than their intake (137, 138, 139, 140, 141, 142, 143, 144, 145).   In Table V the results of 954 daily balance studies taken from the literature are compared with the average storage in the fetus as determined by chemical analysis of 96 fetuses of various ages (144, 145).   From this it may be observed that the fetal requirements are insignificant during the first half of intrauterine life but progressively increase in the second half of gestation.   Over two-thirds of the nitrogen retained by the full term child is stored during the last trimester and almost one-half in the last month.   The fetal storage (58.58 gm.) however, is but a small part of the 514.9 gm. retained by the mother.   If the nitrogen content of the placenta (17 gm.) plus that of the fetus is deducted from the total stored by the mother, it will be found that the average maternal organism retains over 438 gm. above the requirements of the fetal tissue. It has been estimated that 17 gm. of nitrogen are added to the breasts and 39 gm. are utilized by the hypertrophied uterus (141). Even after allowing for these additions, there remain over 370 gm. of nitrogen otherwise stored in the body of the pregnant woman. This storage begins soon after the first trimester and increases at the rate of about 60 gm. per month throughout the remainder of pregnancy (see Table V).

TABLE V

NITROGEN STORAGE

(Macy and Hunscher)

	MONTH							
	3	4	5	6	7	8	9	10
Total storage for mother and fetus, gm.....	79.5	77.3	133	205.5	266.6	327.5	418	514.9
Total fetal storage, gm..............	0.12	0.65	3.04	8.59	14.95	15.47	31.61	58.58
Mother's daily increment, gm............	+2.84	−0.15	+1.99	+2.59	+2.18	+2.18	+3.23	+3.46

As in experimental animals, there is a tendency toward a negative balance in pregnant women late in the first and early in the second trimester. This can hardly be attributed to the needs of the fetus since very little nitrogen is retained by either the fetus or the placenta at this time. On the other hand, it may be due to the activity of the chorion, to nausea and vomiting, to the disturbed carbohydrate metabolism of early pregnancy or to an increase in metabolism resulting from overactivity of the thyroid gland. After the fourth month, all observers find a retention which increases as pregnancy advances. At first this is related to the hypertrophy and hyperplasia of the breasts, uterus and other tissues which add to the weight of the maternal organism. Later, as has been noted, some of the stored nitrogen is retained by the fetus but, even in the last month when the fetus stores 27 gm. or almost half of its total nitrogen, the mother retains an additional 70 gm.

The average daily increment which is added to the mother's store of nitrogen is also shown in Table V. In all but the fourth month, the balance is positive and, for the entire period included in the tabulation, the average daily increment is 2.28 gm. and this increases to 3.23 gm. in the ninth and 3.46 gm. in the tenth months. The degree of retention naturally may be influenced by the character and quantity of the protein in the diet. Eighty per cent of the cases included in the above study had nitrogen intakes of 10–18 gm. and retentions of 1.5 to 2.7 gm. daily (145).

One group of investigators observed the same subject during several pregnancies. In her. there was a total storage of 446 gm. during the last 145 days of

TABLE VI

NITROGEN STORAGE

(Hunscher et al.)

Total nitrogen stored in the last 145 days of pregnancy		+446.2 gm.
Nitrogen lost in parturition:		
Intake	+18.05 gm.	
Urine	−5.84 gm.	
Feces	−0.40 gm.	
Blood	−25.75 gm.	
Placenta	−20.11 gm.	
Placental Blood	−20.28 gm.	
Amniotic Fluid	−0.08 gm.	
Vomitus	−0.24 gm.	
Fetus	−58.5 gm.	
Total Loss	113 gm.	−113 gm.
Balance after parturition		+333.2 gm.
After deducting 182.82 gm. (milk N) there was a negative balance of 44.64 gm. for the first 9 days postpartum, the period of greatest involution of the uterus		44.64 gm.
Balance for lactation		+288.38 gm.
For the following 43 days of lactation, there was a negative balance of		−38.3 gm.
Surplus at end of 52 days postpartum		+250.06 gm.

pregnancy (147). On an average daily intake of 19.01 gm. of nitrogen, 13.98 gm. or 73+% was excreted in the urine, 1.96 gm. or 10+% was passed with the feces and 3.06 gm. or 16% was retained. The high storage in this instance was attributed either to an unusually generous food consumption or to the presence of a somewhat depleted maternal body produced by frequent pregnancies and long lactations. The results of the nitrogen balance studies in this particular individual during parturition, the first 9 days of the puerperium and during the following six weeks of lactation are shown in Table VI. From this table, it may be noted that, in spite of a daily consumption of 115 gm. of protein of good biological value, there was a negative balance throughout the entire postpartum period under observation. The early and large losses of 5 gm. daily no doubt were due chiefly to involution of the uterus. For the following six weeks the tendency also was toward a negative balance which, although slight, indicated an insufficient intake. **Preparation for the loss caused by the milk secretion, accordingly, must be made through ample storage during pregnancy if depletion of the body during lactation is to be avoided.** That this was ample in the subject studied, is shown by the excess of 250 gm. of nitrogen present in her body after she had nursed her baby for more than two months.

While the various requirements of pregnancy are indications for an ample protein intake, it is a question whether the amount of protein consumed in this instance was not excessive since the patient gained over 30 pounds and her child was somewhat overweight at birth. Perhaps it might have been just as well had the nitrogen intake been diminished somewhat below 19 gm. daily during pregnancy and increased slightly above this figure during lactation. The high intake also may account for the passage of more than 10% of the nitrogen with the feces. While this figure seems to be the usual one for nitrogen balance studies, other workers have noted greater absorption during pregnancy and instances are recorded in which all but 3 to 7% of the nitrogen intake was absorbed (137, 138).

The manner in which the nitrogen which is not utilized by the products of conception nor by the uterus and mammary glands, is stored during pregnancy is not known. The total amount of plasma protein is somewhat increased but the increase is less than that of the plasma volume. As a result of this dilution, the percentage of plasma protein is somewhat lower than it is in the non-pregnant state. There is also a change in the protein fractions. Fibrinogen is definitely increased while globulin undergoes but slight change and albumin is frequently lowered.

Although the nitrogen content of the intestinal excretion remains constant during pregnancy, that of the urine is considerably diminished and the diminution is particularly marked in the urea fraction which becomes lower and lower as pregnancy advances. Part of the absorbed nitrogen which customarily is deaminized and excreted in the urine as urea is retained and utilized by the growing fetus. Because the total nitrogen is diminished, the percentage of ammonia is relatively increased. Creatin, which ordinarily does not appear in the urine on a meat-free diet, is present in small amounts during pregnancy, irrespective of the diet and its occurrence has been attributed to the activity of the uterus.

CARBOHYDRATE METABOLISM. Intermittent glycosuria is not uncommon in pregnant women (149, 150). Repeated observations made upon the same individuals in a carefully studied series of pregnancies showed sugar in the urine at some time during the antepartum period in 35% of the cases and repeated recurrence of glycosuria in 18% (150). That this tendency to glycosuria is not due to temporary hyperglycemia is demonstrated by the fact that simultaneous blood and urine analyses failed to reveal an increase in the blood sugar at the time glucose was found in the urine. Blood sugar levels, on the other hand, tend to fall slightly as pregnancy progresses and average 85–80 mg. per 100 cc. throughout gestation. Following delivery, there is noted a slight rise which gradually increases to an average of 94 mg. six months postpartum (150).

Glycosuria, occurring in pregnant women without an increase in the blood sugar, indicates a **lowered renal threshold** as does also the action of phloridzin. This drug, which normally increases the permeability of the kidneys to glucose, causes glycosuria in pregnant women when given in doses ordinarily too small to have any effect (151).

A **lessened ability of the liver to store glycogen** likewise may contribute to the lowered carbohydrate tolerance of pregnancy (152). Evidence of this is furnished by the observation that adrenalin, which causes a breakdown of liver glycogen to glucose, also induces glycosuria in pregnant women when administered in doses otherwise too small.

Increased activity of the anterior lobe of the hypophysis also has been suggested as the cause of certain cases of intermittent glycosuria during pregnancy. In these the increased pituitary secretion is thought to depress the action of insulin and thereby diminish the oxidation of carbohydrates. As a result, the ingestion of 100 gm. of glucose is followed by glycosuria and a sustained but moderate elevation in the blood sugar level (153, 154, 155).

Regardless of the cause, a lowered tolerance for carbohydrates is a common accompaniment of pregnancy and any great increase in the intake of starches and sugars, may lead to the appearance of glucose in the urine. So constant is the occurrence of reducing bodies in the urine after the ingestion of 100 gm. of glucose that the inability to tolerate this amount of carbohydrate has been made the basis of a test of pregnancy.

The fetal drain on the carbohydrates of the mother, together with the increased metabolism of pregnancy, reduces the antiketogenic substances of the blood and their replacement may be delayed because of the diminished storage of glycogen in the liver. At the same time, the lipids of the maternal blood are increased and the alkali reserve is reduced. Such a set-up may readily lead to a disturbance of the ketogenic-antiketogenic relationship and thereby favor the production of a ketosis. As a result, acetone bodies are always present in the urine when the vomiting of pregnancy becomes excessive. For the same reason, the occurrence of pregnancy in a diabetic woman is a grave complication in which great care must be taken to avoid the too rapid withdrawal of carbohydrates and an excessive increase in the fats of the diet.

Lactose may also appear in the urine toward the end of pregnancy and during lactation (156). It most frequently occurs a day or two before delivery and is almost always present on the third and fourth days postpartum (150). The abrupt cessation of suckling likewise is productive of an abundant lactosuria. On the other hand, its occurrence in lactating animals is arrested by the removal of the breasts (157).

FAT METABOLISM. During pregnancy, the fats are more thoroughly absorbed from the intestines, as is shown by the diminution in the unabsorbed fats, fatty acids and soaps in the feces (158). With this greater absorption, there is a 50% increase in the fatty substances of the blood, the change being most pronounced in the plasma, less marked in the whole blood and insignificant in the red cells (159, 160, 161, 162, 163). Plasma neutral fat is more than doubled (129%) and smaller but appreciable increases occur in the plasma phospholipid (27%) and free cholesterol (22%) (162) (Table VII). The earliest evidence of this lipemia of pregnancy is an increase in the neutral fat of the plasma which occurs in the first trimester (160). A rise in the plasma cholesterol is demonstrable as early as the 15th week and continues to its maximum, 33.8% above normal, at 26–35 weeks after which it falls to 27.9% at term. Following delivery, there is a constant decrease which amounts to 21.2% of the term figure eight weeks postpartum (164). The ratios of phospholipid to cholesterol and of cholesterol ester to total cholesterol are but slightly altered in the plasma of pregnant women (162, 165).

TABLE VII

PLASMA LIPIDS IN PREGNANCY

(Boyd)

	TOTAL LIPID	NEUTRAL FAT	PHOSPHO-LIPID	ESTER CHOLESTEROL	FREE CHOLESTEROL
Non-pregnant state, mgm. per 100 cc.....	617	154	195	53	128
Pregnancy at term, mgm. per 100 cc......	900	353	248	65	140
Increase in pregnancy..................	46%	129%	27%	22%	9%

The deposition of fat in the fetus rises from an insignificant figure in the first half of pregnancy to 1.8% of the total fetal bulk at seven months and 11.75% at term. Since this great increase in the fat requirements of the fetus occurs at the time when the accumulation of maternal cholesterol is falling off, it is reasonable to assume that the fetal lipids are taken directly or indirectly from the surplus fatty substances of the mother's blood. In addition to aiding in the fat metabolism of the fetus, the lipemia of pregnancy also may be a preparatory factor in the production of milk. This conclusion is supported by the observation that the maternal blood lipids decrease at term and during lactation, and the decrease is more rapid in women who suckle their children than in those who do not. While fetal metabolism and lactation no doubt create a need for more fatty substances in the maternal blood, this need is not the cause of their increased production since the period of accumulation is far in advance of the time of their utilization. Perhaps the causative factor may be revealed by a study of the other conditions in which lipemia occurs. In this connection, it may be stated that the fat changes in the blood of pregnant women have been compared with those observed in diabetes, nephritis, chronic alcoholism and persistent hemorrhage (161, 162).

During pregnancy, a high fat intake causes a greater increase in the acetone bodies of the blood than is produced in the absence of gestation (166). Similarly, a carbohydrate-free diet which does not lead to the appearance of ketone in the urine in the non-pregnant state is followed by a ketonuria and this ketonuria can be checked by the addition of starches and sugars. It has been suggested, therefore, that an unusually large amount of carbohydrate is required for the combustion of a given quantity of fat (167). This conclusion, however, has been opposed on the ground that the increased metabolism of pregnancy and the large loss of anti-ketogenic material to the fetus, may well explain the increased tendency to ketone production (168). Be that as it may, it should be remembered that carbohydrates cannot be withdrawn too vigorously nor fats increased too extensively during pregnancy without producing a ketonuria.

CALCIUM AND PHOSPHORUS METABOLISM. Animals who have borne young have less calcium and phosphorus than do those who have never been pregnant. Pregnancy and lactation, therefore, are drains upon the mother's store of these elements. In the intervals between pregnancy, however, the diminished store of calcium is replenished but tends to remain below its former level. If the amount of phosphorus is insufficient in the diet and the quantity of calcium is ample, the calcium utilization is only equivalent to that of the deficient phosphorus and vice versa. To avoid a negative balance in animals, it has been found that the calcium and phosphorus intake must be increased 10 to 20% in pregnancy and over 100% in lactation (169, 170).

The amount of calcium in the bodies of the young ordinarily has no relation to the diet of the mother since the offspring of animals on a calcium-deficient diet do not differ greatly in growth and calcification from those born to adequately nourished mothers (169). The deficit of calcium, however, is cumulative in succeeding pregnancies and, as a result, subsequent litters are complicated by stillbirths and increasing degrees of calcium insufficiency in the young (171).

In parts of India and China, the shortage of calcium in the diet is so great that very little reserve is stored in the osseous system. When women with these abnormally low stores of calcium become pregnant, accordingly, the drain of pregnancy and lactation leads to the development of osteomalacia, the incidence of which among parous women in certain districts is 1 to 3 per cent. After the second pregnancy, these osteomalacic mothers no longer are able to furnish the necessary calcium to their offspring. Such children, accordingly, are osteoporotic at birth and later develop rickets (172, 173) which may be accompanied by hypoplasia of the enamel of the teeth and defective dentine formation (174). While calcium deficiencies of such extreme degrees seldom if ever occur in this country, insufficiencies of a lesser degree, however, may be observed. In this connection, it is of interest to note that Roentgen studies of the bones at birth are said to show better ossification when the mother's diet contains adequate amounts of this element (175). It likewise has been suggested that the hardness or softness of the newborn infant's cranium is related to the mother's calcium balance (176, 177, 178). Of 200 skulls examined, 18.3% were soft and 30.5% were hard. In the cases of soft skulls, the mother's diet was found to have been deficient while the reverse was true when the skulls were hard. This increased calcification of the cranial bones may protect the head from injury during parturition and may thereby lessen the liability to intracranial hemorrhage. On the other hand, the diminished malleability of the skull bones interferes with moulding of the head and, in this manner, may make parturition more difficult for the mother and more dangerous for the child.

Sheep at times have a "toxemia" during pregnancy which is said to be due to calcium deficiency (179, 180), and a similar belief is held by some with regard to pregnancy toxemia in women (181).

TABLE VIII

STORAGE OF CALCIUM

	MONTH							
	3	4	5	6	7	8	9	10
Fetus, gm. (Givens and Macy)...........	0.012	0.119	0.948	2.654	3.629	6.890	10.428	22.528
Mother and child, gm. (Macy and Hunscher)...............................	0.112	0.308	4.22	8.68	10.61	15.82	22.40	29.26
Daily increment, gm....................	0.004	0.007	0.162	0.159	0.069	0.186	0.235	0.245
Daily intake, gm......................	0.96	1.15	1.98	1.5	1.3	1.5	1.4	1.4

In Table VIII, are shown the average amounts of calcium deposited in 96 fetuses of various ages (182), together with the daily and monthly calcium storage and daily intake in 118 balance studies (183). About 3 gm., or less than 1/7 of the total fetal calcium at term, is deposited in the fetus during the first two trimesters. This amount is doubled in the eighth month and tripled in the ninth. Over half of the total calcium of the full term fetus is laid down in the tenth month. Infants born prematurely, accordingly, are handicapped by a calcium shortage which predisposes them to the development of rickets (184, 185).

After having a negative balance in the third and fourth months, the mother stores calcium at the rate of 4–7 gm. monthly. The maternal storage, therefore, exceeds the fetal requirements until the last month is reached when the fetus utilizes almost twice as much calcium as the mother retains. This rather heavy withdrawal from the mother's reserve, however, is accomplished without serious consequences to her osseous structures if the storage of calcium in the trabeculae of her bones has been adequate in the preceding months of gestation. From the above tabulation, it may be seen that an average intake of about 1.4 gm. per day furnishes sufficient calcium for this purpose. It does not, however, provide much of a reserve for lactation. The daily allowance, therefore, should be increased while the mother is nursing her child.

Blood studies show that the calcium of the serum remains within normal limits throughout pregnancy. Repeated examination of the same subject, on the other hand, reveals a tendency toward a slight lowering of the calcium values as the end of gestation approaches and a rapid return to higher levels after parturition.

One hundred twenty-six balance studies and 24 fetal phosphorus estimations are summarized in Table IX (183). The average maternal storage of over 64 gm.

TABLE IX
PHOSPHORUS STORAGE
(Macy and Hunscher)

	MONTH							
	3	4	5	6	7	8	9	10
Fetus, gm....................		0.10	0.30	1.65	2.36	3.91	6.38	13.68
Mother, gm....................	3.25	10.98	23.18	30.24	38.25	49.06	57.09	64.79
Daily increment, mg............	0.116	0.276	0.436	0.252	0.286	0.386	0.287	0.275

is almost five times the amount retained by the full-grown fetus. This was accomplished on a diet which contained a daily average of about 2 gm. of which 250 to 400 mgm. were retained. The storage of phosphorus in amounts considerably in excess of the fetal needs is somewhat similar to the nitrogen retention previously described. No doubt much of it, like the nitrogen, is utilized in the maternal tissue accretions which accompany pregnancy.

IRON METABOLISM. The mother's supply of iron may be altered in a number of ways during pregnancy. First of all, the small amount of iron in many articles of food may lead to a deficiency in the diet. The intake of vitamin B complex likewise may be insufficient as is common in tropical countries. If the diet is satisfactory, vomiting in the first trimester may interfere with intake and absorption or the gastric hypochlorhydria of pregnancy may diminish the liberation and utilization of iron in the food. In addition to these difficulties, some hemolysis also occurs in order that iron from the maternal red blood cells may be made suitable for passage through the placenta to the fetus. The augmented blood volume with its concomitant increase in red cells and hemoglobin also increases the maternal need for iron as does the growth of the uterus and other tissues during pregnancy.

TABLE X
IRON STORAGE
(Macy and Hunscher)

	MONTH							
	3	4	5	6	7	8	9	10
Fetus, mg.............................			10.3	25.4	39.5		227.6	246.2
Mother and child, mg..................	57.4	192.4	340.2	477.4	565.0	681.0	754.3	799.1
Daily increment, mg..................	2.0	4.8	5.3	4.9	3.1	4.1	2.6	1.6

In the 23 balance studies which furnished the data for Table X, the mean maternal retention was 799.1 mg. at the end of gestation. This was 553 mg. above the amount of iron found in the average tenth month fetus. Of the total 246 mg. retained by the fetus, all but 39.5 mg. were stored in the last trimester.

Since a large part of this fetal iron is stored in the liver in anticipation of the relative iron shortage of early life, prematurely born infants are not prepared to meet the demands of this period and, as a result, develop anemia unless sufficient iron is added to their diet (186, 187). *but they're not able to use what they have.*

BASAL METABOLISM. Systematic observations of the basal metabolic rate in the same individuals at regular intervals throughout the greater part of pregnancy show a drop to around -10% in the third and fourth months. This drop is followed by a consistent rise of 1% to 2% every three weeks until it reaches 5% to 10% above normal at term. Following delivery, the rate falls abruptly for five or six weeks after which it gradually returns to normal (72, 188, 189, 190, 191, 192, 193, 194). The progressive rise during the antepartum period corresponds to the time of greatest maternal weight gain and the period of greatest fetal growth. It, accordingly, has been attributed to these factors alone. In support of this theory, it has been contended that the rate obtained by dividing the total heat produced per hour by the combined surface areas of mother and child is within normal limits (194). On the other hand, the correctness of adding the calculated fetal area to that of the mother as a means of ascertaining total surface area for metabolic rate calculating purposes has been questioned (195). As a result, it is claimed that there is a definite increase in metabolism above that associated with the increases in fetal and maternal tissues (195, 196). The increased basal metabolism in the latter part of gestation may be compensated by the diminished muscular activity. (See Metabolism, Chapter VI.)

REFERENCES

1. STIEVE, H.: Ueber die Neubildung von Muskelzellen in der Wand der schwangeren menschlichen Gebärmutter. Zentralbl. f. Gyn., 1932, 56, 1442.
2. HELIE: Recherches sur la disposition des fibres musculaires de l'utérus développee par la grossesse. Paris, 1864.
3. HOFBAUER, J. I.: A Specialized Type of Muscle in the Human Pregnant Uterus. J. A. M. A., 1929, 92, 540.
4. RUDOLPH, L. AND IVY, A. C.: The Coördination of the Uterus in Labor. Am. Jnl. Obs. & Gyn., 1931, 21, 65.
5. STIEVE, H.: Der Verschluss der schwangeren Gebärmutter und seine Eröffnung während der Geburt. Zentralbl. f. Gyn., 1928, 52, 218.
   Ueber Schwangerschaftsveränderungen des Halsteiles der menschlichen Gebärmutter. Anatomischer Anzeiger, Verhandl. d. anat. Gesellsch., 1927, 36, 51.
6. GAY, F. P.: Tissue resistance and immunity. (Harvey lecture.) J. A. M. A., 1931, 97, 1193.
7. STIEVE, H.: Die Schwangerschaftsveränderungen der menschlichen Scheide. Anatomischer Anzeiger Verhandl. d. anat. Gesellsch., 1925, 34, 80.
8. DÖDERLEIN: Das Scheidensekret, Leipzig, 1892.
9. KESSLER, R. AND UHR, E.: Biologie und Chemismus der Scheide bei Schwangeren. Arch. f. Gyn., 1927, 129, 844.
10. SEITZ, L.: Die Follikelatresie während der Schwangerschaft, insbesondere die Hypertrophie und Hyperplasie der Theca interna-Zellen (Theca Luteinzellen) und ihre Beziehungen zur Corpus luteum-Bildung. Arch. f. Gyn., 1905, 77, 203.
11. WALTHARD, K. M.: Ueber die histologischen Veränderungen des Ovariums während der Gravidität. Ztschr. f. Geburtsh. u. Gyn., 1923, 86, 74.

12. FELLNER, O. O.: Ueber die Tätigkeit des Ovarium in der Schwangerschaft (interstitielle Zellen). Monatschr. f. Geburtsh. u. Gyn., 1921, 54, 88.
13. MILLER, J. R., KEITH, W. M. AND ROUNTREE, L. G.: Plasma and Volume Changes in Pregnancy. J. A. M. A., 1915, 65, 779.
14. MOHNERT, A.: Ueber das Blutvolumen in der Schwangerschaft. Arch. f. Gynak., 1921, 144, 168.
15. BOHNEN, P. AND BOORMANN, K.: Untersuchungen über die Vermehrung der Blutmenge in der Schwangerschaft. Arch. f. Gyn., 1925, 126, 144.
16. DIECKMANN, W. J. AND WEGNER, C. R.: The Blood in Normal Pregnancy. I. Blood and Plasma Volumes. Arch. Int. Med., 1934, 53, 71.
17. PLASS, E. D. AND BOGERT, J.: Plasma Protein Variations in Normal and Toxemic Pregnancies. Bull. J. Hopk. Hosp., 1924, 35, 361.
18. PLASS, E. D. AND MATTHEWS, C. W.: Plasma Protein Fractions in Normal Pregnancy, Labor and Puerperium. Am. J. O. & G., 1926, 12, 346.
19. DIECKMANN, W. J. AND WEGNER, C. R.: Studies of the Blood in Normal Pregnancy. IV. Percentages and Grams per Kilogram of Serum Protein and Fibrin and Variations in Total Amount of Each. Arch. Int. Med., 1934, 53, 353.
20. FOSTER, D. P. AND WHIPPLE, G. H.: Blood Fibrin Studies. II. Normal Fibrin Values and the Influence of Diet. Am. J. Physiol., 1922, 58, 379.
21. FOSTER, D. P.: A Clinical Study of Blood Fibrin with Observat ons in Normal Persons, Pregnant Women and in Pneumonia and Liver Disease. Ar ch Int. Med., 1924, 34, 301.
22. LITZENMEIER, G.: Untersuchungen über die Senkungsgeschwindigkeit der roten Blutkörperchen. Arch. f. Gyn., 1920, 113, 608.
23. DIECKMANN, W. J. AND WEGNER, C. R.: Studies of the Blood in Normal Pregnancy. II. Hemoglobin, Hematocrit and Erythrocyte Determinations and Total Amount of Variation of Each. Arch. Int. Med., 1934, 53, 188.
24. ROWE, A. W.: The Metabolism of Pregnancy. VII. The Blood Morphology. Am. J. Physiol., 1931, 96, 112.
25. SKAJAA, K.: Variations in Cell Volume of Blood in Pregnancy Toxemia and in Labour. Acta obst., et gynec. Scandinav., 1929, 8, 371.
26. KUHNEL, P.: Untersuchungen über die Physiologische Schwangerschaftsanämie. Ztschr. f. Geburtsh u. Gynak., 1927, 90, 511.
27. WINTROBE, M. M.: Blood of Normal Young Women Residing in Subtropical Climates. Arch. Int. Med., 1930, 45, 287.
28. DIECKMANN, W. J. AND WEGNER, C. R.: Studies of the Blood in Normal Pregnancy. III. Hemoglobin and Cell Volume Coefficients; Erythrocyte Volume, Hemoglobin Content and Concentration; Color, Volume and Saturation Indexes. Arch. Int. Med., 1934, 53, 345.
29. HUGGETT, A. S.: Foetal Blood-Gas Tensions and Gas Transfusion through the Placenta of the Goat. J. Physiol., 1927, 62, 373.
30. EASTMAN, N. J., GEILING, E. M. K. AND DeLAWDER, A. M.: Foetal Blood Studies. IV. The Oxygen and Carbon-Dioxide Dissociation Curves of Foetal Blood. Bull. J. Hopk. Hosp., 1933, 53, 246.
31. DIETRICH, H. A.: Studien über Blutveränderungen bei Schwangeren, Gebärenden und Wöchnerinnen. Arch. f. Gyn., 1811, 94, 383.
32. BAER, J. L.: The Leucocytes in Pregnancy, Labor and the Puerperium. Surg. Gyn. & Obs., 1916, 23, 567.
33. CAREY, J. B. AND LITZENBERG, J. C.: Total Leukocyte Counts in Human Blood during Pregnancy. Ann. Int. Med., 1936, 10, 25.
34. ZANGEMEISTER, W.: Die Beschaffenheit des Blutes in der Schwangerschaft und der Geburt. Ztschr. f. Geb. u. Gyn., 1903, 49, 92.
35. THOMPSON, W. L.: The Blood in Pregnancy. J. Hopk. Hosp. Bull., 1904, 15, 205.
36. OBERST, F. W. AND PLASS, E. D.: Water Concentration of the Blood during Pregnancy, Labor and the Puerperium. Am. J. O. & G., 1936, 31, 61.

37. DIECKMANN, W. J. AND WEGNER, C. R.: Studies of the Blood in Normal Pregnancy. V. Conductivity, Total Base, Chloride and Acid Base Equilibrium. Arch. Int. Med., 1934, 53, 527.

38. OARD, H. C. AND PETERS, J. P.: The Concentration of Acid and Base in the Serum in Normal Pregnancy. J. Biol. Chem., 1929, 81, 9.

39. SIEDENTOPF, H. AND EISSNER, W.: Die wahre Blutreaktion während Schwangerschaft und Geburt. Ztschr. f. Geburtsh. u. Gyn., 1929, 96, 76.

40. STANDER, H. J., EASTMAN, N. J., HARRISON, E. P. H. AND CADDEN, J. F.: The Acid-Base Equilibrium of the Blood in Eclampsia. J. Biol. Chem., 1930, 85, 233.

41. KYDD, D. M., OARD, H. C. AND PETERS, J. P.: The Acid-Base Equilibrium in Abnormal Pregnancy. J. Biol. Chem., 1932, 98, 241 and 261.

42. MYERS, V. C., MUNTWYLER, E. AND BILL, A. H.: The Acid-Base Balance Disturbance of Pregnancy. J. Biol. Chem., 1932, 98, 253, 267.

43. PLASS, E. D. AND OBERST, F. W.: Respiration and Pulmonary Ventilation in Normal, Non-Pregnant, Pregnant and Puerperal Women. Am. J. O. & G., 1938, 35, 441.

44. BOKELMANN, O. AND ROTHER, J.: Ztschr. f. Geb. u. Gyn., 1928, 93, 87.

45. HINSELMANN, H. AND HAUPT, W.: Die Registrierung der Angiospasmen. Deutsch. med. Wchnschr., 1921, 47, 590.

46. HINSELMANN, H.: Der Einfluss der Schwangerschaft auf den Gefässtonus. Arch. f. Gyn., 1922, 117, 161.

47. KYRIELEIS, W. AND SCHROEDER, C.: Über funkionelle Veränderungen am Netzhautgefäss system normaler Schwangerer während der letzten Schwangerschaftsmonate. Arch. f. Augen heilk., 1931–32, 105, 110.

48. MYLIUS, K.: Spastische und telanische Netzhautveränderungen bei der Eklampsie. Ber. u. d. Versamml. d. deutsch ophth. gesellsch., 1929, 47, 379.

49. BARCROFT, J.: Fetal Circulation and Respiration. Physiological Rev., 1936, 16, 103.

50. HARE, D. C. AND KARN, M. N.: An Investigation of Blood Pressure, Pulse-Rate and the Response to Exercise during Normal Pregnancy and Some Observations after Confinement. Quart. J. Med., 1928–29, 22, 381.

51. HENRY, J. S.: The Effect of Pregnancy upon Blood Pressure. J. Obs. & Gyn. Br. Emp., 1936, 43, 908.

52. STANDER, H. J. AND CADDEN, J. F.: The Cardiac Output In Pregnant Women. Am. J. O. & G., 1932, 24, 13.

53. EISMAYER, G. AND POHL, A.: Untersuchungen über den Kreislauf und den Gasstoffwechsel in der Schwangerschaft bei Arbeitsversuchen. Arch. f. Gyn., 1934, 156, 428.

54. BURWELL, C. S. AND STRAYHORN, D.: The Influence of Pregnancy on the Course of Heart Disease. South. M. J., 1936, 29, 1194.

55. LARCHER, J. F.: De l'hypertrophie normale et temporaire du coeur liée a la gestation. Paris, 1868.

56. MUELLER, W.: Die Massenverhältnisse des Menschlichen Herzens. Hamburg & Leipzig, 1883.

57. DREYSEL, M.: Ueber Herzhypertrophie bei Schwangeren und Wöchnerinnen. Münch. Med. Abh. Erste Reihe, No. 3. München, 1891.

58. CLAUSER, F.: Cuoro e stato puerperale. Ann. di ostet. e ginec., 1927, 49, 173.

59. BINHOLD, H.: Das Herzvolumen in der Schwangerschaft. Arch. f. Gyn., 1933, 154, 251.

60. SMITH, S. C.: Observations on the Heart in Mothers and the New-Born. J. A. M. A., 1922, 79, 3.

61. JENSEN, F. G. AND NORGAARD: Studies on Functional Cardiac Diseases and Essential Hypertrophy, in Normal Pregnant Women. Acta obst. et gynec. Scandinav., 1927, 6, 239.

62. CARR, F. B. AND PALMER, R. S.: Observations on Electrocardiography in Heart Disease Associated with Pregnancy With Especial Reference to Axis Deviation. Amer. Heart J., 1933, 8, 238.

63. GAMMELTOFT, S. A.: Heart in Pregnancy. Surg., Gyn. & Obs., 1928, 46, 382.

64. BLAND, E. F. AND WHITE, P. D.: The Clinical Significance of Lead III of the Human Electrocardiogram. Am. H. J., 1931, 6, 333.
65. BURWELL, C. S.: The Placenta As a Modified Arteriovenous Fistula Considered in Relation to the Circulatory Adjustments to Pregnancy. Am. J. Med. Sc., 1938, 195, 1.
66. BARCROFT, J.: Alterations in the Volume of the Normal Spleen and Its Significance. Am. J. Med. Sc., 1930, 179, 1.
67. ZHURAKOVSKI, M. K.: On the Changes in the Form of the Thorax; Power of Inspiration and Expiration and the Vital Capacity of the Lungs in Pregnant and Lying-In Women. St. Petersburg, B. M. Volf, 1893.
68. MACKENZIE, J.: Heart Disease and Pregnancy. London, 1821, p. 13.
69. THOMSON, K. J. AND COHEN, M. E.: Studies on the Circulation in Pregnancy. II. Vital Capacity Observations in Normal Pregnant Women. Surg., Gyn. & Obs., 1938, 66, 591.
70. ROWE, A. W., ALCOTT, M. D. AND MORTIMER, E.: The Metabolism in Pregnancy. II. Changes in the Basal Metabolic Rate. Am. J. Physiol., 1925, 71, 667.
71. ENRIGHT, L., COLE, V. V. AND HITCHCOCK, F. A.: Basal Metabolism and Iodine Excretion during Pregnancy. Am. J. Physiology., 1935, 113, 221.
72. MAGNUS-LEVY, A.: Stoffwechsel und Nahrungsbedarf in der Schwangerschaft. Ztschr. f. Geb. u. Gyn., 1904, 52, 116.
73. ZUNTZ, L.: Respiratorischer Stoffwechsel und Athmung während der Gravidität. Arch. f. Gyn., 1909–10, 90, 452.
74. ROWE, A. W., GALLIVAN, D. E. AND MATTHEWS, H.: Metabolism in Pregnancy. The Respiratory Metabolism and Acid Elimination. Am. J. Physiol., 1931, 96, 101.
75. PLASS, E. D. AND OBERST, F. W.: Respiration and Pulmonary Ventilation in Normal Non-Pregnant, Pregnant and Puerperal Women. Am. J. O. & G., 1938, 35, 441.
76. HOFBAUER, J.: Structure and Function of the Ureter during Pregnancy. Jnl. of Urol., 1928, 20, 413.
77. SCHUMACHER, P.: Die Schwangerschaftsveränderungen der ableitenden Harnwege im Röntgenbild. Arch. f. Gyn., 1930, 143, 28.
78. ARZT, F.: Further Observations on the Gastric Juice in Pregnancy. Am. J. O. & G., 1930, 20, 382.
79. ALVAREZ, W. C. AND HOSOI, K.: Reversed Gradients in the Bowel of Pregnant Animals. Am. J. O. & G., 1930, 19, 35.
80. BAER, J. L., REES, R. A. AND ARENS, R. A.: Appendicitis in Pregnancy—With Changes in Position and Axis of the Normal Appendix in Pregnancy. J. A. M. A., 1932, 98, 1359.
81. SCHAEFER, W.: Zur Physiologie und Pathologie der Gallenblase in Schwangerschaft, Geburt und Wochenbett, unter besonderer Berücksichtigung der Steinentstehung in dieser Periode. Arch. f. Gyn., 1932, 150, 696.
82. DREYFUSS, E.: Beiträge zur Frage der Osteophytenbildung in der Schwangerschaft. Arch. f. Gyn., 1921, 115, 126.
83. DIBBELT, W.: Die Bedeutung der Kalksalze für die Schwangerschafts-und Stillperiode und der Einfluss einer negativen Kalkbilanz auf den mütterlichen und kindlichen Organismus. Beitr. z. path. Anat. u. z. allg. Path., 1910, 48, 147.
84. GIVENS, M. H. AND MACY, I. G.: The Chemical Composition of the Fetus. J. Biol. Chem., 1933, 102, 7.
85. BORKELMANN, O. AND SCHERINGER, W.: Beitrag zur Kenntnis der Schilddrüsenfunktion und des Jodstoffwechsels in der Gestation Arch. f. Gyn., 1930, 143, 512.
86. EUFINGER, H., WIESBADER, H. AND SMILOVITS, N.: Die Beeinflussung der Froschlarvenmetamorphose durch Schwangerenblut. Arch. f. Gyn., 1930, 143, 338.
87. UKITA, T.: On the Influence of Complete Thyroidectomy during Pregnancy upon the Development of the Fetus and on the Duration of Gestation. Acta Scholae Med. Univ. Imp. Kioto, 1919, 3, 287.

88. MARINE, D.: Parathyroid Hypertrophy and Hyperplasia in Fowls. Proc. Soc. Exp. Biol. & Med., 1913, 11, 117.

89. HAMILTON, B., DASEF, L., HIGHMAN, W. J. AND SCHWARTZ, C.: Parathyroid Hormone in the Blood of Pregnant Women. J. Clin. Invest., 1936, 15, 323.

90. FROMMER, V.: Experimentelle Versuche zur parathyreoidealen Insuffizienz in Bezug auf Eklampsie und Tetanie, mit besonderer Berücksichtigung der antitoxischen Funktion der Parathyreoideae. Monatschr. f. Geburtsh. u. Gyn., 1906, 24, 748.

91. COMTE, L.: Contribution a l'étude de l'hypophyse humaine. Thèse de doctorat, Lausanne, 1898.

92. ERDHEIM, J. AND STUMME, E.: Über die Schwangerschaftsveränderung der Hypophyse. Beitr. z. path. Anat. u. z. allg. Path., 1909, 46, 1.

93. RASMUSSEN, H. T.: The Weight of the Principal Components of the Normal Hypophysis Cerebri of the Adult Female. Am. J. Anat., 1934, 55, 252.

94. ALPERS, B. J. AND PALMER, H. D.: The Cerebral and Spinal Complications occurring during pregnancy and puerperium: Critical Review with illustrative cases. J. Nerv. & Ment. Dis., 1929, 70, 465.

95. SEVERINGHAUS, A. E.: Cellular Changes in The Anterior Hypophysis With Special Reference to Its Secretory Activities. Physiol. Rev., 1937, 17, 556.

96. TURNER, C. W. AND GARDINER, W. U.: The Relation of the Anterior Pituitary Hormones to the Development and Secretion of the Mammary gland. Mo. Agr. Exper. Sta. Res. Bull., 1931, 158, 5.

98. COLLIP, J. B.: Further Observation on the Ovary-Stimulating Hormone of the Placenta. Canad. M. A. J., 1930, 22, 761.

99. FEVOLD, H. L. AND HISAW, F. L.: Interactions of Gonad-stimulating Hormones in Ovarian Development. Am. J. Physiol., 1934, 109, 655.

100. ASCHHEIM, S. UND ZONDEK, B.: Die Schwangerschaftsdiagnose aus dem Harnnachweis des Hypophysenvorderlappenhormons. Klin. Wchnschr., 1928, 7, 1404 and 1453.

101. SMITH, O. W., SMITH, G. V. S., JOSLIN, E. P., AND WHITE, P.: Prolan and Estrin in the Serum and Urine of Diabetic and Non-Diabetic Women during Pregnancy, with Especial Reference to Late Toxemia of Pregnancy. Am. J. Obs. & Gyn., 1937, 33, 365.

102. BERBLINGER, W.: Die Korrelativen Veränderungen an der Hypophyse des Menschen. Klin. Wchnschr., 1928, 7, 9.
Die Störungen der inneren Sekretion der Keimdrüsen und die Sexual Hormone. Klin. Wchnschr., 1928, 7, 1673 & 1721.

103. BELL, W. B.: The Pituitary Body. Brit. M. J., 1909, 2, 1609.

104. MacCORQUODALE, D. W., THAYER, S. A., AND DISY, E. A.: The Isolation of the Principal Estrogenic Substance of the Liquor Folliculi. J. Biol. Chem., 1936, 115, 435.

105. SMITH, G. V. S. AND SMITH, O. W.: Studies in the Urinary Excretion of Oestrin, With Especial Reference to the Effects of the Luteinizing Hormone and Progestin. Am. J. Physiol., 1931, 98, 578.

106. PINCUS, G.: The Metabolism of the Ovarian Hormones, especially in Relation to the Growth of the Fertilized Ovum. Cold Spring Harbor Symposia on Quantitative Biology, 1937, 5, 44.

107. SMITH, G. V. S., SMITH, O. W. AND PINCUS, G.: Total Urinary Estrogen, Estrone and Estriol During a Menstrual Cycle and a Pregnancy. Am. J. Physiol., 1938, 121, 98.

108. COHEN, S. L., MARRIAN, G. F. AND WATSON. M.: Excretion of Oestrin during Pregnancy. Lancet, 1935, 1, 674.

109. GOLDBERGER, M. A.: Biologic Assay of Estrogenic Factors in Pregnancy Urine. Am. J. Obs. & Gyn., 1937, 33, 1093.

111. ALLEN, E.: The Menstrual Cycle of the Monkey. Contrib. to Emb. Carnegie Inst., 1927, 19, 1.

112. HISAW, F. L. AND LEONARD, S. F.: Relation of the Follicular and Corpus Luteum Hormones in the Production of Progestational Proliferation of the Rabbit's Uterus. Am. J. Physiol., 1930, 92, 574.

113. CORNER, G. W.: The Nature of the Menstrual Cycle. Medicine, 1933, 12, 61.
114. REYNOLDS, S. R.: Hormonic and Physical Factors in Uterine Growth. Cold Spring Harbor Symposia on Quantitative Biology. 1937, Vol. 5, 84.
115. REYNOLDS, S. R.: The Nature of Uterine Contractility. Phys. Rev., 1937, 17, 304.
116. TURNER, C. W. AND ALLEN, E.: The Normal and Experimental Development of the Mammary Gland in the Monkey. Proc. Am. Assn. Anat., Anat. Rec., 1933, 55, 80.
117. BROWNE, J. S. L., HENRY, J. S. AND VENNING, E. M.: The Corpus Luteum Hormone in Pregnancy. J. Clin. Invest., 1937, 119, 417.
    The Significance of Endocrine Assays in Threatened and Habitual Abortion. Tr. Am. Gyn. Soc. 1939.
118. CORNER, G. W.: The Rate of Secretion of Progestin by the Corpus Luteum. Cold Spring Harbor Symposia on Quantitative Biology., 1937, 5, 62.
    Ovarian Hormones and Experimental Menstruation. Am. J. Obs. & Gyn., 1939, 38, —.
119. CORNER, G. W. AND ALLEN, W. M.: Physiology of the Corpus Luteum. Am. J. Physiol., 1929, 88, 326.
120. WEISBADER, H., ENGLE, E. T. AND SMITH, P. E.: Menstrual Bleeding After Corpus Luteum Excision Followed by Estrin or Progestin Therapy. Am. J. Obs. & Gyn., 1936, 32, 1039.
121. SMITH, G. V. S. AND SMITH, O. W.: The Rôle of Progestin in the Female Reproductive Cycle. J. A. M. A., 1931, 97, 1857.
122. LOEB, L.: The Experimental Production of the Maternal Part of the Placenta in the Rabbit. Proc. Soc. Exp. Biol. & Med., 1908, 5, 102.
123. WESTMAN, A.: Studies of the Function of the Mucous Membrane of the Uterine Tube. Acta Obst. & Gyn. Scandin., 1930, 10, 288.
124. ALLEN, W. M. AND CORNER, G. W.: Physiology of the Corpus Luteum. Normal Growth and Implantation of Embryos After Very Early Ablation of the Ovaries. Am. J. Physiol., 1929, 88, 340.
125. MIKLOS, L.: Experimentelle Verlängerung der Schwangerschaft mit Corpus Luteum-Extracten. Centralbl. f. Gyn., 1930, 54, 1755.
126. KNAUS, H.: Experimentelle Untersuchungen zur Physiologie und Pharmakologie der Uterus-muskulatur in der Schwangerschaft. Arch. f. exper. Path. u. Phar., 1927, 124, 152.
127. REYNOLDS, S. R. AND ALLEN, W. M.: The Effect of Progestin-Containing Extracts of Corpora Lutea on Uterine Motility in the Unanesthetized Rabbit with Observations on Pseudo Pregnancy. Am. J. Physiol., 1932, 102, 39.
128. ALLEN, W. M.: Some Effects of Estrin and Progestin in the Rabbit. Cold Spring Harbor Symposium on Ouantitative Biology, 1937, 5, 66.
129. NAHM, L. J. AND McKENZIE, F. F.: The Cells of the Adrenal Cortex of the Ewe During the Estrual Cycle and Pregnancy. Mo. Agr. Exp. Sta. Res. Bull., 251, 1937.
130. ZWEMER, R. L.: A Study of Adrenal Cortex Morphology. Am. J. Path., 1936, 12, 107.
131. HOERR, N.: The Cells of the Suprarenal Cortex in the Guinea Pig. Their Reaction to Injury and Their Replacement. Am. J. Anat., 1931, 48, 139.
132. HAGEMAN, O.: Ueber Eiweissumsatz während der Schwangerschaft. Arch. f. anat. u. Physiol., 1890, 56, 577.
133. VER ECKE, A.: Les échanges materials dans leur rapports avec les phases de la vie sexuelle. Mémoires courronnés et autres memoires publ. par l'acad. roy. de med. de Belg., 1901, 15, No. 7.
134. JAGEROOS, B. H.: Studien über den Eiweiss-Phosphor-u. Salz-umsatz während der Gravidität. Arch. f. Gyn., 1902, 67, 517.
135. BAR, P.: Leçons de pathologie obstetricale, 1907, 2, 271.
136. MURLIN, J. R.: Metabolism of Development. II. Nitrogen Balance during Pregnancy and Menstruation of the Dog. Am. J. Physiology., 1910–11, 27, 177.

137. ZACHARJEWSKY, A. W.: Ueber den Stickstoffwechsel während den letzten Tagen der Schwangerschaft und den ersten Tage des Wochenbettes. Ztschr. f. Biol., 1894, 12, 368.
138. SLEMONS, J. M.: Metabolism During Pregnancy, Labor and the Puerperium. Johns Hopk. Hosp. Rep., 1904, 12, 111.
139. HOFFSTRÖM, K. A.: Eine Stoffwechseluntersuchung während der Schwangerschaft. Skandinav. Arch. f. Physiol., 1910, 23, 316.
140. LANDSBERG, E.: Untersuchungen über den Stoffwechsel von Stickstoff, Phosphor und Schwefel bei Schwangeren. Ztschr. f. Geburt. u. Gynak., 1912, 71, 163.
141. WILSON, K. M.: Nitrogen Metabolism during Pregnancy. Johns Hopkins Hosp. Bull., 1916, 27, 121.
142. COONS, C. M. AND BLUNT, K.: The Retention of Nitrogen, Calcium, Phosphorus and Magnesium by Pregnant Women. J. Biol. Chem., 1930, 86, 1.
143. SANDIFORD, I., WHEELER, T. AND BOOTHBY, W. M.: Metabolic Studies During Pregnancy and Menstruation. Am. J. Physiol., 1931, 96, 191.
144. HUNSCHER, H. A., DONELSON, E., NIMS, B., KENYON, F. AND MACY, I. G.: Metabolism of Women during the Reproductive Cycle. V. Nitrogen Utilization. J. Biol. Chem., 1933, 99, 507.
145. MACY, I. G. AND HUNSCHER, H. A.: An Evaluation of Maternal Nitrogen and Mineral Needs during Embryonic and Infant Development. Am. J. O. & G., 1934, 27, 878.
146. HUNSCHER, H. A., HUMMEL, F. C., ERICKSON, B. N. AND MACY, I. G.: Metabolism of Women during the Reproductive Cycle. VI. A Case Stucy of the Continuous Nitrogen Utilization of a Multipara during Pregnancy, Parturition and Lactation. J. Nutrit., 1935, 10, 579.
147. HUMMEL, F. C., HUNSCHER, H. A., BATES, M. F., BONNER, P., MACY, I. G. AND JOHNSON, J. A.: A Consideration of the Nutritive State in the Metabolism during Pregnancy. J. Nutrition, 1937, 13, 263.
148. SLEMONS, J. M.: The Involution of the Uterus and Its Effect upon Nitrogen Output of the Urine. Bull. Johns Hopk. Hosp., 1914, 25, 195.
149. CRON, R. S.: Glycosuria during Pregnancy. Am. J. O. & G., 1920, 1, 276.
150. ROWE, A. W., GALLIVAN, D. E. AND MATTHEWS, H.: Metabolism in Pregnancy. V. The Carbohydrate Metabolism. Am. J. Physiol., 1931, 96, 94.
151. NÜRNBERGER, L.: Ueber die Verwendbarkeit der renalen Schwangerschaftsglykosurie zur Frühdiagnose der Gravidität. Deutsche Med. Wchnschr., 1921, 47, 1124.
152. SCHMIDT, H. R.: Zuckerstoffwechsel in der Schwangerschaft mit besonderer Berücksichtigung von Organanalysen bei Hunden. Zentralbl. f. Gyn., 1927, 51, 1107.
153. WALLIS, R. L. M. AND BOSE, J. P.: Glycosuria in Pregnancy. J. Obs. & Gyn. Brit. Emp., 1922, 29, 274.
154. HOUSAY, B. A. AND LEBOIR, L. F.: Action diabetigène antehypophysaire independante des surrenales. Compt. Rend. Soc. de Biol., 1935, 120, 670.
155. RUSSELL, J. A.: The Relation of the Anterior Pituitary to Carbohydrate Metabolism. Physiol. Rev., 1938, 18, 1.
156. HOFMEISTER, —: Ueber Laktosurie. Ztschr. f. Physiol. Chem., 1877, 1, 101.
157. DE SINETY, —: Sur l'ablation des mammales chez les animaux par rapport à la lactation et à la fécondation. Compt. rend. de la Soc. Biol., 1873, 25, 387.
158. FERRONI: Gli acidi grassi, i Saponi nella feci. I grassi neutri, della gravide e della puerpere sane. Ann. de Ost. e Ginec., 1905, 1, 86.
159. HERMANN, E. AND NEUMANN, J.: Ueber den Lipoidgehalt des Blutes normaler und schwangerer Frauen sowie neugeborener Kinder. Biochem. Ztschr., 1912, 43, 47.
160. SLEMONS, J. M. AND STANDER, H. J.: The Lipoids of Maternal and Fetal Blood at the Conclusion of Labor. Johns Hopkins Hosp. Bull., 1923, 34, 7.
161. TYLER, M. AND UNDERHILL, F. P.: The Influence of Pregnancy upon the Lipoids of the Blood. J. Biological Chem., 1925, 66, 1.
162. BOYD, E. M.: The Lipemia of Pregnancy. J. Clin. Investig., 1934, 13, 347.

163. GARDNER, J. A. AND GAINSBOROUGH, H.: The Cholesterol Metabolism during Pregnancy. Lancet, 1929, 1, 603.

164. DIECKMANN, W. J. AND WEGNER, C. R.: Studies in the Blood in Normal Pregnancy. VI. Plasma Cholesterol in Milligrams per Hundred Cubic Centimeters. Grams per Kilogram and Variations in Total Amounts. Arch. Int. Med., 1934, 53, 541.

165. KAUFMAN, C. AND MUHLBACK, O.: Ueber Cholesterinbilanzen in der Schwangerschaft und im Wochenbett. Ztschr. f. d. ges. exper. med., 1933, 89, 200.

166. BOKELMANN, O. AND BOCK, A.: Beitrag zum intermediären Fettsstoffwechsel in der Schwangerschaft. I. Nährungsfett und Acetonkörper. Arch. f. Gyn., 1926–27, 129, 541.

167. KLEESATTEL, H.: Ueber das Zustandekommen und den Ablauf der Acetonurie während der Schwangerschaft. Arch. f. Gyn., 1926, 127, 717.

168. HARDING, V. J. AND ALLIN, K. D.: Ketosis in Pregnancy. J. Biol. Chem., 1926, 69, 133.

169. SHERMAN, H. C., MacLEOD, F. L.: The Calcium Content of the Body in Relation to Age Growth and Food. J. Biol. Chem., 1925, 64, 429.

170. GOSS, H. AND SCHMIDT, C. L. A.: Calcium and Phosphorus Metabolism in Rats during Pregnancy and Lactation and the Influence of the Reaction of the Diet Thereon. J. Biol. Chem., 1930, 86, 417.

171. DAVIDSON, H. R.: J. Agric. Sci., 1930, 20, 233.

172. MAXWELL, J. P., HU, C. H. AND TURNBULL, A. M.: Fetal Rickets. J. Path. Bacteriol., 1932, 35, 419.

173. MAXWELL, J. P.: Further Studies in Adult Rickets (Osteomalacia) and Foetal Rickets. Proc. Roy. Soc. Med., 1935, 28, 265.

174. RECTOR, J. M.: Prenatal Influence in Rickets. J. Pediat., 1935, 6, 161 & 167.

175. COONS, C. M. AND BLUNT, K. J.: The Retention of Calcium Phosphorus and Magnesium by Pregnant Women. J. Biol. Chem., 1930, 86, 1.

176. ABELS, H. AND KARPLUS, D.: Uber die Bedeutung der angeborenen Osteoporose für die Rachitisentstehung. Ztschr. f. Kinderhlk. 1927, 44, 365.

177. TOVERUD, K. U. AND TOVERUD, G.: Studies on the Mineral Metabolism During Pregnancy and Lactation. Biochem. J., 1932, 26, 1424.

178. FINOLA, G. C., TRUMP, B. S. AND GRIMSON, M.: Bone Changes in the Fetus Following the Administration of Dicalcium-Phosphate and Viosterol to the Pregnant Mother. Am. J. Obs. & Gyn., 1937, 34, 955.

179. FRASER, A. H. H., GODDEN, W. AND THOMSON, W.: Vet. J., 1933, 89, 404.

180. HOPKIRK, C. S. M., Austral. Vet. J., 1934, 10, 59.

181. THEOBALD, G. W.: The Causation of Eclampsia. Observations and Experiments. Lancet, 1930, 1, 1115.

182. GIVENS, M. H. AND MACY, I. G.: The Chemical Composition of the Fetus. J. Biol. Chem., 1933, 102, 7.

183. MACY, I. G. AND HUNSCHER, H. A.: An Evaluation of Maternal Nitrogen and Mineral Needs during Embryonic and Infant Development. Am. J. Obs. & Gyn., 1934, 27, 878.

184. HAMILTON, B.: The Calcium and Phosphorus Metabolism of Prematurely Born Infants. Acta Pediat., 1922, 2, 1.

185. COONS, C. M., SCHIEFELBUSCH, A. T., MARSHALL, G. B. AND COONS, R. R.: Studies in Metabolism during Pregnancy. Okla. Agr. Exp. Stat. Bull. No. 223, 1935.

186. COONS, C. M.: Iron Retention by Women during Pregnancy. J. Biol. Chem., 1932, 97, 215.

187. COONS, C. M. AND COONS, R. R.: Some Effects of Cod Liver Oil and Wheat Germ on the Retention of Iron, Nitrogen, Phosphorus, Calcium and Magnesium during Human Pregnancy. J. Nutrition, 1935, 10, 289.

188. CARPENTER, T. M. AND MURLIN, J. R.: Energy Metabolism of Mother and Child. Arch. Int. Med., 1911, 7, 184.

189. HASSELBACH, K. A.: Ein Beitrag zur Respirationsphysiologie der Gravidität. Skand. Arch. Physiol., 1912, 27, 1.

190. BAER, J. L.: Basal Metabolism in Pregnancy and the Puerperium. Am. J. Obs. & Gyn., 1921, 2, 249.

191. ROOT, H. F. AND ROOT, H. K.: The Basal Metabolism during Pregnancy and the Puerperium. Arch. Int. Med., 1923, 32, 411.

192. PLASS, E. D. AND YOAKUM, W. A.: Basal Metabolism Studies in Normal Pregnant Women with Normal and Pathologic Thyroid Glands. Am. J. Obs. & Gyn., 1929, 18, 556.

193. ROWE, A. W., GALLIVAN, D. E. AND MATTHEWS, H.: The Metabolism of Pregnancy. VI. The Respiratory Metabolism and Acid Elimination. Am. J. Physiol., 1931, 96, 101.

194. SANDIFORD, I., WHEELER, T. AND BOOTHBY, W. M.: Metabolic Studies during Pregnancy and Menstruation. Am. J. Physiol., 1931, 96, 191.

195. ROWE, A. W. AND BOYD, W. C.: Metabolism in Pregnancy. IX. The Foetal Influence on the Basal Rate. J. Nutrition, 1932, 5, 551.

196. BRODY, S.: Nutrition. Ann. Rev. Biochem., 1934, 3, 295.

CHAPTER VIII

DIAGNOSIS OF PREGNANCY

The existence of pregnancy is recognized by its subjective and objective effects.

The subjective manifestations or symptoms of pregnancy are:

1. Amenorrhea.
2. Morning sickness.
3. Bladder irritability.
4. Enlargement of the breasts.
5. Enlargement of the abdomen.
6. Quickening.
7. Lightening.

The objective manifestations or signs of pregnancy are:

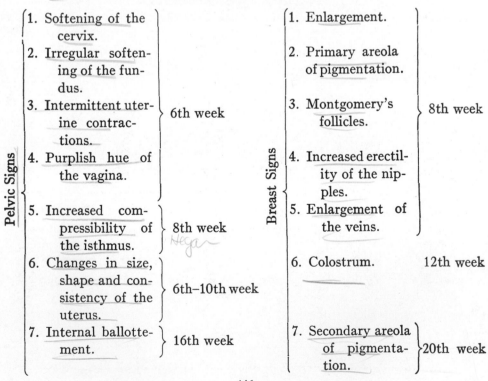

Pelvic Signs

1. Softening of the cervix.
2. Irregular softening of the fundus.
3. Intermittent uterine contractions.
4. Purplish hue of the vagina.
} 6th week

5. Increased compressibility of the isthmus. } 8th week

6. Changes in size, shape and consistency of the uterus. } 6th–10th week

7. Internal ballottement. } 16th week

Hegar

Breast Signs

1. Enlargement.
2. Primary areola of pigmentation.
3. Montgomery's follicles.
4. Increased erectility of the nipples.
5. Enlargement of the veins.
} 8th week

6. Colostrum. 12th week

7. Secondary areola of pigmentation. } 20th week

Abdominal signs

1. Intermittent uterine contractions.
2. Progressive enlargement of the uterus. } 16th week
3. Uterine souffle.
4. Fetal heart sounds
5. Fetal shock sounds.
6. Funic souffle. } 18th week
7. Progressive enlargement of the uterus.
8. Fetal movements.   20th week
9. External ballottement.   22nd week
10. Fetal outline.   24th week

Laboratory Tests

1. Aschheim-Zondek.
2. Friedman. } 5th–6th week
X-ray findings   12th–16th week

SYMPTOMS OF PREGNANCY

AMENORRHEA or the cessation of menstruation is the earliest symptom of pregnancy. In a young, healthy woman, who previously has been regular, the skipping of a period always leads to a suspicion of pregnancy. This symptom, therefore, is one of the best subjective evidences of pregnancy. Its value is increased by the failure of menstruation to appear in successive months, by the absence of other causes of amenorrhea and by the recognition of additional symptoms and signs which correspond to the duration of the suppressed menstruation.

Unfortunately, many conditions may give rise to amenorrhoea. Some of these are: chlorosis, pernicious anemia, tuberculosis, thyroid disorders, hypopituitarism, fear of possible pregnancy after exposure, emotional shock, change in environment or climate, and the menopause.

Occasionally, the first menstrual period is not entirely skipped and a small amount of bleeding occurs about the time that the regular flow is expected. This may be due to a threatened abortion or may be similar to the physiological bleeding that occurs in some animals when the maternal vessels are eroded by the invading trophoblast, or when blood which has been extravasated into the uterine glands is discharged into the uterine cavity.

Women with amenorrhea from other causes may conceive and, when they do, the possibility of pregnancy is not considered until other symptoms and signs appear. During lactation, for example, conception occasionally takes place prior to the return of menstruation, and the patient may be pregnant several months before this possibility is suspected.

MORNING SICKNESS is present in about 50 per cent of all pregnancies. At times, it is very mild and consists only of nausea accompanied by infrequent vomiting. Occasionally, however, this symptom is more troublesome, and almost daily vomiting occurs. In rare instances, the vomiting may become excessive and may threaten the patient's life. It then is known as hyperemesis gravidarum, a condition which will be discussed in the chapter on the Toxemias of Pregnancy. Morning sickness appears soon after the first period is skipped and grows worse for about one month, after which it gradually diminishes and finally disappears at the end of the first trimester.

The value of this symptom is greatly lessened by the fact that many other conditions cause nausea and vomiting.

BLADDER IRRITABILITY is quite constant in the second and third months, following which it is relieved as the uterus rises out of the pelvis. When lightening occurs near the end of pregnancy, pressure of the presenting part on the bladder again causes an increase in the frequency of urination.

This symptom, together with morning sickness, clinches the diagnosis for most women who merely suspected pregnancy when amenorrhea was first noted. Such certainty is not warranted by experience and competent obstetricians refuse to make a positive diagnosis until more satisfactory evidence is available.

BREAST CHANGES. In a woman who has never been pregnant, enlargement of the breasts and increased pigmentation around the nipples are somewhat significant, while the appearance of colostrum is very suggestive of pregnancy. On the other hand, no reliance may be placed upon these changes in multiparae, since the breast secretion may continue for a considerable time after weaning.

ENLARGEMENT OF THE ABDOMEN, as evidenced by increasing tightness of the clothing, often is a valuable symptom of pregnancy, particularly when the enlargement is progressive and is accompanied by a continuing amenorrhea. Too great reliance, however, should not be placed on this combination of subjective findings, since obesity and amenorrhea, as well as ovarian tumors and amenorrhea, are not uncommon.

QUICKENING, or the perception of fetal movements by the mother, usually is noted in all pregnancies that continue to term. As a rule, this symptom is observed a short time before the end of the fifth month, when the patient feels a flutter within her abdomen unlike anything that she has ever felt before. Occasionally, however, the patient may think that she "feels life" or quickening in the absence of pregnancy. Other conditions, therefore, simulate this symptom and lessen its value.

LIGHTENING is the term applied to the descent of the presenting part into the pelvis in the last month of pregnancy. It commonly occurs about two weeks before the onset of labor in primigravidae and often is absent until labor is established in multiparae. The patient usually states that the child is lower. She breathes more easily and notices that her clothing is looser. At the same time, edema and varicosities of the lower extremities are more marked and bladder irritability returns.

SIGNS OF PREGNANCY

Pelvic Signs

SOFTENING OF THE CERVIX, Goodell's sign, is due to the increased congestion that is observed early in all pregnancies. This change is sufficiently marked by the sixth week to render the cervix as soft as the lips, whereas the nonpregnant cervix has a consistency resembling that of the tip of the nose. A similar change in the cervix, that occurs in inflammatory and other congestive conditions, is confusing and greatly lessens the value of this sign. It therefore may be regarded as a possible but not probable evidence of pregnancy.

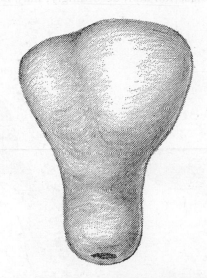

FIG. 79. Irregular softening of the uterus.

IRREGULAR SOFTENING OF THE UTERUS. About the sixth week, bimanual examination shows the uterus to be irregularly softened, as though it were developing unequally. One side seems softer and larger than the other and between these areas of differing density the impression noted by the examining finger is suggestive of a furrow (1) (Fig. 79).

This peculiar softening is felt in some women even though they are not pregnant. If, therefore, the patient has not been previously examined, it should be interpreted with caution. On the other hand, when the physician knows from previous examinations that the patient's uterus does not ordinarily show such a softening, the presence of this sign is quite indicative of pregnancy.

INTERMITTENT UTERINE CONTRACTIONS—Braxton Hicks' sign. The uterus contracts intermittently throughout pregnancy and these contractions may be felt on bimanual palpation within a few weeks after conception takes place (2).

Owing to the firmer consistency of the uterus during a contraction, the examining fingers should not be withdrawn until sufficient time for relaxation has elapsed; otherwise, the early signs in the uterus may be missed.

Since intermittent contractions occasionally occur in other conditions, the diagnosis of pregnancy cannot be made with certainty when they are detected, unless other and better evidence is at hand.

PURPLISH HUE OF THE VAGINA—Chadwick's sign. If any or all of the previously described signs are felt, the vagina may be inspected for the characteristic change in color that occurs early in pregnancy (3). This consists of a purplish discoloration of the anterior vaginal wall and cervix. It, like Goodell's sign, is the result of marked congestion and, accordingly, may be present in conditions other than pregnancy.

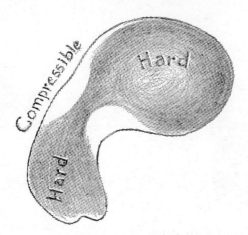 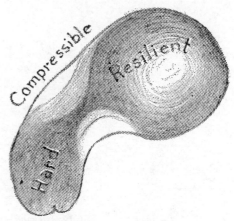

FIG. 80. Increased compressibility of the isthmus during contraction (Jewett).

FIG. 81. Increased compressibility of the isthmus during relaxation (Jewett).

INCREASED COMPRESSIBILITY OF THE ISTHMUS—Hegar's sign. Between the sixth and eighth week, bimanual examination shows an increased compressibility of the isthmus of the uterus (4) (Figs. 80 and 81).

Two fingers are introduced into the vagina and, after locating the cervix, they make slight pressure against the anterior wall of the uterus between the cervix and fundus while the fingers of the other hand indent the abdominal wall and make pressure on the posterior surface of the uterus at the same level. Often, the fingers come so near to each other that the uterus seems to be absent in this region, and the cervix and fundus give the impression of being two distinct entities, rather than opposite poles of the same organ (Fig. 82).

While these findings may be present in other conditions, similar compressibility of the isthmus is so rarely found outside of a uterine gestation that this sign is generally regarded as the best early pelvic evidence of pregnancy and, aside from the Aschheim-Zondek test and the x-ray findings, is the most reliable sign of pregnancy before the fetal heart tones are heard.

The more marked compressibility of the lower segment permits greater flexibility of the cervix and, at times, the latter may be moved without a corresponding movement of the fundus (5).

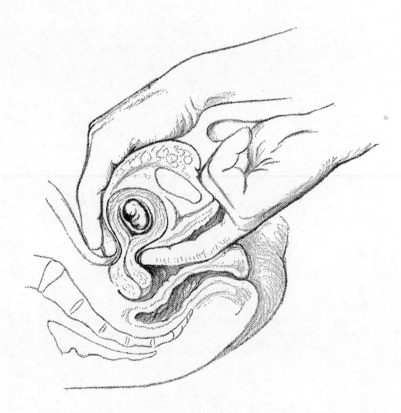

FIG. 82. Hegar's sign. Bimanual examination.

CHANGES IN THE SIZE, SHAPE AND CONSISTENCY. While none of the signs discussed are positive, when taken collectively they are quite reliable if the changes correspond to the duration of pregnancy that is indicated by the history. In doubtful cases, another examination should be made two or three weeks later. Should the additional changes then found correspond to the progressive alterations that are characteristic of that stage of pregnancy, a positive diagnosis may be made.

INTERNAL BALLOTTEMENT—vaginal rebound sign. After the fetus has grown sufficiently to be palpable on vaginal examination, a sudden tap on the presenting part causes it to rise in the amniotic fluid and then rebound so that it in turn taps the examining finger. This sign is first obtained in the fourth month and is almost certain evidence of pregnancy. In rare instances, however, it may be simulated by a pedunculated fibroid with ascites and other equally unusual combinations of conditions. Accordingly, it cannot be classed as positive but is regarded as the most certain of the probable signs (Fig. 83).

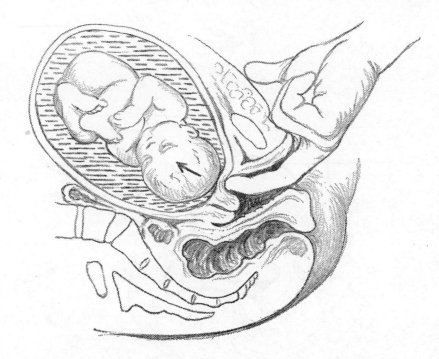

FIG. 83. Internal ballottement.

Breast Signs

ENLARGEMENT of the breasts, due to a deposition of fat and an increase in the glandular elements, is an almost constant accompaniment of pregnancy.

PRIMARY AREOLA OF PIGMENTATION. In most pregnancies, the pigmented area surrounding the nipples becomes darker and is particularly noticeable in brunettes (Fig. 84).

MONTGOMERY'S FOLLICLES are hypertrophied, sebaceous glands that project above the surface of the primary areola (Fig. 85).

INCREASED ERECTILITY OF THE NIPPLES is observed early in pregnancy (Fig. 86).

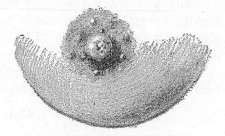

FIG. 84. Primary areola.   FIG. 85. Montgomery's follicles.

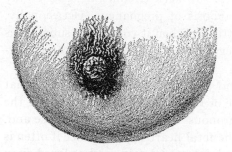

FIG. 86. Erectility of the nipples.   FIG. 87. Enlarged veins.

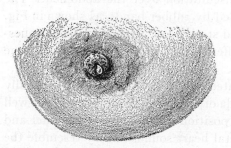

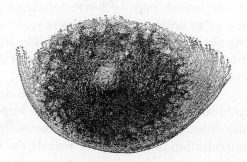

FIG. 88. Colostrum.   FIG. 89. Secondary areola
(*American Text Book of Obstetrics*).

ENLARGEMENT OF THE VEINS usually is observed in the early months and like the other early breast signs may also occur when the woman is not pregnant (Fig. 87).

COLOSTRUM. A thin secretion may be expressed from the ducts of the nipples about the end of the first trimester. It is a good sign of pregnancy in primigravidae, but occasionally occurs in women who are not and never have been pregnant (Fig. 88).

THE SECONDARY AREOLA OF PIGMENTATION consists of the mottled area of slightly lighter pigment changes which surround the primary areola and is observed in the fifth month. Like colostrum, it is a good but not infallible sign in primigravidae (Fig 89).

The breast signs, taken collectively in women who have not been pregnant before, constitute a fairly dependable, probable sign of pregnancy.

Abdominal Signs

INTERMITTENT UTERINE CONTRACTIONS, which were distinguishable as early as the sixth week by bimanual examination, may be felt through the abdominal wall after the uterus rises out of the pelvis. In such circumstances, they are much more valuable as an aid in the diagnosis of pregnancy. Occasionally, however, the uterus may contract intermittently when it contains a submucous fibroid. This sign, therefore, cannot be regarded as positive evidence of pregnancy.

THE UTERINE SOUFFLE is a soft sound similar to a cardiac murmur that may be heard over the large vessels on one or both sides of the uterus after the sixteenth week (6) This sound is synchronous with the maternal pulse and, accordingly, is easily differentiated from the fetal heart tones Since it often is heard over large abdominal tumors, too much reliance should not be placed upon a uterine souffle as a probable sign of pregnancy.

THE FETAL HEART SOUNDS constitute the best sign of pregnancy (6, 7). These sounds may be heard by direct auscultation over the abdomen. The use of an ordinary bell stethoscope, steadied by rubber bands, as shown in Fig. 90, likewise is very satisfactory. The head stethoscope, however, is an unquestionably superior instrument since it offers the added advantage of bone conduction.

The fetal heart is heard after the eighteenth week and its sounds normally are transmitted through the anterior scapula of the child. When the fetus is well developed, therefore, palpation shows the position of the anterior shoulder and auscultation in this vicinity reveals the fetal heart sounds. They resemble the ticking of a watch and their rate is much faster than the maternal pulse. Usually, it is from 120 to 150 per minute. Under conditions unfavorable to the child, the rate may be under 100 or over 160. Accordingly, the fetal heart sounds enable us not only to diagnose positively the existence of a pregnancy, but they also signify that the fetus is alive and, at times, they give warning of impending danger.

The rapid rate of the fetal heart serves as a satisfactory means of differentiating this sign from the uterine souffle. If the mother's radial pulse is felt at the same time that the physician listens to the fetal heart, he will have no difficulty in making the diagnosis.

FETAL SHOCK SOUND. The sound made by a sudden movement of the fetus is characteristic in the middle of pregnancy. To one familiar with this sound, the fetal shock sign is a positive indication that the woman is pregnant and that the child is alive.

FUNIC SOUFFLE. Occasionally, a rapid murmur, synchronous with the fetal heart tones, may be heard (9). This sound comes from the vessels in the umbilical cord and usually is first heard somewhat later than the fetal heart. When present, it is a positive sign of pregnancy.

PROGRESSIVE ENLARGEMENT OF THE UTERUS on abdominal palpation is a probable sign if the enlargement occurs at the rate customarily observed during pregnancy. When palpation at the fourth month and again four weeks later shows the progressive enlargement that is characteristic of pregnancy, the diagnosis may be made with a fair degree of certainty.

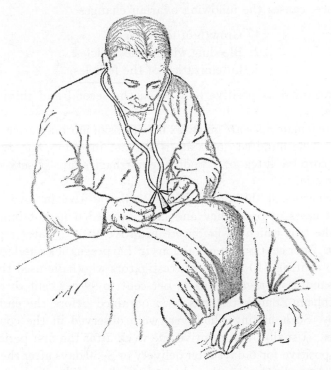

FIG. 90. Listening to the fetal heart tones with an ordinary stethoscope held in place by rubber bands.

ACTIVE FETAL MOVEMENTS can be felt by abdominal palpation about the fifth month. Unlike the symptom known as quickening, this objective evidence of fetal movements is a very valuable aid in the diagnosis of pregnancy, and in the hands of an experienced man is regarded as a positive sign.

EXTERNAL BALLOTTEMENT or passive fetal movements may be obtained during the fifth month and thereafter. Like internal ballottement, this is a very valuable and probable sign of pregnancy. It is obtained by gently tapping the fetus, after which the latter rebounds and returns the tap to the palpating fingers. When the fetus is so well developed that it almost completely fills the uterus, this sign cannot be obtained except in cases of breech presentation in which the more mobile head is ballottable in the fundus of the uterus.

FETAL OUTLINE. After the sixth month, the fetus may be sufficiently well outlined by abdominal palpation to justify a positive diagnosis of pregnancy. As the child grows, its outline becomes more and more clearly defined. Accordingly, this sign is more easily detected in the latter months.

URINE TESTS FOR PREGNANCY

THE ASCHHEIM-ZONDEK TEST is dependent upon the presence of a pituitary-like substance in the urine of the pregnant woman, which, when injected into immature mice, causes the following ovarian changes:

1. Growth of the follicles.
2. Bleeding within the follicles.
3. Luteinization of the follicles.

The test is regarded as positive only when the second and third changes are demonstrable.

Immature female mice are given six injections of morning urine over a period of two days. One hundred hours after the first injection, the ovaries are examined. If corpora lutea or corpora hemorrhagica are observed a positive diagnosis is made.

The originators of this test found it to be positive in seventy-six out of seventy-eight cases of pregnancy and later succeeded in obtaining a positive reaction in the two which at first were negative (9). A later report of their work shows 97.7 per cent positive reactions in 296 pregnancies and four erroneous results in 333 controls (10). Other investigators who have used the method in several thousand cases regard it as 98 per cent to 99 per cent correct (11, 12).

The Aschheim-Zondek test has been obtained before the end of the first lunar month. Such findings, however, were observed in the course of other investigations. Usually, it is positive one week after the first period is skipped and remains positive for 6 days after delivery or 8–30 days after the death of the fetus (12a). Accordingly, it is thought to depend upon the placenta or its derivatives rather than the presence of a living fetus. This opinion is further substantiated by the fact that the test is positive in cases of hydatidiform mole and chorionepithelioma.

FRIEDMAN TEST. The substitution of rabbits for mice has simplified the original technic. In the rabbit, ovulation does not occur until after coitus. The ovaries of an unmated female, therefore, do not contain corpora lutea or corpora hemorrhagica. Friedman, accordingly, assumed that the gonadotropic substance in the urine of pregnant women would cause these changes in the follicle and in a fairly large series of cases found that a diagnosis of pregnancy could be made in this manner.

Ten to twelve cubic centimeters of urine are injected into an unmated mature female rabbit on two successive days. Forty-eight hours after the first injection, the ovaries are examined for corpora lutea and corpora hemorrhagica. If they are found, a positive diagnosis is made. This test, accordingly, can be done in less time than the original one and apparently is equally reliable (13).

MAZER TEST. Within one week after the first skipped period, the amount of ovarian hormone present in the urine is sufficient to cause estrus changes in castrated animals.

In the Mazer test, adult castrated female mice are given five injections of urine, after which a vaginal spread is made. If it shows a preponderance of non-nucleated squamous epithelium and an absence of leukocytes, a positive diagnosis is made (14).

ROENTGEN RAY DIAGNOSIS OF PREGNANCY. Ossification centers appear very early in embryonic life and have been demonstrated as early as the sixth week (15). These, however, are so faintly shown on x-ray films that their detection in the pregnant woman is almost impossible before the 14th to 16th week, when a positive diagnosis can be made by this means (16, 17, 18, 19). Later, the outline of the fetal skeleton is easily discernible and, as a result, the x-ray is one of the best aids in differentiating pregnancy from a large tumor. In addition, it is an excellent means of determining presentation, position and posture, multiple pregnancy and dead fetus.

DURATION OF PREGNANCY. Although ovulation unquestionably takes place about the middle of the intermenstrual period, the exact date of its occurrence is not known. The beginning of pregnancy, accordingly, cannot be estimated from the rather indefinite time that the egg leaves the ovary. Likewise, the date of the fruitful coitus usually is unknown and therefore cannot be used in estimating the approximate time of fertilization. Since pregnancy begins with fertilization, and we have no means of knowing when this event occurs, the exact length of pregnancy cannot be determined.

Most women know the date of the onset of the last menstruation. Although this date is not very closely related to the time of ovulation and fertilization, it usually is the most accurate time available for the estimation of the duration of pregnancy. The duration of pregnancy, accordingly, is generally regarded as ten lunar months or 280 days after the beginning of the last menstrual period. This figure represents the average of a large number of observations in which full term pregnancies varied considerably in duration.

The average length of pregnancy after the date of the fruitful coitus is approximately 270 days. Here again considerable variation is observed, and students of the subject have placed the lower and upper limits between 230 and 329 days (20, 21, 22, 23, 24, 25, 26).

THE ESTIMATION OF THE EXPECTED DATE OF CONFINEMENT may be made by counting forward 280 days from the beginning of the last period. This date is easily calculated by the use of Naegele's rule in which we add 7 days to the onset of the last menstruation and count backward three months.   For example, if the beginning of the last period was July 4th, seven days would be added and three months deducted.   The expected date would then be the 11th day of April. The date thus determined is correct in only 10 per cent of the cases.   About 50 per cent of the remainder, deliver within one week of this estimated time.

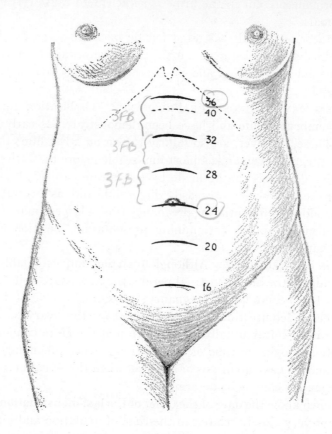

FIG. 91. The height of the fundus at the various weeks of pregnancy.

Many women believe that labor will begin about four and a half months after they first feel life.   This conclusion, however, is not supported by the experience of most obstetricians.   The onset of quickening, accordingly, is not very highly regarded as a means of estimating the duration of pregnancy.

In the last half of pregnancy, the height of the fundus may be of value. It is at the umbilicus at the sixth month or 24th week and is three finger-breadths above this point at the seventh month.   Four weeks later, the fundus rises another three finger-breadths and at the 36th week is slightly below the ensiform cartilage (Fig. 91).

A more accurate means of estimating the duration of pregnancy is to <u>de-</u>
<u>termine the size of the child by the method of Ahlfeld</u> and, from its size, calculate
the age according to Haas's rule.   One end of a pelvimeter is inserted into the
vagina and held against the presenting part while the other indents the upper
abdominal wall and rests upon the fundus of the uterus (Fig. 92).   Two centi-

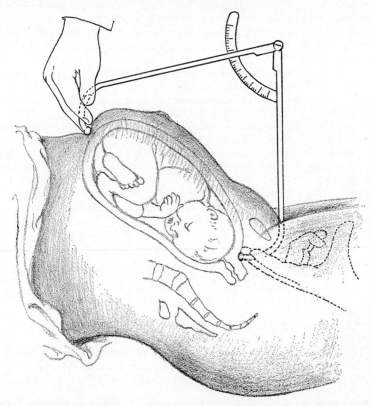

FIG. 92. Ahlfeld's method of measuring the length of the fetal ovoid.   After deducting 2 cm. for
the thickness of the abdominal wall and uterus, the remainder is multiplied by two to obtain the length
of the fetus.

meters are deducted from the measurement thus obtained to allow for the thickness of the abdominal wall and uterus.   The result is the length of the fetal ovoid.
This figure multiplied by two is the length of the fetus, since the latter is twice as
long as the fetal ovoid.   According to Haas's rule the fetal length is the square
of the month in centimeters up to the fifth month, after which it is five times the
month.   The length of the fetus, divided by five, therefore, is the approximate
duration of pregnancy.

Delicate women and those in ill health have a tendency to fall into labor
before the expiration of the customary 280 days, as do many women who are
compelled to work hard during pregnancy.   On the other hand, comfortable
surroundings and a sedentary life with little or no exercise are conducive to
protracted gestation.

REFERENCES

1. VON BRAUN, R.: Ueber Frühdiagnose der Gravidität. Zentralbl. f. Gyn., 1899, 23, 488.
2. HICKS, J. BRAXTON: Selected Essays and Monographs, chiefly from English Sources. New Sydenham Society, 1901, 173, 21.
3. CHADWICK, J. R.: The Value of the Bluish Coloration of the Vaginal Entrance as a Sign of Pregnancy. Tr. Am. Gyn. Soc., 1886, 11, 399.
4. REINL, C.: Ein neues sicheres diagnostisches Zeichen der Schwangerschaft in den ersten Monaten. Prag. med. Wchnschr., 1884, No. 26, 253.
5. McDONALD, E.: The Diagnosis of Early Pregnancy. Am. J. Obs., 1908, 57, 323.
6. Kegardec (quoted by Williams). Memoire sur l'auscultation appliquée à l'étude de la grossesse. Paris, 1822.
7. MAIOR, M.: Bibliothèque universelle des sciences, belles-lettres et arts. Geneva, 1818.
8. KENNEDY, E.: Observations on Obstetric Auscultation. N. Y., 1843, p. 139.
9. ASCHHEIM, S. AND ZONDEK, B.: Schwangerschaftsdiagnose aus dem Harn (Durch Hormonnachweis). Klin. Wchnschr., 1928, 1, 8.
10. ASCHHEIM, S.: Meine Schwangerschaftsdiagnose durch Hormonnachweis im Harn. Zeitschr. f. Artzl. Fortbild., 1929, 1, 5.
    Die Schwangerschaftsdiagnose aus dem Harn durch Nachweis des Hypophysenvorderlappenhormons, weitere praktische und theoretische Ergebnisse. Zentralbl. f. Gyn., 1929, 53, 15.
11. EHRHARDT, K.: The Aschheim-Zondek Pregnancy Reaction. Report based on Two Thousand Controlled Aschheim-Zondek Pregnancy Tests. S. G. & O. 1931, 53, 486.
12. WIESNER, B. P.: Report of Pregnancy Diagnosis Station. Brit. Med. J., 1933, 2, 296.
12a. GOLDBERGER, M. A., SALMON, U. J. AND FRANK, R. T.: Value of the Friedman Test in the Diagnosis of Intra-uterine and Extra-uterine Pregnancy. J. A. M. A., 1934, 103, 1210.
13. FRIEDMAN, M. H. AND LAPHAM, M. E.: A Simple, Rapid Procedure for the Laboratory Diagnosis of Early Pregnancies. Am. J. O. & G., 1931, 31, 405.
14. MAZER, C. AND HOFFMAN, J.: The Three Hormone Tests for Early Pregnancy. J. A. M. A., 1931, 96, 19.
15. HESS, J. H.: Diagnosis of the Age of the Fetus by the Use of Roentgenograms. Ill. M. J., 1918, 33, 73.
16. EDLING, L.: Ueber die Anwendung des Roentgenverfahrens bei der Diagnose der Schwangerschaft. Fortschr. a. d. geb. Roentgenstrahlen, 1911, 17, 345.
17. ALBERT-WEIL, E.: Un cas de Grossesse Diagnostiquée par la Radiographie. Paris Med., 1917, 7, 314.
18. BARTHOLOMEW, R. A., SALE, B. E. AND CALLOWAY, J. T.: Diagnosis of Pregnancy by the Roentgen Ray. J. A. M. A., 1921, 76, 912.
19. PETERSON, R.: Value of Pneumoperitoneal Roentgenography in Obstetrics and Gynecology. J. A. M. A., 1922, 78, 397.
20. LÖWENHARDT, P.: Die Berechnung und die Dauer der Schwangerschaft. Arch. f. Gyn., 1872, 3, 456.
21. AHLFELD, F.: Beobachtungen über die Dauer der Schwangerschaft. Monatschr. f. Geburtsk., 1869, 34, 180.
22. SCHLICHTING, F. X.: Statistisches über den Eintritt der ersten Menstruation und über Schwangerschaftsdauer. Arch. f. Gyn., 1880, 16, 203.
23. ISSMER, E.: Ueber die Zeitdauer der menschlichen Schwangerschaft. Arch. f. Gyn., 1889, 35, 310.
24. EDEN, T. W.: Duration of Pregnancy in its Medico-legal Aspect. Lancet, 1923, 1, 1199.
25. McCAFFREY, L. E.: Prolonged and Shortened Gestation Periods from Medical and Medico-legal Standpoints. Am. J. O. & G., 1925, 10, 107.
26. ENGLEMAN, F.: Die Begutachtung der Schwangerschaftsdauer vor Gericht in Alimentationsprozessen. Zentralbl. f. Gyn., 1927, 51, 30.

CHAPTER IX

THE MANAGEMENT OF PREGNANCY

The profound changes which take place in the maternal organism during pregnancy call for early, constant and careful supervision during the antenatal period. The life-saving effect of such care is shown by all maternal and infant mortality statistics. This supervision should begin soon after the first period is skipped. It should include a careful history, a thorough physical examination and a consideration of the following items:

1. Diet
2. Weight
3. Care of the bowels
4. Care of the kidneys
5. Care of the teeth
6. Clothing
7. Exercise and rest
8. Care of the breasts
9. Sexual intercourse
10. Return visits
11. Danger symptoms and signs

History. Much that will be helpful in the management of pregnancy and labor can be learned from the patient's history. Since the sequellae of certain illnesses cause grave complications in pregnancy, a knowledge of the previous illnesses and their sequellae should lead to the early recognition and, at times, to the prevention of some of the complications of pregnancy. The history of previous labors also should better enable us to plan the proper management of the coming labor. With this in mind, the onset, character, length and termination of each labor are ascertained and an attempt is made to learn the size and condition of each child at birth. If a normal-sized living child came through the pelvis without difficulty, it is reasonable to assume that the pelvis is ample and that a similar outcome may be expected in the coming labor. A careful history is so important that it seems appropriate to discuss more fully the various subdivisions included in the following history outline:

161

HISTORY OUTLINE

A. PAST HISTORY
1. Age
2. Duration of marriage
3. Diseases:
    Rickets
    Scarlet fever
    Tuberculosis
    Rheumatic fever
    Cardiac disease
    Syphilis
    Other serious illness
4. Surgical conditions
    Pelvic operations
    Abdominal operations
5. Menstrual history:
    Onset
    Frequency
    Duration
    Amount of flow
    Date of last period

B. PREVIOUS PREGNANCIES
1. Date of termination
2. Period of gestation
3. Complications:
    Bleeding
    Headache
    Edema
    Visual disturbances
    Albuminuria
    Elevated blood pressure
    Diminished output of urine
    Convulsions

C. PREVIOUS LABORS
1. Spontaneous or induced
2. Duration
3. Character

4. Termination:
    Spontaneous
    Operative
5. Complications
6. Puerperium:
    Hemorrhage
    Infection
    Other complications

D. PREVIOUS CHILDREN
1. Date of birth
2. Weight at birth
3. Alive at birth
4. Dead at birth
    When did fetal movements cease?
5. Premature or full term
6. Breast fed, how long?
7. Artificially fed
8. Age and condition at present time
9. If dead, age and cause of death

E. PRESENT PREGNANCY
1. Date and character of last menstruation
2. Date of quickening
3. Estimated date of confinement
4. Complications:
    Nausea and vomiting
    Bleeding
    Headache
    Edema
    Visual disturbances
    Elevation of blood pressure
    Albuminuria
    Shortness of breath

WHAT IS THE PATIENT'S AGE? If she is in her late thirties and is pregnant for the first time, the relative importance of the child is increased. In other words, the fact that she may never become pregnant again may influence one's judgment in the interests of the child in a manner which might not be considered in younger women who may have other children.

HOW LONG HAS SHE BEEN MARRIED? A lapse of several years between marriage and the first pregnancy, provided the lack of fertility has not been due to the use of contraceptives, may be associated with underdevelopment of the uterus, uterine and ovarian tumors or pelvic inflammatory disease, any one of which might give rise to difficulty during pregnancy and parturition.

HAS SHE HAD RICKETS? Was she a breast or a bottle-fed baby? Was she backward in learning to walk? Is she bow-legged or does she have other evidences of rickets? Because of the effect of rickets on the bony pelvis, any woman with a rachitic history should be suspected of having a marked contraction of the pelvis. In such women, accordingly, contracted pelvis should be ruled out by pelvimetry and x-ray examination at least six weeks before the end of gestation in order that cases of marked cephalo-pelvic disproportion may be terminated by Cesarean section before or at the onset of labor, before the membranes rupture and without the need for a vaginal examination immediately preceding the operation. Early recognition of the difficulty will thus result in the operation being performed under the most favorable circumstances.

HAS SHE HAD SCARLET FEVER? If so, were there renal complications? Many women who, in the course of pregnancy, show an elevation of blood pressure with or without albuminuria, often give a history of having had scarlet fever. Such patients, accordingly, require careful supervision.

HAS SHE HAD TUBERCULOSIS OR HAS SHE BEEN EXPOSED TO TUBERCULOSIS? Is there a history of loss in weight, night sweats, cough, etc.? Have any of her immediate family had tuberculosis? In all suspicious cases, an x-ray examination of the chest is indicated. Early recognition of tuberculosis affords both the internist and the obstetrician an opportunity to do much for the patient. Modern methods of therapy instituted at the right time greatly increase the patient's chance of recovery. On the other hand, the condition may be aggravated if the tuberculosis is not discovered until late in pregnancy or after the child is born.

HAS SHE HAD TONSILLITIS, CHOREA OR RHEUMATIC FEVER? The frequent occurrence of cardiac lesions complicating these conditions should direct our attention toward the possibility of cardiac disease whenever a patient has had tonsillitis, chorea or rheumatic fever.

HAS SHE SUFFERED FROM CARDIAC DISEASE?   Is there a history of shortness of breath, cyanosis, palpitation, rapid or irregular pulse?   Cardiac disease is a treacherous complication of pregnancy and should be recognized early in gestation in order that proper hygienic and therapeutic measures may be taken before a serious accident occurs.

HAS SHE HAD SYPHILIS?   Is there a history of miscarriages, eruption or falling hair?   Has she taken medicine for a long time?   Has she ever had intravenous injections?   Because the evidences of syphilis often are obscured in women, the best way to detect the presence of this complication is by the use of the Wassermann reaction routinely at the first visit of every new pregnancy case.

HAVE THERE BEEN OTHER SERIOUS ILLNESSES? Has she ever been sick enough to require bed rest or hospitalization?   If so, the character of the illness should be ascertained and the possible effects of its sequellae on pregnancy should be considered.

HAS SHE BEEN OPERATED UPON?   If so, what operation was done?   Has she been pregnant since the operation?   Was the uterus involved in the procedure?   Did it leave a scar in the uterus or was the uterus fixed to the abdominal wall?   Either of these might cause complications in pregnancy or labor.   Was a vaginal plastic operation done?   If so, the possibility of serious injury to the reconstructed pelvic supports by the passage of the child's head must be considered.   Was the cervix amputated?   Following amputation of the cervix, premature interruption of pregnancy or difficult labor may occur.   Was a Cesarean section done?   After this operation, the risk of rupture of the uterus during pregnancy and, more particularly, in the course of labor, should be kept in mind.

MENSTRUAL HISTORY.   Ascertain the date of the first menstruation, the interval between periods, the duration, amount of flow and the date of the beginning of the last menstruation.   The onset of puberty and the character of the menstrual cycle may give some clue to endocrine disfunction, the recognition of which may be helpful in the management of pregnancy and labor.   From the date of the last menstruation, the expected date of confinement is calculated.

HAS THE PATIENT BEEN PREGNANT BEFORE?   If so, when and how did each pregnancy terminate?   Whenever a history of abortion or premature labor is obtained, an effort should be made to learn the cause of the interruption of pregnancy in order that a recurrence of this accident may be prevented.   Were any of the previous pregnancies complicated by bleeding?   What was the cause of the bleeding? At what time did it occur? How was it treated? Was there any evidence of toxemia such as edema, visual disturbances, an elevated blood pressure, albuminuria or convulsions? Whenever a history of a previous toxemia is obtained, more careful supervision of the hygiene of pregnancy is indicated.

PREVIOUS LABORS. Were the previous labors spontaneous or induced? If induced, what was the indication for this procedure? How long did each labor last? What was the character of the labor pains? Did labor terminate spontaneously or was it terminated by operative intervention? If an operation was done, ascertain, if possible, the indication for and character of the procedure used. Was the labor complicated in any way? Did she bleed much after the delivery? Did she have chills and fever in the puerperium? How long did she remain in bed after each baby was born? Has her health been good since the birth of her children?

PREVIOUS CHILDREN. How many children has the patient had? What was their weight at birth? Were all of them born alive? If a child was born dead, did the fetal movements cease before labor began or were they lost in the course of the delivery? What was the cause of the child's death? Was the Wassermann reaction obtained? Was an autopsy done? Were all of the previous children born at term? If a child was born prematurely, what was the cause of the interruption of pregnancy? Were the children breast or artificially fed? If artificially fed, what was the cause of the failure of lactation? Ascertain the age and health of each child at the present time. If any are dead, what were their ages at the time of death and the causes thereof?

PRESENT PREGNANCY. From the date of the beginning of the last menstruation, the probable date of confinement is estimated. In this connection, the time of the fruitful coitus may also be of value. Has morning sickness been disturbing? Nausea and vomiting should receive prompt attention in order that they may not develop into hyperemesis gravidarum. Has there been any bleeding? Whenever there is a history of a threatened abortion, the patient should be cautioned to avoid all of the exciting causes of premature interruption of pregnancy. Has there been any evidence of toxemia such as headache, edema and visual disturbances? If so, more careful supervision is indicated. The blood pressure should be taken, the urine examined and the patient weighed more frequently than is the custom in a normal pregnancy. Has there been shortness of breath? This symptom also calls for a change in the patient's routine as well as a thorough investigation of the circulatory system.

OUTLINE OF PHYSICAL EXAMINATION

A. **Pulse, Temperature, Respiration**
B. **Blood Pressure**
C. **Weight**
D. **Survey of**
 Skin and nutrition
 Mouth, teeth and tonsils
 Thyroid
 Heart and lungs
 Breasts
 Extremities
E. **Abdominal Examination**
 Uterus—Axis
   Size
   Shape
   Contractions
   Fluid content
   Tumors
 Fetus—Presentation, Position and
    Posture
   Size
   Movements
   Head—Mobility
     Consistency
     Size
     Relation to pelvic
      inlet
  Heart sounds

F. **Vaginal Examination**
 Cervix—Position
   Length
   Consistency
   Dilatation
 Uterus—Consistency
   Size
   Shape
   Position
 Signs of pregnancy
 Presenting part
 Pelvic tumor
 Smears for gonococcus
G. **Pelvic Measurements**
 Intercristal
 Interspinous
 External conjugate
 Diagonal conjugate
 Transverse of outlet
 X-ray examination
H. **Urinalysis**
 Amount in 24 hours
 Specific gravity
 Albumin, Sugar
 Pus cells, Casts
I. **Blood Examination**
 Cell counts
 Hemoglobin
 Wassermann reaction

PHYSICAL EXAMINATION. After taking the history, a complete physical examination is made. This should include the various items tabulated in the above outline. From the obstetrical standpoint, the abdominal and vaginal examinations, together with the measurements of the pelvis, are most important. To avoid repetition, the reader is referred to the following chapter for the method of determining presentation, position and posture by palpation and to Chapter XIV for an explanation of the other items concerning the uterus and fetus which are included under the heading of abdominal examination.

In the early months of pregnancy, the vaginal examination, unless it is most gently done, may cause an abortion. For this reason, the physician should limit his manipulations to those which are necessary to make the diagnosis of pregnancy and to rule out malposition of the uterus. Six weeks before the estimated date of confinement, a final vaginal examination is indicated. At this time, the parts are considerably relaxed and thorough palpation without much discomfort is possible. It is then that an effort should be made to feel the promontory of the sacrum and measure the length of the diagonal conjugate diameter, the most valuable of all pelvic measurements. **If this measurement is under 11 cm. in length, the size of the pelvis should be determined by one of the more accurate x-ray techniques.** No vaginal examination should be made during the last month of gestation without aseptic precautions. At that time, rectal examination usually is satisfactory if the diagonal conjugate has been previously measured. Likewise, vaginal examination should not be employed in the presence of vaginal bleeding at any period of pregnancy, unless strict aseptic precautions are followed. The technique used under such circumstances is described in Chapter XIV.

Urinalysis is of value in the detection of nephritis, diabetes and pyelitis, all of which might be serious complications in the pregnant woman. In addition, examination of the urine is very helpful in the diagnosis and management of toxemia of pregnancy.

Because of the fetal drain upon the mother's stores of iron, the erythrocyte count, hemoglobin determination and examination of the blood cells are valuable aids in the early detection of anemia. As has been stated, the Wassermann reaction is the best means of diagnosing syphilis in the pregnant woman. It should be determined as early as possible in pregnancy in order that the fetuses of infected women may have the benefit of thorough antenatal treatment. The blood should be tested for the Rh factor. If it is Rh negative and the father's blood is Rh positive and the mother is pregnant for the first time, it is quite probable that this will be her only living child. She accordingly, should be given the same consideration as is shown to the elderly primipara who can have only one child. In this circumstance, conditions which place the life of the fetus in jeopardy should be treated by those procedures which will give the fetus the best chance of survival. Elective cesarean section often may be justifiable.

DIET. It usually is said that no special diet is required during pregnancy. If the patient is accustomed to eat nutritious and easily digestible food in properly balanced proportions, no change in her dietary routine should be necessary. Many women, however, do not eat properly and most of them take an excess of food. Because of the better utilization of food and because of the increase in the appetite, the danger of overeating is ever present. The ill effects of too much food, therefore, are encountered more often in this country than are those of too little food. Excessive weight gains are common and, in these overweight women, the tendency toward toxemia and difficult labors is increased. Although it is generally believed that the size of the fetus is not influenced by the size of the mother's diet, the author and an increasing number of other obstetricians are satisfied that the birth of overly large children can be prevented in the majority of instances by limiting the food intake to actual requirements, and increasing the exercise whenever the weight of the pregnant woman becomes excessive. Restriction of the diet to the point of depletion, on the other hand, results in the birth of undersized and premature infants. Likewise an insufficiency of certain essential food elements may lead to deficiency diseases in the mother, the most common of which is anemia. From the foregoing discussion it is evident that the diet during pregnancy merits serious consideration. In order that the food intake may be ample but not too abundant, and, at the same time, properly balanced, the dietary habits of each patient should be studied and regulated to suit the needs of pregnancy.

According to balance studies, an average intake of 2500 calories is required during pregnancy for a woman weighing 70 kg. and actively engaged in the care of her home (1, 2). Smaller women require less as do women living in elevator apartments in which the household duties are lighter. The caloric intake may be reduced slightly below this average in the early months and allowed to increase gradually until it exceeds this figure by several hundred calories at the eighth month. Because of the diminished muscular activity, near the end of gestation, the needs of the mother are then decreased in spite of the rapid growth of the fetus. For this reason, the diet should be reduced again in the last months of pregnancy. Irrespective of the amount of food prescribed, its effect should be checked at frequent intervals by observation of the patient's weight and by paltation of the fetus. At no time should the gain in weight exceed one pound per week and the size of the fetus, on palpation, should correspond to the period of gestation. During lactation, half of the caloric intake is returned in the milk. Since the average daily milk secretion is 500–600 cc. in the first month, 800 cc. in the second, and almost 900 cc. by the fifth month, the need for an additional intake while the baby is nursing is self-evident (3).

Proteins. To the nitrogen required for the maintenance of the maternal organism during pregnancy, there must be added the needs of the fetus (60 gm.), the placenta and membranes (19 gm.), uterus (39 gm.), and breasts (17 gm.), a total of at least 135 gm. Such a storage requires the daily utilization of about one-half gram of nitrogen above the metabolic needs of the non-pregnant woman. Unfortunately, the calculation of the additional protein requirements is not so simple. Nitrogen also is stored in the form of plasma proteins (increased 18 per cent), in the cellular elements of the blood (increased 20 per cent) and in the other tissue accretions of pregnancy. Accordingly, a minimum storage of at least 250 gm. or almost 1 gm. of nitrogen per day is essential. As was stated in the discussion of protein metabolism (Chapter VII), the average total storage of nitrogen according to balance studies is 514.9 gm. or 1.8 gm. (11 gm. protein) per day. Since this additional requirement is easily covered by the surplus nitrogen in the ordinary diet, there seems to be little need for an increase in the protein intake above the customary 70–100 gm. consumed daily by the average individual, provided the energy requirements are satisfied (1, 2). Because of the need of maintaining the serum proteins at a level sufficiently high to prevent a disturbance in water balance, an adequate protein intake is most essential, especially in the latter part of pregnancy. Lactation, on the other hand, requires progressively increasing amounts of nitrogen. Unless these are supplied by the food, the surplus acquired during pregnancy is rapidly depleted. If little or no surplus has been accumulated during the antenatal period and the diet is inadequate, the amount of breast secretion will be slight because of the fact that the concentration of proteins in the milk tends to remain constant. Inadequate proteins in the diet of lactating women, accordingly, have little effect on the protein concentration of the milk but they cause a lowering of the milk output to the level that corresponds to the protein supply. This, however, may be prevented by adding to the diet. Since half of the additional nitrogen is returned in the milk, two gm. of protein should be added to the diet for every gram of protein in the milk (4).

Carbohydrates are a source of energy during pregnancy and are required in increasing amounts as gestation progresses. The daily intake averages 150 gm. up to the 13th week and increases thereafter to 225 gm. at the end of pregnancy (1). In the early months, ample carbohydrates seem to lessen nausea and vomiting. On the other hand, a reduction of the intake to 150–200 gm. is said to prevent the interruption of pregnancy in certain cases of habitual abortion (5).

Fats. The accumulation of lipoids in the blood increases throughout pregnancy and neutral fat is more than doubled at term. Balance studies show that patients do satisfactorily on an average intake of slightly over 100 gm. daily (2) but fats are useful as a vehicle for some of the essential vitamins and they aid in the fat metabolism of the fetus, the fat content of which increases from 1.8 per cent in the 7th month to 11.75 per cent at term. Excessive amounts of fat, however, should be avoided because they tend to disturb the normal ketogenic-antiketogenic ratio.

Water. About 1 cc. of liquid is ingested for each calorie of food taken. This amounts to about $2\frac{1}{2}$ liters per day. Such quantities of fluid, however, cannot be given to all patients since a disturbance in water balance may occur and lead to retention. For this reason, **the weight and urinary output should be observed at frequent intervals in order that occult edema may be detected and relieved by catharsis and restriction of the fluid intake.**

Calcium. The calcium content of the fetus averages about 23 gm. at birth. This represents an average utilization of 0.08 gm. daily throughout pregnancy. Almost two-thirds of the total deposition, however, takes place during the last month. If one-third of the calcium intake is assimilated, the diet during the last two months would have to provide at least 0.8 gm. of calcium daily. When this is added to the maintenance requirement for good health a total of 1.45 gm. should be contained in the food at least during the last trimester of pregnancy. Balance studies show a storage of calcium slightly above the fetal needs on a daily intake ranging from 0.96 to 1.98 gm. and averaging 1.4 gm. (6, 7). It would seem, therefore, that at least one gram of calcium should be provided during the early months and $1\frac{1}{2}$ gm. in the last trimester. The effect of marked calcium and vitamin D deficiencies was discussed in Chapter VII. Although osteomalacia and fetal rickets are not uncommon in certain parts of India and China, they are extremely rare in this country. Evidences of lesser deficiencies usually are slight. It has not been proven that dental caries is due to a fetal drain upon the mother's calcium (8, 9, 10) but the effect of a calcium-deficient diet upon the subsequent development of rickets in the child is established (11). Granted that the feeding of an excess of calcium and vitamin D does favor the birth of children with an increased amount of calcium in their bones, it is doubtful whether an increase in the hardness of the fetal head is desirable. **Hard heads lead to obstetric difficulties and are easily fractured.**

Adequate calcium and phosphorus are necessary for successful lactation. About four times as much calcium must be taken with the food as is contained in the milk secreted (12). When this is added to the maintenance requirements of the lactating mother, one to two gm. of calcium should be taken daily for a milk yield of from 500–1000 cc.

Iron. As was noted in Chapter VII, the average fetus at birth contains 246 mg. of iron of which all but 40 mg. are acquired during the last trimester. An additional 553 mg. are stored by the mother in the course of pregnancy. The diet, accordingly, should provide about 800 mg. during gestation or almost 3 mg. above the 15 mg. per day ordinarily required in the non-pregnant state. In order that the mother's stores may be spared, a daily ration sufficient to provide for the absorption of 18–20 mg. of iron is indicated. The supply of vitamin B complex likewise should be adequate and this should preferably be obtained in its natural state from the natural foods. In addition, occasional blood studies are indicated and whenever the hemoglobin falls below 10 gm. per 100 cc., (70 Sahli), some preparation of iron should be given or, better still, the latter may be given prophylactically.

Vitamin A. Experiments on rats have shown that diets deficient in vitamin A lead to the birth of a high percentage of deadborn and stunted off-spring (13) and during a drought in California, it was observed that the calves of cows deprived of vitamin A during pregnancy succumbed in one to five days after birth from diarrhea while the young of properly fed mothers were not so afflicted (14). In this connection, it is of interest to recall the discussion in Chapter V on the permeability of the placenta to vitamin A. Very little if any of this vitamin passes through the placental barrier and it is not abundant in the newborn infant. In addition to its possible deleterious effect on the fetus, lack of vitamin A may be a predisposing factor in the etiology of puerperal infection. Animals deprived of vitamin A show a greater incidence of puerperal infection than do those on a complete diet (15) and, in a series of 550 pregnant women, in which alternate patients were given an extra amount of vitamin A in the last month of pregnancy, the 275 who were on the vitamin-rich diet had a morbidity of 1.1 per cent while the morbidity of those not so treated was 4.7 per cent (16).

Since a daily intake of 1400–2000 international units has been found to be necessary for the prevention of measurable signs of deficiency, 3000 units are regarded as the desirable minimum for an adult weighing 70 kilograms (17). Because of the added needs of pregnancy, it has been estimated that at least 5000 I.U. should be taken daily throughout gestation (18). Due to the fact that only 50 per cent of the carotene in fat-free diets is absorbed while 80–90 per cent is utilized when the diet contains a moderate amount of fats, the need for fat as a vehicle is apparent (19).

Vitamin B complex. When vitamin B_1 is withheld completely during the first half of pregnancy in animals, all fetuses are aborted and its withdrawal after the middle of gestation leads to the birth of offspring lacking in vigor (85, Chapter V). Saturation studies show that more vitamin B is required to saturate and keep saturated the pregnant woman than is necessary in the non-pregnant state (20). Latent beri-beri and pellagra are often brought out by pregnancy in those districts in which these deficiency diseases are prevalent (21). Polyneuritis also is a not infrequent complication of hyperemesis gravidarum whenever the vomiting is allowed to continue long enough to cause an avita-minosis (22). The lack of certain elements of vitamin B complex is also thought to be a factor in the etiology of hemorrhagic disease of the newborn (23), the incidence of which is very high in cases of fetal rickets which are born to osteo-malacic mothers (24). Pregnancy likewise makes extra demands on the other factors of the vitamin B complex and a deficiency in some of these is thought to be responsible for gestational anemia. In India, where macrocytic anemia commonly develops during pregnancy, it has been observed that monkeys fed on a diet similar to that of the native Indian women develop megaloblastic hyper-plasia of the bone marrow which can be cured by the addition of the heat stable factor of yeast. Since yeast, liver and other meats, when added to the ordinary diet, have a similar effect on the same type of anemia in pregnant women, this condition is thought to be caused by an inadequacy of vitamin B complex in the diet (25, 26, 27). From the foregoing discussion, it may be seen that ample supplies of vitamin B complex should be included in the diet of pregnant and lactating women and from 150 to 250 I.U. have been recommended by the League of Nations Health Organization (18).

Vitamin C. That there is an increased need for vitamin C in pregnancy is shown by the observation that the level of ascorbic acid in the blood decreases as gestation advances. Irrespective of the diet, the amount present at term (43 mg.) is little more than half that present in the earlier months (0.72 mg.) and it is difficult to maintain the normal level of 1 mg. per 100 cc. unless the diet is supplemented by additional ascorbic acid (28). From this it may be seen that the ascorbic acid of the blood does not respond so promptly to dietary additions of vitamin C late in pregnancy as it does in the non-pregnant state. Latent scurvy in the fetus has been suggested as a factor in the etiology of cerebral and other hemorrhages which occur during or soon after birth and play no small part in neonatal mortality statistics (29). Even though the concentration of ascorbic acid in the mother's blood may be relatively low at term, that of the fetus usually is well above 0.5 mg. per 100 cc. (28). While the amount of vitamin C present may be sufficient to protect the maternal organism against scurvy, it may not be adequate for good health since scurvy is not the first evidence of deficiency (30). Although 33–64 mg. per 100 cc. have been found to be the minimum requirement in 100 pregnant women, not less than 100 mg. of ascorbic acid or 2000 I.U. of vitamin C daily are recommended during pregnancy (31). Whenever vomiting or diarrhea interfere with the taking of sufficient food to provide the required amount of ascorbic acid, parenteral administration of 100 mg. daily are recommended until the difficulty is corrected and oral administration may be resumed.

Vitamin D. Pregnant animals fed ample rations of vitamin D give birth to larger pups and both the mothers and their young have a higher calcium and phosphorus content than those on corresponding diets without Vitamin D. By promoting the assimilation of calcium and phosphorus by the mother, accordingly, vitamin D helps to prevent the fetal drain on the maternal stores of these elements (32). Deficient vitamin D likewise is thought to increase the tendency toward the subsequent development of rickets and dental caries in the offspring (11). On the other hand, animals given an excess of viosterol during pregnancy do not readily become pregnant again (33), their pregnancies may be prolonged and their nasal tissues may show evidence of atrophic rhinitis (34). In addition, there is the danger of causing so great a calcification of the cranial vault that molding of the head during parturition may be impossible. Because of these dangers, caution should be used in the administration of vitamin D to women during pregnancy. If sunshine is available, the time-honored custom of having the patient spend part of each day out of doors in the sunshine is a safer means of promoting calcium and phosphorus metabolism. During the winter months, when overcast days are so common, the diet, however, may be fortified with vitamin D.

Vitamin E. Animals on a diet deficient in vitamin E may not conceive. If they do, the fetuses often are aborted (35, 36). In these cases, it is thought that a lack of vitamin E is responsible for a failure of placental function. Similarly, satisfactory conceptions and normal pregnancies have been obtained by the giving of this vitamin to sterile animals with ovarian disfunction (37). Vitamin E also has been successfully used in the treatment of habitual abortion (38, 39). Vitamin E is widely distributed in grains, vegetables, meat, milk and butter. It usually, therefore, is taken in sufficient amounts in the ordinary well-balanced diet. The fact that it may deteriorate when the fat vehicle becomes rancid may, in some instances, lead to a deficiency. The use of wheat germ oil is still in its experimental stage but some reports give promise of its usefulness in certain cases of habitual abortion.

In summarizing these data, it may be stated that the daily requirements of the pregnant woman are: 70–100 gm. of protein, 150–250 gm. of carbohydrate, 100 gm. of fat, 1–1½ gm. of calcium, 18 mg. of iron, 5000 I.U. of vitamin A, 150–250 I.U. of vitamin B, 2000 I.U. of vitamin C or 100 mg. of ascorbic acid, 340 I.U. of vitamin D. The caloric intake should average 2200–2500 calories in the first half of pregnancy and 2500–2800 calories in the second half for an actively employed woman weighing about 150 pounds. Increased or decreased allowances should be made for patients over or under this figure. Alterations also are indicated when the weight gains observed during pregnancy are abnormal. The requirements thus summarized are fulfilled by the following dietary recommendations:

Foods which must be taken each day. Milk—3 glasses (600 cc.); orange juice—1 glass (200 cc.); butter—5 squares (50 gm.); whole wheat bread—4 slices (100 gm.); cheese—25 gm. and one egg. These articles should be included in the daily diet of every pregnant woman and should be taken in the amounts specified except in the case of bread which may be varied according to the changes in weight that occur. It is well to divide the milk between the three meals, taking a glass at the beginning of each meal. In addition, the milk should be somewhat masticated as is the custom with soups and broths. It then becomes a part of the meal and less of the other foods will be taken.

Foods rich in protein. Meat (beef, lamb, mutton, liver, ham, chicken) or fish are to be taken daily in 100 gm. portions up to the eighth month after which they are to be given every other day. Fish and liver are each recommended at least once a week. Two eggs may be substituted for the meat portion at any meal. On the meat-free days in the last two months, the protein requirements are met by increasing the vegetables rich in protein such as beans and peas and by doubling the daily allotment of cheese. In addition to being rich in protein, cheese also has a high content of calcium and iron. It, therefore, is a valuable food particularly in the last trimester. If the patient gains in weight too rapidly, cottage cheese is preferable to the other varieties since its low fat content adds less to the caloric intake. Care should be taken to avoid too low a protein intake because of its possible effect on water retention.

Foods rich in carbohydrate. One of the following items should be taken at two of the three daily meals throughout pregnancy: potato (100 gm.); beans— canned (100 gm.); beans—Lima (100 gm.); beans—dry (25 gm.) (to be baked); peas (100 gm.); sweet corn (100 gm.); macaroni (50 gm.); rice (50 gm.); corn meal (50 gm.); oatmeal (50 gm.) shredded wheat (50 gm.). A small serving or half portion of any of these may be used in the place of bread.

Other vegetables. Twice daily, the diet should contain a large serving of a leafy green vegetable and another large serving of a root or other vegetable as noted under the two following headings. One or the other of these should be taken in its raw state. These materials add to the vitamins and bring the minerals up to their required levels. It, therefore, is important that they be taken in adequate amounts.

Leafy vegetables. Beet tops, Brussel sprouts, cabbage, chard, dandelion greens, endive, kale, lettuce, spinach and water cress are recommended as leafy vegetables and should be included in two meals each day.

Root and seed vegetables such as asparagus, broccoli, beets, carrots, cauli-flower, onions, parsnips, string beans, tomatoes and turnips are to be served in 100 gm. portions twice daily.

Because of their high vitamin A content, either lettuce, spinach or chard should be given at least once daily. Likewise, one meal each day should include carrots, string beans or tomatoes.

Fruits. An apple, a pear, a fig, four dates, a bunch of grapes, a banana, a portion of cherries, blackberries, raspberries, strawberries, a dish of prunes, peaches, apricots, one slice of canned pineapple or one-half grapefruit twice daily are to take the place of the ordinary rich pastries and desserts.

This diet provides approximately 83 gm. of protein, 207 gm. of carbohydrate, 96 gm. of fat, 1.4 gm. of calcium, 17.5 mg. of iron and about 2000 calories. On the meat-free days, in the latter months of pregnancy, it contains 20 gm. more of carbohydrate and 17 gm. less of protein. If the patient gains too rapidly, **a portion or all of the bread may be omitted and other carbohydrates are to be diminished.** Should more energy be required, on the other hand, an increase in the carbohydrates is indicated. The food tables on pages 175, 176 and 177 will be useful in the preparation of modified diets.

FOOD TABLE

	PRO-TEIN	CARB.	FAT	CALC.	IRON	VITAMINS					CALO-RIES
						A	B	C Ascor-bic Acid	D	G	
	Gm.	Gm.	Gm.	Gm.	Mg.	I.U.	I.U.	Mg.	I.U.	U.	
Required	70 to 100	150 to 225	100	1 to 1.5	18 to 20	3000 to 5000	150 to 250	100	340	—	2200 to 2800

Foods Necessary Each Day

	PROTEIN	CARB.	FAT	CALC.	IRON	A	B	C	D	G	CALORIES
Milk (3 gl.), 600 cc.......	20.69	31.35	25.	.739	1.25	1752	13.8	4.2	16.8	214	432
Orange juice (1 gl.), 100 cc..	.96	13.90	.24	.029	.48	91	40.	63.2	—	15	61
Butter, 5 squares..........	.5	—	40.5	.008	.1	2530	—	—	18.	—	357
Bread, whole wheat (4 slices), 100 gm..........	9.70	49.7	.9	.031	.8	15	75.	—	—	160	244
1 egg..................	6.7	—	5.75	.0315	1.56	770	16.	—	24.	45	73
Cheese, 25 gm............	6.45	—	6.75	.19	.32	932	—	—	—	18	88
Total..................	45.	94.95	79.34	1.0285	4.51	6090	144.8	67.4	58.8	452	1255

Foods Rich in Protein

	PROTEIN	CARB.	FAT	CALC.	IRON	A	B	C	D	G	CALORIES
Beef, 100 gm.............	20.9	—	15.3	.013	3.0	60	30.	1.6	—	60	129
Lamb, 100 gm............	19.7	—	12.7	.011	2.9	—	119	2.5	—	—	192
Mutton, 100 gm..........	19.8	—	12.4	.011	2.9	31	119	2.5	—	—	192
Ham, 100 gm............	15.3	—	20.8	.023	2.14	—	90	1.9	—	—	263
Liver, 100 gm............	19.	—	5.3	.011	8.2	52600	150	24.	10.	800	123
Chicken, 100 gm..........	21.5	—	2.5	.01	3.	—	—	—	—	—	108
Eggs (2).................	13.4	—	10.5	.063	3.1	1540	32	—	48.	99	147
Average................	18.5	—	11.3	.02	3.	+	+	—	+	+	165

Foods Rich in Carbohydrate

	PROTEIN	CARB.	FAT	CALC.	IRON	A	B	C	D	G	CALORIES
Potato (1), 100 gm........	2.0	19.1	.1	.013	1.02	56	30	16	—	15	85
Beans, dry, 25 gm. Bkd....	5.6	14.9	.45	.037	2.5	+	4	—	—	—	86
Beans canned, 100 gm.....	6.9	19.6	2.2	—	—	—	15	—	—	—	122
Beans, lima (fresh), 100 gm.	7.5	23.5	.8	—	2.4	—	—	23	—	100	131
Macaroni, 50 gm..........	6.7	37.	.45	.011	.6	—	—	—	—	—	171
Peas fresh, 100 gm........	7.	17.7	.4	.028	2.	1940	120	4.8	—	100	100
Rice, 20 gm..............	1.6	4.7	.06	.0022	.18	—	—	—	—	—	69
Sweet corn, 100 gm........	3.7	20.5	1.2	.006	.47	—	66	3.5	—	—	107
Corn meal, 50 gm.........	4.6	37.7	.95	.008	.45	—	—	—	—	16	178
Oat meal, 50 gm..........	8.	33.7	3.6	.0325	2.4	70	42	—	—	+	200
Shredded wheat, 50 gm....	5.25	38.9	.7	.021	2.25	—	—	—	—	—	185
Average................	5.35	24.3	.99	.0176	1.43	+	12+	16+	—	+	130

Cheese

	PROTEIN	CARB.	FAT	CALC.	IRON	A	B	C	D	G	CALORIES
American, 50 gm..........	14.8	—	19.2	.465	.65	++	—	—	—	+	227
Cottage, 50 gm...........	11.6	—	.5	.041	.65	+	—	—	—	+	51
Cream, 50 gm............	12.9	—	16.8	.465	.65	++	—	—	—	+	208
Roquefort, 50 gm.........	11.3	—	14.8	.465	.65	++	—	—	—	+	179
Swiss, 50 gm.............	13.8	—	17.4	.465	.65	++	—	—	—	+	217
Average................	12.9	—	13.7	.38	.65	++	—	+	—	+	176

	PRO-TEIN	CARB.	FAT	CALC.	IRON	VITAMINS					CALO-RIES
						A	B	C Ascor-bic Acid	D	G	
	Gm.	Gm.	Gm.	Gm.	Mg.	I.U.	I.U.	Mg.	I.U.	U.	
Required	70 to 100	150 to 225	100	1 to 1.5	18 to 20	3000 to 5000	150 to 250	100	340	—	2200 to 2800

Leafy Green Vegetables

	PROTEIN	CARB.	FAT	CALC.	IRON	A	B	C	D	G	CALORIES
Cabbage, 100 gm..........	1.4	5.6	.2	.046	.43	900	25	20.	—	30	28
Chard, 100 gm............	1.4	4.4	.2	.15	3.09	23000	+	—	—	—	25
Dandelion, 100 gm........	2.7	8.8	.7	.084	3.05	28000	++	8	—	75	51
Lettuce, 65 gm............	.78	1.88	.13	.011	.325	945	9.6	.3	—	24	11.7
Spinach, 100 gm..........	2.3	3.2	.3	.078	2.55	2630	20.	++	—	100	24
Water cress, 100 gm.......	1.7	3.3	.3	.157	2.97	+++	60.	24.	—	60	23
Average.................	1.7	4.53	.3	.087	2.069	+++	27	++	—	58	27.1

(Lettuce, Spinach, Chard, or Dandelion should be taken at least once daily)

Root and Seed Vegetables

	PROTEIN	CARB.	FAT	CALC.	IRON	A	B	C	D	G	CALORIES
Asparagus, 100 gm........	2.2	3.9	.2	.021	1	350	—	12	—	—	26
Beans, string, 100 gm......	2.4	7.7	.2	.055	1.16	600	50	1	—	25	41
Beets, 100 gm.............	1.6	9.6	.1	.028	.85	—	70	2.7	—	24	45
Carrots, 100 gm..........	1.2	9.3	.3	.045	.62	1900	60	1.	—	30	45
Cauliflower, 100 gm.......	2.4	4.9	.2	.122	.94	38	110	19.	—	60	30
Onion, 100 gm............	1.6	9.9	.3	.041	.48	25	40	2.6	—	10	48
Parsnip, 100 gm...........	1.5	18.2	.5	.06	.77	30	++	5.	—	12	83
Tomato, 100 gm..........	.9	3.9	.4	.011	.44	1100	40	12.9	—	17	22
Turnip, 100 gm...........	1.1	7.1	.2	.056	.52	—	40	17.	—	—	34
Average.................	1.6	8.2	.27	.048	.75	1200+	60	+	—	25	36+

(String Beans, Carrots, or Tomatoes should be taken at least once daily)

Fruits

	PROTEIN	CARB.	FAT	CALC.	IRON	A	B	C	D	G	CALORIES
Apple, 250 gm............	1.00	35.0	1.25	0.175	.90	250	40	.1	—	25	157
Apricots, 100 gm.........	1.10	13.4	—	0.013	.60	3700	±	.8	—	42	56
Banana, 100 gm..........	1.20	13.0	.60	.008	.65	333	30	1.0	—	25	100
Blackberries, 150 gm......	1.95	17.8	1.50	.048	1.35	420	17	—	—	—	94
Cherries, 100 gm.........	1.10	14.8	.50	.019	.40	300	+	3.1	—	—	62
Dates (4), 33 gm..........	.70	26.1	.90	.023	1.20	50	10	—	—	—	113
Grapefruit (½), 150 gm....	.75	15.2	.30	.031	.40	±	40	39.	—	40	66
Grapes (1 bunch), 150 gm..	1.50	21.6	1.80	.027	1.10	22	±	1.5	—	—	108
Peach (1), 100 gm.........	.50	12.0	.10	.010	.33	70	10	1.0	—	—	50
Pear (1), 100 gm..........	.70	15.8	.40	.015	.32	8	30	1.0	—	22	69
Pineapple canned (1 slice), 65 gm...................	.26	23.6	.45	.005	.24	18	25	6.76	—	—	100
Prunes (4), 33 gm.........	.70	24.4	—	.019	.95	300	22	—	—	+	100
Strawberries (1 cup), 175 gm....................	1.40	14.1	1.05	.059	1.19	±	+	80.5	—	±	71
Average.................	.99	18.9	.80	.035	.74	++	28	+	—	31	88

176

FOOD TABLE—*Concluded**

	PRO-TEIN	CARB.	FAT	CALC.	IRON	VITAMINS					CALO-RIES
						A	B	C Ascorbic Acid	D	G	
	Gm.	Gm.	Gm.	Gm.	Mg.	I.U.	I.U.	Mg.	I.U.	U.	
Required	70 to 100	150 to 225	100	1 to 1.5	18 to 20	3000 to 5000	150 to 250	100	340	—	2200 to 2800

Summary

	PRO-TEIN	CARB.	FAT	CALC.	IRON	A	B	C Ascorbic Acid	D	G	CALO-RIES
STAPLE foods taken each day	45.	94.95	79.34	1.0285	4.51	6090	144.8	67.4	58.8	452	1255
PROTEIN foods once daily	18.5	—	11.3	.02	3.	+	+	—	+	+	165
CARBOHYDRATE foods twice daily	10.36	49.	3.	.035	2.85	—	—	16+	—	—	260
VEGETABLES, leafy, twice daily	3.40	9.	.6	.174	4.138	1787+	54.	+	—	116	54
VEGETABLES, root, etc., twice daily	3.2	16.4	.54	.096	1.5	1200+	120	10+	—	50	72
FRUITS twice daily	1.98	37.8	1.60	.07	1.48	+	56	+	—	62	176
Total	82.44	207.1	96.38	1.42	17.48	9077+	374.8	93.4+	58.8	680	1982

* Values taken from Sherman, Chemistry of Foods, 1938 and Nutritional Abstracts and Reviews.

Hot breads, rich pastry and fried or highly seasoned foods should be avoided entirely and the use of **salt and sodium compounds** should be restricted as much as possible.

It is better to take the large meal in the middle of the day. This should include at least one raw leafy vegetable with one or two cooked vegetables in addition to the more concentrated foods. Eating between meals is to be avoided except in the early months when it may be indicated as part of the treatment of morning sickness.

During the first trimester, many patients do better on a diet rich in carbohydrates. This is particularly true if morning sickness is troublesome. An abundance of potatoes, rice, bread, cereals, sugar, wholesome candy, figs, dates and preserves is indicated at this time. Frequent small meals also are helpful when nausea and vomiting are excessive. As soon as the nausea disappears, however, these carbohydrate additions and the increased frequency of the meals should be discontinued, in order that an excessive gain in weight may be avoided.

In the second trimester, a balanced regimen with careful attention to the mineral and vitamin requirements is essential. Instead of the almost exclusive bread, butter, meat and potato diet which is so common in many American homes, liberal quantities of milk and vegetables should be added. The weight changes observed at the monthly examination will serve as a guide to the patient's needs. Ordinarily, a gain of over three pounds per month is due to over-indulgence in carbohydrates and fats and their reduction is indicated.

During the third trimester, strict observance of the preceding recommendations is necessary in order that toxemia and overgrowth of the child may be avoided. As has been stated, it is well at this time to replace part of the proteins of meat, fish and eggs with those contained in vegetables. In the last two months, women do better if they take meat, fish and eggs only every other day.

As the uterus enlarges, smaller meals, taken more frequently, may add to the patient's comfort.

The appearance of any of the symptoms or signs of toxemia calls for special dietary instructions which are discussed in the chapter on toxemia. If there is any doubt in this connection, a diet composed exclusively of milk or of milk and vegetables without salt is indicated until a diagnosis can be made.

Most authorities claim that the size of the child cannot be influenced by dietary measures. While the author has not attempted to reduce the weight of any children below normal limits, he has observed in a number of cases that an exclusively milk diet during the last months usually is followed by the birth of a small child—5 to 6 pounds. He likewise has found that the development of excessively large children, as a rule, can be prevented by proper regulation of the diet.

WEIGHT. The patient should be weighed at each prenatal visit. An excessive gain in weight may be due to too great an increase in adipose tissue or to fluid retention. An effort should be made to keep the gain under four pounds per month. This usually can be accomplished by following the dietary recommendations previously given. As therein stated, carbohydrates, particularly bread, sugar, candies and pastries must be restricted or entirely eliminated when there is a tendency toward obesity. If the gain has been very rapid and excessive, water retention should be considered. Fluid elimination is then to be favored by the use of a saline cathartic and restriction of liquids. Recurrence of the retention usually can be controlled by having the patient limit her fluid intake to an amount equal to or slightly under the output of the preceding 24 hours. This step may be simplified if she will keep a daily fluid intake and output record. In addition, the salt intake should be rigidly restricted and all patients with water retention should be more carefully supervised in order that other evidences of toxemia may be detected at their onset.

CARE OF THE BOWELS. During pregnancy, constipation is a common complaint which becomes aggravated as the enlarging uterus interferes with the functioning of the gastro-intestinal tract. Because it favors the development of toxemia, prompt and effective measures should be taken to combat this troublesome symptom.

The diet should contain large amounts of cellulose to give bulk to the feces. It likewise is advisable to substitute fruits for the usual desserts because of their well known laxative properties. An apple or several figs should also be taken before retiring.

The great lack of fluids, so common in the diet of most women, is to be corrected by the use of eight glasses of liquids daily unless a rapid gain in weight occurs and water retention is suspected. In this event fluids are to be restricted. The patient likewise should try to form the habit of having an evacuation at a regular time each day. A good plan is to have her go to the toilet a short time after breakfast even though the inclination to move the bowels is not present.

The faulty posture necessitated by the ordinary toilet seat may be corrected by the use of a small box or bench placed in front of the toilet and used as a footstool.

While these more natural methods are being tried, the use of mineral oil, agar agar, or milk of magnesia may be necessary to secure the essential daily bowel movement. Stronger drugs are not to be recommended as they may cause an interruption of the pregnancy and their continued use interferes with the program above outlined.

CARE OF THE KIDNEYS. Owing to the extra load that is placed on the kidneys during pregnancy, these important organs of elimination require special attention. As a prophylaxis against possible renal damage, foci of infection in the teeth and tonsils should be removed as soon after they are discovered as possible.

The extra burden on the kidneys is often increased by allowing the other emunctories to become sluggish. A daily evacuation of the bowels, therefore, is essential and measures that will promote the activity of the sweat glands are indicated. One of the best means of aiding all of the emunctories is the ingestion of ample quantities of fluids. As most women take an insufficient amount of water, the great need for this essential dietary requirement must be explained to them in order that their daily quota of eight glasses of liquids may be taken. Observation of the total urinary output is a good index of the total fluid intake. It therefore is recommended that the patient keep a record of the fluid intake and measure all of the urine passed in the twenty-four hours preceding each prenatal visit. If the amount excreted falls below two quarts, she should be encouraged to take more liquids unless the fluid intake is measurably greater than the output and an excessive gain in weight indicates a disturbance in water balance. A total output of less than 1000 cc. suggests the possibility of toxemia with its accompanying renal injury.

The urine should be examined at each return visit during pregnancy, and because the danger of toxemia progressively increases as term is approached, more frequent observations and urinalyses during the seventh, eighth and ninth months are necessary. Urinalysis should include the taking of the specific gravity, testing for albumin and sugar, and a microscopic examination for casts and pus cells. If albumin is found, its quantitative estimation with an Esbach albuminometer is indicated.

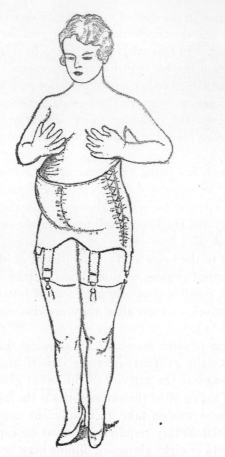 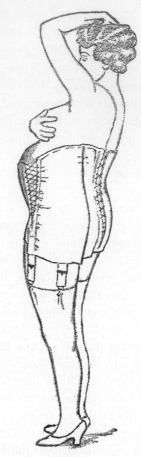

FIG. 93. Front view of maternity corset.   FIG. 94. Back and side view of maternity corset.

CARE OF THE TEETH. Dental caries is common during pregnancy. The teeth, therefore, should be examined by a dentist in the early months and any dental work that is necessary should be permitted.

Infected teeth are a menace and pregnancy is not a contraindication to their removal.

It is advisable to use an alkaline mouth wash in the morning and at night, and the customary cleansing of the teeth after each meal must not be neglected.

Many who are interested in this subject believe that the diet plays an important part in the frequent occurrence of dental caries during pregnancy. If their theory is correct, a balanced diet, such as has been recommended, with an abundance of milk and vegetables, is important. When milk and sunshine are not available, calcium and viosterol should be prescribed.

CLOTHING. The clothing should be loose, comfortable, attractive and up-to-date. Pregnancy is not the time for a cloistered existence in the worn-out garments of yesterday. Since most women feel better when they are well dressed,

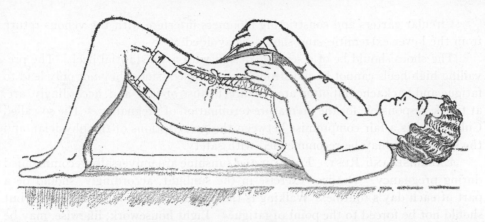

FIG. 95. Putting on the maternity corset in the dorsal posture with the hips elevated. The lacings at the side and back should be tightened from below upward while the patient is standing. After the corset is adjusted so that it is almost too snug for comfort, these are tied and the zipper or hooks in front are loosened. The patient then assumes the position illustrated and fastens the front opening by joining the hooks from below upward or by pulling up the zipper. This posture causes the presenting part to fall away from the pelvis, and the fastening of the corset while the patient is in this position, accordingly, aids in preventing the previously described pressure effects. If a maternity corset is well designed and properly adjusted, the patient will be more comfortable while wearing it and will continue its use even in the seclusion of her own room. When the garment is uncomfortable, it either is not properly designed or needs readjustment.

the daily quota of fresh air, sunshine and exercise will be more cheerfully accepted if the patient is attractively attired. Each year, as the styles change, the designers of women's clothing plan some of their models for the maternity figure; it therefore is possible for the woman who is pregnant to dress according to the prevailing style and at the same time respect the demands of pregnancy.

There should be no constricting bands about the waist, and pressure over the breasts and nipples is to be avoided. These recommendations, however, do not prohibit the wearing of a snug, supporting brassiere and a well designed and properly adjusted maternity corset.

A maternity corset not only aids in disguising the pregnancy figure but also is of great value in preventing a number of the complications of pregnancy (Figs. 93, 94 and 95). It should support the abdominal wall, the spinal column and the pelvic girdle. By supporting the abdominal wall, it holds the growing uterus in place. Thus the feeling of weight and discomfort is lessened and, at the same time, interference with the return circulation from the lower extremities is diminished. Accordingly, edema of the ankles and varicosities occur much less frequently when a good maternity corset is worn. If the garment is properly adjusted and worn faithfully after the fifth month, the contour of the abdominal wall will be better preserved and striae gravidarum seldom will be seen. With the back supported, the change in posture due to the forward displacement of the uterus is less fatiguing and many backaches are eliminated. Similarly, support of the pelvic girdle prevents sacroiliac strain with its accompanying pain and backache.

Circular garters and constricting bloomers interfere with the venous return from the lower extremities and should be avoided.

The shoes should be of a sensible design with a substantial heel. The prevailing high heels cannot be too strongly condemned, since they not only lead to fatigue and backache but often are the direct cause of falls and, accordingly, are, at times, responsible for the premature termination of pregnancy. The so-called Cuban heel is a fair compromise between the prescriptions of the physician and the stylist and may be recommended with safety.

EXERCISE AND REST. Fresh air and sunshine are universally recommended during pregnancy. Outdoor exercise in the sunlight, accordingly, should be a part of each day's routine. Walking is the best and safest form of exercise but should not be forced to the point of fatigue. Light housework, likewise, may be done without harm.

The more strenuous sports, such as tennis, rowing, swimming and horseback riding are contraindicated. Usually, the habits of the individual patient may be used as a guide, provided the more vigorous forms of exercise are excluded and fatigue is avoided. Motoring over smooth roads for short distances is safe. On the other hand, long journeys by auto, train and steamship should not be undertaken during pregnancy as they frequently cause abortion and premature labor.

In the last months, a daily walk out of doors is especially indicated to prepare the mother for her labor and aid in preventing the pregnancy from going beyond term.

Eight hours of sleep in a well ventilated room are necessary. In addition, a rest of one hour after the noon meal is beneficial. All depressing and exciting influences are to be avoided as the tendency toward emotional instability is increased during pregnancy. In the last months, an additional pillow, placed under the shoulders, will make the patient's breathing easier and aid in promoting restful sleep.

CARE OF THE BREASTS. As previously stated, compression of the breasts and nipples is to be avoided. The breasts, however, are much more comfortable when they are supported by a good brassiere. Such a garment acts as a sling and should lift each breast upward and inward toward the opposite shoulder. This action is greatly favored when the brassiere is fastened in front and from below upward. While the desired effect tends to make the breasts more prominent, this is not a disadvantage during pregnancy, since by so doing it aids in giving the front line a straight contour, a factor which is most helpful in disguising the pregnancy figure. The application of liquid vaseline or cocoa butter to the nipples softens the integument and serves as a prophylaxis against fissures from nursing.

SEXUAL INTERCOURSE may cause an abortion in the early months or premature labor in the latter part of pregnancy, and in the event that either of these accidents occurs the risk of infection is greatly increased. Abstinence, accordingly, is recommended during the first three and the last two months. If, at any time, interruption of the pregnancy is threatened, coitus should be avoided throughout the remainder of the gestation.

RETURN VISITS. Because of the changes that take place throughout the pregnancy, the patient should return to her physician at least once a month in the first and second trimesters, and every two weeks thereafter until the last month, when her visits should be made at intervals of one week. **At each of these visits she should be weighed, the blood pressure taken and a urinalysis made.** In addition, an abdominal examination made at the time of alternate visits will give a fair conception of the progress of the pregnancy.

DANGER SYMPTOMS AND SIGNS. The patient should return at once or communicate with her physician if any of the following symptoms develop:

1. Excessive vomiting.
2. Vaginal bleeding.
3. Persistent headaches.
4. Edema (Are her rings too tight?).
5. Diminished urinary output.
6. Visual disturbances.
7. Drainage of amniotic fluid.
8. Excessive gain in weight.

REFERENCES

1. SANDIFORD, I., WHEELER, T. AND BOOTHBY, W.: Metabolic Studies during Pregnancy and Menstruation. Am. J. Physiol., 1931, 96, 191.
2. COONS, C. M.: Dietary Habits during Pregnancy. J. Am. Dietet. Assn., 1933–34, 9, 95.
3. SCHOEDEL, J.: Die Trinkmenger der Brustkinder in der ersten 5 Libensmonaten. Monatschr. f. Kinderhlk., 1933–34, 59, 201.
4. HUNSCHER, H. A., DONELSON, E., NIMS, B., KENYON, F. AND MACY, I. G.: Metabolism of Women during the Reproductive Cycle. V. Nitrogen Utilization. J. Biol. Chem., 1932–33, 99, 507.
5. WILLIAMS, C. P.: Carbohydrate Metabolism in Cases of Unexplained Miscarriages. Lancct, 1933, 2, 858.
6. GIVENS, M. H. AND MACY, I. G.: The Chemical Composition of the Fetus. J. Biol. Chem., 1933, 102, 7.
7. MACY, I. G. AND HUNSCHER, H. A.: An Evaluation of Maternal Nitrogen and Mineral Needs during Embryonic and Infant Development. Am. J. Obst. & Gyn., 1934, 27, 878.
8. MULL, J. W., BILL, A. H. AND KINNY, F. M.: Variations in Serum Calcium and Phosphorus during Pregnancy. II. The Effect on the Occurrence of Dental Caries. Am. J. Obs. & Gyn., 1934, 27, 679.
9. ZISKIN, D. E. AND HOTELLING,   : Effects of Pregnancy, Mouth Acidity and Age on Dental Caries. J. Dent. Res., 1937, 16, 507.
10. ROSEBURY, T. AND FOLEY, G.: Studies in the Rat of Susceptibility to Dental Caries. J. Dent. Res., 1932, 12, 463.
11. TOVERUD, K. U. AND TOVERUD, G.: Studies on the Mineral Metabolism during Pregnancy and Lactation and Its Bearing on the Disposition to Rickets and Dental Caries. Acta Paediat., 1931, 12, Suppl. II, page 5.
12. GARRY, M. B. AND STIVEN, D.: A Review of Recent Work on Dietary Requirements in Pregnancy and Lactation with an Attempt to Assess Human Requirements. Nutrit. Obst. & Rev., 1935–36, 5, 855.

13. MASON, K. E.: Reproductive Function in Female Rats on Low Levels of Vitamin A. Anat. Rec., 1934, 58, Suppl. p. 80.
14. HART, G. H., MEAD, S. W. AND GUILBERT, H. R.: Vitamin A Deficiency in Cattle under Natural Conditions. Proc. Soc. Exper. Med., 1933, 30, 1230.
15. GREEN, H. N.: Proc. Roy. Soc. Med., 1935, 28, 1400.
16. GREEN, H. N., PINDAR, D., DAVIS, G. AND MELLANBY, E.: Diet as a Prophylactic Agent against Puerperal Sepsis with Special Reference to Vitamin A as an Anti-Infective Agent. Br. M. J., 1931, 2, 595.
17. BOOHER, L. E.: Vitamin Requirements and Practical Recommendations for Vitamin A Intake. J. A. M. A., 1938, 110, 1930.
18. LEAGUE OF NATIONS HEALTH ORGANIZATION. Report on the Physiological Basis of Nutrition. Geneva, 1935.
19. WILSON, H. E. C., DASGUPTA, S. M. AND AHMAD, B.: Studies on the Absorption of Carotene and Vitamin A in the Human Subject. Indian J. M. Res., 1937, 24, 807.
20. WESTENBRINK, H. G. H. AND GOUDSMIT, J.: Investigations on the Relation between Intake and Excretion of Aneurin in the Case of Normal Subjects and Pregnant Women. Arch. Néerland Physiol., 1938, 23, 79.
21. SEBRELL, W. H.: Vitamins in Relation to the Prevention and Treatment of Pellagra. J. A. M. A., 1938, 110, 1665.
22. STRAUSS, M. B. AND McDONALD, W. J.: Polyneuritis of Pregnancy. A Dietary Deficiency Disorder. J. A. M. A., 1938, 110, 1665.
23. MOORE, C. U. AND BRODIE, J. L.: The Relation of Maternal Diet to Hemorrhage in the Newborn. Am. J. Dis. Child., 1927, 34, 53.
24. MAXWELL, J. P.: Vitamin Deficiency in the Antenatal Period. Its Effect on the Mother and the Infant. J. Obs. & Gyn. Br. Emp., 1932, 39, 764.
25. WILLS, L. AND BILIMORA, H. S.: Studies in Pernicious Anemia of Pregnancy. Indian J. Med. Res., 1932, 33, 20, 291.
26. WILLS, L.: The Nature of the Hemopoietic Factor in Marmite. Lancet, 1933, 224, 1283.
27. HELSOM, K. O. AND SAMPLE, A. B.: Macrocytic Anemia in Pregnant Women with Vitamin B Deficiency. J. Clin. Invest., 1937, 16, 463.
28. TEEL, H. M., BURKE, B. S. AND DRAPER, R.: Vitamin C in Human Pregnancy and Lactation. I. Studies during Pregnancy. Am. J. Dis. Child., 1938, 56, 1004.
29. TOVERUD, K. U.: Etiological Factors in Neonatal Mortality with Special Reference to Cerebral Hemorrhage. Acta Paediat., 1935–36, 18, 249.
30. SZENT-GYÖRGYI, A.: Les Propriétés Therapeutiques des Vitamins. Presse Med., 1938, 46, 995.
31. GAEHTGENS, G.: Der Tagesverbrauch an Vitamin C in der Schwangerschaft. Arch. f. Gyn., 1937, 164, 571.
32. NICHOLAS, H. O. AND KUHN, E. M.: The Rôle of Calcium, Phosphorus and Vitamin D in Pregnancy. J. Clin. Investig., 1932, 11, 1313.
33. SWANSON, W. W. AND IOB, L. L.: Calcium and Phosphorus Content of the Offspring after Feeding Vitamin D to the Mother Rat. Am. J. Dis. Child., 1935, 49, 43.
34. OKUSHIMA, A.: Experimentalle Studien über den Einfluss von Uberdosierung von Vitamin D Präparaten auf das Nasengewebe. Mit. med. Akad., Kioto. 1937, 20, 1541 and 1732.
35. SURE, B.: Dietary Requirements for Reproduction. III. The Existence of the Reproductive Dietary Complex (Vitamin E) in the Ethereal Extracts of Yellow Corn, Wheat Embryo and Hemp Seed. J. Biol. Chem., 1924–25, 62, 371.
36. THOMAS, B. H., CANNON, C. Y., McNUTT, S. H. AND UNDERBJERG, G.: Variations in the Reproductive Behavior of Different Species of Mammals Restricted to Vitamin E Deficient Rations. J. Nutrition, 1938–15, Suppl. 10.
37. STRASSL, : Das Sterilitätsproblem und Abortosan, E. Berl. Münch. tierarztztl. Wchnschr., 1938, No. 27, 395.
38. VØGT-MOLLER, P.: Die Behandlung des habituellen Aborts mit Weizenkeimöl (E-Vitamin). Klin. Wchnschr., 1936, 15, 1883.
39. CURRIE, D. W.: Vitamins in Habitual Abortion. Br. M. J., 1936, 1, 752.

CHAPTER X

PRESENTATION, POSITION AND POSTURE

PRESENTATION is the relation of the long axis of the fetus to the long axis of the mother. In general, there are two presentations—longitudinal and transverse, depending on whether the long axis of the fetus is parallel with, or at right angles to the long axis of the mother (Figs. 96 and 97).

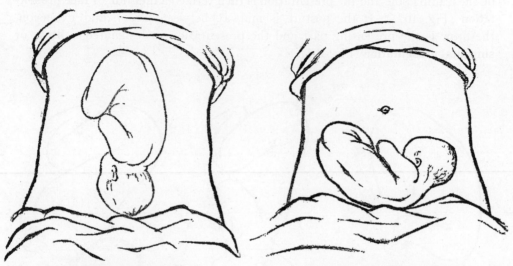

FIG. 96. Longitudinal presentation.   FIG. 97. Transverse presentation.

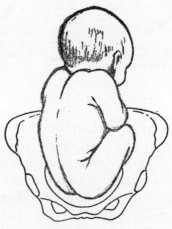

FIG. 98. Cephalic presentation.   FIG. 99. Pelvic or breech presentation.

Longitudinal presentations likewise are either cephalic or pelvic, according to the fetal pole which is in relation to the mother's pelvis (Figs. 98 and 99).

THE PRESENTING PART is that portion of the fetus which is lowest in the pelvis. It accordingly is the part which is first felt by the examining fingers when a vaginal examination is made. In cephalic presentations, the presenting part varies with the posture of the child.

POSTURE OR ATTITUDE is the relation of the fetal parts to each other. The posture or attitude of the fetus may be responsible for three different presenting parts in cephalic presentations. When the head is well flexed, the vertex or occiput presents, and the presentation is known as a **vertex** or **occipital presentation** (Fig. 100). Marked extension of the head causes the chin or mentum to be the leading pole and the presentation is then termed a **mentum** or **face presentation** (Fig. 102). If the posture is midway between flexion and extension, the brow is the presenting part and the presentation is designated a **brow** or **sincipital presentation** (Fig. 101).

FIG. 100. Flexion.   FIG. 101. Partial extension.   FIG. 102. Extension.
Vertex presentation.   Brow presentation.   Face presentation.

POSITION is the relation of the presenting part to the quadrants of the mother's pelvis. Four positions usually are described, according to the quadrant of the mother's pelvis in which the presenting part is found. In vertex presentations, the occiput may lie in the left anterior, right anterior, left posterior, or right posterior quadrants. The presentations then are designated respectively: Left Occipito Anterior (Fig. 103), Right Occipito Anterior (Fig. 104), Left Occipito Posterior (Fig. 105), or Right Occipito Posterior (Fig. 106). For the sake of simplicity, transverse positions of the vertex are not included. They, however, are the most common and occur in about 60 per cent of all cases (2a).

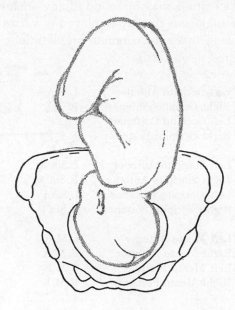

FIG. 103. Left Occipito Anterior. L.O.A.

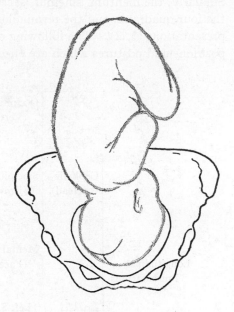

FIG. 104. Right Occipito Anterior. R.O.A.

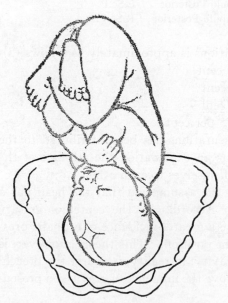

FIG. 105. Left Occipito Posterior. L.O.P.

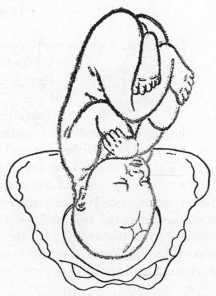

FIG. 106. Right Occipito Posterior. R.O.P.

Similarly, the mentum, sinciput, sacrum or scapula may be found in any one of the four quadrants and the terminology is analogous to that employed in vertex presentations (1, 2).   The following outline includes the common presentations, positions and postures which are encountered in obstetrics:

Posture   *Position*

		Left Occipito Anterior	L.O.A.
	Occipital	Right Occipito Anterior	R.O.A.
	(Vertex)	Left Occipito Posterior	L.O.P.
		Right Occipito Posterior	R.O.P.
Cephalic	Sincipital	Left Sincipito Anterior	L.Sin.A.
(Head)	(Brow)	Right Sincipito Anterior	R.Sin.A.
		Left Sincipito Posterior	L.Sin.P.
		Right Sincipito Posterior	R.Sin.P.
	Mental	Left Mento Anterior	L.M.A.
	(Face)	Right Mento Anterior	R.M.A.
		Left Mento Posterior	L.M.P.
		Right Mento Posterior	R.M.P

Pres *Part*

Presentation

Longitudinal Presentations

Pelvic	Left Sacro Anterior	L.S.A.
(Breech)	Right Sacro Anterior	R.S.A.
(Sacral)	Left Sacro Posterior	L.S.P.
	Right Sacro Posterior	R.S.P.

Transverse Presentations

Scapular	Left Scapulo Anterior	L.Sc.A.
(Shoulder)	Right Scapulo Anterior	R.Sc.A.
	Left Scapulo Posterior	L.Sc.P.
	Right Scapulo Posterior	R.Sc.P.

The frequency of the various presentations is approximately as follows (3):

Vertex, 96 per cent

Breech, 3 per cent

Face, 0.5 per cent

Transverse, 0.5 per cent

The higher incidence of cephalic presentations has been attributed to the effect of gravity.   Another theory offers as an explanation the attempt of the uterine and fetal ovoids to accommodate themselves to each other.

THE GRAVITY THEORY is based upon the assumption that the head has a greater specific gravity than the breech.   Accordingly, the center of gravity should be nearer the head and should cause a greater incidence of cephalic presentations when the woman is in the upright position.   This theory, however, is weakened by the fact that the center of gravity, in reality, is nearer the breech. Much work has been done to prove or disprove the influence of gravity on presentation, but up to the present time the question remains unsettled (4, 5, 6, 7, 8, 9, 10).

THE ACCOMMODATION THEORY.   According to this theory the uterus and fetus are regarded as two similarly shaped ovoids.   The outer or uterine ovoid, being contractile, tends to force the inner or fetal ovoid into the most adaptable position.   The fetal ovoid likewise is active and assumes that position in which it best fits the uterine cavity.   Since the widest diameter of the flexed fetus is nearest the breech, this pole of the fetal ovoid will lie in the widest diameter of the uterus, i.e., near the fundus (11, 12, 13, 14).   Cephalic presentations, therefore, are favored by the conditions that normally are present when a woman goes into labor.   On the other hand, interference with the mechanism of adaptation favors the more frequent occurrence of other presentations.   Some of the conditions which may thus disturb the accommodation of the two ovoids are:

1. Small child in a relatively large uterus, as in hydramnios or premature labor.
2. Dead fetus.
3. Multiple pregnancy.
4. Fibroid tumors of the uterus.
5. Atony of the uterus, as in multiparae.

The frequency of the various positions in occipital presentations as shown by abdominal palpation and vaginal examination is as follows:

Left Occipito Anterior	70 per cent
Right Occipito Posterior	17 per cent
Right Occipito Anterior	10 per cent
Left Occipito Posterior	3 per cent

These figures or others quite close to them have been accepted by most obstetricians for many years.   With the development of better roentgen ray facilities, however, their accuracy is being questioned.   Those who have studied the cephalo-pelvic relationship by the more accurate Roentgen methods, believe that the head enters the pelvis transversely in a large proportion of all cases.   In one series of 200 observations made early in labor, the head was transversely placed in 60 per cent of the cases.   It was found to lie obliquely in 34.5 per cent and occupied an anteroposterior position in 5.5 per cent (2a).   While the number of observations in the series is small, the superiority of this method over the means formerly used in the determination of the generally accepted statistics gives special significance to these observations and leads to the conclusion that the figures now accepted will have to be revised when a larger number of the more accurate Roentgen observations is available.   In the 200 cases studied by this means, the following frequency of the various positions was noted:

L.O.A.	9.5%	L.O.P.	9.5%	L.O.T.	40.5%	Total Left Positions..............	59.5%
R.O.A.	6.5%	R.O.P.	9. %	R.O.T.	19.5%	Total Right Positions.............	35. %
Total	16. %		18.5%		60. %	Occiput Directly Anterior.........	5.5%

According to this study, transverse positions are more common than oblique positions and posteriors occur almost as often as anteriors. The head also is directed toward the left 50 per cent more frequently than toward the right.

This series of observations, as well as others of a similar nature, seems to indicate that the shape of the pelvic inlet is a factor in determing the position of the head early in labor. In the typical female (gynecoid) pelvis, transverse positions are most common (69 per cent) but anterior positions occur more often (21 per cent) than do posteriors (10 per cent) (see Fig. 796, p. 654). Transverse positions also are most common (71 per cent) in the masculine (android) type of pelvis but posterior positions (20.5 per cent) are over twice as frequent as anteriors (8.5 per cent) (see Fig. 797). As might be expected, the long narrow inlet of the ape-like (anthropoid) pelvis has fewer transverse positions (37.5 per cent) and, not infrequently, is associated with directly anterior positions of the occiput (17 per cent) (see Fig. 798). Because of the sacral promontory, however, the occiput is seldom found posteriorly in these antero-posterior positions of the head (2a).

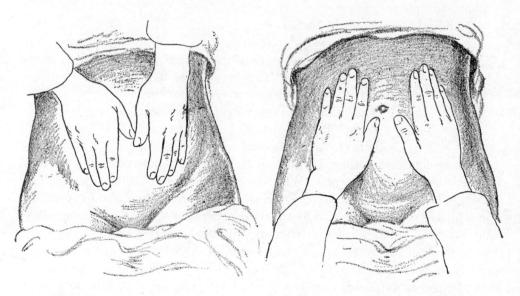

FIG. 109. Abdominal palpation. Comparison of the two sides of the abdomen.

FIG. 110. Abdominal palpation. Comparison of the two sides of the abdomen, position of hands reversed.

DIAGNOSIS

The diagnosis of presentation, position and posture may be made by abdominal and vaginal examination, or by the use of the Roentgen rays.

ABDOMINAL PALPATION. Proficiency in abdominal palpation requires practice and the employment of a definite routine (13, 15). After the examiner warms his hands, he places them gently upon the abdominal wall and, before attempting to feel the parts of the fetus, pauses for a brief interval in order that the patient may become accustomed to their presence. He then compares the two sides and the two poles of the uterus. Since absolute characteristics of the various fetal parts often are difficult to make out, it is better to rely upon these comparative findings.

PALPATION OF THE TWO SIDES. The whole hands, placed equidistant from the midline, gently palpate and compare the two sides of the abdomen (Figs. 109 and 110). That side which is the more resistant, smoother and more convex contains the dorsum of the child, and the opposite one is the site of the irregular small parts. The discovery of an actively mobile small part is an absolute characteristic of the side of the ventrum and when such a part is felt on one side, the dorsum, naturally, is on the opposite. In difficult cases, it may be helpful to ask the patient where the fetal movements are most pronounced. If the ventrum is assumed to be on that side, more careful palpation may then reveal the actual location of the dorsum and the small parts.

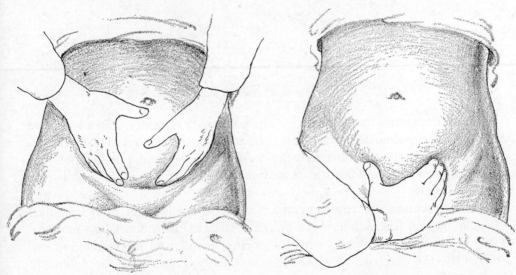

FIG. 111. Abdominal palpation Palpation of the lower pole.

FIG. 112. Abdominal palpation. Palpation of the lower pole with one hand.

PALPATION OF THE LOWER POLE. The entire palmar surfaces of both hands make gentle pressure over the lower abdomen without, at first, attempting to feel any part of the child. Soon the abdominal muscles relax and deeper palpation is possible. The patient is then asked to inhale and exhale and, with each expiration, the finger-tips are gently depressed on each side of the symphysis (Fig. 111). In this manner, the characteristics of the lower pole are easily felt and its consistency, regularity, shape and mobility are noted (Fig. 112).

PALPATION OF THE UPPER POLE. The examiner's position is now reversed and the upper pole is palpated in a similar manner. Its consistency, regularity, shape and mobility are then compared with the findings obtained on palpation of the lower pole (Figs. 111, 112 and 113).

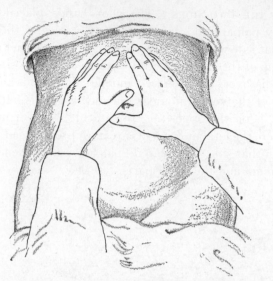

FIG. 113. Abdominal palpation. Palpation of the upper pole.

CHARACTERISTICS OF THE HEAD. The pole which is harder, smoother, more globular and more mobile is the head. In addition to these relative characteristics, a sulcus is often felt between the dorsum and the head. If this pole can be moved from side to side without movement of the trunk, the diagnosis of a head is absolute.

CHARACTERISTICS OF THE BREECH. The pole which is softer, more irregular, less globular and less mobile is the breech. It lacks the independent mobility of the head and is continuous with the dorsum without an intervening sulcus. Frequently, the diagnosis of a breech may be strengthened by the finding of small parts in its vicinity.

PALPATION OF THE CEPHALIC PROMINENCE. The location of the cephalic prominence indicates the attitude or posture of the fetus. When the child is flexed, the cephalic prominence is on the side opposite the dorsum, while in extension it is on the same side as the dorsum. The examiner faces the lower extremities and places his hands over the lower pole equidistant from the midline. He then depresses the fingers of each hand at the same rate until the head is felt (Fig. 114). That portion of the head which is first felt is the cephalic prominence and the side on which it is felt is the side of the cephalic prominence. Occasionally, the cephalic prominence may be easily palpated even though the dorsum cannot be made out. In these circumstances, the experienced physician might conclude that the dorsum is on the opposite side because that is its usual relation to the cephalic prominence. Such a conclusion, however, is not warranted because it may lead him to miss the diagnosis of a face presentation. If the

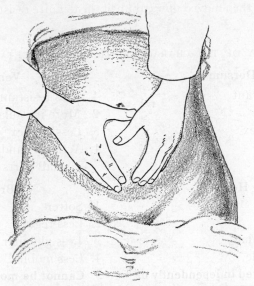

FIG. 114. Abdominal palpation.   Palpation of the cephalic prominence.

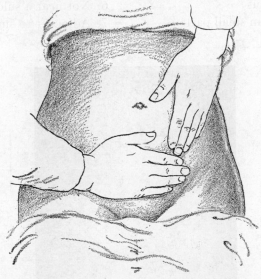

FIG. 115. Abdominal palpation.   Palpation of the anterior shoulder.

beginner finds it difficult to distinguish the cephalic prominence, and he is able to palpate both sides of the head, the fact that most of the head is on the same side of the cephalic prominence should aid in the diagnosis.

PALPATION OF THE ANTERIOR SHOULDER aids in determining the position of the fetus. If the child is in flexion, the anterior shoulder is near the midline in all anterior positions and away from the midline when the position is posterior. One hand is placed over the dorsum and the other palpates the head as in Fig. 115. The latter is then moved upward until the definite resistance of the anterior shoulder is felt.

SUMMARY OF THE CHARACTERISTICS OF THE FETAL PARTS

Dorsum
1. More resistant
2. Smoother
3. More convex

Ventrum
1. Less resistant
2. More irregular
3. Less convex
4. Actively and passively **mobile** small parts palpable

Head
1. Harder
2. Smoother
3. More globular
4. More mobile
5. **Can be moved independently of the trunk**
6. Near a sulcus
7. Remote from small parts

Breech
1. Softer
2. Less regular
3. Less globular
4. Less mobile
5. **Cannot be moved independently of the trunk**
6. Not near a sulcus
7. Adjacent to small parts

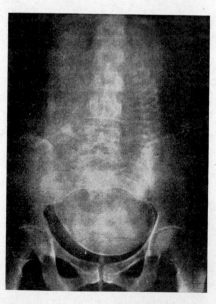

Fig. 116. The x-ray findings in an L.O.A.

VAGINAL EXAMINATION during the latter part of pregnancy is very useful in determining the presentation of the child, and the beginner will find it the easiest method of making the diagnosis after the cervix is somewhat dilated. The head is differentiated from the breech by the fact that it is smoother, harder, more globular, and more mobile. Often, the sagittal suture and the anterior or posterior fontanel may be felt. When they are made out, the diagnosis of a cephalic presentation is certain, and the direction of the sagittal suture, together with the relation of the fontanels to the quadrants of the mother's pelvis, indicates the position of the child.

X-RAY FINDINGS. In addition to its value as an aid in the early diagnosis of pregnancy, the x-ray serves as a means of accurately determining the presentation, position and posture (16) (Fig. 116). Its greatest use is in those cases in which the inexperienced physician suspects an abnormal presentation. Likewise, whenever an excess of fluid, multiple pregnancy or a thick, fat abdominal wall interferes with palpation, the x-ray will be helpful to even the experienced obstetrician.

REFERENCES

1. INTERNATIONAL MEDICAL CONGRESS: Uniformity in Obstetrical Nomenclature. Am J. O., 1889, 20, 1084.
2. BAR: Rapport sur l'unification de la nomenclature obstétricale. Obstétrique, 1903, 8, 103.
2a. CALDWELL, W. E., MOLOY, H. C. AND D'ESOPO, D. A.: A Roentgenologic Study of the Mechanism of Engagement of the Head. Am. J. O. & G., 1934, 28, 824.
3. MARKOE: Observations and Statistics on Sixty Thousand Labors. Bull. Lying-in Hospital, N. Y., 1909, 6, 101.
4. COHNSTEIN, J.: Die Aetiologie der Normalen Kindeslage. Monatschr. f. Geburtsk., 1868, 31, 141.
5. DUNCAN, J. M.: The Position of the Fetus. Researches in Obstetrics. Edinburgh, 1868, p. 14.
6. VEIT, G.: Die Lagenverhältnisse bei Früh und Zwillingsgeburten. Scanzoni's Beiträge zur Geburtsk. u. Gyn., 1860, 4, 279.
7. SCHATZ, R.: Ueber den Schwerpunkt der Frucht. Zentralbl. f. Gyn., 1900, 24, 1033. Die Ursachen der Kinderslagen. Arch. f. Gyn., 1904, 81, 541.
8. SEITZ, L.: Ueber den Einfluss der Schwerkraft auf die Entstehung der Schädellagen. Arch. f. Gyn., 1908, 86, 114.
9. BARNUM, J.: The Effect of Gravitation on the Presentation and Position of the Fetus. J. A. M. A., 1915, 64, 498.
10. GRIFFITH, W. S. A.: An Investigation of the Causes which Determine the Lie of the Foetus in Utero. J. Obs. & Gyn. Brit. Emp., 1915, 27, 105.
11. DUBOIS, P.: Mémoire sur la cause des présentations de la tête. Mem. Acad. de Méd., 1833, 2, 265.
12. SIMPSON, J. Y.: The Attitude and Positions, Natural and Preternatural, of the Fetus in Utero, Acts of the Reflex or Excito-Motory System. Monthly J. Med. Sc., 1849, 9, 423, 639, 863.
13. PINARD, A.: L'accommodation foetale. Traité du palper abdominal. Paris, 1878.
14. SELLHEIM, H.: Experimentelle und vergleichend physiologische Untersuchungen über die "Entwicklung" der typischen Fruchtlage. Arch. f. Gyn., 1917, 106, 1.
15. CREDE U. LEOPOLD: Die Geburtshülfliche Untersuchung. Leipzig, 1892.
16. PORTES AND BLANCHE: Le Radiodiagnostic obstétrical. Gyn. et Obs., 1924, 10, 332.

CHAPTER XI

THE ESSENTIAL FACTORS IN LABOR

LABOR or parturition is the process by which the mature products of conception are separated and expelled from the maternal organism. In every labor there are three essential factors: 1. **The expelling powers**; 2. **The passages**; 3. **The passenger.**

THE EXPELLING POWERS

The forces responsible for the expulsion of the fetus and placenta are derived from the following sources:

1. The involuntary uterine contractions.
2. The voluntary bearing-down efforts.
3. The contraction of the levator ani muscles.

THE UTERINE CONTRACTIONS are **involuntary** and their independence of the central nervous system is shown by the fact that cases of paraplegia, following spinal cord lesions, fall into labor in the usual manner (1, 2, 3, 4, 5). Similarly, the action of the uterus is not disturbed by the use of spinal anesthesia. On the other hand, uterine contractions may be inhibited for brief intervals by factors not associated with the uterus, and the cessation of labor for a short time after the arrival of the obstetrician is a common observation.

The uterus contracts **intermittently** but **regularly** throughout labor. At first, the interval between contractions is about twenty minutes. This period gradually diminishes and, during the height of the expulsive efforts, the contractions recur as often as every two minutes.

Early in labor, the **duration** of the uterine contractions is about thirty seconds. Later they are more prolonged and may last one minute or longer.

The **intensity** of the contractions likewise increases as labor progresses and the force transmitted by them to a hydrostatic bag placed in the parturient canal has been shown to increase from 80 to 250 mm. of mercury. The latter figure, however, includes the effect of the increases in the intra-abdominal pressure which are caused by the bearing-down efforts. When this apparatus is connected with a tambour, tracings on a smoked drum produce the curve illustrated in Fig. 117. This curve shows a gradual increment with a sustained acme and a more rapid decrudescence (6). Palpation of the uterus during a contraction gives a similar impression. At first the contraction is very weak. It then gradually increases in intensity until the acme is reached, when, for a few seconds, the sustained effect of its greatest effort may be felt. Following this, a rather rapid diminution in the intensity of the contraction is evident as the increasing relaxation of the uterus is palpated.

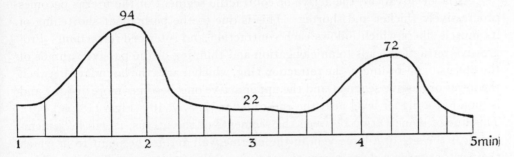

FIG. 117. Curve of the uterine contractions in the first stage of labor (Schatz).

Although the arrangement of the muscle fibers of the uterus is not clearly understood, its behavior during labor favors the belief that the fibers which have a more or less circular arrangement form the greater part of its walls and roof. This conception results from the observation that the anteroposterior and transverse diameters are diminished during a contraction while at the same time

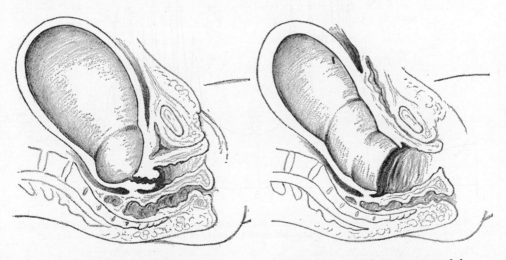

FIG. 118. Upper and lower segments of the uterus early in labor (Schroeder).

FIG. 119. Upper and lower segments of the uterus late in labor (Schroeder).

the uterus is elongated. That longitudinal fibers are also present is evident from the fact that the isthmus and cervix are drawn upward as labor progresses. Accordingly, a uterine contraction acts in two distinct ways: First, contraction of its circular elements diminishes the transverse and anteroposterior diameters, thereby narrowing and elongating the fetal ovoid. Second, the longitudinal fibers draw the weak lower segment and cervix upward over the lower pole of the elongated ovum.

As labor advances, the active or contractile segment of the uterus becomes progressively thicker and shorter. This is due to the permanent shortening of its muscle fibers which follows each contraction and is termed **retraction.** Progressive retraction leads to an elongation and thinning of the passive isthmus of the uterus. Accordingly, the **retraction ring,** which marks the boundary between the lower or passive segment and the upper active one, becomes more distinct and is found at a higher level near the end of labor (7, 8, 9, 10) (Figs. 118 and 119). This line of demarcation between the segments of the uterus, it will be remembered, is the site of a large vein in the uterine wall and is the point from which the peritoneum is reflected from the anterior wall of the uterus to the bladder.

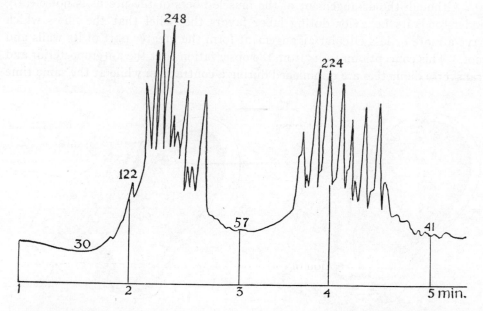

Fig. 120. Curve of the expulsive efforts in the second stage of labor. The deep oscillations indicate the voluntary efforts and are superimposed upon the curve of the uterine contraction (Schatz).

THE VOLUNTARY EFFORTS. During the stage of expulsion, the force of the involuntary uterine contractions is supplemented by voluntary bearing-down efforts similar to those employed in the mechanism of defecation. The patient takes a deep inspiration, holds her breath and contracts all of the abdominal muscles with the result that the intra-abdominal pressure is markedly increased.

In this manner, the uterus is compressed on all sides and the expelling forces are greatly augmented. Figure 120 is a graphic representation of these voluntary efforts. The narrow but deep oscillations that are superimposed on the curve of the uterine contractions show the effects of the intermittent increases in the intra-abdominal pressure.

The voluntary efforts are due to a reflex which is inaugurated by the pressure of the presenting part or membranes on the pelvic floor, and is the same reflex that is set up during the act of defecation. Spinal and caudal anesthesia destroy this reflex and, accordingly, eliminate all bearing-down efforts. Although spinal anesthesia does not interfere with the uterine contractions, most women who are confined under its influence must be delivered by forceps. The voluntary efforts, therefore, are usually essential to a spontaneous termination of labor.

CONTRACTIONS OF THE LEVATOR ANI MUSCLES. Throughout most of labor, the levatores ani are more or less passive. When the presenting part is being forced through the vulvovaginal ring, contraction of these muscles, in the intervals between the pains, aids in causing recession of the head and thus facilitates the temporary restoration of the circulation. After the occiput has passed from beneath the pubic arch, extension of the head likewise is assisted by the contraction of the muscles of the pelvic diaphragm. A similar action also aids the voluntary efforts in the expulsion of the placenta after it has been separated and forced into the vagina.

THE PASSAGES

THE PELVIS is the bony basin in which the trunk terminates and through which the weight of the body is transmitted to the lower extremities. It is made up of the two ossa innominata, the sacrum and the coccyx, the details of which need not be reviewed.

Within this bony girdle, the cavity is divided by the linea terminalis into the major (false) pelvis and the minor (true) pelvis. Since the latter is the canal through which the child must pass during parturition, it is of vital interest to the obstetrician and, accordingly, will be considered in detail. Because of its irregular shape, a clear conception of the pelvic cavity can be gained only by a careful study of its contour at different levels. These include the inlet, the outlet and the planes of greatest and least dimensions.

THE SUPERIOR APERTURE (inlet, brim, superior strait) of the true pelvis is slightly wider than it is deep, and is somewhat heart-shaped owing to the indentation of its posterior aspect by the sacral promontory. It is bounded posteriorly by the base of the sacrum, anteriorly by the pubes and laterally by the linea terminalis (Fig. 121). Six landmarks are usually considered in connection with the pelvic inlet. These are the symphysis pubis in front, and the promontory of the sacrum behind, together with the two sacroiliac joints and the two iliopectineal eminences. Four diameters are formed by joining certain of these landmarks.

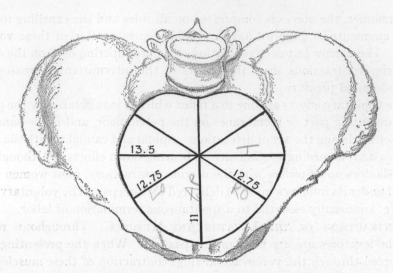

FIG. 121. The superior aperture or pelvic inlet. Anteroposterior diameter, 11 cm. Transverse diameter, 13.5 cm. Right oblique diameter, 12.75 cm. Left oblique diameter, 12.75 cm.

1. THE ANTEROPOSTERIOR diameter of the inlet (conjugata vera) extends from the promontory of the sacrum to the symphysis pubis. It is the shortest diameter and measures 11 cm.

2. THE TRANSVERSE or widest diameter is somewhat nearer to the promontory than to the symphysis and extends from a point midway between the sacroiliac joint and the iliopectineal eminence on one side to a similar point on the other. It is the longest of the inlet diameters and measures 13.5 cm.

3. THE RIGHT OBLIQUE diameter passes from the right sacroiliac joint to the left iliopectineal eminence. It is 12.75 cm. long and takes its name from the posterior landmark.

4. THE LEFT OBLIQUE diameter connects similar landmarks on the opposite side and is also 12.75 cm. in length.

Below the superior aperture the pelvic cavity expands and reaches its greatest dimensions at a plane which passes through the middle of the posterior surface of the symphysis in front and the junction of the second and third pieces of the sacrum behind (Fig. 122).

THE PLANE OF GREATEST DIMENSIONS is almost circular in shape and is bounded laterally by the junction of the upper and middle thirds of the obturator foramina (Fig. 122). Because the extremities of the oblique diameters terminate on each side in the obturator foramina, they usually are not considered in this plane. Accordingly, only two diameters are described.

1. THE ANTEROPOSTERIOR diameter of the plane of greatest dimension extends from the symphysis to the junction of the second and third segments of the sacrum and is 12.75 cm. long.

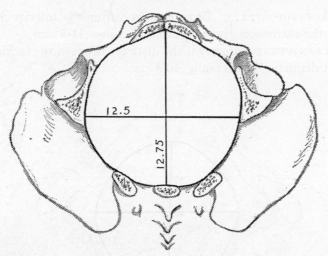

Fig. 122. The plane of greatest dimensions. Anteroposterior diameter, 12.75 cm. Transverse diameter, 12.5 cm.

2. THE TRANSVERSE diameter is slightly shorter, 12.5 cm., and represents the distance between the most widely separated point on the lateral aspects of this plane.

Due to the forward curvature of the lower portion of the sacrum and the inward slope of the lateral walls of the pelvis, the pelvic cavity diminishes in size to reach its greatest contraction at the plane which passes through the sacrococcygeal joint, the ischial spines and the inferior margin of the symphysis (Fig. 123).

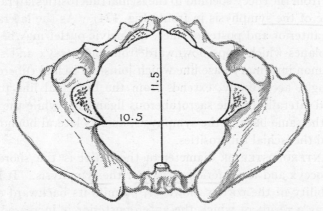

Fig. 123. The plane of the least pelvic dimensions. Anteroposterior diameter, 11.5 cm. Transverse diameter, 10.5 cm.

THE PLANE OF LEAST DIMENSIONS is irregularly oval and is notched on each side by the spine of the ischium (Fig. 123). As in the preceding plane, only two diameters are considered.

1. THE ANTEROPOSTERIOR diameter passes from the inferior margin of the symphysis to the sacrococcygeal joint, and measures 11.5 cm.

2. THE TRANSVERSE diameter is the distance between the ischial spines and is the shortest diameter in this plane, 10.5 cm.

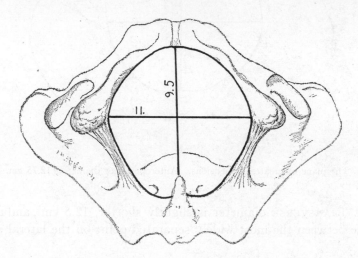

FIG. 124. The pelvic outlet.   Anteroposterior diameter, 9.5 to 11.5 cm.   Transverse diameter, 11 cm.

THE INFERIOR APERTURE (inferior strait, outlet) is a quadrilateral figure which extends from the coccyx behind to the ischial tuberosities laterally and to the inferior surface of the symphysis in front (Fig. 124).   As the lateral landmarks are below the anterior and posterior ones, the pelvic outlet may be described as two inclined planes which slope downward from the coccyx and symphysis to meet at a common imaginary base line which joins the ischial tuberosities.   The posterior triangle, accordingly, extends from the bisischial line to the coccyx and is bounded laterally by the sacrotuberous ligaments, while the anterior one extends from the same base to the symphysis, and its lateral boundaries are the pubic rami and the ischial tuberosities.

1. THE ANTEROPOSTERIOR diameter of the outlet is the shortest distance between the coccyx and the inferior surface of the symphysis.   It measures 9.5 cm.   The mobility of the coccyx, however, permits its backward displacement during labor, as a result of which the anteroposterior is increased about 2 cm. to a length of approximately 11.5 cm.   Accordingly, the anteroposterior diameter, when viewed from the obstetrical standpoint, extends from the sacrococcygeal joint to the lower margin of the symphysis.   Since the outlet is made up of two triangular, inclined planes with a common base, a better conception of the sagittal dimension may be gained if the anteroposterior diameter or perpendicular

of each triangle is considered. The perpendicular of the posterior triangle is 9 cm. long and is known as the **posterior sagittal** diameter, while the shorter perpendicular of the anterior triangle is 6 cm. in length and is termed **the anterior sagittal** (Fig. 125).

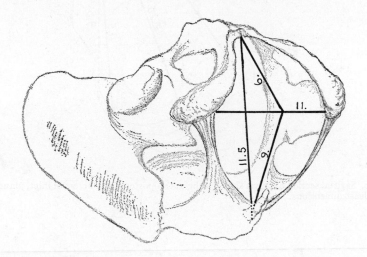

Fig. 125. Oblique view of the pelvic outlet. Anteroposterior diameter, 11.5 cm. Transverse diameter, 11 cm. Anterior sagittal diameter, 6 cm. Posterior sagittal diameter, 9 cm.

2. THE TRANSVERSE diameter of the outlet extends from the inner surface of one ischial tuberosity to the inner surface of the other and measures 11 cm. It commonly is designated as the **bisischial** diameter.

With the shape and location of these planes in mind, the pelvic cavity may be described as an irregular, curved cylinder, the anterior and posterior surfaces of which are unequal and correspond in length to the symphysis, 4.5 cm., and the sacrum, 12 cm. The inlet of this cylinder looks forward and upward so that its axis, if prolonged, would pierce the umbilicus. It therefore meets the horizon at an angle of 60°, while the anteroposterior diameter of the outlet has an inclination of about 10° (Fig. 127).

THE AXIS OF THE PELVIS is a curved line which joins the centers of a number of imaginary planes that pass through various levels of the pelvis. Its shape, accordingly, is somewhat similar to the curve of the sacrum (Fig. 128).

THE CURVE OF CARUS is the arc of a circle, the radius of which is half the length of the conjugata vera and the center of which is the middle of the posterior surface of the symphysis. This curve is not the pelvic axis, nor is it the parturient axis. Because it follows the direction of the lower portion of the parturient axis, it is useful in describing the latter part of the mechanism of labor. The curve of Carus is shown in Figure 129.

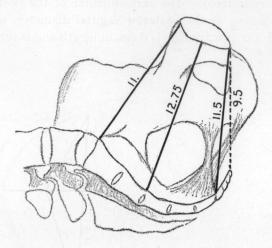

FIG. 126. Sagittal section of pelvis showing the anteroposterior diameters of inlet, plane of greatest and plane of least dimensions.

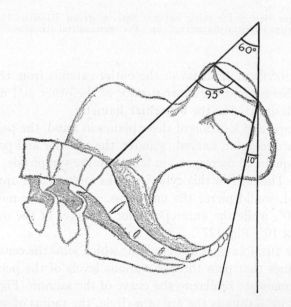

FIG. 127. Thei nclination of the pelvis. When the patient is in the dorsal posture, the pelvic inlet meets a line which is perpendicular to the horizon at an angle of 60°. If the patient were in the erect posture, the inlet would meet the horizon at an angle of 60° and the outlet would meet it at an angle of 10°.

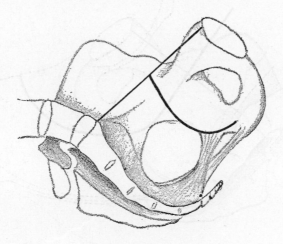

FIG. 128. The pelvic axis

FIG. 128. The pelvic axis

The PELVIC AXIS is the direction that the child follows as it passes through and out of the pelvis. The upper portion is a straight line and corresponds to a downward prolongation of the axis of the inlet to a point about 3 cm. above the tip of the sacrum. From this point it follows the pelvic axis and the curve of Carus as the soft parts of the outlet form a trough through which the child passes in the latter part of labor (Fig. 130).

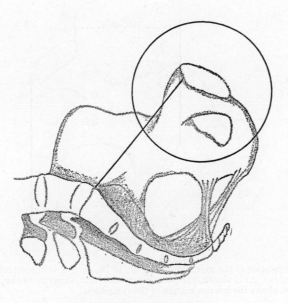

FIG. 129. The curve of Carus.

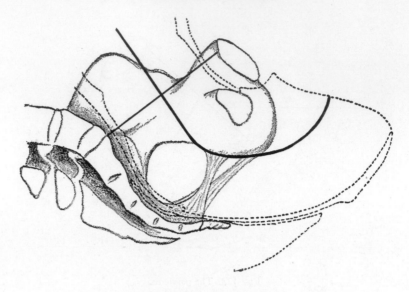

FIG. 130. The parturient axis.

THE PARTURIENT AXIS is the direction that the child follows as it passes through and out of the pelvis. Its upper portion is a straight line and corresponds to a downward prolongation of the axis of the inlet to a point about 5 cm. above the tip of the sacrum. From this point it follows the pelvic axis and the curve of Carus as the soft parts of the outlet form a trough through which the child passes in the latter part of labor (Fig. 130).

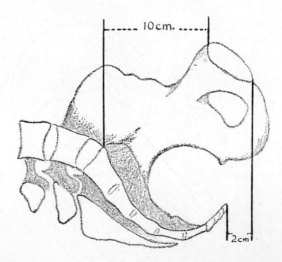

FIG. 131. The relation of the promontory and tip of the coccyx to the superior and inferior margin of the symphysis pubis. As is shown, the promontory is 10 cm. superior to the symphysis and the tip of the coccyx is 2 cm. above the inferior margin of the symphysis.

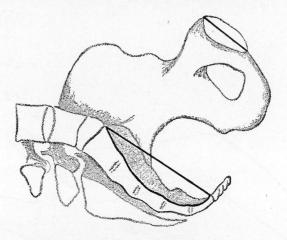

FIG. 132.   The anterior wall of the pelvis (symphysis) is 4.5 cm. while the posterior wall (sacrum) is 12 cm. when the sacral curve is followed and 10 cm. in a straight line from the promontory to the sacrococcygeal joint.

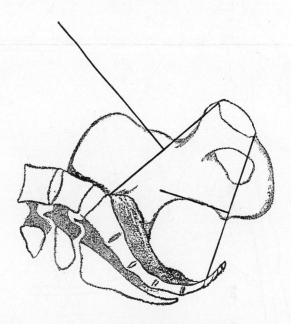

FIG. 133. Axis of inlet and axis of outlet.

It should be remembered that the promontory of the sacrum is about 10 cm. above the superior surface of the symphysis (Fig. 131).   Likewise, the tip of the coccyx is approximately 2 cm. above the inferior margin of the symphysis.

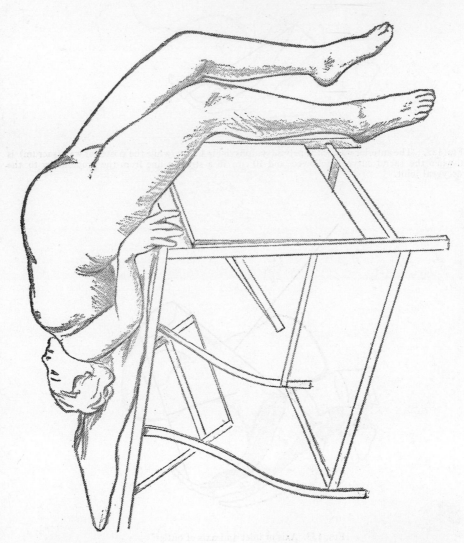

FIG. 134. The Walcher position.

PELVIC JOINTS

The pubic bones are held together by a mass of fibrocartilage, the **symphysis pubis,** and the pubic ligaments.   During pregnancy, the symphysis becomes considerably widened and much more mobile.

The coccyx is attached to the tip of the sacrum by the **sacrococcygeal** joint, which, in young women, is easily movable and, accordingly, is displaced backward during parturition.

Posteriorly, the sacrum is attached to the ossa innominata by the **sacroiliac joints** and the anterior and posterior sacroiliac ligaments.   Like the symphysis, these joints are considerably relaxed during pregnancy and, at the time of labor, permit the pelvic girdle to rotate on the sacrum.

Because of the mobility of the sacroiliac joints, it is possible to rotate the superior surface of the symphysis away from the promontory and thereby increase the anteroposterior diameter of the inlet.   Practical application of this principle is utilized in the **Walcher position**, which is used to increase the size

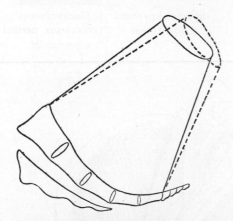 

Fig. 135. The anteroposterior diameter of the inlet is lengthened by hyperextension of the thighs (Walcher position).

Fig. 136. The anteroposterior diameter of the outlet is lengthened by hyperflexion of the thighs.

of the inlet in the treatment of pelvic dystocia (11).   The patient is placed on the edge of the table with the thighs extended.   The weight of the lower extremities then rotates the symphysis downward, away from the promontory, and thereby increases the length of the anteroposterior diameter (Figs. 134 and 135).

The opposite of the Walcher position is utilized as a means of increasing the anteroposterior diameter of the outlet (Fig. 136).   With the patient in the dorsal posture, the thighs are flexed until the knees touch the chest.   The inferior surface of the symphysis is thus rotated upward away from the tip of the sacrum and this, accordingly, results in a considerable increase in the anteroposterior and posterior sagittal diameters.

PELVIC MUSCLES

The muscles of the pelvis fall into three groups:

Those that line the lateral wall of the pelvis
{ psoas
  pyriformis
  obturator internus

Those that cross the pelvic outlet and enter into the formation of the pelvic diaphragm
{ levator ani
  coccygeus

Those that lie beneath the pelvic diaphragm

In the posterior triangle { —sphincter ani

In the anterior triangle

deep perineal compartment { compressor urethrae
                            transversus perinei profundus

superficial perineal compartment { ischiocavernosus
                                    bulbocavernosus
                                    transversus perinei superficialis

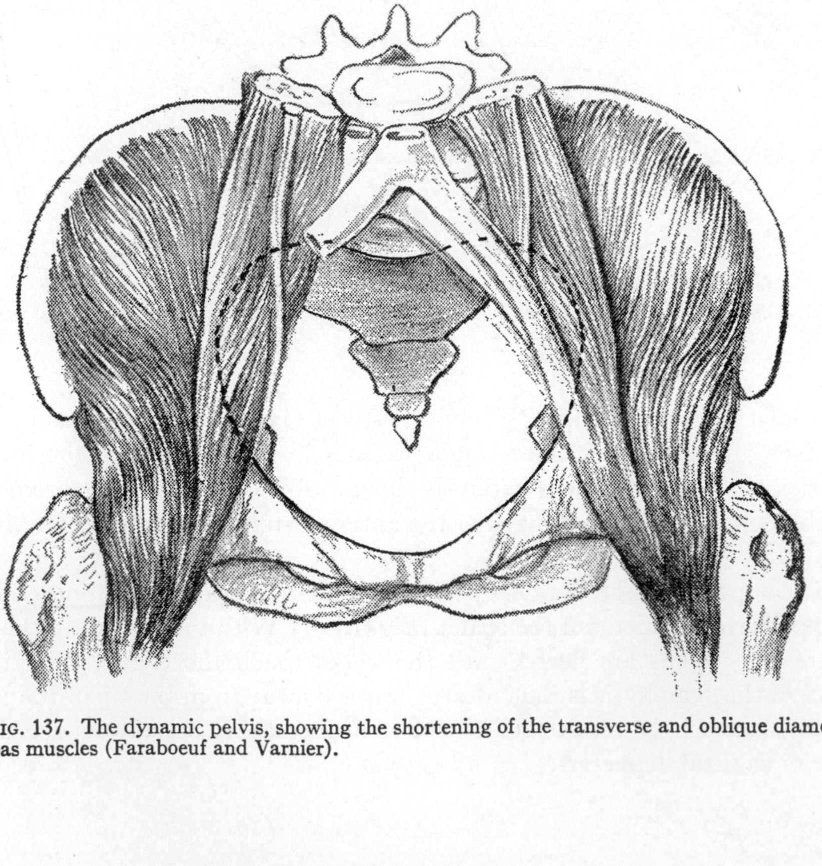

FIG. 137. The dynamic pelvis, showing the shortening of the transverse and oblique diameters by the psoas muscles (Faraboeuf and Varnier).

THE PSOAS MUSCLE arises from the bodies and transverse processes of the last dorsal and all of the lumbar vertebrae, and with the iliacus is inserted into the lesser trochanter of the femur. It is adjacent to the sacral promontory posteriorly and crosses the lateral margin of the posterior half of the superior aperture (Fig. 137). This muscle, accordingly, diminishes the posterior extremity of the oblique diameter and, with its fellow of the opposite side, cuts an

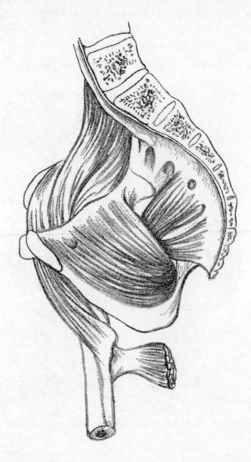

FIG. 138. The muscles on the lateral wall of the pelvis (Luska)

almost equal amount from each end of the transverse diameter. The inlet of the dynamic pelvis, therefore, is somewhat smaller than that of the static pelvis. The action of the psoas muscle is to flex the femur. When the Walcher position is used, it therefore contracts to counteract the hyperextension of the thighs and, as a result, lessens to some extent the advantage that is gained by this procedure.

THE PYRIFORMIS originates from the sacrum, lateral to the second, third and fourth foramina, and is inserted into the great trochanter of the femur. It lies on the posterior wall of the bony pelvis and forms a small portion of the posterior lateral aspect of the pelvic floor before it passes out through the greater sacrosciatic foramen (Fig. 138).

THE OBTURATOR INTERNUS takes its origin from the inner surface of the obturator membrane and the adjacent bony margin of the obturator foramen as far back as the anterior edge of the sciatic notch. Its fibers pass downward and backward beneath the white line and converge to form a tendon which, after leaving the pelvis through the lesser sacrosciatic foramen, is inserted into the great trochanter (Fig. 138).

This muscle, like those described above, acts as a pad for the bony walls of the pelvis and, accordingly, slightly diminishes the size of the pelvic cavity.

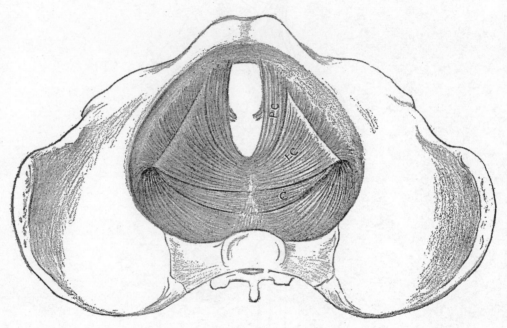

FIG. 139. The muscles of the pelvic diaphragm as seen from above. *PC*, pubococcygeus. *IC*, iliococcygeus. *C*, coccygeus.

THE LEVATOR ANI arises from the posterior surface of the pubis in front, the white line laterally and the spine of the ischium behind (12). It is inserted into the coccyx and the anococcygeal body and some of its anterior fibers join with those of the opposite side to encircle the posterior wall of the anus. The parts of the levator ani are designated as the pubococcygeus and the iliococcygeus, according to their site of origin (Fig. 139).

The **pubococcygeus** originates from the posterior surface of the pubis about 3.5 cm. below the pelvic brim and 1 cm. external to the midline, and passes downward, backward and inward to be inserted into the coccyx and anococcygeal body. Its internal portion is slightly thicker and gives off a few fibers posterior to the vagina, to which it is united by firm connective tissue attachments. This part of the pubococcygeus interdigitates with its fellow of the opposite side to encircle the posterior wall of the anus and is called the **puborectalis** (Fig. 139).

The **iliococcygeus** or obturator coccygeus comprises the greater part of the levator ani muscle and has its origin in the thickened portion of the obturator fascia which is known as the white line. It slopes downward, inward and backward and is inserted into the side of the coccyx.

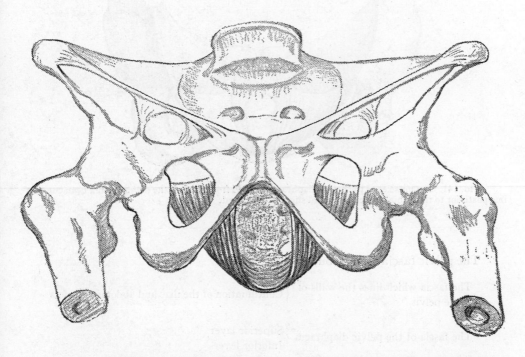

FIG. 140. The muscles of the pelvic diaphragm as seen from the front and below (Dickinson).

The **coccygeus** arises from the spine of the ischium and is inserted into the lower lateral margins of the sacrum and coccyx.

The levator ani muscles act as a constrictor of the anus and vagina. Together with the coccygei, they form a muscular sling which closes the pelvic outlet, excepting at its anterior extremity, where a U-shaped opening, 2.5 cm. wide and 5 cm. long, extends from the anus to the symphysis (Figs. 140 and 141). These muscles, accordingly, enter into the formation of the pelvic diaphragm which supports and resists the intra-abdominal pressure.

The muscles below the pelvic diaphragm will be considered in connection with the fascial planes between which they are found.

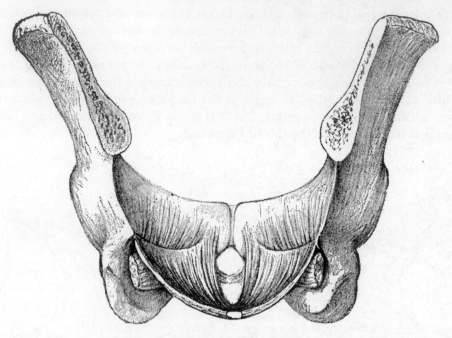

FIG. 141. The muscles of the pelvic diaphragm viewed from behind, the pelvis having been cut on a line posterior to the ischial spines and tilted slightly backward.

PELVIC FASCIA

The pelvic fascia may be outlined as follows:

The fascia which lines the walls of the pelvis { Continuation of the iliac and abdominal fascia

The fascia of the pelvic diaphragm { Superior layer / Inferior layer

The fascia above the pelvic diaphragm (endopelvic fascia or the suspensory apparatus of the bladder, vagina, uterus and rectum) { Vesical portion / Vesicovaginal septum / Rectovaginal septum / Rectal sheath / Uterine portion

The fascia below the pelvic diaphragm {

Posterior triangle { Anococcygeal body

Anterior triangle { Superior layer of the triangular ligament / Inferior layer of the triangular ligament / Deep layer of the superficial fascia or Colles's fascia / Perineal body

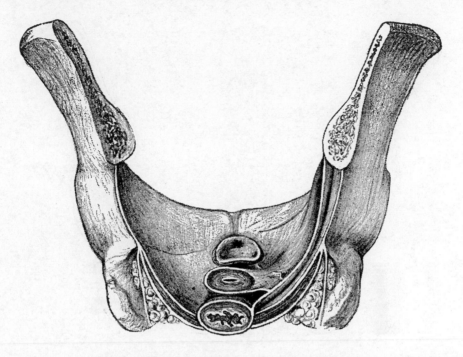

Fig. 142. Superior and inferior fascia of the pelvic diaphragm on the left side. The endopelvic fascia is on the right side.

THE FASCIA WHICH LINES THE WALLS OF THE PELVIS. The fascia from the iliac regions and the abdominal wall continues downward into the pelvis to cover the internal surface of the obturator internus and pyriformis muscles, after which it is attached to the sacrum, the sacrotuberous ligament and the inferior margins of the ischiopubic rami. In the anterior triangle of the pelvic outlet, it is reflected across the pelvis as the triangular ligament. This structure will be further considered in the description of the fascia below the pelvic diaphragm.

THE FASCIA OF THE PELVIC DIAPHRAGM. At the white line the fascia, covering the obturator internus, gives off a mesial reflexion which splits to envelop the muscles of the pelvic diaphragm (Fig. 142).

The upper layer of this fascial sling covers the levator ani and coccygeus of each side and is attached posteriorly to the fascia over the pyriformis. It is known as the **superior fascia** of the pelvic diaphragm (rectovesical fascia).

The under surface of the levator ani and coccygeus is covered by the **inferior fascia,** which also forms the roof and internal wall of each ischiorectal fossa.

THE FASCIA ABOVE THE PELVIC DIAPHRAGM (endopelvic fascia). Above the superior fascia of the pelvic diaphragm, the pelvic viscera are imbedded in

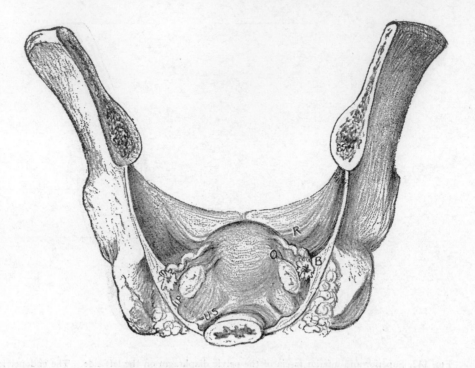

Fig. 143. Section similar to Figures 141 and 142, showing the uterus, tubes, ovaries and their ligaments in place.   R, round ligament; B, broad ligament; US, uterosacral ligament; O, ovarian ligament; IP, infundibulo pelvic ligament.

the subperitoneal tissue in which they were developed.   This tissue is condensed to form fascial sheaths in the region of the vagina, lower uterine segment, rectum and base of the bladder and is attached in places to the superior fascia of the pelvic diaphragm.   Its firmest attachment, however, is along the white line and in the neighborhood of the ischial spines (Fig. 142).

The **vesical portion** of the endopelvic fascia covers the under surface of the bladder and forms the lateral and anterior ligaments of that organ.

The **uterine portion** extends from the lateral surface of the pelvis in the region of the white line and ischial spine to the side of the uterus, where it joins the dense fascial layer which surrounds the lower uterine segment.   This is the broadest band of the endopelvic fascia and forms the supporting structure of the broad ligament.

The **vesicovaginal septum** lies between the bladder and the anterior wall of the vagina and is firmly united to each of these structures.   As it continues upward, it serves to attach the bladder to the lower uterine segment.

The **rectovaginal septum** is between the rectum and the posterior wall of the vagina and is continuous below with the perineal body.

The **rectal sheath** passes behind the rectum and is attached to its wall.

These visceral lamellae and their lateral attachments receive denser connective tissue elements and muscle fibers which pass to the pelvic viscera and are thereby strengthened. Through their intercommunication and attachments to the anterior, posterior and lateral walls of the pelvis, they act as a suspensory apparatus which supports the pelvic viscera and maintains the normal relationship between these structures. If, in the course of labor, this suspensory apparatus is injured in one or more of its elements the adjacent viscera may descend through the vaginal orifice as a cystocele, rectocele, or uterine prolapse.

THE PELVIC FLOOR. The superior and inferior layers of the fascia which enclose the levator ani and coccygeus muscles enter into the formation of the pelvic floor or diaphragm. Anteriorly, this diaphragm arises slightly external to the symphysis and 3.5 cm. below the pelvic brim. Laterally, its line of origin extends downward and backward toward the ischial spine, where it is 5.5 cm. beneath the superior strait. Posterior to the spine of the ischium, its fascia becomes continuous with the fascia over the pyriformis and is attached to the sides of the sacrum and coccyx. The two halves of the pelvic diaphragm are united between the coccyx and anus to form the anococcygeal body and thereby close the pelvic outlet except in its anterior aspect (Figs. 139, 140 and 141). The pelvic floor, accordingly, forms a trough which, like the ways of a ferry-boat, guides the child along the path of least resistance through the outlet of the pelvis. A knowledge of the shape, position and structure of the pelvic diaphragm, therefore, is essential to a clear understanding of the mechanism of labor.

THE FASCIA BELOW THE PELVIC DIAPHRAGM. Beneath the inferior fascia of the pelvic diaphragm, the structure of the posterior triangle of the outlet differs from that of the anterior. At the anterior extremity of the posterior sagittal diameter the anus passes through the U-shaped opening in the levator sling and may be regarded as the point of division between the two triangles of the outlet.

THE POSTERIOR TRIANGLE OF THE OUTLET. Between the tip of the coccyx and the anus is the dense anococcygeal body. It slopes downward and forward and is formed by a union of the two halves of the pelvic diaphragm and the attachments of the **sphincter ani externus** to the coccyx. The latter muscle surrounds the anus and is imbedded anteriorly in the perineal body. On each side of the anus, the deep ischiorectal fossa extends from the sacrum to a point about 5 cm. anterior to the bisischial diameter and is limited above by the white line. Its roof and internal boundary, accordingly, are the inferior fascia of the pelvic diaphragm while the obturator fascia forms its external border. This cavity is filled with fatty connective tissue which is continuous with the subcutaneous fat layer (Fig. 144).

THE ANTERIOR TRIANGLE OF THE OUTLET is closed by several layers of fascia and the perineal muscles, except at the points where they are perforated by the urethra and the vagina (Fig. 145). From above downward, the constituents of these various layers are:

1. The two layers of the triangular ligament with their enclosed muscles—compressor urethrae and transversus perinei profundus.

2. The contents of the superficial perineal compartment—ischiocavernosus, bulbocavernosus and transversus perinei superficialis.

3. Colles's fascia.

4. Panniculus adiposus.

5. Integument.

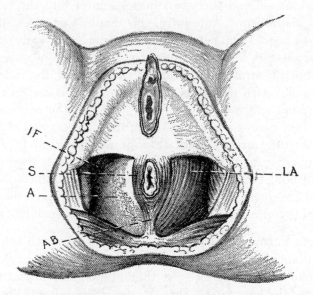

FIG. 144. The posterior triangle of the pelvic outlet. S, sphincter ani externus; AB, anococcygeal body; IF, ischiorectal fossa; A, inferior fascia of the pelvic diaphragm (anal fascia); LA, levator ani; the anal fascia has been removed on this side.

THE TRIANGULAR LIGAMENT (urogenital diaphragm) is the continuation of the obturator fascia which crosses the anterior triangle of the pelvic outlet. It is composed of two layers which are attached laterally to the ischiopubic rami. These extend from the lateral aspect of the pubis on each side to the bisischial line, where they are joined with each other and with Colles's fascia below.

In the midline, the triangular ligament is perforated by the urethra and vagina, lateral to which it is firmly attached to the various elements of the pelvic diaphragm. External to these attachments it forms the floor of the anterior extensions of the ischiorectal fossae.

Between the superior and inferior layers of the triangular ligament is the deep perineal interspace which contains the urethra, the internal pudic vessels and nerves, the deep transversus perinei, and the compressor urethrae muscles (Fig. 145).

THE DEEP TRANSVERSUS PERINEI MUSCLE arises from the ramus of the ischium and extends transversely across the posterior part of the deep perineal interspace to be inserted into the central portion of the perineal body (Fig. 145).

THE COMPRESSOR URETHRAE arises from the ischiopubic rami and, passing transversely, some of its fibers join their fellows of the opposite side in front of and behind the urethra, while others are attached to the lateral walls of the vagina (Fig. 145).

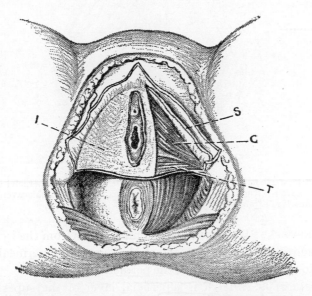

FIG. 145. Anterior triangle of the pelvic outlet. Right side shows inferior layer of triangular ligament. Left side shows inferior layer of triangular ligament removed. *S*, inferior layer of triangular ligament removed. *I*, inferior layer of triangular ligament in place. *T*, deep transversus perinei muscle. *C*, compressor urethrae muscle.

COLLES'S FASCIA is the deep layer of superficial fascia which lies below the triangular ligament and is attached at the sides to the rami of the pubes and ischia. It is continuous with the deep layer of the superficial abdominal fascia and extends backward to the posterior limits of the triangular ligament with which it is joined (Fig. 146).

Between the inferior layer of the triangular ligament and Colles's fascia is the superficial interspace which contains the cavernosus bodies of the clitoris, Bartholin's glands and the superficial perineal muscles—ischiocavernosus, bulbocavernosus and transversus perinei superficialis.

THE ISCHIOCAVERNOSUS MUSCLE arises on the mesial surface of the ischial ramus and passes obliquely forward to be inserted into the fascia on the inferior surface of the clitoris (Fig. 146).

THE BULBOCAVERNOSUS, or sphincter vaginae, has its origin in the central tendon of the perineum and passes forward around the lateral half of the vagina to be inserted into the fibrous sheath of the clitoris (Fig. 146).

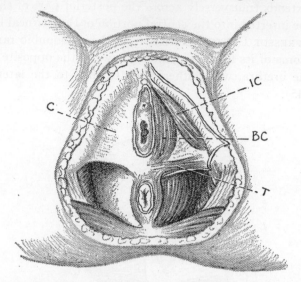

FIG. 146. Anterior triangle of the pelvic outlet. Left side shows superficial interspace; Colles's fascia has been removed. Right side shows Colles's fascia (*C*). *IC*, ischiocavernosus muscle; *BC*, bulbocavernosus muscle; *T*, transversus perinei superficialis.

THE TRANSVERSUS PERINEI SUPERFICIALIS arises from the ischial tuberosity and extends across the posterior part of the superficial perineal interspace to be inserted into the central tendon of the perineum (Fig. 146).

THE PANNICULUS ADIPOSUS, superficial layer of the superficial fascia, is external to the fascia of Colles and is similar to the panniculus that is found beneath the skin in other parts of the body. It is continuous with the adipose tissue that fills the ischiorectal fossae posteriorly, and anteriorly enters into the formation of the mons and labia majora.

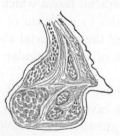

FIG. 147. Sagittal section of the perineal body (Dickinson).

INTEGUMENT. Superficial to the panniculus adiposus is the integument which laterally is thrown into folds to form the labia.

THE PERINEAL BODY is the triangular portion of the perineum which lies between the vagina and the anus. It consists of the various fascial layers and is crossed by the perineal muscles which are joined in the common central tendinous raphe (Fig. 147). Accordingly, the median portion of the perineal body contains all of the fascial elements from the endopelvic fascia above to the superficial fascia below.

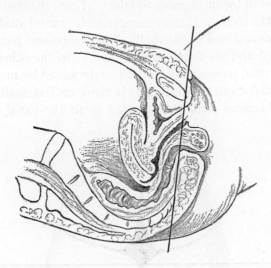

FIG. 148. Pelvic floor in the nonpregnant woman.

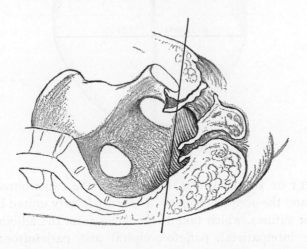

FIG. 149. Pelvic floor at the end of pregnancy. Note the marked projection below a line joining the tip of the coccyx and the inferior margin of the symphysis.

Throughout pregnancy, the pelvic floor and urogenital diaphragm undergo vascular and other changes which cause them to project as much as one inch below their customary level in the nonpregnant state (13, 14), (Figs. 148 and 149).

THE PASSENGER

The passage of the fetus through the birth canal is influenced by the head, the shoulders and the hips.

THE FETAL HEAD, because of its size and relative rigidity, is the most important fetal factor in the mechanism of labor. From the obstetrical standpoint, it is divided into the larger and more compressible cranial vault, and the smaller incompressible face and base of the skull. The component parts of the latter are quite firmly united and are fairly well ossified. On the other hand, the bones of the former are thin, poorly ossified and loosely joined by membranous attachments. The cranial vault, accordingly, is more or less malleable and, in the course of labor, becomes somewhat molded to fit the canal through which it must pass.

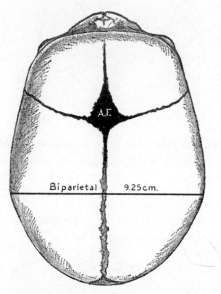

FIG. 150. The anterior fontanel (*A.F.*).

THE VAULT OF THE CRANIUM is formed by the two frontal, two parietal, two temporal and the occipital bones. These are loosely united by membranous attachments or sutures, which take their names from the adjoining bones. In obstetrics, the interparietal, parieto-occipital and parietofrontal sutures are commonly known as the sagittal, lambdoidal and coronal sutures. At the points of intersection, these membranous attachments become considerably enlarged to form the fontanels, the most important of which are the anterior and the posterior.

THE ANTERIOR OR LARGE FONTANEL, or bregma, is situated at the point of junction of the two parietal and the two frontal bones. It is a diamond-shaped figure in which four suture lines intersect (Fig. 150).

THE POSTERIOR OR SMALL FONTANEL is situated at the junction of the two parietal and the occipital bones. It is triangular in shape and is formed by the intersection of three suture lines (Fig. 151).

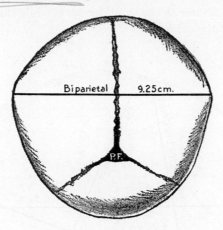

FIG. 151. The posterior fontanel (*P.F.*).

SAGITTAL FONTANELS occasionally result from failure of ossification in the course of the sagittal suture. When present, they may be mistaken for the more important fontanels and lead to considerable confusion (11) (Fig. 152).

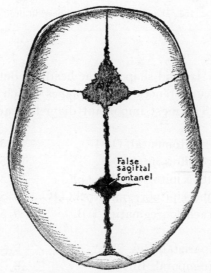

FIG. 152. Sagittal fontanel.

The sutures and fontanels not only contribute to the malleability of the head but also serve as valuable landmarks which aid in the diagnosis of the presentation, position and posture.

The cranial vault is divided into the vertex, the occiput and the sinciput. The vertex is that portion which lies between the anterior and posterior fontanels and extends laterally to the parietal eminences. The occiput is the region of the occipital bone and is posterior to the small fontanel while the sinciput lies between the large fontanel and the orbits.

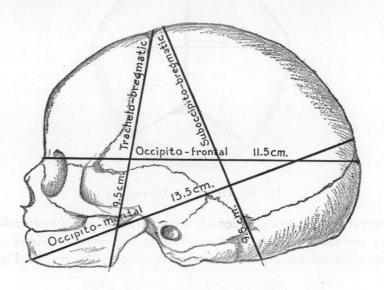

FIG. 153. Diameters of the fetal head in profile.

DIAMETERS. The size and shape of the head are determined by measuring the diameters and circumferences of the planes which are concerned in the mechanism of labor. The most important diameters are:

1. Occipitomental, O.M.   13.5 cm.
2. Occipitofrontal, O.F.   11.5 cm.
3. Suboccipitofrontal, S.O.F.   10.5 cm.
4. Suboccipitobregmatic, S.O.B.   9.5 cm.
5. Trachelobregmatic, T.B.   9.5 cm.

6. Biparietal, Bip.   9+ cm.
7. Bitemporal, Bit.   8   cm.
8. Bimastoid, Bim.   7   cm.

THE OCCIPITOMENTAL DIAMETER, O.M., 13.5 cm., is the largest diameter of the fetal head and extends from the mentum to the posterior fontanel (Fig. 153).

THE OCCIPITOFRONTAL DIAMETER, O.F., 11.5 cm., is measured from the root of the nose to the occiput (Fig. 153).

THE SUBOCCIPITOFRONTAL DIAMETER, S.O.F., 10.5 cm., extends from the junction of the neck and occiput to the brow (Fig. 157).

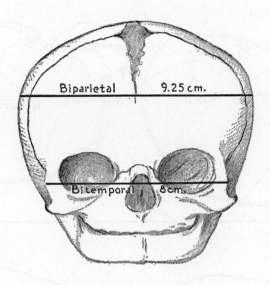

FIG. 154. Biparietal and bitemporal diameters.

THE SUBOCCIPITOBREGMATIC DIAMETER, S.O.B., 9.5 cm., is measured from the junction of the neck and occiput to the bregma (Fig. 153).

THE TRACHELOBREGMATIC DIAMETER, T.B., 9.5 cm., extends from the anterior junction of the neck and lower jaw to the bregma (Fig. 153).

THE BIPARIETAL DIAMETER, Bip., 9+ cm., is the distance between the two parietal eminences (Figs. 154, 150 and 151).

THE BITEMPORAL DIAMETER, Bit., 8 cm., extends from one temporal suture to the other (Fig. 154).

THE BIMASTOID DIAMETER, Bim., 7 cm., connects the two mastoid processes.

PLANES AND CIRCUMFERENCES. Further information concerning the size and shape of the head is gained from a study of its most important planes.

THE OCCIPITOMENTAL PLANE is a cross-section of the head in the occipito-mental diameter. It is the largest of the head planes and has a circumference of 38 cm. The occipitomental, 13.5 cm., and the biparietal, 9+ cm., are its chief diameters (Fig. 155).

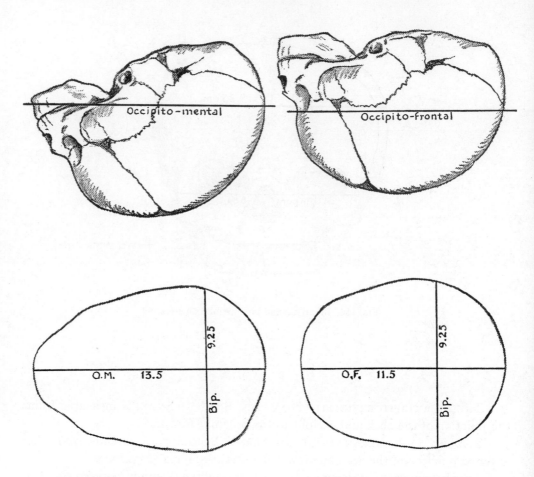

FIG. 155. The occipito-mental plane.   FIG. 156. The occipito-frontal plane.

THE OCCIPITOFRONTAL PLANE passes through the occipitofrontal diameter, 11.5 cm., and the biparietal, 9+ cm. Its circumference is 34 cm. (Fig. 156).

THE SUBOCCIPITOFRONTAL PLANE is a cross-section of the head in the sub-occipitofrontal diameter, 10.5 cm. Its transverse diameter is the biparietal 9+ cm. and its circumference measures 31 cm. (Fig. 157).

THE SUBOCCIPTOBREGMATIC PLANE extends through the suboccipito-bregmatic, 9.5 cm. and the biparietal, 9+ cm., diameters, and has the smallest circumference, 29 cm., of any of the important head planes. It is almost circular in shape and is the plane which passes through the pelvis in the normal mechanism of labor (Fig. 158).

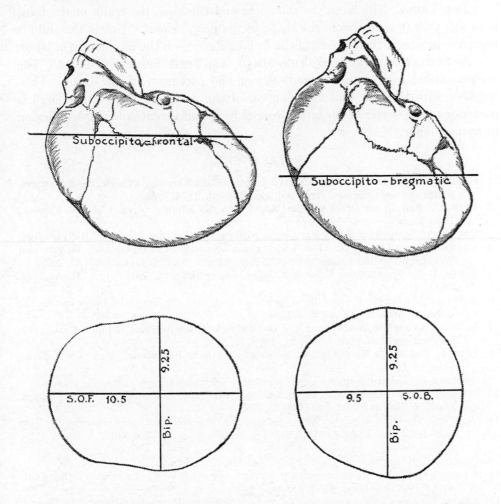

FIG. 157. The suboccipito-frontal plane. FIG. 158. The suboccipito-bregmatic plane.

THE SHOULDERS. Owing to their mobility, the relative position of each shoulder may be altered during labor and it is the rule for one shoulder to occupy a lower level in the pelvis than the other. The anatomical circumference of the shoulders, therefore, is larger than the shoulder plane which actually passes through the birth canal. However, the diminution of the transverse diameter never is sufficient to make it shorter than the anteroposterior. The circumference of the shoulders is 38 cm. and the bisacromial diameter measures 12 cm.

THE HIPS. Due to the greater rigidity of the pelvis, the anatomical plane of the hips corresponds to that plane which is a cross-section of the body through the pelvis and the great trochanters. Its circumference is 31 cm. and the intertrochanteric diameter measures 10 cm.

THE TRUNK. Between the shoulders and the hips, the trunk of the fetus is so soft that it conforms to the shape of the pelvic canal. Unless the child is excessive in size, it therefore has little or no influence on the mechanism of labor.

ARTICULATION BETWEEN THE HEAD AND THE SPINAL COLUMN. The occipito-atloid articulation permits flexion and extension of the head. This, together with the fact that the junction of the neck and base of the skull is posterior to the center of the latter, results in the occurrence of complete flexion in normal labor.

REFERENCES

1. GOLTZ, F.: Ueber den Einfluss des Nervensystems auf die Vorgänge während der Schwangerschaft und des Geburts. Arch. f. d. ges. Physiol., 1874, 9, 552.
2. REIN, G.: Beitrag zur Lehre von der Innervation des Uterus. Arch. f. d. ges. Physiol., 1880, 23, 68.
3. ROUTH, A.: Parturition during Paraplegia, with cases. Tr. Obs. Soc. Lond. 1897, 39, 191.
4. KRUEGER AND OFFERGELD: Der Vorgang von Zeugung Schwangerschaft, Geburt und Wochenbett an der ausgeschalteten Gebärmutter. Arch. f. Gyn., 1907, 83, 257.
5. ELKIN, D. C.: Spontaneous Labor in a Case of Decentralized Uterus. J. A. M. A., 1922, 78, 27.
6. SCHATZ, F.: Ueber die Formen der Wehencurve und über die Peristalik des menschlichen Uterus. Arch. f. Gyn., 1886, 27, 284.
7. ASCHOFF: Ueber die Berichtigung und Notwendigkeit des Begriffes Isthmus uteri. Verhandl. d. deutsch. path. Gesellsch., 1908, 12, 314.
8. VEIT, J.: Das untere Uterinsegment und seine praktische Bedeutung. Zentralbl. f. Gyn., 1914, 38, 1369.
9. ZWEIFEL, P.: Ueber das untere Uterinsegment. Zentralbl. f. Gyn., 1914, 38, 1376.
10. SCHMIDT, H. R.: Anatomische Untersuchungen zur Frage des unteren Uterinsegmentes. Ztschr. f. Geburtsh. u. Gyn., 1923, 85, 233.
11. WALCHER, G.: Die Conjugata eines engen Beckens ist keine konstante Grösse, sonder lässt sich durch die Körperhaltung der Trägerin verändern. Zentralbl. f. Gyn., 1889, 13, 892.
12. DICKINSON, R. L.: Studies of the Levator Ani Muscle. Am. J. Obs., 1889, 22, 897.
13. WEBSTER, J. C.: The Floor in Relation to Pregnancy. Researches in Female Pelvic Anatomy. Edinb. & Lond., 1892, 93.
14. STIEVE, H.: Scheidenwand und Scheidenmund während und nach der Geburt. Jahrbuch f. Morph. u. Mikros. Anat. Ztschr. f. mikr.-anat., 1928, 13, 441.
15. LEA, A.: The Sagittal Fontanelle in the Heads of Infants at Birth. Tr. Obs. Soc., Lond., 1898, 40, 263.

WILLIAM SMELLIE
1697–1763
London

Smellie was an outstanding obstetrician and a noted teacher.

He was one of the first to make use of the manikin in the teaching of obstetrics (1739).

In 1744 he introduced the steel lock (English lock) forceps and 7 years later added the pelvic curve. Priority regarding the latter invention, however, has been claimed for Pugh (1740) and Leveret (1747).

Smellie's "Midwifery" published in 1753 contained an excellent description of the mechanism of labor and gave directions for the safe use of forceps.   This work together with the two volumes of case histories and his large anatomical tables (1754) were invaluable sources of obstetric information. Through his teaching and that of his pupils Smellie had a great influence on modern obstetrics.

CHAPTER XII

THE MECHANISM OF LABOR

There are three stages in the mechanism of labor:

THE FIRST STAGE is the **stage of dilatation.** It is concerned with the obliteration of the cervical canal and the dilatation of the external os.

THE SECOND STAGE is the **stage of expulsion.** It begins when the cervix is fully dilated and ends with the delivery of the child.

THE THIRD STAGE is the **placental stage.** It has to do with the separation and expulsion of the placenta.

THE FIRST STAGE OF LABOR

The first stage begins with the onset of labor and ends when the cervix is sufficiently dilated to permit the passage of a full term child.

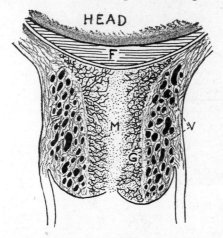 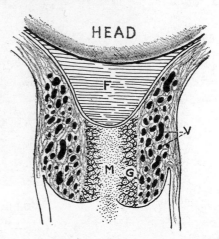

FIG. 159. The condition of the cervix at term (Stieve). Beginning changes in the cervix in the first stage of labor. *F*, forewaters; *M*, mucus; *G*, glands; *V*, vessels.

FIG. 160. The condition of the cervix early in labor (Stieve). Early labor pains are separating the mucus and glands from the cervix.

The factors that are responsible for the phenomena observed in this stage are:

1. The preliminary changes in the cervix which favor dilatation.
2. The hydrostatic action of the bag of waters.
3. The intermittent uterine contractions.

CHANGES IN THE CERVIX. During pregnancy, the cervix undergoes progressive softening and all of its constituents are altered to facilitate dilatation. The mucosa shows a marked proliferation with a very considerable increase in its glandular elements. The latter are dilated and contain a mucous secretion, which also fills the cervical canal. This fragile, spongy layer does not long resist the forces of labor and, accordingly, is largely expelled with the mucous plug. There likewise are marked vascular changes which, at the end of pregnancy, convert the wall of the cervix into a mass of blood spaces and make it yield more readily to the forces that bring about dilatation (Figs. 159, 160, 161 and 162).

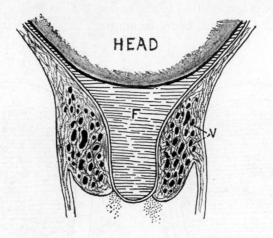

FIG. 161. The condition of the cervix later in the first stage. The forewaters have reached the external os and the hydrostatic pressure being equal in all directions, forces the blood out of the cavernous spaces in the cervical wall (Stieve).

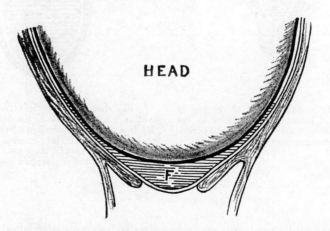

FIG. 162. The cavernous spaces are emptied by the hydrostatic pressure of the forewaters and the canal of the cervix is obliterated. During this process, the mucosa is partially expelled with the mucous plug (Stieve). *F*, forewaters.

In addition, the muscle fibers are diminished in number, and alterations in the connective tissue, similar to those found in all of the pelvic organs, greatly lessen the normal tendency of these structures to resist dilatation (1).

THE HYDROSTATIC ACTION OF THE BAG OF WATERS. As long as the membranes remain intact, the contents of the uterus may be regarded as an elastic sac filled with fluid, and any force applied to that sac acts in accordance with the laws of hydrostatic pressure. When the upper or active segment of the uterus contracts, its force is transmitted to the amniotic fluid and is distributed equally in all directions. This fluid, being incompressible, is displaced in the path of

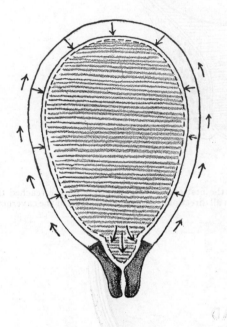 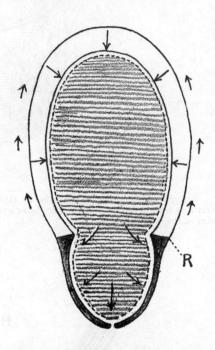

FIG. 163. Hydrostatic action of the bag of waters. Onset of labor; fluid displaced in the direction of the lower uterine segment and cervix. Shaded area is lower segment and cervix.

FIG. 164. Hydrostatic action of the bag of waters. A later phase in the first stage of labor. Hydrostatic bag distending lower uterine segment and dilating the cervix. Shaded area is the lower segment and cervix. Also note the progressive thickening of the segment as labor advances.

least resistance and the elastic sac, accordingly, becomes distended in the region of the weak passive lower uterine segment and cervix. The intact membranes, with their contained liquor amnii, therefore, act as a fluid wedge which exerts a downward and lateral pressure on the isthmus and cervical canal (Figs. 163 and 164). As labor advances, the membranes become stretched and protrude through the progressively dilating cervix until the force of the uterine contractions becomes sufficiently strong to cause their rupture.

THE BALL VALVE ACTION OF THE HEAD.   In most labors, premature rupture of the membranes is prevented by the descent of the head, which acts as a ball valve.   The full force of the uterine contractions is then distributed through the amniotic fluid to the head instead of against the membranes in the cervical canal and the pressure of the fluid below the presenting part, the forewaters, is thereby diminished (Fig. 165).   If the head does not fit well into the pelvis and lower

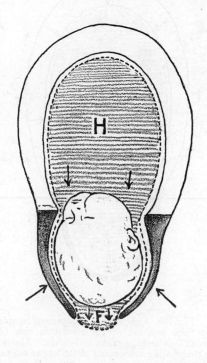

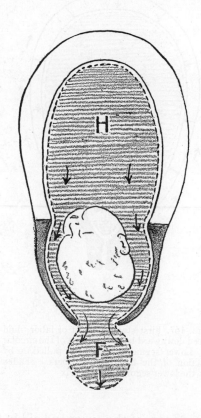

FIG. 165. Ball valve action of the head.   The head snugly fits the lower uterine segment and, acting as a ball valve, lessens the pressure between it and the membranes, i.e., in the forewaters. Watch glass protrusion of the membranes.   H, hindwaters; F, forewaters.

FIG. 166. Absence of ball valve action of the head.   The head does not fit the lower uterine segment and, as a result, the pressure is the same in both the hind and forewaters.   Glove finger protrusion of the membranes.   H, hindwaters; F, forewaters.

uterine segment, it cannot act as a ball valve and the pressure of the forewaters is then the same as the pressure above the presenting part (Fig. 166).   The presence of a good ball valve is indicated when the membranes protrude in the shape of an inverted watch glass, while a poor ball valve causes a glove finger protrusion of the membranes into the vagina.

THE UTERINE CONTRACTIONS. The principal action of the uterine contractions is to constrict that part of the ovum which is in the upper segment of the uterus. This causes a downward displacement of the amniotic fluid and a bulging of the elastic membranes in the region of the isthmus and cervix. Contractions of the longitudinal fibers likewise pull the isthmus and cervix up over

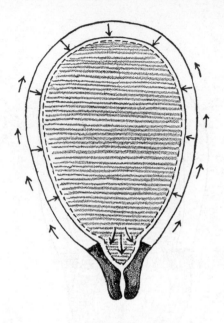 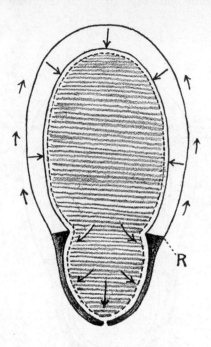

FIG. 167. First stage. Onset of labor, fluid displaced downward by contraction of the circular layer. Lower segment and cervix pulled up by contraction of the longitudinal fibers. Shaded area is the lower segment and cervix.

FIG. 168. First stage. Effacement complete Note the position of the retraction ring (R). Shaded area lower segment and cervix. Also note the progressive thickening of the upper segment as labor advances.

the lower pole of the ovum and aid in the mechanism of dilatation. This action of the uterus also elevates the bladder and anterior vaginal wall, thereby drawing upward the anterior segment of the pelvic floor. Retraction of the musculature of the upper segment causes the retraction ring to rise and, as a consequence, effects the same changes that are produced by contraction of the longitudinal fibers (2).

If the membranes rupture before the cervix is fully dilated, the expansile fluid wedge is replaced by the head of the child. In these circumstances, the presenting part is forced downward as the yielding cervix is pulled up by the contraction of the longitudinal fibers and further retraction of the upper segment. The hard head is a poorer dilator and causes greater trauma to the cervix as

well as an increase in the intensity of the pain of the first stage of labor.   On the
other hand, the pressure of the head on the lower uterine segment frequently
stimulates the uterus to contract more vigorously so that the mechanical disadvantage of early rupture of the membranes is partially offset by an increase in
the strength and frequency of the expelling forces.

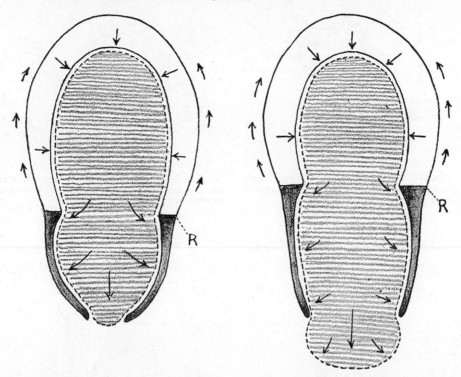

FIG. 169. First stage. External os dilating
as the cervix and lower segment are being pulled
upward over the bag of waters, which exert a
downward and lateral pressure.   Note the position of the retraction ring (R).   Shaded area is
the lower segment and cervix.

FIG. 170. First stage.   Cervix fully dilated.
Note the position of the retraction ring (R).
Shaded area is the lower segment and cervix. Note
the increasing thickness of the upper segment as
labor progresses.

From the foregoing description it will be seen that the preparation of the
cervix for the passage of the child takes place from above downward.   This
preparation is divided into two phases:
    1. Effacement of the cervical canal (Figs. 167 and 168).
    2. Dilatation of the external os (Figs. 169 and 170).
    The **stage of effacement** begins with the onset of labor and ends when the
portio vaginalis is completely obliterated (Figs. 167 and 168).   As the isthmus
becomes elongated and the internal os dilates, the latter is pulled upward and the
canal of the cervix is incorporated into the lower uterine segment.   The cervical
canal, accordingly, becomes progressively shorter until nothing remains but the
undilated external os.   Effacement of the cervix is then said to be complete.

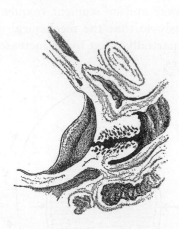

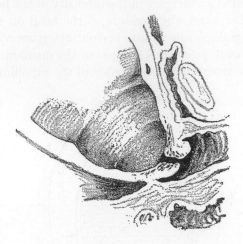

FIG. 171. First stage. Onset of labor. Note the relation of bladder, lower segment and cervix to the symphysis.

FIG. 172. Lower segment, bladder and internal os pulled upward with partial obliteration of cervical canal.

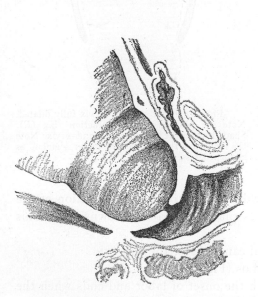

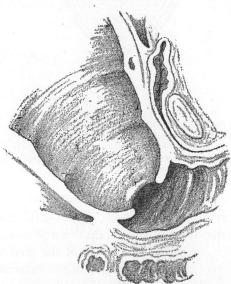

FIG. 173. Bladder, lower segment and internal os pulled farther upward. Complete obliteration of cervical canal.

FIG. 174. Bladder, lower segment and internal os still higher. External os dilating.

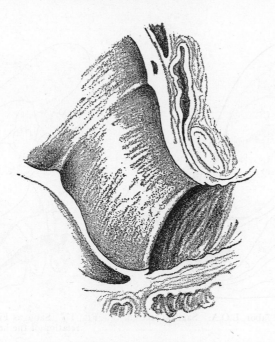

FIG. 175. Bladder above the symphysis, contraction ring 10 cm. above external os. External os fully dilated, 9 cm. Throughout the mechanism of the first stage, the anterior wall of the vagina and the structures in front of and above it have been pulled upward.

The **stage of dilatation** follows effacement. At this time, the cervical margins become thinner and the external os is gradually dilated until its diameter is large enough to permit the passage of a full term child, 9–10 cm. (Figs. 169 and 170).

In women who have borne children, the cervical canal is somewhat dilated at the onset of labor. As labor progresses, however, effacement of this partially dilated canal takes place in the usual manner, and it is completely obliterated before further dilatation occurs.

THE SECOND STAGE OF LABOR

Since L.O.A. is a common presentation and position, its mechanism will be described to illustrate the various movements of the child as it passes through the pelvis.

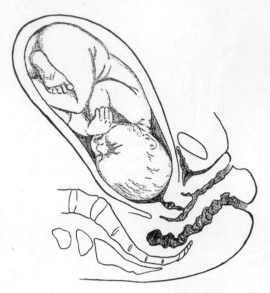

FIG. 176. Onset of labor, L.O.A.   Sagittal section.

FIG. 177. Same as Figure 176 showing the relation of the head to the pelvis.

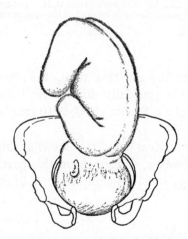

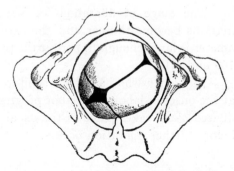

FIG. 178. Front view of L.O.A. in relation to the pelvis at the beginning of labor.

FIG. 179. Onset of labor, L.O.A. as visualized from below.

The head enters the pelvis with the sagittal suture in the right oblique diameter and the occiput in the left anterior quadrant of the mother's pelvis (Figs. 176, 177, 178 and 179).   DESCENT is constant throughout the mechanism, during which the head passes through the following movements: FLEXION, INTERNAL ROTATION, EXTENSION, RESTITUTION, and EXTERNAL ROTATION. For the sake of clearness these will be described separately.   They, however, overlap each other as the mechanism of labor progresses.

Flexion

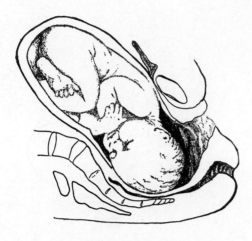

FIG. 180. L.O.A.   Flexion of the head.
Sagittal section.

FIG. 181. L.O.A.   Same as Figure 180 showing
the relation of the head to the pelvis.

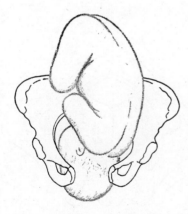

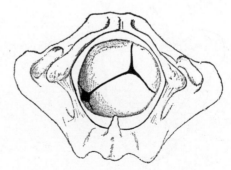

FIG. 182. L.O.A.   Front view of flexed
head in relation to the pelvis.

FIG. 183. L.O.A.   Flexion as visualized
from below.

FLEXION.   As soon as sufficient resistance is encountered, the head becomes so flexed that the chin is in contact with the sternum and, as a consequence, the suboccipitobregmatic plane takes the place of the occipitofrontal as the largest plane that is to pass through the pelvis.

Internal Rotation

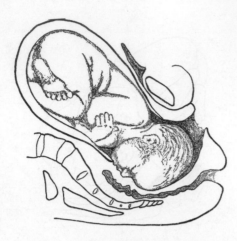

FIG. 184. L.O.A. Internal rotation of the head. Sagittal section.

FIG. 185. L.O.A. Same as Figure 184 showing the relation of the head to the pelvis.

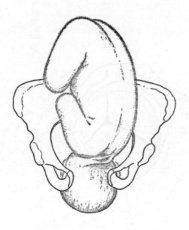

FIG. 186. L.O.A. Front view after internal rotation

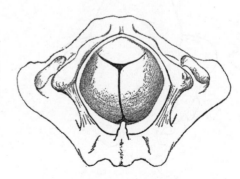

FIG. 187. L.O.A., after internal rotation as visualized from below.

INTERNAL ROTATION. When the occiput reaches the pelvic floor, it is rotated 45° to the right and anteriorly, and comes to lie beneath the symphysis pubis. This brings the sagittal suture into relation with the anteroposterior diameter of the outlet.

Extension

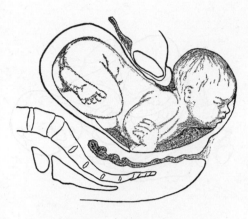

FIG. 188. L.O.A. Extension of the head. Sagittal section.

FIG. 189. L.O.A. Same as Figure 188 showing the relation of the head to the pelvis.

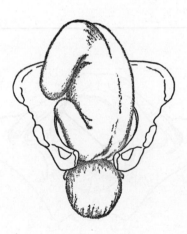

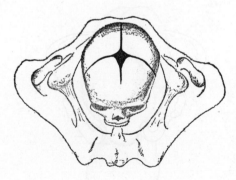

FIG. 190. L.O.A. Front view of extension.

FIG. 191. L.O.A. Extension as visualized from below.

EXTENSION. After the occiput passes out of the pelvis, the nucha becomes arrested beneath the pubic arch and acts as a pivoting point while the sagittal suture, large fontanel, brow, orbits, nose, mouth and chin are born by extension. As a result, the largest diameter which passes through the vulvovaginal orifice is the suboccipito frontal, 10.5 cm.

Restitution

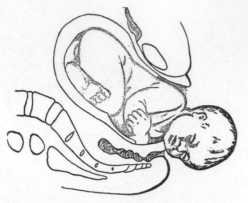

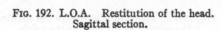

FIG. 192. L.O.A.   Restitution of the head.   Sagittal section.

FIG. 193. L.O.A.   Same as Figure 192 showing the relation of the head to the pelvis.

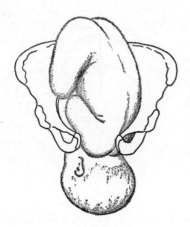

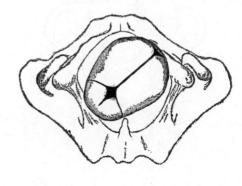

FIG. 194. L.O.A.   Front view after restitution.

FIG. 195. L.O.A.   Restitution as seen from below

RESTITUTION.   As soon as the head is released from the grasp of the vulvovaginal ring, the neck untwists and restitution occurs.   The occiput, accordingly, turns 45° to the left to its original position and the sagittal suture comes to lie obliquely.

External Rotation

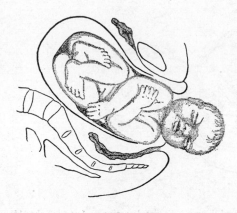

FIG. 196. L.O.A.   External rotation of the head.
Sagittal section.

FIG. 197. L.O.A.   Same as Figure 196 showing
the relation of the head to the pelvis.

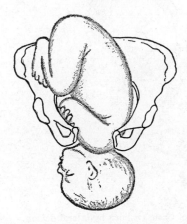

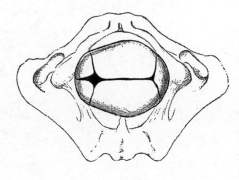

FIG. 198. L.O.A.   Front view after external
rotation.

FIG. 199. L.O.A.   External rotation as seen
from below.

EXTERNAL ROTATION.   When the anterior shoulder meets the resistance
of the pelvic floor on the right side, it is shunted downward, forward and inward
to the symphysis.   This causes the occiput to rotate 45° more to the left.

Birth of the Shoulders

FIG. 200. L.O.A. Birth of the shoulders by lateral flexion. Sagittal section. Anterior shoulder passes out beneath the symphysis.

FIG. 201. Posterior shoulder, following the curve of Carus, is born by lateral flexion.

BIRTH OF THE SHOULDERS. The anterior shoulder comes into view beneath the symphysis, where it is arrested while the posterior shoulder is being born by lateral flexion (Fig. 200). Following the birth of the shoulders, the remainder of the trunk is expelled in the direction of the curve of Carus (Fig. 201).

OUTLINE SUMMARY OF L. O. A. MECHANISM

Descent is constant

FLEXION — The head engages with the sagittal suture in the right oblique diameter and the occiput in the left anterior quadrant of the mother's pelvis.

INTERNAL ROTATION — The occiput rotates 45° to the right and anteriorly to the symphysis.   This brings the sagittal suture into the anteroposterior diameter of the outlet.

OA

EXTENSION — The occiput passes out beneath the pubic arch and the nucha pivots under the symphysis, after which the small fontanel, sagittal suture, large fontanel, brow, orbits, nose, mouth, and chin are born by extension.

RESTITUTION — The neck untwists and the occiput turns back 45° to the left.

EXTERNAL ROTATION — As the anterior shoulder rotates 45° to the left, the occiput turns 45° more to the left.

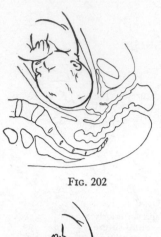  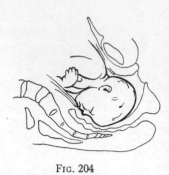

FIG. 202   FIG. 203   FIG. 204

FIG. 208   FIG. 209   FIG. 210

 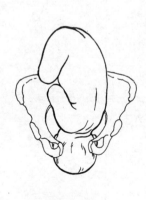

FIG. 214   FIG. 215   FIG. 216

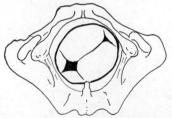 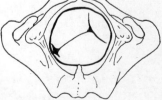 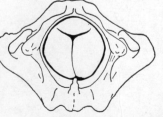

FIG. 220   FIG. 221   FIG. 222

OF L.O.A. MECHANISM

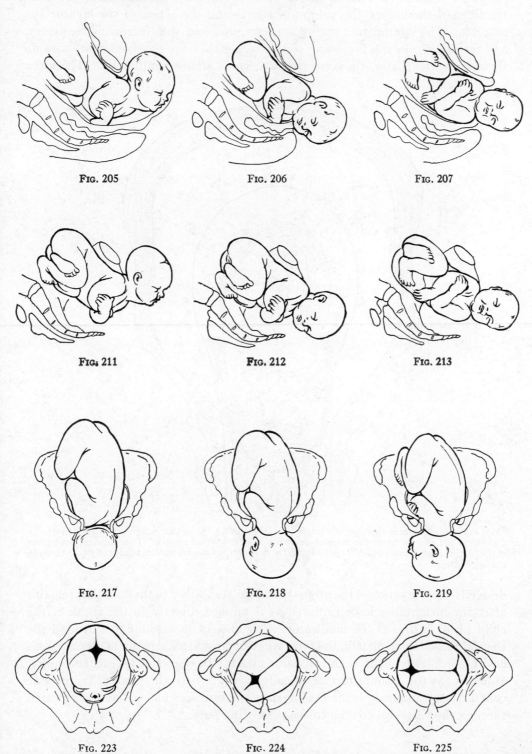

FIG. 205   FIG. 206   FIG. 207

FIG. 211   FIG. 212   FIG. 213

FIG. 217   FIG. 218   FIG. 219

FIG. 223   FIG. 224   FIG. 225

THE EXPULSIVE FORCES of the second stage are derived from the contractions of the uterus, the voluntary efforts and the action of the levator ani muscles. The intermittent uterine contractions recur with increasing frequency and intensity. In the beginning of this stage, they are observed every two or three minutes. Later, the contractions become almost continuous. The force

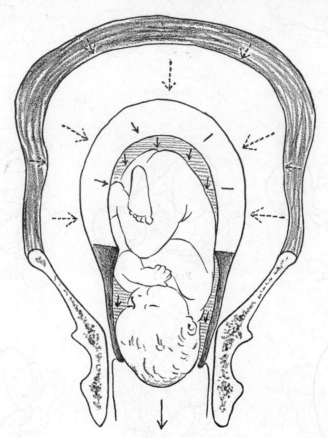

FIG. 226. Diagram showing the action of the forces in the second stage. Contraction of the abdominal muscles increases the intra-abdominal pressure—dotted arrows. This augments the force of the uterine contractions which is applied directly to the fetus, or is transmitted indirectly to it through the hindwaters.

derived from the action of the uterus is transmitted either to the fluid that remains after the membranes have ruptured or is applied directly to the trunk of the child (3, 4, 5, 6). If the hindwaters are sufficient in amount to surround the the child's body completely, the force will be transmitted equally in all directions and, accordingly, will drive the presenting part in the direction of least resistance. However, as the amount of fluid usually is insufficient, the force of the uterine contractions commonly is directed against the buttocks and is then transmitted through the vertebral column to the presenting part.

The voluntary contraction of the abdominal muscles increases the intra-abdominal pressure and constitutes a bearing-down effort. This increased intra-abdominal pressure is applied to the external surface of the uterus through the walls of which it is transmitted to the uterine content. The voluntary efforts, accordingly, greatly augment the force of the uterine contractions. Without their help, spontaneous delivery often is impossible, as is evidenced by the observation that artificial aid is necessary in almost all cases of labor conducted under the influence of spinal anesthesia (Fig. 226).

The effect of the levator ani muscles in labor is largely passive. During the latter part of the second stage, however, their contraction may aid in the extension of the head. They also assist in the expulsion of the placenta after it has been forced into the vagina.

Comment on the Mechanism

DESCENT. In the captions beneath the preceding illustrations, it was stated that descent is constant. It is constant, however, only in the sense that additional progress is made with each contraction. Strictly speaking, therefore, the head advances with each contraction and recedes in the interval of relaxation. This is advantageous to both the mother and the child, since the pressure on the child's head and the maternal soft parts is intermittently relieved and the circulation is restored after each pain. Accordingly, circulatory disturbances in the child's brain are minimized, and pressure necrosis of the maternal tissues is avoided.

ENGAGEMENT. In a left occipito anterior, the head engages in the pelvis with the occiput in the left anterior quadrant and the sagittal suture is in relation to the right oblique diameter. Engagement is complete when the biparietal and suboccipito bregmatic diameters (the engaging diameters for an L.O.A.) pass through the pelvic inlet. This event is recognized by the relationship of the presenting part to the plane of the ischial spines. Ordinarily, the bony presenting part (not the caput succedaneum) is within 1 cm. of the level of the ischial spines when the head is engaged.

As was previously stated (p. 189), stereoscopic roentgenograms show that the head enters the pelvis most frequently in the transverse position. If, at the onset of labor, the uterus can come forward sufficiently with each pain to bring its axis into relation with the axis of the pelvic inlet, the head will present with the sagittal suture midway between the symphysis and the promontory. It then descends in this position until the resistance of the coccyx and pelvic floor is met. Thereafter the sagittal suture is rotated forward so that the biparietal diameter becomes parallel with the various planes of the pelvis as the head passes through the parturient canal. When the head descends in this manner, it is said to be in **synclitism,** the planes of the head being parallel with the planes of the pelvis throughout the mechanism (Fig. 227a).

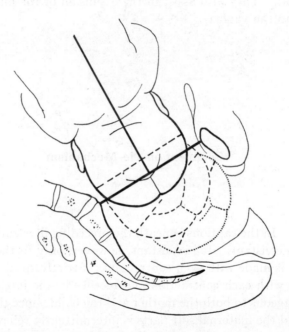

FIG. 227 a. Synclitism or parallelism between the planes of the fetal head and those of the pelvis The head enters the pelvic inlet with the sagittal suture midway between the symphysis and the prom ontory.

In most instances, however, the uterus cannot become perpendicular to the pelvic inlet because of the tenseness of the abdominal wall. The head then enters the pelvis with the sagittal suture somewhat nearer to the symphysis than to the promontory and the posterior parietal bone becomes the presenting part (6a). As the uterus contracts and drives the head against the anterior wall of the pelvis, the angulation of the neck favors rotation of the parietal bone posteriorly toward the sacrum. This mechanism continues until the anterior parietal bone is forced into the pelvis. The sagittal suture, accordingly, is rotated posteriorly until the presenting part passes the plane of the ischial spines and meets the resistance of the pelvic floor. It then is forced anteriorly as the biparietal diameter is brought into a parallel relationship with the planes of the remainder of the parturient canal (Fig. 227b) (6a) (6b). This mechanism is known as **asynclitism.** As a result of it, the posterior parietal eminence enters the pelvis first and the widest diameter passes through the inlet diagonal to rather

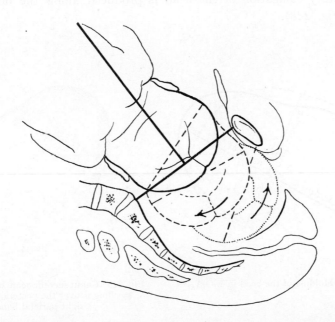

FIG. 227 b. Asynclitism. The head enters the pelvis obliquely with the sagittal suture nearer to the symphysis. As it is forced through the lower segment and cervix the contour of these structures causes the head to rotate backward until the cephalic planes come into parallel relationship with the planes of the lower segment and cervix. After the biparietal diameter passes below the influence of the cervical resistance the sagittal suture rotates anteriorly to come into parallel relationship with the lower part of the parturient canal.

than parallel with the plane of the superior strait. The advantage thus gained permits the passage of a somewhat larger diameter than might be possible if the head entered the pelvis with its planes parallel to those of the inlet. In other words, the mechanism is analagous to that which is used when one takes a table through a door that is too small for it, by first passing one end diagonally through the opening and then the other, instead of trying to force both ends through at the same time.

MOLDING. As labor progresses, the shape of the child's head is altered in order that it may become better adapted to the passages.   This alteration in the fetal skull is known as molding and is dependent upon the width of the sutures and the softness of the bones that make up the cranial vault.   Usually the two parietal bones and the cranial portion of the frontal and occipital bones are only partially ossified, so that their shape may be easily changed in the course of labor. Likewise, broad sutures permit the bones to override each other and thus reduce the size of the head circumference that is to pass through the pelvis.   In an L.O.A., the suboccipitobregmatic circumference, accordingly, is diminished and a compensatory elongation of the head is produced along the occipitomental diameter (Fig. 228).

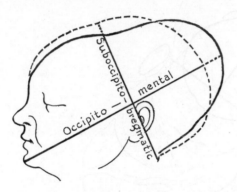

FIG. 228. Molding of the head in L.O.A.

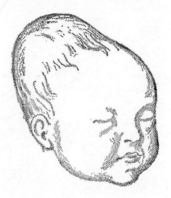

FIG. 229. Caput succedaneum in L.O.A.   The swelling is over the posterior part of the right parietal bone.

CAPUT SUCCEDANEUM. As the head makes pressure against the margins of the cervix and the resisting pelvic soft parts, the return circulation in the scalp is interfered with.   That portion of the child's scalp which is not subjected to pressure thus becomes edematous and is known as the caput succedaneum. After the birth of the child, the original presentation and position may be determined from the location of this edematous swelling.   In an L.O.A., it is found over the posterior part of the right parietal bone (Fig. 229).

FLEXION. As soon as sufficient resistance is encountered, flexion occurs and the suboccipitobregmatic plane is substituted for the occipitofrontal as the largest head plane that is to pass through the pelvis (Figs. 230 and 231).   This may take place at the brim or may be delayed until the head reaches the pelvic floor. It is due to the fact that the force transmitted through the vertebral column to the base of the skull is applied nearer to the occiput. The head may be regarded as a lever of unequal arms, the longer of which extends from the brow to the occipito-atloid articulation and the shorter is the remainder of the occipitofrontal diameter. While the resistance to the passage of the head is equal on each side, its effect on the side of the longer lever arm is greater, and, as a result, the shorter or occipital side advances more rapidly so that flexion is increased (Figs. 230 and 231). The advantage gained by flexion will be appre-

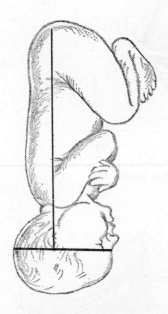

FIG. 230. Relation of the head to the spinal column at the onset of labor.

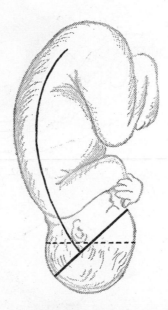

FIG. 231. Relation of the head to the spinal column after flexion has occurred.

ciated when one considers that the suboccipitobregmatic diameter, 9.5 cm., is substituted for the occipitofrontal, 11.5 cm., and the head is thereby made 2 cm., or almost 1 inch, smaller in its longest dimension.

INTERNAL ROTATION. When the presenting part meets the resistance of the pelvic floor, the mechanical principle of a body being driven against an inclined plane operates, and the head is shunted downward, forward and inward, just as a ferry-boat, on meeting one of its ways, is directed toward the center of its wharf (5, 7, 8).

This step in the mechanism is of great advantage in that it brings **the long diameter** of the fetal head plane into a position parallel with the long **diameter** of the pelvic outlet and allows the occiput to pass under the pubic arch and out of the pelvis.

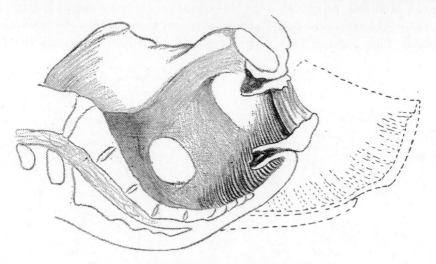

FIG. 232. The pelvic floor before labor.

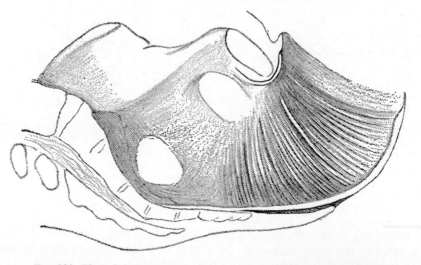

FIG. 233. The pelvic floor as it is altered during the movement of extension.

Another interesting explanation of the phenomenon of internal rotation is that offered by Sellheim, who suggested that the pelvis is a curved cylinder into which is forced another cylindrical body, the child, which may be bent more easily in the region of the neck (9). As a result, in order that the inner cylinder may conform to the shape of the outer, the head must rotate until the back of the neck fits the small curve (under-surface of the symphysis) of the outer cylinder.

Rotation is essential to allow the occiput to pass out of the pelvis beneath the pubic arch. In addition, it facilitates expulsion of the head by bringing the long diameter of the latter into relation with the longest diameter of the outlet.

EXTENSION. The head continues to descend and, after forcing the coccyx backward, makes pressure against the maternal soft parts anterior to it. As the latter yield, the parturient canal dilates and the trough through which the head must pass looks forward and upward (Figs. 232 and 233). The head from now on travels along the axis of this trough, which is parallel to the curve of Carus. The chief factor, then, that is responsible for extension, is the shape of the newly formed parturient canal.

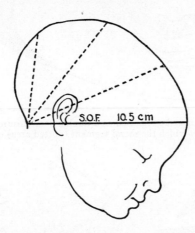

FIG. 234. Diagram showing the largest diameter (S.O.F., 10.5 cm.) which passes through the vulvovaginal orifice as the head is born by extension.

If the levators are capable of acting during extension, they may, by contracting against the brow and face, lift the latter forward and assist in extending the head.

The occiput, passes out of the pelvis and allows the nucha to pivot beneath the symphysis. This placing of the pivoting point at the junction of the occiput and neck greatly lessens the diameters that pass across the fourchette during extension. When the brow is born, the suboccipitofrontal diameter, 10.5 cm., and the circumference of its plane are passing through the vulvovaginal ring. As this is the greatest circumference born during extension, laceration is most likely to occur at this time (10) (Fig. 234).

RESTITUTION. When the head, which is in the right oblique diameter, reaches the pelvic floor, the shoulders are entering the pelvis in the opposite or left oblique diameter, and they remain in this position while the head is being

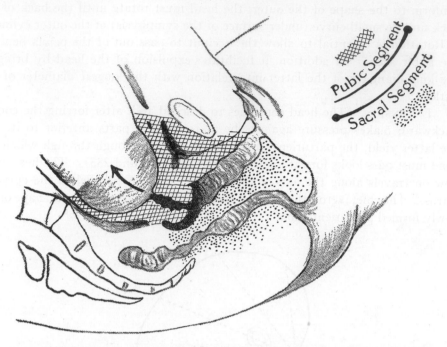

FIG. 235. The pelvic floor may be regarded as a double door closure. The pubic segment (cross hatched area) opens upward after which the sacral segment (dotted area) opens downward.

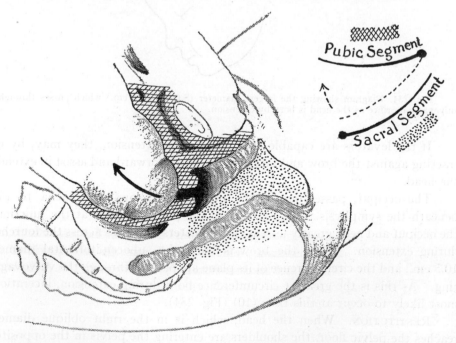

FIG. 236. As the lower segment and internal os are pulled upward, the bladder and pubic segment are elevated.

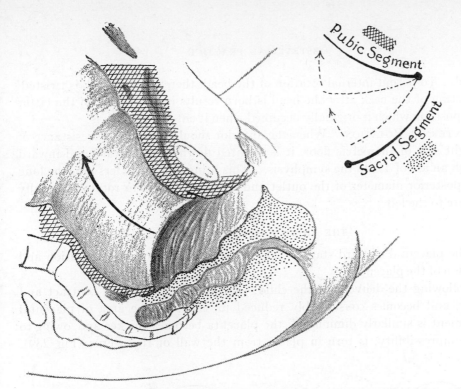

FIG. 237. When the cervix is fully dilated, the bladder is well above the symphysis and the pubic or upper "door" is open. No substitute for this mechanism is known and for that reason, it is good obstetric practice to await full dilatation before attempting an operative delivery.

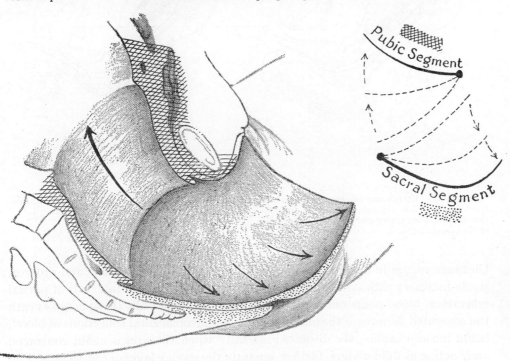

FIG. 238. Downward pressure forces open the sacral segment or lower "door" and fully prepares the passages for the delivery.

rotated.   To permit internal rotation of the head, therefore, the neck is twisted.
Untwisting of the neck after the head is born results in restitution of the latter
to the position which it originally occupied when it entered the pelvis.

EXTERNAL ROTATION.   When the anterior shoulder meets the resistance of
the right side of the pelvic floor, it is shunted downward, forward and inward
through an arc of 45° to the symphysis.   This brings the shoulders into the long
anteroposterior diameter of the outlet and causes the head to rotate externally
45° more to the left.

THE THIRD STAGE OF LABOR

The placental or third stage of labor is concerned with the separation and
expulsion of the placenta.

Following the delivery of the child, the uterus continues to contract and
retract, and becomes considerably reduced in size.   As the area of placental
attachment is similarly diminished, the placenta becomes thicker and, owing to
its incompressibility, is torn in places from the wall of the uterus (Fig. 239).

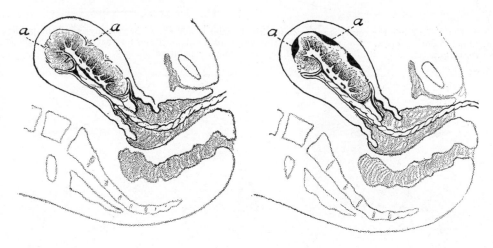

FIG. 239. Uterus and placenta early in the   FIG. 240. Separation of the placenta.   Formation
third stage.   Note the almost complete oblitera-   of retroplacental collections of blood at a, a.
tion of the uterine cavity and beginning separation
of the placenta at a, a.

Cleavage occurs in the fragile spongy layer of the decidua basalis and progressively increases with successive uterine contractions.   In the intervals of partial
relaxation, blood pours out from the denuded areas and fills the spaces beneath
the separated surfaces of the placenta.   These retroplacental collections of blood,
being incompressible, are displaced laterally when the uterus again contracts,
and, acting as fluid wedges, further separate the spongy layer of the decidua (Fig.
240).   Continuation of this process leads to coalescence of the fluid-filled spaces

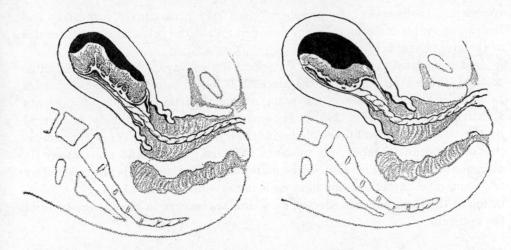

FIG. 241. Separation of the placenta.   Coalescence   FIG. 242. Separation of the placenta.   Periphery
of the retroplacental collections of blood.   of the placenta resisting separation.

and causes the central portion of the placenta to bulge into the uterine cavity as
the more firmly attached periphery resists cleavage (Figs. 241 and 242).   Finally,
the pressure becomes too great and the margins give way as a gush of blood from

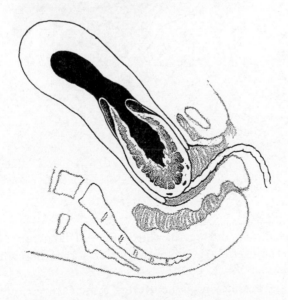

FIG. 243. Separation of the placenta.   Periphery separated.

the uterus and vagina indicates the complete separation of the placenta (Figs.
243 and 244).   Usually, therefore, the third stage of labor is not accompanied
by visible bleeding from the placental site until the separation of the placenta is

complete.   If, however, the periphery gives way prematurely, persistent and increasing visible bleeding from the denuded area is the rule and constitutes one of the great hazards of the third stage.

The expulsion of the placenta may occur in two ways.   In one, the Schultze method, the central portion of the placenta is forced into the vagina and leads to an inversion of the walls of the ovum, so that the fetal surface of the placenta is delivered first (11) (Fig. 245).   The maternal surface, accordingly, is covered by the enveloping membranes of the inverted ovum.   In the other type of expulsion, Duncan's method, the placenta is folded on itself and presents by its margin as it is born (Fig. 246).   The maternal surface usually is not covered by the membranes, and the ovum likewise is not inverted (5, 12, 13, 14, 15).   Separation of the membranes is effected by a similar cleavage in the spongy layer of the decidua.

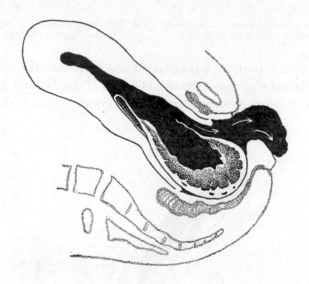

FIG. 244. Gush of blood after complete separation of the placenta.

The forces which act during the third stage of labor are: the contraction and retraction of the uterus, the voluntary efforts and the contractions of the levator ani muscles.

Contraction and retraction of the uterine musculature results in separation of the placenta and assists in its expulsion.   After separation is complete, these contractions force the placenta into the lower uterine segment or vagina and occasionally accomplish its complete expulsion.   Usually, however, the voluntary efforts are necessary to deliver the placenta.   If the latter is low in the vagina, contraction of the levator ani muscles also aids in its expulsion.

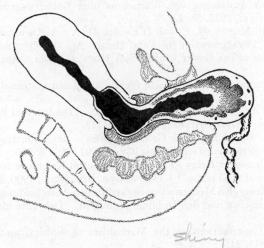

shiny

FIG. 245. Expulsion of the placenta.   Schultze mechanism.

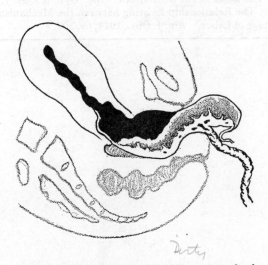

Dirty

FIG. 246. Expulsion of the placenta.   Duncan mechanism.

REFERENCES

1. STIEVE, H.: Die Enge der menschlichen Gebärmutter, ihre Veränderungen während der Schwangerscnaft, der Geburt und des Wochenbettes und ihre Bedeutung.   Jahrbuch f. Morph. u. Mikr. Anat., 1928, 14, 549.
2. SCHMIDT, H. R.: Anatomische Untersuchungen zur Frage des unteren Uterinsegmentes. Ztschr. f. Geburtsh. u. Gyn., 1923, 85, 233.
3. LAHS, H.: Die Theorie der Geburt.   Bonn, 1877, 19.
4. OLSHAUSEN, R.: Beitrag zur Lehre vom Mechanismus der Geburt auf Grund Klinischer Beobachtungen und Erfahrungen   Stuttgart, 1901.

5. WARNEKROS, K.: Geburt und Nachgeburtsperiode im Röntgenbilde.   München, 1925, 15.
6. SELLHEIM, H.: Zur Auffassung von Warnekros über Geburtsmechanik.   Monatschr. f. Geburtsh. u. Gyn., 1922, 58, 237.
6a. CALDWELL, W. E. MOLOY, H. C. and D'ESOPO, D. A.: A Roentgenologic Study of the mechanism of Engagement of the Fetal Head.   Am. J. Obs. and Gyn., 1934, 28, 824.
6b. ——— The Rôle of the Lower Uterine Soft Parts in Labor.   Am. J. Obs. and Gyn., 1939, 37, 618.
7. VARNIER, H.: Accommodation de la tête foetale au bassin maternal.   Obstétrique Journalière, Paris, 1900, p. 131.
8. PARAMORE, R. H.: A Critical Inquiry into the Causes of the Internal Rotation of the Foetal Head.   J. Obs. & Gyn. Brit. Emp., 1909, 16, 213.
9. SELLHEIM, H.: Die Beziehungen des Geburtskanales u. des Geburtsobjektes zur Geburtsmechanik.   Beiträge zur Geburtsh. u. Gyn., 1907, 11, 1 & 120.
10. JONES, J.: Some Causes of Delay in Labor with Special Reference to the Function of the Cervical Spine of the Foetus.   J. Obs. & Gyn. Brit. Emp., 1906, 10, 407.
11. SCHULTZE, B. S.: Ueber den Mechanismus der spontanen Ausscheidung der Nachgeburt und über den Credéschen und den Dubliner Handgriff.   Deutsche med. Wchnschr., 1880, 6, 677, 690.
12. DUNCAN, J. M.: Contributions to the Mechanism of Natural and Morbid Parturition.   Edinburgh, 1875, 246.
13. WEIBEL, W.: Studien über die Nachgeburtsperiode auf Grund röntgenographischer Darstellung.   Arch. f. Gyn., 1919, 111, 413.
14. TUCKER, E. A.: The Birth of the Secundines.   Am. Gyn. & Obs. J., 1898, 12, 569.
15. FREELAND, J. R.: The Relationship Existing between the Mechanism and Management of the Third Stage of Labor.   Am. J. Obs., 1914, 69, 302.

CHAPTER XIII

CLINICAL COURSE OF LABOR

Sometime within two weeks of labor's onset, **lightening** occurs in **most** women who are pregnant for the first time. The patient then experiences a feeling of pelvic pressure and often states that the child is lower. Coincidentally, an appreciable diminution in her waist line is observed and breathing becomes less difficult. These striking manifestations of the change that has taken place within her abdomen lead her to regard the onset of labor as imminent and this apprehension, together with the growing irritability of the uterus, causes some women to overestimate the importance of the intermittent uterine contractions which, at this time, recur with greater frequency and intensity. Occasionally, such contractions are accompanied by more or less pain for several days before the actual onset of labor and thus further add to the apprehension of the patient and her family. These **false pains** are **irregular** and on careful study will be found to differ from those of true labor.

FIRST STAGE. With the onset of labor, **intermittent pains** are felt in the **lumbar region.** At first, they recur at regular intervals of from twenty to thirty minutes and are not sufficiently severe to interfere with the performance of the patient's usual household duties.

Soon the **mucous plug** is forced from the cervical canal and slight bleeding from the injured cervix and separated membranes gives to the vaginal discharge a pink or red discoloration—**the show.**

As labor progresses, the pains gradually **increase in frequency and severity** until the patient is forced to discontinue her activities and lean over a chair or table during each uterine contraction. Later, her suffering becomes so intense that she no longer can control herself and, with each pain, she cries out in despair. As she is unable to appreciate the progress accomplished by these painful contractions, she then feels that her suffering is in vain and appeals for help.

SECOND STAGE. Shortly after the cervix is fully dilated, the membranes rupture and a gush of fluid leads the patient to believe that the end of her suffering is near. As the presenting part makes pressure on the pelvic floor with each succeeding contraction, she takes a deep breath and bears down. At this time,

263

the head, pressing on the rectum, produces a false desire to defecate and she may call for a bed pan. At first, the bearing down pains are more or less under the control of the will. Later, they become involuntary and even though her suffering may be intense, she is unable to restrain the vigorous expulsive efforts.

PERINEAL STAGE. As the sensitive perineum is distended, the cry becomes an agonizing shriek. Bulging of the perineum is soon followed by the appearance of the child's scalp in the vulvovaginal slit (Fig. 247). More and more of

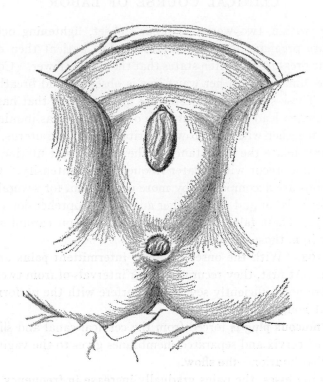

FIG. 247. Bulging of the perineum. Scalp showing.

the head shows with each successive pain, while in the interval between contractions, the presenting part recedes to be concealed again within the vaginal canal. Further progress results in dilatation of the anus and eversion of its anterior wall through the anal orifice (Figs. 248 and 249).

The perineal body becomes thinned out and elongated as it is forced downward and forward by the advancing head so that ultimately, the fourchette is

8 to 10 cm. in front of the rectum and is on a line with but 9 to 10 cm. below the inferior margin of the symphysis (Figs. 247 to 250).

When the vulvovaginal dilatation is sufficient to permit the passage of the biparietal diameter, the head fails to recede in the interval between contractions (Crowning Fig. 250), and marked extension results in the passage over the fourchette of the brow, orbits, nose, mouth and chin (Fig. 251). Usually, the soft parts are unable to withstand the extreme stretching necessary for the

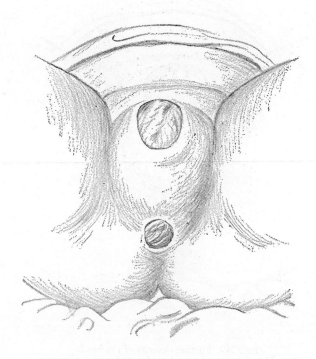

FIG. 248. Scalp protruding through the vulvovaginal ring.

passage of the suboccipitofrontal diameter and more or less laceration of the perineum occurs at this time (Fig. 251).

After the chin is out, the perineum retracts and the head falls back toward the anus (Fig. 252).

RESTITUTION. The neck now untwists and the occiput turns 45° to one side to take the same relative position that it occupied at the onset of labor (Fig. 253).

EXTERNAL ROTATION. Soon further turning of the head is observed as the shoulders are rotated into the anteroposterior diameter of the outlet (Fig. 254).

BIRTH OF THE SHOULDERS. The anterior shoulder then appears beneath the pubic arch and is arrested until the posterior shoulder is born. The remainder of the child is delivered almost immediately by lateral flexion and is followed by a gush of hindwaters.

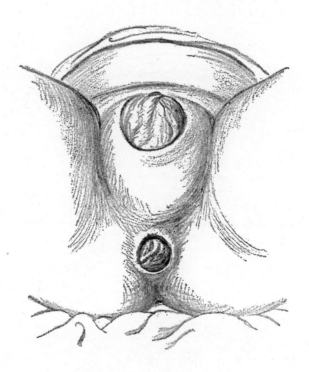

FIG. 249. Further descent of the head.
Note dilated anus and eversion of anterior wall of rectum.

THIRD STAGE. For a short time after the delivery of the child, the pains cease and the patient passes into a light sleep. The uterus, greatly reduced in size, lies well below the umbilicus. Within a few minutes, it intermittently grows hard and soft as contractions are resumed. As a rule, little or no bleeding is apparent until the placenta is separated. The latter event is then followed by a gush of blood from the vagina and a rising of the fundus to or near the umbilicus. If the separated placenta is not expelled by the force of the uterine contraction which completed its separation, the patient again bears down and the increased intra-abdominal pressure, together with the contractions of the levator ani muscles, effects its delivery.

DURATION OF LABOR.   The length of labor averages 12 hours in multiparae and 18 hours in primiparae.

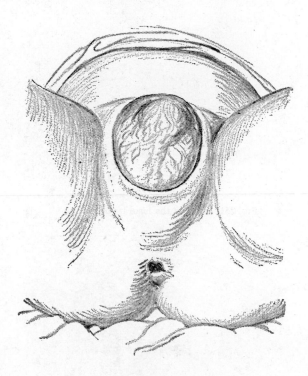

FIG. 250. Crowning.

The average of the first, second and third stages are, in multiparae, 11, $\frac{3}{4}$ and $\frac{1}{4}$ hours respectively, and in primiparae, 16, $1\frac{3}{4}$ and $\frac{1}{4}$ hours.

It is not uncommon to find marked variations in the length of labor.   Primiparae may deliver within one hour or their labor may last for several days.   Most of them, however, have labors somewhat near the averages given.   Multiparae, on the other hand, are most variable and in them the possibility of a rapid delivery always is considered by the experienced obstetrician (1, 2, 3, 4).

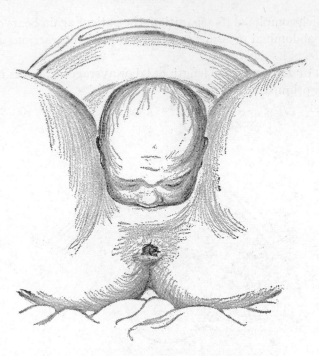

FIG. 251. Birth of the head by extension.

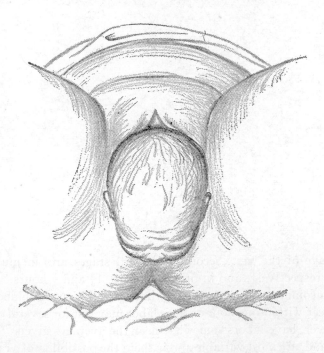

FIG. 252. The head dropping backward towards the rectum.

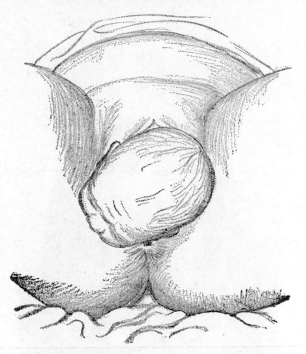

FIG. 253. Restitution.   Occiput turns to the left.

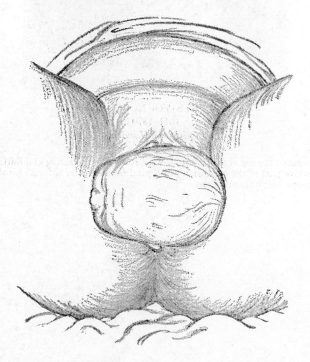

FIG. 254. External rotation.   Occiput turns an additional 45° to the left.

SIR JAMES YOUNG SIMPSON
1811–1870
Edinburgh, London

Simpson introduced the use of chloroform for the relief of pain during childbirth.
He took an active part in the expansion of hospital facilities and through his statistical investigations greatly improved hospital conditions.

CHAPTER XIV

MANAGEMENT OF LABOR

FIRST STAGE

Because of the need of aseptic precautions in the conduct of labor, delivery in a well conducted hospital is desirable. This is particularly true when the patient is having her first baby. Multiparae, on the other hand, often may be confined in their homes with but slight added risk if proper facilities are provided and the attendants employ a technic which approximates that followed in hospital practice. Regardless of the environment, an aseptic conscience is necessary if the perils of childbed fever are to be avoided.

For confinement in the home, certain preliminary preparations are essential.

The obstetrician's bag should contain:

2 scissors
6 artery clamps
2 tissue forceps
2 sponge forceps
1 uterine dressing forceps
4 curved round needles
4 large Hagedorn needles
1 needle holder
2 lateral retractors
1 Sims' speculum
2 rubber catheters
1 obstetric forceps
1 pelvimeter
1 2-cc. hypodermic syringe
2 large hypodermic syringes
1 ether mask
blood pressure apparatus
stethoscope
2 tubes sterile catgut
2 pieces sterile umbilical tape
silkworm gut sutures
silver nitrate 1 per cent

cap
mask
operating suit
rubber apron
2 sterile gowns
4 sterile sheets
2 pr. sterile leggings
6 sterile towels
3 large sterile gauze packs
1 sterile delivery pad
4 pr. sterile gloves
4 oz. lysol
6 oz. alcohol
8 oz. ether
bichloride of mercury tablets
ampules of gynergen
ampules of pituitary extract
ampules of 1 per cent novocaine with
    adrenalin
ampules of 50 per cent glucose
2 sterile hand brushes
sterile orange stick.

The patient should procure the following articles:

> 2 rubber sheets 1 x 2 yards
> 5 hand basins
> 1 two-quart fountain syringe
> bed pan
> 1 pt. alcohol
> 4 oz. lysol
> 4 oz. green soap
> bichloride of mercury tablets
> 1 lb. carton of cotton
> ample towels, sheets and nightgowns.

LYING-IN ROOM. The selection of a large, bright, well ventilated room convenient to bathing and toilet facilities will greatly aid all who are concerned with the conduct of labor and add to the comfort of the mother during her convalescence.

DELIVERY BED. The bed should have a rather firm mattress. If the latter sags, it may be stiffened by placing a table leaf on top of the springs. The mattress is protected from soiling by a large rubber covering placed under a freshly laundered muslin sheet. Over the latter, a smaller rubber and a second muslin sheet are so arranged that they may be easily removed after the completion of labor.

SCRUB TABLE. A small table, protected by several newspapers and covered with freshly laundered towels, is used by the physician in the preparation of his hands if the bathroom is not convenient. On it are arranged two sterile basins of warm water that has been boiled, another which contains a 1–1000 solution of bichloride of mercury, a bottle of 70 per cent alcohol, green soap and two sterile hand brushes which, with a sterile orange stick, are placed between the folds of a sterile towel.

STERILE TABLE. A sterile sheet is placed over another table which has been similarly prepared. On it are placed the sterile instruments, sterile gown, sterile gloves, sterile leggings, sterile drape sheets, sterile towels, sterile gauze and a sterile basin containing 1 per cent lysol solution. These sterile materials are then covered by another sterile sheet to protect them from subsequent contamination.

FALSE PAINS. The onset of true labor must be differentiated from the false pains that not infrequently are present in the last weeks of pregnancy. The latter give rise to much anxiety and accomplish nothing. When they are present, the patient should be informed that she is not in labor, and that she need not expect to give birth until pains of the right kind begin. If these false pains interfere with her rest at night, she should be given morphine ¼ gr. on retiring. This is desirable because true labor pains may begin on the following day and it is important that the patient shall have had a good night's sleep before going into labor.

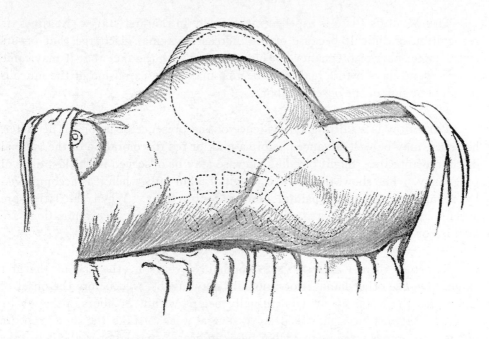

Fig. 255. Change in the contour of the abdomen resulting from the contraction of the uterus During a labor pain, the uterus assumes the position indicated by the dotted lines, i.e., perpendicular to the plane of the pelvic inlet.

THE DIAGNOSIS OF TRUE LABOR is made from the following signs:

> Regular, intermittent, painful uterine contractions
> Lightening
> Expulsion of the mucous plug
> The show
> Rupture of the membranes
> Dilatation of the cervix

TRUE LABOR PAINS recur at **regular intervals** and **progressively increase in frequency and intensity.** They last from **30 to 90 seconds** and are **accompanied by uterine contractions** which may be seen or palpated by the attendant shortly before any pain is perceived by the patient (Fig. 255). **A pain, therefore, may easily be predicted by early recognition of the uterine contraction.** The gradual **increment** of the contraction with its **more rapid decrudescence** likewise is characteristic.

LIGHTENING is common in primiparae but rarely is observed in multiparae. It likewise takes place within two weeks before the onset of labor. As an indication of the onset of labor, this symptom, accordingly, is of slight value. When it occurs, however, labor usually may be expected within a short time.

THE MUCOUS PLUG is expelled rather early in the first stage. At times its recognition is difficult because of the increased vaginal discharge that occurs in the latter part of pregnancy. This, together with the fact that it may come away several days before real labor begins, makes the expulsion of the mucous plug a poor sign of the onset of labor.

THE SHOW is a fairly good evidence of the presence of labor. The latter, however, may be well advanced before a pink or red discoloration of the vaginal discharge appears. Slight bleeding likewise may be observed in the last days of pregnancy. The show, therefore, is a sign of labor only when it is accompanied by **regular, intermittent, painful uterine contractions.** When the latter are absent, however, labor is regarded as imminent, and vaginal examinations are avoided or made only under the strictest aseptic precautions.

RUPTURE OF THE MEMBRANES commonly occurs at the end of the first stage. On the other hand, it occasionally may be observed before the onset of labor. In the latter event, labor usually begins within 24 hours, although its onset, in rare instances, may be delayed several weeks. Like the show, rupture of the membranes without real labor pains indicates that labor is about to take place. For this reason, and because of the greater danger of infection after the membranes have ruptured, strict asepsis must be followed in all such cases.

DILATATION OF THE CERVIX. In primiparae no dilatation may be observed for several hours after the onset of labor. On the other hand, the cervix may be considerably dilated in multiparae during the last few weeks of pregnancy. To be of value, therefore, this sign must be accompanied by true labor pains.

Having decided that the patient is in labor, a careful examination should be made to determine the condition of the mother, the character of her labor, and the degree of progress. If she has not been seen during her pregnancy, this survey should include the taking of the pulse, temperature, respiration and blood pressure, examination of the heart, an abdominal examination, mensuration of the pelvis and a vaginal examination.

THE PULSE, TEMPERATURE, RESPIRATION AND BLOOD PRESSURE FINDINGS give valuable information concerning her physical condition and should be taken every 4 hours throughout labor. If they are normal, the usual routine followed in a complete physical examination may be omitted, provided auscultation of the heart fails to show evidence of an organic lesion.   Should any of these findings be abnormal, a more complete physical examination is indicated.

Abdominal Examination

A systematic abdominal examination in every case will give complete findings, and assure an accurate diagnosis.   The following outline may at first seem time-consuming.   By constant repetition, however, its use will become automatic and will take no longer than a superficial routine.

I. THE CHARACTERISTICS OF THE CHILD
    1. Presentation, position and posture
    2. Size
    3. Fetal movements
    4. Fetal head   { size
                   relation to pelvic inlet
                   consistency
                   mobility
    5. Fetal heart

II. THE CHARACTERISTICS OF THE UTERUS
    1. Axis
    2. Size
    3. Shape
    4. Contractions
    5. Fluid content
    6. Tumors

III. THE CHARACTERISTICS OF THE ABDOMINAL WALL
    1. Scars of previous operations
    2. Condition of the musculature
    3. Amount of fat
    4. Hernia   { umbilical
                inguinal
                femoral
                postoperative

Characteristics of the Child

PRESENTATION, POSITION AND POSTURE are diagnosed by following the routine described in Chapter X, page 190.   Figure 256 shows the outline of the child in L.O.A. as visualized through the abdominal wall.   The touch picture (Fig. 257) is much less distinct but serves very well to identify the presentation and position if all of the findings shown in the accompanying outline are obtained.

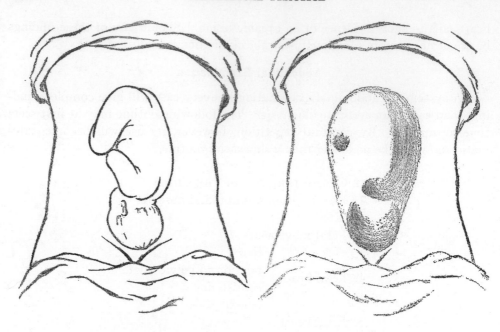

FIG. 256. L.O.A. as visualized through the abdominal wall.

FIG. 257. Touch picture in L.O.A.

PALPATION FINDINGS IN L.O.A.

1. Dorsum—*on the left side, near the midline and easily felt.*
2. Small Parts—*on right side, away from the midline and felt with difficulty.*
3. Lower Pole—the head
{
harder
more globular
less irregular
more mobile
near a sulcus
may be moved independently
}
4. Upper Pole—the breech
{
softer
less globular
more irregular
less mobile
not near a sulcus
may not be moved independently
near small parts
}
5. Cephalic Prominence—*on the right side.*
6. Anterior Shoulder—*on the left side, near the midline and easily felt.*

Comment on Abdominal Palpation

Comparison of the two sides of the abdomen shows the left to be more resistant, smoother and more convex. The back, therefore, is on the left side. Usually its outline may easily be made out near the midline. The right side is less resistant, more irregular and may contain palpable extremities of the fetus. It, accordingly, contains the small parts. The mass in the lower pole of the uterus feels harder, smoother and more globular than that in the upper. It, consequently, is the head and the softer, less regular breech is in the fundus. The cephalic prominence is readily distinguished to the right of the midline, i.e., on the side opposite the dorsum. The anterior shoulder is easily palpated near the midline on the left side (1, 2).

SIZE OF THE CHILD. The beginner should attempt to determine the size of every child. In this way he soon will become familiar with the dimensions of a normal child and will at once be suspicious whenever he feels a very large or a very small fetus. A fair idea of the actual length of the child may be gained by the use of Ahlfeld's method, which is illustrated on page 159.

FETAL MOVEMENTS may be either passive or active. When a small part is palpated, it usually can be moved and often moves of its own accord. Active fetal movements are an absolute sign of a living child.

FETAL HEAD. Careful palpation of the fetal head gives valuable information concerning its size, consistency, mobility and the presence or absence of over-riding.

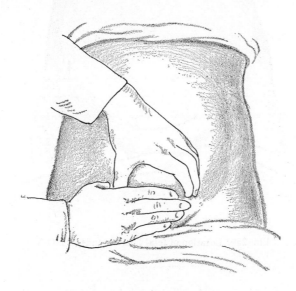

FIG. 258. Method of determining overriding of the fetal head.

Size of the head. Mensuration of the head, except by x-ray, is unsatisfactory. Direct palpation gives the best impression of its size. This step in the routine, therefore, should be practised in every case in order that the beginner may become familiar with the size of the normal head. He then will be on his guard whenever it is abnormally large or small.

Overriding is detected by forcing the head against the pelvic brim and palpating the degree to which the head extends beyond the symphysis (Fig. 258). In the presence of disproportion the overriding is marked.

Consistency of the head. This also is difficult to determine. With practice, however, it is possible to differentiate a hard head from a malleable one, an important consideration when molding is to be a factor in the mechanism.

Mobility of the head is present at the onset of most multiparous labors. In primiparae, on the other hand, the head is fixed when labor begins. **Absence of fixation at the onset of labor in a primipara indicates the possibility of dystocia.**

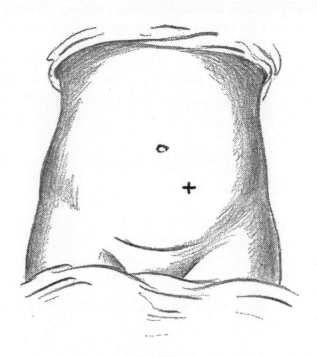

Fig. 259. Location of fetal heart sounds in L.O.A.

FETAL HEART. The sounds of the fetal heart may be heard by direct or indirect auscultation. If the ordinary stethoscope is used, adventitious sounds are eliminated by holding the instrument close to the skin with rubber bands as shown in Figure 90, page 155. Bone conduction greatly augments the fetal heart sounds when a head stethoscope is used. For this reason, the latter is recommended by most good obstetricians.

In flexion cases, the sounds are transmitted through the scapula and therefore are best heard in the region of the anterior shoulder. In extension attitudes, on the other hand, the fetal heart is transmitted through the thorax. A diagnosis of presentation, position and posture should never be based on the location of the fetal heart sounds alone. The site of the punctum maximum, however, may be used to corroborate the findings obtained by palpation. If the latter are indefinite, it is better to remain in doubt until the course of labor or findings more reliable than the location of the fetal heart sounds justify the making of a definite diagnosis.

In an L.O.A. the fetal heart is best heard below the umbilicus, near the midline, on the left side, i.e., over the anterior shoulder (Fig. 259).

Characteristics of the Uterus

AXIS OF THE UTERUS. The position of the uterine axis is important, and should be observed both during relaxation and contraction. Normally, it is near the midline and during a contraction it tends to assume a position perpendicular to the plane of the pelvic inlet. Obliquity of the uterus interferes with flexion and may change a vertex into a brow or face presentation. The same complication sometimes arises when the uterine axis lies too far forward, as in a pendulous abdomen. Marked disproportion likewise may be accompanied by a pendulous abdomen. **In a primipara, therefore, a pendulous abdomen calls for careful mensuration of the pelvis to rule out pelvic dystocia.**

SIZE OF THE UTERUS. The size of the uterus is measured with a pelvimeter according to Ahlfeld's method, page 159, or it may be determined with reference to the umbilicus or ensiform cartilage. When measured with the pelvimeter, the fundus at term is 27 cm. above the symphysis. If a tape measure is used, it usually is 35 cm. above this landmark. A large uterus indicates the possibility of a multiple pregnancy, an excessive amount of amniotic fluid, or a large child. Since the first two of these are frequent causes of breech and transverse presentations, their presence should lead the examiner to be on the lookout for these abnormalities.

SHAPE OF THE UTERUS. The shape of the uterus at term is ovoid. A broad, squat uterus at or near the level of the umbilicus should lead the examiner to consider the possibility of a transverse presentation.

CONTRACTIONS OF THE UTERUS. The character, frequency, duration and strength of the uterine contractions are carefully studied. The importance of this detail cannot be overestimated. If the beginner will time and chart the contractions of the uterus in a few primiparous labors, he will gain an experience which will be invaluable throughout his obstetric life. This will help him not only to differentiate between false and true labor, but will be very useful in the administration of drugs for the relief of pain and will also aid in the treatment of uterine inertia.

FLUID CONTENT OF THE UTERUS. An excessive amount of amniotic fluid is a frequent cause of abnormal presentations. Whenever it is present, therefore, the possibility of breech and transverse must be considered and the attendant should be constantly on the lookout for prolapse of the cord.

TUMORS OF AND ADJACENT TO THE UTERUS usually are easily felt. The commonest of these are fibromyomata. Occasionally, they are as large as a fetal head and, as a result, make the diagnosis of presentation quite difficult.   More frequently they are smaller and resemble somewhat the characteristics of the small parts.   The small parts may be differentiated from movable fibroids in two ways.   First, small parts are actively mobile; second, they may be displaced over a wide area, while fibroids even though they may be mobile cannot be displaced to any great degree.

Characteristics of the Abdominal Wall

SCARS FROM A PREVIOUS OPERATION should lead to a careful interrogation of the patient as to the nature of that operation.   Midline scars below the umbilicus usually signify that a gynecological procedure has been done.   Whenever a history of the latter is obtained, the possibility of fixation of the uterus, together with its danger of dystocia, must be considered.

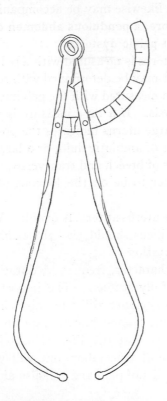 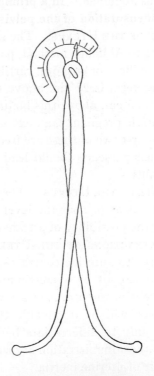

FIG. 260. Martin Pelvimeter.   FIG. 261. Budin Pelvimeter.

ABDOMINAL MUSCULATURE.   Relaxed abdominal muscles frequently occur in multiparae.   They lead to pendulous abdomen and weakening of the voluntary efforts.   When the abdominal wall is lax and flabby, therefore, the possibility of abnormal presentations and delay in the second stage must be borne in mind.

THE AMOUNT OF FAT.   A fat abdominal wall greatly interferes with palpation and auscultation.   The diagnosis in such cases is difficult and often must be postponed until a vaginal examination is made.

HERNIA.   Umbilical, inguinal, femoral and postoperative herniae occasionally are observed in pregnancy and labor.   When they are found, an abdominal binder may prove serviceable as a protective measure and, in all cases of recent operation, its prophylactic use is imperative.

Pelvimetry

Mensuration of the pelvis is referred to in obstetrics as pelvimetry.   The measurements usually made are:

The interspinous diameter, 25 cm.
The intercristal diameter, 28 cm.
The intertrochanteric diameter, 31 cm.
The right and left oblique diameters, 22 cm.
The external conjugate diameter, 21 cm.
The diagonal conjugate diameter, 12.5 cm.
The bisischial diameter, 11 cm.

Pelvimetry usually is done about six weeks before confinement and need not be repeated during labor.   Of course, if the patient is first seen when she is in labor, the pelvis must be measured at this time.

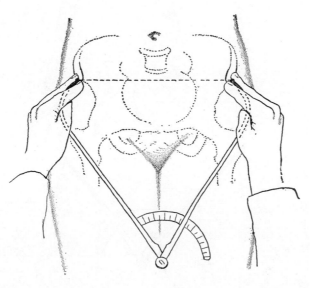

FIG. 262. The interspinous diameter, 25 cm.   It extends between the outer surfaces of the anterior superior spines.

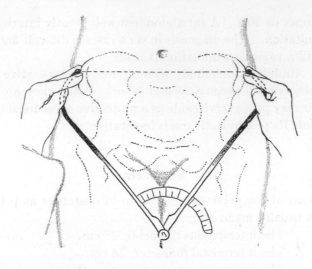

FIG. 263. The intercristal diameter, 28 cm. It is measured from the outermost part of one iliac crest to a similar point on the other.

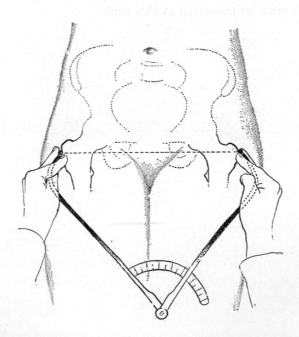

FIG. 264. The intertrochanteric diameter, 31 cm. It is the distance between the two great trochanters.

The **interspinous diameter** extends from the anterior superior spine of the ilium on the one side to the same landmark on the opposite side. It is obtained by placing the ends of a pelvimeter on the outside of the anterior superior spines (Fig. 262). Normally, the interspinous diameter is about 25 cm.

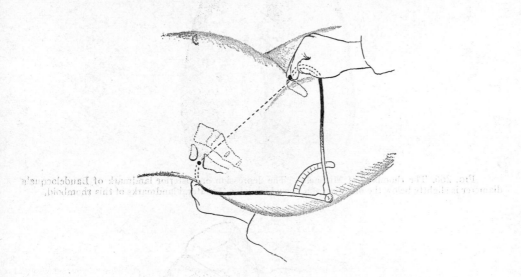

FIG. 265. The external conjugate or Baudelocque's diameter, 21 cm. It extends from the depression below the last lumbar spine to the anterior superior surface of the symphysis pubis.

The **intercristal diameter** is the distance between the outermost parts of each iliac crest. Figure 263 shows the method of obtaining this measurement. Its average length is about 28 cm.

The **intertrochanteric diameter** extends from the great trochanter on one side to the great trochanter on the other (Fig. 264). It is about 31 cm. long.

The **oblique diameters** are measured from the posterior superior spine of one side to the opposite anterior superior spine. These diameters are about the same length, 22 cm.

The **external conjugate or Baudelocque's diameter** extends from a depression beneath the last lumbar spine to the anterior superior surface of the symphysis pubis (3) (Fig. 265). It is about 21 cm. long. The posterior landmark may easily be found by locating the dimples which mark the attachment of the fascia over the posterior superior spine and are the lateral extremities of the rhomboid of Michaelis. When they are connected by an imaginary line, the depression under the last lumbar spine will be found near the point which bisects this imaginary line. Usually it is about 0.5 cm. below the point of bisection (Fig. 266).

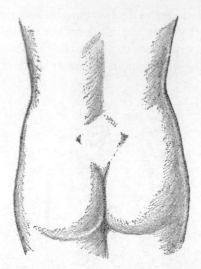

Fig. 266. The rhomboid of Michaelis. The depression or posterior landmark of Baudelocque's diameter is slightly below the bisection of a line which joins the lateral landmarks of this rhomboid.

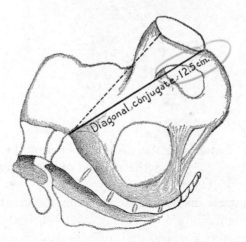

Fig. 267. Diagonal conjugate, 12.5 cm. It is the distance between the promontory of the sacrum and the inferior margin of the symphysis pubis.

The diagonal conjugate is best measured six weeks before the end of pregnancy. When the patient is not seen until after she has gone into labor, this measurement may be omitted if the external conjugate is normal and the head is well in the pelvis, as shown by abdominal and rectal examination. The diagonal conjugate extends between the promontory of the sacrum and the inferior margin of the symphysis pubis (4) (Fig. 267). Its average length is about 12.5 cm. and it is obtained by palpating the promontory of the sacrum with the second finger of one hand, and marking off with the finger of the other the point which comes in contact with the inferior margin of the symphysis pubis. The distance

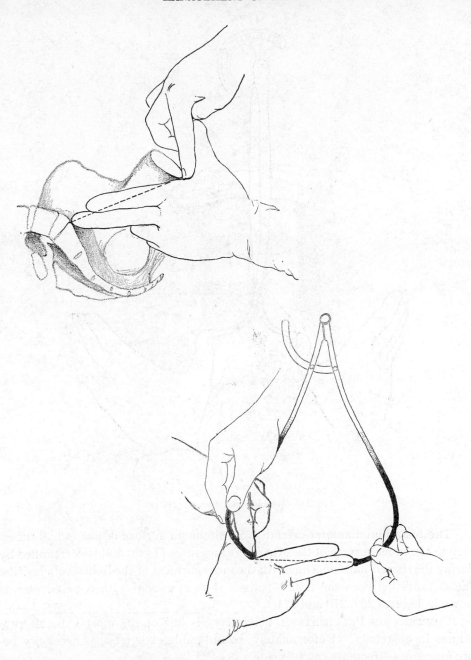

Fig. 268. Measuring the diagonal conjugate.

between these two points is then measured with a caliper (Fig. 268).   This measurement gives the best evidence of the length of the true conjugate, which may
be estimated by deducting 1.5 cm. from the diagonal conjugate.

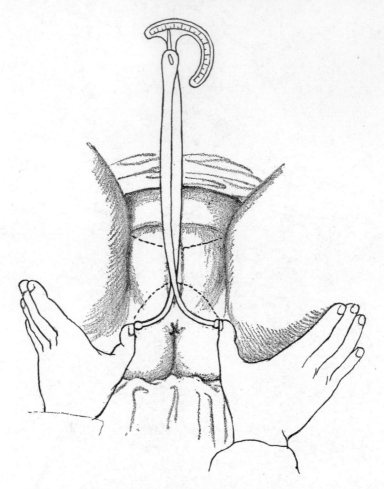

Fig. 269. The bisischial diameter, 11 cm.

The bisischial diameter extends from the inner surface of one ischial tuberosity to the inner surface of the other. It measures 11 cm. and is determined by placing the thumb-nails on a line with the inner surfaces of the ischial tuberosities. The distance between the thumb-nails is then measured with a pelvimeter as shown in Figures 269, 270 and 271.

COMMENT ON PELVIMETRY. Pelvimetry is one of the most valuable procedures in obstetrics. Unfortunately, considerable experience is necessary before exact measurements can be made.

The beginner soon learns to measure accurately the interspinous, intercristal and intertrochanteric diameters. These, however, vary considerably with the amount of fat, the thickness of the bones and their relation to the brim of the pelvis. Unless they are markedly shortened, therefore, conclusions should not be drawn from them alone (5).

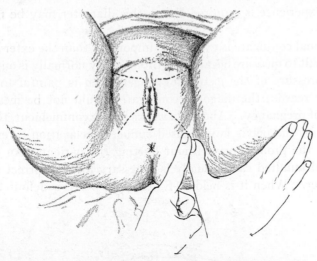

FIG. 270. Checking the location of the inner surface of the left tuberosity. After placing the thumbs in the position shown in Figure 269, the left thumb is removed and with the forefinger of this hand, the inner surface of the left tuberosity is palpated to ascertain whether it is on a line with the right thumb nail.

The external conjugate or Baudelocque's diameter is a more important measurement because it gives valuable information concerning the anteroposterior or shortest diameter of the pelvic inlet. When it is below 18 cm., the pelvis usually is contracted, and a more accurate idea concerning the degree of contraction must be obtained by measuring the diagonal conjugate. Unfortunately,

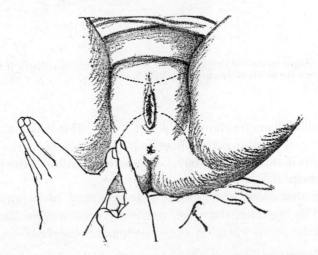

FIG. 271. Checking the location of the inner surface of the right tuberosity. After placing the thumbs in the position shown in Figure 269, the right thumb is removed and with the forefinger of this hand, the inner surface of the right tuberosity is palpated to ascertain whether it is on a line with the left thumb nail.

considerable experience is required before this diameter may be measured correctly (6, 7).

The diagonal conjugate is even more important than the external conjugate. It, too, is difficult to measure because the promontory normally is out of reach and because the pressure of the examining finger often is painful to the patient. For the latter reason, the diagonal conjugate should not be measured in the early months of pregnancy. About six weeks before confinement, the changes in the soft parts of the pelvis have caused sufficient relaxation to enable the examiner to feel the promontory without hurting the patient. An experience of at least several hundred cases usually is necessary for the correct measurement of this diameter. When it is below 11.5 cm., the pelvis is definitely contracted

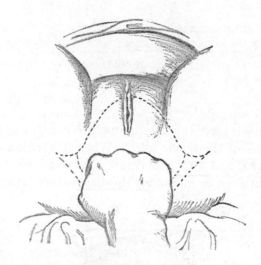

Fig. 272. A simple method of determining the width of the pelvic outlet. If the fist, so placed can be forced between the ischial tuberosities, the outlet is ample.

The bisischial diameter should be above 8 cm. If it is not, the routine suggested under Funnel Pelves is recommended. Unfortunately, the beginner cannot measure this diameter accurately. He therefore will find the method shown in Figure 272 helpful.

From this discussion it is evident that accuracy in pelvimetry requires experience. The beginner, therefore, must rely upon a consultant to rule out contraction of the pelvis whenever the following are observed:

1. Lack of fixation of the head at the onset of labor in a primipara.
2. Overriding of the head in a primipara who is in labor.
3. Pendulous abdomen in a primipara.

Even the experienced obstetrician is unable to judge accurately whether a head will or will not pass through the borderline pelves which are intermediate between the normal and the greatly contracted pelves. It therefore would be better if every woman could have her pelvis measured accurately by one of the more satisfactory roentgen ray techniques. This is particularly advisable in the borderline group. In any case, therefore, in which the promontory can be felt on vaginal examination or in which the external conjugate diameter is 18 cm. or under, an accurate roentgenogram measurement of the pelvis is indicated. For this purpose, the precision stereoscopic roentgenogram technic of Caldwell and Moloy or the use of Thoms' grid method is recommended

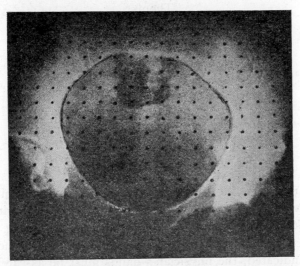

FIG. 272 a. Measurement of the pelvic inlet by the Thoms method. The distance between any two adjacent dots represents 1 cm.

ROENTGEN RAY MENSURATION OF THE PELVIS. By the use of a precision stereoscopic apparatus, the pelvis may be accurately visualized (5a). In this way, the contour of the inlet, outlet and sacro-sciatic notch may be revealed. When such facilities are not available, the size of the pelvic inlet may be accurately determined by the method of Thoms in which the distortion seen in the ordinary x-ray film is corrected by the use of a grid (Fig. 272a) (5b). After placing the patient in a semi-recumbent position, the relation of the superior strait to the sensitive film is established. An exposure is then made and the patient is removed without disturbing the film. A lead plate perforated at 1 cm.

intervals is then interposed in the same position as that occupied by the superior strait of the patient and a second exposure is made. Development of the sensitive plate shows the pelvic inlet as in the usual anteroposterior roentgenogram and measurements are made directly in centimeters.

Lateral exposure made in a similar manner will give the necessary information concerning the promontory, true conjugate and sacro-sciatic notch.

This method also has been used to determine the size of the fetal head and, as a result, has been doubly useful in cases of cephalo-pelvic disproportion. In addition, the period of gestation may be estimated from the size of the occipito-frontal diameter at various stages of pregnancy by the use of the following table (5c) (5d):

RELATION OF WEIGHT AND LENGTH TO OCCIPITOFRONTAL DIAMETER
(Thoms)

Occipitofrontal Cm.	Weight Gm.	Occipitofrontal Cm.	Length Cm.
8–9	1200–1500	7.5–9.5	35–40
9–10	1500–2000	9.5–10.5	40–45
10–11	2000–2500	10.5+	45–50
11+	2500–3000	11+	50–55

Vaginal Examination

Vaginal examinations increase the risk of infection. For this reason, most obstetricians rely upon rectal and abdominal findings. The beginner, however, will have to make use of the vaginal route while he is acquiring the experience necessary for accuracy in abdominal and rectal touch. Whenever a vaginal examination is indicated, the physician's hands must be as carefully prepared as they are for an abdominal operation and the vulva should receive as rigid a preparation as the nature of the parts will permit.

PREPARATION OF THE HANDS:
1. Trim the finger nails.
2. Scrub the hands and forearms with green soap for 5 minutes. Rinse frequently in running water if the latter is available.
3. Cleanse the finger nails with a sterile orange stick.
4. Repeat the scrubbing of the hands.
5. Immerse the hands in 70 per cent alcohol for 3 minutes.
6. Immerse in 1–1000 bichloride of mercury solution for 5 minutes.
7. Dry on a sterile towel, powder with sterile talcum and draw on dry sterile gloves as shown in Figures 273 to 276.

Method of Putting on Sterile Gloves

manner: Fill the gloves with sterile tap-water, the water thus distending and putting them in a mass, and immersing in boiling water for at least ten minutes. Transfer to a basin of bichloride solution and then carefully wrung out. After turning

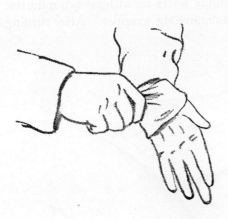 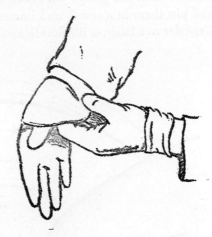

FIG. 273. The fingers of the right hand hold the turned back cuff of the left glove while the left hand is introduced.

FIG. 274. The fingers of the left hand under turned back cuff of right glove hold it while the right hand is introduced.

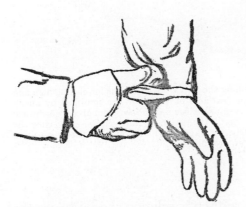 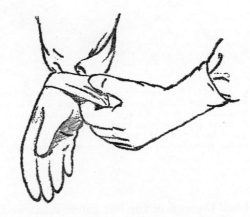

FIG. 275. The cuff of the left glove is pulled over the left sleeve of sterile gown.

FIG. 276. The cuff of the right glove is pulled over the right sleeve of sterile gown.

If wet sterile gloves are to be used, they may be prepared in the following manner: Fill the gloves with water to exclude air from the fingers; then wrap and pin them in a towel, and immerse in boiling water for at least ten minutes. Transfer to a basin of bichloride solution and remove the wrapper.   After turning

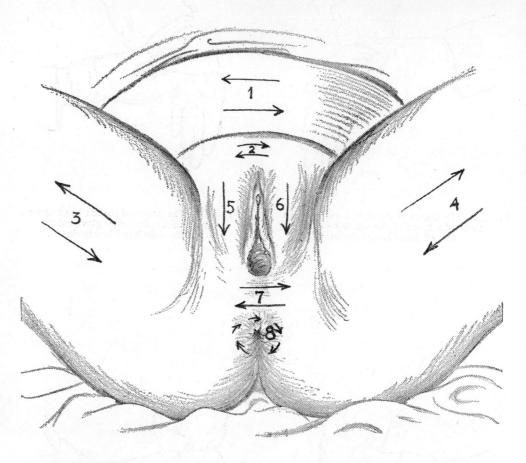

Fig. 277. Diagram showing the method of scrubbing the vulva.   Cleanse the lower abdomen and mons by scrubbing transversely—*1* and *2*.   The inner surfaces of the thigh are scrubbed by an up and down motion—*3* and *4*.   The skin lateral to the vaginal orifice is scrubbed from above downward to avoid contamination from the rectum—*5* and *6*.   Scrub the perineum transversely—*7*.   After the gauze has touched the region of the anus it must not be used again—*8*.   Throughout the preparation of the vulva, avoid contamination of the vagina by the droppings.

back the cuff of the left glove, fill it with antiseptic solution and introduce the left hand as shown in Figure 273.   If the finger tips do not fit properly they should not be touched with the ungloved right hand.   The right hand is then introduced in a similar manner (Fig. 274) and the fingers are worked on with sterile gauze.

PREPARATION OF THE VULVA:

1. Place the patient on a douche pan and shave or clip the pubic hair. Avoid contamination of the vagina by the droppings.
2. Scrub the lower abdomen, mons, inner surface of the thighs and vulva with sterile gauze or cotton and green soap as shown in Figure 277.
3. Repeat scrubbing.
4. Spray on the parts, 70 per cent alcohol or 1–1000 chlorothymol solution (chlorothymol 1 gm., glycerin 100 cc., alcohol 200 cc., water to 1000 cc. (8)).
5. If alcohol is used, rinse with 1–1000 bichloride of mercury solution.

After separating the labia with the thumb and forefinger of one hand (Fig. 278), the first two fingers of the other hand are introduced into the vagina and

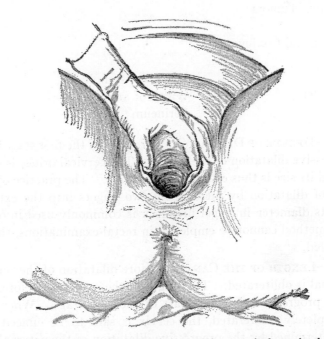

FIG. 278. Separation of the labia before making a vaginal examination.

---

[1] 4 per cent mercurochrome in water may be used as a spray and may also be instilled into the vagina. When it is used, however, the examination should not be made until ½ to 1 hour has elapsed after completing the instillation (9).

the various items given in the following outline are considered:

$$
\text{Cervix} \begin{cases} \text{Degree of dilatation} \\ \text{Length of cervical canal} \\ \text{Position} \\ \text{Thickness and consistency} \\ \text{Scars of previous lacerations} \end{cases}
$$

$$
\text{Membranes} \begin{cases} \text{Intact} \\ \text{Ruptured} \end{cases}
$$

$$
\text{Presenting Part} \begin{cases} \text{Diagnosis} \\ \text{Relation to quadrants of the pelvis} \\ \text{Relation to ischial spines} \\ \text{Malleability} \\ \text{Size} \end{cases}
$$

Pelvic Tumors

Diagonal Conjugate

$$
\text{Outlet} \begin{cases} \text{Length of symphysis} \\ \text{Width of arch} \\ \text{Perineum} \end{cases}
$$

CERVIX—DEGREE OF DILATATION.   Progress in the first stage is determined by the progressive dilatation of the cervix.   The cervical orifice is outlined with one finger and its size is thus estimated (Fig. 279).   The practice of ascertaining the amount of dilatation by introducing two fingers into the external os and designating its diameter in finger-breadths is commonly used in obstetrics but because this method cannot be employed in rectal examinations, the former one is recommended.

CERVIX—LENGTH OF THE CANAL.   Before dilatation of the cervix is appreciable, its canal is obliterated.   The length of the cervix, therefore, is helpful in studying the progress in the early part of the first stage.   When the cervical canal is completely obliterated, the cervix is said to be effaced and further progress is determined by the progressive dilatation of the external os.

CERVIX—POSITION.   Marked displacement of the cervix is evidence of a serious abnormality.   When the cervix is displaced anteriorly and lies near to the symphysis, the presence of a tumor in the cul-de-sac must be ruled out.   On the other hand, a cervix near the promontory of the sacrum may indicate the possibility of dystocia from fixation of the uterus.

CERVIX—THICKNESS AND CONSISTENCY.   The thickness and consistency of the cervix often give a clue to the type of first stage that may be anticipated. Its characteristic consistency, however, can be learned only by experience. Normally, it resembles somewhat the feel of a flabby, paralyzed muscle.   Such a cervix usually is easily dilatable, and when this condition is present, the first stage seldom lasts longer than the average 16 hours, if the pains are satisfactory and no disproportion is present.   Occasionally, its margins may be tough and unyielding.   A leather-like cervix of this type does not dilate readily and is an indication that the first stage may be prolonged.

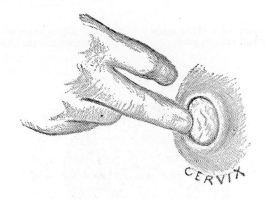

FIG. 279. Finger encircling the external os to determine the degree of dilatation.

CERVIX—SCARS OF PREVIOUS LACERATIONS.   Extensive scars from previous cervical lacerations may interfere with dilatation and, not infrequently, tear again.   The subsequent laceration often is more extensive and may give rise to considerable hemorrhage.   The possibility of hemorrhage, therefore, should always be considered and preparations for its treatment must be made.

MEMBRANES.   When the membranes protrude through the cervix like the finger of a rubber glove, the ball valve action of the presenting part is poor and the possibility of disproportion or abnormal presentation should be considered (Figs. 280 and 281).   Unruptured membranes usually bulge through the external os and are easily detected.   If they are not felt, a diagnosis of rupture of the membranes is not justifiable until an effort has been made to feel them during a contraction.   The discharge of a vernix stained amniotic fluid naturally indicates that they no longer are intact.   Since the amniotic fluid is alkaline and the vaginal secretion is acid, a piece of sterile litmus paper placed in the vagina may aid in the diagnosis.

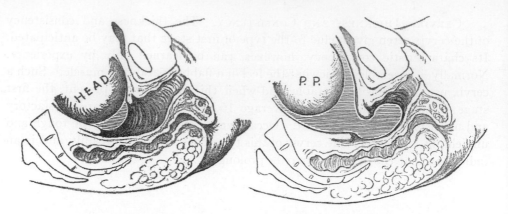

FIG. 280. Watch glass protrusion of the membranes when the ball valve is good.

FIG. 281. Glove finger protrusion of the membranes when the ball valve is poor.

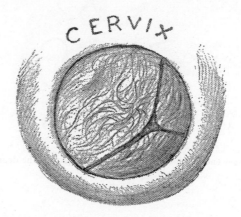

FIG. 282. Touch picture in L.O.A.   The sagittal suture is in the right oblique diameter and the small fontanel is in the left anterior quadrant.

Vaginal Touch Picture in L.O.A.

1. The broad dome of the cranial vault is

    a. hard
    b. smooth
    c. convex
    d. indented by sutures and fontanels

2. The sagittal suture is in the right oblique diameter of the mother's pelvis.

3. The small fontanel is in the left anterior quadrant.

4. The large fontanel, if felt, is in the right posterior quadrant.   Usually, it is not felt.

PRESENTING PART—DIAGNOSIS. The characteristics of the different presenting parts are described in the discussion of the various presentations and positions. In an L.O.A., the broad dome of the vertex or occiput presents. It is hard, smooth and convex, and is indented by the sutures and fontanels (Fig. 282). Of the latter, the sagittal suture and small fontanel are the most important. The small and large fontanels are differentiated by the fact that the former has three sides and three sutures, while the latter has four sides and is entered by four sutures. If the molding of the head is marked, overlapping of the sutures may make it difficult to distinguish the triangular and quadrilateral shapes of these fontanels. By tracing the sagittal suture from one fontanel to the other, and allowing the finger to pass a short distance beyond each, it will be observed that the suture line passes beyond one but not the other. Palpation of this suture between the frontal bones identifies the anterior fontanel and the lack of a similar suture in the occipital bone makes clear the diagnosis of the posterior fontanel. Recognition of these landmarks is easy if the examination is made soon after the membranes rupture. They may, however, be obscured by the development of a caput succedaneum when the membranes have been ruptured for some time.

FIG. 283. Relation of the head to the ischial spines. The suboccipito bregmatic diameter has passed through the inlet (1) when the presenting part reaches the level of the spines (2).

PRESENTING PART—RELATION TO THE QUADRANTS OF THE PELVIS. The relation of the presenting part to the mother's pelvis indicates the position of the child. In an L.O.A., the small fontanel, being nearer the occiput, is in the left anterior quadrant and the sagittal suture is in relation to the right oblique diameter (Fig. 282). If these landmarks cannot be distinguished, late in labor, the location of the posterior ear will show the position of the occiput.

PRESENTING PART—RELATION TO THE ISCHIAL SPINES. The relation of the presenting part to the plane of the ischial spines shows the location of the engaging diameters with respect to the brim of the pelvis. When the **broad dome** of the fetal skull is felt at or near the level of the ischial spines in vertex presentations, the engaging diameters (S.O.B. and Bip.) have already passed through the pelvic brim, and inlet dystocia no longer need be feared (Fig. 283). If, however, the broad dome of the vertex is distorted into an irregular or lopsided mass, the marked molding of pelvic disproportion must be considered and dystocia, accordingly, cannot be ruled out.

PRESENTING PART—MALLEABILITY. Molding of the head is dependent on its malleability. When molding of the head is necessary, therefore, this step in the routine vaginal examination is important. It is determined by observing the width of the sutures and fontanels and noting the consistency of the bones of the cranial vault. Hard bones, with closed sutures and very small fontanels, permit little or no molding. Such a head, accordingly, will have greater difficulty in passing through the pelvis than will one that is more malleable.

PELVIC TUMORS. Tumors in or adjacent to the uterus may be felt on vaginal examination. These, however, are often mistaken by the beginner for parts of the fetus. Whenever the cervix is abnormally placed the possibility of a tumor in the cul-de-sac must be kept in mind.

DIAGONAL CONJUGATE. If the patient is seen for the first time when she is in labor, and the presenting part is movable and above the level of the ischial spines, it is well to feel for the promontory of the sacrum in order that the possibility of contracted pelvis may be ruled out. When the promontory can be felt, the diagonal conjugate should be measured (Figs. 267 and 268, page 284).

OUTLET. Before withdrawing the examining fingers, the length of the symphysis is noted. The fingers are then spread apart transversely to determine the width of the pubic arch. If the subpubic angle is acute, the outlet is contracted (See Funnel Pelvis, page 662). Finally, an attempt should be made to estimate the consistency of the perineum. A tough, unyielding perineum does not dilate easily and may require an episiotomy. Preparations for the repair of an extensive laceration always are indicated in such cases.

Rectal Examination

If the patient has been examined in the latter part of pregnancy, labor may be conducted without the risk of a vaginal examination, provided the attendant is sufficiently experienced in abdominal and rectal touch. Because the latter may be done with very little risk to the patient and does not require any preparation of the physician's hands other than the use of gloves, it is recommended that the beginner make a rectal after every vaginal examination until he feels that he is able to make out the necessary findings by rectal touch. After this, the rectal examination is to be tried first and his findings are then to be checked by a vaginal examination. Within a short time, he should become sufficiently expert to substitute rectal for vaginal examination in a large percentage of his cases.

If, for any reason, an accurate diagnosis cannot be made from these examinations, further efforts to ascertain more accurate data may be postponed until the membranes rupture or until intervention is indicated. In those cases in which the possibility of disproportion is feared, contracted pelvis should be ruled out as early as possible by an experienced obstetrician.

If everything seems satisfactory, the patient should be informed of the favorable outlook. Prognosis as to the duration of labor, however, always must be guarded, because accuracy in this regard is dependent upon such variable conditions that mistakes are common. It is better to tell the patient that her child is lying in a favorable position and that the pelvis seems to be ample, but that one cannot foretell the frequency and strength of the uterine contractions and, as a consequence, the duration of labor cannot be predicted.

Management of the remainder of the first stage may be considered under the following headings:

1. Measures used to accelerate labor.
2. Care of the bladder and rectum.
3. Food requirements.
4. Rest and the relief of pain.
5. Return visits.

MEASURES USED TO ACCELERATE LABOR. The sooner the uterus acquires its proper rhythm, the sooner may the patient be put to bed and given those sedative drugs which not only alleviate her suffering but facilitate the dilatation of the cervix. As most patients have stronger and more frequent uterine contractions when they are on their feet, it is advisable to have them walk about and perform their usual household duties. Contractions also may be safely stimulated by the use of a warm enema. On the other hand, oxytocic drugs are dangerous and should not be given in a normal labor.

CARE OF THE BLADDER. A distended bladder is painful and interferes with the mechanism of labor. Since the patient experiences great difficulty in emptying her bladder after it has become distended, she should be directed to void every two hours. If this plan is followed, distention seldom will occur and the need for catheterization will be minimized.

CARE OF THE RECTUM. As stated previously, a warm enema frequently accelerates the uterine contractions. By emptying the rectum early in labor, it also prevents fecal contamination during the stage of expulsion.

FOOD REQUIREMENTS. Ample nourishment is essential to the maintenance of the patient's strength throughout labor. On the other hand, nausea and an inability to take food are common complaints. In spite of these, however, the physician should explain the need for food and, if necessary, he must insist on the taking of adequate nourishment. Carbohydrate calories are best tolerated and should be given at intervals of two to three hours. Toast, rice, baked or boiled potato and the various prepared cereals are the best foods. Broths and milk are not sufficient to maintain the patient through a long labor. They accordingly should not be given in the early part of the first stage but may be given within several hours of the anticipated time of delivery, because a full stomach may interfere with the giving of an anesthetic. Dehydration is combated by the taking of ample fluids.

REST AND THE RELIEF OF PAIN are secured by the use of sedative drugs after labor is definitely established. In the early part of the first stage, morphine and scopolamine are recommended (10). These drugs, however, cannot be given too soon because they may stop the uterine contractions. Their use late in labor likewise is inadvisable on account of the possible danger to the child. Relief from pain in the latter part of the first stage, however, may be secured by the use of one of the barbiturates.

RETURN VISITS. In the early part of labor, the constant presence of the physician is not necessary. If the patient is a primipara, he may leave her for three or four hours provided he is prepared to return at once should she need him. Subsequent return visits are made at similar intervals until the cervix is 7 cm. in diameter, after which he should plan to remain in the patient's home. With a multipara he always must be prepared for a rapid delivery and must alter the preceding routine to suit the particular circumstances of each case. The patient should be instructed to call him if the pains become stronger and recur at five minute intervals, if the membranes rupture, or if she has a hemorrhage.

After three or four hours he returns and interrogates the patient concerning the condition of her labor during his absence. He checks up on the amount of food that has been taken and satisfies himself that his directions with regard to the bladder and rectum have been followed. The temperature, pulse and respiration are again taken and a second examination is made. Usually, enough information may be gained by introducing one finger into the rectum and noting the degree of dilatation and the amount of progress of the presenting part. If sufficient information cannot be obtained in this manner, an aseptic vaginal examination may be repeated. When the cervical canal is obliterated and the external os is 2 to 3 cm. in diameter, i.e., about the size of a twenty-five cent piece, the frequency and strength of the uterine contractions are noted for the purpose of ascertaining whether sedatives may be given with safety. If the contractions recur at five to six minute intervals and are strong, the patient is put to bed and the uterus is again carefully felt during several pains.

Should the recumbent posture have no effect on the uterine contractions, 100 mg. demerol intramuscularly and $\frac{1}{200}$ gr. scopolamine are given hypodermically. Before these drugs are administered, however, some nourishment should be given as the action of the sedatives may interfere with the taking of food for several hours. In addition to relieving the patient's suffering these sedatives favor dilatation. It is a common observation among those who follow this routine that if demerol and scopolamine do not weaken the uterine contractions, their use generally shortens the first stage of labor. The physician waits a short time to see that his patient is comfortable after the administration of these sedatives and again leaves her with the advice that she is to continue her food and the care of the bladder as previously recommended.

About four hours later, he again visits the patient and after taking the pulse, temperature and respiration, notes the progress of labor. A check-up on his previous recommendations is then made and the patient is encouraged by a sympathetic discussion of all of the favorable findings that are revealed by his examination.

When the cervix is 7 cm. in diameter or larger, the physician should not leave the patient unless there is some one in attendance who is competent to recognize and treat any emergency or summon him if his presence is needed. Should the membranes rupture before the cervix is fully dilated, a vaginal examination is indicated, since abnormalities may then be most easily detected. If they are still intact, when the cervix is fully dilated, artificial rupture of the membranes is indicated. To avoid prolapse of the cord, this is done in the interval between the pains rather than during a contraction and only a small perforation is made. The beginner may have some difficulty in determining whether the cervix is fully dilated. If he has felt the margin of the progressively dilating os throughout the labor, and can no longer feel it, he may safely conclude that the cervix is fully dilated and rupture the membranes. In case of doubt, on the other hand, it is better to wait until the membranes appear at the vulva before rupturing them.

SECOND STAGE

The following items are important in the conduct of the second stage:

1. Vaginal examination.
2. Encouragement of the voluntary efforts.
3. Auscultation of the fetal heart sounds.
4. The use of anesthesia.
5. The employment of an aseptic technic.
6. The prevention of laceration.
7. Management of coils of cord around the neck.
8. Management of the shoulders.

VAGINAL EXAMINATION. Immediately after the membranes rupture a careful vaginal examination is indicated. Even the beginner will then find it easy to diagnose face, breech and transverse presentations, since the tissues over the presenting part will not have had sufficient time to become edematous and obliterate the usual landmarks. Early recognition of an abnormality likewise makes possible its prompt correction before molding of the uterus takes place. Perhaps the best example of the value of this measure is that offered by prolapse of the cord. If an examination is made immediately after the membranes rupture, a prolapsed cord may be detected sufficiently early to save the child. Even when experienced men substitute rectal for vaginal examination, they do not hesitate to use the latter immediately after the membranes rupture in all doubtful cases. Every hour that elapses after the membranes rupture in abnormal cases is an hour of neglect, since the difficulties encountered in the diagnosis and correction of abnormalities multiply with the delay.

FIG. 284. Squat position.

ENCOURAGEMENT OF THE VOLUNTARY EFFORTS. At the onset of each contraction the patient is instructed to take a deep inspiration, hold her breath and bear down just as in defecating. The intra-abdominal pressure is thus directed against the uterus and aids considerably in the expulsion of the child. Crying out, on the other hand, is a forced expiration and lessens the expulsive efforts by causing the intra-abdominal pressure to act in the opposite direction. If the attendant will anticipate such a forced expiratory effort and urge his patient to bear down each time that she otherwise would cry out, the value of the voluntary efforts will be greatly augmented. Anesthesia not only relieves the patient's suffering but is helpful in carrying out this routine, provided it is not used to the extent that it weakens the uterine contractions.

During the second stage of labor, the patient would naturally assume the squat position if she were allowed to follow her own inclination (Fig. 284). In this posture, the symphysis is brought closer to the ensiform cartilage and the thighs are forced against the abdominal wall. Thus, not only is the intra-abdominal pressure increased but the weak part of the abdominal wall is supported by the lower extremities. At the same time, upward rotation of the symphysis results in a considerable increase in the anteroposterior diameter of the outlet. All of these advantages are lost when the patient lies on her back during the second stage. In this respect, the ancient midwife did better than the modern obstetrician. She provided a stool which, to a large extent, retained the advantages of the squat position. When the true etiology of puerperal infection became known and the value of an aseptic technic began to be appreciated, the dorsal position gained in favor because it was easier to preserve an aseptic routine with the patient in this position. It is possible, however, to retain all of the advantages of the squat posture and at the same time use the dorsal position if pullers and a snug abdominal binder are utilized (11). By

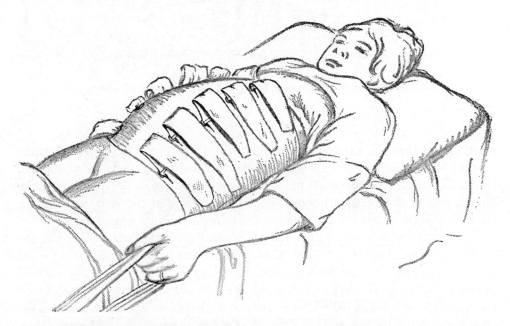

FIG. 285. Abdominal binder and pullers used to retain the advantages of the squat position, although the patient lies on her back in bed.

pulling on the ends of a sheet placed around the foot of the bed and bracing her feet, the patient brings the ensiform cartilage and symphysis closer together. Flexion of the thighs by the attendants causes the symphysis to undergo further

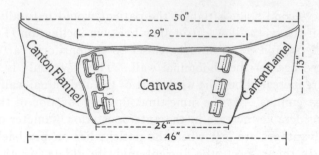

FIG. 286A. Details of the part of the abdominal binder which is placed under the patient and to which the tails shown in Figure 286B are attached.

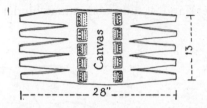

286B. Details of the part of the abdominal binder which is placed over the abdomen.

rotation and thus the anteroposterior diameter of the outlet is elongated, while support of the abdominal wall is obtained by adjusting an inelastic abdominal binder in the interval between pains (Figs. 285 and 286). By employing the binder, pullers and the instructions concerning the use of the voluntary efforts, the second stage of labor may be shortened to about half its usual length.

AUSCULTATION OF THE FETAL HEART SOUNDS gives the best evidence of the child's condition (Fig. 287). Because most instances of fetal distress occur in the second stage and because the requisites for operative interference are fulfilled at this time, the fetal heart sounds should be listened to after each uterine contraction. A rate below 100 or over 160, or an irregular rhythm, indicates the presence of fetal distress and calls for a change in the routine conduct of labor.

ANESTHESIA. Chloroform, ether, nitrous oxide, ethylene, and spinal and local anesthesia with novocaine have been used in labor. See Chapter 46 page 894.

Chloroform has the advantage that the patient may go under and come out of its influence rapidly (12). It also is serviceable in securing the relaxation that at times is necessary for operative deliveries. On the other hand, chloroform is dangerous when given over a long period.   Even for short anesthesias, the margin of safety is so slight that only those trained in its use are justified in giving this anesthetic during labor.

Ether does not act so rapidly and for this reason is less satisfactory, but its greater safety makes it the best general anesthetic for our purposes (13, 14). The anesthetic is given by means of an Allis inhaler during each uterine contraction and is removed in the interval between pains.   It usually is started when the scalp of the child is seen in the vulvovaginal slit, and is deepened as the head is being born.

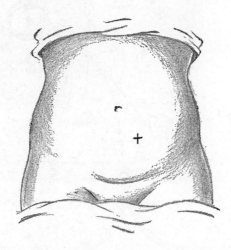

Fig. 287. The location of the fetal heart sounds in L.O.A.

Nitrous oxide has the advantage that it may be given over longer periods. It therefore is used throughout the second stage and often is started before dilatation of the cervix is complete (15, 16, 17).   Nitrous oxide is expensive and requires a special apparatus and a trained anesthetist.   For these reasons, its use is limited largely to hospital practice.

The explosive nature of ethylene restricts its field of usefulness to special institutions which are equipped to combat this dangerous characteristic of an otherwise admirable anesthetic (18).

Spinal anesthesia has been used in the latter part of the first and throughout the second stage of labor (19, 20).   Its administration is technically difficult, but when given properly is said to be quite safe.   It has the further disadvantage of destroying the voluntary efforts and, as a result, even multiparae, under spinal anesthesia, usually are unable to deliver without artificial aid.

Local infiltration anesthesia, when properly used, eliminates the worst pains of labor without interfering with the natural expulsive efforts (21). It accordingly has no ill effect in the third stage and permits the repair of lacerations or episiotomy wounds without further anesthesia. The technic of its administration is shown in Figure 288.

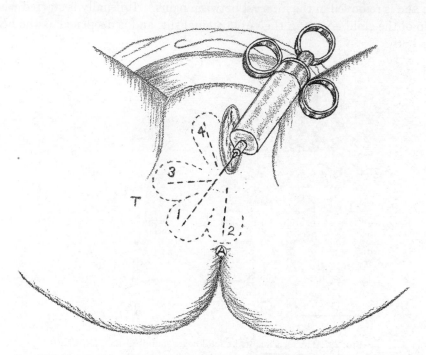

Fig. 288. Local infiltration anesthesia. A small amount of 1% procaine and 1–200,000 adrenaline in normal saline solution is injected just below the fourchette. Through this anesthetized area, a 20 gage needle is passed to a point midway between the anus and the ischial tuberosity, 1. After aspirating to determine whether a vein has been entered, 10 cc. of the anesthetic solution are injected. The needle is again introduced at the original site and similar injections are made along the radiating lines indicated by 2, 3 and 4. The opposite side is infiltrated in a similar manner.

ASEPTIC TECHNIC. As soon as the head begins to distend the perineum, preparations for delivery are made. The vulva is again sprayed with 70 per cent alcohol or 1–500 chlorothymol (if alcohol is used it is followed by an irrigation of bichloride solution). The physician then puts on a cap, mask, sterile gown, sterile gloves and drapes the patient as shown in Figure 289. In addition, the parts are frequently swabbed with chlorothymol or 0.5 per cent lysol solution as the head successively advances and recedes with each uterine contraction.

PREVENTION OF LACERATION. While it is impossible to prevent the almost inevitable laceration that accompanies the delivery of the first child, the following measures will greatly lessen the degree of trauma:

FIG. 289. Method of draping the patient for delivery.   Sterile sheet under the patient, sterile leggings on legs and sterile sheet over lower abdomen.

1. Avoid too rapid descent of the head by:
   a. Proper management of the voluntary efforts.
   b. The use of anesthesia.
   c. Retardation of the head with the hand.
2. Favor flexion until the occiput is born.
3. Favor extension after the nucha impinges under the symphysis.
4. Deliver by Ritgen's maneuver between the pains.
5. Make use of prophylactic median perineotomy or lateral episiotomy when extensive laceration seems inevitable.

AVOID TOO RAPID DESCENT OF THE HEAD.   As soon as the scalp appears in the vulvovaginal ring, the progress of the head should be carefully observed.   If it descends too rapidly, the binder and pullers are removed and the patient is urged to stop bearing down.   Should this prove ineffectual the force of the intra-abdominal pressure may be almost completely eliminated by having her pant.   Anesthesia also helps to control the action of the voluntary efforts and, to some extent, lessens the force of the uterine contractions.   The progress of the head likewise may be quite satisfactorily managed by placing the hand against the scalp and retarding its advance whenever descent is too rapid.   In this manner it is possible to prevent the sudden expulsion of the child with its resulting extensive laceration of the maternal soft parts.

FAVOR FLEXION.   When the vulvovaginal ring is about 7 cm. in diameter, slight downward pressure on the presenting part increases flexion and allows the nucha to impinge beneath the symphysis. As a result, the diameters which pass through the vulvovaginal orifice have their origin in the suboccipital region and, accordingly, are the smallest possible head diameters that can be born. This maneuver must not be used unless the physician has full control of the situation since it is to be followed immediately by extension of the head, otherwise more extensive laceration of the perineum may result.

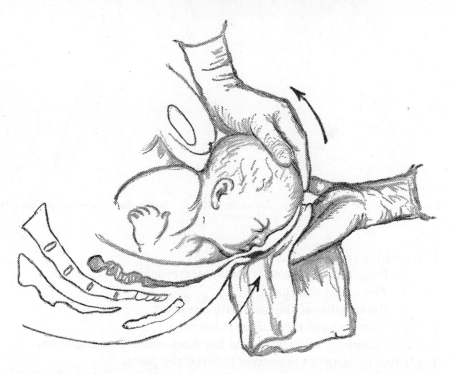

FIG. 290. Delivery of the head in the interval between the pains by the Ritgen's maneuver.

FAVOR EXTENSION. After the nucha comes under the symphysis the hand which is placed over the head to control its progress favors extension by directing the brow upward toward the symphysis.

DELIVERY BY RITGEN'S MANEUVER. When the suboccipitofrontal plane of the head is about to be born, the patient is told to stop bearing down and to pant. The anesthesia is deepened and the head is held back by the physician's hands until the uterine contraction which would have accomplished its delivery ceases. With the other hand protected by a sterile towel, pressure is made through the maternal soft parts behind the rectum, and the face and brow are forced upward (22). Thus the head is born between the pains when the parts are relaxed and the tendency toward laceration is reduced to the minimum (Fig. 290).

MANAGEMENT OF COILS OF CORD AROUND THE NECK. Following the birth of the head, the secretions are wiped from the nose and mouth. After immersing the first two fingers of the right hand in an antiseptic solution, they are introduced into the vagina above the child's neck and a search is made for coils of cord. When found they are pulled over the child's head. Should this be impossible, the cord is severed between two clamps, and the shoulders are artificially extracted.

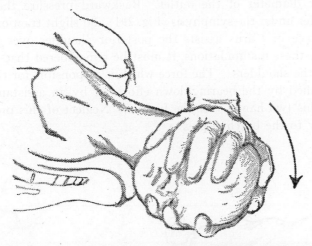

Fig. 291. Management of the shoulders. One hand above and the other below the head make slight downward traction to guide the anterior shoulder under the pubic arch. The force which delivers the shoulders should come from above either through a bearing down effort or suprapubic pressure.

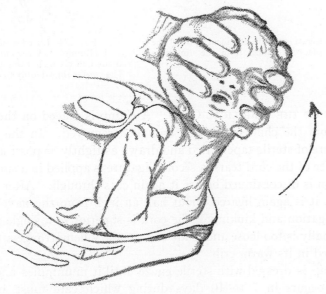

Fig. 292. Management of the shoulders. The head, grasped as in Figure 291, is carried upward along the curve of Carus to guide the birth of the posterior shoulder. The shoulders should not be delivered by traction; otherwise the brachial plexus may be injured.

MANAGEMENT OF THE SHOULDERS. Provided the mother is not under the influence of a general anesthetic and the child's color is good, it is well to wait for spontaneous delivery of the shoulders. This may be accelerated by encouraging the patient to continue her bearing-down efforts. If the cord has been cut or if the child's condition is poor, artificial aid is indicated. With one hand above and the other below the child's head, the physician guides the shoulders into the anteroposterior diameter of the outlet. Backward pressure then brings the anterior shoulder under the symphysis (Fig. 291) and slight traction in the direction of the curve of Carus assists the posterior shoulder over the perineum (Fig. 292). In these manipulations, it must be remembered that the physician merely guides the shoulders. The force which is responsible for their expulsion must be furnished by the bearing-down efforts or by an assistant who makes pressure with his two hands over the fundus. Neglect of this precaution may result in injury to the brachial plexus.

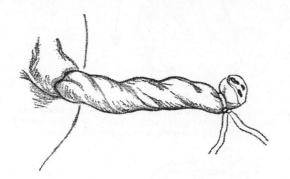

FIG. 293. Ligation of the umbilical cord. The first ligature is placed 2 inches from the umbilicus and tied tightly.

FIG. 294. Ligation of the umbilical cord (Bumm). A second knot is tied about half an inch from the umbilicus. The cord is thus doubly tied and kinked.

LIGATION OF THE UMBILICAL CORD. A clamp is placed on the cord about two inches from the child's abdomen and then removed. In the groove thus made, a ligature of sterile tape is tied and drawn as tightly as possible (Fig. 293). If the substance of the cord tears, a second ligature is applied in a similar manner but the tension is discontinued before it again cuts through. After bending the cord on itself, it is again ligated about half an inch from the navel (Fig. 294). This double ligation and kinking of the cord is superior to a single tie since the latter occasionally is too loose and leads to secondary hemorrhage after the child has been placed in its warm crib.

The stump is dressed with sterile gauze until it mummifies and separates. This usually occurs in 7 to 10 days during which care must be taken to avoid infection. Many devices have been designed to clamp the cord and hasten its separation. Among these the Ziegler clamp is best known and most generally used. By the use of the improved instrument a satisfactory result is obtained within a few days (22 a).

CARE OF THE CHILD'S EYES. A fair percentage of the inmates of institutions for the blind are there because proper care of the eyes was neglected at the time of their birth (23). On the other hand, gonorrheal ophthalmia almost never occurs when Credé's prophylactic recommendations are followed (24). The possibility of gonorrheal ophthalmia, therefore, is so great and its consequences are so serious that prophylaxis against this complication is imperative in every case regardless of the parent's status. The lids are spread apart and from a medicine dropper 1 per cent silver nitrate or freshly prepared 20 per cent argyrol is dropped into the eyes. If a stronger silver preparation is used, it must subsequently be washed out with boric acid solution to prevent the occurrence of a chemical ophthalmia.

THIRD STAGE

The third stage of labor usually is short and uncomplicated. On the other hand, it may be accompanied by severe bleeding and may give rise to great anxiety. The conduct of the third stage, therefore, should receive most careful attention. When it is complicated by hemorrhage, the management of the placenta differs from that followed in the usual cases which are free from bleeding, until the gush of blood shows that the separation of the placenta has been completed. The points of difference are shown in the following outline:

(A) **Management of a Non-bleeding Third Stage**

1. Await the signs of separation:
   a. Rise of the uterus which becomes ball-like in shape.
   b. Further protrusion of cord.
   c. Gush of blood.
   d. Loss of expansile impulse in cord.
   e. Cord not pulled into vagina when uterus is elevated.
2. Artificially express the placenta by the modified Credé maneuver.
3. Carefully examine the placenta to rule out the retention of placental fragments.
4. Massage the fundus and administer oxytocic drugs to prevent postpartum hemorrhage.
5. If the placenta does not separate in 1 hour, try the typical Credé procedure.

(B) **Management of a Bleeding Third Stage**

1. Differentiate between bleeding from the placental site and bleeding from lacerations in the birth passages.
2. Massage the uterus continually.
3. Prepare for a manual removal of the placenta.
4. Separate and expel the placenta by Credé's maneuver.
5. If Credé's maneuver fails, manually remove the placenta.
6. Carefully examine the placenta to rule out the retention of placental fragments.
7. Massage the uterus and administer oxytocic drugs to prevent postpartum hemorrhage.
8. Transfuse whenever the blood loss has been excessive.

Management of a Non-bleeding Third Stage

THE SIGNS OF PLACENTAL SEPARATION. In the absence of bleeding, the conduct of the third stage is largely a matter of watchful waiting until the placenta is separated. Immediately after the delivery of the child, a sterile towel is placed over the abdomen and the height of the fundus is noted. When separation is complete, the placenta passes into the lower uterine segment and thereby causes an **elevation of the fundus** (25, 26). At the same time the uterus becomes more **globular in shape**. Palpation of a ball-like uterus at or near the level of the umbilicus accordingly indicates the presence of the placenta in the lower uterine segment or vagina. For the same reason, **further protrusion of the cord** may be observed.

When separation is complete, **a gush of blood** commonly occurs. This, however, may also result from a premature peripheral detachment of the placenta. Other signs of separation, therefore, should be sought whenever a gush of blood takes place. If they are not found, the plan of treatment is changed to that recommended for a bleeding third stage.

Palpation of **a placental tumor** above the symphysis, at times, is difficult and for this reason is a less valuable sign. When the placenta is attached to the uterus or is still within its upper segment, pressure made on the fundus is transmitted through the fluid contained within the placenta to the umbilical cord. If the distal end of the cord is clamped, such pressure then results in an expansile impulse. During the early part of every third stage each uterine contraction acts in a similar manner and causes the cord to become more tense. The loss of this **expansile impulse,** therefore, is an indication that the placenta has been separated and is in the lower uterine segment. Finally, **failure of the cord to be pulled back into the vagina** when the uterus is artificially elevated clinches the diagnosis of complete separation. (This maneuver should not be employed if the cord has become contaminated by passing over the anus.)

ARTIFICIAL EXPULSION OF THE PLACENTA. As soon as the signs outlined show conclusively that separation of the placenta is complete, the fundus of the uterus is massaged until it contracts. The placenta is then expressed artificially by making pressure in the axis of the pelvic inlet as shown in Figure 295. This procedure, if done properly and at the right time, terminates the third stage with safety long before it otherwise would occur.

EXAMINATION OF THE PLACENTA. The maternal surface of the placenta is examined to make certain that no cotyledons have been left within the uterus. The margins of the fetal surface are then carefully searched for evidence of torn vessels. Discovery of the latter indicates the retention of an accessory lobe. **A retained cotyledon or accessory lobe may give rise to an alarming hemorrhage at any time during the puerperium.** Placental fragments of an appreciable size, therefore, are to be removed at once. Before introducing the hand into the uterus for the removal of such retained fragments, the gloves and gown that were worn during the delivery should be replaced by **clean, sterile ones and the** vulva should again be cleansed with lysol or chlorothymol solution

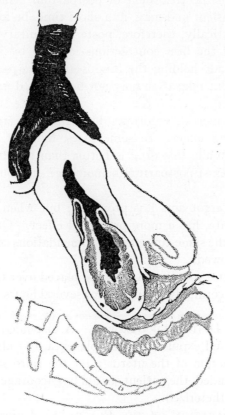

FIG. 295. Artificial expulsion of the placenta after it has separated, by the modified Credé procedure.   This should never be done unless the uterus is well contracted, as it might otherwise cause inversion of the uterus.

PREVENTION OF POSTPARTUM HEMORRHAGE is accomplished by the following:

1. Massage of the uterus.
2. Oxytocic drugs: posterior pituitary extract, ergotamine tartrate, or fluid
     extract of ergot.
3. The use of an ice bag over the fundus.
4. The avoidance of a distended bladder.

MASSAGE OF THE UTERUS.   **Someone competent to massage the uterus
should hold the fundus for at least one hour after the placenta is born.   If at
any time the uterus relaxes, the fundus should be vigorously massaged until it
again becomes firm.**   This is, without question, the best means of preventing
postpartum hemorrhage and should not be discontinued even for a few minutes
within the required hour after the completion of the third stage.

OXYTOCIC DRUGS. Posterior pituitary extract promptly causes firm contractions of the uterus. This rapid and vigorous action, accordingly, makes it a most valuable drug in the treatment of postpartum hemorrhage. The effect, however, is quite transient and may, in a short time, be followed by relaxation. When used prophylactically, therefore, posterior pituitary extract gives a false sense of security and the firm contractions induced by it, at times, lead the attendant to discontinue holding the fundus as above recommended, with the result that a subsequent relaxation may not be detected until its accompanying hemorrhage is observed.

Ergonovine (ergometrin, ergotrate, basergin), an ergot derivative has a rapid but more lasting effect. In some cases, however, the uterus does not respond to its use. While this drug is better than posterior pituitary extract in the prophylaxis against postpartum hemorrhage, it should not take the place of massage.

Fluid extract of ergot acts less promptly, but when freshly prepared, it, like ergotamine tartrate, has a more prolonged effect. One dram by mouth is usually given and at the same time the recommendations concerning the holding of the fundus are followed.

ICE BAG OVER THE FUNDUS. An ice bag placed over the fundus also has an oxytocic effect and, accordingly, is applied for several hours following the delivery of the placenta.

AVOIDANCE OF A DISTENDED BLADDER. A distended bladder not only retards the separation and expulsion of the placenta, but also interferes with the contraction and retraction of the uterus after the third stage. Whenever the bladder becomes distended, the patient should be encouraged to void and if necessary she should be catheterized.

FAILURE OF SEPARATION OF THE PLACENTA. Unfortunately, in rare instances, the separation of the placenta may be considerably delayed. If the signs of separation have not appeared after one hour an attempt is made to accelerate the third stage by the use of the true Credé maneuver, following which the remainder of the placental stage is conducted according to the principle recommended under the management of a bleeding third stage. It is unwise to leave the placenta within the uterine cavity for more than three or four hours, since its separation may, at any time, be accompanied by a profuse hemorrhage. Should the placenta be allowed to remain in the uterus, someone qualified to remove it manually must be in constant attendance.

Management of a Bleeding Third Stage

DETERMINATION OF THE SOURCE OF THE BLEEDING. Each contraction of the uterus separates more of the placenta and, accordingly, results in greater hemorrhage. A bleeding third stage that is due to hemorrhage from the placental site, therefore, is characterized by a progressive increase in the amount of blood lost. On the other hand, third stage bleeding that is due to a laceration in the

birth passages is greatest immediately following the birth of the child and thereafter progressively diminishes as clots form and partially control the hemorrhage.
Bleeding of the latter type is managed according to the site and extent of the
laceration (see Repair of Lacerations, page 825), and the third stage is conducted
as in the non-bleeding variety, if the amount of blood lost is not excessive.

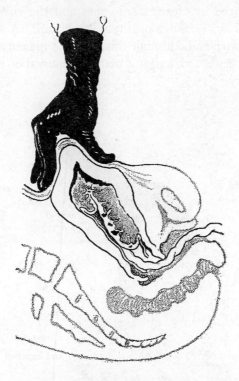

FIG. 296. Credé's procedure. Sagittal section.

MASSAGE OF THE UTERUS by stimulating contractions hastens the separation
of the placenta and lessens to some extent the amount of hemorrhage from the
placental site. The uterus, therefore, should be vigorously massaged while
complete separation of the placenta is awaited. Although this measure is simple
and without risk, it should not be relied upon too long since the constant loss of
blood throughout the third stage may exsanguinate the patient. Careful observation of the amount of blood lost and its effect on the patient's pulse should lead
to the employment of a more satisfactory method before the patient's condition
becomes serious.

PREPARATION FOR A MANUAL REMOVAL OF THE PLACENTA. Since a manual removal of the placenta often may be necessary if an unsuccessful attempt to complete the separation causes a profuse hemorrhage, the physician should always prepare for a manual removal before he attempts the Credé procedure. This precaution is essential because unsuccessful attempts to complete the separation by Credé's method may so increase the bleeding that time will not then permit proper aseptic preparations. The gloves and gown that were worn during the delivery are replaced by clean, sterile ones and the vulva is again cleansed with 1 per cent lysol or 1–500 chlorothymol solution. A sterile towel is then placed over the abdomen and, through this, Credé's maneuver is tried with one hand while the other is kept clean for a manual removal of the placenta, should the latter be necessary.

FIG. 297. Credé's procedure. The placenta is separated and expelled just as the pit is forced from a cherry.

CREDÉ'S MANEUVER. The fingers of one hand are placed behind the fundus and, with the thumb in front, the uterus is grasped and compressed from one side to the other (27). By thus squeezing the fundus and at the same time making pressure in the axis of the pelvic inlet, the placenta is separated and expressed in a manner similar to that used in pitting a cherry (Figs. 296 and 297). This maneuver never should be tried when the uterus is relaxed. If the latter is not in contraction, the manipulations should be preceded by massage until firm contractions are induced.

Unfortunately, this procedure may, at times, be unsuccessful in the hands of the beginner, and in addition may greatly increase the amount of bleeding. In such circumstances, he should not wait too long before manually removing the placenta.

MANUAL REMOVAL OF THE PLACENTA is a dangerous procedure because of the greatly increased risk of infection (28). For this reason, proper preliminary preparations should be made before the Credé maneuver is attempted. Sufficient time then may be taken to carry out a satisfactory aseptic technic. As stated above, the hand, before entering the uterus, must be covered with a clean, sterile glove since the gloves used during the delivery might easily have become contaminated. Before introducing the sterile gloved hand, it is dipped into 1 per

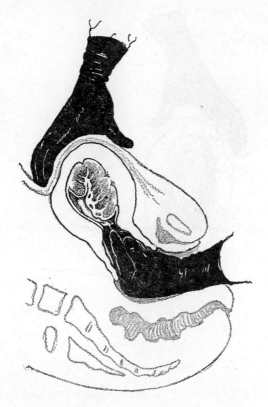

FIG. 298. Manual removal of the placenta. Method of introducing the internal hand and making pressure on the fundus with the external hand.

cent lysol or 1–500 chlorothymol in order that the advantage of antisepsis may be added when it passes through the lower vagina, which always is more or less contaminated. The whole hand is passed into the uterus, and the fundus is forced downward by making pressure with the external hand through the abdominal wall (Fig. 298). After locating the margin of the placenta, a plane of cleavage is found and, by a side to side motion of the fingers, separation of the placenta is continued until the latter is completely freed from its attachment to the uterus (Fig. 299). It then is removed as the internal hand is withdrawn. The separation should be completed before any of the placenta is removed; otherwise a part may be retained. Attention to this detail greatly simplifies the procedure since it is much more difficult to separate remnants of the placenta after the latter has been partially removed.

FIG. 299. Manual removal of the placenta. Technic of separating the placenta before it is removed.

EXAMINATION OF THE PLACENTA. The placenta, after its removal, is carefully examined to determine whether any part of it has been retained. In case of doubt, the uterine cavity is again explored and retained fragments are removed. In this connection, it is well to bear in mind the irregular and jagged contour of the placental site in order that unnecessary manipulations may be avoided.

PREVENTION OF POSTPARTUM HEMORRHAGE is accomplished as in the non-bleeding third stage.

TRANSFUSION. Whenever the amount of blood lost reaches the neighborhood of 1000 cc. or causes the patient to show signs of hemorrhage, an immediate transfusion is indicated. This measure is particularly valuable as a prophylaxis against infection following manual removal of the placenta.

REFERENCES

1. PINARD, A.: L'Accommodation foetale. Traité du palper abdominal. Paris, 1878, 110.
2. CREDÉ, C. U. LEOPOLD, J.: Die Geburtshüfliche Untersuchung. Leipzig, 1892, 8.
3. BAUDELOCQUE, J. L.: L'Art des accouchements. 1789, 76.
4. SMELLIE, W.: Treatise on the Theory and Practise of Midwifery with Collection of Cases. London, 1779.
5. SCHEFFER, R.: Ueber das Verhältniss des Abstandes der Spinae und Cristae ilium zu dem Querdurchmesser des Beckeneinganges. Monatschr. f. Geburstk. u. Frauenk., 1868, 31, 299.
6. SKUTSCH, F.: Die praktische Verwerthung der Beckenmessung. Deutsche. med. Wchnschr., 1891, 17, 700.
7. THOMS, H.: The Diagnosis of Disproportion. S. G. & O., 1931, 52, 963.
8. BECK, A. C.: Chlorothymol as an Antiseptic in Obstetrics. Am. J. O. & G., 1933, 26, 885.
9. MAYES, H. W.: The Use of Mercurochrome in the Preparation for Delivery. Long Island Med. J., 1927, 21, 146.
10. GAUSS, C. J.: Geburten im künstlichem Dämmerschlaf. Arch. f. Gyn., 1906, 78, 579.
11. BECK, A. C.: Abdominal Binder as a Substitute for Pituitary Extract in Second Stage of Labor. J. A. M. A., 1924, 83, 753.
12. SIMPSON, J. Y.: Anaesthesia. Philadelphia, 1849, 83.
13. SIMPSON, J. Y.: Notes on the Employment of the Inhalation of Sulphuric Ether in the Practise of Midwifery. Monthly J. Med. Sc., 1847, 7, 639, 721, 794.
14. CHANNING, W.: Cases of Inhalation of Ether in Labor. Boston, 1847.
    A Treatise on Etherization in Child-birth. Illustrated by five hundred and eighty-one cases. Boston, 1848.
15. WEBSTER, J. C.: Nitrous Oxid Gas Analgesia in Obstetrics. J. A. M. A., 1915, 64, 812.
16. LYNCH, F. W.: Eutocia by Means of Nitrous Oxid and Oxygen Analgesia,—A Safe Substitute for the Freiburg Method. Ill. M. J., 1915, 27, 257.
17. DAVIS, C. H.: Painless Childbirth, Eutocia and Nitrous Oxid-Oxygen Analgesia. Chicago, 1916.
18. HEANEY, N. S.: Ethylene in Obstetrics. J. A. M. A., 1924, 83, 2061.
19. COSGROVE, S. A.: Spinal Anaesthesia in Obstetrics. Am. J. Surg., 1928, 5, 602.
20. LABAT, G.: Regional Anaesthesia. Philadelphia, 1923, 436.
21. GELLHORN, G.: Local Anaesthesia in Gynecology and Obstetrics. S. G. O., 1927, 45, 105.
22. RITGEN, F.: Ueber sein Dammschutzverfahren. Monatschr. f. Geburtsk. u. Frauenk., 1855, 6, 321.
22a. ZIELER, C. E.: A New All Metal Umbilical Cord Clamp. Am. J. Obs. & Gyn., 1936, 32, No. 5, 884.
23. CARROLL, J. J.: Why Does Ophthalmia Neonatorum Continue to Cause so much Blindness? Maryland M. J., 1909, 52, 489.
24. CREDÉ, C.: Die Verhütung der Augenentzündung bei Neugeborenen. Berlin, 1884.
25. PINARD, A.: Du palper pendant la delivrance normale. Traité du palper abdominal. Paris, 1884, p. 241.
26. SCHROEDER, C.: Beitrag zur Physiologie der Austreibungs- und Nachgeburtsperiode. Ztschr. f. Geburtsh. u. Gyn., 1885, 11, 421.
27. CREDÉ, C.: Ueber die zweckmässigste Methode der Entfernung der Nachgeburt. Arch. f. Gyn., 1881, 17, 260.
28. HEIDLER, H. U. STEINHARDT, B.: Ueber die manuelle Placentarlösung. Würzb. Abhandl., 1927, 4, 227.

CHAPTER XV

THE PUERPERIUM

The term puerperium is applied to the six or eight weeks following labor which are required for the involution of the maternal organism.

INVOLUTION OF THE UTERUS. Immediately after the delivery of the placenta, the firmly contracted uterus measures 19 x 12 x 8 cm. and weighs 1,000 gm. (Fig. 300). The picture of congestion which was characteristic of pregnancy is converted into one of ischemia as the vigorous contractions of the uterine mus-

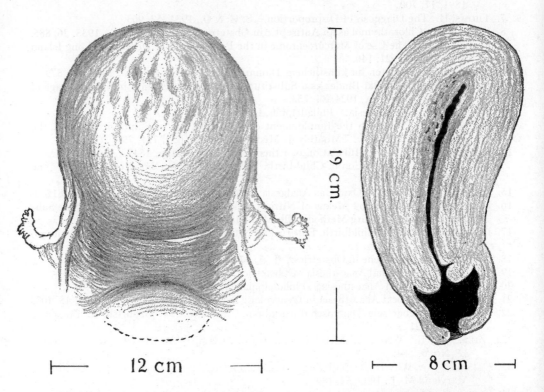

FIG. 300. Front view of the uterus immediately after delivery. ×½.

FIG. 301. Section of the uterus immediately after delivery. Compare Figures 300 and 301 with Figures 302 and 303. ×½.

culature squeeze the blood out of its walls. Its color, accordingly, changes from purplish red to a pale pink and the veins of the broad ligament become markedly distended. In the region of the fundus, indentations on the smooth outer surface mark the points of peritoneal attachment to the underlying structures.

On section, the anterior and posterior walls are in apposition and the cavity is quite smooth except at the former placental site where numerous projections of tissue make this area irregular and jagged. In the early part of involution, the uterus differs markedly in its two segments. Above the retraction ring it is firmly contracted and measures 4 cm. in thickness. As a result, the walls are in contact with each other and almost completely obliterate the uterine cavity. Below the ring, it is soft, flabby and congested, and its cavity is large enough to permit the introduction of several fingers (1) (Fig. 301).

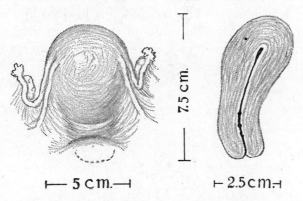

FIG. 302. Front view of uterus six weeks after delivery. ✕½.

FIG. 303. Section of uterus six weeks after delivery. ✕½. Compare Figures 302 and 303 with Figures 300 and 301.

These striking variations in the upper and lower segments illustrate the effect of the physiological changes which occurred in the uterus during pregnancy and labor. Throughout pregnancy, the muscle fibers of the upper segment underwent a most remarkable hypertrophy. The cervix and lower segment, on the other hand, became vascular and congested. While some muscle fibers of the latter were hypertrophied, others disappeared and the connective tissue was greatly altered. Throughout pregnancy, therefore, the upper segment was prepared for its active, dynamic part in labor while the lower segment was made ready by congestion and softening for its more or less passive rôle of dilatation. During labor, the relatively weakened muscles of the lower segment and cervix, unable to withstand the pressure transmitted against them from the stronger upper segment, became paralyzed and were no longer able to resist dilatation. The physiology of involution, as might be expected, is the reverse of that observed in pregnancy. In the upper segment, atrophy is the chief factor, while hypertrophy, hyperplasia and the restoration of muscular tone characterize the changes that take place in the cervix and lower uterine segment.

At the end of six weeks the uterus measures 7.5 x 5 x 2.5 cm. and weighs 40 to 60 gm. (Figs. 302 and 303). In women who nurse their infants the involution of the uterus is so marked that it is known as the hyperinvolution of lactation. This rapid reduction in size and weight is due largely to atrophy of the mucsular elements (Fig. 304).   By teasing out muscle fibers from uterine tissue macerated in acid, their length has been shown to be 158μ on the first day, 82μ in one week and 24μ at the end of the fifth week, while their width was 12μ on the first day and 6μ after five weeks (2).   Two-thirds of the entire weight loss is accomplished by the end of the fourteenth day and over half of this extensive atrophy takes place within the first week.   It is thought that autolysis of the cytoplasm is responsible for this remarkable change and that the albuminous material is ex- creted largely by the kidneys.   This conclusion is justified by the fact that the urinary nitrogen is considerably in excess of the nitrogen intake after the first day or two of the puerperium, but is unchanged if the uterus is removed by hysterectomy after cesarean section (3).

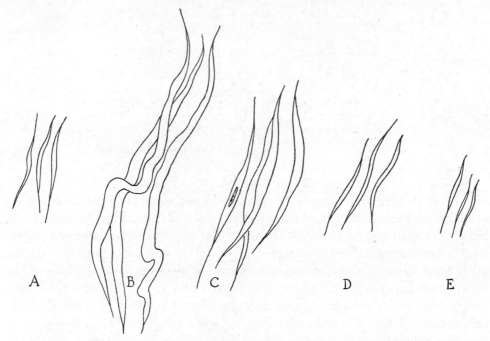

FIG. 304. Muscle fibers before, during and after pregnancy (Sanger). A. Before pregnancy. B. 8 months.   C. 3 days postpartum.   D. 35 days postpartum.   E. 55 days postpartum.

CHANGES IN THE UTERINE VESSELS.   Thrombosis and organization take place in the sinuses while the arteries become hyalinized and obliterated.   In the course of the latter process, smaller vessels develop within and largely replace the older ones (4) (Fig. 305).

CHANGES IN THE ENDOMETRIUM.   In the third stage of labor, separation of the placenta and membranes is effected by cleavage in the spongy layer of the decidua.   The basal or inactive zone soon becomes infiltrated with leuko- cytes, and within a few days the necrotic decidual remnants are cast off.   Coin-

cidently with and following these changes, the glandular epithelium in the inactive
layer proliferates to form a new covering for the endometrium which, except at

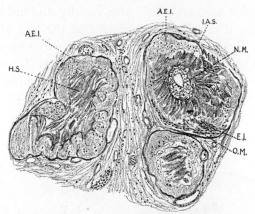

FIG. 305. Changes in the uterine vessels (Goodall).   Three vessels from the remote subplacental
area.   Two have not developed a new vessel in the interior of the old one but the third has done so.
A.E.I. Degenerated elastica interna which can be followed completely about the vessel.   *E.I.* Hyper-
trophic elastica interna with remains of the old media, *O.M.*, lying to its exterior.   *I.A.S.* Interarterial
space filled with a hyaline almost nuclear free substance.   *H.S.* The same hyaline substance filling the
whole lumen of the old vessel.   *N.M.* New media.

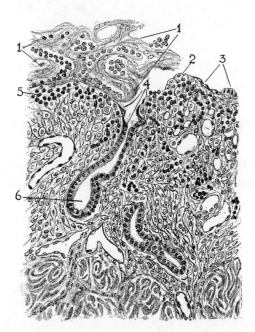

FIG. 306. Regeneration of the endometrium (Bumm).   *1.* Necrotic decidua.   *2.* Exposed raw
surface.   *3.* Regenerating epithelium.   *4.* Epithelium growing out from the glands.   *5.* Granulation
zone.   *6.* Gland.

the placental site, is almost completely regenerated within one week.   This
process is analogous to that which is observed in the regenerative phase of the
menstrual cycle (5, 6) (Fig. 306).

CHANGES IN THE PLACENTAL SITE. After the placenta is expelled, the placental site is about 10 x 7 cm. and is more irregular and jagged than the remainder of the uterine surface. This area rapidly diminishes to 3 or 4 cm. in two weeks and is less than 2 cm. in diameter at the end of involution. The histological changes in this region have been most carefully studied and it has been observed that the decidual elements and thrombosed veins of the placental site are cast off after they have been undermined by the adjacent, newly formed endometrium (7).

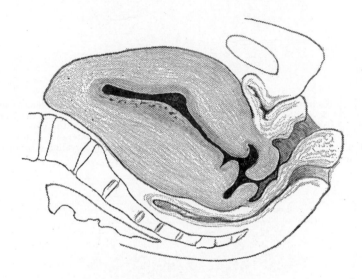

FIG. 307. Sagittal section showing the uterus immediately after delivery (Webster).

CHANGES IN THE CERVIX. The cervix and lower uterine segment are relaxed, congested and edematous, and their cavity is quite patulous up to the level of the contraction ring. The collapse of the walls results in either an infolding or eversion of the cervix so that on vaginal examination its cavity seems to be shortened. If, however, the cervical lips are pulled down by tenacula, the true length of this portion of the uterus is appreciated. Within a short time the line of demarcation between the upper contractile and lower inactive segments disappears and the cervix no longer feels like a separate structure. For several days the external os is large enough to admit two fingers but by the end of the first week it is so contracted that difficulty is encountered in introducing a single finger.

Microscopically, the cervix, immediately after delivery, is the seat of such marked edema, congestion and hemorrhage that its usual constituents cannot be easily distinguished. Within a few days this picture disappears and regeneration of the muscle and connective tissue follows.

CHANGES IN THE VAGINA.   The vagina remains capacious for a considerable time after delivery due to the marked relaxation of the surrounding structures, and, although its walls are in apposition, the introitus for some time tends to gape, especially when the intra-abdominal pressure is increased by a bearing-down effort or coughing.   After several months, the relaxation disappears and the vagina returns to its nonpregnant, multiparous proportions.   While the pelvic floor ultimately regains most of its former tone, it occasionally remains somewhat relaxed and weakened, with the result that the tendency to sag may persist for some time.   Often, six months are necessary for the complete restoration of the pelvic supports.   Lacerations heal rapidly if they are not infected, and tags of the hymen mark the site of its former location.   These are known as carunculae myrtiformes.

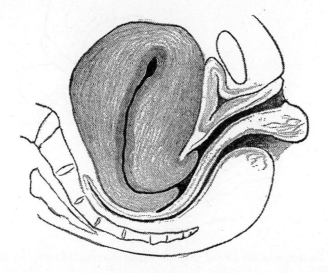

FIG. 308. Involution of the uterus.   Sagittal section showing the uterus $1\frac{1}{2}$ days after delivery (Webster).

CHANGES IN THE ABDOMINAL WALL.   Following labor, the abdominal wall is lax and is noticeably weak in the midline where the recti muscles may be rather widely separated.   This condition of relaxation continues for some time and may become permanent, with the result that the lower abdominal wall bulges when the mother stands erect.   The purplish striae lose their color and although they become somewhat diminished in size, they remain as silvery white, scarlike marks of the previous abdominal enlargement.

BREAST CHANGES.   The changes in the breast will be discussed in the chapter on Lactation which follows.

CLINICAL MANIFESTATIONS OF THE PUERPERIUM

POSTPARTUM CHILL.   At times a postpartum chill occurs shortly after the completion of the third stage.   It has no clinical significance and disappears within a few minutes.

PULSE.   Normally, it is customary to observe a drop in the pulse rate within a short time after the child is born.   The pulse usually ranges from 60 to 70 but may fall as low as 40.   In view of this common occurrence of bradycardia the physician should have in mind the possibility of cardiac failure or hemorrhage whenever the pulse rate is rapid in the early hours of the puerperium.

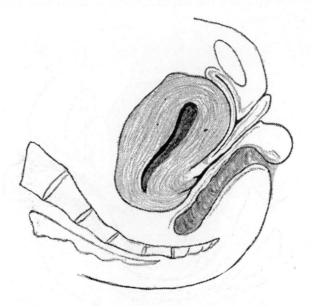

FIG. 309. Involution of the uterus.   Sagittal section showing the uterus on the sixth day after delivery (Webster).

TEMPERATURE.   For 24 hours the temperature may be slightly elevated, but after the first day, it usually remains around 99°F.   Of the various morbidity standards that have been proposed, the most widely accepted one is a temperature of 100.4° on two successive days after the first.   The attempt, however, to classify febrile reactions in the puerperium as excusable and non-excusable leads to much confusion.   As the physician's technic improves, the number of his patients whose temperatures remain around 99° increases, and his ideas concerning the non-infective nature of elevations in temperature are altered.   One of the best examples of the growing tendency to regard all febrile reactions as manifestations of infection is offered by the abandonment of the former belief that a temperature rise on the third day, the so-called milk fever, is due to the onset of lactation.

BLOOD CHANGES. The blood becomes concentrated with the result that the cellular constituents and hemoglobin seem to be increased. During labor and immediately thereafter, a definite leukocytosis is demonstrable and a white count of over 15,000 is not unusual. This leukocytosis rapidly disappears and the number of white cells is quite normal by the fifth day.

THE LOCHIA. For several days following delivery, the vaginal discharge is made up largely of blood and blood clots—lochia rubra. It then becomes paler and brown owing to the alterations in the blood elements which, at this time, are relatively diminished—lochia serosa. About the tenth or twelfth day a predominance of leukocytes gives it a yellowish white appearance—lochia alba. The latter persists for several weeks and may continue for even longer periods if infection is present.

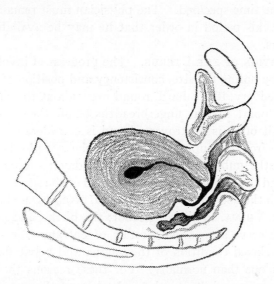

FIG. 310. Involution of the uterus. Sagittal section showing the uterus on the fifteenth day after delivery.

The microscopic constituents of the lochia are red and white blood cells, epithelial cells, fragments of the degenerating decidua, and bacteria. While cultures made from the uterine cavity usually are free from pathogenic bacteria, those taken from the vagina frequently show the presence of streptococci within a few days after delivery.

URINE. A trace of albumen and casts are not infrequent urinary findings on the first day. They, however, rapidly disappear and by the third day are not found in catheterized specimens. The total output is greater but the tendency toward bladder distention is increased. This is due to the laxness of the abdominal walls, the dorsal position in bed, the after-effects of pressure on the neck of the bladder and urethra, and to lacerations in the lower birth passages. Owing to the autolysis of the uterus and other pelvic structures during the process of involution, the nitrogen excretion is considerably above the nitrogen intake.

AFTER-PAINS. Women who have had a rapid labor occasionally complain of rather severe, painful uterine contractions for 24 to 48 hours after delivery. These are not unlike labor pains and are particularly noticeable when the child suckles.

POSTPARTUM CARE

CARE IMMEDIATELY AFTER THE DELIVERY. Immediately following the delivery of the placenta, the first consideration is the condition of the uterus. For at least one hour the attendant must hold the fundus and make it contract, whenever it relaxes. Should this duty be assigned to the nurse, she must understand that the holding of the fundus is not to be discontinued for even a few minutes during the time specified. The physician must remain at the patient's home throughout this period in order that he may be available if postpartum hemorrhage occurs.

DAILY PALPATION OF THE UTERUS. The progress of involution is followed from day to day by noting the size, consistency and position of the uterus. Immediately after delivery, it is a hard, round mass about the size of a fetal head and extends to a point several fingerbreadths below the umbilicus. Twenty-four hours later, it often is dextroverted and is considerably higher. At that time the distance from its superior surface to the symphysis is about 13 cm., i.e., slightly above the umbilicus. On the seventh day it is found midway between the latter point and the symphysis, and at the end of the second week it no longer can be felt through the abdominal wall (Figs. 307, 308, 309 and 310).

CARE OF THE VULVA. Following labor, the birth passages are the seat of lacerations, which serve as possible portals of entrance for virulent bacteria. In addition, the relaxed condition of the vagina and pelvic floor leaves the introitus more patulous than normally. For these reasons the vulva should be regarded as an open wound during the early days of the puerperium and every precaution should be taken to protect it against infection.

During this time the patient lies between two sterile or freshly laundered sheets and the vaginal discharge is allowed to drain onto a sterile absorbent pad which is placed beneath her buttocks. The so-called vulva pads, or guards, and antiseptic irrigations are not used until the introitus is again closed.

After forty-eight hours, sterile vulva pads may be used to absorb the lochia. These are changed three or four times daily, or oftener if necessary. Each time that the guards are changed and after urination and defecation, the vulva is cleansed with 0.5 per cent lysol or 1–1000 chlorothymol solution. In the course of this routine, great care should be taken to avoid contamination from the rectum.

As infection may be introduced by the patient's fingers, she should be instructed to keep her fingers away from the vulva. Vaginal douches likewise may carry infection into the birth passages and, for this reason, they are contraindicated during the early part of the puerperium.

CARE OF THE BLADDER. The bladder should be emptied every six or eight hours. To accomplish this, the patient is placed upon a bed pan and encouraged to void routinely even though she has no desire to urinate. If difficulty is experienced in emptying the bladder, an abdominal binder may be adjusted and she may be allowed to change her position. After the second day, the use of a half sitting posture often is helpful. Should the bladder become distended catheterization under the strictest aseptic precautions is indicated. The passage of a catheter before the distention becomes pronounced often will save the need for its frequent repetition, since a bladder that once becomes overdistended often must be catheterized repeatedly before the patient again is able to empty it herself.

REST AND EXERCISE. Most patients do better if they remain in bed a week or ten days after labor. During the first four or five days it is well to limit visitors to members of the immediate family. Well intentioned friends often cause much trouble. They tire the patient and contribute to her nervous unrest. Adherence to this recommendation will be followed by a more rapid convalescence and a much better milk supply.

During the patient's stay in bed she should turn from side to side frequently and do the exercises shown in Figures 311 to 318. Sitting up in bed may be permitted on the fourth or fifth day and in from three to five days later she may sit in a chair. The abdominal exercise and walking on all fours as shown in Figures 316 and 318 should be continued until the abdominal wall has regained its tone and the uterus is completely involuted. The latter routine not only favors involution but greatly diminishes the tendency toward retroversion.

CARE OF THE BOWELS. Constipation is favored by the dorsal posture and the lax abdominal walls that customarily are observed after delivery. Mineral oil or milk of magnesia, accordingly, should be administered several times daily. On the second day, a soapsuds enema may be given and repeated on alternate days until the patient gets out of bed. After the first week, the rectum should be thoroughly emptied by enemata on every third day, even though the patient has daily, spontaneous evacuations. This measure aids in the involution of the rectovaginal septum and acts as a prophylaxis against rectocele.

Hemorrhoids often become painful during the puerperium. When they are troublesome, the patient is placed in the knee-chest position for a few minutes. The sphincter is then gently stretched and the hemorrhoids are replaced. Their retention within the rectum is aided by inserting a plug of gauze lubricated with vaseline. While this is in place, the patient is instructed to lie on her abdomen and refrain from any bearing-down efforts. At the same time, the plug is held in place with her hand until she becomes accustomed to its presence, after which its retention is effected by the use of a T-binder.

FIG. 311. First day: Raise head, touching chin to sternum.

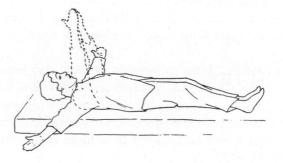

FIG. 312. Second day: Abduction and adduction of arms.

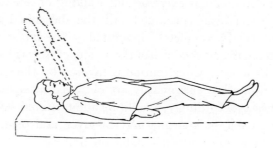

FIG. 313. Third day: Arms over head.

FIG. 314. Fourth day: Flexion of lower extremity.

FIG. 315. Sixth day: Flexion of both lower extremities.

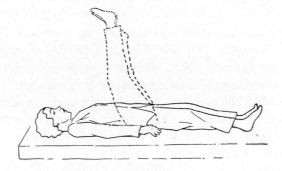

FIG. 316. Eighth day: Flexion of both thighs with legs extended.

FIG. 317. After tenth day: Knee-chest position.

FIG. 318. After two weeks: Walking on all fours.

DIET.   A very light diet is best in the early part of the puerperium.   As the patient convalesces, additions are made from day to day until the end of the first week when a full diet is indicated.   Broths, milk, cereal, soft boiled or poached eggs, tea and toast are given during the first two or three days, after which nourishing, easily digestible food is added according to the patient's desires. The heavier foods are withheld until she is allowed out of bed.

RELIEF OF PAIN AND SLEEPLESSNESS.   After-pains are relieved by the use of an ice bag or $\frac{1}{4}$ gr. of morphine.   If the latter is given, the child should not be allowed to suckle until the drug has been excreted.   Nervous patients may receive sedatives for the first day or two, after which their care should consist largely of isolation from visitors and the general measures mentioned below.

CARE OF THE BREASTS.   On the second or third day, engorgement of the breasts often is very painful.   The measures employed for the relief of this condition are discussed in the following Chapter on Lactation.

GENERAL CARE.   The comfort of the patient and the success or failure of lactation often depend upon the character of the nursing attention given her during the puerperium.   The value of a cheerful, competent and considerate nurse cannot be overestimated.

The temperature, pulse and respiration are taken every four hours in order that those complications which are accompanied by a febrile reaction may be recognized at their onset.   This is particularly valuable in the treatment of mastitis.   An abundance of fresh air likewise is advisable and, if possible, the patient's bed should be moved near a window so that she may receive the benefit of direct sunlight.   A daily sponge bath and frequent changing of the bed linen likewise adds much to her comfort.

VAGINAL EXAMINATION.   At the end of the second or third week, a vaginal examination is made to determine the degree of involution and the position of the uterus in order that the proper treatment of subinvolution, retroversion and relaxation of the supporting structures may be instituted early.   A final examination is made when involution is complete at the end of six to eight weeks.

REFERENCES

1. WEBSTER, J. C.: Researches in Female Pelvic Anatomy, Edinburgh, 1892, 1.
2. SANGER, M.: Die Rückbildung der Muscularis des puerperalen Uterus.   Beitr. z. path. Anat. u. Klin. Med. von Wagner's Schülern, 1887, 134.
3. SLEMMONS, J. M.: Involution of the Uterus and Its Effects upon the Nitrogen Output of the Urine.   Johns Hopkins Hosp. Bull., 1914, 25, 195.
4. GOODALL, J. R.: The Involution of the Puerperal Uterus.   Studies from the Royal Victoria Hospital, Montreal, 1910–9, No. 3.
5. WORMSER, E.: Die Regeneration der Uterus schleimhaut nach der Geburt.   Arch. f. Gyn., 1903, 69, 449.
6. TEACHER, J. H.: On the Involution of the Uterus Post Partum.   J. Obs. & Gyn. Brit. Emp., 1927, 34, 1.
7. WILLIAMS, J. W.: Regeneration of the Uterine Mucosa after Delivery with Special Reference to Placental Site.   Am. J. Obs. & Gyn., 1931, 22, 664.

CHAPTER XVI

LACTATION

THE MAMMARY GLANDS are composed of from 15 to 20 lobes, each of which is itself a compound racemose gland. The individual lobes are subdivided into many lobules and these in turn contain numerous acini. The latter are joined by ducts which connect with one another to form the lobules and finally unite into a single duct for each lobe. These ducts pass through the nipple and terminate in minute openings on its surface (Fig. 319). Each acinus is lined by a single layer of low cuboidal cells and is surrounded by a capillary network.

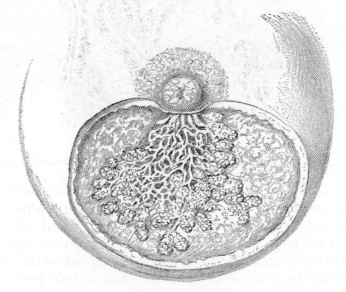

FIG. 319. Section of the mammary glands (Jewett).

PRELIMINARY DEVELOPMENT. At puberty, as has been noted, the breasts become enlarged and assume their characteristic form. The previously inconspicuous nipples grow more prominent and signs of development appear in the rudimentary glands. Under the stimulus of recurring menstrual cycles, the duct system develops extensively and considerable alveolar proliferation takes place. Pregnancy greatly accelerates these changes and the resulting alterations in the breasts constitute some of the earliest evidences of gestation. By the third month, colostrum is produced and may be expressed from the nipples throughout the remainder of pregnancy.

PAINFUL ENGORGEMENT. For two or three days following delivery, the breasts secrete colostrum in increasing amounts. On the second day, in multiparae, and on the third, in primiparae, they become markedly engorged and are firm, tense and tender, a condition to which the term "painful engorgement" is appropriately applied. This is due to lymphatic stasis and is not caused by retention of milk within the glands.   Often the lymph channels leading to the axillae are swollen and distinctly palpable, as are the enlarged and painful axillary nodes.   In from 36 to 48 hours, the pain disappears as the swelling spontaneously subsides.

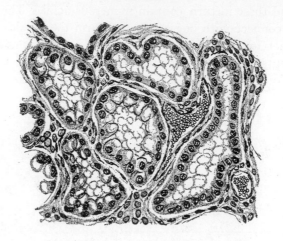

FIG. 320. Microscopic section of functioning gland (Bumm).

LACTATION.   Soon after the onset of painful engorgement on the second or third day after parturition, true milk is secreted.   During the period of activity, the capillaries and lymphatics are engorged; the low cuboidal cells of the acini increase in size and project into the lumen.   At the same time, minute globules of fat appear in the cytoplasm and collect at the distal ends of the cells.   Eventually the peripheries of the secreting cells rupture and the products of their activity are discharged into the cavity of the acinus (1, 2, 3, 4) (Fig. 320).   Most of the milk is formed during the act of suckling and the relative proportion of its constituents varies somewhat with the beginning and end of each nursing period. Almost without exception, every woman who gives birth to a child lactates. The breasts, likewise, show similar activity whenever pregnancy is interrupted after the fourth or fifth month.   Once lactation is established, however, the stimulus of suckling is necessary to its continuance.   When the child is removed from the breasts and the latter are not stimulated by stripping of the nipples or by the use of a breast pump, lactation ceases.   While stimulation of this character is necessary and suckling on both sides is desirable, the child may be kept off one breast without harm as long as suckling on the other breast is continued. Lack of nourishment, as well as emotional disturbances, also have a deleterious effect on the milk secretion.

CAUSE OF LACTATION.   The fact that each of conjoined twins secretes milk, even though only one may be pregnant, indicates that the cause of lactation is probably hormonal and accumulating evidence points to the ovaries and the pituitary as the probable source of the hormones which are responsible for mammary development and activity. Unfortunately, most of the research on this subject has been done on lower animals of different species in which the response to hormone stimulation sometimes varies with the species. Notwithstanding this objectionable feature, the information thus obtained is sufficient, when considered together with known clinical facts, to clear up many points connected with the development and activity of the breasts.

Ovarian Influence. Removal of the ovaries in young animals prevents the changes that customarily take place in the breasts at puberty (5) and castration after puberty is followed by glandular atrophy. The administration of **estrin,** on the other hand, forestalls this atrophy in castrated animals and stimulates the growth and development of the breasts in those that are immature. The follicular hormone has been shown to be responsible for the development of the duct system in all experimental animals. While this substance is capable of inducing alveolar proliferation in some species (6, 7, 8, 9, 10, 11), its effect on the glandular development in others is slight (12, 13, 14) and, in still others, it seems to be incapable of causing any alveolar proliferation (15, 16, 17). Although lobule-alveolar growth may at times be induced by estrin, more marked development of the glandular system follows the combined use of progestin and estrin. This effect upon the glandular portion of the breasts, however, cannot be obtained unless preliminary treatment with the estrogenic factor is employed (13, 16, 18). **It, accordingly, may be stated that the follicular secretion causes the ducts to develop and that the combination of the two ovarian hormones is probably necessary for the further development of the lobule-alveolar system to the extent seen in mid pregnancy.**

Pituitary Influence. Hypophysectomy, in lactating animals (19, 20, 21, 22), is followed by the cessation of the milk secretion (19, 20, 21, 22) and removal of the pituitary, late in pregnancy, prevents lactation (19, 20, 24, 25). Implants and extracts of the anterior lobe, on the other hand, have been successfully used to awaken the secretory activity of the breasts after they have been subjected to preliminary preparation with the ovarian hormones (26, 27, 28, 29) and the administration of the same extract has prevented the decrease in the flow of milk which is observed in advanced lactation (25). It, therefore, is generally accepted that **the actual secretion of milk is dependent upon a stimulus which arises in the anterior lobe of the hypophysis.** From extracts of this gland, there has been prepared a purified lactogenic principle which has been termed, **prolactin** (30) and **galactin** (31). While this purified substance is capable of maintaining and reviving lactation in some hypophysectomized animals (32), in others it is ineffectual (33).

Adrenal Influence. Animals adrenalectomized late in pregnancy fail to lactate sufficiently to rear their litters (34, 35) and the milk secretion cannot be increased to normal by maintenance doses of cortical extract. When salt is given with small amounts of cortical substance, on the other hand, lactation is not inhibited.   Since adrenalectomy is accompanied by a great loss of fluid and sodium from the blood serum, the latter probably is unable to supply the large fluid requirements of lactation.   This salt and water imbalance, therefore, rather than the loss of a possible lactogenic adrenal substance, may be the primary difficulty when the adrenals are removed (36).   In this connection, it is interesting to note that after hypophysectomy the administration of adrenal cortical substance, together with prolactin from the pituitary, induces lactation while prolactin is ineffectual when used alone (37, 38, 39).   This observation indicates a definite relationship between the pituitary and adrenal cortex in the control of lactation (40).

INITIATION OF LACTATION.   Although breast development is sufficiently advanced by the middle of pregnancy to permit the secretion of milk, lactation does not occur until after the birth of the fetus and placenta.   Something connected with the pregnant state, therefore, must inhibit the lactogenic action of the hypophysis.   When estrin is given to induce breast development, its withdrawal is followed by the secretion of milk (7).   The follicular hormone, accordingly, has been suggested as the inhibiting factor which is present during gestation.   This deduction is also supported by the failure of the lactogenic hormone to stimulate lactation when it is given simultaneously with large amounts of estrin (11) and is further substantiated by the observation that lactation is inhibited in normal parturient females by the injection of the estrogenic hormone (41, 42).

The anterior pituitary-like gonadotrophic hormone, found in the placenta and in the blood and urine of pregnant women, also is said to inhibit lactation (21).   This action usually is attributed to stimulation of the follicle with its resulting increased estrin formation.   However, since the inhibiting effect of the anterior pituitary-like substance can be obtained in spayed as well as in normal lactating animals, the lactogenic inhibition cannot be ascribed entirely to the increased production of follicular hormone.   **The presence of these hormones in the placenta may explain the part played by this organ in the inhibition of lactation.**   When the fetus is removed from pregnant experimental animals and the placenta is left in situ, the secretion of milk, which ordinarily occurs after the removal of the products of conception does not take place.   The same inhibition of lactation is observed when placental fragments are retained after delivery as it also is when the placenta is left within the abdomen in an abdominal pregnancy (43).

From the foregoing data, it has been suggested that the **high concentration of the ovarian and placental hormones in the blood during pregnancy, inhibits the production and action of the lactogenic pituitary hormone, prolactin, but, after the evacuation of the uterus these inhibiting hormones are so diminished that the pituitary functions without restraint and, as a result, its action upon the mammary glands is not hindered.**   The observation that artificial distention of the uterus with paraffin after the removal of the products of conception by

Cesarean section is not followed by milk secretion, has led to the suggestion that the distention of the uterus during pregnancy may also be an inhibiting factor and that the reduction in the tension upon the uterine wall which follows evacuation of the uterus may be a factor in the liberation of prolactin from the pituitary (33). In support of both of these hypotheses, it may be stated that the amount of milk is decreased and the lactation period is shortened when a lactating woman becomes pregnant. On the other hand, the fact that nursing mothers continue to lactate after they become pregnant and cows give milk during gestation, has led some observers to question the inhibiting influence of the placenta and pregnancy. No doubt lactation continues in such circumstances because the stimulating effect of suckling is greater than the inhibiting influence of the placenta and pregnancy.

MAINTENANCE OF LACTATION. It is a well-known clinical fact that the milk secretion stops soon after suckling is discontinued. That this is due to the loss of nipple stimulus rather than to an accumulation of milk within the breast has been shown by animal experimentation. The main milk ducts on one side of lactating rats were tied off while on the other side the nipples were excised. Thus suckling was continued on the obstructed side but was impossible on the other. After two weeks, active milk secretion was demonstrated on both sides. From this observation, it may be concluded, first, that the accumulation of milk in the obstructed glands did not arrest their secretory activity and, secondly, that the stimulation of suckling on only one side was beneficial to both sides. Thus lactation is maintained by a reflex which is not entirely local and is not confined exclusively to the gland suckled. It is quite probable that the stimulus of suckling causes the hypophysis to secrete prolactin which is then carried to and affects all of the breasts (33). The centrifugal part of this reflex arc, accordingly, is hormonal. The fact that sympathectomized animals do not lactate well (44) indicates that the centripetal portion of the arc may be along the path of the sympathetic nervous system. In support of a possible connection between the sympathetic system and the nipples, it may be recalled that suckling, in the early days of the puerperium, causes rather strong contractions of the uterus which, because of their accompanying pain, are known as "after pains." These pains also may be due to a stimulus which arises in the nipple and is carried to the uterus by the sympathetic system.

HUMAN MILK is a bluish white emulsion of fat suspended in a solution of protein, carbohydrate and inorganic salts. The three essential food elements, protein, carbohydrate and fat, are present in sufficient quantities to make milk the most satisfactory available food. With the exception of iron and vitamins B^2 and D, it also contains adequate inorganic salts and vitamins for the growing child. The relative amounts of these various constituents vary with the beginning and end of each nursing period. At the end of the period, a slight increase in carbohydrate and protein and a considerable increase in fat is observed (45). Variations also occur with the duration of the entire lactation. Specimens analyzed during the first week, accordingly, may be quite different from those obtained several months later (46, 47). Human milk is approximately seven parts water and one part solids and its specific gravity is 1.030.

	Human Milk Average Percentage	Cow's Milk Average Percentage	Cow's Colostrum Average Percentage
Water	87.09	87.41	74.61
Solids	12.91	12.59	25.33
Fat	3.90	3.66	3.59
Sugar	6.04	4.50	2.67
Casein	1.03	3.50	4.04
Albumin	1.20	0.53	13.60
Ash	0.3	0.70	1.56

PROTEINS. The protein content of human milk is about 2 per cent of the total and is made up of casein, lactalbumin and lactoglobulin. Of these, lactoglobulin is insignificant in amount while lactalbumin and casein occur in the ratio of 1 to 0.8. When the gastric juices precipitate the casein of human milk, the presence of this relatively high proportion of soluble lactalbumin causes the curd to come down in fine flocculi. Cow's milk, on the other hand, contains over three times as much casein and less than half the soluble albumin. Rennet and the gastric acid, accordingly, precipitate out its casein as a tough solid curd. The proteins of milk, unlike those of colostrum, are not coagulated by heat.

CARBOHYDRATES. The carbohydrate fraction is about 6 per cent of the total and is made up of the polysaccharide lactose. It is this sugar which is fermented by contaminating bacteria to form lactic acid when milk sours.

FATS. The glycerides of oleic, palmitic, myrestic, stearic, linoleic, lauric, butyric and caproic acids make up the fats of milk and are responsible for about 4 per cent of its total bulk. They are suspended as fine globules in freshly secreted lacteal fluid but on standing they soon separate and rise to the surface as cream.

INORGANIC ASH. The inorganic substances which make up less than $\frac{1}{2}$ per cent of the total consist largely of phosphorous, calcium, potassium, sodium, magnesium and iron. Of these, calcium and phosphorous are the most abundant and their oxides account for two-thirds of the entire ash. Only 0.1 per cent of the ash, on the other hand, is composed of iron oxide. An exclusive milk diet, accordingly, would soon lead to iron deficiency were it not for the fact that this important mineral is stored in considerable amount in the child's liver during antenatal life.

A SELECTIVE SECRETORY ACTIVITY must be ascribed to the breasts. Casein does not occur in the blood and, aside from very small amounts that may be present in the sebaceous glands, it is not present in other parts of the body. This important and abundant milk protein, accordingly, must be elaborated by the epithelium of the acini. While lactalbumin is similar to serum albumin in all other respects, its behavior toward polarized light is different.   If, therefore, it is not synthesized by the mammary epithelium, it must be changed in some way as it passes through the gland.   Lactoglobulin, on the other hand, is identical with the euglobulin of the blood.   As milk sugar differs from the other carbohydrates found in the body, lactose also must be the product of a selective activity on the part of the breasts.   The same may be said of the fats and minute globules of fat may be demonstrated in the epithelial cells during the period of activity. The breasts also possess the power to exclude or control the passage of certain substances from the blood as is shown by the fact that the common inorganic mineral constituents of the milk differ widely in amount from those of the blood. Certain drugs, on the other hand, pass through the breast and may affect the nursing child.   Most important of these is opium and its derivatives.   For this reason care must be exercised in giving this drug to a lactating mother.   Other drugs which may pass into the milk are quinine, salicylates, iodides, bromides, atropine, mercury, arsenic, lead and alcohol.

COLOSTRUM, as previously stated, is secreted by the breasts during pregnancy.   This substance may be expressed from the nipples as early as the third month and is more abundant on the first two days of the puerperium.   It is a sticky, yellowish fluid which contains the characteristic phagocytic cells—colostrum corpuscles—within which fat globules are included.   Colostrum is richer in proteins and total solids than true milk.   The presence of large amounts of globulin, 8 per cent, is largely responsible for this great difference.   Lactoglobulin, apparently, is identical with the euglobulin of the blood, the element which is closely associated with the protective antibodies.   As might be expected, therefore, the quantity of antibodies in colostrum varies with its globulin content. Because euglobulin is present in only minute quantities at birth and because of the large amount of globulin in colostrum, it has been suggested that colostrum is a fruitful source of protective antibodies (48, 49, 50, 51).   Comparison of newborn infants who were fed colostrum with those who were not, however, fails to support this hypothesis (52).   Unlike milk, colostrum is coagulated by heat.

MANAGEMENT OF LACTATION

In spite of the fact that human milk is the ideal food for the average child, the care of the breasts is often neglected with the result that the secretion of milk either diminishes or entirely disappears.   The chief factor in the loss of the milk secretion is the failure of the mother to suckle her child regularly.   The management of lactation, therefore, should be directed toward those things which favor suckling.   They include:

1. Relief of painful engorgement.
2. Prevention and cure of fissures.
3. A satisfactory schedule of nursing.
4. Adequate diet for the mother.
5. Avoidance of emotional disturbances.
6. Prevention and cure of mastitis.

PAINFUL ENGORGEMENT disappears of its own accord in from thirty-six to forty-eight hours. During that time much relief will be experienced by proper support of the breasts. Figures 321 and 322 show a sling which carries each breast upward and inward. Such a support, when properly adjusted, relieves most of the pain. Should further treatment be required, an ice-bag may be applied to the breasts for alternating two hour intervals. In rare instances, however, a hypodermic of morphine may be necessary to relieve the pain of a markedly engorged breast.

PREVENTION AND CURE OF FISSURES. During the prenatal period, the integument of the nipples is softened by the daily application of an emollient such as mineral oil, olive oil, or cocoa butter. After the child is born, fissures may be prevented by avoiding excessive nursing, and by exposing the bare nipples to the air without any protective covering.

During the first two days, before the true milk is secreted, the hungry child nurses more vigorously in one minute than it does in ten at the end of a week after the milk secretion is established. If it is allowed to remain on the breasts too long at this time, the nipples become so fissured that they are not fit for use when the milk does come in on the third day. During this period, therefore, the child should be allowed to suckle for but a few minutes every six hours and on one breast only. Attention to this detail will prevent the majority of fissured nipples

Following each nursing, the nipples should be cleansed with a sterile solution and exposed to the air until they are dry. Before covering the nipples with the nightgown or bed linen they should be protected from irritation by the use of sterile gauze or a lead nipple shield. The latter accessory should not be used for more than two weeks.

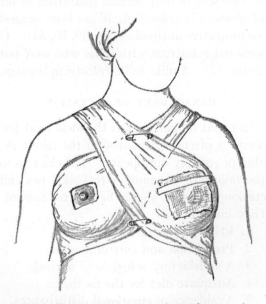

FIG. 321. Breast sling, front view.

Prompt recognition and treatment of fissures leads to their rapid cure. Like other wounds, they heal much better when they are kept at rest. If, therefore, the fissure is on one side only, the child should be taken from that breast for a period of 24 to 48 hours, during which the fissure heals completely. Various applications have been recommended for fissured nipples. None of them, however, is necessary any more than they are required in the management of a clean surgical wound in other parts of the body. Experience has shown that exposure to the air with complete rest leads to a rapid cure. When both nipples are fissured, sterile glass shields should be used during the nursing period to protect them from the added trauma of suckling. If the fissures are annular and do not respond to this routine, it may be necessary to keep the child away from both breasts for several days. While asepsis is essential in the care of the nipples at all times, it is particularly necessary when fissures are present since infection not only may delay healing but it may lead to the development of mastitis.

NURSING SCHEDULE. As has been stated, all mothers have milk but many of them lose it soon after the onset of lactation because the necessary stimulus of suckling is not employed at regular intervals. The child is placed on alternate breasts for a few minutes every six hours until the milk secretion is established on the third day. After this it nurses on alternate breasts twenty minutes every three hours. If there is an abundance of milk and the child gains rapidly, the interval between nursing may be lengthened to four hours and one of the night feedings may be omitted.

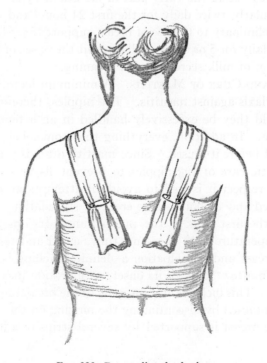

FIG 322. Breast sling, back view.

DIET OF THE MOTHER.   No special dietary routine is required during lactation if the mother is accustomed to a balanced diet.   The attendant should
make certain, however, that her diet is a balanced one; otherwise the quality
and quantity of the milk may be affected.   See diet, Chapter IX.

AVOIDANCE OF EMOTIONAL DISTURBANCES.   Contentment is essential to
lactation.   In the dairying industry, this fact receives great consideration and
an employee who is not kind to the cattle is immediately discharged.   A cheerful
nurse and cheerful surroundings will do much to prolong lactation.   On the other
hand, worry and emotional disturbances diminish and sometimes even stop the
secretion of milk.

CARE AFTER WEANING.   When the child is removed from the breasts, the
loss of the suckling reflex soon leads to a cessation of lactation and the breasts
dry up.   This usually takes place within a week and ordinarily requires no artificial
aid.   Sometimes, however, the glands become overdistended and painful.   Should
this occur, a breast sling or strapping with adhesive tape will give relief.   If the
support thus attained does not accomplish the desired result, the pain may be
alleviated by one or two hypodermic injections of morphine.   Massage and the
use of a breast pump or stripping of the nipples usually are contraindicated since
the stimulating effect of these measures prolongs the lactation and the trauma
that they may produce favors the production of mastitis.   Should the breasts
continue to secrete, atropine, or camphor in oil may be used to diminish or arrest
the flow of milk.   When the child is stillborn or when an indication for drying
up the breasts arises during the early part of lactation, $1\frac{1}{2}$ cc. of camphor in oil
is given intramuscularly twice daily for the first 24 hours and once daily for the
next three days preliminary to the use of breast support (53, 54, 55).   Stilbestrol
mg. 5 three times daily for 5 or 6 days will prevent the onset of lactation and will
hasten the cessation of milk secretion after weaning.

PREVENTION AND CURE OF MASTITIS.   A minimum handling of the nipples
is the best prophylaxis against mastitis.   The nipples, therefore, should not be
fingered, nor should they be excessively handled in an attempt to make a reluctant child nurse.   In addition, everything that comes in contact with them
should be sterilized before it is used.   Since mastitis often is preceded by fissured
nipples, prophylactic care of the nipples to prevent fissures may also prevent
mastitis.   In this respect it is well to avoid all attempts at nursing when the
nipples are retracted and do not become erect on stimulation.   Mastitis usually
is observed after the first week of the puerperium.   Its onset is marked by a
sudden rise in temperature.   At the same time, a red and tender area may be
observed in the breast and on palpation a definite swelling is felt.   If mastitis
is recognized within a few hours of its onset, suppuration may be prevented by
prompt treatment.   This includes rest, support of the breasts and the application
of cold.   Rest is obtained by discontinuing the nursing on the side affected.   At
the same time, the breast is supported by several strips of adhesive plaster ad-

justed in the manner shown in Fig. 323, and an ice-bag is placed over the area involved for alternating periods of two hours. Penicillin 30,000 units every 3 hours and x-ray therapy may also prevent the formation of a breast abscess. If the condition is not improved within a week, a hot water bottle is used in place of the ice-bag, and when the abscess points, it is incised radially and drained. The incision should be wide and deep in order that adequate drainage may be secured. The gloved finger also breaks up any suppurating pockets that may be felt within the depth of the gland and a firm gauze pack is then introduced. The latter should be firm enough to cause any adjacent areas of suppuration to break into the original cavity and thus prevent the occurrence of multiple recurring abscesses. The gauze is removed at the end of one week, after which the cavity is lightly packed and allowed to close.

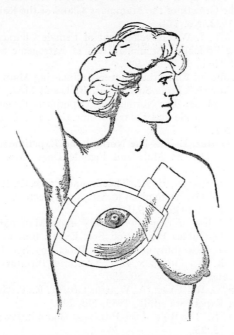

FIG. 323. Method of strapping the breasts in the treatment of mastitis.

REFERENCES

1. STEINHAUS, J.: Die Morphologie der Milchabsonderung. Phys. abth. suppl., p. 54, Arch. f. anat. u. phys., 1892.
2. PIZZOZERO, G. AND OTTOLENGHI, D.: Histologie der Milchdrüse. Merkel and Bonnets Ergeb. d. Anat. u. Entwick., 1899, 9, 252.
3. BASCH, K.: Die Physiologie der Milchabsonderung. Ergeb. des Phys., 1903, 2, 326.
4. BROUHA: Recherches sur les Diverses Phases du Développement et de l'activité la mamelle. Arch. de Biol., 1905, 21, 459.
5. HALBAN, J.: Ueber den Einfluss der Ovarien auf die Entwicklung des Genitales. Monatschr. f. Geburtsh. u. Gyn., 1900, 12, 496.

6. HATERIUS, H. O.: The Effect of Placental Extract on Mammary Glands of Male Guinea Pigs. Proc. Soc. Exper. Biol. and Med., 1928, 25, 471.

7. LOQUER, E., BORCHARDT, E., DINGEMANSE, E. AND deJONGH, S. E.: Ueber Weibliches (sexual)-hormon, menformon. Deutsch. Med. Wchnschr., 1928, 54, 465.

8. NELSON, W. O. AND SMELSER, G. K.: Studies on the Physiology of Lactation. II. Lactation in the Male Guinea Pig and Its Bearing on the Corpus Luteum Problem. Am. J. Physiol., 1933, 103, 374.

9. TURNER, C. W. AND ALLEN, E.: The Normal and Experimental Development of the Mammary Gland of the Monkey. Proc. Am. Assn. Anat., Anat. Rec., 1933, 55, 80.

10. TURNER, C. W. AND GOMEZ, E. T.: The Experimental Development of the Mammary Gland of the Monkey. Mo. Agr. Exper. Sta. Res. Bull., 1934, No. 206.

11. NELSON, W. O.: The Endocrine Control of the Mammary Gland. Physiological Review. 1936, 16, 488.

12. PARKES, A. S.: Functions of the Corpus Luteum; Relation of Oestrin to Luteal Phase, of Oestrus Cycle. Proc. Roy. Soc. Lond. sB., 1930, 107, 188.

13. TURNER, C. W. AND FRANK, A. H.: The Effect of the Ovarian Hormones Theelin and Corporin upon the Growth of the Mammary Gland of the Rabbit. Mo. Agr. Exper. Sta. Res. Bull., 1932, No. 174.

14. FRAZIER, C. N. AND MU, J. W.: Development of Female Characteristics in Adult Male Rabbits following Prolonged Administration of Estrogenic Substances. Proc. Soc. Exper. Biol. and Med., 1935, 32, 997.

15. BRADBURY, J. T.: Studies of Endocrine Factors Influencing Mammary Development and Secretion in the Mouse. Proc. Soc. Exper. Biol. and Med., 1932, 30, 212.

16. TURNER, C. W. AND DeMoss: The Normal and Experimental Development of the Mammary Gland. I. The Male and Female Domestic Cat. Mo. Agr. Exper. Sta. Res. Bull., 1934, No. 207.

17. TURNER, C. W. AND GOMEZ, E. T.: The Normal and Experimental Development of the Mammary Gland. II. The Male and Female Dog. Mo. Agr. Exper. Sta. Res. Bull., 1934, No. 207.

18. ASDELL, S. H. AND SEIDENSTEIN, H. R.: Theelin and Progestin Injections on Uterus and Mammary Glands of Ovariectomized and Hypophysectomized Rabbits. Proc. Soc. Exper. Biol. and Med., 1935, 32, 931.

19. NELSON, W. O.: The Effect of Hypophysectomy upon Mammary Gland Development and Function in the Guinea Pig. Proc. Soc. Exper. Biol. and Med., 1935, 33, 22.

20. McPHAIL, M. K.: Hypophysectomy of the Cat. Proc. Roy. Soc. Lond. sB., 1935, 117, 45.

21. SELYE, H., COLLIP, J. B. AND THOMSON, D. L.: Anterior Pituitary and Lactation. Proc. Soc. Exper. Biol. and Med., 1933, 30, 588.

22. HILL, R. T., TURNER, C. W., UREN, A. W. AND GOMEZ, E. T.: Hypophysectomy of the Goat. Mo. Agr. Exper. Sta. Bull., 1935, No. 230.

23. ALLEN, H. AND WILES, J.: The Rôle of the Pituitary Gland in Pregnancy and Parturition. J. Physiol., 1932, 75, 23.

24. PENCHARZ, R. I. AND LONG, J. A.: Hypophysectomy in the Pregnant Rat. Am. J. Anat., 1933, 53, 117.

25. STRICKER, P. AND GRUETER, F.: Action du lobe anterior de l'hypophyse sur la montée laiteuse. Compt. Rend. Soc. de Biol., 1928, 99, 1978.

26. CORNER, G. W.: Hormonal Control of Lactation. I. Non-effect of the Corpus Luteum. II. Positive Action of Extracts of the Hypophysis. Am. J. Physiol., 1930, 95, 43.

27. NELSON, W. O. AND PFIFFNER, J. J.: An Experimental Study of the Factors Concerned in Mammary Growth and in Milk Secretion. Proc. Soc. Exper. Biol. and Med., 1930, 28, 1.

28. TURNER, C. W. AND GARDNER, W. U.: The Relation of the Anterior Pituitary Hormones to the Development of the Mammary Gland. Mo. Agr. Exper. Sta. Res. Bull., 1931, No. 158.

29. ASDELL, S. A.: The Effect of the Injection of Hypophyseal Extract in Advanced Lactation. Am. J. Physiol., 1932, 100, 137.

30. RIDDLE, O., BATES, R. W. AND DYKSHORN, S. W.: The Preparation, Identification and Assay of Prolactin—a Hormone of the Anterior Pituitary. Am. J. Physiol., 1933, 105, 191.

31. GARDNER, W. U. AND TURNER, C. W.: Mo. Agr. Exper. Sta. Res. Bull., 1933, No. 196.

32. HOUSSAY, B. A.: Secrétion lactée provoquée par l'extrait antéhypophysaire chez le chien. Compt. Rend. Soc. de Biol., 1935, 120, 496? 502?

33. SEYLE, H., COLLIP, J. B. AND THOMSON, D. L.: Nervous and Hormonal Factors in Lactation. Endocrinology, 1934, 18, 237.

34. CARR, J. L.: The Effect of Swingle's Extract upon Lactation in the Adrenalectomized White Rat. Proc. Soc. Exper. Biol. and Med., 1931, 29, 131.

35. GAUNT, R.: Adrenalectomy in the Rat. Am. J. Physiol., 1933, 103, 494.

36. GAUNT, R. AND TOBIN, C. E.: Lactation in Adrenalectomized Rats. Am. J. Physiol., 1936, 115, 588.

37. NELSON, W. O. AND GAUNT, R.: Initiation of Lactation in the Hypophysectomized Guinea Pig. Proc. Soc. Exper. Biol. and Med., 1936, 34, 671.

38. GOMEZ, E. T. AND TURNER, C. W.: Initiation and Maintenance of Lactation in Hypophysectomized Guinea Pigs. Proc. Soc. Exper. Biol. and Med., 1936, 35, 365.

39. NELSON, W. O. AND GAUNT, R.: The Adrenals and Pituitary in Initiation of Lactation. Proc. Soc. Exper. Biol. and Med., 1937, 36, 136.

40. NELSON, W. O.: Studies on the Physiology of Lactation. VI. The Endocrine Influences concerned in the Development and Function of the Mammary Gland in the Guinea Pig. Am. J. Anat., 1937, 60, 341.

41. SMITH, G. V. AND SMITH, O. W.: The Inhibition of Lactation in Rabbits with Large Amounts of Estrin. Am. J. Physiol., 1933, 103, 356.

42. ROBSON, J. M.: The Action of Oestrin on the Mammary Secretion. Quart. J. Physiol., 1935, 24, 337.

43. MACGREGOR, A.: Abdominal Pregnancy near Term, Operation and Hormonal Studies of Blood and Urine with Placenta Left in Situ. Am. J. O. & G., 1937, 34, 1030.

44. CANNON, W. B. AND GUGHT, E. M.: A Belated Effect of Sympathectomy on Lactation. Am. J. Physiol., 1931, 97, 319.

45. LOWENFELD, M. F., WIDDOWS, S. T., BOND, M. AND TAYLOR, E. I.: A Study of the Variations in the Chemical Composition of Normal Human Colostrum and Early Milk. Biochem. J., 1927, 21, 1.

46. HOLT, E., COURTNEY, A. M. AND FALES, H. L.: A Chemical Study of Woman's Milk, especially Its Inorganic Constituents. Am. J. Dis. Child., 1915, 10, 229.

47. WIDDOWS, S. T., LOWENFELD, M. F., BOND, M. AND TAYLOR, E. I.: A Study of the Composition of Human Milk in the Later Periods of Lactation and a Comparison with That of Early Milk. Biochem. J., 1930, 24, 327.

48. CROWTHER, C. AND RAISRICK, H.: A Comparative Study of the Proteins of the Colostrum and Milk of the Cow and Their Relation to Serum Proteins. Biochem. J., 1916, 10, 438.

49. HOWE, P. E.: An Effect of the Ingestion of Colostrum upon the Composition of the Blood of Newborn Calves. J. Biol. Chem., 1921, 49, 115.

50. FAMULENER, L. W.: The Transmission of Immunity from Mother to Offspring. J. Infect. Dis., 1912, 10, 322.

51. LEWIS, J. W. AND WELLS, J. G.: The Function of Colostrum. J. A. M. A., 1922, 78, 863.

52. KUTTNER, ANN AND RATNER, BRET: The Importance of Colostrum to the Newborn Infant. Am. J. Dis. of Child., 1923, 35, 413.

53. LIEGNER, B.: Die Wirkung des Kampfers auf die laktierende Brust. Zentralbl. f. Gyn., 1933, 57, 244.

54. PHILPOTT, N. W.: Intramuscular Injections of Camphor in the Treatment of Engorgement of the Breasts. Canad. M. A. J., 1929, 20, 494.

55. MCNEILE, L. G.: Breast Care with Special Reference to the Use of Camphor in Oil in the Suppression of Milk Secretion after Stillbirths and at the Time the Infant Is Weaned. Western J. Surg. Obst. & Gyn., 1935, 43, 61.

CHAPTER XVII

POSTERIOR POSITIONS OF THE OCCIPUT

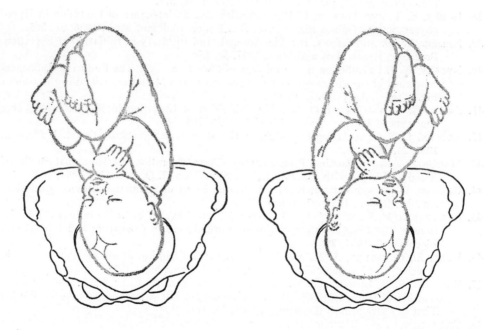

FIG. 324. Left Occipito Posterior, L.O.P.   FIG. 325. Right Occipito Posterior, R.O.P.

In posterior positions of the occiput, the presenting part is in one of the posterior quadrants of the mother's pelvis. Right positions are five times as common as left. In the following descriptions, left occipitoposterior is dealt with because sagittal section illustrations of L.O.P., when arranged in sequence, are more satisfactory than those of R.O.P.

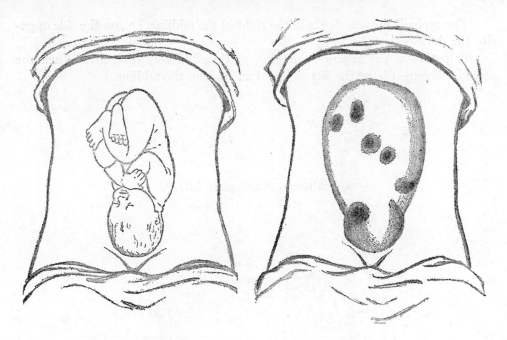

FIG. 326. L.O.P. as visualized through   FIG. 327. Touch picture in L.O.P.
the abdominal wall.

PALPATION FINDINGS IN L.O.P.

1. Dorsum—**on the left side, away from the midline** and **felt with difficulty.**
2. Small Parts—**on the right side, cross the midline** and **felt with ease.**
3. Lower Pole—the head.
4. Upper Pole—the breech.
5. Cephalic Prominence—on the right side.
6. Anterior Shoulder—**on the left, away from the midline** and **felt with difficulty.**

COMMENT ON ABDOMINAL PALPATION

Comparison of the two sides of the abdomen shows the left to be more resistant, smoother and more convex.   The back, therefore, is on the left side, although its outline may be made out with difficulty.   If definitely outlined, it is found to be remote from the midline.

The right side is less resistant and more irregular.   It accordingly contains the small parts which usually are easily felt and appear to cross the midline.

The mass in the lower pole of the uterus feels harder, smoother and more globular than that in the upper—it is the head.   The softer, less regular breech is in the fundus.

The cephalic prominence is to the right of the midline, i.e., on the side opposite the dorsum.

Palpation of the anterior shoulder, at times, is very difficult. When the shoulder is felt, it is on the left side and away from the midline.

Auscultation Findings in L.O.P.

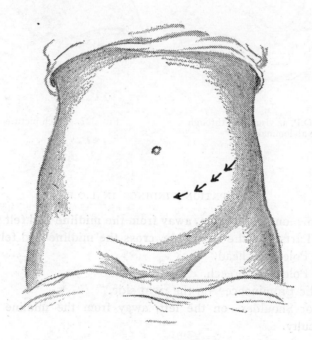

FIG. 328. The varying positions of the fetal heart as an L.O.P. rotates anteriorly.

The fetal heart sounds often are indistinct in posterior positions of the occiput and, in rare instances, they may not be heard even though the condition of the child is good. Usually in L.O.P., they are best heard on the left side and away from the midline, i.e., in the left flank. As labor progresses and the anterior shoulder rotates toward the midline, the fetal heart tones follow the direction indicated in Fig. 328.

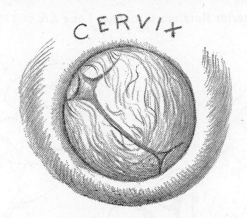

FIG. 329. Vaginal touch picture in L.O.P. The sagittal suture is in the left oblique diameter and the small fontanel is in the left posterior quadrant.

Vaginal Findings in L.O.P.

1. The sagittal suture is in the left oblique of the mother's pelvis.
2. The small fontanel is in the left posterior quadrant.
3. The large fontanel is in the right anterior quadrant.
4. Both fontanels may be at or near the same level in the pelvis.
5. If these landmarks are obscured, the location of the posterior ear will reveal the position of the occiput.

Comment on Vaginal Examination

The hard, smooth head is felt through the vagina. It is identified by the sutures and fontanels which indent the cranial vault. The sagittal suture is easily recognized in relation to the left oblique diameter. Frequently, both the large and small fontanels may be felt, indicating imperfect flexion. The small fontanel is in the left posterior quadrant and the large one is felt in the opposite anterior quadrant.

When an extensive caput succedaneum obliterates these landmarks, palpation of the posterior ear reveals the location of the occiput. In all doubtful cases, much difficulty will be avoided if the posterior ear is located before an operative delivery is attempted.

MECHANISM OF LABOR—L.O.P.

In posterior positions of the occiput, the head may rotate anteriorly to the symphysis through a long arc of 135°, or it may rotate posteriorly through a short arc of 45° to the hollow of the sacrum. Two definite mechanisms, accordingly, are possible.

Anterior Rotation through a Long Arc of 135°

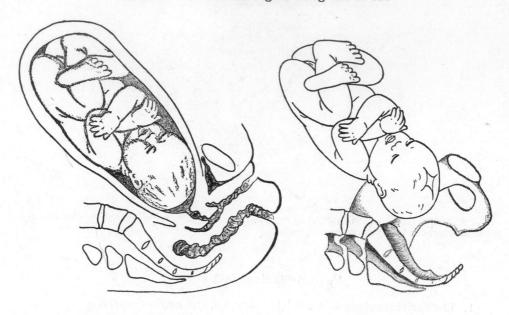

FIG. 330. Onset of labor in L.O.P.
Sagittal section.

FIG. 331. L.O.P. Same as Figure 330 showing
the relation of the head to the pelvis.

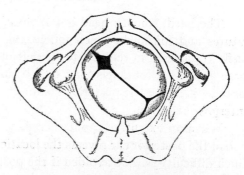

FIG. 332. Front view of L.O.P. in relation
to the pelvis at the beginning of labor.

FIG. 333. Onset of labor, L.O.P., as visualized
from below.

The head enters the pelvis with the sagittal suture in the left oblique diameter and the occiput in the left posterior quadrant of the mother's pelvis.

DESCENT is constant throughout the mechanism if no obstruction is encountered.

Flexion Imperfect.

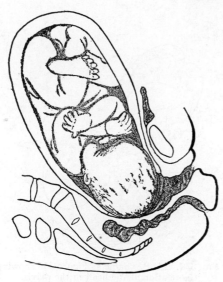

FIG. 334. L.O.P. Imperfect flexion of the head. Sagittal section.

FIG. 335. L.O.P. Same as Figure 334 showing the relation of the head to the pelvis.

FIG. 336. L.O.P. Front view of imperfectly flexed head in relation to the pelvis.

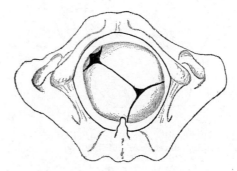

FIG. 337. L.O.P. Imperfect flexion as visualized from below.

As soon as sufficient resistance is met, the head attempts to flex but often it is only partially successful until the presenting part meets the resistance of the pelvic floor. Because of this imperfect flexion the head, at first, is relatively larger, and the largest plane that passes through the pelvis is greater than the suboccipitobregmatic. This larger plane, however, is replaced by the suboccipitobregmatic when the head is forced against the pelvic floor and, as a result, becomes completely flexed.

Internal Rotation.

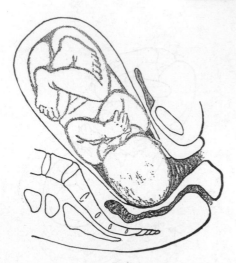

FIG. 338. L.O.P.   45° anterior rotation of occiput to L.O.T. Sagittal section.

FIG. 339. L.O.P.   Same as Figure 338 showing the relation of the head to the pelvis.

FIG. 340. L.O.P.   Front view after 45° of rotation of the head and shoulders make the L.O.P. an L.O.T.

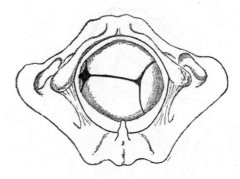

FIG. 341. L.O.T. as visualized from below.

INTERNAL ROTATION.   After the occiput reaches the pelvic floor it is rotated anteriorly 135° and comes to lie beneath the symphysis pubis.   For purposes of illustration, the 135° rotation will be divided into three parts of 45° each.   The figures above show the first 45° of this rotation which makes the L.O.P. an L.O.T., i.e., the sagittal suture is rotated into the transverse diameter of the pelvis.

A large percentage of vertex presentations enter the pelvis with the sagittal suture lying transversely.   Their mechanism, therefore, begins as an L.O.T. and the subsequent steps are similar to those about to be described.

Internal Rotation Continued.

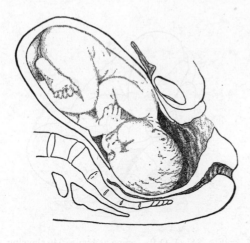

FIG. 342. L.O.P.   45° additional rotation of the occiput to L.O.A.   Sagittal section.

FIG. 343. L.O.P.   Same as Figure 342 showing the relation of the head to the pelvis.

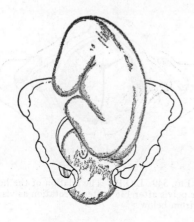

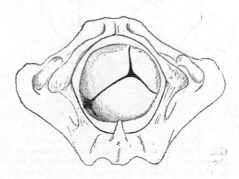

FIG. 344. L.O.P.   Front view after 45° additional rotation of the head and shoulders to L.O.A.

FIG. 345. L.O.A.   The new position after 90° of anterior rotation from the original L.O.P., as visualized from below.

INTERNAL ROTATION CONTINUED.   An additional 45° anterior rotation of the occiput and the shoulders converts the L.O.T. into an L.O.A.   In other words, after the first 90° of rotation have occurred, the occipitoposterior becomes an occipito-anterior in every sense and the mechanism from this point on is the same as that of an L.O.A.

Internal Rotation   Concluded.

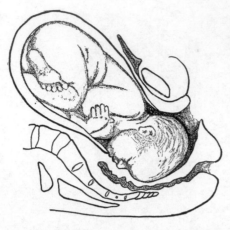

FIG. 346. L.O.P.   45° additional anterior rotation of the occiput to the symphysis.   Sagittal section.

FIG. 347. L.O.P.   Same as Figure 346 showing the relation of the head to the pelvis.

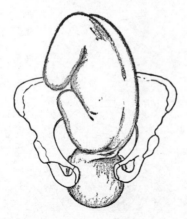

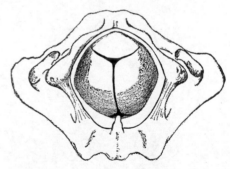

FIG. 348. L.O.P.   Front view showing rotation of the occiput without further rotation of the shoulders.   The shoulders are entering the pelvis in the left oblique diameter, as did the sagittal suture in the original L.O.P.

FIG. 349. L.O.P.   The relation of the head to the pelvis after 135° anterior rotation as visualized from below.

INTERNAL ROTATION CONCLUDED.   As the occiput is rotated through the final 45° to reach the symphysis pubis, the shoulders enter the pelvis in the left oblique diameter.   It should be noted that this is the same diameter that was occupied by the sagittal suture in the first stage of the L.O.P. mechanism.   In other words, the shoulders have rotated 90° but because the bisacromial diameter cannot turn so readily in the pelvis, they do not participate in the final 45° of rotation.   They therefore remain in the left oblique diameter until the anterior shoulder meets the resistance of the pelvic floor, just as in an L.O.A.

Extension.

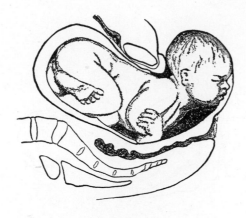

FIG. 350. L.O.P.   Extension of the head. Sagittal section.

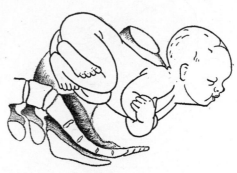

FIG. 351. L.O.P.   Same as Figure 350 showing the relation of the head to the pelvis.

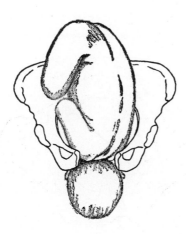

FIG. 352. L.O.P.   Front view of extension.

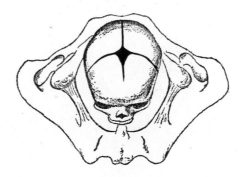

FIG. 353. L.O.P.   Extension as visualized from below.

EXTENSION.   The occiput passes out of the pelvis and the nucha becomes arrested under the symphysis where it acts as a pivoting point while the remainder of the head is born by extension.   By this movement the small fontanel, sagittal suture, large fontanel, brow, orbits, nose, mouth, and chin pass successively over the fourchette.

Restitution.

FIG. 354. L.O.P.   Restitution of the head.   FIG. 355. L.O.P.   Same as Figure 354 showing
            Sagittal section.   the relation of the head to the pelvis.

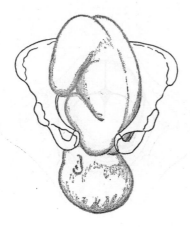

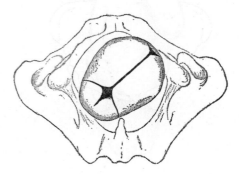

FIG. 356. L.O.P.   Front view of restitution.   FIG. 357. L.O.P.   Restitution as seen
                                                                 from below.

RESTITUTION.   Immediately after the birth of the head, the neck untwists and the occiput rotates 45° to the left.   This brings the sagittal suture into an oblique position, just as occurred in the restitution of an L.O.A.

External Rotation.

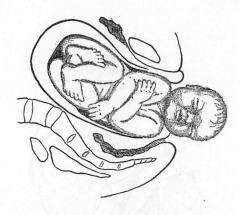

FIG. 358. L.O.P. External rotation of the head. Sagittal section.

FIG. 359. L.O.P. Same as Figure 358 showing the relation of the head to the pelvis.

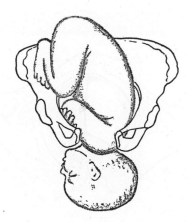

FIG. 360. L.O.P. Front view of external rotation.

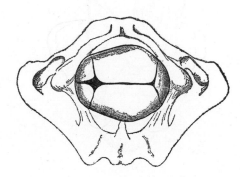

FIG. 361. L.O.P. External rotation as seen from below.

EXTERNAL ROTATION. The anterior shoulder, on meeting the resistance of the pelvic floor on the right side, is shunted downward, forward and inward. This causes 45° additional rotation of the occiput to the left.

Posterior Rotation Through a Short Arc of 45°

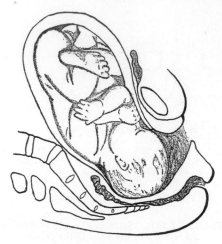

FIG. 362. L.O.P.   The occiput rotates 45° to the hollow of the sacrum.   Sagittal section.

FIG. 363. L.O.P.   Same as Figure 362 showing the relation of the head to the pelvis.

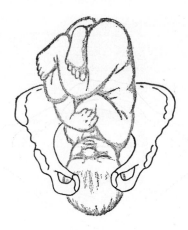

FIG. 364. L.O.P.   Front view of posterior internal rotation.

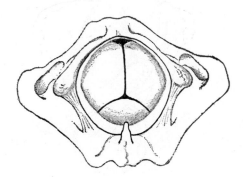

FIG. 365. L.O.P.   Posterior rotation of the occiput as visualized from below.

INTERNAL ROTATION.   Up to the stage of internal rotation the mechanism is the same as that described under anterior rotation through a long arc of 135°. The head enters the pelvis with the sagittal suture in the left oblique diameter and the occiput in the left posterior quadrant.   Imperfect flexion takes place and the presenting part descends below the level of the ischial spine, after which posterior rotation occurs.   The occiput turns 45° to the hollow of the sacrum and, as a result, the sagittal suture is brought into relation with the anteroposterior diameter of the outlet.

Flexion

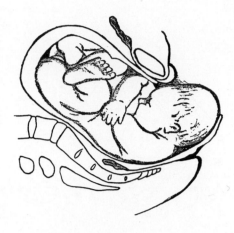

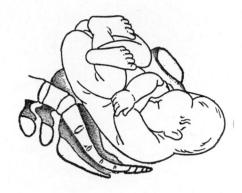

FIG. 366. L.O.P. A point anterior to the large fontanel impinges and flexion occurs.

FIG. 367. L.O.P. Same as Figure 366 showing the relation of the head to the pelvis.

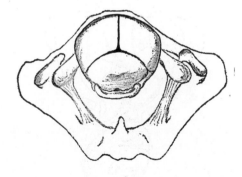

FIG. 368. L.O.P. Front view of flexion in posterior mechanism.

FIG. 369. L.O.P. Flexion in posterior mechanism as seen from below.

FLEXION. Descent continues until a point anterior to the large fontanel becomes impinged beneath the symphysis. Following this, the large fontanel, sagittal suture, small fontanel, and occiput are born successively by flexion.

Extension

EXTENSION. After the birth of the occiput, extension takes place as the nucha pivots on the perineum and the brow, orbits, nose, mouth and chin are born.

Restitution

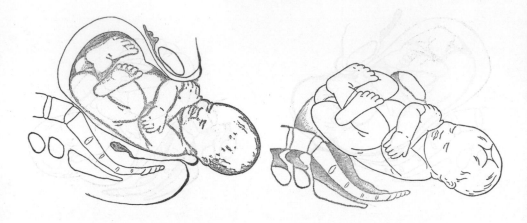

FIG. 370. L.O.P. Restitution in posterior mechanism. Sagittal section.

FIG. 371. L.O.P. Same as Figure 370 showing the relation of the head to the pelvis.

 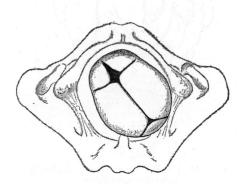

FIG. 372. L.O.P. Front view of restitution in posterior mechanism.

FIG. 373. L.O.P. Restitution in posterior mechanism as seen from below.

RESTITUTION. The head, no longer held by the vulvovaginal ring, turns back to its original position, as a result of the untwisting of the neck. This brings the occiput into relation with the left posterior quadrant of the pelvic outlet and causes the sagittal suture to occupy an oblique position.

External Rotation

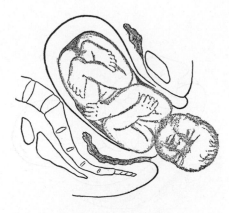

FIG. 374. L.O.P.   External rotation in posterior mechanism.   Sagittal section.

FIG. 375. L.O.P.   Same as Figure 374 showing the relation of the head to the pelvis.

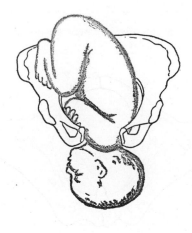

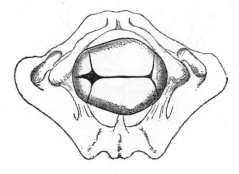

FIG. 376. L.O.P.   Front view of external rotation in posterior mechanism.

FIG. 377. L.O.P.   External rotation in posterior mechanism as seen from below.

EXTERNAL ROTATION. As the anterior shoulder turns to the right in the direction of the symphysis, the occiput is rotated an additional 45° anteriorly, and the sagittal suture comes to lie transversely.

Uncommon Posterior Short Arc Mechanism

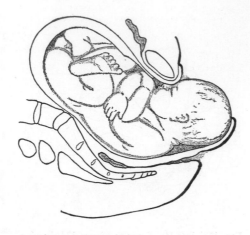

FIG. 378. L.O.P.   The root of the nose pivots beneath the symphysis and flexion occurs.

FIG. 379. L.O.P.   Same as Figure 378 showing the relation of the head to the pelvis.

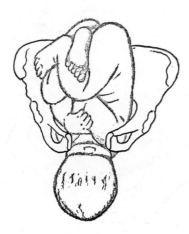

FIG. 380. L.O.P.   Front view of unusual flexion, posterior mechanism.

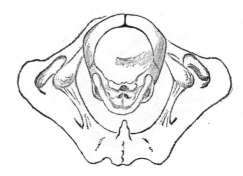

FIG. 381. L.O.P.   Unusual flexion in posterior mechanism as seen from below.

At times, the head may descend so far that the brow passes out of the pelvis. The root of the nose then pivots beneath the symphysis and a much larger diameter—the occipitofrontal, 11.5 cm.—must pass across the fourchette as the head is born by flexion. Prior to and after this step, the mechanism is the same as that described under posterior rotation through a short arc.

Anterior Long 135° Arc Rotation

FLEXION IMPERFECT
The head engages with the sagittal suture in the left oblique and the occiput in the left posterior quadrant of the mother's pelvis.

INTERNAL ROTATION
The occiput rotates 135° anteriorly to the symphysis. This brings the sagittal suture into the anteroposterior of the outlet.

Descent is con- stant

EXTENSION
The occiput passes out beneath the pubic arch and the nucha pivots under the symphysis after which the small fontanel, sagittal suture, large fontanel, brow, orbits, nose mouth and chin are born by extension.

RESTITUTION
The neck untwists and the occiput turns backward 45° to the left.

EXTERNAL ROTATION
As the anterior shoulder rotates 45° to the left the occiput turns an additional 45° posteriorly.

Posterior Short 45° Arc Rotation

FLEXION IMPERFECT
The head engages with the sagittal suture in the left oblique and the occiput in the left posterior quadrant of the mother's pelvis.

INTERNAL ROTATION
The occiput rotates 45° posteriorly to the hollow of the sacrum, and the sagittal suture comes to lie in the anteroposterior of the outlet.

FLEXION
A point anterior to the large fontanel pivots and the large fontanel, sagittal suture, small fontanel and occiput are born by flexion.

Descent is con- stant

EXTENSION
As soon as the occiput is born, the head undergoes extension over the perineum, and the brow, orbits, nose, mouth and chin are born.

RESTITUTION
The neck untwists and the occiput turns anteriorly and to the left 45°.

EXTERNAL ROTATION
As the anterior shoulder rotates 45° to the right, the occiput turns an additional 45° to the left and anteriorly.

Pictorial Summa

ANTER

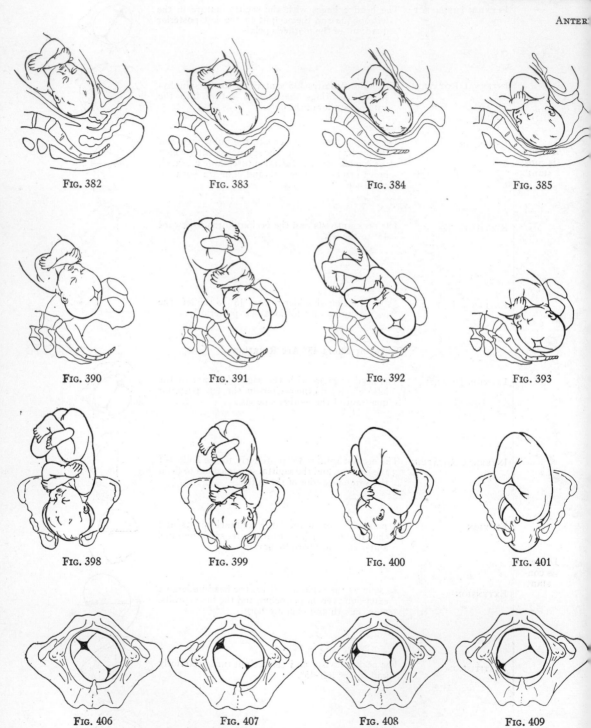

FIG. 382   FIG. 383   FIG. 384   FIG. 385

FIG. 390   FIG. 391   FIG. 392   FIG. 393

FIG. 398   FIG. 399   FIG. 400   FIG. 401

FIG. 406   FIG. 407   FIG. 408   FIG. 409

LOP Mechanism

OTATION

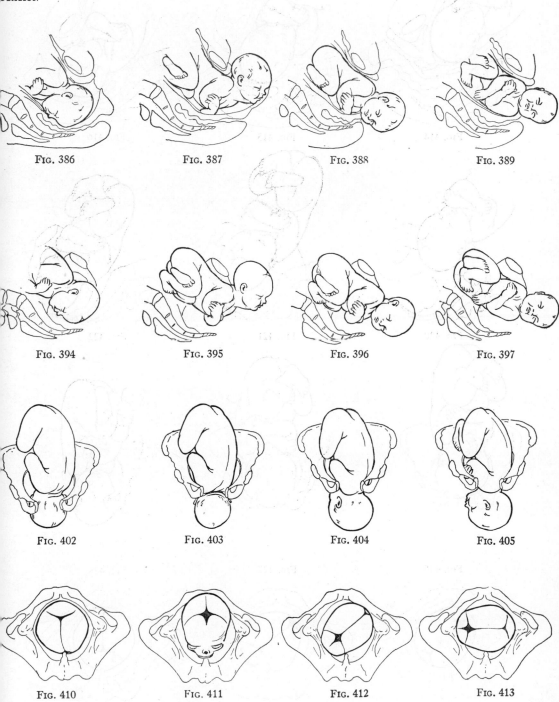

FIG. 386   FIG. 387   FIG. 388   FIG. 389

FIG. 394   FIG. 395   FIG. 396   FIG. 397

FIG. 402   FIG. 403   FIG. 404   FIG. 405

FIG. 410   FIG. 411   FIG. 412   FIG. 413

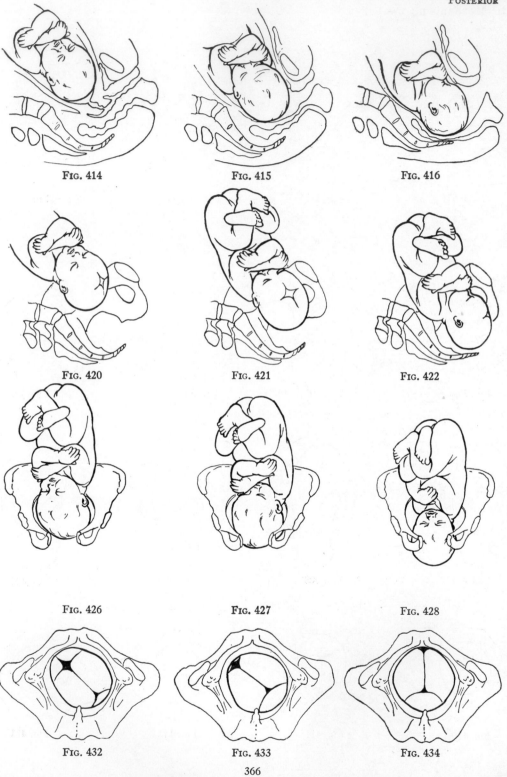

FIG. 414   FIG. 415   FIG. 416

FIG. 420   FIG. 421   FIG. 422

FIG. 426   FIG. 427   FIG. 428

FIG. 432   FIG. 433   FIG. 434

ROTATION

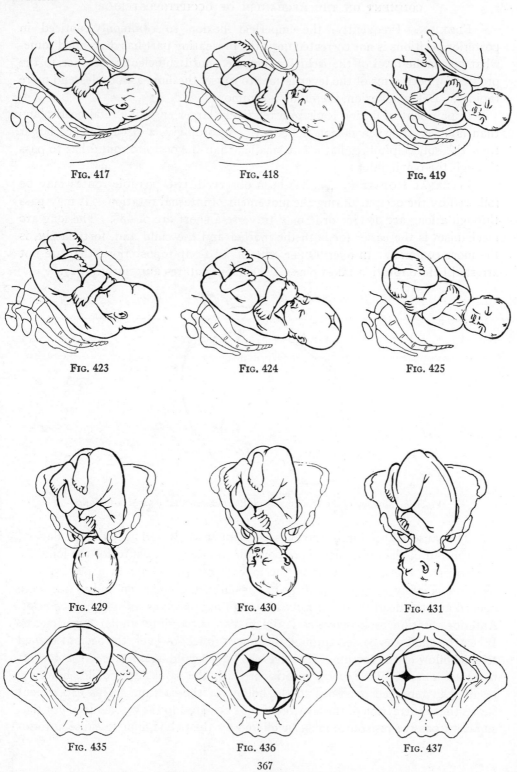

FIG. 417   FIG. 418   FIG. 419

FIG. 423   FIG. 424   FIG. 425

FIG. 429   FIG. 430   FIG. 431

FIG. 435   FIG. 436   FIG. 437

COMMENT ON THE MECHANISM OF OCCIPITOPOSTERIOR

FLEXION. Frequently, the imperfect flexion so commonly noticed in posterior positions is not corrected until the presenting part has descended somewhat below the level of the ischial spines, i.e., until sufficient resistance to the progress of both arms of the lever is met to cause theshort arm to descend more rapidly. Delay in flexion, therefore, is common.

Impairment of flexion leads to a relatively larger engaging fetal head plane than is observed when flexion is perfect. Accordingly, a circumference larger than the suboccipitobregmatic but smaller than the occipitofrontal has to pass through the pelvic inlet.

INTERNAL ROTATION. As has been observed, two possible routes may be followed by the occiput during the movement of internal rotation. It may pass through a long arc of 135° or it may traverse a short arc of 45°. The long arc mechanism is the easier for both the mother and the child and, fortunately, is the more common. In over 90 per cent of all occipitoposteriors, that are not arrested before rotation takes place, the occiput rotates anteriorly (1, 2).

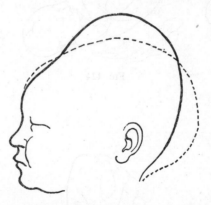

FIG. 438. Molding of the head in an occipito posterior that rotates posteriorly.

The cause of anterior rotation has led to much study and no little speculation. The contour of the pelvic floor is responsible in a large measure for the long arc mechanism. We know this from the following experiment: In a patient who died immediately after the delivery of her child, the abdomen and uterus were opened and the dead child was forced through her pelvis as an occipitoposterior. Anterior rotation took place, as it did in two succeeding similar experiments. When the child was passed through the fourth time, however, the occiput turned to the hollow of the sacrum. The use of a larger child again caused the occiput to rotate anteriorly. Several repetitions with the same large child, however, resulted in repeated rotations to the hollow of the sacrum. This experiment shows that contraction of the levatores is not essential to the mechanism, but that sufficient passive resistance must be offered by the pelvic floor to cause anterior rotation. When this resistance is overcome by frequent births, the occiput turns posteriorly. In practice, the same observations have been noted repeatedly. Seldom is posterior rotation seen in a primipara when the child is normal in size and the pelvic floor is normally resistant. Most posterior rotations occur in multiparae with relaxed floors. If this unusual mechanism is observed in a primipara, the child's head is either very small or very large, or the mother has an abnormal pelvis (3).

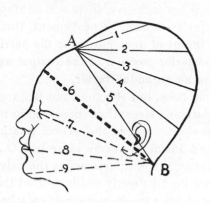 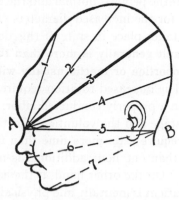

FIG. 439   FIG. 440

FIG. 439. When a point anterior to the large fontanel (A) impinges beneath the symphysis, the diameters 1, 2, 3, 4, and 5 are born in succession. The point (B) then pivots on the perineum and the diameters 6, 7, 8, and 9 are delivered. The heavy dotted line 6 represents the largest diameter which passes through the vulvovaginal orifice.

FIG. 440. When the root of the nose impinges beneath the symphysis, the diameters 1, 2, 3, 4, and 5 are born by flexion. The one represented by the heavy line 3 is the longest and it is much longer than the greatest diameter in Figure 439. Lacerations, accordingly, are more extensive. After the diameter 5 is out, the point B pivots on the perineum and the diameters 6 and 7 and delivered.

EXTENSION. In those occipitoposteriors that rotate anteriorly, extension takes place for the reasons that were discussed under the mechanism of anterior positions. When the occiput rotates posteriorly, a point anterior to the large fontanel pivots beneath the symphysis, and flexion follows. This step in the mechanism is accompanied by much greater difficulty, and causes the head to mold in the manner shown in Figure 438. As a result, further descent of the head is delayed for some little time. Accordingly, whenever arrest takes place after the child's head is visible through the vulvovaginal ring, it is a good plan to be on the lookout for this possibility. In properly conducted labors, spontaneous delivery usually takes place with little added trauma, as the diameters that pass across the perineum are but slightly larger than those observed in the more common mechanism (1) (Fig. 439), and they are further shortened by molding of the head (Fig. 438). When the root of the nose becomes the pivoting point, as it frequently does in instrumental deliveries, the occipitofrontal diameter—11.5 cm.—must pass across the perineum (4, 5) (Fig. 440). The occipitofrontal circumference is too large for the already stretched maternal soft parts and can be born only at the expense of extensive trauma to them (Fig. 440). In these circumstances, a complete tear is not infrequent.

MATERNAL DIFFICULTIES IN THE ANTERIOR ROTATION MECHANISM

It frequently is stated that difficulty may be anticipated even in the presence of the favorable anterior long arc mechanism. Theoretically, at least, one might expect the imperfect flexion to hinder the entrance of the head into the pelvis and the long 135° rotation to retard its exit.

If the pelvis is normal and the child's size is not excessive, there will be ample room for the increased diameters caused by faulty flexion. Engagement, therefore, takes place in spite of this defect. **If the head does not enter the pelvis, the fault generally is more than that of a posterior position of the occiput and disproportion or inertia usually will be found as an added factor.**

The increased rotation requires additional time, but this need not be excessive in a properly conducted labor. If the patient's strength is conserved in the first stage and the voluntary efforts are properly directed in the second, **rotation will require little more time than is consumed during the same stage in L.O.A.** Less than one hour additional is necessary after the occiput reaches the pelvic floor. On the other hand, if the labor has not been properly conducted, so that the patient is mentally and physically exhausted when the second stage is reached, engagement will be delayed and rotation not only will be retarded, but may even be completely arrested. The difficulty then is due not to the occipitoposterior position alone but is the result largely of inertia caused by poor management of the labor.

One who routinely makes use of his knowledge of the physiology of labor has little to fear from posterior positions of the occiput, as the powers usually are more than adequate to overcome the added difficulties caused by this position. Failure to apply such knowledge or interference with these physiological principles by the injudicious use of sedative drugs will lead to apprehension in many cases (2).

MATERNAL DIFFICULTIES IN POSTERIOR ROTATION

When the occiput rotates posteriorly, nature's ability to correct its mistakes is put to a severe test. The head descends satisfactorily until it begins to appear at the vulvovaginal ring. Advance then is slower than one would expect from the character of the pains. **In spite of strong contractions and excellent voluntary efforts, progress for a time seems to be almost completely arrested.** Flexion at this low level is extremely difficult. It will occur, however, in most instances, if the attendant is willing to give nature a little more time than customarily is allowed for the completion of labor.

If delivery is spontaneous, the laceration produced is not much greater than that noted in the anterior mechanism. Lacerations, however, are extensive if the posterior mechanism is followed in instrumental deliveries. Often the attendant feels that anterior rotation has occurred and that an easy, low forceps extraction is better than waiting for nature to complete the perineal stage. In these circumstances, the difficulty of extraction should lead him to suspect that the occiput is posterior.

The maternal difficulties in anterior rotation may be summarized as a somewhat prolonged labor with a slight increase in the need for operative interference. Posterior rotation causes a rather delayed perineal stage and occasionally calls for instrumental delivery, which usually is difficult and is accompanied by much trauma, unless the occiput is rotated anteriorly before the extraction is attempted.

TREATMENT OF L.O.P.

Spontaneous delivery is the rule in posterior positions of the occiput. Such an outcome, therefore, should be patiently awaited and measures that will protect the patient against fatigue and exhaustion should be employed in anticipation of a long labor.

Pseudo Labor. If, before the onset of true labor, the patient suffers from false labor pains, care should be taken to see that these do not undermine her morale and sap her strength. Sufficient morphine or codeine should be given each night to insure a full night's sleep. Morphine gr. $\frac{1}{4}$ or codeine gr. 1, given hypodermically on the night before the onset of real labor, often is better than the most skillful forceps extraction after the patient is exhausted.

Onset of Labor. At the onset of actual labor, measures that stimulate uterine contractions should be employed. Since drugs for this purpose usually are dangerous, they are mentioned only to be condemned. Ergot and posterior pituitary extract act too vigorously and have killed innumerable babies and ruptured many uteri. It is thought by some that quinine in 5 gr. doses has merit, although it has been reported as an occasional cause of fetal death. A warm enema often is followed by an increase in the frequency and intensity of the pains and is without risk. The patient should be urged to walk about or pursue her lighter household duties. This augments the uterine contractions while rest in bed, on the other hand, has the opposite effect and, if permitted too early in labor, weakens and retards the pains.

Rest. As soon as the labor has progressed sufficiently to permit the use of morphine and scopolamine (without weakening the uterine contractions), these drugs should be given, since they not only relieve the patient's suffering but seem to favor dilatation of the cervix. When the cervix is about 2 cm. in diameter and strong pains recur at 5 to 6 minute intervals, the patient is put to bed. If rest in bed is followed by weaker and less frequent contractions, the drugs should be withheld and the patient should be encouraged to walk about again. If, on the other hand, the recumbent posture has no effect on the labor, morphine gr. $\frac{1}{6}$ and scopolamine gr. $\frac{1}{200}$ should be given hypodermically. Frequently, the patient rests and often sleeps in the intervals between pains without any appreciable lessening in the strength of the uterine contractions.

FOOD.   As a preventive of fatigue, food is fully as important as rest.   Since carbohydrate calories are best tolerated, starches and sugars should be forced at the beginning of labor and repeated at least every two hours.   Later in the first stage, milk, orange juice with sugar, and broth may be substituted for the heavier foods used early in labor.   No nourishment should be given during the last hour of the first stage and throughout the second stage, as it may give rise to troublesome vomiting during the induction of anesthesia.

SECOND STAGE

ENCOURAGE THE VOLUNTARY EFFORTS.   As soon as the cervix is completely dilated, the membranes are ruptured artificially, a snug abdominal binder is adjusted, pullers are attached to the bed, and throughout each contraction the patient is encouraged to hold her breath and bear down as in defecation.   If thus managed, only a few pains are necessary to drive the presenting part to the pelvic floor and to complete the rotation of the occiput.   Should progress be delayed, the powers may be augmented by making rectal pressure on one of the levators or directly over the coccyx during each contraction.   This advice concerning the proper use of the voluntary efforts should be given at the onset of the second stage, when the patient has the strength to take advantage of such instruction. **Fifteen minutes devoted to careful direction of the powers at the beginning of the second stage are more valuable than two hours of harsh exhortations after the patient has become fatigued.**

ANESTHESIA

Anesthesia during the pains relieves the suffering in the perineal stage and shortens the remainder of the labor.   After the scalp shows at the vulvovaginal ring, the anesthetic is given during each uterine contraction.   Freed from her suffering, the patient relaxes the pelvic floor and bears down more vigorously, thus accelerating the birth of the head.   Local anesthesia also is of great value.

If labor is conducted in the manner just described, most occipitoposteriors are delivered spontaneously and seldom give cause for anxiety.   Occasionally, faulty powers or poor cooperation on the part of the patient may lead to inertia and exhaustion.   If these complications arise during the first stage, the patient is given a complete rest by the use of morphine gr. $\frac{1}{4}$ hypodermically, in the hope that labor may progress normally after a refreshing sleep.

Inertia or exhaustion during the second stage is an indication for the delivery of the child.

Whenever artificial termination of labor in the second stage is indicated, the procedure used will depend on the location and position of the presenting part:

OCCIPITOPOSTERIOR AT THE BRIM, i.e., before engagement has taken place, is best treated by internal version and extraction, provided disproportion is not present and no other contraindication to version exists.   Occipitoposterior at the brim with disproportion calls for the consideration of a low cesarean section, if the previous conduct of labor does not render suprapubic delivery too dangerous.

OCCIPITOPOSTERIOR AT OR BELOW THE LEVEL OF THE ISCHIAL SPINES may be delivered by forceps extraction. Prior to applying forceps, the exact position of the occiput must be ascertained and, if rotation is not complete, the occiput should be rotated manually (5, 6, 7). Occasionally, the head again turns back to the original position before the forceps can be applied. When this occurs, manual rotation is repeated, and an assistant prevents a recurrence of the posterior position by making sufficient pressure over the uterus to force the occiput farther into the pelvis and against the pelvic floor.

When manual rotation cannot be accomplished, two procedures may be tried:

1. If the occiput can be partially rotated so that the sagittal suture lies transversely, one blade of the forceps may be applied over the brow and the other under the mastoid. After this oblique application, gentle traction is made and the blades are then unlocked. Repetition of this intermittent locking and unlocking of the blades with each traction frequently causes complete anterior rotation (Figs. 954 and 955, page 812).

2. The head may also be rotated by the forceps, after which they are re-applied and extraction is accomplished as in forceps for an occipito-anterior (Figs. 942 to 953, pages 807–811). Fortunately, the need for either of these procedures is rare. The oblique application renders the extraction difficult and may injure the child's head and the mother's pelvic floor. The double application is not so difficult, but rotation of the head by forceps does great damage to the pelvic supporting structures and extensive injury to the anterior wall. Marked cystocele commonly follows the use of this method by those who are not expert. **The beginner will do well to avoid either and call for the assistance of a more experienced obstetrician whenever he cannot rotate the head manually.**

REFERENCES

1. VARNIER: Les occipito-postérieures. Obstétrique Journalière, Paris, 1900, 181.
2. PLASS, E. D.: A Statistical Study of 635 Labors with the Occiput Posterior. Johns Hopkins Hosp. Bull., 1916, 27, 164.
3. THOMS, H.: A Type of Pelvis Intimately Associated with Occipito-Posterior Position. S. G. O., 1933, 56, 97.
4. WEISS, O.: Zur Behandlung der Vorderscheitellagen. Samml. Klin. Vortr. n. F., 1892, No. 60, 601.
5. MÜLLER, A.: Ueber hintere Hauptslagen und Scheitellagen. Monatschr. f. Geburtsh. u. Gyn., 1898, 7, 382 & 534.
6. DE LEE, J. B.: The Treatment of Occiput Posterior Position After Engagement of the Head. S. G. O., 1928, 46, 696.
7. DANFORTH, W. G.: The Treatment of Occipito-posterior Positions with Especial Reference to Manual Rotation. Am. J. O. & G., 1932, 23, 360.

JEAN LOUIS BAUDELOCQUE
1746–1810

Baudelocque measured the external conjugate, Baudelocque's diameter, and invented the first pelvimeter. He was a distinguished obstetrician and eminent teacher. In his excellent book on obstetrics, "L'art des accouchements" 1789, he advanced our knowledge of the mechanism of labor, introduced pelvimetry, and described methods of converting face into vertex presentations.

MARIE-LOUISE LACHAPELLE
1769–1821
Paris

Mme. Lachapelle was an illustrious midwife who contributed much toward the advancement of obstetrics.

Although Baudelocque was responsible for the theoretical instruction at the newly formed Maternité, Lachapelle had charge of the practical work. She soon became famous for her clinical instruction and her pupils were well known throughout France.

Mme. Lachapelle is said to have supervised the delivery of over 50,000 women and thereby gained an experience which enabled her to write "Practique des accouchements" which was completed by her cousin, Dr. Dugès. This work was translated into German and as a result had a great influence in Germany as well as in France.

Lachapelle reduced the 94 theoretical presentations suggested by Baudelocque to 22, and her deductions are the basis of our present teaching in this regard.

CHAPTER XVIII

FACE PRESENTATION

ANTERIOR POSITIONS OF THE FACE

A FACE PRESENTATION is a longitudinal presentation in which the head becomes extended so that the face presents and the chin or mentum is the leading pole.

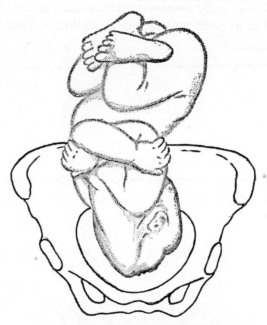

FIG. 441. Right Mentum Anterior, R.M.A.

ETIOLOGY. Primary face presentations are extremely rare and, in practice, the possibility of their occurrence is disregarded. The author has seen but one instance of face presentation before the onset of labor, the diagnosis of which he was able to confirm by the x-ray. In that case, spontaneous flexion occurred when the patient went into labor and the child was born as a vertex. Usually, face presentation is secondary to a previous vertex, and is the result of some condition which interferes with the normal flexion mechanism. The etiological factors which may interfere with flexion and cause face presentation may be fetal or maternal.

The fetal causes are of two varieties. Those conditions which are responsible for a protrusion on the anterior surface of the neck and thus prevent flexion: as numerous coils of umbilicial cord about the neck, or a thyroid tumor (1). The

375

second fetal etiological factor is an abnormal elongation of the occipital arm of the head lever, as in dolichocephaly (2, 3, 4, 5).　Both of these possibilities are extremely rare.　In several instances of children born with thyroid enlargement and in many cases having numerous coils of cord about the neck, not a single face presentation has occurred in the writer's experience.　Dolichocephaly unquestionably may cause a face presentation, but its occurrence as a primary condition is questioned by many obstetricians.　While primary dolichocephaly is rare, if it occurs at all, secondary dolichocephaly is common and results from the molding that takes place in the mechanism of a face presentation.

The commonest maternal etiological factor is a faulty axis of the uterus. When the uterus is markedly dextroverted or sinistroverted, or when the axis is displaced forward as in pendulous abdomen, flexion is disturbed and extension

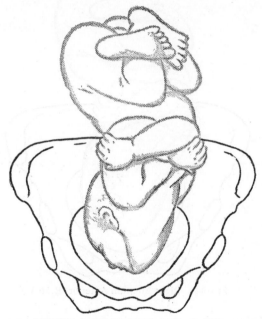

Fig. 442. Left Mentum Anterior, L.M.A.

may occur (6).　The frequency of lateral displacements of the uterus and pendulous abdomen in multiparae accounts for the fact that most face presentations occur in women who have borne children (7).

FREQUENCY.　Face presentation occurs about once in every 250 labors and usually is secondary to a vertex (8).　As L.O.A. and R.O.P. are the commonest vertex presentations, the face positions which result from their extension are the most frequent.　Accordingly, 85 per cent of all face presentations are almost equally divided between R.M.P. and L.M.A.

In anterior positions of the face, the mentum is the leading pole and is in one of the anterior quadrants of the mother's pelvis.　Right Mentum Anterior will be described, as the illustrations show the mechanism to better advantage.

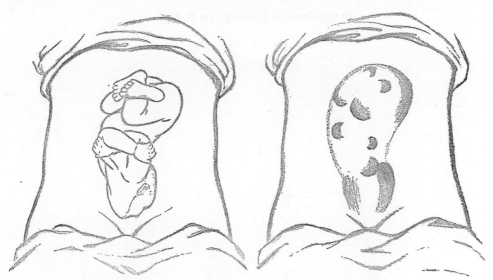

FIG. 443. R.M.A. as visualized through the   FIG. 444. Touch picture in R.M.A.
                abdominal wall.

PALPATION FINDINGS IN R.M.A.

1. Dorsum—to the left, away from the midline, felt with difficulty and
   CONCAVE.
2. Small Parts—to the right, cross the midline, and felt with ease.
3. Lower Pole—the head.
4. Upper Pole—the breech.
5. Cephalic Prominence—is marked and is on the left, i.e., ON THE SAME
   SIDE AS THE DORSUM.
6. Anterior Shoulder—on the left, near the midline, and easily felt.

COMMENT ON ABDOMINAL PALPATION

Simultaneous palpation of the two sides of the abdomen shows the left to
be more resistant and smoother.   The back, therefore, is on this side even though
its entire outline cannot be felt.   Usually, the upper part of the dorsum is more
easily detected and is found to be remote from the midline.   The side on which
the dorsum is felt also is more or less concave.

The less resistant and more irregular right side contains the small parts,
which are easily felt and seem to cross the midline.

The harder, smoother, and more globular mass in the lower pole is the head,
while the softer, more irregular and less globular upper pole indicates the presence
of the breech.

The cephalic prominence is **very marked** and is felt **on the same side as the
dorsum,** a finding which establishes the diagnosis of extension rather than flexion.

The anterior shoulder is felt with ease on the left side, near the midline.

Auscultation Findings in R.M.A.

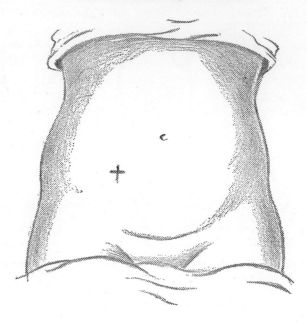

FIG. 445. Location of the fetal heart in R.M.A.

The fetal heart sounds in anterior positions of the face are transmitted through the anterior chest wall, rather than through the scapula. In R.M.A., accordingly, the fetal heart is heard very distinctly on the right side, near the midline (Fig. 445).

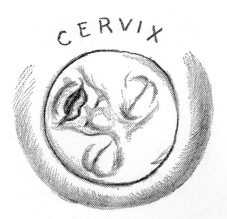

FIG. 446. Vaginal touch picture in R.M.A.

Vaginal Findings in R.M.A.

1. The customary hard, smooth dome of the vertex is not felt.   (Fig. 446).

2. No sutures nor fontanels are palpable.

3. A soft, irregular mass perforated by an opening is detected and the alveolar ridges—the anlagen of the teeth—may be felt within this opening.

4. The orbits and nose are readily distinguished, if these landmarks have not been altered by edema.

5. The malar eminences are prominent and when joined to the mouth by imaginary lines form a triangle, the mouth angle of which points toward the chin (Figs. 447 and 448).

6. The mentum is in the right anterior quadrant.

7. The facial axis lies in the left oblique diameter.

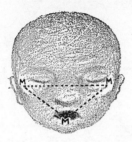
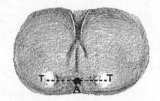

FIG. 447. Mouth perforating soft irregular face.   The mouth angle of an imaginary triangle points toward the mentum.

FIG. 448. The anal orifice perforating the soft, irregular breech.   The anus bisects the bisischial line.

Comment on Vaginal Examination

Absence of a hard, smooth dome, indented by sutures and fontanels, leads one to suspect that he is not dealing with a vertex presentation.   The presenting part is soft, irregular, and perforated by an opening.   It therefore must be either a face or a breech.   When the examination is made soon after the membranes have ruptured, a diagnosis of face presentation may easily be made by distinguishing the orbits and the nose.   If, however, a number of hours have elapsed since the rupture of the membranes, the marked edema that occurs over the presenting part may render the diagnosis more difficult.   In these circumstances, the mouth is distinguished from the anal orifice by the fact that it contains the anlagen of the teeth—the alveolar ridges.   When the mouth is joined by imaginary lines to the malar eminences and they are themselves joined by another imaginary line, a triangle is formed.   On the other hand, a straight line is formed when the ischial tuberosities and the anal orifice are connected, and this line is bisected by the anus (Figs. 447 and 448).   The mentum is in the right anterior quadrant and the axis of the face is in the left oblique diameter.

MECHANISM OF LABOR—R.M.A.

Extension

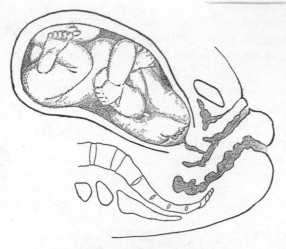

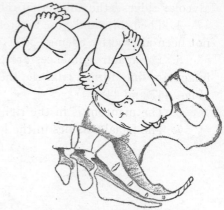

FIG. 449. An L.O.P. has become extended and is now an R.M.A. Sagittal section.

FIG 450. R.M.A. Same as Figure 449 showing the relation of the face to the pelvis.

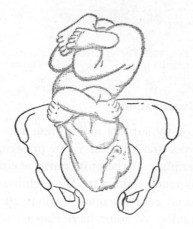

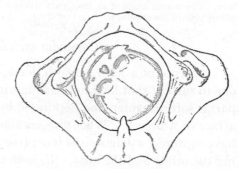

FIG. 451. R.M.A. Front view in relation to the pelvis.

FIG. 452. R.M.A. as visualized from below.

EXTENSION. As a result of some interference with a normal flexion mechanism, the head, which at the onset of labor presented as an L.O.P., becomes deflexed and finally extended so that it passes through the pelvis face first. The mentum is the leading pole and lies in the right anterior quadrant while the axis of the face is parallel with the left oblique diameter. This substitution of extension for flexion causes the trachelobregmatic diameter, 9.5 cm., to take the place of the suboccipitobregmatic, 9.5 cm.

Descent

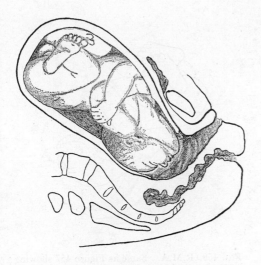

FIG. 453. R.M.A. nearing the pelvic floor.
Sagittal section.

FIG. 454. R.M.A. Same as Figure 453 showing
the relation of the face to the pelvis.

FIG. 455. R.M.A. nearing the pelvic floor.
Front view.

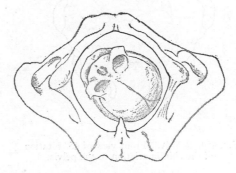

FIG. 456. R.M.A. nearing the pelvic floor as
visualized from below.

DESCENT occurs as in vertex presentations, but the mentum is the leading
pole and the facial axis is in the left oblique diameter.

Internal Rotation

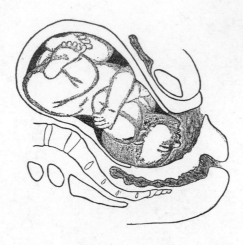

Fig. 457. R.M.A. 45° anterior rotation of the mentum. Sagittal section.

Fig. 458. R.M.A. Same as Figure 457 showing the relation of the face to the pelvis.

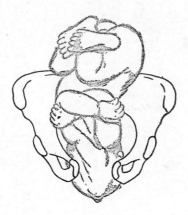

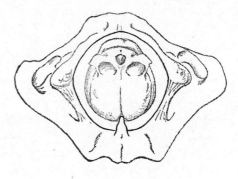

Fig. 459. R.M.A. Front view of 45° rotation of the chin in relation to the pelvis.

Fig. 460. R.M.A. Anterior rotation of the face as visualized from below.

INTERNAL ROTATION.   Since the mentum and facial axis are subject to the same mechanical influence that affected the occiput and the sagittal suture in an L.O.A., they act in a similar manner.   After the chin meets the resistance of the pelvic floor, it rotates 45° anteriorly to the symphysis and the facial axis comes into relation with the anteroposterior diameter of the outlet.

Flexion

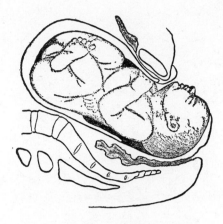

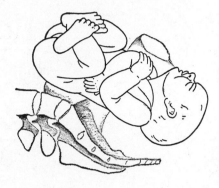

FIG 461. R.M.A. Flexion of the head.
Sagittal section.

FIG. 462. R.M.A. Same as Figure 461 showing
the relation of the face to the pelvis.

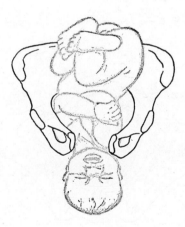

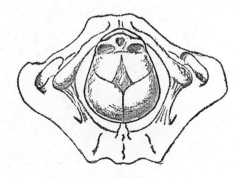

FIG. 463. R.M.A. Front view of flexion in relation
to the pelvis.

FIG. 464. R.M.A. Flexion as visualized
from below.

FLEXION.   Descent continues until the chin escapes beneath the pubic arch, when the undersurface of the mandible becomes arrested under the subpubic ligament.   The head then pivots about this point and the mouth, nose, orbits, brow, large fontanel, sagittal suture, small fontanel, and occiput are born by flexion.

Restitution

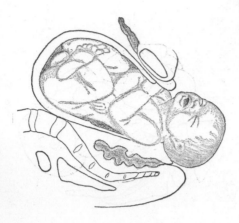

FIG. 465. R.M.A.   Restitution of the head. Sagittal section.

FIG. 466. R.M.A.   Same as Figure 465 showing the relation of the head to the pelvis.

FIG. 467. R.M.A.   Front view of restitution.

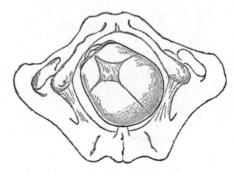

FIG. 468. R.M.A.   Restitution as seen from below.

RESTITUTION. As soon as the head is released from the grasp of the vulvovaginal ring, it drops backward toward the anus and, as a result of the untwisting of the neck, the mentum turns 45° to the right to assume a position similar to that occupied by it in the beginning of the face mechanism.

External Rotation

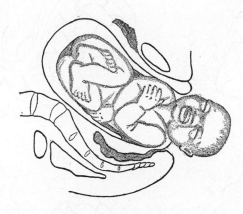

FIG. 469. R.M.A. External rotation. Sagittal section.

FIG. 470. R.M.A. Same as Figure 465 showing the relation of the face to the pelvis.

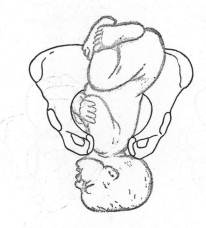

FIG. 471. R.M.A. Front view of external rotation.

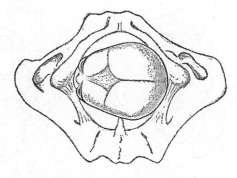

FIG. 472. R.M.A. External rotation as seen from below.

EXTERNAL ROTATION. When the anterior shoulder meets the resistance of the pelvic floor on the left side and is rotated toward the symphysis, the mentum turns an additional 45° to the right.

Pictorial Summary

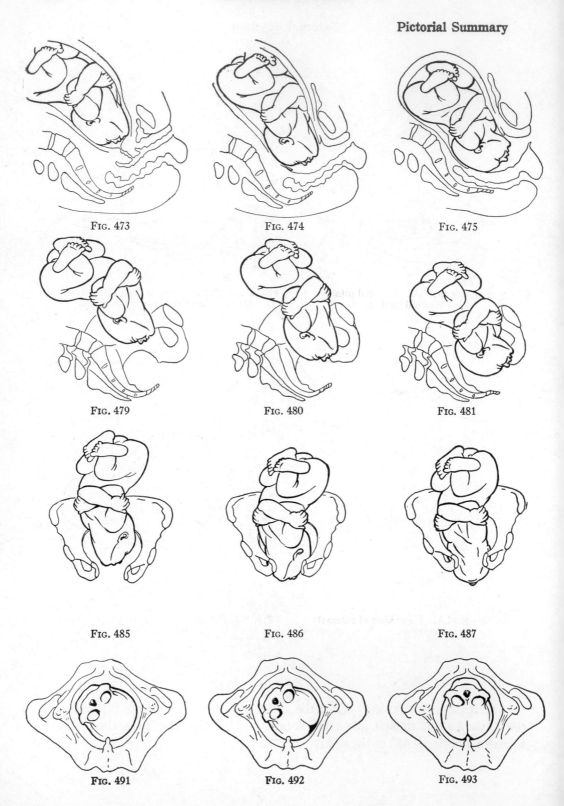

FIG. 473

FIG. 474

FIG. 475

FIG. 479

FIG. 480

FIG. 481

FIG. 485

FIG. 486

FIG. 487

FIG. 491

FIG. 492

FIG. 493

of RMA Mechanism

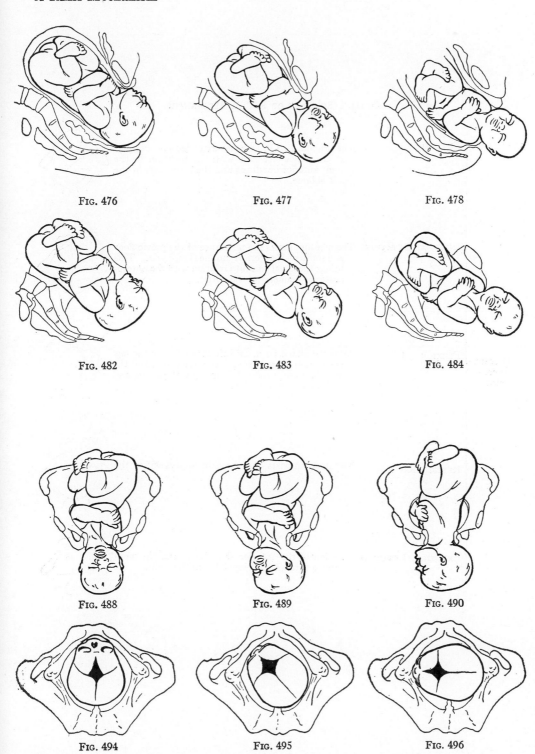

FIG. 476   FIG. 477   FIG. 478

FIG. 482   FIG. 483   FIG. 484

FIG. 488   FIG. 489   FIG. 490

FIG. 494   FIG. 495   FIG. 496

OUTLINE SUMMARY OF R.M.A. MECHANISM

EXTENSION   The original L.O.P. becomes extended and engages
                      in the pelvis face first with the mentum in the
                      right anterior quadrant and the facial axis in the
                      left oblique.

INTERNAL ROTATION   The mentum meets the resistance of the pelvic floor
                      and rotates 45° anteriorly to the symphysis.   This
                      brings the facial axis into relation with the antero-
                      posterior diameter of the outlet.

Descent   FLEXION After the chin is born, the inferior surface of the jaw
is con-   becomes impinged beneath the pubic arch and the
stant   mouth, nose, orbits, brow, sagittal suture and
                      occiput are born by flexion.

RESTITUTION   The neck untwists and the chin rotates 45° to the
                      right.

EXTERNAL ROTATION Rotation of the anterior shoulder causes the men-
                      tum to turn an additional 45° to the right.

COMMENT ON THE MECHANISM OF ANTERIOR FACE PRESENTATIONS

Owing to some interference with the normal flexion mechanism, a previous L.O.P. is extended and becomes an R.M.A. This may occur without much difficulty or it may cause considerable delay, due to the fact that after the head becomes partially extended and the brow presents, further descent is impossible because in brow presentations the occipitomental diameter is too large to pass through a normal pelvis. Usually, however, complete extension ultimately takes place and descent of the face continues without much difficulty. Once extension is completed, the chin descends more rapidly than does the occiput in a vertex presentation, since in a face case the presenting part is somewhat wedge-shaped.

ENGAGEMENT. The face engages with the mentum as the leading pole in the right anterior quadrant and with the facial axis in the left oblique diameter. As the distance from the face to the parietal eminences is greater than the distance from the occiput to the same landmark, the face must descend considerably below the level of the ischial spines before we may conclude that the engaging diameters—trachelobregmatic, 9.5 cm., and the biparietal, 9.25 cm.—have passed through the inlet.

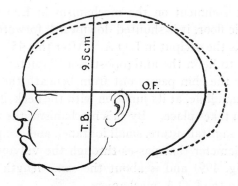

FIG. 497. Molding in an R.M.A.

MOLDING OF THE HEAD. In the mechanism of an R.M.A., the engaging diameters are somewhat diminished with a compensatory increase in the occipitofrontal diameter. These changes in contour are due to the same factors that were described under Molding in an L.O.A. (Fig. 497).

CAPUT SUCCEDANEUM. An edematous swelling is observed over most o the face in extension cases. The eyelids, alae of the nose, and lips become so thickened that the child at birth presents a hideous appearance. Usually, however, the edema disappears within a few days and the contour of the face becomes quite normal (Fig. 498).

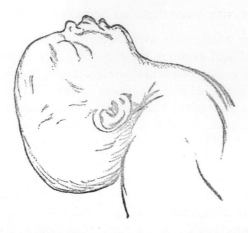

FIG. 498. Distortion of the features resulting from face mechanism.

INTERNAL ROTATION. Since the mentum is the leading pole and the facial axis is the longest diameter, these two entities follow the same course that the occiput and sagittal suture followed in L.O.A., for the same reasons that were mentioned under the comment on the mechanism in L.O.A. When the mentum reaches the pelvic floor, it is shunted downward, forward and inward to the symphysis, just as was the occiput in L.O.A. After this 45° of anterior rotation, the facial axis comes to lie in the anteroposterior diameter of the pelvic outlet.

FLEXION. After the chin passes out from beneath the pubic arch, the inferior surface of the mandible, at its junction with the neck, impinges beneath the symphysis and flexion takes place. By this mechanism, the mouth, nose, orbits, brow, large fontanel, sagittal suture, small fontanel, and occiput are successively born The largest diameter that passes through the vulvovaginal orifice is the trachelo-occipital (Fig. 499) and is about the same length as the suboccipito-frontal, its analogue in the L.O.A. mechanism.

RESTITUTION. Following the birth of the head, the neck untwists and the mentum turns 45° to the right to occupy a position s milar to that occupied by it when the face engaged.

EXTERNAL ROTATION. Due to internal rotation of the anterior shoulder toward the symphysis, the mentum turns an additional 45° to the right.

DANGERS OF ANTERIOR POSITIONS OF THE FACE

As was previously mentioned, some difficulty may be experienced during the period of transition from a posterior vertex to an anterior face. Once the extension is complete, however, and an anterior face is produced, the trouble is over. The tendency toward early rupture of the membranes is greater than in vertex cases. Accordingly, a prolongation of the first stage might be anticipated. In

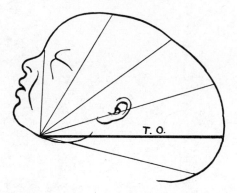

Fig. 499. The largest diameter is the trachelo occipital.

practice, the delay, if any, is hardly noticeable, as the narrow face, like the sharp edge of a wedge, passes through the pelvis more rapidly than does the blunt occiput in a vertex presentation.   This factor probably is an aid in both the first and second stages.   The poorer fit between the face and the pelvis might lead us to expect more frequent prolapse of the cord and dry labor, with a greater possibility of interference with the uteroplacental circulation.   While the danger to the child is slightly increased because of these possibilities, the risk of asphyxia is greatly over-estimated.   After birth the head falls backward as though the neck were broken (Fig. 498).   This, together with the marked edema of the face, disappears within a short time.

TREATMENT OF ANTERIOR POSITIONS OF THE FACE

Spontaneous delivery gives such good results for both mother and child, that an expectant plan is recommended as a routine just as in L.O.A. (9).   **In other words, anterior positions of the face do not require interference, unless a definite maternal or fetal indication, other than face presentation, arises.**   When such an indication is present, labor should be terminated by that means which is best suited to the conditions that are then found.

Anterior Face high in the pelvis should be delivered by version and extraction whenever an indication for interference arises.

Anterior Face below the level of the ischial spine is best treated by extraction with forceps applied to the sides of the face along the mento-occipital diameter.

POSTERIOR POSITIONS OF THE FACE

In the following description, Right Mentum Posterior will be discussed because it can be more satisfactorily illustrated than Left Mentum Posterior. Since it results from the extension of an L.O.A., it also occurs more frequently than L.M.P.

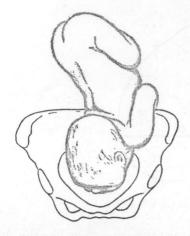

FIG. 500. Left Mentum Posterior, L.M.P.

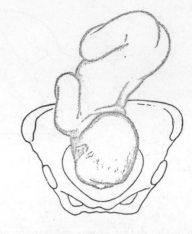

FIG. 501. Right Mentum Posterior, R.M.P.

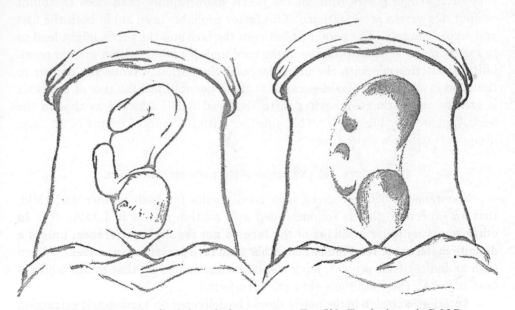

FIG. 502. R.M.P. as visualized through the
abdominal wall.

FIG. 503. Touch picture in R.M.P.

PALPATION FINDINGS IN R.M.P.

1. Dorsum—to the left, near the midline, easily felt and is concave.
2. Small Parts—on the right, away from the midline, and felt with difficulty.
3. Lower Pole—the head.
4. Upper Pole—the breech.
5. Cephalic Prominence—is marked and is on the left side, i.e., ON THE SAME SIDE AS THE DORSUM.
6. Anterior Shoulder—on the right, near the midline and easily felt.

COMMENT ON ABDOMINAL PALPATION

The resistance is greater on the left side.   It may, therefore, be concluded that the back is on this side.   Usually, the dorsum can be made out without difficulty, particularly in the region of the fundus, where the definite outline of the back may be felt near the midline.   The concavity of the dorsum is marked and, accordingly, is readily detected in posterior face presentations.

The less resistant and more irregular right side contains the small parts These are well away from the midline and often are difficult to feel.   The head is easily made out as the lower pole and a very marked cephalic prominence is felt on the same side as the dorsum.   When the mentum is posterior, it is easier to diagnose a face presentation than when the mentum is anterior.

Auscultation Findings in R.M.P.

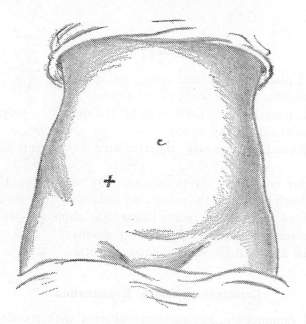

Fig. 504. Location of the fetal heart in R.M.P.

The fetal heart sounds are transmitted through the anterior shoulder to the lower right quadrant of the mother's abdomen.   Accordingly, the punctum maximum is heard on the right side, near the midline (Fig. 504).

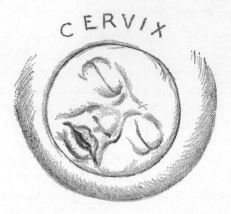

FIG. 505. Vaginal touch picture in R.M.P.

Vaginal Findings in R.M.P.

1. The hard dome of the vertex cannot be felt.
2. It is impossible to detect sutures or fontanels.
3. The soft, irregular face, perforated by the mouth, is palpated. In the mouth, the alveolar ridges may be felt.
4. The orbits and nose are easily differentiated if the edema over these parts is not extensive.
5. The malar eminences are prominent. By connecting the two malar eminences with each other and the mouth, an imaginary triangle is formed, and the mouth angle of this triangle points toward the chin (Fig. 447).
6. The mentum is in the right posterior quadrant.
7. The facial axis is in the right oblique diameter.

Comment on Vaginal Examination

On vaginal examination, the customary vertex with its sutures and fontanels is absent and in its place the soft, irregular face, perforated by the mouth, is felt. Should the examination be made a number of hours after the membranes have ruptured, the face may be confused with the breech. If the examiner will remember that the anus bisects the bisischial line, no great difficulty will be experienced in making a correct diagnosis. By connecting the malar eminences with each other and the mouth, a triangle is formed, and since the mouth angle of this triangle points toward the mentum, the examiner may conclude from its location that the chin is in the right posterior quadrant of the mother's pelvis.

MECHANISM OF LABOR—R.M.P.

Common Anterior Long Arc Mechanism
Extension

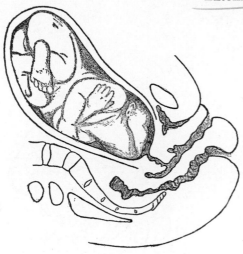

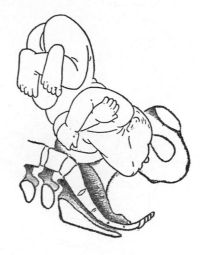

FIG. 506. An L.O.A. has become extended and is now an R.M.P.   Sagittal section.

FIG. 507. R.M.P.   Same as Figure 506 showing the relation of the face to the pelvis,

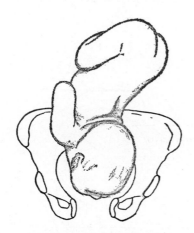

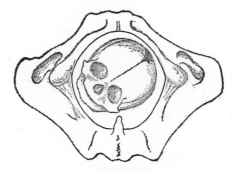

FIG. 508. R.M.P.   Front view in relation to the pelvis.

FIG. 509. R.M.P. as visualized from below.

EXTENSION.   A previous L.O.A. has become extended and is now a Right Mentum Posterior.   The face engages with the mentum in the right posterior quadrant and the facial axis in the right oblique diameter.   Descent is retarded considerably while the head becomes markedly molded in order that the vertex may pass under the anterior portion of the pelvic inlet.

Descent

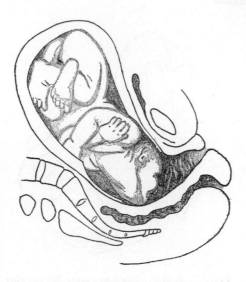

FIG. 510. R.M.P. descending to the pelvic floor.

FIG. 511. R.M.P. Same as Figure 510 showing the relation of the head to the pelvis.

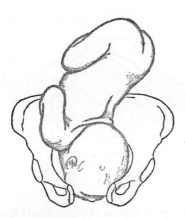

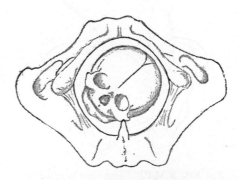

FIG. 512. R.M.P. Front view.

FIG. 513. R.M.P. as visualized from below.

DESCENT is delayed while the head undergoes the essential molding which is necessary in most posterior face cases. Eventually, however, the chin reaches the pelvic floor and the next step in the mechanism—internal rotation—begins.

Internal Rotation

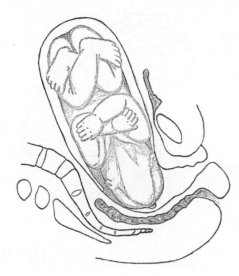

Fig. 514. R.M.P.   45° anterior rotation of the
mentum to R.M.T.   Sagittal section.

Fig. 515. R.M.P.   Same as Figure 514 showing
the relation of the face to the pelvis.

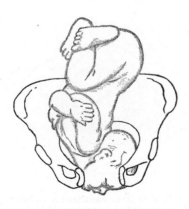

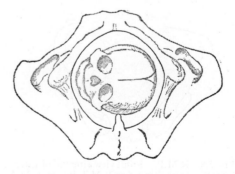

Fig. 516. R.M.P.   Front view of 45° rotation
in relation to the pelvis.

Fig. 517. R.M.P.   45° rotation of the chin as
visualized from below.

INTERNAL ROTATION.   After considerable delay during which excessive
molding of the head occurs, the chin finally reaches the pelvic floor and rotates
anteriorly through an arc of 135° to reach the symphysis pubis.   The first 45°
of this rotation brings the facial axis into the transverse diameter of the pelvis
and produces a Right Mentum Transverse.

Internal Rotation Continued

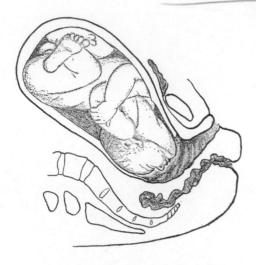

FIG. 518. R.M.P.   45° additonal anterior rotation, changing the R.M.T. into an R.M.A.   Sagittal section.

FIG. 519. R.M.P.   Same as Figure 518 showing the relation of the face to the pelvis.

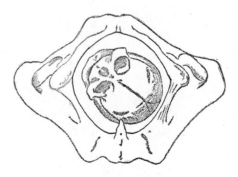

FIG. 520. R.M.P.   Front view after 90° of anterior rotation have changed an R.M.T. into an R.M.A.

FIG. 521. R.M.P. as visualized from below, following 90° of rotation to R.M.A.

INTERNAL ROTATION CONTINUED.   An additional 45° anterior rotation changes the previous R.M.T. into an R.M.A.   Just as in posterior positions of the occiput after rotation of 90° has taken place, the mechanism is the same as that of anterior positions.   The mentum is now in the right anterior quadrant and the facial axis is in the left oblique diameter of the mother's pelvis.

Internal Rotation Concluded

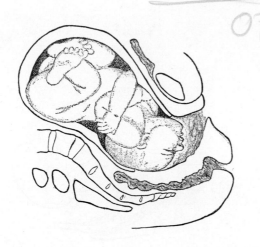

FIG. 522. R.M.P. The mentum rotates the final 45° anteriorly to the symphysis. Sagittal section.

FIG. 523. R.M.P. Same as Figure 522 showing the relation of the face to the pelvis.

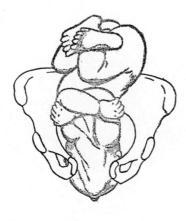

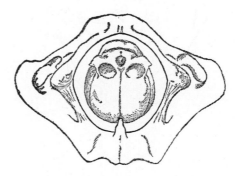

FIG. 524. R.M.P. Front view after 135° of anterior rotation.

FIG. 525. R.M.P. as visualized from below after 135° of anterior rotation.

INTERNAL ROTATION CONCLUDED. After a final 45° of anterior rotation, the chin reaches the symphysis and the facial axis is in the anteroposterior diameter of the outlet.

Flexion

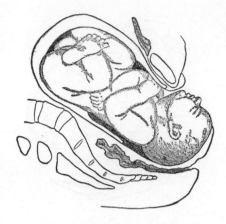

FIG. 526. R.M.P.   Flexion of the head.
Sagittal section.

FIG. 527. R.M.P.   Same as Figure 526 showing
the relation of the head to the pelvis.

FIG. 528. R.M.P.   Front view of flexion.

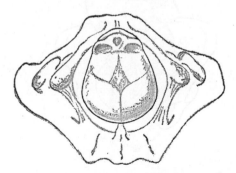

FIG. 529. R.M.P.   Flexion of a rotated posterior
face as seen from below.

FLEXION.   As in anterior face, the chin is born and the mandible becomes impinged beneath the pubic arch, following which the mouth, nose, orbits, brow, large fontanel, sagittal suture, small fontanel, and occiput pass over the fourchette.

Restitution

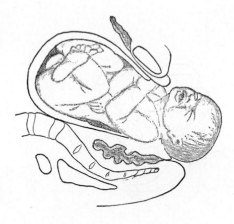

Fig. 530. R.M.P.   Restitution of the head.
Sagittal section.

Fig. 531. R.M.P.   Same as Figure 530 showing
the relation of the head to the pelvis.

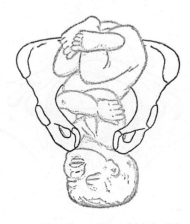

Fig. 532. R.M.P.   Front view of restitution.

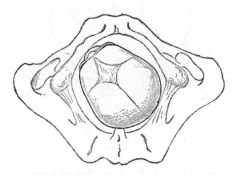

Fig. 533. R.M.P.   Restitution as seen
from below.

RESTITUTION.   Following the delivery of the head, the mentum turns 45°
to the right as the result of the untwisting of the neck.

External Rotation

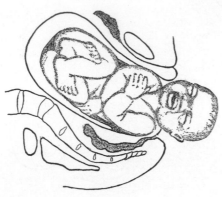

FIG. 534. R.M.P.   External rotation of the head after anterior rotation.   Sagittal section.

FIG. 535. R.M.P.   Same as Figure 534 showing the relation of the head to the pelvis.

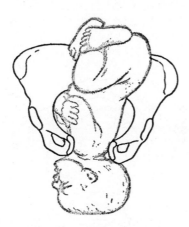

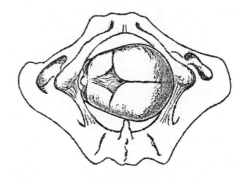

FIG. 536. R.M.P.   Front view of external rotation.

FIG. 537. R.M.P.   External rotation as seen from below.

EXTERNAL ROTATION.   When the anterior shoulder rotates 45° to the symphysis, the mentum turns an additional 45° to the right.

OUTLINE SUMMARY OF R.M.P. MECHANISM

	EXTENSION	The original L.O.A. becomes extended and is engaged in the pelvis as a face presentation, R.M.P. The mentum is in the right posterior quadrant and the facial axis is in the right oblique.
	INTERNAL ROTATION	The mentum meets the resistance of the pelvic floor and rotates anteriorly 135° to the symphysis. This brings the facial axis into relation with the anteroposterior diameter of the outlet.
Descent is constant	FLEXION	After the chin is born, the under surface of the mandible impinges beneath the subpubic ligament and the mouth, nose, orbits, brow, large fontanel, sagittal suture, small fontanel and occiput are born by flexion.
	RESTITUTION	The neck untwists and the mentum rotates 45° to the right.
	EXTERNAL ROTATION	An additional 45° rotation to the right results from internal rotation of the anterior shoulder.

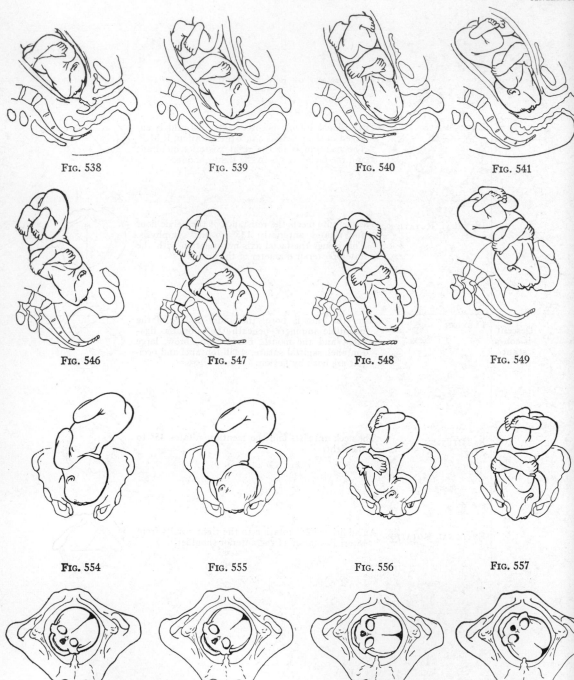

FIG. 538   FIG. 539   FIG. 540   FIG. 541

FIG. 546   FIG. 547   FIG. 548   FIG. 549

FIG. 554   FIG. 555   FIG. 556   FIG. 557

FIG. 562   FIG. 563   FIG. 564   FIG. 565

RMP Mechanism

TATION

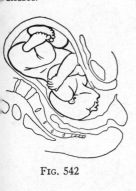

FIG. 542

FIG. 543

FIG. 544

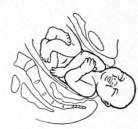

FIG. 545

FIG. 550

FIG. 551

FIG. 552

FIG. 553

FIG. 558

FIG. 559

FIG. 560

FIG. 561

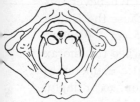

FIG. 566

FIG. 567

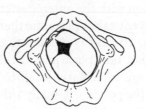

FIG. 568

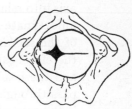

FIG. 569

Posterior Internal Rotation

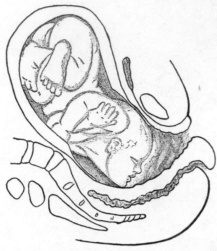

FIG. 570. R.M.P. 45° posterior rotation of the mentum to the hollow of the sacrum. Sagittal section.

FIG. 571. R.M.P. Same as Figure 595 showing the relation of the face to the pelvis.

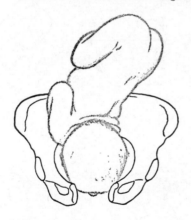

FIG. 572. R.M.P. Front view of 45° posterior rotation.

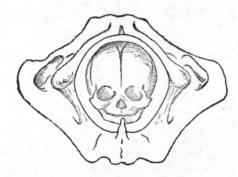

FIG. 573. R.M.P. The mentum in the hollow of the sacrum as visualized from below.

INTERNAL ROTATION. The first part of the mechanism is similar to that described under anterior rotation. Instead of rotating anteriorly, however, the mentum turns 45° posteriorly to the hollow of the sacrum, thus bringing the facial axis into relation with the anteroposterior diameter of the pelvis. Whenever this unfortunate event takes place, further progress is impossible because the length of the sacrum, 10 cm., is greater than the length of the neck, 5 cm. Flexion, therefore, cannot take place and further descent is possible only when the thorax and the head are sufficiently small to permit the thoracobregmatic diameter to pass through the pelvis. Usually this is impossible and impaction, accordingly, is the rule whenever the mentum rotates into the hollow of the sacrum.

COMMENT ON THE MECHANISM OF POSTERIOR POSITIONS OF THE MENTUM

A previous anterior vertex becomes extended to form a posterior face. As in anterior face presentations, difficulty may be encountered before the extension is completed. Following complete extension, progress is delayed for some time to permit the marked molding that is necessary in posterior face cases.

ENGAGEMENT. In R.M.P. the face engages with the mentum as the leading pole. It is in the right posterior quadrant and the facial axis is in the right oblique. For the reason mentioned in the preceding paragraph, engagement usually is considerably delayed.

MOLDING OF THE HEAD. In the mechanism of an R.M.P., marked molding takes place. As a result, the trachelobregmatic diameter, 9.5 cm., is shortened and the occipitofrontal, 11.5 cm., undergoes a compensatory lengthening. Since

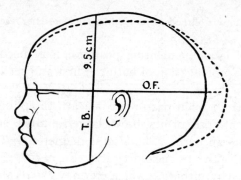

FIG. 574. Molding in an R.M.P.

the bones of the face are quite rigid, this elongation must take place in the posterior part of the cranial vault. Consequently, a secondary dolichocephaly often is produced. When a child is delivered by a posterior face mechanism, the top of the head, accordingly, is markedly flattened as is shown in Fig. 574.

CAPUT SUCCEDANEUM. The edematous swelling that is observed over the presenting part is particularly pronounced in posterior face presentations, due to the fact that the membranes usually rupture early and labor is quite prolonged (Fig. 575).

INTERNAL ROTATION. After considerable delay, the mentum meets the resistance of the pelvic floor and rotates anteriorly 135° to the symphysis or posteriorly 45° to the hollow of the sacrum. Posterior rotation is rare but always leads to impaction, if the child is not unusually small. When anterior rotation takes place, the mechanism is similar to that of an anterior face, after the chin has rotated 90°. In these cases, then, the mentum rotates 135° to the symphysis and the facial axis comes into relation with the anteroposterior diameter of the outlet.

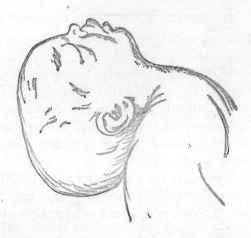

FIG. 575. Distortion of the features resulting from posterior face mechanism.

The progress of labor in mentum posterior may become arrested at any stage. Accordingly, prolongation of both the first and second stages of labor is commonly observed.

FLEXION. After the chin passes out beneath the pubic arch, flexion takes place, and the mouth, nose, orbits, brow, large fontanel, sagittal suture, small fontanel and occiput are born. The largest diameter that passes through the vulvovaginal orifice is the trachelo-occipital (Fig. 576). It is about the same length as the suboccipitofrontal, which, it may be recalled, was the largest diameter in the L.O.A. mechanism.

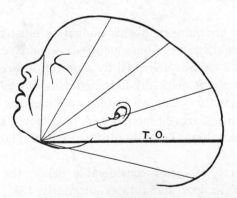

FIG. 576. The largest diameter is the trachelo-occipital.

RESTITUTION. Following the birth of the head, the mentum turns 45° to the right as a result of the untwisting of the neck.

EXTERNAL ROTATION. With the internal rotation of the anterior shoulder, the mentum turns an additional 45° to the right.

DANGERS OF POSTERIOR POSITIONS OF THE FACE

While anterior positions of the face give rise to little or no apprehension, posterior positions are a constant source of anxiety until rotation has occurred. Before rotation is possible, the mentum must be driven well down upon the pelvic floor. Since the vertex of the skull cannot pass the anterior wall of the pelvis until considerable molding has taken place, this is an extremely difficult task. Likewise, the neck must be greatly elongated before the mentum can reach the level necessary for rotation. In addition, early rupture of the membranes is common, and, as a result, the uterus may become molded about the child, thus increasing the length of an already prolonged labor.

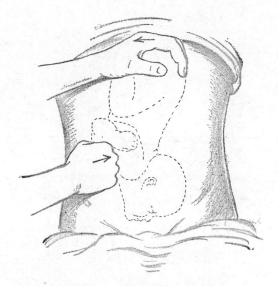

Fig. 577. Schatz maneuver. Pressure is made against the thorax with one hand while the other pulls the breech in the opposite direction.

Great as are the difficulties that arise in mentum posterior when the chin rotates anteriorly, they are insignificant when compared with those that follow posterior rotation. Whenever the mentum rotates into the hollow of the sacrum, nature makes one of the greatest errors possible in obstetrics. In these circumstances, the child dies and the mother is subjected to the risk of rupture of the uterus, since, as a rule, neither spontaneous nor instrumental delivery is possible (8, 9, 10).

FETAL DANGERS. The poor fit between the face and the pelvis may lead to early rupture of the membranes and interference with the uteroplacental circulation. The same condition also leads to prolapse of the cord. Asphyxia, therefore, is possible at any time. In practice, however, this seldom happens when the chin is anterior for the reason that the labor is not particularly retarded.

On the other hand, when the chin is posterior, the fear of asphyxia is well justified, since long, dry labors with molded uteri are not uncommon before anterior rotation occurs. If the chin rotates to the hollow of the sacrum, the death of the child is inevitable.

As the cervix is dilated by pressure of the presenting part, marked edema of the face is produced, and the face of the child at birth is horribly disfigured. This, together with the tendency of the head to fall backward as though the neck were broken, may lead the parents to hope for its death. Fortunately, they may be assured that the deformity is only temporary and will disappear entirely within a short time.

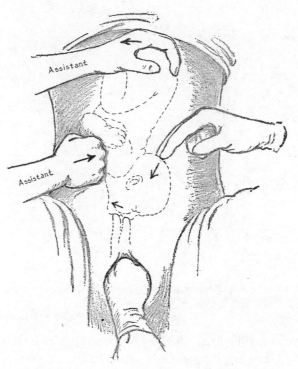

FIG. 578. Ziegenspeck maneuver. Two fingers of one hand pass through the cervix and make upward pressure successively on the mentum, canine fossae and brow as the external hand presses downward on the occiput. At the same time, an assistant does the Schatz maneuver.

TREATMENT OF POSTERIOR POSITIONS OF THE MENTUM

Although most posterior positions of the face ultimately are delivered through the natural passages, the labor is so prolonged and the possibilities of dangerous complications are so great that it seems best to interfere routinely in all posterior face cases (10).

If the membranes are intact, an attempt is made to flex the head by the method of Schatz, which aims to convert the dorsal concavity into a convexity

(11). This is accomplished by making pressure against the thorax with one hand while the other pulls the breech in the opposite direction (Fig. 577). Owing to the fact that the face is usually below the pelvic brim, this procedure seldom is successful. However, since it can be attempted without harm, it may be tried.

As soon as the membranes rupture, flexion is easily brought about by either the Ziegenspeck or Thorn maneuvers. In the Ziegenspeck procedure (Fig. 578) two fingers of one hand are passed through the cervix and make upward pressure successively on the mentum, canine fossae and brow as the external hand presses downward on the occiput. At the same time, an assistant manipulates the trunk according to the method of Schatz. The technic of Ziegenspeck has the advantage that it enables the operator to interfere relatively early in labor when the cervix is only two fingers dilated.

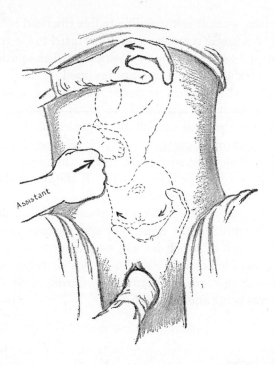

FIG. 579. Thorn maneuver. An assistant makes pressure against the thorax as the operator pulls the breech in the opposite direction and favors flexion by pulling down the brow and forcing the face upward with the fingers and thumb of the internal hand.

The Thorn operation for conversion of a face into a vertex presentation requires a less expert assistant but cannot be done until the cervix is almost fully dilated (12). According to this method, the assistant makes pressure against the thorax while the operator pulls the breech in the opposite direction and at the same time manipulates the head with the internal hand as shown in Fig. 579.

If these procedures are tried under anesthesia **within a reasonable time after the rupture of the membranes,** the potentially difficult mentum posterior may be easily changed into an occipito-anterior.   Following flexion, the occiput should be crowded into the pelvis and held in this position until labor is resumed. Any obliquity of the uterus that is present should be corrected by the use of a binder in order that the face presentation may not recur.   If the membranes have not ruptured, when the diagnosis of mentum posterior is first made, interference should be postponed until they rupture spontaneously or until the cervix is fully dilated.

If the membranes rupture early in labor, before the cervix is sufficiently dilated to permit engagement of the head after flexion has been accomplished, a bipolar podalic version may be necessary to prevent a recurrence of the posterior face.

In neglected cases, when it is impossible to flex the head by a Ziegenspeck or Thorn maneuver, the mentum may be manually rotated to the front.   When this is done, the chin must be held in its new position until the patient comes out of her anesthetic and uterine contractions are resumed.

If the head cannot be rotated or flexed, pubiotomy, cesarean section or a destructive operation must be considered (13).   Of these, pubiotomy, followed by manual anterior rotation and extraction, is preferable if the child is in good condition and the operator is competent.   Cesarean section on such a badly neglected case can be done only with great risk to the mother.   When this procedure is selected, the low technic is indicated.   If the classical operation is done it should be followed by a hysterectomy.

.   As all of these operations are last resort measures, it sometimes is better to allow the labor to continue in the hope that spontaneous rotation may occur. The author recalls a case in which he was preparing to do a pubiotomy on a patient in whom it was impossible for him to flex or rotate the face but who rotated and delivered the face spontaneously during a fit of vomiting that occurred while she was being anesthetized.

BROW PRESENTATION

Since extension seldom occurs before the onset of labor, brow presentation is usually encountered after true labor pains have begun and, as a rule, is but a transitory stage between flexion and extension.   All face cases, therefore, are brows at some time during the process of deflexion.

DIAGNOSIS.   Vaginal examination shows the head to be presenting with the large fontanel easily palpable.   As the finger passes over the brow in the opposite direction, the supra-orbital ridges may be felt and palpation of the root of the nose between the two orbits clinches the diagnosis (Fig. 580).

MECHANISM.   In the mechanism of a brow presentation, the occipitomental diameter must enter the pelvis as did the trachelobregmatic in a face and the suboccipitobregmatic in a vertex.   As this diameter is larger than any of the diameters of the pelvis, impaction is certain to result unless spontaneous or

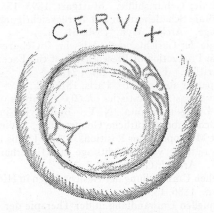

FIG. 580. Vaginal touch picture in brow presentation.

artificial flexion or extension is brought about. A few cases have been recorded in which the head was sufficiently malleable to permit the marked molding that is necessary for an infrapelvic delivery of a brow presentation. As a result of this molding, the occipitomental diameter may be sufficiently diminished to permit its passage through the pelvis (Fig. 581).

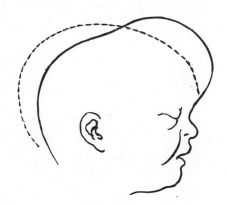

FIG. 581. Molding of the head in brow presentation.

TREATMENT OF BROW PRESENTATION

TREATMENT. As soon as the membranes rupture, all brow cases should be either flexed or extended. If this cannot be done, cesarean section or perforation is indicated, depending upon the conditions that are present.

REFERENCES

1. MORSE, A. H.: Bilateral Congenital Caput Obstipum. S. G. O., 1915, 20, 74.
2. HECKER, C.: Zwei neue Beobachtungen über die Schädelform bei Gesichts- und Stirnlagen. Arch. f. Gyn., 1870, 2, 429.

3. ZWEIFEL, P.: Lehrbuch der Geburtshülfe. Stuttgart, 1895, 155.

4. JELLINGHAUS: Ueber fötale Schädelformen mit Berücksichtigung der Heckerschen Aetiologie der Gesichtslage. Arch. f. Gyn., 1896, 51, 33.

5. GESSNER: Zur Aeteologie der Gesichtslage. Zeitschr. f. Geburtsh. u. Gyn., 1897, 37, 302.

6. DUNCAN, J. M.: On the Production of Presentation of the Face. Mechanism of Natural and Morbid Parturition. Edinburgh, 1875, 218.

7. PINARD, A.: Traité du palper abdominal. Paris, 1878, 32.

8. MARKOE, J. W.: Observations and Statistics on 60,000 Labors occurring in the Service of the Society of the Lying-in Hospital, N. Y. Bull. Lying-in Hosp., 1909, 6, 101.

9. BOER, L. J.: Sieben Bücher über natürliche Geburtshülfe. Wien, 1834, 96.

10. REED, C. B.: Persistent Mentoposterior Positions. Am. J. Obs., 1905, 51, 615.

11. SCHATZ, F.: Die Umwandlung von Gesichtslage zu Hinterhauptslage durch alleinigen äusseren Handgriff. Arch. f. Gyn., 1873, 5, 306.

12. THORN, W.: Zur manuellen Umwandlung der Gesichtslagen in Hinterhauptslagen. Ztschr. f. Geburtsh. u. Gyn., 1886, 13, 186.

Die Stellung der manuellen Umwandlung in der Therapie der Gesichts- und Stirnlagen. Samml. Klin. Vortr. n. F., 1902, No. 339, 745.

13. MORSE, A. H.: Pubiotomy in Face Presentations. S. G. & O., 1912, 14, 165.

CHAPTER XIX

BREECH PRESENTATION

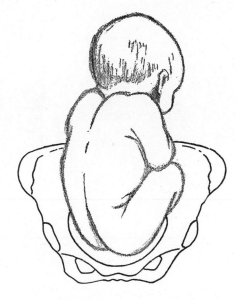 

FIG. 582. Right sacrum anterior, R.S.A.   FIG. 583. Left sacrum posterior, L.S.P.

A breech presentation is one in which the pelvis of the child is the leading pole. In the nomenclature, it is designated as a sacral presentation, and the position of the sacrum is the determining factor in the terminology. Accordingly, a Right Sacrum Anterior is a breech presentation in which the sacrum is in the right anterior quadrant of the mother's pelvis.

ETIOLOGY. In the chapter on Presentation, Position and Posture, the chief reason given for the greater prevalence of cephalic presentations was the tendency for the fetal and uterine ovoids to adapt themselves to each other. A breech presentation, therefore, may be caused by anything that interferes with this mechanism of adaptation, such as prematurity, dead fetus, an excess of amniotic fluid, multiple pregnancy, fibroids of the uterus, contracted pelvis and hydrocephalus.

FREQUENCY. Breech presentations occur about once in every sixty full term pregnancies. If premature deliveries are included, the breech presents in about 3 per cent of all labors. Anterior positions are much more common than posteriors. In the following discussion, the diagnosis and mechanism of Right Sacrum Anterior will be described. From this description, the student or practitioner should be able to work out for himself the diagnosis and mechanism of posterior positions.

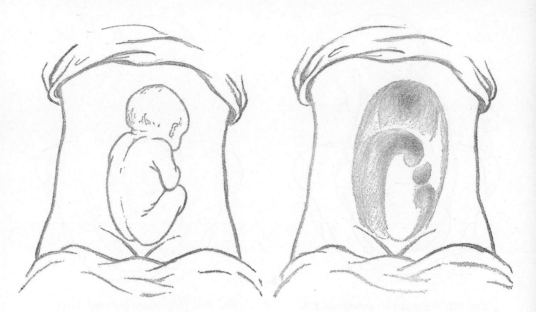

FIG. 584. R.S.A. as visualized through the   FIG. 585. Touch picture in R.S.A.
abdominal wall.

Palpation Findings in R.S.A.

1. Dorsum—**on the right, near the midline, and felt with ease.**
2. Small Parts—**to the left, away from the midline and felt with ease.**
3. Lower Pole—the breech.
4. Upper Pole—the head
$$\begin{cases} \text{harder} \\ \text{more globular} \\ \text{less irregular} \\ \text{near a sulcus} \\ \text{more mobile} \\ \text{moves independently} \\ \textbf{Ballottable} \end{cases}$$
5. Anterior Shoulder—**is near the midline, above the umbilicus** and **is usually on the right side.**

Comment on Abdominal Palpation

Frequently, in breech presentations, the findings on abdominal palpation are obscured by the condition which caused the breech.   This is particularly true if the cause is an excess of fluid, prematurity, dead fetus or multiple pregnancy. If the picture is not thus obscured, the right side is found to be more resistant, smoother and more convex.   From this it may be concluded that the dorsum is on the right and the small parts are on the left.   Comparison of the upper and lower poles reveals the head to be in the upper pole, because it is harder, more globular, less irregular, more mobile, near a sulcus, may be moved independently of the trunk and is **ballottable.**   Occasionally, the findings may be so obscured that only ballottement is obtainable.   **Whenever a ballottable mass is felt in the fundus of the uterus, the tentative diagnosis of a breech should be considered until the membranes rupture and vaginal examination rules out breech presentation.**   The anterior shoulder is felt near the midline above the umbilicus and usually on the right side.   Occasionally, due to obliquity of the uterus, it may be on the left side.

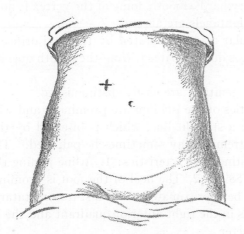

Fig. 586. Location of the fetal heart in R.S.A

Auscultation Findings in R.S.A.

The fetal heart sounds are best heard on the right side, near the midline and above the umbilicus (Fig. 586).   If the uterus is sinistraverted, the fetal heart may be heard more distinctly on the left side.   Occasionally, the heart sounds are best heard in the lower right quadrant, just as in R.O.A.   For this reason, too much reliance should not be placed on the location of the fetal heart sounds as a diagnostic measure.

FIG. 587. Vaginal touch picture in R.S.A.

Vaginal Findings in R.S.A.

1. The customary hard, smooth dome of the vertex is not felt.

2. Sutures and fontanels are absent.

3. A soft, irregular mass, perforated by the anal orifice, is palpated. Absence of alveolar ridges differentiates it from the mouth opening in a face presentation (Fig. 587).

4. The external genitalia are easily distinguished.

5. The tuberosities of the ischium are prominent and when connected with the anal orifice form a straight line, which is bisected by the anus (Fig. 588).

6. The lower extremity may sometimes be palpated. The foot differs from the hand in three distinct characteristics: 1. A line joining the tip of the toes is a straight line (Fig. 589). 2. The heel of the foot is prominent (Fig. 590). 3. The great toe cannot be approximated to the last tarsometatarsal joint (Fig. 591).

7. The sacrum is in the right anterior quadrant and the genital groove is in the left oblique diameter.

8. The anterior hip is in the left anterior quadrant and the intertrochanteric diameter is in the right oblique.

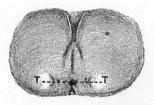

FIG. 588. Anal orifice perforating soft, irregular breech and bisecting a line which joins the tuberosities of the ischium.

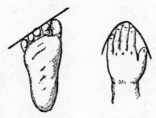

FIG. 589. When the tips of the toes are joined, a straight line is formed.

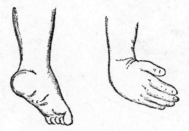

FIG. 590. The foot has a heel.

FIG. 591. The great toe cannot be approximated to the last metatarsophalangeal joint.

COMMENT ON VAGINAL EXAMINATION

If a vaginal examination is made soon after the membranes rupture, no difficulty will be encountered in making a diagnosis of breech presentation. In neglected cases, when the examination is made a number of hours after the membranes have ruptured, many of the landmarks may be so obscured that the soft mass, which contains an opening, may be confused with a face presentation. The differentiation is easy if the relation of the anus to the ischial tuberosities is remembered. Whenever a foot is down, it must be differentiated from a hand. If the examiner will look for the absolute points of difference between a hand and a foot. mentioned under item 6, the differentiation will be easy.

MECHANISM OF THE HIPS—R.S.A.

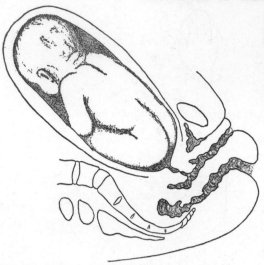

FIG. 592. R.S.A. Onset of labor. Sagittal section.

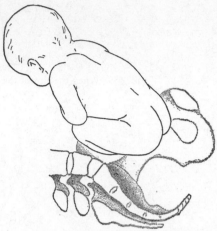

FIG. 593. R.S.A.   Same as Figure 592 showing the relation of the breech to the pelvis.

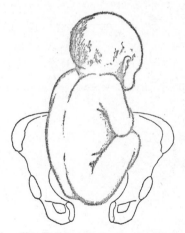

FIG. 594. R.S.A.   Front view in relation to the pelvis at the onset of labor.

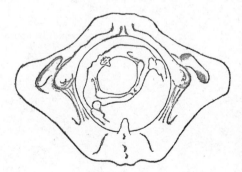

FIG. 595. R.S.A. as visualized from below.

DESCENT is constant throughout the mechanism and the breech enters the pelvis with the sacrum in the right anterior quadrant and the genital groove in the left oblique diameter.   These landmarks, which are useful from the standpoint of nomenclature, are misleading in a study of the mechanism of labor.   Since the anterior hip is that part of the breech which is lowest in the pelvis and the intertrochanteric diameter is the longest diameter of the breech circumference, these two landmarks will follow movements similar to those taken by the occiput and sagittal suture in L.O.A., and the mentum and facial axis in L.M.A.

Internal Rotation

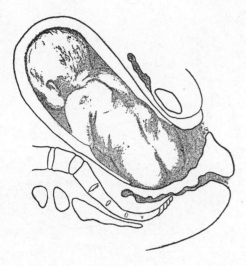

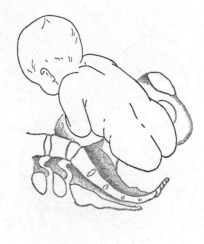

FIG. 596. R.S.A.   Internal rotation of anterior hip.
Sagittal section.

FIG. 597. R.S.A.   Same as Figure 596 showin
the relation of the breech to the pelvis.

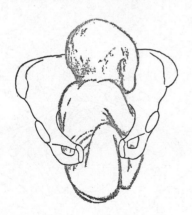

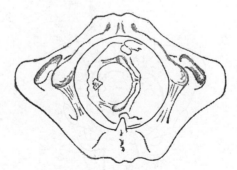

FIG. 598. R.S.A.   Front view of anterior rotation.

FIG. 599. R.S.A. as visualized from below.

INTERNAL ROTATION.   The anterior hip meets the resistance of the pelvic
floor on the left side, and is shunted downward, forward and inward 45° to the
symphysis.   This brings the intertrochanteric diameter into the anteroposterior
of the outlet.

Lateral Flexion

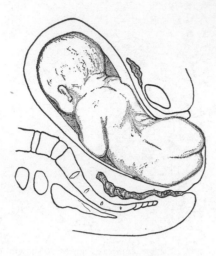

FIG. 600. R.S.A.   Lateral flexion.
Sagittal section.

FIG. 601. R.S.A.   Same as Figure 600 showing
the relation of the breech to the pelvis.

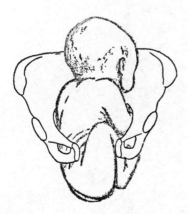

FIG. 602. R.S.A.   Front view of lateral flexion.

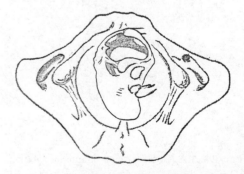

FIG. 603. R.S.A.   Lateral flexion as
visualized from below.

LATERAL FLEXION.   The anterior hip appears in the vulvovaginal ring and
a point just above the pelvic girdle becomes impinged beneath the symphysis.
The posterior hip is then born by lateral flexion.

MECHANISM OF THE SHOULDERS—R.S.A.

Engagement

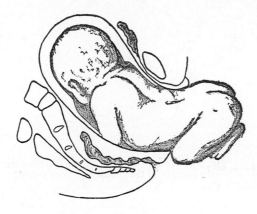

FIG. 604. R.S.A. Engagement of the shoulders. Sagittal section.

FIG. 605. R.S.A. Same as Figure 604 showing the relation of the shoulders to the pelvis.

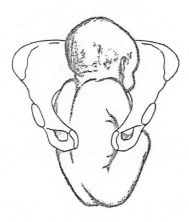

FIG. 606. R.S.A. Front view of engagement of the shoulders.

FIG. 607. R.S.A. Diagram of the shoulders as visualized from below.

ENGAGEMENT of the shoulders is similar to that described for the hips. The anterior shoulder enters the pelvis in the left anterior quadrant and the bisacromial diameter is in the right oblique of the mother's pelvis.

Internal Rotation

FIG. 608. R.S.A. Internal rotation of the anterior shoulder. Sagittal section.

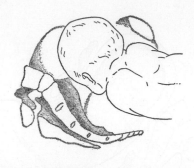

FIG. 609. R.S.A. Same as Figure 608 showing the relation of the shoulders to the pelvis.

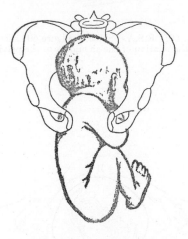

FIG. 610. R.S.A. Front view of internal rotation.

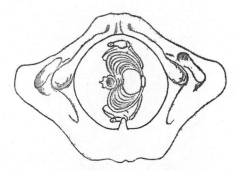

FIG. 611. R.S.A. Diagram of the shoulders as visualized from below.

INTERNAL ROTATION. The anterior shoulder meets the resistance of the pelvic floor and is rotated 45° to the symphysis. The bisacromial diameter then comes into relation with the anteroposterior of the outlet.

LATERAL FLEXION. Theoretically, the anterior shoulder should appear in the vulvovaginal ring, as a point just above the shoulder becomes impinged beneath the symphysis, and it should remain in this position until the posterior shoulder is born by lateral flexion. This step in the mechanism usually does not occur because the weight of the trunk prevents lateral flexion. If the body is supported during this stage of the mechanism, however, nature will be observed to deliver the shoulders as described.

MECHANISM OF THE HEAD—R.S.A.

Flexion

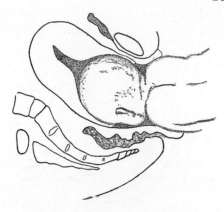

FIG. 612. R.S.A. Flexion and engagement of the aftercoming head. Sagittal section.

FIG. 613. R.S.A. Same as Figure 612 showing the relation of the head to the pelvis.

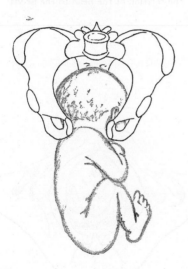

FIG. 614. R.S.A. Front view of engagement of the head.

FIG. 615. R.S.A. Diagram of the aftercoming head engaging, as visualized from below.

FLEXION AND ENGAGEMENT. As the forces from above act upon the after-coming head, its flexion is increased and the head enters the pelvis with the chin against the sternum. The occiput is in the right anterior quadrant and the sagittal diameter is in relation to the left oblique of the pelvis. (Often, the head may enter the pelvis transversely. In these circumstances the mechanism is the same, except for the fact that an additional 45° rotation is necessary to bring the sagittal diameter into the left oblique).

Internal Rotation

FIG. 616. R.S.A. Internal rotation of the aftercoming head. Sagittal section.

FIG. 617. R.S.A. Same as Figure 616 showing the relation of the head to the pelvis.

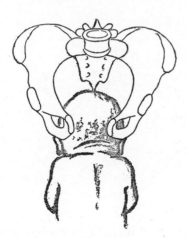

FIG. 618. R.S.A. Front view of internal rotation of the head.

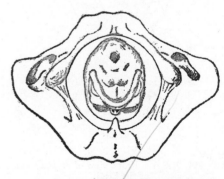

FIG. 619. R.S.A. Diagram of rotation of the aftercoming head, as visualized from below.

INTERNAL ROTATION. At the outlet, the brow rotates 45° to the right and to the hollow of the sacrum. This causes the occiput to rotate 45° to the left and to the symphysis and brings the sagittal diameter into relation with the antero-posterior of the outlet.

Flexion

Fig. 620. R.S.A. Birth of the aftercoming head by flexion. Sagittal section.

Fig. 621. R.S.A. Same as Figure 647 showing the relation of the head to the pelvis.

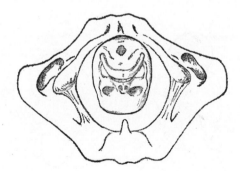

Fig. 622. R.S.A. Flexion of the head as visualized from below.

FLEXION. The nucha becomes arrested under the symphysis and the chin, mouth, nose, orbits, brow, large fontanel, sagittal suture, small fontanel, and occiput are born by flexion.

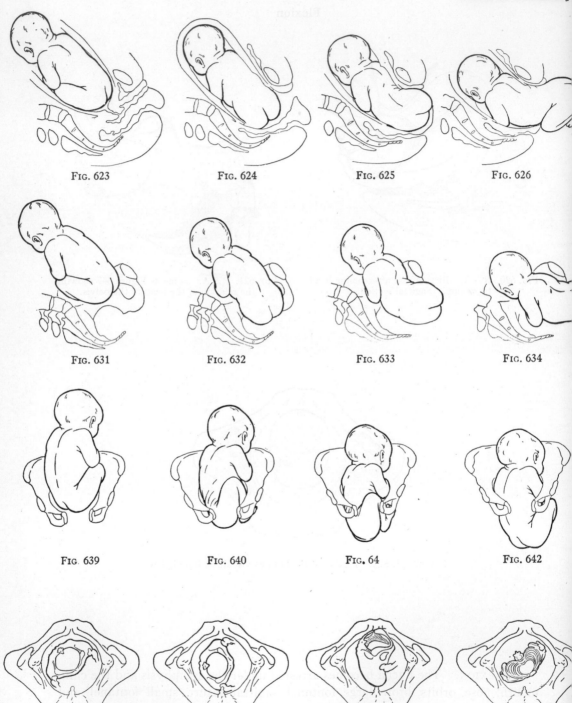

FIG. 623   FIG. 624   FIG. 625   FIG. 626

FIG. 631   FIG. 632   FIG. 633   FIG. 634

FIG. 639   FIG. 640   FIG. 64   FIG. 642

FIG. 646   FIG. 647   FIG. 648   FIG. 649

of R S A Mechanism

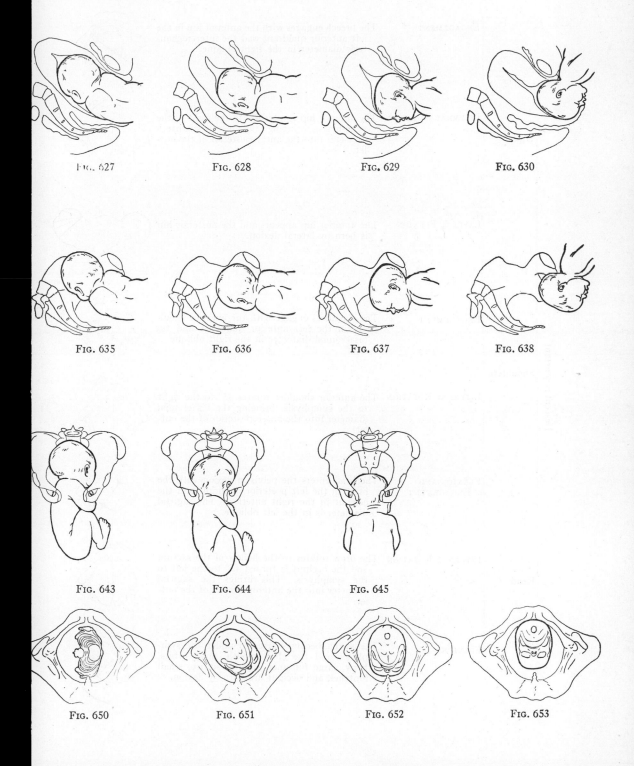

FIG. 627   FIG. 628   FIG. 629   FIG. 630

FIG. 635   FIG. 636   FIG. 637   FIG. 638

FIG. 643   FIG. 644   FIG. 645

FIG. 650   FIG. 651   FIG. 652   FIG. 653

Outline Summary of R S A Mechanism

Hips

ENGAGEMENT   The breech engages with the anterior hip in the left anterior quadrant and the intertrochanteric diameter in the right oblique.

INTERNAL ROTATION   The anterior hip rotates 45° to the right to the symphysis, bringing the intertrochanteric diameter into the anteroposterior of the outlet.

LATERAL FLEXION   The anterior hip appears and the posterior hip is born by lateral flexion.

Shoulders

ENGAGEMENT   The shoulders engage with the anterior shoulder in the left anterior quadrant and the bisacromial diameter in the right oblique.

INTERNAL ROTATION   The anterior shoulder rotates 45° to the right to the symphysis, bringing the bisacromial diameter into the anteroposterior of the outlet.

Head

FLEXION AND ENGAGEMENT   The head enters the pelvis in flexion with the brow in the left posterior quadrant and the occiput in the right anterior. The sagittal diameter is in the left oblique.

INTERNAL ROTATION   The brow rotates to the hollow of the sacrum and the occiput is turned 45° to the left to the symphysis. This brings the sagittal diameter into the anteroposterior of the outlet.

FLEXION   The nucha becomes arrested under the symphysis and the chin, mouth, nose, orbits, brow, large fontanel, sagittal suture, small fontanel, and occiput are born by flexion.

Descent is constant

FIG. 654. Complete breech.

FIG. 656. Frank breech.

FIG. 655. Footling.

In a breech presentation, the legs may be flexed on the thighs and the thighs flexed on the trunk so that the feet and the buttocks present.   This is known as a complete breech (Fig. 654).

Occasionally, the foot is the leading pole; in this case the breech is called a footling (Fig. 655).

Less frequently, the legs may be extended on the thighs, which are flexed on the trunk so that the feet are adjacent to the upper surface of the shoulders. In these circumstances, the buttocks present and the condition is designated a frank breech (Fig. 656).

COMMENT ON THE MECHANISM OF LABOR—R.S.A.

ENGAGEMENT.   Whether the breech be complete, frank or a footling, the pelvic girdle is the largest circumference that must pass through the pelvis. Accordingly, a breech is not considered engaged until the intertrochanteric diameter has passed through the pelvic inlet.   In our description of the mechanism, therefore, this long diameter of the pelvic girdle and that portion of it which is at all times lowest in the pelvis, i.e., the anterior hip, are followed through the pelvis.   The pelvic girdle, accordingly, engages with the anterior hip in the left anterior quadrant and the intertrochanteric diameter in the right oblique for the same reason that the occiput and sagittal suture occupied similar positions in an L.O.A. (Just as in vertex cases, the breech, at times, engages in the transverse diameter).

INTERNAL ROTATION. The anterior hip meets the resistance of the pelvic floor on the left side and moves 45° toward the symphysis for the same reason that internal rotation occurs in anterior positions of the occiput. This brings the longest diameter of the pelvic girdle into the anteroposterior of the outlet.

LATERAL FLEXION. The anterior hip descends until it appears in the vulvo-vaginal ring, after which it becomes arrested and a point above the superior surface of the pelvic girdle impinges beneath the symphysis. The posterior hip, following the curve of Carus, is then born by lateral flexion and the largest diameter that passes through the vulvovaginal ring is somewhat less than the intertrochanteric.

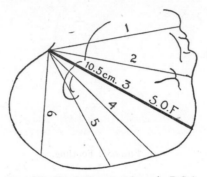

FIG. 657. Head diameters born in R.S.A.

SHOULDER MECHANISM. The shoulders follow the same mechanism as was described for the hips. If the trunk is not supported, lateral flexion may not be so marked as in the hip mechanism and both shoulders may be born at the same time. In these circumstances, the bisacromial diameter is the largest that passes over the fourchette, instead of a diameter somewhat smaller than that observed when lateral flexion takes place.

MECHANISM OF THE AFTERCOMING HEAD. The head usually engages in flexion with the sagittal diameter in the left oblique, although it may, at times, enter the pelvis transversely. The lowest part that comes into contact with the walls of the pelvis is the brow, which is rotated to the hollow of the sacrum for the same reason that the occiput turns posteriorly in the unusual mechanism of posterior positions of the occiput. In other words, the passage of the breech, trunk, and shoulders so diminishes the resistance of the pelvic floor that it no longer influences internal rotation. As a result of posterior rotation of the brow, the occiput turns 45° anteriorly to the left and comes to lie beneath the symphysis, while the sagittal diameter of the head is brought into relation with the antero-posterior of the outlet.

FLEXION. The nucha becomes impinged beneath the symphysis and the head is born by flexion. The diameters that successively distend the vulvo-vaginal ring are the same as those that were observed in anterior positions of the occiput, but their order is reversed. The aftercoming head, therefore, should not cause more trauma than does the head in an occipito-anterior position of the vertex (Fig. 657).

MOLDING. Pressure of the uterus upon the head, as the breech is driven through the pelvis, causes a flattening of the vertex and, as a result, gives the head a characteristic appearance (Fig. 658).

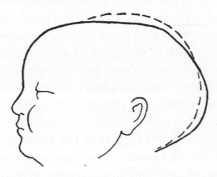

FIG. 658. Characteristic appearance of the head born by the breech mechanism.

POSTERIOR POSITIONS OF THE SACRUM are less common than anterior. On abdominal palpation, the findings are similar to those noted in sacrum anterior, except for the fact that the abdominal characteristics of a posterior position of the dorsum are found.

Posterior positions of the breech usually rotate anteriorly, if they are left to nature. Since the occiput almost always rotates to the front further comment on the mechanism, is not necessary.

PROGNOSIS

MATERNAL DIFFICULTIES. The breech does not fit the pelvis as well as does the vertex. Consequently, early rupture of the membranes is common, and molding of the uterus about the child's body is not infrequent. As a consequence, the dilatation of the cervix may be delayed. In frank breech cases, molding of the uterus is much more common. In addition, the extended legs, acting somewhat as splints, also interfere with lateral flexion and retard the delivery. The birth of the soft breech causes less trauma to the maternal soft parts than does the hard head in vertex presentations. In addition, the diameters that pass through the vulvovaginal ring are the same as those observed in vertex cases. The breech mechanism, therefore, should not cause unusual trauma. On the other hand, if the breech is artificially extracted before the cervix is fully dilated, deep cervical lacerations result from pulling the hard head through the unprepared cervix. This is especially true when the latter becomes constricted about the child's neck. Any effort to deliver the head quickly, because of possible asphyxia, may also cause extensive perineal lacerations. It may therefore be stated that breech presentations cause little trauma to the cervix and perineum if the interests of the child are disregarded and the delivery is left entirely to nature. As this, usually, is unjustifiable, extensive lacerations of the cervix and perineum are bound to follow a rapid extraction done for the sake of the child. The chief maternal dangers, therefore, are trauma and infection from operative interference.

FETAL DIFFICULTIES. The poor fit between the breech and the pelvis leads to an increase in the incidence of dry labor, which interferes with the uteroplacental circulation and may cause asphyxia. For the same reason, prolapse of the umbilical cord may occur. The latter is observed in about 4 per cent of all breech labors and breech presentation is the cause of about one-fourth of all prolapsed cords. While either of these events may lead to asphyxiation, death more commonly is due to compression of the umbilical cord by the aftercoming head as the latter passes through the pelvis. On this account, operative interference may be indicated and the artificial delivery, which is intended as a life-saving measure, may cause injury to the child. Fracture of the humerus, clavicle, femur, spine, or skull, dislocation of the shoulders or cervical vertebrae, brachial plexus paralysis, intracranial hemorrhage and brain lesions, accordingly, are not uncommon (1, 2, 3, 4, 5). Because of these difficulties, the child's chance of survival, when it is born breech first, is much less than in vertex cases. The fetal mortality is about 10 per cent in all cases. If the child is large, the risk is greater, because of the delay in the delivery of the aftercoming head and the increased difficulty of operative interference. Since the shoulder circumference is less than that of the head in premature infants, arrest of the head at the cervix is common in such cases. This delay in the passage of the aftercoming head makes breech delivery extremely hazardous in premature labors (5a).

TREATMENT

BEFORE LABOR. Because of the increased risk of breech presentation to the child, external version is indicated during the prenatal period (6, 7, 8, 9, 10). If this procedure is attempted without the use of anesthesia, and if the manipulations are gentle, it may be done without risk. Although nature frequently corrects a breech presentation in the latter weeks of pregnancy, a careful external version, unquestionably, lessens the risk to the child. Occasionally, the breech presentation recurs after an external cephalic version has been done and the procedure has to be repeated.

FIRST STAGE OF LABOR. Early in labor, external cephalic version may again be tried. At this time, it is much more difficult but occasionally is successful. This procedure should not be attempted if the membranes are ruptured, or if the presenting part is in the pelvis. Anesthesia likewise should not be used, as the manipulations, if sufficiently vigorous, might then cause separation of the placenta.

In those cases in which external version is unsuccessful or not attempted, management of the first stage is similar to that employed in vertex presentations. The establishment of real labor is promoted by the use of a warm enema and by having the patient walk about until true labor pains come with sufficient frequency to permit the giving of sedatives. Morphine and scopolamine are of inestimable value, since they facilitate the dilatation of the cervix and **rest in bed favors the preservation of the membranes.**

SECOND STAGE OF LABOR. When the membranes rupture, a **vaginal examination is made** to verify the diagnosis and rule out prolapse of the umbilical cord.

As soon as the cervix is fully dilated, the patient is transferred to a table and preparations for a breech extraction are made. A snug abdominal binder is then adjusted and with the aid of this and pullers the patient is encouraged to bear down with each labor pain. At the same time, the condition of the child is followed by auscultation of the fetal heart in the interval between uterine contractions. As long as the heart sounds remain within normal limits, labor is allowed to continue until the umbilicus appears.

When the umbilicus is born, the cord is pulled down in order that the operator may constantly feel its pulsations. If the child's condition remains good, **spontaneous delivery is awaited,** and no interference is indicated other than support of the body as it is born (1).

Should the pulsations change, labor must be terminated by extraction of the remainder of the child. Adherence to this routine results in the spontaneous delivery of many multiparae. In primiparae, on the other hand, assistance generally is needed. As a rule, it is not difficult because by the time that the indication for interference arises, the arms are flexed and may be easily delivered.

BREECH EXTRACTION

REQUISITES FOR BREECH EXTRACTION. The following requirements must be fulfilled before extraction of the breech is attempted:

1. The cervix must be fully dilated.
2. The inlet of the pelvis must be ample.
3. The outlet must be ample.
4. The soft parts of the outlet must be manually dilated or ironed out. A mediolateral episiotomy often is indicated.
5. The bladder must be emptied by catheterization.
6. The rectum must be emptied by a previous enema.
7. The patient must be on a table.
8. An assistant must be at hand to make suprapubic pressure. **Traction must not be made without accompanying suprapubic pressure.**

9. Anesthesia by a competent anesthetist must be available.
10. The child must be alive.
11. Aseptic precautions must be observed.

COMMENT ON THE REQUISITES FOR BREECH EXTRACTION

1. **The cervix must be fully dilated.** This requisite is self-evident. When neglected, it results in the death of the child and extensive cervical lacerations. If the external os is not large enough to permit the passage of the aftercoming head, the cervix should be manually dilated or incised before the extraction is attempted.

2. **The inlet of the pelvis must be ample.** Few complications in obstetrics can cause the operator more chagrin than arrest of the aftercoming head which results from contraction of the pelvic inlet. Previous mensuration of the pelvis will prevent such an unfortunate occurrence. In this connection, it must be remembered that the aftercoming head does not have the advantage of the molding which is seen in vertex mechanisms. Consequently, a pelvis which might permit the spontaneous delivery of a well molded vertex may require perforation of an aftercoming head before the delivery can be effected.

3. **The outlet must be ample.** Not only is there danger of loss of the child when the bony outlet is contracted, but the need for more room in the posterior sagittal region results in extensive laceration. A complete tear, therefore, is a common complication of breech extraction in funnel pelves.

4. **The soft parts of the outlet must be dilated.** When breech extraction is started before the breech is born, it usually is possible "to iron out" or manually dilate the pelvic floor sufficiently to minimize the trauma that otherwise might result from the extraction. If this cannot be accomplished, a deep medio lateral episiotomy should be made in order that the pelvic floor may offer no obstruction when that part of the extraction which requires haste is reached. Attention to this detail will result in the saving of many breech babies.

5. **The bladder must be emptied.** Before attempting the extraction, the bladder should be catheterized with a sterile rubber catheter. Glass catheters should never be used in obstetric practice.

6. **The rectum must be emptied.** To prevent contamination of the operative field, the rectum should be emptied by an enema. Usually, this has been done earlier in the labor; in these circumstances it need not be repeated.

7. **The patient must be on a table.** Throughout most of the extraction, downward traction is made in the axis of the pelvic inlet. When the patient is lying in bed such traction is impossible. The advantage of having the patient on a table, accordingly, is obvious. If an emergency arises and the patient cannot be transferred to a table, she should be placed across the bed with her buttocks at the edge and her feet supported by two chairs in order that proper traction may be made.

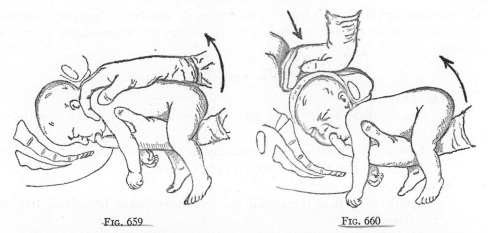

FIG. 659   FIG. 660

FIG. 659. Mauriceau-Smellie-Veit maneuver.   Suprapubic pressure must be made by an assistant, while the operator keeps the head flexed with the fingers of one hand in the mouth or canine fossae and with the other makes enough traction to guide the child out of the pelvis.

FIG. 660. Wigand-Martin maneuver.   Suprapubic pressure is made with one hand while the other keeps the head flexed and guides it out of the pelvis.

8. **Suprapubic pressure is necessary.**   In the Mauriceau maneuver, the fingers of one hand are passed into the mouth or canine fossae and keep the head flexed while the other hand makes traction on the shoulders (11, 12) (Fig. 659). Before making any traction, an assistant should be shown how to make pressure on the fundus of the uterus.   Traction from below without suprapubic pressure interferes with the flexion of the child and may result in extension of the arm over the head or partial extension of the aftercoming head.   These complications sometimes lead to great difficulty and therefore should be avoided whenever possible.   If an assistant is not available, the operator himself should make suprapubic pressure with one hand while he guides the child with the other, as in the Wigand-Martin maneuver (13) (Fig. 660).

9. **Anesthesia is necessary.**   If possible, a competent anesthetist should be at hand.   While manual dilatation of the outlet is being effected, and during the manipulations required for Pinard's maneuver, the anesthesia should be deep enough to produce relaxation.   It then should be lightened sufficiently to allow the patient to assist the extraction with her own bearing-down efforts.   After the mouth is born, she should be so lightly anesthetized that she may be able, within a very short time, to complete the delivery by her voluntary efforts. Excellent results are obtained by the use of local anaesthesia.

10. **The child must be alive.**   If, for any reason, the delivery is so delayed that there is no possibility of the child's survival, the need for haste no longer exists and care should be taken to preserve the maternal soft parts.   If it is certain that the child is dead, perforation of the aftercoming head is indicated.

11. **Asepsis.**   The patient's vulva and the physician's hands must be rendered as sterile as possible before breech extraction is attempted.   In addition,

the operator should rinse his hands in an antiseptic solution at frequent intervals in the course of the extraction, because the possibility of contamination is always present.

INDICATIONS FOR BREECH EXTRACTION

MATERNAL:

    Time indication—2 hours plus $\frac{1}{2}$ hour in the second stage without progress.

    Emergency indication—any maternal emergency which is accompanied by more risk than is a breech extraction.

FETAL:

    Before the birth of the umbilicus—fetal heart below 100, above 160, or irregular.

    After the birth of the umbilicus—any change in the rate or regularity of the pulsations in the umbilical cord.

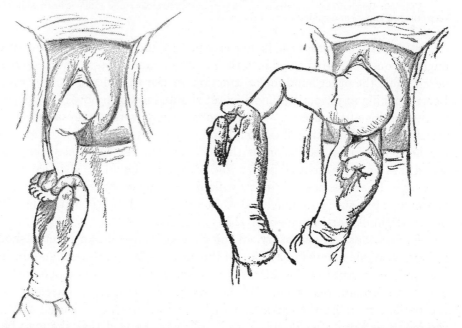

FIG. 661. Traction in the direction of the axis of the pelvic inlet assisted by suprapubic pressure.

FIG. 662. Delivery of the posterior foot while elevating the anterior.

The maternal indications for breech extraction arise from a delay in the progress of labor or some emergency condition in the mother.

Since a prolongation of labor is more common in the frank breech cases, the time indication for interference usually arises in this variety of breech presentation. If all of the requisites have been fulfilled and arrest in the progress takes place after the patient has had an average second stage, termination of the labor by breech extraction is justifiable.

The condition of the mother in some cases may be such that a continuation of the labor after the requisites for extraction are fulfilled will be accompanied by greater danger than is entailed by breech extraction. In these circumstances, extraction of the breech is indicated. This indication, therefore, may arise in labor complicated by cardiac failure, pneumonia, tuberculosis, and other systemic diseases. In the presence of great hemorrhage, extraction may be the means of meeting the emergency, as in premature separation of a normally implanted placenta. **A breech extraction should not be attempted in placenta previa,** because it may cause rupture of the uterus.

Fetal embarrassment is common in all varieties of breech presentation, and is the usual indication for breech extraction. Before the umbilicus is born, the child's condition is followed by auscultation of the fetal heart following each uterine contraction. If the rate falls below 100, goes above 160 or becomes irregular, and **the requisites for breech extraction are fulfilled,** an immediate extraction is indicated. After the umbilicus is born, any change in the rate or regularity of the pulsations in the umbilical cord warrants an immediate breech extraction.

FIG. 663. With the thumbs over the buttocks, traction is continued until the umbilicus appears.

BREECH EXTRACTION. When one of the indications for delivery of the child by breech extraction arises, a foot is brought down, and traction is made in the axis of the pelvic inlet, while an assistant makes pressure over the fundus in the same direction (Fig. 661).

The posterior foot is delivered by flexing the leg on the thigh. If this cannot be accomplished, traction may be aided by the introduction of a finger into the posterior groin (Fig. 662).

After the breech is born, a thumb is placed over each buttock and traction is continued in the same direction until the umbilicus appears (Fig. 663).

The cord is now pulled out and its pulsations are noted. If the rate is normal and regular, no great haste is required for the completion of the delivery. Traction in a downward direction is continued until the anterior scapula is observed beneath the pubic arch.

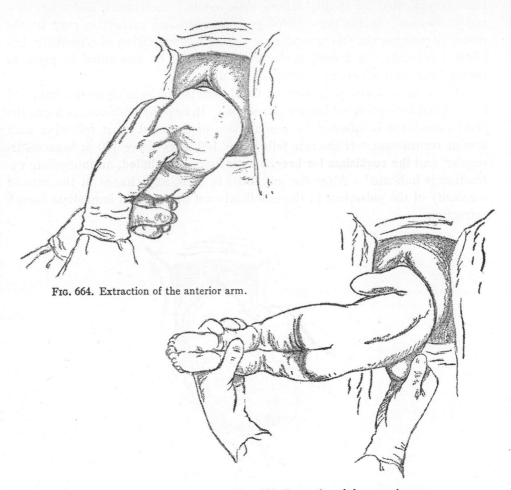

FIG. 664. Extraction of the anterior arm.

FIG. 665. Extraction of the posterior arm.

The anterior arm is extracted by passing the finger along the arm to the elbow and forcing it down over the chest (Fig. 664). Care should be taken to avoid fracture of the humerus at this stage. By splinting the arm between the thumb and forefinger, and making pressure only in the region of the elbow, fracture is prevented. If any difficulty is encountered, it may be better to extract the posterior arm first.

After the anterior arm is delivered, the child's trunk is slightly elevated to bring the posterior shoulder farther down in the pelvis. The hand is then passed over the scapula to the elbow of the posterior arm and the latter is brought down over the chest (Fig. 665).

In those cases in which the anterior arm is not delivered first, its extraction is once more attempted after the posterior arm is born. If this is again unsuccessful, the body is gently circumducted by carrying the feet downward and then upward through an arc of 180° toward the groin which is on the same side as the dorsum. The opposite hand simultaneously rotates the posterior scapula forward. The anterior shoulder is thus carried into the hollow of the sacrum and its extraction is thereby facilitated. When this procedure is used, however, great care must be taken to avoid injury of the brachial plexus.

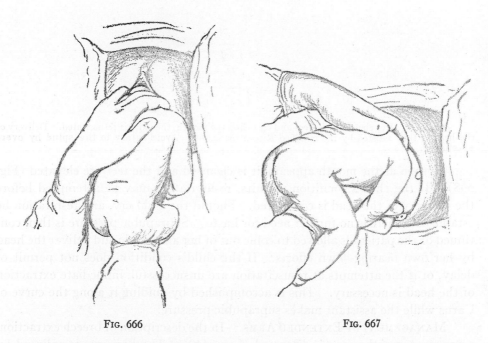

FIG. 666.   FIG. 667.

FIG. 666. The Smellie-Veit or Mauriceau maneuver, directing the descent of the head which is delivered as a result of suprapubic pressure made by the assistant.
FIG. 667. While maintaining flexion, the body is elevated and the chin and mouth are born as the face passes along the curve of Carus.

Following the delivery of the shoulders, the child is placed astride the arm of the operator, and a finger is introduced into the mouth to keep the head flexed. Two fingers of the other hand are then placed over each shoulder and sufficient traction is made to guide the head through the pelvis. The force that delivers the head, however, must be furnished almost entirely by suprapubic pressure (Figs. 666 and 667). This method of breech extraction is known as the Smellie-Veit or Mauriceau maneuver.

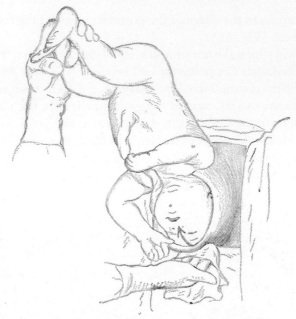

FIG. 668. After elevating the feet and cleansing the mouth, the child is resuscitated. **Delivery of the head is then assisted by the modified Ritgen maneuver. Avoid injury to the spine by over-extension.**

As soon as the mouth appears, it is cleansed and the feet are elevated (Fig. 668). If the child's condition permits, resuscitation may be attempted before the delivery of the head is completed. Should the child cry, and respiration be established, there is no further need for haste. Suprapubic pressure is then continued or the patient is allowed to come out of her anesthetic and deliver the head by her own bearing-down efforts. If the child's condition does not permit of delay, or if the attempts at resuscitation are unsuccessful, immediate extraction of the head is necessary. This is accomplished by guiding it along the curve of Carus while the assistant makes suprapubic pressure.

MANAGEMENT OF EXTENDED ARMS. In the description of breech extraction, management of the arms is discussed (page 440). The humerus is splinted by the thumb and fingers, and pressure is made in the region of the inner surface of the elbow. This causes the arm to flex on the forearm, after which it is brought down over the face and chest. If this maneuver is difficult, it may be facilitated by pushing the head upward sufficiently to release the small parts which may be caught between the head and the pelvic brim.

MANAGEMENT OF NUCHAL ARMS. Should the extended arms become lodged below the occiput and around the neck, their management often is extremely difficult. If the child's trunk is rotated slightly in the direction of the hand that is to be dislodged, the manipulations may be made more easily. If these manipulations cannot then be carried out, greater pressure should be used, even though it results in fracture of the humerus, as a fracture is preferable to the loss of the child (Fig. 669).

FIG. 669. Rotation of the trunk to release a nuchal arm.

MANAGEMENT OF FRANK BREECH. When the legs are extended on the thighs in frank breech presentations, labor is interfered with by the tendency of the uterus to mold itself over the child and by the increased difficulty of lateral flexion which results from the splint-like action of the lower extremities. In general, two plans may be followed in the management of such cases. In one, the frank breech is broken up and a foot is brought down by Pinard's maneuver. With two fingers of one hand, the anterior thigh is forced outward in the direction of the dorsum (Fig. 670). This causes the leg to flex and brings the anterior foot within the grasp of the operator's fingers (Fig. 671). Gentle traction on the foot then accomplishes its delivery (Fig. 672).

In the other plan, the frank breech is allowed to deliver as such. If assistance is required, a finger is placed in the anterior groin and traction is made until the breech has descended sufficiently to permit a finger of the other hand to be placed in the posterior groin (Fig. 673).

When a frank breech is broken up by Pinard's maneuver, the labor progresses more rapidly and traction on the foot can easily be made if interference is indicated (14). A footling presentation, however, is not so good a dilator as the frank breech, and the possibility of the aftercoming head being held back by the cervix is the chief disadvantage. On the other hand, while the frank breech is a better dilator, it frequently causes a delay in the labor. Extraction likewise is much more difficult than in a footling presentation, should an indication for interference arise.

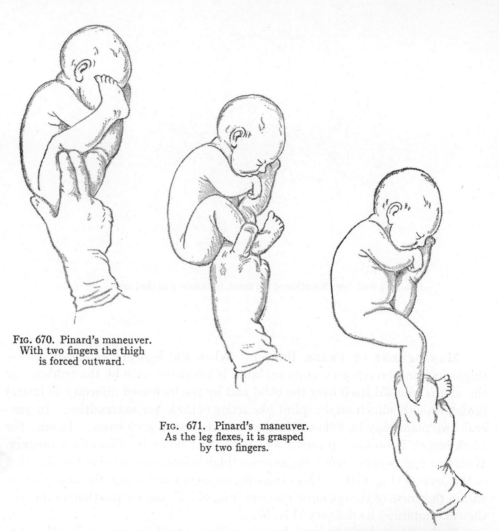

FIG. 670. Pinard's maneuver.
With two fingers the thigh
is forced outward.

FIG. 671. Pinard's maneuver.
As the leg flexes, it is grasped
by two fingers.

FIG. 672. Pinard's maneuver.
Traction on the foot completes the maneuver.

It is impossible to recommend the proper procedure in all cases. Knowing the advantages and disadvantages of each method, however, the choice can be made to suit the individual circumstance. In general, it may be said that it is a good plan to break up a frank breech by Pinard's maneuver whenever a delay in the progress of labor is observed and the breech is high.   Because the difficulties are increased by molding of the uterus, this should be done as soon after the membranes are ruptured as the decision to interfere can be made.

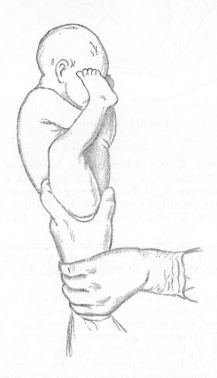

FIG. 673. Traction on frank breech by a finger placed in the groin.   Never use two fingers as they may cause dislocation of the hip.

MANAGEMENT OF POSTERIOR POSITIONS OF THE BREECH.   As spontaneous rotation of a posterior breech is the rule, this event is to be awaited, unless an indication for delivery arises.   Should extraction be necessary, the trunk can be easily rotated.   If the occiput turns to the hollow of the sacrum, and cannot be rotated anteriorly, it is delivered by the Prague maneuver (15, 16) (Fig. 674).

BREECH PRESENTATION IN ELDERLY PRIMIPARAE.   When breech presentation occurs in an elderly primipara, cesarean section is indicated before or early in labor, because of the great risk to the child.   Here, the indication is fetal and is based upon the assumption that the elderly primipara has little chance of again becoming pregnant (17, 18).

FIG. 674. Prague maneuver.

REFERENCES

1. GORDON, C. A., GARLICK, R. AND OGINZ, P.: An Analysis of 3,301 Breech Deliveries in the Hospitals of Brooklyn, N. Y.   Am. J. O. & G., 1934, 28, 140.
2. HOLLAND, E.: Cranial Stress in the Foetus during Labor and on the Effects of Excessive Stress on the Intracranial Contents.   J. O. & G., Brit. Emp., 1922, 29, 551.
3. CAPON, M. B.: Intracranial Traumata in the Newborn.   J. O. & G., Brit. Emp., 1922, 29, 572.
4. CROTHERS, B.: Injury to the Spinal Cord in Breech Extraction as an Important Cause of Foetal Death and of Paraplegia in Childhood.   Am. J. M. Sc., 1923, 165, 94.
5. MORTON, D. G.: Fetal Mortality and Breech Presentation.   Am. J. O. & G., 1932, 24, 853.
5a. BECK, A. C.: The Obstetricians Responsibility for the Hazards of the First Few Days of Life, with Special Reference to Anoxia and Prematurity.   Am. J. O. & G., 1946, 51, 173.
6. GIBBERD, G. F.: An Investigation into the Results of Breech, Labor and of Prophylactic External Cephalic Version during Pregnancy; with a Note on the Technic of External Version.   J. O. & G., Brit. Emp., 1927, 34, 509.
7. BARTHOLOMEW, R. A.: Prophylactic External Version.   Am. J. O. & G., 1927, 14, 648.
8. McGUINNESS, F. G.: Prophylactic External Cephalic Version in Breech Presentation.   Can. Med. Assn. J., 1928, 18, 289.
9. KING, E. L. AND GLADDEN, A. H.: The Fetal Mortality in Breech Presentations.   Is Prophylactic External Version Advisable?   Am. J. O. & G., 1929, 17, 78.
10. STUDDEFORD, W. E.: Breech Presentations and Their Delivery.   J. A. M. A., 1932, 99, 1820.
11. MAURICEAU: Le moyen d'accoucher la femme, quand l'enfant presente un ou deux pieds les premiers.   Traité des Maladies des Femmes Grosses, 1740, 7th ed., p. 280.
12. SMELLIE, W.: The First Class of Preternatural Labors; When the Feet, Breech or Lower Parts of the Foetus Present.   A Treatise on the Theory and Practice of Midwifery. 1774, 8th ed., 195.
13. WINCKEL: Zur Beförderung der Geburt des Nachfolgenden Kopfes mit Demonstration. Verhandl. d. deutsch. Gesellsch. f. Gyn., 1888, 2, 19.
14. AHLFELD, F.: Ueber Behandlung der gedoppelten Steisslagen reifer Kinder bei Erstgebärenden.   Arch. f. Gyn., 1873, 5, 174.
15. KIWISCH, F. H.: Die Geburtskunde, Erlangen, 1851.
16. PUGH, B.: A Treatise on Midwifery, Chiefly with Regard to the Operation with Several Improvements in that Art.   London, 1754.
17. IRVING AND GOETHALS: Elimination of the Second Stage of Labor in Breech Presentations. Am. J. O. & G., 1926, 11, 80.
18. PIPER, E. B. AND BACHMAN, C.: The Prevention of Fetal Injuries in Breech Delivery. J. A. M. A., 1929, 92, 217.

CHAPTER XX

TRANSVERSE PRESENTATION

In a TRANSVERSE PRESENTATION, the shoulder is the presenting part, and the long axis of the fetus is at right angles to that of the mother. Anterior and posterior positions are determined by the location of the dorsum while the situation of the head establishes the position as a right or left. A left scapulo-anterior, therefore, is a transverse presentation in which the shoulder is the presenting part, the dorsum is directed anteriorly, and the head is on the left side.

ETIOLOGY. The commonest cause of transverse presentation is a lack of adaptation between the fetal and uterine ovoids. It accordingly is most commonly found in association with prematurity, dead fetus, lax uterus, multiparity, an excess of amniotic fluid, contracted pelvis, and multiple pregnancy (1, 2, 3).

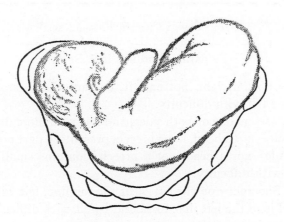

FIG. 675. Right Scapulo Anterior, R.Sc.A.

FREQUENCY. Transverse presentation occurs slightly less than once in every 200 labors. Owing to the laxness of the uterine musculature in women who have given birth to a number of children, this complication is much more common in multiparae. When it is observed in a primipara, contracted pelvis always must be ruled out as the etiological factor. In over 10 per cent of all twin labors one of the fetuses lies transversely (2, 3).

447

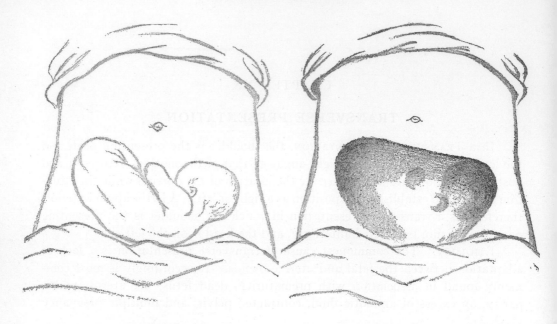

FIG. 677. L.Sc.A. as visualized through the abdominal wall.

FIG. 678. Touch picture in L.Sc.A

Palpation Findings in L.Sc.A.

1. Dorsum—not on right, not on left, lies anteriorly, crosses the midline, and is felt with difficulty.
2. Small Parts—on one or both sides, and felt with difficulty.
3. Lower Pole—not a head, not a breech, presenting part not felt.
4. Upper Pole—not a head, not a breech, contains small parts which are felt with difficulty.
5. Anterior Shoulder—on the left, near the midline, felt with difficulty.
6. The head is in the left iliac fossa and is felt with difficulty.
7. The fundus is lower than normal. Often it is at or near the level of the umbilicus.

Comment on Abdominal Palpation

Comparison of the two sides is unsatisfactory as they seem to be equally resistant. Small parts may be felt on one or both sides near the fundus of the uterus. Often, however, the uterus is so tense that the small parts cannot be distinguished. Absence of anything resembling a head or breech in the lower pole should suggest the possibility of a transverse presentation. This suspicion is strengthened by finding the head in the left iliac fossa. Unfortunately, in many cases, the latter evidence is obscured by the tenseness of the uterus. The most valuable finding is the detection of a so-called **squat uterus**. Whenever the fundus is at or near the level of the umbilicus and the previous items in our palpation routine are doubtful or impossible to make out, transverse presentation should be suspected until proved otherwise by further investigation.

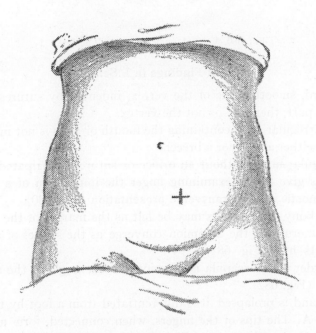

FIG. 679. Location of the fetal heart sounds in L.Sc.A.

Auscultation Findings in L.Sc.A.

The fetal heart sounds are transmitted through the dorsum and shoulder to the lower left quadrant of the mother's abdomen. Because of the ease with which they are located on the left side and near the midline, auscultation often leads to the erroneous diagnosis of an L.O.A.

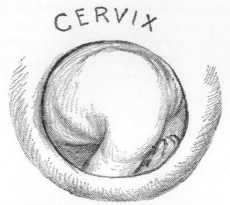

FIG. 680. Vaginal touch picture in L.Sc.A.

Vaginal Findings in L.Sc.A.

1. The hard, smooth dome of the vertex, indented by sutures, is not felt. The presenting part, therefore, is not the vertex.

2. A soft, irregular mass containing the mouth or anus is not made out. It accordingly is neither a face nor a breech.

3. An irregular mass, without an orifice or sutures, is palpated.

4. The ribs give to the examining finger the impression of a **gridiron, an absolutely diagnostic sign of transverse presentation** (Fig. 680).

5. Several bony prominences may be felt as the margin of the scapula, the clavicle, the humerus and the acromion converge as the spokes of a wheel converge toward its hub (Fig. 681).

6. The border of the scapula is anterior and the angle of the axilla points toward the left (Fig. 682).

7. If the hand is prolapsed, it is differentiated from a foot by the following characteristics: A. The tips of the fingers, when connected, form a curved line (Fig. 683).   B. No heel is present (Fig. 684).   C. The thumb can be made to touch the base of the little finger (Fig. 685).

8. An attempt to shake hands with the prolapsed member shows it to be a right hand.

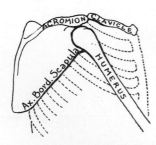

FIG. 681. Radiating bony prominences.

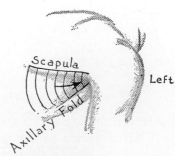

FIG. 682. The scapula is anterior and the angle of the axilla points to the left—L.Sc.A.

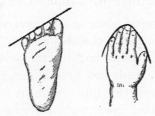

FIG. 683. The tips of the fingers, when joined, form a curved line while a straight line is formed by the toes.

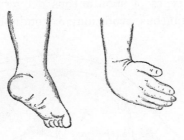

FIG. 684. No heel is felt.

FIG. 685. The thumb may be made to touch the base of the little finger.

Comment on Vaginal Examination

Early in labor, the presenting part is high and may not be felt unless the whole hand is introduced into the vagina. Later, the irregular shoulder, with its absolute characteristics, may be made out. When neither sutures nor an opening can be felt in an irregular presenting part, a shoulder presentation should be suspected and careful search for the characteristic gridiron feel of the ribs should be made to clinch the diagnosis. Palpation of the axilla shows the position of the dorsum and the head. If the scapular border is anterior, the back is in front. Since the angle of the axilla always points toward the head, it is directed to the left in an L.Sc.A. (Fig. 682). When a hand is prolapsed, it may be differentiated from a foot by the absolute points of difference between these two structures. The presence of a hand, however, does not make the diagnosis of a transverse presentation certain, as a hand may occasionally be prolapsed in a vertex presentation. By attempting to shake hands with the prolapsed member, it is possible to tell whether it is a right or a left hand. In left anterior positions, the right hand is down.

MECHANISM OF LABOR—L.SC.A.

In practice the mechanism of labor in a transverse presentation is not considered, since impaction is the rule if the abnormality is not corrected. In this event, the shoulders are driven somewhat into the pelvis, and the neck becomes greatly elongated, while the head and breech remain above the pelvic brim (Fig. 686). As labor continues, the upper segment is retracted until the child lies wholly within the thinned out lower uterine segment. Often, the latter ruptures and the fetus passes through the rent into the peritoneal cavity.

Theoretically, three types of spontaneous delivery are possible: 1. spontaneous version; 2. spontaneous evolution; 3. conduplicatio corpore.

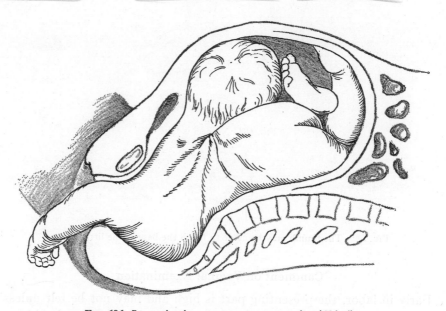

FIG. 686. Impaction in a transverse presentation (Chiari).

SPONTANEOUS VERSION may occur during the latter months of pregnancy and early in labor before the membranes rupture. The transverse presentation then becomes a vertex or a breech and the subsequent mechanism of labor is that of the new presentation. While this fortunate event occasionally does occur in multiparae, the possibility of its happening is not to be awaited in any transverse presentation unless the child is premature or very small.

SPONTANEOUS EVOLUTION. Here the first part of the mechanism is similar to that described under impaction. The neck becomes so elongated that the shoulders slip into the pelvis and the arm passes out of the vagina. The thorax then descends and is followed by the breech, after which the head is born as in a breech presentation. This mechanism is very rare and is possible only when the child is dead or the pelvis is large (4, 5, 6) (Figs. 688, 689, 690, 691).

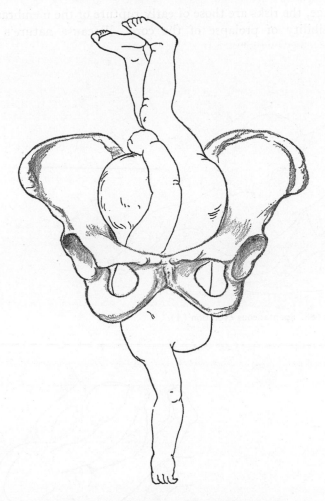

FIG. 687. Conduplicatio corpore (Kleinwachter).

CONDUPLICATIO CORPORE. The first part of the mechanism is similar to that previously described. The back then becomes bent upon itself and is delivered while the head is pressed into the abdomen. The greatly compressed and doubled up remainder of the child is then expelled (7) (Fig. 687). This mechanism is possible only when the child is small and after considerable maceration has taken place.

PROGNOSIS

The dangers of transverse presentation are slight if the condition is recognized and treated early in labor. If neglected, however, transverse becomes a formidable complication and may cause the death of the mother and the child.

In the first stage, the risks are those of early rupture of the membranes together with the possibility of prolapse of the cord. Because nature's hydrostatic

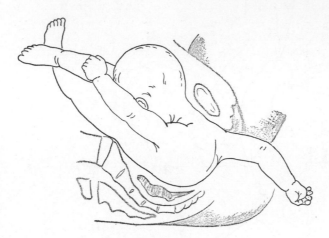

FIG. 688. Spontaneous evolution (A).

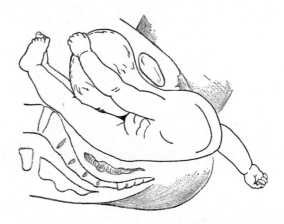

FIG. 689. Spontaneous evolution (B).

dilator is not replaced by a descending presenting part, the stage of dilatation may be greatly prolonged even in multiparae. In the second stage, the danger of impaction and rupture of the uterus is always to be feared. The risk of operative interference depends upon the procedure employed and the conditions that are present when it is done. It accordingly varies from the negligible risk of an external version done early in labor to the great danger of uterine rupture from version or embryotomy performed late in labor. Rupture of the uterus is

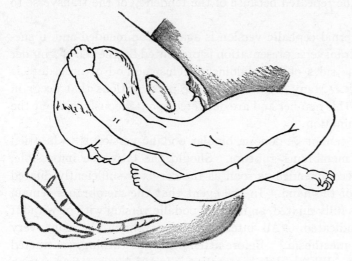

FIG. 690. Spontaneous evolution (C).

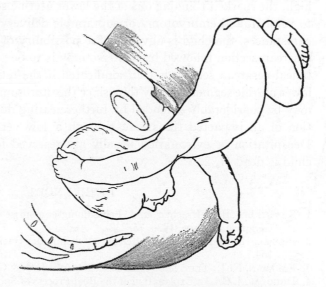

FIG. 691. Spontaneous evolution (D) (Webster).

followed by shock, hemorrhage or peritonitis, any one or all of which may cause the death of the mother.

The child, if neglected, dies from asphyxia. When version is done in neglected cases, fractures, paralyses, and brain hemorrhage may result.

TREATMENT

Before labor, external version is indicated. It usually can easily be performed but often must be repeated because of the tendency of the transverse to recur.

Early in labor, external cephalic version is again recommended and, if successful, recurrence of a transverse presentation is prevented by the use of a binder and pads applied to the sides of the abdomen. This method of procedure is simple and without risk. Many of the transverse presentations that occur in our clinic are treated in this manner and are delivered spontaneously without the need for a vaginal examination.

If external version cannot be done, a bipolar podalic version is to be tried immediately after the membranes rupture. Should the latter be impossible, an internal version is recommended as soon as the cervix is sufficiently dilated to permit the passage of the hand. In the event that the membranes remain intact until the cervix is fully dilated, an internal podalic version with or without breech extraction is indicated. (All internal versions should be done very slowly and under **deep anesthesia**.) Before attempting the turning, contracted pelvis must be ruled out. When pelvic contraction is found, low cesarean section is the operation of choice. If the shoulder is impacted and the retraction ring is high, the marked thinning out of the lower uterine segment is a contraindication to version, and embryotomy or suprapubic delivery is advised. If, in such circumstances, the child is alive and the possibility of infection is not too great, a cesarean section followed by hysterectomy is to be preferred. Low or extraperitoneal cesarean section is contraindicated if the retraction ring is high and the lower uterine segment is very thin, since the uterus may be ruptured or the incision may be considerably extended by further tearing during the turning and extraction of an impacted transverse through a low vertical or transverse incision. Decapitation or evisceration usually are reserved for those cases in which the child is dead (1, 2, 3).

REFERENCES

1. KAMNIKER, H.: Ursachen und Behandlungsergebnisse der Querlagen. Monatschr. f. Geburtsh. u. Gyn., 1926, 75, 233.
2. PUPPEL, E. AND MÜNZEL, W.: Beitrag zur Klinik der Querlagen. Arch. f. Gyn., 1931, 145, 164.
3. EASTMAN, N. J.: Transverse Presentation. Am. J. O. & G., 1932, 24, 40.
4. DOUGLAS, J. C.: An Explanation of the Real Process of Spontaneous Evolution of the Fetus. Dublin, 1819.
5. STEPHENSON, H. A.: The Mechanism of Labor in Spontaneous Evolution. Johns Hopkins Hosp. Bull., 1915, 26, 331.
6. EASTMAN, N. J.: Spontaneous Evolution of the Fetus in Transverse Presentation. Am. J. O. & G., 1933, 25, 382.
7. KLEINWÄCHTER: Beitrag zur Lehre von der Selbstentwicklung. Arch. f. Gyn., 1871, 2, 111.

CHAPTER XXI

COMPOUND PRESENTATION AND PROLAPSE OF THE UMBILICAL CORD

Compound presentations are those in which one or more small parts present with the head or breech. They occur once in every 300 labors.

PRESENTATION OF A HAND OR ARM WITH THE HEAD

Presentation of the hand or arm with the head is the commonest variety. Frequently, only the fingers may be felt alongside the head, but, occasionally, the whole hand and even part of the arm may be prolapsed (1, 2) (Fig. 692).

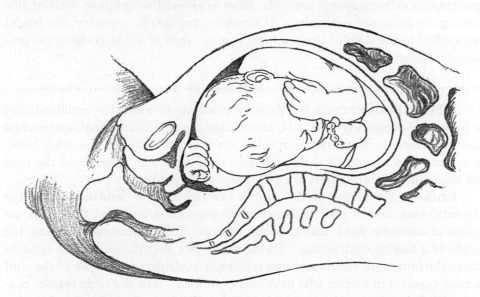

Fig. 692. Presentation of a hand and arm together with the head (Braun's section).

ETIOLOGY. Those conditions which prevent a close approximation of the presenting part to the pelvis are the underlying causes of a compound presentation. They are: contracted pelvis, faulty axis of the uterus, multiple pregnancy, large head, abnormal presentation and an excess of amniotic fluid.

DIAGNOSIS. On vaginal examination, the extremity may be felt alongside or below the head. Its characteristics, as described under transverse and breech presentations, serve to differentiate the hand from the foot, and thus prevent the erroneous diagnosis of a breech presentation. The possibility of a transverse presentation likewise is ruled out by palpating the head and its sutures.

MECHANISM OF LABOR. Prolapse of an extremity increases the engaging diameters and often leads to considerable dystocia. The presenting part, accordingly, remains high until the death of the child reduces these diameters sufficiently to permit their passage through the pelvis. If the child is small, however, labor may not be obstructed. Prolapse of the cord is common and a change in the original presentation occasionally takes place.

TREATMENT. Before attempting to reposit the prolapsed extremity, the promontory of the sacrum should be sought in order that the possibility of contracted pelvis may be ruled out. In the absence of pelvic contraction the extremity is replaced under deep anesthesia. Following reposition, the head should be forced into the pelvis to prevent a recurrence. If the arm subsequently prolapses, a version is recommended. In the event that reposition is impossible, as frequently is the case when the arm is extended over the back of the neck, internal podalic version is indicated. When the head is low in the pelvis and spontaneous delivery seems probable, labor is allowed to continue without disturbing the prolapsed extremity. If forceps extraction is necessary, the blades are applied to the sides of the head and care is taken to avoid grasping the prolapsed member.

FUNIC PRESENTATION AND PROLAPSE OF THE UMBILICAL CORD

A FUNIC PRESENTATION is a primary condition in which the umbilical cord is below the presenting part. It accordingly may be found in this abnormal position before the membranes rupture. PROLAPSED CORD, on the other hand, is secondary to rupture of the membranes (Fig. 693). In either case, the cord lies below the presenting part after the membranes rupture.

ETIOLOGY. Prolapse of the cord is favored by: low implantation of the placenta, long cord, a poor fit between the presenting part and the pelvis, an excess of amniotic fluid, and artificial rupture of the membranes during the height of a uterine contraction. Owing to the fact that the head often remains above the brim until the membranes rupture in multiparae, prolapse of the cord is more common in women who have borne children. For the same reason, contracted pelvis, abnormal presentation and multiple pregnancies are frequent etiological factors (3, 4, 5).

EFFECT ON LABOR. Prolapse of the cord does not alter the mechanism of labor and is without effect on the mother if interference, in the interest of the child, is not attempted. Compression of the cord between the child and the pelvis is a frequent cause of fetal asphyxia and is responsible for the high fetal mortality that follows this accident. The danger obviously is much greater in head presentations.

DIAGNOSIS. Since prompt treatment is imperative, a vaginal or rectal examination is indicated immediately after the membranes rupture. If the presenting part is not engaged before this event takes place, a search for a prolapsed cord is essential. The same is urgently recommended whenever auscultation shows evidence of fetal embarrassment soon after the membranes rupture. The finding of a pulsating cord-like mass in the cervix or vagina establishes the diagnosis. An inexperienced physician may mistake the pulsations which sometimes are felt in the cervix for those of a prolapsed umbilical cord. Comparison of the rate of these pulsations with the mother's pulse and the fetal heart sounds will reveal the true nature of the condition since the cord pulsations are synchronous with the fetal heart rate.

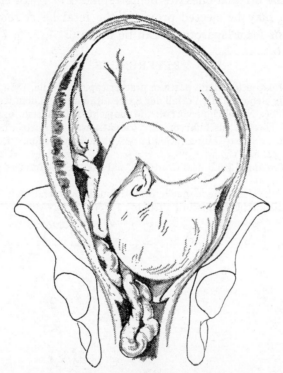

FIG. 693. Prolapse of the umbilical cord (Bumm).

TREATMENT. If the cord is still pulsating when the diagnosis is made and the cervix is fully dilated, version and extraction is indicated. In the absence of a fully dilated cervix, the cord should be reposited. Even though the pulsations cannot be felt, the same routine is recommended whenever the conditions indicate that the cord has been prolapsed for only a short time. Occasionally, the fetal heart sounds and pulsations in the cord return to normal when the compression is thus relieved (4, 6). If, however, the pulsations have ceased, and the cord has been prolapsed for a considerable time, the accident is disregarded and labor is allowed to continue its natural course.

In the hands of a beginner, reposition is quite difficult. For every loop that he replaces two or more seem to come down, and he soon becomes discouraged. If the patient is anesthetized, the chance of success will be greater. Should the use of an anesthetic be impossible, the knee-chest position will be found very helpful. The whole hand is introduced into the vagina and loosely twists the cord, which is reposited in the uterus, and the presenting part is then forced into the pelvis to prevent a recurrence. If the patient is not anesthetized, she should be encouraged to pant during the manipulations in order that the bearing-down efforts may be eliminated, as it is these that cause other loops to prolapse while the original ones are being replaced (7). In elderly primiparae, cesarean section may be elected provided the fetal heart remains satisfactory until preparations for a laparotomy can be made (3, 4, 5, 6, 7).

REFERENCES

1. LAUE, R.: De prolapsu foetalium partium praeter caput. Halle, 1856.
2. PERNICE, H.: Die Geburten mit Vorfall der Extremitäten neben dem Kopfe. Leipzig, 1858.
3. BRANDIS, E.: Ueber Nabelschnurvorfall. Monatschr. f. Geburtsh. u. Gyn., 1929, 82, 208.
4. SCHILLER, W.: Ueber Nabelschnurvorfall. Monatschr. f. Geburtsh. u. Gyn., 1931, 88, 52.
5. ANDÉRODIAS, MAHON AND DAGORN: Sur la procidence du cordon. Bull. Soc. d'obs. et de gyn., 1933, 22, 537.
6. KURZROCK, J.: Prolapsed Umbilical Cord; an Analysis of One Hundred Cases. Am. J. O. & G., 1932, 23, 403.
7. ZANGEMEISTER, W.: Ueber die manuelle Reposition der vorgefallenen Nabelschnur. Münchener Medizinische Wchnschr., 1920, 67, 1375.

CHAPTER XXII

MULTIPLE PREGNANCY

The term "MULTIPLE PREGNANCY" is applied to the condition in which more than one fetus is in the uterus.

FREQUENCY. Twin pregnancies are quite common, triplets infrequent and quadruplets extremely rare. The ratio of multiple to single pregnancies is 1 to 89 for twins, 1 to 7900 for triplets and 1 to 371,000 for quadruplets (1). It has been suggested that the ratio for twins is 1 to 80, for triplets, 1 to 80^2 (6400) and for quadruplets, 1 to 80^3 (512,000). Several authentic cases of sextuplets are recorded. One of these was the fourth pregnancy in a negress who previously had given birth to two sets of triplets and one of quadruplets. All of the six infants were born alive but none survived the fourth day (2).

VARIETIES OF TWINS. Twins may develop from single or double ova. When they are derived from a single ovum, they are identical, homologous or monozygotic and the fetal membranes consist of double amnions surrounded by a single chorion, unless the twinning is due to fission of a very early ovum in which case double chorions may be present (Fig. 694).

Double ovum twins differ from each other as do other brothers and sisters in the same family. They have double amnions, chorions and placentae. Frequently, the latter fuse and are mistaken for a single placenta. The adjacent chorions likewise may fuse, but either this layer of fused chorions or the original two layers of chorion separate the adjacent amniotic membranes (Fig. 695). Double ovum twins are about five times as common as the uniovular variety (3, 4).

Comparison of the physical characteristics is best made between the ages of 2 and 4 years. Monozygotic twins are of the same sex and are identical or mirror images of each other. Features including eyes, ears, teeth, hair, skin and anthropological measurements are alike. Finger and sole prints are similar or mirror images of each other. In 48% left and right handedness are present. This of course is due to the fact that the location of one motor area is the mirror image of the other (4a).

ETIOLOGY. Double ovum twins result from the fertilization of two separate ova expelled from one or both ovaries at the same period of ovulation.

The single ovum variety arises from: (a) fission of the blastoderm; (b) double gastrulation, or (c) fission of the bilateral halves of a single embryonic axis, and is due to some retarding influence (4). In animals, twins and double monsters have been produced at will by changing the environment of the egg (5).

Heredity is recognized as a factor in the etiology of multiple pregnancies, and the tendency toward twins is greater when this hereditary influence is on the maternal side (6).

Two ova expelled at the same ovulation may be fertilized within a short time of each other.   A multiple pregnancy of this type is known as SUPER-FECUNDATION.   That this does occur is shown by the much quoted case of a white woman, who, after having had coitus with a white and a black man, gave birth to twins of different colors.   Fertilization of two ova derived from different

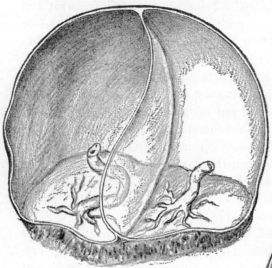

FIG. 694. Membranes in single ovum twins. The transparent partition between the two cavities is made up of two layers of amnion.   Often, these are fused.

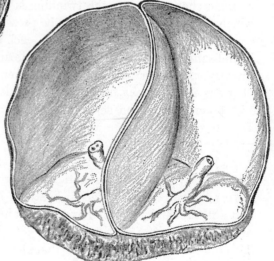

FIG. 695. Membranes in double ovum twins The partition between the two cavities is made up of a fused single or double layer of opaque chorion in addition to the double layer of amnion.

ovulations is termed SUPERFETATION.   The possibility of its occurrence is questioned by most authorities (7).

FETAL DEVELOPMENT.   Twins usually are smaller than other infants and, occasionally, one weighs considerably less than the other.

One fetus may die and be expelled, or, as more commonly happens, it may remain in the uterus throughout pregnancy.   In the latter event, it is compressed by the developing ovum and is known as a fetus papyraceous.

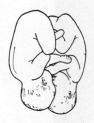

FIG. 696. Two head presentations, 38 per cent.

FIG. 697. Head and breech presentations, 35 per cent.

FIG. 698. Two breech presentations, 10 per cent.

Rarely, a single ovum twin may develop faster than its companion, with the result that the latter is deprived of its share of nourishment and becomes stunted. The weaker embryo may atrophy and at birth appear as a shapeless mass with rudimentary limbs, and without a head or heart—an acephalic or acardiac monster.

SYMPTOMS. The early nausea and vomiting of pregnancy are much more troublesome than in single pregnancies. Likewise, the tendency toward deficiency diseases and toxemia is much greater and a higher incidence of albuminuria and eclampsia is observed. Owing to the excessive enlargement of the uterus, pressure symptoms are more pronounced and appear earlier. Accordingly, edema and varicosities of the lower extremities as well as bladder irritability and dyspnea are common complaints. The uterus may be further distended by hydramnios, a complication frequently observed in multiple pregnancies.

PRESENTATION OF TWINS. The mechanism of adaptation is interfered with in twin pregnancies, and, as a result, malpresentations are common. In the following table, transverse presentation occurs in slightly over 15 per cent of all cases (8):

Presentations	*Relative Frequency*	
Two heads (Fig. 696)	38 per cent	
Head and breech (Fig. 697)	35 per cent	
Two breeches (Fig. 698)	10 per cent	
Head and transverse (Fig. 699)	9 per cent	
Breech and transverse (Fig. 700)	5 per cent	} 15 per cent
Two transverses (Fig. 701)	1-per cent	

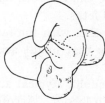
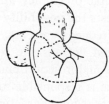
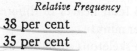

FIG. 699. Head and transverse presentations, 9 per cent.

FIG. 700. Breech and transverse presentations, 5 per cent.

FIG. 701. Two transverse presentations, 1-per cent.

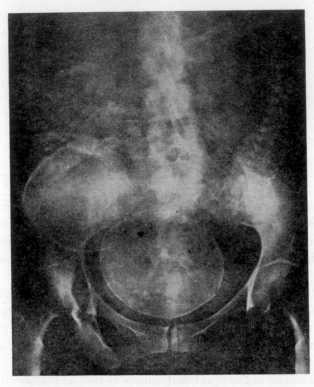

FIG. 702. X-ray picture of twin skeletons.   If the film is indistinct both lateral and dorsal postures should be used.

DIAGNOSIS. Twins are suspected whenever the uterine enlargement is excessive and a multiplicity of small parts is felt. They may be positively diagnosed by the following abdominal findings:

1. Two heads, two breeches and one or two backs.

2. Two fetal hearts in different locations and differing in rate by at least ten beats per minute.

3. Two skeletons as shown by the x-ray (Fig. 702).

4. Palpation of a second child within the uterus after one has been delivered.

Careful palpation should lead one to suspect twins whenever they are present and a positive diagnosis may then be made by either palpation, auscultation, or the use of the x-ray (Fig. 702). Unfortunately, the attendant often is not aware of the presence of a multiple pregnancy until after one child is born and the large size of the uterus suggests the possibility of a second fetus.

LABOR. Premature labor frequently occurs. This, together with the fact that twins usually are undersized, lessens the complications that might arise from the increased frequency of malpresentations.

Overdistension of the uterus is responsible for the infrequent, atypical and ineffectual uterine contractions that are characteristic of twin labors. Accordingly, the first stage is usually prolonged.

In the second stage, progress is similar to that observed in single pregnancy labors until the first child is born. The uterine contractions then cease for a few minutes, after which labor is resumed and the second child is promptly expelled unless a malpresentation causes dystocia. In over 85 per cent of twins the second child is born within one hour after the birth of the first. Occasionally, however, labor is not resumed for some time and the cervix contracts below the presenting part of the second twin. The first stage must then be repeated to redilate the cervix, and labor, accordingly, may be greatly prolonged. Twelve to twenty-four hours, or even several days, may elapse between the birth of the two fetuses.

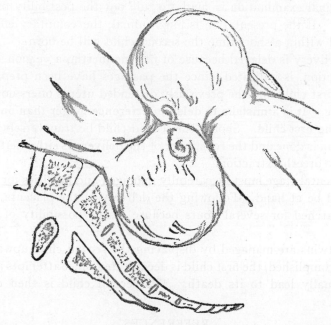

FIG. 703. Locked twins.

Locked twins are seldom encountered within the lifetime of a busy obstetrician (Fig. 703). When this complication does occur, spontaneous delivery is impossible unless the twins are extremely small.

Faulty uterine contractions may cause delay in the separation of the placenta and lead to hemorrhage after it has been expelled. Occasionally, the placenta is partially separated before the second child is delivered, and, in rare instances, has been born immediately after the birth of the first child.

PROGNOSIS. During pregnancy, the discomforts which result from overdistension of the uterus are a source of much complaint and the greater incidence of toxemia causes a slightly increased maternal risk.

In labor, the frequent occurrence of malpresentations increases the need for operative interference with its greater risk of infection. This, together with the tendency toward postpartum hemorrhage, makes labor in twin births more serious than in single pregnancies.

Prematurity, underdevelopment, toxemia, malpresentation and operative interference add to the fetal risk, so that the fetal mortality is almost three times as great as in single births. Twin infants usually are several hundred grams lighter than single pregnancy children. The weight of prematurely born twins, therefore, is not a good index of their chance of survival.

TREATMENT. If the first child presents by the vertex or breech, labor is managed expectantly until after the first twin is born. Following its delivery, the cord is severed between two ligatures and the resumption of uterine contractions is awaited. After twenty minutes, the membranes are ruptured and a careful vaginal examination is made to rule out the possibility of transverse presentation. If the presentation is longitudinal, the voluntary efforts are encouraged and within a short time the second child will be born.

When delivery is delayed because of uterine inertia, a version, followed by breech extraction, is indicated, since the passages have been prepared by the birth of the first child and the previously distended uterus offers no obstruction to the turning. It is a mistake to delay interference longer than one hour after the birth of the first child. Should the second child lie transversely, an internal podalic version is done and the remainder of the delivery is either left to nature or completed by breech extraction.

The placental stage must be carefully managed and facilities for packing the uterus should be at hand. Following the delivery of the placenta, the fundus should be watched for several hours because of the possibility of postpartum hemorrhage.

Locked twins are managed by displacing the second child upward. If this cannot be accomplished, the first child is decapitated, since attempts at extraction would eventually lead to its death. The second child is then delivered by forceps (9).

REFERENCES

1. VEIT, G.: Beiträge zur Geburtshilflichen Statistk.   Monatschr. f. Geburtsk. u. Frauenk., 1855, 6, 127.   i
2. KERR, J. W. AND COOKMAN, H.: A Remarkable Case of Multiple Pregnancy.   Med. Press. & Circ., 1903, 1, 537.
3. OREL, H.: Ueber die Häufigheit eineiiger Zwillinge.   Arch. f. Gyn., 1927, 129, 719.
4. NEWMAN, H. H.: The Experimental Production of Twins and Double Monsters in the Larvae of the Starfish Patiria Miniata, Together with a Discussion of the Causes of Twinning in General.   J. Exp. Biol., 1921, 33, 321.
   Studies of Human Twins.   Biol. Bull, 1928, 55, 283 & 298.
   The Physiology of Twinning, Chicago, 1922.
4a. GUTTMACHER, A. F.: An Analysis of 521 Cases of Twin Pregnancy.   Am. J. O. & G., 1937, 34, 76; also Am. J. Phys. Anthrop., 1934, 19, 391.
5. STOCKARD, C. R.: Developmental Rate and Structural Expression: An Experimental Study of Twins, Double Monsters and Single Deformities, and the Interaction among Embryonic Organs during their origin and development.   Am. J. Anat., 1921, 28, 115.
6. DAVENPORT, C. B.: Heredity of Twin Births.   Proc. Soc. Exp. Biol. & Med., Vol. 17.
7. MEYER, A. W.: The Occurrence of Superfetation.   J. A. M. A., 1919, 72, 769.
8. LEONHARDT: Ueber die Kindeslagen bei Zwillingsgeburten, D. I., Berlin, 1897.
9. AHLFELD, F.: Beiträge zur Lehre von den Zwillingen.   Arch. f. Gyn., 1876, 9, 196.

CHAPTER XXIII

DISEASES OF THE DECIDUA AND FETAL MEMBRANES

ACUTE INFLAMMATION OF THE DECIDUA. When the segmenting ovum becomes implanted in an endometrium that is the seat of an inflammatory lesion, the characteristics of that lesion are passed on to the developing decidua. If the process is acute, the ovum either is not implanted or is aborted at an early stage. Acute inflammation of the decidua, therefore, usually originates after implantation has occurred and most often is due to intrauterine manipulations done for the purpose of interrupting pregnancy. The decidua, however, occasionally is involved in some of the acute infectious diseases (1, 2), and in the early weeks of pregnancy may be invaded by the gonococcus (3).

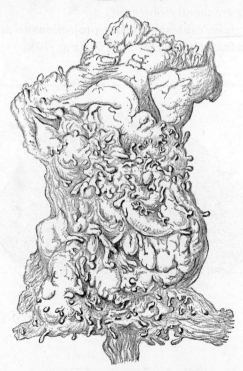

FIG. 704. Decidua polyposa (Bulius).

The tissues become thickened and congested. On microscopic examination, an infiltration with leukocytes and plasma cells is observed together with the other characteristic findings of an acute inflammatory reaction. Pregnancy, as a rule, is spontaneously terminated, and, following evacuation of the uterus, the pathological course is similar to that observed in puerperal infection.

467

The symptoms vary with the virulence of the infection. Often, after attempts at criminal abortion, the febrile reaction is marked and a fatal outcome not infrequently is observed.

TREATMENT is expectant and is similar to that recommended in the Chapter on Puerperal Infection.

HYPERPLASIA OF THE DECIDUA. At times, the decidua, instead of growing progressively thinner, becomes abnormally thickened. This hyperplasia may be diffuse or localized. In the diffuse variety all of the elements of the decidua participate and it occasionally reaches a thickness of $1\frac{1}{2}$ to 2 cm. Hemorrhage into the substance of the decidua and beneath the fetal membranes is common. As a result, layers of fibrin form about the chorionic villi, and interfere with the nutrition of the ovum, after which the embryo dies and the products of conception are cast off in an early abortion. Occasionally, however, they may be retained within the uterus. In this event the embryo is absorbed. If the condition is less marked and pregnancy is not interrupted, slight bleeding, particularly in the latter months, is frequently observed.

Localised hyperplasia causes polyp-like projections to appear on the surface of the decidua—**decidua polyposa** (4, 5, 6, 7) (Fig. 704).

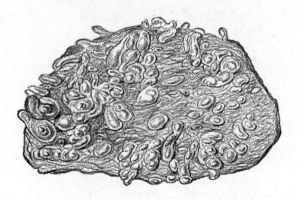

FIG. 705. Endometritis decidua cystica (Breus).

Hyperplasia of the glandular elements occasionally takes place and gives rise to a profuse, clear secretion which may trickle out of the cervix or may collect under the membranes and be discharged at intervals in variable amounts—**hydrorrhea gravidarum.**

If the ducts become occluded, retention cysts form and give to the decidua a nodulated appearance—**endometritis decidua cystica** (8) (Fig. 705).

HYDATIDIFORM MOLE

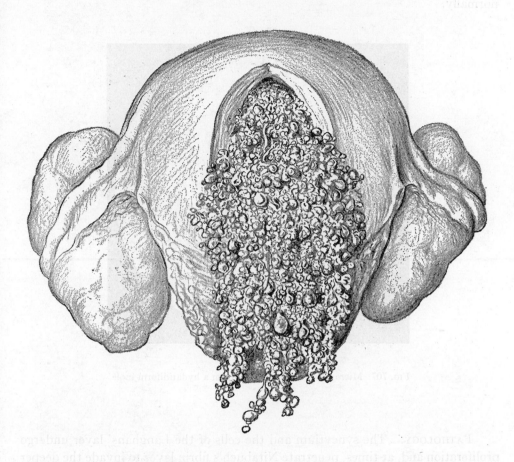

FIG. 706. Uterus containing an hydatidiform mole, together with double lutein cystomata of the ovaries.

HYDATIDIFORM MOLE (vesicular mole, myxoma chorei) is a cystic degeneration of the chorionic villi which is characterized by a proliferation of the epithelial elements, obliteration of the terminal vessels and degeneration of the stroma with the formation of cysts which are attached, like clusters of currants, to the villous trunks (Fig. 706). This change usually takes place early in pregnancy when the ovum is more or less surrounded by chorionic villi and, except in rare instances, involves the entire periphery of the egg.

ETIOLOGY. Hydatidiform mole occurs about once in three thousand pregnancies (9, 10). The exact nature of its cause is not known. It may be said, however, that its origin is in the ovum itself because of the fact that in some twin pregnancies one ovum may show hydatidiform changes while the other develops normally.

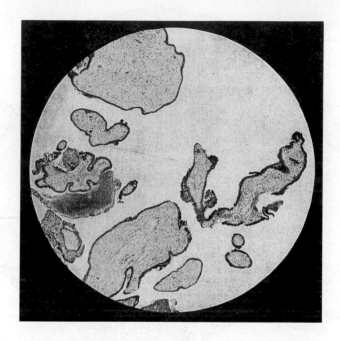

FIG. 707. Microscopic-section of villi from a hydatidiform mole.

PATHOLOGY. The syncytium and the cells of the Langhans' layer undergo proliferation and, at times, penetrate Nitabuch's fibrin layer to invade the deeper parts of the decidua and endometrium. The terminal vessels are obliterated and disappear, while the stroma degenerates and is largely replaced by fluid which, contrary to former belief, is not mucin. The villi, accordingly, are the seat of numerous cyst-like swellings that vary from microscopic proportions to the size of large grapes. These are attached to one another by slender cords and somewhat resemble bunches of grapes (10, 11, 12, 13, 14) (Fig. 707). Hydatidiform moles grow rapidly and are potentially malignant. The entire mass often reaches the size of a five months pregnancy. Usually, the embryo dies and, as a rule, is absorbed.

Frequently, but not invariably, one or both ovaries become polycystic and may become as large as an orange. The individual cysts are lined by lutein cells and contain a clear fluid (15, 16). After the removal of the mole these tumors undergo spontaneous involution (17). During the process of involution, however, the gonadotrophic substances stored in them may give rise to a positive A.Z. test.

SYMPTOMS. Nausea and vomiting are more pronounced. In addition to the usual symptoms of pregnancy the essential symptoms are: 1. Rapid enlargement of the uterus; 2. Bloody vaginal discharge; 3. Expulsion of grape-like cysts from the uterus. Following a period of amenorrhea, a blood stained vaginal discharge appears and the uterus is found to be enlarged out of proportion to the period of gestation. The bloody discharge and uterine enlargement continue for some time, after which intermittent, cramp-like pains are felt and the abnormal ovum is expelled. Occasionally, the invading chorionic elements pass through the entire wall of the uterus (18). Symptoms of perforation and internal hemorrhage then are added to those above enumerated. Frequently a rise in blood pressure, albuminuria and other evidences of toxemia are present. Prolonged bleeding may lead to anemia.

DIAGNOSIS. Fetal movements are not felt and the fetal heart sounds cannot be heard, but the Aschheim-Zondek test is strongly positive and urine diluted as much as ten times often will produce characteristic changes in the ovaries of injected animals (18a). Frequently, the blood pressure is elevated and albuminuria is present. Vaginal examination shows a blood stained vaginal discharge and a uterus which often lacks the consistency characteristic of a normal pregnancy and as a rule is larger than might be expected for the period of gestation. Not infrequently, a cystic ovary may be palpated in the cul-de-sac. If the cervix is open, grape-like vesicles may be felt and removed.

PROGNOSIS. Hemorrhage, perforation of the uterus and infection are the chief dangers and formerly were responsible for a maternal mortality of 10 per cent (10). In from 5 to 16 per cent (10) of the cases recorded in the literature, chorionepitheliomata developed after hydatidiform mole.

TREATMENT. As soon as the diagnosis is made, the uterus should be emptied. Because of the possible thinning of the uterine wall it is best to remove the mass with the finger (never with the curette) and even then great care must be taken to avoid rupturing the uterus. Blood transfusion before, during, and after operation may be of great value. The lutein cystomata are disregarded, as they undergo involution following the evacuation of the uterus. Increase in the size of the cysts after the mole is removed may indicate the presence of chorionepithelioma (18b). Subsequent monthly Aschheim-Zondek tests are to be made. If at any time the test is positive it should be repeated with urine diluted up to ten times. A reaction with well diluted urine is strongly suspicious of beginning chorionepithelioma and calls for a diagnostic curettage. In the event that the material thus obtained shows evidence of chorionepithelioma an immediate hysterectomy is indicated.

CHORIONEPITHELIOMA

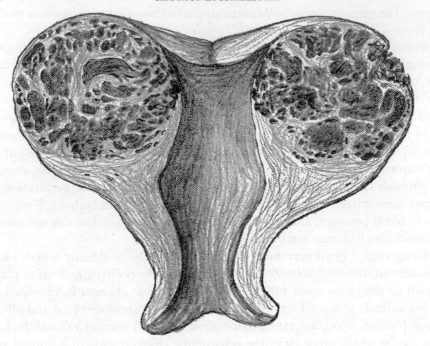

FIG. 708. Uterus containing a chorionepithelioma.

CHORIONEPITHELIOMA is the term given to a malignant new growth which develops in the uterus after an abortion, hydatidiform mole or a full term pregnancy. It is characterized by a lawless proliferation of retained chorionic elements which invade the uterine wall and undergo metastases to remote organs (Fig. 708).

FREQUENCY AND ETIOLOGY. The occurrence of chorionepithelioma is extremely rare after a normal pregnancy. It, however, follows hydatidiform mole much more often and has been reported in 5 to 16 per cent of such cases (10, 19). On the other hand, about 50 per cent of all chorionepitheliomata are preceded by hydatidiform mole. In rare instances, it may arise from a teratoma and, accordingly, can occur in the male (20).

PATHOLOGY. On inspection, the uterus reveals a soft red and somewhat friable mass which may be easily differentiated from the remainder of the uterine wall. Cross-section of the tumor shows it to be made up of clotted blood separated by irregular strands of tissue. Microscopically, the blood clots appear to be of various ages and peripheral to them are collections of proliferating cells

analogous to those found in the Langhans' layer of the chorionic villi.   Masses
of nucleated protoplasm, suggestive of syncytium, invade the uterine musculature

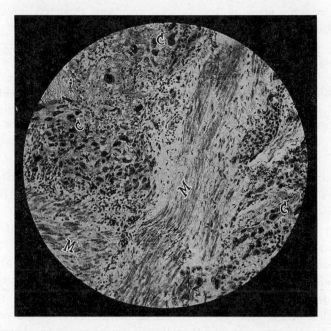

Fig. 709. Microscopic picture of a chorionepithelioma.   *C*, chorionic elements; *M* muscle.

and venous spaces (Fig. 709).   As a result, both types of cells are carried by the
blood stream to the lungs where metastatic tumors rapidly develop.   In addition,
metastases to the vagina, kidneys, spleen, ovaries and brain are frequently
observed (19, 20, 21, 22)

SYMPTOMS.   Following pregnancy, abortion or the removal of a hydatidiform
mole, hemorrhage may occur some little time after the disappearance of the
lochia rubra.   It often is rather profuse and frequently recurs at intervals of a
few days.   In many cases, all symptoms are absent until metastases appear.
Cough and hemoptysis then lead to an examination of the chest, and a diagnosis
of pneumonia usually is made.   Within a short time, the patient dies and autopsy
reveals the true nature of the disease.   Occasionally, a metastatic mass may
be felt in the vagina and direct the attention of the physician toward the possibility of chorionepithelioma.

DIAGNOSIS.   Atypical bleeding after a pregnancy, and particularly after a
hydatidiform mole, calls for an Aschheim-Zondek test and a diagnostic curettage.

The same hormone test should be done at monthly intervals after the removal
of every hydatidiform mole.   Should the test be positive, a diagnostic curettage
is recommended.

TREATMENT. If the curettings show chorionepithelioma immediate hysterectomy is indicated. Regression of lutein cysts after removal of a chorionepithelioma is a favorable omen (18b). Even though metastases are present, hysterectomy is advised, since recoveries have been reported under these circumstances (20, 23, 24, 25, 26).

HYDRAMNIOS

HYDRAMNIOS. An excessive amount of amniotic fluid is known as hydramnios. It may be acute or chronic. In the acute variety the fluid accumulates rapidly and gives rise to distressing symptoms within a few days. The chronic form, on the other hand, develops gradually in the latter half of pregnancy.

FREQUENCY. Mild hydramnios, in which two or three liters of fluid are present, occurs about once in 200 pregnancies. Total quantities of 10 to 30 liters have been reported but are rare.

ETIOLOGY. Excessive amounts of amniotic fluid accumulate in certain fetal and maternal conditions:

Fetal Anomalies. Anencephalus and spina bifida are commonly associated with hydramnios. In these conditions, the excess of liquor amnii is thought to result from loss of the cerebrospinal fluid through the exposed meninges or from stimulation of the kidneys by irritation of the unprotected centers in the brain and cord. Various other fetal malformations have been observed (27, 28).

Multiple Pregnancies, particularly single ovum twins, frequently are accompanied by an excess of amniotic fluid (28). Often, the increase is limited to the amnion of the larger child.

Obstruction to the umbilical circulation due to knots, twists or thrombosis may cause an exudation of fluid from the cord and placenta. and has been offered as a possible explanation in some cases (29, 30).

Maternal cardiac and renal disease, at times, leads to edema of the placenta and filtration into the amniotic cavity. These conditions, accordingly, have been considered as etiological factors.

Many cases of hydramnios occur in which no cause is demonstrable. Likewise, hydramnios frequently does not accompany the etiological factors that have been mentioned. For these reasons, much more investigation is necessary before anything very definite may be said concerning the true cause or causes of this condition.

SYMPTOMS. Pressure symptoms are increased and add to the patient's discomfort. Bladder irritability, constipation, dyspnea and edema of the lower extremities, accordingly, are common complaints. In marked hydramnios, particularly when the condition is acute, the distended uterus greatly interferes with respiration. As a result, dyspnea, cyanosis, palpitation and even cardiac failure may occur.

Pregnancy usually is spontaneously terminated as a result of the over-distention of the uterus. For the same reason, uterine atony is common and leads to a prolongation of the labor. Abnormal presentations likewise are frequent but the small size of the child lessens the difficulty that might otherwise arise from this source. Following the delivery of the placenta, retraction and contraction of the uterus often is inadequate and leads to postpartum hemorrhage. Fetal anomalies are common (31).

When the membranes rupture, the sudden gush of fluid often carries the cord with it. Because of the danger of premature labor and prolapse of the cord, the risk to the fetus is greatly increased.

TREATMENT. Minor degrees of hydramnios require no treatment in the course of pregnancy. During labor, the possibility of atony, malpresentation, prolapse of the cord and postpartum hemorrhage must always be kept in mind. When the distention is excessive and the respiratory difficulty is marked, rupture of the membranes is indicated. Because of the frequent occurrence of malforma-tions, an x-ray examination should be made even before the symptoms become alarming. If a serious anomaly is found, the membranes are ruptured regardless of the severity of the hydramnios (32). Labor follows within a short time and, as previously stated, may be prolonged because of the uterine atony. Prepara-tion should be made to combat postpartum hemorrhage in order that no time may be lost if the uterus fails to control the bleeding from the placental site.

OLIGOHYDRAMNIOS

OLIGOHYDRAMNIOS. When the amount of amniotic fluid is greatly dimin-ished, the condition is known as oligohydramnios. In extremely rare instances, only a few drams of liquor amnii are present.

Little is known concerning the etiology of this condition, but fetal anomalies are commonly found in association with it. Adhesions between the amnion and the fetus formerly were thought to cause serious deformities. The latter, however, are now regarded as the result of imperfect development early in pregnancy due either to defective germ plasm or injury (33).

The uterus is smaller than normal and pressure symptoms, as a rule, are less marked. Pregnancy may be considerably prolonged. In one of the author's cases, labor did not begin until five weeks after the expected date of confinement and the child weighed only three pounds. Aside from its small size, it had the general appearance of a child several months old.

PROGNOSIS for the mother is good but the child often shows the effect of the lack or absence of amniotic fluid.

ANOMALIES AND DISEASES OF THE PLACENTA

ANOMALIES IN SIZE. Normally, the placenta is irregularly circular in shape and measures 15 to 20 cm. in diameter. It is about 2.5 cm. thick and weighs approximately 500 gms., or about one-sixth the weight of a full term fetus.

Occasionally, underdevelopment of the placenta is observed, and its size may be reduced as much as one-half. This lack of growth usually is due to undernourishment resulting from local conditions within the uterus or from general systemic diseases. The fetus, as a rule, is small but occasionally may be normal in size or larger.

Large placentae are associated with oversized fetuses, and fetal and maternal diseases. In fetal syphilis, the relative size of the placenta is greatly increased and it not infrequently weighs one-fourth as much as the child. Edema of the fetus and placenta likewise causes a disturbance in the normal relationship and such placentae occasionally weigh more than the fetus. Whenever the placenta is large it should be examined for evidence of erythroblastosis fetalis. This is especially true if the vernix has a bile stained appearance and the child develops jaundice.

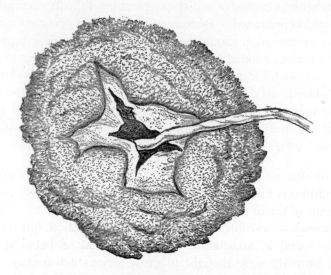

Fig. 710. Placenta membranacea (von Weiss).

PLACENTA MEMBRANACEA. Persistence of well developed villi in the chorion laeve causes the placenta to surround the ovum almost completely. It then is thin and membranous. This rare condition may be due to poor development of the blood supply in the decidua serotina which necessitates the persistence of the villi in the chorion laeve, or it may result from an abnormally good circulation in the decidua capsularis which causes the adjacent villi to continue their growth and development (Fig. 710).

Because of the placenta's extensive attachment, placental elements often are found at or near the internal os. Symptoms suggestive of low implantation and placenta previa, accordingly, may be associated with this anomaly. The third stage is prolonged and is accompanied by hemorrhage, as a result of which manual removal of the placenta may be necessary.

attached to the membranes. This ovule is connected with the main mass of the placenta by vessels which are comparatively large. Such accessory lobes are knowingly retained in the uterus. It can be removed after the expulsion of the afterbirth, and it is a great source of danger during the puerperium. If the membranes are carefully examined, it can almost always be carefully removed to avoid the dangers due to the retention of this portion of the retained placental tissue.

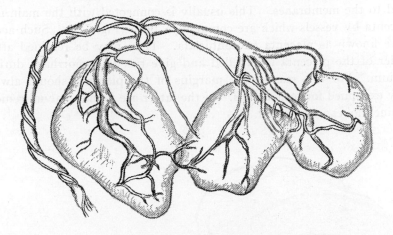

FIG. 711. Placenta tripartita (Hyrtl).

MULTIPLE PLACENTAE.   Rarely, the placenta may be divided into two or more lobes, each of which has a distinct circulation of its own.   The vessels collect at the periphery, and the main trunks finally unite to form the cord. According to the number of lobes, the terms duplex or bipartita, and triplex or tripartita are applied to such placentae (Fig. 711).   Often an accessory lobe is

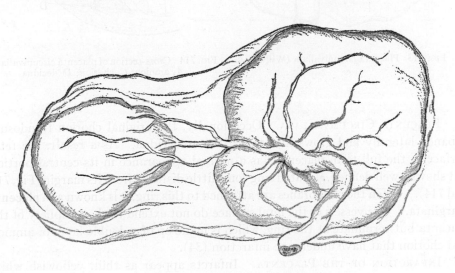

FIG. 712. Placenta succenturiata

attached to the membranes. This usually is connected with the main mass of the placenta by vessels which are common to both (Fig. 712). Such accessory lobes are known as **placenta succenturiata.** They may be retained after the remainder of the placenta is expelled and give rise to hemorrhage during the puerperium. For this reason, the margins of the placenta should always be carefully examined for torn vessels. If the latter are found, manual removal of the retained lobes is indicated.

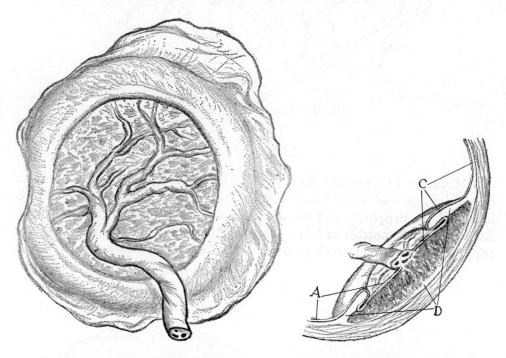

FIG. 713. Placenta circumvallata (Williams).   FIG. 714. Cross-section of placenta circumvallata. *A*, amnion; *C*, chorion; *D* decidua.

PLACENTA CIRCUMVALLATA. Occasionally, the original chorion frondosum expands laterally and grows into the adjacent decidua. As a result, the fetal surface of the full term placenta has a normal appearance in its central portion but shows a well defined, elevated ring some little distance from its margin (Fig. 713 and 714). When the membranes are attached to this ring, it is known as a **placenta marginata.** The vessels of the fetal surface do not extend to the periphery of the placenta but terminate at the ring, which is made up of a double layer of amnion and chorion that have undergone infarction (34).

INFARCTION OF THE PLACENTA. Infarcts appear as thin, yellowish white areas of varying size on the fetal surface of the placenta. They are usually limited to the region adjacent to the chorionic plate, but may occasionally be found on the maternal surface as distinct white areas which penetrate deeply and, at times, involve a considerable portion of the placenta.   Red infarcts also are observed.   They usually are formed on the maternal surface and extend well into the substance of the placenta.

Small infarcts are present in all mature placentae.   Larger ones, measuring 1 cm. or more, occur in over 60 per cent of all full term pregnancies.

Infarct formation has been regarded as an evidence of senility and as such is considered physiological when it occurs in the last month of pregnancy.   The vessels of the villi undergo obliterative endarteritis as a result of which the cellular elements adjacent to the syncytium become necrotic.   The syncytium, which is partially nourished by the blood in the intervillous spaces, at first is not affected.   Later, it also degenerates and the dead villi appear as deeply staining hyaline areas.   Fibrin then collects about their periphery and joins them into a firm mass.   Ultimately, all traces of the villi are lost and the infarcts appear as a laminated fibrinoid structure.   The origin of infarcts may also be traced to changes in the blood in the intervillous spaces.   In places, particularly near the chorionic plate, the circulation becomes sluggish and the blood coagulates. Fibrin thus forms about the villi and interferes with their nutrition with the result that they degenerate and are included in the fibrinoid mass which makes up the infarct.   They also may follow occlusion of the vessels supplying isolated areas of the decidua basalis, which results in necrosis of the decidua.   The nutrition of the villi being thus interfered with, their stroma cells undergo necrosis even though the vessels are distended with blood and show no change.   Later, the degenerative changes involve the syncytium and the entire villi then become a part of the fibrinoid structure which replaces the tissues originally included in the area adjacent to the altered decidua.   Another mode of origin has been described in which collections of blood in the intervillous spaces clot and become changed into fibrin.   Degeneration of the surrounding villi follows, after which the latter become fused to form a capsule for the infarct (35, 36, 37, 38).

Small infarcts have no clinical significance.   Large ones may interfere with the nutrition of the fetus and lead to its underdevelopment or death.   In some cases of nephritis, a considerable portion of the placenta undergoes infarction and death of the fetus is common.

CYSTS OF THE PLACENTA.   Large cysts are rare.   Smaller ones, on the other hand, are frequently observed on the fetal surface of the placenta.   They are filled with a clear or sanguineous fluid or contain a somewhat gelatinous material. On section, the lining membrane is made up of fibrin and large epithelioid cells derived from the trophoblastic elements which penetrate the decidual septa and cause liquefaction of the tissues ivanded (39).   Placental cysts have no effect on pregnancy or labor.

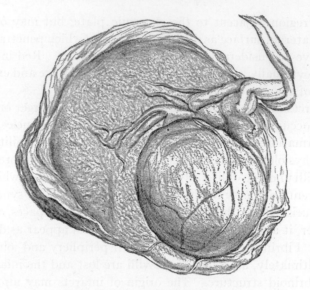

FIG. 715. Chorioma angiomatosum.

SOLID TUMORS OF THE PLACENTA seldom are observed.   They usually are
made up of chorionic elements, fibrous tissue and blood vessels, hence the name
chorioma angiomatosum or fibrosum (Fig. 715).   Unless they occupy a considerable portion of the placenta, such tumors have no effect on pregnancy.   Large
growths may give rise to dystocia or cause difficulty in the third stage of labor
(40, 41).

INFLAMMATION OF THE PLACENTA.   In intrapartum infections, inflammation

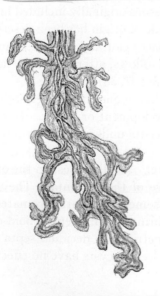

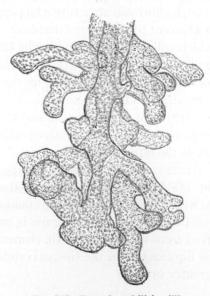

FIG. 716. Teased normal villi.   FIG. 717. Teased syphilitic villi.

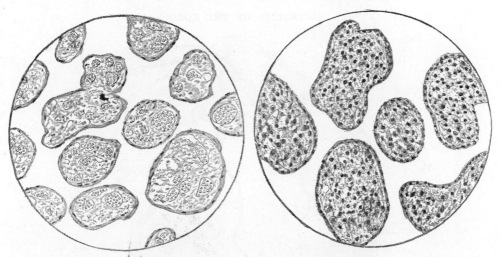

FIG. 718. Microscopic section of normal villi.   FIG. 719. Microscopic section of syphilitic villi.

of the decidua may extend to the fetal portion of the placenta. The placenta likewise may be infected in prolonged dry labors. In either event, a fetal bacteriemia may result and cause the death of the child within a few days after delivery (42).

SYPHILIS OF THE PLACENTA. The syphilitic placenta is pale, yellowish gray in appearance and often weighs one-fourth as much as the child. The villi are greatly enlarged and show less branching than normal (Figs. 716 and 717). On section, their ends are clubbed, the vessels are diminished in number, and their stroma has a more granular appearance (43) (Figs. 718 and 719). The picture of lues, according to some authorities, is characteristic and from it they are willing to make a diagnosis of fetal syphilis. In support of this view, it may be stated that spirochetes may be demonstrated in such placentae (44, 45). On the other hand, it often is impossible to find a characteristic lesion in the placenta even though the fetus is definitely syphilitic.

TUBERCULOSIS OF THE PLACENTA is rare. When it occurs, the lesions usually are found in the maternal tissues, i.e., between the villi and in the decidua basalis. Occasionally, the tubercle bacillus invades the villi and produces characteristic lesions within the chorionic elements (46, 47).

PLACENTA ACCRETA. In rare instances, the decidual elements may be lacking to such an extent that large numbers of villi penetrate the uterine musculature and cause a firmer attachment of the placenta. In the third stage, therefore, the normal mechanism of separation which produces a cleavage in the spongy layer of the decidua is absent. Attempts to remove the placenta manually some hours after the termination of the second stage show the firmness of its attachment and the futility of continuing the manipulations. As hysterectomy gives the best results, the uterus should be removed as soon as the diagnosis is assured (48, 49, 50).

ANOMALIES OF THE CORD

FIG. 720. Velamentous insertion of cord.

VARIATIONS IN INSERTION. The umbilical cord usually is eccentrically placed on the fetal surface of the placenta. Less frequently it is attached to the margin and produces the so-called battledore placenta. Much less commonly the vessels may pass for some distance between the chorion and the amnion before they join to form the cord (Fig. 720). This is known as a **velamentous insertion** and has considerable clinical significance. The placenta and child may be smaller than normal. If the free vessels extend across the internal os and rupture during labor, the resulting hemorrhage may cause the death of the fetus (51, 52, 53).

VARIATIONS IN THE LENGTH OF THE CORD. The umbilical cord varies from a few centimeters to almost 200 cm. in length. These extreme figures are rare. Its average length is about 50 cm. An extremely short cord may cause asphyxia, or separation of the placenta. These same accidents may result when the cord is coiled about the fetus and is thus relatively shortened (54, 55).

TORSION AND KNOTS OF THE CORD. The fetal movements not infrequently produce multiple twists in the cord. Although torsion to a surprising degree often occurs without affecting the child, the twists may be so numerous and so tight as to cause the death of the fetus. Knots in the cord likewise may result from movements of the child. When they become tightly drawn, the child dies from asphyxia.

REFERENCES

1. Slavjansky, K.: Zur Lehre von den Erkrankungen der Placenta. Arch. f. Gyn., 1873, 5, 360.
2. Klotz, H.: Beiträge zur Pathologie der Schwangerschaft. Arch. f. Gyn., 1887, 29, 448.
3. Maslowsky, W.: Zur Aetiologie der vorzeitigen Ablösung der Placenta vom normalen Sitz. (Endometritis decidualis gonorrhoica.) Monatschr. f. Geburtsh. u. Gyn., 1896, 4, 212.
4. Strassmann, H.: Eine Eigenthümliche Hyperplasie der Decidua. Monatschr. f. Geburtsk., 1862, 19, 242.
5. Bulius, G.: Ueber Endometritis decidua polyposa et tuberosa. München Med. Wchnschr., 1896, 43, 537.
6. Ahlfeld, F.: Ueber Endometritis decidualis tuberoso-polyposa. Arch. f. Gyn., 1876, 10, 168.
7. Nyulasy, F. A.: Polypoid Endometritis, a Complication of Pregnancy and the Puerperium. J. O. & G. Brit. Emp., 1909, 16, 9.
8. Breus, C.: Ueber cystöse Degeneration der Decidua Vera. Arch. f. Gyn., 1882, 19, 483.
9. Williamson, H.: The Pathology and Symptoms of Hydatidiform Degeneration of the Chorion. Tr. Obs. Soc. Lond., 1899, 41, 303.
10. Findley, P.: Hydatidiform Mole, with a Report of Two Cases and Clinical Deductions from Two Hundred and Ten Reported Cases. Am. J. O., 1903, 47, 380.
    Hydatidiform Mole—An Analysis of 300 Cases. Am. J. O., 1917, 75, 968.
11. Marchand, F.: Ueber den Bau der Blasenmole. Zeitschr. f. Geburtsh. u. Gyn., 1895, 32, 405.
12. Neumann, J.: Beitrag zur Kenntnis der Blasenmolen und des "malignen Deciduoms". Monatschr. f. Geburtsh. u. Gyn., 1897, 6, 17 & 157.
13. Larrier, L. et Brindeau, A.: Nature de la Môle Hydatiforme. Rev. de Gyn., 1908, 12, 203.
14. Meyer, A. W.: Hydatidiform Degeneration with deductions from over one hundred and fifty new cases. Am. J. O., 1918, 78, 641.
15. Pick, L.: Zur Frage der Eierstocksveränderungen bei Blasenmole. Zentralbl. f. Gyn., 1903, 27, 1033.
16. Stoeckel, W.: Ueber die cystische Degeneration der Ovarien bei Blasenmole, zugleich ein Beitrag zur Histogenese der Luteinzellen. Beitr. z. Geburtsh. u. Gyn., 1902. Fritsch Festschrift, 136.
17. Santi, E.: Zur Rückbildung der Lutein cystome nach Blasenmole. Ztschr. f. Geburtsh. u. Gyn., 1910, 67, 667.
18. Wilton, W.: Hydatids, Terminating Fatally by Haemorrhage. Lancet, 1840, 1, 691.
18a. Mathieu, A.: Hydatidiform Mole and Chorio-Epithelioma. S. G. & O., 1939, 68; Abstracts, p. 52 & 181.
18b. Okazaki, S.: Jap. J. O. & G., 1940, 23, 230.
19. Marchand, F.: Ueber das maligne Chorion-Epitheliom nebst Mittheilung von 2 neuen Fällen. Ztschr. f. Geburtsh. u. Gyn., 1898, 39, 173.
20. Teacher, J. H.: Chorion Epithelioma Malignum. Tr. Obs. Soc. Lond., 1903, 45, 253.
21. Sänger, M.: Ueber Sarcoma uteri deciduo-cellulare und andere deciduale Geschwülste. Arch. f. Gyn., 1893, 44, 89.
22. Williams, J. W.: Deciduoma Malignum. Johns Hopkins Hosp. Rep., 1895, 4, 461.
23. Vineberg, H.: Clinical Data on Chorio-epithelioma with End-results of Operative Treatment. S. G. & O., 1919, 28, 123.
24. Cazin, M.: Des Déciduomes Malins. Étude Clinique et Anatomo-pathologique. La Gynécologie, 1896, 1, 15.
25. Chrobak, R.: Demonstration eines per vaginam exstirpirten uterus. Centralbl. f. Gyn., 1896, 20, 1281.
26. Von Franqué, O.: Ueber eine bösartige Geschwulst des Chorion nebst Bemerkungen zur Anatomie der Blasenmole. Ztschr. f. Geburtsh. u. Gyn., 1896, 34, 199.

27. Küstner, O.: Ueber eine noch nicht bekannte Entstehungsursache amputirender amniotischer Fäden und Stränge. Ztschr. f. Geburtsh. u. Gyn., 1890, 20, 445.
28. Wilson, T.: Hydramnion in Cases of Uniovial or Homologous Twins. Tr. Obs. Soc. Lond., 1899, 41, 235.
29. Levison, F.: Bidrag til Laren ond Foetorandet och den abnorme Töröyelse af delles Mängde (Fruchtwasser und Hydramnios). Arch. f. Gyn., 1876, 9, 517.
30. Fehling, H.: Ueber die physiologische Bedeutung des Fruchtwassers. Arch. f. Gyn., 1879, 14, 221.
31. Vogt: Die Lebenaussichten der Kinder bei Hydramnion. Monatschr. f. Geburtsh. u. Gyn., 1925, 70, 322.
32. Beck, A. C.: A Case Illustrating the Value of the X-ray as an Aid in the Management of Polyhydramnios. Am. J. O. & G., 1929, 18, 257.
33. Streeter, G. L.: Focal Deficiencies in Fetal Tissues and Their Relation to Intrauterine Amputation. Contrib. to Embryol. No. 126, Carnegie Inst., 1930, 22, 1.
34. Williams, J. W.: Placenta Circumvallata. Am. J. O. & G., 1927, 13, 1.
35. Eden, T. W.: A Study of the Human Placenta, Physiological and Pathological. J. Path. & Bact., 1895, 5, 265.
36. Williams, J. W.: The Frequency and Significance of Infarcts of the Placenta, Based upon the Microscopic Examination of Five Hundred Consecutive Placentae. Am. J. O., 1900, 41, 775.
37. Siddall, R. S. and Hartman, F. W.: Infarcts of the Placenta: A Study of Seven Hundred Consecutive Placentas. Am. J. O. & G., 1926, 12, 683.
38. McNalley, F. P. and Dieckmann, W. J.: Hemorrhagic Lesions of the Placenta and their Relation to White Infarct Formation. Am. J. O. & G., 1923, 5, 55.
39. Paddock, R. and Greer, E. D.: The Origin of the Common Cystic Structures of the Human Placenta. Am. J. O. & G., 1927, 13, 164.
40. Margeson, R. D.: Placental Tumor. Bost. Med. & Surg. J., 1920, 182, 200.
41. Siddall, R. S.: Chorioangiofibroma (Chorioangioma). Am. J. O. & G., 1924, 8, 430.
42. Slemmons, J. M.: Placental Bacteremia. J. A. M. A., 1915, 65, 1265.
43. Fränkel, E.: Ueber Placentarsyphilis. Arch. f. Gyn., 1873, 5, 1.
44. Trinchese, J.: Ueber den Zeitpunkt der luetischen Infektion des Fötus und dessen klinische Bedeutung. Arch. f. Gyn., 1913, 18, 201.
45. Philipp, E.: Die Diagnose der Lues bei Mutter und Kind. Zentralbl. f. Gyn., 1928, 52, 416.
46. Warthin, A. S.: Tuberculosis of the Placenta. J. Infec. Diseases, 1907, 4, 347.
47. Norris, C. C.: Gynecological and Obstetrical Tuberculosis. New York & London, 1931, 31.
48. Polak, J. O. and Phelan, G. W.: Placenta Accreta; Its Incidence, Pathology and Management. S. G. & O., 1924, 38, 181.
49. Klaften, E.: Beiträge zur Lehre von der Placenta accreta. Arch. f. Gyn., 1928, 135, 190.
50. Feiner, D.: Placenta Accreta. Am. J. O. & G., 1931, 22, 312.
51. Peiser, E.: Verblutungstod der Frucht unter der Geburt infolge Ruptur einer Umbilicalarterie bei Insertio velamentosa. Monatschr. f. Geburtsh. u. Gyn., 1898, 8, 619.
52. Kosmak, G. W.: Intrauterine Rupture of a Velamentous Umbilical Cord. Am. J. O. & G., 1922, 4, 619.
53. Ottow, B.: Interpositio velamentosa funiculi umbilicalis, eine bisher übersehene Nabelstranganomalie, ihre Entstehung und klinische Bedeutung. Arch. f. Gyn., 1922, 116, 176.
54. Brickner, S. M.: A New Symptom in the Diagnosis of Dystocia Due to a Short Umbilical Cord. Am. J. O., 1902, 45, 512.
55. Gardiner, J. P.: Delayed Labor Caused by a Shortened or Short Umbilical Cord. J. A. M. A., 1932, 98, 598.

CHAPTER XXIV

ABORTION

The term abortion is used to designate the expulsion of the products of conception before the fetus is viable. Any interruption of pregnancy prior to the 28th week, therefore, is known as an **abortion**. Some authorities, however, restrict the use of this term to the first twelve weeks and refer to the premature termination of pregnancy after the placenta is formed as a miscarriage.

Because the expression, "criminal abortion," as applied to an illegal interference with gestation is often contracted to the single word "abortion," most women attach considerable opprobrium to the general use of this term. Should the physician ask a reputable woman if she has had an abortion, she may become indignant. On the other hand, reference to a possible miscarriage may be made without offense since the latter expression, in the minds of most women, implies a spontaneous and not a criminally induced interruption of pregnancy.

Abortions not infrequently occur very early and are mistaken for delayed menstruations. Others cause such slight symptoms that a physician is not called. In addition, many are illegally induced and, as a result, are concealed in every possible manner. As a consequence, only those abortions which give rise to troublesome symptoms and are not associated with a criminal operation are recorded. In 87,061 pregnancies reported to a number of birth control clinics where concealment is unnecessary, 8.2% aborted spontaneously and in 3.7% abortion had been induced (1, 3, 4, 5, 6).

The relative frequency of spontaneous and induced abortions as well as the time of their occurrence in hospital practice is shown in Table I (7). From this,

TABLE I

1000 ABORTIONS

(Simons)

MONTH	SPONTANEOUS	SELF-INDUCED	CRIMINAL	% TOTAL
1	64	25	3	9.2
2	249	158	18	42.8
3	203	119	17	34.
4	33	34	8	7.5
5	35	18	2	5.4
6	7	2	0	0.9

it may be observed that more abortions occur in the first eight weeks than at any other time and that very few pregnancies end in abortion after the first trimester.

ETIOLOGY. The causative factors in abortion are being studied more seriously than in former years in the hope that adequate prophylactic measures may be found to prevent its all too frequent occurrence. Students of the subject have attempted to place these etiological factors into three general groups:

1. Those that cause the death of the embryo or fetus.
2. Those that produce abnormal conditions of the endometrium and decidua.
3. Those that cause the uterus to empty itself.

Unfortunately, it is impossible, with our present methods of investigation, to determine, in most instances, which of these three events occurs first. The uterus may try to empty itself, as is evidenced by the presence of cramp-like pains and bleeding. If allowed to continue, the blood supply to the decidua is altered and the resulting impairment of nutrition not only leads to changes in the decidua, but causes alterations in the fetal membranes, and anomalies or death of the embryo. When the products of conception are expelled, careful search often fails to show whether the death of the ovum occurred first and caused the uterine contractions, or whether the uterine contractions preceded the changes in the decidua and embryo. On the other hand, if prompt therapeutic measures are employed, and the threatened abortion is arrested, pregnancy often goes to term and results in the birth of a normal child. All obstetricians have seen many threatened abortions arrested and the pregnancies go to term without affecting the child in any way. In these cases, it would seem that the primary event was the attempt on the part of the uterus to empty itself. The present tendency to minimize this factor and place the blame upon the ovum or the decidua is often the excuse given by the negligent practitioner when he is accused of having failed to arrest a threatened abortion.

Since it is impossible to tell which of the three factors is the primary event, it seems better to state that abortions may be caused by:

1. Acute infectious disease.
2. Systemic diseases.
3. Toxemia of pregnancy.
4. Certain poisons.
5. Local conditions affecting the uterus.
6. Trauma.
7. Emotional disturbances
8. Faulty diet.
9. Endocrine dysfunction.
10. Oxytocics.
11. Diseases of the decidua and fetal membranes.
12. Anomalies of the ovum.
13. Incompatibility of the blood of husband and wife

INFECTIOUS DISEASES. The profound toxemia which accompanies acute infectious diseases often has a disastrous effect upon the products of conception. This, together with the accompanying hyperpyrexia, causes premature interruption of pregnancy in a large percentage of the gestations which are complicated by **malaria, typhoid fever, cholera, small pox, scarlet fever, influenza** and **pneumonia** (8, 9, 10). When the infection is severe, as it was in the influenza epidemic of 1918, at least half of the pregnancies terminate in abortion. In lobar pneumonia, the diminished oxygen and the increased carbon dioxide content of the blood are injurious to the fetus. In addition, carbon dioxide is said to stimulate uterine contractions. Lobar pneumonia, because of the toxemia, hyperpyrexia and cyanosis, which almost invariably accompany it, is especially apt to bring on an abortion or premature labor and the added strain caused by the emptying of the uterus greatly adds to the risk of this dangerous complication.

Although measles seldom is encountered as a complication of pregnancy, when it does occur, the possibility of abortion is great and over 50 per cent of such gestations end in this manner. The same thing is true, to a lesser extent, of scarlet fever, and, to a greater extent, of smallpox. Perhaps no other infection is as harmful to a pregnancy as is the hemorrhagic type of the latter disease. In hemorrhagic smallpox, spontaneous interruption invariably takes place. While the discrete variety of this disease is less severe than the confluent form after the first trimester, even mild infections, when they occur before the third month, cause abortion in the majority of cases.

Syphilis has been termed the arch-destroyer of fetal life and **is one of the commonest causes of interruption in the second half of pregnancy.** It, however, seldom or never causes an early abortion Because syphilis is an outstanding factor in the etiology of "dead fetus," all abortuses after the fourth month and every stillborn fetus, whether born prematurely or at term, should be subjected to a careful study to rule out this disease. Such a study should include microscopic examination of the fetal organs and placenta for the organisms and the characteristic histologic findings of syphilis, dark field search for treponema pallidum in scrapings from the umbilical vein wall, roentgen ray study of the fetal long bones and Wassermann and Kahn tests upon the mother, father and other children in the family.

SYSTEMIC DISEASES. The oxygen deprivation which accompanies **severe anemia** and **cardiac decompensation** may lead to the death of the fetus and abortion at any time during gestation (11). The same outcome frequently is observed in the last half of pregnancy when the latter is complicated by **nephritis** and **vascular-renal** disease. In these conditions, the abortions often are due to marked infarction and premature separation of the placenta.

TOXEMIA. The late toxemia of pregnancy frequently causes the death of the fetus and interruption of pregnancy in the last trimester. Although eclampsia is accompanied by a high maternal death rate, it is responsible for an even higher fetal loss. The manner in which the products of conception are affected is not understood. Perhaps, when more is known concerning the etiology and pathology of the so-called toxemia of pregnancy, its effect upon the placenta and fetus will be revealed.

POISONS. **Lead, carbon dioxide, histamine and other poisons** are recorded as etiological factors (12, 13, 14). These toxic agents may act upon the products of conception directly or they may first cause damage to the maternal circulation at or near the placental site. Following injury to the endothelium, thrombosis of the larger vessels is observed and hemorrhage occurs from the thin-walled capillaries and sinuses. As a consequence of these changes, degeneration and separation of the trophoblast take place. Occasionally, as in the case of lead, the primary lesion is located in the trophoblast, the degeneration of which may be sufficiently marked to cause the death of the ovum. Such lethal changes in the trophoblast can be brought about by amounts of lead which are too small to cause the death of the mother.

LOCAL CONDITIONS AFFECTING THE UTERUS. Fibromyomata, malformations, ovarian tumors, retroversions, adhesions and other abnormal local conditions frequently are blamed for abortion. Their importance, however, is greatly overestimated. On the other hand, if they prevent the normal development of the uterus, the latter may empty itself. Fibroid tumors, when they encroach upon the uterine cavity, may interfere with the circulation in and development of the decidua. When the ovum becomes implanted in such a decidua, abortion may occur. The contractions which result from the effort of the uterus to expel such submucous tumors also are a factor in the production of premature interruptions of pregnancy. On the other hand, a uterus may be markedly distorted by the growth of multiple fibroids and still carry a pregnancy to term. While the incidence of abortion probably is higher in marked malformations of the birth passages than in normal uteri, pregnancy in a malformed uterus usually continues to term and, in a surprisingly large number of cases, the abnormality is not recognized until after the baby is born. Retroversion, if long standing, may cause alterations in the circulation which favor interruption of pregnancy. When pregnancy occurs in a retroverted uterus, however, the tendency is for the uterus to come forward as it enlarges if no adhesions are present. As a result, most pregnancies complicated by retroversion go to term without difficulty. If, on the other hand, the retroversion is adherent, the inability of the uterus to expand in a satisfactory manner usually results in the expulsion of the products of conception. Deep cervical lacerations and high amputation of the cervix not infrequently cause the interruption of pregnancy soon after the middle of gestation. The same may be said of uterine fixation. After this operation the pregnant uterus usually is unable to expand satisfactorily and it, accordingly, empties itself.

TRAUMA. Instrumentation within the uterus is quite likely to cause an interruption of pregnancy. At times, however, even this may fail to bring about an abortion. One of the author's cases had been curetted three times during the early months of pregnancy after which the patient went to term and gave birth to a normal child. On the other hand, attempts to elicit Hegar's sign or even the slightest pressure during a gentle vaginal examination may cause the uterus to expel its content in a woman with a tendency to abort. Under this heading might be listed the following **exciting causes** which occasionally cause abortion: **a fall or blow on the abdomen, running up and down stairs, surf bathing, excessive vomiting, convulsions, horseback riding, golf, tennis, long journeys by auto, train or steamship and excessive coitus.** In this connection, it is surprising to note how much some pregnant women can stand without aborting and how little it takes to cause an abortion in others. Usually when abortion follows one of these exciting causes, there is present some underlying condition which predisposes to the interruption of pregnancy.

EMOTIONAL DISTURBANCES. Severe, sudden emotional disturbances sometimes are responsible for the premature termination of pregnancy. Earthquakes and other general catastrophes, accordingly, are said to increase the frequency of abortion. Likewise any profound shock, such as a bad fright or the deep grief occasioned by a death in the family, may precipitate the interruption of pregnancy. In these circumstances, however, some other condition usually serves as an underlying etiological factor since most pregnant women who are subjected to severe psychic shock suffer no ill effects therefrom at least as far as their pregnancies are concerned.

FAULTY DIET. Deficient diets in general and those which are deficient in calcium, iodine and the vitamins, in particular, may cause abortion (15). As was mentioned in the discussion of the diet during pregnancy (Chapter IX), some cases of abortion were thought to have been prevented by diminishing the carbohydrate intake of certain women who habitually abort when taking an excess of starches and sugar (16). Sea-coast Indians whose diet consists largely of iodine-rich sea food seldom give birth to dead fetuses. On the other hand, stillbirths have been observed six times more frequently in women not given iodine in the prenatal period than in those so treated (17). Experiments on animals have shown that diets deficient in **vitamin A** lead to the birth of deadborn and stunted offspring (18, 19). Similarly, the withholding of **vitamin B** in the first half of pregnancy caused the abortion of all fetuses and its withdrawal after the middle of gestation led to the premature birth of offspring lacking in vigor. In a series of 120 pregnant women who were given adequate vitamin B during pregnancy, there was no evidence of threatened abortion, while $4\frac{1}{2}$ per cent of a control group on an ordinary diet showed signs of threatened abortion (20). Deprivation of **vitamin E,** the fertility vitamin, in animals usually leads to a failure of conception but, if conception does take place, abortion is the rule (18, 21, 22, 23, 24, 25). The interruption of pregnancy in such instances is thought to be due to a pathologic development of the fetal portion of the placenta and changes in the decidua.

ENDOCRINE DISFUNCTION. Removal of the **corpus luteum** in the early weeks of pregnancy is followed by spontaneous evacuation of the uterus. This accident, however, may be prevented by the injection of sufficient amounts of progestin. **Progestin** also is thought to be of value in the treatment of certain cases of threatened abortion later in pregnancy (26). Estrin, in large doses, causes abortion in some animals (27, 28, 29). It is thought that such abortions are due to atrophic changes in the villi caused by the pressure which results from excessive hyperemia (28). Women who abort and those who go into labor prematurely sometimes show an excess of estrogenic substances in the blood and urine (30).

Hypothyroidism, likewise, is accompanied by a tendency toward premature interruption of pregnancy and the use of thyroid extract has been found to be effectual in some instances of habitual abortion (31, 32, 33, 34).

In **diabetes,** the products of conception are unfavorably affected by the disturbed carbohydrate metabolism, the changes in the alkali reserve and the altered function of the endocrine glands which is associated with the characteristic pancreatic pathology. As a result, almost half of the pregnancies complicated by diabetes prior to the introduction of insulin, terminated in abortion or death of the fetus. While the proper use of this discovery has eliminated most of the risk to the mother, it has only partially reduced the harmful effect of diabetes on the products of conception. It may be possible that the function of progestin is altered by the increased production of prolan with a resulting imperfect development of the decidua. Diminished glycogen in the pregravid endometrium and decidua may also interfere with the nutrition of the early ovum and hypoglycemic states probably prevent the adequate storage of carbohydrates in the placenta and fetal liver. The occurrence of an acidosis likewise may have a disastrous effect upon the products of conception. After the middle of pregnancy, there is a tendency to overgrowth and death of the fetus due possibly, as some investigators have suggested, to the accompanying decided increase in prolan (35, 36).

OXYTOCICS. **Ergot, posterior pituitary extract, quinine** and numerous less potent drugs have been employed to bring on an abortion by causing uterine contractions. Usually, however, they are unsuccessful. In this connection, it is of interest to note that large doses of estrin have been employed to sensitize the uterus preliminary to the use of posterior pituitary extract. Even this combination invariably fails when the fetus is alive and the gestation is normal. On the other hand, abortion has been produced in animals by large doses of estrogenic substance. In these, the evacuation of the uterus was due more to the effect of the hormone on the decidua and trophoblast than to its action on the uterine musculature (28).

DISEASES OF THE DECIDUA. As has been noted, many of the conditions previously mentioned may cause alterations in the decidua and the fetal membranes and thus produce abortion. In addition, inflammation of the endometrium and subsequent deciduitis are responsible for a limited number of interrupted pregnancies.

DEFECTIVE GERM PLASM. Careful examination of the products of conception at the time of abortion reveals a defective development of the human ovum in 80 per cent of the cases which date from the first month and 50 per cent of those which occur after the second month (38, 39). The developmental defect may be restricted to the trophoblast covering of the ovum which gives rise to the fetal membranes or to the embryonic area or it may involve both parts of the egg. Defects of the trophoblast are less frequent and are less important than embryonal defects since the embryo should not be injured if half of the trophoblast is good (Streeter). This imperfect development of the ovum may be due primarily to inherent defects in the sex cells or it may result secondarily from the action of one or more of the above-mentioned factors after implantation has taken place. That the germ plasm alone may be responsible for the unfortunate outcome in such cases is proven by the occurrence of a single dead embryo among several living fetuses in the litter of an animal which commonly has multiple pregnancies. In the human being, an excellent illustration of this effect is afforded by the presence in a twin pregnancy, of an hydatidiform mole and a normal fetus which goes to term. When the fault is inherent in the germ plasm, an abnormal spermatazoon, a defective ovum or an incompatibility between the sex cells, may result in incomplete embryological development and early death of the fertilized ovum.

SPERMATOZOA. Microscopic studies of the semen from the male members of relatively infertile couples often show a large proportion of the spermatozoa to be defective morphologically. When the wives of such men become pregnant, abortion is observed more frequently than in ordinary cases (41, 42). Similar observations have been made in animals and, in one instance, an 18 months old bull with genital hypoplasia and morphologically defective spermatozoa was bred over a period of six months to twenty cows which, in each instance, either failed to conceive or aborted (43). Insemination observations on human beings have also revealed the fact that morphologically normal motile spermatozoa may be incapable of fertilizing normal ova. In a series of cases in which such spermatozoa failed to fertilize the ova of normal women, the same women were afterwards impregnated by the insemination of spermatozoa from other males (44).

Ova. Although microscopic studies of human ova are rare, it is believed that they, too, may be defective. An otherwise normal ovum may be immature or too old and thus may lack the vitality necessary to its continued development. The fertilization of a post-mature ovum, accordingly, may account for the frequency of abortion in those women who have abnormally long menstrual cycles.

Incompatibility of the Spermatozoon and Ovum. The spermatozoon and ovum also may be normal but incompatible. Some apparently normal married couples cannot procreate because the wife fails to conceive or aborts. Occasionally, when the male member of such a union subsequently marries another woman and the wife takes another husband, healthy children are born to the new unions (45).

Incapatability of the Blood of Husband and Wife. An agglutinogen, the Rh factor, in human blood which gives rise to the formation of immune isoantibodies and sometimes causes serious transfusion reactions may be responsible for the death of the fetus and abortion. When the mother's blood is Rh negative and that of the father is Rh positive, the fetal blood may be Rh positive and may be hemolized as a result of immune isoantibodies which are formed in the maternal blood. This hemolysis may cause fetal death or abortion or it may lead to the development of erythroblastosis fetalis (7a, b, c).

Habitual Abortion. Some women abort repeatedly without any apparent cause. The number of these unfortunate cases is growing smaller as our knowledge advances. The removal of foci of infection, the administration of thyroid extract or iodine, and the correction of dietary deficiencies have prevented some of the abortions previously classified as habitual.

PATHOLOGY

In some instances, as previously stated, the primary lesion in an abortion may be an alteration in the maternal endothelium at the placental site. This is followed by thrombosis of the larger vessels and hemorrhage into the spongy layer of the decidua basalis. As a result, more or less separation of the ovum takes place, degenerative changes appear in the trophoblast and, ultimately the embryo dies. In other cases, the abortion may be preceded by the death of the fetus and, in still others, the initial phenomenon may consist of unusually strong intermittent uterine contractions. As a rule, one of these possibilities leads to another and, in many cases, all three are present by the time the products of conception are expelled.

Before the eighth week, the ovum is more or less loosely imbedded within the endometrium and is covered by the thin decidua capsularis which bulges into the uterine cavity. At first it lies free within the egg chamber. Soon thereafter some of the villi become attached to the decidua basalis. These anchoring villi grow more numerous as pregnancy advances so that by the end of this period, the ovum is rather firmly attached to the uterine wall. Because of the lack of fixation in the very early weeks of pregnancy and because the imperfect development of the circulatory system may easily lead to impairment in nutrition, interruption of pregnancy not infrequently occurs soon after the first period is skipped. Such an early abortion usually is accompanied by the expulsion of the entire ovum together with the endometrium. Since it follows soon after the expected date of the skipped period, the patient usually considers such an abortion to be a delayed but profuse menstruation. Later in this period, the increased thinning of the decidua capsularis favors its rupture. This lack of protection offered by the developing decidua, together with the insecure attachment of the ovum, then leads to the expulsion of the entire egg, as may be observed when it is examined under water. **During the first eight weeks, accordingly, abortion is more apt to be complete than later in pregnancy** (Fig. 721 a & b).

Between the 8th and 12th weeks, the chorion adjacent to the decidua basalis undergoes great development and, by means of its numerous anchoring villi, becomes more firmly attached. The better-developed fetal circulation also furnishes ample nourishment to the products of conception. Rupture of the decidua capsularis, likewise, is less apt to occur since the ovum is now in contact with the decidua vera of the opposite side. The incidence of abortion, accordingly, grows less as pregnancy nears the end of this period. Because of the firm attachment of the anchoring villi, however, there is a tendency for the fetus to be cast off without the chorionic elements which frequently are retained even though the expelled gestation sac is unruptured. **Abortions which occur between the 8th and 12th weeks, therefore, are prone to be incomplete.** Regardless of the better attachment of the placental elements, however, the entire ovum may at times be expelled. Examination of such an abortus shows more or less atrophy of the villi over a large part of its surface.

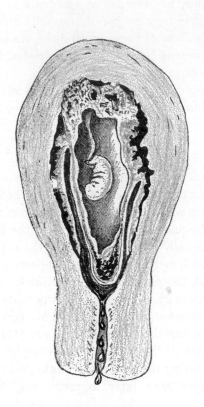 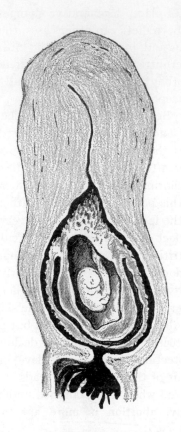

FIG. 721a. Abortion at the 8th week. First stage. Hemorrhage into the decidua (Bumm).

FIG. 721b. Abortion at the 8th week. Second stage. Ovum lies in the lower uterine segment. Cervical canal is obliterated (Bumm).

When the intact gestation sac is expelled, the behavior of the uterus is somewhat similar to that observed in a full term labor. As the abortion progresses, the cervical canal is pulled up and is finally obliterated. Following obliteration of the cervix, dilatation progresses until the external os is large enough to permit the passage of the products of conception. Spontaneous dilatation, therefore, is preceded by a preliminary preparation which cannot be duplicated by artificial means. If the pregnancy has advanced to a stage in which the delivery of the placenta or fetal head requires an opening in excess of 1 cm., this spontaneous dilatation must be awaited or a cutting operation must be employed.

By the 12th week, the chorion frondosum is well differentiated and the ovum is firmly attached to the wall of the uterus. After this time, abortion occurs less frequently than in the first trimester. There is, on the other hand,

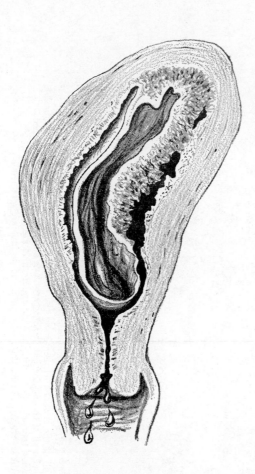 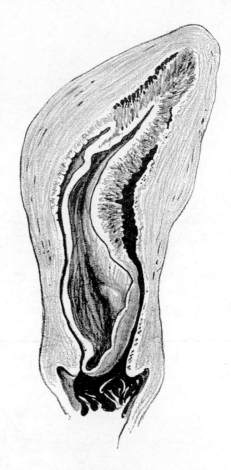

FIG. 722a. Abortion at the 12th week.   First stage.   FIG. 722b. Abortion at the 12th week.   Later stage.
Hemorrhage into the placenta (Bumm).   Cervical canal obliterated (Bumm).

a change in the endocrine system near the end of the third month when the function of the corpus luteum is partly taken over by the placenta.   Should this transfer of function be faulty, abortion may occur in spite of the better fixation of the ovum.   From this standpoint, therefore, the end of the first trimester may be considered a critical period.

After the third month, the egg is less apt to be expelled in its entirety. Usually the fetus comes away first and the placenta is subsequently separated and cast off.   The mechanism, accordingly, simulates that observed in labor but there is a greater tendency toward partial or total retention of the placenta (Fig. 722 a & b).

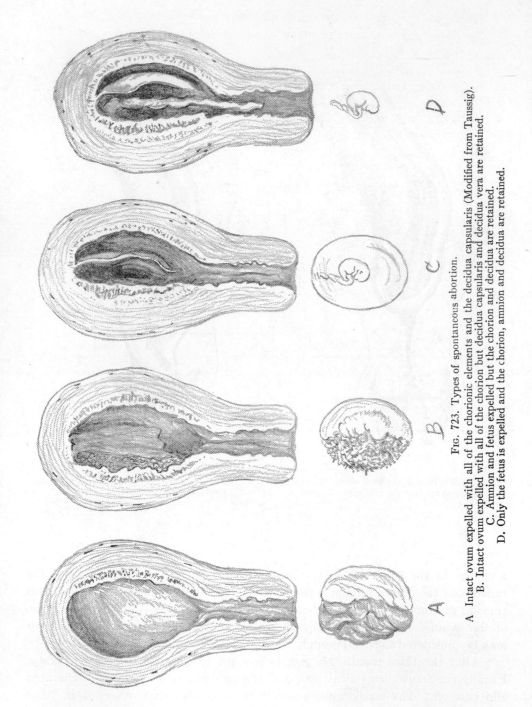

Fig. 723. Types of spontaneous abortion.

A Intact ovum expelled with all of the chorionic elements and the decidua capsularis (Modified from Taussig).
B. Intact ovum expelled with all of the chorion but decidua capsularis and decidua vera are retained.
C. Amnion and fetus expelled but the chorion and decidua are retained.
D. Only the fetus is expelled and the chorion, amnion and decidua are retained.

From the foregoing discussion, it may be stated that the evacuation of the uterus in a spontaneous abortion may be accomplished in several ways:

1. **The entire ovum, together with the decidua, may be expelled at the same time.** This often occurs in very early interruptions of pregnancy and were it not for the increased bleeding which accompanies it, such an abortion might be mistaken for a delayed menstruation (Fig. 723a). Unfortunately, the tendency toward this type of expulsion rapidly diminishes as pregnancy advances and it seldom is seen after the eighth week. The simultaneous evacuation of the ovum and decidua is followed by rapid regeneration of the endometrium without sequellae.

2. **Expulsion of the intact ovum without the decidua** also may occur (Fig. 723b). Although this type of evacuation may take place at any time during pregnancy, its frequency also is greatest in the early weeks. Because of the delayed separation and expulsion of the decidua, the clinical course may be somewhat longer than that which accompanies the first mechanism. The bleeding which results from the retained decidua, however, seldom is profuse and spontaneous evacuation of the retained tissue eventually occurs. As a consequence, this also is a favorable method of spontaneous evacuation.

3. **The unruptured gestation sac may be expelled with retention of a portion of the chorion frondosum and most of the decidua** (Fig. 723c). In such circumstances, more time is required for the separation of the chorionic elements and the accompanying hemorrhage may be severe enough to require intervention. Because of this possible outcome, every abortus should be examined under water to rule out the possibility of retained chorionic tissue. Since the anchoring villi become more numerous after the sixth week, this and the following mechanism are the commonest methods of evacuation after the second month.

4. **The decidua capsularis and chorion leve often rupture and allow the amniotic fluid and fetus to escape but the chorion frondosum and decidua are retained** just as is commonly observed in parturition (Fig. 723d). If the placenta is well-formed, it may separate after a brief interval and be expelled, as in a full-term labor. On the other hand, a part or all of the chorionic elements may adhere to the uterus and be retained for a considerable time. As long as such tissue remains within the uterus, bleeding may occur. Even when there is no appreciable loss of blood, the possibility of a profuse and even fatal hemorrhage must be kept in mind until the uterus is completely evacuated.

Occasionally, the extruded ovum contains only clear amniotic fluid and the remnants of a degenerated embryo or umbilical cord—a so-called **blighted ovum.** When the course is prolonged, the blood which is discharged into the spongy layer of the decidua basalis clots about the degenerating chorionic villi on the surface of the ovum. As the separation continues, more bleeding takes place and this again coagulates on top of the previous clot. Thus the abortus eventually comes to consist of layers of coagulated blood which surround trophoblastic elements in various stages of degeneration. The entire mass may then be expelled from the uterine cavity or it may remain within the uterus for a number of months. In the latter circumstance, the ovum itself becomes compressed and markedly degenerated. As a consequence, it is difficult to differentiate the products of conception from the blood masses with which they are intermingled. Abortuses of this nature are designated as **blood or fleshy moles.**

At times, the amniotic fluid is absorbed and the fetus is considerably compressed. It is then known as a **fetus compressus.** Less frequently, the fetal remnants are so dried out and compressed that they become parchment-like in appearance—**fetus papyraceous.** More frequently and especially in the later stages of pregnancy, **the dead fetus undergoes maceration** in the amniotic fluid. As a result of this change, the external layer of the skin becomes detached or peels off readily, exposing the underlying shiny red corium. The sutures of the fetal skull also are greatly softened and permit marked overriding of the bones of the cranial vault. The fetal head, accordingly, loses its characteristic shape and tends to become more or less collapsed. The general softening and distortion is so great that it may be recognized by roentgenologic examination. Such an examination clearly reveals overriding of the cranial bones and distorted relationships of other parts of the fetus which could not possibly occur during fetal life.

CLINICAL COURSE

VARIETIES. Abortions are classified according to their clinical course as follows:

1. Threatened
2. Imminent
3. Inevitable
4. Complete
5. Incomplete
6. Missed

THREATENED ABORTION. Slight bleeding with or without pain in the early months of pregnancy is referred to as a threatened abortion.

SYMPTOMS. There is a history of amenorrhea and other symptoms of pregnancy corresponding to the period of gestation.

Vaginal bleeding is always present and occurs with or without apparent cause. The blood loss may be so slight that the discharge is described as a pinkish discoloration or a spotting. On the other hand, rather profuse, bright red bleeding may take place.

Pain may or may not be present and may follow or precede the onset of the bleeding. It usually is intermittent and indicates the presence of uterine contractions. If the pain becomes severe and progressively increases in intensity, the threatened abortion rapidly changes to an imminent or inevitable one.

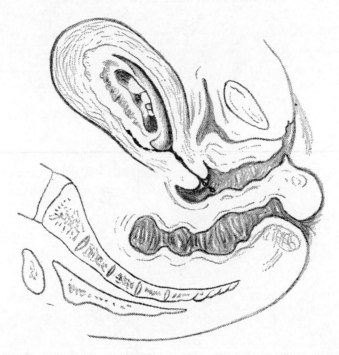

FIG. 725. Threatened abortion. The cervix is closed and its canal is not obliterated.

EXAMINATION shows the uterus to be soft and the other signs of pregnancy corresponding to the period of gestation are evident. The cervix is closed and its canal is not shortened (Fig. 725).

TREATMENT. In those cases in which the bleeding is slight and the pain is not suggestive of an ectopic gestation, vaginal examination is contraindicated, as the gentlest manipulation may aggravate the condition.

The patient should be kept in bed and given opiates hypodermically. Morphine gr. $\frac{1}{4}$, is preferable and is repeated in six hours if the bleeding continues. Should this cause vomiting, codeine gr. $1\frac{1}{2}$, may be substituted. Progestin in doses of 1 rabbit unit several times daily also is indicated.

All napkins are to be saved so that the amount of blood lost in twenty-four hours may be properly estimated.

If the bleeding persists, but is not alarming, expectant treatment, as outlined, is to be continued, provided the amount of blood lost each day is observed and its effect on the mother is followed by hemoglobin and red cell determinations. As long as the Aschheim-Zondek test for pregnancy remains positive, the possibility of a successful outcome should be awaited, unless other conditions demand intervention.

After the cessation of symptoms, rest in bed is indicated for several days, during which cathartics and enemata should be avoided.

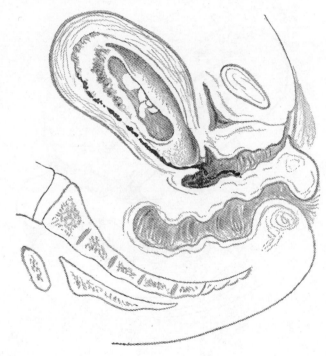

FIG. 726. Imminent abortion. Cervical canal obliterated; external os dilating.

Following recovery, all patients should be careful to avoid any of the exciting etiological factors previously mentioned.

If the bleeding is severe, an aseptic vaginal examination is indicated. When the cervix is found to be obliterated or open, the treatment is that recommended for imminent or inevitable abortion. Should the cervix be closed, the vagina is packed firmly with sterile gauze saturated with 4% mercurochrome solution. Unfortunately, the pack usually causes the cervix to dilate and, as a result, the abortion becomes imminent or inevitable.

IMMINENT ABORTION. When the cervical canal is obliterated or the external os is dilated, the abortion is imminent (Fig. 726).

Symptoms. The symptoms are those of pregnancy together with vaginal hemorrhage and cramp-like pains.

As a rule, the bleeding progressively increases and at times reaches alarming proportions. Pallor, rapid thready pulse, cold extremities, air hunger and even death may result from the hemorrhage.

The pain is colicky and increases in severity as the condition progresses.

Examination shows the usual findings of hemorrhage and pregnancy, together with obliteration of the cervical canal or dilatation of the external os (Fig. 726).

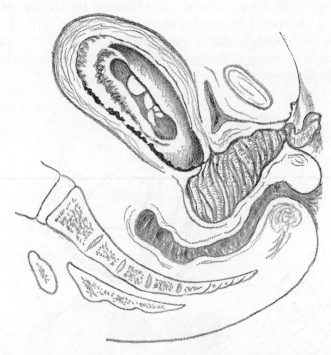

Fig. 727. Imminent abortion. Vagina packed with 4 per cent mercurochrome gauze.

Treatment. The treatment in imminent abortion depends upon the amount of hemorrhage, the duration of pregnancy, the condition of the cervix, and the wishes of the patient.

If the bleeding is not excessive, an expectant plan may be followed. The possibility of an alarming hemorrhage taking place at any time must be kept in mind. Expectant treatment, therefore, is permissible only in a hospital where careful and constant observation is possible, and the facilities for an emergency operation are always at hand. When the condition has progressed to the stage of an imminent abortion, it usually is best to consider emptying the uterus. Very often, this may be accomplished by the injection of posterior pituitary extract.

If the bleeding is excessive, the uterus should be emptied at once. In the event that the external os is not dilated, it is to be opened sufficiently to admit a large curet, the finger or an ovum forceps. For this purpose Hegar dilators are recommended.

When conditions are not satisfactory for the performance of an immediate operation, a mercurochrome-saturated gauze pack is introduced into the cervix and vagina to control the hemorrhage and hasten the dilatation (Fig. 727). Often, the products of conception come away with the pack when it is removed and, as a result, the necessity for further operative treatment is eliminated.

Since imminent abortion, in most cases, cannot be arrested, the radical plan of emptying the uterus or packing the vagina is to be favored, unless the wishes of the patient justify a trial of expectancy. In the latter circumstances, the attendant must be prepared to respond immediately, if a sudden hemorrhage demands prompt intervention.

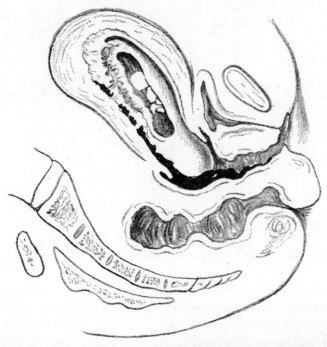

FIG. 728. Inevitable abortion. The membranes bulge through the dilated cervix.

INEVITABLE ABORTION. Abortion is inevitable when the membranes are ruptured or when the ovum protrudes through the dilated cervix (Fig. 728).

SYMPTOMS. The symptoms are the same as those described under Imminent Abortion.

EXAMINATION shows the evidences of pregnancy and an open cervix through which the products of conception bulge. If the membranes have ruptured, the cervix may vary in length and dilatation.

TREATMENT. When the bleeding is not excessive, an expectant plan may be followed in the hope that spontaneous, complete evacuation of the uterus may take place. This outcome often may be hastened by the injection of posterior pituitary extract. The patient, however, must be kept under constant observation and facilities for immediate intervention must be at hand, should excessive bleeding occur. Naturally, such a plan can be followed only in a hospital.

If these requirements cannot be carried out, or if the hemorrhage is profuse, the uterus should be emptied at once.

Before the 8th week, a curet or small ovum forceps is used.

After the 8th week, the products of conception are first separated by the finger (Fig. 729) and then removed by ovum or sponge forceps.

When the cervix is too small, it is dilated with Hegar dilators.

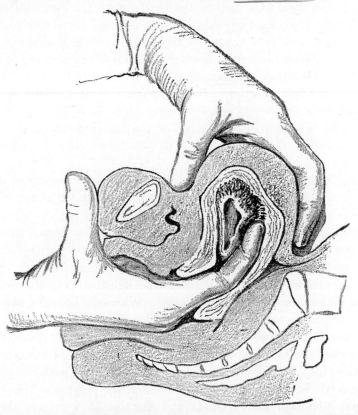

FIG. 729. Separation of the products of conception by the finger. The external hand forces the fundus of the uterus down over the finger which is introduced into the uterine cavity.

If, for any reason, an immediate operation cannot be carried out, the vagina and cervix are packed to control the hemorrhage until the uterus can be emptied.

INCOMPLETE ABORTION. An abortion is incomplete when only a part of the products of conception is expelled. Usually, the fetus comes away and the remainder of the ovum, with the decidua, is left behind. Its occurrence is more frequent after the 8th week because of the better attachment of the chorionic villi.

SYMPTOMS. Bleeding in varying amounts continues until the retained secundines are expelled spontaneously or artificially removed.

TREATMENT. The material expelled at every abortion should be carefully examined under water. If the ovum is complete, no further local treatment is indicated. When examination shows the products of conception to be incomplete, pituitary extract should be given and in those cases in which its use is not followed by expulsion of the retained fragments, the uterus should be emptied with the curet in the early months and with the finger after the third month.

Should operative intervention be decided upon in any abortion that is not septic, it is better to elect a method that will empty the uterus at once. This will minimize the amount of blood loss and reduce the risk of infection.

The use of a pack is restricted to those cases in which infection is present or in which the circumstances will not permit immediate emptying of the uterus.

COMPLETE ABORTION. Expulsion of the entire products of conception is known as a complete abortion. Its occurrence is more common before the eighth week.

SYMPTOMS. Following the passage of the intact ovum and decidua, the pain and hemorrhage cease, but a slight, blood-stained vaginal discharge usually persists for several days.

In **septic abortions,** the possibility of opening up new avenues of entrance for the pyogenic organisms already present must be kept in mind. For this reason and because of the danger of breaking down the wall of leucocytes with which Nature attempts to localize the infection, intrauterine manipulations should be restricted as much as possible. Unless the hemorrhage demands interference, such cases do better if all local treatment is avoided. Should the ovum be separated and block the drainage through the cervical canal, however, its removal with ovum forceps is indicated. When the bleeding requires intervention in the presence of infection, the vagina is packed with mercurochrome-saturated gauze to control the hemorrhage and aid cervical dilatation. Often the entire ovum comes away when the pack is removed 24 hours later. If it does not, the products of conception are gently removed with ovum forceps as soon as the cervix is sufficiently dilated to permit the passage of this instrument. **Instrumental dilatation of the cervix and the use of a curette are distinctly contraindicated in the presence of infection** (19, 20, 21). Unless hemorrhage is present, septic abortions are best treated by rest in bed with an abundance of fresh air and sunshine, a nourishing diet and small transfusions of 200–300 cc. given every four or five days. In addition to this established conservative routine, the use of sulphanilimide as recommended in the treatment of puerperal infection is advisable.

The treatment of abortion may be summarized under three general headings: A. The conservative or expectant routine, B. The radical or immediate evacuation plan and C. The intermediate plan which includes certain principles from each of the other two.

A. **The conservative or expectant plan** consists in leaving the case entirely to Nature in the hope that the products of conception will be spontaneously separated and expelled. Uterine contractions are awaited or preferably are stimulated by the use of posterior pituitary extract and natural dilatation of the cervix is anticipated. After the passages have been thus prepared, Nature is expected to separate and expel the entire ovum from the uterine cavity. This routine accordingly, is analagous to that which is followed in a spontaneous full-term labor. Following it, as in the case of labor at term, there should be no infection and regeneration of the endometrium should follow its natural course. The patient whose abortion has been so treated, accordingly, should be able to become pregnant again and should carry her future pregnancy to a successful termination provided the cause of the abortion is eliminated.

Unfortunately, the clinical course of most abortion cases differs from that of a normal labor with respect to the onset, continuance and amount of the hemorrhage. In early interruptions of pregnancy, bleeding usually occurs early and progressively increases until the uterus is completely evacuated. If, therefore, Nature could be relied on to empty the uterus completely before the patient bleeds to death or before the bleeding becomes alarming, this method would be the procedure of choice in all cases. Because alarming hemorrhage at times occurs and because the patient occasionally may bleed to death, reliance upon the expectant plan alone is not justifiable. In every case, daily inspection of the soiled napkins and daily hemoglobin estimations must be made. Whenever the blood loss becomes excessive, the conservative plan should be abandoned for either the radical or intermediate routine. **With this modification, the conservative routine becomes one of watchful expectancy or judicious neglect and, when so modified, is to be preferred over the other routines whenever the bleeding is not excessive or whenever infection is present.**

B. **The radical routine** consists in the immediate artificial evacuation of the uterus. It includes (1) artificial dilatation of the cervix if the cervix is not open, (2) thorough separation of the chorionic elements from the uterus and (3) complete removal of all of the products of conception. The procedures which are best suited to the accomplishment of these three fundamental considerations vary as follows with the period of gestation:

(a) **Before the 8th week,** curettage or dilatation with Hegar dilators and curettage.

(b) **From the 8th to the 12th week,** dilatation with Hegar dilators, separation of the ovum with the finger and its removal with the ovum forceps.

(c) **After the 12th week,** separation of the placenta with the fingers and removal of the uterine contents with placenta forceps. If the cervix is not sufficiently dilated to permit the withdrawal of the placental mass or the fetal head, preliminary opening of the cervix should be effected by the use of an anterior vaginal hysterotomy.

(a) The first of these recommendations—**curettage or dilatation with Hegar dilators and curettage**—is a simple procedure and, in the absence of infection, is accompanied by very little risk, provided the operation is done under strict aseptic precautions and the anesthetic is given by a competent anesthetist. In emergency operations done on patients who recently have taken nourishment, the stomach should be washed preliminary to the giving of an anesthetic or the operation should be done under local anesthesia. Posterior pituitary extract likewise should be administered immediately before the curette is introduced, in order that the slight risk of perforating the wall of the uterus may be reduced.

(b) From the 8th to the 12th week, the chorionic elements are so extensive and their attachment is so firm that their complete removal with a curette often is impossible. **For this reason, it is better to separate the ovum with the finger and then remove it with ovum forceps.** Naturally, the cervix must be sufficiently patulous to permit the passage of the finger. If it is not, dilatation is accomplished by means of graduated metal sounds—Hegar dilators. Here again, all intrauterine manipulations should be preceded by an injection of posterior pituitary extract in order that the hemorrhage incident to the operation may be lessened and the risk of perforating the uterus may be minimized. While this method of procedure is contraindicated in the presence of infection, removal of the products of conception with ovum forceps when they interfere with drainage by blocking the cervical canal is not only permissible but desirable.

(c) After the first trimester, the placenta is well formed and its increasing bulk must be considered as pregnancy progresses. As a consequence, preliminary separation by the finger under the guidance of the sense of touch is essential. Although the placenta may be broken up by digital manipulation, the cervical opening must be large enough not only for the introduction of the finger but it must be sufficient to permit the withdrawal of the large placental fragments. Owing to the progressive growth of the fetal head, its removal also becomes an increasingly difficult problem as gestation advances. For these reasons, dilatation adequate to the proper evacuation of the uterus cannot be accomplished by any method of artificial means without causing serious injury to the cervix. **After the third month, therefore, it is best to control the hemorrhage with a pack and await spontaneous dilatation. If this plan is contraindicated, the cervical opening should be enlarged by means of an anterior vaginal hysterotomy prior to the necessary intrauterine manipulations.** When infection is present, all intrauterine manipulations should be avoided unless the ovum is blocking the canal of the cervix and can be removed with ovum forceps.

Pituitary extract is of great value in the therapy of abortion. When the expectant plan is followed, its use often hastens the expulsion of the ovum and assists in controlling the hemorrhage. After the cervix is dilated, an injection of pituitary extract serves as a prophylaxis against perforation whenever instrumentation is required.

THE SUBSEQUENT TREATMENT of all abortion cases should not be neglected. Hemoglobin and red cell determinations often show the loss of more blood than is suspected. Postabortal care, therefore, must include the employment of suitable blood building measures. In this connection, transfusion is of great value and, whenever infection is anticipated, its use is imperative. Rest in bed for at least one week is indicated and the patient should be kept under observation until involution is complete.

MISSED ABORTION. Retention of the products of conception for some time after the death of the ovum is known as a missed abortion.

SYMPTOMS. Prior to the death of the ovum, the symptoms of pain and hemorrhage often are similar to those described under threatened and imminent abortion. After the death of the ovum, the breasts become smaller and a persistent brownish vaginal discharge is observed.

EXAMINATION shows a retrogression in the signs of pregnancy. The uterus ceases to grow and lacks its customary soft consistency. Often, a doughy feel is detected. The cervix is closed, and a dirty, brownish discharge may be seen coming from it. Naturally, the Aschheim-Zondek test is negative.

TREATMENT. Soon after the fetus dies, the estrin of the maternal blood is diminished or disappears entirely (46). Lack of this sensitizing agent which prepares the uterine muscle for the stimulating action of posterior pituitary hormone has been suggested as a cause of missed abortion. These hormones, accordingly, have been employed to bring about evacuation of the uterus. Large doses of estrin given intramuscularly and followed by posterior pituitary extract are reported to have caused the expulsion of the products of conception in forty-eight out of a series of fifty-five cases. Estradial benzoate in 2 mg. doses is given intramuscularly every 8 hours or stilbestrol in doses of 1 mg. is taken orally for 7 or 8 days. Four 1 cc. injections of posterior pituitary extract are administered on the 5th day and repeated 3 days later if necessary. The older the fetus before its death and the more recent the death of the fetus the easier is it to evacuate the uterus by this method (47, 47a). Our own experience seems to confirm the value of this routine. It is applicable not only in those cases in which the fetus dies before the period of viability but may also be used in the treatment of dead fetus in the latter months of pregnancy. Should this method fail, the uterus is to be emptied by that procedure which is best suited to the conditions that are present. Dilatation and curettage are used before the eighth week. After the eighth week, dilatation and separation with the finger, followed by removal with ovum forceps is recommended. If the pregnancy is too far advanced for the use of the Hegar dilators, the cervix is opened by means of an anterior vaginal hysterotomy. Packing the vagina to secure dilatation greatly increases the risk of infection and should not be considered in the treatment of missed abortion.

TREATMENT OF HABITUAL ABORTION. As was stated in the discussion of the etiology of abortion, the interruption of pregnancy sometimes occurs repeatedly in the same woman, without any apparent cause. Often, however, the etiological factor may be revealed by a thorough investigation. For this reason, in all so-called habitual or recurrent abortions, a most careful history of the husband and wife is essential. All of the causative factors enumerated in the section on etiology must be considered and the products of conception should be subjected to a careful microscopic examination. Because syphilis, diabetes and nephritis often are overlooked, these possibilities are to be ruled out by the customary laboratory tests. The basal metabolic rate likewise should be taken in order that the presence or absence of hypothyroidism may be ascertained. The possibility of a dietary deficiency and of foci of infection in the teeth and tonsils as etiologic factors also are to be considered.

Following such an abortion, at least six months or preferably one year should elapse before the patient again becomes pregnant. During this time, both she and her husband should be given a well-balanced diet which, for at least several months prior to the date of the contemplated pregnancy, should contain an abundance of vitamin E. After conception takes place, all of the exciting causes of abortion are to be avoided. If cramp-like pains or bleeding occur, she should be put to bed and given morphine gr. $\frac{1}{4}$ and one rabbit unit of progestin hypodermically b.i.d. It is well for the patient to have on hand at all times one or two $\frac{1}{4}$ gr. morphine tablets in order that sedative therapy may be commenced before her physician arrives. Meticulous care is to be given to the diet as recommended in the Chapter on the Management of Pregnancy. In this connection, it should be remembered that iron, calcium and iodine may be indicated. Satisfactory reports concerning the use of thyroid extract, progestin and wheat germ oil as prophylactic agents have appeared in the literature. Thyroid extract is recommended in doses of 0.1 gm. t.i.d. for the first $4\frac{1}{2}$ months, 0.2 gm. thereafter until the 8th month and 0.3 gm. for the remainder of pregnancy (48). Progestin is given in doses of one rabbit unit twice daily until the symptoms cease and thereafter twice weekly up to the 32nd week (50, 51). When wheat germ oil is used, the fact that it loses its potency within eight weeks of its manufacture should lead the physician to obtain a fresh preparation. Three doses of 4 drachms each are recommended during the first 24 hours after the onset of symptoms and this is to be followed by one drachm daily (52, 53, 54).

MORTALITY. It has been estimated that the death rate from abortion is 1.2 per cent. By using this figure and his own estimate of the total number of abortions, Taussig concludes that 8000 to 10,000 die annually from abortion in the United States. He also calls attention to the fact that, for every death resulting from abortion, several women are disabled or rendered sterile or, at a subsequent pregnancy, suffer from the after-effects of the abortion. Realization of these sequellae induced the Russian government to change its attitude toward legalized abortion. Although the death rate from abortions performed by the Russian experts was very low, the after-effects could not be prevented and these led to the abandonment of legalized abortion in Russia.

REFERENCES

1. Pierce, C. C.: Contraceptive Services in the United States. Human Fertility, 1943, 8, 91.
2. Plass, E. D.: Quoted by Taussig.
3. Taussig, F. J.: Abortion, Spontaneous and Induced. St. Louis, 1936, p. 26.
4. Wiehl, D. G.: A Summary of Data on Reported Incidence of Abortion. Milbank Memorial Fund Quarterly, 1938, 16, 80.
5. Stix, R. K.: The Medical Aspects of Variations in Fertility. Am. J. O. & G., 1938, 35, 571.
6. Galloway, C. E.: Discussion of Simon's Paper. Am. J. O. & G., 1939, 37, 848.
7. Simons, J. H.: Statistical Analysis of One Thousand Abortions. Am. J. O. & G., 1939, 37, 840.
7a. Levine, P.: The Role of Iso-immunization in Transfusion Accidents in Pregnancy and in Erythroblastosis Fetalis. Am. J. O. & G., 1941, 42, 165.
7b. Landsteiner, K. and Wiener, A. S.: Studies on an Agglutinogen (Rh) in Human Blood Reacting with Anti Rhesus Sera with Human Isoantibodies. J. Exp. Med., 1941, 74, 309.
7c. Levine, P., Burnham, L., Katzin, E. M. and Vogel, P.: The Role of Iso-immunization in the Pathogenesis of Erythroblastosis Fetalis. Am. J. O. & G., 1941, 42, 309.
8. Das, S.: Malaria and Abortion. Calcutta Med. J., 1923, 18, 348.
9. Laffont and Mélé: Infection éberthienne et grossesse; avortement spontané au 5, mois; mort de l'enfant, présence de Typhoid bacilles d'Ebert dans le sang du coeur de l'enfant. Bull. Soc. d'obs. et gyn., 1928, 17, 573.
10. Harris, J. W.: Influenza Occurring in Pregnant Women. J. A. M. A., 1919, 72, 978.
11. Fellner, O.: Herz und Schwangerschaft. Monatschr. f. Geburtsh. u. Gyn., 1901, 14, 370.
12. Bell, W. Blair: The Specific Action of Lead on the Chorion Epithelium of the Rabbit, Contrasted with the Action of Copper, Thallium and Thorium. J. O. & G. Brit. Emp., 1925, 32, 1.
13. Datnow, M. M.: An Experimental Investigation Concerning Toxic Abortion Produced by Chemical Agents. J. O. & G. Brit. Emp., 1928, 35, 693.
14. Hofbauer, J.: Experimental Studies on Toxemias of Pregnancy; Can Histamine Poisoning be Regarded as Etiologic Factor? Am. J. O. & G., 1926, 12, 159.
15. Macomber, D.: Effect of a Diet Low in Calcium on Fertility, Pregnancy and Lactation in the Rat. J. A. M. A., 1927, 88, 6.
16. Williams, C. P.: Carbohydrate Metabolism in Cases of Unexplained Miscarriages. Lancet, 1933, 2, 858.
17. Kemp, W. N.: The Stillbirth Problem in Relation to Iodine Deficiency. Bull. Vancouver M. A., 1933, 10, 52.
18. Evans, H. M. and Bishop, K. S.: On The Existence of a Hitherto Unrecognized Dietary Factor Essential for Reproduction. Science, 1922, 56, 650.
19. Mason, K. E.: Reproductive Function in Female Rats on Low Levels of Vitamin A. Anat. Rec., 1934, 58, Suppl. p. 80.
20. Tau, E. M. and McNeile, O.: Relation of Vitamin B Deficiency to Metabolic Disturbances During Pregnancy and Lactation. Am. J. O. & G., 1935, 29, 811.
21. Sure, B.: Dietary Requirements for Reproduction. II. The Existence of A Specific Vitamin for Reproduction. J. Biol. Chem., 1924, 58, 693.
    (Also): Dietary Requirements for Reproduction. III. The Existence of the Reproductive Dietary Complex (Vitamin E) In the Ethereal Extract of Yellow Corn, Wheat Embryo and Hemp Seed. J. Biol. Chem., 1924-25, 62, 371.
22. Evans, H. M.: Spontaneous Deciduomata in Pseudopregnancy with Low Vitamin E. Am. J. Physiol., 1928, 85, 149.
23. Urner, J. A.: The Intrauterine Changes in the Pregnant Albino Rat (Mus Norvegicus) Deprived of Vitamin E. Anat. Rec., 1931, 50, 175.
24. Young, J.: The Habitual Abortion and Stillbirth Syndrome and Late Pregnancy Toxemia. Vitamin E and the Prolan-progesterone Mechanism. Br. M. J., 1937, 1, 953.
25. Thomas, B. H., Cannon, C. Y., McNutt. S. H. and Underbjerg, G.: Variations in the

Reproductive Behavior of Different Species of Mammals Restricted to Vitamin E Deficient Rations. J. Nutrition., 1938, 15, Suppl. 10.

26. MASON, L. W.: Sex Hormone Factor in Recurrent Abortion and Sterility. Am. J. O. & G., 1938, 35, 559.

27. PARKESAS, A. S. AND BILLERBY, C. W.: Studies on the Internal Secretions of the Ovary. II. The Effects of Injection of the Oestrus-Producing Hormone During Pregnancy. J. Physiol., 1926, 62, 145.

28. KELLY, G. L.: The Effect of Injections of Female Sex Hormone (Oestrin) on Conception and Pregnancy in the Guinea Pig. S. G. & O., 1931, 52, 713.

29. WADE, M. J. AND DOISY, E. A.: The Prolonged Administration of Theelin and Theelol to Male and Female Rats and Its Bearing on Reproduction. Endocrinology, 1935, 19, 77.

30. SHUTE, E.: Antiproteolytic Properties of Human Blood Serum In Cases of Miscarriage and Premature Labor. J. O. & G. Brit. Emp., 1937, 45, 253.

31. HUNTINGTON, J. L.: Incidence of Miscarriage in Private Obstetrical Practice with a Discussion of the Pathology. N. Y. State Med. J., 1922, 22, 559.

32. WHITE, A.: The Effect of Thyroid and Ovarian Gland Extracts in Cases of Previous Miscarriage and Stillbirth. Brit. Med. J., 1924, 1, 190.

33. LeLORIER AND MAYER, M.: Avortements à répétition et insuffisance thyroïdienne: succès du traitement opothérapique. Bull. Soc. d'obst. et de gynec., 1935, 24, 122.

34. WERBATUS, E.: Die Behandlung des habituellen Aborts mit Thyreoidentabletten. Arch. f. Gyn., 1936, 160, 589.

35. SMITH, O. W. AND SMITH, G. V. S.: Prolan and Estrin in the Serum and Urine of Diabetic Women During Pregnancy, With Special Reference to Late Pregnancy Toxemia. Am. J. O. & G., 1937, 33, 365.

36. WHITE, P.: Diabetes Complicating Pregnancy. Am. J. O. & G., 1937, 33, 380.

38. MALL, F. P.: On the Frequency of Localized Anomalies in Human Embryos and Infants at Birth. Am. J. Anat., 1917, 22, 49.

39. MALL, F. P. AND MEYER, A. W.: Studies on Abortions: A Survey of Pathological Ova in the Carnegie Collection. Contrib. to Embryol. 56, Carneg. Inst. Wash., 1921, 12.

41. MOENCH, G. L.: Do Sperm Morphology and Biometrics Really Offer A Reliable Index of Fertility? Am. J. O. & G., 1933, 25, 410.

42. MONTGOMERY, T.: Lesions of the Placental Vessels: Their Effect Upon Fetal Morbidity and Mortality. Am. J. O. & G., 1933, 25, 320.

43. WILLIAMS, W. W. AND SAVAGE, A.: Observations on the Seminal Micropathology of Bulls. Cornell Veterinarian, 1925, 15, 353.

44. SEYMOUR, F. I.: Sterile Motile Spermatozoa Proved by Clinical Experimentation. J. A. M. A., 1939, 112, 18.

45. HENKEL, M.: Habitueller Abort und Habituelle Frühgeburt. Med. Klinik., 1929, 25, 1765.

46. SPIELMAN, F., GOLDBERGER, M. H. AND FRANK, R. T.: Hormone Diagnosis of Viability of Pregnancy. J. A. M. A., 1933, 101, 266.

47. ROBINSON, A. L., DATNOW, M. M. AND JEFFCOATE, T. N. A.: Induction of Abortion and Labor by Means of Estrin. Br. M. J., 1935, 1, 749.

47a. JEFFCOATE, T. N. A.: Missed Abortion and Missed Labor. Lancet, 1940, 1, 1045.

48. WERBATUS, E.: Die Behandlung des habituellen Aborts mit Thyreoidintabletten. Archives für Gyn., 1936, 150, 589.

50. WEINZIERL, E.: Zur Frage des habituellen Abortes. Med. Klin., 1933, 29, 563.

51. KROHN, L., FALLS, F. H. AND LACKNER, J. E.: On the Use of the Lutein Hormone, Progestin, in Threatened and Habitual Abortion. Am. J. O. & G., 1935, 29, 198.

52. VOGT-MOLLER, P.: Treatment of Sterility and Habitual Abortion with Wheat-germ and Wheat-germ Oil (Vitamin E). Acta Obst. et Gyn Scandinav., 1933, 13, 219.

53. WATSON, E. M. AND TEW, W. P.: Wheat Germ Oil (Vitamin E) Therapy in Obstetrics. Am. J. O. & G., 1936, 31, 352.

54. SHUTE, E.: Wheat Germ Oil Therapy. Am. J. O. & G., 1938, 35, 249.

55. TAUSSIG, F. J.: Abortion and Its Relation to Fetal and Maternal Mortality. Am. J. O. & G., 1937, 33, 711.

CHAPTER XXV

ECTOPIC GESTATION

An Ectopic Gestation is one in which the fertilized ovum is implanted and develops outside of the uterine cavity. When it is wholly outside of the uterus, the pregnancy is known as extrauterine.

The site of implantation determines the variety. Extrauterine pregnancies, accordingly, are classified as **tubal, ovarian,** and **abdominal.** The same classification is applied to ectopic gestations but the latter also includes pregnancies in the interstitial portion of the tube and in a rudimentary horn of a bicornate uterus.

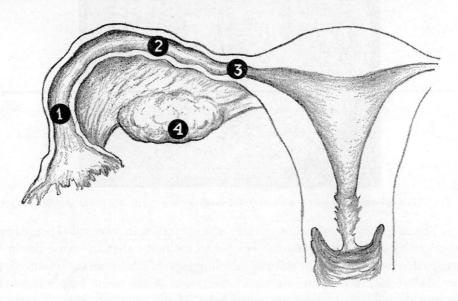

FIG. 730. Varieties of ectopic pregnancy. *1.* Ampullar.   *2.* Isthmal.   *3.* Interstitial.   *4.* Ovarian.

TUBAL PREGNANCY

Implantations in the tube are much more frequent than the other varieties and occur about once in every 300 pregnancies (1).

Tubal pregnancies are most frequently **ampullar,** somewhat less often **isthmal,** and rarely **interstitial** (2, 3, 4) (Fig. 730).

Etiology. Normally, fertilization is believed to take place in the outer third of the tube. All pregnancies, accordingly, are tubal for a short time. Why a few should become implanted in the tube is not definitely known. It is

511

generally taught that the passage of the ovum through the tube is delayed or arrested by certain pathological conditions. Among these are:

1. The loss of the cilia normally present on the lining epithelium (5).
2. Obstructions or pockets formed by adhesions between folds of the endo-salpinx commonly seen after a previous inflammation (6) (Fig. 731).
3. Diverticula in the tubes (7).
4. Obstructions due to peritubal adhesions or adjacent tumors.

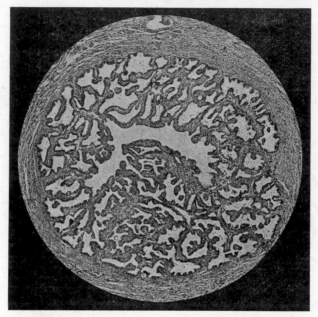

FIG. 731. Adhesions between the folds of the endosalpinx as a result of a previous inflammation.

The absence of these various causes of obstruction, in some tubal pregnancies examined after operative removal, has led to the belief that the cause lies in the fertilized ovum itself. Premature development of the erosive action of the trophoblast may be responsible for implantation of the ovum before it reaches the uterine cavity. It has been suggested that the zona pellucida protects the tube and uterus from the trophoblast as long as it surrounds the dividing cells. Soon after its disappearance, the trophoblast erodes the maternal tissues and implantation follows. If the zona pellucida, which normally is intact when the ovum reaches the uterine cavity, disappears prematurely, or if the progress of the ovum is delayed until this protective structure normally disintegrates, implantation may take place within the tube.

PATHOLOGY. The decidual reaction in the tube, at best, is very imperfect and often is almost entirely absent (8, 9). The tube, therefore, lacks an adequate mechanism of defense against the erosive action of the trophoblast. As a result, the ovum rapidly burrows its way through the mucous membrane and becomes imbedded in the underlying muscle. Further progress, however, is somewhat retarded by a peripheral zone of fibrin, with degenerating muscle and connective tissue elements, which is comparable to the Nitabuch fibrin layer found in intrauterine pregnancy.

After closure of the site of implantation, the tissues which separate the ovum from the tubal lumen act as a pseudocapsularis and bulge into the cavity of the tube (Fig. 732). Later, if rupture does not occur, this structure fuses with the mucosa and obliterates the tube lumen in the region adjacent to the growing ovum.

Fig. 732. Cross-section of a tubal pregnancy.

As development continues, the trophoblast, unhampered by a retarding decidua, penetrates the surrounding musculature and ultimately perforates the peritoneal covering of the tube—**intraperitoneal rupture**—or ruptures through the pseudocapsularis into the tube lumen from which the products of conception are partially or completely expelled into the abdominal cavity—**tubal abortion.** Rarely, it may rupture between the folds of the broad ligament; in this event it is known as an **intraligamentous rupture.** These occurrences are observed early in pregnancy, usually before the tenth week. In very rare instances, the ovum remains within the tube and continues as an advanced extrauterine pregnancy.

Engorgement of the vessels is marked and hemorrhage occurs between the muscle bundles. The entire tube is congested and enlarged. At first, its musculature becomes hypertrophied, but later, if the pregnancy reaches an advanced stage and rupture does not occur, the muscle elements undergo atrophy.

Death of the ovum is common and is followed by absorption or the formation of a mole similar to that observed in missed abortion. It may, however, survive rupture or abortion, or, as previously stated, may continue to live within the tube. After term is reached in the latter cases, the fetus dies and becomes calcified to form a lithopedion, or its fatty tissues undergo alteration with the result that it is changed into a greasy waxlike mass—adipocere (10).

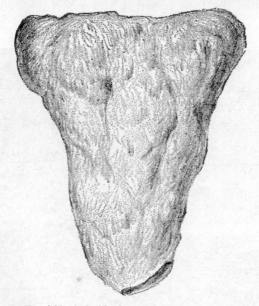

FIG. 733. A decidual cast of the uterine cavity.

The uterus contains a typical decidua which disintegrates in the spongy layer and is cast off soon after the ovum dies. If the pregnancy goes to term, it s expelled by the pseudo labor that occurs at this time. Often, the decidua co:mes away in a single piece as a cast of the uterine cavity (Fig. 733). Hypertrophy of the uterine musculature occurs just as in a normal pregnancy and, if

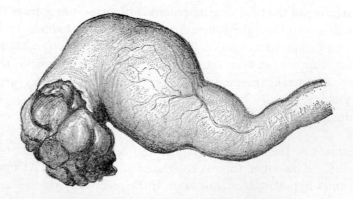

FIG. 734. Abortion of an ampullar pregnancy.

the gestation continues to term, the uterus reaches the size of a four months pregnancy.

AMPULLAR PREGNANCY

Implantation into the outer third of the tube is known as an ampullar pregnancy and may end in one of three ways:

1. Internal rupture into the tube lumen followed by abortion into the peritoneal cavity (Fig. 734).
2. External rupture into the abdomen.
3. Continuation of the pregnancy in its original site.

INTERNAL RUPTURE into the tube lumen, followed by abortion into the abdominal cavity, is the commonest termination. Usually, the ovum dies and is absorbed, unless it is removed. If there remains attached to the tube sufficient placental tissue to nourish the fetus, it may continue as a secondary abdominal pregnancy.

EXTERNAL RUPTURE into the abdomen occurs not infrequently and, as a rule, is followed by the death of the ovum. In rare instances, however, the latter lives and pregnancy continues to term.

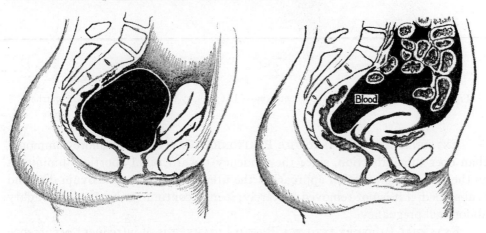

FIG. 735. Hematocele.   FIG. 736. Diffuse hemorrhage.

Following all types of rupture and abortion, hemorrhage into the peritoneal cavity occurs. This may be gradual and frequently is walled off to form a hematocele (Fig. 735). Diffuse hemorrhage usually is profuse and may cause death in a short time (Fig. 736). If the patient survives, the clots ultimately are absorbed unless they become infected; in this event suppuration may occur with rupture and drainage into the vagina, bladder, rectum or through the abdominal wall.

CONTINUATION OF THE PREGNANCY within the tube is extremely rare. In most cases in which rupture does not take place, the ovum dies and a fleshy mole is formed. Should the ovum live, late secondary rupture may occur. A few instances of full term intratubal pregnancies have been recorded.

ISTHMAL PREGNANCY

When the site of implantation is in the isthmal portion of the tube, four possibilities are to be considered:

1. External rupture into the peritoneal cavity (Fig. 737).
2. External rupture into the broad ligament.
3. Internal rupture followed by abortion into the abdomen.
4. Retention of the ovum in its original site of implantation.

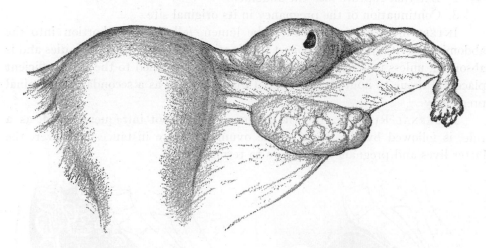

FIG. 737. Isthmal pregnancy.   Specimen removed at autopsy following death from hemorrhage.

EXTERNAL RUPTURE INTO THE PERITONEAL CAVITY occurs more commonly than does tubal abortion, since the tendency toward tubal abortion diminishes as the site of implantation approaches the uterus.   Usually, the ovum dies and is absorbed, if it is not removed.   Rarely, it may continue to live as a secondary abdominal pregnancy.

EXTERNAL RUPTURE INTO THE BROAD LIGAMENT is of infrequent occurrence and commonly is followed by the death of the ovum and the formation of a broad **ligament hematoma.**   If the blood supply is not too greatly disturbed, the ovum may live and go to term within the layers of the broad ligament, or the latter may rupture and result in a secondary abdominal pregnancy.

INTERNAL RUPTURE, accompanied by abortion into the peritoneal cavity, is followed by the death of the ovum, except in the very rare cases in which the latter continues as a secondary abdominal pregnancy (Fig. 738).

RETENTION OF THE OVUM in its original site is infrequent.   Should this occur, the ovum may die and be absorbed, or it may continue as an advanced extrauterine pregnancy.   The latter possibility is extremely rare.   Late rupture of the tube may occur at any time and result in a secondary abdominal pregnancy.

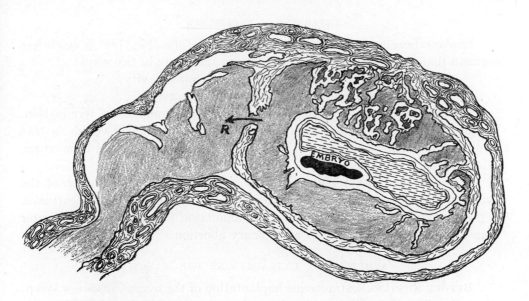

Fig. 738. Internal rupture of the pseudo capsularis in a tubal pregnancy (Litzenberg).

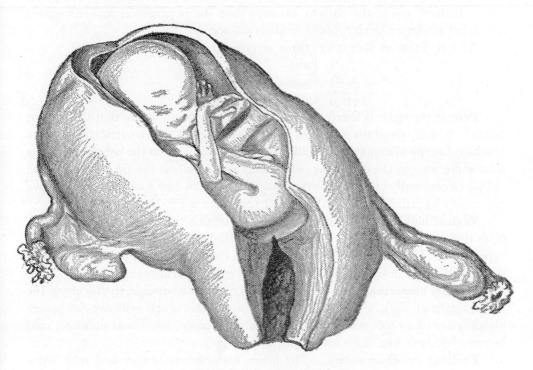

Fig. 739. Interstitial pregnancy.

INTERSTITIAL PREGNANCY

Implantation in the interstitial portion of the tube (Fig. 739) is much less common than the other two varieties and may terminate in two ways:

1. External rupture into the abdominal cavity.
2. External rupture into the uterine cavity.

RUPTURE INTO THE PERITONEAL CAVITY is the commonest termination. Because the site of implantation is also the seat of many blood vessels, a tear through this portion of the uterus not infrequently causes a fatal hemorrhage before a laparotomy can be done.

RUPTURE INTO THE UTERINE CAVITY is followed by the expulsion of the ovum and usually is mistaken for a uterine abortion. Following the extrusion of the products of conception, however, the amount of blood lost is much greater than that usually observed after an ordinary abortion.

SYMPTOMS OF EXTRAUTERINE PREGNANCY

BEFORE RUPTURE, extrauterine implantation of the ovum causes few symptoms other than those observed in a normal pregnancy. Slight pain may be felt in the lower abdomen and vaginal examination may show the uterus to be a trifle enlarged and somewhat softened. The affected tube usually is not palpable (11). In most cases, the patient assumes that she is pregnant and disregards any other symptom until rupture or abortion occurs.

AT THE TIME OF RUPTURE, three symptoms are outstanding:

1. Pain
2. Vaginal bleeding
3. Internal hemorrhage

Pain at the onset is sharp and tearing, and may be so severe that the patient faints. A dull, constant soreness follows as a result of the irritation of the free blood in the abdomen. This blood soon accumulates in the pelvis and forms a sensitive mass in the cul-de-sac, which may cause pain at the time of defecation (12). Occasionally, the intermittent contractions of the tube and uterus give rise to colicky pains which continue until the ovum is expelled.

Vaginal bleeding. Separation of the decidua in the uterus causes bleeding from the vagina (13, 14, 15). This usually is slight and often is referred to as a "spotting". Like menstrual blood, it does not clot. Sooner or later, the decidua is expelled either in shreds or as a cast of the entire uterine cavity.

Internal hemorrhage into the peritoneal cavity or between the layers of the broad ligament always occurs. If it is profuse, the usual evidences of severe bleeding are observed: pallor, rapid and thready pulse, low blood pressure, cold extremities, syncope, restlessness and air hunger.

Findings on examination. The lower abdomen is tender and may show rigidity, particularly on one side. The uterus is slightly enlarged and somewhat softened, but lacks a compressible isthmus. Tenderness on motion is constant and **the cervix is extremely sensitive when it is suddenly moved forward.**   In the interstitial variety, the bulging cornua of the uterus may be detected, but usually is mistaken for a fibroid.   Palpation of the fornices is painful and often reveals the presence of a tender, boggy mass on one side.   If a pelvic hematocele forms, the uterus is displaced upward and forward, and fluctuation in the cul-de-sac is detected.

The pulse is elevated and a slight rise in temperature occurs.   A leukocytosis of about 12,000 is common.   The white cell count may vary at different intervals during the day and such a **fluctuating leukocyte count** is suggestive of recurring hemorrhages (15).   The red cells vary according to the severity of the hemorrhage and the hemoglobin later is similarly affected.   As a result of the shock and internal hemorrhage, the blood pressure may be lowered to 100 or under.   The sedimentation time is relatively slow in the early stages of all ectopics but may later become rapid if suppuration takes place.

The Aschheim-Zondek test is positive as in a uterine pregnancy and continues so for several days after the death of the ovum.

FOLLOWING RUPTURE, the symptoms depend upon the fate of the ovum. If the ovum survives, they are those of an abdominal pregnancy and will be discussed under that heading.   Usually, the products of conception die and are absorbed.   While this is taking place, a mass may be felt on vaginal examination. In time, this grows gradually smaller, and after several months disappears entirely unless it becomes infected.   When infection takes place, the usual evidences of an inflammatory condition are present: elevation in temperature, leukocytosis, pain, tenderness and a rapid sedimentation rate.   Should suppuration occur, fluctuation may be felt.

DIAGNOSIS

Sterility, particularly of the one-child type, or a previous pelvic inflammation or operation on the tubes not infrequently precedes an extrauterine pregnancy.

The history of a skipped period followed by vaginal spotting should suggest the possibility of an ectopic gestation.   The addition of severe pain with fainting and evidence of internal hemorrhage indicates its probability and the diagnosis is made almost certain when examination in such cases shows lower abdominal tenderness, a sensitive cervix and a tender mass on one side.

Many ectopic pregnancies, however, lack this tragic picture and the diagnosis, accordingly, is quite difficult.   A tubal pregnancy is differentiated from an uncomplicated abortion by the fact that the vaginal hemorrhage contains no clots and seldom is profuse.   In addition, the aborting uterus shows the usual signs of pregnancy with a more or less open cervix.   Should a curettage be done, the curettings in an ectopic contain decidual cells only, while in an abortion both decidual cells and chorionic villi are found.

Septic abortion, complicated by parametritis or a pelvic abscess, may be confused with an ectopic gestation. In differentiating between these conditions, the sedimentation rate is helpful since in septic abortions it is rapid while in an ectopic it is relatively slow. If fluctuation in the cul-de-sac is present, aspiration of a small amount of the fluid with a syringe will show either pus or blood and clarify the diagnosis. The differentiation between extrauterine pregnancy and other gynecological conditions is discussed fully in all works on gynecology.

TREATMENT

Before, at the time of, or immediately after rupture or abortion, laparotomy is indicated. This should be done as quickly as is consistent with modern aseptic surgery. While preparations for operation are being made, the patient should be morphinized and kept in the Trendelenberg posture. With the patient maintained in this position, the abdomen is opened and the affected tube is brought into view. The uterine and ovarian ends of the tubal circulation are quickly clamped and the entire tube is removed. The abdomen is then closed without drainage and without attempting to remove the clots from the pelvis. **No additional surgery that is not immediately necessary is justifiable at this time.** If the patient's condition is good, however, the vessels may be ligated individually and the usual salpingectomy technic may be followed. In these

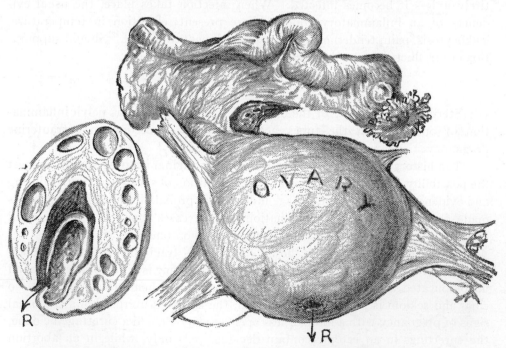

Fig. 740. Ovarian pregnancy (Cullen). *R*, site of rupture.

circumstances, it is good practice to remove the blood clots and do a more careful operation. Blood transfusion and hypodermoclysis are indicated before, during and immediately after the operation. Shock is further combated by a continuance of the Trendelenberg posture, artificial heat and morphine. During convalescence blood building measures are recommended.

OVARIAN PREGNANCY

In very rare cases, fertilization takes place in the ruptured graafian follicle before the ovum is expelled (16, 17, 18). The segmenting egg then becomes implanted in the lutein and theca layers of the imperfectly developing corpus luteum. In true ovarian pregnancies, therefore, the ovum is surrounded by ovarian tissue, and the fallopian tubes show no evidence of extrauterine gestation (18) (Fig. 740). Such pregnancies continue longer than do the tubal implantations and a small number of them are recorded as having gone to term (19, 20, 21).

The symptoms and treatment are similar to those of tubal and abdominal pregnancy.

ABDOMINAL PREGNANCY

Primary abdominal pregnancy is so rare that only a few cases have been recorded (22). On the other hand, secondary abdominal pregnancies are more common, and follow rupture or abortion of a tubal, ovarian or secondary intraligamentous pregnancy. The intact gestation sac then continues to develop among the abdominal viscera, and the placenta remains attached to the tube and the structures adjacent to it.

Vaginal bleeding at the time of the primary rupture occurs in about one-third of all cases even though the ovum continues to live. Fetal movements often are painful to the mother and are easily palpated through the abdominal wall. Rupture of the sac may occur at any time and cause severe abdominal pain and internal hemorrhage. Usually the fetus dies shortly after the occurrence of this accident.

If the pregnancy continues to term, the patient has **pseudo labor** and the decidua is expelled from the uterus. Within a short time the fetus dies, and becomes partially calcified to form a lithopedion, or its tissues undergo the change which results in adipocere formation. Occasionally, the fetus is partially absorbed and its bones are expelled through the intestines, bladder and umbilicus.

DIAGNOSIS

Whenever the small parts are close to the examining hand on abdominal palpation, the uterus should be outlined by percussion. If abnormal areas of tympany indicate the presence of the intestines in front of the uterus, the possibility of an abdominal pregnancy should be considered. In addition, there **may** be a history of an early tubal rupture or abortion and painful fetal movements. Vaginal examination shows the uterus to be on one side of the gestation sac.

TREATMENT

Laparotomy is indicated as soon as the diagnosis is made. If, in the interests of the child, it is desirable to postpone operation, the latter should be done about two weeks before term.

Bleeding from the placental site offers the greatest danger and rare judgment is required in the management of the placenta. Since the usual mechanism for the control of hemorrhage from the placental site is absent in extrauterine pregnancy, the vessels which supply this region should be ligated before the placenta is disturbed. Whenever the blood supply through the placental site is accessible, the placenta, accordingly, is removed. If the insertion of the placenta is such that preliminary control of the blood supply is impossible, its removal is contraindicated and great care should be used to avoid disturbing the placental attachments. In the latter circumstances, the abdomen is closed without drainage and the placenta is left to be absorbed. Should hemorrhage from a partly detached placenta occur, the sac is sutured to the margins of the wound and packed with sterile gauze. Marsupialization also is recommended whenever drainage is required because of the presence of infection (23, 24).

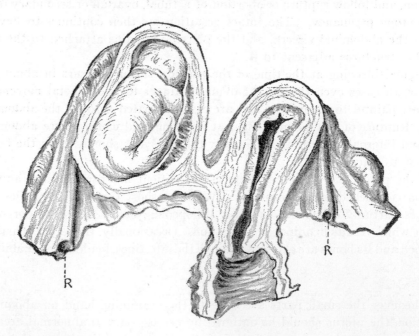

Fig. 741. Pregnancy in the rudimentary horn of a bicornate uterus. R, round ligaments. Note that the round ligament on the right side is external to the gestation sac.

PREGNANCY IN THE RUDIMENTARY HORN OF A BICORNATE UTERUS

When the ovum becomes implanted in the rudimentary horn of a bicornate uterus, the conditions are similar to those found in tubal pregnancies (See Fig. 774, page 495). Such pregnancies are very rare and usually rupture early in the second trimester. As in interstitial pregnancy, the bleeding is so profuse that death often occurs before the abdomen can be opened (Fig. 741). Rarely, the pregnancy goes to term (25).

THE TREATMENT is surgical. At operation, the rudimentary horn is identified by the presence of the round ligament external to the gestation sac, a point which differentiates this condition from an interstitial pregnancy. Following the removal of the gestation sac and the rudimentary horn, the abdomen is closed without drainage. If the diagnosis is made before rupture occurs, this operation is accompanied by slight risk. On the other hand, when it is done after rupture has taken place, 15 per cent to 20 per cent of the mothers die (26).

REFERENCES

1. SCHUMANN, E.: Extra Uterine Pregnancy, Phila. 1921, 18.
2. HARTMANN, H. AND BERGERET, A.: Quelques Remarques à Propos de 186 Cas Consecutifs de Grossesse Extra-uterine. Ann. de Gyn. et d'Obs., 1919, 13, 321.
3. OASTLER, F.: Ectopic Pregnancy. Surg. Gyn. & Obs., 1917, 24, 224.
4. FOSKETT, E.: A Study of 117 Cases of Ectopic Gestation. Am. J. Obs., 1916, 74, 232.
5. TAIT, L.: Lectures on Ectopic Pregnancy and Pelvic Haematocele, 1888.
6. OPITZ, E.: Ueber die Ursachen der Ansiedlung des Eies im Eileiter. Ztschr. f. Geburtsh. u. Gyn., 1902, 48, 1.
7. LANDAU, T. U. RHEINSTEIN, J.: Beiträge zur pathologischen Anatomie der Tube. Arch. f. Gyn., 1891, 39, 273.
8. YOUNG, J.: The Anatomy and Histology of the Pregnant Tube. Edinb. Med. J., 1909, n. s., 3, 118.
9. NOVAK, E. AND DARNER, H. L.: The Correlation of Uterine and Tubal Changes in Tubal Gestation. Am. J. O. & G., 1925, 9, 295.
10. KÜCHENMEISTER: Ueber Lithopädien. Arch. f. Gyn., 1881, 17, 153.
11. BOLDT, H. J.: The Diagnosis of Extra-uterine Pregnancy. Arch. Diag., 1908, 1, 32.
12. POLAK, J. O.: Observations on Two Hundred Twenty-seven Cases of Ectopic Pregnancy. Am. J. Obs., 1915, 71, 946.
13. TAYLOR, H. C.: Cases of Ectopic Pregnancy at the Roosevelt Hospital. Med. & Surg. Rep. Roosevelt Hosp., 1915, 147.
14. SAMPSON, J. H.: The Influence of Ectopic Pregnancy on the Uterus, with Special Reference to Changes in its Blood Supply and Uterine Bleeding. S. G. & O., 1914, 18, 587.
15. FARRAR, L. P.: The Value of the Leukocyte Count as an Aid to Diagnosis in Ectopic Gestation. Surg. Gyn. & Obs., 1925, 41, 655.
16. THOMPSON, J. F.: Ovarian Pregnancy with Report of a Case. Am. Gyn., 1902, 1, 1.
17. MALL, F. P. AND CULLEN, E. K.: An Ovarian Pregnancy Located in the Graafian Follicle. Surg. Gyn. & Obs., 1913, 17, 698.
18. SPIEGELBERG, O.: Eine ausgetragene Tuben-Schwangerschaft. Arch. f. Gyn., 1870, 1, 406.
19. LEOPOLD, G.: Ovarialschwangerschaft mit Lithopädionbildung von 35-jähriger Dauer. Arch. f. Gyn., 1882, 19, 210.
20. WYNNE, H. M. N.: Ectopic Pregnancy. Johns Hopkins Hosp. Bull., 1919, 30, 15.
21. SANTI, A. J.: Ein Fall von ausgetragener Eierstockschwangerschaft und ähnliche Fälle aus der Literatur. Acta Gyn. Scand., 1928, 8, 207.

22. REIFFERSCHEID, K.: Primäre Abdominalschwangerschaft beim Menschen. Zeitschr. f. die ges. Anat., 1922, 63, 554.
23. SITTNER, A.: Ergebnisse der in den letzten 20 Jahren durch Koeliotomie bei lebendem Kinde operirten Fälle von vorgeschrittener Extrauterinschwangerschaft. Arch. f. Gyn., 1907, 84, 1.
24. BECK, A. C.: Treatment of Extra-uterine Pregnancy after the Fifth Month. J. A. M. A., 1919, 73, 962.
25. BECKMANN, W.: Weiterer Beitrag zur Gravidität im rudimentären Uterushorn. Ztschr. f. Geburtsh. u. Gyn., 1911, 68, 600.
26. KEHRER, E.: Das Nebenhorn des Doppelten Uterus. Heidelberg, 1900.

J. BRAXTON HICKS
1823–1897
London

Hicks was a well known obstetrician and teacher who served as obstetrical physician to Guy's Hospital from 1859 to 1882.

In 1863 he introduced the combined method of podalic version which has been so successfully used in the treatment of placenta praevia.

CHAPTER XXVI
TOXEMIAS OF PREGNANCY

HYPEREMESIS GRAVIDARUM

The ovum, which is slightly larger than a pinhead when the first period is skipped, becomes as large as a marble in two weeks and reaches the size of a small egg by the end of the second month. Such rapid growth requires great expansion of the original site of implantation and an abundance of nutrient embryotroph, both of which necessitate a marked destruction of maternal tissues. The waste material which results from this destruction of decidual elements, together with buds of trophoblast that have gained entrance to the maternal circulation and the metabolic products from the ovum itself, may well have a toxic effect on the mother in the early months of pregnancy. About 50 per cent of all pregnant women, accordingly, are mildly toxic and complain of nausea and vomiting in the first trimester. As the conflict between the trophoblast and the decidua becomes less active with the formation of the placenta, not only is the amount of decidual detritus lessened but the maternal organism acquires an increased ability to care for this and other toxic materials that are derived from the products of conception. By the third month, therefore, morning sickness usually ceases. Rarely, the nausea and vomiting may become excessive. It then is known as **hyperemesis gravidarum** or **pernicious vomiting**.

ETIOLOGY. All cases of hyperemesis gravidarum have the toxic basis just described. Something additional, however, is necessary to produce the characteristic excessive vomiting. This may be: a neurotic temperament, a disturbed carbohydrate metabolism, or an excessive or unusual toxemia.

NEUROTIC VOMITING. Women with a neurotic temperament suffer from an exaggeration of the usual nausea and vomiting of pregnancy. Fear of vomiting then leads to the refusal of nourishment and as a result the tendency toward inanition is increased. This variety of hyperemesis, while basically a mild toxemia, is due chiefly to the superimposed neurotic element. Although it is the commonest type of pernicious vomiting, it seldom is encountered among clinic patients.

VOMITING DUE TO FAULTY CARBOHYDRATE METABOLISM. If, for any reason, the carbohydrate intake is inadequate, inanition rapidly develops and increases the tendency to vomit. Basically again, there is a mild toxemia which normally would have caused only morning sickness. In addition, either the usual disturbance in the carbohydrate metabolism is aggravated or the carbohydrate intake is voluntarily or involuntarily diminished (1, 2). This type of hyperemesis often is an added menace in the neurotic variety where, in addition to the diminished carbohydrate intake which results from the vomiting itself, the fear of vomiting leads the patient to refuse nourishment. A vicious circle soon results from this combination as the vomiting and refusal of food lead to starvation which then causes more vomiting and further starvation.

TOXIC PERNICIOUS VOMITING is very rare. Occasionally, there develops in early pregnancy a toxemia which causes persistent vomiting and ends fatally within a short time unless the pregnancy is terminated. Nothing is known concerning the specific substance which is responsible for this grave condition aside from the fact that it probably has its origin in the products of conception (3).

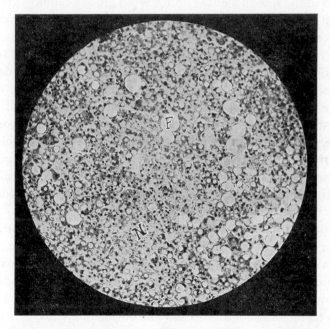

FIG. 742. Section of liver from a case of hyperemesis gravidarum. *N*, necrosis; *F*, fatty change.

PATHOLOGY. When hyperemesis gravidarum results fatally, the liver is affected. Diffuse, fatty changes are the commonest lesions and are found in those patients who ultimately die of inanition (Fig. 742). In typical toxic pernicious vomiting, the liver shows necrosis in the center of the lobule and resembles the picture seen in chloroform and phosphorus poisoning (4, 5, 6, 7, 8).

SYMPTOMS. Soon after the onset of morning sickness, vomiting in the patient with a neurotic temperament becomes persistent and great difficulty is experienced in retaining any food in the stomach. Even water often is not tolerated. The patient becomes dehydrated, her breath frequently has an acetone odor, and in due time she shows the effects of inanition. Due to the resulting vitamin deficiency, muscular weakness, loss of reflexes and other evidences of polyneuritis may be observed (9). Occasionally retinal hemorrhages occur and indicate the possibility of concomitant hemorrhages in the brain (10). After some weeks, death occurs from starvation. In the typical toxic variety, a more rapid termination is common. The usual morning sickness becomes excessive. Within a short time, jaundice develops and the vomitus has a coffee-ground appearance Coma occurs in a few days and is soon followed by death.

As a result of the concentration of the blood which accompanies dehydration, the hemoglobin and plasma proteins are relatively high but return to ordinary values after treatment is instituted. When the condition is long standing, however, the proteins of the blood may be destroyed. In such circumstances, their values may be low in spite of the dehydration. Low plasma protein values, accordingly, have a grave prognostic significance (11). Ordinarily, there is an increase in the non-protein nitrogen and uric acid of the blood but these fall following the active administration of fluids. The persistent vomiting and the diminished salt intake likewise cause a reduction in the chlorides (12) and the blood sugar also is somewhat lowered (13). Wide fluctuations are observed in the carbon-dioxide combining power of the blood (14, 15). Because of inanition, the diminished alkali reserve of pregnancy is further reduced but this may be somewhat compensated by the loss of hydrochloric acid which results from the excessive vomiting. As a consequence, the acid base equilibrium is unstable, fluctuating toward the side of acidosis at one time and toward alkalosis at another. Insufficient carbohydrates to meet the metabolic requirements of pregnancy lead to utilization of body fats and the appearance of acetone bodies in the urine. Acetonuria, accordingly, is a common finding in hyperemesis and it increases with the severity of the disease. On the other hand, acetone and diacetic acid disappear rapidly from the urine when the vomiting ceases and the carbohydrate intake is adequate.

DIAGNOSIS. After making a diagnosis of pregnancy, other causes of vomiting are ruled out. At first toxic hyperemesis cannot be differentiated from the other varieties. After a few days of observation under proper management, however, it is possible to make the diagnosis from the way the patient responds to treatment. Suggestion, with proper feeding and intravenous injections of glucose, has a favorable effect upon neurotic and starvation vomiting but gives no relief in the toxic variety. The course in the latter is altered only by therapeutic abortion.

TREATMENT. The essentials in the treatment of pernicious vomiting are:

1 Isolation
2. Suggestion
3. Rest
4. Adequate fluid intake
5. The administration of carbohydrates (glucose)

ISOLATION. Whenever the vomiting of pregnancy becomes pernicious, temporizing measures are to be discontinued and immediate isolation of the patient is recommended. Every one but the nurse and physician must be excluded from her room. This applies particularly to the husband, mother, and other members of the family. Before attempting to treat a case of hyperemesis the physician should obtain from the husband his promise to cooperate in this respect until recovery is assured. Strict isolation of this type seldom can be carried out in the home. Hospitalization, therefore, is advisable. As much depends upon the efficiency and attitude of the nurse, an older nurse, who has had successful experience with similar cases, should be employed.

SUGGESTION. Every possible means is employed to assure the patient of her ultimate recovery. Suggestion likewise should be liberally and seriously added to all therapeutic measures that are employed. No doubt, the success that followed the use of the numerous drugs that formerly were recommended for this condition was due largely to the fact that the physician himself believed in them and succeeded in making his patient share this belief.

REST in bed in a quiet, well ventilated room is essential. No food or fluids of any kind are to be given by mouth for 24 hours and sedatives in the form of bromides and chloral are administered with the solutions used for proctoclysis. If necessary luminol may be given hypodermically.

FLUID INTAKE. Each day, 3000 cc. of fluid should be administered. This may be divided and given intravenously by hypodermoclysis, and by proctoclysis. When the patient is again able to take nourishment by mouth without vomiting, fluids should be forced by this route.

THE ADMINISTRATION OF CARBOHYDRATES—INTRAVENOUS INJECTIONS. One thousand cc. of 10 per cent or 500 cc. of 20 per cent glucose are given intravenously three times daily. These solutions are prepared by adding freshly distilled water and buffer solution to the concentrated glucose that is purchased in ampules. Each injection must be given slowly and should consume at least one to two hours. The fluids overcome the dehydration; salt combats the chloropenia and sugar spares the proteins, protects the liver, overcomes inanition and reduces the tendency to acidosis. During the administration of this therapeutic measure, the physician and nurse should emphasize its curative properties and assure the patient that not many injections will be necessary to effect a complete cure.

PROCTOCLYSIS. Glucose and bromides are given in salt solution in the form of a Harris drip. This solution is prepared by adding 50 gm. of glucose and 100 gr. of bromide to each 1000 cc. of saline used. After cleansing the rectum with a low enema, a rectal tube is passed into the sigmoid and connected with an enema can. The fluid in the container is maintained at a temperature of 110°–115° and is kept on a level with the colon. By this method the patient is able to absorb the fluids continuously without discomfort.

DUODENAL FEEDING.   If intravenous therapy is difficult or contraindicated, 50 cc. of a 20 per cent solution of glucose may be given every half hour through a duodenal tube which is left in place for 24 hours.   Vitamin B complex, in the form of yeast, and vitamin C as orange juice, also are administered in this manner.

The good results reported from the use of adrenal cortical substance warrant a trial of this hormone whenever vomiting becomes excessive (16, 17).   If food by mouth is tolerated, one 3 gr. tablet is given three times daily.   After the first week, the dose may be doubled if the vomiting has not ceased.   When necessary, one ampoule (1 cc.) is injected hypodermically t.i.d.   Following the cessation of vomiting, oral administration of the extract is substituted for the hypodermic injection.   Vitamin B (thiamin) intramuscularly and vitamin C (ascorbic acid) intravenously are also recommended (18, 19, 20).   Thiamin is particularly indicated in those cases which show evidence of polyneuritis and ascorbic acid should be given whenever symptoms of scurvy appear.

After 24 hours of isolation, rest, and intensive intravenous, subcutaneous and rectal therapy, an effort is made to show the patient that she has improved. This should not be difficult since the vomiting usually is considerably diminished when nothing is taken by mouth.   The patient often will ask that some of the treatment be discontinued.   Her request may be granted if she is able to take nourishment by mouth and retain it for two hours.   Should the result of such a test be unsatisfactory, the routine is continued for another 12 or 24 hours after which the test is repeated.   The severe vomiting which may accompany hyperthyroidism should not be mistaken for hyperemesis gravidarum.   It usually responds to Lugol's solution given in 10 m. doses t.i.d. (21, 22).

When the above recommendations are seriously carried out, most patients improve rapidly and are able to take ample quantities of fluids and carbohydrates by mouth.   Small, frequent feedings of dry foods, rich in carbohydrates, are then given.   These include popcorn, puffed rice, toast, zwieback, dry cereals, soda biscuits, boiled rice and baked potato.   Fluids are best tolerated between meals. Often, water is distasteful and carbonated waters, ginger ale, or other liquids that the patient desires may be substituted.   Carbohydrate, amino acid and vitamin C sometimes are easily administered by adding glucose and gelatin to orange juice.   Glucose and gelatin in the proportion of one tablespoonful of each to a glass of orange juice seem to be well tolerated when taken in this manner.

In rare instances, this routine may fail either because the physician and nurse have not been successful from the standpoint of psychotherapy or because the vomiting is of the true toxic variety.   In either event, therapeutic abortion is indicated.   This is especially true in the presence of continued loss of weight, a persistently rising non-protein nitrogen and uric acid of the blood, retinal hemorrhage and marked jaundice.   The uterus should be emptied by the curet before the eighth week.   From the eighth to the twelfth week, the cervix is opened with

Hegar dilators, after which the ovum is separated by the finger and removed with ovum forceps. After the third month, anterior vaginal hysterotomy is advised.

ACUTE YELLOW ATROPHY

Acute yellow atrophy is a very rare disease. The fact that the majority of the cases reported in the literature have occurred in pregnant women has led to the belief that some toxin associated with pregnancy may be responsible for the liver changes. The exact nature of this toxin, however, is not known.

Acute yellow atrophy usually is observed in the last half of pregnancy and is characterized by a remarkably rapid alteration in the liver, which occasionally is diminished to half its normal size. These changes are due to extensive necrosis which usually is limited to the central portion of the lobules. In severe cases, however, almost the entire lobule may be involved, but the interlobular tissues and vessels remain more or less unaltered.

The symptoms are similar to those observed in the toxemias of pregnancy. Severe headache, abdominal pain, and vomiting are commonly noted at the onset. These are followed by drowsiness and jaundice of a varying degree. Within a short time, the patient becomes delirious and after a day or two goes into coma which terminates in death. Occasionally, convulsions occur and the condition is confused with eclampsia. Recovery rarely is observed. The liver is tender and, on percussion, is markedly diminished in size. The fetus dies in the course of the disease, and often is expelled prematurely before the death of the mother occurs.

Study of the blood shows a hypoglycemia and a decrease in urea with an increase in non-protein nitrogen, uric acid, and amino acid. The decrease in urea and the increase in non-protein nitrogen reduces the ratio of urea to non-protein nitrogen well below the low levels usually found in pregnancy. A decrease in the alkali reserve also is observed and this becomes more marked as the condition progresses (23).

TREATMENT of this serious complication is unsatisfactory. Intensive glucose therapy similar to that recommended in hyperemesis gravidarum is advised. Interruption of the pregnancy and eliminative measures also are indicated.

PREECLAMPSIA AND ECLAMPSIA

Certain symptoms and signs which occur in the latter part of some gestations are thought to be due to a toxin or toxins peculiar to pregnancy. Hence the terms, "the toxemia" and "the toxemias" of late pregnancy. What the specific toxin or toxins are is unknown. In fact, it is not certain that these symptoms and signs really are due to any toxin. If they are, the manner in which the latter acts is not understood. Although autopsy findings in the severe fulminating cases are fairly well known, the intermediate stages which lead to this ultimate pathological picture are the subject of much conjecture. For the sake of simplicity, therefore, it seems best to consider all of the so-called toxemias of late pregnancy as a single entity which reaches the acme of its development when convulsions occur, the different types being merely differences in the degree of the same disease.   The condition then may be regarded as mild or severe.

In the mild cases, the symptoms come on gradually and can be controlled, to a large extent, by rest, diet, and other therapeutic measures.   If, however, they persist for a long time before the pregnancy is terminated, residual vascular and renal damage may remain after delivery.   In such circumstances, it would seem that the etiological factor is capable of only slight but prolonged action or that the vascular and renal lesions were present before the onset of pregnancy or that the patient has a predisposition toward them.

The severe cases, on the other hand, develop rapidly and usually resist all therapeutic efforts except the interruption of pregnancy.   Convulsions almost always occur unless the fetus dies or unless the pregnancy is spontaneously or artificially terminated.   In them, the causative agent apparently acts quickly and powerfully with the result that the maternal organism is overwhelmed within a short time.

According to this simple classification, one or more of the ordinary symptoms or signs, occurs in every case but, depending upon the severity, these may or may not culminate in convulsive seizures.   Any or all of them, therefore, may be regarded as danger signals of impending convulsions.

DANGER SYMPTOMS AND SIGNS.   The most common of these symptoms and signs which may be premonitory to the occurrence of convulsions are:

1. A rise in blood pressure
2. Albuminuria
3. A rapid gain in weight
4. Edema
5. Headache
6. Diminished urinary output
7. Visual disturbances
8. Epigastric pain

ELEVATION OF BLOOD PRESSURE.   An elevation in the blood pressure is one of the earliest and most important evidences of toxemia. Occurring in 98 per cent of all toxemic patients, it likewise is the most constant.   Systolic hypertension not infrequently is observed several days before any other symptom.   For this reason, the blood pressure should be determined at monthly intervals throughout the first seven lunar months, bi-weekly during the next six weeks and every week in the last month and a half of pregnancy.   Whenever it rises above 140 mm., the possibility of impending eclampsia must be ruled out.   Since the systolic pressure is more sensitive to change, it becomes elevated much earlier than does the diastolic and, as a consequence, is more useful in the early detection of toxemia. The diastolic pressure, on the other hand, follows the systolic in the more severe cases but, because of its tendency to remain stable, slight diastolic rises have greater significance whenever they occur.

In the severe cases, the elevation usually is sudden and rises rapidly in spite of rest in bed and other therapeutic measures. Just before the onset of convulsions, it may reach or even exceed 200 mm. After recovery and delivery of the child, the blood pressure falls with almost equal rapidity and, in 75 per cent of all eclamptic patients, is normal by the tenth day postpartum. Very rarely, convulsions occur without hypertension.

In the mild cases, the rise in the systolic pressure is less marked and its increase is more gradual. Seldom does the elevation exceed 160 mm. Of greater significance is the fact that it usually responds readily to rest, diet and eliminative treatment. In other words, the increased tension can be controlled sufficiently to justify the use of an expectant routine with the hope that the pregnancy may terminate spontaneously. Unfortunately, the hypertension persists in many of these mild cases and this persistent elevation of the blood pressure is especially common when the toxemia is of long duration. About 60 per cent of the women who have persistent postpartum hypertension, later show evidences of residual vascular or renal damage. In some of them, however, the lesion probably was present before the onset of pregnancy.

ALBUMINURIA. Like hypertension, albuminuria is an early evidence of toxemia. Usually, it follows the elevation in blood pressure. At first, only a trace of albumin may be detected in the urine but, depending upon the severity of the toxemia, it either gradually or rapidly increases. For this reason, quantitative estimations by means of the Esbach tube are most helpful. Because of the importance of albuminuria, the urine should be examined at frequent intervals throughout pregnancy and the same schedule which was recommended for the blood pressure determinations during the antenatal period is suggested.

In the severe cases, the urine is loaded with albumin and, occasionally, boils solid. The heat and acetic test usually is faintly positive within a few days after an elevation of the blood pressure is first detected. Subsequently, the amount of albumin in the urine increases rapidly. Within 24 hours, one gm. to two gm. per liter may be observed and, shortly before the onset of convulsions, it may reach eight to ten gm. While albuminuria is almost invariably present in all severe toxemias, occasionally the amount of albumin is much less than might be expected from the severity of the symptoms.

In the mild cases, the albuminuria may be slight or absent. Albumin usually is detected in the urine some little time after the onset of hypertension and then may appear only as a trace. The amount increases very gradually and seldom reaches more than one to two gm. per liter. Like the blood pressure in these mild cases, the albuminuria responds well to treatment and often disappears entirely when the patient's regimen is readjusted.

FLUID RETENTION is one of the commonest findings in the toxemia of late pregnancy. The accumulation of fluid in the interstitial tissue causes a rather rapid gain in weight and should be suspected whenever the gain exceeds one pound per week during the latter months of pregnancy. For this reason, the patient should be weighed monthly for the first seven lunar months, bi-monthly during the next six weeks and every week during the last month and a half of pregnancy. Fluid retention may also manifest itself in the form of edema. The patient's shoes then become too small and her rings too tight. The ankle edema of toxemia should not be confused with that which results from the pressure effects of a normal pregnancy. In the latter, it is more marked on one side than on the other and is not accompanied by swelling of the fingers.

In the severe cases, edema usually is detected within a short time after the initial rise in the blood pressure. It rapidly increases and may involve the labia majora and the tissues of the abdominal wall. The fingers are swollen and show deep furrows beneath the tight finger rings. Just before and following the onset of convulsions, the face becomes puffy and distorted beyond recognition. This puffiness of the face is unlike the usual type of facial edema and resembles a generalized urticaria. Following delivery, the edema disappears within a few days. Occasionally, convulsions may occur without any apparent fluid retention.

In the mild cases, edema usually is restricted to the ankles and the fingers. Its increase is very gradual and it subsides rapidly under appropriate treatment.

HEADACHE is a frequent symptom of toxemia. It usually is observed after hypertension, albuminuria and edema have appeared. This type of headache is persistent and increases in severity as the toxemia becomes more intense.

In the severe cases, it resists all treatment and may be present several days before the onset of convulsions. Occasionally caphalalgia may be the only symptom and may therefore cause the attending physician to take the blood pressure and look for albumin in the urine.

In the mild cases, the headache is less severe and responds to the ordinary treatment for toxemia.

DIMINISHED URINARY OUTPUT. A diminished urinary output is common. Whenever the total quantity passed in 24 hours falls below one quart and the fluid intake is known to have been ample, the attending physician should be on the look-out for other evidences of toxemia. Measurement of the 24 hour urinary output, accordingly, is indicated at monthly intervals for the first seven lunar months, bi-weekly during the next six weeks and every week in the last month and a half of pregnancy.

In the severe cases, the diminution in the urinary output often is marked and, at the time of convulsions, the output may be only a few ounces in 24 hours or a complete suppression may occur.

In the mild cases, the urinary excretion may be but little less than normal and is evident only when accurate records of fluid intake and output are kept.

VISUAL DISTURBANCES usually are an indication of the severity of the toxemia. Narrowing of the vessels, however, may be observed by ophthalmological examination before the vision is affected. When the changes are sufficiently marked to cause a disturbance in vision, the toxemia is either of the very severe type or has progressed to a rather late stage. The vision then becomes blurred and specks appear before the eyes. Complete amaurosis not infrequently occurs shortly before the onset of convulsions. Examination of the fundus reveals a generalized narrowing and localized spastic constriction of the retinal arterioles as the earliest changes that are demonstrable in toxemia. For this reason, search for angiospastic lesions of the retinal arterioles is indicated whenever hypertension is present during pregnancy. Later retinal edema, hemorrhage and exudate appear as the toxemia increases in severity. The retina becomes detached in a small percentage of cases. In these instances, re-attachment usually takes place within ten days after the termination of pregnancy.

EPIGASTRIC PAIN. Pain may be felt in the epigastrium when the toxemia is severe. This symptom is of value because it usually is first noted only a short time before the onset of convulsions. When epigastric pain occurs, therefore, the possibility of convulsions occurring within a few hours must always be considered and seldom will any method of interrupting the pregnancy, other than Cesarean section, forestall their occurrence.

SYMPTOMS DURING AND FOLLOWING A CONVULSIVE ATTACK. Immediately preceding the onset of convulsions, the patient's expression becomes fixed as she appears to stare at some distant object. Her eyes roll from side to side and finally turn upward. The pupils are dilated. The nostrils quiver. Her mouth is drawn spasmodically to one side and the tongue, forced between the teeth, is bitten. Jerky lateral movements of the head follow as the neck muscles participate in the spasm. The muscular contractions then become generalized and extend to the trunk and extremities. The arms are in pronation and the fingers close tightly about the thumbs. Tonic contractions of the respiratory muscles stop the breathing and cause deep cyanosis. Soon the tonic spasms pass off and are succeeded by clonic convulsions in which the whole body becomes involved in a series of violent, jerky movements. Respiration, now partially restored, is stertorous as the air is forced through the blood-tinged, frothy saliva which drips from the mouth. This horrible picture lasts for a few minutes and, just as the attendant decides that death is inevitable, the severity of the contractions diminishes, several deep inspirations are taken and the cyanosis disappears. The patient looks about her vaguely and seems to be confused. In a short time, her mind clears and she is able to converse intelligently, but has no recollection of the seizure through which she has passed. After a variable interval, the convulsive stage returns and is again followed by a deeper and more prolonged stupor. Unless prompt treatment is inaugurated, the eclamptic attacks recur with increasing frequency and, within a short time, the coma between convulsions becomes so deep that the patient no longer regains consciousness.

Although the so-called toxemias which occur late in pregnancy have been considered as varying degrees of the same entity, the onset of convulsions is such a critical event that most clinicians divide their late toxemias into those which have convulsions—**eclampsia** and those which do not—**preeclampsia**.

PREECLAMPSIA

PREECLAMPSIA, as the term implies, is that form of toxemia which ultimately may develop into eclampsia, unless the fetus dies or the pregnancy is terminated or unless the clinical course is altered by appropriate treatment. It occurs during the last half of pregnancy and is most frequently observed in the last trimester. Preeclampsia manifests itself by the occurrence of one or more of the following signs and symptoms: an elevation in the blood pressure, albuminuria, edema, headache, visual disturbances, a diminished urinary output and epigastric pain. Of these, hypertension, albuminuria and edema are the most common. Some patients may show only a slight elevation in blood pressure; in others, there may be added a trace of albumin and fluid retention, as indicated by a somewhat excessive gain in weight. These **mild cases** are quite common. They usually are easily controlled and, accordingly, cause little anxiety. On the other hand, they require careful observation because of the possibility of their becoming severe at any time. The **severe cases** occur much less frequently and respond less readily to treatment. In some of them, nothing short of the induction of labor is able to forestall the onset of convulsions.

DIAGNOSIS. Since one or more of the chief manifestations of preeclampsia, **hypertension, albuminuria** and **edema**, commonly occurs in other conditions, it is difficult at times to make the diagnosis with certainty. If the other conditions such as glomerulo-nephritis or essential hypertension were recognized before the onset of pregnancy, the problem is greatly simplified. Sometimes, however, the pathology develops in the course of but independent of pregnancy, as in the case of acute nephritis and pyelitis. In other instances, the patient may have an inherent predisposition toward such a condition as essential hypertension which is brought out by the extra load of pregnancy and, accordingly, becomes manifest for the first time during gestation. The possibility that preeclampsia may cause residual vascular renal damage also complicates the picture and makes the ultimate differentiation still more perplexing. Finally, it must be remembered that pre-eclampsia may be superimposed upon any of these other pathological entities. This form of toxemia, therefore, should be kept in mind whenever hypertension, albuminuria or edema is discovered, irrespective of some other underlying cause and the attendant should be on the lookout for additional symptoms and signs which may indicate that a preeclampsia is developing in the presence of one of these other conditions. The diseases from which preeclampsia should be differentiated are: acute glomerulo-nephritis, chronic glomerulo-nephritis, nephrosis, pyelitis, essential hypertension and nephrosclerosis.

Acute glomerulo-nephritis is rather rare as a complication of pregnancy. If it occurs early in gestation, the accompanying albuminuria, edema and hypertension should not be attributed to preeclampsia since the latter develops in the last half of pregnancy and especially in the last trimester, except when it occurs as a complication of hydatidiform mole. When the nephritis comes on late in gestation, it may well be confused with preeclampsia. The history of a recent infection, the presence of many red blood cells in the urine and the finding of an increase in the non-protein nitrogen of the blood should help in the differentiation of the two conditions.

Chronic glomerulo-nephritis also may be evident from the history. This may show that the patient has had scarlet fever or some other infection which was followed by the various manifestations of nephritis. A history of repeated premature stillbirths or abortions after the middle of pregnancy is suggestive, especially if syphilis can be ruled out. This is particularly true when the duration of pregnancy was shortened with each successive gestation. If the condition is sufficiently advanced, impairment of the kidney's ability to concentrate leads to polyuria and a lowering of the specific gravity of the urine. Faulty renal function also is revealed by the urea clearance and concentration tests. In well-advanced cases, the urea nitrogen of the blood also is increased and typical changes in the fundus oculi are observed. A large percentage of the cases seen in an obstetric clinic, however, have not progressed to the stage in which the blood chemistry and functional tests are altered. As a result, a differential diagnosis often is impossible in the course of pregnancy unless the patient is seen early in the gestation or unless the history is significant. In such circumstances, the true nature of the condition may not be revealed until other evidences of nephritis appear, months or even years after the termination of the pregnancy.

Nephrosis rarely occurs as a complication of pregnancy and seldom must be differentiated from preeclampsia. The presence of edema and marked albuminuria are confusing but the absence of an elevation of the blood pressure should suggest the correct diagnosis since hypertension is the most constant manifestation of preeclampsia. Because of the large amounts of albumin which are lost in the urine, the plasma proteins are rather rapidly diminished and a reversal of the albumin-globulin ratio takes place. Doubly refractile cholesterol ester bodies are found in the urine and hypercholesterolemia also is a common finding, values of 800 mg. per 100 cc. having been recorded.

Pyelitis. Occasionally, routine urinalysis during pregnancy shows a rather marked albuminuria due to pyelitis which might lead the attending physician to suspect preeclampsia. In such cases, there usually is a history of a chill followed by an elevation in the temperature and severe pain in the region of one or both kidneys. The blood shows a moderate leucocytosis and microscopic examination of the sediment from a catheterized specimen of urine reveals large numbers and clumping of white blood cells. The latter finding, together with an absence of an elevation in the blood pressure, should clear up the diagnosis.

Essential Hypertension. Because an elevated blood pressure occurs so commonly in preeclampsia, essential hypertension complicating pregnancy often is confused with this form of toxemia. If the history shows that the condition was present before the onset of pregnancy, or if the hypertension was detected early in gestation, preeclampsia can be ruled out unless the possibility of its being superimposed upon the underlying vascular condition is considered. When essential hypertension appears for the first time late in gestation, as the result of the load of pregnancy in a woman who is predisposed to this vascular change, the differential diagnosis is not so easy. The blood pressure is high, and albuminuria is slight or absent. Aside from the presence of pressure edema, marked fluid retention is not apparent. In long-standing cases, the heart is enlarged and changes in the retinal vessels are demonstrable.

Nephrosclerosis frequently is one of the sequellae of late toxemia and often develops in the course of essential hypertension. It, therefore, is a common complication of pregnancy and, in many instances, may be confused with preeclampsia. A history of its presence before conception or the development of symptoms early in pregnancy, should lead to the elimination of preeclampsia as a possibility. Nephrosclerosis usually manifests itself before the sixth month and is aggravated as pregnancy advances. While the blood pressure is high, in the mild cases the albuminuria usually is slight. If the condition is sufficiently advanced, the specific gravity of the urine is lowered and gradual loss of the concentrating power of the kidneys is revealed by the concentration test. In the malignant form of nephrosclerosis, evidences of renal impairment are more marked and the retention of non-protein nitrogen in the blood occurs early. Albuminuric retinitis is frequent and its substitution for the retinal arteriosclerosis seen in benign nephrosclerosis is an indication of the change from a benign to a malignant condition.

TREATMENT

PROPHYLACTIC. Experience has shown the great value of certain prophylactic measures which are now a part of all good prenatal routines. These include **attention to the emunctories, regulation of the diet, exercise,** and **frequent prenatal visits to the physician.**

ATTENTION TO THE EMUNCTORIES. Throughout pregnancy, a daily bowel movement is necessary. This is especially true during the last trimester. Adequate fluids and an anti-constipation diet, together with mineral oil and milk of magnesia, usually are sufficient. If, however, constipation can be combatted in no other way, more drastic measures must be used.

REGULATION OF THE DIET. The concentrated foods should be replaced to a considerable extent by vegetables in the last months of pregnancy and the total salt intake should be restricted to 4–5 gm. daily (See recommendations concerning diet in Chapter IX). Over-eating is to be avoided. At each pre-natal visit, the patient should be weighed and, if the rate of gain is greater than $3\frac{1}{2}$ lbs. per month, the dietary habits must be carefully studied and altered to suit each case. Restriction of the diet to fruits and vegetables on alternate days is one of the simplest ways to handle the problem of over-eating. Three glasses of milk daily are necessary. If these are taken at the beginning of each meal, the danger of over-feeding by this measure will be largely eliminated.

EXERCISE. The patient should be encouraged to walk out of doors daily. If the gait is brisk and is accompanied by deep breathing, much benefit will be derived from this form of exercise. For half an hour each day, she should expose her skin to the rays of the sun. In the winter months, when overcast days are common, vitamin D is indicated.

RETURN PRENATAL VISITS. The patient should return to her physician **monthly for the first seven months, bi-weekly during the next six weeks and every week in the last month and a half of pregnancy.** At each visit she should be interrogated concerning the possible occurrence of headache, edema, visual disturbances and diminished urinary output. In this connection, it is well to have the patient measure the entire urinary output for the twenty-four hours preceding each visit. The blood pressure should be taken and the urine should be examined. The possibility of fluid retention also is to be considered. Its detection will be made easier if the patient is weighed in the physician's office. **Whenever the weight gain is excessive, each day's fluid intake should be reduced below the previous day's output.**

When the blood pressure suddenly rises above 140 mm. in a woman whose pressure previously had remained well below 140, the possibility of preeclampsia is to be considered. The management of her case should then consist of rest in bed, restriction of the diet to five pints of milk daily and the securing of copious evacuations of the bowels by the use of citrate of magnesia or magnesium sulphate. The blood pressure and the amount of albumin in the urine are to be estimated every 24 hours. In addition, the weight should be taken daily and a record kept of each day's intake and output of fluids. If an increase in the weight or a positive water balance indicates fluid retention, the total amount of liquids taken each day should be kept below the previous day's output. After twenty-four hours, the patient is again seen and a careful search is made for other evidences of toxemia. A fall in blood pressure, together with an absence of other symptoms and signs, should lead to less apprehension. Vegetables are then added to the diet. Because of the tendency toward fluid retention, salt is restricted to 2–4 gm. daily and the proteins are maintained above 80 gm. per day. Blood pressure, albumin, weight and water balance observations are continued for the next two days. If, at the expiration of that time, no evidence of toxemia is present, the ordinary routine recommended in the chapter on prenatal care is resumed with the exception that salt is restricted, proteins are maintained and the fluid intake is kept below the output.

In case the blood pressure fails to fall but does not increase, the routine instituted at the onset of preeclampsia is continued for another twenty-four hours, after which milk and vegetables are given on alternate days. During this time, care should be taken to follow the directions outlined in the previous paragraph concerning the salt, protein and fluid intake. Continued observations, at intervals of two days for a period of at least one week, are then indicated. If no other evidences of toxemia appear at that time, the ordinary pregnancy routine is again followed.

When the blood pressure at the end of twenty-four hours rises in spite of rest in bed, a milk diet, catharsis, etc., the suspicion of impending eclampsia is strengthened and more frequent observations are necessary. Blood pressure determinations, together with urinalysis and a search for other symptoms should be made at least every twelve hours until it is established that eclampsia is imminent or until the patient improves. During this time, the milk diet and daily purge are continued. A sudden, pronounced rise in blood pressure, a marked increase in the albuminuria or the observation of greater edema of the fingers and face, indicate the necessity for the interruption of pregnancy. Labor, accordingly, is induced at once by that method which is best suited to the conditions that are present and which will insure the most rapid emptying of the uterus. If it appears that the toxemia is progressing so rapidly that delivery from below cannot be accomplished before the onset of convulsions, Cesarean section under local anesthesia should be considered.

PROGNOSIS. Less than seven per cent of the toxemic patients treated in our clinic according to the routine outlined, required induction of labor and only 0.3 per cent of them developed convulsions. If the toxemia is detected sufficiently early, therefore, the immediate risk for the mother should not be very great. On the other hand, there is said to be considerable danger of residual vascular renal damage if the condition is allowed to continue over a long period and some observers have shown sequellae of this character in as high as 60 per cent of their non-convulsive toxemic cases. For this reason and because the immediate prognosis is always improved by the termination of pregnancy, the gestation should be interrupted more frequently than is the custom at the present time. This is particularly true when the toxemia occurs in multiparae who are within a few weeks of term. In them, the risk from induction is so slight that the artificial termination of pregnancy is often less dangerous than the residual damage which results from waiting for a spontaneous delivery.

ECLAMPSIA

ECLAMPSIA is the term applied to the acute toxemia—occurring during pregnancy, labor or the puerperium—which culminates in convulsions. The convulsive seizures have already been described on page 534. In most instances, they are preceded by one or more of the following prodromata: hypertension, albuminuria, edema, headache, visual disturbances, diminished urinary output and epigastric pain. In other words, eclampsia (a shining forth), usually follows the symptoms and signs of preeclampsia but, because the evidences of the latter are relatively mild and those of the former are terrifying, the convulsions appear to burst forth like lightning out of a clear sky, without any preliminary warning.

FREQUENCY. The incidence of convulsive toxemia is difficult to determine. Because the majority of cases are transferred from their homes to hospitals, eclampsia is not uncommon in the latter institutions, where it is noted in about 1 per cent of all pregnancy admissions. In general practice, on the other hand, it is encountered much less frequently, probably about once in every 500 pregnancies. In Denmark, where satisfactory statistics as to hospital and home practice are available, a ten year survey revealed 1282 cases of eclampsia to 737,701 deliveries, an incidence of one case of eclampsia to every 575 births, or 1.74 per 1000 confinements (24). Due to better prenatal care, this serious complication has been prevented to such an extent in recent years, that its occurrence is now rare in the experience of those practitioners who give careful attention to the management of all pregnancies (25, 26).

MONTH OF PREGNANCY. Eclampsia is a disease of the last half of pregnancy. Statistical analyses, however, show that about one case in every 500 occurs before the fifth month (27). When preeclampsia or eclampsia is encountered early in gestation, it usually is a complication of hydatiform mole. While convulsive toxemia is considered a disease of the last half of pregnancy, it does not occur with equal frequency in the different months of this period but its incidence increases as gestation progresses, as is shown by the following summary of 306 cases:

2–3 months	1 case
5–6 months	13 cases
6–7 months	39 cases
7–8 months	53 cases
8–9 months	85 cases
9 months to term	115 cases

GRAVIDA. Sixty-eight per cent of all cases of convulsive toxemia occur in primigravidae. On the other hand, the incidence in primigravidae is 3.7 per 1000 against 0.75 per 1000 multiparae. In women who are pregnant for the first time, accordingly, the risk of eclampsia is five times as great as in those who already have had children (24, 29, 30, 31).

MULTIPLE PREGNANCY. Twin pregnancies are more frequently complicated by toxemia than are single ones. Approximately every fifteenth case of eclampsia occurs in a multiple pregnancy (32).

SEASON AND CLIMATE seem to have some influence on the occurrence of eclampsia. Warm climates have a lower incidence and southern countries are freer from toxemia than are their northern neighbors. In the vicinity of New

York, the greatest number of cases is observed during the months of March and April (33). That this is due to seasonal changes, however, has been disputed and the high incidence of eclampsia in early spring has been explained by the greater number of primigravidae who reach the last trimester of pregnancy at that time, due to the relatively larger number of marriages contracted in May and June.

ILLEGITIMACY. In a European survey, 10.9 per cent of all the births recorded were found to be illegitimate and 21.3 per cent of all the cases of eclampsia occurred in these unmarried mothers. Since the rates of its occurrence in unmarried women and married women were 3.38 and 1.53 per 1000, respectively, eclampsia may be said to be twice as frequent in illegitimate pregnancies. This higher incidence has been attributed to the greater mental anxiety of the unmarried prospective mother. The difference, however, has recently been shown to be due largely to the fact that a much higher percentage of illegitimately pregnant women are primigravidae (24).

ETIOLOGY. From the fact that eclampsia occurs only in association with the pregnant state and improvement often follows the death of the fetus, it is believed to be due primarily to some disturbance which is initiated by the **living products of conception.** The specific cause, however, is unknown.

Many theories as to its etiology have been advanced and much research has been done to prove that it is due to one or more of the following: infection, autointoxication, syncytial elements in the blood, decomposition products from the placenta, fetal metabolic products, faulty maternal metabolism, mammary toxins, anaphylaxis, endocrine disfunction, water retention, arteriolar spasm and deficient oxidation. Eclampsia, accordingly, has been called the disease of theories. The present status of the water retention and arteriolar spasm theories will be discussed in connection with the pathogenesis of convulsive toxemia.

INFLUENCE OF DIET. During the World War blockade, eclampsia was less prevalent in Germany than in former years (34, 35). This has been attributed to the dietary changes that resulted from the shortage of meats and fats. Not only were the latter largely eliminated, but the use of vegetables was considerably increased. If these deductions are correct, they substantiate the belief held by older physicians that a vegetable diet is advisable in the last trimester of pregnancy. Milk always has been regarded as the ideal food in impending eclampsia. Possibly vegetables and milk supply certain food elements which are essential to the prevention of toxemia and which are deficient in the ordinary diet.

EFFECT OF CONSTIPATION. That inadequate elimination through the intestinal tract is a contributing etiological factor is supported by the frequent history of constipation immediately preceding the onset of toxemic symptoms. Use of this knowledge is always employed in the prophylaxis of eclampsia and attention to the bowels is one of the chief recommendations in the hygiene of pregnancy.

PATHOGENESIS. In most cases of preeclampsia and eclampsia, there is a definite **disturbance in water balance** which manifests itself in the rapid gain in weight and edema which are so often observed. Accompanying this tendency toward fluid retention, the plasma proteins are diminished below the lowered values of pregnancy and the albumin-globulin ratio is considerably reduced as a result of a fall in albumin and a rise in globulin (36, 37, 38). The greatest change is noted in the albumin fraction due to the loss of albumin through the kidneys and its possible leakage into the tissue spaces of the body which may result from a general increase in capillary permeability. It is quite possible that the alterations in the glomerular capillaries which permit the passage of the smaller albumin molecule are only a part of a general vascular change which permits leakage of albumin into the tissue spaces throughout the body (38, 39, 40).

The lowering of the plasma proteins naturally causes a drop in the osmotic pressure of the blood and favors the retention of fluid in the tissues. The finding of low serum protein values in edematous patients, accordingly, has led to the suggestion that the disturbance in water balance may be secondary to a diminution of the proteins of the blood and that the primary cause of the toxemia is a deficient protein intake (41). Although the importance of maintaining the proteins of the blood at a satisfactory level cannot be denied, this is not the only factor to be considered, as is shown by the disappearance of edema in some toxemic women without any change in the low protein values.

Retention of fluids is also associated with salt retention. The giving of sodium either as sodium chloride or as sodium bicarbonate, therefore, increases any edema that may be present and this is especially true if the plasma proteins are low (42). Some observers are of the opinion that early in the toxemia, the kidney is unable to function normally with respect to the balancing of the electrolytes. In other words, they believe that there is a tendency toward the retention of sodium ions which at first favors an increase in the blood volume and, subsequently, as a result of the abnormal diffusion of sodium ions into the tissue spaces, leads to retention of fluid in the interstitial tissues and a withdrawal of fluids from the cells of the body. They attempt to explain the disturbance in water balance largely on this basis rather than from the standpoint of the change in plasma proteins and, in some instances, have shown that the edema may be reduced by forcing fluids and giving a neutral or acid ash diet which will insure a minimum sodium intake (43).

These observations on the disturbance in water balance support the **water balance theory** concerning the pathogenesis of eclampsia. According to this theory, originally proposed by Zangemeister, some unknown factor causes a change in the walls of the capillaries which increases their permeability and leads to the passage of substances such as serum albumin, which normally are held back. The osmotic pressure relationships are thereby changed and the absorption of fluids from the tissue spaces is diminished. The resulting retention of fluids within the tissues ultimately leads to edema and involvement of the brain causes convulsions and coma. This theory does not explain the visceral lesions so often seen in eclampsia. Though its advocates claim that an increased capillary resistance resulting from retention of the surrounding fluids is responsible for the rise in blood pressure, such an explanation is hardly acceptable since similar and more marked accumulations of fluid in the tissues take place in nephrosis without their having any effect on the blood pressure. It may also be stated that eclampsia sometimes occurs without edema and these cases often are the most serious.

A better and more inclusive explanation of the pathogenesis of eclampsia is offered by the **arteriolar spasm theory.** This also assumes the presence of some unknown factor which causes a spasm of the arterioles in different parts of the body. The arteriolar spasm deprives the capillary cells of their oxygen supply and thereby increases the permeability of the capillaries. For the reasons mentioned in connection with the previous theory, fluid is then retained in the tissue spaces. In other words, the arteriolar spasm theory includes all that is contained in the disturbed water balance theory but more satisfactorily explains the visceral lesions. In the different organs of the body, the character of the lesion varies with the terminal circulation in the organs. At first, the parenchymal cells which are dependent for nourishment upon the involved vessels, together with the cells of the terminal capillaries, undergo degeneration. When the circulation is restored, after cessation of the spasm, thrombosis and hemorrhage into the surrounding tissues take place (44, 45, 46, 47).

These changes in the arterioles can be demonstrated by ophthalmoscopic examination of the fundus oculi (48, 49, 50, 51). At first, spastic constrictions of the retinal arterioles are seen. These tend to be localized. One artery may be affected more than another and the irregularities in the calibre of the vessels change in position every few minutes. Later, the constriction ceases to shift and becomes more marked. Following this, a suggestion of edema is observed in the immediate vicinity of the vessels. Hemorrhage and exudate ultimately occur if the toxemia progresses in severity. The eye findings are so characteristic that the interruption of pregnancy is indicated whenever their progression cannot be arrested by conservative treatment. Evidence of vascular spasm also has been demonstrated in the capillaries at the bases of the nails (46). In the following description of the lesions found in the brain, liver and kidneys, it may be seen that the pathology in these vessels may well follow arteriolar spasm.

BRAIN. The brain may show no gross lesion other than anemia of the cortex. Often, however, edema is present and multiple minute hemorrhages are common. On section, punctiform hemorrhagic spots frequently are distributed diffusely throughout the cortex and, in places where these are grouped, such areas may reach a diameter of .5 to 1 cm.

Microscopic examination of these altered areas shows the hemorrhage to be associated with small foci of softening in which the arteries reveal evidence of degeneration. In the walls of the latter, fatty change is observed and their lumina often contain hyaline thrombi. In some places, the endothelial cells are necrotic while, in others, they are well preserved. Most of the ganglion cells in these foci have disappeared and those that remain are pyknotic and shrunken. The glia cells, likewise have disappeared. At the periphery of the foci and in the perivascular spaces, red blood cells have accumulated as a result of diapedesis from the adjacent vessels (52).

The area of parenchymal damage is more extensive than that supplied by the injured vessel, a finding which points to a greater ischemia than could have been produced by the vascular changes noted. This observation has led to the assumption that the primary disturbance is an arteriolar spasm which is somewhat more extensive than the final vessel lesion. Because the ganglion cells are particularly sensitive to oxygen deprivation and, because of the extent of the vascular spasm, the resulting ischemia produces a relatively widespread necrosis of the parenchyma. The vessel wall, at the same time, is similarly but less extensively affected. Finally, when the circulation is restored, red blood cells escape and thrombosis occurs as a result of the changes in the endothelium (52).

KIDNEYS. Renal involvement is noted in almost every case of eclampsia. The kidney is enlarged and, on section, its cortex is pale and cloudy. The tubules, particularly in their convoluted portions, show degenerative lesions which vary from simple cloudy swelling to complete necrosis. The epithelial swelling often is sufficient to obliterate the lumina which otherwise may be filled with precipitated albumin and desquamated necrotic epithelium. These changes are similar to those produced by poisonous chemicals but are thought by some to be caused by the anemia which follows spasm of the arterioles.

Glomerular changes likewise are demonstrable. The glomeruli are slightly enlarged and have a somewhat hyaline appearance. The capillaries are practically empty and their walls show considerable thickening of the basement membrane (53, 54, 55, 56, 57, 58, 59). When stained to bring out the basement membrane, the capillary walls are found to be greatly altered due to an extensive and peculiar laminated thickening of the basement membrane. This is unlike the homogenous swelling of edema and is thought to be the result of an actual increase in substance. Because of these thick bands of homogenously stained material between the rows of epithelial and endothelial cells, many of the capillary tufts have a hair pin or wire loop appearance. Little or no change is noted in the endothelial cells aside from the fact that their nuclei are sometimes slightly increased in number. Largely as a result of the massive thickening of the basement membrane, the capillary lumina are considerably narrowed and in places where the thickened walls are in contact, they seem to be occluded (56, 58, 59). These changes differ from those of acute glomerulonephritis in that the glomeruli in eclampsia are smaller, the basement membrane is thicker and there is an absence of polymorphonuclear leucocytes, intracapillary fibers and epithelial crescents. Likewise, in glomerulonephritis the endothelial nuclei are surrounded by much more cytoplasm (56, 59). It has been suggested that the capillary changes may be caused by the toxin of eclampsia (56). It also is possible that they may result from spasm of the afferent arterioles.

Occasionally, symmetrical necrosis of the cortex is found. In these cases, there is almost complete necrosis of the cortices of both kidneys with thrombosis of the intralobular arteries and usually of the vasa afferentia also. Sometimes, the thrombosis extends into the glomerular capillaries. It is thought that the vascular change is primary and that the necrosis follows infarction (56). Clinically, the patients with cortical necrosis of this type have hematuria, polyuria or complete anuria.

The question naturally arises, "Do the acute changes customarily found in eclampsia cause permanent renal damage?" "The picture is quite different from ordinary glomerulonephritis in its pathogenesis but the end result is obstruction of the glomerular capillaries and tubular atrophy. On the basis of the anatomical structure, one would expect to find hypertension and renal insufficiency clinically" (55). Although all symptoms and signs usually disappear rapidly after recovery and delivery, in about 20 per cent of the cases of eclampsia, elevation in the blood pressure and albuminuria persists and an even higher percentage of pre-eclamptics show these evidences of residual damage. The lesion found in such cases seems to be analagous to that which develops in the course of essential hypertension. It, accordingly is primarily a vascular one and the ultimate picture is that of nephrosclerosis.

LIVER. The liver is larger and softer than normal and usually is pale yellow in color. Often irregular patches of purplish discoloration may be seen beneath the capsule. The cut surface has a mottled appearance due to areas of hemorrhage and necrosis which, on microscopic examination, are found to involve the periphery of the lobules (60, 61). Thrombi also are seen in the smaller portal vessels. The fact that this lesion is so common and is seldom found in other conditions has led some observers to regard hemorrhage and necrosis of the periphery of the liver lobules as the characteristic lesion of eclampsia (61, 62, 63, 64, 65). Other writers, while agreeing that these findings often are observed believe that the lesion, in eclampsia, does not always have this relationship to the lobule. Similar changes have been observed occasionally in the central and frequently in the mid-zonal regions, especially when the degeneration was extensive (66, 67, 68, 69). In one report of 38 autopsy examinations, focal necrosis indiscriminately scattered in the liver substance, without predilection for any particular zone of the lobule, was noted in 26 cases (68). There is, however, a distinct predilection for the subcapsular regions and the right lobe seems to be affected more often than the rest of the liver (69, 70). This frequent involvement of the right lobe has been attributed to the fact that the blood current, in the portal circulation from the stomach, duodenum and jejunum, goes to that portion of the liver (70). In general, the pathology in the liver may

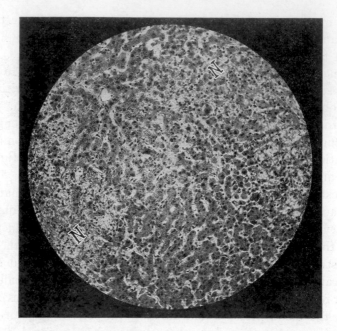

FIG. 743. Liver in eclampsia. N, necrosis at periphery of the lobules.

be summarized as portal thrombosis, periportal hemorrhage and necrosis and focal necrosis in the liver substance, without respect to the center or periphery of the lobule.

It has been suggested that the so-called typical liver lesion begins as a thrombosis of the smaller portal vessels and that this is followed by necrosis of the adjacent liver cells and hemorrhage into the necrotic zone. The tendency toward thrombosis is thought by some to be due to the effect of placental proteins and tissue fibrinogen taken up from the alimentary tract. Support is given to this hypothesis by the observation that tissue fibrinogen injected into the circulation within a short time after the ingestion of a meat meal causes similar lesions in the livers of dogs (70). In this connection, it may be stated that the clotting time is so shortened in eclampsia that it sometimes is difficult to do a satisfactory phlebotomy without using more than one vein. No doubt, this is partly due to the fact that fibrinogen is increased even above the higher values which are normal for pregnancy. These liver changes also have been attributed to arteriolar spasm which is thought to cause necrosis of the adjacent hepatic cells and alterations in the vessel walls which lead to thrombosis and hemorrhage into the surrounding tissues.

HEART. In many cases, the heart fails to show any pathological changes. In others, there is a tendency toward petechial hemorrhages and myocardial degeneration (79).

LUNGS. Congestion and edema are common findings in the lungs and petechial hemorrhages also are observed. Very often, bronchopneumonia results from aspiration (69).

Punctate hemorrhages occasionally are found in the bladder, gastro-intestinal tract and adrenals. The adrenal cortex in particular may show evidences of the vascular changes previously mentioned in other organs.

TREATMENT

Although the interruption of pregnancy and its consequent removal of the cause of the toxemia is the anchor to windward upon which we should depend for safety whenever conservative treatment fails to arrest the progress of the disease, it must be remembered that **after the onset of convulsions, the patient is a poor risk for any operative procedure.** Induction of labor and attempts to hasten the delivery by operative means, therefore, are contraindicated after the toxemia has reached the convulsive stage. Treatment after that time, accordingly, is directed toward the relief of the symptoms of toxemia rather than the removal of its cause and the interruption of pregnancy should be postponed until the patient has recovered sufficiently to stand whatever operative interference is necessary to accomplish this end.

MORPHINE. A hypodermic injection of morphine gr. $\frac{1}{2}$ is given as soon as possible after the onset of the first convulsion and repeated in $\frac{1}{4}$ gr. doses at hourly intervals until the convulsions cease or the respirations are lowered to 12 per minute (9). Seldom are more than three or four injections required, if the treatment is begun early and includes a large phlebotomy.

PHLEBOTOMY. Soon after the first injection of morphine has been given, a large bore paraffin-coated needle is inserted into the median basilic vein and 1000 cc. of blood are withdrawn. By noting the pulse and blood pressure, the loss of too much blood is avoided. Only rarely is it necessary to discontinue the procedure before the desired 1000 cc. are removed. In our experience, phlebotomy of less than 600 cc. seldom is of value.

If the procedure is done before or during labor, the blood is typed and a suitable donor is held in readiness should hemorrhage in the third stage require transfusion.

PROTECTION AGAINST EXTERNAL STIMULI. Due to the increased irritability of the nervous system, convulsions often are precipitated by very slight external stimuli. The patient, therefore, must be protected in every possible way against unnecessary irritation. She is placed in a darkened room from which all noise is excluded and those in attendance are requested to refrain from conversation within her hearing. Since most of the therapeutic and diagnostic measures formerly employed often cause convulsions, they should be abandoned. It accordingly is advisable to avoid frequent blood pressure determinations, catheterizations, gastric lavage and enemata. In other words, the patient is treated in this respect just as is a patient suffering from strychnine poisoning.

COLONIC IRRIGATION.   A colonic irrigation is given immediately after the completion of the blood letting and is repeated daily.   If the patient regains consciousness at any time, elimination is further assisted by the oral administration of two ounces of castor oil.

MAGNESIUM SULPHATE.   Usually the convulsions cease within a short time after these measures are instituted.   Should they continue, however, 20 cc. of a 10 per cent solution of magnesium sulphate are given intravenously or into the muscle (71).

INDUCTION OF LABOR.   Labor often occurs spontaneously in the course of eclampsia.   If it does not, the interruption of pregnancy is recommended as soon as the patient has recovered sufficiently to stand the procedure.   In two of our cases, eclampsia recurred two and four weeks after the initial attacks.   Labor, accordingly, should be induced within four or five days after the cessation of convulsions.

RESULTS OF TREATMENT.   This plan has been followed in 129 cases in our clinic with a maternal mortality of 7.7 per cent.   In 70 per cent no convulsions were observed after the completion of the phlebotomy (72).

STROGANOFF'S ROUTINE.   One of the most successful methods of treating eclampsia is that advocated by Stroganoff (73).   The patient is placed in a dark, quiet room and subjected to as little external irritation as possible.   Small amounts of chloroform are administered during all examinations and treatments. An injection of morphine gr. $\frac{1}{4}$ is given as soon as possible and repeated three hours later.   These are supplemented by the use of 20–40 gr. of chloral hydrate per rectum 2, 7, 13 and 21 hours after admission.   Following the third convulsion, phlebotomy is done.   The amount of blood withdrawn, however, is much less than that recommended in the routine which has been so successful in our clinic.   The pregnancy is not interrupted and labor is not accelerated except for a definite indication other than eclampsia.

MAGNESIUM SULPHATE ROUTINE.   In some clinics, repeated intravenous injections of magnesium sulphate have also given very good results (19).   Twenty cubic centimeters of a 10 per cent solution of magnesium sulphate are given as soon after the first convulsion as possible and repeated every hour until the convulsions are controlled.   After their cessation, the injections are repeated whenever a rise in blood pressure seems to indicate the imminence of another attack.

In addition, 1000 cc. of 10 per cent intravenous glucose are given to those patients who have little edema, while in the presence of marked edema, 50 cc. of a 50 per cent solution are used.   This measure is thought to be particularly important if there is a scanty urinary output, a low CO_2 combining power, and especially if delivery is imminent or an operative procedure is contemplated.

Chloral gr. 20 and sodium bromide gr. 60 are given per rectum if the patient is comatose or very restless and the blood pressure is falling.   Following each convulsion, oxygen inhalations are employed until the breathing is normal.   If the patient is in labor, the pain is relieved by the use of nitrous oxide and, whenever progress is delayed in the second stage, low forceps or version and extraction are used.

COMMENT ON THE TREATMENT OF ECLAMPSIA.   Until the cause of eclampsia is known and more has been learned concerning its pathology, the treatment of this alarming complication of pregnancy cannot be placed upon a scientific basis and must remain more or less empirical.   For this reason, the routines vary in different clinics according to the ideas and experiences of those who, by trial and error, attempt to solve the problem.   While the interruption of pregnancy no doubt removes the primary cause of the toxemia, most observers are agreed that the time for operative intervention has passed when convulsions have occurred.   On the other hand, they also agree that labor should be induced as soon as the patient has recovered sufficiently to stand the procedure.   There may, of course, be circumstances which might justify operative intervention even though the patient is having convulsions.   For instance, if she is an elderly primipara and delivery can be effected soon after the onset of convulsive seizures, even Cesarean section may be considered justifiable in the interests of the child, since the fetal mortality in eclampsia is extremely high irrespective of the routine followed.   In this connection, it may be stated that, in the days when the interruption of pregnancy was the first consideration in the treatment of eclampsia, the maternal mortality was highest in the cases which were terminated by Cesarean section.   In our clinic, we never resort to a Cesarean section unless the patient is in labor and has cephalo-pelvic disproportion or unless some other indication, aside from eclampsia, is present.   In other words, we usually regard eclampsia as a contraindication to Cesarean section.   Whenever this operation is employed, it should be done under local anesthesia.

While there is no lack of agreement as to the need for sedation, the method of its accomplishment differs in different clinics.   Morphine, chloral, magnesium sulphate and the barbiturates are used most frequently for this purpose.   For a number of years, we relied upon $\frac{1}{4}$ gr. of morphine every hour until the convulsions ceased or until the respirations were lowered to 12 per minute.   In the course of this experience, it occasionally was found that the convulsions could not be controlled by this routine but that they ceased when the dose was increased to $\frac{1}{2}$ grain.   For this reason, we now give $\frac{1}{2}$ gr. of morphine as the initial dose and have found that further use of the drug seldom is necessary.   Luminal, sodium pentobarbiturate, etc. have also been recommended as sedatives in eclampsia.

Most observers have also noted that the patient should be protected, as much as possible, from external stimuli.   All agree that she should be in a darkened room from which all unnecessary noise is excluded.   While the various routines differ as to the advisability of catheterization, blood pressure determinations, gastric lavage and colonic irrigations, all of them attempt to restrict these sources of irritation as much as possible.

The other measures which are used in most of the routines have one thing in common in that they all serve to dehydrate the interstitial tissues. Whether this is accomplished by the use of phlebotomy, concentrated glucose, magnesium sulphate, tapping of the spinal fluid or veratrum viride, the success of the routine usually depends upon the accomplishment of this purpose. Concentrated glucose stimulates the kidneys and draws the fluids from the tissue spaces into the circulation. It, at the same time, is a source of food and is of value when the patient has not taken nourishment for some time. Intravenous glucose, accordingly, is one of the most valuable measures employed in the treatment of eclampsia. Magnesium sulphate intravenously and intramuscularly serves as a sedative and also draws the fluid from the interstitial tissues into the circulation. The results from its use have been most satisfactory in some localities. Repeated spinal taps of 50–60 cc. every 4–6 hours are said to lessen the cerebral tension and aid in arresting the convulsions. In some clinics, the use of this procedure is recommended most highly. While veratrum viride was employed more extensively in former years, its use at the present time has been abandoned except in a few localities where it is said to prove very successful. It also depletes the circulation by causing intense perspiration. Like veratrum viride, phlebotomy also has been given up by many clinicians. Most men, however, still feel that its use is advisable in certain cases which fail to respond to other therapeutic measures. They also seem to look with favor upon this ancient therapeutic measure in postpartum eclampsia and in cases complicated by edema of the lungs. Many years ago, we limited the use of phlebotomy to similar cases and then concluded that if phlebotomy is good after the stage of extremis, it should also be good before this critical period is reached, provided the patient is not suffering from anemia. With this idea in mind, we decided to take off a large amount of blood as soon as possible after the first convulsion occurs and, up to the present time, not only have we failed to regret this action but from our results, we believe that it can be recommended to others. In this connection, it may be stated that the good results which we have obtained are due, in our opinion, to two considerations, first, the fact that the phlebotomy was done early and second, that at least 600 cc. and preferably 1000 cc. were withdrawn.

REFERENCES

1. DUNCAN, J. W. AND HARDING, V. J.: A Report on the Effect of High Carbohydrate Feeding on the Nausea and Vomiting of Pregnancy. Can. Med. Assn. J., 1918, 8, 1057.
2. TITUS, P. AND DODDS, P.: The Etiologic Significance of Lowered Blood Sugar Values in Vomiting of Pregnancy. Am. J. O. & G., 1928, 16, 90.
3. DUNCAN, J. M.: Clinical Lecture on Hepatic Disease in Gynecology and Obstetrics. Med. Times & Gaz. Lond., 1879, 1, 57.
4. LINDEMANN, W.: Zur Pathologischen Anatomie des unstillbaren Erbrechens der Schwangeren. Centralbl. f. Allg. Path. u. Path. Anat., 1892, 3, 625.
5. STONE, W. S.: Toxemia of Pregnancy. Am. Gyn., 1903, 3, 518.
6. WILLIAMS, J. W.: Pernicious Vomiting of Pregnancy. Johns Hopkins Hosp. Bull., 1906 17 7[1]

Further Contributions to Our Knowledge of the Pernicious Vomiting of Pregnancy. J. O. & G., Brit. Emp., 1912, 22, 245.

7. EWING, J.: The Pathological Anatomy and Pathogenesis of the Toxemia of Pregnancy. Am. J. O., 1905, 55, 145.

8. WINTER, G.: Zur Aetiologie der Hyperemesis gravidarum. Zentralbl. f. Gyn., 1907, 31, 1497.

9. STRAUSS, M. B. AND MCDONALD, W. J.: Polyneuritis of Pregnancy. J. A. M. A., 1933, 100, 1320.

10. TILLMAN, A. J. B.: Two Fatal Cases of Hyperemesis Gravidarum with Retinal Hemorrhages. Am. J. O. & G., 1934, 27, 240.

11. VAN WYCK, B. A.: The Treatment of Hyperemesis Gravidarum. Am. J. O. & G., 1931, 21, 243.

12. HARDING, V. J. AND VAN WYCK, H. B.: The Use of Fluids in the Treatment of Hyperemesis Gravidarum. Am. J. O. & G., 1926, 11, 1.

13. TITUS, P. AND DODDS, P.: The Etiological Significance of Lowered Blood Sugar Values in Vomiting of Pregnancy. Am. J. O. & G., 1928, 16, 90.

14. PECKHAM, C. H.: Observations on Sixty Cases of Hyperemesis Gravidarum. Am. J. O. & G., 1929, 17, 776.

15. GLASSMAN,   : A Study of Hyperemesis Gravidarum with Special Reference to Blood Chemistry. Surg. Gyn. & Obs., 1938, 66, 858.

16. FREEMAN, W., MELICK, J. M. AND MCCLUSKY, D. K.: Suprarenal Cortex Therapy in the Vomiting of Pregnancy. Am. J. O. & G., 1937, 33, 618.

17. SPITZER, W.: Hyperemesisbehandlung mit Vitamin B_1, ein Beitrag zur Frage des Kohlenhydratstoffwechsels bei Schwangerschaftshypovitaminosen und der Nebennierenrindenhormon. Zentralbl. f. Gyn., 1938, 62, 1433.

18. STAHLER, F. B.: Hypovitaminosen in der Schwangerschaft. Munch. Med. Wchnschr., 1937, 84, 327.

19. IRVING, F. C.: The Treatment of Severe Vomiting of Pregnancy by the Use of the Levine Tube and Vitamin B Complex. Med. Rec. & Annals, 1937, 31, 416.

20. DICKER, S.: Treatment of Vomiting of Pregnancy by Ascorbic Acid (Vitamin C). Schweiz. Med. Wchnschr., 1937, 67, 74.

21. FALLS, F. H.: Hyperthyroidism Complicating Pregnancy. Am. J. O. & G., 1929, 17, 536.

22. FITZGERALD, J. E. AND WEBSTER, A.: Hyperemesis Gravidarum: A Clinical Study of 396 Cases. Am. J. O. & G., 1938, 36, 460.

23. STANDER, H. J. AND CADDEN, J. F.: Acute Yellow Atrophy of the Liver in Pregnancy. Am. J. O. & G., 1934, 28, 61.

24. HAUCH, E. AND LEHMAN, K.: Investigations into the Occurrence of Eclampsia in Denmark during the years 1918–1927. Acta Obstet. et Gyn. Scandinavia, 1934, 14, 425.

25. MCPHERSON, R.: A Consideration of the Pregnancy Toxemia Known as Eclampsia. Am J. O. & G., 1922, 4, 50.

26. LICHTENSTEIN: Zur Klinik, Therapie und Aetiologie der Eklampsie, nach einer neuen Statistik bearbeitet auf Grund von 400 Fällen. Arch. f. Gyn., 1912, 95, 183.

27. EBELER, F.: Ueber Früheklampsie. Ztschr. f. Geb. u. Gyn., 1916–17, 79, 536.

28. GOEDECKE: Klinische Beobachtungen über Eklampsie. Ztschr. f. Geb. u. Gyn., 1901, 45, 44.

29. BÜTTNER, O.: Statistik und Klinik der Eclampsie im Grossherzogtum Mecklenburg-Schwerin. Arch. f. Gyn., 1903, 70, 322.

30. HAMMERSCHLAG: Die Eklampsie in Ostpreussen. Monatschr. f. Geb. u. Gyn., 1904, 20, 475.

31. MEYER-WIRZ: Klinische Studie über Eklampsie. Arch. f. Gyn., 1904, 71, 15.

32. ZANGEMEISTER, W.: Die Lehre von der Eklampsie. Leipzig, 1926.

33. HARRAR, J. A.: Concerning One Hundred and Fifty Cases of Eclampsia in the Lying-in Hospital of New York. Bull. Lying-in Hosp., N. Y., 1905, 2, 72.

34. WARNEKROS, K.: Kriegskost und Eklampsie. Zentralbl. f. Gyn., 1916, 40, 897.

35. VARO, B.: Krieg und Eklampsie. Zentralbl. f. Gyn., 1920, 44, 522.

36. ZANGEMEISTER, W.: Der hydrops gravidarum sein Verlauf und seine Beziehungen zur Nephropathie und Eklampsie. Ztschr. f. Geb. u. Gyn., 1919, 81, 491.
37. PLASS, E. D. AND BOGERT, L. J.: Plasma Protein Variations in Normal and Toxemic Pregnancies. J. Hopk. Hosp. Bull., 1924, 35, 361.
38. EASTMAN, N. J.: The Serum Proteins in The Toxemias of Pregnancy. Am. J. O. & G., 1930, 19, 343.
39. DOMAGK, G.: Bei der Eklampsie Auftretende Endothelveränderungen und Ihre Bedeutung. Klin. Wchnschr., 1925, 4, 1011, No. 21.
40. JAFFÉ, R.: Beiträge zur Frage der apoplektischen Blutung (an Hand eines Falles von Eklampsie. Zentralbl. f. Gyn., 1927, 51, 1387.
41. STRAUSS, M. B.: Observations on the Etiology of the Toxemias of Pregnancy. The Relationship of Nutritional Deficiency Hypoproteinemia and Elevated Venous Pressure to Water Retention in Pregnancy. Am. J. Med. Sc., 1935, 190, 811.
42. STRAUSS, M. B.: Production of Acute Exacerbation of Toxemia by Sodium Salts in Pregnant Women with Hypoproteinemia. Am. J. Med. Sc., 1937, 194, 772.
43. McPHAIL, F. L.: Water Exchange in Relation to the Toxemias of Pregnancy. West. J. Surg., Obst. & Gyn., 1939, 47, 306.
44. FAHR, T.: Die Eklampsie. Bonn, 1924, p. 200.
45. HINSELMANN, H.: Die Eklampsie. Bonn, 1924, p. 361.
46. IRVING, F. C.: The Vascular Aspect of Eclampsia. Am. J. O. & G., 1936, 31, 466.
47. EASTMAN, N. J.: The Vascular Factor in the Toxemias of Late Pregnancy. Am. J. O. & G., 1937, 34, 549.
48. MYLIUS, K.: Funktionelle Veränderungen am Gefässsystem der Netzhaut. Berlin, 1928.
49. VOLHARD: Die Pathogenese der Retinitis albuminurica. Zentralbl. f. d. ges. Ophth., 1929, 21, 129.
50. WEGENER, H. P.: Arterioles of the Retina in Toxemia of Pregnancy. J. A. M. A., 1933, 101, 1380.
51. MUSSEY, R. D.: The Relation of Retinal Changes to the Severity of the Acute Toxic Hypertensive Syndrome of Pregnancy. Am. J. O. & G., 1936, 31, 938.
52. DEVRIES, E.: Acute Diseases of the Brain Due to Functional Disturbances of the Circulation. Arch. of Neurol. & Psychiatry, 1931, 25, 227.
53. LÖHLEIN, M.: Zur Pathogenese der Nierenkrankheiten. Deutsche. Med. Wchnschr., 1918, 44, 1187.
54. FAHR, T.: Über Nierenveränderungen bei Eklampsie. Zentralbl. f. Gyn., 1920, 44, 991.
55. FAHR, T.: Über die Nierenveränderungen bei der Eklampsie und ihre Abgrenzung gegen andere Formen des Morbus Brightii. Zentralbl. f. Gyn., 1928, 52, 474.
56. BELL, E. T.: Renal Lesions in the Toxemias of Pregnancy. Am. J. Path., 1932, 8, 1.
57. BAIRD, D. AND DUNN, J. S.: Renal Lesions in Eclampsia and Nephritis in Pregnancy. J. Path. & Bact., 1933, 37, 291.
58. ZIMMERMAN, H. M. AND PETERS, J. P.: Pathology of Pregnancy Toxemias. J. Clin. Invest., 1937, 16, 397.
59. KELLAR, R. J., Arnott, W. M. AND MATTHEW, D.: Observations on the Morbid Histology of the Kidney in Eclampsia and other Toxemias of Pregnancy. J. O. & G. Brit. Emp., 1937, 44, 320.
60. PILLIET, A. H. AND L'ÉTIENNE, A.: Lesions du Foie dans L'eclampsie avec Ictere; Leurs Rapports avec les Lesions Hepatiques de L'éclampsie Vulgaire. Nouv. Arch. d'Obs. et de Gyn., 1889, 4, 312.
61. SCHMORL, G.: Zur Lehre von der Eklampsie. Arch. f. Gyn., 1902, 65, 504.
62. HEINRICHDORFF, P : Die anatomischen Veränderungen der Leber in der Schwangerschaft. Zeitschr. f. Geb. u. Gyn., 1912, 70, 620.
63. CEELEN, W.: Über eklamptische Leberveränderungen. Virchow's Arch. f. Path. Anat. u. Phys., 1910, 201, 361.
64. KONSTANTINOWITSCH, W.: Beitrag zur Kenntnis der Leberveränderungen bei Eklampsie. Beitr. z. path. Anat. u. z. allg. Path., 1907, 40, 483.

65. FAHR, T.: Die Path-anatomischen Veränderungen der Niere u. Leber bei der Eklampsie. Hinselmann: Die Eklampsie. Bonn, 1924, p. 200.

66. BELL, J. W.: Postmortem Findings in Ten Cases of Toxemia of Pregnancy. Am. J. O. & G., 1926, 12, 792.

67. THEOBALD, G. W.: Hepatic Lesions Associated with Eclampsia and Those Caused by Raising Intra-abdominal Pressure. J. Pathology & Bacteriology, 1932, 35, 843.

68. DAVIDSON, J.: Eclampsia and Puerperal Toxemia: A Study of the Histological Changes Occurring in Liver and Kidneys. The Edinburgh Obst. Soc., 1930–31, p. 24.

69. SISON, H.: A Clinicopathologic Study of Eclampsia Based upon Thirty-eight Autopsied Cases. Am. J. O. & G., 1931, 22, 35.

70. DIECKMANN, W. J.: Further Observations on the Hepatic Lesion in Eclampsia. Am. J. O. & G., 1929, 18, 757.

71. LAZARD, E. M., IRWIN, J. C. AND VRUWINK, J.: The Intravenous Magensium Sulphate Treatment of Eclampsia. Am. J. O. & G., 1926, 12, 104.

72. BECK, A. C.: The Conservative Treatment of Eclampsia. Am. J. O. & G., 1924, 7, 677 & 730.

73. STROGANOFF: My Improved Method of the Prophylactic Treatment of Eclampsia. J. O & G. Brit. Emp., 1923, 30, 1.

CHAPTER XXVII

MEDICAL AND SURGICAL COMPLICATIONS OF PREGNANCY

DISEASES OF THE RESPIRATORY SYSTEM

UPPER RESPIRATORY INFECTIONS are a decided menace during pregnancy. Because the pyogenic organisms present in the nose and throat may give rise to a serious puerperal infection, even the mild cases constitute a source of danger at the time of labor. This relationship between infections of the upper respiratory tract and puerperal infection is well shown by the fact that the latter condition with its consequent increased maternal morbidity and mortality is most frequent during January, February, March and April, the months in which respiratory infections are most prevalent (Fig. 744).

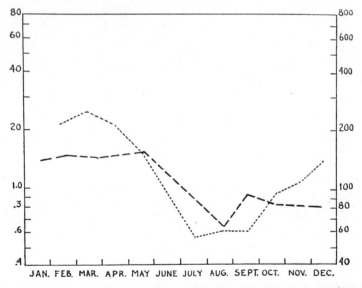

FIG. 744. Curves of maternal mortality (broken line) and pneumonia deaths (dotted line).

ORDINARY "COLDS" last longer and cause greater discomfort during pregnancy. As term approaches, they become a real hazard. Not only is the risk of pneumonia greatly increased whenever anesthesia is required, but many cases of serious puerperal infection owe their origin to this source. Because of the consequences that may follow such infections, women who are pregnant should not associate with others who have a "cold". If the husband or other members of the family are afflicted, isolation from them is desirable. Whenever infection of the upper respiratory tract does occur, an effort should be made to shorten the course of the disease. If it persists, complications are to be suspected and the possibility of reinfection from other members of the family must be ruled out.

INFLUENZA. Pregnant women are unusually susceptible to influenza, which often leads to abortion or premature labor, and not infrequently is complicated by a fatal bronchopneumonia.

In the last influenza epidemic, about 25 per cent of the pregnancies were spontaneously interrupted and a like number of mothers died. Most of the deaths, however, were due to a complicating pneumonia. When the latter complication develops, the maternal mortality rises to over 50 per cent and about half of the pregnancies terminate in abortion or premature labor, an accident which adds greatly to the risk. The child often is stillborn. Occasionally, it may die soon after birth from septicemia or bronchopneumonia (1, 2, 3, 4, 5, 6, 7, 8). Encephalitis in the newborn following influenza in the last trimester of pregnancy has been reported (9).

During pregnancy, isolation from those known to have influenza is imperative. When the disease develops in a woman who is pregnant, she should be kept in bed from its onset and the toxemia should be combated by the use of such eliminative measures as will not cause the induction of labor. **Morphine in sufficient amounts to prevent abortion or premature labor likewise is indicated.** If labor does occur, the second stage should be shortened by forceps extraction under local anesthesia.

LOBAR PNEUMONIA. The dangers usually encountered in lobar pneumonia are increased during pregnancy by the tendency toward abortion and premature labor. This unfortunate accident occurs in the majority of cases and is thought to be due to profound toxemia, high temperature and anoxemia. When the pregnancy is thus prematurely terminated, a large percentage of the mothers succumb because of the severe strain of labor on the already weakened circulation. Death of the child also is common.

Because of the seriousness of this complication all upper respiratory infections, as above stated, should be carefully managed with a view to warding off a possible pneumonia. After pneumonia develops, oxygen and morphine are indicated to prevent the interruption of pregnancy, and pituitary extract, which sometimes is given for the relief of distention, is contraindicated. The treatment otherwise is the same as that followed in nonpregnant cases.

If the pneumonia patient falls into labor, the strain of the bearing-down efforts on the embarrassed circulation should be eliminated by artificial delivery. As soon as the cervix is fully dilated and the head descends well below the ischial spines, the child is extracted by forceps. Local anesthesia, by means of novocaine infiltration of the perineum, is preferable to the use of a general anesthetic.

PULMONARY TUBERCULOSIS. Women suffering from active tuberculosis often grow worse during and after pregnancy. Morning sickness and the early metabolic disturbances may have a deleterious effect in the first trimester, after which apparent improvement occasionally is observed. During labor, the violent action of the diaphragm and the loss of blood that occurs at this time may again cause an aggravation of the disease. The strain of lactation also is detrimental (10, 11, 12, 13, 14). Because of these added difficulties, therapeutic abortion was recommended by most of the older authorities (15, 16). Recently, however, extensive joint studies by obstetricians and phthisiologists have cast considerable doubt on the wisdom of this advice (17, 18, 19, 20, 21, 22, 23, 24, 25, 26, 27).

It has been noted in large groups of patients suffering from tuberculosis that mild early cases improve at about the same rate under proper hygienic treatment, irrespective of the presence or absence of pregnancy, and that the progress of advanced lesions is not affected by emptying the uterus. In other words, follow up records in nonpregnant and pregnant women show the disease to run parallel courses in the two groups. It may therefore be said that those best qualified to render an opinion on the subject are skeptical of the good that may result from therapeutic interruption of pregnancy.

Since it was formerly thought that pregnancies up to the fifth month should be interrupted, and those beyond the fifth month allowed to continue, it may be possible that the relatively poor results following therapeutic abortion were due to the fact that the operation was done at too late a date, when the interruption of pregnancy itself was a rather formidable procedure. Curettage before the eighth week, on the other hand, is accompanied by very little risk even in the presence of tuberculosis. In spite of the statistical evidence above referred to, therefore, it seems justifiable to empty the uterus in active cases if the diagnosis can be made before the eighth week, whenever the patient's circumstances do not permit adequate care of the tuberculosis (27a).

When the pregnancy is not interrupted, the tuberculosis must be very carefully treated. Best results are obtained in well equipped sanatoria where accurate observations as to the course of the disease may be followed by such therapeutic measures as are indicated. Probably more women would be saved if greater care were given to the treatment of the tuberculosis and less attention paid to the complicating pregnancy.

The bearing-down efforts of labor, accompanied as they are by wide excursions of the diaphragm, are harmful in that they interfere with the principle of keeping the diseased lungs at rest. For this reason, the second stage should be shortened by forceps extraction after the perineum has been infiltrated with novocaine. Continuous caudal analgesia by eliminating the bearing down reflex entirely should be ideal for labor complicated by tuberculosis. Likewise, in some cases, it may be advisable to avoid the strain of the entire labor, and cesarean section under local anesthesia may be indicated.

Lactation is harmful to both the mother and the child. Accordingly, the infant should not be allowed to suckle.

As the tubercle bacillus seldom passes through the placenta, the offspring of most tuberculous mothers are free from the disease at birth. After birth the child must be rigidly isolated from its mother in order that contact infection may be avoided.

BRONCHIAL ASTHMA. During pregnancy, an asthmatic patient may be relatively free from attacks. Less commonly, on the other hand, an aggravation of the symptoms is observed and, in rare instances, the manifestations of the disease may be present only when the patient is pregnant. The attacks usually are most severe in the first half of gestation, during which spontaneous abortion occasionally occurs. Children of such patients likewise are hypersensitive and commonly have eczema and food idiosyncrasies. Sooner or later about half of them develop asthma (28, 29, 30).

The treatment consists in the control of the attacks by small doses of adrenalin or ephedrine. Careful search should be made to ascertain the substances to which the patient is hypersensitive and they should be eliminated from her food and environment. Attempts at immunization during pregnancy are inadvisable. Only in very rare instances is therapeutic emptying of the uterus justifiable (31).

REFERENCES

1. WOOLSTON, W. J. AND CONLEY, D. O.: Epidemic Pneumonia (Spanish Influenza) in Pregnancy. Effects in 101 Cases. J. A. M. A., 1918, 71, 1898.
2. HARRIS, J. W.: Influenza Occurring in Pregnant Women. J. A. M. A., 1919, 72, 978.
3. BLAND, P. B.: Influenza in its Relation to Pregnancy and Labor. Am. J. Obs., 1919, 79, 184.
4. FARRAR, L. K. P.: The Visitations of Influenza and its Influence upon Gynecologic and Obstetric Conditions. Am. J. Obs., 1919, 79, 229.
5. KOSMAK, G. W.: The Occurrence of Epidemic Influenza in Pregnancy. Am. J. Obs., 1919, 79, 238.
6. WELZ, W. E.: Influenza Complicating Pregnancy and Labor. Am. J. Obs., 1919, 79, 247.
7. TITUS, P. AND JAMISON, J. M.: Pregnancy Complicated by Epidemic Influenza. J. A. M. A., 1919, 72, 1665.
8. ABT, I. A.: Influenza in a Newly Born Infant. J. A. M. A., 1919, 72, 980.
9. STEWART, W. B.: Encephalitis in Children, Apparently Congenital and Following Maternal Influenza. Am. Jnl. Med. Sciences, 1934, 188, 522.
10. BACON, C. S.: The Essentials of Sanatorium Treatment of Tuberculous Gravidae and Puerperae and Their Children. J. A. M. A., 1913, 61, 750.
11. NORRIS, C. C. AND MURPHY, D. P.: Pregnancy in the Tuberculous With the Report of 166 Cases. Am. J. Obs. & Gyn., 1922, 4, 597.
12. ROBINSON, A. L.: The Influence of Childbearing upon Pulmonary Tuberculosis. J. Obs. Gyn. of the Brit. Emp., 1931, 38, 338.
13. RIST, E.: Relation of Pregnancy to General Diseases; Tuberculosis. Brit. Med. J., 1927, 2, 247.
14. STEWART, D. A.: Tuberculosis and Maternity. Public Health J., 1918, 9, 221.
15. TREMBLEY, C. C.: Tuberculosis and Pregnancy. J. A. M. A., 1909, 52, 989.
16. NORRIS, C. C.: Pregnancy in the Tuberculous. Am. J. Obs., 1916, 73, 997.

17. FORSSNER, H., SUNDELL, C. AND KJELLIN, G.: Les relations entre l'état de gestation et la tuberculose. Rev. de la tuberculose, Paris, 1924, 3s, 5, 730.
18. BRIDGMAN, E. W. AND NORWOOD, V.: Pulmonary Tuberculosis and Pregnancy. Johns Hopkins Hosp. Bull., 1926, 38, 83.
19. HILL, A. M.: Sanatorium Provision in the United States for the Pregnant Tuberculous Woman. Am. Rev. Tuberc., 1927, 16, 157.
20. HILL, A. M.: A Statistical Study of the Relationship between Pregnancy and Tuberculosis. Am. Rev. Tuberc., 1928, 17, 113.
21. BECKMAN, M. AND KIRCH, A.: Tuberculose und Schwangerschaft. Arch. f. Gyn., 1928, 135, 438.
22. BARNES, H. L. AND BARNES, R. P.: Pregnancy and Tuberculosis. Am. J. Obs. and Gyn., 1930, 19, 490.
23. BLISNJANSKAJA, A.: Tuberkulose und Schwangerschaft. Arch. f. Gyn., 1931, 146, 302.
24. JENNINGS, F. L., MARIETTE, E. S., LITZENBERG, J. C.: Pregnancy in the Tuberculous. Am. Rev. Tuberc., 1932, 25, 673.
25. JENNINGS, F. L. AND MARIETTE, E. S.: A Biometric Study of Pregnancy and Tuberculosis. Am. Rev. Tuberc., 1932, 25, 687.
25a. MARIETTA, E. S., LARSON, L. M., AND LITZENBERG, J. C.: The Treatment of the Tuberculous Woman During Pregnancy. Am. J. Med. Sc., 1942, 203, 866.
26. SCHULTZE-RHONHOF, F. AND HANSEN, K.: Kritische Bemerkungen zur Frage "Tuberkulose und Schwangerschaft". Med. Klin., 1933, 29, 765.
27. DURYEA, A. W.: Pregnancy and Bilateral Phrenic Exairesis Postpartum; Case Report. Am. Rev Tuberc., 1931, 24, 256.
27a. ALEXANDER, J.: In the Discussion of a Paper on Tuberculosis and Pregnancy. Am. J. O. & G., 1937, 34, 284.
28. SPAIN, W. C. AND COOKE, R. A.: Studies in Specific Hypersensitiveness. J. Immunol., 1924, 9, 521.
29. CLARKE, J. A., DONNALLY, H. H. AND COCA, A. F.: Studies in Specific Hypersensitiveness. J. Immunol., 1928, 15, 9.
30. WILLIAMSON, A. C.: Pregnancy concomitant with Asthma or Hay Fever. Am. J. Obs. & Gyn., 1930, 20, 192.
31. VIGNES, H.: Asthme et Gestation. Gaz. Med. de France, 1930, 3, 65.

DISEASES OF THE BLOOD AND CIRCULATORY SYSTEMS

ANEMIA. The concentration of hemoglobin and red blood cells often is considerably lowered during pregnancy but returns to normal within a short time after delivery (1, 2, 3, 4, 5, 6, 7). This usually is due to the physiological dilution which accompanies the increase in blood volume and, as such, it probably has no pathological significance. In the discussion of the changes in the maternal organism (Chapter VII) it was stated that the hemoglobin and the cell volume were increased 13 and 20 per cent respectively but that these important constituents of the blood failed to keep pace with the 23 per cent increase in total volume. As a result of their less rapid increase, therefore, the concentrations of erythrocytes and hemoglobin are somewhat reduced and an anemia seems to have occurred. Because more hemoglobin and red cells are circulating during gestation, this so-called "physiological anemia of pregnancy" reveals itself only when the blood is examined and does not cause symptoms. In other words, the reduction in these essential elements of the blood is only a relative one and a true anemia does not exist. If, as is thought, the circulation of the blood is increased during pregnancy, the hemoglobin and red cell mass available to a given tissue in a given time is greater than normal, even though the concentration of these constituents is reduced.

Not only do these changes facilitate the normal functioning of the blood but the increase in volume also helps to compensate for the blood which is lost during parturition and aids in the restoration of the normal blood values thereafter. The presence of an excess of fluids in the tissue spaces and in the circulating blood thus enables the parturient woman to withstand blood losses which, otherwise, would prove fatal and the increase in hemoglobin and red cells in the diluted blood leads to the rapid return of normal values when the blood again becomes more concentrated.

In addition to the blood loss which accompanies parturition, the fetal demands for iron, particularly in the last three months, are a drain upon the mother's resources. That this demand is met without harm is shown by the fact that the hemoglobin concentration is greater at term than it was several months previously.

If the diet is adequate and the blood-building mechanism is capable of functioning normally, the pregnant woman should have no difficulty in maintaining her blood in a satisfactory condition. In spite of the frequently lowered values for hemoglobin and the erythrocyte count, therefore, the blood picture in most women returns to normal within a relatively short time after delivery. On the other hand, the great demands of these circulatory changes, together with the fetal drain upon the maternal stores of iron, call for careful management during pregnancy in order that there may be no break-down in the mechanism by which these needs are met and in order that any interference with its functioning that may occur, may be detected and corrected in its incipiency.

For this reason, a survey of the blood should be made early in pregnancy and again at the beginning of the last trimester. If the hemoglobin is below 10 gm. per 100 cc. (about 70 %) or the cell volume falls to 33 vol %, or the erythrocytes drop below 3,500,000, some form of anemia should be suspected and blood studies similar to those ordinarily used in the differentiation of the anemias are indicated. While these arbitrary values do not necessarily indicate the presence of anemia, their use should lead to the discovery of any true anemia which may be present. In such cases, the blood findings most commonly observed are those of the hypochromic microcytic type of anemia and, less frequently they resemble those found in the hyperchromic variety.

<u>Hypochromic microcytic anemia</u> may be present before the onset of pregnancy or it may develop in the course of gestation. The factors which favor its development or aggravation in the pregnant woman are:

1. The demands of pregnancy which underlie the changes previously noted.
2. The demands of the fetus for iron.
3. A possible deficient iron intake.
4. A possible deficient iron assimilation due to a defective gastric secretion.
5. A possible deficiency of protein and vitamins.

In from 50–75 per cent of the patients with hypochromic anemia during pregnancy, the hydrochloric acid of the gastric secretion is reduced or totally absent (8). Study of the balance figures given in Chapter VII and of the food values noted in the discussion of the diet during pregnancy shows that a well-chosen balanced diet contains little more than the required amount of iron. Women in the economic class which cannot afford iron-containing foods in sufficient amounts and those whose pregnancies follow in too rapid succession to enable them to replenish their depleted stores of iron, therefore, are especially liable to this form of anemia and this is particularly true if the hydrochloric content of their gastric secretion is low. In this connection, it is interesting to note that one group of observers gave 0.5 gm. of ferrous sulphate daily to 100 women throughout the last three months of pregnancy and noted that the hemoglobin was above 70 at term in every case while 24 per cent of 100 alternate patients who received no additional iron had hemoglobin findings of 70 or under (9).

Hypochromic anemia is best treated prophylactically. Proper hygiene and a balanced diet should prevent its occurrence during pregnancy. Women who cannot afford the essential iron-containing vegetables and meats should be given some preparation of iron at least during the last three months. Those who already have this type of anemia are best treated before they become pregnant. Recognition of the disease early in gestation permits early regulation of the diet and hygiene together with the early use of iron. While iron is regarded as specific in secondary anemia, it often has little or no effect when hypochromic anemia occurs as a complication of pregnancy. The addition of diluted hydrochloric acid is also indicated in those cases in which a deficient gastric secretion is found. If these measures prove ineffectual or if the condition is discovered too late in pregnancy to permit its adequate treatment before the onset of labor, repeated transfusions should be given.

Hyperchromic macrocytic anemia is very rare as a complication of pregnancy. Occasionally, however, there develops in pregnant women a condition which is quite like pernicious anemia except that nervous manifestations and remissions do not occur. The red cell count is extremely low and the color index high. Blood smears show many poikilocytes, normoblasts and megaloblasts. The bone marrow is hyperplastic and the skin has a lemon-yellow tint not unlike that seen in true pernicious anemia. While this condition is rare in the United States, it occurs in about 3 per cent of all maternity admissions in

India and is responsible for one-third of all deaths occurring in hospital maternity practice in that country (10, 11). The onset is sudden and the course is progressive until the pregnancy is terminated after which recovery rapidly takes place. Weakness, sore mouth, vomiting, diarrhea, rapid pulse and dyspneia are common complaints and edema and albuminuria often are observed. Frequently, the exertion of labor is too much for the weakened circulatory system and, as a result, a large percentage of the mothers die during parturition. The fetal mortality is also high and such children as survive usually are small but their hemoglobin is normal at birth.

Monkeys fed on a diet similar to that eaten by the native patients suffering from typical macrocytic anemia develop megaloblastic hyperplasia of the bone marrow. The condition alike in women and in monkeys is cured by the administration of marmite, the active factor being heat stable, thus suggesting that macrocytic anemia of pregnancy is due to a dietetic inadequacy of some factor closely associated with vitamin B_2 (13, 14, 15) It also is thought that this type of anemia may be due to a deficiency of the intrinsic factor contained in the gastric juice (16).

Prophylaxis in the form of proper hygiene and a balanced diet is also the best treatment for hyperchromic anemia. After the disease has occurred, yeast and liver extract are indicated. In urgent cases, the latter should be given intramuscularly. At times, transfusions also are necessary.

LEUKEMIA. Pregnancy complicated by leukemia is rare (17). Of twenty-six cases collected by Hofstein, ten were acute and sixteen chronic (18). In the acute cases, nine mothers died and only two infants survived. The sixteen chronic myologenous leukemias had twenty-six pregnancies which resulted in the birth of only fifteen living children. Seven of these mothers died. As roentgen-ray therapy may have a deleterious effect on the fetus, early interruption of the pregnancy is indicated.

PURPURA HEMORRHAGICA is also a rare but serious complication and causes the death of the mother and child in the majority of cases Hemorrhage at the time of delivery is greatly to be feared, and preparations for the treatment of intrapartum and postpartum bleeding should be made in anticipation of this complication. Repeated transfusions should be considered (19, 20, 21, 22, 23).

PREGNANCY AFTER SPLENECTOMY. Following the removal of the spleen, women may conceive and carry their pregnancies to term without particular risk. Soon after the middle of gestation, a general adenopathy is observed and some of the glands reach a diameter of 2 cm. These glandular enlargements disappear after the child is born.

CARDIAC DISEASE. The 23 % increase in blood volume, the 50 % increase in cardiac output, the 15–20 % gain in weight and the increased metabolism, cause an increase in the work of the heart during pregnancy (24, 25, 26). Cardiac disease, therefore, may be a source of considerable anxiety whenever it is present in a woman who becomes pregnant (27).

Slightly over 1% of the patients who apply for obstetric care in localities where rheumatic fever, tonsillitis and chorea are prevalent, have seriously damaged hearts and, in almost 95% of these, the difficulty is due to rheumatic heart disease.

Because the age incidence of **cardiovascular syphilis** and **coronary artery disease** does not correspond with the period of greatest fertility, these cardiac complications are very rarely encountered during pregnancy.

Congenital heart disease complicating pregnancy also is rare. When the congenital anomaly does not result in the establishment of a communication between the right and left side of the heart or between the pulmonary artery and aorta, it usually is of little consequence. Cases of defective interventricular septa and patent ductus arteriosis, even though there is no history of previous disability, may develop sudden unexpected and alarming symptoms immediately following delivery. The respirations and pulse are greatly increased in rate without evidence of venous congestion and the patient apparently dies of asphyxia and exhaustion. This outcome seems to follow rapid evacuation of the uterus as is the case in Cesarean section and version and extraction, rather than normal spontaneous delivery (28).

On the other hand, cardiac disease is often suspected when it does not exist. The rotation and displacement of the heart incident to the changes in the diaphragm cause a great increase in functional murmurs which often are mistaken for evidence of serious organic lesions. Unless they occur in diastole, or are accompanied by enlargement of the heart or other evidence of true cardiac disease, too much significance should not be attached to the murmurs ordinarily heard during the latter part of gestation.

Mitral insufficiency is a relatively benign lesion and seldom leads to decompensation in the pregnant woman. For this reason, it usually receives little consideration and rarely gives cause for anxiety (28, 29).

Mitral stenosis, on the other hand, is the most common of the serious lesions. It is observed in 70–90% of the seriously damaged hearts encountered during pregnancy and, unless properly managed, decompensation frequently occurs. Mitral stenosis, accordingly, is responsible for the majority of the maternal deaths that result from cardiac disease.

Although the patient with mitral stenosis is particularly susceptible to fibrillation, pregnant women with this lesion seldom show evidence of **auricular fibrillation.** Absence of this complication is all the more striking because operative interference and the strain of labor should favor its development. Similarly, the association of fibrillation and congestive failure which so commonly occurs in mitral stenosis is relatively rare during pregnancy. In a large series of cases, less than 3% developed fibrillation while almost 20% had congestive failure. Perhaps, as has been suggested, the average pregnant woman is not old enough to have heart muscle that is susceptible to auricular fibrillation (28). Fibrillation, when it does occur, however, is a very serious complication (30).

While **paroxysmal tachycardia** is not regarded seriously in patients with sound hearts, it can be a dangerous complication of mitral stenosis and may accompany or precipitate congestive failure. Fortunately, it also occurs relatively rarely and is encountered in less than 2% of all cases of mitral stenosis complicating pregnancy (28).

Congestive heart failure is the commonest serious complication that may occur and was observed in almost 20% of the cases in the series previously mentioned. While the risk of a break in compensation is somewhat less in young women, it is almost double this figure in those who have passed the age of thirty-five (28). In the cases in which congestive failure occurs, the limit of cardiac reserve usually is reached during the course of pregnancy and the break in compensation is observed before the onset of labor. **Seldom, therefore, does congestive failure develop during or after parturition in a woman who never previously has shown evidence of decompensation** (28).

Congestive heart failure usually comes on rather suddenly after exertion or in the course of some intercurrent disease. While it may develop at any time during pregnancy, the incidence of its occurrence is rather low up to the 6th month after which it rises rapidly to reach a peak in the 8th month. Soon thereafter the tendency toward a break in compensation rapidly diminishes (28) (Fig. 744a). The danger of congestive failure, accordingly, rises and falls to some extent with the rise and fall in the blood volume.

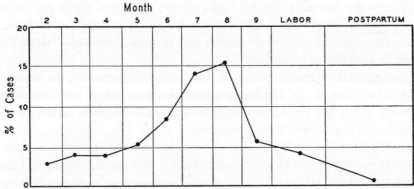

FIG. 744 a. Incidence of cardiac failures in the various months of pregnancy (Carr and Hamilton).

At one time, mitral stenosis was so feared that women with this lesion were warned to remain single. If they married, the prevention of conception was recommended and when they became pregnant, abortion was advised.   This attitude, however, is not justifiable at present since 70 to 90% of all pregnancies complicated by mitral stenosis terminate spontaneously without difficulty, while only 5 to 8% of the mothers die (31, 32, 33, 34).   If the cases are seen from the beginning of gestation and classified according to their response to physical effort, it will be found that those that are well compensated assume very little added risk provided they are kept under close supervision (35).   While mitral stenosis unquestionably is a serious complication, the prognosis depends more upon the cardiac reserve than upon the nature of the lesion.   The great problem, therefore, is to determine the amount of reserve rather than the type of lesion and, from this, to decide upon the proper management with regard to pregnancy.   Many tests for this purpose have been devised but none seems to be as acceptable as the history of the patient's response to the various circumstances which tax this reserve.   Irrespective of the type of lesion, it is most important in all cardiac cases to find out whether the patient has ever had a break in compensation.

If there never has been a break in compensation, pregnancy should add very little risk to that which already is present, provided the patient is a young woman.   After the age of thirty-five, however, pregnancy is to be discouraged, even in this otherwise favorable group.

If there is a clear history of previous congestive failure, an effort should be made to ascertain the circumstance to which the cardiac response was inadequate, in order that some conclusion may be drawn as to the patient's reserve. When cardiac failure occurs in the course of a strenuous game of tennis in a woman who never has had a break in compensation, the reserve may be better than that of the patient who is unable to withstand the efforts of ordinary life. While pregnancy increases the risk in all women who have had a previous break in compensation, the risk is so great in those who are unable to stand the strain of every day activity that they should not become pregnant and, if they do, therapeutic abortion is indicated.

When congestive failure occurs in the course of pregnancy, the same reasoning should be followed.   If the break occurs as a result of an inability to respond to ordinary effort, the gestation should be terminated as soon as the patient has recovered from the break in compensation.

For the purpose of facilitating the study of patients with organic heart disease, the following classification according to their cardiac functional capacity has been suggested (33):

CLASS I.—*Those in whom fatigue, palpitation or dyspnea are not caused by ordinary activity.*

CLASS II A.—*Those in whom fatigue, palpitation or dyspnea are caused by ordinary activity.*   (Such patients have shortness of breath after climbing stairs or after walking against a wind or up grades or after such things as housecleaning or lifting heavy articles. These patients would by some be said to be "fairly well compensated.")

CLASS II B.—*Those in whom fatigue, palpitation or dyspnea are caused by less than ordinary activity.* (Such activities would be climbing two flights of stairs or walking at an ordinary rate for half a mile. These patients might be called "somewhat decompensated.")

CLASS III.—*Those in whom fatigue, palpitation or dyspnea are caused by the least physical activity.* (Such patients are unable to walk a city block or to climb one flight of stairs or to do any housework. They might be said to be "definitely decompensated." Even while at rest, such patients may show symptoms or signs of cardiac insufficiency.)

While it is safest to regard all patients who have a history of previous congestive failure as unfitted for pregnancy and to do a therapeutic abortion if they do become pregnant (28), it has been found that the treatment need not be so radical if the patient is given the advantage of competent supervision by a cardiologist and an obstetrician. In such circumstances, **the cases in class I** seldom have difficulty. **Those in Class II A**, require greater vigilance but most of them do fairly well. **Class II B patients,** on the other hand, need more frequent and more prolonged bed rest and offer a fair chance of having difficulty. They therefore may require operative intervention. Even under the care of the expert cardiologist and obstetrician, **those in class III** may not be able to withstand the extra load of pregnancy. Some of them, accordingly, must be aborted, or if they are near term, delivery by Cesarean section, under ether or preferably local anesthesia, often is required (36).

The management of pregnancy in a woman who has a mitral stenosis or any other form of serious heart disease calls for careful supervision of her activities to avoid a break in compensation and constant watchfulness to detect the earliest evidence of impending decompensation. **Regardless of how well a patient has done in the past, cardiac cases in pregnancy are treacherous.** Even the most favorable sometimes end tragically. For this reason, all of them deserve respect and consideration both from the patient and from her physician. Each case should be treated individually without too much regard being paid to her classification status, since the latter may change as the pregnancy advances. In addition, the patient should, if possible, be under the observation of a cardiologist and an obstetrician.

Since congestive failure usually follows overexertion or intercurrent infection, these harmful influences must be guarded against at all times. **The cardiac patient therefore should avoid lifting, climbing, running and any activity that may lead to fatigue.** Lifting heavy articles or one of her children may overtax her reserve as may the exertion of running after a child, or for a street car or bus. Stair-climbing also may prove disastrous. For this reason, it is advisable to have the patient live on the ground floor or in an elevator apartment. If this is impossible, and it is necessary for her to go up and down stairs, she should take one step at a time as a baby does and should rest for a few seconds several times on her way up. Hill climbing, likewise, is to be forbidden. While walking on the level, and the lighter household duties are not contraindicated, **nothing should be done in a hurry.** Even though she may not be fatigued, the patient should sit or lie down for brief rest periods in the course of whatever activity she undertakes. Scrubbing, washing and ironing, moving furniture and similar exertions, must be avoided at all times. Even the limited liberties allowed early in pregnancy are to be further curtailed in the last trimester, at which time the rest periods should be increased. Rest is so important that specific directions, in this respect, are essential. **At least 8 or 10 hours of sleep each night are necessary and the patient should lie down for half an hour after each meal as well as at such other times as may be necessary to prevent fatigue.** Fatigue must be avoided. Should it occur, absolute rest in bed is imperative. Because emotional disturbances may lead to a break in compensation, the relatives should be warned of this possibility in order that they may protect her from anything which may lead to an emotional outburst. Sexual intercourse also must be avoided.

The part played by intercurrent infection in the production of congestive failure is so important that the cardiac patient must guard against such infections in every possible manner. When epidemics of upper respiratory infection are prevalent, she should remain at home and be isolated from such members of the family as are suffering from the disease. **Should she develop a cold, sore throat, rhinitis or tonsillitis, she should remain in bed until her recovery is complete.**

Decompensation. Clinical observation of the respirations, pulse, heart beat, color and general appearance of the patient, may suggest the possibility of beginning congestive failure and the finding of persistent râles over the lung bases should confirm this suspicion. In order that such early evidence may not be overlooked, all patients with seriously damaged hearts should be seen several times monthly in the early months and weekly in the last trimester. In addition, they should be cautioned to report to their physician if they experience attacks of coughing, breathlessness, smothering, cyanosis or hemoptysis. When the condition is recognized early, rest in bed, morphine and digitalis are indicated. Should edema of the lungs occur, 500 cc. of blood are withdrawn by phlebotomy. Complete and rapid digitalization is secured by giving 30 min. of a standardized parenteral digitalis preparation intramuscularly or intravenously every four hours until the patient has received 15 min. for every 10 lbs. of body weight. Following digitalization, a sustaining dose of 20 min. daily is required to compensate for the amount excreted. Those who become decompensated during pregnancy, not infrequently again show evidence of a break in compensation before, during or immediately after labor (37). When such patients have fully recovered from a break in compensation, the uterus should be emptied, unless they are able to remain in the hospital or under hospital conditions throughout the remainder of their pregnancies. Before the third month, the uterus is emptied by means of dilatation and curettage or by the use of ovum forceps. After the third month, abdominal hysterotomy and sterilization under local anesthesia is the method of choice. If decompensation occurs near the end of pregnancy, an abdominal Cesarean section followed by sterilization under novocaine infiltration anesthesia, should be done as soon as the patient recovers sufficiently to stand the operation. **It is a great mistake to operate while the heart is decompensated.** Operative interference in every case, therefore, should be postponed until the patient has recovered from the break in compensation or until the maximum improvement is obtained. Following delivery, the patient should be morphinized for several days after which her convalescence is to be managed in the usual way.

If no untoward signs have appeared during pregnancy, spontaneous labor may be permitted. Morphine and scopolamine are valuable in the stage of dilatation, and mediolateral episiotomy under local anesthesia is recommended to shorten the second stage. Should signs of decompensation arise after the cervix is fully dilated and the head has passed the level of the ischial spines, extraction with forceps is indicated.

During and immediately following the third stage, a break in compensation frequently is observed. When this unfortunate event occurs after the placenta is delivered, a phlebotomy is recommended unless contraindicated by the amount of blood lost during labor (28, 29, 30, 31, 32, 33, 34, 35, 36, 37).

ALTERATIONS IN BLOOD PRESSURE. A moderate hypotension is not uncommon during the greater part of most pregnancies, and has no clinical significance. Hypertension, on the other hand, is abnormal and calls for a prompt and careful search for its cause. Whenever the pressure reaches 140, an impending eclampsia should be suspected until it can be eliminated by the routine suggested in the preceding chapter on Toxemia.

VARICOSE VEINS. The veins of the lower extremities and vulva not infrequently are the site of varicosities which, at times, are quite troublesome. Hemorrhoids also are common during and after pregnancy. The cause of these venous enlargements is thought to be due to several factors: pelvic engorgement, relaxation of the vein walls, increased blood volume and interference with the return circulation which may result from pressure of the pregnant uterus. When the varicosities are first observed, all constricting bands about the thighs should be removed and a properly fitted maternity corset should be worn according to the instructions given under prenatal care (page 98). At night the foot of the bed is elevated and several times during each day relief is afforded by the supine posture with the legs held at right angles to the trunk. If these measures fail, an elastic bandage or stocking should be put on before the patient gets out of bed and worn throughout the day. **Varicosities of the vulva** seldom cause trouble during pregnancy but may give rise to considerable hemorrhage should they rupture in the course of labor.   In the latter circumstances, the bleeding can usually be controlled by mass ligation.   **Varicose veins of the vulva never should be removed during pregnancy.**

HEMORRHOIDS are treated by similar postural measures and replacement of the dilated veins.   When they become greatly swollen, cold applications often give relief and their replacement is facilitated by the use of the knee-chest position.   After reposition, a vaselin gauze plug is partially introduced into the rectum and held in place by the patient.   Mineral oil by mouth is indicated to prevent constipation and keep the stool soft.

EDEMA is common in the latter months of pregnancy.   It usually is demonstrable only in the lower extremities and, as a rule, the swelling is greater on one side.   Fluid retention should be suspected whenever the gain in weight exceeds one pound per week in the latter months.   Swelling of the fingers, as shown by an increasing tightness of the rings, and puffiness of the face often are the result of a serious toxemia.   Whenever edema is demonstrable, the possibility of toxemia, cardiac failure and nephritis calls for careful investigation to rule out these complications.

PHLEBITIS.   Thrombosis of the pelvic veins and the larger venous trunks of the thigh is rare during pregnancy but not infrequently is encountered in the puerperium as a complication of puerperal infection.   When it does occur, the part involved is kept at rest and treated by the application of heat and cold. Manipulations are to be avoided because of the danger of embolism.   Occasionally, hemorrhoids become thrombosed and, on account of the pain, require incision.   Similarly, thrombi may form in varicose veins of the legs, but these usually cause little trouble and require no treatment.

REFERENCES

1. LYON, E. C.: Anemia in Late Pregnancy.   J. A. M. A., 1929, 92, 11.
2. GALLOWAY, C. E.: Anemia in Pregnancy.   Am. J. Obs. & Gyn., 1929, 17, 84.
3. BLAND, P. B., GOLDSTEIN, L. AND FIRST, A.: Secondary Anemia in Pregnancy and in
    Puerperium; a study of 300 patients.   Am. J. Med. Sc., 1930, 179, 48.
    "Physiological" Anemia of Pregnancy; study of 1000 patients.   Surg., Gyn. and Obs..
    1930, 50, 429.
4. ROWLAND, V. C.: Anemia of Pregnancy.   J. A. M. A., 1933, 100, 537.
5. DIECKMANN, W. J. AND WEGNER, C. R.: Studies of the Blood in Normal Pregnancy.   II.
    Hemoglobin, Hematocrit, and Erythrocyte Determinations and Total Amount of
    Variations of Each.   Arch. Int. Med., 1934, 53, 188.
6. ADAIR, F. L., DIECKMANN, W. J. AND GRANT, K.: Anemia in Pregnancy.   Am. J. Obs. &
    Gyn., 1936, 32, 560.
7. WATSON, H. J.: The Blood Pictures of Pregnancy.   Am. J. Obs. & Gyn., 1938, 35, 106.
8. STRAUSS, M. B. AND CASTLE, W. B.: Studies of Anemia in Pregnancy.
    I. Gastric Secretion in Pregnancy and the Puerperium.   Am. J. Med. Sc., 1932, 184, 655.
    II. The Relationship of Dietary Deficiency and Gastric Secretion to Blood Formation
    during Pregnancy.   Am. J. Med. Sc., 1932, 184, 663.

9. Corrigan, J. C. and Strauss, M. B.: Prevention of Hypochromic Anemia in Pregnancy. J. A. M. A., 1936, 106, 1088.
10. McSwiney, S. A.: The Anemia of Pregnancy. A Study of 43 Cases. Indian Med. Gaz., 1927, 62, 487.
11. Balfour, M. I.: The Anemia of Pregnancy. Indian Med. Gaz., 1927, 62, 491.
12. Mudaliar, A. L. and Rao, K. N.: Interim Report on "Pernicious Anemia of Pregnancy". Indian J. Med. Research, 1932, 20, 435.
13. Wills, L. and Bilimora, H. S.: Studies in Pernicious Anemia of Pregnancy. Indian J. Med. Research, 1932, 33, 20, 291.
14. Wills, L.: The Nature of the Hemopoietic Factor in Marmite. Lancet, 1933, 224, 1283.
15. Helsom, K. O. and Sample, A. B.: Macrocytic Anemia in Pregnant Women with Vitamin B Deficiency. J. Clin. Invest., 1937, 16, 463.
16. Strauss, M. B. and Castle, W. B.: Studies of Anemia in Pregnancy. III. The Etiologic Relationship of Gastric Secretory Defects and Dietary Deficiency to the Hypochromic and Macrocytic (pernicious) Anemia of Pregnancy and the Treatment of These Conditions. Am. J. Med. Sc., 1933, 185, 539.
17. Kosmak, G. W.: Splenic Leucemia Associated with Pregnancy. Am. J. Obs. and Gyn., 1921, 1, 485.
18. Hofstein, J.: La Leucémie comme indication d'interruption de la grossesse. Gynec. et obst., 1932, 25, 45.
19. Vignes, H. and Stiassnie: Purpura récidivant au cours de trois gestations successives Progres. Med., 1921, 36, 167.
20. Mosher, G. C.: The Complication of Purpura with Gestation. Surg., Gyn. and Obs., 1923, 36, 502.
21. Morgan, G.: Course of Pregnancy, Labour and Puerperium in Chronic Purpura Hemorrhagica. J. Obs. & Gyn. Brit. Emp., 1923, 30, 438.
22. Rushmore, S.: Purpura Complicating Pregnancy. Am. J. Obs. & Gyn., 1925, 10, 553.
23. Liebling, P.: Purpura Hemorrhagica Complicating Pregnancy. Am. J. Obs. & Gyn., 1926, 11, 847.
24. Neubauer, W.: Blutmengenbestimmung vor, während und nach der Geburt. Deutsch. Med. Wchnschr., 1923, 49, 520.
25. Gammeltoft, S. A.: The Heart in Pregnancy. Surg. Gyn. & Obs., 1928, 46, 382.
26. Stander, H. J., Duncan, E. E. and Sisson, W. E.: Heart Output During Pregnancy, Am. J. Obs. & Gyn., 1926, 11, 44.
27. Fellner, O.: Herz und Schwangerschaft. Monatschr. f. Geburtsh u. Gynaek., 1901, 14, 370 and 497.
28. Carr, F. B. and Hamilton, B. E.: Five Hundred Women with Serious Heart Diseases Followed Through Pregnancy and Delivery. Am. J. Obs. & Gyn.,
29. Halban, J.: Herzkrankheiten und Schwangerschaft. Wien klin. Wchnschr., 1928, 41, 628.
30. Robinson, A. L.: The Effect of Parturition on the Heart. Lancet, 1927, 1, 170.
31. Corwin, J., Herrick, W. W., Valentine, M. and Wilson, J. M.: Pregnancy and Heart Disease. Am. J. Obs. & Gyn., 1927, 13, 617.
32. Hamilton, B. E. and Kellogg, F. S.: Cardiac Disease in Pregnancy. J. A. M. A., 1928, 91, 1942.
33. Pardee, H. E. B.: Experiences in the Management of Pregnancy Complicated by Heart Disease. Am. J. Obs. & Gyn., 1929, 17, 255.
34. Reid, W. D.: The Heart in Pregnancy. J. A. M. A., 1930, 95, 1468.
35. MacKenzie: Heart Disease and Pregnancy, 1921.
36. Pardee, H. E. B.: The Cardiac Functional Capacity As An Aid To Prognosis During Pregnancy. Am. J. O. & G., 1937, 34, 557.
37. Daly, P. A.: The Heart in Pregnancy. J. A. M. A., 1924, 82, 1439.

DISEASES OF THE DIGESTIVE SYSTEM

PTYALISM.   At times, the secretion of the salivary glands becomes excessive and, in rare instances, may reach 1000 cc. daily.   It often occurs in neurotic women and, as a result, is extremely difficult to relieve.   Careful attention to the hygiene of the mouth, alteration of the diet and atropine are helpful in some cases.

DENTAL CARIES.   The teeth should be examined by a dentist early in every gestation and again four months later, in order that necessary dental work may not be neglected.   Ample exposure to the sun's rays and a diet rich in calcium are likewise indicated.   In the latter connection, three glasses of milk should be taken daily.   If these essentials cannot be carried out, calcium gluconate and viosterol may be substituted.   In addition to the usual cleansing of the teeth after meals, an alkaline mouth wash should be used in the morning and at night.

GINGIVOSTOMATITIS.   Inflamed, tender gums that bleed when touched occasionally are present during pregnancy and are treated by the use of an astringent mouth wash and massage of the gums with sodium perborate.

GASTRO-INTESTINAL DISTRESS.   The changes in the gastric secretions so commonly observed during pregnancy may be responsible for the gastro-intestinal distress which frequently is troublesome during gestation.   Careful study of each case will reveal the nature of the disturbance and suggest the appropriate treatment.   Very often a hypochlorhydria is responsible for the difficulty.

CONSTIPATION.   During pregnancy, when all of the emunctories should functionate efficiently to eliminate the waste products of both the fetus and its mother, the intestinal tract frequently is sluggish.   As a result, the patient not only suffers from the customary immediate results of intestinal stasis, but at any time may have her life or that of her child placed in jeopardy by the remote consequences of accumulating toxins.   Since, in most cases, constipation is merely an accentuation of the faulty function that antedates conception, each patient should receive careful instruction as to the care of the bowels.

The diet should contain an abundance of fruits and vegetables.   Those which leave considerable residue are especially recommended unless flatulence is an accompanying symptom.

Lack of fluids leads to a diminished fluidity of the intestinal contents and, accordingly, is an important factor in the etiology of constipation.   The tendency of most women to drink an insufficient amount of liquids, therefore, should be combated by insisting that at least eight glasses of fluid be taken daily and a definite schedule should be arranged for this purpose.   Water before breakfast and again at night has the desired effect and does not inconvenience the patient.   At least one or two glasses, therefore, should be taken soon after arising and just before retiring.

It is well also for the patient to acquire the habit of regularity. Since the most natural time for defecation is soon after a meal, she should go regularly to stool a short time after breakfast even though the inclination to move her bowels, at first, is not present. Faulty construction of most toilet seats may be overcome by having the patient place her feet on a box or bench that stands about eight inches above the floor.

If these measures are not entirely effective, mineral oil, milk of magnesia, or agar-agar may be taken as often as is necessary to secure proper daily evacuations. In some cases, because of long continued neglect of these important hygienic measures, more drastic drugs may be required. Phenolphthalein, senna, or cascara are then used temporarily until the patient becomes accustomed to this routine.

APPENDICITIS is not uncommon in pregnancy. After the third month, the growing uterus gradually displaces the appendix upward until it reaches the level of the iliac crests (1) (Fig. 745). The customary right-sided pain likewise is somewhat higher than in nonpregnant cases and the point of tenderness also follows the upward displacement of the appendix. This upward displacement of the appendix, together with the intermittent uterine contractions, greatly interferes with nature's walling-off process and frequently leads to general peritonitis following the rupture of a suppurating appendix. The mortality, after this accident, accordingly, is very high.

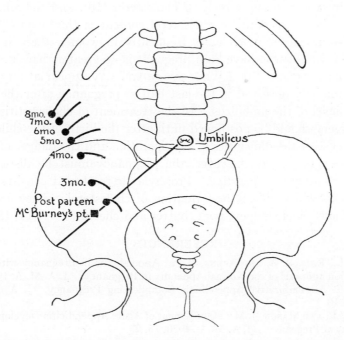

FIG. 745. Diagram showing the level of the appendix at the various months of pregnancy (Baer)

In acute appendicitis, removal of the appendix before rupture is imperative and an exploratory laparotomy is indicated whenever the diagnosis is in doubt. Following operation, the patient should be thoroughly morphinized for several days to prevent abortion or premature labor.

After the appendix has ruptured, the problem is much more difficult and a successful outcome is dependent upon drainage and the prevention of the interruption of pregnancy. Handling of the uterus, accordingly, is to be avoided as much as possible during the operation and the postoperative routine should include the administration of morphine in $\frac{1}{4}$ gr. doses every four to six hours, in order that premature labor may be avoided (1, 2, 3, 4, 5).

DISEASES OF THE LIVER. The changes which take place in the liver as a result of the toxemia of pregnancy were described in the chapter on Toxemia (page 545).

JAUNDICE may occur as a symptom of pernicious vomiting, acute yellow atrophy or the late toxemia of pregnancy. In these circumstances, its appearance is an unfavorable sign and should not be mistaken for catarrhal jaundice, a condition which is seldom seen in pregnancy. In the early days of the puerperium, chloroform poisoning should be suspected whenever icterus appears within the first week after the use of chloroform during labor.

CHOLELITHIASIS formerly was thought to occur more frequently in women who have borne children (6, 7). This relationship with pregnancy was attributed to the hypercholesterolemia (8, 9) which is present at that time, since gallstones usually are made up largely of cholesterin (10), and the amount of the latter in the bile varies with the cholesterol content of the blood (11, 12). Although gallstones occur much more frequently in women than in men, their occurrence in women who have been pregnant is no greater than in women who have not been pregnant (7a). While symptoms may appear at any time, they are more commonly observed in the last half of pregnancy after the uterus has reached the level of the umbilicus. In the treatment of cholecystitis and cholelithiasis, surgery should be postponed until after the birth of the child whenever possible because of the difficulties of the operation and the danger of premature delivery. In severe cases, however, the pregnancy must be disregarded and surgical intervention is imperative. Prophylactic treatment consists in restricting those foods which aid in the formation of cholesterol. They are: fats, egg yolk, fried foods, liver, kidney, pork, butter and cheese (4, 13, 14, 15).

REFERENCES

1. BAER, J. L., REIS, R. A. AND ARENS, R. A.: Appendicitis in Pregnancy with Changes in Position and Axis of the Normal Appendix in Pregnancy. J. A. M. A. 1932, 98, 1359.
2. BABLER, E. A.: Perforative Appendicitis Complicating Pregnancy. J. A. M. A., 1908, 51, 1310.
3. COCKE, N. P. AND MASON, J. M.: Management of Acute Appendicitis Developing in Latter Weeks of Pregnancy. J. A. M. A., 1920, 75, 95.

4. MUSSEY, R. D. AND CRANE, J. F.: Operations of Necessity during Pregnancy. Arch. Surg., 1927, 15, 729.

5. WILSON, R. A.: Acute Appendicitis Complicating Pregnancy, Labor and the Puerperium. Surg. Gyn. & Obs., 1927, 45, 620.

6. SCHROEDER, H.: Beitrage zur Aetiologie und Statistik der Cholelithiasis. Strassburg, 1892.

7. MENTZER, S. H.: A Clinical and Pathologic Study of Cholecystitis and Cholelithiasis. Surg. Gyn. & Obs., 1926, 42, 782.

7a. ROBERTSON, H. E. AND DOCHAT, G. R.: Pregnancy and Gallstones. S. G. & O., 1944, 78, abstracts, 193.

8. CHAUFFARD, A., LAROCHE, G. AND GRIGAUT, A.: Evolution de la cholestérinémie au cours de l'état gravidique et puerpéral. Obstetrique, Paris, 1911, n.s., 4, 481.

9. SELMONS, J. M. AND CURTIS, C. S.: Cholesterol in the Blood of Mother and Fetus: A Preliminary Note. Am. J. Obs., 1917, 75, 569.

10. MENTZER, S. H.: The Pathogenesis of Biliary Calculi. Arch. Surg., 1927, 14, 14.

11. FASIANI, G. M.: Expériences préliminaires sur les rapports entre le contenu de cholestérine dans le sang et dans le bile. Arch. ital. de biol., 1915, 63, 136.

12. D'AMATO, L.: Uebt das in der Nahrung enthaltene Cholesterin einen Einfluss auf die Cholesterinausscheidung in der Galle aus? Biochem. Ztschr., 1915, 69, 217.

13. PETERSON, R.: Gallstones during Pregnancy and the Puerperium. Surg. Gyn. & Obs., 1910, 11, 1.

14. FERGUSON, L. K. AND PRIESTLEY, J. T.: The Relation of Gall Bladder Disease to Pregnancy with Special Relation to the Factor of Hypercholesterolemia. Am. J. Obs. & Gyn., 1928, 16, 82.

15. FRIGYESI, J.: Schwangerschaft und Gallensteinkrankheit (Cholelithiasis und Gestationsperioden); der Zusammenhang swischen Gestation und Gallensteinkrankheit. Med. Klin., 1927, 23, 1844, 1886, 1926.

DISEASES OF THE URINARY SYSTEM

NEPHRITIS may develop at any time during pregnancy, or pregnancy may occur in a woman who already has nephritis. The symptoms and signs not infrequently simulate those of toxemia. Often, they are mild at first but, as the pregnancy advances, they become greatly aggravated and seriously affect the mother and child. The blood pressure is elevated from the beginning and, as gestation progresses, gradually increases to 200 mm. or over. Although appropriate treatment frequently causes a temporary fall, it seldom can be brought within normal limits. The urine contains casts and albumin in amounts varying from a trace to 1–2 gms. Recurring headaches also are common and edema not infrequently is observed. At times, the vision is affected and evidences of albuminuric retinitis are revealed by the ophthalmoscope. Uremic convulsions and coma rarely occur. Occasionally, all symptoms are absent and the condition is not recognized unless blood pressure determinations and urinalyses are made.

Premature labor and death of the fetus in the last half of pregnancy are common, and often are preceded by marked infarction of the placenta. Following delivery, some improvement in the blood pressure and albuminuria may be noted. Frequently, however, these signs persist. With each subsequent pregnancy, the nephritis becomes aggravated and severe symptoms as well as premature labor and death of the fetus occur at an earlier date.

DIAGNOSIS. If the patient has been under observation from the beginning of her pregnancy, and symptoms or signs appear in the early months, nephritis is easily differentiated from impending eclampsia by the fact that the latter condition is peculiar to the last half of pregnancy. Should the first evidence of nephritis appear in the latter months, the differential diagnosis is much more difficult. Prompt improvement or arrest in the progress of the symptoms following appropriate treatment helps to rule out impending eclampsia, and the more delicate functional tests differentiate a true nephritis from pregnancy toxemia. The latter has no effect on the urea clearance and creatinin tests, which are considerably altered in nephritis. The kidneys, in well advanced cases, likewise show an inability to concentrate and the secretion of phenolsulphonphthalein is delayed. Blood chemistry reveals an increase in urea nitrogen and uric acid.

PROGNOSIS. The immediate danger to the mother is not very great. A fairly large percentage of pregnancies, however, terminate prematurely or the fetus dies. Even when the gestation continues to term, the child is slightly under weight and often does not do well on its mother's milk. It is thought that pregnancy has a deleterious effect on nephritis and, accordingly, somewhat reduces the life expectancy of the mother.

TREATMENT. Women with severe nephritis should receive instructions in the use of contraceptives. If pregnancy occurs, therapeutic abortion and sterilization are indicated. Less severe cases, that respond well to therapeutic and dietetic measures, as well as those that develop in the last half of pregnancy, are allowed to continue but are kept under close observation. The diet is modified to suit each individual's needs as shown by the blood pressure and urine findings. Rest in bed for prolonged periods may aid in the prevention of a premature delivery. Occasionally, women who have lost several successive children, and who are willing to assume the additional risk, may be subjected to cesarean section under local anesthesia several weeks before term, if the child is living at that time.

PYELITIS complicates pregnancy about once in every one hundred cases (1, 2). It is due to a hematogenous, lymphatic or ascending infection of the upper urinary tract by colon bacilli and usually follows urinary and intestinal stasis.

During pregnancy, considerable dilatation of that portion of the ureter which lies above the pelvic brim is often demonstrable and is particularly frequent on the right side (3, 4, 5, 6). It is thought that pressure of the growing uterus, or the kinking, twisting and congestion caused by the pregnancy changes that take place in the parametrium, bladder, ureter and cervix interfere with the urinary flow. The resulting urinary stasis, accordingly, favors the growth of the colon bacilli which are latent in the urinary passages or gain entrance to the latter by hematogenous or lymphatic invasion from a sluggish intestinal tract (7, 8, 9, 10, 11).

The onset frequently is accompanied by a chill and temperature elevation of from 103°–105°. Severe pain is felt in the lumbar region and tenderness may be elicited over the kidney. Nausea and vomiting are common and the patient may complain of pain on one side of the lower abdomen. As the symptoms are more commonly observed on the right side, the attack may simulate, in some respects, acute appendicitis. The white blood cells are increased to around 15,000 and microscopic examination of a catheterized specimen of urine reveals many clumps of pus cells. While the symptoms often are referable to only one side, catheterization of the ureters in those cases which do not improve under ordinary medical treatment may show the condition to be bilateral. Nitrogen retention as shown by blood chemistry studies indicates involvement of the kidney parenchyma. In such cases the prognosis is poor unless the course can be altered by treatment.

Pyelitis usually responds well to treatment without any ill effect on the mother or the child. There is, however, a possibility of more or less permanent injury, and urological examinations made several months after delivery occasionally disclose evidence of a hydro-ureter, hydronephrosis and stricture, even though the patient is symptomatically cured (12, 13, 14). Rarely, the condition progresses in spite of all therapeutic measures and spontaneous premature labor follows, or interruption of the pregnancy is required.

TREATMENT. The patient is kept in bed and instructed to lie on the side which is free from symptoms. In addition, the foot of the bed is elevated at least twelve inches. This posture often gives considerable relief within a few hours. Fluids are forced and the urine is rendered alkaline by the administration of sodium bicarbonate and potassium citrate. After the urine has been alkaline for several days, hexamethylenamine gr. 10 and acid sodium phosphate gr. 20 are given every four hours for six doses, in place of the alkalinizing drugs. Following this, the use of the sodium bicarbonate and potassium citrate is resumed. Ammonium mandelate and the ketogenic diet which have been used successfully in the treatment of pyelitis are not ordinarily used during pregnancy because of the fear that either of these may further lower the alkaline reserve. Sulphanilimide, on the other hand, has been successfully employed in the treatment of pyelitis complicating pregnancy. Because of its effect on the liver and the blood, however, it should be used only after other methods have failed and it should be discontinued as soon as any untoward effects are observed. Among these are jaundice, diarrhea, mental aberrations, rapid reduction in hemoglobin and agranulocytosis. Should the medical treatment, as above outlined, prove ineffectual, catheterization of the ureter, followed by lavage with weak silver nitrate solution, is indicated. This may be repeated in three to four days or the catheter may be left in place for twenty-four or forty-eight hours to facilitate drainage. In very rare instances in which the condition progresses after all of the foregoing measures have been tried, interruption of pregnancy is indicated (5, 8, 12, 15, 16, 17).

575...

RENAL TUBERCULOSIS is seldom seen in pregnancy, but when a woman suffering from it becomes pregnant, the disease is aggravated (18). If only one kidney is involved, immediate nephrectomy is advised, as pregnancy does not add to the risk of operation and the danger of abortion is not very great (1). When both kidneys are involved, the interruption of pregnancy may be indicated. Following nephrectomy for renal tuberculosis, three years should elapse before pregnancy is permitted (18, 19).

HEMATURIA during pregnancy may be due to renal damage resulting from toxemia, new growths or tuberculosis, or may be a symptom of calculi. Whenever blood is found in the urine a careful urological examination is indicated.

NEPHROLITHIASIS. During pregnancy, urinary calculi apparently give little trouble; otherwise this complication would be more frequently discovered. Possibly, the increasing use of roentgen rays and ureteral catheterization in pyelitis of pregnancy may reveal a greater incidence of calculi.

If the condition is latent or the symptoms are mild, palliative treatment is recommended and operation is deferred until after pregnancy. Hexamethylenamine and acid sodium phosphate are given and the patient is encouraged to take large quantities of fluids. Severe symptoms, on the other hand, may require immediate operation and pyelotomy, nephrotomy, or nephrectomy may be necessary. The risk of these surgical measures is no greater than that which ordinarily accompanies these procedures, but after the sixth month, the danger of interrupting the gestation must be considered (20).

PREGNANCY AFTER NEPHRECTOMY. Many cases of pregnancy after nephrectomy have been reported and in most of them no great difficulty was encountered, aside from the occurrence of a slight albuminuria in the latter months. Pregnancy and labor, accordingly, should be allowed to take their natural courses, but under strict supervision. If renal insufficiency or infection develops, or symptoms of toxemia appear, the uterus should be emptied (19, 21, 22).

REFERENCES

1. STEVENS, W. F.: Urology in Women. J. A. M. A., 1923, 81, 1917.
2. CRABTREE, E. G. AND PRATHER, G. C.: Clinical Aspects of Pyelonephritis in Pregnancy. New Eng. J. Med., 1930, 202, 356.
3. HODGES, F. M.: Pyelitis of Pregnancy. Am. J. Roentgenol., 1922, 9, 352.
4. DUNCAN, J. W. AND SENG, M. I.: Factors Predisposing to Pyelitis in Pregnancy. Am. J. O. & G., 1928, 16, 557.
5. KRETSCHMER, H. L., HEANEY, N. S. AND OCKULY, E. A.: Dilatation of the Kidney Pelvis and Ureter During Pregnancy and the Puerperium. J. A. M. A., 1933, 101, 2025.
6. CARSON, W. J.: Dilatation of the Ureter in the Female; Autopsy Findings. J. Urol., 1927, 18, 61.
7. OPITZ, E.: Die Pyelonephritis gravidarum et puerperarum. Ztschr. f. Geburtsh. u. Gyn., 1905, 55, 209.
8. DANFORTH, W. C.: Pyelitis of Pregnancy with Especial Reference to its Etiology. Surg. Gyn. & Obs., 1916, 22, 723.

9. FALLS, F. H.: A Contribution to the Study of Pyelitis in Pregnancy. J. A. M. A., 1923, 81, 1590.
10. LUCHS, L.: Uber den Infectionsweg der Schwangerschaftspyelitis. Arch. f Gyn., 1926, 27, 149.
11. INGRAHAM, C. B.: Pyelitis in Obstetrical and Gynecological Patient. Colorado Med., 1929, 26, 15.
12. CORBUS, B. C. AND DANFORTH, W. C.: Pyelitis in Pregnancy. J. Urol., 1927, 18, 543.
13. CRABTREE, E. G.: Stricture Formation in the Ureter Following Pyelonephritis of Pregnancy. J. Urol., 1927, 18, 575.
14. DODDS, G. H.: The Immediate and Remote Prognosis of Pyelitis of Pregnancy and the Puerperium. J. Obs. & Gyn., Brit. Emp., 1932, 39, 46.
15. SEXTON, W. G.: Pyelitis in Pregnancy. J. Urol., 1922, 7, 481.
16. PUGH, W. S.: Pyelitis of Pregnancy. Its Treatment with the Indwelling Catheter. J. Urol., 1927, 18, 553.
17. McCLELLAND, J. C.: Pyelitis of Pregnancy. Canad. M. A. J., 1925, 15, 494.
18. BALDWIN, H. A.: Surgery of the Kidneys; based on case records of ten years. Ohio M. J., 1912, 8, 563.
19. MATTHEWS, H. B.: Pregnancy after Nephrectomy. J. A. M. A., 1921, 77, 1634.
20. HEINECK, A. P.: Nephrolithiasis and Pregnancy. Am. J. O. & G., 1923, 6, 191.
21. POUSSON, A.: The Future of the Nephrectomized. Am. J. Urol., 1913, 9, 113.
22. SCHMIDT, L. E.: Nephrectomy During Pregnancy. Surg. Gyn. & Obs., 1915, 21, 679.

DISEASES OF THE DUCTLESS GLANDS

THYROID ENLARGEMENT is demonstrable in the majority of pregnancies and disappears soon after delivery (1, 2, 3, 4). Similarly, the basal metabolic rate is increased and readings of +20 are not uncommon (4, 5, 6, 7).

COLLOID GOITER. In those regions in which goiter is endemic, this complication is very often seen during pregnancy. The enlargement is diffuse and seldom causes pressure effects. If accompanied by marked hypothyroidism, spontaneous interruption of pregnancy may occur. The children often have congenital goiter or are cretins, and the prophylactic use of iodine in the form of syrup of hydriodic acid min. 10 twice weekly is recommended for all pregnant women living in goiter communities, not only to relieve the maternal symptoms, but to prevent the occurrence of goiter in the offspring (6, 8, 9).

ADENOMATOUS GOITER without hyperthyroidism occasionally is observed. While enlargement during gestation is not so frequent in this type of tumor, its irregular nodules may make pressure on the trachea and cause dyspnea during pregnancy and labor (10, 11).

HYPERTHYROIDISM. Fortunately, women with exophthalmic goiter and toxic adenomas have a diminished fertility (12). When such patients do become pregnant, the condition usually is aggravated and abortion is not uncommon (11, 13, 14). The severe vomiting that accompanies thyrotoxicosis may be mistaken for hyperemesis gravidarum. Iodine therapy and surgical treatment of the thyroid by those properly qualified to do thyroid surgery has greatly lessened the risk of this complication and therapeutic abortion is limited to those cases which are not within the reach of a competent thyroid surgeon (11, 14). The severe vomiting, which, at times, is confused with hyperemesis gravidarum, usually responds to iodine therapy (5).

PREGNANCY FOLLOWING PARTIAL THYROIDECTOMY occasionally is complicated and, accordingly, requires constant supervision because of the possibility of abortion, toxemia and the recurrence of the symptoms of thyrotoxicosis. Anomalies of the fetus likewise are occasionally observed. For these reasons, pregnancy should be avoided for at least two years after operation and then is permissible only in those cases in which a complete cure has been effected (15).

HYPOTHYROIDISM, at times, is observed in pregnancy. Its symptoms of obesity, mental dullness, constipation, somnolence and low basal metabolic rate call for proper thyroid medication. Some cases of habitual abortion have been attributed to this condition and have been cured by the administration of thyroid extract (16).

TETANY. Animals which are unaffected by partial removal of the parathyroid bodies show tetany when they become pregnant. It therefore is believed that the work of these glands is increased during the pregnant state and that parathyroid deficiency is responsible for tetany (17, 18, 19).

Tetany occasionally is observed in pregnant women. It usually appears in the latter half of gestation and tends to recur with succeeding pregnancies (20). Parathormone controls the condition (21). One to three cc. of dihydrotachysterol given daily to increase calcium absorption and phosphorus excretion has a more lasting effect than parathormone (21a, 21b).

Altered calcium metabolism during pregnancy has been offered as the cause of cramp-like pains in the legs, insomnia, paresthesia and edema, and relief of these symptoms has resulted from calcium therapy. Milk, leafy vegetables, fruit, sunlight, viosterol, cod-liver oil, and calcium by mouth are recommended (22).

DIABETES. Untreated diabetics seldom become pregnant for the following reasons: first, the disease usually occurs after or late in the child-bearing period of a woman's life (23), second, juvenile cases when not treated with insulin, usually die before they reach marriageable age and third, the amenorrhea and other menstrual disturbances which frequently accompany diabetes indicate associated endocrine disfunction which may well cause sterility (24).

The discovery of insulin has changed the situation considerably. Its use not only prolongs the life of juvenile diabetics into the childbearing period but often leads to the establishment of regular menstruation in those cases which have an amenorrhoea and other menstrual disturbances (25, 26, 27, 28). By increasing fertility and prolonging the lives of diabetic children, insulin accordingly has led to a great number of pregnancies complicating diabetes. In the

London Hospital, the incidence of this complication has increased from 2 to 15% since the beginning of the insulin era (29). Although this probably was partly due to better diagnostic methods, it clearly shows that the problem of diabetes and pregnancy is becoming increasingly important.

In preinsulin days, the association of pregnancy and diabetes was a very serious one and the prognosis for mother and child was bad. In 66 cases collected by Williams (30), 27% of the mothers died in labor or within two weeks and 23% succumbed within two years. About one-eighth of the pregnancies ended in abortion or premature labor and one-third of those that continued to term resulted in stillbirths. Since mild cases usually recovered and were not reported, the end results recorded by Williams probably were worse than those that actually occurred in ordinary practice (31). Maternal and fetal deaths, however, were so common that therapeutic abortion frequently was recommended. **By the use of insulin, the risk to the mother has been largely eliminated, but the danger to the child is still considerable** (28).

Effect of pregnancy upon diabetes. (a) **Tolerance.** Pregnancy, which is a great strain upon the metabolism of carbohydrates for the non-diabetic woman is a far greater carbohydrate strain for the diabetic. A greatly lessened tolerance for carbohydrates, accordingly, should be expected in diabetes complicated by pregnancy. This is true in the early months but because of other factors, tolerance remains stationary in the second trimester and either increases or diminishes in the third (28, 32).

The increased tolerance for carbohydrate observed after the middle of pregnancy has been attributed to the presence of the fetal pancreas. In support of this view, it may be said that animals from which the pancreas is removed late in pregnancy fail to develop hyperglycemia or glycosuria until after the birth of their young (33, 34, 35). It also has been shown that insulin, injected into the fetus of a goat far advanced in pregnancy, is followed by a lowering of the blood sugar of the mother (36). Further support of the supposed beneficial effect of the fetal pancreas is afforded by the observation that those diabetic women who show a lessened hyperglycemia in the latter half of pregnancy often have an increase in their blood sugar after the fetus dies (37). On the other hand, all of these observations may be explained on the basis of a greater utilization of glucose due to its passage through the placenta and utilization by the fetus. In addition, the weight of evidence indicates, as was shown in Chapter V, that insulin does not pass through the placenta, a conclusion which is substantiated by the observation that the carbohydrate tolerance of depancreatized dogs receiving insulin remains unchanged when the animals become pregnant (38, 39, 40).

(b) **Acidosis.** Because of the growing products of conception and the hyperactivity of the thyroid, a rise in the metabolic rate is a normal accompaniment of pregnancy. As a consequence, the strain of the increased load upon the altered carbohydrate metabolism readily leads to a diminished alkali reserve with the result that ketosis during gestation is easily produced by starvation, by diets rich in fat and by the diminution in the food intake incident to nausea and vomiting of pregnancy (41, 42). The pregnant diabetic, therefore, is especially susceptible to ketosis since she already has a metabolic derangement which is characterized by a defective utilization of carbohydrate and an incomplete combustion of fat (31). Coma, accordingly, may develop at any time with astonishing rapidity. The increased mobilization of glycogen, together with the more rapid burning up of sugar in the muscles which accompanies the severe muscular efforts of parturition, may lead to exhaustion of the available carbohydrate. Acidosis and coma, therefore, are particularly apt to occur in the course of labor. As labor progresses, a complicating coma usually deepens and treatment often is unsatisfactory. With the delivery of the child, however, chemical recovery may be effected (28).

(c) **Hypoglycemia.** Hypoglycemia usually is the result of poor treatment and occurs when the dosage of insulin is increased in the presence of a low renal threshold. During labor, it results from the increased utilization of carbohydrates and in the puerperium, from lactation (28).

Effect of diabetes upon the course of pregnancy. (a) **Abortion** still occurs in a fair proportion of well-treated cases and is recorded in 16% of the pregnancies treated since the discovery of insulin in the Joslin Clinic which, prior to that time, showed 25% early interruptions of pregnancy (28). The cause of this accident is not definitely known. Hypoglycemia, acidosis, dietary deficiencies and a lack of glycogen in the decidua have been suggested.

(b) **Stillbirths.** Even though insulin therapy unquestionably prevents the intrauterine death of many infants, the Joslin cases show a stillbirth incidence of 25% after and 29% before the insulin era. Of the 271 pregnancies which occurred in 191 diabetic women of this series, however, the stillbirth rate among those patients who were under direct supervision was only one-third that of pre-insulin days and was but twice that of non-diabetic pregnancies (28). It has been suggested that an excessive secretion of prolan may be responsible for this high fetal death rate since the administration of prolan to pregnant rabbits has been followed by a prolongation of pregnancy and the death and maceration of giant post-mature rabbit fetuses (43, 44).

(c) **Overgrowth of the fetus.** When the gestation continues to term, the children of diabetic mothers often are considerably larger than normal and the tendency toward overweight is so striking that the birth of a very large child always leads to the suspicion of diabetes (45, 46, 47). This overgrowth of the fetus has been attributed to maternal hyperglycemia. It, however, also occurs in patients who are well supervised. As the greatest growth of the fetus takes place in the last two months and as a marked progressive increase in prolan has been observed in some diabetics at this time, overactivity of the pituitary gland has been offered as a cause of the tendency toward gigantism (43).

(d) **Toxemia.** Toxemia and eclampsia occur much more frequently in pregnancy complicated by diabetes and the incidence of eclampsia in the Joslin series of 271 pregnancies in 191 diabetic mothers was 5 per cent (28). The possibility of the development of toxemia is even greater in patients who survive juvenile diabetes. In this connection, it is interesting to note that a progressive increase in prolan, together with a diminishing estrin secretion, has been observed in diabetics who ultimately became toxic (43)..

(e) **Hydramnios.** Hydramnios occasionally is observed in pregnancy complicated by diabetes, and fetal diuresis resulting from hyperglycemia has been suggested as the cause of the excess of amniotic fluid (31). In one instance, intermittent hydramnios was observed whenever the patient neglected to follow her diabetic regimen (48).

Diagnosis. During pregnancy the tolerance for carbohydrates is so lowered that this fact has been made the basis for several pregnancy tests. In addition, carbohydrate metabolism may be further altered by other factors which commonly occur at this time, such as hyperactivity of the thyroid, pituitary and adrenal glands, as well as starvation and glycogen depletion. Glycosuria not due to diabetes accordingly is frequently observed and repeated urinalyses during pregnancy have revealed glucose varying in amounts from a trace to several per cent in as high as 66% of pregnancy women (49).

Occasionally, glucose found in the urine during pregnancy may be the result of a lower renal threshold. This type of glycosuria is recognized by the absence of an accompanying hyperglycemia and by its persistence even though insulin is given. When the latter is used injudiciously in such cases, there accordingly is danger of producing hypoglycemia and acidosis.

The non-diabetic glycosuria which is observed rather commonly in pregnancy and often recurs in succeeding gestations, is differentiated from true diabetic glycosuria by blood sugar determinations, by tolerance tests and by the usual symptoms of diabetes—polyuria, polydipsia, polyphagia, loss of weight, etc. The finding of over 140 mg. of glucose per 100 cc. of blood after fasting, or 170 mg. at any time, should lead to a suspicion of diabetes. If the blood is examined at intervals of one, two and three hours following the ingestion of 50 gm. of glucose after fasting, and the blood sugar does not return to its normal level in the last specimen, diabetes is present.

The following tolerance test has been suggested: 200 gm. of glucose from carbohydrate, protein and fat are given daily for two or three days. Twenty-four hour specimens of urine are collected and the total excretion of sugar per day is calculated. For the next two or three days, the same type of diet is repeated but increased so that its glucose content is 300 gm. In non-diabetic glycosurias, approximately the same percentage of sugar will be excreted in the urine. Diabetics, on the other hand, show the percentage of glucose found in the urine to be markedly increased as more carbohydrate is added to the intake (50).

Treatment. Since pregnancy normally is a great strain upon the carbohydrate metabolism, its effect upon the defective metabolism of carbohydrate in the diabetic calls for constant supervision whenever a woman with diabetes becomes pregnant. The possible occurrence of acidosis, glycogen depletion and hypoglycemia should be kept in mind and guarded against at all times. **Great caution, accordingly, must be exercised in withdrawing carbohydrates and adding fats.** Sufficient carbohydrates are given to provide for the increase in the metabolism of the mother and for the glycogen needs of the fetus, while the glycosuria is controlled by means of insulin.

In the first trimester, vomiting may lead to carbohydrate starvation. At this time, therefore, it is best to prescribe frequent small meals. Nourishment at one or two hour intervals is recommended in conjunction with the administration of insulin every three hours in doses which vary with the degree of glycosuria: 20 units if the Benedict test is red, 15 units if it is orange, and 10 or 5 if yellow or green. Under these conditions, 150 gm. of carbohydrate, 60 gm. of protein and 60 to 80 gm. of fat may be taken with safety (28). If because of nausea or vomiting, the ingestion of food is difficult or impossible, small intravenous injections of glucose are indicated.

In the second trimester, spontaneous improvement may occur (29) and the developing pregnancy often requires an increase in the food intake. The diet accordingly is augmented and not infrequently, the amount of insulin may be diminished.

In the third trimester, the basal metabolic rate is at its highest and the alkali reserve at its lowest level. Acidosis and coma, accordingly, must be guarded against. As the fetus now needs 50 gm. of glucose daily (31), the carbohydrates are increased to 175–200 gm. If more insulin seems to be required, great caution should be exercised in increasing the dose because of the low renal threshold (51, 52). Small quantities of sugar, accordingly, should be present in the urine at this time. Frequent blood sugar determinations, likewise, are indicated, if the occurrence of hypoglycemia is to be recognized and hypoglycemic shock prevented (28).

During labor, the severe muscular exertion depletes the glycogen reserve in the maternal tissues. The carbohydrate and insulin requirements throughout and immediately after labor, accordingly, must be determined in each case by frequent blood sugar estimations if serious complications are to be avoided.

Even though all therapeutic measures are thus carefully controlled, insulin shock and coma may at times occur (32). In a normal labor, 200–300 gm. of carbohydrate are required. If delivery is effected by surgical means, the routine used is similar to that followed in other operations performed upon diabetics. During the first 24 hours of the puerperium, 100 gm. of carbohydrate are given by mouth or intravenously and insulin is used at three hour intervals in amounts corresponding to the previously mentioned Benedict reactions (28).

Interruption of pregnancy. Diabetics should be advised to avoid conception. If they become pregnant, however, therapeutic abortion is not indicated except in the severe cases in which the diabetes cannot be controlled. The high incidence of fetal death and overgrowth of the child justify the premature termination of pregnancy between two weeks and one month before term, whenever palpation or x-ray examination shows an excessive growth of the fetus (28, 53). Should subsequent research verify the observation that increasing prolan and diminishing estrin are indicative of approaching fetal death or gigantism, such estimations may likewise be of great assistance (43). In such cases diethylstilbestrol and progesterone in 15 mg. doses given intramuscularly daily reduced the fetal mortality in the Joslin clinic (43a). The method of interrupting pregnancy will depend upon the circumstances present in each case. **If a short labor is anticipated,** as in the case of a multipara with a short open cervix, induction by one of the vaginal methods is recommended. **If a long labor is anticipated,** Cesarean section under local anesthesia is to be chosen as the best means of prematurely terminating the pregnancy. Cesarean section, accordingly, is to be preferred in the case of the primipara with a long closed cervix, and it likewise should be the method of choice in those cases in which sterilization is indicated as it is in all serious diabetics.

Labor. Since fear, muscular exertion, trauma and anesthesia affect carbohydrate metabolism, labor should be made as easy as possible by the use of morphine and scopolamine, and should be terminated by low forceps under novocaine infiltration anesthesia with the avoidance of all possible trauma. If, because of obstetric difficulties, the danger of prolonged labor or excessive size of the child, Cesarean section is done, local anesthesia should be used since ether and chloroform are contraindicated in the presence of diabetes (28, 31, 32, 53, 54, 55, 56, 57, 58).

As the diabetic woman resists infection poorly (59, 60), strict aseptic precautions must be followed throughout labor.

Hypoglycemia in the newborn child must be thought of as some neonatal deaths have been attributed to this cause (61). Feedings of 10% sugar solution should be started soon after birth and continued at two hour intervals. Should symptoms of hypoglycemia appear, 10 cc. of 10% glucose is to be given subcutaneously (62).

Inheritance. It is believed that diabetes is inherited as a Mendelian recessive trait. The child cannot inherit the disease from one diabetic parent alone but only from two diabetics, a diabetic and a hereditary carrier or two hereditary carriers. The children of all diabetics, however, will be hereditary carriers of the disease. Assuming that 25% of our population must be carriers, the possibility of inherited diabetes is at least 25% whenever a diabetic mother has a child (28). This hereditary factory deserves important consideration whenever a woman with diabetes consults her physician concerning the advisability of her becoming pregnant, or the justification for abortion if she is already pregnant.

ADDISON'S DISEASE. Removal of the adrenal bodies causes death of experimental animals in six to ten days. When the same experiment is done during pregnancy, death does not occur so soon and several are reported to have survived for six weeks or more after the operation (63). Possibly the products of conception take on the function of the suprarenal cortex, which is shown to be the essential element by the fact that injections of extracts made from adrenal cortex prevent death in adrenalectomized animals.

Addison's disease as a complication of pregnancy is seldom observed (64). When it does occur, the usual pigment changes are intensified. Gestation has little effect on the course of the disease if the latter is in the early stage. When it has progressed to the point of marked asthenia, however, spontaneous interruption of the gestation may occur. The ultimate prognosis is bad but improvement has been reported during pregnancy, only to be followed by death soon after delivery. The use of cortical extract may prove beneficial, at least during pregnancy (65).

REFERENCES

1. ENGELHORN: Ueber Schilddrüsenveränderungen in der Schwangerschaft. Verhandle, d. deutsch. Gesellsch. f. Gynäk., 1911, 14, 675.
2. MARINE, D.: The Thyroid Gland in Relation to Gynecology and Obstetrics. Surg. Gyn. & Obs., 1917, 25, 272.
3. DALY, P. AND STROUSE, S.: The Thyroid During Pregnancy. J. A. M. A., 1925, 84, 1798.
4. DAVIS, C. H.: Thyroid Hypertrophy and Pregnancy. J. A. M. A., 1926, 87, 1004.
5. FALLS, F. H.: Hyperthyroidism Complicating Pregnancy. Am. J. Obs. & Gyn., 1929, 17, 536.
6. PLASS, E. D. AND YOAKAM, W. A.: Basal Metabolism Studies in Normal Pregnant Women with Normal and Pathologic Thyroid Glands. Am. J. Obs. & Gyn., 1929, 18, 556.
7. SANDEFORD, I., WHEELER, T. AND BOOTHBY, W. M.: Metabolic Studies During Pregnancy and Menstruation. Am. J. Physiol., 1931, 96, 191.
8. MARINE, D. AND KIMBALL, O. P.: The Prevention of Simple Goiter in Man. J. A. M. A., 1921, 77, 1068.
9. YOAKAM, W. A.: The Thyroid Gland in Pregnancy: A Clinical Study in a Region of Endemic Goiter. Am. J. Obs. & Gyn., 1928, 15, 617.
10. MÜLLER, B.: Das Verhalten der Glandula thyreoidea im endemischen Kropfgebiet des Kantons Bern zu Schwangerschaft, Geburt, und Wochenbett. Zeitschr. f. Geburtsh. u. Gynak., 1913, 75, 264.
11. MUSSEY, R. D. AND PLUMMER, W. A.: Treatment of Goiter Complicating Pregnancy. J. A. M. A., 1931, 97, 602.

12. MUSSEY, R. D., PLUMMER, W. A. AND BOOTHBY, W. M.: Pregnancy Complicating Exoph-thalmic Goiter. J. A. M. A., 1926, 87, 1009.
13. SEITZ, L.: Die Störungen der inneren Sekretion in ihren Beziehungen zu Schwangerschaft, Geburt and Wochenbett. Verhandl, d. Deutsch. Gesellsch. f. Gynäk., 1913, 15, 213.
14. GARDINER-HILL, H.: Pregnancy Complicating Simple Goiter and Grave's Disease. Lancet, 1929, 1, 120.
15. WILLIAMSON, A. C.: Pregnancy Following Thyroidectomy. Am. J. Obs. & Gyn. 1927, 14, 196.
16. LITZENBERG, J. C. AND CAREY, J. B.: The Relation of Basal Metabolism to Gestation Am. J. Obs. & Gyn., 1929, 17, 550.
17. FROMMER, V.: Experimentelle Versuche zur parathyreoidealen Insuffizienz in Bezug auf Eklampsie und Tetanie mit besonderer Berücksichtigung der antitoxischen Funktion der Parathyreoideae. Monatschr. f. Geburtsh. u. Gynäk., 1906, 24, 748.
18. ADLER, L. AND THALER, H.: Experimentelle und Klinische Studien über die Graviditäts-tetanie. Ztschr. f. Geburtsh. u. Gynäk., 1908, 62, 194.
19. MACCALLUM, W. G. AND VOEGTLIN, C.: On the Relation of Tetany to the Parathyroid Glands and to Calcium Metabolism. J. Exp. Med., 1909, 11, 118.
20. THOMAS, H. M.: Tetany in Pregnancy. Johns Hopkins Hosp. Bull., 1895, 6, 85.
21. COLLIP, J. B.: The Extraction of a Parathyroid Hormone which will Prevent or Control Parathyroid Tetany and which Regulates the Level of Blood Calcium. J. Biol. Chem. 1925, 63, 395.
21a. HOLZ, F. AND ROSSMAN, E.: Schwangerschaft und Tetanie. Ztschr. f. Geburtsh. u. Gyn., 1938, 116, 187.
21b. ANDERSON, G. W. AND MUSSELMAN, L.: The Treatment of Tetany in Pregnancy. Am. J. Obs. & Gyn., 1942, 43, 547.
22. HARLTEY, E. C.: the Tetanoid Syndrome in Obstetrics. Am. J. Obs. & Gyn., 1930, 19, 54.
23. JOSLIN, E. P.: The Treatment of Diabetes, London, 1928.
24. PARISOT, J.: Les troubles de la fonction génitale chez les diabetiques; leur pathogénie. Bull. et mem. soc. med. d. hop. de Paris, 1911, 32, 95.
25. JOSLIN, E. P., ROOT, H. F., AND WHITE, P.: The Growth, Development and Prognosis of Diabetic Children. J. A. M. A., 1925, 85, 420.
26. ALLEN, F. M. AND SHERRILL, J. W.: Clinical Observations with Insulin; Use of Insulin in Diabetic Treatment. J. Metab. Res., 1922, 2, 803.
27. FITZ, R. AND MURPHY, W. P.: Diabetes, Insulin and Pregnancy. Boston Med. and Surg J., 1925, 193, 1092.
28. WHITE, P.: Pregnancy Complicating Diabetes. Surg. Gyn. and Obs., 1935, 61, 324.
29. SKIPPER, E.: Diabetes Mellitus and Pregnancy. Quart. J. Med., 1933, 2, 353.
30. WILLIAMS, J. W.: The Clinical Significance of Glycosuria in Pregnant Women. Am. J. Med. Sc., 1909, 137, 1.
31. LAMBIE, C. G.: Diabetes and Pregnancy. J. Obs. & Gyn. Brit. Temp., 1926, 33, 563.
32. PECKHAM, C. H.: Diabetes Mellitus and Pregnancy. Bull. Johns Hopkins Hosp., 1931, 49, 184.
33. CARLSON, A. J. AND DRENNAN, F. M.: The Control of Pancreatic Diabetes in Pregnancy by the Passage of the Internal Secretion of the Pancreas of the Fetus to the Blood of the Mother. Am. J. Physiol., 1911, 28, 391.
34. CARLSON, A. J., ORR, J. S., AND JONES, W. S.: The Absence of Sugar in the Urine after Pancreatectomy in Pregnant Bitches near Term. J. Biol. Chem., 1914, 17, 19.
35. LAFON, G.: Sur le passage de la secretion interne du pancreas du fetus a la mere. Compt. rend. Soc. biol. Par., 1913, 75, 266.
36. PACK, G. T. AND BARBER, D.: The Placental Transmission of Insulin from Fetus to Mother. Am. J. Obs. & Gyn., 1928, 16, 115.
37. HOLZBACH, E.: Die Blutzuckerkurve einer pankreasdiabetischen Schwangeren. Zentralbl. f. Gynak., 1926, 50, 2610.
38. ALLEN, F. M.: Experimental Studies in Diabetes. Am. J. Physiol., 1920-21, 54, 451.
39. MARKOWITZ, J. AND SOSKIN, S.: Pancreatic Diabetes and Pregnancy. Am. J. Physiol., 1926-7, 79, 553.

40. MACLEOD, J. J. R.: Carbohydrate Metabolism and Insulin, London, 1926.
41. HARDING, V. J. AND ALLEN, K. D.: Ketosis in Pregnancy. J. Biol. Chem., 1926, 69, 133.
42. STANDER, H. J., EASTMAN, N. J., HARRISON, F. P. H. AND CADDEN, J. F.: The Acid Base
    Equilibrium of the Blood in Eclampsia. J. Biol. Chem., 1929, 85, 233.
43. SMITH, G. V. AND SMITH, O. W.: Excessive Gonad-Stimulating Hormone and Sub-normal
    Amounts of Oestrin in the Toxemias of Late Pregnancy. Am. J. Physiol., 1934, 107,
    128.
43a. WHITE, PRECILLA: Pregnancy Complicating Diabetes. J. A. M. A., 1945, 128, 181.
44. SNYDER, F. F.: The Prolongation of Pregnancy and Complications of Parturition in the
    Rabbit Following Induction of Ovulation near Term. Bull. Johns Hop. Hosp., 1934,
    54, 1.
45. SPRINGER, A.: Zur Frage: Diabetes und Schwangerschaft. Zentralbl. f. Gynak., 1924,
    48, 2642.
46. BIX, H.: Ueber Beziehungen zwischen mütterlichen Diabetes und Riesenkindern. Med.
    Klin., 1933, 29, 50.
47. DAMELIN AND FOUQUIAU: Dystocie par excès de volume dufoetus et diabète. Bull. Soc.
    d'Obst. de Par., 1910, 13, 159.
48. LABBÉ, M. AND COUVELAIRE, A.: Insulin in Treatment of Diabetes in Pregnant Women.
    Bull. Acad. de Med. Paris, 1925, 94, 1016.
49. CHASE, L. A.: Glycosuria in Pregnancy. Canad. M. Ass. J., 1932, 26, 297.
50. WOODYATT, R. T.: Diabetes in Pregnancy. Adair & Steiglitz, Obstetric Med., Phila.
    1934.
51. VIGNES, H. AND BARBARA, G.: Glycosuria and Diabetes in Connection With Pregnancy.
    Presse Méd., 1924, 32, 1018.
52. HÖST, H. F.: Carbohydrate Tolerance in Pregnancy. Lancet, London, 1925, 1, 1022.
53. RONSHEIM, J.: Diabetes and Pregnancy. Am. J. Obs. & Gyn., 1933, 25, 710.
54. RAVENO, W. S.: Insulin in Diabetic Coma Complicating Pregnancy. J. A. M. A., 1923,
    81, 2101.
55. EHRENFEST, H.: Carbohydrate Metabolism During Pregnancy and the Value of Insulin
    to the Obstetrician. Am. J. Obs. & Gyn., 1924, 8, 685.
56. WIENER, H. J.: Diabetes Mellitus in Pregnancy. Am. J. Obs. & Gyn., 1924, 7, 710.
57. PARSONS, E., RANDALL, L. M. AND WILDER, R. M.: Pregnancy and Diabetes. Med. Clin.
    N. Am., 1926, 10, 679.
58. LAWRENCE, R. D.: Improvement in a Pregnant Woman Due to Fetal Insulin. Quart.
    J. Med., 1929, 22, 191.
59. LIEPMANN, W.: Diabetes Mellitus und Metritus dissecans, nebst einem Beitrag zur Pathol-
    ogie der Metritis dissecans. Arch. f. Gyn., 1903, 70, 426.
60. WALKER, A.: Diabetes Mellitus and Pregnancy. J. Obs. & Gyn. Brit. Emp., 1928, 35,
    271.
61. GORDON, W. H.: Fetal Hypoglycemia due to Hyper insulinism. J. Mich. M. Soc., 1935,
    34, 167.
62. RANDALL, L. M. AND RYNEARSON, E. H.: Successful Treatment of Spontaneous Hypo-
    Glycemia of Infant of a Diabetic Mother. Proc. Staff Meetings Mayo Clinic, 1935,
    10, 705.
63. ROGOFF, J. M. AND STEWART, G. N.: The Influence of Pregnancy upon the Survival Period
    in Adrenalectomized Dogs. Am. J. Physiol., 1926–1927, 79, 508.
64. FITZ-PATRICK, G.: Addison's Disease Complicating Pregnancy, Labor, or the Puerperium.
    Surg. Gyn. and Obs., 1922, 35, 72.
65. ROWNTREE, L. G., GREENE, C. H., SWINGLE, W. W. AND PFIFFNER, J. J.: Addison's
    Disease Experiences in Treatment with Various Suprarenal Preparations. J. A. M.
    A., 1931, 96, 231.

NERVOUS AND MENTAL DISEASES

PSYCHOSES. Faulty elimination, worry, loss of sleep, the thought of the added responsibility of motherhood, toxemia, the fear and exhaustion of labor and puerperal infection may lead to mental disorganization in those who, through inheritance or faulty training in childhood, have an unstable nervous system. Often such individuals, though able to withstand the customary shocks of ordinary life, are unequal to the assaults of childbearing and, accordingly, show the first evidence of a psychosis during or soon after pregnancy. Because of their association with pregnancy, therefore, these cases frequently are incorrectly designated as gestational or puerperal psychoses, when, as a matter of fact, they differ from the usual mental diseases in no way other than that they are precipitated by pregnancy. In other words, they would have developed sooner or later in the absence of pregnancy had a sufficiently strong exciting cause arisen. The term "puerperal insanity", therefore, should be restricted to those psychoses in which toxemia and infection are alone responsible for the mental disturbance, and many psychiatrists prefer to call even these forms of insanity toxic or infectious psychoses, since they also are not peculiar to pregnancy.

TOXIC OR INFECTIOUS EXHAUSTION PSYCHOSES (Confusional Insanity). Psychoses are commonly observed in the puerperium following a toxemia of pregnancy or a puerperal infection. In the course of the latter, the patient is unable to sleep and becomes unusually nervous, irritable and anxious, or depressed. Often she develops an antipathy toward her child and may even disown it, or the same mental aberration may lead to an aversion for her husband. Later, confusion, clouding of consciousness, illusions, hallucinations of sight and hearing, delusions and motor excitement are noted. The prognosis in this type of insanity is usually favorable and recovery often follows soon after the source of the infection is removed. Death, however, may occur from sepsis or from exhaustion due to motor excitement and insomnia.

AFFECTIVE DISORDERS are the commonest type of psychoses seen during pregnancy itself. Depression usually is observed after the fifth month and grows progressively worse as the gestation advances. The patient, greatly worried concerning her condition and fearing labor and the added cares of motherhood, becomes gloomy and despondent, and shows an indifference toward those things which formerly were sources of pleasure and satisfaction. She loses interest in her family and household, has no desire for food, is unable to sleep and develops delusions in the form of ideas of humility or self-accusation. She accordingly feels that she is unworthy to become a mother or that in doing so she is committing a grievous sin. A suicidal tendency likewise is not uncommon. The prognosis usually is good and disappearance of the symptoms often begins as soon after delivery as the patient realizes that she has passed safely through her pregnancy and is again restored to health.

SCHIZOPHRENIA   Occasionally, pregnancy may precipitate catatonic or paranoid types of schizophrenia.   The former is preceded by a change in disposition, indifference and insomnia.   Speech becomes incoherent, movements are disordered and impulsive reactions are common.   This phase of excitement is followed by the stage of catatonic stupor in which the patient fails to react to external stimuli.   She refuses to speak, declines to take nourishment, and her attitude toward the outside world is one of extreme indifference.   The paranoid type is similar to that seen in nonpregnant women and is characterized by delusions of persecution, which often are centered about the husband.   Because of these, the tendency toward homicide is always present and requires constant watchfulness on the part of the attendants.   The outlook in these cases is similar to that of schizophrenia in general.

A fair conception of the mental complications of pregnancy may be gained from the Bellevue Hospital report (1) of 114 cases which were classified as follows:

	TOTAL	DEATHS	IMPROVED	RECOVERED		
				no.	per cent	
1. Manic-depressive psychosis..................	52	5	7	40	77	(a)
2. Dementia praecox.........................	18					(b)
3. Epileptic psychosis.........................	3			3	100	
4. Alcoholic psychosis........................	1			1	100	
5. Intellectual and mental deficiency psychosis.....	4			4	100	
6. Infective exhaustion psychosis................	31	9	3	19	61	(c)
7. Transient attacks of excitement and confusion...	5			5	100	(d)

a. Of the fifty-two manic-depressive cases, only four began in the latter months of pregnancy and all but one of the remainder developed during the puerperium.   Thirteen had had previous attacks not associated with childbirth and two suffered from recurrences with each successive pregnancy.   The five deaths were due to intercurrent disease.

b. Six of the eighteen in the dementia praecox group showed evidence of the disease in a milder form for some time before conception took place and were aggravated by the pregnancy.

c. Three of the thirty-one infective exhaustion psychoses developed during pregnancy, five at the time of labor and the remainder during the puerperium.

d. One of these had five mental breakdowns in as many pregnancies.

TREATMENT.   In view of the fact that most of the psychoses which are observed during or after pregnancy are the result of an underlying nervous and mental instability, proper prenatal hygiene might prevent mental breakdown at that time.   After making a thorough examination early in pregnancy, the attending physician should assure the patient that a successful outcome may be anticipated. If any unfavorable findings are noted, their significance must be withheld from her until later in the pregnancy when she will have acquired sufficient confidence in her physician to feel that he will guide her safely through her confinement in spite of the difficulty. Of course, the husband should be acquainted with the true condition if it is felt that his apprehension will not be transmitted to the patient. She likewise should be protected as much as possible from those friends who may discuss the possible dangers of childbirth. Frequent visits to the obstetrician, and adherence to the suggestions made in the chapter on the hygiene of pregnancy, will do much to preserve her mental equilibrium.

The actual treatment of any psychosis should be in the hands of a psychiatrist, and, because of the expense and difficulty in obtaining satisfactory attention at home, it usually can be better carried out in an institution. The measures followed include the use of mild sedatives, regulation of the bowels, an abundant diet, consisting of nutritious food given in small amounts four or five times daily instead of the usual two or three hearty meals, fresh air, outdoor exercises, and constant observation by a competent attendant to see that these measures are carried out and to protect the patient from injuring herself and others. In the infective exhaustion psychosis, every effort should be made to eliminate all foci of infection.

The question of abortion occasionally is considered but rarely is it indicated (2). Unquestionably, women who are subject to exacerbations of their psychoses should not become pregnant and if they do conceive, constant attention should be given toward the prevention of worry, fear, insomnia, toxemia and a difficult labor. In some cases, cesarean section, at times, may be advisable. When the latter operation is done, it should be accompanied by sterilization (3).

ENCEPHALITIS LETHARGICA. Owing to the predilection of this disease for young adults, pregnant women may occasionally have lethargic encephalitis and, for the same reason, the latter is more frequently observed in primigravidae. The mortality during pregnancy is about twice as high as that observed in non-pregnant women. This would seem to indicate that pregnancy has a bad influence on the course of the disease, but some observers feel that the usual group statistics are not trustworthy because of the variations in the virulence of different epidemics (4). Since labor, in some instances, has been observed to have an unfavorable effect, it may be possible that the interruption of pregnancy itself is the chief cause of the higher death rate in puerperal cases. This deduction is further supported by the observation that those cases which were artificially terminated did not do so well as the ones in which the gestation was allowed to continue to term. Pregnancy usually is not disturbed by this complication. In severe cases, however, interruption may occur. Labor is often painless and spontaneous delivery may take place without warning from the patient. As previously stated, parturition sometimes causes a change for the worse.

Transmission of the disease to the fetus is possible but rarely occurs and the infants usually are healthy at birth.

Pregnancy is thought to increase the incidence of Parkinson's syndrome (5) and, when it occurs in a woman who already is the subject of parkinsonism, the latter condition may be aggravated.

Ordinarily, interruption of the pregnancy is not indicated. Because parkinsonism may begin in a subsequent pregnancy, women who have had encephalitis should not be allowed to conceive for several years. Those who already have developed Parkinson's syndrome likewise should not become pregnant for a similar period.

CHOREA, though rarely observed in obstetric practice, occasionally is a grave complication. This is particularly true when the condition appears for the first time during pregnancy. Although chorea gravidarum formerly was thought to be due to a toxemia, extensive reviews of reported cases show it to be similar to Sydenham's chorea in the majority of instances. It is most frequently encountered in young women who are pregnant for the first time. Over half of the cases give a history of an attack prior to pregnancy and more than one-third have had rheumatic fever. Cardiac disease is common and is noted in one-third of the recorded cases, as well as in 87 per cent of those that come to autopsy (6).

The symptoms may be mild but often are so severe that the violent and persistent choreiform movements disturb the patient's rest and interfere with her ability to take nourishment, with the result that exhaustion is inevitable. The prognosis is grave. About one mother out of eight dies. Many of the fetuses are stillborn or die soon after birth and those that survive may be defective (7). Recurrences are frequently observed in subsequent pregnancies.

Treatment of chorea complicated by pregnancy includes rest in bed, isolation, careful feeding and the use of sedative drugs. Intravenous injections of magnesium sulphate often have a quieting effect when most other sedatives fail. Improvement also has been observed after the use of arsphenamine. Abortion is not to be considered in the mild cases and is of questionable value in the severe ones. The latter not only are not improved, but often rapidly progress to a fatal termination after the pregnancy is interrupted. If it is deemed advisable to empty the uterus, induction of abortion or premature labor is preferable to a surgical procedure in which the cervix or uterus is incised.

EPILEPSY. Pregnancy is said to have a bad effect on epilepsy. In some cases, however, freedom from attacks is experienced throughout gestation. Occasionally, epileptic seizures are mistaken for eclampsia and the patient is unnecessarily subjected to the therapeutic routine indicated in convulsive toxemia. On the other hand, it must be remembered that a woman subject to epilepsy may also develop eclampsia and require the treatment recommended for that condition. Abortion and sterilization may be considered from the eugenic standpoint, but seldom are justified on purely medical or obstetrical grounds. The management of epilepsy during pregnancy is similar to that employed in nonpregnant women. Each patient must be individualized and special attention should be given to diet, elimination, rest and the avoidance of worry and fatigue.

TUBERCULOUS MENINGITIS. Because of its extreme rarity, tuberculous meningitis is seldom diagnosed correctly during pregnancy. In the early months, the clinical picture may be suggestive of pernicious vomiting and later it may be regarded as eclampsia. Its effect on pregnancy is not unfavorable and does not increase the tendency toward abortion or premature labor. The incidence of tuberculosis in the offspring, however, is greater than that observed in pulmonary tuberculosis. Cesarean section has been recommended in the treatment of this complication (8).

ANTERIOR POLIOMYELITIS. Pregnancy seems to have little effect on the course of anterior poliomyelitis. The gestation, accordingly, should not be interrupted unless its presence increases the severity of the complications. Encroachment of the uterus on the diaphragm in the latter months may add to the difficulties that arise when the disease causes diaphragmatic paralysis and may require premature emptying of the uterus. In the absence of disproportion, labor likewise is uneventful. It is generally thought that the transmission of poliomyelitis to the fetus does not occur, but that the child does receive an immunity from its mother (9, 10, 11).

The advisability of future pregnancies in women who have recovered from this disease has been questioned. When the muscles involved in the bearing-down efforts are paralyzed, it would seem that subsequent labors might be complicated. Experience, however, has shown that such patients are delivered at term without difficulty. Subsequent pregnancies, therefore, are not contra-indicated.

MYELITIS. Degenerative changes in the spinal cord analogous to those seen in toxic and infectious conditions are sometimes observed during pregnancy and are known as gestational myelitis. Vitamin deficiency may be a factor. In experimental avitaminosis degenerative and hemorrhagic lesions similar to those found in myelopathy of pregnancy have been observed (14a). Pain, spastic weakness in the lower extremities, and bladder symptoms are commonly observed. Paralysis and loss of sensation may develop, and, as a result, the patient complains that she no longer feels the fetal movements. The disease usually is seen in the latter half of pregnancy and improvement often follows delivery or the emptying of the uterus. Recurrences are commonly observed in subsequent pregnancies. Therapeutic abortion is indicated and future pregnancies should be avoided (12, 12a, 13, 14, 14a).

MULTIPLE SCLEROSIS is aggravated by pregnancy and women who are in the stage of remission have their improvement checked by the acute exacerbations that commonly develop in the course of pregnancy and the puerperium. Death may occur during or soon after labor. Since the prognosis in multiple sclerosis is bad, it would seem that in some cases the deleterious effect of pregnancy should be eliminated by early evacuation of the uterus. For the same reason, women who have multiple sclerosis should be warned against the added dangers of pregnancy.

POLYNEURITIS occasionally is observed to follow excessive vomiting in the early months of pregnancy and, in the past, was considered a manifestation of toxemia (15, 16, 17, 20). Recently, however, the great similarity between the degenerative nerve changes noted in polyneuritis of pregnancy and those found in beriberi has suggested the possibility that it might also be due to a dietary deficiency (18, 19). This hypothesis is further supported by the analogous findings that are observed in Korsakoff's syndrome, which is now regarded as a vitamin deficiency disease, based on chronic alcoholism.

Symptoms of polyneuritis usually are noted in the lower extremities and follow the prolonged and excessive vomiting that occasionally is encountered in early pregnancy. At first, they may be mild and limited to a single nerve trunk. The muscles supplied by this nerve show progressive weakness and become soft and flabby. As the paralysis increases in extent, other nerves are involved and the symptoms then vary with the location of the lesion. Mental disturbances occur in the majority of severe cases. These consist of disorientation, misidentification, loss of memory for recent events, and confabulations in which the loss of memory for connected description of past and present events leads to delusions of various kinds. The prognosis is bad and, as a result, it was formerly recommended that the uterus be emptied immediately whenever the first sign of polyneuritis appeared in any case of pernicious vomiting (16, 17, 20). The fact that in some instances the paralysis continues to progress even after an abortion has been done seems to discredit this recommendation. Recently it has been advised that the idea of interrupting the pregnancy be abandoned and that measures be taken to supply that food which will meet the dietary deficiency (18, 19). Vitamins B_1 and B_2, accordingly, should be given. It is recommended that 10–50 times the daily requirements of vitamin B_1 be given by adding 18 mg. of Vegex to the diet and administering 10 mg. of crystalline vitamin B_1 (21, 22, 23). If no improvement follows their use, liver extracts by mouth and by injection should be tried. When persistent vomiting interferes with the feeding regimen advised, the essential vitamins may be given through a duodenal tube.

REFERENCES

1. GREGORY, M. S.: Mental Disease Associated with Childbearing. Am. J. Obs. & Gyn., 1924, 8, 420.
2. SINGER, H. D.: Mental Disease and the Induction of Abortion. J. A. M. A., 1928, 91, 2042.
3. ROBINSON, A. L.: The Effect of Reproduction upon Insanity. J. Obs. & Gyn., Brit. Emp., 1933, 40, 39.
4. ROQUES, F.: Epidemic Encephalitis in Association with Pregnancy, Labour and the Puerperium—a Review and Report of Twenty-one Cases. J. Obs. & Gyn., Brit. Emp., 1928, 35, 1.
5. BLAND, P. B. AND GOLDSTEIN, L.: Pregnancy and Parkinsonism. J. A. M. A., 1930, 95, 473.
6. WILSON, P. AND PREECE, A. A.: Chorea Gravidarum, a Statistical Study of 951 Collected Cases, 846 from the literature and 105 previously unreported. Arch. Int. Med., 1932, 49, 471 & 671.
7. VIGNES, H.: La chorée des femmes enceintes. Rev. gén. de clin. et de thérap., 1929, 43, No. 49, 801.
8. GAUJOUX, E. AND BOISSIER, A.: A propos d'un cas de méningite tuberculeuse durant la grossesse. Rev. franc. de gynéc. et d'obst., 1931, 26, 591.
9. MILLER, N. F.: Anterior Poliomyelitis Complicating Pregnancy. J. Mich. S. M. S., 1924, 23, 58.
10. McGOOGAN, L. S.: Acute Anterior Poliomyelitis Complicating Pregnancy. Am. J. Obs. & Gyn., 1932, 24, 215.
11. BRAHDY, M. B. AND LENARSKY, M.: Acute Epidemic Poliomyelitis Complicating Pregnancy. J. A. M. A., 1933, 101, 195.
12. HAMILL, R. H.: A Case of Myelitis Following Labor; Death; Autopsy. Am. J. Obs., 1895, 32, 106.
12a. SPITZER, W.: Arch. f. gyn., 1932–33, 152, 517.
13. GUEISSAZ, E.: Un cas de myélite gravidque. Gynéc. et Obst., 1925, 11, 446.
14. ALPERS, B. J. AND PALMER, H. D.: The Cerebral and Spinal Complications Occurring During Pregnancy and Puerperium; critical review with illustrative cases. J. Nerv. & Ment. Dis., 1929, 70, 606.
14a. NEEDLES, W. AND DAVISON, C.: Diseases of the Spinal Cord in Pregnancy. Am. J. Obs. & Gyn., 1938, 35, 52.
15. WHITFIELD, D. W.: Peripheral Neuritis Due to the Vomiting of Pregnancy. Lancet, 1889, 1, 627.
16. BERKWITZ, N. J. AND LUFKIN, N. H.: Toxic Neuronitis of Pregnancy: A Clinicopathological Report. Surg., Gyn. & Obs., 1932, 54, 743.
17. WILSON, K. M. AND GARVEY, P.: Polyneuritis Gravidarum a "Presumable" Toxemia of Pregnancy. Am. J. Obs. & Gyn., 1932, 23, 775.
18. STRAUSS, M. B. AND McDONALD, W. J.: Polyneuritis of Pregnancy. A Dietary Deficiency Disorder. J. A. M. A., 1933, 100, 1320.
19. LUIKART, R.: Avitaminosis as a Likely Etiologic Factor in Polyneuronitis Complicating Pregnancy, with the Report of a Case. Am. J. Obs. & Gyn., 1933, 25, 810.
20. BURNETT, S. G.: Toxic Palsies Complicating Pregnancy. Med. Herald, 1916, 35, 1.
21. STÄHLER, F. B.: Hypovitaminosen in der Schwangerschaft. Münch. med. Wchnschr., 1937, 38, 327.
22. VAN DER HOEVEN, P. A.: Polyneuritis of Pregnancy and Korsakoff's Psychosis. Nederl. Tijdschr. v. geneesk, 1938, 82, 873.
23. GOODHART, R. AND JOLLIFF, N.: Effects of Vitamin B, Therapy on Polyneuritis of Alcoholic Addicts. J. A. M. A., 1938, 110, 414.

INFECTIOUS DISEASES

SMALLPOX is one of the worst complications that may occur during pregnancy.   Death of the mother and child is invariable in the hemorrhagic type and frequently occurs when the lesions are confluent.   In the discrete variety, on the other hand, the prognosis is not so grave.   The possibility of spontaneous interruption of pregnancy likewise varies with the severity of the disease.   It is inevitable in hemorrhagic smallpox and not infrequent in the confluent variety, but seldom occurs after the third month in discrete cases.   Up to the third month abortion is the rule even when the disease is mild (1).

Transmission of smallpox to the child is common and infants have been born with eruptions or the scars of such lesions.   A child born in the course of the disease, however, may not be infected but apparently has a temporary immunity, since such children do not contract smallpox when they are placed on the breast. Vaccination of these children likewise does not take at first but later is successful. Women who are vaccinated during pregnancy do not transmit their immunity to the child (2).

Infection and hemorrhage are the chief dangers that accompany abortion and labor.   Vaginal examinations, therefore, should be restricted and preparations for the control of hemorrhage should be made at the onset of labor.

MEASLES very rarely is observed during pregnancy.   When it does occur, the high temperature which is characteristic of the disease in adults often leads to abortion and premature labor.   This tendency toward the interruption of pregnancy is responsible for the loss of over half of the fetuses (3) and, because of secondary infection, the risk of pneumonia and postabortal or postpartum infection is greatly increased.   Congenital anomalies, particularly eye defects may occur when rubella complicates pregnancy in the early months (3a).

SCARLET FEVER seldom is encountered as a complication of pregnancy.   In the early months the patient may abort; otherwise the course is similar to that usually observed and the child shows no evidence of the disease at birth.   At the time of labor and during the puerperium, it is much more serious, because streptococci may then gain entrance to the puerperal wounds in the genital tract.   In the treatment of the severe cases, convalescent serum is recommended. When the latter is given, however, the possibility of a serum reaction must be considered.   Transfusion from a scarlet fever patient is advisable whenever a suitable donor is available.

DIPHTHERIA, when properly treated, does not have an unfavorable effect on pregnancy.   In the event of abortion, or spontaneous labor, the added strain upon an embarrassed circulation may prove troublesome.   In addition, the presence of the diphtheritic and secondary infections greatly increases the risk of puerperal infection. The throat condition, therefore, should be eliminated as soon as possible by the use of antitoxin and every precaution should be taken to guard against contamination of the genital passages. Vaginal examinations and instrumentation, accordingly, are to be avoided. Unfortunately, however, the cardiac condition sometimes is such that artificial delivery is imperative.

TYPHOID FEVER. Pregnancy occasionally is complicated by typhoid fever. If abortion or premature labor does not occur, the course of the disease is not altered. Children born to mothers who recover from typhoid in the early part of their pregnancy are normal. If, on the other hand, the complication occurs in the last trimester, the child usually is underdeveloped. Unfortunately, interruption of pregnancy frequently takes place. This may be due to the hyper-pyrexia or it may result from the effect of the infection on the fetus itself, since a number of instances are recorded in which the bacilli were recovered from the child at birth (4, 5, 6). When the pregnancy is terminated in the course of the disease, great care must be taken to prevent puerperal infection. Careful attention to the usual aseptic details is necessary and vaginal examinations, accordingly, should be limited.

MALARIA. The effect of malaria on pregnancy depends upon the severity of the disease and the adequacy of its treatment. The more virulent forms frequently cause abortion, premature labor and fetal death. Only rarely, however, is the organism transmitted to the fetus (7, 8, 9). Less severe cases, particularly when they are well treated, go to term without serious complications. Old infections have a tendency to relapse in the latter part of pregnancy and during the puerperium (10). While the disease seldom is transmitted to the fetus, children born to mothers suffering from malaria often are underdeveloped and not infrequently die during the neonatal period.

Quinine in therapeutic doses prevents rather than causes abortion (11). Its administration, therefore, is doubly indicated during pregnancy. Since the oxytocic effect of quinine is dependent upon the concentration of the drug in the blood, it should not be given intravenously and massive doses are contraindicated. Two to five grs. are recommended every two to four hours instead of the larger doses usually given at less frequent intervals. In malarial districts and whenever a latent infection is suspected, the prophylactic use of quinine in the latter part of pregnancy and immediately after labor may prevent a relapse. Some of the synthetic preparations are thought to be as efficacious as quinine and are said to be without toxic effect. They therefore might well be used during pregnancy (12).

SYPHILIS is one of the commonest causes of fetal death in the latter half of pregnancy and is encountered in about 6% of clinic and 1% of private obstetrical cases (13, 14, 15, 16, 17).

Effect of syphilis on the mother. As in the non-pregnant woman, the response of the maternal organism to infection usually is mild. Primary lesions are rarely observed. This may be due to their concealed location or they may be suppressed by some factor in pregnancy which apparently has a beneficial effect on maternal lues. When they do occur, they may be multiple and often are small and atypical. Occasionally, however, the opposite is true particularly if the infection occurs after the early months of pregnancy. Because of the increased congestion of the parts, the chancres at this time may be larger, more indurated and may last much longer than usual. They sometimes persist for several months and occasionally remain after secondaries appear. Secondary manifestations usually are also mild and the rash may be so slight as to pass unnoticed. Frequently the syphilitic roseala, if present at all, disappears within a surprisingly short time. Because of the increased blood supply, the local secondary lesions which may appear upon the vulva—condylomata lata—also are larger, more numerous and tend to become ulcerated. Occasionally they resemble carcinomata and the diagnosis of the true condition is not revealed, unless blood for a Wassermann is taken or a biopsy is done. Secondary infection not infrequently occurs, with the result that the discharge from these lesions becomes very irritating. In the majority of instances, however, the disease is latent and its symptoms are so mild that, unless routine serological studies are made, about 75% of syphilitic pregnant women are unaware of the infection until a miscarriage, a premature stillbirth or the birth of a living syphilitic infant directs attention to this complication. This altered response to infection during pregnancy has also been observed in laboratory animals. Although non-pregnant rabbits may be easily inoculated with the treponema pallidum, such inoculations during pregnancy often are unsuccessful and, when infection does result, it frequently is mild and atypical (18).

The mildness or absence of symptoms during pregnancy, together with the results of laboratory experiments on animals, seems to indicate that during pregnancy there exists some protecting factor which may inhibit or suppress the action of the organisms of syphilis (19, 20). Should this be so, it may help to explain the lower incidence of cardiovascular and neurosyphilis in the female sex, and particularly in those who have been pregnant since infection (21, 22, 23, 24, 25, 26, 27). In this connection also may be mentioned the observation that women with latent syphilis sometimes respond better to treatment when they are pregnant (28).

The effect of syphilis on the fetus. The response of the products of conception to infection is as severe as that of the maternal organism is mild. Protected as it is in the early months, the fetus continues to develop normally until about the middle of pregnancy, when it apparently is overwhelmed by the invading hordes of spirochetes which then pass through the altered placental barrier. Unless the organisms have been attenuated by long contact with the mother's protecting mechanism, this general invasion of the helpless fetus soon leads to its destruction. In women who have been recently infected, death and expulsion of the fetus is commonly noted in the 5th and 6th months. More latent cases carry their pregnancies longer but ultimately terminate in premature and full-term stillbirths or in the birth of living syphilitic infants. Each succeeding pregnancy, therefore, tends to continue longer than its immediate predecessor until a living luetic child is born. Although subsequent gestations may go to term and the infants may live, in the majority of instances they ultimately show the usual manifestations of lues.

The frequent occurrence of late abortion due to syphilis has led to the erroneous impression that recurring abortions at any period are due to this disease. Statistical studies of early abortions in syphilitic and non-syphilitic women show the incidence of pregnancy interruptions in the first trimester to be about equal in both groups. Likewise, examination of the products of conception expelled at early abortions, fails to reveal evidence of syphilis and those who have demonstrated spirochetes in fetal tissue have not been able to find the organism during the early months (29). While early abortion may occur in a syphilitic mother just as in any other woman, it therefore is a mistake to regard such early interruptions of pregnancy as due to syphilis. This early fetal protection against invasion by the mother's spirochetes may, in the very early weeks of pregnancy, be due to the same factor which enables the ovum to become imbedded in the decidua. In other words, the erosive action of the trophoblast may also have a spirocheticidal effect (20). Later, when this action of the chorionic elements is diminished or lost, the well-defined and active syncytium and Langhans cells, which cover the villi, may serve as an efficient barrier to the invasion of the organisms of syphilis. After the middle of pregnancy, on the other hand, the Langhans cells are less and less in evidence and, as the gestation progresses, they finally disappear, leaving only the thin and senile syncytium as a protecting cover (20). It therefore is not surprising that fetal infection is common after the 5th month. In a series of 75 stillbirths, in which the treponema pallidum was demonstrated, the smallest fetus weighed 100 gm., the average weight at the end of the 4th month and only three were in the 5th month (Table I).

TABLE I

WEIGHTS AND AGES AT WHICH SPIROCHETES WERE RECOVERED FROM 75 DEAD SYPHILITIC FETUSES
(McCord)

NUMBER OF FETUSES	GRAMS	WEEKS
5	100–500	16–24
6	500–1000	24–28
13	1000–1500	28–32
19	1500–2000	32–34
23	2000–2500	34–36
8	2500–3000	36–40
1	3000–3500	40

When the barrier against invasion is thus removed, in the latter half of pregnancy, the organisms may enter the fetal circulation directly or they may pass through the umbilical vein wall from the placental lymph channels, since spirochetes frequently can be demonstrated in the wall of the umbilical vein. Regardless of the method of transmission, they soon pass to most of the fetal organs and have been recovered from the brain, heart, lungs, liver, kidneys, ovaries and adrenals.

Diagnosis of syphilis in the mother. As has been stated, primary lesions may be suppressed. When they do occur, they frequently are concealed. Very few women, accordingly, give a history of a chancre. Secondary manifestations also are often overlooked. The previous pregnancy history, on the other hand, is very important in the diagnosis of maternal lues and every stillbirth or abortion after the middle of pregnancy should be regarded with suspicion. Reliance upon the history alone will, in the majority of cases, result in a failure of diagnosis until the fetus is destroyed. Because the usual evidences are mild or masked in most women and because the disease tends to be latent during pregnancy, the practical way to recognize syphilis in pregnancy is by the routine use of the serological tests. If these tests are not employed as a routine, the majority of cases will go unsuspected until a late abortion, premature stillbirth or the birth of a living syphilitic infant demonstrates the tragic consequence of this neglect.

The unfortunate emphasis placed upon the so-called false positive reaction of pregnancy by some eminent obstetricians has done great and unjustifiable harm. Careful investigation of all strongly positive Wassermann cases, with apparently negative histories, sooner or later reveals sufficient clinical evidence to support the diagnosis of syphilis. If the reaction is positive, the test should be repeated and, in the event that a second strongly positive result is obtained, immediate, thorough and continued treatment is indicated. A false negative reaction unfortunately occurs in about 10% of all syphilitic gestations. This misleading finding may cause a false sense of security unless a careful search is made for other evidences of lues in all late interruptions of pregnancy. In such a search, the husband and other members of the family should be included. The placenta, the umbilical cord and the fetus should also be examined microscopically for organisms and the characteristic changes of syphilis. In these and other doubtful cases, a provocative injection of arsphenamine may lead to a positive reaction four or eight days later.

Diagnosis of syphilis in the infant at birth. Whether to treat or not to treat the newborn infant of the syphilitic mother is a most perplexing problem, the solution of which may be aided by the following procedures:

1. The cord Wassermann.
2. Examination of the placenta.
3. Dark field examination of umbilical cord scrapings.

4. Roentgen examination of the long bones.
5. Repeated Wassermann tests after the first month.
6. Repeated and frequent search for the customary lesions of congenital lues.

Cord Wassermann. Blood for a Wassermann test should be taken from the mother and from the umbilical cord at the time of delivery in order that the strength of the reaction of each may be compared; otherwise, the cord Wassermann is unreliable and does not justify the bother and expense of its performance. Since the reagin from the mother's blood may pass through the placental filter, a non-infected child may have a strongly positive reaction at the time of birth. In a large series of cases, 17.6% of the newborn infants with positive cord Wassermanns were not syphilitic (30). It likewise is possible that the cord Wassermann may be negative and the child have syphilis as was observed in 13.7% of the negative cord Wassermann cases in the same series. If, on the other hand, the maternal and fetal bloods are compared and the fetal blood Wassermann is repeated in all positive cases, the serological reactions will give a very good indication of the presence or absence of syphilis in the child.

Examination of the placenta. There is a marked lack of agreement among different pathologists as to the criteria necessary for a positive diagnosis of placental syphilis and extensive work with this procedure has failed to establish its value. In 20% of the cases in which the placenta was reported as normal, the Johns Hopkins clinic found the child to be luetic and 12.1% of the placentas diagnosed as syphilitic were from cases which gave birth to non-infected children (30). Another investigator (31), in a series of 1085 cases in which the Wassermann was strongly positive, was able to make a definite diagnosis of placental syphilis in only 43 even though 427 of his patients had had no treatment and 386 had received less than 7 injections of arsphenamine. Among 679 instances in which the child was born alive, the placenta was positive in only 3 and doubtful in 23 others notwithstanding the fact that the mothers were poorly treated or had no treatment at all. A positive diagnosis of placental syphilis, accordingly, should be supported by additional evidence of lues before either the mother or the child is condemned to the rigid routine of antiluetic treatment.

Dark field examination of umbilical cord scrapings offers great promise in the diagnosis of congenital lues (32). As soon after birth as possible, the umbilical vein is opened throughout the entire length of the cord. After removing the blood, the vein wall is scraped with a clean scalpel at intervals of several inches. The material so obtained is then diluted with normal salt solution and examined for spirochetes. Should the organisms be found, a positive diagnosis is justifiable and the inauguration of vigorous antisyphilitic treatment is indicated. This procedure should be done within eight hours after birth, or, better still, immediately after the conclusion of the delivery.

Roentgen ray examination of the long bones often shows syphilitic osteo-chondritis (33 & 34). In this condition, the line of demarcation between the epiphysis and the diaphysis—Guérin's line—which normally is .5 to 1 mm. in width, is considerably enlarged and frequently reaches a thickness of 2 to 3 mm. In addition to a definite broadening of this area, it also has an irregular or jagged outline. Unfortunately, the intermediate stages may give rise to roentgen findings which are difficult to differentiate from other conditions. One of these is the possible deposition of the heavy metals used in the prenatal treatment. Another is the picture of a premature scurvy which might result from a prenatal vitamin C deficiency. If the x-ray findings are definite, a positive diagnosis on this evidence alone is justifiable and the immediate treatment of the infected child is indicated. Negative roentgenological findings, on the other hand, do not rule out the possibility of congenital syphilis.

The Wassermann reaction in the blood of the newborn child is similar to that of the cord blood. Its use within the first few days after birth, accordingly, is open to the criticism already mentioned. If, however, the cord blood is strongly positive, repeated Wassermann tests in the newborn child may help to show whether the reaction was due to syphilis or merely to a transfer of the reagin from the mother's blood. After the first month, serological studies on the child become increasingly valuable. In all negative cases, therefore, they should be repeated at monthly intervals until the child is three months old and every three months subsequently during the first two years of life.

Repeated search for the lesions of congenital lues should be made in all infants who are apparently free from syphilis. Such children during the first year also should be given the benefit of one or more examinations by a pediatrician who is familiar with the stigmata of this disease. Only in this way will the shocking examples of neglected syphilis be recognized and treated.

If the comparison of the blood from the umbilical cord with that of the mother at the time of birth indicates the presence of syphilis in the child, or if the dark field examination of umbilical cord scrapings shows spirochetes or if the roentgen examination of the long bones is definitely positive, a diagnosis of syphilis is justifiable and immediate treatment is indicated. In the absence of these positive findings, infants born to adequately treated mothers should not be condemned as syphilitic and subjected to the prolonged therapy of this disease. On the other hand, it is well to keep such children under observation for a number of years.

The criteria for a diagnosis of lues in the newborn infant of untreated and poorly treated syphilitic mothers, who have a strongly positive Wassermann at the time of delivery, need not be so rigid. These children should be placed on antisyphilitic treatment at once, regardless of the presence or absence of definite evidences of the disease.

Treatment. Because the fetus is fairly well protected against invasion during the first half of pregnancy, vigorous prophylactic treatment is given in the early months with a view to preventing syphilis in the fetus by eradicating the mother's spirochetes before the placental barrier loses its effectiveness. Likewise, treatment is continued in the second half for the purpose of curing any possible fetal involvement that may result from inadequate early therapy or from a lighting-up of the mother's infection. Adequate treatment, therefore, implies thorough treatment begun in the early months and continued throughout the remainder of pregnancy.

Arsphenamine or neoarsphenamine and bismuth are employed as in ordinary syphilis and at least 15 injections of each drug at weekly intervals are necessary to insure a good result. When a total of 4 to 5 gm. of arsphenamine or the equivalent amount of neoarsphenamine are used in this manner, 90% of the children should be born alive and free from syphilis. If the mother's syphilis is longstanding, the chance of a good result is increased. This is especially true when the disease has been fairly well treated before conception or when the Wassermann reaction becomes negative during pregnancy. On the other hand, the possible development of congenital lues must not be overlooked in women whose Wassermann is negative at the time of conception. Every woman who has had syphilis, accordingly, should be treated throughout every pregnancy, irrespective of her former treatment and serological findings, even though her previous children are not syphilitic.

Although it is desirable to begin treatment in the first trimester and continue it throughout pregnancy, vigorous treatment in the last month often is surprisingly efficacious. If the patient first appears at this time, neoarsphenamine should be given twice a week or arsphenamine weekly until the child is delivered. The use of only 4 or 5 injections of these drugs is of inestimable value in that it makes easier the neonatal control of congenital lues and occasionally results in the birth of a non-syphilitic infant.

Since pregnant women tolerate these drugs almost as well as non-pregnant syphilitics, the dangers of their use during pregnancy have been overestimated. Occasional severe reactions and very rarely death from hemorrhagic encephalitis may occur when the treatments are given by one who is ignorant of possible obstetrical complications and lacks a knowledge of the action of arsphenamine (34a). The treatment, accordingly, is begun with half the usual dose and is gradually increased to the amount customarily used—.6 gm. of arsphenamine or .9 gm. of neoarsphenamine. If the blood pressure is taken, the urine is examined and a knowledge of the patient's reaction to previous injections is obtained, a competent physician should not hesitate to give the unborn syphilitic fetus the advantage of this prenatal treatment (35, 36, 37, 38, 39).

Penicillin apparently is a safe and effective therapeutic agent for the treatment of syphilis during pregnancy. If subsequent reports concerning its use are as favorable as those which have appeared, all other methods of treatment of syphilis during pregnancy will probably be abandoned in its favor.

A total of 2.4 million Oxford units are injected intramuscularly over a period of 7 to 9 days. On the first day, 10,000 units are given every 3 hours. The dose is doubled on the 2nd day and 40,000 units are administered thereafter at 3 hour intervals until a total of 2.4 million units is reached.

The patient is kept under close observation throughout the remainder of her pregnancy, and quantitatively titered serological tests are made monthly. If no diminution in the reagin titer is observed after 3 months, or if the reagin titer increases at any time, or if clinical evidence of syphilis reappears, a similar course of penicillin should be given. Should it be impossible to obtain satisfactory quantitative serological tests it may be well to repeat the penicillin therapy at some time during the latter part of pregnancy.

Serological response to treatment with penicillin varies with the duration of the disease before treatment is instituted. In early syphilis the response is more rapid than in latent cases. In all favorable cases however, the quantitatively titered serological tests should show a diminishing titer within 3 months and sustained negative reactions should be observed after 6 months. Because of the persistence of the syphilis reagin which passes through the placenta, many non-syphilitic infants show positive Wassermann reactions at birth. In such cases the titer gradually diminishes and by the end of one month the reaction usually is negative. It may however persist for another 30 days. When it is positive, quantitatively titered serological tests should be continued and roentgenograms of the long bones should be taken in order that congenital syphilis may be diagnosed and treated early.

The end results reported to date show that penicillin is superior to any other therapy for the prevention of congenital syphilis. When syphilis complicating pregnancy is satisfactorily treated by this method over 95% of the infants should be born free from syphilis. Because of its greater effectiveness and because of its freedom from the risk to the mother which accompanies the use of the arsenicals, penicillin should replace the arsenicals in the treatment of syphilis during pregnancy (39a, 39b, 39c).

GONORRHEA. Since 80 to 95 per cent of the men in large cities have gonorrhea at some time in their lives (40), the transmission of the disease to their wives is not uncommon and its association with pregnancy is noted in from 1 to 5 per cent of obstetric cases. The influence of this complication on gestation depends upon whether the patient is infected before, during or after conception.

Before conception. Should the gonorrheic woman escape the sterility which so commonly follows this disease, the latent infection in her cervix may become aggravated and produce a troublesome discharge when she becomes pregnant. The tendency toward a recurrence of a Skenitis or a Bartholinitis is not so great but occasionally is observed. In addition to these exacerbations of an inactive infection, pregnancy may be influenced by the sequelae of a cured gonorrhea. Adhesions of the folds of the endosalpinx have already been mentioned in the etiology of ectopic gestation and the peritoneal adhesions which remain after a gonorrheal peritonitis may be the cause of pelvic and abdominal pain during pregnancy. In this connection, however, it may be said that laparotomy during pregnancy and at the time of cesarean section often reveals many adhesions which never caused symptoms.

During conception. If the infection occurs within a short time of impregnation, the course of the disease is similar to that observed in nonpregnant women. Should it advance beyond the internal os, and cause an endometritis before or shortly after the fertilized ovum reaches the uterine cavity, abortion results and the risk of salpingitis is greatly increased.

After conception. Gonorrheal infections that occur after the first month of pregnancy usually are limited to the structures situated below the internal os until abortion or labor terminates the gestation and permits extension of the gonorrhea to the endometrium, endosalpinx and pelvic peritoneum. The plug of mucus in the cervix and internal os is an efficient barrier against the upward invasion of the gonococcus, unless nature's mechanism of defense is broken down by injudicious therapeutic measures. Because of the effect of pregnancy on the tissues of the pelvis, infection at this time differs from that observed in the nonpregnant woman in that the vulva and vagina may be involved, in addition to the usual sites—the urethra, Bartholin's glands and the cervix.

VULVITIS, which seldom occurs in adult gonorrheal infections, is not uncommon during pregnancy and the inflammatory reaction may be so severe that rest in bed is required until it subsides.

URETHRITIS is not unlike that ordinarily observed and usually clears up within a short time. Latent infection in Skene's tubules is common.

BARTHOLINITIS. Involvement of Bartholin's glands is not infrequent and follows the usual course. During labor, the abscess may rupture and increase the risk of disseminating the infection.

VAGINITIS. During pregnancy the vaginal mucous membrane not infrequently participates in the gonorrheal inflammation and, as a result, is thickened, red, and has a granular appearance. It is bathed in a profuse, purulent discharge which is foul and irritating to those parts of the vulva with which it comes into contact.

ENDOCERVICITIS always is present and gives rise to a profuse, purulent discharge which, no doubt, is partly responsible for the severity and persistence of the vaginal mucous membrane changes.

ENDOMETRITIS does not occur unless the infection is present early in the gestation. Postabortal and postpartum involvement of the endometrium is common after the termination of pregnancy.

SALPINGITIS is extremely rare. It may be due to a preëxisting infection or one that occurs at or near the time of conception. The condition naturally is unilateral and usually is due to an exacerbation of a subacute unilateral salpingitis that was present before the onset of pregnancy. If pus forms, the prognosis is bad and death occurs in most cases unless the diagnosis is made early and surgical treatment is instituted (41).

TREATMENT. Since the sulfa drugs are not contraindicated during pregnancy they should prove to be very valuable in the treatment of gonorrhoea complicating pregnancy. The disease is self limiting and its cure ordinarily is effected by the development of tissue resistance and encapsulation of the organism. Whatever is done, therefore, in the way of treatment, must not interfere with nature's curative efforts and above all must not break down the barrier in the cervical canal which prevents extension above the internal os. All therapeutic measures, accordingly, should be gently applied and the use of irritating drugs is contraindicated. Since the gonococcus is readily killed by the milder antiseptics, any benefit that is to be derived from a direct attack on the organism may be secured by the use of the weaker chemicals. In the acute stage, the patient is put to bed and given a bland diet. Fluids are forced and the urethritis is combated by the use of urinary antiseptics. Local cleanliness is essential and, if vulvitis is present, warm applications and occasional irrigations with a warm, mildly antiseptic solution may be beneficial. Bartholinitis is treated in a similar manner. Should suppuration occur, incision and drainage are indicated. Immediately after opening the abscess, the skin adjacent to the incision is protected by vaselin and the cavity is gently packed with gauze saturated with pure carbolic acid. After several minutes, the latter is removed and a loose packing of iodoform gauze is introduced. During pregnancy, this is a more satisfactory method than excision of the gland (42). Vaginitis, unless it is severe, does not require treatment. If severe, the parts are exposed at weekly intervals and painted with 20 per cent argyrol. Daily instillations of the same drug may also be used. Several ounces of a 10 per cent solution are drawn up into a soft rubber ear syringe and then gently forced into the vagina, after which the silver solution is retained by holding the labia together for ten minutes. Insufflations of a dusting powder, made up of equal parts of Fuller's earth and boric acid, also are beneficial (43). Following the use of these drugs, a tampon is inserted and retained for forty-eight hours. The treatment of cervicitis is the greatest problem, since it is here that strenuous measures do more harm than good. It usually is considered better to avoid treatment in this region, as attempts to introduce drugs into the cervical canal may cause an abortion and thereby spread the infection which is buried in the inaccessible cervical glands. Topical applications of 25 per cent argyrol are permissible but the use of the cautery during pregnancy is to be questioned. The latter measure, however, has been used by some men without deleterious effect at this time (44). The treatment of postabortal and postpartum infection is similar to that discussed in the Chapter on Puerperal Infection.

TRICHOMONAS VAGINITIS. During pregnancy, vaginitis associated with the parasitic protozoon **Trichomonas vaginalis** is often very troublesome. The patient has an annoying vaginal discharge and complains of an irritation or itching of the vulva and vagina. Examination through a speculum shows a peculiar type of inflammation that is most marked in the posterior fornix and on the posterior lip of the cervix. The mucous membrane is red and granular in appearance and is bathed with a profuse, **frothy,** white or yellowish discharge. When this secretion is sponged off from the inflamed surfaces, minute hemorrhagic areas often are exposed. Hanging drop preparations made from fresh material reveal spindle shaped, mobile organisms somewhat larger than leukocytes. That vaginitis of this type is followed by increased morbidity in the puerperium has not been agreed upon by all observers (45, 46).

Many drugs have been recommended in the treatment of trichomonas vaginitis. After carefully cleansing and drying the mucous membrane, it is swabbed with any one of the following preparations: 1–1000 hexylresorcinol, 5 per cent mercurochrome, 1 per cent aqueous gentian violet, dilute Lugol's solution or 1 per cent aqueous picric acid. A boroglyceride tampon, 10 per cent, is then introduced and kept in the vagina for twenty-four hours (45, 46, 47, 48, 49). Following the removal of the tampon, a douche of 1–5000 bichloride of mercury is to be taken. The foregoing treatments should be given every three days and should be supplemented by daily bichloride douches. If it is inconvenient for the patient to follow this routine, the condition may be controlled by the insertion of a 1 per cent picric acid suppository at night and the taking of a lactic acid douche on the following morning (50). This should be repeated for five successive days.

MONILIA VULVOVAGINITIS. Vaginitis during pregnancy may be associated with the growth of organisms of the Monilia group (51). Microscopic examination of fresh and stained material obtained from such cases shows mycelial threads and budding elements, both of which are gram-positive. The lower part of the vagina is intensely reddened and, at times, thrushlike, whitish patches may be observed. A thin, acid discharge, containing white flakes, is characteristic. Burning or smarting on urination and itching of the vulva are common complaints. Spontaneous relief follows the birth of the child. At the time of delivery, the child may become infected and, as a result, may subsequently develop oral thrush. Gentian violet, 1 per cent aqueous solution, seems to be specific and several daily applications of this dye give prompt relief. Alkaline douches likewise are beneficial.

REFERENCES

1. GUÉIREL: Variole et grossesse. Ann. de gynéc. et d'obst., Paris, 1907, 4, 137.
2. URNER, J. A.: Some Observations in the Vaccination of Pregnant Women and Newborn Infants. Am. J. Obs. & Gyn., 1927, 13, 70.
3. KLOTZ, H.: Beiträge zur Pathologie der Schwangerschaft. Arch. f. Gyn., 1887, 29, 448.
3a. ALBAUGH, C. H.: Congenital Anomalies Following Maternal Rubella in Early Weeks of Pregnancy. J. A. M. A., 1945, 129, 719.

4. Lynch, F. W.: Placental Transmission, with Report of a Case During Typhoid Fever. Johns Hopkins Hosp. Rep., 1902, 10, 283.
5. Hicks, H. T. and French, H.: Typhoid Fever and Pregnancy with Special Reference to Foetal Infection. Lancet, 1905, 1, 1491.
6. Wing, E. S. and Troppoli, D. V.: The Intra-uterine Transmission of Typhoid. J. A. M. A., 1930, 95, 405.
7. Buckingham, E. W.: Transplacental Malarial Infection. China Med. J., 1925, 39, 1140.
8. Blacklock, D. B. and Gordon, R. M.: Malaria Infection as it Occurs in Late Pregnancy; Its Relation to Labor and Early Infancy. Ann. Trop. Med. & Parasit., 1925, 19, 327.
9. Wislocki, G. B.: Observations on the Placenta from a Case of Malaria. Johns Hopkins Hosp. Bull., 1930, 47, 157.
10. Clark, H. C.: The Diagnostic Value of the Placental Blood Film in Aestivo-autumnal Malaria. J. Exp. Med., 1915, 22, 427.
11. Taboloff, V. S.: Can Quinine be Used During Pregnancy? Vrach. Gaz., 1931, 35, 1763.
12. Green, R.: A Report of Fifty Cases of Malaria Treated with Atebrin, a New Synthetic Drug. Lancet, 1932, 1, 826.
13. Williams, J. W.: The Value of the Wassermann Reaction in Obstetrics, Based upon the Study of 4547 Consecutive Cases. Johns Hopkins Hosp. Bull., 1920, 31, 335.
14. Beck, A. C.: A Preliminary Report on the Treatment of Syphilis Complicating Pregnancy. Am. J. Obs. & Gyn., 1921, 2, 416.
15. King, E. L.: Syphilis and Pregnancy. New Orleans M. & S. J., 1924, 76, 526.
16. McCord, J. R.: Syphilis of the Placenta in the Negro. A Study Based on 1000 Consecutive Cases. Am. J. Obs. & Gyn., 1926, 11, 850.
17. Spiegler, R.: Lues und Schwangerschaft Erwiderung. Monatschr. f. Geburtsh. u. Gyn., 1932, 91, 340.
18. Brown, W. H. and Pearce, L.: On the Reaction of Pregnant and Lactating Females to Inoculation with Treponema Pallidum. Am. J. Syph., 1920, 4, 493.
19. Kemp, J. and Shaw, C.: Effect of Administration of Theelin Upon Course of Experimental Rabbit Syphilis. Am. J. Syph., Gonor. and Ven. Dis., 1938, 22, 9.
    Also: Effects of Placental Extract on Course of Experimental Rabbit Syphilis. Ibid., 1938, 22, 368–380.
20. Beck, A. C. and Daily, W. T.: Syphilis in Pregnancy. A. A. A. S. Publication No. 6, 1938.
21. White and Jones: Quoted by White, P. D.: Heart Disease, N. Y., 1937, p. 272.
22. Clawson, B. J. and Bell, E. T.: The Heart in Syphilitic Aortitis. Arch. of Path., 1927, 4, 922.
23. Moore, J. E., Danglade, J. H. and Resisinger, J. C.: Diagnosis of Syphilitic Aortitis Uncomplicated by Aortic Regurgitation or Aneurism. Arch. Int. Med., 1932, 49, 753.
    Treatment of Cardiovascular Syphilis. Arch. Int. Med., 1932, 49, 879.
24. Moore, J. E.: Studies in Asympotomatic Neurosyphilis III. The Apparent Influence of Pregnancy on the Incidence of Neurosyphilis in Women. Arch. Int. Med., 1922, 30, 584.
25. Gärtner, W.: Ueber die Häufigkeit der progressiven Paralyse bei kultivierten und unkultivierten Völkern. Eine statistische, biologische und Immunitätsuntersuchung über die Syphilis. Zeitschr. f. Hyg. u. Infekionskr., 1921, 92, 341.
26. Turner, T. B.: Race and Sex Distribution of the Lesions of Syphilis in 10,000 Cases. Bull. Johns Hopkins Hosp., 1930, 46, 159.
27. Solomon, H. C.: Pregnancies as a Factor in the Prevention of Neurosyphilis. Am. J. Syph., 1926, 10, 96.
28. Cole, H. N., Usilton, L. J., Moore, J. E., O'Leary, P. A., Stokes, J. H., Wile, U. J., Parran, T. and Vonderlehr, R. A.: Cooperative Clinical Studies in the Treatment of Syphilis: Syphilis in Pregnancy. J. A. M. A., 1936, 106, 464.
29. McCord, J. R.: A Study of 200 Autopsies Made on Syphilitic Fetuses. Am. J. Obs. & Gyn., 1929, 18, 597.

30. McKelvey, J. L. and Turner, T. B.: Pregnancy and Syphilis: An Analysis of the Outcome of Pregnancy in Relation to Treatment in 943 Cases. J. A. M. A., 1934, 102, 503.

31. McCord, J. R.: Syphilis of the Placenta: The Histological Examination of 1085 Placentas of Mothers With Strongly Positive Blood Wassermann Reactions. Am. J. Obs. & Gyn., 1934, 28, 743.

32. Ingraham, N. F.: Congenital Syphilis: Diagnosis by Dark Field Examination of Scrapings From the Umbilical Cord. J. A. M. A., 1935, 105, 560.

33. Shipley, P. G., Pearson, J. W., Weech, A. A. and Greene, C. H.: X-ray Pictures of the Bones in the Diagnosis of Syphilis in the Fetus and in Young Infants. Johns Hopkins Hosp. Bull., 1921, 32, 75.

34. McLean, S.: The Osseous Lesions of Congenital Syphilis: Summary and Conclusions in 102 Cases. Am. J. Diseases of Child., 1931, 41, 1411.

34a. Plass, E. D. and Sacks, M.: Syphilis in Pregnancy. Am. J. O. & G., 1942, 43, 484.

35. Beck, A. C.: The Management of Syphilis Complicating Pregnancy. N. Y. State J. Med., 1926, 26, 102.

35a. Beck, A. C. and Daily, W. T.: Syphilis in Pregnancy. Pub. No. 6, Am. Assn. Adv. Science.

36. Bartholomew, R. A.: Syphilis as a Complication of Pregnancy in the Negro. Analysis of Three Hundred Cases. Results of Antisyphilitic Treatment; Dark Field Examination as an Aid in Diagnosis of Fetal Syphilis at Necropsy. J. A. M. A., 1924, 83, 172.

37. Reinberger, J. R. and Toombs, P. W.: End-results of 10 years' Study of Treatment of Pregnancy Syphilis in Trimesters. South. M. J., 1933, 26, 532.

38. Gammeltoft, S. A.: Ueber einen Fall von Encephalitis hämorrhagica nach Salvarsanbehandlung während der Schwangerschaft. Acta. Obs. et Gynec. Scand., 1930, 9, 167.

39. McCord, J. R.: Two Hundred and Forty-three Fetal Autopsies. A Syphilitic Study. J. A. M. A., 1927, 88, 626.

39a. Ingraham, N. R., Stokes, J. H., Bierman, H. and Lentz, J. W.: Penicillin Treatment of the Syphilitic Pregnant Woman. J. A. M. A., 1946, 130, 683.

39b. Goodwin, M. S. and Moore, J. E.: Penicillin in Prevention of Prenatal Syphilis. J. A. M. A., 1946, 130, 688.

39c. Speiser, M. D. and Thomas, E. W.: Regarding the Unusual Effect of Penicillin Therapy upon the Uterus. J. Ven. Dis. Inform., 1946, 27, 20.

40. Pelouze, P. S.: Gonorrhea in the Male and Female. Philadelphia, 1931.

41. Heyer, E.: Adnexentzündung während der Schwangerschaft. Monatschr. f. Geburtsh Gyn., 1927, 76, 243.

42. Balard, P.: Conduite à tenir dans les collections suppurées de la vulve et du vagin pendant la grossesse et l'accouchement. Rev. Franc. de gynéc. et d'obst., 1926, 21, 465.

43. Schumann, E. A.: The Relation of Venereal Diseases to Childbirth. Am. J. Obs. & Gyn., 1924, 8, 257.

44. Brown, G. V.: Chronic Endocervicitis; its Sequelae and Treatment. South. M. J., 1931, 24, 122.

45. Cornell, E. L., Goodman, L. J. and Matthers, M. M.: The Culture Incidence and Treatment of Trichomonas Vaginalis. Am. J. Obs. & Gyn., 1931, 22, 360.

46. Bland, P. B., Wenrich, D. H. and Goldstein, L.: Trichomonas Vaginitis in Pregnancy. S. G. & O., 1931, 53, 759.

47. Greenhill, J. P.: Vaginal Discharge Due to Trichomonas Vaginalis. Am. J. Obs. & Gyn., 1928, 16, 870.

48. Davis, C. H. and Colwell, C.: Trichomonas Vaginalis, Donné, Preliminary Report on Experimental and Clinical Study. J. A. M. A., 1929, 92, 306.

49. Klugman, S. J.: Trichomonas Vaginalis Vaginitis. S. G. & O., 1930, 51, 552.

50. Goodall, J. R.: A Specific Treatment for Trichomonas Vaginitis. Lancet, 1933, 2, 648.

51. Plass, E. D., Hesseltine, H. C. and Borts, I H.: Monilia Vulvovaginitis. Am. J. Obs. & Gyn., 1931, 21, 320.

PELVIC NEOPLASMS

FIBROMYOMATA OF THE UTERUS, at times, are a source of real danger during pregnancy, labor and the puerperium. Small tumors are very common but have no clinical significance. Those which are large enough to become a potential menace are noted once in every one hundred and fifty admissions to maternity hospitals (1, 2, 3).

THE EFFECT OF PREGNANCY ON FIBROIDS. Under the stimulus of pregnancy, myomata often become greatly enlarged and show hypertrophy similar to that observed in the uterine wall. Most of the increase in the size of these tumors, however, is due to edema which, at times, becomes marked and

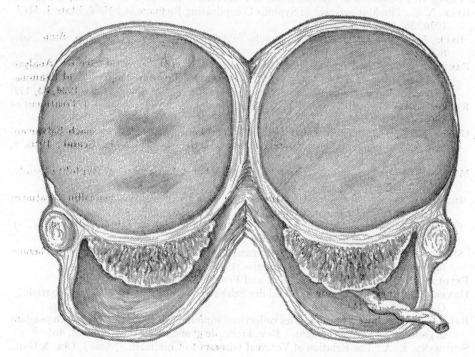

FIG. 746. Red degeneration of a fibroid in pregnancy. During the sixth month this patient had severe abdominal pain and tenderness with an elevated pulse, temperature and leukocyte count.

causes such softening that the usual fibroid consistency is lost. Alterations in the circulation occasionally lead to degenerative changes, and the so-called red degeneration is most commonly observed at this time. The latter condition usually occurs about the middle of gestation and in most cases is limited to the subserous growths. On cross-section, such degenerating tumors reveal areas of partial necrosis which, as a result of hemolysis, become beefy-red in appearance—hence the name, red degeneration. Clinically, this change in fibromyomata is characterized by severe pain, localized tenderness, a rise in the temperature, elevation of the pulse and a moderate leukocytosis (Fig. 746).

Because of the peritoneal symptoms, it may be confused with acute appendicitis, ruptured extrauterine pregnancy or a twisted ovarian cyst. Formerly, red degeneration always was an indication for surgical intervention. Experience, however, has shown that the symptoms usually disappear under expectant treatment, and laparotomy, accordingly, is seldom necessary (4, 5, 6, 7).

THE EFFECT OF FIBROIDS ON PREGNANCY depends largely on their size and location. A subserous sessile tumor in the fundus often undergoes considerable increase in size without having much influence on the gestation. The uterine contractions may, however, force it nearer and nearer to the surface until it is pedunculated. Pedunculated growths occasionally become twisted and undergo necrosis. They then require surgical removal. On rare occasions, fundal myomata may also lead to backward displacement and subsequent incarceration in the pelvis. In such circumstances, pressure symptoms are common and these, together with the possibility of abortion, may make laparotomy imperative. Interstitial tumors seldom have any influence on pregnancy unless they are located in the lower uterine segment, cervix or broad ligament. Submucous growths encroach upon the uterine cavity and, as a result, often are responsible for a poor development of the decidua in their neighborhood. They therefore may be the indirect cause of an imperfect implantation of the ovum and consequently may be a factor in the etiology of abortion, low implantation of the placenta, placenta previa, and adherent placenta, all of which have a higher incidence in fibroid cases. If the tumors are large and alter the shape of the uterine cavity, they also interfere with the mechanism of adaptation and cause a more frequent occurrence of breech and transverse prresentations.

Tumors in the lower segment, cervix and broad ligament, as well as those that are adherent in the pelvis, may prevent the entrance of the presenting part into the pelvic cavity at the time of labor. The danger of this type of dystocia, however, has been greatly overestimated since such tumors not infrequently are drawn upward above the pelvic brim as the cervix dilates. This favorable course naturally is impossible when the obstructing fibroids are adherent, or located on the posterior aspect of the lower uterine segment or cervix. In addition to the difficulties that may arise from an unfavorable location of the tumor, there is a distinct tendency toward uterine inertia in most fibroid cases, with the result that labor often is prolonged. Similarly, the alterations in the uterine wall interfere with the separation and expulsion of the placenta, and proper retraction of the placental site after the third stage. Postpartum hemorrhage, therefore, may be a cause of great anxiety when fibroids are present.

To summarize the effects of this complication, it may be said that early in pregnancy abortion is the chief danger and occurs in about one-fourth of the cases. Later, spontaneous interruption is less common but must always be kept in mind. Premature labor likewise is rather frequent and is responsible for a considerable part of the high fetal mortality that is encountered in fibroids

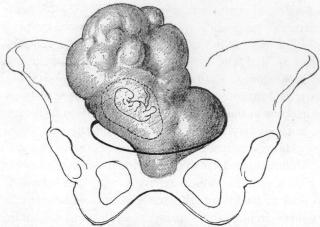

FIG. 747. Multiple fibroids complicating an early pregnancy (Bumm). **Compare with Figures 748 and 749.**

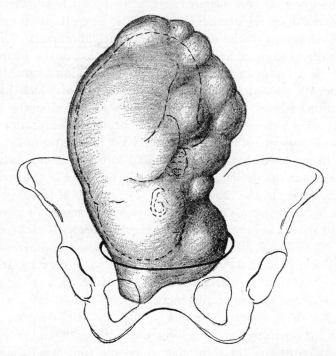

FIG. 748. Multiple fibroids complicating pregnancy (Bümm). **Note the change in the position and size of the tumors as gestation advances.**

complicating pregnancy (1, 2, 8). Labor is more difficult and prolonged because of the frequency of abnormal presentations, early rupture of the membranes, uterine inertia, and the occasional dystocia due to the presence of large fibroids in the pelvis. In the third stage, the separation and expulsion of the placenta may be interfered with and postpartum hemorrhage, due to inertia and faulty retraction of the uterus, sometimes occurs. The puerperium occasionally is complicated by degeneration of the tumor, and inadequate drainage, which, at times, is caused by the presence of fibroids, may add to the risk if infection has occurred. Rarely, a submucous tumor may at this time be forced through the cervix and become necrotic.

TREATMENT. This catalogue of the rather formidable potential dangers of fibroids complicating pregnancy might lead to the conclusion that pregnancy

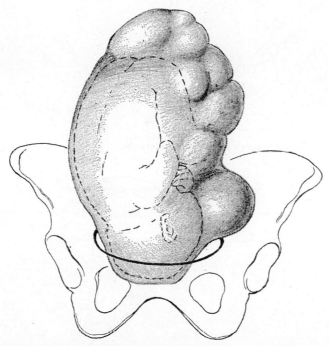

FIG. 749. Multiple fibroids complicating pregnancy (Bumm). As a result of labor, the large fibroid which originally was in the pelvis has been pulled up above the brim thus enabling the head to enter the pelvis.

should be avoided, and, if it does occur, therapeutic abortion should be done. Experience, however, does not justify such a recommendation, and abortion has no place in the treatment of this complication. If the attending physician is aware of the condition and gives his patient the advantage of careful supervision throughout labor and the puerperium, spontaneous delivery will occur in the majority of cases and the need for surgical intervention will be greatly diminished. The risk of interruption of the pregnancy is combated by warning the patient of this possibility and cautioning her concerning the exciting causes of abortion and premature labor. Coitus, strenuous exercise, over-exertion, long automobile rides and railroad or steamship journeys, accordingly, should be avoided. It is recommended that the knee-chest position be assumed several times daily to

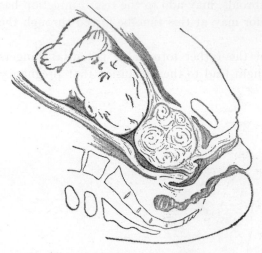

Fig. 750. A large fibroid in the pelvis but situated anteriorly.

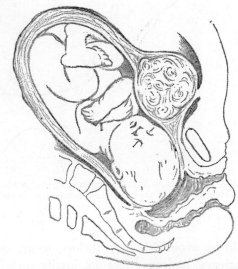

Fig. 751. The same large fibroid pulled above the pelvic brim as the cervix dilates.

avoid impaction of large fibroids in the pelvis and to prevent circulatory stasis. Pain or bleeding calls for immediate rest in bed and morphinization. Should interruption of pregnancy occur, great care must be taken to guard against infection.

If a pedunculated tumor becomes twisted, myomectomy is indicated. Red degeneration usually responds to expectant treatment. This consists of rest in bed, morphinization and the use of an ice-bag over the area involved. Should operative intervention be necessary, hysterectomy is preferable to myomectomy. The latter operation, however, can be done without great risk of interrupting the

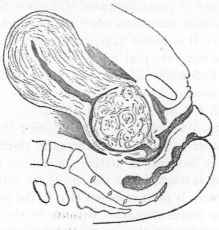

FIG. 752. The same large fibroid interfering with **drainage after delivery.**

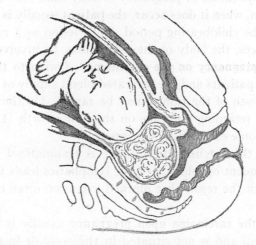

FIG. 753. A large fibroid in the pelvis interfering with the engagement of the head. **Note the** anterior displacement of the cervix. Because this tumor is situated posteriorly, it cannot be pulled above the promontory. Suprapubic delivery, accordingly, is necessary. Following delivery, myomectomy **or** hysterectomy is indicated, since such a tumor will greatly interfere with drainage, if it is not removed.

pregnancy, if it seems desirable to avoid sacrificing the uterus. In such cases, thorough morphinization for several days after operation is essential.

Labor is also managed conservatively but under most rigid aseptic conditions. Should a large tumor obstruct the passages, suprapubic delivery will be necessary if the growth is intraligamentous, adherent or fails to be drawn upward as the cervix dilates. **When a cesarean section is done, the obstructing tumor should be removed by myomectomy or hysterectomy.** Here, again, removal of the uterus is preferable, but myomectomy can be done if that procedure seems desirable. Red degeneration occurring in the puerperium may require operation, and hysterectomy, at times, is advisable when a fibroid becomes infected. The latter operation, however, is contraindicated if the infection is not localized in the tumor, and is especially dangerous when the parametrium is involved. In the latter circumstances, it is better to rely on repeated blood transfusions and the various supportive measures that are recommended in the management of puerperal infection. Following delivery, the fibroids often undergo atrophy as the uterus becomes involuted so that their future care is not much of a gynecological problem (1, 2, 3, 4, 5, 6, 7, 8, 9, 10, 11, 12).

CARCINOMA OF THE UTERUS rarely occurs during the third decade of life and is encountered rather infrequently in the early thirties. After the age of thirty-five, however, the incidence of uterine malignancy increases rapidly with each year until its peak is reached near the end of the fifth decade (13). Pregnancy, on the other hand, is most common late in the second, throughout the third and early in the fourth decades. Because of the difference in the age incidence of the two conditions, therefore, carcinoma of the uterus is not encountered as a complication of pregnancy oftener than once in 2000 cases (14). For the same reason, when it does occur, the patient usually is a multipara and is well advanced in the childbearing period. The lesion as a rule is cervical but, in very rare instances, the body of the uterus may be involved.

The effect of pregnancy on the carcinoma. Owing to the relatively early age of these cancer patients and the increased blood supply of the uterus, during pregnancy, the growth of the tumor may be rapid. On the other hand, pregnancy may have a retarding influence on the new growth (15, 16) just as it is thought to retard some extragenital cancers (17).

During labor, the carcinomatous tissue is traumatized by the presenting part and the consequent opening up of the lymphatics leads to dissemination of the cancer cells with the result that marked extension often occurs in the puerperium.

The effect of the carcinoma upon pregnancy usually is most unfavorable. If the lesion is small and is not situated in the body or in the cervical canal, pregnancy may go to term and end with a spontaneous labor. When the cervical canal or the body of the uterus is involved, abortion is common. Not infrequently, the lesion and the pregnancy progress simultaneously. In such circumstances, more or less vaginal bleeding takes place and this often simulates that of a threatened abortion or premature labor. Occasionally, the hemorrhage is so profuse that placenta previa is suspected. By the end of gestation, the cervix is markedly infiltrated and the characteristic softening of a normal pregnancy is replaced by indurated, unyielding tissue which resists dilation and obstructs the passage of the child. As a consequence, dilation of the cervix is retarded and sometimes is impossible. When the presenting part does pass through the greatly altered cervix, extensive lacerations are the rule and even rupture of the uterus may occur. Serious hemorrhage, accordingly, is an almost constant accompaniment of labor complicated by carcinoma of the cervix. If the patient survives the delivery, the pyogenic bacteria present in the malignant growth are widely distributed over the newly traumatized areas and cause an overwhelming puerperal infection.

Diagnosis. The customary bleeding which accompanies carcinoma of the cervix often is mistaken for a threatened interruption of pregnancy. Such cases are kept in bed and vaginal examinations are avoided with the result that the true condition is not discovered for some time. The great difference in the consistency of the softened uninvolved portion of the cervix and that of the indurated new growth, as shown by bimanual examination, should lead to early diagnosis of the carcinoma. Inspection of the cervix likewise is helpful and, in all suspicious cases, a biopsy is indicated. As previously stated, placenta previa may be considered when a severe hemorrhage occurs in the latter part of pregnancy. Vaginal touch again is helpful since the indurated carcinomatous mass cannot be mistaken for the extremely soft cervix of a placenta previa.

Prognosis. Excessive bleeding may occur at any time during pregnancy. Owing to the great danger of extensive cervical laceration and rupture of the uterus, fatal hemorrhage is especially liable to occur during labor in the advanced cases which go to term and are delivered through the natural passages. Infection, for the same reason, may occur and is a frequent cause of primary mortality. Survival after treatment directed toward the cure of the carcinoma naturally depends upon the extent of the lesion and the duration of the pregnancy. Early cases in the early part of pregnancy have a fair chance of cure and statistics showing 66% of five year survivals are reported (18). In the latter half of pregnancy, the prognosis for ultimate cure is poor.

Treatment. Early in pregnancy. If the lesion is small and is recognized early in pregnancy, two methods of treatment are available: abdominal hysterectomy followed by irradiation or irradiation alone. The radical operation of Wertheim has given very good results in cases of this type (18). Following removal of the uterus, the pelvis should be irradiated by means of the deep x-ray. When irradiation alone is employed, the pregnancy is ignored and radium is applied to the cervix for 3000 to 4000 mg. hours. Similar irradiation of the pelvis with radium or deep x-ray is essential. As a consequence of this treatment, the fetus dies and is usually expelled spontaneously. If abortion does not occur, the products of conception subsequently are artificially removed. The management of more extensive lesions early in pregnancy is limited to irradiation therapy alone without consideration of the pregnancy. Because of the great risk of infection and dissemination of cancer cells, the uterus should not be emptied prior to the application of radium.

In the middle of pregnancy, irradiation alone is the method of choice. The largest amount of radium available should be applied over the lesion for not over 3500 mg. hours, avoiding, if possible, the cervical canal. By using a large amount of radium, the duration of the treatment is lessened and the necessity for prolonged packing of the vagina is avoided. These precautions, together with the administration of progestin and morphine for several days, should greatly diminish the risk of abortion, a factor of great importance to the mother as well as to the child. When term is reached, delivery by a classical Cesarean section is advisable in order that the recently diseased and irradiated cervix may not be traumatized. This should be followed by deep x-ray irradiation of the pelvis.

While the effect on the fetus of radium used in this manner has not been investigated, a few cases are reported in which no serious injury to the child was observed (19). On the other hand, the ill-effects of irradiation during pregnancy have been reported rather frequently and, according to one collective review, 74 women who went to term after having been subjected to radium and x-ray therapy gave birth to 25 deformed children, 17 of whom were microcephalic idiots (20). These end results would seem to favor the sacrifice of the child by abdominal hysterotomy as soon as the irradiation is completed and the risk of infection is eliminated but it must be remembered that they are derived from a collective study in which the maldevelopment of the infants may have been caused by irradiation earlier than the middle of pregnancy. By the fifth month, the fetus is suspended in a relatively large amount of amniotic fluid, and, since it often presents as a breech, the fetal head should be more than 5 cm. (the minimum distance for safety) above any radium which might be applied to the cervix.

Late in pregnancy the same plan may be followed unless the gestation is so near to term that labor may begin before the desired effect of irradiation has been obtained. In such circumstances the possibility of the onset of labor and the delivery of a full-term child through the carcinomatous cervix presents a rather perplexing problem. If no ulceration nor infection is present, the child should be delivered by a classical Cesarean section and, ten days later, the cervix and pelvis should be thoroughly irradiated.

In the presence of infection and ulceration, abdominal Cesarean section with supracervical hysterectomy and followed by irradiation of the pelvis and cervical stump probably is the best method of meeting the situation. Suprapubic delivery avoids trauma to the diseased cervix and thereby prevents the spread of infectious material and cancer cells. Hysterotomy removes the potentially infected uterus which because of a breaking down of the uterine wound or a damming-up of the lochia might rupture into the peritoneal cavity and cause a fatal peritonitis. Following operation, the stump of the cervix and the pelvis are subjected to thorough irradiation with radium and deep x-ray.

During labor, if the growth is small, delivery through the natural passages should not be difficult since most women in this age group are multiparae. Such a lesion, however, offers the best prospect of cure and this chance of ultimate eradication of the disease unquestionably will be vitiated by the dissemination of cancer cells that is certain to follow the mechanism of the first stage of labor and the pressure of the presenting part on the cervix. Delivery by classical Cesarean section, therefore, is to be preferred whenever the possibility of infection can be ruled out. Ten days after operation, radium should be applied to the cervix and the pelvis irradiated with deep x-ray.

Should the involvement of the cervix be sufficient to prevent dilatation or obstruct the passage of the child, incision of the cervix and attempts at delivery through the pelvis are contraindicated. The danger of hemorrhage, rupture of the uterus and infection is so great that Cesarean section followed by supra-cervical hysterectomy and subsequent irradiation of the pelvis and cervical stump is a much safer procedure (17, 19, 21, 22, 23).

OVARIAN TUMORS rarely are observed as a complication of pregnancy. When present, however, they constitute a serious menace.

During pregnancy, growth of the uterus greatly increases the risk of torsion, the occurrence of which is noted in about 20 per cent of all cases while the usual incidence of this accident is only 8 per cent (24, 25, 26). As a twist in the pedicle most frequently accompanies the ascent of the uterus out of the pelvis, 50 to 60 per cent of all torsions occur in the third and fourth months (27). The symptoms are constant severe pain, vomiting and distention. Because they simulate the findings in intestinal obstruction, the latter condition often is suspected. Usually, there also is considerable shock, which should indicate the possibility of an abdominal calamity. In addition to torsion, other accidents common to ovarian cysts occasionally are observed, and it is generally stated that dangerous complications may be looked for in at least one-fourth of all cases. Abortion and premature labor likewise are not infrequent (25, 28, 29).

In labor, the hazards are much greater. Here, the presence of a tumor in the pelvis often causes marked dystocia, and rupture of the uterus or rupture of the cyst may occur. Even though delivery without these accidents eventually does take place, the tumor frequently is injured (24, 25). When not treated by operative interference over 20 per cent of the mothers die and half of the children are lost. Surgical intervention, on the other hand, has reduced the maternal mortality to about 3 per cent (29, 30, 31).

During the puerperium, involution of the uterus greatly increases the tendency toward torsion which occurs in 40 per cent of the cysts noted at this time (24). Hemorrhage into the tumor, necrosis and suppuration may follow injury received during labor and add to the risk of the puerperium. The latter accidents are most common when the cysts are intraligamentous or adherent in the pelvis.

The frequency of these serious accidents justifies surgical intervention in all cases. **Early in pregnancy** laparotomy for the removal of the tumor is recom-

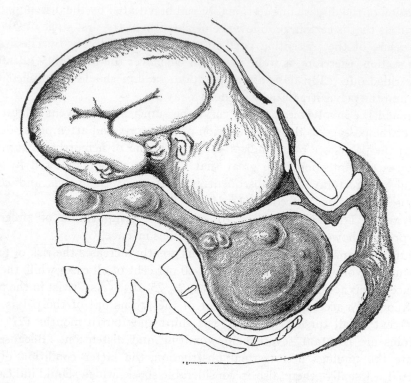

FIG. 754. Ovarian cyst complicating pregnancy (Bumm). This large tumor in the pelvis will interfere with the descent of the head in the course of labor and cause serious dystocia.

mended. Because of the danger of abortion, however, the operation should be postponed, if possible, until after the third month, and should be followed by thorough morphinization of the patient for several days. **In the latter part of pregnancy,** cesarean section, accompanied by removal of the cyst, is indicated (29, 32, 33, 34). If the presence of an obstructing tumor is not discovered until after the patient has been in labor sufficiently long to complete the dilatation of the cervix, the abdomen is opened to permit dislodgement of the tumor and, while the operator holds it out of the pelvis, an assistant delivers the child from below by forceps or version and extraction (35, 36). Following delivery of the child, the tumor is removed. This technic is much safer than cesarean section in those cases which have been neglected until the cervix is fully dilated. Whenever cesarean section is performed on potentially infected women, the uterus should also be removed. As the accidents described above occur with diminishing frequency **after the sixth month,** it often is advisable to postpone operation until the child is sufficiently developed to warrant its delivery by cesarean section.

This recommendation is made in the interests of the mother as well as of the child, since removal of the tumor at this time requires eventration of the enlarged uterus, and its subsequent replacement within the abdomen may be extremely difficult or even impossible. Likewise, a late operation may leave a large laparotomy wound that is too weak to stand the strain of labor. Should spontaneous delivery occur and the ovarian tumor be discovered **in the puerperium,** its surgical removal is indicated as soon after the diagnosis is made as the condition of the patient will permit. Induction of labor, forceps, version, and tapping of the cyst are absolutely contraindicated in the treatment of this condition.

REFERENCES

1. PINARD, A.: Fibromes et Grossesse. Ann. de gynéc., 1901, 56, 165.
2. PIERSON, R. W.: Fibromyomata and Pregnancy, a Study of 250 Cases. Am. J. Obs. & Gyn., 1927, 14, 333.
3. WATSON, B. P.: Pregnancy and Labor Complicated by Fibroid Tumors. Am. J. Obs. & Gyn., 1932, 23, 351.
4. FAIRBAIRN, J. S.: A Contribution to the Study of One of the Varieties of Necrotic Change, the Socalled Necrobiosis in Fibryomyomata of the Uterus. J. Obs. & Gyn., Brit. Emp., 1903, 4, 119.
5. IVENS, F.: Five Specimens Illustrating Necrobiotic Changes in Fibroids Associated with Pregnancy. J. Obs. & Gyn., Brit. Emp., 1922, 29, 639.
6. BLAND, P. B.: Uterine Myomata and Pregnancy with Special Reference to Tumor Necrosis. S. G. & O., 1925, 40, 367.
7. POLAK, J. O.: Influence of Fibroids in Pregnancy and Labor. S. G. & O., 1928, 46, 21.
8. LYNCH, F. W.: Fibroid Tumors Complicating Pregnancy and Labor. Am. J. Obs., 1913, 68, 427.
9. SPENCER, H. R.: Tumors Complicating Pregnancy, Labour, and the Puerperium. Lancet, 1920, 1, 411.
10. LITZENBERG, J. C.: Myomata of the Uterus and Pregnancy. Surg. Clinics of N. A., 1923, 3, 1285.
11. VAUDESCAL, R.: Myomectomy During Pregnancy. Brit. Med. J., 1928, 2, 793.
12. CAMPBELL, R. E.: Pregnancy and Labor Complicated by Myomatous Tumors of the Uterus. Am. J. Obs. & Gyn., 1933, 26, 1.
13. PACK, G. T. AND LEFEVRE, R. G.: Age and Sex Distribution and Incidence of Neoplastic Diseases at Memorial Hospital, New York City, With Comments on Cancer Ages. J. Cancer Res., 1930, 14, 167.
14. TAGLIAFERRO, P.: Cancro dell'utero in gravidanza. Ann. di. ostet. e ginec., 1935, 57, 1089.
15. WEIBEL, W.: 25 Jahre "Wertheimscher" Carcinom operation. Arch. f. Gyn., 1928, 135, 1.
16. STÖCKL, E.: Kollumkarzinom und Schwangerschaft. Ztschr. f. Beb. u. Gyn., 1932, 101, 437.
17. SMITH, F. R.: The Effect of Pregnancy on Malignant Tumors. Am. J. O. & G., 1937, 34, 616.
18. PEHAM AND AMREICH: Operative Gynecology, 1934, 2, 392.
19. NEILL, W.: Pregnancy Complicated by Carcinoma of the Cervix. Am. J. O. & G., 1935, 30, 414.
20. MURPHY, D. P.: The Outcome of 625 Pregnancies in Women Subjected to Pelvic Radium and Roentgen Irradiation. Am. J. O. & G., 1929, 18, 179.
21. PORTES, L., DENABIAS AND COUVELAIRE: Combined Treatment of Uterine Cancer During Pregnancy and Parturition. Gynéc. et Obst., 1924, 10, 105.
22. BAER, J. L.: Carcinoma of the Cervix Complicated by Pregnancy. Surg. Cl. N. A., 1936, 16, 51.

23. DANFORTH, W. C.: Carcinoma of the Cervix during Pregnancy. Am. J. O. & G., 1937, 34, 365.
24. McKERRON: Pregnancy, Labour and Childbed with Ovarian Tumors. London, 1903.
25. PATTON, C. L.: Ovarian Cysts Situated Above the Superior Pelvic Strait, Complicated by Pregnancy with a Report of 3 Cases and a Review of 321 Cases Collected from the Literature. S. G. & O., 1906, 3, 413.
26. CAVERLY, C. E.: Ovarian Cyst Complicating Pregnancy. Am. J. Obs. & Gyn., 1931, 21, 566.
27. RUSHMORE, S.: Ovarian Cyst with Twisted Pedicle Complicating Pregnancy–Operation. Report of One Case and Review of the Literature. S. G. & O., 1909, 9, 551.
28. WILLIAMS, J.: Ovarian Tumour with Pregnancy. Lancet, 1897, 2, 129.
29. NORRIS, R. C.: Ovarian Neoplasms Complicating Pregnancy and Labor. Am. J. Obs., 1913, 68, 420.
30. GRAEFE, M.: Zur Ovariotomie in der Schwangerschaft. Zeitschr. f. Geburtsh. u. Gyn., 1905, 56, 499.
31. MARSHALL, G. B.: Ovarian Tumours Complicating Pregnancy, Labour, and the Puerperium with Notes on 8 Recent Cases and Special Reference to Treatment. J. Obs. & Gyn., Brit. Emp., 1910, 17, 81.
32. LITZENBERG, J. C.: Ovarian Cysts Complicating Pregnancy. Am. J. Surg., 1927, 3, 506.
33. LYNCH, F. W.: Fibroids and Ovarian Cysts Complicating Pregnancy. Calif. & West. Med., 1931, 35, 415.
34. INGRAHAM, C. B.: Ovarian Tumors Complicating Pregnancy, with a Report of 6 Cases. Am. J. Obs. & Gyn., 1925, 10, 815.
35. BEACH, R. M.: The Management of Ovarian Tumors Complicating Pregnancy, Labor and the Puerperium. Am. J. Obs., 1916, 73, 1029.
36. SPENCER, H.: Tumors Complicating Pregnancy, Labour and the Puerperium. Lancet, 1920, 1, 475.

CHAPTER XXVIII

THE PATHOLOGY OF LABOR

When the factors concerned in the process of parturition are normal and properly coördinated, labor is physiologic or normal and is known as eutocia. On the other hand, anomalies of the powers, passages, or passenger, acting singly or conjointly, may lead to pathologic or abnormal labor, and it is then termed dystocia.

ANOMALIES OF THE POWERS

Normally, the uterine contractions are regular and progressively increase in frequency and intensity throughout labor. If the passages are ample and the passenger is not at fault, they bring about a gradual dilatation of the cervix in the first stage and aid in the expulsive efforts of the second, with the result that the average child is born within twelve hours in multiparae and eighteen hours in primiparae. Unfortunately, the action of the uterus at times is atypical and may give rise to considerable difficulty.

PRECIPITATE LABOR. Strong uterine contractions occasionally lead to such a rapid delivery that the labor is designated as precipitate. This usually occurs in multiparae in whom the soft parts offer little or no resistance. The child, accordingly, is born without sufficient warning to permit the usual preparations and its rapid passage through the pelvis may cause intracranial injury, rupture of the cord and extensive laceration of the maternal soft parts.

Whenever there is a history of precipitate labor, the attending physician should guard against its repetition by administering an anesthetic as soon as he is certain that the contractions of the uterus are typical of true labor. To accomplish this, it may be necessary to hospitalize the patient near the end of pregnancy.

INERTIA UTERI is the term applied to feeble and ineffectual uterine contractions. If the atypically weak action of the uterus is present from the onset of labor, the inertia is known as primary, in contrast with secondary inertia, which always is preceded by normal labor pains.

Primary inertia. Weak and ineffectual uterine contractions from the onset of labor are rather frequent and primary inertia is probably the commonest factor in prolonged and difficult labors. The cause of this condition is one or more of the following:

1. Atypical development of the uterine musculature may be responsible for a more or less imperfect action of the uterus, as is observed in bicornate uteri,

621

and the cases of hypoplasia which are associated with prolonged sterility and funnel pelvis. In the latter group, the patients often are unable to conceive for several years after marriage and examination before pregnancy shows their uteri to be small and acutely anteflexed with relatively long cervices. The first stage of labor in such individuals often is prolonged and by the time that the cervix is fully dilated and the presenting part reaches the pelvic floor, the patient is too exhausted to mold the head through her contracted bony outlet.

2. **Overdistention of the uterus,** resulting from the presence of a multiple pregnancy or hydramnios, has an effect similar to that which is produced in other hollow viscera when their muscular walls are overstretched. Weak and ineffectual pains, accordingly, are commonly observed in twins and are responsible for much of the added difficulty that is encountered in such cases.

3. **Rapidly succeeding pregnancies** have a similar effect on the muscle of the uterus and, even though the resistance of the maternal soft parts becomes less and less with the birth of each child, the tendency toward a prolonged labor may increase because of the atypical action of the uterine musculature.

4. **Tumors in the wall of the uterus,** by interfering with the coördinating and conducting apparatus, may cause alterations in the strength, frequency and duration of the contractions, and their presence may so disturb the muscular arrangement as to cause atypical labor pains. Multiple fibromyomata, accordingly, are frequent causes of uterine inertia.

5. **Debilitating conditions,** such as profound anemia, antepartum hemorrhage, prolonged fevers, and chronic wasting diseases may also have a deleterious effect on the action of the uterus in labor and thereby cause inertia.

6. **Inhibition of the uterine contractions** sometimes results from fright or an emotional upset. This type of inertia is most often seen in young, neurotic primigravidae who greatly fear the pains of labor, and it is particularly frequent in such individuals when the severity of their suffering is increased by early rupture of the membranes.

7. **Rest in bed, obliquity of the uterus,** and **pendulous abdomen,** by lessening the pressure of the presenting part on the lower uterine segment, remove one of the factors which is known to have a stimulating effect on uterine contractions. When these are allowed to continue, the frequency and intensity of the labor pains are less than they otherwise would be and, as a result, they may be said to contribute to the prolongation of labor.

8. **Heredity** likewise plays a part in the etiology of uterine inertia. Some women who cannot be placed in any of the foregoing groups have prolonged labors just as did their mothers and other relatives. Because no other cause of dystocia is demonstrable in these cases, heredity may be considered the underlying factor.

SYMPTOMS. The contractions of the uterus are infrequent, short and lack the characteristic feel of a true labor pain, in which the contraction curve has a gradual increment, a sustained acme and a rather rapid decrudescence. They accordingly are ineffectual, and vaginal or rectal touch reveals little or no progress in the obliteration and dilatation of the cervix and only slight bulging of the membranes with each pain. On the other hand, the suffering may be out of proportion to the strength of the uterine contractions. Labor, therefore, is prolonged and the lack of progress leads the patient to believe that her suffering is in vain. Discouraged and impatient with her physician, she begs for relief and often demands operative intervention. As a result, nervous and physical exhaustion is not infrequent and may require artificial termination of the labor. If she is not delivered and the presenting part is low in the pelvis, pressure necrosis may result and cause the formation of fistulae between the vagina and bladder or rectum. Uterine inertia in the third stage interferes with proper retraction and leads to excessive hemorrhage from the placental site.

TREATMENT. The underlying principles which govern the management of primary inertia are:

1. Stimulation of the uterine contractions.
2. The use of supportive measures.
3. The administration of sedatives to prevent nervous and physical exhaustion.

Stimulation of the uterine contractions. The measures which have been recommended to stimulate labor pains are: The administration of castor oil, quinine, pituitary extract, ergot, a warm enema, keeping the patient on her feet, rupture of the membranes, the introduction of a hydrostatic bag into the lower segment of the uterus and tamponade of the vagina. Under certain circumstances, many of these possibly have a place in the treatment of inertia. Several of them, however, are not without great danger and should be employed in only those cases which justify their use.

Ergot in the form of the extract or fluid extract at one time was a favorite means of stimulating labor pains. Unfortunately, it causes tetanic contractions and favors molding of the uterus about the child, with the result that fetal death and rupture of the uterus not uncommonly follow its use (Fig. 755). These accidents have been so frequent that ergot has been abandoned, excepting as a means of controlling hemorrhage after the birth of the placenta and in the rare condition known as ablatio placentae.

Pituitary extract. The history of ergot in obstetrics is being repeated in the case of posterior pituitary extract. Hypodermic injections of this powerful oxytocic preparation likewise may cause intrauterine asphyxia and are responsible for many maternal deaths from rupture of the uterus (1, 2, 3). Whenever it is used the initial dose should not exceed 1 min. This is gradually increased to 3 min. It ordinarily should be used only after labor has progressed sufficiently to permit forceps extraction. In other words, pituitary extract usually is not given until the cervix is fully dilated and the head has descended below the level of the ischial spines. Its administration likewise should be preceded by preparation for forceps extraction in order that no time may be lost in completing the delivery, should this drug act unfavorably and jeopardize the life of the mother or child. In addition chloroform or ether should be at hand in order that the patient may be anesthetized immediately and the uterus relaxed if the drug causes spastic uterine contractions.

Hydrostatic bag. Uterine contractions may be stimulated and dilatation of the cervix favored by the introduction of a hydrostatic bag into the lower uterine segment. This measure, however, is accompanied by the risks of infection, anesthesia, rupture of the membranes and displacement of the presenting part with its accompanying danger of prolapse of the cord and malpresentation. It therefore has a limited field of usefulness and should be employed only in those cases in which the membranes have ruptured and the condition of the mother justifies the risks incident to its use.

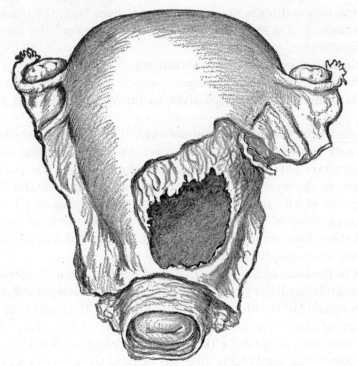

FIG. 755. Rupture of the uterus resulting from ergot administered in the course of labor (Edgar).

Tamponade of the vagina with sterile boroglyceride gauze also acts as a stimulant and seems to aid dilatation of the cervix when the latter is thick and edematous. Its use, however, greatly increases the risk of infection and, for this reason, is seldom justifiable.

Artificial rupture of the membranes. The observation that uterine contractions often are stronger after the waters break has led to the recommendation that the membranes be ruptured artificially to stimulate labor pains in uterine inertia. While the desired effect often is obtained, in some cases the contractions come on less frequently after the waters are broken and labor is thus retarded. In addition to this possibility, the loss of the amniotic fluid causes greater suffering and, by adding to the risk of infection, molding of the uterus and intrauterine asphyxia, further complicates an undesirable situation. For these reasons, preservation of the membranes usually is to be favored and their rupture is justifiable only in those cases in which their abnormal adherence to the lower uterine segment hinders dilatation of the cervix.

Quinine, castor oil, and a **warm enema** are commonly used for their stimulating effect in uterine inertia. Quinine is given in five grain doses at two hour intervals until ten or fifteen grains are taken and seems to be efficacious in some cases. While it is said to be harmless, a few instances of fetal death from its use are recorded. Castor oil and a warm enema, at times, have a stimulating effect and, since they are harmless, their use is recommended in all cases.

Keep the patient on her feet. The recumbent posture allows the presenting part to fall away from the lower uterine segment and, as a result, one of nature's best stimulating measures is lost. On the other hand, when the patient is kept on her feet as long as possible, the pains are stronger and more frequent. It therefore is desirable to have her walk about or at least avoid lying down until true labor is established.

Supportive measures. Since no one can foretell the duration of labor at its onset, adequate fluids and nourishment should be given to prevent dehydration, acidosis and exhaustion. Frequent, small but substantial meals are necessary from the onset and should be continued throughout the greater part of the first stage. For this purpose, carbohydrates in the form of easily digestible starches and sugar are most desirable, and, if the patient is unable to retain sufficient food of this character, repeated intravenous injections of 10 or 20 per cent glucose solution should be given (4).

The use of sedatives. Almost as important as fluids and nourishment is the judicious use of sedatives. If the inertia prolongs the labor for several days, the patient should receive enough sedatives each night to insure at least eight hours of restful sleep. For this purpose 15 grs. of chloral, or a hypodermic injection of morphine gr. $\frac{1}{4}$ and scopolamine gr. $\frac{1}{200}$ are given. Additional sedatives may be required during the day whenever her physical condition begins to show the effect of the tedious labor. The rest induced by sedative drugs not only improves her physical and mental condition, but often has a favorable influence on labor itself, and a sound sleep not infrequently is followed by vigorous uterine contractions (5, 6).

In order that the application of the foregoing principles may be better understood, the treatment of primary inertia will now be considered in some of the circumstances commonly encountered in practice. If the patient is seen for the first time in the evening, and her uterine contractions are weak, irregular and ineffectual, she should be reëxamined two or three hours later. In the event that the pains have not then increased in frequency and intensity, and rectal examination shows no progress, enough sedatives to induce sleep are indicated. On the following morning at 6 a.m., an ounce of castor oil is administered. One or two hours later, the patient is urged to take a substantial carbohydrate breakfast and walking is encouraged. At 8 a.m., the first five grains of quinine are given and the stimulating effect of a warm enema is tried. Posterior pituitary extract in 1 min. doses may be used if the precautions previously noted are respected. The patient is then informed that her contractions are not typical of true labor but that sooner or later the right kind of pains will come on and when they do labor should progress to a satisfactory conclusion. Nourishment and fluids are given at two or three hour intervals throughout the day and, if possible, her time is to be occupied with the lighter of her usual household duties. The bladder likewise should be emptied every three or four hours and if the patient is unable to void, catheterization is indicated whenever evidence of distention is present. After the onset of typical labor pains that progressively increase in frequency and intensity, the further management of the case is similar to that previously described under the conduct of a normal labor.

If the inertia persists, the patient should be visited several times during the day to see that the instructions above mentioned are carried out and to give her the encouragement that comes from a sympathetic interest in her case. Should it continue into the second night, sufficient sedatives are again administered to induce a restful sleep, but on the following day, the castor oil and quinine are withheld. Otherwise the management of the case is similar to that above outlined. Ultimately, the action of the uterus will become typical and labor will progress satisfactorily. The problem, therefore, is to prevent physical and mental exhaustion while awaiting this happy outcome. Should the membranes remain intact and no disproportion or other anomaly be present, this expectant plan may be followed for several days provided the pulse and temperature do not become elevated.

A rapid pulse and a rise in temperature are indications for the use of additional sedatives if the cervix is not dilated enough to permit artificial termination of the labor. When, on the other hand, labor has progressed sufficiently to permit artificial delivery, operative interference is indicated and the procedure elected will depend on the conditions that are present.

Rising pulse and temperature, cervix fully dilated, head above the spines, membranes intact. When the cervix is fully dilated and the head is above the ischial spines, the membranes are ruptured and the child is delivered by version and extraction.

Rising pulse and temperature, cervix fully dilated, head below the spines, membranes intact. If the cervix is fully dilated and the head is below the ischial spines, the membranes are ruptured and small doses of posterior pituitary extract are given, or the child is extracted by forceps.

Rising pulse and temperature, cervix partially dilated, membranes intact.
If the cervix is not fully dilated, and manual dilatation or incision of the cervix
is practicable, one of these procedures is done and the child is then delivered by
forceps or version and extraction, according to the relation of the presenting
part to the ischial spines.

When the membranes are ruptured, the patient's suffering is aggravated and
the risk of infection is increased. The uterus likewise may become molded about
the child and cause intrapartum asphyxia. The combination of uterine inertia
and dry labor, accordingly, is rather serious and frequently requires artificial aid.
Even after the membranes rupture, however, the expectant plan merits further
consideration. Small doses of posterior pituitary extract may be used if previous recommendations as to dosage and availability of anesthetics are followed.
If, after a fair trial, no progress is observed, a hydrostatic bag may be introduced
into the cervix to stimulate contractions and facilitate dilatation. Following the
expulsion of the bag, labor should be managed in the usual manner.

Membranes ruptured, cervix thick and edematous. If the cervix is thick
and edematous, packing of the vagina with sterile boroglyceride gauze is recommended. This not only stimulates uterine contractions, but changes the character of the cervix and often facilitates dilatation.

Membranes ruptured, cervix fully dilated, head at or below the spines.
After the cervix is fully dilated and the head has reached the level of the ischial
spines, small doses of pituitary extract are given. If they fail to stimulate contractions and cause the head to descend, delivery with forceps is indicated.

Child dead, cervix only partly dilated. If the child dies before the cervix is
fully dilated, perforation of the head allows the presenting part to descend farther
into the cervical ring and often greatly accelerates labor. This procedure is
particularly indicated when the pulse becomes rapid and the temperature is
elevated before the cervix is fully dilated, and is preferable to incision of the
cervix whenever intrapartum infection is suspected.

Rising pulse and temperature, membranes ruptured. Acceleration of the
pulse and fever are an indication for termination of the labor, just as in the cases
in which the membranes are not ruptured, and the method of delivery will depend
upon the conditions that are present.

Control of hemorrhage. Following delivery in all cases of inertia, the
possibility of postpartum hemorrhage must be kept in mind. Prophylactic use
of ergot and pituitary extract immediately after the placenta is expressed is
indicated and sterile gauze packs for tamponade of the uterus should be at hand.

Secondary inertia. The uterine contractions sometimes become feeble and
inefficient after they have been strong, regular and effective. When the action
of the uterus thus diminishes in strength after true labor has been in progress,
the condition is known as secondary inertia.

Normal contractions of the uterus after primary inertia may be of short
duration because of the inherent defects in the uterine musculature. The

causes of primary inertia, therefore, may be factors in the etiology of secondary inertia.   In addition, anything which obstructs the progress of labor or leads to its prolongation may cause the uterus to become thus fatigued, such as multiple pregnancy, hydramnios, dry labor, molding of the uterus around the child, rigid cervix, rigid perineum, malpresentation, contracted pelvis, large child, and pelvic tumors which obstruct the passages.

SYMPTOMS.   The contractions, at first, are typical of normal labor and continue with increasing frequency and intensity until the uterine muscle becomes fatigued.   The pains then grow feeble and infrequent and, after a time, they become irregular.   In some instances, labor ceases entirely and the patient falls asleep.   When she awakens, the uterus usually resumes its rhythmic contractions, and labor progresses normally if the advance of the presenting part is not retarded by some obstruction.

TREATMENT.   The treatment of secondary inertia may be considered under the following headings:

1. The correction of any abnormality that obstructs labor.

2. The use of sedatives to secure rest.

3. The employment of stimulating measures when the inertia occurs late in labor.

4. Artificial aid after the requisites for the various operative procedures have been fulfilled.

Contracted pelvis, large child and pelvic tumors should be handled in the manner recommended for these conditions in their respective chapters.   **Abnormal presentations** likewise are corrected as soon as conditions permit.   It is amazing to note the change in the uterine contractions that follows the bringing down of a foot in a frank breech and the effect of flexion or anterior rotation in a posterior face presentation.   Often, within a short time after the patient comes out of her anesthetic, normal contractions are resumed and labor terminates with surprising rapidity.

Sedatives.   Much time can be saved by the prompt recognition of secondary inertia.   When it occurs in the first stage of labor, the necessary rest is secured by the administration of chloral or morphine and scopolamine in sufficiently large doses to put the patient to sleep.   After a good rest, frequent, vigorous and effectual contractions are resumed with the result that labor progresses in the normal manner.

Stimulating measures.   If secondary inertia appears late in labor, when only a relatively few good contractions are needed to complete the delivery, the fatigued uterus is stimulated by the use of oxytocic drugs.   Because the action of the latter may prove harmful, they should be employed only after labor has reached that stage which will permit rapid artificial delivery.   After the cervix is fully dilated, therefore, pituitary extract may be given whenever no disproportion is present, and the head is low enough in the pelvis to allow its immediate extraction by forceps should the injections cause violent contractions of the uterus and jeopardize the life of the child.

Artificial delivery is indicated at any time after the cervix is fully dilated. If the head is above the spines of the ischium, version and extraction should be the procedure of choice, while extraction by forceps is recommended when inertia appears after the cervix is fully dilated and the head has descended below the level of the spines.

SPASMODIC CONTRACTIONS OF THE UTERUS

CLONIC SPASMS, occasionally, are due to the irritation which results from too frequent vaginal examinations, intrauterine manipulations and attempts to deliver the child through an undilated cervix.

TONIC CONTRACTION, TETANUS UTERI, usually is due to the violent efforts of the uterus to overcome some obstruction to the passage of the child. Occasionally, however, it may be caused by the injudicious use of ergot or posterior pituitary extract.

SYMPTOMS. Clonic spasms often follow each other in rapid succession and then cease for a time. Tetanus uteri, on the other hand, is a continuous spasm. The uterine contractions having grown increasingly frequent, finally become continuous. Although the action of the uterus is vigorous, it fails to cause any advance of the presenting part and labor remains at a standstill. The lower segment grows progressively thinner as the retraction ring is drawn upward and the fundus is retracted to form a thick, muscular hood which in marked cases lies entirely above the fetus and may be mistaken for a large fibroid. Either type of spasm is accompanied by intense pain and tenderness over the uterus. Because of the increased tension and greater sensitiveness of the uterine wall, palpation of the fetal parts is impossible, but the difference in the consistency of the uterus above and below the high retraction ring renders the diagnosis easy. The pulse and temperature are elevated. The tongue is dry and the lips are cracked as a result of dehydration. Vaginal examination shows the vagina and cervix to be dry, hot and swollen and since the child usually is dead, evidence of maceration may be detected. If the uterus does not rupture, the mother may die from exhaustion.

TREATMENT. Morphine gr. $\frac{1}{4}$ to $\frac{1}{2}$, atropine gr $\frac{1}{120}$ and 1 cc. of 1–1000 adrenalin solution should be tried in clonic spasms (7, 8, 9). If they are not effective, an anesthetic may be given for a short time. Tonic spasm calls for correction of the condition which is responsible for the dystocia and immediate delivery. In vertex cases, craniotomy is advisable. Transverse presentation is best treated by decapitation or evisceration. If the dilatation of the cervix is not sufficient, multiple incisions may be necessary before the foregoing procedures can be carried out. Whenever cesarean section is elected in place of one of the destructive operations, it should be followed by hysterectomy if the condition of the patient permits.

Molding of the uterus, retraction ring dystocia. Occasionally, the uterus molds itself about the irregular fetal ovoid and prevents descent of the child. More rarely, contraction of Bandl's ring may similarly grasp the child and interfere with delivery. As a rule, both of these conditions occur in dry labors and are usually recognized after operative delivery is attempted. When the true state of affairs is recognized, adrenalin and deep anesthesia may bring about sufficient relaxation to permit delivery (7, 10, 11, 12). Often, molding of the uterus is responsible for the arrest of a frank breech presentation. In such cases, the bringing down of a foot by Pinard's maneuver releases the impaction and leads to a satisfactory continuation of the labor.

HOUR-GLASS UTERUS. Following the delivery of the child, contraction of the uterus below the placenta may lead to the formation of an hour-glass uterus and the retention of the placenta. This complication usually follows the use of ergot or pituitary extract when it is given to hasten the separation of the placenta. If neither of these drugs is used until after the placenta is born, hour-glass contraction seldom is encountered. When it does occur, deep anesthesia and manual dilatation of the ring are necessary before removal of the placenta is possible.

SPASM OF THE CERVIX very rarely occurs. It may, however, be observed in dry labors, particularly after artificial attempts to accelerate the delivery have increased the irritability of the cervix and lower uterine segment. The stage of dilatation is delayed and examination shows the cervix to be tense and unyielding, while forcible attempts to hasten the dilatation are painful. Sedatives, and, in rare instances, a very short anesthesia may relieve the condition, after which a hydrostatic bag may be introduced to facilitate dilatation. If the spasm occurs late in the first stage, multiple incisions of the cervix may be sufficient to permit artificial delivery (13).

FAULTY BEARING-DOWN EFFORTS. Not infrequently, the voluntary efforts are feeble and ineffectual. This condition may be the result of weak abdominal muscles and is commonly seen in multiparae who have borne many children. It may also be due to the sedative action of drugs that are used for the relief of pain in the first stage. If morphine and scopolamine are continued too long in the stage of dilatation, their effect not only deadens the reflex that is essential to good expulsive efforts, but leads to mental confusion and thus renders the patient incooperative. Anesthesia has a similar effect. When started too early in labor it may diminish the bearing-down pains. Spinal anesthesia and caudal anesthesia completely obliterate this reflex and render the abdominal muscles useless during labor. Those who advocate spinal anesthesia, accordingly, resort to the use of forceps almost routinely even in their multiparous labors. If the first stage is prolonged and not properly conducted, the resulting fatigue leads to poor use of the abdominal muscles and ineffectual bearing-down efforts. The same may be said of all cases in which labor is obstructed.   Faulty bearing-down efforts, accordingly, are to be avoided by careful management of the first stage and the restriction of sedative drugs and anesthesia to their proper use.   Advantage should be taken of an abdominal binder, pullers and the practical application of the physiological principles involved in the voluntary efforts.   As soon as the cervix is fully dilated, therefore, a snug abdominal binder is adjusted and the patient is shown how to use her pains (14).

If the head is below the level of the ischial spines and all of the requisites for forceps extraction are fulfilled, the child may be delivered artificially.   Some men prefer to give small doses (3 m.) of pituitary extract in these circumstances. Whenever the latter drug is used, preparations for operative delivery must be made before it is given; otherwise the child may be lost, if the contractions of the uterus become vigorous and interfere with the uteroplacental circulation.

REFERENCES

1. Bell, W. Blair: The Pituitary Body and the Therapeutic Value of the Infundibular Extract in Shock, Uterine Atony and Intestinal Paresis.   Brit. Med. J., 1909, 2, 1609.
2. Mundell, J. J.: Pituitrin in Labor.   Am. J. Obs., 1916, 73, 306.
3. Mendenhall, A. M.: Solution of Pituitary and Ruptured Uterus.   J. A. M. A.,1929, 92, 1341.
4. Bailey, H.: The Long Labors.   Am. J. O. & G., 1928, 16, 324.
5. Beck, A. C.: Is Interference Justifiable After 24 Hours of Labor When No Other Indication is Present?   Am. J. O. & G., 1922, 4, 623.
6. Bourne, A. and Bell, A. C.: Uterine Inertia.   J. O. & G., Brit. Emp., 1933, 40, 423.
7. Rucker, M. P.: The Treatment of Contraction Ring Dystocia with Adrenalin.   Am. J. O. & G., 1927, 14, 609.
8. Schickelé, M.: Les contractions spasmodiques, troubles d'innervation.   Bull. Soc. d'obs. et de gyn., 1927, 16, 291.
9. Fink, K.: Spasmen im Durchtrittschlauch intrapartum.   Monatschr. f. Geburtsh. u. Gyn., 1927, 75, 365.
10. Weiss, J.: Tetanospasmodic Uterine Rings, with a Report of Four Cases.   Am. J. O. & G., 1933, 26, 346.
11. Dickinson, R. L.: Cesarean Section for Impassable Contraction Ring.   Surg. Gyn. & Obs., 1910, 11, 377.
12. White, C.: On Contraction and Retraction Rings.   Am. J. O. & G., 1926, 11, 364.
13. Greenhill, J. P.: Dystocia Due to Constriction of One Thigh by Cervix in a Cephalic Presentation.   J. A. M. A., 1922, 78, 98.
    Zur Frage des Muttermundskrampfes.   Zentralbl. f. Gyn., 1929, 53, 1316.
14. Beck, A. C.: Abdominal Binder as a Substitute for Pituitary Extract in Second Stage of Labor.   J. A. M. A., 1924, 83, 753.

CHAPTER XXIX

FAULTY PASSAGES—SOFT-PART DYSTOCIA

DEVELOPMENT OF THE MÜLLERIAN DUCTS. Complete or incomplete failure of fusion of the müllerian ducts and other malformations of the genital tract lead to a variety of abnormalities which may complicate labor. For this reason, it is desirable to review briefly the development of the female genital tract.

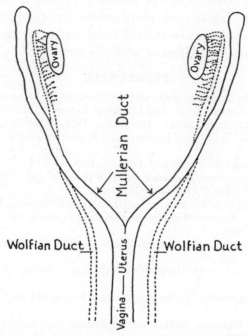

FIG. 756. Diagrammatic representation of the müllerian ducts in relation to the wolffian duct.

The early embryo (10–11 mm.) shows a shallow longitudinal depression in the coelomic epithelium on the lateral surface of each mesonephros near its cephalic extremity. As this groove deepens, its margins protrude and finally fuse to form the müllerian duct, the blind caudal extremity of which penetrates more deeply into the mesenchyme and passes caudally on the outer side of the wolffian duct. Near the caudal extremity of the mesonephros, it crosses the latter and progresses backward until it reaches the posterior wall of the urogenital sinus (Fig. 756).

About the tenth week, fusion of this blind end with its fellow of the opposite side is observed, and thereafter progresses cranially to form the uterovaginal canal. The caudal extremity of the latter soon shows marked changes in its epithelium which becomes stratified and completely fills the lumen up to the

632

site of the future cervicovaginal junction (1).   This caudal portion of the uterovaginal canal thus is converted into a solid cord of cells (the müllerian segment
of the vagina) which later fuses with the stratified epithelium of the sinovaginal
bulbs (Fig. 757).

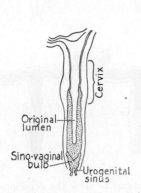

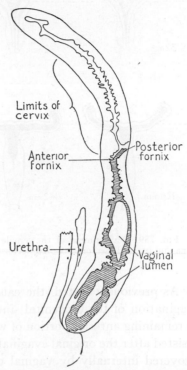

FIG. 757. Development of the uterovaginal
canal (Koff).   Note the stratification of the epithelium and the obliteration of the lumen at its
caudal extremity which fuses with the evaginated
epithelium from the sinovaginal bulbs.

FIG. 758. Reappearance of the vaginal lumen
at a later stage in the development of the vagina
(Koff).

DEVELOPMENT OF THE VAGINA.   The sinovaginal bulbs are bilateral, bulb-
shaped evaginations of the posterior wall of the urogenital sinus in the region
of the wolffian duct orifices.   Their lining membrane also becomes stratified and
undergoes marked proliferation which causes considerable increase in the size of
the bulbs and obliteration of their small cavities.   These masses of epithelium
later fuse with the solid epithelial cord that has replaced the caudal portion of the
uterovaginal canal to form the primitive vaginal plate (2).

Continued proliferation of the epithelium leads to an invasion of the surrounding mesenchyme and increases the size of the vaginal plate in all dimensions
(Fig. 757), with the result that the posterior wall of the urogenital sinus is thus
invaginated to form the caudal segment of the hymen.   After the eighteenth
week, the central cells of the vaginal plate degenerate and are discharged through
the hymen.   Similar canalization proceeds caudocranially and the vaginal lumen
is completely established by the twentieth week (Fig. 758).

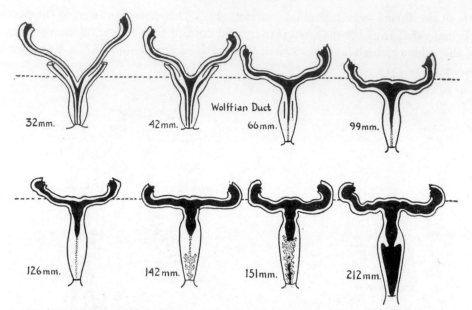

FIG. 759. Development of the female genital tract. Scheme to show the development of the vagina and uterus based on wax plate reconstructions and dissections of fetuses (Hunter).

As previously stated, the caudal expansion of the vaginal plate causes an invagination of the urogenital sinus to form the caudal segment of the hymen, the remaining anterior portion of which is derived from the lateral lips that have persisted after the original evagination of the sinovaginal bulbs (2). It therefore is covered internally by vaginal cells derived from the sinovaginal bulbs and externally by epithelium from the urogenital sinus, while between the two is an intervening stroma derived from the mesenchyme.

DEVELOPMENT OF THE UTERUS. The fused portions of the müllerian ducts, which form a single uterovaginal canal cranially, give rise to the uterus and about four-fifths of the vagina (2). The upper extremity of this canal remains stationary at the level of the first sacral vertebra and its lower limit corresponds to the fourth piece of the sacrum (3). Growth, accordingly, keeps pace with the development of the sacrum. This growth, however, is confined largely to the caudal portion and, as a result, is observed mostly in the developing vagina and cervix (Fig. 759).

After the twentieth week, the cervix is observed to grow much more rapidly than the body so that at birth it comprises at least two-thirds of the entire uterus (Fig. 760). This marked development is thought to be influenced by a hormone from the placenta or some maternal gland since the cervix becomes relatively and absolutely smaller soon after birth (3, 4).

The condensation of mesenchyme around the fused müllerian ducts forms a squat hour-glass structure, the constricted portion of which represents the dividing line between the body and the cervix. The upper limit of this organ, at first, is V-shaped as a result of the divergence of the free portions of the ducts. At this time, the wolffian ducts are still present and the round ligament attachments are adjacent to them. Following the disappearance of the wolffian ducts, the round ligaments become directly attached to the oviducts slightly beyond the upper limits of the primitive uterus. As development proceeds, the uterine wall encroaches more and more on the free portions of the oviducts and finally absorbs them as far as the attachment of the round ligaments. As a result, the round ligaments are now attached to the uterus on its ventrolateral borders. Growth and development of the muscle leads to the formation of a well marked fundus and the loss of the notch which marked the upper limit of the fused müllerian ducts.

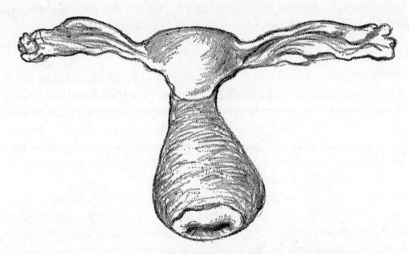

FIG. 760. The uterus at the eighth month of fetal life (Hunter).

The mesenchyme in the fused portions of the urogenital folds undergoes condensation which is continued laterally to the free portions of the ducts. The cells become arranged into an outer subserous layer, a middle muscular zone and an inner layer from which the mucosa forms. Branches from the blood vessels of the broad ligament grow between the outer and middle layers and form a vascular network.

About the middle of fetal life, muscle fibers make their appearance at the periphery of the middle layer and rapidly involve the whole uterine wall (5), the greatest activity being observed in the cervical region. Shortly before birth, the muscular elements extend into the subserous layer and form a loose meshwork about the vessels in this region.

The lumen of the uterus, at first, is circular and later, due to its lateral expansion, becomes oval. As growth continues, the walls become somewhat folded upon each other so that the lumen, in cross-section, appears as a wave-like slit. Secondary longitudinal folds later appear and from them smaller accessory folds arise. As the uterus enlarges, these folds become flattened in the region of the body but are retained in the cervix. Long, transverse folds added to these longitudinal ones cause broad swellings which project into the lumen of the cervix. Because of the lack of room in the cervical lumen, these tend to become oblique and are the forerunners of the plicae palmatae. Their absence in the upper portion of the cervix makes that region appear like the body. It therefore becomes the so-called isthmus of the uterus, which, macroscopically, resembles the cervix, but microscopically is like the body of the uterus. Portions of the deepest infoldings are cut off and give rise to the glands of the cervix. The cervical epithelium is columnar in type and shows evidence of secretory activity. In the region of the external os, degenerative changes are observed and parts of the original epithelium are cast off—congenital erosion. Soon after birth, these areas of erosion are reëpithelialized by squamous-like cells from the stratified vaginal epithelium (3, 6).

DEVELOPMENT OF THE TUBES. The oviducts or fallopian tubes are formed from the unfused portions of the müllerian ducts. As their length increases more rapidly than that of the other structures in this portion of the urogenital folds, the tubes soon become coiled within their peritoneal coverings. On the other hand, the development of this portion of the müllerian system lags and, as a result, the oviducts wander caudally to occupy a somewhat transverse position in the region of the fourth lumbar segment.

From the lips of the original abdominal ostium at the cranial extremity of each duct, several projections develop and persist as the fimbriated extremity of the tube. The single layer of columnar epithelium, which lines the ducts from the beginning, persists and in the latter part of fetal life becomes ciliated. At an early age, folds of the lining membrane and its underlying stroma project into the tube lumen and, as development proceeds, give to the latter its characteristic appearance.

About the eleventh week, the loose mesenchyme adjacent to the duct epithelium assumes a concentric arrangement and, within a short time, is divided into an inner layer of round cells and an outer spindle celled layer, the anlagen of the submucosa and muscularis. Soon after the middle of fetal life, muscle fibers, arranged in a circular manner, may be observed and later inner and outer longitudinal layers are developed.

DEVELOPMENT OF THE EXTERNAL GENITALIA. In the very early embryo (3 mm.), a conical eminence—the genital tubercle—appears on its ventral surface between the umbilical cord and the base of the tail (7) (Fig. 761). With continued growth, this tubercle comes to occupy almost the entire area between these landmarks, and its caudal surface is indented by a shallow longitudinal depression—the urethral groove (8 mm.) (Fig. 762). As development progresses, this groove grows broader and deeper at its distal extremity.   The urethral portion of the cloacal membrane then ruptures (12–13 mm.) and the urethral groove is transformed into a gutter-like primitive urogenital opening which communicates with the urogenital sinus.   Later (16–17 mm.), a pair of rounded lateral ridges appear on each side of the genital tubercle—the labioscrotal swellings—which unite caudally to form the posterior commissure (18 mm.).

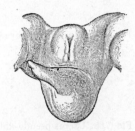

FIG. 761

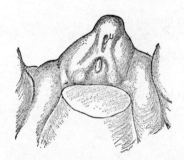

FIG. 762

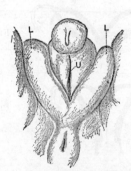

FIG. 763

FIG. 761. Genital tubercle in an 8 mm. embryo (Keibel and Mall).
FIG. 762. Genital tubercle in an embryo 16.8 mm. (Spaulding).   U, urethral groove.
FIG. 763. Development of external genitalia in an embryo 49 mm. (Spaulding).   U, urethral groove; L, labioscrotal fold.

Further development of the primary genital tubercle results in the formation of the shaft and glans of the clitoris.   The folds or margins of the urethral groove do not unite as in the male but develop into the labia minora and surround the urethrovaginal orifice.   Likewise, the labioscrotal swellings fail to fuse except at their posterior extremities and persist as the labia majora (8) (Fig. 763). On the following pages 494 and 495 many of the anomalies of development are diagrammatically shown.

FIG. 764. Uterus unicornis

FIG. 765. Uterus didelphys or duplex separatus.

FIG. 766. Uterus pseudo-didelphys

FIG. 767. Uterus bicornis duplex.

FIG. 768. Uterus bicornis septus.

FIG. 769. Uterus septus bilocularis.

FIG. 770. Uterus subseptus uniformis

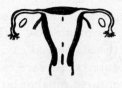

FIG. 771. Uterus subseptus biforis suprasimplex unicorpus.

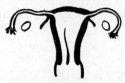

FIG. 772. Uterus infraseptus biforis.

FIG. 773. Uterus bicornis unicollis.

FIG. 774. Uterus bicornis with rudimentary horn.

FIG. 775. Uterus bicornis subseptus unicollis.

FIG. 776. Uterus subseptus unicollis.

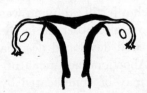

FIG. 777. Uterus arcuatus.

PREGNANCY IN A RUDIMENTARY HORN. The cavity of a rudimentary horn frequently does not communicate with the other horn or with the cervix. Pregnancy, therefore, usually occurs as a result of external migration of the ovum and spermatozoon (Figs. 774 and 778). For the same reason, the ovum must either remain within the rudimentary horn or be expelled into the abdominal cavity. Since the muscular wall usually is poorly developed, rupture takes place early in pregnancy and the symptoms are similar to those of a ruptured tubal or interstitial pregnancy (9, 10, 11). The treatment is immediate removal of the ruptured horn by laparotomy.

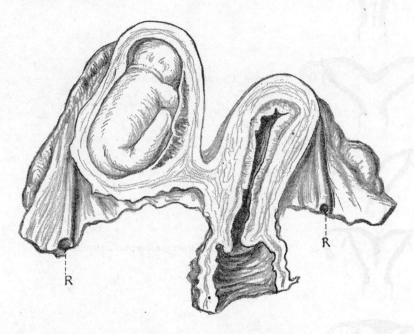

FIG. 778. Pregnancy in the rudimentary horn of a bicornate uterus. Note the absence of any communication with either the nonpregnant horn or the cervix.

UTERUS BICORNIS. Pregnancy may take place in either horn of a bicornate or double uterus and rare instances are reported in which a fertilized ovum was implanted in each side. The usual pregnancy changes are also observed in the nonpregnant horn, which hypertrophies and acquires a well developed decidua that is expelled at the time of or shortly after labor. Abortion and premature labor occur with slightly increased frequency. Labor may be complicated by inertia, breech and transverse presentations, and obstruction due to the enlarged nonpregnant horn. Frequently, the delivery is spontaneous and the condition is not recognized until the patient is examined in the puerperium (12, 13).

Labor should be conducted in an expectant manner. Abnormal presentations, however, must be corrected and if the nonpregnant horn obstructs delivery, cesarean section may be indicated. When the latter operation is done, it should be followed by hysterectomy. If it is desirable to preserve the child-bearing function, the nonpregnant horn should be removed, since its retention after cesarean section may interfere with drainage and lead to difficulty in the puerperium.

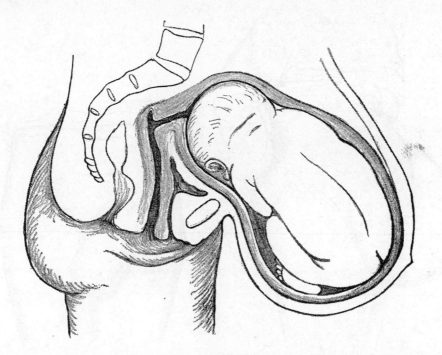

FIG. 779. Pendulous abdomen complicating pregnancy.

ANTERIOR DISPLACEMENT OF THE UTERUS, PENDULOUS ABDOMEN. Marked anterior displacement of the uterus is frequent among multiparae. Owing to the separation of the recti and the laxness of the abdominal muscles which results from frequent childbearing, the uterus falls forward and gives rise to the condition known as pendulous abdomen (Fig. 779). Disproportion between the presenting part and the pelvis likewise may cause the uterus to become acutely anteflexed and it also occasionally may form part of the contents of a ventral or inguinal hernia (14, 15) (Figs. 780 and 781).

Pendulous abdomen is responsible for much difficulty in labor. In the first stage, the posterior displacement of the cervix retards its dilatation while the faulty axis of the uterus favors deflexion of the head and may even cause complete extension. Due to the anterior displacement of the uterus, the force of the contractions is misdirected and the presenting part, instead of being driven into the pelvic brim, is forced against the sacral promontory. The relaxed abdominal walls likewise are responsible for weak and ineffectual bearing-down efforts which further complicate the stage of expulsion.

During pregnancy, the tendency toward a pendulous abdomen should be corrected by the use of a properly adjusted maternity corset (Figs. 93, 94 and 95).

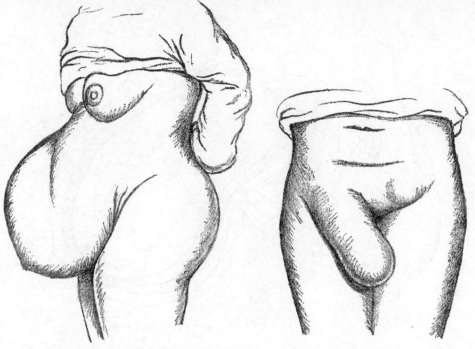

FIG. 780. Pregnant uterus protruding in a
ventral hernia.

FIG. 781. Pregnant uterus in an inguinal
hernia (Eisenhart).

Immediately after the onset of labor, the possibility of disproportion must be ruled out. This is particularly true in all primiparous labors, since the firm abdominal walls of young women who are pregnant for the first time does not permit anterior displacement of the uterus unless the presenting part cannot enter the pelvis. **Usually, therefore, pendulous abdomen in a primipara is evidence of disproportion.**

Dystocia from other causes should be corrected and, in the cases of marked disproportion, suprapubic delivery is indicated.

Pendulous abdomen and anterior displacement of the uterus are best corrected by the use of a snug abdominal binder throughout labor (Fig. 285). If, for any reason, such treatment cannot be carried out, the thighs should be flexed on the trunk while the patient lies on her back, or the squat position may be used. In either of these positions, the thighs splint the abdominal wall and help to hold the uterus in position during the contractions.

POSTERIOR DISPLACEMENT OF THE UTERUS is common in the early months of pregnancy and usually is spontaneously corrected as the enlarging uterus rises out of the pelvis soon after the first trimester.   If it is adherent, however, the fundus projects downward and backward and, with the progress of pregnancy, gives rise to marked pressure symptoms.   The vesical irritability noted early in gestation becomes aggravated and difficulty is experienced in emptying the

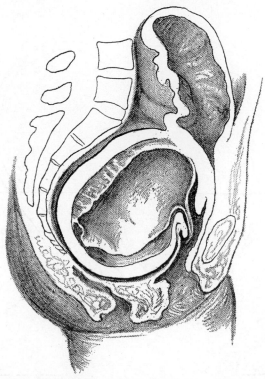

FIG. 782. Incarceration of an adherent retroverted pregnant uterus.   Pressure on the vesical neck is causing bladder distension (Schwytzer).

bladder.   Pressure on the vesical neck favors retention of urine and ultimately becomes sufficient to cause marked distention.   In such circumstances, dribbling of urine or paradoxical incontinence causes the patient to consult her physician. Constipation and backache also are troublesome.   If the condition is not relieved, rupture of the bladder and sloughing of the uterus may take place (Fig. 782). Spontaneous abortion is common.   Rarely, the anterior wall of the uterus becomes greatly elongated and, by projecting upward into the abdominal cavity, allows the pregnancy to continue (Fig. 783).   The cervix is then displaced anteriorly and lies above the symphysis while the posterior wall of the uterus is wholly within the pelvic cavity.   Delivery in such circumstances is impossible and the uterus inevitably ruptures (16, 17, 18)

Spontaneous correction of non-adherent retrodisplacement of the uterus is favored by the knee-chest position early in pregnancy and the continued use of the latter for a few minutes each night and morning for several weeks usually corrects the condition. Manual reposition and the use of a pessary, accordingly, are seldom necessary. When the uterus is adherent, laparotomy is indicated before the symptoms of incarceration become marked. If sacculation takes place and the pregnancy goes to term, the child should be delivered by cesarean section.

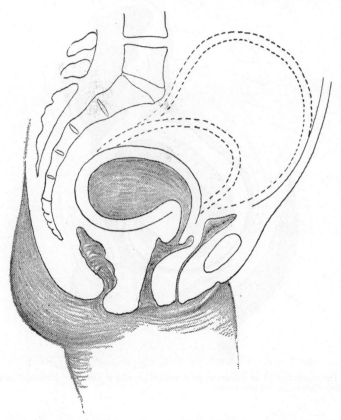

FIG. 783. Sacculation in a pregnant, adherent, retroverted uterus. Note the elongation of the anterior uterine wall (Oldham).

DYSTOCIA DUE TO NEW GROWTHS in and adjacent to the uterus has been discussed in Chapter XXVII.

DYSTOCIA DUE TO VENTROFIXATION OF THE UTERUS. Abdominal operations done for retroversion may result in fixation of the uterus to the anterior abdominal wall. When pregnancy occurs in such a uterus, its posterior wall becomes elongated to enclose most of the gestation sac, while the anterior wall remains short and thick. The cervix, accordingly, is displaced posterioriy and often lies above the promontory (Fig. 784).

Dilatation of the cervix is rendered much more difficult, and serious dystocia is common. Similar difficulties are encountered after anterior vaginal fixation and the interposition operation.

Because of the dystocia which follows fixation of the uterus, cesarean section with sterilization is indicated. In some cases, however, spontaneous dilatation of the cervix does occur and delivery through the natural passages is possible. Because of the great difficulties that must be overcome in the latter cases, cesarean section is preferable whenever the length of labor, the previous vaginal manipulations, and the hours that the membranes have been ruptured do not offer a serious contraindication (19, 20, 21).

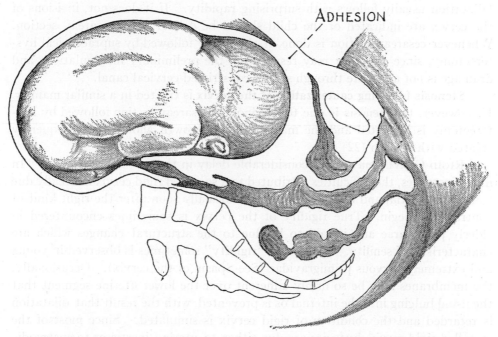

ADHESION

FIG. 784. Pregnancy after ventrofixation of the uterus. The cervix is displaced posteriorly and lies above the promontory. The anterior wall is short and thick while marked elongation of the posterior wall has occurred.

STENOSIS AND ATRESIA OF THE CERVIX. Changes in the cervix due to inflammation, scar tissue formation and new growths may cause stenosis of the cervix and, if the condition progresses after conception takes place, actual atresia may develop. **Old lacerations of the cervix** sometimes give rise to tough cicatrices which may cause delay in the first stage. Usually, however, extensively scarred and hypertrophied cervices undergo great softening during pregnancy and, as a rule, dilate much more readily than might be anticipated. Occasionally, such tears extend and may lead to troublesome hemorrhage.

The operation of trachelorrhaphy may alter the cervix and interfere with dilatation. Sooner or later, however, the canal opens along the scars on each side of the cervix and delivery is accomplished. Following labor, such cases require immediate resuturing to restore the continuity of the cervical canal and prevent serious hemorrhage.

Amputation of the cervix, particularly the high operation, is frequently followed by miscarriage or premature labor. When the pregnancy goes to term, stenosis or even atresia may be noted. As a result the external os often is difficult to find on vaginal examination. Inspection through a speculum, however, usually will reveal it as a slight projection or dimple. In cases of atresia, the dimple should be perforated and stretched slightly by the finger or a small clamp. Dilatation usually follows with surprising rapidity. If it does not, incisions of the cervix are indicated or the child should be delivered by cesarean section. Whenever cesarean section is done, it should be followed by supracervical hysterectomy, since infection may result from the preliminary manipulations and drainage is not adequate through such a constricted cervical canal.

Stenosis following cauterization of the cervix is treated in a similar manner. If, however, the stenosis is due to carcinoma, cesarean section followed by hysterectomy is indicated and the malignant new growth should be subsequently treated with radium (22).

RIGID CERVIX may cause considerable delay in the first stage of labor. In many instances, the difficulties attributed to a so-called rigid cervix are really due to uterine inertia, and dilatation proceeds normally soon after the right kind of contractions begin. True rigidity of the cervix is sometimes encountered in elderly primiparae and is said to be due to the structural changes which are characteristic of senility. Spasmodic "rigidity" sometimes is observed in young and extremely nervous primigravidae (See Spasm of the cervix). Occasionally, the membranes may be so firmly adherent over the lower uterine segment that the usual bulging into the internal os is prevented, with the result that dilatation is retarded and the condition of rigid cervix is simulated. Since most of the so-called rigid cervix dystocias are due either to uterine inertia or to spasmodic "rigidity", the use of sedatives as recommended in the preceding chapter is indicated (23, 24).

RIGID PERINEUM. The perineum may lack the normal succulence which permits the usual stretching that is observed as the head is being born. This condition of rigidity is noted in primiparae and is more common in those who are over 35 years of age. A plastic operation on the posterior vaginal wall also may be responsible for an unyielding perineum. Not infrequently, the pain caused by the pressure of the presenting part is followed by attempts on the part of the patient to hold back and retard the descent of the head. The lack of advance then simulates that observed when the perineum is rigid. Sufficient anesthesia, however, to relieve the suffering is followed by normal progress of labor. Rigid perineum causes considerable delay in the second stage, adds to the risk of fetal death and greatly increases the danger of extensive laceration. It is readily recognized on vaginal examination and is treated by mediolateral episiotomy.

A BARTHOLIN CYST OR ABSCESS may be present at the time of labor. If it is large enough to obstruct the passage of the child, or if it is in danger of rupture, aspiration is indicated. In the case of an abscess, great care should be taken to prevent the spreading of the infection to the upper birth passages.

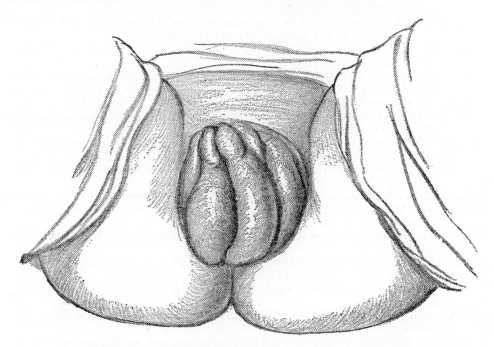

FIG. 785. Extensive edema of the vulva complicating pregnancy.

EDEMA OF THE VULVA. Eclampsia, the pressure effects of a prolonged labor, and the repeated use of irritating antiseptics sometimes cause marked edema of the vulva. The extremely swollen labia are tense and bulge well beyond the adjacent integument so that they completely close the vulvovaginal opening. Vaginal examination, accordingly, is more difficult and the progress of labor may be interrupted. Deep tears are common and gangrene may follow. If necessary, the edema fluid may be liberated by multiple incisions. Since the prolonged pressure caused by the increasing serous exudate lowers the resistance of the tissues, great care must be taken to guard against infection when the incisions are made as well as during the perineal stage of labor (Fig. 785).

GRANULOMA INGUINALE. The lesions of granuloma inguinale may be sufficiently extensive to interfere with the progress of labor. Because of the presence of secondary infection, vaginal examinations should not be made and cesarean section should not be considered. Delivery through the natural passages is possible and should be awaited (25).

REFERENCES

1. TOURNEUX, J. AND LEGAY, C.: Développement de l'utérus et du vagin depuis la fusion des conduits de Müller jusqu'à la naissance. Cong. périod. internat. de sc. med. Comptrend, 1884, Copenhagen, 1886, i sec. d'anat.
2. KOFF, A. K.: Development of the Vagina in the Human Fetus. Contrib. to Embryol., Carnegie Inst., No. 140, 1931, 24, 61.
3. HUNTER, R. H.: Observations on the Development of the Human Female Genital Tract. Contrib. to Embryol., Carnegie Inst., No. 129, 1930, 22, 91.
4. SCAMMON, R. E.: Prenatal Growth and Natal Involution of the Human Uterus. Proc. Soc. Exp. Biol. & Med., 1926, 23, 687.
5. CLARK, H. R.: A Contribution to the Origin of the Uterine Muscle in Relation to Blood Vessels. J. O. & G. Brit. Emp., 1911, 20, 85.
6. FELIX, A.: Keibel & Mall, 1912, 2, 925.
7. KEIBEL, F.: Zur Entwicklungsgeschichte des menschlichen Urogenitalapparates. Arch. f. Anat. u. Entwick., 1896, 55.
8. SPAULDING, M. H.: The Development of the External Genitalia in the Human Embryo. Contrib. to Embryol., Carnegie Inst., No. 61, 1921, 13, 67.
9. SÄNGER: Ueber Schwangerschaft im rudimentären Nebenhorn bei Uterus duplex. Zentralbl. f. Gyn., 1883, 7, 324.
10. KEHRER: Das Nebenhorn des doppelten Uterus. Heidelberg, 1900.
11. BECKMANN, W.: Weiterer Beitrag zur Gravidität im rudimentären Uterushorn. Zeitschr. f. Geburtsh. u. Gyn., 1911, 68, 600.
12. BETTMAN, M.: A Case of Labor in a Bicornate Uterus. Johns Hopkins Hosp. Bull., 1902, 13, 56.
13. MILLER, N. F.: Clinical Aspects of Uterus Didelphys. Am. J. O. & G., 1922, 4, 398.
14. ADAMS, S. S.: Hernia of the Pregnant Uterus. Am. J. O., 1889, 22, 225.
15. EISENHART, H.: Fall von hernia inguinalis cornu dextri uteri gravidi. Arch. f. Gyn., 1885, 26, 439.
16. OLDHAM, H.: Case of Retroflexion of the Gravid Uterus During Labour at Term. Tr. Obs. Soc. Lond., 1860, 1, 317.
17. DÜHRSSEN, A.: Ueber Aussackungen Rückwärtsneigungen und Knickungen der schwangeren Gebärmutter. Arch. f. Gyn., 1899, 57, 70.
18. CAMPBELL, J.: Rupture of an Incarcerated Retroverted Gravid Uterus. Recovery. J. O. & G., Brit. Emp., 1908, 14, 403.
19. ANDREWS, H. R.: On the Effect of Ventral Fixation of the Uterus upon Subsequent Pregnancy and Labor Based on the Analysis of 395 Cases. J. O. & G., Brit. Emp., 1905, 8, 97.
20. WILLIAMS, J. W.: Dystocia Following Ventral Suspension and Fixation of the Uterus. Tr. Southern Surg. & Gyn. Assn., 1906, 19, 237.
21. WEIBEL, W.: Ueber Schwangerschaft und Geburt nach Interpositio uteri vesico-vaginalis. Arch. f. Gyn., 1916, 105, 65.
22. AHLSTRÖM, G.: Zwei Kaiserschnitte wegen narbiger Verengerung der weichen Geburtswege. Mitth. a. d. Gyn., Klin. d. Prof. O. Engström, 1904, 6, 289.
23. OING, M.: Schnurfurchenbildung am Neugeborenenschädel infolge Rigidität des Muttermundes. Zentralbl. f. Gyn., 1929, 53, 150.
24. MATHIEU, A. AND SCHAUFFLER, G. C.: The Rigid and Stenosed Cervix in the First Stage of Labor. Am. J. O. & G., 1928, 16, 390.
25. WILSON, L. A.: Pregnancy and Labor Complicated by Granuloma Inguinale. J. A. M. A., 1930, 95, 1093.

CHAPTER XXX

FAULTY PASSAGES—CONTRACTED PELVES

At birth the various parts of the bony pelvis are represented by cartilaginous structures which contain ossification centers in various stages of development. The sacrum is made up of twenty-one osseous segments which are joined by cartilage. Likewise, only partial ossification of the ilium, ischium and pubis has occurred but these too are united by cartilage in the region of the acetabulum. The acetabulum, accordingly, is largely cartilaginous as are also the crests of the ilia and the rami of the pubes and ischia. The bodies of the sacral vertebrae are not united until the seventh year, while ossification of the sacrum and os innominatum is not complete until after the twentieth (1) (Figs. 786 and 787).

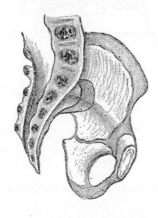
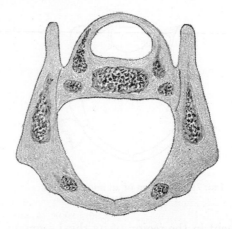

FIG. 786. Sagittal section through the pelvis of a newly born child showing the relative proportion of bone and cartilage (Williams).

FIG. 787. Section through an infantile pelvis showing the relative proportion of bone and cartilage (Williams).

Not only is the infant's pelvis more plastic, but its shape differs from that of the adult. The sacral portion is narrower and has a diminished vertical concavity. The promontory is much less marked and the horizontal rami of the pubes are shorter. Because of these differences, the pelvic inlet is narrower and more circular in shape, the tranverse and anteroposterior diameters being almost equal in length. The cavity likewise is more funnel-shaped and terminates in an outlet which is considerably constricted by a more acute pubic arch. Even at this time, however, the effect of sex is noticeable in that the female infant's pelvis has a wider pubic arch, larger sacrosciatic notches and a broader cavity (2, 3).

DEVELOPMENT OF THE PELVIS

The change from the fetal form to that of the adult is brought about by inherent developmental and mechanical factors. The former cause a marked broadening of the sacrum, a widening of the inlet and an increase in the subpubic angle. By some, they are thought to be the chief cause of the changes seen in the adult pelvis (4). The mechanical factors consist of a downward pressure exerted by the weight of the trunk, and an upward and lateral pressure from the femora together with the peculiar response of the various parts of the pelvis to these forces. Since the center of gravity is anterior to the promontory, the weight of the child's trunk exerts a downward and forward pressure on the body of the first sacral segment. This tends to rotate the sacrum on its transverse axis. The strong ischiosacral ligaments, however, prevent such a rotation, with the result that the promontory is forced forward and the somewhat plastic sacrum is

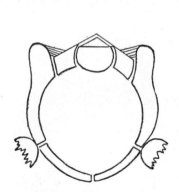

FIG. 788. Diagram of an infant's pelvis (Schroeder).

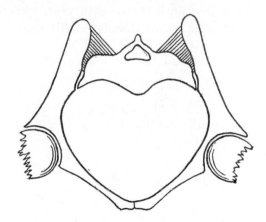

FIG. 789. Diagram of an adult pelvis (Schroeder).

bent in the region of its third segment. This action, accordingly, is responsible for the indentation of the pelvic inlet by the sacral promontory and causes a considerable increase in the vertical concavity of the sacrum. Because of the wedge-like articulation between the sacrum and innominate bones, the body weight likewise acts to displace the entire sacrum downward and forward, but this action is resisted by the posterior iliosacral ligaments. The resulting pull exerted on the posterior superior spines tends to rotate the innominate bones outward, as a consequence of which they are bent rather acutely in the region between the sacroiliac articulations and the acetabula. The pelvic inlet is thereby increased transversely and diminished anteroposteriorly (Figs. 788 and 789).

These mechanical factors unquestionably have a marked effect when disease of the osseous system renders the pelvic bones unusually plastic. They accordingly help to explain the mode of formation of some of the contracted pelves.

In the absence of such disease, however, their effect has been overestimated and plausible as they may seem, belief in their influence is weakened by the observation that sexual and racial characteristics apparently are not greatly altered by them.

CHARACTERISTICS OF THE MALE AND FEMALE PELVIS

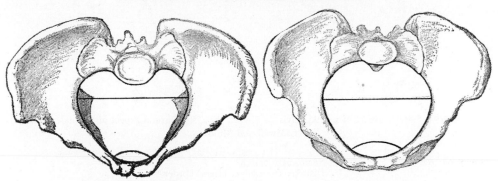

FIG. 790. Inlet of a male pelvis (Caldwell and Moloy).

FIG. 791. Inlet of a female pelvis (Caldwell and Moloy).

Male		Female
Heart shaped	Shape	More oval
Shorter	Anteroposterior diameter	Longer
More posterior	Transverse diameter	Less posterior
Straighter, more angular	Anterior iliac portion	Broad, gracefully curved
Shorter	Posterior iliac portion	Longer
Short, broad, stout	Region from iliopectineal eminence to apex of sacrosciatic notch	Longer, not so broad, not so stout

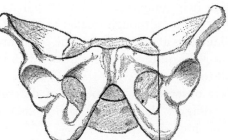 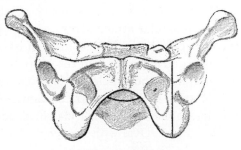

FIG. 792. Anterior aspect of a male pelvis (Caldwell and Moloy).

FIG. 793. Anterior aspect of a female pelvis (Caldwell and Moloy).

Male		Female
Long, heavy, juts forward	Symphysis	Short, light, does not protrude so much
Narrow	Subpubic angle	Wide
Longer	Descending pubic rami	Shorter
Arise from lower border of pubes		Arise from lower lateral borders of pubes
Edges straight		Edges roll out
Pass directly downward at an acute angle		Curve outward
Gothic arch		Norman arch
Narrow	Outlet	Wide
8 cm.	Bisischial diameter	11 cm.
101 mm.	Depth of pelvis (iliopectineal line to tuberosities)	90 mm.

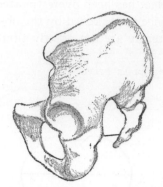
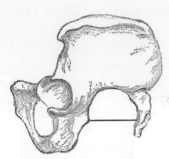

FIG. 794. Lateral aspect of a male pelvis   FIG. 795. Lateral aspect of a female pelvis
(Caldwell and Moloy).

Male		*Female*
Long, narrow	Sacrosciatic notch	Wide
Short	Distance from lower lateral border to ischial spine	Long
Short	Sacrospinous ligament	Long
Short	Posterior sagittal diameter	Long
Narrower		Broader
Longer		Shorter
Straighter	Sacrum	More concave
Heavier		Lighter

SEXUAL DIFFERENCES are present even in the fetus. They, however, are pronounced in adult life and are sufficiently characteristic in many cases to aid the anthropologist in the diagnosis of sex. In general, the male pelvis is heavier, deeper and narrower. The bones of which it is composed are larger and have heavier muscular attachments. The pelvic cavity, although smaller at the inlet, becomes greatly diminished in all of its diameters at the outlet. The pubic arch is longer and narrower, and the subpubic angle is quite acute in contrast with the broad arch of the female pelvis (Figs. 790 to 795).

RACIAL CHARACTERISTICS likewise are observed in the pelves of different peoples. They have been classified according to the shape of their inlets as:

    1. Oval with transverse lengthening—platypellic.

    2. Round—mesatipellic.

    3. Oval with anteroposterior lengthening—dolichopellic.

The oval pelvis with transverse lengthening is said to be characteristic of the females of the more highly civilized races. It is found predominantly among Caucasians and Mongolians. The round or mesatipellic type is characteristic of Kaffirs and Malayans, while the aboriginal Australians have elliptical pelves with anteroposterior lengthening (5, 6).

From the foregoing discussion, it will be seen that race, sex, developmental and mechanical factors play some part in the formation of the adult pelvis. If these are properly coordinated, the pelvis is normal. Unfortunately, however, this necessary coordination often is lacking and, as a result, many variations are observed. The normal shape of the pelvis may be retained but its size may be increased or greatly diminished. A lag in the development of some of the constituents likewise may cause an alteration in its form. Often, too, it seems that the underlying factors which are responsible for the sexual characteristics fail to function normally, with the result that the female pelvis frequently develops certain of the male characteristics. It accordingly is extremely difficult to classify pelvic anomalies (7, 8, 9).

Formerly, all classifications of abnormal pelves were based upon the rather rare specimens that from time to time were obtained from anatomical and autopsy material. Most often, the deductions, concerning the frequency of each variety and its effect on labor, were made from pelvic measurements taken during life. Because such measurements often are inadequate and vary within wide limits, the prognosis as to delivery through the natural passages in all but the markedly abnormal cases cannot be definite.

The addition of the x-ray to our facilities now enables us to measure the inlet accurately and offers a suitable means of studying variations in form and structure. While the number of x-ray observations is not sufficient to justify a final classification of abnormal pelves based only upon such studies, they do warrant the conclusion that many of the former deductions dependent upon pelvimetry are erroneous (10). As the newer evidence accumulates, the entire subject of contracted pelvis, accordingly, will have to be revised. Preliminary to such a revision, it has been suggested that pelves be classified as follows (11):

A. Gynecoid
   Oval with transverse diameter increased
   Ordinary female pelvis
   1. Narrow outlet
   2. Moderate outlet
   3. Wide outlet
   4. Large
   5. Small

B. Android
   Heart shaped
   Female pelvis with male characteristics
   1. Narrow outlet
   2. Moderate outlet
   3. Wide outlet
   4. Large
   5. Small

C. Anthropoid
   Oval with anteroposterior diameter increased
   Female pelvis with characteristics of the
      anthropoid ape
   1. Narrow outlet
   2. Moderate outlet
   3. Wide outlet
   4. Large
   5. Small

D. Platypelloid
   Female pelvis flattened
   1. Narrow outlet
   2. Moderate outlet
   3. Wide outlet
   4. Large
   5. Small

E. Asymmetrical pelvis
   1. Narrow outlet
   2. Moderate outlet
   3. Wide outlet
   4. Large
   5. Small

In this classification, the shape of the inlet is the chief characteristic but other points of difference are also considered. These include the length, curvature and inclination of the sacrum, the breadth and depth of the sacrosciatic notch, the depth of the pelvis from the tuberosities to the iliopectineal line and the length, width and character of the pubic arch (11).

The chief points of difference among these types are found in the variations in the two segments of the inlet which are divided by the widest transverse diameter of the superior aperture. The posterior segment or that portion which is behind the widest transverse diameter is regarded as the dominant factor and determines the type to which the pelvis belongs.

FIG. 796. Gynecoid pelvis (Caldwell and Moloy).

The **gynecoid** pelvis is the true female pelvis and is the commonest type found in women (Fig. 796). Its inlet is round or oval with the transverse diameter slightly larger than the anteroposterior. The widest transverse diameter is considerably anterior to the promontory and as a consequence **the dominant posterior segment is broad and deep.** Anteriorly the lateral walls curve gently towards the symphysis to form a rather broad and well rounded fore-pelvis. The sacrosciatic notch and the posterior iliac portion of the inlet at the apex of the notch are average in size but the sacrum slopes backward and produces a wide sacrosciatic aperture thus increasing the space in the posterior pelvis. The descending rami of the pubes are given off from the lower lateral aspect of each pubic bone to form a wide pubic arch, the angle of which is equal to or greater than a right angle. The fetal head usually enters this type of pelvis transversely and engages in slight asynclitism, the mechanism being that which was described as normal in Chapter XII. Because of its spacious posterior segment and its roominess in general the gynecoid pelvis causes little or no difficulty in labor.

The **android** pelvis represents the masculine and funnel pelves of other classifications (Fig. 797). Due to the fact that the promontory deeply indents the inlet the latter is often described as heart shaped. It also has been termed wedge shaped because its more or less straight lateral walls converge anteriorly to form a relatively narrow and rather sharply angulated fore-pelvis. The widest transverse diameter is close to the promontory and as a result **the dominant posterior segment is shallow.** The sacrosciatic notch is narrow and the sacrum tends to be inclined forward with the result that the space in the entire posterior pelvis is relatively shallow. The descending rami spring from the under surface of the pubic bones and give rise to a narrow pubic arch. The subpubic angle accord-

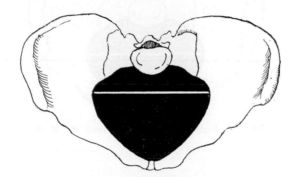

FIG. 797. Android pelvis (Caldwell and Moloy).

ingly is narrow and the lateral walls tend to converge with the result that the transverse diameter of the outlet is short. The symphysis is long, the bones are heavy and the pelvic cavity is deep.

Although the general tendency is for the head to enter an android pelvis transversely, posterior positions of the occiput occur rather frequently in this type of pelvis. The shallow posterior segment and the straight walled narrow fore-pelvis make engagement difficult while the lack of room posteriorly may interfere with the mechanism of labor after the head has passed through the inlet. The head frequently becomes arrested transversely in the midpelvis, and dystocia at the outlet is not uncommon. These difficulties coupled with the fact that the android pelvis occurs relatively frequently make this type of pelvis the commonest pelvic cause of difficult labor.

The **platypelloid** pelvis is characterized by short anteroposterior and wide transverse diameters (Fig. 798).   The shape of its inlet therefore is that of a narrow transverse ellipse with the widest transverse diameter about equidistant from the symphysis and promontory.   Because of its short anteroposterior diameters both **the anterior and posterior segments are relatively shallow.**   This pelvis is the simple flat pelvis of the old classifications but its occurrence is much less frequent than was formerly believed.   The fetal head enters the inlet transversely in marked asynclitism and the mechanism of labor is essentially that which is described subsequently in the discussion of the simple flat pelvis.

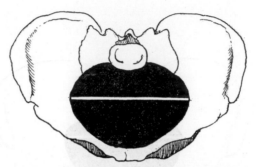

FIG. 798. Platypelloid pelvis (Caldwell and Moloy).

In the **anthropoid** pelvis the anteroposterior diameter of the inlet is long while the transverse is relatively or absolutely shortened (Fig. 799).   The shape of the superior aperture accordingly is that of a longitudinal ellipse.   Because its widest transverse diameter is considerably in front of the promontory **the posterior segment is deep.**   The sacrosciatic notch is wide and the sacrum is more or less vertical and often contains 6 segments.   This variety of pelvis occurs almost as frequently as the android type and corresponds to some of the pelves which used to be classified as assimilation pelves.   The head enters the pelvis obliquely and is posterior more frequently than anterior.   Arrest of the posteriorly placed occiput at the outlet and delivery as a persistent occipito posterior occasionally occurs.

As was previously stated this morphologic classification is complicated by the fact that the characteristics of one type may be combined with those of another. A pelvis accordingly may have a dominant gynecoid posterior segment with an android anterior segment in which case it would be classified as a gynecoid android pelvis and the mechanism of labor might well be altered as a result of this change in morphology. The intermingling of the characteristics of the different parent types gives rise to many combinations such as: gynecoid anthropoid; gynecoid flat; android gynecoid; anthropoid gynecoid; etc. (11a).

The incidence of the occurrence of the various parent types is shown in Table I.

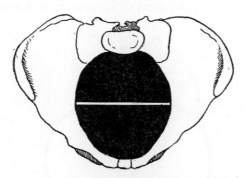

Fig. 799. Anthropoid pelvis (Caldwell and Moloy).

TABLE I
RELATIVE FREQUENCY OF THE VARIOUS TYPES OF PELVES
(Caldwell, Moloy and Swenson)

Anthropoid	22.7%
Gynecoid	50.6%
Android	22.4%
Asymmetrical	1.8%

The **asymmetrical** types usually are due to shortening of the posterior iliac segment on one side with an associated narrowing of the corresponding sacrosciatic notch.

Owing to the fact that sufficient x-ray observations have not been recorded to permit a full discussion of the various types and their effect on labor, it still is necessary to consider abnormal pelves from the standpoint of pelvimetry. In the following discussion, however, no attempt will be made to adhere to any of the older classifications and, wherever the newer x-ray methods have revealed pelvimetric errors, these will be noted. The different varieties of abnormal pelves, therefore, will be taken up in the order of their frequency. Following the consideration and management of the more common types, the rarer varieties will be described.

GENERALLY CONTRACTED PELVIS

GENERALLY CONTRACTED, JUSTO-MINOR PELVIS (Gynecoid, Small). In a generally contracted pelvis, the contraction is proportionate in all of the diameters, excepting the anteroposterior, which usually are shortened to a slightly greater degree. It therefore is a miniature of a normal pelvis that is somewhat flattened in its conjugate diameters (5, 12) (Figs. 800, 801, 802). While all of the bones are small and slender, the sacrum is particularly shortened and, owing to the less perfect development of its alae, is also somewhat narrowed.

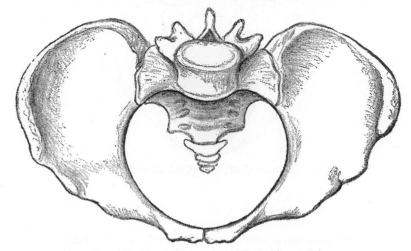

FIG. 800. Generally contracted, justominor pelvis.

FIG. 801. Sagittal section of a generally contracted pelvis (solid black) compared with the sagittal section of a normal pelvis (dotted lines).

FIG. 802. Pelvic inlet of a generally contracted pelvis (solid black) compared with that of a normal pelvis (dotted lines).

The generally contracted pelvis is the commonest type of pelvic deformity (13) encountered in this country and is usually found in small-boned, undersized women. In the opinion of most authorities, it is due to faulty development and by some is regarded as an evidence of degeneration that has resulted from the poor hygienic conditions commonly found in crowded cities.

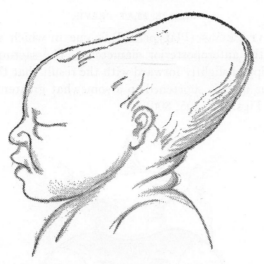

FIG. 803. Molding of the head due to a generally contracted pelvis.

DIAGNOSIS. Pelvimetry shows all of the diameters to be proportionately diminished with slightly greater shortening of the diagonal and external conjugates. As the degree of contraction never is extensive in nonrachitic pelves of this type, evidence of rickets should be looked for whenever the diagonal conjugate is below 9.5 cm. The rhomboid of Michaelis is small and narrow, and the diminutive nature of the other bones is apparent. Often the radius can be spanned by the extended thumb and little finger.

Typical Measurements of a Generally Contracted Pelvis

Interspinous diameter	22 cm.
Intercristal diameter	24.5 cm.
Intertrochanteric diameter	27.5 cm.
External conjugate	17 cm.
Diagonal conjugate	10.5 cm.
Bisischial	9.5 cm.

EFFECT ON LABOR. The mechanism of labor is essentially the same as that observed in a normal pelvis. Early and **marked flexion** assists engagement. In those cases in which the contraction is sufficient to cause dystocia, this often is overcome by further **molding of the head** with the result that it is greatly elongated along the occipitomental diameter (Fig. 803). Extreme flexion and marked molding, accordingly, are nature's means of overcoming the difficulties that may arise from a generally contracted pelvis.

The justo-minor characteristics are combined with those of flat, funnel, rachitic, and rachitic flat pelves in the generally contracted flat, generally contracted funnel, generally contracted rachitic and generally contracted flat rachitic pelves respectively.

SILMPE FLAT PELVIS

A SIMPLE FLAT PELVIS (Platypelloid) is one in which the contraction is limited largely to the anteroposterior diameters. The sacrum is nearer to the symphysis and is tipped slightly forward with the result that the anteroposterior measurement of the inlet is shortened to a somewhat greater degree than that of the outlet (14) (Figs. 804, 805, 806).

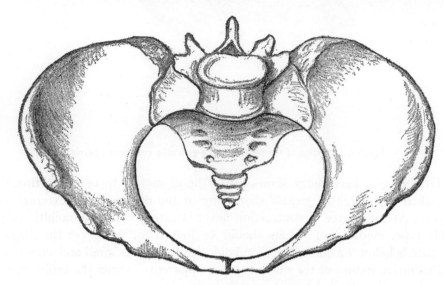

FIG. 804. Simple flat pelvis.

FIG. 805. Sagittal section of a simple flat pelvis (solid black) compared with the sagittal section of a normal pelvis (dotted lines).

FIG. 806. Pelvic inlet of a simple flat pelvis (solid black) compared with that of a normal pelvis (dotted lines).

European observers state that this type of contraction is more common than any other variety (14, 15). In this country, however, pelvimetry shows the incidence of its occurrence to be less than that of generally contracted and funnel pelves (13). According to the more accurate x-ray measurements, it is quite rare and the pelvis which usually is diagnosed as flat is, in reality, a female pelvis with masculine characteristics (android) (10, 11). The etiology of the nonrachitic flat pelvis is not definitely known. Overloading of the spinal column in early life is thought by some to cause a forward displacement of the sacrum which results in a flattening of the pelvis. From this standpoint, prolonged standing and the carrying of heavy burdens during childhood are mentioned as the commonest etiological factors. Others believe that the deformity is due largely to changes in the ossa innominata and, as similar findings are noted in rachitis, they consider the latter to have a causative relationship (16). Since the pelves of newborn children occasionally are somewhat flattened, the simple flat pelvis also has been regarded as a congenital defect (2).

DIAGNOSIS. Simple flat pelves frequently occur in women of large stature. The general appearance, accordingly, may prove deceptive unless the back is examined and the rhomboid of Michaelis is found to be flattened. Pelvimetry shows the transverse diameters to be approximately normal while the external and diagonal conjugates are contracted.

Typical Measurements of a Simple Flat Pelvis

Interspinous diameter	25	cm.
Intercristal diameter	28	cm.
Intertrochanteric diameter	31	cm.
External conjugate	18	cm.
Diagonal conjugate	10.5	cm.
Bisischial	10	cm.

EFFECT ON LABOR. The head enters the pelvis in a transverse position with the biparietal diameter occupying the roomier lateral aspect of the pelvis, while the shorter bitemporal is in relation to the contracted true conjugate, flexion is imperfect and the occipitofrontal plane rather than the suboccipito bregmatic descends into the pelvis by a movement known as asynclitism. The anterior parietal bone lies over the pelvic inlet and the sagittal suture is nearer to the sacrum (Fig. 807). The posterior parietal bone, accordingly, is arrested by the promontory while the anterior one is forced into the pelvic cavity. Levelling then takes place as the sagittal suture is rotated forward and the previously arrested parietal bone slips past the promontory. The advantage of this mechanism is similar to that gained by turning a table on its side and carrying it obliquely through a small doorway. Asynclitism of this type is known as Naegele's obliquity (Figs. 807, 808, 809).

The posterior parietal bone may present at the brim, and a similar mechanism is followed. This is known as Litzmann's obliquity (Fig. 810). Further advantage is gained by the marked molding of the head, which gives it a very asymmetrical shape (Fig. 811). Occasionally, a spoon-shaped fracture in the parietal region results from the pressure of the head against the promontory (Fig. 812).

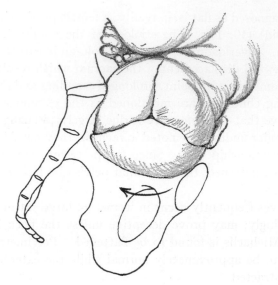

FIG. 807. Naegele's obliquity, anterior parietal presentation (Bumm). The sagittal suture lies near the sacrum and the posterior parietal bone is arrested by the promontory.

FIG. 808. Naegele's obliquity, anterior parietal presentation (Bumm). The anterior parietal bone has descended into the pelvis and the sagittal suture is being rotated anteriorly as the posterior parietal bone passes by the promontory.

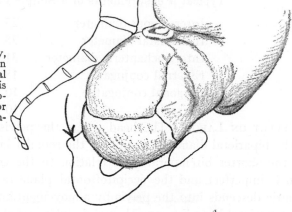

FIG. 809. Naegele's obliquity, anterior parietal presentation (Bumm). Levelling is complete, both parietal bones are now in the pelvis and the resistance of the pelvic floor is causing the occiput to rotate anteriorly. The subsequent mechanism is similar to that observed in a normal pelvis.

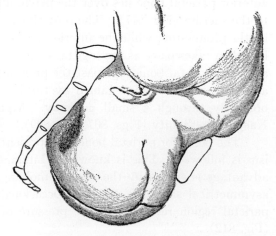

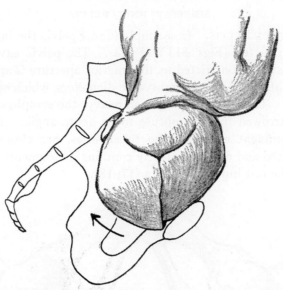

FIG. 810. Litzmann's obliquity, posterior parietal presentation (Bumm). The sagittal suture lies near to the symphysis and the anterior parietal bone is arrested by the pubic bones.

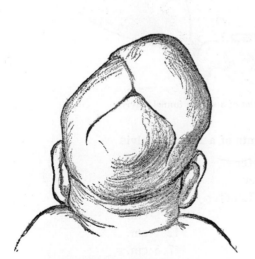

FIG. 811. Molding of the head due to a simple flat pelvis.

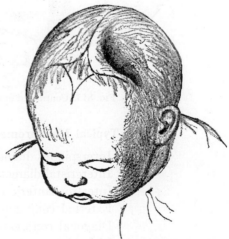

FIG. 812. Spoon-shape fracture in the parietal region due to pressure of the head against the promontory of a simple flat pelvis.

The characteristics of a flat pelvis are combined with those of generally contracted, rachitic and generally contracted rachitic pelves in the generally contracted flat, flat rachitic and generally contracted flat rachitic pelves respectively.

SIMPLE FUNNEL PELVIS.   In a simple funnel pelvis the inlet is normal but the outlet is contracted (Figs. 813 and 814).   The pelvic cavity, accordingly, becomes progressively constricted as the inferior aperture is approached.   This is particularly noticeable in the transverse diameters, which often are the only ones contracted.   The bones are large and heavy; the symphysis is long and the pubic arch is narrowed from an obtuse to an acute angle.   The spines of the ischium are prominent and, like the tuberosities, are closer together.   The sacrum is elongated and not infrequently contains six segments as a result of the assimilation of the last lumbar vertebra (17, 18).

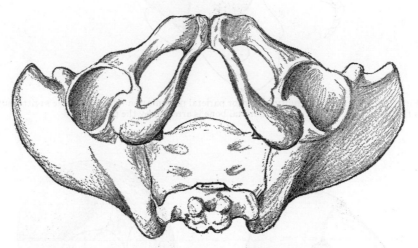

FIG. 813. Contracted outlet of a simple funnel pelvis.

Typical Measurements of a Funnel Pelvis

Interspinous diameter	25	cm.
Intercristal diameter	28	cm.
Intertrochanteric diameter	31	cm.
External conjugate	20	cm.
Diagonal conjugate	12	cm.
Bisischial	7.5	cm.
Posterior sagittal	8	cm.

Simple funnel pelvis of a slight degree is common and is found in about 5 per cent of women.   It is second in frequency among the contracted pelves and constitutes about one-third of all anomalies of the bony pelvis.   The exact cause of this developmental defect is not known.   Assimilation of the last lumbar vertebra alters the sacroiliac joint with the result that the lateral walls of the pelvic outlet converge (17).   The suggestion has been made that it is due to an

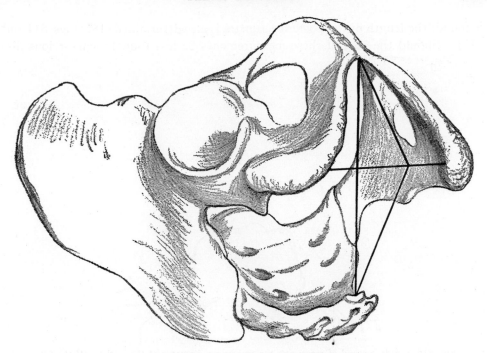

FIG. 814. Oblique view of the outlet showing the anterior and posterior sagittal diameters.

inversion of the male and female characteristics, which results in a male type in the ischiopubic portion without change in the female characteristics of the iliosacral region (8).

DIAGNOSIS. If the outlet of the pelvis is measured routinely, funnel pelvis is readily recognized by the narrowness of the pubic arch. The length of the bisischial diameter always is 8 cm. or less. Whenever contraction of this degree

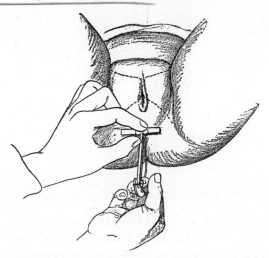

FIG. 815. Method of measuring the posterior sagittal diameter.

is found, the length of the posterior sagittal is also determined (18) (Figs. 814 and 815). Should the sum of these measurements be less than 15 cm. serious dis-

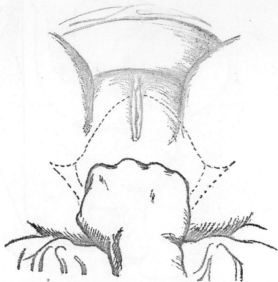

FIG. 816. Crude method of measuring the transverse diameter of the outlet. If the fist can be forced between the tuberosities of the ischium, the outlet is ample.

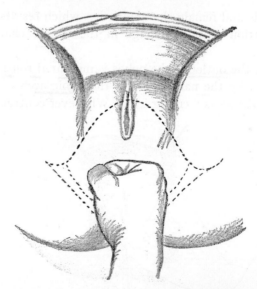

FIG. 817. Crude method of measuring the posterior sagittal diameter. If the fist can be forced into the pelvis, posterior to the bisischial line, as illustrated, the posterior sagittal diameter is ample.

proportion may be expected (19). If the examiner lacks the experience necessary to assure accuracy in taking these measurements, the crude method illustrated (Figs. 816 and 817) will be of value until he becomes more skilful.

EFFECT ON LABOR. Contraction of the bony outlet offers a serious obstacle to the progress of the presenting part and additional time is required for adequate molding of the head. In the meantime, the prolonged arrest of the head upon the maternal soft parts may cause necrosis. When delivery ultimately does occur, the presenting part is forced backward because of the narrowness of the pubic arch and the perineum is deeply torn (Figs. 818, 819, 820, 821). Posterior rotation of

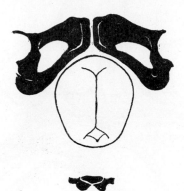

FIG. 818. Head passing out of a normal outlet.

FIG. 819. Head passing out of a funnel pelvis in which the posterior sagittal is ample.

FIG. 820. Head cannot pass out of this funnel pelvis because the posterior sagittal diameter is too small.

the occiput likewise is more common in funnel pelvis. Because of the delay encountered during the perineal stage of labor, operative interference often is necessary and extensive lacerations, which not infrequently involve the sphincter and rectum, are common. Hyperflexion of the thighs lengthens the anteroposterior diameter of the outlet. Its use, accordingly, increases the space posteriorly and facilitates delivery through a funnel pelvis (Fig. 821). Contraction of the posterior sagittal diameter, in addition to shortening of the bisischial, increases the difficulty and cesarean section is indicated when the sum of these two measurements is less than 15 cm.[19]

The funnel characteristics are combined with those of the generally contracted pelvis in a generally contracted funnel pelvis.

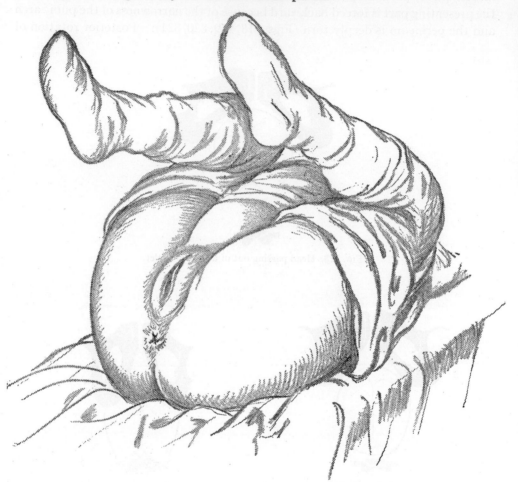

FIG. 821. Extreme flexion of the thighs on the trunk carries the inferior margin of the symphysis forward and away from the tip of the sacrum. This increases the length of the anteroposterior diameter of the outlet and the accompanying increase in the posterior sagittal permits the head to pass out of the pelvis. See Figure 136, page 209.

RACHITIC PELVES

RACHITIS interferes with the process of ossification with the result that the bones, at first, are abnormally soft and yielding. Marked deformities, accordingly, may arise from the action of the mechanical factors which normally alter the shape of the pelvis during infancy. If, at this time, the body is kept in the erect or sitting posture, its weight forces the promontory downward and forward, and thus shortens the anteroposterior diameter of the pelvic inlet. For the same reason, the lower part of the sacrum tends to rotate backward. The latter action, however, is resisted by the strong sacrospinous and sacrotuberous ligaments, with the result that the softened sacrum is bent backward more sharply in the region of its fourth segment. Less commonly this increase in the vertical concavity is not observed and the sacrum is found to be even straighter than normal. The bodies of the vertebrae also extend anteriorly beyond their lateral masses and convert the normal lateral concavity into a convexity. In some cases, the body of the first segment is out of line with the remainder of the sacrum and projects forward to form a false promontory. The sacrum, therefore, tends to rotate anteriorly on its transverse axis; its vertical concavity is accentuated and the lateral concavity is changed to a convexity. In addition to these characteristics, a rachitic pelvis is more delicately formed and is broader, shorter and thinner.

The posterior iliosacral ligaments exert a greater pull upon the posterior superior spines of the ilia as the promontory is displaced forward and the resulting closer approximation of the spines causes the iliac crests to flare outward. The anterior superior spines, accordingly, are relatively more widely separated and the interspinous diameter either approaches, is equal to, or is greater than the intercristal. The relationship between the sacral, iliac and pubic segments of the innominate bones is also altered. Instead of being about equal in length as they are in the normal pelvis, the iliac segment is markedly shortened while the sacral extremity is slightly diminished and the pubic portion remains unchanged (16). This change, together with the somewhat greater angulation of the iliopectineal line anterior to the sacroiliac synchondrosis, causes still greater shortening of the anteroposterior diameter of the inlet.

Owing to the fact that the child cannot walk, the upward and inward pressure of the femora is absent and, as a result, the pubic arch is relatively much wider than normal. The bisischial diameter, therefore, is longer than might be expected from the other measurements.

By pelvimetry and vaginal examination, the following characteristics of rickets may be observed:

1. The interspinous diameter approaches, is equal to, or is greater than the intercristal.

2. The vertical concavity of the sacrum either is increased or is eliminated to form almost a straight line.

3. The lateral concavity of the sacrum is converted into a convexity.

4. The inlet is diminished in size as is shown by great shortening of the diagonal conjugate.

5. The bisischial diameter is relatively large.

The usual types of rachitic pelves are:
1. Flat rachitic
2. Generally contracted rachitic
3. Generally contracted flat rachitic
4. Pseudo-osteomalacic

FLAT RACHITIC PELVIS

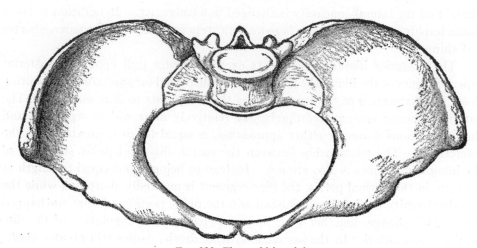

FIG. 823. Flat rachitic pelvis.

FIG. 824. Sagittal section of a flat rachitic pelvis (solid black) compared with that of a normal pelvis (dotted lines).

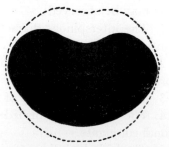

FIG. 825. Inlet of flat rachitic pelvis (solid black) compared with that of a normal pelvis (dotted lines).

FLAT RACHITIC PELVIS. A flat rachitic pelvis is one in which the characteristics of rickets are present and the inlet is contracted in its anteroposterior diameters only. The superior strait, accordingly, is more or less kidney-shaped (Figs. 823, 824, 825).

DIAGNOSIS. The external and diagonal conjugates are small and the bisischial diameter is large. All other measurements approximate the normal dimensions, but the interspinous approaches, is equal to, or exceeds the intercristal. The sacrum is convex laterally and its vertical concavity is either increased or obliterated. There is a history of rachitis in infancy and other evidences of the disease may be manifest in the skull, vertebral column, chest and lower extremities.

Typical Measurements of a Flat Rachitic Pelvis

Interspinous diameter	27	cm.
Intercristal diameter	27	cm.
Intertrochanteric diameter	30	cm.
External conjugate	17.5	cm.
Diagonal conjugate	10.5	cm.
Bisischial	12	cm.

GENERALLY CONTRACTED RACHITIC PELVIS. In this type of contraction, the rachitic characteristics are combined with those of the justo-minor pelvis, The inlet, accordingly, is proportionately diminished in all of its diameters and the outlet, although contracted, is wider than might be expected from the other measurements.

DIAGNOSIS. All of the measurements are proportionately shortened but the interspinous approaches, equals or exceeds the intercristal and the bisischial is relatively large for the other diameters. The sacrum is convex laterally and is either markedly curved vertically or is almost straight. Characteristics of rickets may be observed in other parts of the body.

GENERALLY CONTRACTED FLAT RACHITIC PELVIS. This is the variety in which the greatest contractions are most commonly found. It combines the characteristics of the flat and generally contracted rachitic pelves. In addition to being generally small, it is excessively contracted in the anteroposterior diameters (Figs. 826, 827, 828).

GENERALLY CONTRACTED FLAT RACHITIC PELVIS

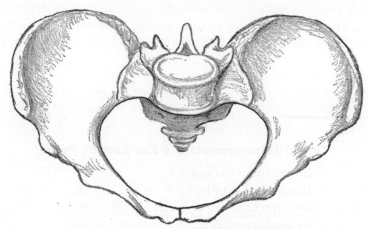

FIG. 826. Generally contracted flat rachitic pelvis.

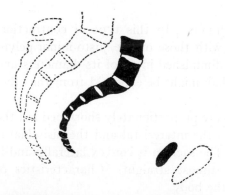

FIG. 827. Sagittal section of a generally contracted flat rachitic pelvis (solid black) compared with that of a normal pelvis (dotted lines).

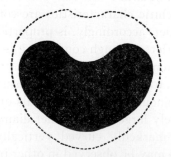

FIG. 828. Inlet of a generally contracted flat rachitic pelvis (solid black) compared with that of a normal pelvis (dotted lines).

DIAGNOSIS. Pelvimetry shows all of the diameters to be small and greater shortening is noted in the external and diagonal conjugates. The usual rachitic relation between the interspinous and intercristal also is observed and the characteristics of rickets are demonstrable in the curvatures of the sacrum.

Typical Measurements of a Generally Contracted Flat Rachitic Pelvis

Interspinous diameter	23 cm.
Intercristal diameter	22 cm.
Intertrochanteric diameter	27 cm.
External conjugate	16 cm.
Diagonal conjugate	9 cm.
Bisischial	10 cm.

PSEUDO-OSTEOMALACIC RACHITIC PELVIS is extremely rare and resembles the picture seen in osteomalacia in which the pubic bones project anteriorly like a beak while the sacrum and lateral walls approach each other and give to the markedly contracted brim a triradiate shape. The sacrum and innominate bones, however, show the usual characteristics of rachitis (Fig. 829).

EFFECTS OF RACHITIC PELVES ON LABOR. In general, the mechanism is similar to that observed in the simpler varieties of contracted pelves. The common occurrence of changes in the spinal column and lower extremities, however, causes alterations in the inclination of the pelvis and leads to more or less asymmetry of the pelvic cavity. These factors, together with the more prominent bodies of the sacral vertebrae, make engagement more difficult. Because of the added difficulties and the greater degree of contraction observed in rachitic pelves, operative interference of a major type is more frequently required. After the head has passed through the narrow inlet, however, the remainder of the labor is facilitated by the relative widening of the outlet.

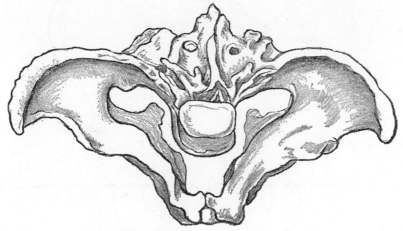

FIG. 829. Pseudo osteomalacic rachitic pelvis. Note the flaring out of the iliac crests (Breus and Kolisko).

ASSIMILATION PELVIS

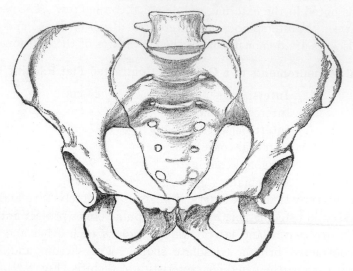

FIG. 830. High assimilation pelvis—inlet almost circular in shape, outlet contracted (Breus and Kolisko).

ASSIMILATION PELVIS is one of the commonest pelvic anomalies. The last vertebra may become assimilated to the sacrum and give to the latter six instead of the usual five segments—high assimilation pelvis. Less commonly, the first piece of the sacrum is missing and becomes a part of the last lumbar vertebra—low assimilation pelvis. Rarely, the last lumbar vertebra is only partially assimilated and but one side takes on the characteristics of the sacral vertebra while the other remains more or less unchanged—asymmetrical assimilation pelvis (20, 21).

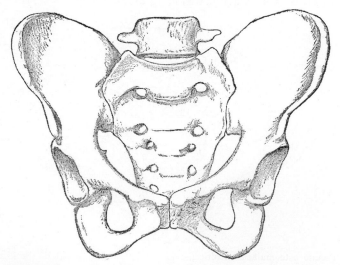

FIG. 831. High assimilation pelvis, with a relative increase in the anteroposterior diameter (anthropoid) (Breus and Kolisko).

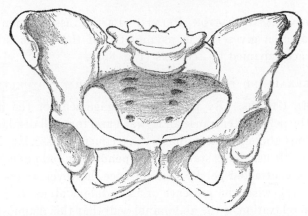

FIG. 832. Low assimilation pelvis—the sacrum has but four segments (Breus and Kolisko).

HIGH ASSIMILATION PELVIS. Assimilation of the last lumbar vertebra causes the sacrum to be longer and broader than usual. The high and less prominent promontory often gives to the inlet an almost circular shape while the outlet is contracted (Fig. 830). Less frequently, a transverse contraction of the inlet is observed and the long anteroposterior diameter then favors engagement of the head in the anteroposterior position (22). The latter variety resembles that of the ape and, accordingly, is referred to as the anthropoid pelvis (11) (Fig. 831).

LOW ASSIMILATION PELVIS. Assimilation of the first part of the sacrum with the lumbar vertebrae results in a short sacrum. This greatly diminishes the depth of the posterior pelvic wall, but has no particular influence on labor (Fig. 832).

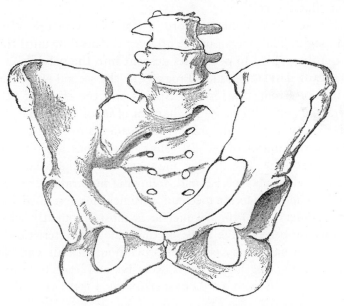

FIG. 833. Asymmetrical assimilation pelvis (Breus and Kolisko).

ASYMMETRICAL ASSIMILATION PELVIS. Partial assimilation of the last lumbar vertebra often gives rise to asymmetry of the pelvic inlet. It may, accordingly, be accompanied by scoliosis (Fig. 833).

MATERNAL AND FETAL DANGERS IN CONTRACTED PELVES

AXIS OF THE UTERUS. By preventing engagement of the head, marked contractions of the pelvis often cause an upward and forward displacement of the uterus. Pendulous abdomen, accordingly, is frequently associated with serious pelvic dystocia and it usually is stated that **a pendulous abdomen in a primipara is significant of a contracted pelvis.** Its absence, however, offers no assurance of engagement. Likewise, the presence of a pendulous abdomen in a multipara so often is due to relaxation of the abdominal wall that this diagnostic point is of little value in women who have had previous labors.

MALPRESENTATIONS are more commonly encountered in women with contracted pelves and the incidence of their occurrence increases with the degree of contraction. Breech presentation occurs twice as frequently and transverse is observed three times as often as in normal pelves. In fact, the occurrence of transverse presentations in primiparae with normal pelves is so rare that a contracted pelvis is always suspected whenever a shoulder presents in the course of a primiparous labor (13).

DELAYED DILATATION OF THE CERVIX. Because the presenting part fits poorly into the pelvic brim, the ball valve action of the head is lost and the full force of the uterine contractions is transmitted to the forewaters with the result that the membranes rupture early in labor. Thus, not only is nature's favorable hydrostatic dilator lost, but the obstructed head is prevented from making pressure on the undilated cervix.

The cervix, accordingly, hangs more or less loosely in the pelvis until the action of the longitudinal fibers pulls it up over the head or until the latter has become sufficiently molded to permit its descent into the pelvis.

SECOND STAGE DIFFICULTIES. Progress in the second stage depends upon the continuance of strong bearing-down pains and the effect of the particular form of contracted pelvis upon the mechanism of labor. For the characteristic effect of each variety of pelvic deformity, the reader is referred to the discussion which follows the description of the different types of contracted pelves. Should the dystocia be excessive, the mother may die from exhaustion or rupture of the uterus, or the child may perish and, following maceration, be expelled.

INERTIA. In addition to the mechanical difficulties described above, uterine inertia often is observed. Primary inertia is most frequently encountered in those women whose pelves have some of the male characteristics. Secondary inertia, on the other hand, may occur in association with all varieties of pelvic deformity in which the length of labor is excessive and leads to fatigue.

PRESSURE NECROSIS AND THE FORMATION OF FISTULAE. The head may become so tightly fixed in a contracted pelvis that it is unable to recede in the intervals between pains. As a result, restoration of the circulation in the soft parts compressed between it and the bony pelvis is impossible and necrosis follows. Within a few days the necrotic tissue sloughs and if it involves the bladder, cervix, rectum or vagina, a vesicocervical, vesicovaginal or rectovaginal fistula is formed. Incontinence of urine and feces accordingly were common sequelae of labors complicated by contracted pelves in preaseptic days when operative interference was infrequent.

RUPTURE OF THE UTERUS. As was mentioned in the discussion of faulty uterine contractions, pelvic dystocia may lead to tetanus uteri, and tetanic contractions, unless they respond to the use of sedatives or anesthesia, favor rupture of the uterus. More frequently, in obstructed labors, the lower uterine segment is progressively elongated with the result that the retraction ring approaches the level of the umbilicus. The lower segment thus is greatly thinned and finally ruptures unless delivery is effected. Palpation of a high retraction ring, therefore, is regarded as evidence of impending rupture of the uterus and constitutes an urgent indication for artificial delivery.

INFECTION. Early rupture of the membranes, repeated vaginal examinations and resort to operative interference individually and collectively increase the risk of infection. If labor is prolonged over several days, the onset of febrile symptoms may even be observed before the child is born. Intrapartum infection always is most serious because, as labor progresses, new avenues are opened for the spread of the invading micro-organisms. Usually, however, the first symptoms appear within a few days after delivery and the complication is diagnosed as postpartum infection, a condition which will be fully discussed in Chapter XXXVII.

PROLAPSED CORD. The poor fit between the head and the pelvis not only leads to early rupture of the membranes but likewise favors prolapse of the umbilical cord. Fetal death resulting from prolapsed cord, accordingly, is much more common in contracted pelvis and is responsible for a fair proportion of the fetal deaths which accompany pelvic dystocia.

ASPHYXIA. Interference with the uteroplacental circulation which results from the premature draining away of the hindwaters and the prolonged pressure of the head against the pelvis and maternal soft parts following the loss of the forewaters leads to intrauterine asphyxia. Because of the early rupture of the membranes in labor complicated by contraction of the pelvis, the risk to the child is much greater than in prolonged labors in which the membranes remain intact.

Temporary distortion of the fetal head often results from the marked molding that is required for its passage through a narrow pelvis. In addition, spontaneous, depressed fracture of the parietal bone is not infrequently observed when the dystocia is due to a flat pelvis. Fractures of the skull and intracranial hemorrhages, however, are most commonly the result of operative interference.

TREATMENT

In former times women having contracted pelves were given a real **test** of labor at the end of their first pregnancies. This test of labor was not considered complete until the cervix had become fully dilated and the patient had had several hours of good second stage pains after rupture of the membranes. If spontaneous delivery failed to occur the child was extracted through the natural passages even though this necessitated the use of a destructive operation. Whenever craniotomy was required the termination of all subsequent pregnancies by cesarean section was recommended. Although this routine subjected the mother to a long, difficult and at times dangerous first labor and entirely disregarded the interests of the first child, it prevented the use of many unnecessary cesarean sections. By enabling the obstetrician to do an elective operation at or before the onset of labor, it also reduced the risk of suprapubic delivery to a minimum whenever this procedure was subsequently required. Obstetric knowledge fortunately has advanced beyond the stage in which a real test of labor is now employed routinely in the management of contracted pelvis. Prognosis as to the possibility of delivery through the natural passages depends upon a knowledge of the three factors essential in labor—the powers, the passenger and the passages. Consideration, therefore, must be given to the **character of the expulsive efforts, the size, position and malleability of the child's head** as well as the **size and shape of the pelvis.**

The size of the pelvis may be estimated by means of pelvimetry, and abdominal palpation gives a fair impression of the fetal head. In addition, attempts to force the head into the pelvis reveal to some extent the cephalopelvic relationship. To these findings may be added the more accurate x-ray measurements of the head and pelvis; the effectiveness of the expulsive efforts, however, cannot be predicted. It often is impossible, therefore, to give a satisfactory prognosis in all but the very slight or very marked degrees of pelvic deformity until after the onset of labor.

In 2,274 labors complicated by contracted pelvis that were studied at the Johns Hopkins Hospital, 221 or 9.7 per cent were delivered by cesarean section (13). With each half centimeter diminution in the diagonal conjugate, there was an increase in the need for suprapubic delivery, which was employed in two-thirds and three-fourths of the cases in which the diagonal conjugate measured 9.5 cm. and 9 cm. respectively. Since the majority of the contracted pelves in this study occurred in Negro women who usually have relatively small children and since over half of the children born to white women were under 3,250 gm., it seems safe to assume that when a white woman has a diagonal conjugate of 9.5 cm. or under, a normal sized child has very little chance of being born alive.

DIAGONAL CONJUGATE BELOW 9.5 CM. Because of the poor chance for a satisfactory outcome when the diagonal conjugate is below 9.5 cm., it is advisable to deliver such cases by elective cesarean section shortly before or at the onset of labor, unless the smallness of the child indicates that it may pass through the pelvis. In the event that the child is dead or the conditions present offer a serious contraindication to suprapubic delivery, craniotomy is recommended, excepting in those cases in which the true conjugate is below 5.5 cm. The indication for cesarean section is then absolute, since delivery from below after craniotomy in such cases is impossible or so difficult that it is extremely dangerous.

DIAGONAL CONJUGATE 9.5 CM. TO 10.5 CM. The possibility of delivery through the natural passages is sufficient to warrant a trial of labor whenever the diagonal conjugate is 9.5 cm. to 10.5 cm. unless the size of the child's head is excessive. Women with pelves in this group are allowed to go into labor and within a few hours after its onset, a careful examination is made to determine the relationship between the head and the pelvis. This is best accomplished by attempting to force the head into the pelvis with one hand while the index finger of the other is introduced into the rectum to note the degree of descent with reference to the level of the ischial spines. If the head cannot be made to enter the pelvis and it is observed to override the symphysis to any great degree, a low cesarean section is done. Should no overriding be detected, labor is allowed to continue and several hours later another attempt is made to force the head into the pelvis. When repeated observations indicate that the head will engage, delivery through the natural passages is awaited. In doubtful cases, it is a mistake to wait too long before deciding between suprapubic and infrapubic delivery. As long as the membranes remain intact, ten to fifteen hours of labor are permissible provided the two flap low cesarean section is done whenever delivery from above is decided upon. If the waters break early, the decision should be made more promptly, because the risk of cesarean section increases with the number of hours that elapse between its performance and the rupture of the membranes. Throughout the trial labor, the tendency should be to favor suprapubic delivery in those cases in which the diagonal conjugate is below 10 cm. and to await infrapelvic delivery if it is over 10 cm. Needless to say, it is essential that all trial labors should be conducted in a hospital under aseptic conditions and without the use of vaginal examinations.

DIAGONAL CONJUGATE 10.5 to 11.5 CM. When the diagonal conjugate is over 10.5 cm. the chance of delivery through the pelvis is much greater. Often the head becomes engaged or can be forced into the pelvis soon after the onset of labor. The management of such cases accordingly offers little difficulty. Sometimes, however, the head remains high and cannot be forced into the pelvis. In such circumstances the trial of labor is continued in the hope that the head may become sufficiently molded to permit its decent into the pelvis. Repeated examinations during this trial period should enable the obstetrician to determine whether suprapubic delivery is indicated before the safe time for cesarean section has elapsed. His decision will depend upon the presentation and position of the head, its relationship to the anterior and posterior segments of the pelvis, the degree of flexion, the size of the fontanels and sutures, the consistency of the cranial vault and the strength of the uterine contractions. A roentgenologic study of the cephalopelvic relationship is helpful but should not take the place of the examination by an experienced obstetrician. If the attendant lacks experience in handling these borderline cases of pelvic dystocia a more experienced man should be called in consultation. Should it be impossible to obtain the service of such an individual a real test of labor may be given. When the head fails to engage after this test craniotomy is recommended, unless the test of labor is completed within the safe period for a cesarean section. If the child is dead or dying craniotomy naturally should be the operation of choice. When the child is in good condition however, it sometimes is necessary because of religious or other reasons to chose the suprapubic route. In these circumstances the low flap technic is superior to the classical operation and a classical cesarean section followed by hysterectomy or possibly the Latzko or Waters operations are preferable to the low transperitoneal procedure.

In order that the difference between a test of labor and a trial of labor may be better understood it may be stated that a **test of labor** is one in which the patient is allowed sufficient labor **to prove** that the child cannot be born alive through the natural passages. Such proof of the inadequacy of the pelvis implies that any impediment offered by an undilated cervix must be removed and that the expulsive forces are not impaired. **A test of labor therefore, is one in which the patient is allowed several hours of good second stage pains after the cervix has become fully dilated.** Such a procedure requires no great skill and its employment as a routine measure is not in accordance with good practice. Ignorant midwives and poorly trained physicians who suspect dystocia only when the patient fails to deliver after several days of labor still resort to the routine use of a test of labor. The careful and well trained physician on the other hand, can decide whether or not to do a cesarean section in most of his cases of contracted pelvis without subjecting them to such a test. The greater the skill of the attendant therefore, the more frequently is a trial of labor substituted for a test of labor.

A **trial of labor** is a labor of sufficient length to enable the attendant to recognize the presence or absence of enough cephalopelvic disproportion to warrant the use of cesarean section. In the event that a cesarean section is contemplated the duration of the labor should not exceed 16 hours if the membranes remain intact and should not continue longer than 4 hours after the membranes have ruptured. During the trial labor the attendant attempts to force the head into the pelvis and as a result of the knowledge thus gained reaches the decision as to whether a cesarean section should or should not be done Fig. 833a.

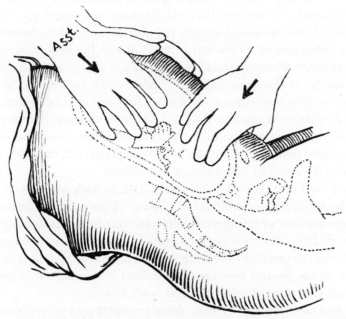

FIG. 833a. METHOD OF DETERMINING WHETHER THE HEAD WILL ENTER THE PELVIS. An assistant makes pressure over the fundus in the direction of the pelvic inlet. The examiner grasps the head with one hand and forcing it backward toward the promintory tries to fit the head into the pelvis. At the same time the relationship of the presenting part to the ischial spines is determined by rectal examination.

FORCEPS. Ordinarily, the use of forceps is not recommended until after engagement has taken place. If this is good practice in the normal case when no disproportion is present, it is especially commendable when the pelvis is contracted and the failure of engagement following a test of labor has demonstrated the need for either reducing the size of the head or delivering from above. Forcible efforts to drag a head through a pelvis that is too small do irreparable damage to the mother and result in the death of the child. Since the infant often is in poor condition by the time that forceps extraction is considered, it is far better to reduce the size of its head deliberately by craniotomy and thereby avoid extensive maternal injury.

It usually is regarded as an essential requisite for the application of forceps that the head must be at or below the level of the ischial spines. When the pelvis is contracted and marked molding is taking place, the caput succedaneum or even the molded vertex may reach this level before engagement is accomplished. For this reason further descent should be awaited before forceps are applied in those cases in which asymmetry or marked molding of the head indicates the presence of pelvic dystocia.

VERSION. The fact that the head in breech presentations enters the pelvis with relatively smaller diameters than those which first meet the resistance of the pelvic brim in vertex cases, formerly led obstetricians to recommend podalic version in the treatment of contracted pelvis. While the aftercoming head may be regarded as more wedge-shaped and in a rapid extraction should enter the pelvis more easily, it does not have the opportunity to become molded and, accordingly, is much less advantageous than an oncoming head. The old recommendation that version be done for moderate degrees of pelvic deformity, accordingly, is not advised, and version and extraction is limited to those emergencies which require rapid delivery before the head is engaged, but in which the head is deemed sufficiently small to pass through the pelvis.

INDUCTION OF PREMATURE LABOR at the 34th to 36th week has been recommended in the treatment of contracted pelvis. This routine, unquestionably, assures a larger number of infrapelvic deliveries, but it also is accompanied by a high fetal mortality (23). In many instances, the child is smaller than anticipated (24) and the problem of rearing a small, premature infant is encountered. Since the risk of the routine previously described is so small, it is preferable to one in which a larger proportion of the infants are lost.

BREECH PRESENTATIONS. The problem in contracted pelvis is considerably more difficult when the child presents by the breech. In these circumstances, the cephalopelvic relationship cannot be ascertained until the aftercoming head reaches the pelvic brim. When pelvic contraction is not recognized until this stage in labor is reached, it is too late to consider suprapubic delivery and the child invariably is lost. This inability to study the fit between the head and the pelvis in breech presentations should lead to a more frequent resort to suprapubic delivery than is recommended in the plan suggested for vertex cases.

REFERENCES

1. ADAIR, F.: The Ossification Centers of the Fetal Pelvis. Am. J. Obs., 1918, 78, 175.
2. FEHLING, H.: Die Form des Beckens beim Fötus und Neugeborenen. Arch. f. Gyn., 1876, 10, 1
3. THOMSON, A.: The Sexual Differences of the Foetal Pelvis. J. Anat. & Physiol., 1899 33, 359.
4. FALK, E.: Die Entwicklung und Form des fötalen Beckens. Berlin, 1908.
5. STEIN, G. W., JR.: Lehre der Geburtshülfe. Elberfeld, 1825.
6. TURNER, W.: The Index of the Pelvic Brim as a Basis of Classification. J. Anat. & Physiol., 1885–86, 20, 125.
7. DERRY, D. E.: Note on the Innominate Bone as a Factor in the Determination of Sex: With Special Reference to the Sulcus Praeauricularis. J. Anat. & Physiol., 1909, 43, 266.
8. HART, D. B.: On Inversion of the Ilium and Sacrum and Ischium and Pubes (Iliosacral and Ischiopubic Bony Segments) as Causes of Deformities of the Female Pelvis. Edinb. M. J., 1916, 16, 9.
9. STRAUS, W. L.: The Human Ilium: Sex and Stock. Am. J. Phys. Anthropol., 1927–28, 11, 1.
10. THOMS, H. C.: The Inadequacy of External Pelvimetry. Am. J. Obs. & Gyn., 1934, 27 270.

11. CALDWELL, W. E. AND MOLOY, H. C.: Anatomical Variations in the Female Pelvis and Their Effect in Labor with a Suggested Classification. Am. J. Obs. & Gyn., 1933, 26, 479.
11a. CALDWELL, W. C., MOLOY, H. C. AND SWENSON, P. C.: The Use of the Roentgen Ray in Obstetrics.
    1. Roentgen Pelvimetry and Cephalometry; Technique and Pelvioroentgenography, Am. J. Roentgenology and Radium Therapy, 1939, 41, 305.
    2. Anatomical Variations in the Female Pelvis and Their Classification According to Morphology, 1939, 41, 505.
    3. The Mechanism of Labor, 1939, 41, 719.
12. DEVENTER, H.: Neues Hebammenlicht, 1728.
13. WILLIAMS, J. W. AND SUN, K. C.: A Statistical Study of the Incidence and Treatment of Labor Complicated by Contracted Pelvis in the Obstetric Service of the Johns Hopkins Hospital from 1896 to 1924. Am. J. Obs. & Gyn., 1926, 11, 735.
14. NAEGELÉ, F. C.: Das schräg verengte Becken nebst einem Anhange über die wichtigsten Fehler des weiblichen Beckens überhaupt. Mainz, 1839.
15. MICHAELIS, G. H.: Das Enge Becken. Leipzig, 1851.
16. BREUS, C. AND KOLISKO, A.: Die Pathologischen Beckenformen. 1900, 1, 534.
17. WILLIAMS, J. W.: Frequency, Etiology, and Practical Significance of Contractions of the Pelvic Outlet. Surg. Gyn. & Obs., 1909, 8, 619.
18. KLIEN, R.: Die geburtshilfliche Bedeutung der Verengerungen des Beckenausgangs, insbesondere des Trichterbeckens. Samml. Klin. Vortr., Leipzig, n.F., No. 169.
19. THOMS, H. K.: A Statistical Study of the Frequency of Funnel Pelves and the Description of a New Outlet Pelvimetre. Am. J. Obs., 1915, 72, 121.
20. PATTERSON: The Human Sacrum. Scientific Trans. Royal Dublin Soc., 1893, 5, 123.
21. EMMONS, A. B.: A Study of the Variations in the Female Pelvis, Based on Observations Made on 217 Specimens of the American Indian Squaw. Biometriak, Cambridge, 1913, 9, 34.
22. FABRE AND BOURRET: Un cas de bassin à diamétre antéropostérieur prédominant. Bull. Soc. d'obs. et de gyn., de Paris, 1913, 16, 108.
23. BANISTER, J. B.: Discussion on the Place of Induction of Premature Labor in the Treatment of Contracted Pelvis. Brit. M. J., 1926, 2, 519.
24. CONNAN, P. AND OWEN-JONES, R.: Observations on the Indications for the Induction of Labor. J. Obs. & Gyn., Brit. Emp., 1927, 34, 83.

CHAPTER XXXI

FAULTY PASSAGES—CONTRACTED PELVES—RARE TYPES

OSTEOMALACIC PELVIS, MALACOSTEON PELVIS. Osteomalacia is rarely encountered in this country. In some parts of Central Europe and China, however, it is quite prevalent and occurs more frequently in adult women and especially in those who are pregnant. While the exact etiology is not known, it is thought to be due to a vitamin and calcium deficiency (1), and possibly is associated with ovarian hyperfunction (2), or hypoadrenalemia (3), since removal of the ovaries and the administration of adrenalin have a favorable influence on the course of the disease.

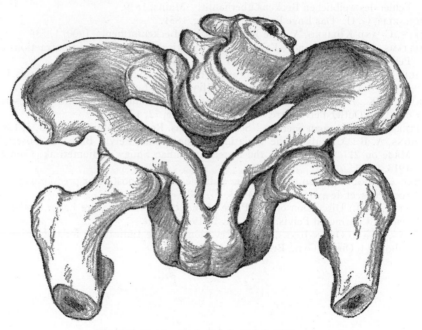

FIG. 834. Osteomalacic Pelvis, Pelvis Malacosteon.

As the disease progresses, the bones become markedly softened and are distorted by the mechanical factors described in the preceding section on rachitic pelves. The weight of the body forces the promontory downward and forward, while the opposing pressure from the femora causes the lateral walls of the pelvis to approach each other, with the result that the inlet becomes markedly contracted. The almost completely obliterated superior aperture is thus converted into a triradiate figure whose anterior arm projects forward like a beak, between the closely approximated pubic portions of the innominate bones. Similar narrowing of the pubic arch causes an extreme shortening of the bisischial diameter.

Pelvimetry and vaginal examination show the absence of the rachitic characteristics and remove all doubt as to the type of pelvic contraction.

EFFECT ON LABOR. In the mild contractions, labor occurring during the acute stage of softening may result in spontaneous delivery as the descending head forces the yielding bony structures aside. In marked cases, delivery through the natural passages is impossible.

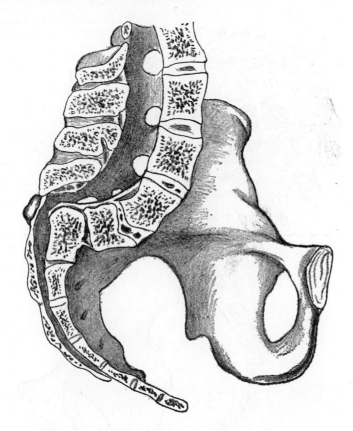

FIG. 835. Spondylolysthetic Pelvis (Kilian).

SPONDYLOLISTHETIC PELVIS. In rare cases of spondylolysis, the interarticular portion of the last lumbar vertebra becomes lengthened, thinned out and bent so that its inferior articular surface is in relation to the superior articular surface of the sacrum, and the body is displaced forward and downward. The anterior surface of the first piece of the sacrum is gradually worn away and ultimately becomes ankylosed to the last lumbar vertebra. Owing to the dipping forward of the vertebral column, a compensatory backward rotation of the pelvis occurs and the pelvic inlet comes to lie parallel to the horizon. Pressure on the sacral promontory likewise causes the sacrum to rotate posteriorly on its transverse axis and, as the coccyx is forced forward, the anteroposterior measurements of the outlet are diminished. As in kyphotic pelvis, this also causes the ischial portions of the innominate bones to come closer together and thereby shortens the bisischial diameter. Although the condition has been described as a slipping forward of the last lumbar vertebra, it is not a true luxation but is due to changes in the bone itself (4, 5).

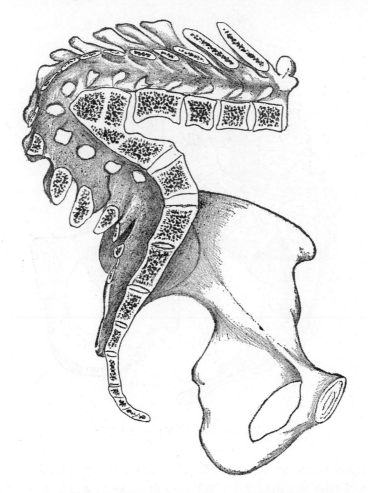

FIG. 836. Kyphotic Pelvis (Breus and Kolisko).

DIAGNOSIS. The figure and gait of women with a spondylolisthetic pelvis are characteristic. There is a marked lordosis in which the ribs come almost into contact with the crests of the ilia (Fig. 835), and when the patient walks, her footprints fall in a straight line without any turning out of the toes. Vaginal examination readily reveals the displaced lumbar vertebrae, and measurement of the distance between the inferior margin of the symphysis and that lumbar vertebra which marks the obstetric inlet of the pelvis gives a clue as to the degree of contraction. When this measurement is 9.5 cm. or under, delivery through the pelvis usually is not possible.

EFFECT ON LABOR. In the mild cases in which spontaneous labor is possible, the mechanism of engagement is similar to that observed in flat pelves, and the passage of the head through the outlet is analogous to that followed in slightly contracted, funnel, or kyphotic pelves.

As stated above, when the obstetric inlet is markedly contracted, cesarean section is indicated.

KYPHOTIC PELVIS is quite rare and occurs about once in every 6,000 labors (6). The effect of a posterior curvature of the spine depends upon the site of the displacement. When the deformity is high, a compensating lordosis in the lumbar region prevents serious alterations in the pelvis. Dorsolumbar and lumbosacral kyphoses, however, are accompanied by marked pelvic deformity. The sacrum then rotates posteriorly on its transverse axis and increases the anteroposterior diameter of the inlet but shortens that of the outlet. This backward displacement of the sacrum likewise spreads the posterior borders of the ilia farther apart with the result that the crests flare outward. For the same reason, the ischia are rotated inward, and marked narrowing of the pelvis is produced in the region of the ischial spines and tuberosities. The sacrum also is longer, narrower and straighter. These changes cause a funnel-shaped pelvic cavity, the oval-shaped inlet of which is greatly lengthened in its anteroposterior diameter while the outlet is markedly contracted in the region of the ischial pines (Fig. 836).

DIAGNOSIS. Marked curvature of the spine is evident. In addition, pelvimetry shows the intercristal diameter to be greater than the intertrochanteric. Both the anteroposterior and transverse measurements of the outlet are markedly diminished while the diagonal conjugate is increased. On vaginal examination, the ischial spines are found to be abnormally near to each other.

EFFECT ON LABOR. Abnormal presentations are slightly more frequent. The large inlet favors engagement but the contracted outlet causes great difficulty, and the head often is arrested by the closely approximated ischial spines. The narrowness of the pubic arch and the diminished posterior sagittal diameter add further to the dystocia if the head is able to pass through the plane of least dimensions. Whenever the bisischial diameter is below 8 cm., great difficulty may be anticipated and cesarean section should be seriously considered (7).

SCOLIOTIC PELVIS. Lateral curvature of the spine in the lumbar region leads to an abnormal position of the sacrum and pelvic deformity. Scoliosis of non-rachitic origin usually is slight and its effect on the pelvis is not sufficient to cause dystocia. On the other hand, curvature due to rachitis may be marked and may cause serious pelvic changes in addition to those which are characteristic of the latter disease. The compensatory tilting of the sacrum in the opposite direction, together with axial rotation toward the affected side, causes a narrowing of that half of the pelvis (Fig. 837).

DIAGNOSIS. Spinal deformity and signs of rachitis usually are present. The rachitic relationship between the spines and crests of the ilia is demonstrated and the sacrum shows the usual characteristics of rachitis. The oblique diameters are unequal and the ischial tuberosity on the side of the curvature is higher.

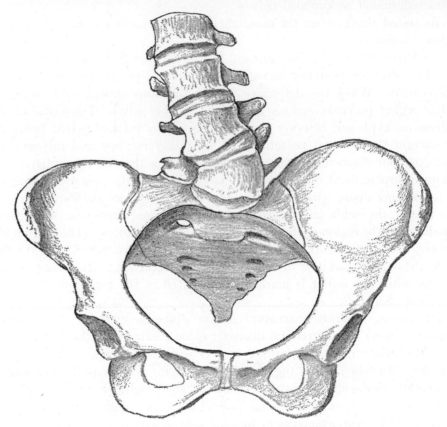

FIG. 837. Scoliotic Pelvis (Breus and Kolisko).

EFFECT ON LABOR. Labor is not affected by the pelvic changes that accompany scoliosis unless the curvature is marked and is due to rachitis. The difficulties then are those of rachitic pelves in general plus the lateral contraction that results from the spinal curvature.

OBLIQUE CONTRACTION DUE TO UNILATERAL LAMENESS. Unilateral lameness leads to oblique contractions of the pelvis when the condition is present in early life. The weight of the trunk is thrown largely on the sound leg with the result that the pelvis on the healthy side is displaced upward, backward and inward. This causes a lateral rotation of the sacrum and tends to diminish the concavity of the iliopectineal line on that side. The pelvic inlet, accordingly, is obliquely contracted (Fig. 838).

Less commonly, an oblique contraction results from a narrowing of the inlet on the affected side due to an arrest in development which results from bone disease on that side. In these cases, the affected leg is ankylosed in adduction and internal rotation (8).

Oblique contraction due to unilateral lameness is not very common and may result from hip joint disease (coxalgic pelvis), unilateral luxation of the femur, infantile paralysis, disease of the knee or ankle and amputation early in life.

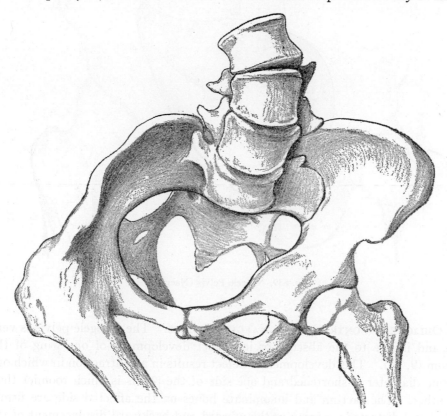

FIG. 838. Coxalgic Pelvis (Bumm).

DIAGNOSIS. In addition to the history of lameness from early childhood, the external oblique diameters are unequal and one iliac crest is higher than the other. The x-ray findings likewise are helpful.

EFFECT ON LABOR. Most cases of oblique contraction due to lameness are mild and have little influence on labor. In the marked contractions, the management should be similar to that outlined for borderline pelvic contractions. Soon after the onset of labor, an attempt should be made to force the head into the pelvis. If this cannot be done, low cesarean section is indicated.

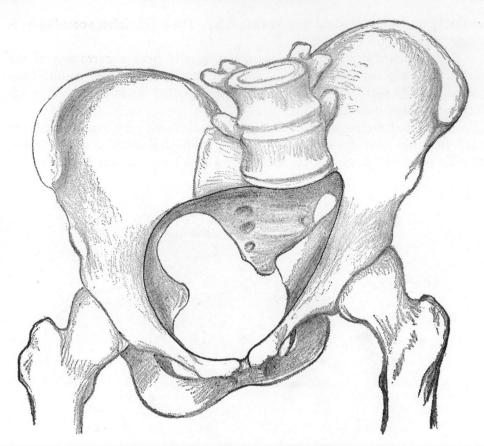

FIG. 839. Naegele Pelvis (Naegele).

OBLIQUELY CONTRACTED OR NAEGELE PELVIS. The Naegele pelvis is very rare and is due to the absence or imperfect development of one wing of the sacrum (9, 10). This developmental defect results in a contraction in which one oblique diameter is shortened and one side of the pelvis is much roomier than the other. The sacrum and innominate bones on the affected side are firmly united and distorted. Owing to the upward and backward displacement of the ilium, its crest is considerably elevated and the contour of the iliopectineal line is changed to almost a straight line in marked contractions.

The outlet is similarly affected and, as a result, the spine and tuberosity of the ischium are higher and are brought almost on a line with the sacrum and symphysis. The symphysis is forced beyond the midline and lies opposite the side involved. Tilting of the pubic arch toward the affected side likewise is observed.

This type of deformity is recognized by the marked shortening of one of the external oblique diameters.   The distance between the ischial tuberosities also is diminished.   On vaginal examination the spine of the ischium on the affected side is higher, nearer to the sacrum, and is on a line with the symphysis and the sacrum.

Considerable dystocia results when this deformity is marked, and the majority of the cases reported in the literature before the days of asepsis terminated fatally.   Spontaneous labor, however, may occur if the child is small (11).

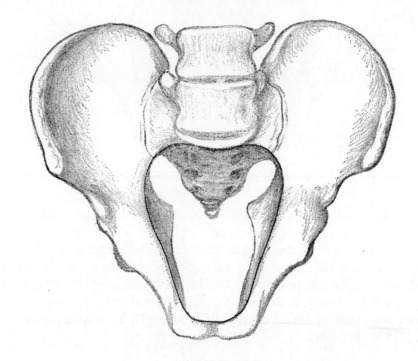

FIG. 840. Robert Pelvis (Robert).

TRANSVERSELY CONTRACTED OR ROBERT PELVIS.   The Robert pelvis is one in which both wings of the sacrum fail to develop, with the result that the transverse diameters are markedly contracted (12) (Fig. 840).   This type of bilateral deformity is extremely rare but is easily recognized by the great shortening of all of the transverse measurements, with little or no change in the external and diagonal conjugates.   Spontaneous delivery of a normal sized child through a typical Robert pelvis is impossible.

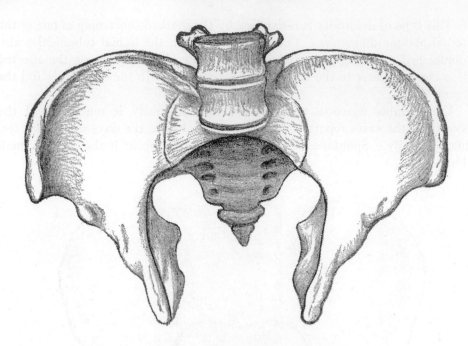

FIG. 841. Split Pelvis (Breus and Kolisko).

SPLIT PELVIS. Failure of union between the pubic bones is known as a split pelvis. This condition is extremely rare and is associated with similar arrested developments of the bladder and lower abdominal wall. Because of the latter, most of the cases die at an early age. If they survive, there is a marked widening of the pelvis. In the few instances of split pelvis in which labors have been reported, delivery through the natural passages took place. Prolapsus is a common sequel of labor in women who have split pelves (13, 14, 15, 16, 17, 18) (Fig. 841).

REFERENCES

1. MAXWELL, J. P. AND MILES, L. M.: Osteomalacia in China. J. Obs. & Gyn., Brit. Emp., 1925, 32, 433.
2. FRAZER, J. R.: The Ovary in Osteomalacia. Am. J. Obs. & Gyn., 1927, 14, 697.
3. BOSSI, L. M.: Nebennieren und Osteomalakie. Zentralbl. f. Gyn., 1907, 31, 172.
4. NEUGEBAUER, F. L.: Spondylolisthésis et spondylizème. Paris, 1892.
5. CHIARI, H.: Spondylolisthesis. Johns Hopkins Hosp. Bull., 1911, 22, 41.
6. KLIEN, R.: Die Geburt beim kyphotischen Becken. Arch. f. Gyn., 1896, 50, 1.
7. NEUGEBAUER, F.: Die heutige Statistik der Geburten bei Beckenverengerung infolge von Rückgratskyphose. Monatschr. f. Geburtsh. u. Gyn., 1895, 1, 317.
8. BRIGGS, H.: The Coxalgic Pelvis. J. Obs. & Gyn., Brit. Emp., 1914, 26, 212.
9. NAEGELÉ, F. C.: Das Schrägverengte Becken, 1839.
10. THOMAS, A.: Das Schrägverengte Becken, Leyden, 1861.
11. WILLIAMS, J. W.: A Clinical and Anatomic Description of a Naegelé Pelvis. Am. J. Obs. & Gyn., 1929, 18, 504.

12. ROBERT, H. L. F.: Ein durch mechanische Verletzung und ihre Folgen querverengtes Becken. Beschrieben und zusammengestellt mit den drei übrigen bekannten querverengten Becken. Berlin, 1853.

13. AYERS, D.: Congenital Exstrophy of the Urinary Bladder and its Complications Successfully Treated by a New Plastic Method. N. Y., 1859.

14. LITZMAN, C.: Das gespaltene Becken. Arch. f. Gyn., 1872, 4, 266.

15. SCHICKELE, G.: Beiträge zur Lehre des normalen und gespaltenen Beckens. Beitr. z. Geburtsh. u. Gyn., 1901, 4, 243.

16. GEMMEL, J. E. AND PATERSON, A. M.: Duplication of Bladder, Uterus, Vagina and Vulva with Successive Full Term Pregnancy and Labor in Each Uterus. J. Obs. & Gyn., Brit. Emp., 1913, 23, 25.

17. WINSLOW, R.: Report of a Case of Exstrophy of the Bladder Operated on Nearly Thirty Years Ago with Subsequent History. Surg. Gyn. & Obs., 1916, 22, 350.

18. MILLER, C. J. AND KING, E. L.: Complete Exstrophy of the Bladder with Split Pelvis as a Complication of Pregnancy. Am. J. Obs., 1918, 78. 267.

HENRICUS VAN DEVENTER
1651–1724
The Hague

Van Deventer did much to improve the status and education of the midwives in Holland.

His book, "Novum Lumen" printed in 1701, accurately describes the pelvis for the first time and discusses the effect of pelvic deformity on labor. In this respect it remained the outstanding work until "Das enge Becken" by Michaelis appeared in 1851.

CHAPTER XXXII

PLACENTA PREVIA AND ACCIDENTAL HEMORRHAGE

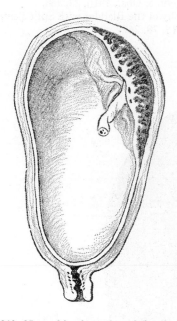 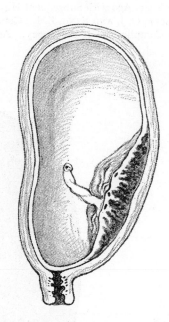

FIG. 842. Normal implantation of the placenta.   FIG. 843. Low implantation of the placenta.

PLACENTA PREVIA. When the placenta is implanted so low that it encroaches upon the internal os, the condition is known as a placenta previa.

True placenta previa is rare and occurs about once in every five hundred obstetric patients. Busy general practitioners, with twenty-five or more years of experience, see only one or two cases during their entire professional lives. In hospital practice, on the other hand, placenta previa is observed in about 0.5 to 1 per cent of all maternity admissions and is encountered much more frequently in multiparae than in primiparae (1).

694

THE VARIETIES of placenta previa are:

1. **Marginal placenta previa** in which only the margin of the placenta may be felt through the cervix—45.6 per cent (2) (Fig. 844).

2. **Partial placenta previa** in which the internal os is partially covered by the placenta—36 per cent (2) (Fig. 845).

3. **Central placenta previa** in which the placenta completely covers the internal os—18.4 per cent (2) (Fig. 846).

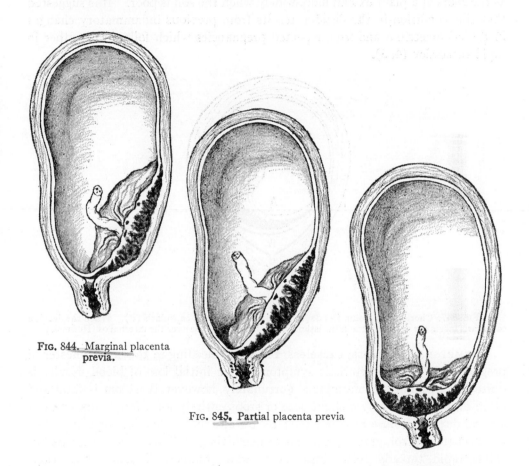

FIG. 844. Marginal placenta previa.

FIG. 845. Partial placenta previa

FIG. 846. Complete placenta previa.

Sometimes the placenta is situated in the lower uterine segment but does not reach the internal os (Fig. 843). It is then designated as a **low implantation** of the placenta, the symptoms of which simulate those of placenta previa but usually are less severe.

ETIOLOGY. Several theories have been offered to explain the cause of placenta previa. The following are the most plausible:

1. Development of the chorion beneath the decidua capsularis so that when the latter joins the decidua vera in the region of the internal os, it carries with it the adjacent chorion (3) (Fig. 847).

2. Implantation of the fertilized egg in a decidua which has a deficient blood supply. As a consequence, the placenta spreads more widely than usual, just as the roots of a plant extend more widely when the soil is poor. It is suggested that this condition in the decidua results from previous inflammatory changes in the endometrium and from repeated pregnancies which follow each other in rapid succession (4, 5).

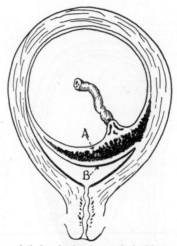

FIG. 847. Chorion frondosum (A) developing beneath decidua capsularis (B). When the decidua capsularis meets the decidua vera in the isthmus, the placenta will be over the internal os (Hoffmeier).

SYMPTOMS. Painless, causeless, recurring bleeding in the last trimester of pregnancy is the characteristic symptom. The initial loss of blood usually is quite profuse and often alarming. Fortunately, however, it seldom is fatal and often diminishes to only a slight ooze or stops entirely for a few hours or even several days. Profuse bleeding then recurs and unless definite steps are taken to effect its control, grave symptoms of hemorrhage follow. These are: pallor, thirst, rapid, thready pulse, restlessness and air hunger. Uterine contractions may begin spontaneously and terminate the pregnancy before the patient bleeds to death. Frequently, however, the outcome is less favorable and the patient dies before the completion of her labor. The bleeding history is so characteristic in placenta previa that in many cases the diagnosis is made from the history alone.

Abdominal examination shows the uterus to have its normal consistency. Intermittent contractions may be present but there is no suggestion of a board-like uterus nor are there definite areas of tenderness, such as are found in ablatio placentae.   The presenting part usually is high, and abnormal presentations are common.   On auscultation, the fetal heart sounds are unchanged but a well marked uterine souffle in the vicinity of the symphysis pubis suggests the presence of a placenta previa.

Vaginal examination reveals a soft, boggy cervix through which placental tissue may be felt.   The feel of placental tissue is quite characteristic and any one may become familiar with it if he will press between his finger fragments of placenta that have been obtained at a normal delivery.   When the cervix is closed, the thick placenta may often be detected between the examining finger and the presenting part.   Examination through the vagina always increases the amount of bleeding, especially when the head is pushed upward.   On the other hand, dislodgment of the presenting part does not cause a gush of blood as frequently is the case in premature separation of the placenta.

PROGNOSIS.   The effect of placenta previa on the mother and the child depends largely upon whether it is complete, partial or marginal, and upon the manner in which it is treated.   If left entirely to nature, a large percentage of the mothers die and a still larger number of children perish.   In good maternity services, the maternal mortality varies from 2 to 10 per cent depending upon the condition of the patients at the time of admission.   If the placenta previa cases occur in a hospital clinic and are seen from the onset by a competent obstetrician, very few mothers are lost.   On the other hand, when patients are almost exsanguinated and infected before admission, the mortality often exceeds 10 per cent.   At least one out of six mothers is lost when the placenta previa is of the complete variety, while the mortality is considerably lower in partial, and almost nil in the marginal placenta previas (1).

The chief danger is antepartum, intrapartum and postpartum hemorrhage. Before and during labor the bleeding comes from the partially denuded placental site.   After delivery, atony of the lower uterine segment and deep lacerations of the cervix are contributing factors.   The increased circulation of the cervix and lower uterine segment renders these structures very friable.   Deep lacerations and even rupture of the uterus, therefore, are not uncommon, particularly when the child is extracted artificially.   The low situation of the placenta also greatly increases the risk of infection and many patients who survive the hemorrhage succumb from puerperal infection.

TREATMENT.   Placenta previa is a most treacherous obstetric complication. Its treatment, therefore, should not be attempted by the average practitioner if a more experienced obstetrician is available.   Likewise, the chance for a good result should not be jeopardized by bungling and injudicious handling of the case before it is turned over to more competent hands.   Often, when the physician is called to see a patient who has had a severe hemorrhage in the last trimester of pregnancy, he immediately makes a vaginal examination (sometimes without proper preparation of his hands or the vulva) and attempts to feel the placenta in the region of the internal os.   His awkward manipulations thus separate more of the placenta and a vigorous hemorrhage follows.   Alarmed by the renewed and profuse bleeding he then introduces a few yards of questionably sterile gauze into the vagina and sends the patient to the nearest hospital.   When first seen by the attending obstetrician, most cases of placenta previa, accordingly, are potentially infected and often exsanguinated.   Poor judgment and bad management by the physician who first attended the patient at home, therefore, are responsible for the death of many women even though they receive the best of care subsequently.   Notwithstanding the advances that have been made in the treatment of placenta previa and accidental hemorrhage, the present high maternal death rate in these conditions will not be lowered until the inexperienced physician realizes that all cases of severe hemorrhage in the last trimester should be transferred **immediately** to the nearest hospital without the usual harmful and unnecessary vaginal examinations.

The underlying principles involved in the treatment of placenta previa are as follows:

1. All bleeding cases in which placenta previa is suspected should be referred at once to one who not only is competent to treat this grave condition, but who can assume the responsibility of a possible fatal outcome.

2. Vaginal examination before referring the patient is unnecessary and dangerous.

3. Because a vaginal examination increases the bleeding, it should not be attempted until after all necessary preparations for the immediate treatment of placenta previa have been made.   These include: the presence of an anesthetist, aseptic preparation of the vulva, aseptic preparation of the physician's hands, sterilization of the instruments necessary for the introduction of a large hydrostatic bag, ample sterile gauze for packing and preparation for possible Braxton Hicks version.

4. Because of the need for these preliminary preparations, suspected pacenta previa cases should not be examined in the home if hospital facilities are available.

5. Transfusion before, during and after operation frequently is necessary and several suitable donors should be kept on hand until all danger of a fatal hemorrhage is past.

6. Active interference is indicated as soon as the diagnosis is made.   **There is no place for expectancy in the treatment of placenta previa.**

7. The methods of interference are: cesarean section, bipolar version, the introduction of a large hydrostatic bag, rupture of the membranes and vaginal tamponade.

CESAREAN SECTION.   Since cesarean section is followed by a high maternal mortality whenever infection is present, suprapubic delivery should not be considered if the patient has been examined vaginally in her home.   This is particularly true after a pack has been inserted into the vagina to control the hemorrhage.   Likewise, cesarean section is to be avoided if the child is too premature to have a good chance of surviving, since women who have had one section often refuse to become pregnant again and, if they do, repeated cesarean sections are necessary.

While most obstetricians agree that cesarean section is contraindicated in the foregoing circumstances, some are more liberal than others in their indications for its use in the treatment of placenta previa.   It offers the best chance for the child and, accordingly, all agree that it is the method of choice whenever an elderly primipara has placenta previa.   Likewise, many feel that in the absence of contraindications, central placenta previa is best treated by this procedure. In partial placenta previa, it also has been suggested as the preferable method if the cervix is not sufficiently dilated to permit Braxton Hicks version or the

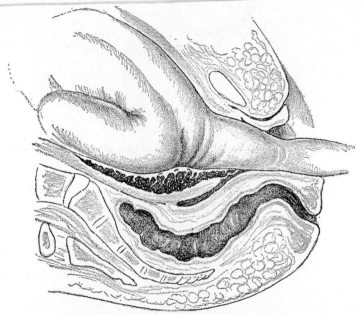

FIG. 848. Hemorrhage controlled by Braxton Hicks version.

introduction of a large bag.   Because cesarean section avoids trauma to the friable cervix and stretching of the atonic placental site, a few very good men in this country also lean toward its routine use in the treatment of all cases (1, 6, 7, 8, 9).

In our clinic all placenta previas, other than those which occur in the elderly primipara, are treated according to the conditions found in each individual patient.   Because most of them have been potentially infected before admission to the hospital, cesarean section seldom is employed.

BIPOLAR VERSION.   Unquestionably, the best vaginal method of handling placenta previa is by the use of bipolar or Braxton Hicks version (10, 11).   Pressure of the thigh and breech upon the bleeding area usually arrests the hemorrhage (Fig. 848).   If it does not, slight traction on the foot is effective.   In no

circumstances should it be followed by breech extraction, as extraction of the
aftercoming head not only tears the soft and boggy cervix, but it may rupture
the uterus through the friable placental site and convert an already serious situation into a tragedy.   Since this tragic accident seldom is observed if spontaneous
delivery of the aftercoming head is awaited, one should be prepared to sacrifice
the child in order that the mother may be saved whenever Braxton Hicks version
is done.   Occasionally, however, the child may be born alive, although the condi-

Fig. 849. The placenta encircling the thigh of a living child that was born after a Braxton Hicks
version was done for a placenta previa.   In spite of the fact that the case was left to nature, the child
was born alive and in good condition.

tions present at the time of the version may lead to the belief that it has no chance
of surviving.   Figure 849 is an illustration of the manner in which the placenta
was born surrounding the thigh and buttocks of a living child in one of our cases
of central placenta previa.   When this patient entered the hospital, the cervix
admitted two fingers and the placenta completely covered the internal os.   As
the mother had four other living children, it was decided that she should not be
subjected to any added risk for the sake of another child.   The interests of the

latter, accordingly, were disregarded and, after cutting through the placenta with scissors, a foot was brought down by bipolar version.   Much to our surprise, the child was born alive in spite of the fact that the placenta completely encircled its thigh and buttocks.

Braxton Hicks version should be the vaginal method of choice whenever the cervix is dilated sufficiently to admit two fingers and the conditions present justify disregarding the child's interest.   These obtain when the child is too premature, or when so much of the placenta is over the internal os as to offer very little chance for its survival.   In some clinics where the Braxton Hicks version is preferred, the maternal mortality is as low as 2 per cent but the infant loss is

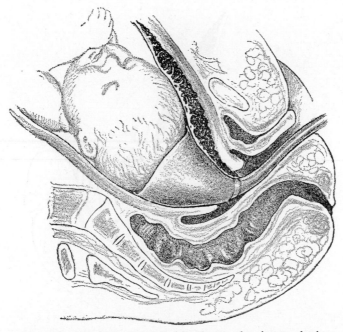

FIG. 850. Hemorrhage controlled by the use of an intraovular bag.

appalling (60 to 75 per cent).   Since one of the requirements of this routine is that breech extraction must be avoided, the good maternal results, in many cases, are obtained at the expense of the child.   Therefore, if the interests of the latter cannot be disregarded, some other method of artificial aid should be chosen as the extraction of a breech following Braxton Hicks version is so dangerous that the saying "Braxton Hicks version and leave the rest to nature" has become an obstetric aphorism.

HYDROSTATIC BAG.   A large hydrostatic bag introduced into the uterus by making pressure over the bleeding area usually arrests the hemorrhage (Fig. 850).   Occasionally, a small weight must be attached to produce the desired effect.   If such a weight is used care must be taken to allow for free play of the attaching cord when the patient moves; otherwise the tension may be sufficient to cause rupture of the uterus through the friable placental site.

The membranes are ruptured, or, if the placenta covers too much of the internal os, it is perforated with scissors and the bag is introduced in the usual manner. When the bag is expelled, descent of the head follows and controls the hemorrhage by making pressure over the bleeding area. Delivery is spontaneous and naturally results in the birth of a living child much more frequently than does the Braxton Hicks routine. Unfortunately, the head is displaced by the bag and a brow, face or transverse presentation may result. In the latter circumstances, the abnormality must be corrected promptly to prevent severe

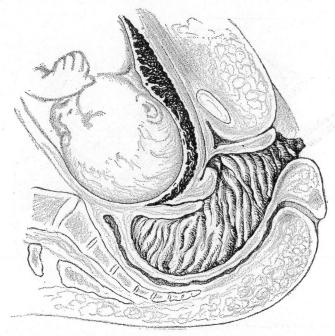

FIG. 851. Hemorrhage controlled by the use of a gauze tampon in the vagina.

hemorrhage from the placental site. These possibilities, together with the chance of prolapse of the cord, always increase the anxiety whenever the bag method is employed. On the other hand, a certain sense of security is felt when a foot is brought down to control the hemorrhage, provided the operator is willing to disregard the child and leave the remainder of the delivery entirely to nature.

As the method of introducing the hydrostatic bag is slightly less safe for the mother, it should not be used when the conditions indicate that the child's chance of survival is poor. Accordingly, it is better to give preference to version in central placenta previa and marked prematurity, and limit the use of a hydrostatic bag to those cases in which only a small part of the os is covered by the placenta or in which a version cannot be done (1, 11, 12).

Some obstetricians prefer to introduce the bag into the uterus without rupturing the membranes.   The extraovular bag seems to control the hemorrhage as well as its intraovular introduction and the risk to the child is somewhat less.   The chief disadvantage of this method is the possibility of profuse hemorrhage when the bag is expelled.   The operator, therefore, must remain with the patient in order that he may do an immediate version as soon as the bag is expelled into the vagina (13, 14).

RUPTURE OF THE MEMBRANES often is sufficient to control the hemorrhage which is due to that type of placenta previa in which only the margin of the placenta is in the vicinity of the internal os.   The efficiency of this method may be increased by the use of constant scalp traction by means of Willett's forceps. If this measure fails, the introduction of a hydrostatic bag will arrest the bleeding.

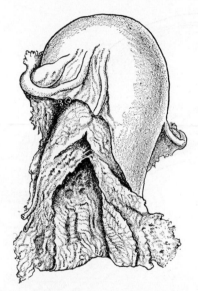

FIG. 852. Rupture of the uterus due to manual dilatation for a placenta previa (Edgar).

TAMPONADE OF THE VAGINA is restricted to those cases in which the cervix is not sufficiently dilated to permit the use of one of the other vaginal procedures (15) (Fig. 851).   At least fifteen yards of twelve-inch moist sterile gauze are used and great care is taken to maintain an aseptic technic.   If the gauze is first saturated with 4 per cent mercurochrome solution, the danger of infection will be lessened.   A firm tampon in the vagina controls the hemorrhage and favors dilatation of the cervix.   After some time, bleeding through the pack may be observed and the procedure must then be repeated, or, if the cervix is large enough, one of the more preferable methods is substituted.

Manual dilatation should not be done in placenta previa.   The soft, boggy cervix is torn rather than dilated by attempts at manual dilatation and such a tear may lead to rupture of the uterus (16, 17) (Fig. 852).

ACCIDENTAL HEMORRHAGE

ACCIDENTAL HEMORRHAGE is the term used to describe the bleeding that results from the premature detachment of a normally implanted placenta, in contrast with the so-called **unavoidable hemorrhage** which is observed in placenta previa. Ablatio placentae (18), abruptio placentae and premature separation of the placenta often are employed as synonyms.

Slight detachment of the placenta with varying degrees of hemorrhage is not uncommon. More marked and complete separation, however, is quite rare and in hospital practice occurs about once in every 200 maternity admissions.

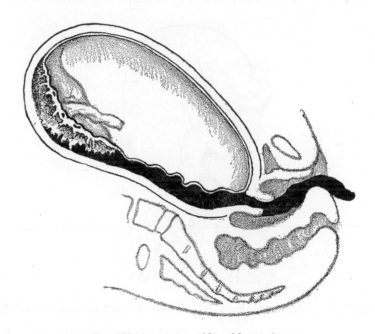

Fig. 853. Apparent accidental hemorrhage.

VARIETIES. Accidental hemorrhage may be apparent (Fig. 853) or concealed.

It is absolutely concealed when the periphery of the placenta remains attached to the uterus with the result that a large retroplacental collection of blood forms and causes an outward bulging of the overlying uterine wall (Fig. 854).

In the relatively concealed varieties, the blood escapes from the placental site and ruptures through the membranes into the amniotic cavity (Fig. 855), or is kept within the uterus by the ball valve action of the head (Fig. 856).

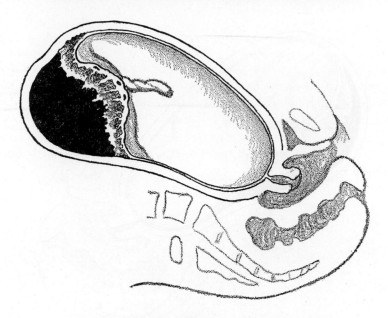

FIG. 854. Absolutely concealed accidental hemorrhage.

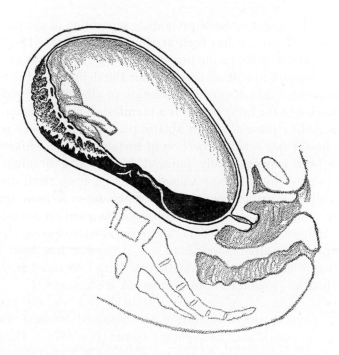

FIG. 855. Relatively concealed accidental hemorrhage. Retained blood concealed within the amniotic cavity.

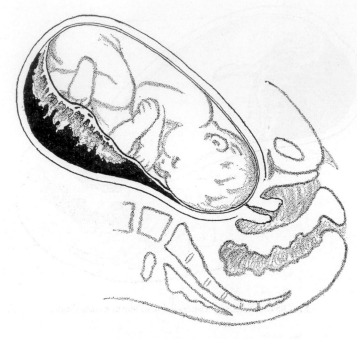

FIG. 856. Relatively concealed accidental hemorrhage.

ETIOLOGY.   The exact cause of premature separation of the placenta is not known.   In rare instances, it has been attributed to trauma (18), a short umbilical cord (19), and a sudden reduction in the size of the uterus as occurs when the membranes rupture in hydramnios or after the delivery of the first child in multiple pregnancies.   The frequent association of albuminuria with accidental hemorrhage has led to the belief that it is a manifestation of toxemia, and lesions somewhat resembling those found in ablatio placentae have been produced experimentally in animals by the injection of histamine (20).   Likewise, similar changes have been experimentally induced by injecting uranium nitrate or bacillus pyocyaneus into pregnant animals suffering from renal damage or in which kidney injury is artificially produced by the use of sodium oxalate (21).

Clinically, anuria not infrequently is observed as a serious complication after premature detachment of the placenta, and renal disease, having the aspects of interstitial nephritis, is often noted (22, 23).   It likewise has been shown that women suffering from toxemia have ablatio placentae four times as frequently as do those in whom the manifestations of toxemia are absent (24).

PATHOLOGY.   The uterus itself is definitely altered in many cases.   Externally, areas of purplish red discoloration are observed beneath its peritoneal covering which, in places, may be slightly fissured (Fig. 857).   The uterine wall is the seat of multiple hemorrhagic extravasations which are most marked near the placental site and in the more superficial or subperitoneal layer.   These

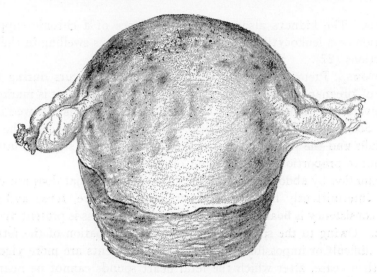

FIG. 857. Uterus removed by hysterectomy from a case of accidental hemorrhage. Note the areas of discoloration beneath the peritoneum (Couvelaire uterus).

intramural hemorrhages surround the smaller veins and separate the muscle fibers, while the neighboring tissues are spread apart by edema (25, 26, 27) (Fig. 858). Hemorrhage into the spongy layer of the decidua causes separation of the placenta with the formation of hematomata on its maternal surface. The broad ligaments are engorged and often are the seat of extensive hemorrhagic

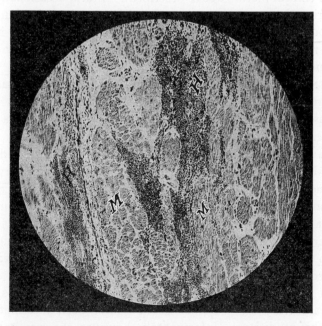

FIG. 858. Hemorrhage between the muscle fibers in a case of uteroplacental apoplexy.

infiltrations. The kidneys also may show evidence of a chronic suppurative inflammation or a leukocytic infiltration with edematous swelling in their interstitial portions (22).

SYMPTOMS. Premature separation of the placenta occurs during the last trimester of pregnancy and in the course of labor. Its onset is marked by a sudden, severe and continuous pain over the uterus which is followed by hemorrhage. Soon, the patient becomes pale, her extremities grow cold, the systolic pressure falls and the pulse becomes rapid and thready as she goes into shock which is out of proportion to the amount of blood lost.

Examination by abdominal palpation shows a uterus that does not contract and relax intermittently but which is extremely sensitive, tense and spastic. Often, its consistency is **board-like** and exquisite tenderness is present over irregular areas. Owing to the spasticity of the uterus, palpation of the fetal parts usually is difficult or impossible. The child's movements are more vigorous at first and then cease, after which the fetal heart sounds cannot be heard. On vaginal examination the placenta cannot be felt and slight upward displacement of the presenting part causes a gush of blood. Repeated examinations show an increasingly tender and more ligneous uterus which, in concealed or partially concealed accidental hemorrhage, may become considerably larger in one or more of its diameters. In the rarer absolutely concealed variety, the bulging, tender placental site may sometimes be felt. Following delivery, the apoplectic uterus often fails to contract and retract, and postpartum hemorrhage adds to the gravity of the clinical picture above described. Anuria occasionally is observed and death during the puerperium may occur from suppression of urine.

THE PROGNOSIS in mild cases is good. When the placenta is completely detached, the risk to the mother is great. The maternal mortality is then 5 to 10 per cent and all of the children are lost.

TREATMENT. Slight degrees of premature separation of the placenta require no special treatment other than rest in bed and careful observation.

Severe cases of accidental hemorrhage should be removed to a hospital and cared for by one who is competent to master obstetric emergencies.

Blood transfusions, before, during and after operation are indicated and a sufficient number of suitable donors should be at hand to furnish all the blood that may be needed until all danger is past. One of our patients was saved by the transfusion of 2500 cc. of blood from three different donors during the brief period of one and one half hours.

Since uterine bleeding usually is best controlled by emptying the uterus, it would seem advisable to hasten the delivery of the child by whatever means are best suited to the condition of the passages in each case. Accordingly, accouchement forcé, the introduction of a hydrostatic bag, forceps, version and extraction, craniotomy and cesarean section have been recommended in the treatment of this condition. Unfortunately, however, the cases most in need of active intervention are profoundly shocked and are poor risks for any operation. Because it is bad surgery to subject a patient already in collapse to the additional shock of a major obstetric procedure, other means of controlling the hemorrhage, therefore, should be tried while measures to combat shock are being employed (28, 29, 30, 31). The membranes are ruptured, a tight abdominal binder is adjusted and small doses of pituitary extract are given at twenty-minute intervals in the hope that the pressure of the child against the placental site may control the hemorrhage (Fig. 859). At the same time, the head of the bed is lowered, the patient is surrounded by hot water bottles and blankets, and a transfusion of 1000 cc. of blood is given. In the great majority of cases improvement is prompt and labor begins within a short time. Expectant treatment, accordingly, is to be continued if careful observation shows that the hemorrhage is controlled. For this purpose the height of the fundus above the symphysis and the girth of the abdomen are measured hourly, the blood pressure and pulse are taken every thirty minutes, and the red blood cells and hemoglobin are estimated repeatedly in order that continued bleeding with concealment in the uterus may not be overlooked.

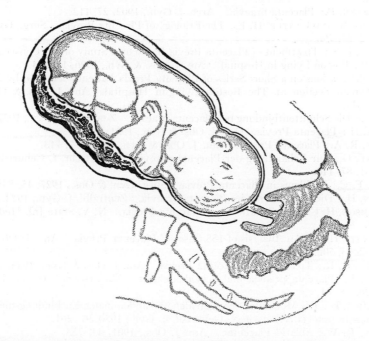

FIG. 859. Hemorrhage controlled by molding of the uterus upon the fetus after rupture of the membranes and the use of pituitary extract

In a small percentage of cases in which the foregoing routine fails to stop the bleeding, the uterus must be emptied. If the cervix is sufficiently dilated to permit delivery after craniotomy, the head of the dead child is perforated and crushed. Should the passages be unprepared, cesarean section under local anesthesia is recommended. Following cesarean section, the uterus may not contract and a quick hysterectomy occasionally is necessary. If the patient's condition is grave, the customary technic is not followed but clamps are placed on the vessels and, after the removal of the uterus, these are allowed to protrude through the abdominal wound and are not released until three days later. This method of doing a rapid hysterectomy with transfusion during the operation will save some of the seemingly hopeless cases.

Following delivery through the maternal passages, a prophylactic pack is placed in the uterus and vagina, as many of the severe types of accidental hemorrhage continue to ooze after the uterus is emptied (26, 28, 29, 30, 31, 32, 33).

REFERENCES

1. PECKHAM, C. H.: A statistical Study of Placenta Previa at the Johns Hopkins Hospital. Am. J. Obs. & Gyn., 1931, 21, 39.
2. BURGER, O. AND GRAF, R.: Zur Statistik der Placenta praevia. Monatschr. f. Geburtsh. u. Gyn., 1907, 25, 49.
3. HOFMEIER, M.: Referate über Placenta praevia. Deutsch. Gesellsch. f. Gyn. 1897, 7, 204.
4. STRASSMANN, P.: Placenta praevia. Arch. f. Gyn., 1902, 27, 112.
5. SOLOMONS, B. AND CANTER, H. E.: The Etiology of Placenta Previa. Surg., Gyn. & Obs., 1932, 54, 790.
6. KELLOGG, F. S.: Treatment of Placenta Previa Based on a Study of 303 Consecutive Cases at the Boston Lying-in Hospital. Am. J. Obs. & Gyn., 1926, 11, 194.
    Observations on a Short Series of Placenta Previa Patients delivered by Abdominal Cesarean Section at The Boston Lying-in Hospital. Am. J. Obs. & Gyn., 1930, 20, 643.
7. FREY, E.: Die Schnittentbindung bei Placenta praevia. Zentralbl. f. Gyn., 1927, 51, 1073.
8. BILL, A. H.: Placenta Previa. Am. J. Obs. & Gyn., 1931, 21, 227.
9. WILSON, R. A.: Placenta Previa. Am. J. Obs. & Gyn., 1934, 27, 713.
10. THIEMKE, G.: Zur Behandlung der Placenta praevia. Monatschr. f. Geburtsh. u. Gyn., 1931, 87, 110.
11. IRVING, F. C.: Problems in Placenta Previa. Surg. Gyn. & Obs., 1927, 45, 834.
12. DEPKEN, H.: Die Behandlung der Placenta praevia. Zentralbl. f. Gyn., 1924, 48, 298.
13. WILLIAMSON, H. C.: The Treatment of Placenta Previa. N. Y. State Jnl. Med. 1929, 29, 936.
14. MOSKOWITZ, H. L.: An Analysis of 158 Cases of Placenta Previa. Am. J. Obs. & Gyn., 1932, 23, 502.
15. McPHERSON, R.: Treatment of Placenta Previa. Am. J. Obs. & Gyn., 1924, 7, 403.
16. MARTIN, E.: Placenta praevia und Scheidenschnitt. Monatschr. f. Geburtsh. u. Gyn., 1926, 78, 61.
17. VON AMMON, E.: Die Mortalität der vaginalen und abdominalen Entbindungsmethoden bei Placenta praevia. Zeitschr. f. Geburtsh. u. Gyn., 1930, 97, 261.
18. HOLMES, R. W.: Ablatio Placentae. Am. J. Obs., 1901, 44, 753.
    The Relationship of Utero-placental Apoplexy to Ablatio Placentae. Am. J. Obs. & Gyn., 1923, 6, 517.
19. GARDINER, J. P.: The Umbilical Cord. Surg. Gyn. & Obs., 1922, 34, 252.
20. HOFFBAUER, J. AND GEILING, E. M. K.: Studies on the Experimental Production of Premature Separation of the Placenta. Johns Hopkins Hospital Bull., 1926, 38, 143.
21. BROWNE, F. J. AND DODDS, G. H.: Further experimental Observations on the Etiology of Accidental hemorrhage and Placental Infarction. J. Obs. & Gyn., Brit. Emp. 1928, 35, 661.

22. BATESWEILER, J.: Ueber die Zusammenhänge der vorzeitigen Placentalösung mit Nierener-krankungen.   Arch. f. Gyn., 1933, 153, 536.
23. KELLOGG, F. S.: Premature Separation of the Normally Implanted Placenta with Special Reference to the Kidney in these cases.   Am. J. Obs. & Gyn. 1928, 15, 357.
24. GOETHALS, T. R.: Premature Separation of the Placenta.   Am. J. Obs. & Gyn. 1928, 15, 627.
25. COUVELAIRE, A.: Deux nouvelles observations d'apopléxie utéro-placentaire.   Ann. de gyn. et d'obs., 1912, 9, 486.
26. WILLIAMS, J. W.: Premature Separation of the Normally Implanted Placenta.   Surg. Gyn. & Obs., 1915, 21, 541.
    Further Observations Concerning Premature Separation of the Normally Implanted Placenta.   J. Obs. & Gyn., Brit. Emp., 1925, 32, 259.
27. WILLSON, P.: Uteroplacental Apoplexy (Hemorrhagic Infarction of the Uterus) in Accidental Hemorrhage.   Surg. Gyn. & Obs., 1922, 34, 57.
28. BURGESS, H. C.: Hemorrhage in the Last Trimester of Pregnancy.   Am. J. Obs. & Gyn., 1925, 10, 49.
29. FITZ GIBBON, G.: A Revised Conception of Antepartum Accidental Hemorrhage.   J. Obs. & Gyn., Brit. Emp., 1926, 33, 194.
30. POLAK, J. O.: Accidental Hemorrhage—Ablatio Placentae.   Am. J. Obs. & Gyn., 1931, 21, 218.
31. IRVING: Paper on Accidental Hemorrhage.   Read at N. Y. Obstetrical Society, 1934.
32. BARTHOLOMEW, R. A.: Premature Separation of the Normally Implanted Placenta.   Am. J. Obs. & Gyn., 1929, 18, 818.
33. DAVIS, M. E. AND McGEE, W. B.: Abruptio Placentae.   Surg. Gyn. & Obs., 1931, 53, 768.

CHAPTER XXXIII

RUPTURE OF THE UTERUS

Rupture of the uterus is a most serious obstetric complication. The frequency of its occurrence in any community varies with the quality of obstetric practice in that locality. When maternity care is of a low grade and complications are neglected, the uterus may rupture as often as once in every 500 labors. On the other hand, in properly conducted obstetric clinics where the patients are given the benefit of competent care throughout pregnancy and labor, this obstetric tragedy is very rarely observed (1).

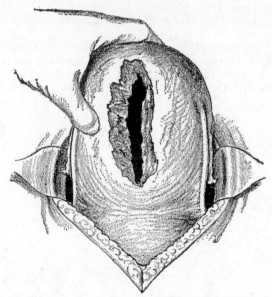

FIG. 860. Rupture of the uterus through a previous classical cesarean section scar at the seventh month.

ETIOLOGY. Rupture during pregnancy is very unusual and nearly always is found at the site of a previous operation or injury. Myomectomy, cesarean section, curettage, perforation by a uterine sound, hydatidiform mole, and manual removal of an adherent placenta have been reported as the causes of the uterine injury which almost invariably precedes spontaneous rupture in the antepartum period (2). Because of its increasing popularity, however, cesarean section is responsible for most ruptures in this group (Fig. 860).

Early in labor, degenerative changes in the uterine musculature and previous extensive cervical lacerations, as well as the conditions above noted, predispose toward rupture in the first stage.

712

Late in labor, rupture of the uterus is the result of dystocia, or injudicious and unskilful operative interference. Under dystocia, contracted pelvis may be listed as the commonest cause. Neglected transverse presentation is next in frequency, and hydrocephalus, brow and posterior face presentations, large child, and pelvic tumors occasionally are recorded as etiologic factors. While forceps deliveries, decapitation, and other destructive operations do, at times, cause rupture, version for neglected transverse presentation and attempts at turning when this procedure is definitely contraindicated are responsible for more ruptured uteri than all other operative measures (3, 4) excepting cesarean section. During recent years, the oxytocic effect of posterior pituitary extract has been the subject of much clinical investigation, and attempts have been made to extend its usefulness beyond the indications that are supported by good judgment. Its use as a panacea for most of the difficulties encountered in labor, accordingly, has caused rupture of the uterus in a great number of cases (5).

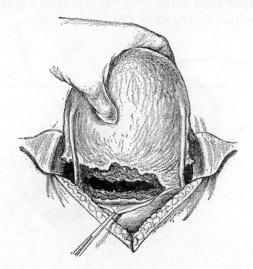

FIG. 861. Transverse rupture in lower uterine segment.

SITE OF RUPTURE. When the uterus ruptures during pregnancy, the lesion is situated in the upper segment and usually is the site of a previous operation or injury. Figure 860 shows a spontaneous rupture at the seventh month that followed a previous cesarean section done according to the classical technic.

Uterine rupture occurring late in labor usually is situated in the lower segment. When the anterior or posterior wall is involved, the tear extends transversely or obliquely, and longitudinally if it is in the region of the broad ligament. The bladder seldom is injured. Figure 861 is an illustration of an oblique tear in the lower segment that was caused by an injudicious version, and Figure 862 shows a longitudinal rupture into the broad ligament which extended from the external os to the round ligament.

SYMPTOMS AND SIGNS.   In pregnancy, the uterus usually ruptures without any premonitory signs, while during labor warning of the impending catastrophe may be given by the occurrence of tetanic contractions and a high Bandl's ring. The symptoms of actual rupture, as a rule, are definite and unmistakable.   At the height of a uterine contraction, the patient complains of a sudden agonizing pain in the abdomen with a feeling that something is tearing.   This is followed immediately by a total cessation of labor and evidence of collapse.   The pulse becomes rapid, weak and imperceptible.   Respirations are labored.   The skin is pale, cold and covered with a clammy perspiration.   The uterus may be felt as a distinct tumor alongside of the child, which is free in the abdominal cavity. Rectal or vaginal examination shows a recession or a change in the presenting part, and further exploration of the birth canal reveals a rent in the uterine wall. Death may follow within a very short time.

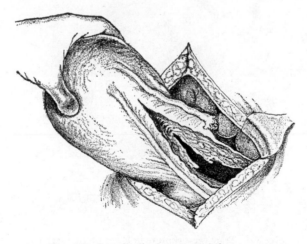

FIG. 862. Longitudinal rupture of the uterus.

If the patient reacts from the initial shock, hemorrhage, either external or internal, may cause a secondary and fatal collapse.   Should she survive the shock and hemorrhage, symptoms of peritonitis appear within a few days and bring about the almost inevitable fatal termination.

Occasionally, the picture is obscured by the tardy appearance of one or more of the classic signs of rupture.   Sooner or later, however, the tragic nature of the accident is revealed, and, unfortunately, in many cases the diagnosis is made too late for anything short of heroic treatment.

PROGNOSIS in rupture of the uterus depends upon the manner in which labor is managed before the accident occurs, in addition to the extent and location of the lesion.   When the tear extends completely through the uterine wall into the peritoneal cavity, the mortality approaches 100 per cent unless the patient is promptly subjected to skilful surgery; in these circumstances the risk is about halved.   Should the previous conduct of labor predispose toward infection, even skilful surgery cannot give an equal chance for recovery.

Incomplete ruptures are much less serious, and under appropriate treatment recovery is the rule.

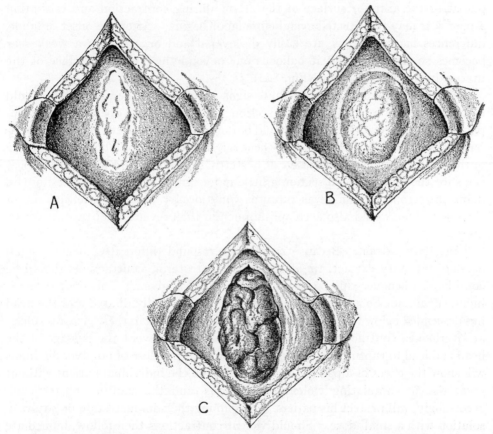

FIG. 863. Partial and complete ruptures of previous cesarean section scars.   A. Thin scar in interval between contractions.   B. Thin scar ballooning out during a pain.   C. Placenta protruding through a ruptured scar.

TREATMENT.   **Prophylactic.** As complete rupture is accompanied by a very high mortality even under the most favorable circumstances, the best treatment for this alarming condition is prophylactic.

Previous cesarean section. Rupture of a previous cesarean scar is not an uncommon event today. In a study of pregnancies following cesarean section, it was found that 4 per cent of 448 women who became pregnant after this operation ruptured their uteri (6). Such a high incidence of this tragic accident should lead us to advise women who have had a cesarean section to remain within a reasonable distance of their obstetric hospital and surgeon during the latter months of all subsequent pregnancies. This is particularly true if the cesarean was done according to the classical technic and **is imperative if the postoperative course was febrile.** Throughout the pregnancy, the site of the previous incision in the uterus should be examined repeatedly for evidence of thinning. By palpating the anterior surface of the uterus during contraction and relaxation a poor scar may be detected even before labor begins. After the onset of labor, differences in consistency are easily discovered and occasionally a weak scar becomes so stretched that it balloons out beyond the adjacent surface of the uterus during a contraction (Fig. 863).

Whenever the scar shows definite signs of weakness, the pregnancy should be terminated by a second cesarean section. If the previous operation was complicated by infection, the section should be done before the onset of labor. Suprapubic delivery likewise is indicated whenever, in the course of labor, any thinning of the old scar becomes manifest. If obstetric surgeons would weigh the indications for the first cesarean section a little more carefully and be less hesitant in doing the second section, fewer ruptures would occur. A more extensive use of the low technic would also accomplish much in the prevention of rupture of the uterus.

Pituitary extract. Because individuals respond differently to even small doses of pituitary extract, the danger of violent uterine contractions should be considered whenever this powerful oxytocic drug is given. This drug, accordingly, should not be administered unless the cervix is fully dilated and the head has descended below the level of the ischial spines. Even in these circumstances, an overlooked contraction of the pelvic outlet may prevent the passage of the head and lead to rupture of the uterus. A small initial dose of not over 3 minims will show the effect of a particular preparation on the individual patient without great risk of stimulating violent contractions, and the cautious obstetrician, accordingly, will protect his patient by beginning the administration of pituitary solution with a small dose. Should violent contractions then follow, immediate delivery is indicated. If delivery cannot be effected, chloroform anesthesia should be used until the effect of the drug wears off.

Bandl's ring. Many years ago Bandl called attention to the marked thinning of the lower uterine segment that precedes spontaneous rupture in cases of dystocia, and showed that a marked elevation of the ring which divides the upper active segment from the lower passive one is an index of this thinning (7). A high ring near the level of the umbilicus, accordingly, is considered an indication

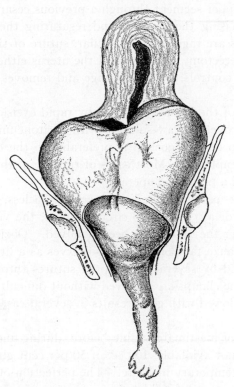

FIG. 864. Impacted transverse presentation wholly within the thinned out lower uterine segment with retraction ring and upper segment riding above the child and resembling a large fibroid.

of impending rupture and calls for prompt delivery, if rupture of the uterus is to be prevented. In these circumstances, the method of operative interference will depend upon the conditions that are present but version is always contraindicated. Figure 864 illustrates the marked thinning of the lower segment that may occur in a neglected transverse presentation.

Version. Rupture of the uterus during version may be avoided by gentle, slow manipulations, by waiting until the patient is deeply anesthetized (never with nitrous oxide) and by reserving version for only those cases in which it is not contraindicated.

AFTER RUPTURE HAS OCCURRED. As soon as the diagnosis of rupture is made, an immediate laparotomy is indicated unless the tear is incomplete (1, 4, 8). While preparing for operation, a transfusion of whole blood is indicated if a suitable donor is available. If the transfusion cannot be given at once, 100 cc. of concentrated 50 per cent glucose are introduced into a vein as a temporary measure. The delivery of the child should be postponed until preparations for the laparotomy have been completed. If the child is free in the abdominal cavity, delivery will be easier after the abdomen is opened.

A tear in the upper segment through a previous cesarean scar sometimes is best treated by excising the old scar and resuturing the uterine wound. As most other ruptures are ragged and irregular, suture of the tear usually is less desirable than hysterectomy. Excision of the uterus either by supracervical or total hysterectomy controls the hemorrhage and removes the menace of an infected uterus.

Quick ligation of the vessels, followed by rapid excision of the uterus without attempting to cover all raw surfaces with peritoneum and reliance upon a large gauze drain to control oozing, is preferable to the finished hysterectomy technic ordinarily employed. Most cases of rupture of the uterus are critically ill and cannot stand a prolonged operation.

Even when the patient's condition seems hopeless, operation should be attempted without delay. In these circumstances, the vessels and the clamps are left in place after the uterus has been removed. Oozing from cut surfaces is controlled by a gauze tampon which also serves as a drain. The abdominal wound is then closed by several interrupted sutures through all of the layers. On the third day, the clamps are removed without difficulty. In our clinic, this technic has been followed with good results in several cases that appeared to be hopeless.

Transfusion is of inestimable value before, during and after operation. If a suitable donor is not available, 100 cc. of 50 per cent glucose should be given intravenously as a temporary measure. The perfection of the method of blood transfusion has been most helpful in many of our tragic obstetric complications.

Incomplete tears are best handled by suturing them through the vagina or or by plugging the rent with a tight uterine pack. If possible, such packs should be saturated with some mild antiseptic solution before they are introduced. Removal of the pack is begun twenty-four hours later. Only about one-third of it should be withdrawn at one time and fresh gauze should be at hand in case renewal of the hemorrhage requires repacking.

REFERENCES

1. DAVIS, A. B.: The Ruptured Uterus. Am. J. Obs. & Gyn., 1927, 13, 522.
2. BAISCH: Ueber Zerreissung der Gebärmutter in der Schwangerschaft. Beitr. z. Geburtsh. u. Gyn., 1903, 7, 249.
3. MERZ, K.: Zur Behandlung der Uterusruptur. Arch. f. Gyn., 1894, 45, 181.
4. FRITSCH, H.: Referat über die Behandlung der Uterusruptur. Verhandl. de deutsch. Gesellsch. f. Gyn., 1895, 1.
5. MENDENHALL, A. M.: Solution of Pituitary and Ruptured Uterus. J. A. M. A., 1929, 92, 1341.
6. HOLLAND, E.: Discussion on Rupture of the Cesarean Section Scar in Subsequent Pregnancy or Labour. Proc. Roy. Soc. Med., 1920, 14, 22.
7. BANDL: Ueber Ruptur des Uterus und ihre Mechanik. Wien, 1875.
8 KERR, J. M.: Rupture of the Uterus and Its Treatment Based on a Series of Fourteen Cases. J. Obs. & Gyn., Brit. Emp., 1908, 14, 1.

CHAPTER XXXIV

INVERSION OF THE UTERUS

Inversion of the uterus is a very serious accident in which the organ is partially or completely turned inside out. Fortunately, it is one of the rarest of obstetric complications.

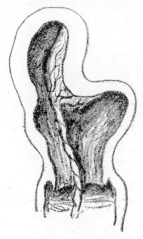

FIG. 865. Beginning inversion.

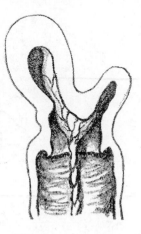

FIG. 866. Partial inversion.

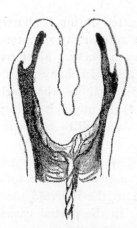

FIG. 867. Cupping of the fundus.

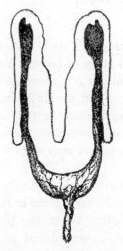

FIG. 868. Complete inversion.

An inversion is termed partial when the fundus dips into the lower segment or protrudes through the cervix, and complete when the entire uterus is inverted. As the cervix seldom is completely involved, most inversions are partial.

The accident of inversion may occur spontaneously. As a rule, however, it is the result of bad management in the third stage of labor and is due to traction on the umbilical cord or attempts at expression of the placenta while the uterus is relaxed. It accordingly is seen almost exclusively in consultation practice among those who are without competent care during confinement (1, 2, 3, 4) (Figs. 865, 866, 867, 868).

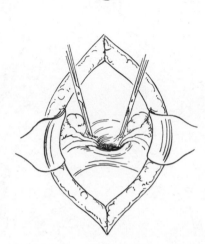

Fig. 868 a. The inverted uterine wall is grasped by Allis clamps and pulled upward (Huntington Irving and Kellogg).

SYMPTOMS. As a rule, the uterus becomes inverted during or shortly after the third stage of labor. Rarely, it occurs without noteworthy symptoms and, as a result, is not recognized for several days or even weeks. Most patients, however, bleed profusely and are profoundly shocked. In many cases, death follows within one or two hours and a large number of those who survive the shock and hemorrhage subsequently die of sepsis. If the uterus is not replaced, the tight cervix may cut off the uterine circulation and lead to gangrene of the fundus.

EXAMINATION shows the absence of the uterus above the pelvic brim and the presence of a large mass in the vagina which, at first, may be mistaken for a large fibromyoma. When the placenta is still attached to the inverted uterus, no difficulty is encountered in making the diagnosis. In the partial variety, the cup-shaped indentation of the fundus is felt through the abdomen.

TREATMENT. The fact that thousands of women are confined annually in good maternity hospitals without the occurrence of this accident proves that prophylaxis is the best treatment. If traction on the cord is avoided entirely and expression of the placenta is attempted only when the uterus is contracted, the majority of uterine inversions will be prevented. After inversion occurs, immediate manual reposition is indicated. Relaxation of the uterus is first secured by the use of adrenalin and deep anesthesia (5). The cervix is then grasped by Jacobs forceps and held by an assistant while the operator passes the fingers of one hand through the relaxed abdominal wall into the cup-shaped depression made by the indentation of the fundus. With the thumb and fingers of the other hand in the vagina, he makes upward pressure on opposite sides of the

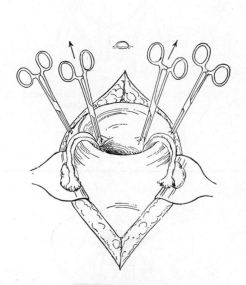

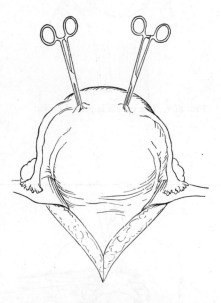

FIG. 868 b. Upward traction by means of the Allis clamps is continued.

FIG. 868 c. Operation completed and the normal shape of the uterus is restored.

uterus near the region of the cervix, so that one side slides up over the other. After reposition, the uterus is packed with 4 per cent mercurochrome gauze. If the placenta is attached, it should not be disturbed until after the uterus has been reposited, unless reposition is impossible without its removal.

If the uterus cannot be easily replaced, the operation should be postponed until after the shock has been overcome by the use of transfusion, artificial heat and the Trendelenberg posture. In the meantime, the bleeding is controlled by the use of moist gauze packs. After all evidence of shock has disappeared, the foregoing manipulations are then tried and, if they fail, reposition may be accomplished by opening the abdomen and pulling the uterus through the inverted lower segment by means of forceps (6) fig. 868 a, 868 b, and 868 c. The Spinelli (7)

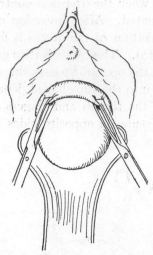

FIG. 869. The cervix is pulled down.

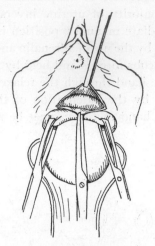

FIG. 870. The vagina is incised and
the bladder is exposed.

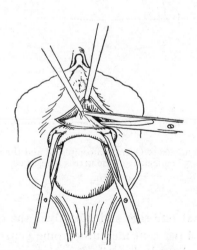

FIG. 871. The peritoneum is incised.

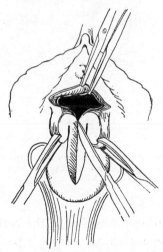

FIG. 872. The cervix and uterus are incised.

operation which is so useful in chronic inversion may also be used when manual
reposition fails.   In this procedure, the bladder is dissected off from the anterior
uterine wall, and the cervix and body of the uterus are cut in the midline (8, 9,
10) (Figs. 869 to 874).   The inversion is then corrected and the wound is closed
as in a vaginal hysterotomy.   In the presence of gangrene, vaginal hysterectomy
is indicated.

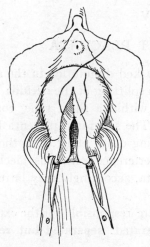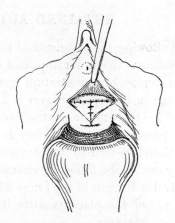

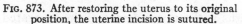

Fig. 873. After restoring the uterus to its original position, the uterine incision is sutured.

Fig. 874. The peritoneum is sutured prior to the approximation of the vaginal incision.

REFERENCES

1. Holmes, R. W.: Inversio Uteri Complicating Placenta Previa; Etiology and Mechanism Considered. Obs., N. Y., 1899, 1, 297.

2. Beckmann, W.: Zur Aetiologie der Inversio uteri postpartum. Zeitschr. f. Geburtsh. u. Gyn., 1895, 31, 371.

3. Vogel, G.: Beitrag zur Lehre von der Inversio Uteri. Ztschr. f. Geburtsh. u. Gyn., 1900, 42, 490.

4. McCullagh, W. McK. H.: Inversion of the Uterus; a Report of Three Cases and an Analysis of 233 Recently Recorded Cases. J. Obs. & Gyn., Brit. Emp., 1925, 32, 280.

5. Urner, J. A.: The Use of Adrenalin in the Treatment of Acute Inversion of the Puerperal Uterus. Am. J. Obs. & Gyn., 1933, 25, 131.

6. Huntington, J. L., Irving, F. C. and Kellogg, F. S.: Abdominal Reposition in Acute Inversion of the Puerperal Uterus. Am. J. Obs. & Gyn., 1928, 15, 34.

7. Spinelli, P. G.: Della inversione uterina. Riv. di ginec. contemp., 1897, 1, pages 1, 17 33, 49.

8. Jones, W. C.: Inversion of the Uterus. Surg., Gyn. & Obs., 1913, 16, 632.

9. Thorn, W.: Zur Inversio Uteri. Samml. Klin. Vortr., Leipzig, 1911, N.F., 625. Gyn. No. 229–231, p. 101.

10. Miller, N. F.: Pregnancy Following Inversion of the Uterus. Am. J. Obs. & Gyn., 1927, 13, 307.

CHAPTER XXXV

RETAINED AND ADHERENT PLACENTA

Following the expulsion of the child, the marked diminution in the area of the placental site is accompanied by more or less splitting of the decidua basalis in the region of the stratum spongiosum and, within a short time, complete cleavage in this spongy layer is accomplished. The separated placenta is then forced by the uterine contractions or by a bearing down effort, into the lower birth passages and ultimately is expelled. Interference with this mechanism may therefore lead to its retention. The placenta, accordingly, may be retained in any one of the following circumstances:

1. Inpairment of the forces which normally are responsible for the expulsion of the placenta after it has been separated: **separated but retained placenta.**

2. Hour-glass contraction of the uterus with imprisonment of the separated placenta within the upper segment: **separated but incarcerated placenta.**

3. Failure of the customary decidual cleavage due either to an abnormal decidua, an anatomical defect in the uterus, or to a lack of the normal contraction and retraction in the third stage: **adherent but separable placenta.**

4. Absence of a normal decidua with direct attachment of the chorionic elements to the uterine musculature: **adherent and inseparable placenta**—placenta accreta.

A separated but retained placenta occurs rather frequently when the third stage of labor is left entirely to Nature and is encountered most commonly in women with lax abdominal walls who have been greatly fatigued by a prolonged labor. It was in these cases that the midwife formerly brought about the placenta's expulsion by irritating the nasal mucous membrane with a feather to induce sneezing. The forced contractions of the diaphragm and abdominal muscles thus increased the intra-abdominal pressure and effected the delivery of the separated placenta from the lower uterine segment and vagina. Natural expulsion was also favored by the use of a tight abdominal binder or by gathering folds of the relaxed abdominal wall within the grasp of the attendant's hand for the purpose of diminishing the capacity of the abdominal cavity.

About the middle of the eighteenth century, The Dublin School of Midwifery recommended the artificial expulsion of the separated placenta. With the fingers behind and the thumb in front of the uterus, pressure in the axis of the pelvic inlet is exerted on the fundus. The uterus thus is used as a piston and forces the placenta out of the birth canal. **This procedure should never be used when the uterus is relaxed. In such circumstances,** the latter is gently massaged until it becomes firmly contracted; otherwise inversion may be produced. Pressure on the fundus as a means of hastening the delivery of the placenta was again advocated by Credé of Leipzig in 1861, after which it became known as Credé's method of expressing the placenta.

While this measure is accompanied by little or no risk when the placenta is separated but retained within the birth passages, its premature use may cause serious bleeding if complete detachment has not occurred. Artificial expression, accordingly, should not be employed until at least one hour has elapsed after the

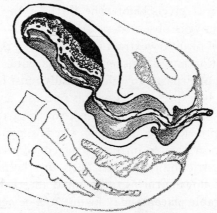

FIG. 874 a. Separated but incarcerated placenta in an hour-glass uterus. Note the thick ridge of muscle tissue beneath the placental site. This must be artificially dilated before the imprisoned placenta can be removed.

birth of the child, unless the signs of separation are present, or unless evidence of increasing hemorrhage is noted. The signs which indicate complete separation of the placenta are:

(a) The rising of the fundus well above the level at which it was noted immediately after the birth of the child;

(b) The change in the shape of the uterus from a somewhat irregularly elongated mass to the more or less ball-like shape which is characteristic of the empty organ;

(c) A gush of blood from the vulvovaginal orifice;

(d) Further protrusion of the umbilical cord;

(e) A loss of the expansile impulse in the cord when pressure is exerted on the fundus of the uterus;

(f) The cord is not drawn back into the vagina when the uterus is elevated.

Although one may wait a number of hours for natural expulsion to take place, such expectancy is quite unnecessary and most inconvenient, since the attendant must preserve an aseptic technique until the placenta is delivered. On the other hand, to leave the patient while the placenta is within the birth canal is to risk the danger of a fatal hemorrhage.

A separated but incarcerated placenta (Fig. 874 a) is very rarely encountered in ordinary obstetric practice. Following an obstructed labor, the placenta may be held within the upper segment by a definite retraction ridge which forms at the isthmus of the uterus. This rigid ring results from a spasmodic contraction and thickening of the uterine musculature and cannot be dilated without the use of deep anesthesia. While it occurs most commonly in obstructed labors, it may also follow early rupture of the membranes in certain cases in which the uterus becomes molded about the child's body. Oxytocic drugs, when administered injudiciously, likewise may aid in the production of this complication. Formerly, when ergot was given before the birth of the placenta, hour-glass contraction of the uterus was observed rather frequently. Even now it occasionally follows the use of pituitary extract when this drug is employed as a means of hastening the separation and expulsion of the placenta.

The constricting ring of spastic muscle naturally must be relaxed and dilated before the placenta can be expressed. For this purpose, a hypodermic injection of 5 mm. of adrenalin, 1:1000, may be tried, or the patient may be deeply anesthetized before expression by means of Credé's maneuver is attempted. Usually, however, it is necessary to introduce the coned fingers of one hand, and manually dilate the constricting ring under deep anesthesia. Successful relaxation has been reported following the use of a spinal anesthetic.

Adherent but separable placenta may be due to a defective decidua in which the customary fragile network of the spongy layer is abnormally dense. Cleavage also may be retarded by an unusually extensive placental attachment. This complication accordingly is encountered more frequently in twin and succenturiate placentae and is a common accompaniment of placenta membranacea. The various congenital anomalies of the uterus and multiple myomata lead to alterations in the contour of the uterine cavity, and are predisposing causes of inertia. They therefore are occasional etiological factors in adherent but separable placenta. The commonest cause of this condition, however, is a lack of the normal contraction and retraction of the uterus in the third stage of labor. This impairment of function often is the result of over-distention of the uterus, prolonged labor or the use of sedative drugs and anesthetics. It likewise may be due to a distended bladder since catheterization frequently is followed by rapid separation and expulsion of the placenta.

Unfortunately, an adherent but separable placenta often becomes partially detached and, as a result, may give rise to bleeding of alarming proportions. If little or no blood is lost, an expectant attitude for at least one hour after the birth of the fetus is advisable. At the expiration of this time, active interference is indicated. On the other hand, immediate intervention is recommended whenever the hemorrhage is profuse. By means of external manipulations, the placenta must then be artificially separated and expressed or it must be removed manually from the uterine cavity.

The external method of artificially separating and expressing the placenta consists of fundal compression through the abdominal wall. With the fingers behind and the thumb in front, the uterus is squeezed successively from side to side after the manner of pitting a cherry (Fig. 874 b). Pressure is then exerted in the axis of the pelvic inlet. This procedure differs from the one previously recommended in that it aims to separate as well as to expel the placenta. If the bleeding is not too severe, manipulations are repeated until the desired result is obtained. At times, however, the hemorrhage may be excessive and necessitate immediate manual removal.

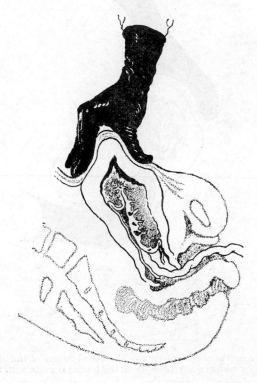

FIG. 874 b. Method of artificially separating and expressing the placenta. Uteru s is first compressed from side to side after the manner of pitting a cherry and then pressure is exerted in the axis o f the pelvic inlet.

The great risk of infection which accompanies manual removal of the placenta makes the use of a strict aseptic technique imperative whenever this operation is done. Since the gown and sterile gloves, which were worn during the delivery, might have become contaminated, they are to be replaced by clean ones, the sterility of which is unquestioned. The vulva, likewise, should again be cleansed with 1:500 chlorothymol solution or painted with half strength tincture of iodine after the patient has been anesthetized. With the thumb and forefinger of the left hand, the labia are then widely separated, and the coned fingers of the right hand, lubricated with 1:500 chlorothymol solution, are passed upward through the vagina and into the uterus (Fig. 874 c). At the same time, counterpressure on the fundus is made with the external hand. By following the cord, the placenta is easily located and its margin readily found. Search

FIG. 874 c. Manual removal of the placenta. The coned fingers of the internal hand are introduced into the uterine cavity while counterpressure on the fundus is made with the external hand.

is then made for a plane of cleavage and, by a side-to-side motion of the fingers, the separation is completed (Fig. 874 d). The detachment should be complete before any of the placenta is removed; otherwise, part of it may be retained. Following complete separation, the uterus is massaged with the external hand and made to expel both the placenta and the internal hand. The placenta should never be removed while the uterus is in a state of relaxation.

After its removal, the placenta is examined carefully in order that the operator may be certain that no part has been left behind. In case of doubt, the uterine cavity should be explored again, and any retained fragments removed manually. In this connection, the operator will avoid unnecessary manipulations if he will have in mind the irregular and jagged contour of the placental site.

Since the external method of separating the placenta may fail to detach it completely and, as a result, may cause such a serious hemorrhage that manual

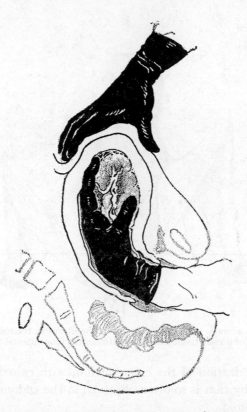

FIG. 874 d. Manual removal of the placenta. After locating the plane of cleavage the separation of the placenta is completed by a to and fro movement of the fingers.

removal may be necessary, the usual aseptic preparation for manual removal always should precede any external attempt to separate the placenta artificially.

Whenever the amount of blood lost is in the neighborhood of 1000 cc., or causes the patient to show signs of hemorrhage, an immediate transfusion is indicated. This measure is particularly valuable as a prophylaxis against the infection which may follow the operation of manual removal.

Adherent and inseparable placenta, placenta accreta, is very rarely encountered even in active obstetric clinics. It results from an almost complete absence of the decidua basalis, as a consequence of which the eroding, chorionic elements penetrate the uterine musculature and firmly fix the placenta to the wall of the uterus (Fig. 874 e).   In one of our cases, the erosive action of these trophoblastic elements was so marked that the villi penetrated the uterine wall almost to its peritoneal covering, and instances have been reported in which complete perforation into the peritoneal cavity has occurred.   This complication is thought to

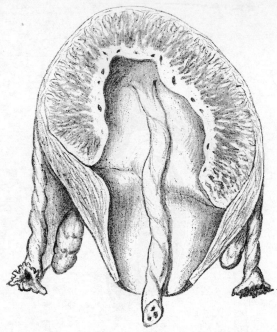

FIG. 874 e. Placenta accreta.   Note the thinness of the uterus in the region of the placental site. In places, less than 2 mm. of muscle tissue intervene between the placenta and the peritoneum.

be favored by cauterization of the endometrium with caustics, repeated curettings, and the atrophy that is so often observed in the endometrium which overlies a submucous fibroid.

Bleeding from the placental site does not occur when the placenta is adherent and inseparable; likewise, all evidences of detachment are absent.   Therefore, whenever the placenta is retained for more than one hour without vaginal bleeding and with a complete absence of the usual signs of separation, placenta accreta should be suspected.   If the Credé procedure is attempted, there is always a possibility of rupturing the uterus in the region of the thinned-out placenta site. For this reason, external manipulations should be most gentle, or, better still, entirely abandoned.   Under strict aseptic precautions, the hand is introduced into the uterine cavity and a search is made for a line of separation.   When such a cleavage zone cannot be found, the diagnosis of placenta accreta rather than adherent but separable placenta is made, and immediate hysterectomy is indicated.   It is the height of folly to attempt to remove piecemeal such a placenta. When this injudicious procedure is tried, serious hemorrhage, shock, perforation of the uterus, or sepsis almost invariably causes the death of the mother.

CHAPTER XXXVI

POSTPARTUM HEMORRHAGE

Excessive bleeding after the placenta is delivered is known as POSTPARTUM HEMORRHAGE. In ordinary obstetric practice, it is one of the commonest causes of death from hemorrhage, but does not occur sufficiently often to impress those in charge of obstetric patients with the need for proper prophylactic care.

VARIETIES. Two general varieties are recognized:
1. Placental site or atonic hemorrhage.
2. Traumatic hemorrhage.

PLACENTAL SITE OR ATONIC HEMORRHAGE. Following the delivery of the placenta, slight bleeding is observed in all cases. An excessive loss of blood, however, occurs about once in every one hundred deliveries if proper precautions are taken, and more frequently when they are neglected (1, 2).

ETIOLOGY. The causes of placental site hemorrhage may be outlined as follows:

1. Uterine inertia due to
$$\begin{cases} \text{Overdistention as in twins} \\ \quad \text{and hydramnios} \\ \text{Prolonged labor} \\ \text{Multiparity} \\ \text{Anesthesia} \end{cases}$$

2. Retention of placental fragments
3. Placenta previa
4. Ablatio placentae
5. New growths of the uterus
6. Precipitate labor
7. Idiopathic

UTERINE INERTIA. Ordinarily contraction and retraction of the uterine muscle fibers constrict and kink the vessels which supply the placental site (Figs. 875 and 876). If the uterus has been overdistended, as in multiple pregnancy or hydramnios, inadequate contraction and retraction may lead to severe postpartum hemorrhage. The same may be said of prolonged labor when it causes fatigue of the uterine muscle. Multiparity, particularly when the pregnancies have been numerous and have followed one another closely, may result in a weakened musculature and, accordingly, contributes its share to the etiology of postpartum hemorrhage. When ether and chloroform are given, especially for operative procedures after prolonged labors, the normal tone of the uterus frequently is lost, and contraction and retraction after the placenta is delivered often are inadequate.

731

RETAINED PLACENTAL TISSUE prevents the proper closure of the adjacent blood sinuses. Such fragments, accordingly, are a menace as long as they remain within the uterus.

PLACENTA PREVIA. When the placental site is in the lower or passive uterine segment, the lack of adequate contractile tissue in this region may lead to hemorrhage.

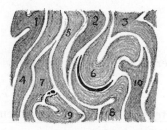

FIG. 875   FIG. 876

FIG. 875. Schematic representation of the muscular elements surrounding the blood vessels before the placenta is separated (Bumm).

FIG. 876. Contraction and retraction of the uterine musculature shown in Figure 875 constricting the vessels after the placenta is removed (Bumm).

ABLATIO PLACENTAE. The hemorrhagic changes observed in the uterine musculature in premature separation of the placenta greatly interfere with its contractility. For this reason, the danger of postpartum hemorrhage is constantly present in uteroplacental apoplexy.

TUMORS not only interfere with the normal muscular action of the uterus, but, at times, they prevent adequate closure of the vessels supplying the placental site and, as a result, are responsible for some cases of postpartum hemorrhage.

PRECIPITATE LABOR. In very rapid labors, profuse hemorrhage may be due to the separation and expulsion of the placenta before the usual retraction can take place. All who have done cesarean sections know that profuse hemorrhage often follows the immediate removal of the placenta while very little bleeding is observed when a few minutes are allowed for retraction of the uterus before the placenta is removed.

IDIOPATHIC POSTPARTUM HEMORRHAGE occurs in some women without any demonstrable cause. Frequently they give a history of repeated hemorrhages following the delivery of all previous children.

SYMPTOMS. Two types of bleeding may be observed. In one, more or less profuse hemorrhage takes place immediately after the placenta is born and continues intermittently as the uterus relaxes after each contraction. In the other, a sudden profuse hemorrhage may occur at any time within several hours after the delivery of the placenta, although the greatest danger is in the first hour. Other symptoms are those of hemorrhage: pallor, thirst, cold extremities, air hunger and syncope. On examination, the pulse is rapid and thready, the blood pressure is low and the uterus may be so relaxed that it no longer is palpable through the abdominal wall. If it is felt, it will be soft and enlarged, and massage of the fundus should stimulate contractions and stop the bleeding.

TREATMENT. The best way to treat postpartum hemorrhage is to prevent its occurrence. The prophylactic treatment, therefore, is most essential, and may be outlined as follows:

1. The uterus should be held by the obstetrician or a competent nurse for at least one hour after the placenta is born. If it relaxes, gentle massage over the fundus will stimulate contractions and prevent bleeding. **There is no substitute for this prophylactic measure,** and nothing should be permitted to interfere with its being carried out.

2. One dram of fluid extract of ergot is given by mouth immediately after the placenta is delivered. The oxytocic action of this drug often is not observed for from ten to fifteen minutes after its administration, but it has a prolonged effect if the preparation used is a good one and is not too old. While vigorous contractions are induced almost immediately by pituitary preparations, the effect wears off rapidly and may be followed by relaxation of the uterus. Injections of pituitary extract, accordingly, may lead to a false sense of security and may, after a short time, be followed by serious bleeding. Their use, therefore, should always be supplemented by one of the ergot preparations. The hypodermic use of ergotrate acts more readily than the fluid extract of ergot and, accordingly, is used as a substitute for the combination of pituitary extract and the fluid extract of ergot.

3. An ice-bag over the fundus tends to favor contractions of the uterus. It accordingly may be used as an additional prophylactic measure.

4. If the examination of the placenta and membranes indicates the retention of placental fragments within the uterine cavity, these should be removed manually under strict aseptic conditions (3).

5. Whenever there is a history of previous postpartum hemorrhage, the intravenous injection of calcium at the onset of labor may be helpful (4, 5).

FIG. 877. The uterus is elevated as one hand makes upward pressure in the region of the symphysis, while the other hand massages the fundus to stimulate uterine contractions and control postpartum hemorrhage.

AFTER HEMORRHAGE HAS OCCURRED. 1. After the hemorrhage has occurred, one hand indents the abdomen in the region of the lower uterine segment and elevates the uterus, while the other vigorously massages the fundus (Fig. 877). At the same time, 1 cc. of pituitary extract or ergotrate is given hypodermically.

2. Should this fail to control the bleeding the uterus is brought forward over the symphysis and massage is continued (Fig. 878).

3. If the uterus is so relaxed that it cannot be felt, the abdomen is massaged deeply with the fists for a few seconds. Often this stimulates the uterus and restores its outline. It is then grasped and vigorously massaged.

4. When necessary, the hemorrhage may be controlled by compression of the aorta (Fig. 879) (6). This not only checks the bleeding, but often is followed by contraction of the uterus, after which the foregoing routine is carried out.

5. Should all of these efforts fail, the introduction of a firm, moist gauze pack is indicated (Fig. 880).

6. If the examination of the placenta shows the retention of placental fragments within the uterus, the uterine cavity should be explored immediately in order that these may be removed (3).

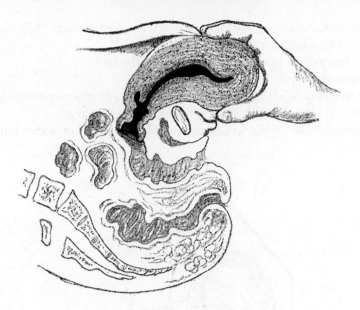

FIG. 878. The uterus is sharply anteflexed over the symphysis while it is being massaged to stimulate contractions.

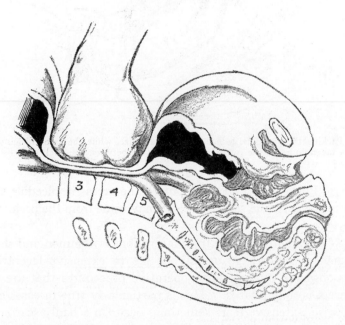

FIG. 879. Compression of the abdominal aorta to control postpartum hemorrhage.

THE ACUTE ANEMIA following postpartum hemorrhage calls for prompt treatment. This should include:

1. The immediate lowering of the head of the bed.
2. Hypodermoclysis.
3. Intravenous injection of 100 cc. of 50 per cent glucose solution.
4. Direct transfusion of as much blood as is necessary.
5. External heat by the use of warm blankets and hot water bottles or an electric heater.

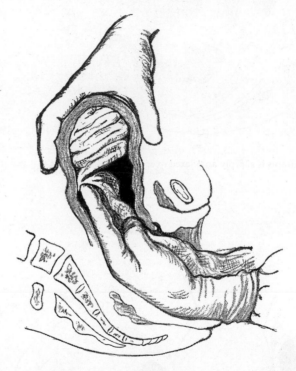

FIG. 880. Packing the uterus with moist, sterilized gauze, while the external hand steadies the fundus. Care is taken to avoid the retention of blood clots between the pack and the uterine wall.

TRAUMATIC POSTPARTUM HEMORRHAGE is the excessive bleeding that results from trauma to the maternal soft parts. It may come from the perineum, vulva, vagina or cervix.

FREQUENCY. Slight bleeding from lacerations is common and should cause no alarm. Severe hemorrhage usually is due to extensive laceration of the cervix and is observed oftenest after operative procedures that are attempted before the cervix is fully dilated. This is particularly true in cases of placenta previa. Likewise, extensive tears sometimes occur in a badly scarred cervix or one that has been previously operated upon. Lacerations near the clitoris and ruptured varicose veins may also bleed profusely.

SYMPTOMS. Profuse hemorrhage following the delivery of the child, and continuing throughout the third stage and after the delivery of the placenta, is due to laceration in the birth passages, when it persists after the uterus is made to contract by massage.

TREATMENT. If, after massage, the uterus is hard and the bleeding continues, immediate exploration is indicated. A quick search of the vulva is made, particularly in the region of the clitoris. Following this, the cervix is forced into the vulvovaginal ring by making pressure on the fundus of the uterus. The anterior and posterior lips are then grasped by sponge forceps, and traction on these facilitates the search for the site of hemorrhage. The introduction of posterior and lateral retractors likewise is helpful in exposing bleeding points, which are then secured by suture ligatures. If immediate suturing of the laceration cannot be carried out because of the lack of the necessary instruments and assistants, a tight, wet pack should be introduced. All packs are removed gradually, one-third in twelve hours and the remainder at the end of one day.

The measures recommended above to combat the acute anemia should be utilized, while preparations are being made for immediate transfusion.

REFERENCES

1. MEYER, K.: Ueber atonische Blutungen an der Universitäts-Frauenklinik München in den letzten 90 Jahren. Arch. f. Gyn., 1930, 142, 226.
2. PECKHAM, C. K. AND KUDER, K.: Some Statistics of Postpartum Hemorrhage. Am. J. Obs. & Gyn., 1933, 26, 361.
3. HABA, A.: Die Behandlung der Placentarperiode mit besonderer Berücksichtigung der Frage der Entfernung der im Inneren zurückgebliebenen Placentarreste. Arch. f. Gyn., 1926, 127, 80.
4. BARDENHAUER, F. H.: Zur Prophylaxe der Nachgeburtsblutung durch Kalzium. Zentralbl. f. Gyn., 1929, 53, 1826.
5. SZENTEH, S.: Die blutstillende Wirkung des Kalziums bei der Geburt und im Wochenbett. Zentralbl. f. Gyn., 1929, 53, 1828.
6. CLASON, S.: Erfolge der manuellen Aortenkompression in blutiger Nachgeburtsperiode. Acta Obs. et Gyn., Scandin., 1933, 13, 127.

OLIVER WENDELL HOLMES
1809–1894
Boston

Holmes in 1843 published the famous paper "The Contagiousness of Puerperal Fever," in which he proved that the disease was transmitted directly or indirectly from one individual to another as was suggested by White (1773) and others. In a later publication, "Puerperal Fever as a Private Pestilence" (1855) he referred to the use by Semmelweis of chloride of lime as a prophylactic wash for the physician's hands.

IGNAZ PHILLIP SEMMELWEIS
1818–1865
Vienna, Budapest

The first division in the Allgemeines Krankenhaus in Vienna in which Semmelweis served as an assistant permitted students to make vaginal examinations without washing their hands even though they came directly from the dissecting room. All of the work on the other service was done by midwives who paid greater attention to personal cleanliness. Semmelweis observed that the maternal mortality was much higher in the first division. In 1847 he also observed that the lesions present in one who died of a wound obtained during dissection were similar to those found in puerperal infection. Following these observations his students were obliged to wash their hands in a solution of chloride of lime before making vaginal examinations with the result that the mortality rate dropped from 9.92 to 3.8 and reached the low rate of 1.27 in the following year. Semmelweis thus proved the cause of puerperal infection to be transmissible and showed how the disease might be prevented by the prophylactic washing of the hands in an antiseptic solution.

CHAPTER XXXVII

PUERPERAL INFECTION

PUERPERAL INFECTION is a wound infection in the birth passages. It often is referred to as puerperal fever, childbed fever, puerperal sepsis, or puerperal septicemia.

FREQUENCY. Puerperal infection is one of the commonest complications of labor and is responsible for a large percentage of all maternal deaths.

ETIOLOGY

Streptococus pyogenes, Staphylococcus aureus, citreus and *albus, Neisseria gonorrhoeae, Diplococcus pneumoniae, Bacillus coli, Bacillus diptheriae, Bacillus pyocyaneus* and *Bacillus welchii* have been found to be the specific causative factors, but, as might be expected, the common pyogenic organisms are most frequently responsible for puerperal infection.

STREPTOCOCCUS PYOGENES. Hemolytic and non-hemolytic, as well as anaerobic and aerobic streptococci are the commonest invaders, and have been shown to be present in the uterus or in the blood stream in about 75 per cent of all infections (1, 2, 3, 4, 5, 6, 7, 8).

STAPHYLOCOCCUS AUREUS, CITREUS AND ALBUS occasionally are found and are particularly virulent when present in the blood stream (9, 10).

THE GONOCOCCUS is not infrequently recovered from the birth passages in puerperal infection and has been reported in as high as 10 per cent of the cases observed in some hospitals (11, 12).

THE COLON BACILLUS is very frequently found in puerperal infection. Because of its low virulence, infections with this organism are mild, but when it is found together with streptococci or staphylococci such mixed infections are more serious (13).

BACILLUS AEROGENES CAPSULATUS is an infrequent cause of puerperal infection. It grows on dead tissue and, accordingly, is found in cases of dead fetus. Invasion of the blood stream by this organism often is fatal (14, 15).

Parturition causes many wounds in the birth canal, and these may serve as portals of entry for the microörganisms above mentioned. On the other hand, the chief factor in the etiology of puerperal infection is the carrier who directly or indirectly transmits virulent bacteria to the birth passages immediately before, during or a few days after labor. Contamination with infectious material may result from the following:

1. Coitus before, or early in labor (16, 17).

2. Vaginal douches before, during or after labor.

3. Fingering of the vulva and vagina by the patient before, during and after labor.

4. Infectious spray from the nose or throat of those in attendance (18).

5. Vaginal examination without proper preparation of the hands and vulva.

6. Delivery or instrumentation without the observance of an aseptic technic.

7. Catheterization and postpartum care of the vulva without similar regard for the possibility of infection.

8. The use by different patients of a common bed pan and other sick room accessories without adequate sterilization of these articles before they are given to the woman who is in labor or who has recently been delivered.

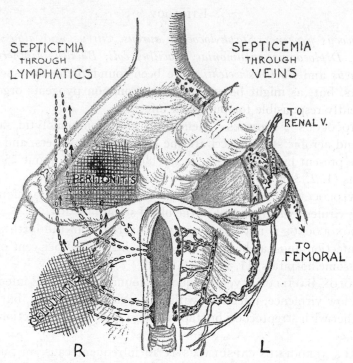

FIG. 881. Diagram showing extension of infection by way of the lymphatics (right) and blood stream (left).

While a study of these various sources of contamination places the responsibility for most cases of puerperal infection upon the physician and nurse, it also must be admitted that the vagina and cervix may harbor mildly virulent bacteria which, under proper circumstances, may cause puerperal infection (19). At times also, auto-infection may occur as the result of a hematogenous invasion of the puerperal wounds by organisms from a focus in some remote part of the body.

In rare instances also, women become infected even when all precautions are taken to prevent contamination.   This is notably true in epidemics of puerperal fever that occasionally are observed in institutional practice (20).   The fact that it sometimes is impossible to eradicate these epidemics without closing the institutions in which they occur proves the inadequacy of sterilization, scrubbing, and the use of antiseptics, when the fundamental principle of isolating all possible sources of infection is disregarded.   Even before the advent of asepsis, this was well known to the conscientious obstetricians who, mindful of the danger of carrying contamination from cases of erysipelas, scarlet fever and puerperal infection to parturient women, refused to treat such conditions while in attendance on labor cases (21, 22, 23, 24).

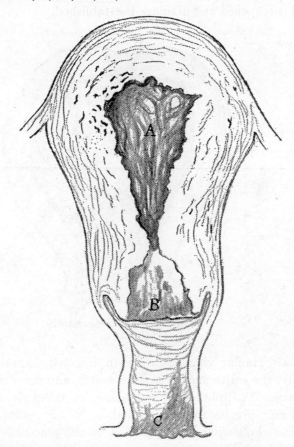

Fig. 882. Superficial infection (Bumm).   A, endometritis; B, cervicitis; C, vaginitis.

PATHOLOGY

Puerperal infection is a wound infection.   The inflammatory process may therefore be local or it may extend through the blood stream or lymphatics to other parts of the body and produce metastatic lesions (Fig. 881).   Local lesions vary from simple infected perineal lacerations to an involvement of the entire birth passages, with extension to the adjacent parametrium and peritoneum.

VULVA. Infected perineal and labial tears are similar in appearance to septic wounds in other parts of the body. They have a grayish yellow granular surface which is covered with a purulent and often foul-smelling discharge. Occasionally, the presence of a grayish membrane may lead to the erroneous diagnosis of a diphtheritic ulcer. The surrounding tissues are swollen, red, and painful. After a few days the inflammatory reaction subsides and gradual healing of the ulcer takes place. If drainage is not interfered with, systemic symptoms usually are absent. When a laceration that has been repaired shows evidence of infection, extension to the adjacent tissues is more marked and a systemic reaction is commonly observed. This, however, soon disappears after the wound is reopened and drainage is established.

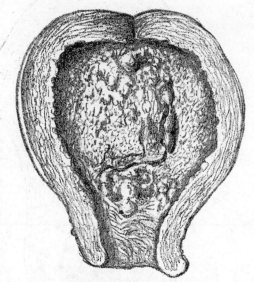

FIG. 883. Septic endometritis.

VAGINA. Similar changes occur in infected lacerations of the vagina. Occasionally, the entire mucosa is red, swollen, and gives rise to a profuse purulent discharge. A diphtheritic membrane, at times, is also observed in this region and may involve the whole canal.

UTERUS. Following the separation of the placenta and membranes, the interior of the uterus is an extensive wound. When this becomes infected, the inflammatory changes may be limited to the placental site or they may affect the entire raw surface of the uterus. The latter condition, PUERPERAL ENDO-METRITIS, varies with the type and virulence of the invading bacteria and the adequacy of the mother's defensive mechanism. In mild cases, it is limited to the thin basal layer of the decidua and the subjacent muscular elements. The endometrial remnants become swollen, necrotic and are bathed in a foul-smelling purulent discharge (Fig. 883). Beneath the necrotic surface, a protective wall of leukocytes prevents further invasion by the infecting microörganisms, while external to this leukocytic barrier, the uterine wall is congested, but otherwise normal (25). This congestion, together with the greater tendency toward relaxation, causes a slight softening and enlargement of the uterus. The lochia are abundant and have a foul odor. Systemic symptoms are common.

A more virulent invading organism or a diminished defensive reaction leads to a rapid invasion of the blood stream or lymphatic extension to the myometrium, parametrium and peritoneum without much alteration in the endometrium. An infection of this type may cause death within a few days and autopsy not infrequently fails to reveal any macroscopic evidence of uterine infection.

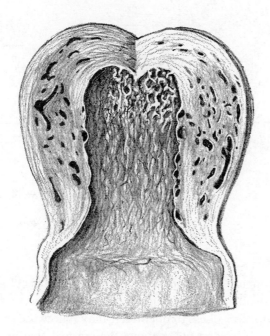

FIG. 884. Thrombophlebitis.

MYOMETRIUM. Metritis is a common complication following infection of the endometrium and often precedes or accompanies parametritis. The muscle wall becomes hyperemic, edematous and infiltrated with round cells, and localized collections of leukocytes may be observed in the deeper layers. At times, these areas break down and form local abscesses. Rarely, portions of the uterine wall become gangrenous and are discharged with the lochia—(METRITIS DESICCANS) (26).

PARAMETRIUM. Extension through the lymphatics to the loose cellular tissue surrounding the uterus occurs in many cases. It usually follows cervical lacerations and, accordingly, is one of the commonest complications. Hyperemia and cellular infiltration are observed and the tissues become swollen by a serous effusion, which later is replaced by a hard and tender exudate (Fig. 885). As the latter increases in size, it fills the broad ligament and fixes the uterus. Such inflammatory masses extend for a considerable distance beneath the peritoneum and ultimately undergo resolution or suppuration. In the former, the exudate is gradually absorbed. The mass then becomes less tender and less fixed, but remains quite hard. Abscess formation is a less frequent termination. When it occurs, rupture usually takes place in the neighborhood of Poupart's ligament. The exudate first extends outward to the wall of the pelvis and then upward

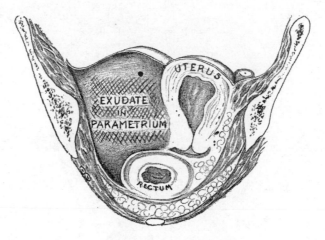

FIG. 885. Pelvic exudate.

between the peritoneum and the abdominal wall. The skin over Poupart's ligament becomes swollen, red and tender, and fluctuation soon indicates the site of the impending rupture. Less frequently, it may follow the course of the uterine vessels to the pelvic brim and point above the crest of the ilium. Rupture into the peritoneal cavity or into the vagina is rare. Such exudates, however, frequently bulge into the posterior vaginal fornix and are artificially drained through a posterior colpotomy incision whenever fluctuation in this region is detected.

PERITONEUM. Extension of the infection through the lymphatics to the peritoneum may take place early or late in the course of a puerperal infection. If the invading organism is a virulent one, or if the patient's defense is weak, peritonitis often occurs with little or no involvement of the intermediate tissues. Frequently, however, it is the last step in the sequence of events which begins with an endometritis and progressively advances through the stages of metritis, and parametritis, and finally terminates in a pelvic peritonitis. Direct extension through the lumen of the tubes is extremely rare.   The lesion may remain local as a pelvic peritonitis or it may spread throughout the abdomen and become a general peritonitis.

When the peritoneum is invaded, the vessels become engorged and give to its surface an injected appearance, while the characteristic peritoneal sheen is replaced by a thin mottling of fibrinous exudate.   Its normally smooth, moist, glistening appearance, accordingly, is lost as the peritoneum becomes dull, red, and thickened.   These changes are accompanied by the secretion of a serous, seropurulent, or purulent exudate which accumulates in the cul-de-sac of Douglas. Temporary paralysis of the intestines favors the formation of adhesions between the sigmoid, cecum, bladder and omentum, as nature attempts to wall off the infection and limit it to the pelvis (Fig. 886).   If this walling-off process is suc-

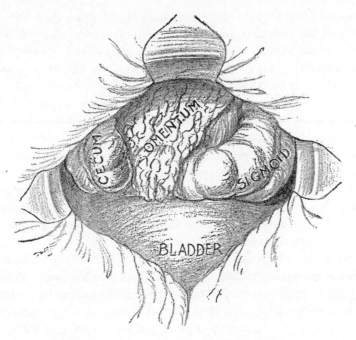

FIG. 886. Localization of peritonitis to the pelvis.

cessful, the inflammation subsequently subsides or suppuration takes place.   In the latter event, the fluctuating mass may bulge into the vagina.   Failure of this effort to prevent a spreading of the infection to the remainder of the peritoneal cavity leads to general peritonitis, a complication which usually terminates fatally.

TUBES AND OVARIES.   Occasionally, the tubes become infected through lymphatic extension, or a perisalpingitis may follow in the course of a pelvic peritonitis.   Similarly, the ovaries may participate in an extensive puerperal infection. Congestion and edema lead to great swelling of these structures and microscopic examination reveals numerous areas of leukocytic infiltration. A puerperal inflammatory process in the tubes and ovaries ultimately subsides or progresses to abscess formation.

PELVIC VEINS. Soon after delivery the uterine sinuses are plugged by large thrombi, which, like granulation tissue in a healthy wound, act as barriers against invasion by pyogenic organisms. These thrombi, however, at times are unable to cope with the more virulent bacteria and invasion of the sinuses in any part of the uterine wall and particularly at the placental site may then take place. The thrombi break down and the vessel walls show evidence of a phlebitis. As the latter advances, new thrombi form in an attempt to limit the infection. These in turn again disintegrate and extension of the inflammatory process in the vessel walls continues. It may extend to the iliac and femoral veins, and occasionally may involve the vena cava. During the course of nature's attempt to limit the phlebitis, minute fragments from the infected thrombi gain access to the blood stream and give rise to a temporary systemic reaction, in the course of which they are either destroyed or cause metastatic abscesses (27).

If the attempt to limit the thrombophlebitis to the uterine wall is successful, the inflammatory process may subside, or the affected areas may break down and cause the formation of small abscesses. Thrombophlebitis often persists for several months and may lead to metastatic lesions which vary according to the organ involved. The most frequent metastases are found in the lungs, where they directly or indirectly cause infarction, lung abscess, pneumonia, pleurisy or pyopneumothorax. Bacterial emboli may also pass through the lungs and cause acute endocarditis and other distant inflammatory lesions. Occasionally, death occurs from the metastatic lesion after the original inflammatory process in the uterus has undergone complete resolution.

FEMORAL VEIN. Extension of a thrombophlebitis to the femoral vein leads to the condition known as PHLEGMASIA ALBA DOLENS (milk leg). A large thrombus forms in the femoral vein and extends for some distance along its lumen. The occlusion of the latter often leads to painful edema of the extremity involved. As this condition may be a part of a more extensive thrombophlebitis, it sometimes proves fatal. Usually, however, patients suffering from phlegmasia alba dolens recover, but their convalescence is protracted. Frequently, the tendency toward varicose veins and edema of the ankle, as well as a somewhat painful extremity, persists for a considerable time. Pressure on the pelvic veins by the exudate which forms in a parametritis may simulate the findings noted in femoral thrombophlebitis. Here the vessel wall is not involved in the inflammatory process and, accordingly, the exciting cause is removed as soon as the exudate is absorbed.

Infection by the gonococcus differs considerably from that caused by other pyogenic organisms. Instead of extending through the lymphatics or the blood stream, a gonorrheal inflammation advances by continuity along the surface of the structures involved (Fig. 887). It usually follows a previously quiescent infection of the cervix or lower birth passages which becomes active soon after delivery and extends to the uterus. In a short time the endosalpinx is involved and a typical gonococcal salpingitis results. The discharge of purulent material from the tube lumen into the peritoneal cavity sets up a local pelvic peritonitis which, as a rule, is adequately walled off by adhesions between the cecum, sigmoid and omentum. General peritonitis, accordingly, is rare in this type of infection and a fatal termination seldom is observed.

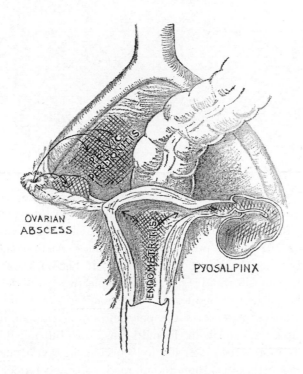

Fig. 887. Diagram showing extension of gonorrheal infection by continuity (Polak).

SYMPTOMS

The patient's reaction to infection of the wounds in her genital tract varies with the site of infection and with the type and virulence of the organism.

VULVA AND VAGINA. Lesions of the vulva and vagina produce slight systemic reactions if the drainage is good. If, however, infection is present in tears that have been repaired, the symptoms may be marked until the wound is again opened. Before drainage is thus reëstablished, the systemic reaction often is as severe as that which accompanies a uterine infection.

UTERINE INFECTION. Within a few days after delivery, the temperature rises above 100.4° and reaches a higher elevation on each successive day. Morning remissions are common and give to the temperature chart an irregular sawtooth appearance (Fig. 888). The pulse likewise is elevated and tends to follow the temperature curve. There may be a feeling of chilliness or a definite rigor

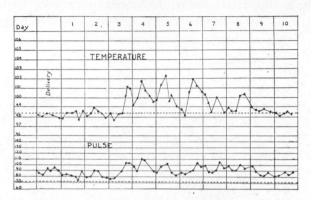

FIG. 888. Temperature chart in mild puerperal infection. Endometritis.

at the onset. Headache, malaise, and loss of appetite are common additional symptoms. In more virulent infections, the patient has a severe chill in from one to four days after labor. This is followed by an elevation in temperature to 103° to 105° and a rise in the pulse to 120 or over. At first the pulse is full and bounding, but, as the infection progresses, it becomes soft and difficult to count. Pallor, cyanosis, rapid respiration, sleeplessness, and delirium indicate the gravity of the patient's condition. A leukocytosis of 18,000 to 24,000 is common and a relative increase in the polymorphonuclear count is observed. Blood cultures usually are sterile in the mild infections, but not infrequently are positive for hemolytic streptococci or staphylococci in the severe ones. Bimanual examination reveals little other than an enlarged, soft, and tender uterus. The lochia may be diminished or profuse, and may have a normal or foul odor. Usually, the symptoms are less severe when the lochia are abundant and foul smelling. Within ten days, the temperature ordinarily subsides and a prompt recovery follows. In the graver infections, a fatal outcome may occur within a few days.

PARAMETRITIS. An increase in the temperature with more marked morning remissions accompanies the development of a pelvic exudate (Fig. 889). The general symptoms above noted continue and the patient complains of pain in the region of the parametrium. Examination shows a large, tender uterus that is fixed by an exudate in the base of one or both broad ligaments. This exudate is felt as a hard, unyielding, sensitive mass which extends from the uterus to the walls of the pelvis.   For a time the mass increases in size and in density.   Subsequently it loses its tenderness and, as gradual absorption takes place, the mobility of the cervix and uterus becomes less restricted.   Suppuration of the exudate is accompanied by a greater spiking of the temperature curve and physical examination reveals a fluctuating mass bulging into the vagina or above Poupart's ligament.

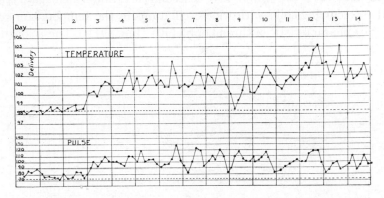

Fig. 889. Temperature chart in puerperal infection with parametrial involvement.

PERITONITIS.   Pain, tenderness and rigidity in the lower abdomen, with a more continuous temperature and a greater acceleration of the pulse, indicate the onset of pelvic peritonitis (Fig. 890).   When the condition becomes general.

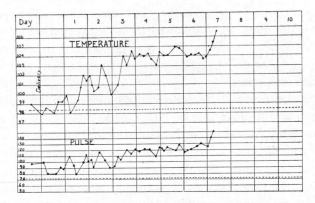

Fig. 890. Temperature chart in a severe puerperal infection with peritonitis.   Death on seventh day.

these symptoms and signs are aggravated and are followed by hiccough, vomiting, distention, and a characteristic pinched expression.   In peritonitis, pressure on the abdomen not only causes pain, but the pain is greater when the pressure is suddenly removed.   This socalled rebound sign is a valuable means of differentiating between parametritis and a beginning peritonitis.   Peritoneal involve-

750   OBSTETRICAL PRACTICE

ment also is accompanied by a change in the blood picture and the polymorpho-nuclear count rises above 90. The prognosis is grave in general peritonitis, and death usually occurs within a few days after its onset.

THROMBOPHLEBITIS. About seven to ten days after delivery, the patient who often has had a relatively low temperature experiences a severe chill which is followed by a marked rise in temperature. Within a few hours the temperature returns to normal, but is soon followed by a second elevation which again is preceded by a chill. Recurring chills with wide oscillations in the temperature curve, accordingly, are characteristic of thrombophlebitis (Fig. 891). These continue for a

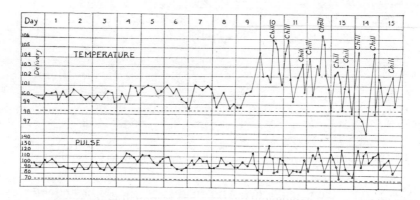

FIG. 891. Temperature chart in puerperal infection with thrombophlebitis (1st. half of chart).

considerable time until recovery takes place or the development of metastatic lesions alters their course. Occasionally, the temperature may remain normal for a period of even ten days, to be followed by an exacerbation as new lesions are formed in remote areas. A patient may thus be confined to her bed for from two to three months as a result of these recurring exacerbations and finally die of a distant metastatic infection.

GONOCOCCIC INFECTION. In puerperal gonorrheal inflammation, the initial elevation in temperature may also be late. About one week after delivery, the temperature suddenly rises and remains elevated for from ten days to two weeks. This late onset differs from the onset of thrombophlebitis in that it, as a rule, is not accompanied by a chill. Pain and tenderness are present and are particularly severe when the tubes become involved. Physical examination reveals the presence of bilateral, tender masses which cause movement of the cervix or uterus to be painful.

PROGNOSIS

The prognosis is favorable in localized infections of the **vulva, vagina,** and **endometrium.** It may, however, be changed at any time by extension of the inflammatory process and the development of more serious complications. Of these, **bacteriemia, peritonitis,** and **thrombophlebitis** are most to be feared (28).

Foul lochia, indicating a **putrid endometritis,** usually are regarded as less dangerous than non-putrid discharges. The prognosis is less favorable when the lochia are scant.

PARAMETRITIS ordinarily is not serious as long as extension to the peritoneum or blood stream does not occur, but the prolonged temperature, together with a still longer persistence of the exudate, confines the patient to her bed for a considerable time.

PERITONITIS, when limited to the pelvis, may run a long course. It usually ends in resolution or abscess formation. Ultimate recovery is the rule, but often is followed by sterility and more or less permanent invalidism. On the other hand, general peritonitis usually is fatal. The rapidity of its development and course depends upon the virulence of the infecting organism in relation to the defensive mechanism.

THROMBOPHLEBITIS likewise may prove fatal. In our clinic, however, the mortality has been lowered by the use of repeated small blood transfusions. Femoral thrombosis usually undergoes resolution and ultimately ends in recovery. The danger of pulmonary embolism is always present and a painful extremity with a tendency toward varicosities is a not infrequent sequela.

TREATMENT

The knowledge that pyogenic bacteria are responsible for puerperal infection makes easy the task of its prevention. If the genital tract is protected against contamination by these organisms, **before, during** and **after labor,** puerperal infections are limited to those rare instances in which auto-infection results from inoculation by the vaginal flora or in which virulent bacteria are carried from distant foci through the blood stream to the genital wounds.

BEFORE LABOR. **Sexual intercourse** in the latter part of pregnancy may be followed by the onset of labor, and the protective properties of the vaginal secretions may not have sufficient time to render innocuous such pyogenic organisms as are introduced into the lower birth passages during coitus. Sexual intercourse, therefore, should be absolutely avoided during the last two months of pregnancy. A **vaginal douche** may have a similar effect. In addition, it dilutes and removes the protective vaginal secretions and, if it contains a strong antiseptic, the resultant injury to the mucosa of the vagina and cervix lowers the resistance of the latter and thereby favors infection.

Vaginal examination immediately before the onset of labor also may be a source of contamination. At this time, therefore, it should be replaced by rectal examination, unless the attendant follows the same aseptic precautions that are used during labor. Since the **general condition of the patient** is a factor in the prevention of infection such measures should be employed as will best fit her for labor and the warding off of a possible infection. These are: the prevention of toxemia, the treatment of any anemia that may be present, an abundance of fresh air and sunshine, sufficient rest, particularly at night, and an adequate, balanced diet which should include leafy green vegetables and other vitamin-containing foods at two out of every three meals (29).

DURING LABOR. Rectal examination should be substituted for vaginal examinations whenever possible. All vaginal examinations must be preceded by proper preparation of the vulva and the hands of the physician (See Management of Labor). The added protection of sterile gloves is indispensable and a mask should be worn over the mouth and nose of all in attendance. The latter is especially necessary if the obstetrician or nurse is suffering from an upper respiratory infection. The physician likewise should not care for such virulent streptococcal infections as erysipelas and attend women in labor at the same time. Similarly, he should wear gloves when opening abscesses and dressing infected wounds, to avoid contamination of his hands and the carrying of the infectious bacteria to his labor cases. While infection usually results from vaginal examinations and manipulations within the birth canal and, accordingly, is diminished as these measures are limited, the prophylaxis against infection in the course of labor should go further than minimizing the number of the examinations, and the conscientious employment of an aseptic technic. Since the incidence of infection is greater when the membranes rupture early in labor, preservation of the membranes until the cervix is fully dilated is desirable.

Infected lacerations of the vulva, vagina, and cervix often are the source of uterine infections. Every effort, therefore, should be made to minimize the trauma of all deliveries.

AFTER LABOR. Because tears of the lower birth passages are more readily contaminated, lacerations of the perineum and vagina should be aseptically repaired immediately after the placenta is born.

If the blood lost during the labor is excessive, it should be replaced by transfusion as a prophylaxis against infection, since it is well known that acute anemia interferes with the body's defensive reaction to infection.

The patient should be cautioned against infecting herself by fingering the vulva after delivery and during the early days of the puerperium. Even the nurse's efforts to keep the vulva clean may result in infection. Judicious neglect is better for forty-eight hours, after which vulval dressings with a mild antiseptic solution may be made. The nurse who carries out the latter should follow an aseptic technic and should wear a mask over her mouth and nose while looking after the toilet of the perineum.

CURATIVE. It must be remembered that recovery is the rule in puerperal infection. The attendant, in his zeal to help, therefore, should guard against interfering with nature's efforts to limit and eradicate the infection.

REST is most essential and is best secured by competent nursing. An intelligent and sympathetic nurse can do much to make the patient comfortable and hasten her recovery.

Food. The diet should consist of ample and easily digestible food. Forced fluids aid in elimination and help to reduce the temperature. Accordingly, an abundance of water and fruit juices is recommended. If the patient is unable to take much nourishment, brandy may be helpful for a few days.

Fresh Air and Sunshine are also very beneficial. The windows should be opened and the patient should be in the sun at least a part of each day. This measure is best carried out by moving the bed to a roof or porch whenever one is available. Such a step improves the patient's morale, increases her appetite and usually is followed by a lessening of the restlessness, and a tendency to sleep better at night.

Antipyretics. Slight elevations in temperature are disregarded. When the fever is high or is continuous, fluids should be forced and the use of tepid sponges add greatly to the patient's comfort. Some physicians give quinine in puerperal infection. Other antipyretic drugs usually are contraindicated.

Elimination. Because of the ever present danger of peritonitis, cathartics are contraindicated. A daily low enema and forced fluids are sufficient and without risk.

Drainage. Elevation of the head of the bed, the Fowler position, favors drainage. This is further assisted by having the patient lie on her side several times daily. When a repaired laceration becomes infected, removal of the sutures secures drainage and often causes a rapid disappearance of systemic symptoms. Pelvic abscesses are evacuated and drained through the vagina or above Poupart's ligament.

Relief of Pain. An **ice-bag,** placed over the uterus, stimulates contractions and relieves pain in that region. Later, ice over the lower quadrants of the abdomen is indicated when parametritis develops. **Morphine or codeine** should be employed if the use of an ice bag fails to give relief.

Ergot. Most of the older obstetricians believed that ergot was valuable in the treatment of puerperal infection because it increased the tone of the uterus. By thus aiding contraction and retraction of this organ, its use was thought to prevent lymphatic extension. In addition to this action, the stimulating effect of ergot preparations on the reticulo-endothelial system also is of value. Small repeated doses of ergot, accordingly, are indicated in all cases of puerperal infection (30, 31, 32).

Blood Transfusion. As previously stated, a large prophylactic transfusion should be given whenever the blood lost during labor is excessive. Small transfusions of from 250 to 350 cc., repeated every fourth or fifth day, are invaluable in the treatment of severe puerperal infections. This measure should be employed early and, if possible, before the onset of alarming symptoms. It is our custom to resort to its use whenever an elevated temperature persists for one week, even though a bacteriemia or thrombophlebitis is not suspected. In bacteriemia and thrombophlebitis, small repeated blood transfusions have saved

many lives.   Consistent repetition of the transfusions at intervals of not over five
days, however, is necessary and they should not be discontinued until recovery is
certain (33).   If transfusions cannot be given, injections of milk or other foreign
protein should be used (34).

SULPHANILIMIDE is of great value in the treatment of such infections as are
due to streptococci.   If the hemoglobin is below 60, the drug should be withheld
until the blood picture is improved by transfusions.   Sulphanilimide is administered in sufficiently large doses to maintain a concentration in the blood of about
10 mg. per 100 cc., as determined by the colorimetric method.   This usually is
accomplished by giving twenty grains every four hours during the day and
night.   After the fourth day or earlier if the temperature subsides, the dose is
reduced to 15 grains and, several days later, to 10 grains every four hours for the
duration of the treatment.   In order that the concentration may be maintained
at a satisfactory level, it is well to give the drug during the night as well as in the
daytime.   For the same reason, the amount of fluids should be somewhat limited.
We have found about 1500 cc. per day to be satisfactory.   While the patient is
taking sulphanilimide, all suphur compounds are contraindicated.   Magnesium
sulphate, therefore, should never be given at this time.   The drug should be
withdrawn whenever any of its toxic symptoms appear.   These are: jaundice,
diarrhea, mental aberrations, agranulocytosis, a marked reduction in hemoglobin
and the appearance of blood in the urine.   Hemoglobin determinations and examinations of the blood for agranulocytosis, accordingly, should be made at
frequent intervals.   Sulphathiazole is preferable in infections which are due to
gonococcus, pneumococcus, staphylococcus and colon bacillus.   If culture shows
any of these organisms instead of streptococci an initial dose of 30 gr. of sulphathiazole is given and this is followed by 15 gr. every 4 hours.

PENICILLIN in doses of 30,000 units is given every three hours intramuscularly as a prophylaxis immediately after all deliveries in which infection is suspected.   In definite cases of puerperal infection the same routine is started as
soon as the condition is detected.   If given early the results usually are excellent.
After suppuration has taken place, penicillin is of little value.   The same may
be said of its use in thrombophlebitis particularly if the administration of
the drug is begun after the disease is well established.

PELVIC EXAMINATION is harmful in that it often is followed by extension
of the infection.   Vaginal examinations, therefore, should be infrequent and
should be as gentle as possible.   After locating the cervix and uterus, the examiner feels for an exudate in the broad ligament.   If a mass is found, he then
attempts to elicit fluctuation.   Further manipulation is unnecessary and may be
dangerous.   General peritonitis and death have followed the usual complete
gynecological examination.

INFECTED PERINEAL TEARS.   When a repaired perineal laceration becomes
infected, removal of the sutures establishes drainage and relieves the symptoms.

The wound is then dressed with a mild antiseptic solution until the danger of extension has passed.

PELVIC ABSCESS.   The presence of a fluctuating mass in the cul-de-sac is an indication for a posterior colpotomy.   After the pus is evacuated, several gauze drains should be inserted into the collapsed cavity and left in place for at least one week.   Posterior colpotomy should be most carefully done.   If pus is not readily obtained, it is better to abandon the operation than to cause a general peritonitis by too vigorous attempts to burrow through the inflammatory tissues in an effort to reach the abscess.   If the abscess points above Poupart's ligament, incision and drainage likewise are indicated.

PERITONITIS.   The onset of peritonitis calls for an alteration in this routine. Everything by mouth is discontinued and enough morphine is given hypodermically to favor adhesion of the sigmoid, cecum and omentum.   Fluids are administered by hypodermoclysis or by the Harris drip, and glucose is given intravenously.   If, after thirty-six hours, the symptoms of peritonitis disappear, the former routine is resumed.

The surgical treatment of peritonitis, complicating puerperal infection, has proved unsatisfactory, and multiple incisions with drainage are no longer used.

PHLEGMASIA ALBA DOLENS.   In addition to the usual routine, the affected extremity is elevated on pillows and the pressure of the bed clothing is relieved by the use of a cradle over the leg.   Likewise, an ice-bag is kept over the femoral vein and sedatives are given whenever necessary to relieve the pain (35).

SURGICAL MEASURES are limited to incision and drainage of pelvic abscesses. Hysterectomy formerly was recommended by some physicians as a means of hastening the recovery in puerperal infection.   Most authorities now believe it to be dangerous and employ this measure only in those cases which are complicated by infected fibromyomata or in which drainage is interfered with, as in fibroids in the lower uterine segment, fixation of the uterus, bicornate uterus, etc.   In addition to hysterectomy, ligation of the infected veins has been advocated in thrombophlebitis, but the better results obtained by the use of blood transfusions have led to the gradual abandonment of this measure (33, 36, 37, 38).

FIXATION ABSCESSES.   In some of the protracted cases of puerperal infection, benefit seems to follow the formation of fixation abscesses.   Since this method of treatment is quite painful, it should not be used until other less disagreeable measures have been tried.   One cc. of turpentine is injected into the subcuticular tissue of the thigh, midway between the skin and the aponeurosis. When fluctuation occurs about one week later, the abscess is incised.   If an inflammatory reaction fails to develop within twenty-four hours, a second injection is recommended (39, 40).

REFERENCES

1. MAYRHOFER, C.: Zur Frage nach der Aetiologie der Puerperalprocesse.   Monatschr. f. geburtsk., 1865, 25, 112.

2. PASTEUR, L.: Septicémie puerpérale. Bull. de l'Acad. de Med. Paris, 1879, 8, 256.
3. DOLÉRIS, J. A.: Essai sur la pathologénie et la thérapeutique des accidents infectieux des suites de couches. Thèse de Paris, 1880, No. 245.
4. WIDAL, F.: Étude sur l'infection puerpérale la phlegmatia alba dolens et l'érysipèle. Thèse de Paris, 1889, No. 123.
5. BUMM, E. U. SIGWART, W.: Untersuchungen über die Beziehungen der Streptococcus zum Puerperalfieber. Beitr. z. Geburtsh u. Gyn., 1904, 8, 329.
6. SCHOTTMÜLLER, H.: Zur Bedeutung einiger Anaeroben in der Pathologie, insbesondere bei puerperalen Erkrankungen. Mitt. a. d. Grenzgeb. d. Med. u. Chir., 1910, 21, 450.
7. SCHWARZ, O. H. AND DIECKMANN, W. J.: Puerperal Infection Due to Anaerobic Streptococci. Am. J. O. & G., 1927, 13, 467.
8. HARRIS, J. W. AND BROWN, J. H.: A Clinical and Bacteriological Study of 113 Cases of Streptococcic Puerperal Infection. Johns Hopkins Hosp. Bull., 1929, 44, 1.
9. BRIEGER, L.: Ueber bakteriologische Untersuchungen bei einigen Fällen von Puerperalfieber. Charité Ann. Berl., 1886, 13, 198.
10. SOMMER, K.: Die puerperale Sepsis. Ztschr. f. Geburtsh. u. Gyn., 1928, 94, 481.
11. KRÖNIG, B.: Vorläufige Mittheilung über die Gonorrhöe im Wochenbett. Centralbl. f. Gyn., 1893, 17, 157.
12. TAUSSIG, F. J.: Gonorrhoeal Puerperal Fever. Am. Gyn., 1903, 2, 334.
13. V. FRANQUÉ, O.: Bakteriologische Untersuchungen bei normalem und fieberhaftem Wochenbett. Zeitsch. z. Geburtsh. u. Gyn., 1893, 25, 277.
14. DOBBIN, G. W.: Puerperal Sepsis Due to Infection with the Bacillus Aerogenes Capsulatus. Johns Hopkins Hosp. Bull., 1897, 8, 24.
15. TOOMBS, P. W. AND MICHELSON, I. D.: Clostridium Welchii Septicemia Complicating Prolonged Labor Due to Obstructing Myoma of the Uterus. Am. J. O. & G., 1928, 15, 379.
16. V. BÜBEN, I.: Die Rolle des Koitus beim vorzeitigen Blasensprung und bei Erkrankungen des Kindbettes. Zentralbl. f. Gyn., 1924, 48, 1310.
17. LIUBIMOWA, M. P.: Zur Frage über den Einfluss des Koitus auf den vorzeitigen Abgang des Fruchtwassers und den Verlauf des Kindbettes. Zentralbl. f. Gyn., 1926, 50, 1466.
18. MELENEY, F. L., ZUNG-DAU ZAU, ZAYTEZEFF, H. AND HARVEY, H. D.: Epidemiologic and Bacteriologic Investigations of the Sloane Hospital Epidemic of Hemolytic Streptococcus Puerperal Fever in 1927. Am. J. O. & G., 1928, 16, 180.
19. WINTER, G.: Ueber Selbstinfektion. Zentralbl. f. Gyn., 1911, 35, 1495.
20. WATSON, B. P.: An Outbreak of Puerperal Sepsis in New York City. Am. J. O. & G., 1928, 16, 157.
21. WHITE, C.: Treatise on the Management of Pregnant and Lying-in Women, London, 1773.
22. GORDON, A.: A Treatise in Epidemic Puerperal Fever, London, 1795.
23. HOLMES, O. W.: Puerperal Fever as a Private Pestilence. Boston, 1855.
24. SEMMELWEISS, I. P.: Aetiologie, Begriff und Prophylaxis des Kindbettfiebers. Leipzig, 1861.
25. BUMM, E.: Histologische Untersuchungen über die puerperale Endometritis. Arch. f. Gyn., 1891, 40, 398.
26. ROTTHAUS, E.: Metritis dissecans. Arch. f. Gyn., 1927, 130, 727.
27. V. BARDELEBEN, H.: Streptococcus und Thrombose. Arch. f. Gyn., 1907, 73, 1.
28. WARNEKROS, K.: Zur Prognose der puerperalen Fiebersteigerungen auf Grund bakteriologischer und histologischer Untersuchungen. Arch. f. Gyn., 1915, 104, 301.
29. GREEN, H. N., PINDAR, D., DAVIS, G. AND MELLANBY, B.: Diet as a Prophylactic Agent Against Puerperal Sepsis, with Special Reference to Vitamin A as an Anti-infective Agent. Brit. M. J., 1931, 595.
30. GUÉRIN, J.: Sur la fievre puerpérale. Bull. Acad. de Med., Paris, 1858, 23, 766.
31. LOUROS, N. U. SCHEYER, H. E.: Ueber eine bisher unbekannte Wirkung der Sekalepräparate. Zentralbl. f. Gyn., 1927, 51, 763.
32. LOUROS, N.: Die Bedeutung des Reticulo-endothelialsystems für das Streptokokkensepsisproblem. Klin. Wchnschr., 1928, 7, 996.

33. POLAK, J. O.: Further Studies in Puerperal Infections and Their Treatment. Am. J. O. & G., 1925, 10, 521.

34. GELLHORN, G.: Milk Injections in Gynecology and Obstetrics. Am. J. O. & G., 1924, 8, 535.

35. VIGNES, H.: Phlegmatia Alba Dolens. Le Concours Medicale, 1923, 45, 3194.

36. JUNG, P.: Die Behandlung der puerperalen Infektion. Deutsch. Med. Wchnschr. 1916, 42, 437.

37. KING, E. L.: Noninterference in Puerperal and Postabortal Infections. J. A. M. A., 1920, 75, 147.

38. BUMM, E.: Die Behandlung des Puerperalfiebers. München Med. Wchnschr. 1921, 68, 1494.

39. SORRENTINO, B.: Le Traitement des Infections Puerpérales en Particulier par les abcès de Fixation. Gyn. et Obs., 1931, 23, 511.

40. VIGNES, H.: L'abcès de fixation dans le traitement de l'infection puerpérale. Progres Méd., 1931, 2, 2096.

CHAPTER XXXVIII

THE ARTIFICIAL INTERRUPTION OF PREGNANCY

Pregnancy may have to be interrupted artificially before the period of viability is reached. Such an interruption is known as a **therapeutic abortion.** It is done only for those conditions in which the continuance of pregnancy jeopardizes the life of the mother, or aggravates the disease from which she suffers.

The treatment of many of the conditions which formerly were aggravated by pregnancy has been improved so much that they are now treated satisfactorily without interfering with the gestation. Therapeutic abortion accordingly is rarely justifiable. When it is indicated, the operation should be performed in a reputable hospital and the written opinion of a competent consultant should be incorporated in the hospital records for the protection of the patient and the physician.

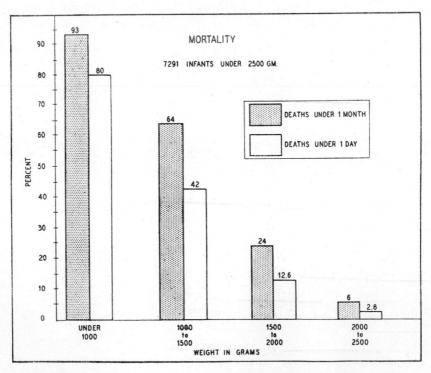

CHART 1. Mortality of infants born prematurely in New York City in 1939.

Occasionally artificial termination of pregnancy is required after the fetus has become viable but has not reached full term.   The procedure employed to induce the uterus to empty itself at this time is termed an **induction of premature labor.**   Because the chance for survival of the prematurely born child increases greatly with every 500 gm. addition in body weight, each additional week of intrauterine life is greatly to its advantage.   As shown in Chart 1, 93% of the infants weighing less than 1000 gm. at birth fail to survive the first month, 64% of those between 1000 and 1500 gm. die within 30 days, while only 24% of the prematurely born infants between 1500 and 2000 gm. are lost.   Before a pregnancy is interrupted prematurely the length of the occipito frontal diameter may be measured by means of roentgen rays and from it the weight of the fetus calculated (see page 290).   The unborn fetus also is entitled to the benefit of consultation with an experienced obstetrician in order that the pregnancy may be prolonged whenever possible until the child's chance for survival is good.

More frequently labor is brought on artificially at or near term.   It then is referred to as an **induction of labor at term.**

Since therapeutic abortion, the induction of premature labor and the induction of labor at term may be done for similar indications arising in different periods of gestation and since all of these procedures are employed for the purpose of interrupting pregnancy the indications for each is included in and discussed under the general indications for the interruption of pregnancy which are:

Diseases of the ovum.
> Hydatidiform mole.
> Hydramnios.
> Habitual death of the fetus.
> Placenta previa.

Diseases peculiar to pregnancy.
> Pernicious vomiting.
> Preeclamptic toxemia.
> Eclampsia.
> Accidental hemorrhage.

Diseases which may be aggravated by pregnancy.
> Cardiac insufficiency.
> Renal insufficiency.
> Hypertension.
> Pulmonary tuberculosis.
> Blood diseases—Pernicious anemia, Leukemia.
> Diseases of glands of internal secretion –Diabetes, Hyperthyroidism.
> Nervous and mental diseases—Chorea, Myelitis, Multiple sclerosis.

Condition which may cause disproportion.
> Large child.
> Small pelvis.
> Pelvic tumors.

HYDATIDIFORM MOLE. The embryo usually has been absorbed or at least is dead when the diagnosis of hydatidiform mole is made. One should have no scruples about emptying the uterus, accordingly, whenever this condition is recognized. The method employed for this purpose will depend upon the condition of the cervix. Removal of the ovum with the finger, ovum forceps and curette as a rule is satisfactory. Occasionally anterior vaginal hysterotomy is necessary.

HYDRAMNIOS. The rapid enlargement of the uterus which accompanies acute hydramnios in the last half of pregnancy sometimes is so marked that · the membranes must be ruptured to relieve the pressure symptoms. When the X-ray reveals the presence of a grave fetal anomaly the gestation should be interrupted even before the maternal symptom become sufficiently severe to warrant the termination of pregnancy.

HABITUAL DEATH OF THE FETUS. In some women death of the fetus before it has reached full term sometimes occurs even though the mother does not have syphilis, nephritis nor any of the other diseases which may cause fetal death. The interruption of pregnancy before the fetus dies accordingly is sometimes indicated. One of my patients in whom seven pregnancies had terminated in the death of the fetus at or near term and in whom no evidence of complicating disease could be found was delivered of a living healthy child by terminating the 8th pregnancy one month before term.

PLACENTA PREVIA. The danger of a fatal hemorrhage resulting from the separation of a placenta which is implanted over the internal os has led to the dictum: "There is no expectant treatment for placenta previa." As soon as the diagnosis of placenta previa is made, therefore, appropriate measures are taken to control the bleeding and terminate the pregnancy. These include, rupture of the membranes with or without scalp traction, packing the cervix and vagina with gauze, the introduction of a large hydrostatic bag into the uterus, Braxton Hicks version and cesarean section. The relative merits of each are discussed in Chapter 32. Fortunately bleeding from this condition usually begins in the last trimester of pregnancy when the child is viable. The child accordingly may have some chance of surviving, but the chance is less than might be expected from the period of gestation. For this reason it should receive the care given to prematurely born infants regardless of its weight at birth.

PERNICIOUS VOMITING. Formerly pernicious vomiting was a rather frequent indication for therapeutic abortion. Today most cases respond satisfactorily to treatment without the interruption of pregnancy. Abortion, accordingly, is very rarely required in the management of this condition at the present time. When indicated, however, it should be performed before the patient's condition becomes too grave to stand the operation. Very early in pregnancy the uterus may be emptied by dilatation and curettage. Later vaginal hysterotomy may be necessary.

TOXEMIA. When preeclamptic toxemia progresses in spite of treatment the interruption of pregnancy is indicated. If the indication for the termination of the gestation arises in the last month, labor is induced by rupture of the membranes provided the requisites for this method of induction are fulfilled. Before the last month the introduction of a bougie or hydrostatic bag is preferred. If the toxemia is fulminating and it seems that convulsions may occur before the pregnancy can be terminated by inducing labor, cesarean section under local anesthesia may be indicated.

After convulsions appear in the course of eclampsia the induction of labor usually is postponed until recovery has occurred. Within a few days after recovery the interruption of pregnancy is recommended; otherwise the convulsive seizures may recur.

ACCIDENTAL HEMORRHAGE. The hemorrhage which accompanies premature separation of a normally implanted placenta often calls for treatment which is not compatible with a continuation of the pregnancy. Whether one follows the conservative plan of giving oxytocic drugs and rupturing the membranes or the radical one of emptying the uterus by cesarean section the pregnancy is interrupted in all severe cases of accidental hemorrhage. Although this condition commonly occurs late in gestation after the period of viability is reached, the fetus usually dies in utero because of the separation of the placenta.

CARDIAC INSUFFICIENCY. Most women with cardiac disease are able to withstand the effects of pregnancy satisfactorily provided they are under the supervision of a competent cardiologist and obstetrician. In our cardiac clinic therefore, pregnancy is seldom interrupted for cardiac disease. Those who are unable to withstand slight activity without showing evidence of congestive failure should be aborted unless they are able to receive expert cardiac guidance. This is particularly true if the difficulty arises early in pregnancy since more marked cardiac insufficiency is to be expected during the critical 6th and 7th months. Although auricular fibrillation is rarely observed in pregnant women, when it does occur the risk is greater than the customary functional classification indicates and warrants early consideration of the interruption of pregnancy. The same may be said of the cardiac patient who becomes pregnant after she has reached the age of 35. In Class III cardiac insufficiencies abortion also is indicated. It should be remembered that surgical intervention is dangerous in the presence of congestive failure. For this reason operative interference should be postponed until the patient has recovered from cardiac failure or has reached the limit of improvement from medical care (1, 2, 3).

RENAL INSUFFICIENCY. Prolonged and marked albuminuria with a tendency to anemia, edema and uremia in nephritis complicating pregnancy does not respond to treatment. Not only is the disease aggravated by pregnancy but death of the fetus frequently occurs. The interruption of pregnancy accordingly is frequently indicated when the mother has nephritis (4).

HYPERTENSION.   Some students of the subject are of the opinion that pregnancy shortens the life expectancy of patients having hypertension.   They advise the avoidance of conception in such cases and recommend abortion if pregnancy occurs.   Should the hypertension be first observed in the last trimester of pregnancy they believe that labor should be induced within four weeks of its discovery.   Other obstetricians incline to a more conservative attitude towards the interruption of pregnancy.

PULMONARY TUBERCULOSIS.   The recent improvement in the treatment of pulmonary tuberculosis has led many phthisiologists to advise against abortion even in the presence of activity.   They believe that the pregnancy may be disregarded if the patient is able to take advantage of proper treatment.   If the disease is active and is recognized before the 8th week of pregnancy, therapeutic abortion is to be considered whenever the patients circumstances do not permit adequate care of the tuberculosis.   Such early pregnancies may be terminated by curettage under local anesthesia with very little risk.

PERNICIOUS ANEMIA AND LEUKEMIA.   Anemia complicating pregnancy usually responds to appropriate treatment.   Women who have pernicious anemia seldom become pregnant, if they do abortion usually is indicated.   The hyperchromic macrocytic anemia which occasionally occurs during pregnancy and resembles pernicious anemia in many respects can be controlled by proper therapy and does not require the termination of pregnancy.   Pregnancy complicated by leukemia also is rare.   When the condition is acute pregnancy is regarded as exceedingly detrimental and early interruption of the gestation is indicated.

DIABETES AND HYPERTHYROIDISM.   While diabetes used to be regarded as a definite indication for abortion the risk has been so diminished by insulin and dietary measures that the interruption of pregnancy in the interest of the mother no longer is considered.   Because the fetus tends to become excessive in size and often dies in utero, pregnancy may be interrupted before term in the interest of the child.   Although hyperthyroidism usually is aggravated by pregnancy the modern treatment of this condition has so lessened the risk that the interruption of pregnancy seldom is considered.

CHOREA, MYELITIS, AND MULTIPLE SCLEROSIS.   Chorea and other nervous and mental diseases which formerly were considered indications for abortion frequently are aggravated rather than improved by the interruption of pregnancy. As a result abortion is seldom done for these conditions.   Myelitis occurring in the latter half of gestation often improves after pregnancy is terminated by the induction of premature labor.   When it recurs early in a subsequent pregnancy abortion is indicated.   Since pregnancy aggravates the condition and brings on acute exacerbations of the disease, women with multiple sclerosis should not become pregnant and if they do early evacuation of the uterus is recommended.

SMALL PELVIS.   Formerly the induction of premature labor at the 34th to

36th week was recommended in the treatment of contracted pelvis.   The high death rate of the premature infants thus obtained together with the greatly diminished risk from cesarean section has led to the abandonment of the induction of premature labor in cases of contracted pelvis.

LARGE CHILD.   When the child is growing too large and the pregnancy has gone beyond the expected date of confinement the induction of labor is indicated. This is particularly true if the pelvis is slightly contracted.

PELVIC TUMORS.   At one time pelvic tumors were considered an indication for therapeutic abortion.   As a result of the improvements made in gynecological surgery the surgical removal of such tumors or cesarean section accompanied by their removal has eliminated this indication for the interruption of pregnancy.

METHODS OF INTERRUPTING PREGNANCY

Pregnancy may be interrupted by inducing the uterus to empty itself, by surgically removing the products of conception or by a combination of the two methods.

The methods which induce the uterus to empty itself stimulate uterine contractions, which by a mechanism analogous to that observed in normal labor first obliterate and dilate the cervix and finally separate and expel the products of conception.   Induction of abortion or premature labor by such means accordingly is time consuming.   Because the mechanism often is inadequate delay and hemorrhage may require further operative intervention to complete the emptying of the uterus.

The surgical removal of the products of conception on the other hand is accomplished by rapid dilatation of the cervical canal or incision of the cervix or uterus and the immediate removal of the products of conception.   Surgical interruptions of pregnancy accordingly are quickly accomplished and are completed without subsequent interference.

The methods of inducting the uterus to expel its contents are:
1. Stimulation of uterine contractions by various drugs.
2. Artificial rupture of the membranes.
3. Destruction of the life of the ovum by roentgen rays.
4. Tamponade of the vagina and cervix.
5. The introduction of a bougie into the uterus.
6. The introduction of a hydrostatic bag into the cervix and uterus.

The surgical methods of interrupting pregnancy are:
1. Dilatation and curettage.
2. Dilatation and removal of the products of conception with ovum forceps.
3. Dilatation followed by digital separation and removal with ovum forceps.
4. Anterior vaginal hysterotomy.
5. Abdominal hysterotomy.

INDUCTION BY DRUGS

STIMULATION OF UTERINE CONTRACTIONS BY MEANS OF OXYTOCIC DRUGS. Ergot, tansy, pennyroyal, aloes, castor oil, quinine and many other so called oxytocic drugs have been used to bring on an abortion, to induce premature labor and to cause the onset of labor at term.   Experience has shown that all of them as well as the estrogenic and posterior pituitary hormones are incapable of inducing abortion or premature labor if the products of conception are alive.   Although large doses of estrogenic substances have been shown to cause abortion in some animals they are ineffectual in the human, unless the ovum is dead.   In cases of missed abortion and dead fetus on the other hand evacuation of the uterus may be accomplished by giving posterior pituitary extract after the uterus has been sensitized with large doses of estrogenic substance.   For this purpose estradial benzoate in 2 mg. doses is given intramuscularly every 8 hours or stilbestrol in doses of 1 mg. is taken orally every 4 hours for 7 or 8 days.   Four 1 cc. injections of posterior pituitary extract at hourly intervals are given on the fifth day and are repeated three days later if necessary.   The older the fetus is before its death and the more recent the death of the fetus the easier it is to evacuate the uterus by this means (5).

Labor at or near term may be induced by the use of castor oil, quinine and posterior pituitary extract.   The use of castor oil and quinine for this purpose is so well known that many women ask for these drugs as soon as the expected date of confinement is reached.   Often they are unsuccessful.   When they succeed on the other hand it is difficult to determine whether the onset of labor is due to natural causes or to their use, since labor's onset follows the mere mention of their use almost as often as it does the taking of the drugs.   Posterior pituitary extract given after the administration of castor oil and quinine has proven quite satisfactory in bringing on labor at full term and the combined use of these drugs has come to be termed the **medical induction of labor.**

The routine usually followed in the medical induction of labor is as follows (6, 7,):

6:00 a.m.   One ounce of castor oil.
7:00 a.m.   Quinine 10 gr. followed by a warm enema.
8:00 a.m.   Pituitary extract 3 m. and repeated at half hour intervals until labor is established or until 6 doses have been given.

Warning.   Posterior pituitary extract acts differently in different women and even when given for the purpose of inducing labor has caused rupture of the uterus, premature separation of the placenta, and sufficient interference with the utero-placental circulation to kill the child.   For this reason the initial dose should not exceed 1 min.   If the tonus of the uterus is not too greatly augmented the amount is gradually increased until 3 min. are given.   The length and strength of each contraction together with the tonus of the uterus in the interval between contractions and the character of the fetal heart sounds rather than the frequency of the labor pains should determine whether the dose is to be increased or discontinued. Whenever this method of induction is used an anesthetic capable of relaxing the uterus, such as ether or chloroform, should be at hand. Because of the violence of the contractions which sometimes are induced by posterior pituitary extract the intranasal application of this hormone has been substituted for its hypodermic administration (8). According to this technic a pledget of cotton is saturated with 1 cc. of posterior pituitary extract and introduced beneath the inferior turbinate bone on one side of the nose. This is withdrawn at the end of an hour and another similar pledget is inserted into the opposite nostril.

INDUCTION BY RUPTURING THE MEMBRANES

ARTIFICIAL RUPTURE OF THE MEMBRANES. Because labor sooner or later is certain to follow rupture of the bag of waters artificial rupture of the membranes has been used for the purpose of inducing abortion and premature labor and to cause the onset of labor at term. Although the interval between the time of rupture and the beginning of labor is seldom over 2 days when induction by this method is attempted at term, the latent period may be greatly prolonged if the method is used prior to the last month of pregnancy. Because of this prolonged latent period and because of the consequent increase in the risk of infection, rupture of the membranes is not recommended for the induction of abortion or for the induction of labor before the last month of pregnancy. On the other hand, it is an excellent method of bringing on labor at or near term when the head is engaged and the cervix is soft and partially taken up. When combined with medical induction it probably is the best means of inducing labor at this time (9, 10, 11, 12, 13, 14). In fact this combination of methods is so satisfactory that it is employed by some obstetricians to bring on labor for no indication other than their own convenience or the convenience of the patient. Although the average length of labor following this type of induction is shortened the number of prolonged labors is increased. Because of this difficulty and because the incidence of intrapartum infection and prolapse of the cord is twice that observed in spontaneous labors (13) the method is not entirely free from danger and should be used only when the induction of labor is definitely indicated.

In order that the risk of prolapse of the cord may be reduced to its minimum the head should be at the level of the ischial spines whenever labor is induced by this method. The frequent failures following attempts to induce labor before term by this means also indicate that its use should be limited to those cases which are at or near the end of pregnancy. In addition the cervix should be soft and its canal should be partially obliterated if the required manipulations are to be accomplished easily and a successful outcome is to be assured.

INDUCTION BY X-RAY

DESTRUCTION OF THE LIFE OF THE OVUM BY X-RAY: The X-ray has been used to produce a therapeutic abortion in women suffering from conditions in which surgical interruption is contraindicated.   Advocates of this method recommend its use only for pregnancies under 14 weeks.   Sufficient radiation (60% of a skin erythema dose given to the center of the uterus) is employed to destroy the life of the ovum which then acts as a foreign body within the uterus and causes the uterus to empty itself.   In 90% of the cases the procedure is said to be successful but three to four weeks elapse between the last treatment and the appearance of the bleeding and cramps which indicate the onset of the impending abortion.   Unfortunately the side effects of the X-rays on the ovaries cause amenorrhea and may be responsible for the development of defective ova (15).   Since local anesthesia may be used in the same group of cases, the surgical interruption of pregnancy under local anesthesia will give better immediate results and little or no danger of late side effects.

INDUCTION BY PACKING VAGINA AND CERVIX

TAMPONADE OF THE VAGINA AND CERVIX.   The bleeding in inevitable and incomplete abortions which are infected is controlled by a firm gauze pack in the vagina and cervix.   When the gauze is removed 24 hours later the cervix usually is found to be dilated and the products of conception often are separated and expelled from the uterus.   Packing the vagina and cervix thus may stimulate uterine contractions and may be used to induce abortion and premature labor.   When the uterus has not started to empty itself however, this method is not so effective and repeated packings may be necessary.   Because of its uncertainty and because the repeated packings greatly increase the risk of infection this method of induction is unsatisfactory.

BOUGIE INDUCTION

THE INTRODUCTION OF A BOUGIE INTO THE UTERUS.   A bougie passed into the uterine cavity between the membranes and the wall of the uterus often will induce the uterus to contract and evacuate the products of conception. The introduction of such a bougie therefore, is used for the purpose of inducing abortion and premature labor and of bringing on labor at term.   The nearer the pregnancy is to term the more successful is this method of induction.   For this reason and because the surgical removal of an early pregnancy is a much better procedure, the use of a bougie to induce an abortion is not recommended. Induction of labor by means of the bougie also is somewhat uncertain and this uncertainty is increased if the pregnancy has not reached full term.   About 90% of all bougie inductions are successful when the child is 2500 gm. or over and failure is to be anticipated in about 20% of the cases in which the fetus is premature or non-viable (16).

TECHNIC OF INTRODUCING A BOUGIE. For this purpose, a new rubber rectal tube is preferable to a silk bougie. The vagina is first prepared by the instillation of 4 per cent aqueous mercurochrome solution. After allowing at least thirty minutes for this antiseptic to become effective the membranes are separated posteriorly by a finger introduced through the cervix. The sterile rectal tube is then gently forced between the separated membranes and the uterine wall until all but a few inches of it are within the uterine cavity. Should the progress of the tube be interrupted by an obstruction, the possibility of detaching the placenta must be considered and the danger of this accident avoided by removing the bougie and reinserting it in the opposite direction. If the internal os is too small, dilatation is effected by the use of Hegar's graduated sounds. Anesthesia seldom is required.

Some operators prefer to expose the cervix and introduce the bougie by sight rather than by touch. After retracting the posterior vaginal wall with a Sims' speculum, the cervix is grasped by a suitable forceps and brought into view. The bougie is then introduced in the manner already described. While this method may lessen the risk of infection, it interferes somewhat with the introduction of the tube and increases the danger of rupturing the membranes prematurely.

DANGERS. The maternal dangers of induction by means of the bougie are: infection, separation of the placenta, rupture of the uterus and premature rupture of the membranes. While the most serious of these seldom are to be considered, if the procedure is carefully done, the possibility of infection cannot be entirely overlooked. The introduction of a bougie, therefore, is not without risk and, in hospital practice, is followed by a morbidity of 18 per cent and a mortality of slightly over 1 per cent (16).

The risks to the child are: premature rupture of the membranes and prolapse of the cord. If the bougie is introduced by touch and the procedure is carried out with care and gentleness, prolapse of the cord seldom occurs and the fetal risk does not greatly exceed that of spontaneous labor.

From the foregoing, it will be seen that the method of inducing labor by means of a bougie has the advantage of simplicity. It therefore should be the method of choice by those who lack obstetric skill, and is often employed by experienced operators in those cases in which a more rapid and more certain method is not indicated. On the other hand, a maternal mortality of slightly over 1 per cent does not justify its indiscriminate use.

BAG INDUCTION

INTRODUCTION OF A HYDROSTATIC BAG INTO THE CERVIX AND UTERUS. Hydrostatic bags of various sizes may be introduced into the cervix and uterus to induce abortion and premature labor and to bring on labor at term. The nearer the pregnancy is to term the more rapid and certain is the induction. Because the surgical removal of the early ovum is more satisfactory, abortion before the 4th month is seldom induced by means of the hydrostatic bag. After the fourth month the bag sometimes is used to secure sufficient cervical dilation to permit manual removal of the products of conception. In such circumstances the operation is done in two stages and the risk of infection is increased. Because of the necessary delay and this added risk of infection anterior vaginal and abdominal hysterotomy usually are preferred by those operators who have the necessary skill to perform these operations. Induction of labor at or near term by the use of a hydrostatic bag has been supplanted by the combination of medical induction and rupture of the membranes. In the event that the latter procedure fails however, labor is induced by means of the hydrostatic bag.

Labor begins within 1 hour after the bag is introduced in about half of the cases and over 90% go into labor within 24 hours (16) (17).

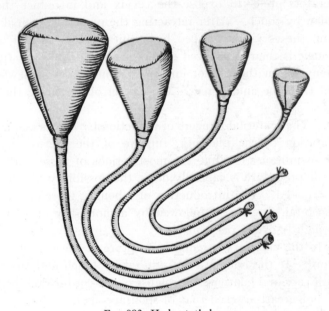

FIG. 892. Hydrostatic bags.

TECHNIC OF INTRODUCING A HYDROSTATIC BAG. The bag most commonly used in this country is made of an inelastic rubber-covered fabric according to the Voorhees modification of the Champetier de Ribes balloon. Four sizes, varying in diameter from 2½ to 10 cm., are available so that the bag may be suited to the size of the cervix (Fig. 892). Generally speaking, the larger ones are preferable when the internal os is sufficiently patulous to permit their introduction. For this reason, all sizes should be sterilized and tested for each case. The bags, accordingly, are distended with sterile water by using a large glass syringe and the number of syringefuls necessary to fill each one is recorded in order that the bag selected may be properly filled when it is in the uterus. After preparing the vagina with 4 per cent mercurochrome solution, the examining

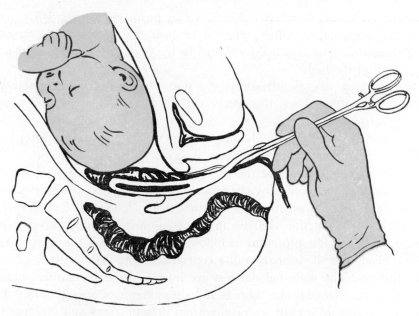

FIG. 893. Introduction of a hydrostatic bag. After testing the bag, it is held by the bag forceps and introduced between the membranes and the uterine wall.

finger separates the membranes posteriorly and the folded bag is introduced by means of a bag forceps (Fig. 893). The forceps are then removed and the bag is held within the internal os by the fingers in the vagina while an assistant injects the necessary syringefuls of sterile solution (Fig. 894). The end is tied

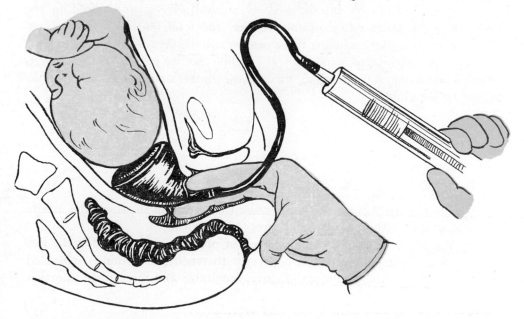

FIG. 894. Introduction of a hydrostatic bag. Following the removal of the forceps, the bag is held in place by the fingers while it is being filled.

and placed in the vagina, where it is retained by means of a small gauze mercuro-chrome-saturated pack. Often, when it is desirable to hasten the induction, a small weight may be attached by a cord to the neck of the bag and suspended over the foot of the bed.

The bag may also be introduced by sight. After introducing a posterior retractor and pulling down the cervix with a suitable forceps, the foregoing routine is carried out.

When a bag 5 cm. or less in diameter is used, labor may cease after the bag is expelled. Examination in such cases shows a well dilated external os but a contraction ring slightly above the site previously occupied by the bag. This complication may be avoided by the removal of the bag and artificial rupture of the membranes as soon as labor is well established. The most certain and most rapid method of induction consists in the combined introduction of a bougie and a bag. When this procedure is followed, labor usually continues after the bag is expelled, and the formation of a contraction ring is prevented.

DANGERS. The maternal dangers are infection and premature rupture of the membranes. In addition, there is an increased risk of operative interference due to the occasional occurrence of abnormal presentations and prolapse of the cord following the introduction of a bag. Because of these increased risks, about one-third of all cases show some morbidity, and death of the mother occurs about once in every hundred bag inductions (4).

The risk to the fetus is considerable. Not only are the membranes rup-tured prematurely, but prolapse of the umbilical cord is not uncommon and displacement of the presenting part may lead to face, brow and transverse presentations. Operative interference, as a result, is often required in the interests of the child. In hospital practice, the fetal mortality may exceed 10 per cent, even after excluding those cases which die because of the underlying condition for which labor is induced (4). While the bag method of induction is a fairly certain one, it is not without risk to the mother and greatly increases the danger to the child.

CURETTAGE

The term curettage is used to describe the operation in which the uterine cavity is scraped with a sharp or dull curet (Fig. 895).

INDICATIONS. Before the eighth week of pregnancy, curettage is the best method of emptying the uterus, whenever a therapeutic abortion is indicated. It also is useful in the treatment of early, inevitable and incomplete abortion.

FIG. 895. Curet.

OPERATIVE TECHNIC. The operation of curettage may be done under gas, ether or local anesthesia. Before starting the anesthetic, the vulva is shaved and cleansed according to the method recommended for an aseptic vaginal examination. The operator then sterilizes his hands and puts on a sterile gown and sterile rubber gloves. As soon as the patient is anesthetized, the vulva is painted with half strength tincture of iodine and draped with a sterile sheet. After injecting iodine into the vagina, the posterior wall is retracted by a Sims' speculum and the cervix, grasped by a double tenaculum, is drawn towards the vulvovaginal orifice. The canal is then sterilized by injecting iodine from a bulb syringe (Fig. 896). Following this, a sound is passed to determine the size and position of the uterine cavity.

If the internal os is too small, it is dilated sufficiently to permit the passage of a curet by means of Hegar's graduated sounds. With a dull and rather large curet, the uterine cavity is then systematically scraped. Throughout the manipulations, great care is taken to avoid perforating the softened wall of the uterus (Fig. 897). Because portions of the ovum may be retained, a narrow strip of gauze, saturated in 4 per cent mercurochrome solution, is packed into the uterine cavity and left for 24 hours. The danger of hemorrhage and perforation

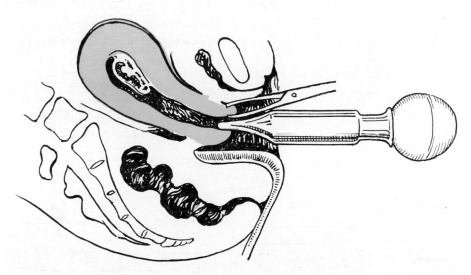

FIG. 896. Sterilization of the cervical canal and uterine cavity by the injection of half strength tincture of iodine. For this purpose, the glass syringe shown is very satisfactory.

is greatly lessened if an ampoule of pituitary extract is given immediately after the cervix is dilated. Following this operation, the position of the uterus often is altered, and manual replacement, while the patient is still anesthetized, is indicated. The curettings should always be examined microscopically.

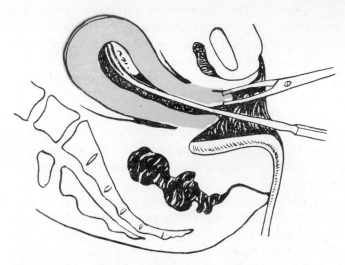

Fig. 897. Curettage. The products of conception are removed by a large, dull curet.

DANGERS. The dangers of curettage are infection, hemorrhage and perforation of the uterine wall. All of these are very slight, if a good technic is followed and the operation is limited to only those cases for which it is best suited. It therefore should not be done in the presence of infection and should be avoided in all therapeutic and inevitable abortions after the eighth week.

DIGITAL REMOVAL OF PREGNANCY WITH OVUM FORCEPS

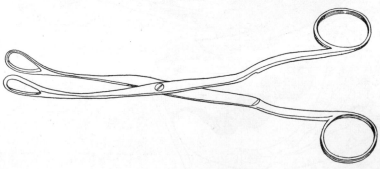

Fig. 898. Ovum forceps.

REMOVAL OF THE PRODUCTS OF CONCEPTION WITH OVIUM FORCEPS. After the eighth week, the products of conception are best removed with ovum forceps (Fig. 898).

INDICATIONS. Therapeutic, inevitable and incomplete abortion are the indications for this operation.

OPERATIVE TECHNIC. Following the essential aseptic preparations and dilatation of the cervix, the ovum forceps are introduced into the uterine cavity and grasp the products of conception. These are then pulled through the dilated cervix, and the uterus is loosely packed with 4 per cent mercurochrome gauze.

DIGITAL SEPARATION OF THE OVUM

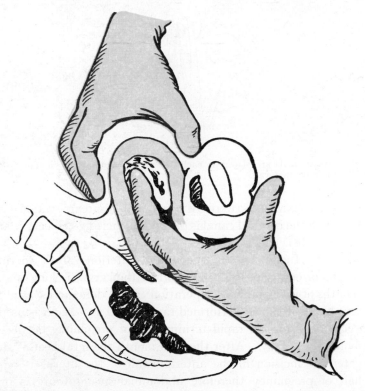

FIG. 899. After the twelfth week, a finger is passed into the uterus for the purpose of separating the products of conception preliminary to the passage of the ovum forceps. While this is being done, the fundus is forced downward and steadied by the external hand.

If the gestation is over twelve weeks, it is better to break up the placental tissue with the finger (Fig. 899) before attempting its removal with ovum forceps. Should it be impossible to secure sufficient dilatation for this purpose, a tight pack, placed in the cervix and upper vagina for 24 hours, often will have the desired effect. For the competent surgeon, on the other hand, anterior vaginal or abdominal hysterotomy is preferable, since the latter procedures are certain and make possible the complete evacuation of the uterus at one sitting.

DANGER. The chief danger is infection. When the operation is done for hydatidiform mole, however, the risk of rupture of the uterus cannot be disregarded.

3-5 mos

ANTERIOR VAGINAL HYSTEROTOMY

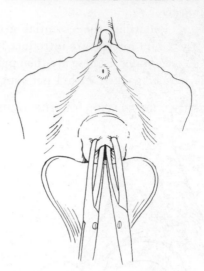

FIG. 900   Two tenacula are placed on each side of the anterior lip.   Traction on these exposes the cervix and anterior vaginal wall.

ANTERIOR VAGINAL HYSTEROTOMY (vaginal cesarean section) is a vaginal operation in which the cervical canal is opened by incising the cervix and anterior wall of the uterus (18).

INDICATIONS.   Incision of the cervix and anterior wall of the uterus is an excellent means of emptying the uterus when the cervix is long and rigid.   In the early months of pregnancy this operation can be done under local anesthesia. In competent hands it can be performed rapidly and as a result is used whenever there is urgent need for the rapid termination of pregnancy between the third and fifth months (19) (20).   After the fifth month the fetal head is so large that a rather extensive incision in the anterior wall of the uterus is required.   In the last half of pregnancy therefore abdominal hysterotomy is preferable if laparotomy is not contraindicated.

OPERATIVE TECHNIC.   After exposing the cervix by means of a posterior retractor, the anterior lip is grasped by two tenacula placed on each side of the midline (Fig. 900).   The anterior vaginal wall is then incised vertically and, by blunt dissection, the bladder is separated from the anterior wall of the uterus (Fig. 901).   With the bladder held out of the operative field by an anterior retractor, the uterus is incised in the midline until the opening is sufficiently large to permit the delivery of the fetal head (Fig. 902).

Following the removal of the placenta, the uterine incision is closed with interrupted sutures (Fig. 903) and the vaginal wall is approximated as in an anterior colporrhaphy (Fig. 904).   A hypodermic injection of pituitary extract

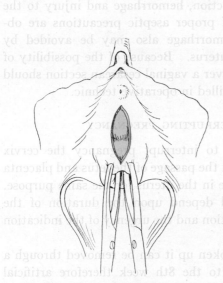

FIG. 901. After incising the anterior vaginal wall in the midline, the bladder is separated from the wall of the uterus by blunt dissection.

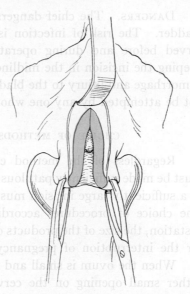

FIG. 902. The bladder is held out of the way by an anterior retractor, while the cervix and anterior wall of the uterus are incised in the midline. At this time, an ampoule of pituitary extract is injected hypodermically.

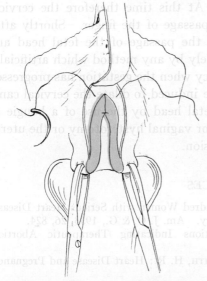

FIG. 903. After removing the products of conception, the uterus and cervix are closed by interrupted chromic catgut sutures.

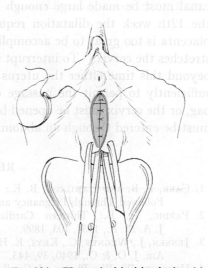

FIG. 904. The vaginal incision is closed by interrupted sutures, after which the uterus is manually reposited.

often lessens the hemorrhage which accompanies and follows the artificial separation of the placenta.

DANGERS. The chief dangers are infection, hemorrhage and injury to the bladder. The risk of infection is slight if proper aseptic precautions are observed before and during operation. Hemorrhage also may be avoided by keeping the incision in the midline of the uterus. Because of the possibility of hemorrhage and injury to the bladder however a vaginal cesarean section should not be attempted by any one who is not skilled in operative technic.

CHOICE OF METHODS OF INTERRUPTING PREGNANCY

Regardless of the method employed to interrupt pregnancy the cervix must be made sufficiently patulous to permit the passage of the fetus and placenta or a sufficiently large incision must be made in the uterus for the same purpose. The choice of procedures accordingly will depend upon the duration of the gestation, the size of the products of conception and the urgency of the indication for the interruption of pregnancy.

When the ovum is small and easily broken up it can be removed through a rather small opening on the cervix. Up to the 8th week therefore artificial dilatation of the cervix with Goodall or Hegar dilators will suffice for the removal of the products of conception with a curette. Between the 8th and 12th week the dilatation should be ample for the introduction of the ovum forceps. By the 12th week the ovum must be separated and broken up with the finger before it is removed with the placenta forceps. At this time therefore the cervical canal must be made large enough for the passage of the finger. Shortly after the 12th week the dilatation required for the passage of the fetal head and placenta is too great to be accomplished safely by any method which artificially stretches the cervix. To interrupt pregnancy when the gestation has progressed beyond this time either the uterus must be induced to dilate the cervical canal sufficiently to permit the passage of the fetal head by the use of a bougie or bag, or the cervix must be opened by anterior vaginal hysterotomy or the uterus must be entered through an abdominal incision.

REFERENCES

1. CARR, F. B. AND HAMILTON, B. E.: Five Hundred Women with Serious Heart Diseases Followed Through Pregnancy and Delivery. Am. J. O. & G., 1933, 26, 824.
2. PARDIC, H. E.: Thirteen Cardiac Conditions Indicating Therapeutic Abortion. J. A. M. A., 1934, 103, 1899.
3. JENSEN, J., WEGNER, C., KEYS, E. H. AND SMITH, H. R.: Heart Disease and Pregnancy. Am. J. O. & G., 1940, 39, 443.
4. HERRICK, W. W.: Phases of Cardiovascular and Renal Disease Indicating Abortion. J. A. M. A. 1938, 103, 1902.
5. JEFFCOATE, T. M. A.: Missed Abortion and Missed Labor. Lancet, 1940, 1, 1045.
6. WATSON, B. P.: Pituitary Extract in Obstetrical Practice. Canadian Med. Assn. J., 1913, 8, 739.

7. WATSON, B. P.: Further Experiments with the Use of Pituitrin for Induction of Labor. Am. J. O. &. G., 1922, 4, 603.
8. HOFFBAUER, J. I. AND HOERNER, J. K.: Nasal Application of Pituitary for Induction of Labor. Am. J. O. & G., 1927, 14, 137.
9. SLEMONS, J. M.: The Induction of Labor at Term. Am. J. O. & G., 1932, 23, 494.
10. EASTMAN, N. J.: The Induction of Labor. Am. J. O. & G., 1938, 35, 721.
11. HOLMAN, A. W. AND MATHIEW, A.: Induction of Labor in Patients with Toxemia or Nephritis. West J. Surg., 1939, 47, 182.
12. McCORD, JR.: Premature Rupture of the Membranes as a Method of Inducing Labor. Am. J. O. & G., 1939, 38, 587.
13. KEETTEL, N. C., DIDDLE, A. W. AND PLASS, E. D.: Premature Elective Rupture of Membranes. Comparative Study. Am. J. O. & G., 1940, 40, 225.
14. TEW, W. P.: Induction of Labor. Canadian M. A. J., 1940, 42, 556.
15. MAYER, M. D., HARRIS, W. AND WIMPFHEIMER, S.: Therapeutic Abortion by Means of X-ray. Am. J. O. & G., 1936, 32, 945.
16. MORTON, D. G.: A Comparison of the Results Obtained in the Induction of Labor by Means of Bougie or Bag. Am. J. O. & G., 1929, 18, 849.
17. IVENS, F., CANTRELL, H. AND REID, J. K.: The Induction of Premature Labor. Lancet, 1925, 2, 493.
18. DÜHRSSEN, A.: Der vaginale Kaiserschnitt. 1896.
19. PETERSON, R.: The Indications for and Technic of Vaginal Cesarean Section. S. G. & O., 1909, 8, 180.
20. MARTIN, E.: Der Scheidenschnitt in der klinischen Geburtshilfe. Monatschr. f. Geburtsh. u. Gyn., 1930, 85, 255.

CHAPTER XXXIX

METHODS USED TO HASTEN OR COMPLETE THE DILATATION OF THE CERVIX

Before considering the procedures used to hasten or to complete the dilatation of the cervix it may be well to recall that the cervix normally is dilated by being pulled up over the presenting part. Its canal accordingly is obliterated from above downward and following this effacement, the external os is gradually enlarged. Since no artificial method of accomplishing the same result has been devised, all so called rapid means of dilatation are contrary to physiological principles. While it is true that the cervix can be forced open, the artificial removal of the cervical barrier can thus be effected only at the risk of causing extensive lacerations and the degree of these lacerations will be inversely proportional to the dilatation produced by Nature's efforts up to the time of intervention. The terms instrumental and manual dilatation therefore are misleading in that the cervix may be more lacerated than dilated.

The procedures which have been recommended to hasten or complete the dilatation of the cervix are:

1. Packing the vagina with gauze.
2. Introduction of a hydrostatic bag.
3. Instrumental dilatation.
4. Manual dilatation.
5. Incisions of the cervix.

PACKING OF THE VAGINA. Formerly uterine contractions were stimulated and cervical dilatation was facilitated by packing the vagina with boro glyceride gauze in certain cases of prolonged labor in which the **cervix was edematous and unyielding.** Tamponade of the vagina to control hemorrhage and hasten the dilatation of the cervix also was employed in the treatment of **placenta previa** (Fig. 851, page 703). Because of the risk of infection this method of hastening cervical dilatation has been abandoned. Its use in placenta previa likewise is limited to those cases in which the hemorrhage might prove fatal before a better method of treatment can be instituted.

INTRODUCTION OF A HYDROSTATIC BAG. A hydrostatic bag introduced into the cervix and uterus stimulates uterine contractions and accelerates dilatation of the cervix (Fig. 893, 894, page 769). This procedure formerly was used by many obstetricians whenever labor failed to begin within 24 hours after **premature rupture of the membranes** and it still is employed for this purpose when medical induction fails. A hydrostatic bag also was used to accelerate labor when the first stage was delayed because of **uterine inertia.** At the present time such cases of inertia are treated by the use of sedatives or uterine contractions are stimulated by other means. In certain instances of **placenta previa** the hemorrhage is controlled and cervical dilatation is favored by the introduction of a large Voorhees bag (Fig. 850, page 701). A small weight attached by a cord to the neck of the bag and suspended over the foot of the bed often increases the efficiency of this method of treating placenta previa. If such a weight is used, care must be taken to allow free play of the attaching cord when the patient moves: otherwise the tension may be too great and the uterus may be ruptured through the friable placental site.

As previously stated the introduction of a hydrostatic bag is accompanied by the risks of infection, displacement of the presenting part which may lead to malpresentation and prolapse of the umbilical cord.

INSTRUMENTAL DILATATION. The so-called rapid dilatation by means of the Bossi four pronged metal dilator was endorsed by many obstetricians around the beginning of this century. With it the cervix could be pried open in thirty minutes. This rapid method of overcoming the cervical barrier accordingly was used **whenever the life of the mother demanded immediate emptying of the uterus.** Because the immediate delivery of the child was at that time regarded as imperative in toxemia complicated by convulsions, eclampsia was the most frequent indication for instrumental dilatation of the cervix in the latter half of pregnancy. Today convulsive toxemia is better treated by more conservative means. For this reason and because of the extensive lacerations which result from its performance, instrumental dilatation of the cervix with the Bossi dilator has been abandoned and its place has been taken by better methods of rapid delivery.

MANUAL DILATATION

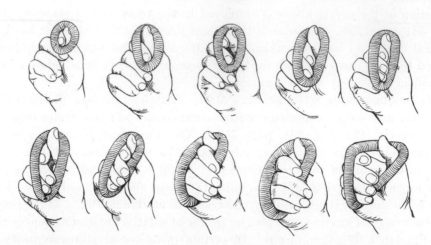

FIG. 905. Manual dilatation of the cervix (Harris). The thumb and forefinger are introduced into the external os and by a movement similar to that used in snapping the fingers, the cervix is slowly stretched. Additional fingers are then introduced and manipulated in a like manner.

MANUAL DILATATION OF THE CERVIX. After labor has progressed beyond the stage of effacement and the external os is several centimeters dilated, dilatation may be completed manually provided the cervix is soft and feels as though it were paralyzed. Under deep ether anesthesia the sterile gloved thumb and fore finger are introduced into the external os and by a movement similar to that used in snapping the fingers the cervix is slowly stretched. As dilatation proceeds, additional fingers are introduced and manipulated in a like manner until the loosely clenched fist can be passed into the uterus with ease (Fig. 905). If delivery is completed by the use of forceps or breech extraction and a rim of cervix remains below the head this should be gently forced over the head before the latter is extracted; otherwise the cervix may be deeply torn and the supporting structures within the pelvis destroyed. Following the delivery of the placenta the cervix should be brought into view with sponge forceps in order that the inevitable laceration may be discovered and repaired. Digital dilatation is time consuming and is so fatiguing that the operator may have to stop in the course of the operation to give his hands a rest (1) (2).

INDICATIONS. The cervix sometimes is dilated manually when the first stage is prolonged as a result of inertia. If uterine inertia is properly treated however the need for this type of interference seldom arises. When the external os is almost but not fully dilated and the condition of the mother or child requires operative delivery, the dilatation occasionally is completed manually. In this connection it may be stated that this operation never should be done for placenta previa because of the great danger of rupturing the uterus.

DANGERS. The chief dangers of manual dilatation are infection, extensive lacerations, hemorrhage and the ill effects of prolonged deep anesthesia in a patient whose condition is unfavorable for even a short anesthetic. Although the extent of the trauma may be diminished by slow and gentle manipulations under deep anesthesia it is almost impossible to dilate the cervix manually as satisfactorily as it is dilated by the natural mechanism. Because of this trauma and the increased risk of infection, manual dilatation for the purpose of accelerating a labor which is progressing normally is not justifiable. If there is a definite indication for hastening the delivery on the other hand deliberate cutting of the cervix is preferable, for the reason that the resulting wounds are clean cut and are placed in the most suitable locations.

INCISIONS OF THE CERVIX

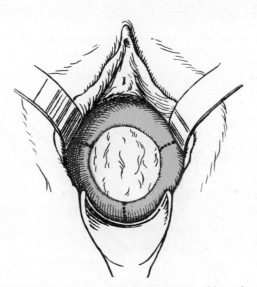

FIG. 906. Incisions of the cervix (Hunt and McGee). After making a deep mediolateral episiotomy the cervix is exposed by wide retraction. The dotted lines on the cervix indicate the site of the proposed incisions at 10, 2 and 6 o'clock.

INCISION OF THE CERVIX, DÜHRSSEN'S INCISIONS. After the cervix is effaced and half dilated the opening may be enlarged by means of incisions made at points corresponding to the position of the numerals 10, 2 and 6 on the dial of a clock (Fig. 906). These incisions are made between previously placed long connection it may be stated that this operation never should be done for placenta previa because of the great danger of infecting the uterus.

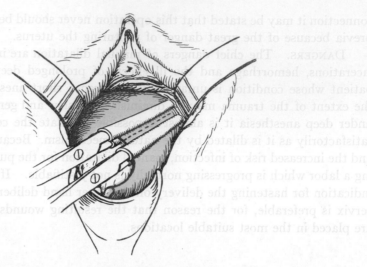

FIG. 907. Incisions of the cervix. Two long clamps are placed on the cervix adjacent to the midline posteriorly. The posterior incision is then made between these clamps. Clamps are similarly placed on the sides of the cervix and the lateral incisions are made. If the lateral incisions are made first bleeding from them may obscure the field of operation and interfere with the making of the posterior incision.

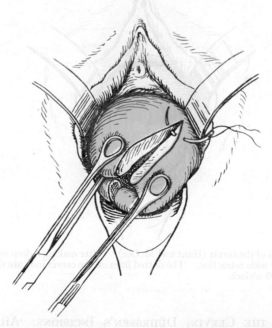

FIG. 908. Incisions of the cervix. Following the delivery of the child and placenta the cervix is again exposed by means of vaginal retractors. Its edges are grasped with sponge forceps and each incision is brought into view and closed with interrupted catgut sutures. To secure good union the tissues at the upper angle should be everted. Each suture is passed down to but not into the lining membrane and tied tightly enough to approximate the tissues without excessive constriction.

clamps and are continued outward to the vaginal fornix (Fig. 907). Because the bladder is pulled upward as effacement takes place, its dissection from the anterior wall of the uterus is not required as in vaginal cesarean section. Immediately after the delivery is completed the cervix is exposed and the wound edges are approximated with interrupted catgut sutures (Fig. 908, 909).

INDICATIONS. The indications for multiple incision of the cervix are similar to those given for manual dilatation. Because clean cut properly placed incisions are more easily repaired and heal better than the lacerations which accompany manual dilatation, deliberate incision of the cervix is the preferable procedure whenever delivery is indicated before the cervix is completely dilated (3) (4). It naturally is essential that the pelvis be ample and that the child can be delivered through the passages after the cervical barrier has been removed.

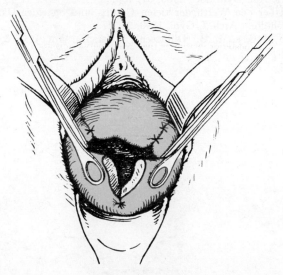

FIG. 909. Incisions of the cervix. Two to four sutures are used for each incision. If the wound has extended beyond the original incision care should be taken to bring the upper angle into view with Allis clamps or traction sutures in order that it may be properly repaired.

DANGERS. If the incisions are too short or are made too soon there is danger that they may be extended in the course of the delivery of the child. In these circumstances the repair of the trauma may be difficult and the hemorrhage may be profuse. For this reason Dührssen's incisions should be made only by a skillful operator and the operation should be performed in a properly equipped hospital. Because the patients who are subjected to this procedure often are dehydrated and exhausted by long labors, shock and post partum hemorrhage may occur. This may be prevented in some instances by the preoperative intravenous administration of glucose, and blood transfusion. In addition suitable donors should be on hand to give blood if it is necessary after the operation. Although the cervix may be opened rapidly by this method the prolonged labor which often precedes this type of intervention predisposes towards infection. If infection is present the healing of the wounds may be interfered with and result in a badly scarred cervix.

While Dührssen's incisions are preferable to manual dilatation they are not to be substituted for Nature's method of dilatation in the average case and should be employed only when the indications for a rapid delivery justify their use.

REFERENCES

1. HARRIS, P. A.: A Method of Performing Rapid Dilatation of the Os Uteri. Am. J. Obs., 1894, 29, 37.
2. EDGAR, J. C.: Advantages of the Bimanual Dilatation of the Pregnant and Parturient Uterus. Tr. Am. Gyn. Soc., 1906, 31, 108.
3. DÜHRSSEN, A.: Über den Werth der tiefen Cervix- und Scheiden-Damm-Einschnitte in der Geburtshülfe. Arch. f. Gyn., 1890, 37, 27.
4. HUNT, A. B. AND McGEE, W. B.: Dührssen's Incisions. Am. J. O. & G., 1936, 31, 598,

CHAPTER XL

FORCEPS

DR. PETER CHAMBERLEN
1601–1683
London

Peter Chamberlen the elder probably invented the obstetric forceps and through his brother Peter the younger the instruments were secretly handed down to Dr. Peter Chamberlen (above) and his sons, Hugh and John.

The secret of the forceps accordingly was kept within the Chamberlen family for several generations and gave them great renown as obstetricians. Because of this prestige they overcame the prevailing prejudice against trained male obstetricians and Hugh Chamberlen not only numbered the ladies of the nobility among his patients but was engaged to attend the queen when the pretender was born in 1688.

In 1699 Hugh Chamberlen was retired to Holland on suspicion of debt where he sold the family secret to Roonhuysen. Knowledge of the instruments soon became public and Chapman in 1735 published an illustrated description of them.

In the 18th century the midwife began to be supplanted by the trained male obstetrician. Stimulated by the obstetric treatise included in Paré's "A Short Compendium on Anatomy" which rejuvenated the operation of version in 1550, men were induced to consider the practice of obstetrics, but their opportunities for clinical experience were very limited. Since no lady would permit the attendance of a man in her bed chamber during her confinement, their practice was largely among prostitutes and women in the lowest social stratum. Gradually however they gained prestige and Julien Clement attended the mistress and later the queen of Louis XIV (1682). Subsequently the trained obstetrician became the fashion among the ladies of the French court. In England a similar trend away from the midwife was stimulated by the Chamberlen family who by the use of their secret means (the obstetric forceps) of delivering difficult cases were able to establish themselves as obstetricians with the better classes. This almost simultaneous employment of trained male obstetricians by the Royal families of France and England was a great boon to obstetrics. At first the physician was engaged to be present at the time of delivery but his services were used only in case of difficulty. Later when women permitted him to make vaginal examinations in the course of labor knowledge of the details of parturition grew rapidly.

FIG. 910. Forceps, showing the cephalic curve.

FIG. 911. Forceps, showing the pelvic curve.

Several hundred varieties of forceps have been described. Many of them, however, differ from one another only in minor details (1). All of the modern instruments consist of two steel parts which cross each other like a pair of scissors and lock at the point of crossing. Each part consists of a handle, shank, lock and blade. The blades usually are fenestrated and have two curves: a **cephalic curve,** which conforms to the shape of the child's head (Fig. 910), and a **pelvic curve,** which follows the direction of the parturient axis (Fig. 911). They are

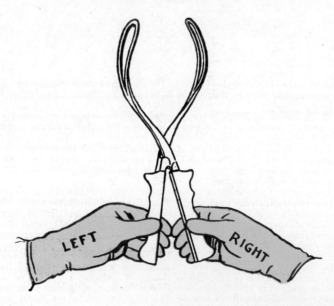

FIG. 912. Forceps partially locked and held in the hands. The right blade is in the right hand and the left blade is in the left hand.

joined by an English sliding lock (Fig. 912), or a French screw lock. When the forceps are locked and held so that the convexity of the pelvic curve is directed downward, the handle of the left blade is in the left hand and the handle of the right blade is in the right hand (Fig. 912). Axis traction forceps are constructed in a similar manner but have additional parts which are termed traction rods (Fig. 913).

USES. Forceps have been recommended as dilators (bad), compressors (bad), levers (bad), rotators (for the expert), and tractors (satisfactory).

The use of forceps as **dilators** is condemned for two very good reasons. First, they tear rather than dilate the cervix, and the resulting extensive cervical laceration often gives rise to alarming hemorrhage. Second, traction on the head, before the cervix is fully dilated, injures the supporting structures of the uterus with the result that a future gynecological operation often is necessary.

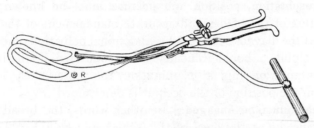

FIG. 913. Axis traction forceps (Jewett).

Forceps likewise should not be used as **compressors,** because of the great danger of injury to the child's brain. On the contrary, the more skilful the operator, the greater is his endeavor to lessen the compression of the child's head. If a head is too large, therefore, forceps are contraindicated and some other operative procedure should be selected.

The to and fro movement of the forceps as **levers** has no place in modern obstetric practice. With the patient completely anesthetized, the possibility of extensive damage to the maternal parts is so great that the use of the lever principle is not justifiable in forceps operations.

Rotation with forceps is not without risk, and irreparable damage to the supporting structures may follow unskilful attempts at instrumental rotation. For this reason, the inexperienced operator should employ manual rotation before applying the blades, and if the head cannot be rotated manually, he should call in someone who is sufficiently expert to do the forceps rotation without serious injury.

Traction was the original use for forceps and still is their most important function. **In the hands of the average practitioner, the use of forceps should be restricted to that of traction.**

REQUISITES. Before extraction with forceps is attempted, certain requisites must be fulfilled:

1. **The cervix must be dilated.** Sufficient dilatation to allow the passage of the child is essential and failure to heed this requirement frequently leads to what is termed **"failed forceps"**. If the head is pulled through a partially dilated cervix, there is great danger of **extensive cervical laceration, hemorrhage,** and **injury to the pelvic supporting structures.** Labor, accordingly, should be allowed to continue until the cervix is pulled up over the head, or, in the event of an emergency that requires immediate delivery, the cervical opening should be sufficiently enlarged by manual stretching or multiple incisions. It is a good plan to try to feel the cervix after the blades have been applied. If it is not completely retracted, the remaining rim of cervix should be pushed up over the head with the fingers before traction is made. Regard for this precaution will prevent injury to the supporting apparatus of the uterus.

2. **The presentation, position and posture must be known;** otherwise a proper application of the blades and accurate management of the extraction is not possible. If the diagnosis is in doubt, abdominal palpation, under anesthesia, will be very helpful. Should difficulty be encountered in distinguishing the sutures and fontanels on vaginal examination, the posterior ear is located and from its location the position of the occiput is determined.

3. **The head must be engaged.** In other words, the broad dome of the cranial vault must be at the level of the ischial spines (Fig. 914). When the caput succedaneum is marked, however, it sometimes is felt below these landmarks and, unless the examiner is on his guard, it may lead to an erroneous conclusion as to the position of the cranial vault (Fig. 915). Again, in cases of marked disproportion, the head may be so irregularly molded that its lower limit is below the level of the ischial spines before engagement has taken place (Fig 916).

Although the presence of the broad dome of the cranial vault at the level of the ischial spines indicates the absence of disproportion at the inlet, this must be regarded as the upper limit for forceps extraction, and the inexperienced operator should remember that the higher the level of the head, the greater are the difficulties for the mother, for the child and for himself. As the danger from delay is less than that which follows unskilful manipulations, he should put off the application of forceps until after the head has descended well below the spines.

4. **The outlet of the bony pelvis must be ample.** When the bisischial diameter is over 8 cm., no great difficulty need be expected. If it is under 8 cm., the sum of the bisischial and posterior sagittal should be over 15 cm. In the absence of trustworthy outlet measurements, a bisischial diameter as large as the folded fist may be regarded as ample.

5. **The membranes must be ruptured.** Application of the forceps over unruptured membranes favors slipping of the blades during traction and increases the risk of premature separation of the placenta.

FIG. 914. Head engaged at the level of the ischial spines.

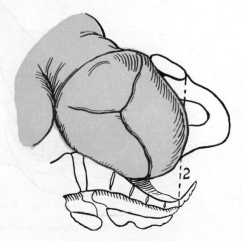

FIG. 915. Head not engaged. Caput succedaneum below the ischial spines.

FIG. 916. Head not engaged but below the spines due to irregular molding.

6. **The child must be alive.** While a destructive operation is to be preferred if the child is dead, it sometimes is extremely difficult to make a certain diagnosis of fetal death. In this connection, it may be stated that the absence of fetal heart sounds is **not** sufficient evidence to warrant perforation. Even if the heart sounds disappear after they have been previously heard, the child may still be alive. In all doubtful cases, therefore, forceps are elected. However, if repeated observations establish the certainty of fetal death, a destructive operation rather than forceps should be done.

7. **The soft-parts must be manually dilated.** Extraction is facilitated and lacerations are minimized by preliminary manual dilatation of the perineum and pelvic floor. After lubricating the sterile gloved hands with tincture of green soap, the soft-parts of the outlet are ironed out in the manner shown in Fig. 917. This procedure must be carried out gently and slowly. In the average primipara, at least 10 minutes are required for its satisfactory completion. When properly done, it is bloodless and the introitus admits the folded fist. If episiotomy is contemplated, the amount of dilatation need not be so extensive. Whenever haste is required, a deep mediolateral episiotomy is indicated.

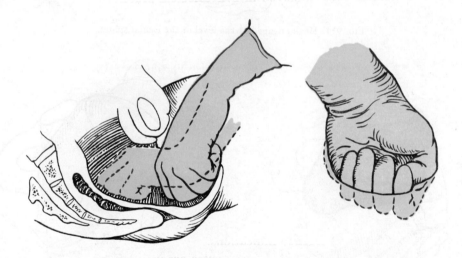

FIG. 917. Manual dilatation or "ironing out" of the perineum (Piper).

8. **The patient must be on a table.** The legs are held by assistants, or, if the latter are not available, stirrups or leg-holders are used. While in emergencies the operation may have to be done with the patient lying across the bed, the disadvantages of this method are so great that it should be avoided whenever possible.

9. **The patient must be anesthetized.**   Sufficient anesthetic is recommended to produce relaxation while the soft-parts are being dilated and during the application of the blades.   On the other hand, as traction is being made, the anesthesia is lightened to permit the return of uterine contractions, and is again deepened when the head is extended across the perineum.   Chloroform is ideal from the obstetric standpoint, but it is dangerous.   The statement that the pregnant woman is immune to the toxic effect of this drug is fallacious.   Its use, therefore, should be avoided unless a competent anesthetist is available.   Gas and ether or ethylene are very satisfactory, if given by a trained anesthetist.   Local anesthesia is adequate for most low forceps operations.   In our clinic, it is given the preference.   The technic of its administration is shown on page 306.

10. **Asepsis must be observed** in the preparation of the patient, the instruments, and the operator.   The technic used in the preparation of the patient should be as rigid as that employed in gynecological practice.   The pubic hair is clipped or shaved and, after being scrubbed with green soap and sterile water, the vulva is swabbed or sprayed with half strength tincture of iodine or 1–500 chlorothymol in 20 per cent alcohol.

The instruments are sterilized by boiling and the operator uses the same preoperative preparation as is used for a laparotomy.   This includes a careful scrubbing of the hands and the wearing of sterile gloves, a sterile gown and a mask which adequately covers the mouth and nose.

11. **The rectum must be empty.**   Usually, the enema recommended earlier in labor is sufficient.   If none has been given and time permits, a soapsuds enema should precede the operation.

12. **The bladder must be empty.**   All forceps cases should be catheterized with a **rubber** (never glass) catheter before the operation is commenced.

INDICATIONS.   The indication for forceps extraction are maternal or fetal, and are either time or emergency indications.

1. **Time indications.**   If all of the requisites are fulfilled and the patient has been in the second stage of labor for two hours without any advance of the presenting part, extraction with forceps is indicated.   This is particularly true when the head is well below the level of the ischial spines.   The common conditions which give rise to the time indication are uterine atony, early rupture of the membranes, posterior positions of the occiput, face presentation, large child and contracted pelvis.   These conditions in themselves are not the indication but they give rise to the delay which is the indication.   As an illustration: it may be stated that only those cases of occipitoposterior which are sufficiently delayed to fall within the time requirement noted are delivered with forceps, if the labor has progressed far enough to fulfill the requisites previously enumerated.

If the head has been in sight on the perineum for one hour, forceps should be applied since the prolonged pressure of the child's head against the pelvic floor is more injurious to its brain than the operation of low forceps required for its delivery.

2. **Maternal emergencies.** Any maternal emergency may justify extraction with forceps if the risk of such interference is less than the risk of waiting for a natural delivery. Some of these emergencies are: maternal exhaustion, cardiac failure, threatened rupture of the uterus, pneumonia, tuberculosis, and, rarely, placenta previa and accidental hemorrhage.

3. **Fetal emergencies.** Fetal embarrassment and prolapse of the umbilical cord are fetal emergencies that may require delivery with forceps.

Fetal embarrassment is detected by the following signs:

1. Irregular fetal heart.
2. Slow fetal heart—below 100 between uterine contractions.
3. Rapid fetal heart—above 160 between uterine contractions.
4. Passage of meconium in vertex presentation.
5. Deep cyanosis of the child's scalp.

At times, it requires rare judgment to decide whether to apply forceps for fetal embarrassment or to await spontaneous delivery. Of the signs mentioned, an irregular heart is the worst, and a slow one is almost as bad. When either or both of these are present, the child should be delivered as soon as possible. If the head is well below the level of the ischial spines even the novice may save the child's life by forceps extraction. On the other hand, when the head is at or near the level of the spines, the risk to the child is so great that interference is not justifiable. In such circumstances, it is better for the inexperienced man to leave the case to nature. Unnecessary injury to the mother will thus be avoided and she may, as a result, give birth to other children with the ease of a multipara. To lose the child is deplorable but it is worse to kill the child and wreck the mother in an effort to save a life that can be saved only by an expert.

A fetal heart rate above 160, and the passage of meconium are much less serious evidences of fetal embarrassment. Often, the fetus may live for hours after the first appearance of these signs. If the head is high, it therefore is better to allow labor to proceed in the hope that sufficient progress may follow and permit easy extraction should the fetal heart become slow or irregular.

Cyanosis of the scalp as the latter protrudes through the vulvovaginal orifice is an indication for an episiotomy with or without forceps extraction, since such a delivery can be effected with almost no risk to either the mother or the child.

Prolapse of the cord usually is better treated by other methods. Occasionally, however, extraction with forceps can be done rapidly enough to save the child.

CONTRAINDICATIONS to the use of forceps are: unengagement of the head, insufficient dilatation of the cervix, hydrocephalus, posterior face or brow presentations, and contracted pelvis.

VARIETIES OF FORCEPS.   Forceps applications are designated according to the level of the presenting part as floating, high, mid and low (Fig. 918).

When the instruments are applied to a head that is floating above the brim, the term **floating forceps** is used.   This variety is mentioned only that it may be condemned.

The term **high forceps** is applied to those cases in which the head is entering the pelvis but is not engaged, i.e., above the level of the ischial spines.   High forceps are difficult, cause great damage to the maternal soft parts, and are dangerous to the child.   For these reasons, other methods of delivery usually are to be preferred.

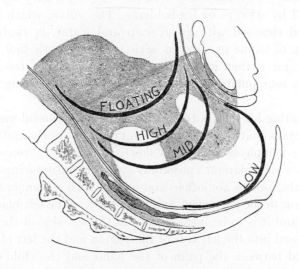

FIG. 918. Diagram showing the level of the head in floating, high, mid and low forceps.

If the head is at or near the level of the ischial spines, the procedure is known as a **mid forceps** operation.   Even this variety entails considerable risk if the operator is inexperienced and, whenever possible, the beginner will do well to postpone the use of instruments until further descent has occurred.

Application of the forceps to a head that is on the perineum or well below the spines, is known as **low forceps.**   This is the commonest variety and may be done with very little added risk to the mother or the child.

APPLICATIONS. Two types of applications are recognized: pelvic and cephalic.

A **pelvic application** is one in which the child's head is more or less disregarded and the blades are so applied that the pelvic curve is in relation to the parturient axis. It is the simplest variety but, at times, the ease of application is more than offset by the increased difficulty encountered in extracting a head that is grasped at a disadvantage.

Cephalic applications are those in which the blades are applied to the sides of the child's head in the most favorable manner, i.e., along the occipito mental diameter.

If the occiput has rotated to the symphysis, a pelvic application is also cephalic.

LOW FORCEPS—OCCIPITO-ANTERIOR. The patient is placed on a table in the dorsal position. Two assistants hold her legs, or, if they are not available, the legs are held by stirrups or leg-holders. The vulva, which has previously been shaved and cleansed with green soap and water, is swabbed with half strength tincture of iodine or sprayed with 1–500 chlorothymol in 20 per cent alcohol. Novocaine is then injected and at least five minutes are allowed to elapse before any manipulations are undertaken. While waiting, the bladder is catheterized.

After lubricating his fingers the operator makes a careful vaginal examination to make certain that the occiput has rotated anteriorly and has come into relation with the symphysis. He then slowly and gently "irons out" the peritoneum or does a mediolateral episiotomy. Before introducing the left blade into the vagina the forceps are locked and held in such a manner that the pelvic curve is in relation to the parturient axis (Fig. 919). The left blade will then be in his left hand and it is to be introduced into the left side of the vagina. The right hand is passed into the left side of the vagina and the left blade held like a pen is introduced between the palm of the hand and the child's head. With the internal hand it is then brought into relation with the ear (Fig. 920). The blade accordingly is applied along the occipito mental diameter (Fig. 921). After introducing the right blade in a similar manner (Fig. 922, 923) the forceps are locked and a tentative traction is made (Fig. 924, 925). Difficulty in locking the forceps indicates a faulty application and calls for their removal and reapplication. Failure of the head to advance with the tentative traction also indicates that something is wrong and shows the need for removal of the instruments and careful search for the difficulty. Such a search frequently will reveal that a mistake in diagnosis has been made. Often the occiput is found to be posterior or the outlet of the bony pelvis is contracted. The tentative traction thus will lead to the discovery of the difficulty before too much force is applied. If the tentative traction results in satisfactory progress intermittent tractions

are continued according to the method of Pajot in which one hand makes outward and upward traction while the other pulls in an outward and downward
direction (Fig. 926, 927). These tractions are made at intervals of one to two
minutes and between them the forceps are unlocked to relieve the pressure on
the child's head. The latter is also protected against compression by placing a
finger or folded towel between the handles while traction is being made.
Throughout the procedure the condition of the child is followed by listening to
the fetal heart in the intervals between tractions. After the occiput is brought

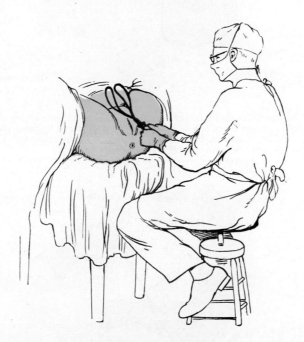

FIG. 919. Low forceps O.A. The operator seated on a stool locks the blades and holds them in
such a position that the pelvic curve is in relation to the parturient axis. The left blades is then in the
left hand and the right blade is in the right hand. After unlocking the forceps the right blade is laid
aside and the left one is ready for introduction into the vagina.

into view the tractions are made in an upward and outward direction to favor
extension of the head (Fig. 928, 929). As soon as the large fontanelle is delivered
over the fourchette the blades are removed in the reverse order to that in which
they were applied. The right one accordingly is removed first by directing its
handle outward towards the mother's left groin (Fig. 930, 931). The left blade is
then removed by lifting it outward in the direction of the right groin (Fig. 932,
933). The delivery of the head is completed by the modified Ritgen maneuver
(Fig. 934, 935).

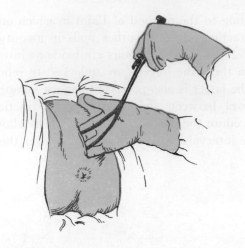

Fig. 920. Low forceps O.A.   Introduction of the left blade.   After passing the right hand into the left side of the vagina the left blade is held like a pen and introduced between the palm of the hand and the child's head.   With the internal hand it is then brought into relation with the ear.   The blade accordingly is applied along the occipito mental diameter.

Fig. 921. Low forceps O.A.   Introduction of the left blade.   Sagittal section showing the technic of applying the left blade along the occipito mental diameter.

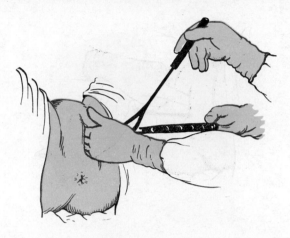

FIG. 922. Low forceps O.A. Introduction of right blade. The left hand is introduced on the right side of the vagina and the right blade held like a pen is passed posteriorly along the palm of the hand in the vagina. It then is applied to the side of the head along the occipito mental diameter. Difficulty in locking the blades indicates a faulty application and calls for their removal and reapplication.

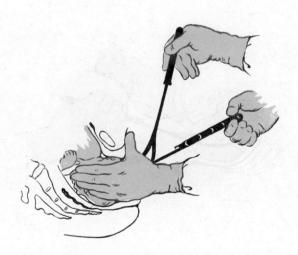

FIG. 923. Low forceps O.A. Introduction of right blade. Sagittal section.

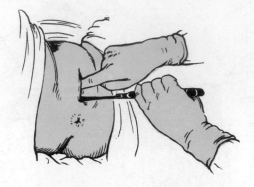

Fig. 924. Low forceps O.A.   Tentative traction.   After listening to the fetal heart sounds to rule out the possibility of pressure on the cord by the forceps a tentative traction is made.   If the head does not advance when the force used is equal to that which customarily results in advance something is wrong and the blades should be removed to permit a careful search for the cause of the difficulty.   It often will be found that a mistake has been made in the diagnosis and the occiput is in the hollow of the sacrum.   Likewise the outlet of the bony pelvis may be contracted.   In either circumstance art rather than force is indicated if injury to the child's head and the maternal soft parts is to be prevented.

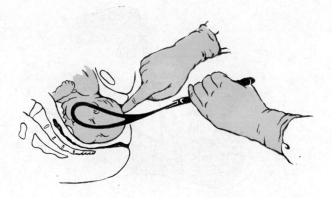

Fig. 925. Low forceps O.A.   Tentative traction.   Sagittal section.

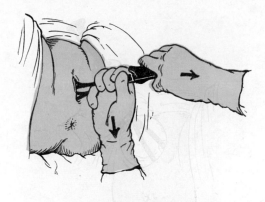

FIG. 926. Low forceps O.A. Pajot's maneuver. The left hand makes outward and upward traction while the right hand pulls in an outward and downward direction. The resultant of these forces draws the head along the parturient axis. Similar tractions are made at intervals of one to two minutes and between them the blades are unlocked to relieve the pressure on the child's head. The latter is also protected against compression by placing a finger or folded towel between the handles while traction is being made. Throughout the procedure the condition of the child is followed by listening to the fetal heart sounds in the interval between tractions.

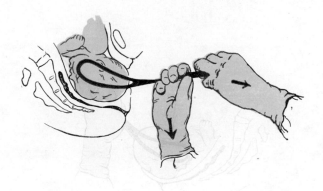

FIG. 927. Low forceps O.A. Pajot's maneuver. Sagittal section.

FIG. 928. Low forceps O.A. Extension of the head. After the occiput is brought into view the tractions are made in an upward and outward direction to cause extension of the head along the curve of Carus.

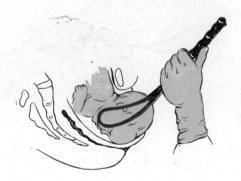

FIG. 929. Low forceps O.A. Extension of the head. Sagittal section.

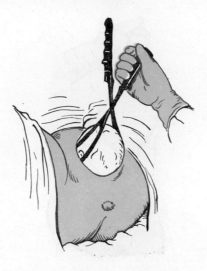

FIG. 930. Low forceps O.A. Removal of the right blade. The forceps are removed in the reverse order to that in which they were applied. The right one accordingly is removed first by directing its handle outward towards the mothers left groin.

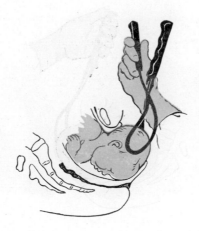

FIG. 931. Low forceps O.A. Removal of the right blade. Sagittal section.

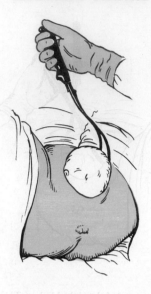

FIG. 932. Low forceps O.A. Removal of the left blade. This is accomplished by directing the handle towards the mother's right groin.

FIG. 933. Low forceps O.A. Removal of the left blade. Sagittal section.

FIG. 934. Low forceps O.A   Delivery of the head by the modified Ritgen maneuver.

FIG. 935. Low forceps O.A.   Delivery of the head by the modified Ritgen maneuver.   Sagittal section.

SUMMARY OF LOW FORCEPS O.A.

FIG. 936. Application of the left blade.

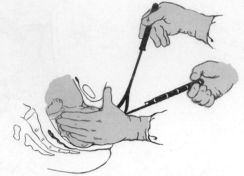

FIG. 937. Application of the right blade.

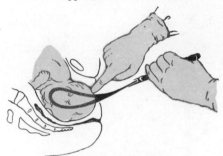

FIG. 938. Tentative traction.

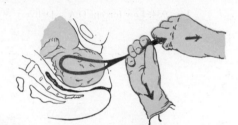

FIG. 939. Pajot's maneuver.

FIG. 940. Extension.

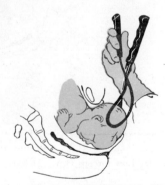

FIG. 941. Removal of the right blade.

FIG. 942. Removal of the left blade.

FIG. 943. Delivery of the head by Ritgen's maneuver.

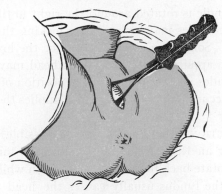

FIG. 944. Forceps L.O.A. The right hand is inserted into the left side of the vagina and locates the posterior ear. The left blade is passed posteriorly into the vagina along the palm of the right hand and is gently rotated so that it comes into relations with the ear. It then is applied along the occipito mental diameter and serves as a guide for the proper application of the right blade. The right blade is introduced in a similar manner and rotated anteriorly until the blades can be easily locked. If the application is properly made the concavity of the forceps looks towards the occiput and the instruments grasp the head along occipito mental diameter.

FIG. 945. Forceps L.O.A. Sagittal section. The concavity of the forceps is directed towards the occiput and the blades are applied to the head in relation to the occipito mental diameter.

FORCEPS EXTRACTION—L.O.A. If possible, the occiput should be rotated to the symphysis and the forceps applied as in O.A. When rotation cannot be brought about, the right hand is inserted into the left side of the vagina and the posterior ear is located. The left or lower blade is then passed posteriorly into the vagina along the palm of the right hand and is gently rotated so that it lies in relation to the occipitomental diameter, i.e., just in front of the ear (Figs. 944 and 945). This is the guide blade and is held in piace by an assistant. With the left hand in the vagina the right blade is introduced and rotated anteriorly until the blades can be easily locked. In this manner, a good cephalic application is made. The procedure from this point is the same as that described under O.A. extraction.

FORCEPS EXTRACTION—R.O.A. In R.O.A., the posterior ear is on the right side. Accordingly, the left hand is introduced into the right side of the vagina to locate this landmark. The right or upper blade, held in the right hand, is inserted and rotated so that it lies in front of the ear. The left blade is then introduced and its handle is rotated around the right until it becomes the lower one, in order that the blades may lock. After locking the blades, extraction is effected as in L.O.A. Some men always introduce the lower or left blade first. This is easier, but the application to the child's head may not be so good since the position of the blades is determined by the position of the sagittal suture, a method which is less accurate than the one which applies the first blade in relation to the posterior ear.

FORCEPS EXTRACTION—R.O.P. Whenever possible, the head should be rotated to an O.A. or an R.O.A. manually before the forceps are applied. If the occiput tends to rotate back to its original position while the blades are being applied, pressure on the fundus usually causes the head to remain in the new position until the blades can be applied.

When manual rotation is unsuccessful, the inexperienced man should call a more skilful operator to help him. Two procedures may be followed in such cases: the double application of the forceps, or manual rotation of the head to a transverse position, followed by an oblique application of the forceps. Either of these, when done by the expert, may be successful. In the hands of the unskilful, either may kill the child and seriously injure the mother.

DOUBLE APPLICATION TO R.O.P. (Scanzoni) (2, 3, 4). The right hand is passed into the vagina on the left side and locates the posterior ear, after which the left blade is applied along the occipitomental diameter. This is held by an assistant while the right blade is inserted on the opposite side and rotated anteriorly until the blades are in a position for locking. The forceps are thus applied to the sides of the child's head with the concavity of the pelvic curve looking toward the sinciput. Before being locked, they are gently depressed in order that they may grasp the head more nearly along the occipitomental diameter (Figs. 946 and 947). The blades are then locked and the handles are elevated to increase the flexion, after which they are swept through a large arc in order that the blades may be kept in the same axis (Figs. 948 and 949).

In the original Scanzoni maneuver, the original R.O.P. was rotated to R.O.A. (Figs. 950 and 951), after which the blades were reapplied and the remainder of the procedure was carried out as in the forceps extraction of R.O.A. (Figs. 952 and 953).

The chief exponents of the Scanzoni operation now recommend that the rotation be continued until the occiput is brought under the symphysis. The handles are then directed obliquely downward. Slight traction is made to prevent backward rotation when the blades are removed. The forceps are then reapplied for the new anterior position. During this step, it is essential to apply first that blade which corresponds to the side toward which the occiput was originally directed, as the application of the other blade may cause a recurrence of the posterior rotation. It also is recommended that no traction be made during the rotation of the head from a posterior to an anterior position.

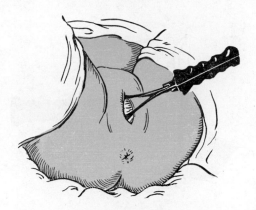

FIG. 946. Double application of forceps (Scanzoni) R.O.P.   The right hand introduced into the left side of the vagina locates the posterior ear.   The left blade is passed between the palm of the right hand and the child's head and is then rotated to a position in front of the ear.   It is to be the guide blade and is held in position by an assistant.   The right blade is introduced on the opposite side and is rotated anteriorly until the blades are in a good position for locking.   Before being locked the forceps are gently depressed in order that they may grasp the head more nearly along the occipito mental diameter.   They are then locked and the handles are elevated to increase the flexion.

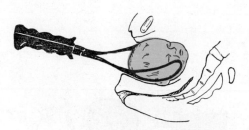

FIG. 947. Double application of forceps (Scanzoni) R.O.P.   Sagittal section.   The forceps are applied along the occipito mental diameter and the concavity of their pelvic curve looks anteriorly towards the brow and face.

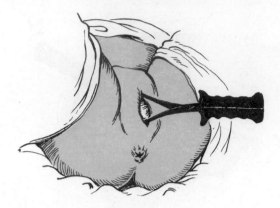

Fig. 948. Double application of forceps (Scanzoni) R.O.P. rotated to R.O.T. After locking the forceps and elevating their handles to increase flexion the latter are swept through a wide arc to the left and posteriorly. When the blades reach a horizontal position the head will have been rotated 45° and the sagittal suture will lie transversely. Note the wide arc through which the handles must pass in order that the blades may remain in the same axis.

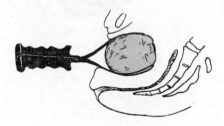

Fig. 949. Double application of forceps (Scanzoni) R.O.P. rotated to R.O.T. Sagittal section. The blades remain in relation to the occipito mental diameter but the concavity of their pelvic curve looks towards the left.

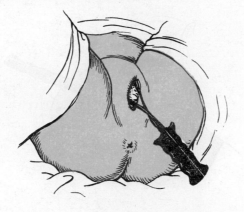

FIG. 950. Double application of forceps (Scanzoni) R.O.P.-R.O.T.-R.O.A. The downward sweep of the handles through a wide arc is continued until the forceps are upside down and the concavity of their pelvic curve points downward and to the left.   This brings the occiput into the right anterior quadrant.   Some obstetricians continue the rotation until the occiput is under the symphysis.

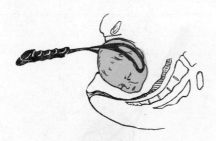

FIG. 951. Double application of forceps (Scanzoni) R.O.P.-R.O.T.-R.O.A. Sagittal section.   With the completion of the rotation the concavity of the pelvic curve of the forceps looks downward and to the left.

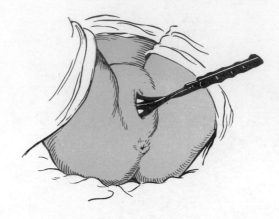

Fig. 952. Double application of forceps (Scanzoni) R.O.P.-R.O.A.-O.A. After removing the blades they are reapplied to the head in R.O.A.   The delivery is then completed as in forceps delivery of an R.O.A.

Fig. 953. Double application of forceps (Scanzoni) R.O.P.-R.O.A.-O.A. Sagittal section. Re-application of blades as in R.O.A.

Summary of Double Application of Forceps in R. O. P.

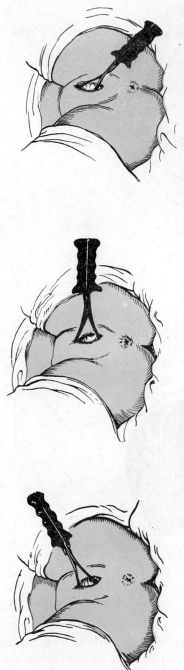

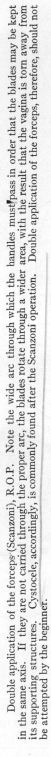

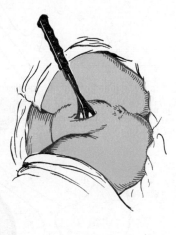

Double application of the forceps (Scanzoni), R.O.P. Note the wide arc through which the handles must pass in order that the blades may be kept in the same axis. If they are not carried through the proper arc, the blades rotate through a wider area, with the result that the vagina is torn away from its supporting structures. Cystocele, accordingly, is commonly found after the Scanzoni operation. Double application of the forceps, therefore, should not be attempted by the beginner.

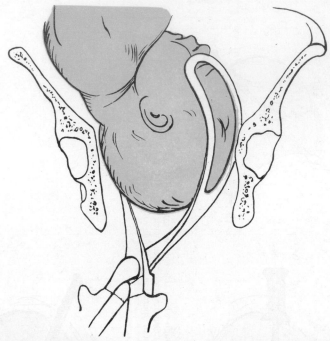

FIG. 954. Forceps oblique application R.O.P.-R.O.T. (Bumm). The head is rotated manually from R.O.P. to R.O.T. The left blade is then applied over the brow and the right blade to the vicinity of the mastoid. After each traction the blades are unlocked and again locked when the next traction is made. Slight rotation is accomplished with each traction so that the occiput finally comes to lie under the symphysis. The delivery is then completed as in O.A.

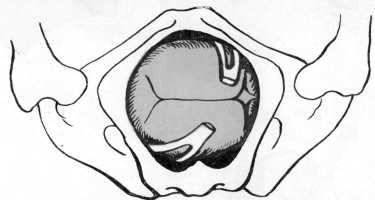

FIG. 955. Oblique application of forceps R.O.P.-R.O.T. Sagittal section. Left blade over brow anteriorly. Right blade over mastoid posteriorly.

OBLIQUE APPLICATION OF FORCEPS. It usually is possible to rotate an occipitoposterior manually into the transverse diameter, even though it cannot be brought forward into the anterior position. In these circumstances, the forceps may be applied obliquely to the fetal head as shown in Figures 954 and 955. After each traction, the blades are unlocked and again locked when the next traction is made. Often, the occiput is rotated to the symphysis in the course of these repeated tractions. While this method is more injurious to the child's head, in the hands of the beginner it does not cause the irreparable damage to the pelvic supporting structures that is certain to follow an inexpert attempt at the Scanzoni operation.

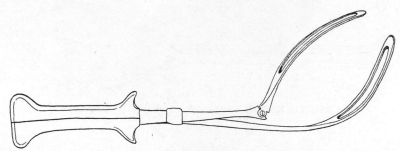

FIG. 956. The Barton forceps.

The Barton forceps (Fig. 956), are used in those cases in which the head is rather high and has not rotated beyond the transverse position (5). The anterior blade is hinged to the shank and is introduced up side down along the posterior aspect of the head. It is then rotated anteriorly into position beneath the symphysis. The posterior blade is passed into the posterior part of the vagina and

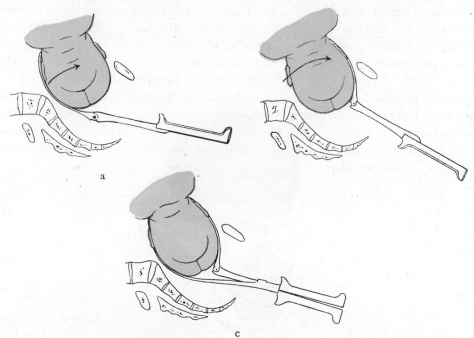

FIG. 957. Application of Barton forceps.   a. The anterior blade is introduced upside down along the posterior aspect of the head. b. The anterior blade is rotated into position beneath the symphysis.   c. The posterior blade is introduced and the forceps are locked.

applied to the posterior surface of the child's head. The sliding lock permits locking of the blades even though one may be higher than the other (Fig. 957). The head is brought down by means of the Pajot maneuver and is then rotated anteriorly.

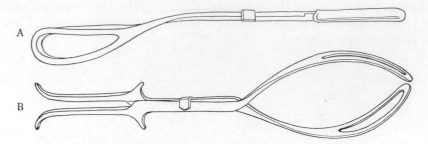

A

B

FIG. 958. The Kielland forceps.   A. Side view.   B. Front view.

The Kielland forceps (Fig. 958) also are recommended in the management of transverse positions of the occiput (6, 7).   This instrument has a very slight pelvic curve and is equipped with a sliding lock which facilitates the articulation of the blades.   After locating the posterior ear and determining the position of the occiput from it, the direction of the proposed rotation is decided upon. The anterior blade is then introduced into the side of the vagina and rotated anteriorly until it comes to lie beneath the symphysis.   Originally this blade was introduced upside down between the head and the symphysis and then rotated 180° to fit the anterior side of the child's head.   Because of the danger of rupturing the lower segment of the uterus by this maneuver the method described first is preferable.   The posterior blade is then applied to the posterior side of the child's head.   Even though one blade is higher than the other locking of the forceps is possible because of the sliding lock.   As traction is made and the head descends rotation usually occurs spontaneously.   If it does not the head is rotated with the forceps.   Like the Scanzoni operation extraction of the head with Kielland forceps requires more than ordinary skill and should not be attempted by the beginner.

FIG. 959. Forceps application in face presentation.   The blades are applied along the occipito mental diameter with the concavity of their pelvic curve looking forward.

FORCEPS EXTRACTION—FACE PRESENTATION. In face presentation the forceps are applied to the sides of the head along the occipito mental diameter with the concavity of their pelvic curve looking forward (Fig. 959). The extraction is accomplished by following the natural mechanism of anterior face cases. If the symphysis is unusually long some difficulty may be encountered and the head may have to be flexed into a vertex presentation. Because forceps rotation of posterior positions of the face causes extensive trauma and because forceps extraction without rotation is impossible the mentum must be manually rotated to an anterior position or the face must be converted to a vertex presentation before forceps are applied in all mentum posterior cases.

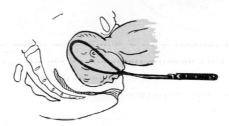

FIG. 960. Forceps applied to the after coming head. The blades are applied along the occipito mental diameter with the concavity of their pelvic curve looking forward.

FORCEPS EXTRACTION OF THE AFTERCOMING HEAD. Occasionally it is necessary to extract the after coming head with forceps. Forceps therefore should always be sterilized and ready for use whenever a breech extraction is done. When used for this purpose the blades are applied along the occipito mental diameter of the after coming head with the concavity of their pelvic curve locking forward (Fig. 960). Piper's forceps (Fig. 961, 962) are excellent instruments for this purpose and are used routinely in all breech cases by some obstetricians (8).

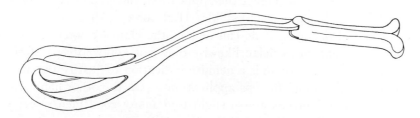

FIG. 961. Piper's forceps for the aftercoming head.

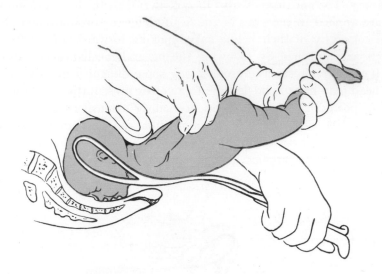

FIG. 962. Piper forceps applied to the aftercoming head while an assistant supports the trunk of the child.

PROGNOSIS.   The maternal dangers of forceps are trauma and infection.   In rare instances, the uterus may be ruptured, or the symphysis separated.   Often, the cervix is extensively torn and injury to the supporting apparatus of the pelvic organs may lead to prolapse of the uterus, cystocele and rectocele.   Forceps so commonly cause extensive tears of the perineum that prophylactic episiotomy is often done.

The fetal risks are: compression of the brain, fracture of the skull, cerebral hemorrhage, tentorial tears, paralysis of the facial nerve, and asphyxia due to compression of a partially prolapsed cord.   Loss of the child, accordingly, is not uncommon and an infant mortality of 3 to 10 per cent (9, 10) has been reported in large series of cases.   The higher the application, the greater is the possibility of serious injury to the mother and child.   High forceps, therefore, are avoided by even the skilful operator, if he can deliver the child by some other means (11).   The competent obstetrician likewise does not apply forceps at the level of the ischial spines unless there is a definite indication to justify the occasional poor result that follows mid forceps applications.   On the other hand, the risks which accompany low forceps are so slight that many good men resort to this procedure in a large proportion of their cases (12).

REFERENCES

1. Das: The Obstetric Forceps, Its History and Evolution. Calcutta, 1929.
2. Smellie, W.: A Treatise on the Theory and Practice of Midwifery. London, 1752.
3. Scanzoni, F. W.: Lehrbuch der Geburtshülfe. II Aufl. 1853, 838.
4. Bill, A. H.: Forceps Rotation of the Head in Persistent Occipito-posterior Positions. Am. J. O., 1918, 78, 791.
5. Barton, L. G., Caldwell, W. E. and Studdeford, W. E.: A New Obstetric Forceps. Am. J. O. & G., 1928, 15, 16.
6. Kielland, C.: Über die Anlegung der Zange am nicht rotierten Kopf mit Beschreibung eines neuen Zangemodelles und einer neuen Anlegungsmethode. Monatschr. f. Geburtsch. u. Gyn., 1916, 43, 48.
7. Eisenberg, C.: Erfahrungen mit der Kiellandschen Zange. Med. Klin., 1924, 20, 1694.
8. Piper, E. B. and Bachman, C.: The Prevention of Fetal Injuries in Breech Delivery. J. A. M. A., 1929, 92, 217.
9. Rittershaus, G.: Zangenfrequenz und Kindersterblichkeit. Monatschr. f. Geburtsch. u. Gyn., 1925, 69, 182.
10. Stander, H. J.: Practical Conclusions Drawn from One Thousand Forceps Deliveries. Johns Hopkins Hosp. Bull., 1930, 47, 323.
11. Baer, J. L., Reis, R. A. and Lutz, J. J.: The Present Position of Version and Extraction. Analysis of the Shifting Incidence of Version and Extraction, High Forceps and Cesarean Section at the Michael Reese Hospital. Am. J. O. & G., 1932, 24, 599.
12. Plass, E. D.: The Relation of Forceps and Cesarean Section to Maternal and Infant Morbidity and Mortality. Am. J. O. & G., 1931, 22, 176.

CHAPTER XLI

VERSION

VERSION or turning is the operation in which one pole of the fetus is substituted for the other, or for a transverse presentation.

Two varieties are described:

1. **Cephalic**—that which results in a cephalic presentation.

2. **Podalic**—that which results in a breech presentation.

According to the method used in the turning, versions also are designated as:

1. **External**—in which the turning is accomplished solely by external manipulations through the abdominal wall.

2. **Combined or bipolar**—in which the version is effected by the combined manipulations of one hand through the abdominal wall and two fingers within the uterus.

3. **Internal**—in which the child is turned largely by means of the whole hand within the uterus.

EXTERNAL VERSION

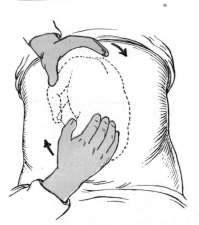

FIG. 963. External version. One hand is placed over the head and the other over the breech. In the interval between contractions and without anesthesia the head is turned in the direction of the occiput and the breech in the direction of the feet. If the manipulations cause pain they should be discontinued.

The term external version is applied to that method in which the turning is accomplished by external manipulations through the abdominal wall (Figs. 963, 964 and 965). It is the safest version.

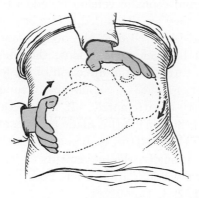

FIG. 964. External version. Should the uterus contract, the turning is discontinued but the child is prevented from returning to its original position; otherwise the turning is continued, the head being forced downward in the direction of the occiput and the breech upward in the direction of the feet.

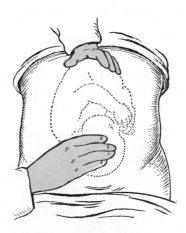

FIG. 965. External version. When the child is brought into relation with the long axis of the uterus the version is completed. After the completion of the version an effort is made to force the head into the pelvis and thereby prevent a recurrence of the previous presentation.

REQUISITES.

1. The membranes must be intact.

2. The presentation, position and posture must be known.

3. The presenting part must be above the brim of the pelvis.

4. All manipulations must be made in the intervals between uterine contractions.

INDICATIONS. External cephalic version is indicated in breech and transverse presentations when they are diagnosed before or early in labor.

TECHNIC. One hand is placed over the occiput and the other grasps the breech. In the interval between contractions, the presenting part is forced upward, and the head is turned in the direction of the occiput and the breech in the direction of the feet (Fig. 963). Should the turning be difficult, version in the opposite direction may be attempted. If the uterus contracts, all manipulations are discontinued, but an effort is made to prevent the child from returning to its original position (Fig. 964). As soon as the uterus is again relaxed, the turning is resumed. Occasionally, the movements of the fetus and thei uterine contractions complete the version, after it has been partially accompl shed by manual manipulations (1, 2, 3, 4).

Following the version, an effort is made to force the head into the pelvis in order that a recurrence of the original presentation may be prevented (Fig. 965). For the same reason, an abdominal binder with pads on one or both sides of the uterus is employed.

DANGERS. Premature separation of the placenta has been mentioned as a possible danger when external version is done. **If anesthesia is avoided** and the operator discontinues his attempts at version whenever the manipulations are difficult or painful, the risk of separating the placenta is negligible. Injury to the cord and interference with the uteroplacental circulation are, theoretically, possible, but they seldom occur in practice. The author has done many external versions for his students in the antepartum clinic without ever having observed any injurious effects.

BIPOLAR VERSION

COMBINED OR BIPOLAR VERSION is the procedure in which the turning is accomplished by the combined manipulations of one hand through the abdominal wall and two fingers within the uterus. It sometimes is referred to as the Braxton Hicks Version and is the most difficult of all versions.

TECHNIC. Two fingers are introduced into the cervix and displace the presenting part upward and toward the occiput, while the external hand turns the breech in the direction of the feet (Figs. 966 and 967). The external hand then forces the feet into the lower uterine segment (Fig. 968), where a foot is grasped. While traction is made on the foot, the head is pushed upward into the fundus of the uterus by the external hand (Fig. 969). Traction is continued until the knee reaches the vulva, when the version may be considered complete (Fig. 970).

When a transverse presentation is treated in this manner, either a bipolar cephalic or a bipolar podalic version may be done. In the former, the shoulder is forced in the direction of the breech, while in the latter, the turning is in the opposite direction. Since the membranes have ruptured in such transverse cases as are treated by bipolar version, it is preferable to bring down a foot in order that the possibility of recurrence of the original transverse presentation may be prevented (5, 6) (Figs. 971, 972, 973 and 974).

ADVANTAGES.

1. Bipolar version may be used after the presenting part has entered the pelvis.

2. It is of value early in labor, i.e., as soon as the cervix admits two fingers.

3. It renders version possible in many cases that are complicated by premature rupture of the membranes.

REQUISITES.

1. The patient must be on a table.

2. She must be **deeply** anesthetized.

3. The membranes must be intact or only recently ruptured.

4. The cervix must be sufficiently dilated to permit the passage of two fingers.

5. The presentation, position and posture must **positively** be known.

6. All aseptic precautions must be observed.

INDICATIONS.

1. Bipolar version is indicated in all transverse presentations in which the membranes rupture early.

2. It is recommended in certain cases of posterior positions of the face when the membranes rupture early.

3. Bipolar version is of great value in the treatment of placenta previa.

DANGERS.

1. There is a slight risk from the use of an anesthetic.

2. Introduction of the fingers into the uterus increases the chance of infection.

3. The uterus may be ruptured if the operation is not **skilfully** performed.

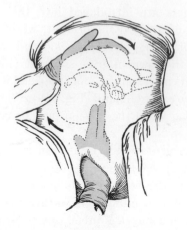

FIG. 966. Combined-bipolar version. The position of the back must be known; otherwise the operation should not be attempted. If necessary the location of the dorsum may be determined by abdominal palpation after the patient has been anesthetized. Two fingers of the hand which corresponds to the side towards which the dorsum is directed are introduced into the uterus and displace the head upward in the direction of the occiput. At the same time the breech is gently forced in the direction of the feet.

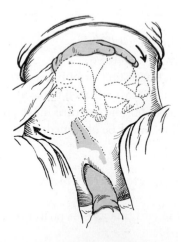

FIG. 967. Combined-bipolar version. If the uterus should contract the manipulations are discontinued until the contraction ceases, but an attempt is made to prevent the child from returning to its original position; otherwise the external hand makes pressure over the breech and forces the feet into the lower uterine segment.

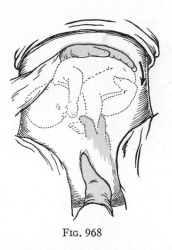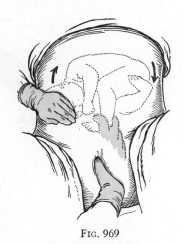

FIG. 968   FIG. 969

FIG. 968. Combined-bipolar version. Downward pressure over the buttocks forces a foot into the region of the internal os where it is grasped by the fingers of the internal hand.

FIG. 969. Combined-bipolar version. Traction is made on the foot while the external hand forces the head upward in the direction of the fundus.

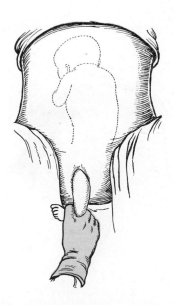

FIG. 970. Combined-bipolar version. If the cervix is sufficiently dilated traction is continued until the knee reaches the vulva. The version is then completed.

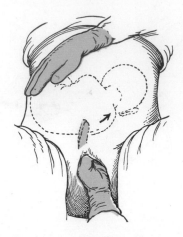

Fig. 971. Combined-bipolar version transverse presentation. Two fingers of the internal hand force the shoulder in the direction of the occiput. At the same time pressure on the breech assists in the turning.

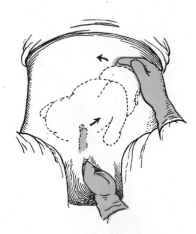

Fig. 972. Combined-bipolar version transverse presentation. As the head is forced in the direction of the fundus by the external hand the fingers of the internal hand search for a foot. The foot is differentiated from a hand by the projecting heel and by the fact that a line joining the tips of the toes would be straight whereas that joining the tips of the fingers would be curved.

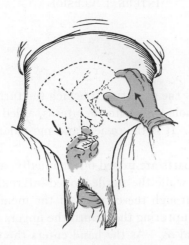

FIG. 973. Combined-bipolar version transverse presentation.   A foot is grasped and pulled down.
At the same time the external hand forces the head into the fundus of the uterus.

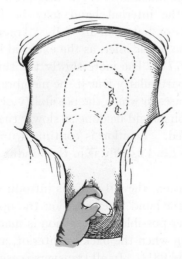

FIG. 974. Combined-bipolar version transverse presentation.   If the cervix is sufficiently dilated
traction is continued until the knee reaches the vulva.   The version is then completed.

INTERNAL VERSION

INTERNAL VERSION is the operation in which the turning is accomplished by the introduction of the whole hand into the uterus, aided by external manipulations with the other hand. It is the easiest and most dangerous of the versions (7, 8, 9, 10).

TECHNIC.   The soft parts are ironed out manually, after which the external hand steadies the fundus, while the sterile-gloved internal hand, lubricated with an antiseptic, is passed through the cervix. If the membranes are intact, care should be taken to avoid rupturing them until the fingers have passed some little distance above the internal os. As the hand enters the uterus, the head is displaced upward and in the direction of the occiput (Fig. 975). The hand chosen for the internal manipulations usually corresponds to the side on which the back is found, i.e., when the back is on the left side, the left hand is used. Should the uterus contract, it is advisable to discontinue all manipulations until it again relaxes. The internal hand searches for one or both feet, and the operator must be certain that he is grasping a foot before the turning is commenced (Fig. 976). Little difficulty will be experienced in this regard if he remembers that the tips of the toes are on a straight line and that the heel projects posteriorly from the foot. If he is in doubt, the internal hand may be introduced farther into the uterus until the thighs or buttocks are felt. Traction on the feet is now made in the direction of the pelvic inlet, as the external hand displaces the head toward the fundus (Fig. 977). The more slowly the turning is done, the safer is the operation. This is particularly true if the membranes have been ruptured over one hour. In those cases in which the possibility of rupture of the uterus is to be considered, the version should be done so slowly that the movements of the arm can hardly be observed. Traction is continued until the knees appear at the vulva; at this time the head usually is in the fundus and the version is completed (Fig. 978).

In transverse presentation, the left hand is introduced when the head is on the right side, and the right hand when it is on the opposite side. Both feet should be grasped whenever possible. If traction is made on only one foot, the lower foot should be chosen when the back is anterior, and the upper when it is posterior (Figs. 979, 980 and 981). In all transverse cases, the turning should be done very slowly and the manipulations of the head by the external hand should be carried out with the greatest care. Whenever the arm is prolapsed, it should not be replaced until a fillet has been attached to the wrist to prevent extension.

ADVANTAGES.

1. Internal version can be done in circumstances in which external or bipolar version is impossible.

2. Recognition of the foot is much easier when the operator's hand is introduced into the uterus.

3. Grasping one or both feet in the hand greatly facilitates the turning.

4. It is the easiest and best means of delivering a child when the head is high and the passages are fully dilated.

REQUISITES.

1. The patient must be on a table.

2. The bladder must be catheterized.

3. The rectum must be empty.

4. The presentation, position and posture must be known.

5. The cervix must be large enough to permit the passage of the whole hand.

6. The pelvis must be ample for the passage of the aftercoming head.

7. The patient must be **deeply** anesthetized.

8. Rigid asepsis must be followed.

9. The child must be alive.

INDICATIONS.

1. Transverse presentation.

2. Posterior positions of the face that have recurred after they have been flexed or rotated anteriorly.

3. Rarely, in compound presentations in which the arm is prolapsed below the head.

4. Delivery of the second child in twins if it has failed to reach the level of the ischial spines within an hour after the birth of the first child.

5. Uterine inertia, causing the head to remain above the level of the ischial spines for two and a half hours after the cervix has been fully dilated. **Disproportion must be ruled out in all of these cases before version is attempted.**

6. Maternal emergencies in which the presenting part is high, the cervix is fully dilated and the mother's condition demands immediate delivery, as in accidental hemorrhage, pneumonia, cardiac failure, etc.

7. Fetal emergencies in which the head is high and the cervix is fully dilated, as in prolapse of the umbilical cord.

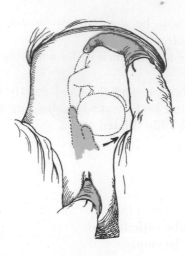

FIG. 975. Internal version. The external hand steadies the uterus while the internal hand is introduced and displaces the head upward and in the direction of the occiput.

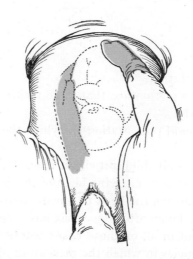

FIG. 976. Internal version. The internal hand searches for one or both feet. The foot is differentiated from the hand by the presence of the projecting heel and by the fact that a line joining the tips of the toes would be straight in contradistinction to the curved line which would join the tips of the fingers.

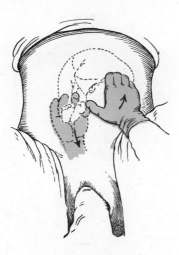

FIG. 977. Internal version.   After grasping both feet with the internal hand **gentle** traction is made in the direction of the pelvic inlet while the external hand forces the head in the direction of the fundus.

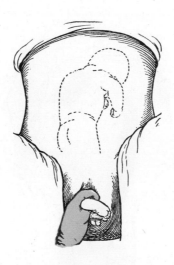

FIG. 978. Internal version.   Traction is continued until the knees are out.   The version is then completed.

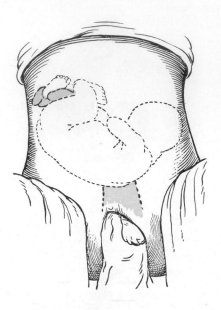

FIG. 979. Internal version transverse presentation L.Sc.A. The internal hand is introduced posteriorly behind the child's body and grasps the lower foot. When the back is posterior, the anterior foot is chosen.

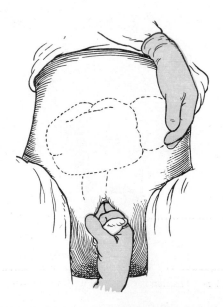

FIG. 980. Internal version transverse presentation L.Sc.A. Gentle traction is made on the posterior foot while the external hand forces the head towards the fundus.

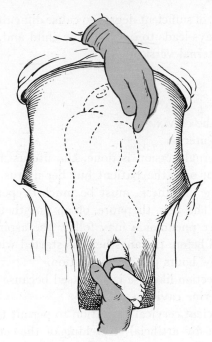

FIG. 981. Internal version transverse presentation L.Sc.A.   Traction on the foot is continued until the knee appears at the vulva.   The version is then completed.

CONTRAINDICATIONS.
1. Membranes ruptured too long.
2. Spastic uterus.
3. A high retraction ring.
4. Contracted pelvis.
5. Hydrocephalus.

Internal version is easiest when the membranes are ruptured in the course of the procedure, or when the operation is done immediately after they rupture spontaneously.   For this reason, the beginner should not attempt a version in any case in which the membranes have been ruptured over one hour.   If the membranes have been ruptured more than one hour and the indication for version arises, he should seek the assistance of a more skilful man, whose experience will enable him to decide whether the turning can be done without risk.

A spastic uterus makes version difficult or impossible and frequently is the cause of its rupture.   If the tight uterus cannot be relaxed by deep anesthesia and adrenalin, a version should not be done.

A high retraction ring indicates excessive thinning of the lower uterine segment.   When the ridge which marks the retraction ring is felt near the level of the umbilicus, version is distinctly contraindicated.

Contracted pelvis, of sufficient degree to cause difficulty in the delivery of the aftercoming head, always leads to death of the child and, for this reason, it is a contraindication to internal version.

DANGERS.

1. Anesthesia.
2. **Infection.**
3. Laceration of the cervix.
4. **Rupture of the uterus.**

Whenever an internal version is done, the uterus must be completely relaxed. Accordingly, not only the patient but her uterus must be anesthetized. To accomplish this, the anesthesia must be much deeper than is necessary for ordinary operations. The risk, therefore, of an anesthetic accident is great in internal version. Since pneumonia may follow the aspiration of vomitus, gastric lavage is indicated before the anesthetic is started whenever the patient has taken food within a few hours prior to operation.

The danger of infection likewise is increased because the hand is carried to a high level in the uterine cavity.

The need for sufficient cervical dilatation to permit the passage of the hand frequently is overcome by artificial stretching of the cervix. In such circumstances, the cervix usually does not stretch, but tears.

Delivery by version and extraction is so easy that this method often is chosen when the uterus is too tight, the lower segment too thin, or the child too large. It accordingly is responsible for many cases of rupture of the uterus. In fact, internal version probably causes more ruptured uteri than all other obstetric operations, excepting labor following a previous cesarean section.

REFERENCES

1. WIGAND, J. H.: Über Wendung durch äussere Handgriffe. Hamb. Med. Mag., 1807, 1 52.
2. PINARD, A.: De la version par les manoeuvres externes. Traite du palper abdominal. Paris, 1889.
3. GIBBERD, G. F.: An Investigation into the Results of Breech Labor and of Prophylactic External Cephalic Version During Pregnancy; with a Note on the Technic of External Version. J. O. & G., Brit. Emp., 1927, 34, 509.
4. BARTHOLOMEW, R. A.: Prophylactic External Version. Am. J. O. & G., 1927, 14, 648.
5. WRIGHT, M. B.: Difficult Labors and Their Treatment. Tr. Ohio Med. Soc., 1854, 59.
6. HICKS, J. B.: On Combined External and Internal Version, London, 1864.
7. PARE, A.: Edition Malgaigne, 1840, III, p. 623.
8. GUILLEMEAU: De l'heureux accouchement des femmes. Paris, 1609.
9. MAURICEAU, F.: Le moyen d'accoucher la femme, quand l'enfant presente un ou deux pieds les premiers. Traite des maladies des femmes grosses. 6 mc. ed., 1721, p. 280.
10. POTTER, I. W.: Version. Am. J. O. & G., 1921, 1, 560.

CHAPTER XLII

CESAREAN SECTION

Abdominal cesarean section is the operation in which the child is delivered through an incision in the abdominal wall and uterus.

Four types of operation are used:

1. Classical cesarean section (The Sänger Operation).
2. Transperitoneal low cesarean section with extraperitoneal closure (The Krönig Operation).
3. Extraperitoneal cesarean section (The Latzko and Waters Operations).
4. Cesarean section followed by hysterectomy (The Porro Operation).

Throughout the ages cesarean section has been one of the most dangerous of all operations. Usually it was considered as a last resort measure and was done only on those women who were certain to die. After the patient had been in labor several days, after the membranes had been ruptured many hours and after many vaginal examinations had been made, the midwife, having exhausted her resources, called in the crude surgeon of the times (1). If the latter individual had sufficient courage he would do a cesarean section with the result that almost 100% of the mothers died. When the medical profession took over the practice of surgery, surgical technic was greatly improved. In spite of this improvement however, cesarean section continued to be a very dangerous operation and up to 100 years ago over 75% of the mothers were lost (2). There are recorded a number of instances in which women were delivered suprapubically as a result of having been gored by a bull and strange as it may seem the results in these accidental cesarean sections which were done by the bull were better than those performed by man since only 40% of the mothers died (3). Are we to conclude from these better results that the bull's horns could make a better incision than the surgeon's scalpel, or that the barnyard was a more suitable operating room than the patient's home? Certainly not. They were due to the fact that the bull unconsciously used better judgment in the selection of his patients. His patients were not dehydrated and starved and exhausted by long labors. In them the cervix was not dilated; the membranes had not ruptured; and no vaginal examinations had been made. In other words the patients were in good general condition and the birth passages were not potentially infected prior to operation.

Some of the fatal cases died of shock. Others who survived the shock, died of hemorrhage. Most of them, however, succumbed to peritonitis. Although bacteriology and asepsis were unknown at that time, the bad results from cesarean section cannot be ascribed entirely to the lack of an aseptic technic since the same surgeons who lost 75% of their cesarean sections were able to do laparotomy for ovarian cyst with a mortality of only 33% (4). Some other factor accordingly must have contributed to the cesarean section mortality. This factor was the open wound in the uterus through which the lochia drained backward into the peritoneal cavity. Because of this factor cesarean section continued to be a most dangerous procedure until Eduardo Porro in 1876 removed the uterus following cesarean section and fixed the cervical stump into the lower angle of the abdominal wound (5). With this technic, drainage of the lochia back into the abdominal cavity was eliminated and the mortality dropped to 20% (6). Unfortunately the Porro operation sacrificed the uterus. Shortly thereafter Kehrer and Sänger devised a method of suturing the uterine wound which prevented the back flow of lochia without the removal of the uterus (7). With the use of these improvements the indications for cesarean section were considerably broadened and its advantages and disadvantages became better understood. It soon was evident that the safe time for performing the operation was **before the onset of labor, before the membranes had ruptured** and **before any vaginal examinations had been made.** As a result of this knowledge some men reported 50, 60 and even 100 cases without a death. When the safe period was ignored however, and the operation was done long after the onset of labor, after the membranes had been ruptured many hours and after a number of vaginal examinations had been made the mortality remained at its former high figure. The difference between the results of operating during the safe period and those of operating in the unsafe one were so great that Schauta formulated the dictum that no cesarean section should be performed for a first child. He suggested that every patient with disproportion be given a thorough test of labor in which the cervix should be allowed to become fully dilated and the patient should have several hours of good second stage pains after the membranes had ruptured. If spontaneous delivery failed to occur after this test of labor, delivery was to be effected from below in every instance even though such a delivery required a destructive operation. Whenever the need for a destructive operation was thus demonstrated all subsequent full term children were to be delivered by elective cesarean section, before the onset of labor, before the membranes had ruptured and without making any vaginal examinations.

While the Schauta dictum was quite satisfactory from the standpoint of the mother it caused the unnecessary loss of many first babies and as a result further attempts were made to improve the technic of the operation. Because the usual cause of death in those women who were operated upon during the unsafe period was peritonitis these efforts naturally were directed toward the prevention of this complication. Since peritonitis might result from the spilling of amniotic fluid at the time of operation or from the subsequent breaking down of the repaired wound in the uterus a true extraperitoneal technic was sought. Soon after the turn of the century such a technic was devised by Frank, Sellheim and Latzko (8, **9, 10**). Because of the difficulty of its performance and believing that the danger from the spilling of amniotic fluid was of minor importance, others made the incision in the uterus through the cervix and isthmus and covered it with previously prepared flaps of peritoneum (11, 12, 13, 14). The latter technic was essentially a transperitoneal operation with a closure of the uterine wound which became extraperitoneal within 24 hours. This procedure protected the patient against peritonitis which might occur as a result of the opening up of an infected uterine wound and greatly improved the results of cesarean section. Its use is accompanied by a mortality of less than 1% when the operation is done in the safe period under local anesthesia. It also permits a considerable trial of labor without much additional risk. When such an operation is done within 16 hours of the onset of labor and within 4 hours of the rupture of the membranes the mortality should not exceed 2% if no vaginal examinations are made. While this improved technic has added greatly to the safety of cesarean section it has fallen considerably short of our expectation in the neglected cases. When the operation is done after 24 hours of labor, after the membranes have been ruptured many hours and after a number of vaginal examinations have been made a much higher mortality must be expected. Because of this high mortality the low transperitoneal cesarean section is contraindicated in the badly neglected cases. For them either a true extraperitoneal procedure as recommended by Latzko or Waters is worthy of consideration or the uterus should be removed following the simple classical operation (10, 15, 16).

INDICATIONS. The simplicity of the classical cesarean section has lead to much abuse with the result that the operation is done for questionable indications. Suprapubic delivery, however, may be indicated in certain cases of the following:

1. Contracted pelvis.
2. Pelvic tumors.
3. Abnormal presentations.
4. Postoperative dystocia.
5. Placenta previa.
6. Accidental hemorrhage.
7. Grave systemic diseases.
8. Fulminating toxemia.
9. Weak scar from previous cesarean section or operation on the uterus.
10. Fetal distress particularly in elderly primiparae.

Contracted Pelvis. Because a child of normal size has but slight chance of being born alive through the natural passages when the **diagonal conjugate is 9.5 cm. or less,** cesarean section should be done as an elective operation at or slightly before the onset of labor in all pelvic contractions of this degree. If the disproportion is not recognized until after the onset of labor the low transperitoneal section with extraperitoneal closure should be the method of choice unless the labor has been long or many hours have elapsed after the membranes have ruptured or a number of vaginal examinations have been made. In the latter circumstances the patient is considered infected or potentially infected and the risk is too great for the classical or low flap operations. Either a true extraperitoneal procedure or the classical technic followed by hysterectomy or a destructive operation is then indicated. Should a bad result follow any of these procedures, as it well may, the blame properly rests with the original attendant who was responsible for the neglect rather than with the obstetric surgeon who attempted to help him out of his difficulties. In extremely rare instances in which a true conjugate below 5.5 cm. makes delivery by a destructive operation impossible, cesarean section is imperative regardless of the presence of contra-indicating circumstances. A true conjugate of 5.5 cm. therefore, is considered an **absolute indication** for suprapubic delivery in contradistinction to the **relative indication** which is said to exist when lesser degrees of contraction cause sufficient dystocia to justify the use of cesarean section but in which delivery by craniotomy would be possible.

Whenever the **diagonal conjugate is over 9.5 cm.** the possibility of delivery through the natural passages is sufficient to warrant a trial of labor. If at any time in the course of this trial labor examination indicates that the head will not come through the pelvis a low transperitoneal section with extraperitoneal closure should be done. The decision to operate or to await delivery through the natural passages must be made before the safe period for cesarean section has passed, i.e., within 16 hours of the onset of labor and within 4 hours of the rupture of the membranes. Naturally the nearer the measurement is to the 9.5 cm. figure, the easier it is to make an early decision. Because the more exact roentgen ray methods enable us to make more accurate measurements of the pelvis and fetal head and because they show the true cephalopelvic relationships their use should be helpful in determining whether or not suprapubic delivery is indicated. On the other hand, such findings are open to misinterpretation unless they are studied by one who is experienced in the special field of obstetric roentgenology. Even when they are properly interpreted in border line cases a trial of labor often is necessary before the decision can be made. Rarely cesarean section is done for contraction at the pelvic outlet. Further information concerning the details of this indication are to be found in the discussion of the treatment of contracted pelvis.

Pelvic Tumors. A large fibromyoma in the lower uterine segment or cervix may obstruct the passages and require delivery by cesarean section. Because such a tumor interferes with postoperative drainage from the uterus, hysterectomy also is indicated unless the tumor can be removed by myomectomy. The passages also may be blocked by a cystic or solid **tumor of the ovary.** Suprapubic delivery accordingly is indicated in such cases and the possibility of rupture of the cyst makes early operation imperative. The low flap technic is used before or soon after the onset of labor and following delivery the tumor is removed to prevent interference with drainage from the uterus. Whenever pregnancy is complicated by **carcinoma of the cervix** the child should be delivered by a classic cesarean section as a preliminary to thorough irradiation. If infection is present hysterectomy should follow the section.

Dystocia from Abnormal Presentations. Occasionally a **neglected posterior face** or **transverse presentation** is best treated by a cesarean section. This is particularly true when the child is alive and the danger from a destructive operation seems to be as great as is that of suprapubic delivery. Because such cases usually are infected or potentially infected the uterus should be removed. Cesarean section may also be indicated **in the elderly primipara who has a breech presentation** especially if the child is large.

Postoperative Dystocia. If the **uterus is fixed to the abdominal** wall as a result of a previous operation the cervix may be displaced posteriorly and come to lie in the region of the promontory. The dystocia thus produced usually makes it necessary to deliver the child by cesarean section. Following operation the abnormal condition of the uterus does not favor good drainage. For this reason and for the purpose of sterilization the uterus should be removed. **Cervical stenosis** resulting from a high amputation or excessive cauterization sometimes requires suprapubic delivery. In such circumstances, hysterectomy should follow the classic technic because the stenosed cervix does not permit good postoperative drainage of the lochia. For further information regarding this indication the reader is referred to the discussion of dystocia in Chapter 29.

Placenta Previa. Cesarean section is being used more and more frequently in the treatment of placenta previa. Because it offers the best chance for the survival of the child it should be the method of choice whenever an elderly primigravida has this complication. It likewise is the method of choice in **central placenta previa** and is recommended in those cases of **partial placenta previa in which the cervix is long and closed.** Whenever cesarean section is done for placenta previa preoperative transfusion is indicated in the interests of both the mother and the child.

Accidental Hemorrhage. Some obstetricians recommend the use of cesarean section in most cases of accidental hemorrhage. Although we prefer the conservative routine described in Chapter 32, suprapubic delivery under local anesthesia is resorted to **whenever the cervix is long and closed** as well as in the occasional instance in which the conservative routine fails to control the bleeding. Occasionally uteroapoplexy may interfere with hemostasis at the placental site and thus require the removal of the uterus.

Grave Systemic Diseases. In certain systemic diseases the risk of cesarean section may be less than the risk of delivery through the natural passages. **Following a break in compensation complicating mitral stenosis** cesarean section occasionally is indicated. This is especially true in primiparae in whom the dilatation of the cervix does not progress satisfactorily. It must be remembered, however, that no operative procedure should be done until the patient has recovered from the decompensation.

Fulminating Toxemia. Although cesarean section is a dangerous method of delivery when the toxemia has reached the stage of convulsions, the uterus sometimes is emptied in this manner before convulsions occur in certain cases of fulminating toxemia. If the symptoms of toxemia progress rapidly in spite of treatment and it seems apparent that convulsions will occur before the uterus can be emptied from below, cesarean section under local anesthesia sometimes is an excellent method of terminating the pregnancy before the onset of convulsions.

Weak Uterine Scar. A weak uterine scar following a previous cesarean section or any other operation on the uterus is an indication for suprapubic delivery. Whenever in the course of pregnancy a thin scar in the uterus can be detected by abdominal palpation the patient should not be allowed to go into labor but should be delivered before its onset by cesarean section. If the previous operation was complicated by infection the wound in the uterus should not be trusted and a cesarean section should be done before labor begins.

Fetal Distress. In certain instances of fetal distress and prolapse of the cord in which the complication cannot be handled satisfactorily from below, cesarean section is sometimes considered in the interest of the child. This is particularly true when the mother is an **elderly primipara.** When a woman who is pregnant for the first time has Rh negative blood and her husband's blood is Rh positive, cesarean section may be indicated in the interest of the child whenever fetal distress is present and this procedure seems to be the safest method of delivery for the child. Often, in such cases, all subsequent pregnancies end in abortion, or stillbirth, or the birth of infants with erythroblastosis who die soon after they are born.

CLASSICAL CESAREAN SECTION

In the classical or Sänger cesarean section the abdomen is entered through a median or paramedian incision. The uterus is incised in the midline and the child usually is delivered feet first. After removing the placenta manually the uterine wound is closed with catgut sutures. Regardless of the method of closure all deep sutures are passed down to but not into the endometrium and an attempt is made to peritonealize the wound by careful approximation of its peritoneal edges with a continuous catgut suture. Details of the technic used in our clinic are shown in figures 982, 983, 984, 985.

Because the classical section does not require the removal of the uterus it formerly was also known as the conservative cesarean section in contradistinction to the Porro operation in which the uterus was sacrificed. Since the transperitoneal low cesarean section and the typical extraperitoneal operations also conserve the uterus the term conservative is confusing and should not be applied to the Sänger operation exclusively.

There are several variations of the classical technic. The location of the abdominal incision usually is determined by the proposed site of the uterine incision. When the incision in the uterus is high, as was customary in former times, two-thirds of the abdominal wound is above and one-third below the umbilicus. Today most obstetricians prefer to make the incision in the uterus as low as possible. The abdominal incision accordingly, is now made entirely below the umbilicus. Some operators use continuous, others interrupted sutures for the closure of the uterine wound. We prefer interrupted sutures and introduce them while we are waiting for the placenta to separate. The normal retraction of the uterus is thereby favored and the danger of hemorrhage from the placental site is greatly diminished. After the interrupted sutures are placed, the wound is separated and the placenta is removed between two of the sutures.

The **advantages** of the classical operation are:

1. It is the simplest of all the cesarean section technics.

2. It can be done more quickly than any other type of operation.

For these reasons it should be the method of choice whenever the condition of the patient makes the duration of the operation an important factor.

The **disadvantages** of the classical operation are:

1. The risk of hemorrhage is greater than in the low transperitoneal section.

2. Distention and postoperative discomfort also are more frequent.

3. There is greater danger of peritonitis should infection be present in the uterus.

4. Postoperative adhesions are not uncommon.

5. There is greater danger of rupture of the uterine scar in subsequent pregnancy and labor.

Because of the danger of peritonitis in potentially infected cases the classical technic should be restricted to those in which the operation is done as an elective procedure before or soon after the onset of labor while the membranes are still intact or have recently ruptured and without any vaginal examinations or manipulations having been made.

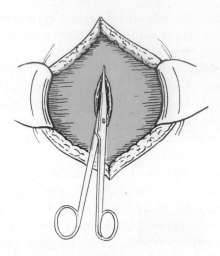

Fig. 982. Classical cesarean section.   The abdomen is entered through a left paramedian incision about five inches long which extends from the symphysis almost to the umbilicus.   As a prophylaxis against hemorrhage 1 cc. of posterior pituitary extract is given before the uterus is opened.   After walling off the abdominal cavity with laparotomy pads a small stab wound is made through the entire uterine wall.   This is then enlarged with scissors until it is ample for the extraction of the child.

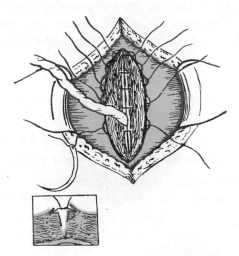

Fig. 983. Classical cesarean section.   The whole hand is introduced into the uterus and the child is extracted feet first.   If there is no bleeding the child is held by the feet for a short time to permit fluid to drain from the nasopharynx and to allow it to take up as much blood as possible from the placental circulation.   The cord is then clamped and cut and the child is turned over to an assistant who is familiar with the methods of resuscitation.   If the incision does not pass through the placental site very little hemorrhage takes place until the placenta separates.   While waiting for its separation interrupted chromic catgut sutures are passed from the peritoneal covering of the uterus through its entire muscular wall down to but not including the endometrium.   These sutures are placed about 1.5 cm. apart and their ends are left long so that they may be clamped and held out of the way by an assistant.

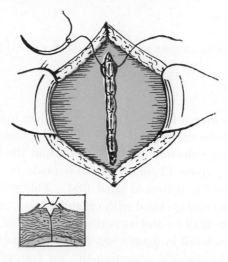

FIG. 984. Classical cesarean section. After all of the deep sutures have been introduced the edges of the wound are separated and the hand is passed into the uterine cavity between the two sutures which are adjacent to the cord. The placenta is then separated and removed. The introduction of the deep sutures before the placenta separates affords time for the uterus to become retracted and thus greatly lessens the risk of hemorrhage from the placental site. Following the removal of the placenta the sutures are tied and a second layer of more superficial sutures is then introduced.

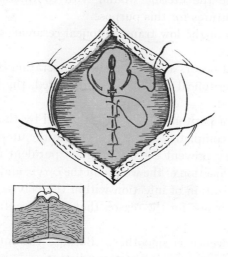

FIG. 985. Classical cesarean section. The peritoneal edges are approximated by a running lock stitch of fine plain catgut.

LOW TRANSPERITONEAL CESAREAN SECTION WITH EXTRAPERITONEAL CLOSURE

The abdomen is entered through a left paramedian incision about five inches long. This extends from the symphysis almost to the umbilicus. After separating the bladder and its reflection of peritoneum from the lower uterine segment and cervix an incision about 12 cm. in length is made in the midline of the denuded area. The child is delivered head first. Following the removal of the placenta the uterine wound is closed with catgut sutures, and extraperitonealized by covering it with the bladder and its peritoneal reflection. The technic used in our clinic is shown in detail in figures 986 to 1008 inclusive.

As was true of the classical operation the low transperitoneal cesarean section has several modifications. In addition to the single bladder reflection flap which is used to cover the wound in the uterus, an upper flap of peritoneum also is sometimes utilized in order that the upper angle of the uterine wound may be covered by a double layer of peritoneum. A transverse or semilunar incision in the uterus also may be employed in place of the original midline uterine incision. Some operators close the uterine wound with continuous while others prefer interrupted catgut sutures for this purpose.

The **advantages** of the low transperitoneal cesarean section with extraperitoneal closure are (13):

1. Any spill that occurs at the time of the operation is confined to the lower abdomen. If the peritoneal cavity is contaminated, the infection, is less liable to become generalized.

2. The danger of peritonitis is also diminished by the fact that the bladder and peritoneal flaps completely seal the wound in the uterus. Should the latter become infected, they prevent the discharge of purulent material into the peritoneal cavity. The location of the wound in the cervix and lower uterine segment likewise favors localization of infection within the pelvis.

3. Hemorrhage is less for the reason that the placental site usually is above the line of incision.

4. The convalescence is smoother. Because the intestines and omentum seldom are seen in a low cesarean section, distention is infrequent.

5. Abdominal adhesions are minimized by the low situation of the uterine wound and its more perfect peritonealization.

6. The scar in the uterus is stronger and rupture in subsequent pregnancies and labors seldom occurs. Because the incision is in the passive segment, the wound heals better than when it is in the contractile portion of the uterus.

The **disadvantages** of the low transperitoneal cesarean section with extra-peritoneal closure are:

1. The low operation is somewhat more difficult than the classical technic.
2. It also requires a slightly longer time than the classical operation.

Because of its many advantages and because the added difficulties are easily mastered the low transperitoneal cesarean section with extraperitoneal closure is preferable in all cases excepting those in which infection is present or in which the element of time is important. This operation accordingly, is used routinely in our clinic.

Just as we regard the low flap operation as the safest type of cesarean section for the average case so also do we believe that local anesthesia is the safest type of anesthesia for the average case. For this reason some of the details of local anesthesia will be discussed and the technic of its administration will be combined with that of the low cesarean section in the illustrations which are to follow (Figs. 986 to 1008, inclusive).

Under procaine anesthesia temperature and pain sensation are lost before the sensations of touch and pressure disappear. For this reason the patient feels the manipulations of the operator without experiencing any pain. In order that her anxiety may not be increased the tissues are handled as gently as possible and wide retraction is avoided. Adhesions are severed with a knife and not separated by blunt dissection. Unnecessary traction on the uterus, sutures and clamps is never permitted. Because the manipulations required for the removal of the child and the placenta sometimes are too vigorous for local anesthesia, brief analgesia is induced with nitrous oxide while these manipulations are carried out.

Unfortunately the drugs which usually are relied upon to relieve the patient's anxiety when local anesthesia is employed, cannot be given preliminary to a cesarean section because of their harmful effect on the child. After the operation is started and shortly before the child is removed from the uterus one-third of a grain of pantopon and 1:200th of scopolamine are given for this purpose.

To obtain the maximum effect with a minimum of drugs three different solutions are used:

Solution (1) consists of 50 cc. of 0.5% procaine without adrenalin. It is employed for the intradermal and subcutaneous infiltrations which anesthetize the site of the incision. Because slight sloughing sometimes occurs when adrenalin is used in these intradermal injections and because prolonged anesthesia in this region is secured by the subsequent deeper nerve blockings, adrenalin is omitted from this first solution.

Solution (2) is prepared by adding 1 cc. of 1-1000 adrenalin to 200 cc. of 1% procaine. This 1% procaine and 1-200,000 adrenalin solution is used only for the deep nerve blocking injections which are made in the vicinity of the semi-

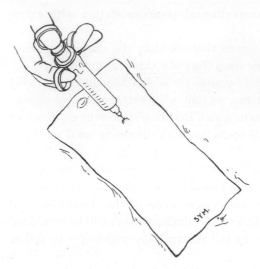

FIG. 986. Low cesarean section. The point of the needle is introduced into the skin slightly to the left of the midline and a small amount of 0.5% procaine (solution 1) is injected intradermally. The needle is then plunged through the entire thickness of the skin and 1 cc. of the solution is forced into the subcutaneous tissues. Adrenalin is not used in the skin injection because it sometimes causes the wound margins to slough.

FIG. 987. Low cesarean section. As anesthesia occurs almost immediately within the intradermal wheal the needle is painlessly reintroduced near its periphery and additional weals and subcutaneous injections are repeated until they extend from the symphysis almost to the umbilicus. About 25 cc. of solution (1) are used to produce the chain of wheals which anesthetize the skin and subcutaneous tissues. After a brief delay to allow for complete anesthesia, the skin and subcutaneous tissues are incised down to the fascia over the rectus muscle.

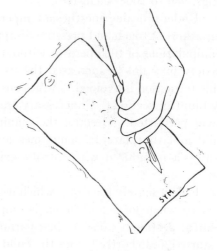

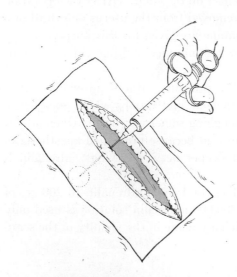

FIG. 988. Low cesarean section. A three-inch 22 gage needle is introduced into the incised tissues as near as possible to the fascia and passed outward to the outer border of the right rectus. After withdrawing the plunger slightly to make certain that a vein has not been entered 2 cc of 1% procaine in 1/200,000 adrenalin (solution 2) are forced into the region adjacent to the linea semilunaris.

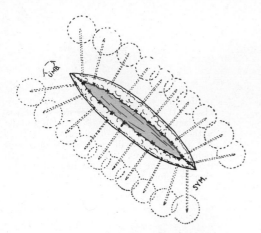

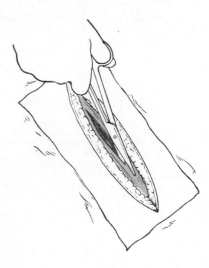

FIG. 989. Low cesarean section. Similar injections are made at intervals of 1 cc. on each side of the wound. At the upper and lower angles the needle is passed obliquely in order that the solution may extend beyond the limits of the proposed incision. If the injections are made correctly a continuous mass of 1% procaine is thus introduced in the region of the lineae semilunares from which it infiltrates through the fascia and blocks the nerves before they give off the terminal branches which supply the abdominal wall from the peritoneum to the skin. After the last injection is given an attendant is instructed to note the time and tell the operator when 10 minutes have passed.

FIG. 990. Low cesarean section. After the required time has elapsed a small incision is made in the fascia with a knife. This is enlarged with scissors. Scissors are used because they may cause discomfort in imperfectly anesthetized tissues which otherwise may be incised painlessly with a knife. Should the use of scissors show the anesthesia to be imperfect a slightly longer interval of waiting is indicated. If the sensitiveness is not then eliminated additional procaine is required. On the other hand, the absence of discomfort when the scissors are used is indicative of perfect anesthesia and the operator may proceed with the assurance that even the peritoneum may be incised without pain.

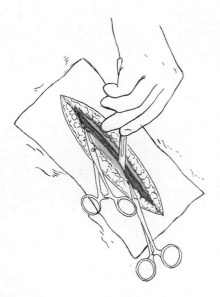

FIG. 991. Low cesarean section. The inner margin of the rectus muscle is separated from its sheath and the peritoneum is exposed. During this step slight traction on the fascia is made with clamps to facilitate the dissection and reveal any possible inadequacy of the anesthesia.

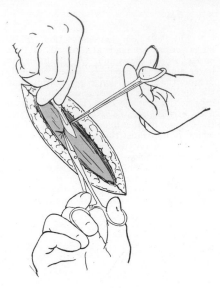

Fig. 992. Low cesarean section. The peritoneum is grasped with clamps and incised. If the blocking of the nerves is satisfactory, as it usually is, this can be done without further use of procaine. If it is not the clamps will cause discomfort and require injection of the peritoneum with 0.5% procaine in 1–200,000 adrenalin (solution 3) before the incision is made.

Fig. 993. Low cesarean section. After incising the peritoneum traction is made on one side at the junction of its middle and lower third and 5 cc. of 0.5% procaine in 1–200,000 adrenalin (solution 3) are injected into the subperitoneal tissues on that side of the bladder. This is followed by a similar injection on the opposite side.

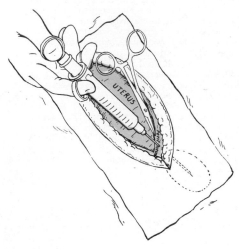

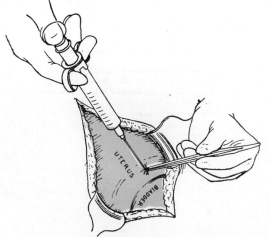

Fig. 994. Low cesarean section. Smooth pointed forceps pick up the peritoneum on the anterior surface of the uterus about 1 inch above the bladder and 10 cc. of 0.5% procaine and 1–200,000 adrenalin (solution 3) are injected beneath the bladder reflection.

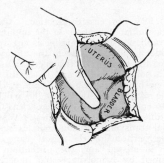

FIG. 995. Low cesarean section. Pressure on the wheal thus made disperses the fluid towards the sides and under the bladder.

FIG. 996. Low cesarean section. The peritoneal reflection is incised transversely and scissors are passed beneath it on one side of the midline. They are then opened and withdrawn.

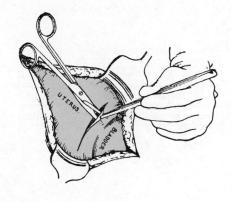

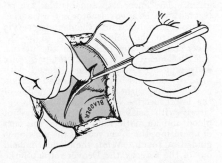

FIG. 997. Low cesarean section. Into the space formed by the blunt scissors dissection, the finger is introduced and by a side to side motion dissects off the peritoneum and bladder from that side of the lower segment and cervix.

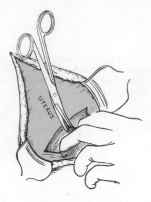

Fig. 998. Low cesarean section. After making a similar dissection on the opposite side the adhesion in the midline is cut and the bladder is pushed off from the anterior surface of the uterus. If the operator uses a smooth pointed forceps and is careful to pick up nothing but the peritoneum at the beginning of the flap dissection he will be certain to enter the proper plane of cleavage and the dissection will be bloodless. When the initial transverse incision includes more than the peritoneum the right plane of cleavage is missed and the dissection is accompanied by hemorrhage and unnecessary trauma to the tissues.

Fig. 999. Low cesarean section. If the patient has been in labor some hours and the membranes have been ruptured for a considerable time an upper flap of peritoneum is similarly prepared by blunt dissection.

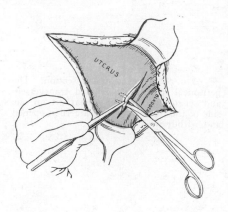

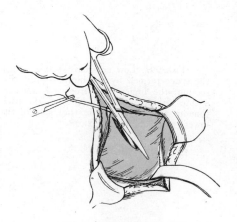

Fig. 1000. Low cesarean section. After the flaps have been prepared ⅓ gr. of pantopon and 1/200th of scopolamine are given. The lower flap and bladder are retracted by a Deaver retractor and a traction suture is introduced into the denuded cervix adjacent to the point which is to be the lower angle of the incision in the uterus. The abdomen is walled off with laparotomy pads and brief analgesia is induced with nitrous oxide and oxygen. A small incision is then made with a knife in the midline of the lower uterine segment and this is enlarged with scissors. If the discharge of blood and amniotic fluid obscures the field of operation, the lower part of the incision is guided by touch. While the bladder is held out of the way by the Deaver retractor the finger of one hand guides the scissors in the direction of the previously placed traction suture.

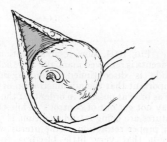

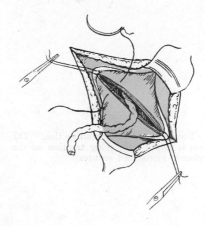

FIG. 1001. Low cesarean section. The left hand is introduced into the uterine cavity and acting as a vectis assists in the delivery of the child's head while the right hand makes downward pressure over the fundus of the uterus. The administration of nitrous oxide is now discontinued. Because the removal of the child sometimes is painful nitrous oxide is used to induce analgesia during the manipulations required for the delivery. The nitrous oxide should be given for a very short interval only, not much over one minute, the aim being to produce analgesia without anesthesia. If too much of the gas is given the patient may pass through a stage of excitement and force the intestines into the field of operation

FIG. 1002. Low cesarean section. Immediately after the delivery of the child 1 cc. of ergotrate is injected hypodermically and interrupted chromic catgut sutures are passed through the entire uterine musculature down to but not including the endometrium. These sutures are placed $1\frac{1}{2}$ cm. apart and are left long.

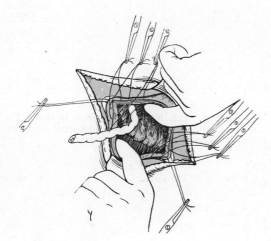

FIG. 1003. Low cesarean section. After the interrupted sutures have been introduced throughout the length of the wound, nitrous oxide is again administered for about 1 minute while the placenta is being removed. During this time the wound edges are spread apart and the hand is introduced between the two sutures which are adjacent to the umbilical cord.

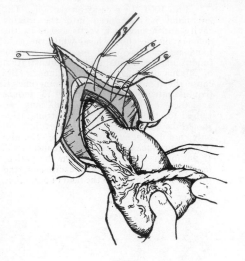

Fig. 1004. Low cesarean section. The placenta is removed manually and the nitrous oxide is discontinued. Here again it is important that the administration of the gas be as brief as possible in order that the patient may not get out of control. While the deep sutures are being introduced time is afforded for proper retraction of the uterus with the result that very little bleeding from the placental site occurs after the placenta is removed.

Fig. 1005. Low cesarean section. The uterus is closed by making traction on the previously introduced sutures.

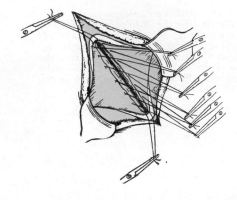

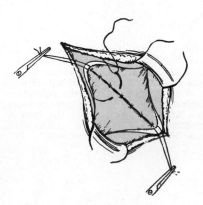

Fig. 1006. Low cesarean section. The sutures are tied and additional ones are introduced wherever necessary.

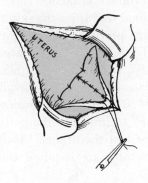

FIG. 1007. Low cesarean section. **The upper flap is brought** down over the upper angle of the uterine wound.

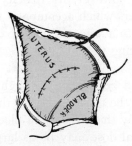

FIG. 1008. Low cesarean section. The lower flap is brought up over the upper one and sutured in place by plain catgut sutures. Within 24 hours the flaps become adherent and thoroughly seal the wound in the uterus from the peritoneal cavity. The abdominal wound is closed in layers. This usually can be done without the use of additional procaine. Should the anesthetic wear off however, the peritoneum is again infiltrated with 0.5% procaine and 1–200,000 adrenalin (solution 3) before it is sutured. It is not necessary to reanesthetize the fascia and skin.

If the patient has been in labor a number of hours or the membranes have been ruptured for sometime or if infection is suspected, a gauze laparotomy pad powdered on both sides with sodium sulfathiazole is left in the uterine cavity with one end in the cervix to facilitate its removal 48 hours later. The raw surfaces beneath the bladder and flaps of peritoneum likewise are dusted with powdered sulfathiazole before the flaps are finally sutured.

lunar lines at the outer border of the recti muscles.   By blocking the nerves
before they give off their terminal branches these injections anesthetize the
entire thickness of the abdominal wall from the skin to the peritoneum inclusive.
In its action on nerve fibers procaine affects the smaller relatively thinly
medullated fibers more readily than it does the larger more thickly medullated
nerves.   For this reason a 0.5% solution is less efficacious in blocking the larger
nerve elements which are adjacent to the lineae semilunares.

Solution (3) is made up of 50 cc. of 0.5% procaine to which 0.25 cc. of 1–1000
adrenalin is added.   It is used to infiltrate the peritoneum on each side of the
bladder and over the lower part of the uterus.   If at any time in the course of
the operation additional injections are required this solution rather than the
stronger one is selected.

DANGERS OF LOCAL ANESTHESIA

The lethal dose of procaine used in the manner described is unknown
for man.   If human susceptibility is similar to that of laboratory animals, at
least 25 gm. would be required to kill a woman weighing 130 lbs.   When the
drug is injected into a vein however, its toxicity is increased almost tenfold
(17, 18).   The greatest dangers which accompany the use of procaine therefore,
are its accidental injection into a vein and its rapid absorption in very vascular
tissues.   The risk of introducing the solution directly into a vein is slight if the
needle and plunger are kept moving throughout the injection.   As an added
precaution the plunger should be withdrawn slightly before the major portion
of the injection is forced into the tissues in order that the entrance of the needle
into a vein may be revealed by the presence of blood in the syringe.

While the supposed lethal dose may be as large as 25 gm. for the average
person, less than 1:10th of this amount of procaine may cause toxic manifestations.   These include nervousness, anxiety, talkativeness, tremor, nausea, vomiting and a fall in blood pressure.   As most of these symptoms also follow the use
of adrenalin some of the unsuccessful results of local anesthesia which are attributed to an unsatisfactory choice of patients or to the employment of a faulty
technic probably are due to the use of too much of one or both of these drugs.
According to the majority of writers not more than 1–1.5 gm. of procaine and 15
min. of adrenalin should be used.   Satisfactory anesthesia can be obtained within
these limits.

ADVANTAGES OF LOCAL ANESTHESIA

1. The chief advantage of local anesthesia lies in the fact that its use is
accompanied by little or no immediate risk of death.   I do not know of nor have I
heard of a single instance in which death occurring during or immediately after a
cesarean section was attributed to local anesthesia.   I am unable to say the same

for any other anesthetic agent. Because of its safety many men prefer this type of anesthesia in cases complicated by toxemia, respiratory infection, diabetes, heart and kidney disease. If it is best in the presence of these serious complications, it should be best for the ordinary cases as well.

2. The general condition of the patient immediately after operation is so good and her convalescence is so much better than after general anesthesia that even the operators who have trouble in obtaining satisfactory anesthesia by means of the local technic are reluctant to discontinue its use.

3. Fluids can be taken by mouth before, during and immediately after operation. Thirst accordingly either does not occur or is easily relieved. Sweating also is seldom observed and the dehydration which is so common after the most major operations is greatly reduced or entirely eliminated.

4. Vomiting during and after operation does not occur unless excessive amounts of the drugs are given. As a result the stomach need not be empty at the time of operation. Because the decision to operate often is made after labor has started and after food has been taken, this freedom from gastric disturbance and its sequelae is one of the chief reasons for the selection of local anesthesia. The absence of vomiting also greatly diminishes the risk of aspiration pneumonia and plugging of the bronchi.

5. Foods are ingested within a few hours after the patient returns to her room. Because of this and because the intestines are seldom seen during the operation distention and gas pains are much less frequent than after general anesthesia.

6. The heat regulating mechanism is not disturbed and abnormal sweating and chilling of the body surface do not occur. Since the respiratory tract is not irritated as it is when inhalation anesthesia is used the bronchial secretion is not increased and latent infection in the lungs is not activated. For this reason and because the absence of vomiting eliminates the danger of aspirating gastric contents, pneumonia and massive collapse of the lungs seldom occur. The lack of respiratory irritation also makes possible the use of cesarean section in women who ordinarily would be considered poor risks because of the presence of an upper respiratory infection.

7. Due to better contraction and retraction of the uterus the danger of hemorrhage from the placental site is less under local than under general anesthesia. The freedom from circulatory disturbance together with this lessened tendency towards hemorrhage greatly reduces the possibility of the occurrence of shock.

8. The gentle handling of the tissues required by the local technic coupled with the fact that the patient is active almost immediately after the operation is finished, diminishes the risk of thrombosis and embolism, postoperative complications which are not infrequent after ordinary cesarean section.

9. If pantopon and scopolamine are not given until the operator is ready to make the incision in the uterus, the child will be in excellent condition at birth. Asphyxia accordingly, is seldom observed and resuscitation is not necessary in those cases in which the condition of the child is satisfactory at the start of the operation.

DISADVANTAGES OF LOCAL ANESTHESIA

The only disadvantages are that it is time consuming, requires gentle handling of the tissues and tries the patience of the operator. With practice it can be mastered easily and the satisfaction of achievement will then reward the surgeon for his perseverance.

WATERS SUPRAVESICAL EXTRAPERITONEAL CESAREAN SECTION

In the Waters extraperitoneal cesarean section an extraperitoneal approach to the cervix and lower uterine segment is afforded by stripping the bladder from the uterus after the perivesical fascia with its attached peritoneum has been dissected off from the bladder fundus. Through a transverse semilunar incision in the exposed lower segment of the uterus the child is delivered as it presents. The uterine wound is closed with continuous catgut sutures and a drain is placed over the sutured area. After reuniting the fascia the abdominal wound is closed in the usual manner (15, 16), (Fig. 1009 to 1018, inclusive).

The **advantages** of the Waters extraperitoneal operation are:

1. The peritoneal cavity is not entered.

2. The danger of peritonitis resulting from the spilling of infected amniotic fluid is eliminated.

3. There is very little danger of peritonitis resulting from a breaking down of the uterine wound.

4. Infected and potentially infected cases may thus be delivered suprapubically without the sacrifice of the uterus.

5. It is said to be superior to the Latzko extraperitoneal cesarean section in that it affords more ample room for the extraction of a large child, it offers less chance for infection of the deep cellular tissues and its use is accompanied by little or no danger of injuring the ureter.

The **disadvantages** of the Waters extraperitoneal operation are:

1. It is a technically difficult procedure which should be done only by those who are skilled in surgical technic.

2. There is the danger that the bladder may be injured. This accident should cause little trouble if the injury is recognized and properly repaired.

3. The peritoneum also may be perforated. This also is of little consequence if it is recognized and repaired before the uterus is incised.

4. The danger of peritonitis developing by lymphatic extension from an infected retained uterus is not eliminated.

5. The risk of postpartum hemorrhage from relaxation of the uterus also is not eliminated.

6. If hemorrhage from a relaxed uterus should occur in the course of the operation this accident may not be observed after the uterine incision is closed. Likewise massage of the uterus and other local intra-abdominal measures used to combat uterine relaxation cannot be employed because the field of operation is extraperitoneal.

From the foregoing considerations the Waters extraperitoneal cesarean section seems to be the preferable operation when cesarean section is indicated in a patient who has been too long in labor, with membranes too long ruptured and with too much vaginal manipulation to justify a low transperitoneal cesarean section with extraperitoneal closure. This of course implies that the operator is familiar with the technic and has the necessary skill to perform the operation satisfactorily.

Because the patient usually has been in labor a long time and may be dehydrated and because the taking of food has not been restricted she is not a good subject for inhalation anesthesia. It therefore may be well to give a hypodermoclysis prior to operation. Sometimes it may be advisable to give a sedative and let her rest for several hours before proceeding with the section. In these neglected cases spinal anesthesia is preferred. One hundred milligrams of novocaine in 4 cc. of spinal fluid are injected through the fourth lumbar space and unless contraindicated the patient is kept flat. Three-quarters of a grain of ephedrin sulphate are given before operation.

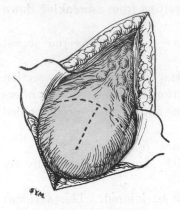

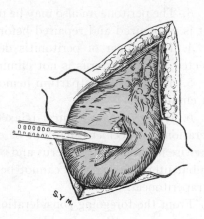

Fig. 1009. Waters supravesical extra-peritoneal cesarean section (After Waters and Eisaman and Austin). Through a left paramedian incision extending from the symphysis almost to the umbilicus, the fascia beneath the rectus muscle is exposed. The bladder is then distended with 200 cc. or more of an aqueous methylene blue solution introduced from a sterile irrigating vessel connected with an indwelling catheter. The vertical arm of a T-shaped incision is made through the perivesical fascia down to the muscular wall of the bladder.

Fig. 1010. Waters supravesical extra-peritoneal cesarean section. By blunt dissection with the handle of a scalpel the peri-vesical fascia is freed from the left side of the bladder fundus and the horizontal arm of the T-shaped incision is completed. During the dissection the vesical vessels which may be seen lying upon the muscularis serve as an aid in the identification of the proper plane of cleavage to be followed.

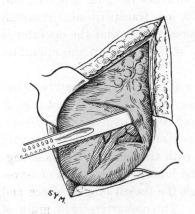

Fig. 1011. Waters supravesical extra-peritoneal cesarean section. With the handle of the scalpel further separation of the fascia is accomplished.

FIG. 1012. Waters supravesical extra-peritoneal cesarean section. Blunt dissection with the finger continues the dissection which was begun with the knife handle.

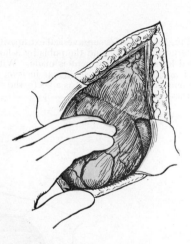

FIG. 1013. Waters supravesical extra-peritoneal cesarean section. The perivesical fascia which has been separated from the bladder fundus is pulled upward while the denuded bladder is pressed downward. This exposes the fold of the bladder reflection of peritoneum at the upper and left side of the bladder. It appears as a hernial pouch, the two layers of which form a whitish line of identification. This white identifying line of the supravesical plica must always be kept in view as the dissection is continued.

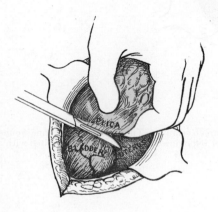

FIG. 1014. Waters supravesical extra-peritoneal cesarean section. The bladder is now emptied and with the finger insinuated behind the peritoneal fold of the uterovesical pouch the vesicouterine plica is cut away from the posterior surface of the bladder, care being taken to avoid cutting the peritoneal fold which forms the whitish line of identification.

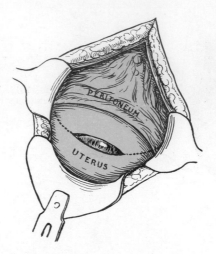

Fig. 1015. Waters supravesical extraperitoneal cesarean section.   The bladder is stripped off from the uterus and held behind the pubis by a large curved retractor.   A small transverse incision in the exposed lower uterine segment is made.   With scissors this is enlarged on each side in an upwardly curved manner to form a semilunar incision sufficiently large to permit the extraction of the child. Using one blade of the forceps as a vectis the child is delivered head first by making downward pressure over the fundus of the uterus.

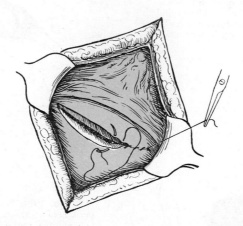

Fig. 1016. Waters supravesical extraperitoneal cesarean section.   The edges of the uterine wound are exposed by grasping them with Allis clamps and after removing the placenta they are united with a continuous chromic catgut suture.

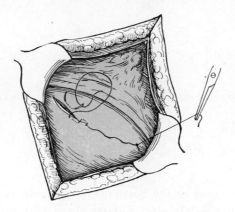

Fig. 1017. Waters supravesical extraperitoneal cesarean section. The sutured uterine wound is buried by means of a second continuous Lembert suture.

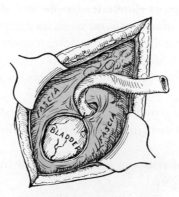

Fig. 1018. Waters supravesical extraperitoneal cesarean section. All bleeding points are ligated and the bladder is refilled to check for damage. It is then emptied and the retrovesical space is drained with a roll of rubber tissue. The transversalis fascia is sutured with interrupted sutures and the remainder of the abdominal wound is closed in the usual manner. A catheter is left in the bladder for 48 hours after operation. The rubber tissue drain is removed in from 2 to 5 days depending upon the patient's condition and the appearance of the wound.

CESAREAN SECTION AND HYSTERECTOMY, THE PORRO OPERATION

Cesarean hysterectomy or the Porro operation is the procedure in which the uterus is removed immediately after a classical cesarean section. Sometimes in frankly infected cases the child may not be removed from the uterus until after the latter organ has been extirpated. Fixation of the cervical stump in the lower angle of the abdominal wound as originally recommended by Porro is seldom practised today (Figs. 1019 to 1029, inclusive).

The **advantages** of hysterectomy after cesarean section are:

1. In neglected labor cases it removes an infected or potentially infected organ from the peritoneal cavity.

2. Removal of the uterus eliminates the danger of peritonitis which follows the breaking down of the uterine wound when an infected uterus is retained.

3. Peritonitis resulting from lymphatic extension also is prevented by removal of the potentially infected uterus.

4. The danger of postpartum hemorrhage from an atonic uterus is eliminated by hysterectomy.

5. Hysterectomy also removes the possibility of poor drainage, degeneration and subsequent complications from uterine tumors when they are present at the time of operation.

The **disadvantages** of cesarean section followed by hysterectomy are:

1. The uterus is sacrificed.

2. In infected cases contamination of the field of operation may give rise to a fatal peritonitis.

3. At times the patient may be in too poor condition to stand the operation.

Because of the advantages enumerated cesarean hysterectomy is superior to either the classical or the low transperitoneal operations in badly neglected cases of labor which are infected or potentially infected. Because it sacrifices the uterus and causes contamination of the peritoneum it probably is less suitable for such cases than the Latzko or Waters operations and Craniotomy, if the operator is competent to do the latter procedures. It sometimes is of great value in the treatment of accidental hemorrhage especially when the condition fails to respond to conservative measures. Naturally the removal of the uterus is indicated following cesarean sections done for dystocia from obstructing tumors.

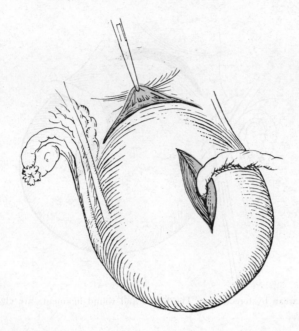

Fig. 1019. Cesarean hysterectomy. After removing the child by classical cesarean section the bladder reflection of peritoneum is dissected off from the uterus

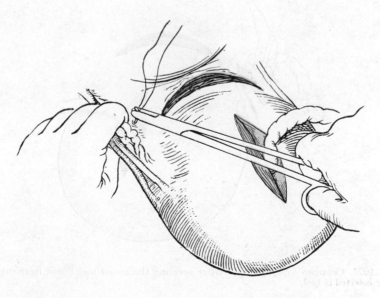

Fig. 1020. Cesarean hysterectomy. With the fingers of one hand the veins in the broad ligament are pulled to one side and into the clear space thus exposed a suture is passed.

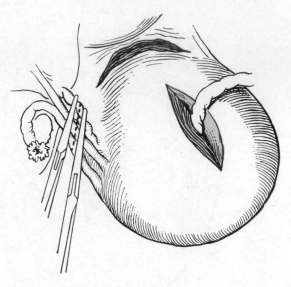

FIG. 1021. Cesarean hysterectomy. The broad and round ligaments are clamped with Kocher clamps.

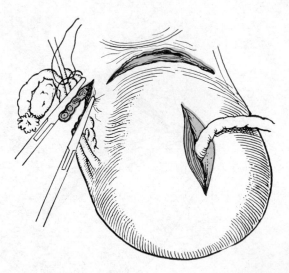

FIG. 1022. Cesarean hysterectomy. After severing the round and broad ligaments the suture previously inserted is tied.

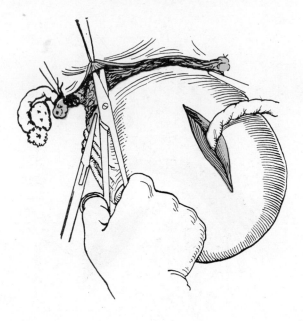

FIG. 1023. Cesarean hysterectomy.   The uterine vessels are exposed by blunt dissection.

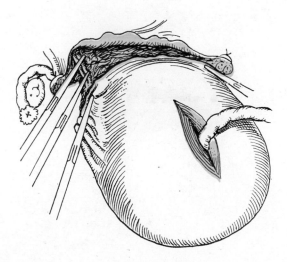

FIG. 1024. Cesarean hysterectomy.   The uterine vessels are secured by two large clamps.

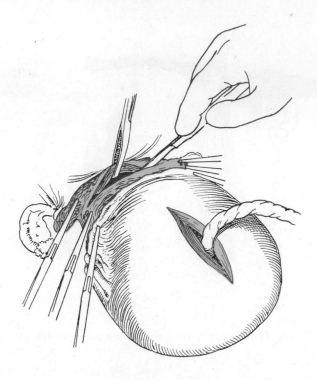

FIG. 1025. Cesarean hysterectomy.   After severing the tissues between the clamps the vessels on the opposite side are similarly clamped and cut.   The uterus is then amputated, the anterior and posterior walls of the stump being grasped with tenaculum forceps.

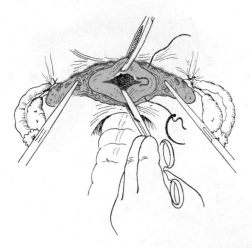

FIG. 1026. Cesarean hysterectomy.   The cervix is closed with interrupted sutures.

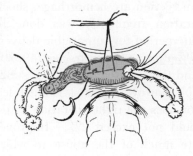

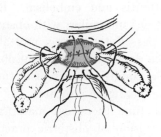

FIG. 1027. Cesarean hysterectomy. The uterine vessels are ligated with suture ligatures and the round ligaments are anchored to the sides of the stump.

FIG. 1028. Cesarean hysterectomy. The raw surfaces are peritonealized by attaching the bladder reflection to the posterior surface of the cervix.

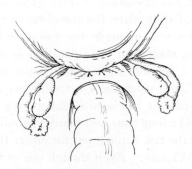

FIG. 1029. Cesarean hysterectomy.
Completion of the operation.

(When cesarean section hysterectomy is done because of the presence of infection or because infection is anticipated, a somewhat higher abdominal incision is made in order that the pregnant uterus may be eventrated. After the uterus is eventrated the abdominal wound is temporarily held together with clamps and covered with a sterile towel. A sheet of sterile rubber tissue is partially cut in its middle portion and the severed edges are clamped tightly about the lower most portion of the uterus in order that the abdominal wall and the field of operation may be protected from the spill of infected amniotic fluid. The uterus is incised and the child is removed as in cesarean section. The protecting rubber tissue is then removed and the hysterectomy is continued.

PROGNOSIS. The chief dangers of cesarean section are hemorrhage, shock, peritonitis and embolism. Because the operation frequently was done by surgeons unfamiliar with obstetrics after the safe period for suprapubic delivery had passed, the average mortality was around 7% up to a few years ago (19, 20). When done by a competent obstetric surgeon and the technic employed is suited to the conditions present at the time of operation, however, the risk is much less than this figure indicates. If the right operator does the right operation at the right time the gross maternal mortality should not exceed 2%. Improved supervision of obstetric practice will eliminate much of the abuse to which cesarean section has been subjected and result in the general attainment of this lower mortality figure. That this is possible is shown by the fact that one large eastern city has succeeded in reducing the mortality from over 6% in 1931 to approximately 1.5% in 1940 (21).

As was noted in the beginning of this chapter the morbidity and mortality following cesarean section depend more upon the hours the patient has been in labor, the hours the membranes have been ruptured and the number and character of vaginal examinations made prior to operation, than upon the operative technic followed. When the operation is done at or soon after the beginning of labor, before or immediately after the membranes rupture and without any vaginal examinations having been made the risk will not be over 1%. If no vaginal examinations are made and the operation is done within 16 hours of labor's onset and within 4 hours of the rupture of the membranes the mortality should not exceed 2 or 3% provided the low technic with extraperitoneal closure is used. Whenever the patient has been in labor over 24 hours and the membranes have been ruptured a long time and many vaginal examinations or manipulations have been made the risk is too great for either the classical or low operation with extraperitoneal closure. Even though one of the true extraperitoneal technics or the Porro operation is employed in such circumstances, a relatively high mortality must be expected. If the child's condition is satisfactory when the operations is begun it should be born alive.

EFFECT OF CESAREAN SECTION ON FUTURE PREGNANCIES AND LABORS. Rupture of the uterus in subsequent pregnancies and labors is possible and occurred in 4% of a series of 448 women who became pregnant after a cesarean section had been done (22). This accident occurs more commonly after labor has started than in the course of pregnancy. If the patient has completely dilated her cervix or is a multipara when the operation is done the risk of rupture of the uterus in a subsequent labor is less than it is in the patient who has a cesarean section performed at or before the onset of a first labor provided no infection is present. The presence of infection at the time of operation naturally interferes with healing of the wound in the uterus and predisposes towards rupture in subsequent pregnancy and labor. Because of the danger of rupture of the uterus, women who have had a cesarean section should remain within a reasonable distance of their obstetric hospital and surgeon during the latter months of all subsequent pregnancies. This is particularly true if the cesarean was done according to the classical technic and **is imperative if the postoperative course was febrile.** Throughout the pregnancy, the site of the previous incision in the uterus should be examined repeatedly for evidence of thinning. By palpating the anterior surface of the uterus during contraction and relaxation a poor scar may be detected even before labor begins. After the onset of labor, differences in consistency are easily discovered and occasionally a weak scar becomes so stretched that it balloons out beyond the adjacent surface of the uterus during a contraction.

Whenever the scar shows definite signs of weakness, the pregnancy should be terminated by a second cesarean section. If the previous operation was complicated by infection, the section should be done before the onset of labor. Suprapubic delivery likewise is indicated whenever, in the course of labor, any thinning of the old scar becomes manifest. If obstetric surgeons would weigh the indications for the first cesarean section a little more carefully and be less hesitant in doing the second section, fewer ruptures would occur. A more extensive use of the low technic may also aid in the prevention of rupture of the uterus (23, 24).

REFERENCES

1. BURTON, J.: New System of Midwifery. London, 1851, p. 264.
2. RADFORD, T.: Observations on the Caesarean Section, Craniotomy and Other Obstetric Operations. 2nd ed., London, 1880, p. 11.
3. HARRIS, R. P.: Cattle-Horn Laceration of the Abdomen and Uterus in Pregnant Women. Am. J. Obs., 1887, 20, 673, 1033.
4. ATLEE, W. L.: A Table of Operations of Ovariotomy from 1701 to 1851. Tr. Am. Med. Ass., 1851, 284, 310.
5. PORRO, E.: Della amputazione utero-ovarica, etc. Milan, 1876.
6. HARRIS, R. P.: The Porro-Caesarean Section in All Countries from Its Introduction to the Close of 1888. Brit. Med. J., 1890, 1, 68.
7. SANGER, M.: Der Kaiserschnitt bei Uterusmyomen, etc. Leipzig, 1882.
8. FRANK, F.: Die suprasymphysare Entbindung und ihr Verhältniss zu den anderen Operationen bei engen Becken. Arch. f. Gyn., 1907, 81, 46.
9. SELLHEIM, H.: Der extraperitoneale Uterusschnitt. Zentralbl. f. Gyn., 1908, 32, 133.
10. LATZKO,   : Über den Extra-peritonealen Kaiserschnitt. Zentralbl. f. Gyn., 1909, 33, 275.
11. KRÖNIG, B.: Transperitonealer, cervicaler Kaiserschnitt. Krönig-Döderlein Operative Gynecology III. Auf. 1912, 879.
12. BECK, A. C.: Observations on a Series of Cases of Cesarean Sections Done at the Long Island College Hospital During the Past Six Years; with an Improved Technic for this Operation. Am. J. O., 1919, 79, 197.
13. BECK, A. C.: The Advantages and Disadvantages of the Two-flap Low Incision Cesarean Section, with a Report of 83 Cases Done by Fifteen Operators. Am. J. O. & G., 1921, 1, 586.
14. DELEE, J. B.: Low or Cervical Cesarean Section. J. A. M. A., 1925, 84, 791.
15. WATERS, E. G.: Supravesical Extraperitoneal Cesarean Section, Am. J. Obs. & Gyn., 1940, 39, 423.

16. EISAMAN, J. R. AND AUSTIN, B.: Extraperitoneal Cesarean Section. The Waters Operation. Penn. M. J., 1942, 45, 813.
17. HIRSHFELDER, A. D. AND BIETER, R. N.: Local Anesthetics. Physiological Rev., 1932, 16, 180.
18. BIETER, R. N.: Applied Pharmacology of Local Anesthetics. Am. J. Surg. 1936, 34, 500.
19. HOLLAND, E.: Methods of Performing Cesarean Section. Brit. Med. J., 1921, 2, 519.
20. GORDON, C. A.: Survey of Cesarean Section in Brooklyn. Am. J. O. & G., 1928, 16, 307.
21. Report of the Committee on Maternal Welfare of the Philadelphia County Medical Society. 1931–1940.
22. HOLLAND, E.: Discussion on Rupture of the Cesarean Section Scar in Subsequent Pregnancy and Labour. Proc. Roy. Soc. Med., 1920, 14, 22.
23. GREENHILL, J. P.: Histologic Study of Uterine Scars After Cervical Cesarean Section. J. A. M. A., 1929, 92, 21.
24. GAMBLE, T. O.: A Clinical and Anatomical Study of Fifty-one Cases of Repeated Cesarean Section with Especial Reference to the Healing of the Cicatrix and to the Occurrence of Rupture Through It. Johns Hopkins Hosp. Bull., 1922, 33, 93.

EDUARDO PORRO
1842–1902
Milan

Porro in 1876 suggested amputation of the uterus after cesarean section with fixation of the cervical stump in the abdominal wound. This greatly diminished the danger of infection and hemorrhage and thereby lessened the mortality rate of cesarean section which previously was almost 100 per cent.

MAX SANGER
1853–1903
Leipzig

Sanger successfully sutured the uterus in cesarean section in 1881. By his method hemorrhage was controlled and the discharge of the lochia into the peritoneal cavity was avoided. He thus prevented hemorrhage and infection without sacrificing the uterus and his operation accordingly became known as the conservative cesarean section.

CHAPTER XLIII

DESTRUCTIVE OPERATIONS

CRANIOTOMY

Craniotomy is the operation in which the skull of the child is perforated. Because it is the first step in all of the destructive procedures which aim to reduce the size of the child's head, the term craniotomy commonly is used to include the latter operations.

INDICATIONS. Perforation of the head is indicated in hydrocephalus and in all prolonged labors in which the child is dead. It also is used as a preliminary to the crushing operations whenever the child is dead and labor is arrested because of contracted pelvis, large child, brow presentation and posterior position of the face. As a result of the advances which have been made in modern obstetrics, the maternal risk of suprapubic delivery has been so lessened that craniotomy on the living child is seldom justifiable. On the other hand, it is a mistake to subject the mother to the great risk which accompanies abdominal delivery in those neglected cases which have had prolonged labors, with many vaginal examinations and in which the membranes have been ruptured for many hours. In these circumstances the child often is in such poor condition that it may die during or soon after a cesarean section. It therefore is far better to anticipate or to await the death of the child and do a craniotomy than to subject the mother to the grave risk of suprapubic delivery for the sake of a child that has little chance of surviving.

Because the crushed head cannot be extracted through a pelvis which is extremely contracted, craniotomy is contraindicated whenever the true conjugate measures 5.5 cm. or less. Pelvic deformity of such great degree requires delivery by cesarean section even though the child is dead and infection is present.

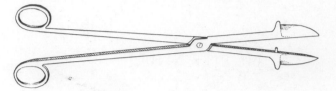

FIG. 1030. Smellie Scissors

FIG. 1031. Naegele's Perforator.

OPERATIVE TECHNIC. The site of the perforation is determined by the conditions present at the time of operation. If the head is well flexed and the attitude of flexion is to be maintained as it is when perforation is not to be followed by crushing and extraction, the region of the posterior fontanelle is the preferable location. The same site is chosen when the disproportion is slight and an easy extraction is anticipated. If there is much disproportion on the other hand a point near the large fontanelle is selected in order that the crushing instruments may be better applied over the face. In brow presentations the frontal bone is perforated; the perforator is passed through the orbit in face cases and perforation of the after coming head is accomplished through one of the posterolateral fontanelles.

To avoid injury of the thinned out lower uterine segment the head is held firmly against the pelvic inlet by an assistant while it is being perforated. In addition to this suprapubic pressure, the head may also be steadied by grasping the scalp with vulsellum forceps. Under guidance of two fingers within the vagina, the spear pointed Smellie scissors (Fig. 1030) or Naegele perforator (Fig. 1031) are forced through the skull at the desired site. The opening is enlarged by separating the blades. They are then withdrawn and reinserted at right angles to the original wound so that a crucial incision is made in the child's skull. Finally the brain is broken up by plunging the closed instrument into its substance in various directions. Because slipping of the perforator may cause injury to the maternal soft parts it should always be held perpendicular to the skull. The fingers in the vagina also should protect the maternal tissues from injury by the sharp edges of the instrument. Following craniotomy the head usually is crushed and extracted by means of the cranioclast, the cephalotribe or the basiotribe.

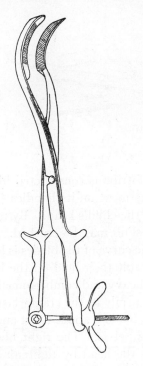

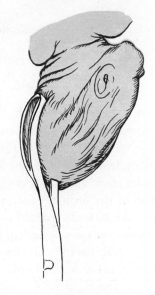

FIG. 1032. Cranioclast.   FIG. 1033. Cranioclast introduced (Bumm).

USE OF THE CRANIOCLAST. The cranioclast is a heavy metal two bladed instrument to the handles of which is fitted a strong compression screw (Fig. 1032). The smaller solid blade is grooved on its inner surface and tends to fit into the larger fenestrated blade. The cranioclast accordingly is capable of grasping the head firmly without slipping and is able to effect considerable reduction in its size.

Guided by the fingers in the vagina, the inner solid blade of the cranioclast is passed through the perforation in the cranial vault in such a manner that the grooved portion is in relation to the occiput. The larger fenestrated blade is then introduced posteriorly and rotated to its final position over the occipital bone (1, 2) (Fig. 1033). If the pin of the lock on the first blade points upward the second blade is passed above the first. If it points downward the second blade must be passed under the first; otherwise they cannot be locked. After locking the blades the compression screw is tightened as much as possible. One hand in the vagina protects the maternal soft parts from laceration by fragments of bone and guides the head through the most favorable mechanism while the other hand makes traction. If the occipital bone tears away, the blades are applied over the face.

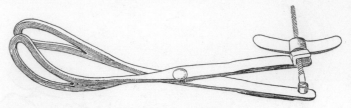

FIG. 1034. Cephalotribe.

USE OF THE CEPHALOTRIBE.   The cephalotribe is constructed like a heavy pair of forceps with a compression screw adjustment on its handles (Fig. 1034). Like the forceps it is applied to the outside of the child's head.   By means of its use the entire head including the base of the skull may be crushed.   To obtain the maximum effect as compressors the cephalic curve of the blades is less marked than is that of the ordinary forceps.   As a result their hold on the head is less secure after the latter is crushed.   While this heavy and cumbersome instrument is a good crusher it does not grasp the head as firmly as the cranioclast and has a tendency to slip in the difficult cases.   The left blade is applied first and naturally is introduced on the left side of the mother's pelvis.   The right blade is then introduced on the right side.   After crushing the head by tightening the compression screw the child is extracted as in a forceps operation.

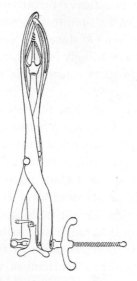

FIG. 1035. Basiotribe.

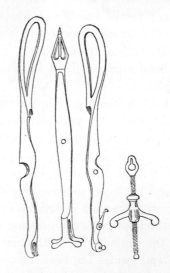

FIG. 1036. The parts of the basiotribe

USE OF THE BASIOTRIBE. The basiotribe is a three bladed instrument consisting of a central part for introduction into the skull and two heavy curved fenestrated blades for application over the occiput and face respectively (Figs. 1035, 1036). All three parts are connected with a compression screw. In the basiotribe are incorporated the good principles of the cranioclast and the cephalotribe. Combining the advantages of both of these instruments it, accordingly, grasps the head as well as the cranioclast and crushes the skull as well as the cephalotribe (3). After perforating the cranial vault, the central blade is passed into the opening and forced to the base of the skull. The shorter and lower of the remaining blades is introduced on the left side of the pelvis (Fig. 1037). The compression screw is attached and tightened until the two blades can be hooked. After hooking the internal and short blades, the compression screw is removed and the long blade is introduced on the right side of the pelvis (Fig. 1038). The compression screw is again applied and tightened until the base of the skull is thoroughly crushed (Fig. 1039). Extraction is accomplished by traction with one hand while the other hand in the vagina guides the head along the parturient axis.

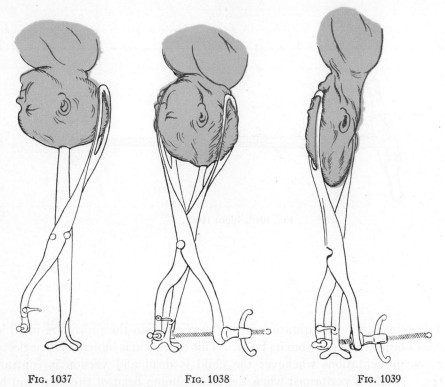

FIG. 1037.   FIG. 1038.   FIG. 1039.

FIG. 1037. The central blade is introduced into the perforation and forced to the base of the skull. The shorter and lower of the remaining blades is introduced on the left side of the pelvis.

FIG. 1038. By means of the compression screw, the two handles are approximated until they may be hooked. The longest blade is then introduced on the right side of the pelvis.

FIG. 1039. Tightening of the compression screw thoroughly crushes the base of the skull.

Following the delivery of the head traction is made on the posterior arm if it can be brought down.   If it cannot, the delivery of the shoulders is facilitated by placing the blunt hook in the posterior axilla and making downward traction with this instrument.

Should difficulty be encountered in the extraction of the child after craniotomy has been done the operator may be tempted to do a version and extraction.   Because the sharp fragments of the perforated and crushed skull may rupture the uterus whenever this procedure is followed **version after craniotomy never should be done.**

CLEIDOTOMY.   Cleidotomy is the operation in which one or both of the clavicles are severed for the purpose of reducing the shoulder circumference. It is indicated when the impacted shoulders of a dead child cannot be easily delivered after an arm is brought down.   While an assistant makes traction on the extracted arm the more accessible clavicle is cut by heavy blunt scissors under the guidance of the fingers in the vagina which at the same time protect the maternal tissues from injury.

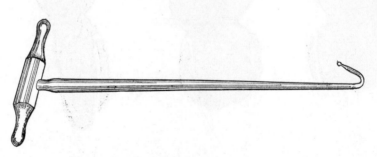

FIG. 1040. Blunt Hook.

DECAPITATION.   Decapitation is the term given to the procedure in which the child's head is severed from its body.   This operation is indicated in neglected transverse presentations whenever the child is dead and version is contraindicated.   It also is performed when the after coming head of the first twin becomes interlocked with the forecoming head of the second.

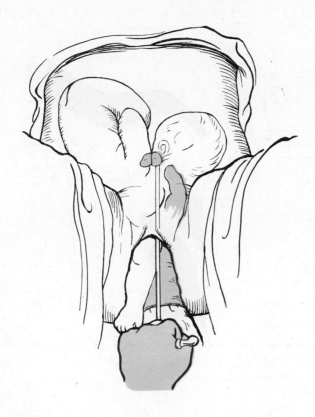

FIG. 1041. Decapitation. Blunt hook applied to the neck in an impacted shoulder presentation.

OPERATIVE TECHNIC. Decapitation is usually performed with a Braun blunt hook (Fig. 1040) or the sickle knife of Schulze. While an assistant makes traction on the prolapsed arm the whole hand is introduced into the vagina and the child's neck is encircled with the fingers behind and the thumb in front. The hook pointing transversely is passed along the palm of the hand and carried over the anterior surface of the neck until its point is above the neck. The point is then rotated posteriorly and pulled down so that the spinal column is within the grasp of the hook (Fig. 1041). With the fingers still in place to protect the maternal soft parts traction is made on the hook which at the same time is rotated from side to side until the vertebral column is divided. The hook is then removed and the soft parts are severed with scissors. Extraction of the body usually is easily accomplished by traction on the prolapsed arm. The after

FIG. 1042. Delivery of the severed head after decapitation.

coming head is delivered by suprapubic pressure while a finger in the mouth guides the neck and chin through the pelvis as shown in figure 1042. During the delivery of the shoulders and later during the delivery of the severed head the maternal tissues are protected from injury by keeping the fingers or thumb over the sharp fragments of the vertebrae.

EVISCERATION. The operation known as evisceration consists in the removal of the abdominal and thoracic viscera for the purpose of reducing the size of the fetal trunk. It sometimes is required when the child's size is excessive but is used most frequently in the treatment of neglected transverse presentations.

OPERATIVE TECHNIC. Under guidance of a hand in the vagina the thorax and abdomen are opened with blunt pointed curved scissors and through this opening the viscera are grasped and removed. The body, thus reduced in size, is then extracted (4). In neglected transverse presentations a blunt hook is passed over the spinal column and rotated until the latter is fractured. The lower half of the body is then pulled down and the fetus is delivered in a manner similar to that observed in spontaneous evolution.

PROGNOSIS. The morbidity and mortality which follows the destructive operations depends upon the degree of disproportion, the condition of the lower uterine segment and the number and character of the vaginal examinations and attempts at delivery made prior to operation. In properly selected cases the risk should not be much higher than that of forceps extraction. If the disproportion is marked on the other hand the risk is greatly increased because of the possibility of trauma and infection. In such cases rupture of the uterus is possible as it also is whenever the labor has been allowed to continue until the lower uterine segment is thinned out excessively. The greatest danger is present in those women in whom trauma and infection have been produced by attempts at delivery before the destructive operation is done. In some clinics accordingly, the mortality is as high as 12% (5) while in others it may be as low as 7% (6). All of the destructive operations, excepting a simple perforation, are major operations and should be undertaken only by those who are skilled obstetricians. Even in the hands of the expert, the uterus may be ruptured when the lower uterine segment is greatly thinned out by long obstructed labor. This risk, together with the danger of infection, hemorrhage and exhaustion, should lead the operator to give a guarded prognosis whenever these operations are done in badly neglected cases. When the conditions are favorable on the other hand the destructive operations are accompanied by very little risk if they are done by a competent man (7).

REFERENCES

1. SIMPSON, J. Y.: Cranioclast. Med. News & Gaz., 1860, Vol. 1.
2. BRAUN, G.: Über das technische Verfahren bei vernachlässigten Querlagen und über Decapitationsinstrumente. Wien. Med. Wchnschr., 1861, 2, 714.
3. TARNIER, A.: Le basiotribe. Ann. de Gyn. ed d'obs. Paris, 1884, 21, 74.
4. MERMAN, A.: Zur Behandlung verschleppter Querlagen. Centralbl. f. Gyn., 1895, 19, 963.
5. KERR, J. M.: Operative Midwifery. 1908, p. 481.
6. BRETSCHNEIDER, R.: Über hundertzweiunddreissig Fälle von Perforation und Extraction mit dem Zweifel'schen Kranio-Kephaloklast. Berlin, 1901, 63, p. 225–247.
7. FISCHER, G.: Some Observations on Craniotomy at the Woman's Clinic at Lund. Acta obs. et gyn. Scand., 1927, 6, 144.

CHAPTER XLIV

REPAIR OF LACERATIONS

CERVICAL LACERATIONS. In all primiparous labors the cervix is torn. Usually the injury is not extensive and union is spontaneous. Extensive lacerations and those that give rise to hemorrhage should be repaired immediately after the completion of the third stage. Persistent, profuse hemorrhage following the delivery of the placenta usually comes from a relaxed placental site or a cervical tear. If examination of the placenta shows that no part of it has been retained, and if the hemorrhage continues after the uterus has been made to

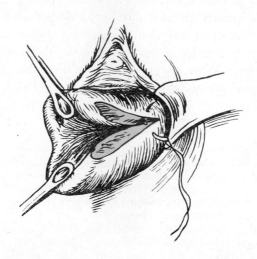

FIG. 1043. Repair of a laceration of the cervix. Pressure on the fundus forces the cervix to the vulvovaginal orifice. Sponge forceps grasp the cervix and expose the tear which is sutured with interrupted catgut sutures.

contract by massage, the cervix should be exposed at once. A Sims' speculum is introduced into the vagina and the friable lips of the cervix are grasped by sponge forceps. The cervix is then pulled down and inspected. The first suture should be inserted a short distance above the upper angle of the wound in order that possible hemorrhage from a retracted vessel may be arrested (Fig. 1043). The edges of the tear are then approximated with interrupted catgut sutures placed about 1 cm. apart and tied only tightly enough to coaptate without constricting the tissues.

PERINEAL LACERATIONS. Most women are torn when their first child is born. In about half of all primiparae, the laceration is rather extensive. If it passes through the external sphincter and rectum, it is termed a complete tear. Should the rectum and sphincter escape injury, the tear is then said to be incomplete. As a prophylaxis against infection all perineal lacerations should be repaired at once. The sutures are introduced immediately after the child is born, when the injury is slight, or after the placenta is delivered when it is more extensive. Should the patient's condition be critical, however, it is better to postpone the repair for a day or two. The beginner also will do well to put off the repair of extensive injuries long enough for him to obtain suitable assistance.

The patient is placed on a table or across the bed, and her legs are held back by a sheet or leg holder. The vulva is then sponged with tincture of iodine, lysol or chlorothymol solution. After putting on clean sterile gloves and a fresh sterile gown, the physician exposes the wound and notes the extent of the injury.

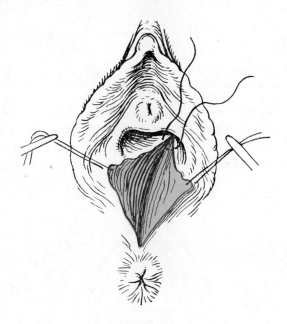

FIG. 1044. Repair of unilateral tear. Latera traction sutures expose the wound and an interrupted suture is placed at the upper angle.

REPAIR OF INCOMPLETE LACERATIONS. The wound is exposed by making traction on two sutures placed at the margins of the torn fourchette (Fig. 1044) and a large piece of gauze, saturated with 1 per cent lysol, is placed against the cervix to keep the field of operation free from the bloody uterine discharge. The upper angle of the wound is then approximated with an interrupted catgut suture. Slight traction on this suture readily exposes the edges that are to be brought

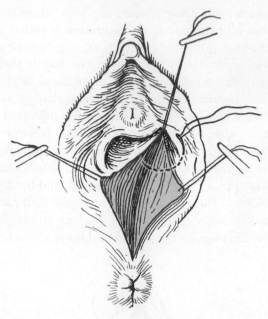

FIG. 1045. Repair of unilateral laceration.   Deep interrupted sutures are passed through the entire tear.   If necessary, the deeper structures may be pulled out and united by buried sutures.

together by the next one, which is inserted about 1 cm. below the first (Fig. 1045).   Exposure for succeeding sutures is gained by successively making traction on the last suture tied.   The deeper structures should be carefully coaptated. Each suture, therefore, takes a large bite of the tissue or better still, the deep

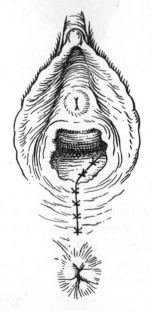

FIG. 1046. Repair of unilateral laceration completed.

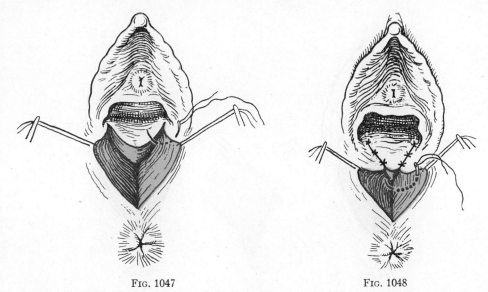

FIG. 1047   FIG. 1048

FIG. 1047. Repair of bilateral laceration.   Lateral traction sutures expose the wound and each angle is closed by interrupted sutures.
FIG. 1048. Repair of bilateral laceration.   The deep structures are united by buried interrupted sutures.

structures are pulled out with tissue forceps and united separately.   The skin or external portion of the tear is brought together with interrupted chromic catgut sutures placed about 1 cm. apart and introduced by means of a large Hagedorn needle (Figs. 1047 to 1050).

After the completion of the repair, the gauze which was placed against the cervix is removed.

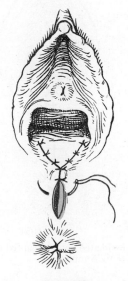

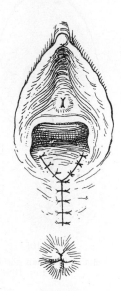

FIG. 1049   FIG. 1050

FIG. 1049. Repair of bilateral laceration.   The skin is approximated by interrupted catgut sutures
FIG. 1050. Repair of bilateral laceration completed.

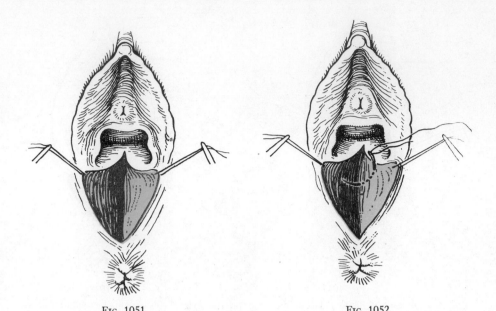

FIG. 1051   FIG. 1052

FIG. 1051. Repair of median perineotomy.   Lateral traction sutures expose the wound.
FIG. 1052. Repair of median perineotomy.   The deep structures are united by buried interrupted catgut sutures.

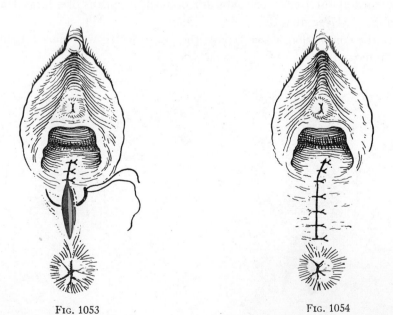

FIG. 1053   FIG. 1054

FIG. 1053. Repair of median perineotomy.   The skin is approximated by interrupted catgut sutures.
FIG. 1054. Repair of median perineotomy completed.

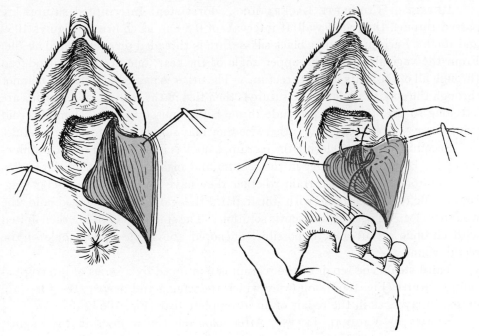

FIG. 1055   FIG. 1056

FIG. 1055. Repair of mediolateral episiotomy. Lateral traction sutures expose the wound.
FIG. 1056. Repair of lateral episiotomy. With a finger in the rectum as a guide, the deep structures are united by interrupted catgut sutures after the upper angle has been repaired with interrupted sutures. After all of the deep interrupted sutures are introduced the finger is withdrawn, the gloves are changed and the sutures are tied.

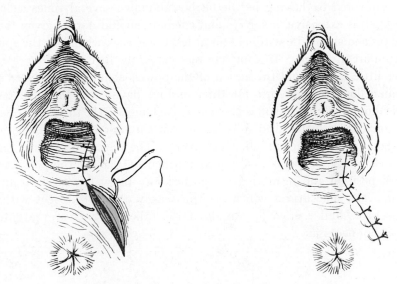

FIG. 1057   FIG. 1058

FIG. 1057. Repair of mediolateral episiotomy. The skin is approximated by interrupted catgut sutures.
FIG. 1058. Repair of lateral episiotomy completed.

REPAIR OF COMPLETE LACERATIONS. **First step:** Interrupted sutures are passed through the rectal wall at intervals of 0.5 cm. as shown in Figures 1059 and 1060.   Each end of a fine black silk suture is threaded on a fine round needle. From the vaginal side of the upper angle of the tear, one needle is introduced through all of the coats into the rectum.   The other is passed in a similar manner through the opposite side.   The suture is then tied in the rectum, and its ends are left long so that they will protrude through the anus.   Care is taken to avoid tying these sutures too tightly; otherwise they may slough out and cause a fistula.

Second step: After closing the rectum, a hook is introduced into each sphincter end.   By placing a finger in the rectum and making traction on the hooks, the operator can easily ascertain whether they have hold of the sphincter (Fig. 1061).   Before proceeding with the repair, the gloves are changed and the wound is cleansed with an antiseptic solution.   The sphincter ends are then united with chromic catgut and, if possible, anchored above the upper angle of the rectal wound.

Third step: The repair of the rectum is reinforced by a series of interrupted catgut sutures (Fig. 1062), following which the vagina and deeper structures are united in layers as in the repair of an incomplete tear (Fig. 1063).

REPAIR OF VAGINAL TEARS.   After exposing the wounds in the vagina, their edges are approximated by interrupted catgut sutures.   Tears in the anterior wall, if repaired, heal well, but if neglected they may lead to cystocele, a condition which, when repaired subsequently, may interfere with future deliveries.

AFTER CARE.   The patient is kept in bed in the Fowler position.   Drainage is likewise favored by having her lie on her abdomen several times a day.   If the laceration is extensive, laxatives and enemata should not be given for three or four days and should be withheld for at least one week whenever the sphincter and rectum are involved.   In complete tear cases, the diet should be one which will leave little residue and the action of the bowels should be inhibited by the use of small doses of paregoric for three or four days.   On the fifth day and thereafter $\frac{1}{2}$ ounce of mineral oil is given after each meal.   At the end of one week, 1 pint of olive oil is introduced into the rectum through a large rubber catheter and two hours later a soapsuds enema is given.   The rectal sutures are removed on the twelfth day.   This is easily accomplished by placing the patient in the knee-chest position and retracting the posterior rectal wall with a virgin Sims' speculum.   The silk sutures which are thus easily exposed are cut with sharp pointed scissors and removed.   As all of the other sutures are catgut, their removal is not necessary.

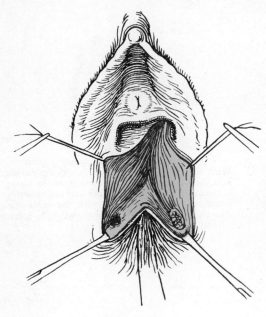

FIG. 1059. Repair of complete laceration. After exposing the wound by the use of lateral traction sutures, Allis clamps are placed on the torn edges of the rectum in order that the upper angle of the tear in the rectal wall may be exposed. A double threaded black silk suture is then passed through all of the coats of the rectum and tied within the rectum.

FIG. 1059

FIG. 1060. Repair of complete laceration. Interrupted black silk sutures are introduced at 0.5 cm. intervals until the rectum is closed. The suture ends are left long and are allowed to protrude through the newly made anal orifice.

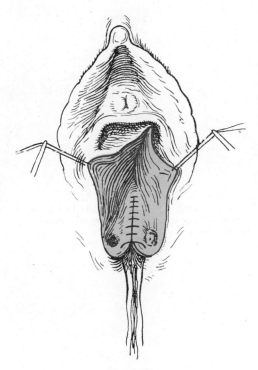

FIG. 1060

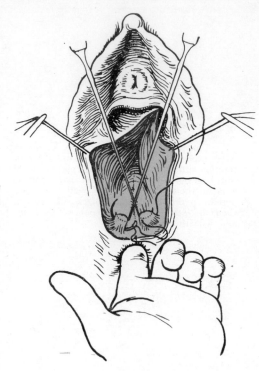

FIG. 1061. Repair of complete laceration.
With a finger in the rectum, hooks are passed
into the sphincter ends. Traction on the hooks
is then felt by the rectal finger and the operator
is assured that he is dealing with the sphincter.
The ends of the muscle are then united by interrupted catgut sutures.

FIG. 1061

FIG. 1062. Repair of complete laceration.
A layer of deep interrupted sutures reinforces the
rectal sutures.

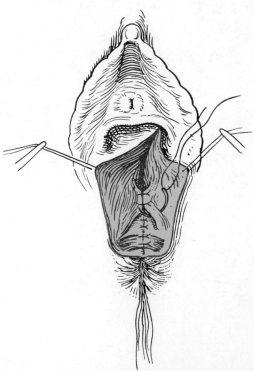

FIG. 1062

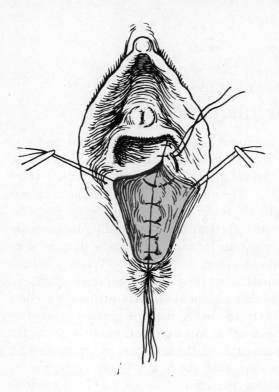

FIG. 1063. Repair of complete laceration. The upper angle and deeper structures
are united as in an incomplete tear.

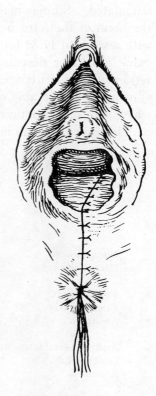

FIG. 1064. Repair of complete laceration completed.

CHAPTER XLV

RESUSCITATION OF THE NEWBORN CHILD

As was noted in Chapter VI, respiratory movements begin early in fetal life. In the animal experiments in which the fetus is artificially delivered into a suitable bath, these movements continue after birth and are not unlike those observed in the newly born infant (1). The mechanism by which the lungs are contracted and expanded, accordingly, is present and functions before the fetus is born and is not inaugurated at birth. Just as in postnatal life, these movements are dependent upon the stimulating influence of carbon dioxide since hyperventilation of the mother leads to apnea in the fetus. While a certain level of CO_2 is essential for the maintenance of these fetal respiratory efforts, an excess sufficient to accelerate the mother's respirations has little or no effect upon the movements of the child. On the other hand, a certain amount of oxygen also is necessary. If a gas mixture of low oxygen content is given, the fetal respiratory movements are depressed, even though those of the mother are stimulated. Studies made on goats show that the mixed blood which goes to the brain of the fetus has an average oxygen content of 5.9 vol.%, in contrast with a value of 17.85 for the arterial blood of the mother (2). This low oxygen value is further decreased when the placental circulation is retarded by the retraction of the uterine musculature at the end of the second stage of labor. Obviously, comparable observations have not been made on the mixed blood which goes to the brain of the human fetus but studies of blood taken from the umbilical cord at birth indicate a similar oxygen shortage (Table I).

TABLE I
UMBILICAL VEIN BLOOD
(Eastman)

	pH	CO₂ CONTENT	CO₂ TENSION	O₂ CONTENT	LACTIC ACID
		Vol. %	Mm.	Vol. %	Mg. 100 cc.
Normal infants Normal delivery	7.36	48.4	36.1	10.5	35.7
Normal infants Forceps delivery Anesthesia	7.20	40.1	44.8	7.3	50.1
Asphyxiated infants Some forceps Anesthesia	7.04	37.5	61.6	1.3	76.5

Persistence of the conditions which are responsible for this anoxemia leads to a still further diminution in the oxygen content of the fetal blood and, in the presence of such marked oxygen deprivation, lactic acid accumulates in increasing amounts. These acid additions combine with buffer sodium and release CO_2 with a resultant lowering of the CO_2 content of the blood. The inadequate diffusion of this liberated CO_2 through the placenta causes an increase in the CO_2 tension and increases the acidity as does the alkali deficit caused by the fixation of base by lactic acid. Thus the pH of the infant's blood may be progressively lowered to or below the limits of tolerance as the asphyxia deepens. When it reaches 7 or under, the child naturally is unable to survive (3, 4, 5).

According to this explanation of the chemical changes associated with asphyxia, the primary and most important alteration is the decrease in the oxygen content of the newborn infant's blood. It has been found that the oxygen content of the umbilical vein blood may be lowered to 5 vol. % without any ill effect. When it falls below this figure, however, the brain cells are affected and clinical evidences of asphyxia appear. If reduced to 1 vol. % or less, the oxygen supply to the respiratory center is inadequate for the basal requirements of the cells and they no longer are able to respond to the stimulus of CO_2 (6).

While the mechanism by which the lungs are contracted and expanded is similar to that observed in postnatal life, the child before birth inhales and exhales amniotic fluid. When it is born, therefore, the condition of the lungs may be similar to that of an immersion victim who is rescued from drowning. Some of the fluid, no doubt, is forced out of the lungs as the body of the child is compressed during the delivery. Much of it, however, may be retained. This is particularly true in the infants who are born by Cesarean section as well as in those delivered rapidly through the natural passages by operative means while the mother is deeply anesthetized. Even though the fluid may be forced out of the lungs, it often accumulates in the nasopharynx from which it is again drawn into the lungs when the child takes its first inspiration. **The first step in the resuscitation of the newborn infant, therefore, should be directed toward the removal of the fluid accumulations in the respiratory passages** just as it is the first step in the resuscitation of the patient suffering from immersion.

Clearing the respiratory passages. Material in the lungs as well as that in the nasopharynx at birth, often will run out of the mouth and nose if the child is inverted. Immediately after birth and preferably before the first inspiration occurs, the trunk of the child is inverted so that the head is dependent. While waiting for the first inspiration, the infant is suspended by the feet and the trachea is stroked toward the head. The material which exudes from the mouth and nose is then wiped away. By the use of this procedure, the fluid which has collected in the lungs as well as that which has accumulated in the nasopharynx is thus removed from the respiratory passages or is sufficiently dependent so that it may not be drawn back into the lungs with the first inspiration. In most instances, this simple measure is all that is necessary to secure the reestablishment of respiration. Its success, however, depends upon its use before the first inspiratory movements are made. On the other hand, if the inversion is too long delayed, the material in the mouth and nasopharynx may be aspirated and cause asphyxia in a child who otherwise is capable of breathing. Inversion of the child as described has been used in our clinic for many years and, in our opinion, is one of the most valuable aids in the resuscitation of the newborn infant. Objection to its use has been made on the ground that it favors intracranial hemorrhage whenever the brain is injured. This disadvantage, however, is slight in comparison with the great advantage to be gained by its use as a means of clearing the respiratory passages.

If, in spite of the inversion of the child, the passages become obstructed, a small rubber catheter is inserted into the larynx under guidance of the finger and the obstructing material is removed by suction. This procedure should always precede any method of artificial respiration since the attempt to force air into a child with obstructed respiratory passages is about as unreasonable as attempting to fill a bottle without removing the cork. In hospital practice, where ample facilities are at hand, material from the nasopharynx may be removed with a soft rubber ear syringe, a goose-neck aspirator designed for this purpose or with a catheter attached to a special glass contrivance which permits the withdrawal of fluid without risk of aspiration by the operator. A still better method consists in exposing the glottis and removing the material from the larynx and trachea by suction under direct vision. The next step in the resuscitation of a newborn infant will depend upon the condition of the child.

If the color, muscle tone and pulsations of the cord are good, it is well to await the natural return of the respiratory efforts. The CO_2 in the child's blood usually is sufficient to stimulate respiration. After all normal and easy operated deliveries, accordingly, Nature should be given a trial before artificial methods are used. This is particularly true if the heart beat at the apex is regular and has not been slowed, if the muscle tone is good and if the reflexes are present. Such infants are able to urinate and resist movements of the head and extremities. At first, they begin to breathe by occasional gasps and, within a short time, regular respiration is established. If it is not, inhalations of oxygen carbon dioxide through a pharyngeal tube or small mask applied over the mouth and nose usually are sufficient to bring about the desired result. Whenever the ribs and epigastrium become retracted during an inspiratory effort, aspiration of the nasopharnyx and trachea should be repeated since this observation indicates an obstruction of the air passages.   Should the apparatus necessary for the giving of oxygen carbon dioxide not be available, as is usually the case in home practice, respiration may be hastened by the following measures if artificial stimulation is found to be necessary after Nature has been given a fair trial:

a. Milking of the trachea while the child is in the inverted position
b. Irritation of the skin over the spine by gently rubbing the finger tips over this area.
c. Flagellation by striking gentle, glancing blows against the buttocks or the soles of the feet.
d. Sprinkling the child with whatever cool fluid is available.

If these measures are carefully employed, no harm will result.   Careless flagellation, however, has been blamed for some injuries which occasionally cause death.   The commonest of these is suprarenal hemorrhage.   While a direct blow over the small of the back might be responsible for such a lesion, it is difficult to conceive how spanking the buttocks with gentle, glancing blows could cause any damage.

If the child is pallid, the muscle tone lost, pulsations in the cord markedly slowed or if the apex beat is slow or irregular, some form of artificial respiration should be used **at once.**   In this connection, it may be well to recall that the chemical changes which occur in asphyxia favor an increase in the CO_2 tension. As a result, **sufficient CO_2 to stimulate respiration probably is always present.** On the other hand, **the oxygen content of the blood is being constantly lowered.** When it drops to 1 vol. %, the oxygen supply is inadequate for the basal requirements of the cells of the respiratory center and they no longer respond to the stimulus of CO_2.   Further reduction of the oxygen supply, therefore, depresses respiration and its increase acts as a stimulant.   This reversal of the customary action of the respiratory center which is brought about by an insufficient supply of oxygen, may be precipitated by the use of ordinary respiratory stimulants in the presence of a severe anoxemia which is approaching the threshold of reversal, because such stimulants cause an increase in oxygen consumption (6).   Carbon dioxide and other respiratory stimulants, therefore, act only in the presence of sufficient oxygen to support the metabolism of cellular activity; otherwise, they may be depressants.   The customary respiratory stimulants, accordingly, should not be used when the respiratory center is approaching the stage of reversal unless an adequate supply of oxygen is available.   Clinical proof of the untoward action of respiratory stimulants is afforded by the not infrequent observation that their use is sometimes followed by a cessation of all respiratory movements and the death of the asphyxiated infant is hastened.   For this reason, atropine, camphor, strychnine, caffein, alphalobelin, coramine and carbon dioxide should not be used unless the respiratory passages are clear and ample quantities of oxygen are taken into the lungs (4, 5). Since the CO_2 tension of the blood in asphyxiated infants is almost double that of those without respiratory embarrassment, the giving of CO_2 seems to be superfluous and may possibly be harmful in asphyxia neonatorum.

In severe cases of asphyxia in which the reflexes are absent and the glottis is relaxed, the baby has a relaxed open larynx which is suitable for intubation. The larynx is exposed by means of a laryngoscope and, after aspiration of the fluid from the passages, a tube is inserted into the trachea. Through this, oxygen and carbon dioxide or oxygen alone are introduced under controlled manometric pressure (7).

In the less severe cases, the reflexes are present and laryngoscopic examination is difficult. Such infants not only are not suitable for intubation but in them intubation usually is unnecessary. After aspirating the fluids from the nasopharynx the lungs are inflated intermittently with oxygen or carbon dioxide by pharyngeal insufflation through a mask which fits over the mouth and nose or through such a mask which contains a rubber breathing tube for insertion into the mouth (8). From the previous discussion of the chemistry of asphyxia, it would seem that CO_2 is unnecessary and that the use of oxygen alone is to be preferred. This conclusion is also supported by favorable clinical experience While the more or less elaborate devices for the performance of artificial respiration are quite satisfactory for hospital practice, they are not sufficiently portable for use in the home. In domiciliary practice, therefore, reliance must be placed on the older and more dangerous methods. All of these procedures may do damage which in itself may cause the death of the child. For this reason, they should not be employed in the cases which may recover without their use.

MOUTH TO MOUTH INSUFFLATION. While mouth to mouth insufflation is advantageous in starting respiration, the risk that accompanies its use is considerable. The abdomen is compressed with the right hand while the attendant places a piece of sterile gauze over the mouth and blows into the respiratory passages. This causes the thorax to expand, after which it is gently compressed with the hand and the insufflation is repeated. Often, one or two insufflations are sufficient to start respiration. There is great danger of injury to the lungs when this procedure is employed and even though respiration is established, such injury may ultimately cause the child's death.

REFERENCES

1. SNYDER, F. F. AND ROSENFELD, M.: Direct Observations of Intrauterine Respiratory Movements of the Fetus and the Rôle of Carbon Dioxide in their Regulation. Am. J. Physiol., 1937, 119, 153.
   Also: Intra-Uterine Respiratory Movements of the Human Fetus. J. A. M. A., 1937, 23, 1946.
2. HUGGETT, A. ST.G.: Fetal Blood-Gas Tensions and Gas Transfusion Through the Placenta of the Goat. J. Physiol., 1926–27, 62, 373.
3. EASTMAN, N. J.: Foetal Blood Studies I: The Oxygen Relationships of Umbilical Cord Blood at Birth. Bull J. Hopk. Hosp., 1930, 47, 221.
4. EASTMAN, N. J. AND MCLANE, C. M.: Foetal Blood Studies II: The Lactic Acid Content of the Umbilical Cord Blood Under Various Conditions. Bull. J. Hopk. Hosp., 1931, 48, 261.
5. EASTMAN, N. J.: Fetal Blood Studies III: The Chemical Nature of Asphyxia Neonatorum and Its Bearing on Certain Practical Problems. Bull. J. Hopkins Hosp., 1932, 50, 39.
6. SCHMIDT, C. F.: The Influence of Cerebral Blood-Flow on Respiration I. The Respiratory Responses to Changes in Cerebral Blood-Flow. Am. J. Physiol., 1928, 84, 202.
7. FLAGG, P.: The Treatment of Postnatal Asphyxia. Am. J. Obs. & Gyn., 1931, 21, 537.
8. KREISELMAN, J., KANE, H. F. AND SWOPE, R. B.: A New Apparatus for Resuscitation of Asphyxiated New-Born Babies. Am. J. Obs. & Gyn., 1928, 15, 552.
9. MURPHY, D. P., WILSON, R. B. AND BOWMAN, J. E.: The Drinker Respirator Treatment of the Immediate Asphyxia of the New-Born. Am. J. Obs. & Gyn., 1931, 21, 528.

CHAPTER XLVI

ANALGESIA, AMNESIA AND ANESTHESIA

While the relief of pain during labor by the use of opium and other substances was attempted in ancient times, it was not until chloroform was used for this purpose about one hundred years ago, that the medical profession was able to alleviate the suffering of childbirth. Because of its toxicity this potent anesthetic agent ultimately was used only during the second or expulsive stage of labor. Shortly after the beginning of this century, morphine and scopolamine were successfully employed to lessen the pain which accompanies the stage of cervical dilatation. Although this method, as originally proposed, proved to be less safe for the mother and child than was anticipated, it stimulated a new and intense interest in the subject of pain relief during labor with the result that the old methods were made less dangerous and many new ones were proposed. Among these were the use of chloroform, ether, nitrous oxide, ethylene, cyclopropane, morphine or pantopon and scopolamine, the barbiturates alone or combined with scopolamine, demerol and scopolamine, paraldehyde, local, paravertebral, presacral, caudal and spinal anesthesia. This long list of agents indicates the praiseworthy zeal which the obstetricians of the present and past generation displayed in their effort to render childbirth painless. It also indicates that the goal towards which all were striving has not been reached. In other words, the perfect method which will give 100% relief from pain without adding to the maternal or fetal risk has not been discovered.

Although the laudable attempt to reach the desired goal with the "twilight sleep" routine deserves credit for having stimulated an interest which led to much achievement, it also introduced the element of amnesia which by diverting attention from the original objective, has had a retarding influence. Soon after this method was introduced it was found that, even though some patients had little relief from pain, these same patients often lost all memory of their suffering. As a consequence, amnesia became as desirable as analgesia and since it was more easily attained than complete analgesia, the true objective of pain relief became a secondary consideration. As the attainment of amnesia became more perfect, patients even demanded that they be put to sleep at the onset of labor and not awakened until after the child was born. Thus was created the impression that labor is an experience concerning which the patient should have no recollection. The recent introduction of continuous caudal anesthesia, by completely relieving the pain of labor in those patients to whom its administration is suited, has demonstrated that women do not object to the retention of their consciousness during the birth of their children if they are free from pain at the time. On the contrary, the conscious experience of childbirth is regarded by many as desirable rather than objectionable. Caudal anesthesia therefore should be credited with having directed the interest of the obstetrician back to the original and true objective of pain relief, even though the technic of its administration may prove to be too complicated for universal application.

Although there is no method that will give 100% pain relief to every woman in labor with absolute safety for the mother and child, it is possible to give every woman some relief, and many women, relief from most of their suffering. It therefore is the physician's duty to give, and the patient's right to demand, such relief as is consistent with safety. The decision as to the method and the extent to which it shall be used, however, should be made by the physician and not by the patient.

MORPHINE AND SCOPOLAMINE

Morphine and scopolamine were used early in this century to produce analgesia and amnesia during labor according to the "dämmerschlaf" or "twilight sleep" technic (1). While the original technic has been abandoned in most clinics it deserves credit for having demonstrated the advantages as well as the disadvantages of these drugs in obstetrics. The experience thus gained also led many obstetricians to modify their routine for the sake of greater safety or to search elsewhere for a better method of pain relief during childbirth.

While different obstetricians have somewhat different routines the following method comes quite close to that which is recommended by most of them. When labor is fairly well established with the pains recurring every 5 minutes and the cervix about 2 cm. in diameter, morphine gr. $\frac{1}{6}$ and scopolamine gr. $\frac{1}{150}$ are given hypodermically. Forty-five minutes later, scopolamine gr. $\frac{1}{200}$ is repeated and after three-quarters of an hour, half of the last dose of scopolamine or $\frac{1}{400}$th gr. is given. The morphine is never repeated unless the labor is prolonged. It likewise is not given within 3 hours of the anticipated delivery. Further administration of the scopolamine depends upon the degree of seminarcosis and the return of the patient's ability to cooperate (2, 3).

When these drugs are given sufficiently early the patient shows little or no evidence of pain during the contractions of the uterus and sleeps in the intervals between them. If started after the labor is well established they have only a slightly depressing effect on the uterine contractions and more than compensate for this disadvantage by having a relaxing effect on the cervix. In satisfactory cases accordingly, the first stage of labor may be accelerated. The patient's inability to cooperate and the partial loss of the bearing down reflex interferes with the progress of the second stage. In many instances it is delayed and the need for operative interference is increased. This however is not a very serious disadvantage since the use of low forceps and episiotomy does not add greatly to the risk in the average maternity hospital. Because the anesthetic used for the operative delivery adds to the depressing effect which morphine and scopolamine have upon the uterus, separation of the placenta may be delayed and hemorrhage during and after the third stage is increased.

The depressing action of this method of pain relief on the respiratory center of the fetus causes a delay in the inauguration of respiration in the newborn child. The danger of apnea and oligopnea in the child following the use of these drugs led to the abandonment of the original "twilight sleep" routine and caused most obstetricians to refrain from using morphine and scopolamine, particularly morphine, within 3 hours of the anticpated delivery of the child.

In addition to its depressing effect on the fetal respiratory center, the morphine and scopolamine method of analgesia and amnesia has two other rather important disadvantages. One is the tendency to cause restlessness and excitement in some patients. Because of this action and because the patient is in a state of seminarcosis, the constant attendance of a nurse is essential. The other disadvantage is the fact that these drugs may stop the labor if they are given too soon. It may aid the beginner to compare the frequency and intensity of the uterine contractions, when the patient is up, with their frequency and intensity when she is lying down. If lying down diminishes the contractions or prolongs the interval between them, the administration of the drugs should be withheld until no change is effected by the recumbent posture.

BARBITURATES

The barbiturates in combination with scopolamine have been used extensively to produce amnesia. Their use is usually supplemented by some form of anesthesia during the actual delivery of the child. Even though the sensation of pain is not eliminated, all memory of the labor may be obliterated. A patient may scream and show every evidence of pain during a uterine contraction and after the labor is over have no recollection of her suffering.

The preparations most commonly used are seconal sodium for rapid action of short duration and pentobarbital sodium or sodium amytal for a more prolonged effect. The dose of seconal is 3 to $4\frac{1}{2}$ grains and that of pentobarbital is $1\frac{1}{2}$ to 3 grains.

When labor is definitely established and the patient begins to complain,

6 grains of pentobarbital sodium are given orally with scopolamine gr. $\frac{1}{150}$ hypodermically. Two hours later, $1\frac{1}{2}$ grains of the barbiturate and $\frac{1}{200}$ gr. of scopolamine are repeated if the patient is awake and answers questions intelligently (4, 5, 6).

The room is darkened and kept quiet. Throughout the labor a nurse must be in constant attendance to guard against the patient's falling out of bed and injuring herself while under the influence of the drugs. Late in the first stage of labor when the cervix is half to three-quarters dilated, some clinics add paraldehyde or ether in oil by rectum. For the delivery of the child, ether, nitrous oxide and ether, spinal and caudal anesthesia are used. Since the cooperation of the patient often is lacking, the delivery of the child usually is accomplished by the use of forceps or some other type of obstetric operation.

In a series of 14,676 deliveries in which the barbiturates were used 85% of the patients had no recollection or only slight recollection of their labors and 62% of the babies breathed immediately after birth (6).

The greatest disadvantage of the barbiturates is their tendency to cause restlessness, excitement and occasionally delirium. In about 15% of the cases this difficulty is quite troublesome. The patient may try to get up or while thrashing about she may fall out of bed. She also may contaminate the vulva by touching the genitalia. Not only is she unable to cooperate but at times she becomes decidedly unmanageable. The bed accordingly should be equipped with padded side boards and constant supervision by a nurse is imperative. Because the patient may mutter incoherently or even scream like a maniac the presence of the relatives should be prohibited. For the control of this excitement, demerol mg. 100 or paraldehyde and ether in oil per rectum are recommended.

The barbiturates are central nervous system depressants. Given orally in therapeutic doses they cause slight slowing of the respiration and little or no change in the circulation. In large doses or when used intravenously they may cause respiratory and circulatory failure, the former preceding the latter by a sufficient interval to permit the use of artificial respiration. A rather marked fall in blood pressure is not uncommon after rapid intravenous administration. Changes in the pulmonary vascular bed which normally is somewhat congested in all pregnancies may cause edema of the lungs (7). As the barbiturates pass through the placenta they may and often do have a depressant effect upon the respiratory center of the fetus. After their use accordingly, the inauguration of respiration in the newborn child may be delayed.

Even when the barbiturates are given orally in the usual doses some slight danger to the mother is present. In 10,097 pentobarbital cases reported by one of the leading exponents of this method, 35 or 1 in 288 had respiratory complications and 3 or 1 in 3366 died (6). One of the deaths occurred on the day of delivery and was due to pulmonary edema and massive collapse of the lungs. The other two succumbed to bronchopneumonia during the puerperium. Although respiratory difficulties may arise in the first stage of labor they usually are encountered in the second stage during the induction of anesthesia by one of the inhalation methods. When they occur the anesthetic should be discontinued, the foot of the bed elevated and the patient turned on her side to favor the escape of edema fluid from her lungs. Mechanical suction and an artificial airway should also be used.

In the large series of barbiturate cases previously mentioned 38% of the infants failed to breathe immediately after birth (6). Although some fetal respiratory difficulty was admitted, the author of the report stated that their stillbirth and neonatal death rates had fallen since the use of the barbiturate routine was inaugurated. He also stated that none of the infants showed signs of mental impairment, such as might be expected had anoxia been present. In the light of our present knowledge concerning the remote ill effects of anoxia, it would be interesting to compare the mentality at school age of the 38% of infants who failed to breathe immediately, with that of a similar number of infants who did breathe immediately after birth (8, 9).

PARALDEHYDE

Paraldehyde is given during labor for its rapid sedative effect. Patients often go to sleep between contractions within 15 to 20 minutes after its administration. The drug is given orally and per rectum with or without preliminary sedation in the form of morphine and scopolamine or the barbiturates. The supplementary use of ether or nitrous oxide and ether for the delivery of the child may be necessary (10, 11, 12, 13, 14, 15).

When the labor becomes decidedly painful, either morphine gr. $\frac{1}{6}$ and scopolamine gr. $\frac{1}{150}$ or pentobarbital sodium gr. 3 or seconal gr. $4\frac{1}{2}$ are given. As soon as the cervix is four to five cm. in diameter, 24 cc. of paraldehyde are given in cold water, swallow by swallow over a period of 15 to 20 minutes. After the first swallow it is advisable to wait five minutes to ascertain whether vomiting will occur. If it does occur not much of the drug will be lost and the stomach will be emptied so that the remainder may be retained. If vomiting persists the drug is given by rectum (11, 12, 13).

Another method of oral administration consists of the use of $4\frac{1}{2}$ gr. of seconal and 20 cc. of mineral oil preliminary to the use of paraldehyde. One-half hour later, five 1.2 gr. capsules of paraldehyde are given orally. These are repeated at hourly intervals if necessary until a total of 16 are taken.

Oral and rectal administration may also be combined. On admission a soap suds enema is given in a sufficient quantity to remove all fecal matter from the rectum. As soon as the patient begins to complain of pain, 20 cc. of paraldehyde are administered orally to women of average weight. If the weight is over 170 lbs., 1 cc. for each 10 lbs. above this weight is added. The paraldehyde is mixed with equal parts of port wine and water and is followed by small sips of the latter. Within 10 minutes the patient becomes drowsy and in a short time sleeps between contractions. When the effect of the drug wears off after 2 to 4 hours, a mixture of paraldehyde and benzyl alcohol is given by rectum. With the patient on her left side 1.2 cc. of paraldehyde for each 10 lbs. of body weight and 1.5 cc. of benzyl alcohol are instilled into the rectum by gravity through a funnel and large catheter which is inserted to a height of 4 inches. As the solution disappears from the funnel, 30 cc. of normal salt solution are added. This instillation is effective for from 3 to 5 hours but may be repeated in $1\frac{1}{2}$ hours if necessary (14, 15).

Although paraldehyde is considered to be one of the safest drugs used for the relief of pain and recovery has followed the administration of as much as 150 gm., deaths have been reported following 31 cc., 50 cc. and as little as 12 cc. In the latter case, a woman weighing 196 lbs. was given 12 cc. of paraldehyde with 6 cc. of benzyl alcohol per rectum when the cervix was fully dilated. She was delivered by forceps and died 18 hours after delivery and $21\frac{1}{2}$ hours after the administration of paraldehyde without having regained consciousness. Autopsy showed acute pulmonary congestion and edema with subpericardial and subplural hemorrhages consistent with asphyxia. The child was asphyxiated at birth and died 31 hours later after having had bouts of cyanosis and convulsions (16).

Restlessness may be a troublesome complication. It may be necessary to restrain the hands by using cuffs attached to the sides of the bed and often the addition of padded sideboards is necessary to prevent the patient from falling out of bed. Because of restlessness and the inability of the patient to cooperate, delivery by forceps under ether anesthesia may be necessary. A fairly large percentage of the infants are affected either by the drug or by the anoxemia which is produced by this method of analgesia and some difficulty in the initiation of respiration may be encountered. Those who advocate the use of paraldehyde however, report no increase in the incidence of stillbirths and neonatal deaths.

DEMEROL

Demerol, a synthetic drug which chemically resembles morphine and atropine has both an analgesic and a spasmolytic action which makes it useful when pain is due to smooth muscle spasm (17). In conjunction with scopolamine it is often used for the relief of pain during childbirth. Accumulating evidence seems to indicate that this combination offers the best means of securing analgesia and amnesia in labor with the least risk to the mother and child. In our experience, it has been possible to relieve the mother of 80% to 90% of her suffering without risk to herself or her child, by the use of demerol and scopolamine throughout the greater part of labor supplemented by local anesthesia for the actual delivery of the child.

Demerol mg. 100 and scopolamine gr. $\frac{1}{150}$ are given intramuscularly when the labor is established and the scopolamine is repeated 45 minutes later in a smaller dose of $\frac{1}{200}$ gr. Subsequently demerol mg. 100 is given every four hours and scopolamine gr. $\frac{1}{200}$ every three hours. Within 15 or 20 minutes the pain is relieved and neither the frequency nor the intensity of the uterine contractions are diminished. In addition, there seems to be a relaxing effect on the cervix. Often one is amazed at the manner in which the cervix melts away under this form of medication. These drugs accordingly not only relieve the pains of labor but they seem to favor dilatation of the cervix and thereby hasten the delivery (18, 19, 20).

While demerol and scopolamine lessen and may even abolish the intense pains of the second stage of labor, it usually is desirable to administer nitrous oxide and ether or employ local anesthesia for the delivery of the child. We have found local anesthesia to be very satisfactory. Because it does not increase the risk of fetal anoxia, it is our method of choice and is used routinely in our clinic. Given in the manner described, these drugs have little or no effect on the fetal or maternal respiratory center. Pulmonary complications in the mother are rare and spontaneous respiration of the child immediately after birth is the rule (21). During the past year the uncorrected combined stillbirth and neonatal death rate of fetuses over 1000 gm. in our clinic was 2.4%, while that of fetuses over 2500 gm. was 1.3%. Since these figures include congenital anomalies, obstetrical accidents etc. it is clear that the demerol and scopolamine which was given to most of the mothers could not have had a bad effect on the fetal respiratory center.

The chief disadvantage of this routine is that it may stop the labor if it is given too soon. To guard against this possibility, it may be well for the beginner to wait until labor is well established before administering the drugs. It also is recommended that he compare the strength and frequency of the contractions when the patient is up with the same when she is lying down. If the action of the uterus is weakened by lying down the drugs should be withheld until the recumbent posture has no effect on the contractions.

LOCAL ANESTHESIA

Local anesthesia of the perineum and vulva may be secured by infiltrating these structures with an anesthetic agent or by blocking the pudendal nerve posterior to the ischial spine (22, 23, 24, 25, 26). It is the simplest and safest method of anesthesia for the spontaneous delivery of the child, for episiotomy, for the repair of perineal lacerations, for low forceps delivery and for breech extraction. Local anesthesia also is the safest method for cesarean section.

When the head appears at the vulva a three inch 20 gage needle is inserted into the distended perineum in the midline just below the fourchette and a small amount of 1% procaine and 1–200,000 adrenaline in normal saline solution is injected beneath the skin. The needle is then passed downward and to one side in the direction of a point midway between the tuberosity of the ischium and the anus (the site of a possible mediolateral episiotomy). After aspirating to determine whether a vein has been entered, 10 cc. of the anesthetic solution are injected along lines radiating from the original site of insertion until that side of the

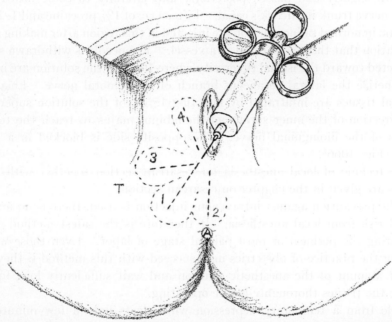

Fig. 1065. Local infiltration anesthesia. A small amount of 1% procaine and 1–200,000 adrenaline in normal saline solution is injected just below the fourchette. Through this anesthetized area, a 20 gage needle is passed to a point midway between the anus and the ischial tuberosity, 1. After aspirating to determine whether a vein has been entered, 10 cc. of the anesthetic solution are injected. The needle is again introduced at the original site and similar injections are made along the radiating lines indicated by 2, 3 and 4. The opposite side is infiltrated in a similar manner.

perineum and inner vulva are infiltrated. The needle is again introduced at the original site of insertion and passed toward the opposite side in a like manner and the injections are repeated on this side to complete the infiltration of the entire perineum and inner vulva (Fig. 1065). A sufficient amount of the solution should be used to produce the desired result, since several ounces may be injected without toxic effect, provided the needle is not in a vein. As intravenous injection is extremely dangerous, the plunger of the syringe should be withdrawn slightly to determine by the presence or absence of aspirated blood whether or not a vein has been entered. When blood is aspirated, the needle should be withdrawn and reinserted to one side of the vein. In addition to the use of a sufficient amount of the solution, it is important to wait five or ten minutes to allow thorough infiltration of the tissues before proceeding with the operation.

Pudendal block is accomplished in the following manner. With a finger in the vagina or rectum to locate the ischial spine and act as a guide, the needle is introduced midway between the anus and the tuberosity of one side and passed in the direction of the ischial spine. After making contact with the spine, it is withdrawn slightly and passed posteriorly and laterally to come into relation with the nerve trunk in Alcock's canal. Fifteen cc. of 1% procaine and 1–200,000 adrenaline in normal saline solution are injected in this region after making certain by aspiration that the needle is not in a vessel. The needle is withdrawn slightly and directed toward the ischial tuberosity where 10 cc. of the solution are injected to anesthetize the lateral cutaneous branch of the femoral nerve. Finally the superficial tissues are infiltrated by injecting 15 cc. of the solution superficially in the direction of the inner surface of the labium majus to reach the terminal branches of the ilioinguinal nerve. The opposite side is blocked in a similar manner (Fig. 1066).

The technic of local anesthesia for cesarean section together with its advantages are given in the chapter on cesarean section.

If the precaution against intravenous injection is used, there is no maternal nor fetal risk from local anesthesia. It therefore is the safest method of pain relief during the perineal or most painful stage of labor. Even those who are beginning the practice of obstetrics may succeed with this method if they use a sufficient amount of the anesthetic solution and wait sufficiently long for it to infiltrate the tissues thoroughly before operating.

Aside from a temporary depression which lasts only a few minutes, the strength of the uterine contractions is not impaired. Because of this and because the patient is conscious and able to cooperate the progress of the second stage is not interrupted. The lack of interference with the action of the uterus also assures prompt separation and expulsion of the placenta with minimum blood loss during and after the third stage of labor.

Because local anesthesia does not increase the tendency toward vomiting which is observed when inhalation methods are used and because the patient is not unconscious, the danger of aspirating regurgitated stomach contents is eliminated. Massive collapse of the lungs and aspiration pneumonia accordingly, are rarely encountered. This fact together with the absence of irritation of the respiratory tract makes local anesthesia the preferable method for the delivery of women who have respiratory infection and cardiac disease. It also is the method of choice in anemia, diabetes, nephritis and toxemia of pregnancy.

The fact that this method of pain relief has no effect on the fetal respiratory center renders it most suitable for premature deliveries. In our clinic this method of anesthesia when combined with episiotomy offers the premature infant the best chance of withstanding the hazards of labor.

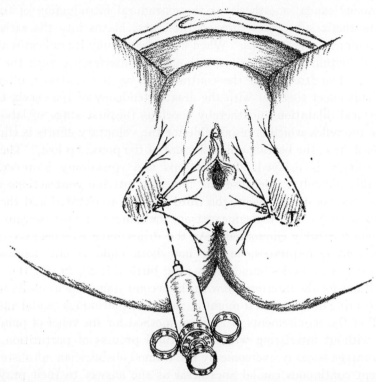

Fig. 1066. Pudendal block. With a finger in the vagina or rectum to locate the ischial spine and act as a guide, the needle is introduced midway between the anus and the tuberosity on one side and passed in the direction of the ischial spine. After making contact with the spine, it is withdrawn slightly and passed posteriorly and laterally to come into relation with the nerve trunk. Fifteen cc. of 1% procaine and 1–200,000 adrenaline in normal saline solution are injected in this region, after making certain by aspiration that the needle is not in a vessel. The needle is then withdrawn slightly and directed toward the ischial tuberosity. Ten cc. of the solution are injected in this region to block the lateral cutaneous branch of the femoral nerve. Finally the superficial tissues are infiltrated by injecting 15 cc. of the solution in the direction of the inner surface of the labium majus to reach the terminal branches of the ilioinguinal nerve. The opposite side is infiltrated in a similar manner.

Careful consideration of all of the methods advocated for the relief of pain during childbirth leads to the conclusion that **local anesthesia combined with demerol and scopolamine is the simplest, the safest and the most satisfactory method for the average woman in the hands of the average practitioner.**

CONTINUOUS CAUDAL ANESTHESIA

Continuous caudal anesthesia or the extradural introduction of fractional doses of anesthetic substances through the sacral hiatus into the sacral canal has many commendable features.   When used successfully it eradicates all of the pain of labor within a few minutes without any interference with the uterine contractions.   The strength of the contractions, on the contrary, often is increased.   This effect together with the greater tendency of the cervix to relax, hastens cervical dilatation and thereby shortens the first stage of labor.   Unfortunately the reflex which is responsible for the voluntary efforts is eliminated with the result that the bearing down element of the powers is lost.   The second stage accordingly is delayed. Low forceps and episiotomy however, easily overcome this difficulty.   Because the increased uterine contractions are not impaired by the anesthetic agent, the third stage is accelerated and the loss of blood is minimized.   For the same reason, the danger of post-partum hemorrhage is almost entirely eliminated.   As the drugs have no effect on the fetal respiratory center, respiration in the new born child is not depressed.   It therefore breathes and cries immediately after birth (27, 28, 29, 30, 31).

Were it not for the interference with the second stage which results from the loss of the bearing down reflex, it might be said that continuous caudal anesthesia satisfied all of the requirements of an ideal method for the relief of pain during childbirth without interfering with the natural process of parturition.   Since this disadvantage is easily overcome by the trained obstetrician, all obstetricians would accept continuous caudal anesthesia as the answer to their prayer if it were not for the fact that the **technic is difficult to master and the margin of safety for the mother is so narrow that constant supervision by one capable of recognizing and treating the first evidence of an untoward reaction is imperative.**

PREMATURE DELIVERIES.   The high degree of relaxation of the lower uterine segment, cervix, vagina and pelvic floor assures the birth of the premature infant's head with minimum trauma to the brain, cranial vessels and skull.   Continuous caudal anesthesia accordingly, is ideal for such cases.

TUBERCULOSIS.   The absence of voluntary efforts without lessening the strength of the uterine contractions enables the mother to complete the first stage and force the head sufficiently low so that it may be easily extracted with forceps.   The violent excursions of the diaphragm which accompany the bearing down efforts accordingly, are eliminated.   The lesion in the lung is thus kept at rest and dissemination of the infection by marked expansion and contraction of the thoracic cavity is avoided. This method of analgesia should prove exceedingly advantageous in the management of labor in a woman who has pulmonary tuberculosis.

ECLAMPSIA. When a woman with eclampsia goes into labor, convulsions are unquestionably stimulated. Because the absence of pain and the elimination of the bearing down efforts removes to a large extent the source of such stimuli, caudal anesthesia should prove valuable during labor in eclampsia.

SELECTION OF PATIENTS

Not all women are suitable subjects for caudal anesthesia. The originators of this technic state that only 60% of the women admitted to a maternity hospital may receive the benefits of their procedure (32).

About 10% of all admissions deliver within 40 minutes either because they are well advanced in labor when admitted or because the strength of the contractions and the lack of resistance of the soft parts make a precipitate labor inevitable. For them caudal anesthesia is not suitable and one of the inhalation anesthetics is preferable.

Another 10% of maternity patients are so nervous and apprehensive and fear the needle injection to such an extent that they are not good subjects for this method.

Deformities or diseases of the spine or central nervous system such as syphilis, tumors which narrow the spinal canal, abnormally low extension of and deformities around the sacral hiatus preclude the use of caudal anesthesia as does a history of epilepsy, hysteria and emotional instability. Such cases make up an additional 10% of admissions.

The balance of the 40% who are not suitable for this method of anesthesia consists of the following:

1. Obese individuals in whom accurate palpation of the hiatus and adequate insertion of the needle into the caudal canal is impossible.
2. Those who have a local infection or a pilonidal cyst at the site of injection.
3. Patients suffering from profound anemia and dehydration.
4. Labor cases having obstetric complications in which the obstetrician prefers to omit the use of caudal anesthesia.

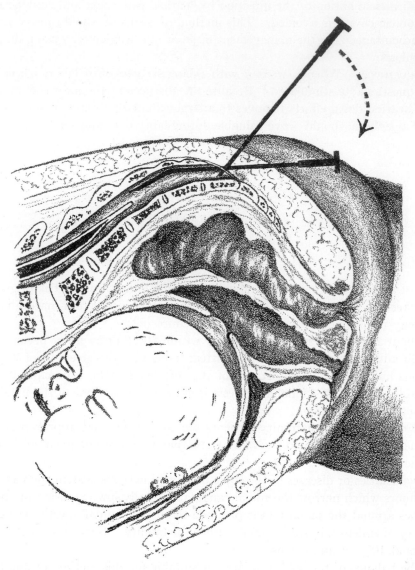

Fig. 1067. Continuous caudal anesthesia. A special malleable rustless steel 19 gage needle is passed through the sacrococcygeal ligament at an angle of 45°. It is then depressed through an arc of 1 to 3 cm. and forced upward slowly in the midline for 1 to 2 inches within the sacral canal. After aspirating to determine whether the dural sac has been entered, 8 cc. of the anesthetic solution is introduced and 10 minutes are allowed to elapse before the injection is completed, to make certain that low spinal anesthesia has not taken place. Following this waiting period, 30 cc. of 1½% metycaine in isotonic solution are slowly injected. An antiseptic ointment is then spread about the collar of the needle.

With the patient in the left lateral Sims position the sacrococcygeal area is cleansed with ether and an antiseptic solution. After placing the middle finger of the left hand on the tip of the coccyx, the thumb locates the sacral hiatus which is about 1½ to 2 inches above the tip of the coccyx.

A skin wheal is made immediately below the hiatus by injecting the anesthetic agent intradermally. The solution is then injected more deeply to secure infiltration of the sacrococcygeal ligament.

A special malleable rustless steel 19 gage needle is inserted in the midline in the direction of the hiatus at an angle of 45 degrees with the skin. As soon as the sacrococcygeal ligament is pierced, the collar of the needle is depressed through an arc of 1 to 3 cm. and the needle is thrust slowly and evenly in the midline for 1 to 2 inches within the sacral canal, where its bevel should lie inferior to the lowest extent of the dural sac. This is determined by measuring on the skin with the stilet the approximate extent of the needle. The point should always be below the level of the second sacral spine (27) (Fig. 1067).

After attaching a syringe, aspiration is attempted. Should spinal fluid be obtained it indicates that the needle has pierced the dura and lies within the subarachnoid space. When this occurs the needle should be withdrawn immediately and the case ruled out for caudal anesthesia. Failure to take this precaution may result in a massive spinal injection of the analgesic drug, the consequence of which would be extremely hazardous, if not fatal. The withdrawal of pure blood indicates that the needle has pierced a blood vessel in the highly vascular peridural space. In this event, the point of the needle should be moved until blood no longer can be obtained. The injection is then continued cautiously.

To doubly safeguard the patient against a massive intraspinal injection, a trial dose of 8 cc. of the solution should be injected and further action delayed 10 minutes to determine that a low spinal anesthesia does not ensue. Loss of motor power in the lower extremities in 10 minutes after injection indicates that the subarachnoid space has not been entered.

The syringe is removed and to the collar of the caudal needle four feet of special rubber tubing is attached, after all air has been excluded by filling it with the metycaine solution. With the palm of the left hand making pressure on the skin area over the dorsum of the sacrum, 30 cc. of 1½% metycaine in isotonic sodium chloride solution are slowly injected. An antiseptic ointment is then generously spread around the collar of the needle.

If the injection is properly carried out, the abdominal uterine cramps are relieved within 5 to 15 minutes. Supplementary injections of 20 cc. are given every 30 to 60 minutes to keep the patient comfortable. The indication for repeating the injection is a descending level of anesthesia below the umbilicus.

The original technic of continuous caudal anesthesia has been modified by the use of a nylon ureteral catheter inserted into the caudal canal through a large caliber needle and through which the anesthetic agent is injected. A 13 gage needle is first inserted into the caudal canal and through it a number 3 nylon ureteral catheter is passed into the caudal canal. Its tip should rest at about the third sacral foramen. After the catheter has been introduced the needle is withdrawn over it by a combined pull and rotation. Tubing is then attached to the catheter and the injections are carried out according to the original technic. This modification was designed to permit greater movement of the patient during labor without the hazard of trauma and breakage of the needle (33) (Fig 1068).

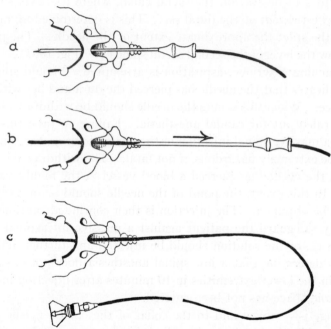

FIG. 1068. Continuous caudal anesthesia. Nylon catheter technic. A 13 gage needle is first inserted into the caudal canal and through it a number 3 nylon ureteral catheter is passed, A. After the catheter has been introduced the needle is withdrawn, B. Tubing is then attached to the catheter C and the injection carried out according to the original technic. Courtesy J. A. M. A.

Because of its potential dangers and because of the skill required for the satisfactory introduction of the needle, the technic of continuous caudal anesthesia should not be attempted without the supervision of one who is thoroughly experienced in its use. The young practitioner accordingly, should not employ this method of analgesia unless he has had an opportunity to become familiar with its use under the guidance of a skillful and experienced man. Since practice makes perfect, the percentage of failure as well as the percentage of serious complications varies inversely with the experience of those who administer this form of analgesia.

COMPLICATIONS

Headache may follow too rapid injection of the anesthetic agent. If it occurs, subsequent injections should be given more slowly.

Backache is complained of by some patients, particularly those who remain on their backs throughout labor. Change of posture is desirable and lying on one side or the other except at the time of delivery will reduce the incidence of this complaint.

Fall in blood pressure due to dilatation of the vessels of the pelvis and lower extremities may exceed 80 to 100 mm. in hypertensive patients, but is much less pronounced in those who have normal blood pressures. In about 20% of such cases the systolic pressure falls 20 mm. or more. Ephedrine 25 mg. accordingly is given intramuscularly or intravenously whenever the blood pressure falls below 90 mm.

Peridural infection seldom is encountered if a careful aseptic technic is followed. It occasionally does occur and may terminate fatally as it did in one of the cases reported by the originators of this method of analgesia.

Intravenous injection is extremely dangerous but seldom occurs if the syringe plunger is withdrawn slightly to determine by the presence or absence of aspirated blood whether or not a vein has been entered. This accident is followed almost immediately by marked disorientation and convulsions. Barbiturates given intravenously may control the convulsions. Just enough should be injected to accomplish this end and avoid overdosage. Rapid vascular absorption may cause an immediate circulatory collapse. For this, ephedrine sulfate, 25 or 50 mg., cardiac and circulatory stimulants, oxygen, plasma and blood transfusion are recommended.

Intradural injection is to be avoided by the use of the safeguards set up to prevent this accident. Chief of these is the tentative injection of 8 cc. of the anesthetic agent instead of the full amount, followed by a waiting period of 10 minutes to learn whether anesthesia from intraspinal injection has occurred. If the injected material enters the spinal canal in spite of the customary precautions, immediate spinal puncture and withdrawal of the anesthetic laden spinal fluid is indicated. Artificial respiration and the administration of oxygen through a trachial tube employed sufficiently early may prevent the tragic consequence of this accident. No time, however, can be wasted since patients have died within two minutes after intradural injection.

From the foregoing discussion it may be concluded that caudal anesthesia is accompanied by potential dangers. Meticulous care in guarding against these dangers may reduce but not entirely eliminate the risk as is evident from the report of the following accidents. The author of this report states that the drug was accidentally injected intradurally and caused sudden respiratory failure in what was approximately their 600th case. The accident occurred in spite of the fact that the injection was made by an experienced man who observed the precautions usually followed to exclude intradermal and intravenous injection. Although the intratrachial oxygen, artificial respiration, lumbar puncture and the withdrawal of spinal fluid with its contained anesthetic resulted in the restoration of spontaneous respiration after 20 anxious minutes, their confidence was so shaken that the routine use of caudal anesthesia was discontinued. The same author states that two well known university hospitals in his locality also abandoned caudal anesthesia because of similar but fatal accidents. In one, the patient died two minutes after the drug was injected. Although the customary safety precautions had been observed, autopsy revealed the presence of the drug in the spinal fluid. In the other, the anesthetist left the patient five minutes after the anesthetic was administered. On his return a few minutes later, the patient was dead (35).

These tragic accidents show how narrow the margin of safety is when caudal anesthesia is used. They also emphasize the importance of restricting its use to those who not only are thoroughly familiar with the technic of its administration but who are competent to recognize and treat the first evidence of danger and who in addition have the time and are willing to give the constant supervision which is so essential. These restrictions unfortunately limit the use of continuous caudal anesthesia and no doubt will prevent its universal adoption. It is to be hoped that the stimulus resulting from this new technic together with the information gained from its new approach to the problem of pain relief may lead to a more practical solution which will give complete relief from the suffering of childbirth without risk to the mother or child.

SPINAL ANESTHESIA

Spinal anesthesia produced by the introduction of an anesthetic agent into the subarachnoid space is sometimes used for the delivery of the child and for some obstetrical operations, including cesarean section. The anesthetic agent is introduced through the third or fourth lumbar interspace and having a higher specific gravity than the spinal fluid its diffusion in the direction of the brain is limited.

After making an intradermal wheal between the third and fourth lumbar spines, 1 to 2 cc. of 1% procaine are injected through the muscle into the deeper structures. A 20 gage needle is then passed through the infiltrated area into the subarachnoid space and a free flow of the spinal fluid is obtained. After dissolving 100 to 150 mg. of procaine in 4 cc. of spinal fluid the solution is slowly injected into the subarachnoid space (36). Relief of pain occurs within 3 to 5 minutes. With the needle left in place the blood pressure is determined at five minute intervals. If the systolic pressure remains above 100 mm. the patient is in no danger. Should it fall below 50 mm. the level of anesthesia is ascertained by pin prick. In the event that anesthesia has extended several segments above the umbilicus, 4 to 5 cc. of spinal fluid should be withdrawn and inhalations of pure oxygen started. A fall in blood pressure below 80 mm. usually is corrected by the intravenous injection of 25 mg. of ephedrine. The Trendelenburg position should not be used for at least 10 minutes and preferably not until the uterus is empty. Intravenous saline solution with or without adrenaline is administered during and following the operation as a prophylaxis against shock.

The relief of pain is prompt and complete and lasts for $1\frac{1}{2}$ to 2 hours. This relatively short action of spinal anesthesia however, renders it unsuitable for the first stage of labor and limits its usefulness largely to the delivery of the child and operative procedures. Because the patient is conscious and free from restlessness and excitement, a good aseptic technic for the delivery or operation may be followed. The uterine contractions are not lessened in frequency and intensity. They accordingly assist in the delivery of the child and minimize the blood loss during and after the 3rd stage. This advantage on the other hand is a distinct disadvantage when uterine relaxation is required. Spinal anesthesia therefore should not be used for internal version and the correction of a face presentation. Ordinarily there is no depression of respiration in the mother and as a result the hazard of fetal anoxia is reduced. Most infants breathe immediately after birth.

The accidents which may occur when spinal anesthesia is used frequently are serious and often cause the sudden death of the patient. They usually are due to carelessness and faulty technic. Because the ill effects are so sudden and so grave and because their prevention requires such careful attention to all of the details of its administration, spinal anesthesia is regarded by many as the most dangerous of all methods of pain relief. This form of anesthesia should be administered only by trained anesthetists who not only are careful to follow the details of the technic but who are capable of immediately detecting and treating any untoward reaction.

The chief dangers are respiratory depression due to depression of the respiratory center or depression of the phrenic and intercostal nerves, and peripheral vascular collapse resulting in shock. Both of these accidents however, can usually be avoided by careful attention to the details of the spinal anesthesia technic.

Headache occurs in about one out of six patients and may be severe and persistent in about half of them. Because the bearing down reflex is interfered with, the voluntary efforts are diminished or eliminated. Anterior rotation of posterior positions of the occiput is more frequently delayed or arrested and operative interference is more often required than when no anesthetic or local anesthesia is used.

Spinal anesthesia is contraindicated in the presence of shock, severe hemorrhage, anemia and low blood pressure. It is preferable to general anesthesia in diabetes, asthma, tuberculosis and other respiratory infections.

CHLOROFORM

Chloroform was one of the first anesthetic agents used to relieve the pains of childbirth. Its use by Queen Victoria's physicians during her eighth confinement gave it vogue and lead to the origin of the term "chloroform a la Reine" which even today is applied to this method of obstetric analgesia. Because it acts rapidly and is pleasant to take, chloroform soon became popular in all countries and this popularity was retained until the turn of the century when it was largely replaced by safer procedures. Owing to the fact that chloroform is much less volatile than ether it still is the preferable anesthetic in the tropics.

Since chloroform is very irritating to the conjunctiva and may even burn the skin, the face is anointed with vaseline and the eyes are covered with rubber tissue prior to its administration. This anesthetic is always administered **drop by drop** (never poured) on an **opened mask** consisting of a few layers of gauze covering a light wire frame. In order that air may enter from below and prevent too great a concentration of the vapors the mask should always be held a little above the face. At the beginning of each contraction of the uterus the mask is placed over the patient's nose and mouth. Within a few seconds the pain becomes deadened and often entirely disappears. As soon as the contraction ceases the anesthetic is removed and the patient is urged to take several deep breaths while she is resting. If chloroform is not given in the interval between contractions fairly satisfactory analgesia will be obtained without excitement and loss of the patient's ability to cooperate.

Because chloroform lessens the strength of the uterine contractions, its administration should not be started until after the cervix is fully dilated and the bearing down efforts have automatically begun to augment the force of each contraction. When crowning takes place or in the event that an episiotomy is to be performed, the anesthetic is deepened slightly to secure greater relaxation of the perineum and enable the obstetrician to deliver the head in the interval between contractions by the modified Ritgens maneuver.

The diminished intensity of the uterine contractions may prolong the third stage of labor and increase the tendency toward postpartum hemorrhage.   For this reason, the anesthetic should be discontinued immediately after the child is born and the separation and expulsion of the placenta awaited before repair of the perineum is attempted.   Many women have died from postpartum hemorrhage because this precaution was not followed.   It is better to administer the anesthetic a second time after the placenta has been expressed and the hemorrhage controlled by retraction and contraction of the uterus than to prolong the anesthetic and increase the risk of third stage difficulties and postpartum hemorrhage.   Removal of the anesthetic immediately after the birth of the child's head also permits the anesthetist to give the mother oxygen inhalations which will greatly benefit the child if the umbilical cord is not tied until it stops pulsating.

Because it is the most potent anesthetic, anesthesia can be induced more rapidly and complete relaxation of the uterus obtained in a shorter time with chloroform than with any other agent.   It therefore is of great value when used as a means of diminishing the violence of the uterine contractions in precipitate labor and after the unwise use of posterior pituitary extract.   It also is the anesthetic of choice for those operations which require complete relaxation of the uterus such as internal podalic version and the decomposition of a frank breech by Pinard's maneuver.

While chloroform is the most potent of the inhalation anesthetics, it also is the most dangerous.   It acts as a depressant of the central nervous system and affects the highest centers first and the medulla last.   In toxic amounts paralysis of respiration occurs shortly before cardiac arrest, but sufficient time elapses between the two events to permit the use of artificial respiration.   Because the margin of safety in this respect is much less than that observed when ether is used, ether has to a large extent replaced chloroform in most hospitals.   In addition to causing sudden death from respiratory and cardiac failure during the administration of the anesthetic, chloroform may also cause death several days later.   In such cases, the picture of a normally convalescing puerpera changes to one of impending tragedy.   Troublesome nausea and vomiting appear on about the third day and are soon accompanied by increasing jaundice.   Within 24 hours the patient goes into coma and dies.   Autopsy then reveals marked central necrosis of the liver.

The early manifestations of chloroform poisoning are treated by the removal of the anesthetic, artificial respiration, the giving of oxygen through a trachial tube and the administration of circulatory stimulants.   The best treatment however is prophylactic and consists of the use of the drop method with an open mask which is never allowed tightly to encircle the mouth and nose.   Late chloroform poisoning is treated by intravenous injections of glucose.   Here again prophylaxis is most important.   If the anesthetic is not given over a long period of time, the danger of liver necrosis is greatly lessened. For this reason, chloroform analgesia (during the uterine contractions only) should be used for only one hour and surgical anesthesia by this agent should not be carried on for more than thirty minutes.

ETHER

Ether, because of its greater safety, has replaced chloroform as an anesthetic agent to a very large extent. It is used alone or with nitrous oxide during the delivery of the child and for most obstetric operations which do not require marked relaxation of the uterus. Mixed with oil it also is given by rectum to secure analgesia during the latter part of the first and early in the second stage of labor. Its pungent irritating odor however makes it unpleasant as an inhalation analgesic and this, together with the fact that its action is rather slow, has prevented light inhalations of ether from becoming popular for prolonged analgesia.

Before administering ether the face should be anointed with oil or vaseline and the eyes should be protected with rubber tissue. If the drug is to be used to produce inhalation analgesia it may be given in two ways. In one a semi-closed inhaler of the Allis type is saturated with ether and placed over the mouth and nose during the contractions only. After removing the mask the patient is encouraged to take several deep inspirations in the interval between pains. In the other, the drug is given by the drop method and an open mask is used. The mask is kept over the mouth and nose continuously. Throughout each labor pain the drops are given rapidly but in the interval between contractions they are reduced to 5–10 per minute. At the end of the second stage of labor surgical anesthesia with relaxation of the perineum is secured by increasing the rate of administration while the child's head is being delivered. After the birth of the head the mask is removed and oxygen inhalations are given until the cord stops pulsating. As noted in the discussion of chloroform the anesthetic should not be continued for the purpose of perineal repair until after the placenta has been expressed and the danger of postpartum hemorrhage from uterine atony eliminated. While the use of ether according to either method as an analgesic is not very satisfactory, its use in combination with nitrous oxide is well suited to the needs of the end of the second stage of labor. As a supplement to the nitrous oxide and oxygen analgesia which is employed late in the first stage and early in the second, it accordingly, is very widely used for the purpose of securing anesthesia and relaxation during the actual delivery of the child.

Rectal ether. Ether administered rectally by the modified Gwathmey technic is a much more suitable analgesic agent than inhalation ether. After giving a cleansing 5% bicarbonate of soda enema, $2\frac{1}{2}$ ounces of ether mixed with

$1\frac{1}{2}$ ounces of mineral oil are injected into the rectum by gravity or by a special pressure apparatus through a rectal tube which has been inserted sufficiently far to pass above the presenting part (about 8 inches). The patient is then kept on her side and requested to pant in order that straining efforts and the expulsion of the drug may be avoided. Pressure likewise is made over the rectum with a pad for the same purpose. Analgesia follows within a few minutes and lasts for several hours at the expiration of which the instillation of ether and oil may be repeated if necessary. This form of analgesia usually is supplemented by inhalations of ether or nitrous oxide and ether for the delivery of the child. Because ether may diminish or even stop the uterine contractions it is advisable to postpone the use of rectal ether until the cervix is 5 to 7 cm. in diameter and precede its use by the employment of morphine and scopolamine or demerol and scopolamine (37, 38, 39).

Like chloroform, ether depresses the central nervous system but because of its lesser toxicity its action is less rapid and as a consequence ether is much safer than chloroform. While cardiac arrest may follow respiratory failure when too much of the drug is given, this event does not occur for some little time after the patient stops breathing. Ample time for the introduction of an artificial airway and the use of artificial respiration and oxygen usually is available with the result that a fatal outcome may be avoided. For this reason the margin of safety is much greater with ether than it is with chloroform.

The chief difficulties with ether are its irritation of the respiratory tract, its tendency to cause vomiting and its depressant effect on the uterine contractions any or all of which may indirectly cause the death of the patient.

Irritation of the respiratory tract may lead to postoperative pneumonia. This is particularly true in patients who are suffering from respiratory disease. Ether accordingly should not be used if the patient has a "cold" or is suffering from bronchitis, tuberculosis or other pulmonary disease.

Vomiting during anesthesia is always a potential danger since aspiration of the vomitus may cause massive collapse of the lungs or pneumonia or both. Ether anesthesia should not be given if the patient has taken nourishment recently unless the stomach contents are first removed by gastric lavage.

Because of its depressant effect on the uterine contractions ether given over long periods may prolong the labor and cause atonic postpartum hemorrhage. As previously stated the anesthetic should be discontinued immediately after the child's head is born and should not be readministered for repair of the perineum until the placenta has been expressed and the danger of postpartum hemorrhage removed.

Ether passes through the placenta and is found in almost as high a concentration in the fetal as in the maternal blood. Apneic infants as well as their mothers show higher concentrations of ether in their bloods than the mother and child do when the newborn infant breathes immediately after birth. The respiratory difficulty in the child accordingly, is thought to be due largely to the direct action of ether on the fetus rather than to interference with the maternal or fetal oxygen supply (40).

NITROUS OXIDE

Nitrous oxide because of its relative safety and rapid action is used as an analgesic agent in the latter part of the first and early in the second stage of labor. Combined with small amounts of ether it also is employed for the delivery of the child and for short obstetrical operations. It is unsuitable for those manipulations which require relaxation of the uterus and is dangerous for the fetus in all prolonged operative procedures.

Successful analgesia depends upon the use of the right mixture of nitrous oxide and oxygen and its administration at the right time in relation to the uterine contractions. **The right mixture of nitrous oxide and oxygen** is determined for each patient by trying first the relatively safe proportion of 80% nitrous oxide to 20% oxygen and gradually increasing the nitrous oxide concentration as may be required to produce the desired effect. Since the gas is given only during the uterine contractions when the circulation through the placental lake is almost completely arrested, the danger to the fetus from such high concentrations is greatly reduced. This danger may be still further diminished by giving oxygen inhalations in the interval between contractions. **The right time of administration** is from the onset of each contraction to the disappearance of the pain. If the anesthetist will keep his hand over the fundus of the uterus he may feel the contraction before the patient feels the pain. In this way he will be able to begin the administration of the nitrous oxide before he would if he relied upon the patient to tell him when each labor pain begins. Should the administration be started after the pain has become acute on the other hand, it may be difficult to secure satisfactory analgesia. The mask is removed or the administration of the drug is discontinued and 100% oxygen is given immediately after the contraction ceases. In other words, analgesia with nitrous oxide is safe for the fetus only when its administration is intermittent and synchronous with the uterine contractions. Used in this manner it is possible to employ concentrations which if given continuously and in the interval between contractions would cause serious anoxemia in the mother and her unborn child.

Towards the end of the second stage of labor when the uterine contractions are intense and come close together it is advisable to add ether to the mixture in order that the concentration of nitrous oxide may be lowered and that of oxygen raised to at least 20%. This not only reduces the risk to the fetus but it favors relaxation of the maternal soft parts during the delivery of the child. The anesthetic should be discontinued immediately after the child's head is born and inhalations of oxygen given until the umbilical cord stops pulsating to counteract a possible anoxemia in the newborn child.

Since the analgesia and anesthesia produced by nitrous oxide is largely due to the effect of oxygen deprivation on the brain cells it naturally follows that the prolonged use of this gas particularly as an anesthetic rather than analgesic agent may affect the fetus. Infants born after nitrous oxide analgesia and anesthesia accordingly do not breathe as readily as do those whose mothers have had no analgesia or anesthesia or who have had local, caudal or spinal anesthesia only. This increased tendency toward respiratory difficulty in the newborn child is still further increased if morphine and scopolamine, the barbiturates or paraldehyde are given prior to the use of nitrous oxide (41, 42, 43).

ETHYLENE

Ethylene is safer for the fetus than nitrous oxide because it is given with a higher percentage of oxygen. Acting more rapidly than ether it is a very satisfactory anesthetic agent for obstetric operations in which it is desirable to vary the degree of anesthesia readily (44, 45).

The intermittent administration of 70% ethylene and 30% oxygen is used to produce analgesia throughout the second stage of labor in institutions which are suitably equipped to eliminate the risk of explosion. For the delivery of the child and for operative procedures, the concentration of ethylene is increased to 85% during the induction of anesthesia and reduced to 80% for its maintenance. In the majority of cases the addition of ether is not necessary for the delivery of the child. Ethylene however does not produce sufficient relaxation for internal version and decomposition of a frank breech.

Because it is given with a relatively high concentration of oxygen, the administration of this gas has much less effect on the fetus than does nitrous oxide with the result that fetal asphyxia is encountered only half as frequently as when nitrous oxide is used (45).

Unfortunately low concentrations of ethylene in air or oxygen are extremely explosive. While the risk of explosion is absent when the high concentrations necessary for anesthesia are used, this danger is always present for a time after the anesthetic is discontinued. As a consequence, the patient must be guarded against such an accident during the period of recovery. For the same reason, the intermittent use of ethylene as an analgesic agent is more dangerous than is its continuous administration to produce anesthesia. Most institutions accordingly, are unwilling to use this gas intermittently for obstetric analgesia.

Ethylene is administered by means of a closed anesthesia apparatus which is so constructed as to eliminate the development of static electric charges which might initiate an explosion. In addition to the anesthesia machine itself, the most dangerous area extends for 1 foot above the patient's face and 2 feet lateral to the mask. Obviously, care should be taken to exclude from the room, open flames, electric cautery, lighted cigarettes, defective electric wiring and nearby electric switches. The humidity also should be kept above 55 to prevent the development and accumulation of static charges.

CYCLOPROPANE

Cyclopropane is a more potent anesthetic agent than either nitrous oxide or ethylene. In 3 to 5 percent mixtures with oxygen it produces analgesia and 20 to 35 percent concentrations are sufficient for anesthesia. It likewise is the most toxic of the gas anesthetics and causes respiratory failure in concentrations of 30 to 40 percent. While somewhat less explosive than ethylene the hazard in this respect is considerable but may be reduced by the addition of helium to the anesthetic mixture (46). All of the precautions mentioned in the discussion of ethylene to guard against explosion should be used.

Success in the use of cyclopropane as an analgesic agent during labor requires the individualization of each case in which it is used. The anesthetist must first ascertain the patient's tolerance and then as with nitrous oxide he must administer the gas promptly at the onset of each labor pain. A 4 to 6 liter bag is filled with cyclopropane at 300 cc. per minute, oxygen at 500 cc. per minute and helium at 700 cc. per minute, i.e., 20% cyclopropane and 33% oxygen diluted with helium. At the onset of each contraction the mask is placed over the patient's face and she is requested to take three deep breaths and hold the last one and bear down. If she becomes drowsy or unconscious the number of inhalations is reduced to two or even one with each pain until the anesthetist learns the patient's tolerance. If she exhales into the bag before her first and after her last breath of cyclopropane, each bag of the specified mixture should give relief for 4 to 6 contractions. For episiotomy and for the delivery of the child the concentration of cyclopropane is increased and that of oxygen reduced by filling the bag with cyclopropane, oxygen and helium at the rate of 700 cc., 500 cc. and 1000 cc. per minute respectively (47). As soon as the child's head is born the cyclopropane is discontinued and oxygen is given until the cord stops pulsating. For the repair, the administration is the same as that employed for ordinary surgical procedures. **Because of its toxicity and explosiveness, cyclopropane should be given only by experienced anesthetists and a standard apparatus should always be used.** When thus administered the risk to the mother and child is slight.

The rapid action of cyclopropane gives it a flexibility well suited to the needs of obstetrics. With it satisfactory analgesia may be secured during the bearing down efforts of the second stage of labor without lessening the strength of the uterine contractions. Anesthesia and relaxation at the time of delivery is easily secured and more prolonged action may also be obtained should it be required for the various obstetric operations and repair of lacerations. The same rapid potent action which makes it flexible and suitable for obstetrics also makes cyclopropane dangerous unless it is properly given (48).

Owing to the fact that pituitary shock is greatly accentuated during or after cyclopropane anesthesia, posterior pituitary extract should not be used when this method of anesthesia is employed (49).

While the amount of oxygen given with cyclopropane is advantageous to the fetus it should be remembered that this potent gas readily passes through the placenta with the result that its concentration in the fetal blood is as high as is that of the mother. Its effect on the respiration of fetus accordingly may be marked and may lead to apnea at birth (50).

REFERENCES

1. GAUSS, C. J.: Geburten im künstlichen Dämmerschlaf. Arch. f. Gyn., 1906, 78, 579.
2. KRIBS, O. S., WULFF, G. L. AND WASSERMANN, H. C.: Scopolamine-Morphine Seminarcosis with Modifications. J. A. M. A., 1936, 37, 1704.
3. BILL, A. H.: Analgesia and Anesthesia and Their Bearing Upon the Problem of Shortened Labor. Am. J. O. & G., 1937, 34, 868.
4. ROBBINS, A. R., McCALLUM, T. T. C., MENDENHALL, A. M. AND ZERFAS, L. Q.: The Use of Sodium Iso-amylethyl Barbiturate (Sodium Amytal) in Obstetrics. Am. J. O. & G., 1929, 18, 406.
5. IRVING, F. C., BERMAN, S. AND NELSON, H. B.: The Barbiturates and Other Hypnotics in Labor. S. G. O., 1934, 58, 1.
6. IRVING, F. C.: Advantages and Disadvantages of the Barbiturates in Obstetrics. Rhode Island M. J., 1945, 28, 493.
7. GRUBER, C. M.: On Certain Pharmacologic Actions of the Newer Barbituric Acid Compounds. Am. J. O. & G., 1937, 33, 729.
8. TOLLEFSON, D. G.: Analgesia and Anesthesia in Labor. West. J. Surg., 1941, 49, 44.
9. SCHREIBER, F.: Apnea of Newborn and Associated Cerebral Injury. Clinical and Statistical Study. J. A. M. A., 1938, 111, 1263.
10. ROSENFELD, H. H. AND DAVIDOFF, R. B.: A New Procedure for Obstetrical Analgesia. New Eng. J. Med., 1932, 207, 366.
11. COLVIN, E. D. AND BARTHOLOMEW, R. A.: The Advantages of Paraldehyde as a Basic Amnesic Agent in Obstetrics. J. A. M. A., 1935, 104, 362.
12. COLVIN, E. D. AND BARTHOLOMEW, R. A.: Improvements in the Paraldehyde Method of Relief of Pain In labor. Am. J. O. & G., 1938, 35, 589.
13. DOUGLAS, L. H. AND LINN, R. F.: Paraldehyde in Obstetrics with Particular Reference to Its Use in Eclampsia. Am. J. O. & G., 1942, 43, 844.
14. KANE, H. F. AND ROTH, G. B.: The Use of Paraldehyde in Obtaining Obstetric Analgesia and Amnesia. Am. J. O. & G., 1935, 29, 366.

15. KANE, H. F. AND ROTH, G. B.: Combined Oral and Rectal Administration of Paraldehyde for the Relief of Labor Pains. Anest. & Analg., 1940, 19, 282.
16. SHOOR, M.: Paraldehyde Poisoning. J. A. M. A., 1941, 117, 1534.
17. BATTERMAN, R. C.: Clinical Effectiveness and Safety of a New Synthetic Analgesic Drug Demerol. Arch. Int. Med., 1943, 71, 345.
18. ROBY, C. AND SCHUMANN, W. R.: Demerol (S-140) and Scopolamine in Labor. Am. J. O. & G., 1943, 45, 318.
19. SCHUMANN, W. R.: Demerol (S-140) and Scopolamine in Labor. Am. J. O. & G., 1944, 47, 93.
20. GILBERT, G. AND DIXON, A. B.: Observations on Demerol as an Obstetrical Analgesic. Am. J. O. & G., 1943, 45, 320.
21. GALLEN, B. AND PRESCOTT, F.: Pethidine as an Obstetric Analgesic; Report on 150 Cases. Brit. M. J., 1944, 1, 176.
22. GREENHILL, J. B.: The Use of Local Infiltration Anesthesia in Obstetrics & Gynecology. Surg. Cl. N. A., 1943, 23, 143.
23. BUXBAUM, H.: Local Anesthesia. Am. J. O. & G., 1944, 48, 90.
24. URNES, N. P. AND TIMMERMAN, H. J.: Breech Delivery; A Comparative Study of Local and General Anesthesia. J. A. M. A., 1937, 109, 1616.
25. BUNIN, L. A.: Effect of Local Anesthesia by Means of Pudendal Nerve Block with Novocaine on Cervical Dystocia Occurring Late in the First Stage of Labor. Am. J. O. & G., 1943, 45, 805.
26. RUCKER, M. P.: Pudendal Block in Obstetrics. So. Med. & Surg., 1944, 106, 407.
27. HINGSON, R. A. AND EDWARDS, W. B.: Continuous Caudal Anesthesia During Labor and Delivery. Anesth. & Analg., 1942, 21, 301.
28. EDWARDS, W. B. AND HINGSON, R. A.: Continuous Caudal Anesthesia in Obstetrics. Am. J. Surg., 1942, 57, 459.
29. SOUTHWORTH, J. L., EDWARDS, W. B. AND HINGSON, R. A.: Continuous Caudal Analgesia in Surgery. Ann. Surg., 1943, 117, 321.
30. PARRETT, V.: Caudal Anesthesia in One Hundred Sixty Obstetric Cases. Am. J. O. & G., 1943, 46, 417.
31. MENGERT, W. F.: Continuous Caudal Anesthesia with Procaine Hydrochloride in 240 Obstetric Patients. Am. J. O. & G., 1944, 48, 100.
32. HINGSON, R. A.: Contraindications and Cautions in the Use of Continuous Caudal Anesthesia. Am. J. O. & G., 1944, 47, 718.
33. ADAMS, R. C., LUNDY, J. S. AND SELDON, T. H.: Continuous Caudal Anesthesia or Analgesia. J. A. M. A., 1943, 122, 152.
34. GREADY, T. G.: Some Complications of Caudal Anesthesia and Their Management. J. A. M. A., 1943, 123, 671.
35. BAPTISTI, A.: Continuous Caudal Analgesia in Obstetrics. Am. J. O. & G., 1944, 48, 103.
36. COSGROVE, S. A., HALL, P. O. AND GLEESON, W. J.: Spinal Anesthesia with Particular Reference to Its Use in Obstetrics. Anesth. & Analg., 1937, 16, 234.
37. GWATHMEY, J. T.: Obstetrical Analgesia; A Further Study Based on More Than Twenty Thousand Cases. S. G. O., 1930, 51, 190.
38. McCORMICK, C. O.: A New Rectal Ether Analgesia Apparatus. Am. J. O. & G., 1930, 20, 411.
39. GWATHMEY, J. T. AND McCORMICK, C. O.: Ether-Oil Rectal Analgesia in Obstetrics. J. A. M. A., 1935, 105, 2044.
40. SMITH, C. A. AND BARKER, R. H.: Ether in the Blood of the Newborn Infant. Am. J. O. & G., 1942, 43, 763.
41. CLIFFORD, S. H. AND IRVING, F. C.: Analgesia Anesthesia and the Newborn Infant. S. G. & O., 1937, 65, 23.

42. SMITH, C. A.: Effect of Nitrous Oxide Ether Anesthesia Upon Oxygenation of Maternal and Fetal Blood. S. G. O., 1940, 70, 787.
43. TURINO, M. D. AND MERWARTH, H. R.: Anoxia Following Nitrous Oxide Anesthesia for Labor. Am. J. O. & G., 1941, 41, 843.
44. HEANEY, N. S.: Ethylene in Obstetrics. J. A. M. A., 1924, 83, 2061.
45. PLASS, E. D. AND SWANSON, C. H.: Ethylene in Obstetrics. J. A. M. A., 1926, 87, 1716.
46. THOMAS, J. I. AND JONES, G. W.: The Value of Helium in the Prevention of Explosions of Anesthetic Mixtures. N. Y. State M. J., 1942, 42, 326.
47. KARP, M. AND RICHARDSON, G. C.: A Technic for Administering Cyclopropane in Obstetrics. Surg. Cl. N. A., 1943, 23, 59.
48. SAHLER, S. L., KELBY, J. F. AND PHILLIPS, R. B.: Cyclopropane Anesthesia at the Rochester General Hospital. J. A. M. A., 1942, 118, 1042.
49. BELINKOFF, S.: Cyclopropane-Pituitrin Incompatibility. Am. J. O. & G., 1944, 48, 109.
50. SMITH, C. A.: The Effect of Obstetrical Anesthesia Upon Oxygenation of Maternal and Fetal Blood with Particular Reference to Cyclopropane. S. G. O., 1939, 69, 584.
51. DOGLIOTTI, A. M.: Anesthesia Narcosis, Local, Regional, Spinal. Debour., Chicago 1939.
52. LUNDY, J. S.: Clinical Anesthesia. Saunders, Philadelphia 1942.
53. LULL, C. B. AND HINGSON, R. A.: Control of Pain In Childbirth. Anesth., Analg., and Amnesia, Philadelphia, Lippincott, 1944.

INDEX